"An admirable compilation; it includes an astonishing number of items ... accurate and clear."

—Henry Steele Commager,
Amherst College

"*An Encyclopedic Dictionary of American History* is a distinguished work. Particularly strong are the many entries on the contemporary scene, on military history, religious denominations, famous sayings, Indians, literature, the states, and Supreme Court decisions. A reference work of this caliber will be indispensable for every student of American history and indeed for every home."

—Morris Gall,
Department Head, Social Studies,
Norwalk (Connecticut) Public Schools

HOWARD L. HURWITZ (Ph.D., Columbia, 1943) has had a long and distinguished career as a history teacher in the New York City public schools. His published works include articles in numerous journals as well as books on American and world history, economics, labor relations, and recently *Donald: The Man Who Remains a Boy*. Dr. Hurwitz is currently Principal of Long Island City High School.

This revised edition contains a Supplement on Contemporary Events beginning on page 741 which updates the original text. The index covers material in both the main text and the supplement.

An
Encyclopedic
Dictionary of

AMERICAN
HISTORY

Revised and Updated

by

HOWARD L. HURWITZ

WASHINGTON SQUARE PRESS
POCKET BOOKS • New York

AN ENCYCLOPEDIC DICTIONARY OF
AMERICAN HISTORY

WASHINGTON SQUARE PRESS paperback edition published
March, 1970
Revised and updated edition published August, 1974

L

Published by
POCKET BOOKS, a division of Simon & Schuster, Inc.,
630 Fifth Avenue, New York, N.Y.

WASHINGTON SQUARE PRESS editions are distributed
in the U.S. by Simon & Schuster, Inc., 630 Fifth Avenue,
New York, N.Y. 10020, and in Canada by Simon & Schuster of Canada, Ltd., Markham, Ontario, Canada.

for
NETTIE

Table of Contents

Foreword

ABOUT THIRTY YEARS AGO, while a graduate student at Columbia University, I wandered into a bookstore and left elated after having purchased a secondhand set of the two-volume *Encyclopedic Dictionary of American Reference* (1901), by J. Franklin Jameson and J. W. Buel. Since I was majoring in American history, I was pleased to add to my personal library a work by distinguished historians who had performed a service for an earlier generation.

A few years later, I was able to make use of the superb five-volume *Dictionary of American History* (1940), edited by James Truslow Adams, supplemented by a sixth volume in 1961. One might assume that with this and other similar dictionaries available to the student of history, the field is rather thoroughly covered.

I believe, however, that many readers will welcome a one-volume dictionary of American history, just as they recognize the values of both an unabridged general dictionary and a more manageable desk version. In short, there is room for both the multi-volume reference work as well as a condensation that can supply authoritative and, at the same time, readable explanations of items in American history encountered by busy people who have neither the time nor the inclination to do extensive research. I have tried to meet such a need in *An Encyclopedic Dictionary of American History*.

Certainly since the time of Jameson and Buel, the province of the historian has expanded greatly. Historians no longer confine themselves to politics and military events. Everything in the past is history. This creates a major problem in a work of this kind. If it is to serve as a concise reference, it must attempt to be simultaneously comprehensive and selective. What, then, does the author leave out? The answer to such a question must necessarily be based upon a series of value judgments. In general, the approach here has been to supply the information most useful to students, teachers and the intelligent non-specialist in the field of American history.

My choice of entries will doubtless satisfy no one completely. Nevertheless, I am assuming that more than twenty-five years of teaching experience have not gone for naught, and that in this time I have become familiar with what information a widely ranging reader of American history is likely to seek in his efforts to understand the American past as a guide to the world in which we live today.

Despite the acknowledged limitations, the range of items is broad, and the space devoted to each is determined by its relative importance or complexity of content. Thus some entries are only a few lines in length; others continue for several pages. In point of time, the entries extend from the earliest trace of contact with America (Vinland) through space exploration (Apollo Project). Categories, too, are numerous, as a glance at the Index will readily reveal.

Certain broad subjects, like "labor," "agriculture," "inventions" and "literature" would not be suitable for coverage in a work of this kind. However, through the treatment of specific items important in such areas, the general details can be quickly assembled. For instance on the subject of "labor," the Dictionary lists "American Federation of Labor and Congress of Industrial Organizations (AFL–CIO)," the "Anthracite Coal Strike (1902)," and similar pertinent references.

Where a work is celebrated I have listed it as a special item (*e.g., Walden*); but I have also included a capsule biography of "Thoreau, Henry David (1817–62)." This is not, however, a biographical dictionary. I have included over 400 brief biographies as an additional convenience to the reader and because there are aspects of our culture (especially in the area of modern science) which cannot be pinpointed in a specific item.

The Index is a vital key to the use of this work, both for the specific details and broader matters. While most items sought by the general reader will be found in their alphabetical places in the body of the volume, the Index contains other thousands of items and names.

The maps which precede the Index range from the period of exploration to the boundaries of our fifty states. They are not likely to discourage use of any of the many historical atlases available to the public; but they offer quick access to historical experiences, including locations of American Indian tribes, major military campaigns, boundary changes as our nation expanded and agricultural and industrial growth.

A user of *An Encyclopedic Dictionary of American History* would, for example, be poorly served if he looked up "Intolerable Acts," significant in the colonial period, and did not find it under the "i's." The Index lists "Intolerable Acts" but tells the reader that he will find it under "Coercive Acts."

I have not used cross-references in the body of the work because they would be so numerous as to be a distraction rather than an aid to the user. Also, the usual cross-references (in capitals, italics or other distracting type faces) tend to hinder the easy reading of the text. If the reader is curious about pursuing an item further, the cross-references are contained in the Index.

Capitals for the first letter in a word have been used only when the item is commonly capitalized by authorities.

It has been my intent to present to the user of this book a ready reference to the study of American history. Its intrinsic value can be derived if its function is recognized as an immediate source of factual identification.

*   *   *

I have drawn on the works of a great many historical scholars and I am grateful to them. To mention them by name would be to recapitulate in part the imposing bibliographies in *A Guide to the Study of The United States of America* (Library of Congress) and the *Harvard Guide to American History* (Harvard University Press).

There are several people who have given generously of their time in reading the manuscript in its entirety and whose scholarship and acumen have helped to shape the final work. I believe that they will see evidence that their criticisms have been given weight in revisions and additions of many items.

I am especially indebted to Dr. Merle Curti, Frederick

Jackson Turner, Professor of History, University of Wisconsin, for his encouragement, careful reading of the manuscript and specific suggestions for improvement of the Dictionary.

Dr. Morris Gall, Department Head, Social Studies, Norwalk (Connecticut) Public Schools, and Dr. John Anthony Scott, Chairman of the History Department, Fieldston School, Riverdale, New York, fingered some gaps in coverage.

Mr. Charles J. Steingart, Head of the English Department, Anna Head School, Oakland, California, read and edited the manuscript with a view to making each item as clear as possible.

Mr. Donald Reis, Editor-in-Chief, Washington Square Press, perceived the problems of item selection and carefully supervised the project.

Mr. Phillip C. Flayderman, formerly of Washington Square Press, started me on the project. The sage advice of Mr. Harry Shefter saved me from errors along the publication road.

My wife, Nettie Schifrin Hurwitz, has shared me with libraries for the past 25 years. She typed drafts of each item, read them critically and willingly handled burdensome details.

*An
Encyclopedic
Dictionary of
AMERICAN
HISTORY*

A

ABC conference (1914). Argentina, Brazil and Chile met with the U.S. at Niagara Falls, Canada, to mediate a dispute between the U.S. and Mexico. The controversy developed when, because of the arrest of an American whaleboat crew at Tampico, Pres. Wilson ordered the marines to take Vera Cruz. The Mexican government's subsequent apology was deemed unsatisfactory by Wilson, and the quarrel took a dangerous turn when it was reported to Wilson that a German ship was bringing munitions to Mexico.

The proposal of the ABC powers to establish a new government in Mexico, following free elections, was rejected by Pres. Huerta. Further mediation, however, became unnecessary when his regime, unable to secure arms or credit from European powers on the eve of World War I, collapsed.

Abilene, Kansas. A cow town on the Kansas Pacific Railway, Abilene was conveniently located for northern buyers and Texas and western breeders. During the peak year of 1871, 700,000 cattle were driven into Abilene for shipment by rail to Kansas City. After that other cow towns sprang up as the Kansas Pacific was extended westward, and Abilene declined in importance. It is remembered in recent history as the boyhood home of Dwight D. Eisenhower, 34th President of the U.S.

ab-initio movement. In 1866 in Texas, Reconstruction measures were snarled in the Texas constitutional convention. Radical unionists held that secession had been null and void from the first (*ab-initio*) and that measures passed by the Texas legislature during the period under the Confederacy were not binding in either public or private relations. Conservatives disputed this point of view. Compromises were made and the views of the ab-initios were largely rejected. Texas, however, repudiated not only her war debts, but also her civil debts which were unrelated to the Civil War.

1

Ableman v. Booth (1859). The U.S. Supreme Court laid down the rule that no state court has the power to release prisoners held in custody under the authority of the U.S.

The decision, delivered by Chief Justice Taney, reversed the judgment by a justice of the Wisconsin Supreme Court releasing a prisoner charged with violating the fugitive slave law. The action of the Wisconsin justice illustrates a rarely attempted type of state court interference with federal courts: the use of the writ of habeas corpus to release persons in federal custody.

Abnaki. Like the Algonquins with whom they were rather close kin in language, these Indians sided with the French against the English colonists. Their name stems from the Algonquian word meaning "easterners." They inhabited Maine but surviving tribesmen now live in Canada.

Abolition. The antislavery movement became a major reform issue from the 1820's to the Civil War. Abolitionists differed over how to rid the nation of slavery but were united in regarding slavery as sinful. The more moderate Abolitionists sought to free slaves by purchasing them from their masters and colonizing them in Liberia and elsewhere. When colonization failed, more radical Abolitionists agitated for immediate emancipation without compensation to slave owners.

An extremist Abolitionist leader, William Lloyd Garrison of Massachusetts, described the Constitution, which guaranteed slavery, as a "covenant with death and an agreement with hell." Among the more moderate Abolitionists were such distinguished preachers as Theodore Parker, William Ellery Channing, Samuel J. May and Henry Ward Beecher.

Although Abolitionists were always a minority, the dedication of thousands of Abolitionists caused the South to fear that slaves might be led to revolt. In the North it was felt that extremists among the Abolitionists might destroy the Union if they were left unchecked.

Abrams v. U.S. (1919). The U.S. Supreme Court affirmed under the Sedition Act (1918) the conviction of a group of Russian emigrants for distributing leaflets opposing American intervention in Russia.

Justice Holmes dissented and with the concurrence of Justice Brandeis wrote: "Only the emergency that makes it immediately dangerous to leave the correction of evil counsels to time warrants making any exception to the sweeping command, 'Congress shall make no law . . . abridging the freedom of speech.'"

academies. They mark a transition from the aristocratic college-preparatory Latin grammar school of colonial times to the democratic high school of today. Franklin's Academy at Philadelphia (1751) was probably the first American academy. Another early academy was the Phillips Academy at Andover, Mass. (1778).

The academy movement spread during the first half of the 19th century and dominated secondary education until after the Civil War. Essentially private institutions arising from a church foundation, or a local endowment, it became customary for towns, counties and states to assist in their support, thus making them semipublic institutions. Practically all charged a tuition fee and most of them had dormitories and boarding halls.

A number of states founded and supported a state system of academies. Massachusetts, in 1797, granted land to approved academies. Georgia, in 1783, established a system of county academies. As early as 1787 New York put its academies under state inspection and, in 1813, extended state aid to them.

The new academies taught Latin and, usually, Greek, adding a number of new subjects —English grammar, arithmetic, algebra, geometry, geography, surveying, natural and moral philosophy. Girls were admitted to the new academies, often in a "female department."

Academies also became training schools for teachers. Before the rise of the normal school they were a main source of supply for elementary teachers.

Academies were in time displaced by the American public high school, the first of which dates from 1821.

Acadia. As a province of the French colonial empire in America, Acadia comprised what is now Nova Scotia, New Brunswick and part of Maine. In the 17th century the land became a battleground between the French and English, changing ownership several times.

It was finally ceded to England in 1713 by the Treaty of Utrecht. The British later accused the Acadians, who were French, of violating their privileges as neutrals. In 1755 they were uprooted and dispersed throughout the English colonies. Their tragic suffering was immortalized in Longfellow's poem *Evangeline.*

Adair v. U.S. (1908). The U.S. Supreme Court declared void the Erdman Act (1898) which prohibited an interstate carrier from dismissing a worker because of union membership.

The case arose when William Adair, representing railroad management, discharged a labor union member. The Court reasoned that the interstate commerce in which the railroad was engaged had no bearing on the relations between the railroad and its employees. It held that the limitation abridged the liberty of contract vital to due process of law provided for in the 5th Amendment.

Adams, Charles Francis (1807–86). Statesman. Born in Boston, Mass., he was the son of Pres. John Quincy Adams. He opposed slavery in the years before the Civil War and founded the *Boston Whig* to oppose conservative Whigs. He was the Republican member of Congress (1859–61) from Massachusetts. As U.S. Minister to England during the Civil War, he handled the *Trent* Affair tactfully and later was one of the arbitrators who settled the *Alabama* Claims Dispute. He edited the family papers: *Works of John Adams* (1850–56); *Memoirs of John Quincy Adams* (1874–77).

Adams, Henry Brooks (1838–1918). Historian. Born in Boston, Mass., he was another of the distinguished Adams family. The son of Charles Francis Adams, he is best remembered for *The Education of Henry Adams* (1906) and *Mont-Saint-Michel and Chartres* (1904). While a professor of history at Harvard, he was editor of the *North American Review* (1869–76). His major works include the *History of the United States During the Administrations of Jefferson and Madison* (9 vols., 1889–91).

Adams, John (1735–1826). Second President of the U.S. (1797–1801). He was born in Braintree (now Quincy), Mass., and was graduated from Harvard (1755). A leader in Massachusetts and delegate to the First Continental Congress (1774), Adams was one of the signers of the Declaration of Independence. An able diplomat, he helped negotiate the treaty of peace with Great Britain (1783). He was the first Vice-President of the U.S. (1789–97).

Adams, John Quincy (1767–1848). Sixth President of the U.S. (1825–29). He was born in Braintree (now Quincy), Mass., and was graduated from Harvard (1787). Son of the second President, he was an experienced diplomat. He served as Minister to Russia (1809–11). He helped negotiate the peace that ended the War of 1812. Sec. of State under Pres. Monroe, he was partly responsible for the Monroe Doctrine (1823). Defeated by Jackson for a second term (1828), he served in House of Representatives (1831–48), where he led the fight against the "gag rule."

Adams, Samuel (1722–1803). Revolutionary leader. Born in Boston, Mass., he was graduated from Harvard. The foremost propagandist of the American Revolution, Adams organized a committee of correspondence in Boston to communicate with the other colonies. Among the first to urge a complete break with Britain, he vigorously opposed the Stamp Act and was a leader of the Boston Tea Party. Adams was a member of the Continental Congress and a signer of the Declaration of Independence. Although his influence waned during the Revolution, he served as Governor of Mass. (1794–97).

Adamson Act (1916). To head off a major railroad strike, Congress passed a law imposing an eight-hour day for railroad workers and providing for a commission to study the railroad employment problem. It was rushed through Congress at the urging of Pres. Wilson, who had been unsuccessful in getting railroad managers to agree to the reduction in working hours demanded by the railroad brotherhoods.

Addams, Jane (1860–1935). Social reformer. Born in Cedarville, Ill., she was graduated from Rockford College, Ill. A settlement worker, she founded Hull House (Chicago, 1889) and made it a model for recreational and educational programs for the poor. She was also an ardent worker for international peace and shared the Nobel Peace Prize with Nicholas Murray Butler (1931). Her written works include *Twenty Years at Hull House* (1910).

Addyston Pipe and Steel Co. v. U.S. (1899). The U.S. Supreme Court ruled that six producers of cast iron pipe had conspired to divide territory among themselves and to fix prices. Their action was held to be a "direct" restraint of commerce in violation of the Sherman Antitrust Act of 1890. This was the first time that the Act was successfully applied

against an industrial combination.

Adkins v. Children's Hospital (1923). The U.S. Supreme Court ruled invalid the minimum wage law for women in the District of Columbia that had been passed by Congress in 1918. The majority decision held that there was no relationship between women's wages and their morals, welfare or health that justified passage of a law which had the effect of destroying the liberty of contract between employers and their women workers. The law was thus held to violate due process guaranteed by the 5th Amendment.

The decision was overruled in *West Coast Hotel Co. v. Parrish* (1937).

admiralty courts. In the colonial period each governor held the position of vice-admiral in his colony. He had the power to establish vice-admiralty courts to judge maritime cases and enforce Navigation Acts. The admiralty courts made no provision for trial by jury for the accused.

Since many arrests were made in colonial ports and waters, the colonial courts claimed jurisdiction and sought to remove the accused from the admiralty courts. This struggle for control of the enforcement of the Navigation Acts continued until the Revolutionary War.

The Constitution (Art. III, Sec. 2, Par. 1) eliminated the

injustice, stipulating that the power of the federal courts was extended "to all cases of admiralty and maritime jurisdiction."

adult education. The education of adults through public lectures took shape in the lyceum movement, beginning in 1826. This developed into the Chautauqua Institution. Universities undertook programs of adult education, beginning with the University of Chicago in 1892, and gave impetus to the University Extension movement. The slogan, "Lifelong Learning," has been popularized by the University of California Extension Division.

Public school systems have also furthered the adult education movement, especially since the end of World War II. The range of courses has been widened so that nearly every adult can find something of interest that he would like to learn.

Adventists. Accepting the doctrine preached by William Miller, that at Christ's second coming in 1844 the earth would be destroyed by fire, many Protestants banded together in a sect called the Adventists. When the event did not occur, the "Millerites," or Second Adventists, met at Albany in 1845 and declared their belief that the visible return of Christ was to be expected, but at an indefinite time. In 1846 the Seventh-Day Adventists adopted the religious observance of the Sabbath from sunset on Friday to sunset on Saturday. They took the position that there would be no resurrection for the wicked until 1,000 years after the second advent. In 1866 as a result of a division over the prophecies of Mrs. Ellen Gould White, a new group of Adventists, the Church of God, was formed.

At present the title Adventists is included in the names of various Protestant sects whose total membership is about 400,000.

Afro-American Unity, Organization for (1964). After his suspension from the Black Muslims in 1964 Malcolm X (Malcolm Little) formed a new organization. He abandoned the concept of total separation of the Negroes from the white population of the U.S. (the philosophy of Elijah Muhammed, head of the Black Muslims) and instead urged black nationalism and united pressure by all oppressed non-white peoples throughout the world as a means of obtaining social and political equality.

Malcolm X, killed by assassins' bullets in 1965, told his followers that the right to use arms in self-defense was one of their "human rights," a right superseding "civil rights."

Agassiz, Jean Louis Rodolphe (1807–73). Naturalist and geologist. Swiss-born, he published works on fossil fishes and glacial action over Europe before coming to the U.S., where he became a naturalized citizen (1861). He was a professor of natural history at Lawrence Scientific School, Harvard (1848–73), where he founded the Harvard Museum of Comparative Zoology (1859). An influential teacher and promoter of scientific study, he was opposed to the Darwinian theory of natural selection.

Agricultural Adjustment Acts (1933–38). The New Deal's approach to the farm problem was to pay farmers to curtail production in order to reduce surpluses and thus raise prices. The first effort in this direction was the Agricultural Adjustment Act (AAA) of 1933. Farmers agreed to curb production voluntarily and in return received special bounty payments. The money for these benefit payments was raised by a processing tax on businesses which handle farm products (*e.g.*, flour mills). In 1936, declaring the law unconstitutional (*U.S. v. Butler*), the Supreme Court ruled that Congress did not have the right to use its taxing power for the benefit of a special class of citizens and that the regulation of agriculture belonged to the states.

The Act of 1936 showed the influence of the droughts of 1934, 1935 and 1936. Its major emphasis was on the conservation of soil, though it contemplated cutbacks in the acreages of commercial cash crops. It was recognized, however, that the weather conditions which had reduced agricultural production between 1934 and 1936 did not constitute a permanent solution to the problem. The droughts also emphasized the need for more specific methods of guarding against shortages in the event of continuing periods of low rainfall.

A new Agricultural Adjustment Act, passed in 1938, continued the policy of making payments to farmers. The emphasis was shifted from mere reduction in utilized acreage to withdrawal of worn-out farm land from cultivation, planting of soil-conserving crops and other conservation measures. Farmers were given "benefit payments" in proportion to the number of acres they voluntarily withdrew from cultivation. Each year the government might fix the total acreage for wheat, corn, cotton, rice and tobacco and then divide the total among individual farmers; or the farmers themselves might decide to set up marketing quotas, limiting the quantities of various basic crops which individual growers could place on the market.

If surpluses appeared in spite of such limitations, the government would buy up supplies of these crops at "parity" prices and place them in storage. The word parity comes from the Latin word *par*, meaning "equal." This suggests that the prices the farmer receives should be "equal" to, or in balance with, the prices he pays. For the purposes of farm legislation, the prices prevailing from 1910–14 were accepted as "normal." The object of farm legislation in recent years has been to raise agricultural prices to a level where they will be in the same relationship to industrial prices as they were in 1910–14. When a farmer sells a bushel of wheat, for example, he should be able to buy approximately as much with the return as was possible in 1910–14.

Surpluses were not to be released until a "lean year," when the market could absorb them without depressing prices. This has been called the "ever-normal granary" plan.

Agricultural Marketing Act (1929). Enacted during the Hoover administration, the Act was intended to encourage the growth of farmers' cooperatives by extending credit to farmers. It also authorized the Federal Farm Board to purchase surpluses of farm produce in an effort to keep prices up.

But the Board's purchases of wheat and cotton were too slight to prevent a disastrous fall in prices. Cotton, for example, fell from 16 cents a pound in 1924 to six cents in 1932; wheat from a dollar a bushel to 38 cents. The creation of farm cooperatives was, however, stimulated by the Act.

Agricultural Revolution. Increased mechanization of agriculture in the U.S. (with a comparable development in Europe) was stimulated by John Deere's steel plow in 1837. In the pre-Civil War period wheat-growing especially was revolutionized by the invention of McCormick's horse-drawn reaper with which a single man could do the work of five men equipped with scythes. In the 1850's mechanical threshers were in use and investment in farm machinery increased greatly.

The revolution extended to the East where farmers realized that they would have to concentrate their production on those materials that could not be so easily transported from the West. Emphasis was placed on preserving perishables such as fresh meats, butter, milk and fruit. Dairying became a big business on eastern farms in the 1850's. Packaging of perishables increased greatly in America in the 1840's with the adoption of the canister or "tin can," an English invention. It enabled eastern farmers to supply not only nearby cities but also men at sea.

Eastern farmers realized that they would have to keep abreast of new developments in farming if they were to remain in business. Accordingly, they developed a keen interest in information about climate, soils, fertilizers and methods of cultivation.

Agriculture, Department of. Created by Congress in 1862, the department was expanded in 1889 and made the eighth executive department of the federal government. The commissioner became the Secretary of Agriculture.

The department disseminates useful information on agricultural subjects. It performs functions relating to research, education, conservation, marketing, regulatory work, surplus disposal and rural development. It makes research results available for practical farm application through extension and experiment station work in cooperation with the states.

Other important functions include administrating the national forests; assisting in the prevention of floods; cooperating with the states through grant-in-aid programs; carrying on the national school lunch program; making loans to farmers who cannot get elsewhere at reasonable terms the credit they need to enable tenants to become farmowners; making loans to farmer cooperatives, nonprofit organizations and commercial concerns for the purpose of financing electric and telephone facilities in rural areas.

Air Force, Department of the. A branch of the military service, the Air Force was incorporated into the Department of Defense by the National Security Act of 1947. The U.S. Air Force (USAF) includes both combat and service aviation forces. It organizes and trains and equips a force for combat operations in aerospace for defense of the U.S. against attack.

The Secretary of the Air Force conducts all affairs of the Department, as may be prescribed by the President or the Secretary of Defense. The Chief of Staff, USAF, as a member of the Joint Chiefs of Staff and the Armed Forces Policy Council, is one of the principal military advisers to the President, the National Security Council and the Secretary of Defense.

airmobile. In 1965 an increase in guerrilla warfare in Southeast Asia led to the formation at Fort Benning, Ga. of a new type of Army division which flies into battle in its own planes and helicopters. It maintains four times as many aircraft as the conventional infantry division.

Aisne Defensive (May 27–June 5, 1918). A German offensive in France, started along the Aisne River, brought the Germans to Château-Thierry on the Marne River, only 37 miles east of Paris. Desperate, Marshal Pétain, Commander-in-Chief of the French armies, asked Gen. Pershing, head of the American Expeditionary Force (AEF) for an American division to hold the Marne crossings. Pershing had been firm in his intention of engaging American troops only as a separate army, but the situation was critical and he assigned the 3rd Division to the task. In bitter fighting the American forces were successful in preventing the Germans from crossing the Marne, stopping them on the north bank of the river.

Other German forces advanced west of Château-Thierry on the road to Paris. The American 2nd Division was thrown across the road and in hand-to-hand fighting halted the Germans.

Aisne-Marne Offensive (July 18–Aug. 6, 1918). A decisive counteroffensive, planned by Marshal Foch of France, forced German withdrawal from a salient between the Aisne and Marne rivers near Soissons. It was a joint operation of French, British, Italian and American forces. The American 2nd Division suffered 5,000 casualties; the 1st, 7,200.

German Chancellor Von Hertling later said: "On the 18th even the most optimistic among us understood that all was lost. . . ."

Aix-la-Chapelle, Treaty of (Oct. 18, 1748). While the treaty ended the War of the Austrian Succession (King George's War), it aroused hostility in America. The New Englanders who had conquered Louisbourg and Cape Breton strongly objected to those provisions of the Treaty that restored these possessions off the east coast of Canada to France.

Alabama. The "Cotton State," in the East South Central group, was first explored by De Soto of Spain in 1539. Before it became part of the Mississippi Territory in 1798, it was settled by the Spanish, French and English. Spain held on to Mobile, a major seaport in Alabama, until 1813 when it was forced to yield the city to the U.S.

Alabama, the 22nd State (named after a tribe in the Creek Confederacy), was admitted to the Union as a slave state, Dec. 14, 1819. Part of the Old South, it seceded from the Union in 1861. Regarded as the "Cradle of the Confederacy," Montgomery, Ala., the state's capital, was the birthplace of the Confederate States on Feb. 4, 1861. Jefferson Davis took the oath as President there and his "first White House" has become a state shrine. The state suffered severe disruption during the Civil War and was readmitted to the Union in 1868.

Alabama's main farm crop is cotton although Birmingham, its largest city, is a steel manufacturing center.

***Alabama* Claims Dispute.** During the Civil War, such Confederate ships as the *Alabama, Shenandoah* and *Florida,* built in British ports, preyed on northern commerce and warships with devastating effect.

International law permitted neutrals to build naval craft for belligerents, but it forbade their being armed. The British got around this by permitting the ships to "escape." They were then outfitted as warships in the Azores and elsewhere. This intervention embittered relations between the U.S. and England during and after the war.

The U.S. claimed over $2 billion (known as the "*Alabama* Claims") for damages resulting from prolongation of the war and higher insurance rates on northern shipping. In the Treaty of Washington (1871) settlement of various disputes between the U.S. and Britain was agreed upon, including arbitration of the *Alabama* Claims. And the following year an international tribunal awarded the U.S. $15,500,000 as result of this arbitration.

"Alabama Letters." Henry Clay, Whig candidate for President in 1844, wrote a series of letters in July modifying the opposition to the annexation of Texas he had previously expressed in his "Raleigh Letter." In an effort to counteract the ardent expansionism of James K. Polk, his Democratic opponent, Clay stated that he would accept the admission of Texas if it could be done "without dishonor, without war, with the common consent of the Union and upon just and fair terms."

Alamance, battle of (May 16, 1771). Back country farmers of North Carolina, known as Regulators, were routed by government militiamen in a battle on the Alamance River. The Regulators had attacked the courts in a protest against taxes but their badly equipped forces were no match for the militia. Many of the Regulators migrated to Tennessee after the defeat.

Alamo. On Feb. 23, 1836, the Alamo mission at San Antonio, Tex., was attacked by Mexicans under Santa Anna. Resistance

was led by Lt. Col. William B. Travis, whose force of almost 200 included James Bowie and David Crockett. Refusing to surrender, they fought against overwhelming odds until Mar. 6, when they were wiped out to the last fighting man. The Mexicans spared 30 noncombatants. "Remember the Alamo" became the battle cry of Texans who, under Sam Houston, defeated Santa Anna at San Jacinto (Apr. 21, 1836) and gained independence for Texas.

Alaska. This largest political division of the U.S., located in the northwestern part of North America, is about two and one-half times the size of Texas. Discovered in 1741 by Vitus Bering, a Dane employed by Russia, the area was settled by Russian fur traders. Soon British and Americans were attracted to it by the furs and fishing.

When it seemed that Britain would seize the territory, Russia opened negotiations with the U.S. for its sale; this culminated in the purchase of Alaska by the U.S., in 1867, for $7,200,-000. Negotiated by Secretary of State Seward, an ardent expansionist, the purchase was ridiculed by some Americans as "Seward's folly" and "Seward's icebox."

In 1896 the discovery of gold in the Klondike and the ensuing "rush" across Alaska brought to a head the Alaska boundary dispute with Canada. Arbitration (1903) favored the U.S. claim that the Russians had been right in defining the southern boundary of Alaska.

Alaska (meaning "the great land" to Aleuts, a branch of the Eskimo race) was organized as a Territory in 1912. Its admission to the Union was complicated by the controversy over statehood for Hawaii. However, it was admitted as the 49th State on Jan. 3, 1959, the first non-contiguous state to enter the Union. Its capital is Juneau.

The principal sources of income of Alaska are fisheries, minerals, timber and furs. The state is a vital outpost in the continental defense system of the U.S.

Albany Plan of Union (1754). When the need for united action against the French and hostile Indians became evident at the beginning of the French and Indian War, the British government summoned representatives of the colonies to a conference at Albany. At this Albany Congress, Benjamin Franklin proposed a plan for uniting the American colonies.

Under the Albany Plan, the Crown would appoint a president general, and each of the colonies would send representatives to a body that would be empowered to deal with the Indians and provide for mutual defense of the colonies. The Plan was rejected both by the colonial legislatures, which felt that it would weaken their powers, and by the English who felt it would diminish the power of the king and Parliament.

Franklin observed about the outcome: "Everybody cries a union is absolutely necessary, but when they come to the manner and form of the union, their weak noddles are perfectly distracted."

"Albany regency." During king-maker Martin Van Buren's stay in Washington from about 1820 to 1848, the political machine in New York's capital which dominated state politics for him was referred to as the "Albany regency." It was established by Van Buren with the help of William L. Marcy and relied on the spoils system for keeping political fences intact.

Albemarle settlements. Grants were issued in 1663 by King Charles II to the Carolina proprietors and increased in 1665 to bring the existing settlement at Albemarle Sound (now in North Carolina) within the limits of Carolina.

The Carolina proprietors, among whom was George Monck, Duke of Albemarle, opposed all moves to establish a "numerous democracy" which they linked with Puritan New England. They hoped to sell parts of their land, keep large estates for themselves and raise crops not yet grown in England or her colonies. Socially, the proprietors hoped to duplicate in the American wilderness the class system and feudal loyalty to superiors which prevailed at home.

Alcott, Louisa May (1832–88). Author. Born in Boston,

Mass., she showed an early talent for writing poems, plays and short stories. In 1867, after service as a nurse in the Civil War, she became editor of a children's magazine, *Merry's Museum*. Her best-remembered novel, *Little Women* (2 vols., 1868, 1869) is autobiographical. The familiar characters of Jo, Amy, Beth and Meg were drawn from her family life. Her other books include *Little Men* (1871) and *Aunt Jo's Scrap-Bag* (6 vols., 1872–82).

Aldrich-Vreeland Emergency Currency Law (1908). In response to the Panic of 1907, legislation was passed to increase elasticity of the currency. It authorized national banks to issue circulating notes based on commercial paper and state, county and municipal bonds for a period of six years. In order to limit the issuance of bank notes on securities other than federal bonds, a graduated tax of up to 10% was levied on such notes.

An important provision was the establishment of the National Monetary Commission, headed by Sen. Nelson Aldrich (R.I.). Its report influenced passage of the Federal Reserve Act of 1913.

Alexanderson, Ernst Frederik Werner (1878–   ). Electrical radio engineer and inventor. Born in Upsala, Sweden, he became a naturalized U.S. citizen (1908). He has been associated almost continuously since 1902 with the General Electric Company at Schenectady, N.Y. His work helped revolutionize the field of radio communications; he also was a pioneer in television. Among his inventions are a high frequency alternator, multiple tuned antenna, vacuum tube radio telephone transmitter and tuned radio frequency receiver.

Algeciras Conference (1906). Pres. Theodore Roosevelt, intervening in the dispute between France and Germany over the Open Door in Morocco, persuaded them to meet at Algeciras, Spain. Although U.S. interests in Morocco were negligible, Roosevelt felt that the conflict might erupt into a general war. In the agreement reached at the Conference, Germany failed to prevent France from gaining a privileged foothold in North Africa. The U.S. Senate ratified the resulting treaty, but noted that this step was taken "without purpose to depart from the traditional American foreign policy. . . ."

Alger, Horatio (1834–99). Writer. Born in Revere, Mass., he was graduated from the Harvard Divinity School. Alger soon gave up a post as Unitarian minister and moved to New York where he acquired a knowledge of children in the city streets through his charitable work. This was reflected in an outpouring of enormously popular novels in which the rags to riches theme was dominant. He fashioned a widely accepted image of the American character in such works as *Ragged Dick* (1867), *Luck and Pluck* (1869) and *Tattered Tom* (1871).

Algonquin. The name applies to a large ethnic stock of related North American Indian peoples and their languages. The Algonquin Indians, original bearers of the name, were among the first fur-trading partners of the French in the St. Lawrence River valley in the 17th century.

Alien and Sedition Acts (1798). Utilizing their control of Congress, staunch Federalists pushed through a series of acts aimed to cripple the young Republican party of Thomas Jefferson.

Under the Alien Acts Pres. John Adams was empowered in peacetime to order any alien from the country and, in wartime, to imprison any alien. French aliens in the U.S., at a time when a war with France was threatening, were forced to flee. Federalists opposed the French Revolution, with which Jeffersonian Republicans sympathized.

The Sedition Act provided severe fines and punishment for anyone speaking, writing or publishing "with intent to defame" the President or other members of the government. Federalist judges jailed and fined 70 men under the Sedition Act. Many Republican papers had to close down.

James Madison called the Sedition Act "a monster that must forever disgrace its parents." Together with Jefferson, he wrote the Virginia and Kentucky Resolutions in protest against Federalist conduct in power.

alien property. The disposition of property held by enemy aliens became a problem after the Revolutionary War. British claims were settled early in the 19th century, and subsequent treaties affirmed the principle that enemy property might not be sold and would be returned at the end of hostilities.

During World War I Congress created the Office of Alien Property Custodian to dispose of property owned in the U.S. by persons residing in enemy countries. Thousands of valuable German chemical patents were sold at nominal prices. In the years between the two World Wars Austrian and Hungarian property owners were compensated in full. The office was active during World War II and was terminated in 1946 when its functions were transferred to the Department of Justice.

Alliance for Progress. Pres. Kennedy announced in Mar. 1961 a program of economic aid for Latin American countries. Pres. Johnson, in 1965, called it "the war on poverty in Latin America."

In Aug. 1961 the U.S. and 19 Latin American nations signed an agreement at Punta del Este, Uruguay, initiating the Alliance. Aiming to eliminate some of Latin America's poverty, the U.S. pledged to contribute—through outright grants, loans and technical assistance—$10 billion over a 10-year period. The countries receiving the aid are to institute tax and land reforms. Aid is denied to any dictatorial regime that comes to power by ousting a duly elected democratic government. Funds have been used to build schools, homes and water systems, to pay for new mobile health units and to arrange for loans to farmers.

It is generally realized that a 10-year term was set for a process that will require a few generations.

Allies. In World War I Russia, France, British Commonwealth, Italy, U.S., Japan, Rumania, Serbia, Belgium, Greece, Portugal and Montenegro (listed in order of total mobilized forces) came to be designated as the "Allies." They opposed the Central Powers—Germany, Austria–Hungary, Turkey and Bulgaria.

In World War II the major Allies were the U.S., Britain and the Soviet Union.

Alouette. A U.S. launch vehicle orbited a Canadian satellite on Sept. 28, 1962, to investigate the ionosphere and to measure the radio noise in space that disrupts long-range communications. It was the first satellite completely designed and built by any nation other than the U.S. or the Soviet Union.

alphabet agencies. The proliferation of new government agencies during the early days of Pres. Franklin D. Roosevelt's New Deal led to the abbreviation of their long titles in newspapers. The Agricultural Adjustment Administration, for example, was known as the "triple A" or AAA. The expression "alphabet agencies" was used, sometimes derisively, in lumping the agencies together.

Altgeld, John Peter (1847–1902). Political leader. Born in Germany, he became the first Democratic governor of Illinois (1892–96) since the Civil War. His pardon of four of the men convicted of complicity in the Haymarket Riot (Chicago, 1886) virtually ended his political career. Altgeld also opposed use of federal troops in the Pullman Strike (1894).

Aluminum Company of America. In 1886 Charles Martin Hall, a chemist, applied for a patent (issued Apr. 2, 1889) for his electrolytic process of making aluminum inexpensively. With the aid of the Mellon interests, he formed the Pittsburgh Production Co. to manufacture aluminum, one of the more common elements in the earth's crust. The company developed into the Aluminum Company of America (Alcoa) in 1907.

Alcoa is the world's largest aluminum producer. It obtains bauxite (the principal ore of aluminum) from mines in Arkansas, Dominican Republic, Jamaica and Surinam. Aluminum is widely used in the manufacture of automobile and aircraft parts, trains, bridges, high tension wires and machine parts. The company manufactures electrical conductor cable, cooking utensils, foil for wrapping foods and chemical products. Its primary aluminum capacity is over 950,000 tons annually.

In 1946 the company was one of the chief targets in the antimonopoly investigations of the Antitrust Division of the Justice Department. It was not dissolved.

Amen Corner. "Boss" Platt of New York, a powerful Republican political leader, held his "Sunday school class" (so-called by the press) in a corner of the Fifth Avenue Hotel (N.Y.C.). When he announced his political decisions there, his underlings would say, "Amen," thus giving the name to this well known meeting place in the 1890's.

Amendments to the Constitution

Dissatisfied with the Articles of Confederation, which required unanimity (for ratifying amendments), the Founding Fathers of the Constitution established in Article V more flexible procedures.

Amendments may be proposed in either of two ways: a two-thirds vote of both Houses of Congress, or on application of two-thirds of the states Congress may call a convention to amend the Constitution.

Amendments may be ratified in one of two ways which Congress may choose: by the approval of the legislatures of three-fourths of the states, or by the vote of conventions in three-fourths of the states.

Congress has fixed the time limit for ratification at seven years, and this time limit has become traditional.

The first 10 amendments are known as the Bill of Rights.

First Amendment (1791). The fundamental freedoms that already existed in the U.S. are guaranteed. Congress is prohibited from establishing a religion, interfering with religious freedom, abridging freedom of speech or press or preventing peaceful assembly for the purpose of petitioning the government and seeking correction of grievances.

Second Amendment (1791). Congress is prohibited from interfering with "the right of the people to keep and bear Arms. . . ." The protection afforded by this Amendment prevents infringement by Congress of the right to bear arms for a lawful purpose, but private citizens do not have the right to carry arms unless authorized to do so by the state. The U.S. Supreme Court upheld

16

a state statute which forbade bodies of men to associate together as military organizations or to drill or parade with arms in cities and towns unless authorized by law (*Presser v. Illinois*, 1886).

Third Amendment (1791). This Amendment, which prohibits peacetime quartering of soldiers without the consent of property owners, is so thoroughly in accord with all our ideals that it does not appear to have been the subject of comment by the courts. It also provides for quartering "in time of war, but in a manner to be prescribed by law." This has never been necessary.

Fourth Amendment (1791). The Amendment protects citizens "against unreasonable searches and seizures" and limits the issuance of warrants to instances where there is "probable cause." It also protects citizens by limiting the scope of the warrant.

The Amendment applies only to governmental action, not to the unlawful acts of individuals in which the government has no part. For example, where officers demand admission to private premises in the name of the law, their subsequent searches are in violation of the Amendment, even though the occupant opens the door to admit them (*Amos v. U.S.*, 1921).

Fifth Amendment (1791). No person shall be punished for a crime unless he has been indicted by a Grand Jury, except those serving in the armed forces or in the militia during wartime or public danger. No person can be tried for the same crime twice; nor shall any person "be compelled in any criminal case to be a witness against himself, nor be deprived of life, liberty, or property, without due process of law; nor shall private property be taken for public use, without just compensation."

This Amendment has been the subject of extensive comment by the courts because of the "due process" clause.

Sixth Amendment (1791). An accused person is guaranteed "the right to a speedy and public trial, by an impartial jury of the State and district wherein the crime shall have been committed. . . ." The accused shall be "informed of the nature and cause of the accusation; to be confronted with the witnesses against him. . . ." and has the right to compel the appearance of witnesses in his favor. The accused also has the right to be defended by a lawyer.

Seventh Amendment (1791). The Amendment provides the right of trial by jury in suits at common law that involve more than twenty dollars. Moreover, it declares that the decision of a jury cannot be disregarded by the judge or any other court unless done so "according to the rules of common law."

The Amendment established the right to a trial by jury in certain civil cases. Its primary purpose was to preserve the historic line separating the province of the jury from that of the judge in accordance with the system of law originating in England. It is, for example, constitutional for a judge, in the course of a trial, to express his opinion upon the facts, provided all questions of fact are ultimately submitted to the jury (*Vicksburg &c. Railroad Co. v. Putnam*, 1886).

Eighth Amendment (1791). The Amendment was intended to prevent unnecessarily long imprisonments by prohibiting "excessive bail"; it also forbade the levying of "excessive fines" and "cruel and unusual punishments." When the Bill of Rights was being debated in Congress, some members objected to the vagueness of the terms "excessive bail," "excessive fines" and "cruel and unusual punishments." The courts have had to determine the meaning of these terms as they apply in individual cases.

Ninth Amendment (1791). The Amendment states that the specific "enumeration . . . of certain rights" does not mean that other rights of the people are being denied or disparaged. The only right which the Supreme Court has explicitly acknowledged as protected by this Amendment is the right to engage in political activity.

Tenth Amendment (1791). The Constitution reserves considerable governmental power for the states. This includes both the powers not granted to the federal government by the Constitution and those the Constitution does not deny to the states. Education, marriage laws, control of crime and health standards are among the concerns of the states.

Eleventh Amendment (1798). Federal courts are excluded from jurisdiction over any suits "against one of the United States by Citizens of another State, or by Citizens or Subjects of any Foreign State."

The need for the Amendment arose when the Supreme Court in *Chisholm v. Georgia* (1793) upheld the right of a British subject to sue the state. Since the state of Georgia refused to appear as a defendant, a judgment by default was entered against the state.

Indignation in Georgia and other states was aroused. Georgia refused to pay the claim. When individuals instituted suits against other states, a constitutional amendment was introduced into Congress depriving the federal courts of all jurisdiction in cases brought against a state by the citizens of other states or of any foreign country. Under the Eleventh Amendment jurisdiction in such suits is held by the courts of the state being sued.

Twelfth Amendment (1804). Henceforth the electors named "in their ballots the person voted for as President and in distinct ballots the person voted for as Vice-President."

The Amendment was made necessary by the confusion in the Electoral College in 1800 when Jefferson and Burr received the same number of electoral votes. It was common knowledge that the Republican electors intended Jefferson to be President and Burr to be Vice-President, but the Federalists took the opportunity of seeking to elevate Burr, who did nothing to discourage their action. The Federalists finally yielded and Jefferson was elected President on the 36th ballot in the House of Representatives (each state having one vote). The 12th Amendment prevents recurrence of this situation.

Thirteenth Amendment (1865). Sponsored by Radical Republicans at the end of the Civil War, the Amendment abolished slavery. It declared that "Neither slavery nor involuntary servitude . . . shall exist within the United States." The Southern states were required to accept it as one of the conditions for regaining admission to the Union.

Fourteenth Amendment (1868). Negroes were granted citizenship during the Reconstruction era. The first of the four sections prohibited the states from abridging the privileges of citizens; "nor shall any State deprive any person of life, liberty, or property, without due process of law; nor deny to any person . . . the equal protection of the laws." The second section penalized any state for withholding the voting privilege by reducing the state's representation in Congress. The third section disqualified from office Confederates who had held federal office before the Civil War, unless Congress specifically lifted the disqualification. Finally, the Amendment guaranteed the Union debt and outlawed the Confederate debt and any compensation for the loss of slaves.

Ratification of the Amendment was made a condition for readmission of the Confederate States to the Union. Although rejected in 1866 by southern states that did not want to disenfranchise their leaders, it was ratified when the legislatures of the southern states were reconstituted under Congress' Reconstruction plan.

The primary purpose of the Amendment was to place the civil rights of the Negro upon a firm basis. But the framers also intended to bring about a revolution in the constitutional system by placing in the hands of Congress the broadest possible power to prevent impairment of the whole body of civil rights, especially those enumerated in the Bill of Rights. Instead of looking to the state legislature for protection of his civil liberty, the citizen, especially the freedman, would henceforth look to Congress or the federal courts.

The Amendment, designed to protect Negroes, has been used in the courts to protect corporations, regarded as "persons" in the eyes of the law, against state action depriving them of property without due process of law.

The primary purpose of the Amendment was brought into play in 1954 and in subsequent civil rights cases when the Supreme Court held that state laws requiring school segregation deprived Negroes of "the equal protection of the laws guaranteed by the Fourteenth Amendment."

Fifteenth Amendment (1870). During the Reconstruction era when Negroes were prevented from voting in certain states such as Louisiana and Georgia, the Radical Republicans in Congress strengthened the provisions of the 14th Amendment with a subsequent Amendment which guaranteed all citizens the right to vote regardless of "race, color, or previous condition of servitude."

Sixteenth Amendment (1913). The Amendment gives Congress the power to levy taxes and collect them. Any income, "from whatever source derived," may be taxed "without regard to any census or enumeration."

The ratification of this Amendment was the direct consequence of the decision in *Pollock v. Farmers' Loan & Trust Co.* (1895) whereby the attempt of Congress the previous year to tax incomes uniformly throughout the U.S. was held by a divided court to be unconstitutional. A tax on incomes derived from property, the Court declared, was a "direct tax" which Congress under the terms of Art. I, Sec. 2, Par. 3, and Sec. 9, Par. 4, could impose only by the rule of apportionment according to population; although scarcely 15 years prior the Justices had upheld (*Springer v. U.S.*, 1881) the collection of a similar tax during the Civil War.

Seventeenth Amendment (1913). Direct election of Senators by the people of the state was established. In the event of a vacancy, the governor may make a temporary appointment until the people fill the vacancy by election.

The ratification of this Amendment was the outcome of increasing popular dissatisfaction with the operation of the originally established method of electing Senators by the vote of the legislatures of the states. As more of the people became eligible to vote, the belief became widespread that Senators ought to be popularly elected in the same manner as Representatives. Support for this view was strengthened as evidence accumulated of deals being made in legislatures over elections to the Senate and deadlocks within legislatures resulting in vacancies remaining unfilled for long periods of time.

Eighteenth Amendment (1919). This Amendment, later repealed by the 21st Amendment, established Prohibition. It forbade the "manufacture, sale, or transportation of intoxicating liquors" in the U.S.

Nineteenth Amendment (1920). The women's suffrage movement was climaxed by success in time for women to vote in the Presidential election of 1920. The Amendment stated that the right to vote "shall not be denied or abridged by the United States or by any State on account of sex."

Twentieth Amendment (1933). The President's term of office was altered to end on Jan. 20 rather than Mar. 4. The Amendment also corrected a situation whereby "lame-duck" Congressmen, defeated for reelection in November, had remained in Congress during the next ("short") session, beginning in December. They had thus legislated for people who had rejected them at the polls. The Amendment provides that each new Congress meet on Jan. 3, without distinction as to "short" or "long" sessions.

Twenty-first Amendment (1933). The 18th (Prohibition) Amendment was repealed. The Amendment provides, however, that states, territories and possessions of the U.S. could prohibit the sale or use of intoxicating liquors within their borders.

Twenty-second Amendment (1951). Limits were placed on the President's term in office: "No person shall be elected to the office of President more than twice. . . ." and the maximum number of years in the Presidency was set at ten. Although Pres. Harry S Truman was exempted from its provisions, since Congress passed the Amendment during his administration, he did not seek a third term.

The Amendment was a post-World War II reaction to the New Deal of Pres. Franklin D. Roosevelt, who had been elected for a third and fourth term.

Proponents of the Amendment contended that it guards against assumption of excessive power by a President. Opponents held that it weakens the power of a President during his second term.

Twenty-third Amendment (1961). Citizens of the District of Columbia were granted the appropriate rights of voting in national elections for President and Vice-President of the U.S. It permits District citizens to elect Presidential electors who are "in addition to those appointed by the States" to the number it would be "entitled if it were a State, but in no event more than the least populous State. . . ."

Before the adoption of the Amendment, the citizens of the District had all of the obligations of citizens, including the payment of federal taxes, but they could not vote in national elections because the Constitution restricted that privilege to citizens who resided in states.

Twenty-fourth Amendment (1964). The Amendment prohibited the denial of the right to vote because of "failure to pay any poll tax or other tax."

Ratification marked the culmination of Congress' efforts to effect elimination of the poll tax as a qualification for voting in federal elections. The Amendment was necessary because Congress did not have the power to establish or alter qualifications for voting for electors for President and Vice-President (Art. II, Sec. 1, Par. 2).

Twenty-fifth Amendment (1967). Presidential succession is established by two major provisions. The first empowers the President, whenever there is a vacancy in the office of Vice-President, to nominate a candidate for the position who would take office when confirmed by a majority vote of both houses of Congress.

The second provision sets up a mechanism by which the Vice-President could become Acting President when the President was disabled. There are two parts to this provision. If the President himself concluded that he was unable to perform the duties of office, he could so advise the President *pro tempore* of the Senate and the Speaker of the House in writing. The Vice-President would then take over as Acting President. This arrangement would prevail until the President advised the congressional officers that he was able to resume his Presidential functions.

If the President were disabled but could not, or did not, take the initiative in transferring his duties to the Vice-President, the Vice-President, acting in concert with a majority of the Cabinet "or of such other body as the Congress may by law provide," could advise the President *pro tempore* and the Speaker that the President was disabled and take over as Acting President.

The President could reclaim the powers of his office by informing the congressional officers that he had overcome his disability. But if the Vice-President and a majority of the Cabinet or of the "other body" did not agree that he had recovered, it would then be up to the Congress to decide the issue by a two-thirds vote of each House.

"**America.**" The national hymn, which begins "My country 'tis of thee," was written by Samuel Francis Smith in 1832. It is sung to the British tune, "God Save the King."

America, discovery of. Long before Leif Ericsson, the Norseman, is said to have reached North America in about the year 1000, America was inhabited by Indians. Columbus and his crew on the *Niña, Pinta* and *Santa Maria* landed in the Bahamas, Oct. 12, 1492, at what is now believed to be Watlings Island (named San Salvador by Columbus). Although Columbus made three subsequent trips, 1493–96, 1498–1500 and 1502–04, he continued to believe that he had reached the Orient.

It remained for Americus Vespucius (Amerigo Vespucci), who claimed to have sighted the mainland of South America in 1499, to call it *Mundus Novus* (New World). His name was given to the land mass in 1507 by the German geographer, Martin Waldesemüller.

Magellan in 1519 penetrated this land mass that blocked the westward route to the Orient by sailing through what is now the Strait of Magellan, at the southern tip of South America. Earlier, in 1513, Balboa had crossed the Isthmus of Panama and caught sight of the "South Sea," which he renamed the Pacific. His discovery made it clear that the American continent was truly a New World and not part of Asia.

Other explorers of America include Cabot, an Italian sailing for Henry VII of England in 1497, who stumbled on what later became Newfoundland and New England. This gave England a claim to large areas of the New World.

Cabral, sailing for Portugal, landed in Brazil in 1500, after being blown off course in a voyage around Africa. Ponce de León in 1513 sailed along the coast of Florida and claimed it for Spain. Cortéz landed on the coast of Mexico in 1519. Pizarro, another Spaniard, led an expedition into the Inca Empire of Peru (1531–35), seizing immense treasures of gold and silver.

De Soto explored the southeastern part of what is now the U.S. (1539–42) and discovered the Mississippi River, the "Father of Waters." Coronado set out northward from Mexico (1540) to find the Seven Cities of Cibola, reputed in fable to have streets paved with gold. He explored what was to become the U.S. southwest. These explorations extended Spain's claims in North America.

French claims to a share of North America were laid by Verrazano, an Italian who sailed along the coast (1524) in the hope of finding a water route to Asia. Cartier, beginning in 1534, explored the Gulf of St. Lawrence and sought to establish a colony on a site later to become Quebec.

In a mere 50 years between 1492 and 1542 the outlines of America began to take shape on maps in which territories were staked out by Spain, Portugal, England and France.

America First Committee. As the U.S. veered toward war in 1940, isolationists organized themselves to oppose American involvement in any way in the war in Europe. The Committee dissolved soon after U.S. entry into World War II.

American Association for the Advancement of Science. Founded in 1848 with William C. Redfield as president, it embraced all science in its scope. The charter of the Association expressed a determination to "advance science in the New World" in every possible way. Meeting annually or semiannually in different American cities, it not only brought scientists together for discussion of papers in particular fields but stimulated investigation and cooperation. By 1954 the original 471 members had increased to over a thousand. The Association developed as a joint endeavor of American and Canadian scientists.

American Automobile Association (AAA). Organized in 1902 to aid in the "development and introduction of the automobile," the AAA has expanded to include hundreds of motor clubs with branches all over the U.S. and in many other parts of the world. Through its affiliates it furnishes road service, travel information and travel service including air and ship connections. In addition, many branches are active in legislative halls seeking to advance the interests of motorists.

American Bible Society. Over a half billion copies of the Scriptures have been distributed by this organization, which was founded in 1816 in New York City. The distribution is worldwide and the texts are translated into many languages. Funds are raised by contributions from churches, individual gifts and membership dues in local societies. The Society's monthly magazine is the *Record.*

American Colonization Society (1817–1912). The chief purpose of the Society was to purchase the freedom of slaves and to colonize them in Liberia. After the abolition of slavery in 1865, the Society continued to aid the free Negroes of Liberia.

American Commonwealth, The (1888). James Bryce, the British diplomat and historian, in a classic work on American government made a contribution to understanding American government and politics greater than that produced by any American. It quickly became a standard text for government courses and started the serious study of American political parties. The work treats public opinion, weaknesses and strengths of democracy, social institutions, courts, railroads, Wall Street, the position of women and some aspects of social life in America.

24

American dream, the. America's unique gift to mankind has been the dream of a land in which life should be fuller for every man. It is a dream that has attracted tens of millions to the U.S. It has been more than a dream of better living. It has been a dream of being able to attain maximum growth as an individual, unrestrained by handicaps which had arisen in older nations where the lines between social classes had become fixed. The historian James Truslow Adams in *The Epic of America* (1931) wrote: "It is a difficult dream for the European upper classes to interpret adequately, and too many of us ourselves have grown weary and mistrustful of it. It is not a dream of motor cars and high wages merely, but a dream of a social order in which each man and each woman shall be able to attain the fullest stature of which they are innately capable, and be recognized by others for what they are, regardless of the fortuitous circumstances of birth or position. . . . And that dream has been realized more fully in actual life here than anywhere else, though very imperfectly even among ourselves."

American Federation of Labor (AFL). The Federation, launched in 1881 and reorganized in 1886, concentrated on skilled workers who were organized into local craft or trade unions. The locals within each industry were formed into a national union ("international"

if Canadian locals were included). The national and international union in turn joined in the AFL, which was supported by a per capita tax levied on local union members.

The main driving force behind the AFL was Samuel Gompers, first president of the organization, who held office, except for a single year, from 1886 until his death in 1924. Gompers made "straight" trade unionism his life work. He refused to waste his time and energy promoting such causes as currency reform, land settlement and the setting up of cooperative enterprises. His one concern was to organize skilled workers into craft unions, to bargain collectively with employers in order to win higher wages, shorter hours and better working conditions.

The AFL refrained from supporting any single political party. It acted upon the principle that labor should "reward its friends and punish its enemies" regardless of political party.

In 1935 a split in the AFL led to the formation of the Congress of Industrial Organizations. The split was repaired in 1955 when the AFL–CIO was formed.

American Federation of Labor and Congress of Industrial Organizations (AFL–CIO). The merger of the AFL and CIO took place on Dec. 5, 1955, after a 20-year schism in organized labor. George Meany, president of the AFL, became president of the new organization. Walter Reuther, CIO president, was chosen to be vice-president and to head the industrial union department of the unified labor federation.

Labor leaders hoped that the merger would end "raiding" and other forms of hostility between rival unions and would lead to greater effectiveness in organizing workers and in gaining labor's objectives. During the early years of the merger, the problem of internal disputes threatened to wreck the Federation. Eleven mergers of national and international unions took place in the decade after 1955. Such consolidation of competing organizations is encouraged by the AFL–CIO.

The AFL–CIO, when it was set up, included 140 national and international unions, comprising about 60,000 locals. In addition, there were 844 locals directly affiliated with the AFL–CIO. By 1966 this number had been reduced to 255. The international unions gained through the transfer process encouraged by the AFL–CIO.

The national unions and their major locals continue to be the real center of power in the American labor movement. It is the nationals and their smaller bodies which carry on the bargaining with employers, enter into contracts and do all the day-to-day tasks of providing services to millions of members. The central officials of the AFL–CIO make recommendations, give help and offer criticisms. They cannot issue orders.

The central organization of the AFL–CIO in Washington, representing 15 million workers and their families, speaks with a powerful voice regarding policies of national interest. Its Committee on Political Action (COPE) is active in the legislative field and in the 1950's and 1960's was active in the medicare and pension plans, aid to education, the war on poverty, housing, civil rights and other programs.

In 1967 Reuther, president of the 1,300,000-member United Automobile Workers (UAW), resigned as a vice-president of the AFL–CIO in a widening rift within the ranks of organized labor.

American Historical Association. Founded by college and university teachers of history in 1884 in Saratoga, N.Y., and incorporated by Congress in 1889, the Association helps to place scholars in teaching positions, encourages scholarly contributions and has sought to raise the level of instruction in the secondary schools through pamphlets published by its Service Center for Teachers of History.

American Labor party. The ALP was formed in New York State in 1936 by labor leaders of the Committee for Industrial Organization, soon to be ousted from the AFL. Sponsorship of the party by the CIO was part of its campaign for reelecting

Pres. Roosevelt and supporting candidates sympathetic to social legislation.

An internal struggle commencing in 1939 between a pro-Soviet faction and anti-Communists led to a split and the formation of the rival Liberal party in 1942. The ALP failed to poll 50,000 votes in the New York election of 1954 and went off the ballot and out of existence in 1956.

American Legion. In 1919 Congress chartered a national association of war veterans. Subsequent revisions of the charter opened the organization to membership by veterans of World War II and the Korean War making it the largest organization of war veterans with a membership of over 2,350,-000.

Over the years the Legion, always active in gaining benefits for veterans, was a strong force in establishing the U.S. Veterans Bureau in 1922 (now the Veterans Administration) and the Servicemen's Readjustment Act of 1944 (GI Bill).

The Legion has an active child care program and sponsors many patriotic activities, including oratorical contests in schools. It maintains a lobby in Washington and in many state legislatures. It can invariably be counted on for leadership and support of laws curbing Communists and "subversive" activity.

American Liberty League. Founded in 1934, its members equated the New Deal with radicalism and opposed most New Deal measures as a threat to property rights. The organization included conservative Democrats who were regarded by New Dealers as reactionaries.

American Medical Association. The AMA was founded in 1847 at a Philadelphia convention of representatives of national medical societies and schools. Generally opposed to group medical practice, it was found guilty by the U.S. Supreme Court, in 1943, of violating antitrust laws on the grounds of preventing activities of cooperative health groups. In 1966 the AMA, with 206,000 members, or more than 70% of all American physicians, went on record in favor of direct billing of the patient under the Medicare program of the Social Security Administration.

American Philosophical Society. Under the leadership of Benjamin Franklin, a number of American scholars organized, in 1743, a society to promote scientific research and to encourage the exchange of information among scientists. The organization now has a worldwide membership limited to 500 and includes the world's leading scientists, scholars and statesmen.

American Protective Association. A secret society was formed in Clinton, Iowa, in 1887, to exploit the bigotry of the rural Middle West and oppose the influence of Roman Catholicism in labor and politics. It split up over support of William McKinley in the 1896 free silver campaign. From that time on its decline was rapid and the organization was defunct by 1911.

American Revolution. The rebellion of the Thirteen Colonies against rule by King George III of England culminated in the establishment and worldwide recognition of the United States of America.

The seeds of the Revolution were planted long before the outbreak of fighting at Lexington in 1775. They sprouted during the long period of "salutary neglect" when English Navigation Laws were indifferently enforced and the colonies developed self-government.

After 1763 the seeds began to germinate, warmed by the new British policy of raising revenue in the colonies to support a standing army. Its aim was to protect the colonies from foreign or Indian attacks and at the same time preserve the expanded empire of Britain. Parliament believed that support of the army should come, at least in part, from the colonies. To this end, the Sugar Act (1764), Stamp Act (1765), Townshend Acts (1767) and other measures were passed by Parliament. Colonial resistance and organization were sparked by the popular cry, "Taxation without representation is tyranny"; but concern about electing representatives to the House of Commons did not go very deep. The real fear was the certainty that England had embarked upon a policy of firm control over colonial economic and political life.

When colonial resistance was met by Parliament's Coercive Acts (1774), the colonies sent representatives to the First Continental Congress. Colonial hopes were still couched in requests to the King for redress of grievances. This was not forthcoming. What did come forth were British regulars at Lexington (Apr. 1775). The Second Continental Congress, which assembled in May 1775, quickly recognized that the subject of independence could no longer be avoided. Attack shifted from Parliament to the King and a Continental army was authorized (June 1775). The Declaration of Independence (July 4, 1776) followed.

The Congress assumed the powers of a national government. While the Revolutionary War was under way, it drafted the Articles of Confederation adopted by the required number of states in 1777. The new, shaky government, threatened by military reverses and feeble financing, was bolstered by the French decision in 1778 to weaken an old enemy by coming to the aid of the embattled American states. By the Treaty of Paris (1783), the independence of the United States was recognized by England.

American system. Henry Clay gave this name to the program

28

he urged in support of the Tariff of 1824. It included a protective tariff to help develop American industry, federal aid for internal improvements such as roads and canals and a centralized banking system. The internal improvements were to be financed in part by revenue from the tariff and sale of public lands. They were to link the industrial East and agricultural West and place the nation on a solid "basis of common interest."

American Telephone and Telegraph Company. Alexander Graham Bell's telephone patent in 1876 led to a quickening of activity in the new field. By 1880 there were 148 telephone companies. Western Union, which had at first turned down Bell's invention as an "electrical toy," entered the field with the American Speaking Telephone Co. It withdrew in 1879, in an out-of-court settlement, when the Bell Co. sued for patent infringement.

The Bell Co., led by Theodore N. Vail, bought up many competitors' franchises and formed the American Telephone and Telegraph Co., a holding company incorporated in New York in 1885. Vail, as general manager, and later as president of the new company, organized the growing telephone system into effective companies. His major purpose in forming A. T. & T. was to establish a long-distance telephone system, begun in 1884, by connecting many operating companies. When Bell patents expired in 1893 and 1894, conditions in the industry again became confused and Vail was active in bringing about a second unification of the industry.

A. T. & T. went on to become the world's greatest public utility enterprise and now operates 76 million telephones and numerous auxiliary services. The instruments and apparatus are manufactured by the Western Electric Co., owned by A. T. & T.

American Tobacco Co. v. U.S. (1911). The U.S. Supreme Court held that the company had sought to restrain trade in violation of the Sherman Antitrust Act. Proceedings against the tobacco trust had been initiated during Theodore Roosevelt's administration and were concluded when Pres. Taft was in office.

Both in this case and in *Standard Oil Co. of New Jersey et al. v. U.S.* (1911), the Court laid down the so-called "rule of reason."

American Veterans Committee (AVC). Dissatisfied with the American Legion's role in seeking special benefits for veterans, a number of ex-soldiers of World War II formed a new veterans' organization in 1943. It holds the position that its members are citizens first and veterans second. It has favored desegregation in the armed forces and support of the United Nations. Veterans of the

Korean War are included in the organization.

American Veterans of World War II and Korea (AMVETS). Although it has not been able to make much of a dent in the strength of the American Legion, it is the second largest veterans' organization with a membership of about 100,000. It was founded in 1944.

Amherst College. Chartered in Amherst, Mass., in 1825, classes actually began in 1821 under the Rev. Zephaniah Swift Moore, a Congregational clergyman, who became its first president.

A small, independent, nonsectarian men's college of the liberal arts and sciences, it has a current enrollment of about 1,000. The college emphasizes a broad general education.

Amistad **Case.** A cargo of 54 slaves left Cuba in 1839 aboard the Spanish schooner *Amistad*. Under the leadership of an African headman, Cinqué, they murdered the captain and three crewmen. Although ordered to return to Africa, the remaining crewmen were able to bring the vessel into Long Island waters where it was boarded by a U.S. Navy officer.

The Negroes were imprisoned in New London, Conn., and charged with piracy. Abolitionists entered the case, which reached the U.S. Supreme Court in 1841. The Negroes were freed since, it was held, they had been illegally kidnapped. They were returned to Africa.

Amnesty Act (1872). The first proclamation of amnesty was issued by Pres. Lincoln, Dec. 8, 1863. Congress had authorized the President to offer full pardon to all persons, except the most prominent Confederate leaders, who would swear an oath of allegiance to the U.S. It was not until 1872, however, that Congress passed a law making almost all former Confederates once more eligible to hold office in the federal or state governments. This Act in effect cancelled a clause in the 14th Amendment that had prevented many southerners from holding office.

Anaconda Copper. The company was first organized for silver mining in 1881. Mining operations in Butte, Mont., however, made it clear that copper was to be the major mineral extracted from the mines. The company then underwent a number of name changes. Since 1955 it has been the Anaconda Company, the world's leading copper producer and refiner.

"anaconda" plan. Early in the Civil War, Gen. Winfield Scott offered a military plan for conquering the Confederacy. It called for the capture of Richmond, the Confederate capital, the blockade of southern ports and control of the Mississippi and Tennessee rivers. The army in the East was to be joined by the Union army in the West after it cut the Confederacy to pieces.

The plan's name is derived from that of the snake that crushes its victims to death.

Ananias Club. Members included all those who were called liars by Pres. Theodore Roosevelt (1901–09) during some of the controversies which marked his exciting administration.

anarchism. Anarchists believe that the state is an intrinsic evil. They want governments to be replaced by free associations of groups and are opposed to private ownership of property. In the U.S. anarchists belonged to the same organizations as socialists until 1883, although socialists advocate a very powerful, completely democratic government which would own the more important means of production.

Factions among anarchists disagree as to how best to bring the state to an end. Some hold that it will disappear through evolution; others favor violence as a means of hastening the state's disappearance.

Josiah Warren, an early 19th-century Boston-born social reformer, is regarded as the founder of philosophical anarchism in the U.S. He influenced Benjamin R. Tucker who became an authority on the works of P. J. Proudhon, the French journalist and politician who gave anarchism its name in 1840. Tucker's publication *Liberty* (Boston, 1891–92; New York, 1892–1908) at first publicized the views of European anarchists in general; later, it reflected the views of Max Stirner (pseudonym for Kaspar Schmidt), the 19th-century German philosopher who advocated violence in ending the state.

Johann Most, a German who came to the U.S. in 1882, became a leading anarchist. He headed a small coterie of foreign-born revolutionists, organized in the Black International, who sought unsuccessfully to infiltrate the American labor movement in the 1880's.

In 1886 anarchists were charged with being implicated in the Haymarket Square bomb explosion. Eight were convicted of the crime although there was no evidence that any of them had thrown the bomb.

Anarchists startled the nation again when Leon Czolgosz, who believed in "propaganda by deed," shot Pres. McKinley, Sept. 6, 1901. A decade earlier, Alexander Berkman, an anarchist, made an unsuccessful attempt on the life of Henry Clay Frick, steel industrialist, who was resisting the Homestead strikers.

In 1917 Emma Goldman, publisher of the anarchist magazine, *Mother Earth*, and Berkman who edited it after a 13-year prison term, were found guilty of interfering with conscription. They were deported to Russia in 1919.

Anderson, Carl David (1905–   ). Physicist. Born in New

York City, he was awarded a Nobel Prize (1936), shared with Victor Franz Hess, for discovery of the positron (positively charged electron) in cosmic radiation. He has been a faculty member at the California Institute of Technology since 1928.

Anderson, Sherwood (1876–1941). Novelist. Born in Camden, O., he later became a newspaper editor in Marion, Va. His reputation as a writer was established with the stories told in *Winesburg, Ohio* (1919). Its short sketches contain keen portraits of people in a small midwestern town. Anderson felt that it was the Industrial Revolution that had depressed the individual and caused the unpredictable behavior that marked so many of his characters. His realism influenced such younger writers of his period as Ernest Hemingway, Thomas Wolfe and William Faulkner.

Anderson v. Dunn **(1821).** The U.S. Supreme Court held that the House of Representatives had the power to punish by arrest and imprisonment a person other than a member for contempt of its authority. In this case an attempt had been made to bribe one of its members.

Andersonville. The Confederate military prison (1864–65) achieved notoriety because of the mistreatment of captured Union soldiers, who were poorly fed and crowded within a stockade where sanitation and lack of medical facilities were appalling. The desperate circumstances of the South during the closing stages of the Civil War help to explain the 13,000 Union dead in the National Cemetery at Andersonville, located about 50 miles southwest of Macon, Ga.

The prison commander, Capt. Henry Wirz, was tried by a military commission after the war and hanged on Nov. 10, 1865. Some researchers have suggested that Wirz was a scapegoat and that prison conditions were largely beyond his control.

Annapolis Convention (1786). Difficulties over commercial relations caused the Virginia legislature to invite the 13 states to send delegates to a convention at Annapolis, Md. Only five of the states sent representatives. They did not undertake full scale deliberations, but instructed Alexander Hamilton of New York to issue a call for a larger meeting at Philadelphia.

The Continental Congress itself affirmed this action by asking the states to send delegates to Philadelphia "for the sole and express purpose of revising the Articles of Confederation." Delegates were sent to what became the Constitutional Convention of 1787.

Antarctica Treaty (1959). The U.S. and 11 other nations, including the USSR, agreed on limiting the use of Antarctica to scientific activities. Military activities are forbidden and nuclear explosions banned. It is the first treaty to guarantee that its terms are not violated; unlimited inspection rights are provided.

Anthony, Susan Brownell (1820–1906). Social reformer. Born in Adams, Mass., she was an active temperance advocate, abolitionist and proponent of Negro suffrage. She is best remembered for her leadership of the successful struggle to attain suffrage for women.

Anthracite Coal Strike (1902). The strike was called by the United Mine Workers of America under the presidency of John Mitchell in protest against low wages, frequent layoffs, excessive accidents and the 10-hour day in the anthracite mines of Pennsylvania.

George F. Baer, spokesman for the operators, refused to meet with the union or accept arbitration. He declared in a statement that helped to put the public on the union side that "God in His infinite wisdom" had given control of the mine properties to the owners who would "protect and care for" the workers.

As the coal shortage began to hurt the public, Pres. Theodore Roosevelt stepped in. He let J. P. Morgan, the financier, know that he planned to seize the mines and operate them in receivership unless the operators agreed to arbitration. This was decisive. The miners, who had been striking since May,

went back to the mines in October.

In Mar. 1903, the President's commission granted a 10% wage increase, reduced the working day to eight and nine hours for different classes of workers and set up a special board to settle disputes arising during the three years in which the award was to remain in force. The operators were not required to recognize the union, but the gains greatly strengthened the United Mine Workers.

Antietam, battle of (Sept. 17, 1862). In one of the bloodiest battles of the Civil War, also known as Sharpsburg, the Confederates under Gen. Lee were forced back across the Potomac River. His attempted invasion of Maryland had been halted at Antietam Creek by Union armies under Gen. McClellan.

Anti-Federalists. Opponents of the Constitution during the struggle over ratification argued that the Constitution would ultimately bring an end to the states, that an aristocracy would develop with little sympathy for the "low-born" and that basic personal rights were not protected by the proposed law.

After adoption of the Constitution during Washington's first administration (1789–93), there was a growth of political parties. The Anti-Federalist party took shape under the leadership of Thomas Jefferson and James Madison. It favored a strict construction of the Constitution, opposed a national bank and favored encouragement of agriculture rather than manufacture.

The Anti-Federalists took the name "Republican" (not to be confused with the Republican party of today that was founded in 1854) to suggest that they were defending self-government against the aristocratic tendencies of the Federalist party. In general, small farmers, frontiersmen, small shopkeepers and city laborers were Republicans. The Republicans were sympathetic to the French Revolution and generally critical of England.

The opposition smeared Jefferson's Republican party by calling it the "Democratic–Republican" party. The term "democratic" soon ceased to be one of opprobrium and the party adopted the hyphenated title. By the time Jackson became President in 1829, the party name was shortened to Democratic party. Today's Democratic party claims to have its origins in this early party in the U.S.

Anti-Masonic party. The nation's first third party set an example for the major parties in 1831 by holding a national convention to choose democratically its candidate for President. William Wirt of Maryland was nominated. Wirt, a distinguished lawyer, hoped to gain the support of the National Republicans, but they disappointed him by nominating Henry Clay. Wirt received only seven electoral votes in the election of 1832.

In 1836 the party nominated William H. Harrison, sharing him with the newly organized Whigs. After the election, won by the Democrat Van Buren, the Anti-Masons joined the Whigs. In 1840 Harrison was again nominated and gained the Presidency.

On the state level an Anti-Masonic party was formed and elected 15 members to the New York State Assembly in 1827. Pennsylvania and Vermont elected Anti-Masonic governors.

Anti-Masonry was a reaction against the secrecy of the fraternal order of Masons. A critic of the Masons in western New York, William Morgan, disappeared mysteriously in 1826 and was never found. A body washed ashore from Lake Ontario was uncertainly identified as Morgan's.

Antinomian controversy. Antinomianism is a theological idea holding that Christians achieve grace through faith and have no need to regard the moral law, especially as laid down in the Old Testament.

According to the standard view of the Covenant of Grace held by the Puritan clergy in the Massachusetts Bay colony, true salvation could be achieved by faith alone, a fundamental Protestant tenet. However, the test of true conversion demanded visible signs of morality along with positive acceptance of the sovereignty of an all-wise and all-powerful God.

This view was challenged by Anne Hutchinson, who held that it placed too much emphasis on "works" and, in effect, denied salvation by faith alone. Relatively late in the controversy, which shook the Bay colony, she held that religious persons could receive revelations and inspiration directly from God.

Her views were opposed by ministers who believed that the clergy alone were the interpreters of the Scriptures and that Antinomianism challenged their authority and invited immorality. She was accused of "Antinomianism" by a synod of ministers, found guilty of errors and banished from the Bay colony (1638).

Antirent War (1839–46). Farmers in New York protested violently against the old patroonships, a system of landholding that had made possible the buildup of huge estates under Dutch and English rule. Resentment against great landowners who collected produce from farmers and a share of any land sold, erupted when heirs of Stephen Van Rensselaer tried to collect $400,000 in back rent in the Albany region. The so-called "Helderberg War" was suppressed by Gov. Seward, who called out the militia.

In Delaware County, law enforcement officers were attacked by farmers disguised as Indians. In 1846 the murder of a deputy sheriff caused Gov. Wright to place the county under martial law. The disturbances led to political reform and a more liberal constitution, adopted in 1846. Large estates were gradually broken up as land purchases without restrictions were made by small farmers.

The revolts were portrayed by James Fenimore Cooper in his novels, *Satanstoe* (1845), *The Chainbearer* (1846) and *The Redskins* (1846).

ANZUS Pact (1951). The U.S. signed a treaty with two nations below the equator, Australia and New Zealand, for their mutual defense in Asia. Each country is pledged to come to the other's aid in case of attack.

Apache. The name Apache, meaning "enemy" in Zuñi, was given to Athapascan-speaking Indian tribes in the Southwest (Arizona and New Mexico). By the 1850's various bands had lived on the frontier of European settlement for 200 years and, as masters in the art of raiding, had remained completely independent. Geronimo, one of their leaders, was not captured until 1886.

Apollo Project. One of the U.S. space projects landed explorers on the moon and brought them safely back to earth. The Apollo spacecraft is designed to carry three astronauts. Two astronauts landed on the moon while the third crewman remained with the parent craft which continued to orbit the moon. The two who landed on the moon did so by means of a lunar excursion module (LEM), a space ferry that took them down to the moon to explore its surface near their landing site, took pictures, collected samples and conducted scientific experiments.

LEM then carried the two astronauts from the moon's surface into lunar orbit and rendezvous with the Apollo. After the two astronauts rejoined the other astronaut in the parent craft, they jettisoned the LEM.

The moon landing was accomplished on July 20, 1969, when Neil A. Armstrong, commander of Apollo 11, set foot on the moon's surface, followed by Col. Edwin E. Aldrin, Jr. The third member of the crew, Lt. Col. Michael Collins, orbited the moon in the command ship which Armstrong and Aldrin rejoined for their return to earth after a one-day stay on the moon.

Appalachia Aid (1965). In an effort to eliminate pockets of poverty in an 11-state area in the Appalachian Mountains, Pres. Johnson signed into law a $1.1 billion aid program. The major thrust of the legislation was to open the region by building new highways as part of a long-term redevelopment program. Grants-in-aid for states willing to provide matching funds were also provided to make possible construction of colleges, vocational schools, sewage-treatment plants and airports.

Appeals, U.S. Courts of. Intermediate appellate courts were created by Congress in 1891 to relieve the Supreme Court of the task of considering all appeals in cases originally decided by the federal trial courts. Courts of Appeals are also empowered to enforce orders of many federal administrative bodies, such as the Securities and Exchange Commission and the National Labor Relations Board. The decisions of the Courts of Appeals may be reviewed by the Supreme Court.

The U.S. is divided into 11 judicial circuits, one of which is the District of Columbia. There is a U.S. Court of Appeals in each circuit and each of the 50 states and territories is assigned to one of the circuits. At present a court may have three to nine circuit judgeships (78 in all), depending upon the amount of work in the circuit.

Appomattox Courthouse. It was at the McClean farmhouse in this village, about 100 miles west of Richmond, Va., that Gen. Lee surrendered the armies of Virginia to Gen. Grant, Apr. 9, 1865.

In accordance with Lincoln's wishes, Grant offered generous terms of surrender. Any Confederate soldier who could establish his claim to a horse or a mule could ride it home and officers could retain their sidearms. About a month later, other Confederate army commanders surrendered and the Civil War was over.

Arabic incident (Aug. 19, 1915). A German submarine torpedoed a British White Star liner, named the *Arabic*, which went down with two Americans aboard. U.S. public opinion was so inflamed that the German ambassador in Washington, Count Von Bernstorff, gave the following reassuring statement to the State Department: "Liners will not be sunk by our submarines without warning and without safety of the lives of noncombatants, provided that the liners do not try to escape or offer resistance."

Arapaho. An Algonquian people, these plains Indians, who ranged from Wyoming to Arkansas, occasionally menaced the Santa Fe trade, but generally were friendly to the whites. The southern Arapaho were removed to Oklahoma in 1867 where they became American citizens in 1892. Some of the surviving members of these Indians live on the Shoshone reservation in Wyoming.

Arbella. John Winthrop, Puritan leader, sailed in 1630 from England to Salem, Mass., on the flagship by that name.

Arbor Day. A tree-planting festival was inaugurated in 1872 in Nebraska through the efforts of Julius Sterling Morton, later Sec. of Agriculture. In 1885 Apr. 22 was officially designated as Arbor Day by the state legislature. Other states followed suit, but observe the festival on different days.

Archangel intervention. Some 5,000 American troops were sent, with Pres. Wilson's approval, to the Russian port of Archangel, on the White Sea, to strengthen the Allied support of the White Russians against the Bolsheviks. They suffered 500 casualties between Sept. 1918 and May 1919.

Archives, National. National documents and records are appraised by a federal agency which disposes of them or, if they are of permanent value, transfers them to the Archives building. The agency arranges the records, publishes guides to their use and exhibits those of historic significance. It reproduces important research materials on microfilm for use throughout the country.

Area Redevelopment Act (1961). Under the ARA Congress authorized federal grants for training or retraining unemployed or underemployed workers in specific areas of the country.

Ariel I. Launched on Apr. 26, 1962, by the U.S. in cooperation with Great Britain, the world's first international satellite provided information on the variation of cosmic rays.

Arizona. The "Grand Canyon State," a Mountain group state, was first settled by aboriginal tribes of advanced culture; the ruins of buildings, pueblos and irrigation canals provide evidence. In the 16th century it was explored by the Spanish who found numerous Indian tribes there such as the Apache, Pima, Mohave, Yuma, Papago, Hopi and Navaho. Today Arizona has more Indians on reservations than any other state.

Arizona (meaning "small springs," perhaps from Pima Indian) was included in the territory of New Mexico, acquired from Mexico by the Treaty of Guadalupe-Hidalgo (1848) at the close of the Mexican War. The southern part, the Gadsden Purchase, was bought from Mexico in 1853.

Arizona became a territory in 1863, after Texan Confederate troops were driven out. It was admitted to the Union as the 48th State on Feb. 14, 1912. Phoenix is the state's capital.

Arizona leads the country in copper production. Manufacturing is its biggest industry, followed by mining and agriculture. The low humidity has made the state popular as a health resort.

Arkansas. The "Land of Opportunity," in the West South Central group, was discovered by De Soto in 1541 and by the French explorers Marquette and Jolliet in 1673. After changing hands several times between France and Spain, the territory passed to the U.S. as part of the Louisiana Purchase (1803). Arkansas (a Sioux Indian name for south wind people) was admitted to the Union as the 25th State, June 15, 1836. At the commencement of the Civil War a state convention

(Mar. 4, 1861) decided not to secede, but Lincoln's call for troops led to reconsideration and Arkansas became a Confederate state on May 6, 1861. Although a state convention in 1864 abolished slavery and repudiated secession, Arkansas was not readmitted to the Union until 1868. Its capital is Little Rock.

Cotton ranks first in value in Arkansas. The state supplies 96% of the nation's high grade domestic bauxite ore and has the only diamond field in the U.S.

"Arkansaw Traveler." Col. Sanford Faulkner was reputed to be the first "Traveler." In moving about in Arkansas during the campaign of 1840, Col. "Sandy" asked directions of a squatter who happened to be playing a fiddle. The ensuing banter led to the Colonel's taking the fiddle and finishing the tune.

The "Arkansaw Traveler" has become part of American folklore. It is both the name of the tune and the story that goes with it. The spirit of the exchange between the "Traveler" who asks foolish questions and the squatter is suggested in this repartee: "Old man, what makes your corn so yellow?" asks the "Traveler." "You fool, you, I planted *yellow* corn," the squatter retorts.

Arlington National Cemetery. War dead of every war in which the U.S. has participated since the Revolution lie in this cemetery in the Virginia hills, directly across the Potomac from Washington, D.C.

The cemetery was established in 1864. It is the site of the Tomb of the Unknown Soldier, which holds the body of an unknown American soldier brought from France during World War I. On Memorial Day 1958, two other unknown soldiers were placed beneath the tomb, one killed in World War II and the other in the Korean War. Pres. John F. Kennedy was buried in the cemetery in 1963.

The land was occupied by Union troops during the Civil War because of its strategic location for the defense of the capital.

Arminianism. Derived from the teachings of the 16th-century Dutch theologian, Jacobus Arminius, the doctrine maintained that man could achieve salvation by faith in God and did not require the intervention of ministers.

For a time in the 1630's, those who subscribed to the doctrine posed a threat to the church-directed Massachusetts Bay community. The "Arminian" heresy was denounced, and those held guilty of believing in it were banished from the colony.

The Antinomian doctrine, which Anne Hutchinson was accused of propagating, was derived from the views of Arminius, who gave man considerable responsibility in determining his own conversion.

Armistice (Nov. 11, 1918). A truce during World War I, preliminary to the peace treaty, was requested by Germany and granted by the Allies. The terms were based on Wilson's Fourteen Points, and stipulated that the freedom of the seas was not to be discussed and Germany would be expected to pay reparations for war damages.

Under the terms, Germany evacuated France, Alsace-Lorraine, Belgium and Luxembourg, the left bank of the Rhine and a buffer zone on the right bank. It also surrendered its arms and all submarines, making it impossible to continue the war. In addition, Germany renounced the treaties of Bucharest and Brest-Litovsk, with Rumania and Russia, respectively.

The Armistice terms were signed by a German delegation, Marshal Foch of France and other Allied officers in a railroad car in the Forest of Compiègne where Hitler was to make the French agree to a humiliating capitulation another war later.

Arms Control and Disarmament Agency, U.S. Established by Congress in 1961, the federal agency is responsible for arms control research and the formulation of disarmament policy. In its advisory capacity to the Sec. of State and the President, it prepares our representatives for U.S. participation in international negotiation for arms control and coordinates public education concerning disarmament.

A major share of the Agency's efforts has gone into the nuclear test ban and disarmament discussions both at the United Nations and at Geneva.

Armstrong, Edwin Howard (1890–1954). Electrical engineer. He was born in New York City. He was engaged in research with Michael Pupin and succeeded him as professor of electrical engineering at Columbia University (1934). The "Father of FM," he developed frequency modulation system of radio, providing freedom from interference and greater range in tone. He made important contributions to military communications during World War II.

Army, Confederate (1861–65). The army of the South during the Civil War was recruited by a draft law and voluntary enlistment. It reached a peak of about 500,000 in 1864 and declined to 175,000 in the final days of the war.

The numerical inferiority of the Confederate army was offset somewhat by the short "interior" lines it defended and by the lack of need to divert men to hold subjugated territory. The Confederate army had a further advantage in that many recruits had been trained from childhood to ride and use firearms.

However, the length of the war and the overwhelming numerical and industrial superiority of the North was too much for the Confederate army. Its superior officer material, the leadership of Generals Robert E. Lee and Joseph E. Johnston and the generally high morale which prevailed except toward the end, were not enough to prevent surrender in Apr.–May, 1865.

Army, Department of the. The Department of War was established by Congress as an executive department in 1789. The Secretary of War was established as its head and his powers were those entrusted to him by the President. Under the National Security Act of 1947, creating the National Military Establishment, the Department of War was designated the Department of the Army and the title of its Secretary became Secretary of the Army. The Department of the Air Force was established as a separate department. Both departments are under the Secretary of Defense.

The Department of the Army trains and equips land forces for the conduct of combat operations in accordance with plans for national security. Command of the Army is exercised by the President through the Secretary of Defense and the Secretary of the Army.

Army, Union (1861–65). At the time of the firing on Fort Sumter, the army of the North could count on some 16,000 men and officers, including those who left to serve in the Confederate Army. During the final two years of the Civil War, however, the Union army was to reach and hold to a peak of 1,000,000.

Recruitment was a continuous problem after the initial enthusiasm for crushing the "secesh." The major burden of meeting Pres. Lincoln's quota calls fell on the governors of the states. They were aided by bounties (cash) paid to volunteers who would otherwise have faced the draft authorized by Congress.

Although the Union army outnumbered the Confederate by two to one, it was handicapped by the lack of decisive leadership. The parade of Lincoln's generals included Mc-Dowell, McClellan, Burnside, Halleck, Hooker and Meade, before halting at Ulysses S. Grant.

Grant's record in the western theater earned him appointment as the Supreme Commanding General of the Union army, Mar. 10, 1864. He immediately launched his "grand movement" which ended in the surrender of the South, Apr.–May 1865.

Army of the Potomac (1861–65). Following the defeat of Union forces at the first battle of Bull Run, the Army of the Potomac (about 125,000 at maximum strength) was organized and trained by Gen. George B. McClellan. Its immediate purpose was to protect Washington, D.C. by guarding against a Confederate invasion across the Potomac. Major offensive actions in which it participated included the un-successful Peninsular Campaign in which McClellan sought to capture Richmond, Va., the capital of the Confederate States.

Arnold, Benedict (1741–1801). Army officer. Born in Norwich, Conn., his name is synonymous with "traitor." During the early years of the Revolutionary War, he distinguished himself in the capture of Fort Ticonderoga (1775), a brave though unsuccessful attack on Quebec (1775), and the defeat of Burgoyne at Saratoga (1777). Disaffection, stemming in part from disappointment over promotion and the need for money to maintain his social position, led to his plan for turning over West Point, a key post on the Hudson River, N.Y., to the British. The plan was exposed by the capture of the British spy, Major John André (1780). During the remaining years of the war, Arnold led British raids in Virginia and Connecticut. He died in London impoverished and disgraced.

Arnold's treason. Plans for the betrayal of strategic West Point on the Hudson were given to Major John André, a British officer, by Brig. Gen. Benedict Arnold on Sept. 21, 1780. When the British ship (*Vulture*) which carried André was forced downstream, he sought to disguise himself and escape to the British lines. He was captured, turned over to the American army and hanged as a spy, Oct. 2, 1780.

Arnold escaped to the British and served with them in raids in Virginia (1780) and Connecticut (1781). After the war, he lived in England where he died in disgrace and poverty (1801).

Aroostook "War" (1839). A bloodless "war" between Maine and Canada arose over the uncertain boundary that had persisted since the Treaty of Paris (1783). When Canadian lumberjacks began operations to build a road along the Aroostook River, American lumberjacks moved in to stop them.

Maine called out her militia and New Brunswick did likewise. Pres. Van Buren sent Gen. Winfield Scott to the area to arrange a truce. A settlement was reached in the Webster-Ashburton Treaty establishing the present line.

"arsenal of democracy." Early in World War II when the U.S. was not yet involved, Pres. F. D. Roosevelt assumed for the U.S. the responsibility of being the "arsenal of democracy." By the end of the war, in addition to supporting its own huge combat forces, the U.S. had loaned and leased $48.5 billion worth of military equipment to 42 countries engaged in fighting Nazism, fascism and Japanese imperialism.

Art, National Gallery of. A bureau of the Smithsonian Institution, the Gallery was created by Congress in 1937 following Andrew W. Mellon's gift to the nation of his important collection of works of art and a monumental gallery building in Washington, D.C. The Gallery is charged with the responsibility of assembling and maintaining a national collection of paintings, sculpture and the graphic arts, representative of the best in the artistic heritage of America and Europe.

Arthur, Chester Alan (1830–86). Twenty-first President of the U.S. (1881–85). He was born in Fairfield, Vt., and was graduated from Union College (1848). Vice-President (Mar. 4–Sept. 19, 1881), he succeeded to the Presidency on the death of James A. Garfield. A collector of the port of New York (1871–78), he surprised politicians by his support of civil service reform when President.

Articles of Confederation (1781–89). The framework of the first U.S. government was established by the Continental Congress during the American Revolution. It was submitted to the states in 1777, but was not ratified until 1781.

Each of the 13 states retained its sovereignty under the Articles, but yielded certain powers to Congress, which became the central government of the Union. It was given jurisdiction over foreign affairs, interstate disputes, national defense, coinage, the postal system and Indian affairs. It could borrow and request money from the states. The sentiment of nationalism was strengthened by the provision that guaranteed to citizens moving from one state to another the privilege of citizenship in the new community.

Under the Articles, executive and legislative power was concentrated in Congress. There was no President of the U.S. and no federal judiciary. Reliance was placed on state courts. Congress lacked the power to tax or to regulate interstate commerce.

Each state had one vote in Congress and important decisions required approval by nine of the 13 states. Amendment of the Articles required unanimous agreement of the states.

The Articles held the states together during the formative period which followed the Revolution. Disputes over commerce, abuse by foreign nations, depreciating currency made it increasingly clear that a mere federation of states could not function as a nation.

Although the Constitutional Convention (1787) met to revise the Articles, the need for a new constitution establishing a stronger central government was apparent to the Founding Fathers.

ASCAP. The American Society of Composers, Authors, and Publishers, most often known by its initials, was established Feb. 13, 1914, in New York City. Victor Herbert was its first director.

"As goes Maine, so goes the Union." Since Maine holds state elections in September, the party winning there hopefully regards it as a barometer of political victory in November. The phrase was coined by the Whig party after its first national victory in 1840.

Ashley, William Henry (1778–1838). Fur trader, explorer and congressman. He was born in Powhatan Co., Va., and later settled in Missouri which he represented in Congress (1831–37). With Andrew Henry, he dispatched expeditions up the Missouri in the 1820's. He abandoned the fixed trading method of operation and arranged annual meetings with trappers at any convenient place. He brought supplies to the "Mountain Men," hardy trappers who had mastered the condition of their chosen life in a vast region comprising present-day Nebraska, Colorado, Wyoming and Utah.

Assiento (1713). As an outcome of the War of Spanish Succession (Queen Anne's War in the New World) Great Britain was awarded a contract allowing the South Sea Co. (formed 1711) to import into the Spanish colonies 4,800 Negroes a year for 30 years and to send one trading ship a year to the Spanish colonies.

Spain did not engage in the slave traffic but rather sold to assientists or private contractors the exclusive right to supply her colonies with slaves (the assiento).

43

Associated Press. A number of New York newspapers in 1848 organized an association for the purpose of collecting and transmitting news as inexpensively as possible. The first members of the AP were the New York *Sun, Herald, Tribune, Journal of Commerce, Courier and Inquirer* and *Express.* Contracts for lower telegraph rates were arranged and other newspapers were admitted to the association. The AP is now one of the largest news gathering services in the world.

Astor, John Jacob (1763–1848). Fur trader and financier. Born in Duchy of Baden, Germany, he migrated to the U.S. (1784) and entered the fur trade in New York City. He expanded his fur trading in the Far West and Mississippi Valley and founded Astoria (1811) at the mouth of the Columbia River, as a trading post. He also acquired heavy real estate interests in New York City. He left a fortune of more than $20 million.

Astor Place riot (May 10, 1849). Partisans of the American actor Edwin Forrest gathered outside the Astor Place Opera House in New York City, where the English actor William Charles Macready was playing *Macbeth.* The police were unable to disperse the mob and the state militia was called out. The riot took 22 lives and caused injuries to 36 others.

Atchison, Topeka & Santa Fe Railroad. Chartered in 1859, the railroad was one of the early transcontinental lines that gave the states and territories west of the Mississippi the connections they needed with the older parts of the country.

The line has been expanded into the largest U.S. railroad system in point of mileage— 12,990 miles. Originally, it was intended to connect Atchison and Topeka, Kan. The main line now runs from Chicago via Kansas City to San Francisco, Los Angeles, Dallas, Ft. Worth and Galveston.

Atlanta Constitution. One of the largest daily newspapers in the southeastern states, it was founded in 1868 by W. A. Hemphill. In 1876 Evan P. Howell became its editor and helped build its reputation. Henry W. Grady became managing editor of the paper in 1880. By the time of his death, in 1889, circulation of the weekly edition (made up chiefly of material from the daily) reached 140,000. This was a peak for circulation of a weekly.

In 1966 the daily circulation of the morning edition of the *Atlanta Constitution* was 210,-668; the Sunday *Atlanta Journal Constitution*, a joint publication of the *Atlanta Constitution* and the *Atlanta Journal* (founded in 1883) 523,238.

Atlantic Cable. Telegraphic communication across the Atlantic connecting the U.S. and England was first completed in 1858 in a project undertaken by Cyrus W. Field. It broke down after a few months and the Civil War intervened, causing a suspension in repair operations.

In 1865 the *Great Eastern*, a steamer, had laid 1,200 miles of cable on the floor of the Atlantic, when the cable snapped. In 1866 the cable laying was completed and communications established.

Atlantic Charter (Aug. 14, 1941). Pres. F. D. Roosevelt met with Prime Minister Churchill of England aboard the British battleship *Prince of Wales*, off the coast of Newfoundland. Although the U.S. had not yet entered World War II, the two leaders signed the Atlantic Charter outlining a program for lasting peace. It called for "final destruction of the Nazi tyranny" so "that all men in all lands may live out their lives in freedom from fear and want." Like the Fourteen Points formulated by Pres. Wilson, it called for equal access by all nations to the raw materials of the world, freedom of the seas, "measures which lighten for peace-loving peoples the crushing burden of armaments" and the "establishment of a wider and permanent system of general security." This last was a reference to the organization of the United Nations which took place four years later at San Francisco.

Atlantic Coast Line Railroad. The road was first chartered in Virginia, 1836, and took its present name in 1900. ACL operates about 5,000 miles of rail extending from Tampa and other Florida points to Norfolk and Richmond, Va. It has access to Washington, D.C.

Atlas. The name is given to a series of rockets used to launch spacecraft into orbit. Atlas D, for example, was used to launch the Mercury spacecraft into earth orbit in 1962.

Atlas-Agena B. Developed by the U.S. Air Force and adapted by the National Aeronautics and Space Administration (NASA) to civilian space programs, the rocket is designed principally for launching heavy communications and other scientific satellites. It was intended for close approach or hard landing in early lunar explorations and became operational in 1961.

atom bomb. On July 16, 1945, the first A-bomb was exploded at Alamogordo, N.M. On Aug. 6, less than a month later, an A-bomb was dropped on Hiroshima, Japan. On Aug. 9 an A-bomb was exploded over Nagasaki. The Japanese surrendered, Aug. 14, and World War II ended.

All of the nations realized that the U.S. held in its grasp "the most terrible weapon ever known in human history," as Sec. of War Henry L. Stimson called it.

The scientific knowledge on which the atomic bomb is based is truly international in its sources. Many great scientists made contributions which led ultimately to the fission ("splitting") of the atom and the conversion of mass into energy. Among the scientists were Albert Einstein (Germany and U.S.), Nils Bohr (Denmark), Ernest O. Lawrence, J. Robert Oppenheimer, Harold Urey (U.S.) and Enrico Fermi (Italy and U.S.).

Pres. F. D. Roosevelt approved work on the atom bomb project in the Office of Scientific Research and Development under Vannevar Bush, shortly before U.S. entrance into World War II. In 1942 the "Manhattan Project" (a code name) for production of the bomb was given to Major Gen. Leslie R. Groves who headed a special unit of the Army Corps of Engineers. Two plants were constructed for making the bomb, one at Oak Ridge, Tenn., and the other at the Hanford Engineer Works in the state of Washington.

After World War II the U.S. announced that it would share the scientific knowledge with other nations only when a plan for controlling the use of atomic energy could be agreed upon in the United Nations.

In 1949 the Soviet Union exploded its first atomic bomb, and during the next two decades the "nuclear club" expanded to include Britain, France and Communist China.

As the cold war became more intense, the U.S. proceeded with development of the hydrogen bomb. Finally developed in 1952, with its estimated force of five million tons of TNT, the hydrogen bomb is 250 times more powerful than the Hiroshima bomb. So high a temperature is needed for the detonation of the H-bomb that it can be produced only by exploding an A-bomb.

Years of negotiation over controls have resulted at various times in suspending testing bombs in the atmosphere, as in 1958 and 1963. Defenders of the 1963 limited nuclear test ban believe that by agreeing to limit testing, the U.S. and Russia acknowledge that there is little possibility of a nuclear "breakthrough" which would end the nuclear stalemate and give any one country definite nuclear superiority.

Atomic Energy Commission (AEC). After the close of World War II, a long-range effort was begun to put the atom to peaceful uses. The AEC was established by the Atomic Energy Act of 1946 (McMahon Act). The Commission is composed of five members appointed by the President by and with the advice and consent of the Senate.

It is a civilian body which has supported a broad research and development program in medicine, agriculture, industrial uses and power production. Much of the work is carried on in cooperation with private organizations.

Atomic radioisotopes are used in the study of diseases while in agriculture they help produce more and better crops and healthier animals. The U.S. has shared its knowledge of radioisotopes with other nations.

A training program of the AEC has brought hundreds of foreign scientists to the U.S. to receive instruction in building atomic reactors and in the use of radioisotopes.

The AEC advises and consults with the Department of Defense on matters relating to military applications of atomic energy.

"atoms for peace" plan. In a speech before the United Nations General Assembly, Dec. 8, 1953, Pres. Eisenhower proposed that all nations with nuclear resources make contributions to set up an atomic energy "pool" or "bank." This would then be used to "serve the peaceful pursuits of mankind" with emphasis on help for undeveloped nations. This plan received the enthusiastic backing of the UN General Assembly and of public opinion and led to formation of the International Atomic Energy Agency (IAEA), a specialized agency of the UN. Seventy nations have joined the IAEA, including both the U.S. and Soviet Union.

Attorney General's list of subversive organizations. In Dec. 1947, Attorney General Tom Clark issued a list of 90 organizations regarded as disloyal to the U.S. It was to be used as a guide for federal agencies in determining the loyalty of their employees.

The list was prepared in accordance with Pres. Truman's executive order of Mar. 22, 1947, providing for strict checkups by the FBI and the Civil Service Commission on the loyalty of federal employees and those whose applications were then being considered. This so-called loyalty order was interpreted as being directed against those who held Communist party membership or were Communist sympathizers.

In 1951, the U.S. Supreme Court ruled that three of the organizations listed had not been given the chance to prove that they were not Communist-controlled.

Audubon, John James (1785–1851). Ornithologist and artist. Born in Haiti, he came to the U.S. in 1803. Unsuccessful in business, he turned to painting birds from life on his various trips, including those down the Mississippi. Engravings of these paintings were made in England, and his European reputation spread to the U.S. Although his work has been criticized from both scientific and artistic points of view, he nevertheless holds a deserved place among America's foremost naturalists. His most famous work is *The Birds of America* (4 vols., 1827–38).

Audubon Societies. Lovers of American wildlife formed associations for its conservation. They took their name from

John J. Audubon, naturalist, whose work *The Birds of America* began to appear in 1827. The first was organized in 1886 by George Bird Grinnell, editor of *Forest and Stream.*

The National Association of Audubon Societies was incorporated in 1905.

Aurora. Founded in 1790 in Philadelphia by Benjamin Franklin Bache, a grandson of Benjamin Franklin, the newspaper, also known as the *General Advertiser,* vigorously supported the Republicans (Jeffersonian), often publishing abusive attacks on the Washington administration. Bache was arrested in 1798 under the Sedition Act for libeling Pres. John Adams.

Austin, Stephen Fuller (1793–1836). Colonizer. Born in southwestern Va., he led in the settlement of Texas by Anglo-Americans and maintained peace and order there. He was imprisoned by the Mexican government (1833–34) for urging the independence of Texas. He was defeated by Sam Houston for the presidency of the Republic of Texas (1836) but became its secretary of state shortly before his death.

automation. Although definitions of automation vary, there is general agreement that the essential feature is the use of one machine for automatic control of another machine. The overall effect of automation is to make possible more and more complex sequences of operation with less and less human assistance. Automation is now being applied with increasing effectiveness to an ever-increasing number of processes, including printing, steel manufacture, preparations of payrolls, accounting, banking operations and navigation.

Automation has been called the "second industrial revolution." There are already factories in operation where automation has enabled a relatively small number of skilled workers to carry on operations which formerly required a full force of production workers.

Many businessmen and engineers who have pioneered in introducing automation believe that any unemployment which may result will be, at most, temporary. In the long run, they maintain, jobs will actually be increased. The Bell Telephone Co., for example, began installing automatic switchboards in the 1920's, but the industry employs far more people than it did a generation ago. Nevertheless, as automation destroys old jobs and creates new ones, many individuals will have to learn new skills.

B

Babbitt (1922). In his novel Sinclair Lewis contributed a new word to the English language, "Babbitt." Lewis satirized small town business as represented by George F. Babbitt, a town booster and joiner whose concentration on business causes him to miss the finer things in life.

Bacon's Rebellion (1676). Frontier farmers in Virginia led by Nathaniel Bacon revolted against Gov. Berkeley. Berkeley had refused to commission Bacon to fight against the Indians who occupied land wanted by the frontier farmers. The colonial governor opposed any attack on friendly Indians who acted as a buffer against Indians further in the interior.

Bacon and his forces entered Jamestown and forced Berkeley to issue the commission. At the same time, the House of Burgesses passed liberal tax and voting laws and eased office holding requirements. Although these became known as "Bacon's Laws," Bacon did not relax in his determination to drive out the Indians.

When Berkeley raised an army against the rebels, Bacon returned again from the frontier fighting and burned Jamestown. Later he died of dysentery. The revolt was then crushed and Berkeley executed 23 of the rebels before commissioners of King Charles II arrived and removed him from office.

Bacon's Rebellion was not a break between colony and mother country which led ultimately to the Revolution of 1776; it was an internal struggle for lands held by the Indians at a time when falling tobacco prices and economic unrest in Virginia led the frontiersman to challenge the colonial government's authority.

Badlands of South Dakota. The steep hills, gullies and fantastic land formations, now part of a national park (Badlands National Monument), impeded travel of fur traders early in the 19th century. They lie in the western part of the state and contain extensive fossil remains of prehistoric animals.

49

Baekeland, Leo Hendrik (1863–1944). Chemist and inventor. Born in Ghent, Belgium, he emigrated to the U.S. (1889). Inventor of a photographic paper (Velox), he sold his rights to Eastman Kodak for $1 million. He is known especially for his discovery of the synthetic resin Bakelite.

Bailey v. Drexel Furniture Co. (1922). The U.S. Supreme Court invalidated the child labor tax provision of the Revenue Act of 1919 which provided for a 10% excise tax upon the annual net profits of mines, factories and other establishments that employed children below the age of fourteen.

The Drexel Furniture Co. had permitted a boy less than 14 years old to work in its factory. It was notified by Bailey, Collector of Internal Revenue, that it would be assessed 10% of its net profits for the year 1919. The company brought suit to recover the amount of the tax.

The Court held that Congress was using the tax to coerce in a matter completely the business of the state government and beyond the taxing power of Congress under the Constitution.

balance of trade. Within any given year a nation buys a certain amount of goods from the outside world and sells a certain amount to the outside world. If it sells more than it buys, it is said to have a "favorable balance of trade." If the reverse is true, its trade balance is said to be "unfavorable." This, however, does not consider significant "invisible" items of trade such as tourist expenditures, loans and grants to friendly foreign governments, insurance payments and payments for shipping services which enter into the more significant balance of payments.

For many years before World War I, the U.S. had a favorable balance of trade. It exported vast quantities of wheat, cotton and other farm products to obtain the foreign exchange needed to pay for merchandise imports and for payments to foreign investors in U.S. factories and railroads.

During World War I many foreign investors sold their holdings in American business and the U.S. government made huge loans to the Allies. Furthermore, between 1918 and 1929, Americans invested billions of dollars in the securities of foreign nations. The U.S. became the world's great creditor nation.

However, a nation which is a world creditor and, therefore, has a strongly favorable balance of invisible items cannot also expect to export more visible items (merchandise) than it imports. Exports and imports must be understood in the sense of all economic transactions, including both visible and invisible items.

Ballinger-Pinchot controversy. In the dispute over conservation of natural resources under

Pres. Taft, Chief Forester of the Department of Agriculture Gifford Pinchot accused Sec. of the Interior Richard A. Ballinger of abusing the powers of his office. He charged Ballinger with making water power sites available for sale to private interests after they had been withdrawn for conservation purposes and with showing favoritism in the granting of coal land claims in Alaska. A congressional investigating committee did not find Ballinger guilty of any misconduct.

Pinchot was forced to resign in 1910. Since he was a friend of Theodore Roosevelt's, this further divided Roosevelt and Taft. As a result of the controversy Taft was made to appear unfriendly to conservation when, as a matter of record, he removed more lands from possible sale to private interests than had Roosevelt in a comparable period.

Ballistic Missile Early Warning System (BMEWS). The U.S. Air Force system of detection extends up to 3,000 miles into space. Units in Alaska pick up and track missiles and satellites for the purpose of warning the Air Defense Command of any hostile attack.

Ball's Bluff, battle of (Oct. 21, 1861). Union forces, on a reconnaissance mission west of Washington, D.C., near Leesburg, Va., were ambushed and defeated by the Confederates. Many were driven over the bluff and killed in hand to hand fighting, including Col. Edward D. Baker, ex-U.S. Senator from Oregon and a close friend of Pres. Lincoln.

The battle, also known as Edward's Ferry, was so badly managed that Gen. C. P. Stone was imprisoned for six months.

The U.S. Congress, Dec. 10, established the Joint Committee on the Conduct of the War to investigate inactivity of the Union armies, the Ball's Bluff defeat and the doings of the generals.

Baltimore & Ohio Railroad. The first line to be incorporated for the purpose of carrying passengers and freight was chartered in Maryland, Feb. 28, 1827. It was built to compete with the Erie Canal which had attracted trade to the northern route to the West. Baltimore merchants sought to recapture the trade that had come to them over the National Road.

The first public passengers were carried over tracks in a horse-drawn car, Jan. 1, 1830. Horses were replaced by steam engines after the *Tom Thumb*, built by Peter Cooper of New York, was used on the line in the summer of 1830. In 1831 the B. & O. advertised for locomotives, offering $4,000 for the best one. The *York*, built by Phineas Davis of York, Pa., won the prize.

The B. & O. has expanded and now operates about 6,000 miles of line between points on the Atlantic seaboard and middle western centers. In 1963 the Chesapeake and Ohio Railway gained majority control of the B. & O.

Bancroft, George (1800–91). Historian, diplomat and statesman. He was born in Worcester, Mass. The publication of his *History of the United States* (1834–76) brought public recognition; its final revision (6 vols., 1883–85) covered the span between the discovery of America and the close of the Revolutionary War. Active in Democratic politics, he was U.S. minister to Great Britain (1846–49) and Germany (1867–74). U.S. Sec. of Navy (1845–46), he established the U.S. Naval Academy at Annapolis.

Bank Holiday (1933). During the Great Depression the number of bank failures mounted steeply. By Mar. 4, 1933, the morning of F. D. Roosevelt's inauguration, most of the banks in the country had been closed by state action. On Mar. 6, by presidential proclamation, Roosevelt suspended all banking operations and gold transactions for four days. Congress rushed through the Emergency Banking Act on Mar. 9, which ratified the President's action and provided for the opening of sound banks. Within two months of the banking holiday, more than 12,000 banks with 90% of the country's bank deposits were back in business.

Bank of Augusta v. Earle (1839). In the chief of the three Comity Cases, Justice Taney, speaking for the U.S. Supreme Court, rejected the argument that a corporation possessed all the legal rights guaranteed to natural persons under the full faith and credit clause of the Constitution. Alabama had attempted to exclude corporations chartered by other states.

The case arose when a citizen of Alabama refused to honor the bills of exchange of a Georgia bank, contending that a "foreign" corporation had no lawful right to enter into a contract within a "sovereign" state. Taney recognized the right of a corporation to do business under interstate comity with other states, but upheld the right of states to exclude corporations by positive action. The Georgia bank was thus prevented from doing business in Alabama.

Bank of Commerce v. New York City (1863). The U.S. Supreme Court held unconstitutional a New York law taxing federal securities held by the bank. The decision was helpful to the federal government at a time when it was seeking to finance the Civil War.

Bank of North America. The first bank to be incorporated by a government of the U.S. was founded and organized by Robert Morris, superintendent of finance, and chartered by the Continental Congress, Dec. 31, 1781. In 1783 it received a charter from Pennsylvania. The Bank helped to finance the

Revolution. Benjamin Franklin, Alexander Hamilton and Thomas Jefferson were among its distinguished depositors and stockholders.

Bank of the United States. The first Bank of the U.S. was chartered by Congress in 1791. Its headquarters were in Philadelphia and branch banks were soon established in port cities from Boston to New Orleans. The Bank was capitalized at $10,000,000 with the federal government subscribing one-fifth of this amount. It served as depository for government funds, lent the government money to meet its short-term obligations and issued notes that served as paper currency. As a commercial bank, it made personal loans and was strongly supported by the mercantile interests in the nation.

The bill which authorized establishment of the Bank had been sponsored by Alexander Hamilton and opposed by Thomas Jefferson and James Madison. The opposition charged that Congress had no right to establish a national bank. Hamilton, however, argued successfully that Congress had the right to regulate currency and the "implied power" to establish a bank to issue that currency.

When the Bank's 20-year charter expired in 1811, it was not renewed by Congress. The Bank had been the government's main fiscal agency and liquidated its assets with a profit to stockholders.

The second Bank of the U.S. was chartered in 1816 for 20 years. The bill was supported in Congress by John C. Calhoun and Henry Clay and was opposed by New England, where state banks were well managed. It was capitalized at $35,000,000 with the federal government again subscribing one-fifth. The Bank was the government's sole depository and issued notes which tended to drive the notes of local banks out of circulation. Five of the Bank's 25 directors were appointed by the President and foreign stockholders were to have no vote in the Bank's affairs.

At first the Bank was too lavish in its loan policy. This policy was changed under the presidency of Nicholas Biddle, beginning in 1823. The Bank, however, had many enemies. Its great power was distrusted by Pres. Jackson, who vetoed the charter's renewal in 1832 on the grounds that it favored the privileged classes. Rival bankers in New York and other cities did what they could to ruin the Bank. Biddle, himself, testifying before Congress indicated that the Bank had enormous power but, generously, did not destroy smaller banks. The Bank went out of business in 1836.

Bank of the U.S. v. Planters' Bank of Georgia (1824). The U.S. Supreme Court decided that if a state became a party to a banking or commercial enterprise, the state could be sued in the course of the business.

The case arose when the Bank of the U.S. sued the Planters' Bank for payment of a note. The state of Georgia held stock in the latter bank.

Baptists. Although Roger Williams has often been regarded as the founder of the first Baptist church in America, at Providence, R.I. (1639), recent Baptist historians have challenged this claim. Baptists believe that immersion is the only mode of administering baptism indicated in the New Testament and reject baptism by the pouring or sprinkling of water over infants. Williams was not rebaptized by immersion. The claim of Isaac Backus, organizer (1756) of the Baptist Church, Middleborough, Mass., as the "real" founder of the Baptist church in America has been advanced.

The views of Baptists subjected them to persecution in New England during the 17th century. Baptists gained strength in New York, Pennsylvania, Maryland and Virginia during the colonial period. They were dominant on the frontier where evangelism affected the uneducated farmer-preachers. Baptists in frontier settlements in the early 19th century opposed the newly formed missions and were known as "Hard Shells," "Old School" or "Primitive Baptists." The growing division over slavery led to the formation of the Southern Baptist Convention in 1845. The Northern Baptist Convention was formed in 1907

and took the name American Baptist Convention in 1950.

After the Civil War, Negroes formed the National Baptist Convention, U.S.A., in 1880, in Montgomery, Ala. The number of Negro Baptists grew rapidly owing to the ease of forming Baptist churches and the dramatic power of the immersion ceremony.

Baptists, with church membership of over 23,000,000, comprise the largest denomination of Protestants in the U.S.

Barbary Wars (1801–05, 1815). The Barbary pirates, aided by the Barbary States (Morocco, Algiers, Tripoli and Tunis) in North Africa, traditionally preyed on the commerce of other nations and exacted tribute from them.

In 1801 the U.S. determined to resist this threat to commerce and attempted to bottle up the pirates in their home ports. Tripoli, troubled by internal dissension, sued for peace in 1805, halting the Tripolitan War. Annual payments by the U.S. ended.

The other Barbary States continued to exact tribute on the pretense that American shipping was being protected from even worse piratical forays. Crews and vessels were captured and ransom was paid. At the end of the War of 1812, the U.S. sought to end these depredations and a strong naval force was sent to the Mediterranean. Algiers was forced to renounce demands for tribute and the

54

other Barbary States fell into line.

barbed wire. The improvement of barbed wire fencing by Joseph F. Glidden, an Illinois farmer and inventor, made possible its manufacture by factory in 1874. The result was a revolution in ranching. By 1890 privately owned ranches were enclosed, ending free grazing, curbing thievery, controlling loss of cattle in blizzards and making possible stock breeding.

Barnard, Henry (1811–1900). Educator. Born in Hartford, Conn., he was a leader in public school movement, especially in Connecticut and Rhode Island. He was the first U.S. Commissioner of Education (1867–70); chancellor of the Univ. of Wisconsin (1858–60); president of St. John's College, Annapolis, Md. (1866–67); and editor of *American Journal of Education* (1855–82).

Barnburners. In the 1840's an antislavery faction in the Democratic party was organized in New York State to oppose the conservative Hunkers. They gained the nickname when it was charged at a New York convention that they were willing to "burn down" the Democratic "barn" to get rid of the proslavery "rats."

The Barnburners joined Free Soilers in support of Van Buren for President in 1848. With the decline of his star many drifted back into Democratic ranks. Others later became active in the newly formed Republican party.

Barnum, Phineas Taylor (1810–91). Showman. He was born in Bethel, Conn. Indelibly linked with the circus, he opened "The Greatest Show on Earth" in Brooklyn (1871); he combined with Bailey (1881) to form Barnum and Bailey Circus. Among his widely promoted triumphs: he exhibited the dwarf Tom Thumb in U.S. and England; he brought Jenny Lind to the U.S. for a concert tour (1850); he imported Jumbo, a huge African elephant bought from the Royal Zoological Society in London (1881).

Barron v. Baltimore **(1833).** The U.S. Supreme Court held that the 5th Amendment was a limitation on the federal and not the state government. It dismissed Barron's claim that the city of Baltimore by diverting certain streams had made his wharf unsuitable for vessels, depriving him of his property without just compensation provided for in the 5th Amendment. The Court ruled that it had no jurisdiction over the action of the local government. It was the last case in which Chief Justice Marshall participated.

Barton, Clara (1821–1912). Humanitarian. Born in Oxford, Mass., she started her career as a schoolteacher (1836–54); she helped on battlefields and in hospitals during the Civil War. In association with the International Red Cross in Europe (1869–73), she aided the wounded in the Franco-Prussian War. She became the first president of the American Red Cross (1882–1904) and was active in establishing the role of the Red Cross in peacetime disasters, such as the Galveston tidal wave (1900).

Bartram, William (1739–1823). Explorer and naturalist. Born in Philadelphia, Pa., he explored the southeastern part of what is now the U.S. (1773–77); made botanical drawings; and collected seeds and specimens. He published an account of his trip, *Travels through North and South Carolina, Georgia, East and West Florida, the Cherokee Country, etc.* (1791), a significant literary and scientific work.

baseball. The origins of the U.S. "national game" are obscure. A game like the one in which the rules have been standardized since about 1900 was played during the early 19th century. Abner Doubleday has been credited with inventing the game in Cooperstown, N.Y., in 1839 and the National Baseball Hall of Fame and Museum was built there in 1939. But historians have not been impressed with the substance of this legend.

The sport took on significant proportions in 1876 when the National League of Professional Baseball Clubs was formed. It had the professional field to itself until 1901 when the rival American League was formed. In 1903 the first World Series between the winning teams in each league was played. There are now twelve teams in each league and they spread from coast to coast.

The game is played on sandlots, parks with baseball fields and on high school and college fields throughout the nation. Boys play it from the time that they are old enough to hold a bat, hit the ball and run the bases. By the time the boys are old enough to have families of their own, they are content to be spectators and urge their sons to play in Little Leagues.

If there is one name that is known to baseball lovers everywhere, including Japan and Latin America, it is George Herman (Babe) Ruth, the Bambino, who established a season home-run record in 1927 by hitting 60 home runs.

basketball. The game is an American invention, devised in 1891 by James A. Naismith, a physical education instructor at YMCA Training College (now Springfield College) in Springfield, Mass. It is now the most widely attended spectator sport in the U.S.

Bastogne. On Dec. 21, 1944, in the Battle of the Bulge, in Bastogne, a town in Belgium, Gen. Anthony McAuliffe was asked to surrender by German officers bearing a message that the Americans were in a hopeless position, caught in a trap.

McAuliffe gave a one-word reply: "Nuts!"

Bataan, battle of (Jan.–Apr. 9, 1942). The peninsula in the Philippines was captured by the Japanese despite stubborn defense by U.S. and Filipino soldiers who were cut off from outside assistance.

The survivors were subjected to the Bataan "Death March" to Camp O'Donnell, a prison in the jungles of Arlac Province. Japanese guards tortured the marchers, nearly mad with thirst and starvation, and murdered those who were not likely to survive.

Gen. Douglas MacArthur led the resistance on Bataan until he was ordered by Pres. F. D. Roosevelt to escape. On his arrival in Darwin, Australia, Mar. 17, MacArthur announced: "I came through and I shall return."

"Battle Hymn of the Republic." With the opening lines, "Mine eyes have seen the glory of the coming of the Lord. . . ." Mrs. Julia Ward Howe, a New Englander, made possible a marching song (1862) that was to inspire Union soldiers during the Civil War. She set the words of her poem to the tune of "John Brown's Body," written some years earlier by William Steffe.

The "Battle Hymn" is regarded as a patriotic song although it is also included in the hymnals of some churches. But the lines, "He hath loosed the fateful lightning of/His terrible swift sword. . . ." have offended some southerners.

Bayard - Chamberlain Treaty (1888). A joint Anglo-U.S. commission headed by Sec. of State Thomas Bayard and Joseph Chamberlain of Great Britain met in 1887 to settle a dispute over Canadian fisheries. A pact was signed, Feb. 15, 1888, but it was rejected by the Senate on Aug. 21 partly because it provided for a reciprocal tariff and partly because anti-British sentiment was high. Senators with election approaching preferred holding the Irish vote to a treaty with Britain.

However, a working arrangement was established whereby Americans were entitled to privileges in the ports of British North America upon the payment of a tonnage fee. The agreement lasted until abrogated by Canada in 1923 in retaliation against the Fordney-McCumber Tariff.

A treaty provision was, in effect, adopted by the Hague Tribunal in 1910 when the U.S. and Britain agreed to arbitration of the continuing controversy over the North Atlantic fisheries. The Canadian definition of bays was upheld.

Bayard v. Singleton (1787). The case decided by the Court of Appeals of North Carolina is significant because it was the first reported in which an act of a state legislature was declared unconstitutional.

The case arose over the sale

of confiscated Tory land. The legislature had passed a law that required courts to dismiss suits against any person holding "enemy alien" land "under a sale from a commissioner of forfeited estates. . . ." The North Carolina court held this law to be void because it violated the constitution of the state, which provided that the plaintiff had a right to a jury trial in a dispute over property.

Bay of Pigs (Apr. 17–20, 1961). About 1,500 Cubans who had fled from the Castro regime sought to liberate Cuba by force in an unsuccessful invasion at the Bay of Pigs on Cuba's southern coast.

The anti-Castro rebels had been armed and trained with unofficial help from the U.S. Central Intelligence Agency (CIA), but they were no match for Castro's army.

The Kennedy administration was criticized for not giving the invaders all-out support. Others said the U.S. should not have lent support at all—that this was contrary to the U.S. "hands-off" policy toward political movements in other countries.

Bay Psalm Book. Except for an almanac, the *Bay Psalm Book* in 1640 was the first book printed in America (Cambridge, Mass.). It contained new versions of all the Psalms. Early editions contained no musical notations, but included instructions as to which tunes should be used for each Psalm.

The full title of the book is *The Whole Booke of Psalmes Faithfully Translated into English Metre.* Stephen Daye was the printer.

On Jan. 28, 1947, one of the few remaining original copies of the book was bought for $151,000, the highest price ever paid for a book, at an auction of the Parke-Bernet Galleries in New York.

"Bear Flag" Republic (1846). The fear of Americans in California that they might be forced to leave by a hostile Mexican government gave rise to the Bear Flag revolt against Mexican rule. It received its name from the design of the flag, which showed a grizzly bear facing a red star, used as its standard.

Before the new republic of California could function, its flag was replaced by the American flag, for the U.S. had declared war on Mexico.

John C. Frémont, who had ostensibly been "exploring" for the U.S., joined the settlers' revolt. He cooperated with U.S. naval forces in California waters.

Beard, Charles Austin (1874–1948). Historian. Born in Knightstown, Ind., he was graduated from DePauw Univ. (1898), earned his Ph.D. at Columbia Univ. (1904) and was a professor of politics at Columbia (1904–17). He made a great impact on the academic fraternity and the general public with his *An Economic Inter-*

pretation of the Constitution (1913). Beard's emphasis on the economic interpretation of American history was expressed in his highly readable *The Rise of American Civilization* (1927), written with his wife, Mary Ritter Beard. In later writings, he modified his emphasis on the economic interpretation. In the World War II period, he lost popularity with liberals because of his espousal of intercontinental isolationism. Beard, nevertheless, is numbered among the great American historians.

"beat generation." The expression has been used to describe a portion of the youth of the affluent 1950's who rebelled against what they regarded as a "sick" society. They included "hipsters," who were sometimes criminal in inclination and engaged in violent revolt, and "beatniks," of middle-class origin, who were descendants of the bohemians of an earlier day. "Beatniks" made known their withdrawal from society by experiments in verse, sometimes intoned to musical accompaniment, and by an inclination to Zen Buddhism.

Both hipsters and beatniks developed a special vocabulary and admired "cool cats" like the anti-hero actors James Dean and Marlon Brando. They held the "squares" of the world—the conformists—in contempt. Critics of the "beat generation," noting the widely expanded economic and cultural opportunities for youth, saw in them a tiresome conformity and re-

garded them as "rebels without a cause."

Beaumont, William (1785–1853). Surgeon. He was born in Lebanon, Conn. While in military service, he was able to observe a patient whose stomach was exposed by a gunshot wound (1822). His work *Experiments and Observations on the Gastric Juice and the Physiology of Digestion* (1833) remains a vital contribution to the knowledge of gastric digestion.

Beecher, Henry Ward (1813–87). Clergyman. Born in Litchfield, Conn., his influence as a Presbyterian minister extended widely from his pulpit in the Plymouth Congregational Church, Brooklyn, N.Y. (1847–87). An antislavery leader, he counseled disobedience to the Fugitive Slave Law, supported woman suffrage and civil service reform. His personal life became a public issue when he was charged (1874) by Theodore Tilton of committing adultery with Mrs. Tilton. The jury was divided but upheld his defense.

Beecher was a brother of Harriet Beecher Stowe, author of *Uncle Tom's Cabin*.

Beecher's Bibles. Preaching that a Sharps rifle in the hands of Free Staters would be more convincing to proslavery forces than any arguments in the Bible, the celebrated Brooklyn (N.Y.) clergyman, Henry Ward Beecher, used the money he

59

raised to ship rifles instead of Bibles to troubled Kansas in 1856. Hence the rifles became known as Beecher's Bibles.

Beef Trust Cases. Attempts were made by Pres. Theodore Roosevelt in 1902 to combat big business monopolies. A number of packing companies, Swift and Armour among them, had combined to form the National Packing Co., which extended its dominance of the industry to stockyards, slaughtering, meat-packing, wholesaling of meat and retail stores. The U.S. Supreme Court handed down an indecisive decision in 1905 and the company was not dissolved. It was not until 1920, following a Federal Trade Commission investigation, that the National Packing Co. disposed of some of its interests and confined itself to meat-packing.

Belknap scandal (1876). Pres. Grant's Sec. of War William W. Belknap was charged with receiving payments from a trader at one of the Army posts. Belknap was impeached by the House of Representatives, but his resignation was accepted by Pres. Grant. He was not convicted by the Senate, which held that it had no jurisdiction over a Cabinet officer who had resigned.

Bell, Alexander Graham (1847–1922). Inventor. Born in Scotland, he came to Boston in 1871 to train teachers of the deaf. His continual work on re-

producing the human voice electrically culminated in the invention of the telephone (1876). Its commercial development started with the Bell Telephone Co. (1877). Among Bell's other inventions were the photophone which transmitted the first wireless telephone message (1880) and improvements on Edison's phonograph. Deeply interested in aviation, he worked with Samuel P. Langley (1834–1906) to solve the problem of stability in a flying machine. He founded the Volta Laboratory to further increase knowledge about the deaf. His wife, Mabel G. Hubbard, had been deaf from childhood.

Belleau Wood, battle of (June 2–July 7, 1918). Gen. Pershing, Commander of the American Expeditionary Forces, assigned the 2nd Division to the French. In hard-fought bloody actions it took Vaux, Bouresches and Belleau Wood (about 50 miles east of Paris), stemming the German advance. The 4th U.S. Marine Brigade, serving with the 2nd—its men known as "Leathernecks" or "Devil Dogs" —won its immortality. The casualties were high, 40% for many of the combat units.

Bellows, George Wesley (1882–1925). Artist and lithographer. Born in Columbus, O., he is known as a leader among the realists; his early paintings were inspired by city crowds. The lithographs of his later years captured the drama of pugilistic scenes. His paintings include

Emma and Her Children (Boston Museum of Fine Arts), *Stag at Sharkey's* (Cleveland Museum), *Up the Hudson* (Metropolitan Museum, N.Y.C.).

Bennett, James Gordon (1795–1872). Editor. Born in Scotland, he emigrated first to Canada (1819) and then to the U.S. Active in newspaper publishing in Boston and New York, he founded the New York *Herald* (1835), a penny paper usually found in the Democratic camp. The *Herald* covered the Civil War in sensational style. Bennett did not give Lincoln his full support until 1864.

His son, James Gordon Bennett (1841–1918) sent Stanley to Africa to find Livingston (1869–71); established (1887) a Paris edition of the New York *Herald*; broke the Gould monopoly of transatlantic cable communication when he joined with John W. Mackay to form the Commercial Cable Co.

Bennington, battle of (Aug. 16, 1777). The defeat of a detachment at Bennington, Vt., ultimately led to the surrender of the British at Saratoga, N.Y. British Gen. Burgoyne had dispatched the force to acquire provisions and strengthen Loyalists in New England. Bennington was some 30 miles southeast of Saratoga. The rout of the Germans, Canadians, Indians and English who comprised the British force encouraged New England farmers to join the American army in Burgoyne's path on his march south from Canada toward Albany.

Benton, Thomas Hart (1782–1858). Statesman. "Old Bullion" was born in Hillsboro, N.C., but settled in Missouri (1815). The first U.S. Senator to serve 30 consecutive years (1821–51), he supported Jackson in the war against the Bank of the United States and secured a change in the ratio of gold and silver from 15 to 1 to 16 to 1. Defeated for the Senate because of his opposition to the slavery provision of the Compromise of 1850, he served in House of Representatives (1853–55). He was opposed to secession.

Benton, Thomas Hart (1889–). Painter. Born in Missouri, he is known for realistic portraiture of people representing ordinary life and occupations of the Middle West. His works include *Cotton Pickers, Lonesome Road*, and *Susanna and the Elders*. His murals include *The Arts of Life in America* (Whitney Museum of American Art, N.Y.C.). He is the grandnephew of Senator Thomas Hart Benton.

Bering Sea dispute. In the 1880's the demand for sealskins stimulated by women's fashions encouraged Canadians to kill seals indiscriminately in the open seas near the U.S. owned Pribilof Islands off the coast of Alaska.

In 1889 Congress authorized the President to seize vessels

encroaching upon American rights in the waters of Bering Sea. When the British objected to these seizures, Sec. of State Blaine did not defend U.S. actions on the basis that the Bering Sea was *mare clausum* (a closed sea), comparable to Chesapeake Bay. He argued that pelagic sealing (killing of seals in the open sea as they come to and from their breeding grounds) was so harmful as to be *contra bonos mores* (against good public morals).

The controversy gave rise to war talk, which subsided when the dispute was submitted to arbitration. A mixed tribunal met at Paris in 1893 and assessed the U.S. for almost a half million dollars in damages for unwarranted seizures of Canadian schooners. The tribunal also sought to limit pelagic sealing. The Paris award has been described by Thomas A. Bailey as "a victory for arbitration and the pacific settlement of disputes—not for the seals."

Berkeley student rebellion. In 1964 the Berkeley campus of the University of California experienced an upheaval unmatched in the history of any major American campus. Faced with curtailment of their varied activities on behalf of civil liberties, students mobilized into the Free Speech Movement (FSM). Their demands widened to the abolition of all university regulation of student political conduct and to student participation in administration decisions affecting their interests.

The student rebellion included resistance to police efforts to remove them during a sit-in in the chief Berkeley administration building and a strike which halted classes for two days.

Berlin, Irving (1888–). Songwriter. Born in Russia, Israel Baline came to the U.S. in 1893. His first big hit was "Alexander's Ragtime Band" (1911). Others in a long parade of successes include: "Oh, How I Hate to Get Up in the Morning," "All Alone," "Remember," "Always," "Russian Lullaby," "White Christmas." He was also a composer of lyrics for musical reviews: *Ziegfeld's Follies* (1912), *This Is the Army* (1942); he also wrote *Annie Get Your Gun* (1947) and *Call Me Madam* (1950).

Berlin and Milan Decrees. During the Napoleonic Wars, Britain blockaded the European coast. In retaliation Napoleon issued a Berlin Decree (Nov. 1806) declaring a "paper blockade" of the British Isles but his navy was too weak to enforce the Decree. In response to another British Order-in-Council, he replied with the Milan Decree (Dec. 1807) which declared that ships lost their neutral character if they obeyed the British Order-in-Council or submitted to search on the high seas by British officers.

Berlin Blockade (1948–49). At the Potsdam Conference Germany was divided into four occupation zones. The city of Berlin, included in the Soviet zone, was occupied by the four powers. The Russians attempted to force the U.S., Britain and France out of Berlin by blockading the city and cutting off supplies. The U.S. and British reply was an "airlift" by which everything from drugs to coal was flown into the Allied section of the city (West Berlin). The Soviet Union lifted the blockade, nominally enforced by East Germany, in May 1949.

Bernstein, Leonard (1918–). Composer and conductor. Born in Lawrence, Mass., he gained national fame as conductor of the New York City Symphony (1945–48) and the N.Y. Philharmonic Symphony (1957–58) and has been its musical director since 1958. He is a music interpreter on television (*Omnibus*, 1957; children's concerts). His compositions include "Clarinet Sonata" (1942), "Kaddish Symphony" (1963) and scores for such shows as *On the Town* (1944) and *West Side Story* (1957).

Bessemer process. Invented by Henry Bessemer in England in 1856, the new method of manufacturing steel revolutionized the industry. A blast of cold air is forced through a hot mass of melting iron. The great heat thus created burns out the impurities in the iron which becomes ready for the addition of carbon, manganese and other substances to make good quality steel. In the U.S., William Kelly of Kentucky arrived at the same principle independently and received a patent in 1857. Bessemer received a U.S. patent in 1865. In 1866 the Bessemer and Kelly interests reached an agreement and paved the way for large-scale steel manufacture by the new method.

A method of making finer steel than that possible with the Bessemer process was developed as early as the 1870's. This is the "open-hearth process." It permitted creation of greater heat and made it easier to draw samples for testing during actual production. The process gave the worker greater control in recombining elements or mixing them with alloying metals. The finer steel was used after 1900 for skyscrapers and automobiles. Much of the Bessemer steel was used before 1900 for making rails for railroad tracks.

Bible reading in public schools. The U.S. Supreme Court in *School District of Abington Township v. Schempp* (1963) held that the Pennsylvania requirement that the school day begin with the reading of 10 verses from the Bible was unconstitutional since it violated the 1st Amendment respecting establishment of religion.

The case arose when the Schempp family of the Unitarian faith sought to enjoin the school district from requiring the Bible readings and recitation of the Lord's Prayer in the public schools attended by their children.

In the majority opinion, Justice Clark observed that since the Pennsylvania statute "requires the reading of the 'Holy Bible' a Christian document, the practice . . . prefers the Christian religion. The record demonstrates that it was the intention of . . . the Commonwealth . . . to introduce a religious ceremony into the public schools. . . ."

Earlier, in *Engel v. Vitale* (1962), the U.S. Supreme Court held that a prayer composed by the N.Y. State Board of Regents, the agency which supervises the public school system, was unconstitutional. The Court ruled that the prayer was religious in nature and the use of the public schools to encourage its daily recitation was inconsistent with the "establishment clause" of the 1st Amendment.

Big Five. At the Paris Peace Conference (1919) after World War I the term referred to Britain, France, Italy, Japan and the U.S.

After World War II the term was sometimes used to refer to Britain, France, Nationalist China, U.S. and U.S.S.R., the five powers accorded veto power in the Security Council of the United Nations.

Big Four. In World War I the term referred to England, France, Italy and the U.S., the powers that defeated Germany. At the Paris Peace Conference (1919) they were represented by David Lloyd George, British Prime Minister; George Clemenceau ("The Tiger"), French Premier; Vittorio Orlando, Italian Prime Minister; and Woodrow Wilson, President of the U.S.

Biglow Papers, The. James Russell Lowell wrote two series of political satires in verse and prose. The first satirized the Mexican War from the viewpoint of New England abolitionists and appeared (1846–48) in part in the Boston *Courier* and in part in the *National Anti-Slavery Standard.* The second satirized the South and contemporary politics during the Civil War and Reconstruction. It appeared in the *Atlantic Monthly* (1861–66).

The series was written in Yankee dialect with Hosea Biglow, a down-east farmer, the chief narrator.

Big Parade, The. Immediately popular in 1925 when it was released, the motion picture dealt with the love lives of two soldiers in World War I. It was written by Laurence Stallings.

"big stick" policy. In 1901 Pres. Theodore Roosevelt quoted approvingly the old proverb: "Speak softly and carry a big stick, and you will go far." Many of the President's critics accused him of practicing the "big stick" policy against Colombia, when he aided the revolutionists in Panama and thus made possible U.S. construction of the Panama Canal. The expression was used to describe Roosevelt's intervention in the Dominican Republic in 1905 and elsewhere in Latin America.

Big Three. In World War II the term referred to the three great Allies—U.S., Great Britain and the Soviet Union—who won the war against the Axis powers—Germany, Italy and Japan.

Bill of Rights. The first 10 Amendments to the U.S. Constitution, adopted Dec. 15, 1791, are usually referred to as the Bill of Rights. It was on the promise of members of Congress that the Amendments would be submitted to the states that ratification of the Constitution was achieved. Those who feared a strong central government argued that without specific guarantees the civil rights and liberties of the people and the states would be at the mercy of the proposed national government. Several states ratified the Constitution with the recommendation that it be amended.

The 1st Amendment indicates by its own language that it is directed only against the federal government, for it begins, "Congress shall make no law. . . ." The other Amendments are couched in terms of general prohibition.

The states, too, have Bills of Rights in their constitutions. Virginia was the first state to adopt a Bill of Rights (1776), largely the work of George Mason. It was based on English common law and basic English documents, including the Bill of Rights (1689). The American Bill of Rights drew on the Virginia Bill of Rights. The general effect of all these Bills of Rights is to affirm the basic freedoms of the American people.

Billy the Kid. The real name of this notorious outlaw of the American Southwest was William H. Bonney (1859–81). He was born in New York City, but his legendary glamor was acquired in Kansas, Colorado and New Mexico.

bimetallism. Up to 1873 the U.S. government used two metals as a basis for its money and the Mint purchased both silver and gold to be coined. In 1873 it ceased to purchase silver. In 1879 it resumed the purchase of small amounts of silver.

Bimetallism became a major political issue in the period after 1873 until it was decisively rejected in the election of 1896. By the opening of the 20th century, the U.S. in common with virtually all other advanced nations of the world was officially on the gold standard.

Biosatellites. In this phase of the U.S. space program a wide variety of plants and animals will be carried into space. They will be used in tests which will study the effects of space (weightlessness, radiation, lack of earth's rotation) upon living things. Biosatellites are expected to supply information about the dangers facing man during prolonged flight in space.

Birth of a Nation, The (1915). Produced by D. W. Griffith, the motion picture presented a strongly pro-South drama of the American Civil War and the period of Reconstruction. It glorified the role of the Ku Klux Klan and generated anti-Negro sentiment. The film so outraged liberals and the pro-Negro organizations that were gaining strength, notably the National Association for the Advancement of Colored People, that violent demonstrations generally marked showings of the film.

The film was recognized as technically a superior achievement in the medium and a disturbing social document. The immensity of its impact stimulated awareness of the social importance of films.

Black, Hugo La Fayette (1886–1971). Jurist. Born in Harlan, Ala., he represented that state as Democratic senator (1927–37). He was appointed to the U.S. Supreme Court (1937) by Pres. F. D. Roosevelt. His appointment was clouded by the revelation that he had once been a member of the Ku Klux Klan, but his record on the bench justified Roosevelt's expectation that he would be progressive. Many of his decisions have had the effect of strengthening the 1st Amendment.

"Black Codes." Laws regulating the status of former slaves were passed in the ex-Confederate states, 1865–66. The most severe of the laws applied to vagrancy. Negroes "strolling about in idleness" were subject to arrest and, if convicted, were sent to work on state chain gangs or contracted out to planters. Other laws granted the Negro the right to sue and be sued and to own property. Nowhere could Negroes hold office, serve on juries, vote or bear arms.

In some states the laws for freedmen, known as "Black Codes," were harshly administered and led to what many in the North believed to be a return to involuntary servitude.

Blackfeet. An Algonquin people, these plains Indians, possessing great herds of horses in the 18th century, dwelt along the eastern base of the Rockies throughout Montana where their descendants now live in diminished numbers. Their Indian name, Siksika, meaning blackfooted people, possibly referred to black-dyed moccasins.

Black Friday (Sept. 24, 1869). A genuine panic was created when Jay Gould and James Fisk sought to corner the available gold supply. They had learned from Pres. Grant that the government was not planning to sell gold on the open market and this gave them their opportunity. They purchased gold and drove the price up so sharply that bankers and merchants who required gold for the settlement of international debts sold stocks and bonds and called in debts in an effort to raise the money to purchase gold.

Grant authorized the sale of $4,000,000 of the Treasury's gold supply, but it was too late to prevent a financial disaster for many. Gould and Fisk learned about this decision of the Treasury in time to sell gold at a profit.

The incident further besmirched the Grant administration.

Black Hawk War (1832). Chief Black Hawk, leader of a faction of Sauk and Fox Indians in northern Illinois and southern Wisconsin, contested the right of other tribesmen to cede land to the white settlers. When hunger caused him and his people to return from Iowa to the disputed area, he was ordered to leave. His failure to comply resulted in the total defeat of the Indians by regular troops and militia. They were driven further west across the Mississippi. Capt. Abraham Lincoln served with the Illinois militia in the war.

Black Muslims (Nation of Islam). Opposed to integration, numbers of Negroes have joined the cult, which is not formally recognized by Moslems and which preaches the separation of the races and Negro nationalism. Leadership was taken over in 1934 by Elijah Muhammed (Robert Poole), born in Georgia. It has headquarters in Chicago, where Mosque No. 1 (of an estimated 50 mosques) is located. The Black Muslims have no political program and do not vote. The cult looks forward to buying or taking over from one to four states so that its members can live apart from the "slave masters" in a separate Negro "nation."

As part of their alienation from the white race, members adopt Arabic names or use their first name with an X, rejecting their surnames as a heritage of slavery.

Members are disciplined to be neat in appearance, and the "laws of Islam" prohibit use of alcohol, gambling, tobacco and narcotics. Also prohibited are the eating of pork, cornbread, kale and, generally, any typical southern Negro food.

The organization says Allah forbids them to bear arms, however, a "Fruit of Islam" paramilitary security guard is trained in judo and karate.

Members are expected to pay a tithe (contribute 10% of their gross income). The size of the membership is an organizational secret. Some estimates have ranged as high as 100,000, but it is probably closer to 8,000.

"Black Power." The civil rights slogan was first chanted on a march by Negroes and whites (June 1966) into Jackson, Miss., led by James Meredith. Roy Wilkins, NAACP's executive director, attacked "Black Power" as "the father of hatred and the mother of violence." Others held that it contained no more sinister meaning than the civil rights slogan "Freedom Now!"; that it is meant to remind the Negro minority of the power of the vote and economic power; that it is a weapon to use against retail stores which refuse to hire Negroes but are anxious to profit from trading with them; that it is an economic weapon used to prevail on interstate firms to stop discriminatory practices in southern areas.

The unity of civil rights organizations was shattered in 1966 by the rising cry of "Black Power." There was a break between the older and more moderate groups (the National Association for the Advancement of Colored People and the National Urban League) and the younger and more radical ones (the Congress of Racial Equality and the Student Nonviolent Coordinating Committee).

Black Republican. Republicans who opposed extension of slavery into the territories were regarded with contempt by Southerners. The term was applied to Abraham Lincoln before he became President and, in the Reconstruction period, to Republicans who favored legislation aiding Negroes.

Black Thursday (Oct. 24, 1929). The wave of stock selling which had continued from the previous day became so great that the bottom seemed to drop out of the market. At noon, a group of bankers met in the office of J. P. Morgan and announced that they were going to support the market by buying stocks. But confidence was not restored and the Great Depression, triggered by the stock market crash, began.

Black Tom explosion (July 30, 1916). The explosion at a munitions plant on Black Tom Island, part of Jersey City, N.J., was traced to German saboteurs. Seven people were killed and 35 injured; damages amounted to $40,000,000. The incident contributed to anti-German feelings a year before U.S. entrance into World War I.

Black Warrior Affair (1854). At a time when there was much agitation in the U.S. for purchase and annexation of Cuba, the *Black Warrior*, an American steamer, was seized, Feb. 28, by Spanish officials in Cuba. The drastic action was based on a technicality that had been ignored some 30 times the vessel had previously touched at Havana.

The American minister to Spain, Pierre Soulé, exceeded his instruction from Sec. of State Marcy and virtually threatened war. The incident was quieted when the *Black Warrior* was released, Mar. 16, and Spain compensated the owners of the vessel for losses.

Bladensburg, battle of (Aug. 24, 1814). Four miles from Washington, in Maryland, an American force of 7,000, made up largely of untrained militia, was routed by 3,000 British regulars during the War of 1812. The defeat opened the way to Washington, D.C. and the burning of the Capitol, the White House, almost all of the public buildings, several private homes and the office of the *National Intelligencer*.

The U.S. government learned as a result of the battle that it could not rely for its defense on raw state militia.

Blaine Amendment. The language of the New York State Constitution, ratified by the voters of the state in 1894, forbids the state and its subdivisions from financially aiding church-related schools "directly or indirectly" (Art. XI, Sec. 4). This provision is the so-called Blaine Amendment; but it is not an amendment at all. It is known as an amendment because, in the early 1870's, Maine's James G. Blaine, then a Congressman, had campaigned for a similar prohibition.

The New York State Constitutional Convention of 1967 voted for repeal of the Blaine Amendment, substituting for it the general wording of the 1st Amendment to the U.S. Constitution barring the "establishment" of religion. The voters, however, rejected the proposed Constitution, submitted to them as a single package, in part at least, because of the controversy over repeal of the Blaine Amendment.

Blaine, James Gillespie (1830–93). Statesman. Born in West Brownsville, Pa., he was graduated from Washington College, Pa. One of the founders of the Republican party, he was unsuccessful in winning the party's nomination for President in 1876 and 1880. He won the nomination in 1884 but lost the Catholic vote and the election when he failed to challenge the Rev. S. D. Burchard, who castigated the Democratic party as "the party whose antecedents are rum, Romanism and rebellion."

The "Plumed Knight" was a member of the U.S. House of Representatives (1863–76), Speaker of the House (1869–75) and U.S. Senator (1876–81). He led the opposition within his party, the Halfbreeds, against the Stalwarts who supported Pres. Grant. Blaine's public image was tarnished by railroad graft scandals which contributed to his defeat by Grover Cleveland in 1884. His reputation as a statesman was enhanced by his service as U.S. Sec. of State (1889–92) when he helped to improve relations with Latin America by establishing the Bureau of American Republics at Washington, D.C.

Blalock, Alfred (1899–   ). Surgeon. Born in Colloden, Ga., he became director of the department of surgery at Johns Hopkins Univ. He is noted for his work in surgical shock and the regulation of blood circulation. As a result of a type of surgery known as the Blalock operation (1944), in which he bypasses the pulmonary artery, he has helped to save thousands of "blue babies."

Bland-Allison Act (1878). Under the Act, the U.S. Treasury was required to purchase not less than $2,000,000 nor more than $4,000,000 of silver a month and have it coined into legal-tender dollars. The law was virtually a subsidy for the silver mining interests who were clamoring for free and unlimited coinage of silver. The Act had been proposed by Rep. Richard ("Silver Dick") Bland of Missouri, but the amendment by Sen. William Allison of Iowa "limited" the coinage of silver. The Act did not satisfy either the silver interests or farmers, who wanted cheaper money.

"Bleeding Kansas." In the pre-Civil War period, 1854 to 1860, Kansas became a battleground. Under the principle of popular sovereignty in the Kansas-Nebraska Act, the voters were to decide whether the territory was to be admitted to the Union as a free or slave state. Rival governments were set up in Kansas and troublemakers on both sides rashly provoked each other.

The New England Emigrant Aid Society financed free-soil migrations to Kansas. These were met on Kansas soil by proslavery Missourians who suspected the New Englanders and other Northern groups of using Kansas as a base for an attack against slavery in the Southwest.

Violence erupted in the Kansas town of Lawrence (the "sack of Lawrence") in 1856, when a force of proslavery men burned down the hotel and destroyed homes and free-soil printing presses. The abolitionist reply was the Potawatomie "massacre" of proslavery men. The Border War continued intermittently until Kansas entered the Union as a free state.

Block Island. Seven miles long and three and one-half miles wide, the island lies 10 miles off the coast of Rhode Island, at the east entrance to Long Island Sound, between Point Judith, R.I., and Montauk Point, N.Y. Its Indian name was Manisses (translated as little god or little island). Its present name was given by the Dutch navigator, Adriaen Block, who explored the coast of Rhode Island in 1614. The island was first settled in 1661 and was admitted to the colony of Rhode Island in 1664. It is now a summer resort with two good harbors and two lighthouses. Weather reports for boating on the northeast coast invariably are given for Cape May (in southern New Jersey) to Block Island.

"Blood is thicker than water." The 17th-century proverb was quoted by Commodore Tattnall, an American commander in Far Eastern waters, to explain why he disregarded U.S. neutrality in coming to the aid of a British squadron in northeast China, June 25, 1859.

Bloody Angle. A salient in Gen. Lee's line, north of Spotsylvania Courthouse, Va., in the Wilderness Campaign, it was overrun by Gen. Grant's troops (May 12, 1864). The Union advance was halted when Lee's forces rallied.

"Blue and Gray." The Union and Confederate armies were popularly referred to by the color of their uniforms during the Civil War. The Union forces wore blue and the Confederates wore gray.

Blue Eagle. The symbol of a blue-colored eagle on a poster displayed by a businessman indicated that he accepted the "codes of fair competition" drawn up under the supervision of the National Recovery Administration (NRA) in 1933. Under the eagle were the words: "Member N.R.A. We do our part."

bluegrass country. Centered about Lexington, Ky., the region is famous for its racehorses and bluegrass used for pasture, hay and lawns.

Early Kentucky pioneers, including Daniel Boone, guided settlers to this region in 1775. It became the objective of a great migration through the Cumberland Gap in the Appalachians.

"Blue Laws" of Connecticut. In the 17th century, laws passed by the General Court of New Haven provided punishment for Sabbath offenders, drunkenness, sex misconduct and similar misbehavior. One such law read: "No one shall run on the Sabbath day, or walk in his garden, or elsewhere, except reverently to and from meeting." Such laws were not confined to any one colony. The laws were published in a history of Connecticut (1781) by the Loyalist clergyman, Samuel Peters.

In the 19th and 20th centuries, laws restricting behavior on Sunday, and other limitations regarded as old fashioned, have been described as "blue laws."

Boas, Franz (1858–1942). Anthropologist. Born and educated in Germany, he came to the U.S. in 1886 and became a professor at Columbia Univ. in 1899. He carried on field studies in North America, Mexico and Puerto Rico (1886–1931). He was a pioneer in statistical analysis of physical measurements of man, and opposed theories of racial supremacy. An authority on linguistics of North American tribes, he was the author of *The Mind of Primitive Man* (1911, 1938); *Race, Language, and Culture* (1940).

Bonus Army (1932). During the Great Depression some 12,-000 unemployed veterans of

World War I assembled in Washington, D.C., to pressure Congress into immediate payment of "bonus" certificates granted in 1924. When Congress defeated the appropriation, the veterans lingered on in the capital. Pres. Hoover ordered their dispersal. Gen. Douglas MacArthur used tear gas, bayonets and tanks to clear the capital.

Bonus Bill. In 1816 John C. Calhoun proposed the building of roads and canals (internal improvements) at federal expense. He urged that it be financed out of the bonus of $1,500,000 that the second Bank of the United States had paid to the government.

New Englanders opposed the bill because they thought that it would hasten the movement of people to the West. The South was divided on the bill. The western and middle states favored it. Pres. Madison vetoed the bill, March 3, 1817, because he doubted that Congress had the power to pay for the building of roads and canals in various states.

Boomers. Would-be settlers on the land that had not been assigned to Indians in Oklahoma (the "Unassigned Lands" or "Old Oklahoma") were called "boomers" because efforts in the 1880's to settle this land threatened a land boom. Federal troops, however, evicted the illegal squatters.

Boone, Daniel (1735–1820). Pioneer, scout and Indian fighter. Born near Reading, Pa., he became a legendary figure in the history of frontier exploration and settlement. He established the Wilderness Trail over the Cumberland Gap and founded Boonesborough, Ky. (1775). Although his stature has been modified by recent scholarship, Boone played an important role in the settlement of Kentucky and the defense of the frontier during the Revolutionary War.

Booth, Edwin Thomas (1833–93). Actor. Born near Bel Air, Md., he became world famous for Shakespearean roles, especially that of Hamlet. Triumphant appearances in Boston and New York (1857) brought him to the top of his profession. He managed the New York Winter Garden and when it burned (1867) opened Booth's Theatre (1869). His brother John Wilkes Booth, the deranged actor, shot Lincoln; however, audiences rallied to support the great tragedian after his brief retirement following the assassination.

Borah, William Edgar (1865–1940). Statesman. Born in Jasper Township, Ill., he won national prominence as prosecutor (1907) of the leader of the Industrial Workers of the World (IWW), William D. Haywood, who was charged with the murder of Idaho Gov. Frank D. Steunenberg. He was Republican senator from Idaho (1907–40). A confirmed isolationist, he opposed U.S. entrance into the League of Nations and the World Court and advocated nonintervention in World War II. A political maverick, he favored most of the New Deal's domestic program.

Border States. Of the slave states that bordered on the North—Delaware, Maryland, Virginia, Kentucky and Missouri—only Virginia seceded from the Union in 1861. The Border States had close economic ties to the North, but their sympathies were strongly southern. They were strategically important to the North during the Civil War.

Border War (1854–59). Settlement of the Kansas territory precipitated a conflict between rival slavery and free-state factions. Intermittent fighting in "Bleeding Kansas" included pitched battles, lynchings, raids, looting and plain murder arising not only from the slave issue but also from land claims-jumping.

In an effort to pack the territorial legislature with proslavery men, thousands of men called "Border Ruffians" by the abolitionist press poured into Kansas from Missouri in 1855. In an election marked by fraud and violence, a proslavery legislature emerged that sought to crush any opposition to slavery. There followed the "sack of Lawrence" in 1856 by proslavery raiders searching for free-soil leaders who had been indicted for treason by the legislature. In a bloody sequel, five men were hacked to death by John Brown and his followers, at Potawatomie. In 1858 this was countered by the massacre of nine free-state men at Marais des Cygnes. A parade of territorial governors seemed too helpless to restore order.

In 1858 the Lecompton Constitution guaranteeing slavery was rejected by Kansas voters. Territorial status was continued until 1861 when Kansas entered the Union as a free state.

Borgne, Lake, battle of (Dec. 14, 1814). Although a victory for the British navy in the War of 1812, the battle led to the British disaster at the battle of New Orleans.

The delay achieved by American gunboats on the lake, a Mississippi inlet east of New Orleans, enabled Andrew Jackson to arrive in the city and, later, to defeat the British army.

boss, political. Party bosses have been of different types in U.S. political history. Some have held elected office and others have worked behind the scenes. In either case, the boss, as the center of political power, controls patronage and influences the passage of legislation. The most notorious municipal boss of the 19th century was William Tweed, who dominated New York City in the 1870's. Another political boss in the same decade was Thomas C. Platt, on the state level in New York. Richard T. Croker of

Tammany Hall held sway in New York City from 1886 to 1902.

In the 20th century the big political bosses have been Boies Penrose of Pennsylvania, about 1904 to 1920; William Hale "Big Bill" Thompson, mayor of Chicago from 1915 to 1923 and 1927 to 1931; Tom Pendergast of Kansas City, Mo., in the 1930's; Edward J. Kelly, who became mayor of Chicago in 1933 and retained the joint position of mayor and boss for 14 years; Ed Crump of Memphis, Tenn., who before 1947 ran for office 23 times without a defeat; and Frank Hague, who became mayor of Jersey City, in 1917, a position which he held for 30 years.

Political bosses have been classified as "urban," "state" or "rural." They have varied in educational background from Penrose, a Ph.D. who wrote some reputable treatises on government, to Hague who was expelled from the sixth grade as incorrigible.

Boston Massacre (Mar. 5, 1770). British soldiers provoked by a Boston mob fired into it, killing or wounding 11 citizens. The soldiers had been called out by a sentry on duty in front of the Customs House when a crowd seemed to menace him.

John Adams, later a leader in the Revolution, defended the officer and soldiers, who were acquitted of murder charges.

The "massacre" was kept alive by the oratory of Samuel Adams and others during the years preceding the American Revolution.

Boston News-Letter, The. The first regularly published American newspaper appeared on Apr. 24, 1704 as a "tiny four-page two-column folder" offering local items such as shipping notices and European news. It enjoyed continuous publication, though under different names, until 1776.

Boston police strike. When the police commissioner refused to recognize the right of the police to join the American Federation of Labor, the Boston police struck for higher pay. The city was left open for rioting and robberies and public safety was endangered. Mayor Andrew J. Peters could not persuade the police commissioner, appointed by the governor, to meet some of the police demands. When Gov. Coolidge failed to act, the mayor used Boston militia units to break the strike.

With the strike virtually over, Coolidge sent in the state militia and declared: "There is no right to strike against the public safety by anybody, anywhere, any time." The statement was made at a time when fears had been aroused by post-World War I labor unrest. It gained national attention and won for Coolidge the Republican nomination for Vice-President in 1920. He became President when Harding died in 1923.

Boston Port Bill. The first of the Coercive Acts became effective June 1, 1774. Under it, Parliament removed the British customhouse from Boston and ordered the port closed to all shipping until the town paid the East India Company for the tea thrown into the harbor, Dec. 16, 1773.

Lord North failed to anticipate the inflammatory effect of this measure on the colonies. It led to the summoning of the Continental Congress.

Boston Tea Party (Dec. 16, 1773). Colonists masquerading as Indians boarded three tea ships of the British East India Company and threw the tea into Boston Harbor.

Colonial merchants feared that the entry of the low-priced tea would establish a monopoly for the British company and deprive them of a lucrative source of revenue. Colonists regarded the tea as symbolic of the growing interference in colonial trade by an increasingly active British government. It was felt that monopolies of other commodities might be established by Parliament if the tea monopoly was not resisted.

Parliament's reply to the destruction of the tea was a series of "Intolerable Acts," including closing of the port of Boston until the tea was paid for. The rest of the colonies rallied to the aid of Boston and brought the American Revolution a step nearer.

bounties. Governments sometimes make payments to stimulate production of certain goods.

By the 1700's the British government was paying bounties to colonists for production of such naval stores as tar, resin and turpentine. The colonial fishing fleet was encouraged by bounties paid on fish and whale oil. Cash payments were also made to stimulate shipbuilding and recruitment of seamen.

During the Revolutionary War Congress paid bounties to men who volunteered for service in the Continental army. The states, too, paid bounties for militia volunteers. Competition between the two forced up the price so that at one time New Jersey was paying a bounty as high as $1,000 for each man.

The practice of bounty payments was continued in the War of 1812, the Mexican War, the Civil War and intermittent Indian wars. During the Civil War, bounty brokers recruited derelicts and then took part or all of the bounty. Desertions from the Union army were high because of bounty jumping. Some men deserted and reenlisted again and again. The cost to the federal government for bounty payments during the Civil War was over $300 million and about the same amount was paid by the states in an effort to meet the draft calls. Bounty payments by the military have not been made since the beginning of World War I.

Bowditch, Nathaniel (1773–1838). Mathematician and astronomer. He was born in Salem, Mass. Prominent among early American intellectuals, he prepared the first American edition of J. H. Moore's *The Practical Navigator* (1799). Over 60 editions of the revised work, *The New Practical American Navigator*, have appeared. He also made charts of New England harbors. He translated La Place's *Mécanique céleste* (1829–39), doubling its size with his annotations—"an epoch in American science." He was actuary of the Massachusetts Hospital Life Insurance Co. in Boston (1823–38).

bowie knife. Highly valued by soldiers and frontiersmen of the Southwest, the knife had a guarded hilt and a straight one-edged blade about 10 inches long. It could be thrown, used for stabbing, skinning animals or eating. Its reputed inventor was Rezin P. Bowie, brother of James Bowie, a hero of the Texas Revolution.

Boxer Rebellion (1900). A secret anti-Western military organization of Chinese (called "Boxers" because their symbol was a clenched fist) attacked missionaries and seized Peking (also Peiping), site of the foreign legations. An international mission of 20,000 men, including 2,500 U.S. soldiers, came to the rescue.

U.S. Sec. of State John Hay persuaded the powers to demand an indemnity, not territory, from the Chinese government. The U.S. gave most of its share back to China and this was used by China to educate selected students in the U.S.

Boy Scouts of America. Intended for boys over 12 years of age, the organization was incorporated in 1919 in the U.S. Since then the movement has spread throughout most of the world. Scouts wear distinctive uniforms but are nonmilitary. There are no racial, religious or political requirements for membership. The unit is the troop headed by a volunteer scoutmaster. Scouts are divided into classes beginning with tenderfoot and advancing through various ranks. They stress outdoor knowledge and skills and perform useful service in civic projects. There are about 5,500,000 members of the organization in the U.S. including adult leaders.

Bozeman Trail. The pioneer John M. Bozeman blazed (1863–65) a Rocky Mountain trail which crossed the Oregon Trail at Fort Laramie and led to the gold mines of Virginia City, Mont. The Sioux Indians, however, attacked the caravans en route and by 1868 forced the abandonment of military posts along the trail.

After the suppression of the Sioux in 1877 the trail was opened again and became part of a cattle route from Texas to Montana.

braceros. By agreement between the U.S. and Mexico, Mexican farmhands are employed as "seasonal" workers in the U.S.

The bracero program was instituted as an emergency measure during World War II when there was a scarcity in the farm-labor market. When the program was terminated in 1946 there was an invasion of Mexican border jumpers working for as little as 10 cents an hour. This occasioned Public Law 78 (1951). Under it up to 450,000 braceros a year were used by a score of states, with California using the most. Braceros (Spanish idiom for manual laborers) were supposed to be employed only where there was a government-certified shortage of labor. They generally worked for less than the minimum wage paid American labor.

Public Law 78 expired at the end of 1964. American farm workers looked upon the braceros as cheap labor who caused them loss of employment. Some farmers contended that the braceros were a certain supply of labor whereas American farm labor was often difficult to recruit for "seasonal" work.

Bradford, William (1590–1657). Pilgrim leader. Born in England, he joined a separatist group in 1606 and sailed for the New World in the *Mayflower* (1620). He was Governor of Plymouth Colony almost every year from 1621 to 1656. With the help of other Pilgrim Fathers he placed it on a sound economic base. His *History of*

Plimmoth Plantation was not published in full until 1856.

Bradstreet, Anne Dudley (c. 1612–72). Poetess. Born in England, she emigrated with her family to Massachusetts Bay in 1630. The first woman poet in America, she is the author of *The Tenth Muse Lately Sprung Up in America* (1650), a book of religious poetry.

"Brain Trust." The advisers of Pres. F. D. Roosevelt included professors and intellectuals who were not members of his Cabinet but who were widely regarded as responsible for the experimental nature of the New Deal. They were placed in various government positions in Washington, D.C. to bring them close to the President. Prominent members of the "Brain Trust" were Raymond Moley, Adolph A. Berle, Jr., Rexford Tugwell, all from the Columbia University faculty, and Harry Hopkins, a New York social worker.

Brandeis, Louis Dembitz (1856–1941). Jurist. Born in Louisville, Ky., he received his law degree from Harvard and practiced law in Boston. A "people's lawyer," he departed from the usual legal citations and drew on the facts of social life to persuade the U.S. Supreme Court of the constitutionality of the Oregon law limiting the working day for women to 10 hours (*Muller v. Oregon,* 1908). As an Associate Justice of the Supreme Court (1916–39), his dissents ranked with those of Justice Holmes in support of civil rights and the common man. His vigorous opposition to monopolies was captured in his books, *Other People's Money* (1914) and *The Curse of Bigness* (1934).

Brandywine Creek, battle of (Sept. 11, 1777). In the battle, Gen. Washington failed to prevent the British under Gen. Howe from taking Philadelphia. His force of 11,000 faced a British army of 15,000 and was almost routed. He was, however, able to retreat to Chester, Pa.

Brannan Plan. A plan for stabilizing the income of farmers was proposed by Sec. of Agriculture Charles Brannan in 1949. Instead of price supports for farm crops, Brannan advocated direct payments to farmers. The Plan was adopted by Congress in 1973.

bread colonies. During the colonial period the Middle colonies—New York, New Jersey, Pennsylvania and Delaware—shipped wheat, flour and loaves of bread in enormous quantities to New England, the southern colonies, the West Indies and Europe.

Bread Riots. During the Panic of 1837 the price of flour rose to $12 per barrel. In February and March the poor of New York broke into flour warehouses and helped themselves.

The state militia quelled the riots.

Bretton Woods Conference (July 1–22, 1944). Representatives of 44 nations met in New Hampshire to plan for postwar international economic cooperation. They set up an International Monetary Fund to stabilize national currencies and an International Bank for Reconstruction and Development to extend loans to nations that needed economic rehabilitation.

Bricker Amendment (1954). Sen. John W. Bricker (O.) proposed an amendment to restrict the treaty-making powers of the President. It would have limited the scope of international treaties to which the U.S. could be a party. Bricker argued that the United Nations was in a position to commit the U.S. to positions which the Congress had not approved and thus deprive the American people of their constitutional rights. It was opposed by Sec. of State John Foster Dulles as "dangerous to our peace and security." The Amendment was rejected by the Senate.

Bridger, James (1804–81). Fur trader, frontiersman and scout. Born in Richmond, Va., he was the first white man to visit the Great Salt Lake (1824). He established Fort Bridger in southwestern Wyoming (1843). A friend of leaders in the westward movement, he guided numerous exploring expeditions including Reynolds' Yellowstone expedition (1859–60), Berthoud's engineering party (1861) and the Powder River expeditions (1865–66).

Brook Farm. A group of transcendentalist intellectuals led by George Ripley founded in 1841 a 200-acre cooperative farm in West Roxbury, Mass. One of its members, Nathaniel Hawthorne, was inspired to write *The Blithedale Romance*, based on his experience in the utopian colony.

Members sought to combine the intellectual life with farming. Although the colony never numbered more than a hundred members, it became a popular center for visitors from Boston. When Charles Fourier's ideas on communal living were adopted, a phalanstery for housing the community was built. It burned down in 1846 and the insolvent community was dissolved.

Brooklyn, N.Y. First settled by Walloons and Hollanders in 1636–37, the town of Breuckelen was formed in 1645 and became coextensive with Kings County in 1683. It is located in the southwest part of Long Island.

Settlement became rapid in the years before the Civil War. The state chartered Brooklyn, the "city of homes and churches," in 1834.

Brooklyn became part of the borough system of New York City, Jan. 1, 1898. New York on Manhattan Island became the Borough of Manhattan; the city areas north and east of Manhattan became the Borough of the Bronx; Queens County became Queens Borough; Richmond County (Staten Island) became Richmond Borough. Each borough has a president with little power. The mayor of New York is the chief executive of the five boroughs. Brooklyn is the largest of the boroughs in population, 2,615,-000.

The boroughs are linked by an intricate system of roads, tunnels and bridges. The latest link, the Verrazano-Narrows Bridge at the entrance of New York Harbor, connecting Brooklyn and Staten Island, was opened Nov. 21, 1964. It has a main span of 4,260 feet and is the longest and heaviest suspension bridge in existence.

Brooks, Phillips (1835–93). Episcopal clergyman. He was born in Boston, Mass. A gifted preacher and spiritual leader, he was consecrated Bishop of Massachusetts (1891). His sermons at Independence Hall, Philadelphia, over Lincoln's body, and at the Harvard Commemoration of the Civil War dead received nationwide attention in 1865. Rector of Trinity Church, Boston (1869–91), he was author of the hymn, "O Little Town of Bethlehem" (1868).

Broun, Heywood (1888–1939). Journalist. Born Matthew Heywood Campbell Broun, in Brooklyn, N.Y., he became a legend in his own time as a liberal, crusading New York columnist. His syndicated feature, "It Seems to Me," appeared in the Scripps-Howard papers (from 1928). He hit hard against social injustice and championed the poor.

Brown, John (1800–59). Abolitionist. Born in Torrington, Conn., he is one of the most controversial figures in American history. He has been denounced as a fanatic whose plots to free the slaves helped plunge the country into the Civil War, and defended as a martyr whose memory is preserved in the marching song "John Brown's Body." High points in Brown's abolitionist crusade include the massacre of proslavery men at Potawatomie, Kan. (1856) and his frustrated attempt to start a general slave insurrection at Harpers Ferry, Va. (1859). Found guilty of treason, he was hanged (Dec. 2, 1859).

Brownists. Robert Browne was a Church of England clergyman of Norwich until 1580 when he began declaiming against the discipline and ceremony of the Church. His name was associated with the religious Separatists of England during the latter part of the 16th century.

The Pilgrim Fathers were Brownists. The Puritans, too, followed Browne's Congregational organization.

Brownsville Riot (1906). Negro soldiers stationed in Brownsville, Tex., incensed by mistreatment by whites, fired indiscriminately at citizens, killing one man. In the investigation that followed it was not possible to identify the Negroes responsible. Pres. Theodore Roosevelt ordered dishonorable discharges for 159 privates and noncommissioned officers of the companies involved.

Brown University. Chartered in 1764 as Rhode Island College, at Warren, R.I., the school moved in 1770 to Providence. It is the seventh oldest college in the nation. The charter provides for absolute liberty of conscience and prohibits religious tests. During the Revolutionary War, the college was closed and used as barracks and hospitals by American and French troops. Although founded by the Baptists, the college maintains its independence and nonsectarian principles. Its present name was adopted in 1804 after gifts from Nicholas Brown, a merchant.

Pembroke College in Brown University, the woman's college, was established in 1891 and later named for the college attended by Roger Williams (Pembroke College in Cambridge University).

The university established a graduate program in 1887. It offers work in the liberal arts and sciences that lead to a B.A. degree in 45 different fields of specialization.

Brown v. Board of Education (1954). The U.S. Supreme Court held unanimously that state constitutional provisions requiring segregation of white and Negro children in public schools on the basis of race denies to such children the equal protection of the laws guaranteed by the 14th Amendment and are void.

This momentous decision arose from litigation in Topeka, Kan., and spurred the Negro civil rights movement. The Court, reversing the "separate but equal" doctrine of *Plessy v. Ferguson* (1896), relied on psychological and sociological studies which indicated that separation of children based on race "generates a feeling of inferiority as to their status in the community" and adversely affects "the educational development" of Negro children.

Bryan, William Jennings (1860–1925). Political leader. Born in Salem, Ill., he moved to Nebraska. He won the Democratic nomination for President in 1896 with his famous "Cross of Gold" speech. Campaigning for free silver, Bryan was defeated by McKinley. He was defeated again in 1900 when he opposed territorial expansion, and lost a presidential campaign for the third and last time in 1908 against Theodore Roosevelt. In 1912 he helped Woodrow Wilson win the nomination and became U.S. Sec. of State (1913–15), breaking with Wilson over U.S. policy following the sinking of the *Lusitania*. His final days were clouded by his opposition to the theory of evolution, when his ignorance of

modern science was exposed in the Scopes Trial (Tenn., 1925).

Bryan-Chamorro Treaty (1916). The pact between the U.S. and Nicaragua gave the U.S. the exclusive right to build a canal through Nicaragua. The U.S. thus prevented construction of a canal rivaling the Panama Canal and allowed for the possibility of additional canal construction at some future time.

The U.S. paid Nicaragua $3 million in consideration of the rights granted, a sum which enabled the Nicaraguan government to meet its obligations to American bankers. Pres. Wilson and Sec. of State William J. Bryan were criticized by *The New York Times* for making the "Dollar Diplomacy" of Pres. Taft and his Sec. of State, P. C. Knox, "more nearly resemble ten-cent diplomacy."

Bryant, William Cullen (1794–1878). Poet and editor. Born in Cummington, Mass., he is best remembered for his poem, "Thanatopsis" (1817). A poet of nature, his work includes "To a Waterfowl," "Green River" and "The Yellow Violet" (1821); "Rizpah," "Autumn Woods" and "A Forest Hymn" (1824–25). On the political side of his life, he edited the New York *Evening Post* (1829–78) and vigorously opposed slavery in the pre-Civil War years. The paper turned from the Democrats to support of the newly formed Republican party. After the Civil War, Bryant broke with the Radical

Republicans and supported Andrew Johnson's Reconstruction policy. He was critical of the Grant administration, but kept the paper in the Republican column.

Buchanan, James (1791–1868). Fifteenth President of the U.S. (1857–61). He was born in Cove Gap, Pa. and was graduated from Dickinson College (1809). He served Pennsylvania as a Democratic member of U.S. House of Representatives (1821–31) and as U.S. Senator (1834–45). He was U.S. Sec. of State (1845–49). As U.S. minister to Great Britain (1853–56), he was out of the country as the slavery controversy boiled. He avoided the use of force when South Carolina seceded, then supported the Union during the Civil War.

Buckshot War (1838). A disagreement over the organization of the Pennsylvania House of Representatives became so violent that the governor called on the Philadelphia militia to restore order. His requisition included buckshot cartridges, thus giving the affair its name. Democrats eventually triumphed.

Bucktails. Disgruntled Tammany politicians, who opposed Gov. DeWitt Clinton's canal policy, organized an opposition party in New York State in the 1820's. Party members wore a deer-tail on their hats, a Tammany symbol.

Buena Vista, battle of (Feb. 22–23, 1847). Although greatly outnumbered, Gen. Zachary Taylor's forces won a brilliant victory in northern Mexico over Santa Anna.

Buffalo Bill. William F. Cody (1846–1917), scout and trooper during the Civil War, earned the nickname by furnishing buffalo meat for food contractors to the Kansas Pacific Railroad in the postwar period. Cody entered show business with a "Wild West" spectacle in 1883.

buffalo chips. The white men who first moved across or settled on the Great Plains used buffalo droppings as fuel.

Buffalo soldiers. Indians called Negro troopers by the name because of the similarity between their tightly curled hair, generally short, and that of the buffalo. White soldiers called them Brunettes. There were two Negro infantry regiments and two Negro cavalry regiments in continuous service in the West during the three decades following the Civil War.

Bulfinch, Charles (1763–1844). Architect. Born in Boston, Mass., his early travels in Europe influenced his style toward the classical architecture of France and Italy. He designed churches in New England; the State House at Hartford, Conn; and the Massachusetts State House on Beacon Hill. He influenced New England domestic architecture—he was the first to use curved staircases. He took over as architect of the Capitol, Washington, D.C., when Benjamin Latrobe resigned in 1817.

Bulge, battle of the (Dec. 1944–Jan. 1945). Attempting the last major offensive of the Germans in World War II, the *Wehrmacht*, under Field Marshal von Rundstedt, counterattacked and created a bulge in the Belgium-Luxembourg sector. The Germans were repulsed and thrown back behind the Siegfried Line, at a cost of 120,000 killed, wounded and prisoners. The U.S. lost 76,-890 killed, wounded or missing. The defeat had a catastrophic effect on German morale. Winston Churchill described the action as "the greatest American battle of the war."

bull-boats. During the 19th century fur traders, imitating the Indians, built staunch craft (about 18 feet long and five feet wide with round bottoms) for use in the rapid, snagfilled, shallow tributaries of the Missouri River. They were made of buffalo skins (preferably of old tough bulls) stretched across a willow frame and had to be taken out of the water and sun-dried frequently to prevent waterlogging. They only lasted for one long trip, but they were more serviceable than other boats for transporting furs on the rivers of the high plains.

"Bull Moose" party. When Theodore Roosevelt, a hunter and exponent of the outdoor life, was asked about his health he replied that he felt "fit as a bull moose." The phrase became the popular name for the Progressive party, which nominated Theodore Roosevelt for President in 1912.

Bull Run, battle of. There were two battles of Bull Run (also called Manassas) during the Civil War. The first Bull Run (July 21, 1861) was the first major action of the war. Confederate forces were stationed in Virginia, within 20 miles of Washington, D.C., along Bull Run Creek, under the command of Gen. Pierre Beauregard.

The Union army under Gen. Irvin McDowell was ordered to march toward Richmond. An early victory seemed possible when the tide turned against McDowell. The routed Union forces fled toward Washington but were rallied for a stand at Centreville, on the outskirts of the capital.

During this action Gen. Thomas Jackson earned the title "Stonewall" for his defense of a Confederate position.

The effect of the Union defeat was to stimulate the confidence of the Confederacy and to confront the North with the hard reality of the struggle to restore the Union.

Second Bull Run (Aug. 27–Sept. 2, 1862) was also a Confederate victory. Union Gen. John Pope undertook a frontal assault on Richmond and was turned back by Gen. Robert E. Lee and "Stonewall" Jackson. The setback left Union soldiers bitter and discouraged under leadership that seemed dwarfed by the brilliance of Confederate generals.

bumboats. Small boats were used to peddle provisions and other goods from harbor ports to vessels at anchor. They were common in the 19th and early 20th centuries in the harbors of Cuba and the Philippines.

Bummers. The nickname was given to the foragers who helped Gen. Sherman's troops to live off the land on their "March to the Sea," through Georgia and the Carolinas, in 1865.

buncombe (sometimes **bunkum**). In the late 1820's when a member of Congress from Buncombe County, N.C. was chided for his irrelevance, he countered: "I am speaking not for you, but for Buncombe." Since then the term has been used to describe effusive talk that has nothing to do with the business at hand.

bundling. During the 17th and 18th centuries sweethearts who were courting were permitted to get into bed together with their clothes on. The custom, carried over from Europe, arose because of lack of space and heat in the poorer houses.

Bunker Hill, battle of (June 17, 1775). Patriots, before the for-mal break with Britain, were sent to fortify Bunker Hill, but took a position on Breed's Hill which was closer to Boston. When Gen. Howe, on orders of Gen. Thomas Gage, sought to dislodge them, his regular troops were turned back by withering fire. It was only when the Americans' powder ran out that they retreated. The American patriots had won a moral victory.

Burlingame Treaty (1868). Because of the need for "cheap labor" in mines and on railroads, under this Treaty the Chinese were given unlimited immigration rights to the U.S. Sec. of State Seward encouraged these arrangements made by Anson Burlingame, who had gained China's confidence during his years there as U.S. Minister. The West, particularly California, applauded the Treaty at the time although the section changed its views within a decade.

Burns fugitive slave case (1854). Aroused by exhortations of Wendell Phillips and Theodore Parker at large meetings in Faneuil and Meionaon Halls on May 26, a Boston mob sought unsuccessfully to prevent a Virginia slave, Anthony Burns, from being returned to his master. The mob broke into the jail and killed the marshal. The fugitive, however, was "protected" by a military force and was escorted to the cutter *Morris* to be returned to the South.

Indictments against Phillips

and Parker were quashed. The next year a fund was raised for the purchase of Burns and he came back to Boston in 1855.

Other rescues of fugitive slaves involved James Hamlet at New York City (1850), Rachel Parker at Baltimore, Shadrach and Thomas Sims at Boston (1851), "Jerry" at Syracuse (1851), the Christiana (Pa.) affair (1851) and the Oberlin rescue (1858).

Burr, Aaron (1756–1836). Political leader. Born in Newark, N.J., he served in the Revolutionary Army and practiced law in New York City. He represented New York in the U.S. Senate (1791–97) and tied with Thomas Jefferson for the Presidency in the election of 1800. He withdrew when the election was thrown into the House of Representatives and became Vice-Pres. (1801–05). A political rival of Alexander Hamilton, whose financial plans he opposed, Burr fought and killed Hamilton in a duel (1804). He proceeded from scheme to scheme for the balance of his life. Charged with treason, he was found innocent of the charge (1807) that he had attempted to wrest the Southwest Territory from Spain in order to set up an independent republic.

Burr-Hamilton duel. Aaron Burr challenged Alexander Hamilton to a duel and shot him through the chest, July 11, 1804, at Weehawken, N.J. Hamilton died the next day and Burr's political future was ended.

Burr had been incensed by Hamilton's part in his defeat in the New York gubernatorial campaign in April and their long-standing differences in the state and nation. It had been rumored that Burr's victory in New York was to be followed by secession of New England and New York. Hamilton and other Federalists, loyal to the Union, allegedly referred to Burr as a traitor.

Hamilton, while opposed to dueling, accepted rather than have his reputation besmirched by any charge of cowardice that might damage his political fortunes.

Burroughs, William Seward (1857–98). Inventor. Born in Rochester, N.Y., he patented the earliest successful adding machine (1892) that recorded both the separate items and the final result.

Burr's Conspiracy. When Burr killed Hamilton in a duel, in 1804, he destroyed himself politically. He embarked on a number of ill-defined plans involving land and empire that he hoped would free him of his debts and bring him power. Burr's plan for detaching the western states from the U.S., with the aid of England, fell through in 1805. He then interested an Irish exile, Harman Blennerhasset, who lived on an island in the Ohio River, in a plan to meet with Gen. Wilkinson, military commandant of Louisiana, in a western adventure involving Spain. Wilkinson betrayed him to Pres. Jefferson and Burr was arrested in Alabama (1807), before he could escape to Spanish territory.

Burr was indicted for treason and tried before Chief Justice Marshall in the U.S. Circuit Court, at Richmond, Va. (1807). In the course of the trial, Marshall on behalf of the accused ordered Pres. Jefferson to appear before the court. Jefferson refused, setting a precedent for future Presidents. Burr was acquitted when the administration lawyers could not prove that he had been personally engaged in actual warlike activity.

business cycles. Swings from good times to bad and back again have occurred throughout most of human history. The business cycle in the modern world extends over a period of years. The pattern is never exactly the same, but economists can identify a number of stages or phases which occur in all cases. *Prosperity* is the period when business is good and getting better. This period is sometimes interrupted by *recession* during which demand falls off and unemployment increases. *Crisis* is the time when business begins to show a downward trend. *Depression* is the period when business is bad and getting worse. *Recovery* is the time when firms find conditions improving somewhat.

Butler, Nicholas Murray (1862–1947). Educator. Born in Elizabeth, N.J., his life re-

volved around Columbia Univ. (N.Y.). He was organizer and first president of Teachers College (1886–91) and president of Columbia Univ. (1902–45). He was Republican nominee for Vice-President (1912); president of the Carnegie Endowment for International Peace (1925–45); and awarded the Nobel Peace Prize (1931), shared with Jane Addams.

Butler's General Order No. 28. Gen. Benjamin F. Butler who commanded Union troops occupying New Orleans issued an order on May 15, 1862, that Southern women who showed their contempt for Union officers and soldiers were to be treated as women of the town. The order made Butler a hated figure in the South and a controversial figure elsewhere.

Butternuts. A reference to the home-dyed clothing of the ignorant rustics of Southern origin who supported the Democratic party during the Civil War, it was used as a term of contempt to describe the "Peace Democrats" in the North. The "Peace Democrats" were more commonly called Copperheads, a term which they naturally resented. They chose to accept Butternuts as a badge of honor, since they regarded themselves as spokesmen for the common people.

Byrd, Richard Evelyn (1888–1957). Polar explorer. Born in Winchester, Va., he was graduated from the U.S. Naval Academy (1912). In charge of the aviation unit in the Navy-Mac-Millan Polar Expedition (1925), he and his pilot Floyd Bennett (1890–1928) were the first to fly over the North Pole (1926). Byrd established "Little America" as his base for explorations of the Antarctic (1928–30, 1933–35) and flew over the South Pole (1929). He was promoted to rear admiral (1930) in recognition of his discoveries and compilation of scientific data in polar regions. His explorations laid the basis for U.S. territorial claims in the Arctic.

C

Cabinet. The members of the chief advisory body to the President, as heads of the executive departments in the federal government, are appointed by him and meet with him regularly to discuss current problems. Unlike their counterparts in the British government, U.S. Cabinet officers are not members of the legislature. However, they may be invited to sessions of congressional committees and questioned.

No specific mention of the Cabinet occurs in the Constitution, but the President "may require the Opinion, in writing, of the principal Officer in each of the executive Departments, upon any Subjects relating to the Duties of their respective Offices" (Art. II, Sec. 2, Par. 1). Pres. Washington originated the tradition of the Cabinet by consulting with the heads of the State, War, and Navy departments and the Attorney General. The term was first used in 1793.

The influence of the Cabinet varies with the President. He is under no obligation to accept the opinion of a Cabinet member in making a decision or to consider the wishes of the entire Cabinet. In recent years Cabinet meetings have been attended by the Vice-President and by various other presidential advisers. The Cabinet member need not confine his advice to the particular department or office which he heads.

The names of the 11 executive departments represented in the Cabinet (1974) are: Department of State, Department of the Treasury, Department of Defense, Department of Justice, Department of the Interior, Department of Agriculture, Department of Commerce, Department of Labor, Department of Health, Education and Welfare, Department of Housing and Urban Development, and Department of Transportation.

Cable Act (1922). Previously the naturalization law had provided that a woman marrying an American citizen automatically acquired citizenship. Under this Act, women no longer either gain or lose U.S. citizenship by marriage. The alien woman who marries an American citizen can, however, acquire citizenship after only three years (rather than five) of residence in the U.S.

Caine Mutiny, The (1951). A novel by Herman Wouk that embodied the new collective ethic by suggesting that the worst sinner was the man who challenged the organization. No matter how cowardly or mad Capt. Queeg was, his executive officer, Lt. Maryk, should not have relieved him of his post. In so doing, Maryk threatened the whole philosophy of command. The true villain, Wouk argued, was not Queeg but the rootless intellectual, Lt. Keefer, who had filled Maryk's mind with subversive doubts about the sacredness of authority.

The book was adapted by the author as the play *The Caine Mutiny Court-Martial* (1954).

Cairo Conference (Nov. 22–26, 1943). Pres. Roosevelt, Prime Minister Churchill and Generalissimo Chiang Kai-shek met in North Africa. Stalin did not attend because the Soviet Union was not then at war with Japan. They announced that Japan would have to surrender unconditionally. "Japan shall be stripped of all the islands in the Pacific which she has seized or occupied since the beginning of the first World War in 1914, and all the territories Japan has stolen from the Chinese, such as Manchuria, Formosa, and the Pescadores, shall be restored to the Republic of China." Korea

was to become free and independent.

Calamity Jane. The nickname was won by pistol-packing Martha Jane (Canary) Burke (c. 1852–1903), a frontier figure in the gold-mining town of Deadwood, Dakota Territory, during the late 1870's. She has been glamorized in western movies and television, but research indicates she was an immoral alcoholic.

Calhoun, John Caldwell (1782–1850). Statesman. Born in Abbeville District, S.C., he was graduated from Yale (1804). The leading political philosopher defending slavery, he represented South Carolina in the U.S. House of Representatives (1811–17). He held the positions of U.S. Sec. of War (1817–25), Vice-Pres. (1825–32), U.S. Senator (1832–43, 1845–50) and U.S. Sec. of State (1844–45). A champion of the Southern cause, Calhoun formulated the doctrine of nullification and resigned as Vice-Pres. when this view of states' rights was disputed by Pres. Jackson. He wanted each section of the country to share equally in federal power and favored independence for the South if control by the majority were imposed on it.

Calhoun's *Disquisition on Government* (1851). Coupled with his *Discourse on the Constitution and Government of the United States* (1851), this posthumously published work ex-

89

pands upon his earlier "South Carolina Exposition." The later works set forth the theory of "concurrent majorities," which would obtain for any special interest group, such as the South, the right to veto an act passed by a majority in Congress. Calhoun's position was that a minority out of power should be able to protect its interests against a section that was in power "by dividing and distributing the powers of government."

California. The "Golden State," a Pacific group state, was first explored by Cabrillo and Ferrelo of Spain in 1542–43. Later the English explorer, Drake, visited the coast. The land was claimed by Spain, but Indian wars and distance prevented successful colonization.

California, although under the jurisdiction of Mexico in 1822, was practically autonomous. American settlers agitated for independence and union with the U.S., which was achieved as an outcome of the Mexican War in 1848. Settlement of the territory was speeded by the California gold rush of 1849.

An antislavery constitution was adopted in 1849 and California (named by the Spanish conquistador, Cortez), as provided in the Compromise of 1850, was admitted to the Union as the 31st State, Sept. 9, 1850.

Within California are located both the highest (Mt. Whitney, 14,495 ft.) and lowest (Death Valley, 282 ft. below sea level) altitudes in continental U.S.

Sacramento is the state's capital. Two of the great cities in the state are Los Angeles and San Francisco. Los Angeles, motion picture capital of the world, is a vast electronic center and a major center for oil refining and aircraft manufacture. San Francisco, a major Pacific coast port, has numerous industries including food processing, chemicals, transportation equipment and electrical machinery.

Irrigation has helped to make California one of the leading agricultural states in the U.S. It produces more fruit and vegetables than any other state. It is second to New York in manufacturing.

California became first in the nation in population, wresting the lead from New York, on July 1, 1964, when the U.S. Bureau of the Census estimated its population at 18,084,000, compared with New York's 17,915,000.

Call It Sleep (1935). One of the highly rated "proletarian" novels of the 1930's, the story by Henry Roth tells of an immigrant childhood in New York's East Side. Reprinted in 1964 as a paperback, the book won a wide audience.

Calvinism. John Calvin, the French theologian of the Reformation, developed a system of Protestant doctrine which held that redemption is for the elect alone, the free gift of God not to be won by good works. Since Calvinism emphasizes virtues of thrift, industry, sobriety and responsibility as essential to the achievement of God's reign on earth, its extension to all spheres of human activity has contributed to the development of a successful industrial economy.

New England Congregationalists and Presbyterians who came to the colonies from England in the 17th century held to much of Calvin's teachings—the sovereignty of God, the depravity of man and predestination. They did not, however, regard themselves as Calvinists, for they stressed the Covenant theology. This placed a higher importance on the individual in attaining salvation. According to the "Covenant" or "Federal" theology of the 17th century, God offered a covenant or contract to anyone who heard His words. The predestined ("elect") accepted the offer. The "elect" were identified by their good behavior and unswerving belief in Christ.

Cambridge Agreement (1629). A group of Puritans under the leadership of John Winthrop, father of Massachusetts, were authorized to transfer the charter from England to the colony provided that they pledged to migrate to New England. The transfer of the charter was intended to prevent non-Puritans in England from gaining control of the Massachusetts Bay Company and thus destroying the godly commonwealth which Winthrop envisaged in the New World.

Camden, battle of (Aug. 16, 1780). British Gen. Cornwallis won a decisive victory over the Continental Army and militia under Gen. Horatio Gates whose defeat meant the loss of South Carolina. In the battle, Baron Johann de Kalb, a French army officer (born in Germany), who had been commissioned a major general in the Continental Army, was killed.

camels. When Jefferson Davis was Sec. of War in Pres. Pierce's Cabinet, he persuaded Congress in 1855 to appropriate funds for the purchase of camels from Egypt. He had them delivered to army forts in the territory acquired from Mexico in the hope that they would be more suitable than pack animals for the desert country. They were not and some were sold to western mining companies, others to circuses. Many roamed wild in the desert until they died.

canal (Panama) tolls controversy. Under the Hay-Pauncefote Treaty (1901) with Great Britain "all nations" were to be required to pay the same tolls for use of the U.S.-owned Panama Canal. In 1912, however, Congress passed an act providing for the operation of the Panama Canal in which a provision exempted American coastal shipping from payment of any tolls. Defenders of the act held that by "all nations" was meant "all other nations."

The British charged the U.S. with violating the Treaty and acting in bad faith. In 1914 Pres. Wilson appeared before Congress personally to ask for repeal of the toll exemption provision. Anglophobes, incited by the Hearst press, opposed repeal, but after bitter debate, Congress approved repeal.

Cantigny, Americans attack at (May 28, 1918). In the first offensive operation undertaken by Americans in World War I the French village, on high ground near Paris, was captured by the U.S. 1st Division. The successful offensive came appropriately at a time when Allied morale was low. To the Germans, who had been scornful of American fighting ability, the American victory at Cantigny was discouraging.

Canton and Enderbury islands. In 1939 the U.S. and Great Britain agreed on a system of joint control of these mid-Pacific islands in the Phoenix group. Each government is represented by an administrative official. The islands are available for communications and for use as airports for international aviation, but only by civil aviation companies incorporated in the U.S. or in any part of the British Commonwealth of Nations. Canton serves as an air stop between Hawaii and Australia. Enderbury is uninhabited.

Canton fur trade. As early as 1784 Americans were carrying on trade with China through the port of Canton. Boston merchants brought the skins of sea otters from the U.S. Northwest coast and other furs valued by the Chinese and traded them for tea. The Canton trade was expanded during the 19th century to include other products.

Cantwell v. Connecticut **(1940).** The U.S. Supreme Court ruled that the 1st Amendment's mandate that "Congress shall make no law respecting an establishment of religion, or prohibiting the free exercise thereof" applied to the states since the 14th Amendment "rendered the legislatures of the states as incompetent as Congress to enact such laws. . . ." The Court reasoned that the fundamental concept of liberty embraced in the 14th Amendment includes the liberties guaranteed by the 1st Amendment. Justice Roberts handed down the decision.

Cape Cod. The sandy peninsula, 65 miles long and one to 20 miles wide, juts out of southeastern Massachusetts into the Atlantic. It has become famous as a landmark and resort area. It was named by the English navigator, Gosnold, in 1602. The Pilgrims landed in 1620 on a site that became Provincetown. Some of the Cape's scenery is being preserved in the Cape Cod National Seashore, established by the federal government in 1961.

Cape Kennedy. The U.S. Air Force Missile Test Center is located at a point in Florida, formerly Cape Canaveral. The area was renamed following Pres. Kennedy's assassination in 1963. From it the nation's first earth satellite was launched, Jan. 31, 1958, the first U.S. manned space flight, May 5, 1961, and the first manned orbital flight, Feb. 20, 1962, by Col. John H. Glenn.

capitalism. Under the economic system which prevails in the U.S. the means of production, such as factories, farms, machines, railroads and mines are generally the property of private owners, who sell their products in the hope of making profits.

During much of the 19th century the principles of laissez-faire dominated the economic philosophy of the U.S. This meant that government should not "interfere" with private businessmen and organizations. Since the latter part of the 19th century, however, and especially since the early 1930's, business in the U.S. has been placed under some forms of government control. For example, the federal and state governments set minimum wage levels which employers are required to meet. The federal government owns a considerable amount of such natural resources as forest lands and carries on such businesses as

the Tennessee Valley Authority and the atomic energy plants. The U.S. is, therefore, said to have a "mixed" economy. It is not "pure capitalism," complete private ownership of the means of production without government interference; but it is a far cry from socialism, or government ownership.

Capper-Volstead Act (1922). Under this law, also known as the Cooperative Marketing Act, farm cooperatives were exempted from the federal antitrust laws.

Cardozo, Benjamin Nathan (1870–1938). Jurist. Born in New York City, he was chief judge, New York State Court of Appeals (1927–32). He replaced Oliver Wendell Holmes as associate justice on the U.S. Supreme Court (1932–38), as an appointee of Pres. Hoover. He joined Justices Brandeis and Stone in the great dissents that became the reasoning of the Court when conservative justices retired and a majority of the Court accepted the New Deal legislation intended to meet the conditions of a changing world. He is author of *The Nature of the Judicial Process* (1921) and *Law and Literature* (1931).

CARE. The Cooperative for American Relief in Europe was formed in 1945, at the end of World War II, to send food parcels to the hungry in France and other liberated countries in Europe. But as recovery progressed the "Europe" in the name was changed to "Everywhere," keeping the CARE acronym intact. Its missions are now active in 37 countries in Africa, Asia, and Latin America as well as Europe.

Carey Act (1894). Yielding to Western pressure for irrigation projects, Congress passed legislation drawn by Sen. Joseph M. Carey (Wyo.) that provided up to one million acres of U.S.-owned desert land within its boundaries to each state that contracted for reclamation of arid regions. Private companies undertook construction of the projects in return for the sale of "water rights" in a region in which farmers are dependent on irrigation.

Carlotta. After the defeat of the Confederacy in 1865 some southerners emigrated to Mexico to establish a colony. They were encouraged by the Emperor Maximilian and the colony was named after the Empress. Its fate was, however, no better than that of the Emperor, who was executed in 1867. The colony, located between Vera Cruz and Mexico City, failed quickly.

Carnegie, Andrew (1835–1919). Industrialist and philanthropist. Born in Scotland, he emigrated to the U.S. in 1848. Starting as a telegrapher, he rose in the ranks of the Pennsylvania Railroad before resigning (1865) to concentrate on the iron and oil businesses. Beginning in 1873,

he devoted himself to the steel industry. Under his leadership, U.S. steel production exceeded that of Great Britain by 1889. He sold his interests to the newly formed U.S. Steel Corp. (1901). Subsequent benefactions included large contributions for public libraries, public education and the Carnegie Endowment for International Peace.

Caroline affair. In 1837 efforts of U.S. partisans to assist Canadian insurgents to overthrow the "tyrants of Britain" led to the burning of the *Caroline*, a small American steamer that had been ferrying supplies across the Niagara River. The ship was moored on the state side of the river, and in the scuffle with Canadian regulars who had come across the river, one American was killed.

The incident was revived when Alexander McLeod was arrested in New York in 1840 and charged with arson and murder for his part in the *Caroline* affair. The British government then admitted that the raid on the *Caroline* had been officially planned. Lord Palmerston, British Foreign Secretary, warned that McLeod's execution would mean war. McLeod was acquitted and the dispute subsided.

Carothers, Wallace Hume (1896–1937). Chemist. Born in Burlington, Ia., he was granted a Ph.D. by Univ. of Illinois (1924). He taught at Illinois and Harvard before joining E.I.

du Pont de Nemours and Co. (1928). His fundamental research program in organic chemistry culminated in the commercial production of nylon fiber. He committed suicide.

Carpenters' Hall. The building at 320 Chestnut Street in Philadelphia in which the first Continental Congress met, Sept. 5, 1774, is preserved as a U.S. landmark. It was lent to the Congress by the Carpenters' Guild, which constructed it as a meeting place in 1770.

carpetbaggers. Newcomers to the South in the Reconstruction era were regarded with contempt. They reputedly could put all their possessions into the common hand luggage of the day, a carpetbag.

Seeking financial gain or public office, some of the carpetbaggers became state legislators or represented the South in Congress. Others were missionaries sent from the North to try to help the freedmen.

When the Reconstruction era came to an end about 1877, most of the carpetbaggers returned to the North.

cartwheels. Westerners have a traditional preference for silver dollars which they call cartwheels. Although comparatively heavy, they have the feel of real money to people in a region in which agitation for free silver reached a peak near the turn of the century.

In recent years there has been a scarcity of the cart-

wheels because of an increase in coin collecting, hoarding and speculation prompted by a silver shortage.

Carver, George Washington (1864–1943). Chemist. Born of slave parents, near Diamond Grove, Mo., he was illiterate until the age of 20. He then went on to gain an M.S. in Agriculture at Iowa State (1896). He worked chiefly at Tuskegee Institute (Ala.) where his research on such common crops as the peanut, sweet potato and soy bean produced their diversified use in plastics, dyes, medicines, lubricants, etc. This helped to end the single-crop economy of the South.

Casablanca Conference (Jan. 14–24, 1943). At this meeting in French Morocco, Pres. Roosevelt and Prime Minister Churchill decided on an invasion of Sicily and Italy. Premier Stalin had been invited, but replied that he could not come because of Soviet military operations at the time.

At Casablanca it was decided to dispatch aid to the Russian front in order to whittle down German manpower and equipment, to take steps to strengthen the Chinese armies of Chiang Kai-shek, to unite various French factions in a common effort against the Axis and to maintain the initiative gained in the closing days of 1942. The Allies called for the "unconditional surrender" of the Axis.

Casket Girls. During the 18th century poor but virtuous

French girls from church charitable institutions were brought to Louisiana to become wives of settlers. The gloomy name is derived quite simply from the fact that the clothes they carried with them were kept in *cassettes* (small chests). In contrast to the prostitutes brought to Louisiana from Paris streets, they provided a respectable family background for Creole descendants.

Cass, Lewis (1782–1866). Soldier, statesman. Born in Exeter, N.H., he moved west and established a law practice in Ohio. He won distinction in the War of 1812, and was Governor of Michigan Territory (1813–31). As Jackson's Sec. of War (1831–36) he directed the Black Hawk War. He was U.S. minister to France (1836–42), U.S. senator from Michigan (1845–48; 1849–57), unsuccessful Democratic candidate for President in 1848 when he lost to Taylor. He resigned as Sec. of State (1857–60) when Pres. Buchanan refused to defend Charleston (S.C.) forts.

Catawba. A Siouan people, the Indians located along the Catawba River in North and South Carolina could almost always be counted on as friends of the English settlers. They were virtually wiped out by mid-18th century due to the ravages of disease, drink and attacks by Shawnee or Iroquois. A few survivors live in South Carolina.

Cather, Willa (1876–1947). Novelist. Born in Winchester, Va., she spent her early years in Nebraska. She was on the staff of the Pittsburgh *Daily Leader* (1898–1901), and was associate editor of *McClure's Magazine* (1906–12) before devoting herself to writing novels. She recollected pioneer past in simple but poignant style in such memorable works as *O Pioneers!* (1913), *My Ántonia* (1918), *Death Comes for the Archbishop* (1927) and *Shadows on the Rock* (1931).

Catholicism in the U.S. The first Catholics to settle in the American colonies reached Maryland in 1634. Their arrival was planned by Sir George Calvert, the first Lord Baltimore, who had embraced Catholicism and sought to establish a religious refuge for English Catholics in America. His sons continued the project.

By the time of the American Revolution there were some 35,000 Catholics in the U.S. whose spiritual needs were ministered to chiefly by Jesuits. Although Catholics were not physically molested in 18th-century America, the overwhelmingly Protestant population was hostile to Rome and anti-Catholic propaganda was spread by Protestant ministers, educators, editors and publishers. Nevertheless, Charles Carroll of Carrollton signed the Declaration of Independence and two other Catholics, Daniel Carroll (Md.) and Thomas

FitzSimons (Pa.) served in the Constitutional Convention.

During the colonial period Catholics established schools and charities. In the early national period Georgetown (D.C.) Academy was established (1791) and opened to both Catholics and non-Catholics. In 1807 there was only one Catholic bishop in the U.S. and under his dominion some 70 priests cared for 70,000 worshipers. By 1830 there were 20 bishops and about 500,000 communicants. In addition, the Catholics had established six seminaries, nine colleges, 33 monasteries and convents, and a sizable number of schools, hospitals and other parochial institutions. A Catholic press, starting with the *United States Catholic Miscellany* (1822), also had come into being, along with a Catholic Tract Society (1827), founded in Philadelphia to combat Protestantism as well as to promote the Church.

About 2,000,000 Irish and German Catholic immigrants came to the U.S. 1830–60. Anti-Catholic prejudice mounted and took shape in the vicious burning of the Ursuline convent at Charlestown, Mass. (1834) and riots in Philadelphia (1844). Political hostility was fanned by the Know-Nothing party.

During the Civil War Catholics fought on both sides and Catholic sisters were active in hospitals.

The Catholic community continued to grow in the post-Civil War period. John McCloskey, Archbishop of New York, became the first American cardinal (1875). There was a great influx of Catholic immigrants in the years from 1881 to 1890, when some 2,000,000 came to the U.S. Another 1,250,000 came in the next decade bringing the total Catholic population in the U.S. to 12,000,000 in 1900.

In 1884 Catholic religious education in the U.S. was spurred by a council in Baltimore which ordered priests to establish elementary schools in each parish. Catholic parents, where schools were available, were expected to send their children to them. Since that time Catholic education has expanded greatly in America although the Church has been unable to provide enough schools for all Catholics seeking entry. There are about 10,000,-000 students in Catholic schools —elementary through college, about one-fifth of the total school enrollment in the U.S.

There are about 23,700 Catholic churches in the U.S. The church organization includes 10 cardinals, 38 archbishops, 235 bishops and nearly 60,000 priests. There are also over 12,000 lay brothers and 176,000 sisters. All meet the spiritual needs of over 48,215,000 Catholics.

Catlin, George (1796–1872). Artist. Born in Wilkes-Barre, Pa., he practiced law until 1823 when he turned to art. He painted portraits of New York notables, including DeWitt Clinton, before deciding, as he later wrote, "to use my art . . . in rescuing from oblivion the looks and customs of the vanishing races of native man in America." He accompanied expeditions to the trans-Mississippi West and in the course of his career painted some 600 portraits of Indians as well as villages, religious ceremonies and other aspects of Indian life. A large collection of his American Indian paintings was presented to the Smithsonian Institution (1879). His published works include *Catlin's North American Indian Portfolio* (1845) and *Life Among the Indians* (1867).

Cato Conspiracy (1739). Negroes at Stono, near Charleston, S.C., armed themselves by robbing a store and set out for Florida. They gathered recruits and murdered whites on the way. A white force was assembled and crushed the conspiracy. The plot cost the lives of 30 whites and 44 Negroes.

cattle kingdom. Cattle in Texas multiplied enormously during the Civil War. When the ranchers on the plains between the Rio Grande and the panhandle discovered that steers worth three to four dollars a head could be sold for ten times this price in Kansas and Missouri, they decided to drive their cattle northward, grazing as they went. The growing eastern demand for beef soon began to attract big-time capital. In the late 1870's, eastern investors formed large cattle-raising companies with huge holdings of land and cattle in Texas, the Dakotas, Nebraska, Kansas, Montana, Wyoming, Colorado and New Mexico.

caucus. The party caucus developed during the First Congress when Federalists met to discuss political programs. When Pres. Washington decided to retire, it was the congressional caucus that chose John Adams as candidate for President. The Republicans were not far behind in their utilization of the caucus and it was the supreme determinant in the choice of the "Virginia dynasty" of Presidents.

Even earlier origins of the caucus have been traced to the ship mechanics or caulkers who met in Boston, early in the 18th century, to endorse candidates for local office.

Although "King Caucus" gave way to the national nominating conventions in the 1830's, the caucus on national, state and local levels is a continuing practice. In varying degrees, it influences party decisions on political programs and the choice of candidates for public office or appointive positions.

Cayuga. The smallest of the five tribes of the Iroquois League, they sided with the British in the American Revolution.

Cayuse. Marcus Whitman hopefully established a mission

among the warlike Indians in Oregon. In 1847, however, following a smallpox epidemic for which they blamed the white men, the Indians destroyed the mission and other white settlements (Cayuse War). The word "cayuse" refers to the popular Indian pony of the Northwest. The Cayuse, of Walilatpuan stock, owned many horses in their heyday. Tribal survivors are found in Oregon.

Centaur. Actually the second stage of a two-stage rocket (the first stage is an Atlas) the launch vehicle for U.S. spacecraft in the 1960's is the first to employ high-energy liquid-hydrogen liquid-oxygen propellant. It can launch a 1,300 pound spacecraft to Venus or Mars or rocket to the moon a 2,300 pound spacecraft.

Central Intelligence Agency (CIA). Established by Congress under the National Security Act of 1947, the Agency coordinates the intelligence activities of government departments in the interest of national security, evaluates intelligence reports and sees that they are made available to the appropriate agency.

Central Pacific Railroad. Chartered in California, June 28, 1861, the Central Pacific met the Union Pacific in Utah, May 10, 1869, at a point designated by Congress. It had laid 689 miles of track from Sacramento over the Sierra Nevada Mountains.

The final spikes connecting the roads symbolized the effect the lines were to have on the growth of the West. Nevada contributed a spike of silver; Arizona a spike of iron, silver and gold; California a spike of pure gold.

The line received the same substantial aid from the U.S. as did the Union Pacific, and the builders solved the labor problem by importing Chinese coolies to supplement the white labor force.

In 1870, the year after the completion of the Union Pacific-Central Pacific, 52,922 miles of railroad had been constructed as compared with only 9,000 miles of railroad in 1850.

Central Treaty Organization (CENTO). As another link in the Western defense chain, the alliance was formed in 1955 to block Soviet moves southward into the oil-rich Middle East. Originally, it was the Middle East Treaty Organization (METO), commonly known as the Baghdad Pact. Both names were dropped in 1959, however, after Iraq (whose capital, Baghdad, had served as METO headquarters) withdrew from the alliance following a revolution.

The three members of the Central Treaty Organization are three nations on the southern border of the USSR—Turkey, Iran and Pakistan—plus Britain. The U.S. is not a full member of CENTO, but an American military mission participates in the work of its military committee.

Century of Dishonor, A (1881). In her book, Helen Hunt Jackson (Mass.) added her strong appeal to the humanitarian campaign for better treatment of the Indians. It helped to bring about passage of the Dawes Severalty Act (1887).

Cerro Gordo, battle of (Apr. 18, 1847). Santa Anna sought to halt the U.S. advance in the Mexican War at a mountain pass between Vera Cruz and Mexico City. He failed to protect the heights overlooking his position and a Mexican force of 13,000 was routed by an American force of 9,000 under Gen. Winfield Scott.

chain stores. A group of stores owned and operated by a single firm are used as a method of retail distribution that currently accounts for over 20% of the total retail trade in the U.S. This percentage of total retail sales is made by multiunit organizations operating 11 or more retail stores.

The Atlantic and Pacific Tea Co., begun as a single store marketing food products in 1859, is the largest chain in the country. The F. W. Woolworth Co., founded in 1879, is the largest variety chain in the U.S. Retail chain stores operate in many areas of business, including food, general merchandise, apparel, gasoline service stations, household appliances, furniture, automobile accessories, etc.

In some states, special "penalty" taxes are imposed on chain stores for the purpose of helping small, owner-run stores compete with them. The federal government sought to curb price discrimination that favored chain stores in the Robinson-Patman Act (1936).

Champagne-Marne offensive (July 15–17, 1918). In his fifth and last offensive German Gen. Ludendorff sought unsuccessfully to capture Reims preparatory to an attack (never carried out) in Flanders against the British Expeditionary Force. Gen. Foch learned of the plans through aerial photography and German deserters and his countermeasures frustrated what the Germans had come to think of as a *Friedensturm* (peace offensive) that would end the war. Three American divisions fought in the Allied defense with the U.S. 3rd Division earning the accolade, "Rock of the Marne."

This offensive and the Aisne-Marne offensive of July 18–Aug. 6 together are often referred to as the Second Battle of the Marne.

"Champ" Clark. James Beauchamp Clark was the Speaker of the House from 1911 to 1919 and a candidate for the Democratic nomination for President in 1912. He dropped the first name James at the age of 24 when he was confused with another James B. Clark. When he found that only Frenchmen could pronounce "Beauchamp," he retained only the last half of his middle name.

Chancellorsville, battle of (May 2–4, 1863). In one of the major battles of the Civil War, Chancellorsville, Va., Union Gen. Joseph Hooker ("Fighting Joe") failed to break through to Richmond. His massive Army of the Potomac retreated to a position north of the Rappahannock River.

The Confederate victory was dampened by the loss of "Stonewall" Jackson, who was shot in the arm by one of his own men and died of pneumonia when his arm was amputated.

Channing, William Ellery (1780–1842). Clergyman. Born in Newport, R.I., he was Minister of the Federal Street Church at Boston (1803–42). Known as the "Apostle of Unitarianism," he dissented from the Calvinist doctrine of the depravity of man and preached the doctrine of man's perfectibility and "breathed into theology a humane spirit." His sermons and writing had wide influence. He abhorred slavery and was a pioneer in the modern movement against war. He influenced American literature through writers closely associated with the Unitarian movement—Emerson, Bryant, Longfellow, Lowell and Holmes.

Chapultepec, Act of (Mar. 3, 1945). With the war in Europe nearing the end, the U.S. met with all of the Latin American countries, except Argentina, at Chapultepec Castle, Mexico City. The Act passed at the Inter-American Conference on Problems of War and Peace made all American republics co-guardians of the Monroe Doctrine (not mentioned by name), even against an American aggressor. This multilateralizing of the Doctrine expanded it into a kind of Pan-American defense doctrine.

Chapultepec, battle of (Sept. 13, 1847). The fortified hill on the outskirts of Mexico City was scaled and taken by Gen. Winfield Scott's forces. It was the prelude to Scott's entrance into Mexico City, from which Santa Anna fled.

Charles River Bridge v. Warren Bridge **(1837).** The U.S. Supreme Court ruled that a charter granted by a state to a private corporation must be strictly construed so as not to work to the disadvantage of the public. Chief Justice Taney delivered the decision.

The Charles River Bridge Co. had been granted a charter by Massachusetts in 1785 authorizing it to operate a toll bridge across the Charles River. In 1828 the Warren Bridge Co. was authorized to build a bridge nearby that was to be toll free after construction costs were paid off. The Charles River Co. unsuccessfully sought an injunction to prevent the building of the new bridge. The Court held that there was nothing in its charter that specifically granted it a monopoly of bridge crossings.

chartered colonies. Two of the early 17th-century colonies in America, Virginia and Massachusetts, were founded by chartered companies whose funds were provided by investors and used to equip, transport and maintain the colonists. Later, when trading companies failed, the king granted charters to proprietors. Such proprietary colonies included Maryland, Pennsylvania and Carolina.

Charters granted by the king to companies or proprietors affirmed the sovereignty of the king over the colonies. The promoters were granted the powers of government and the colonists were to enjoy the liberties of English subjects.

The chartered colonies had a governor and council appointed by the company or proprietor. The colonists elected a house of representatives. In Virginia this was the House of Burgesses. The chartered colonies, except for Rhode Island and Connecticut, soon became royal colonies (Virginia, for example, in 1624). Pennsylvania and Maryland remained proprietary colonies, except during intervals of royal control.

Charter Oak. In 1687 Sir Edmund Andros, governor of the Dominion of New England, demanded that Connecticut give up the liberal charter it had received from Charles II in 1662. He did so on the authority of James II, who sought to curb the colonies. Tradition has it that the charter was hidden in the hollow of an oak in Hartford.

Charter of Liberties (1683). Popular opposition of the New York colony to Gov. Dongan forced James, Duke of York, to instruct Dongan to call a representative assembly. Among the laws it passed was a charter of liberties lodging legislative power in the governor, council and assembly; extending the ballot to all freeholders; outlining the principles of land holding, inheritance and court procedures; and guaranteeing freedom of worship and trial by jury.

When the Duke became King in 1685 he turned against the New York colony, ordering the abandonment of the representative assembly. The charter was never fully confirmed.

Chase, Salmon Portland (1808–75). Statesman. Born in Cornish, N.H., he was Republican governor of Ohio (1855–60) and U.S. senator (1849–55; 1860). He opposed the fugitive slave laws and was known in Ohio as the "attorney general for runaway Negroes." Appointed Lincoln's Sec. of Treasury (1861–64), he originated the national banking system. He split with Lincoln and resigned but supported Lincoln for President in 1864 and was appointed Chief Justice of the U.S. Supreme Court. He upheld Republican Reconstruction laws.

Chase impeachment trial (1805). U.S. Supreme Court Justice Samuel Chase, a Federalist, had antagonized the Republicans who came into power under Jefferson, when as a circuit judge he had abused them from the bench. They decided to impeach him in order to bring the other Federalist judges into line.

The House impeachment proceedings went badly and Chase was acquitted of all eight charges. Had Chase been convicted, it seems likely that Republicans would have proceeded against other Federalist judges and the position of the judiciary would have been undermined.

Château-Thierry, battle of (June 3–4, 1918). When the Germans advanced to the Marne at Château-Thierry, within 37 miles of Paris, French Gen. Petain asked Gen. Pershing for an American division to hold the Marne crossings. Although Pershing had intended to keep the American troops as a separate army, the situation was critical and he assigned the U.S. 2nd and 3rd Divisions. In early June, they turned the Germans back in bitter hand-to-hand fighting at Château-Thierry.

Chautauqua movement. John H. Vincent, a Methodist minister, established a Sunday-school institute to include both religious and secular subjects at a camp site on Lake Chautauqua, N.Y. (1874). It became a permanent summer colony offering a range of religious, cultural and recreational activities.

The Chautauqua Library and Scientific Circle was formed in 1878 to meet the needs of those who could not attend the institute, but who wished to read and discuss books recommended by the directors. Occasionally, a lecturer was sent to a group.

"Chautauqua" was used in the first decade of the 20th century to describe traveling groups who offered lectures and concerts, usually in a large tent, in towns all over the U.S. The term has since been appropriated by various religious groups to describe their programs.

checks and balances. The Founding Fathers were mindful of extremes in government. They recalled the abuse of power by the King of England in his relationship with Parliament and the contrasting weakness of Congress under the Articles of Confederation with virtually no provision for an executive or judiciary. They sought therefore in the Constitution to separate the powers of the executive, legislature and judiciary so that while they could work together, no one branch of the federal government would become too powerful at the expense of the other. With this in mind, they provided a system of checks and balances.

For example: either branch of Congress can halt legislation by refusing to approve the action taken by the other; the President has the right to make treaties, but the treaty must be ratified by a two-thirds vote of the Senate; although there is no direct constitutional provision to this effect, the Supreme Court has assumed the power to declare laws of Congress unconstitutional.

Cherokee. The most advanced of the Indians in the South, the Cherokee practiced farming and lived in permanent villages. They met the white man for the first time when De Soto explored the Southeast (1540).

Generally, the Cherokee sided with the British against the French, but in 1760 they were provoked into war with the colonists. During the Revolutionary War they attacked frontier patriots. In 1827 they established the Cherokee Nation under a constitution. By this time they had built roads, schools and churches and adopted a system of government modeled on that of the U.S.

Sequoya, a Cherokee warrior who was crippled in a hunting accident, produced a workable alphabet of Cherokee characters in 1821. The Cherokees studied it with such enthusiasm that within a matter of months thousands could read and write. A printing press was obtained and in 1828 the Cherokees began the publication of a weekly newspaper.

They were, however, forced out of Georgia and, after a terrible march, reached the Indian Territory (later Oklahoma) in 1838, where they formed one of the Five Civilized Tribes. Their leader at this time and until 1861 was Chief John Ross.

During the Civil War their allegiance was divided between North and South. At the close of the war they freed their Negro slaves and admitted them to tribal citizenship. Finally, they sold their western territorial extension, known as the "Cherokee Strip" (1892), disbanded as a tribe (1906) and became U.S. citizens. Descendants live west of the Mississippi and a few are on a North Carolina reservation.

Cherry Valley massacre (Nov. 11, 1778). Col. John Butler, leading loyalists and Indians under Joseph Brant, a Mohawk chief, attacked and defeated an American outpost in Cherry Valley, N.Y. Some 40 survivors who had surrendered were massacred.

Chesapeake **Affair** (1807). During the Napoleonic Wars, Britain's need for seamen in her navy led to her halting and searching American ships for English seamen who had deserted. The new U.S. frigate *Chesapeake*, whose guns were not completely mounted, was attacked and forced to surrender to search by the British ship *Leopard*, off the coast of Virginia. The British removed one English deserter and three Americans who had served in the English navy.

The incident aroused war fervor in the U.S., but it was channeled into "peaceful coercion" by Pres. Jefferson when the British offered to make reparations. It was not until 1811, however, that two of the American seamen were returned (one had died) to the U.S.

Chesapeake & Ohio Railway Co. Originally the 22-mile Louisa Railroad, the line was chartered in Virginia (1837) and eventually gave Virginia and Ohio direct connections between Norfolk and Cincinnati. It now operates over 5,000 miles of road extending from southern West Virginia, eastern Kentucky and southern Ohio, east to tidewater at Hampton Roads, and north and west to Toledo, Detroit, lower Michigan, Cincinnati and Chicago. The Canadian Division is an important link between the West and Buffalo.

In 1965 directors of the C. & O. and the Norfolk and Western Railway announced that they had approved plans to merge. The proposed merger was linked to the potential acquisition of five other major eastern railroads. These are the Erie-Lackawanna, the Delaware & Hudson, Boston & Maine, the Reading and the Central Railroad of New Jersey. The amalgamation, if approved by stockholders and the Interstate Commerce Commission, would make the entire system the largest in the U.S. in terms of mileage and revenues.

Cheyenne. An Algonquian people, the most hostile of the plains Indians, they opposed western settlement, especially after 1861 when treaties were violated by Pikes Peak gold miners. An indiscriminate massacre of the Cheyenne by federal troops at Sandy Creek, Colo. (1864) led to the most bitter Indian wars in the West. The Cheyenne helped to destroy the commands of Capt. Fetterman (Dec. 21, 1866) and Gen. Custer (June 26, 1876).

The northern Cheyenne are still found in Montana. Southern Cheyenne survive in Oklahoma.

Chicago, Milwaukee, St. Paul & Pacific. Originally chartered as the Milwaukee Road to cross Wisconsin, the line has become a transcontinental system with 10,599 miles of road. It now runs from Chicago, Milwaukee and the Twin Cities (Minneapolis and St. Paul) through South Dakota and Washington to Seattle and other Pacific Coast points.

Chicago fire (Oct. 8–9, 1871). The fire devastated an area three and one-half miles square, left almost 100,000 persons homeless and consumed 17,450 buildings. Property loss was estimated at $200,000,000. First incorporated as a village in 1833, by 1871 Chicago had become a city built of wood. Even the sidewalks were of pine and a dry season preceding the fire made the city a virtual tinderbox. The origins of the holocaust are unknown, although tradition has it that a Mrs. O'Leary upset a lamp while milking her cow.

Chicago Tribune. The paper known at first as the *Chicago Daily Tribune* was founded June 10, 1847. It was in financial difficulty until Joseph Medill and five partners took it over in 1855. Medill made the paper a profitable and lively news medium. He gained control of its stock in 1874 and directed the newspaper until his death in 1899, when it was published by his son-in-law Robert W. Patterson.

Medill was one of the major advocates of Lincoln for President and the *Tribune* became a great national paper during the Civil War. From the beginning, it was hostile toward the South, urged active prosecution of the war, and spoke for the Radical Republicans. After the war, the paper opposed Pres. Grant's administration. Its editorial page continued to command the respect which it had won in the period of the Civil War. During the Spanish-American War, however, its jingoistic news columns echoed the *New York World's* and the *New York Journal's* Cuban services. It was ranked among the four outstanding papers of Chicago journalism—the *Tribune, Daily News,* the *Inter Ocean* and the *Times-Herald* (later *Record - Herald*) — during the period (1892–1914) which covered the rise and fall of yellow journalism.

In the 20th century the *Tribune,* competing with Hearst's *Chicago American,* became more sensational. Republican in politics, it conducted numerous civic crusades.

In the 1930's the *Tribune,* whose owners also controlled the *New York Daily News,* became the second largest paper in the U.S. Its circulation reached one million in 1940. By the beginning of that year four American Sunday papers were in the million class: the *New York Daily News,* the *New York Mirror,* the *Chicago Tribune* and the *Philadelphia Inquirer.* In 1967 the *Tribune's* daily circulation was 827,524, its Sunday edition, 1,152,118.

Chickamauga, battle of (Sept. 19–20, 1863). Confederate Gen. Bragg confronted Union Gen. Rosecrans and Gen. Thomas at Chickamauga Creek, Tenn. Gen. Rosecrans was forced to retreat to Chattanooga, but Gen. Thomas stood his ground, earning the title "Rock of Chickamauga," and preventing the complete rout of the Union army. The heavy losses on both sides discredited both Bragg and Rosecrans.

Chickasaw. Loyal supporters of the English during the colonial period, the Muskhogean tribe lived in northern Mississippi and part of Tennessee until their removal to the Indian Territory (Oklahoma) in the 1830's. There they joined the Five Civilized Tribes. In the Civil War they served in the Confederate army. At the close of the war they freed their Negro slaves. After dissolving their tribal government, they became U.S. citizens in 1906. The Chickasaws, many of whom intermarried with whites, live on in Oklahoma.

"chicken in every pot." Republican campaigners in the election of 1928 adopted such slogans as "A chicken in every pot, a car in every garage!" They sought to convince voters that with a Republican in the White House the prosperity of the Coolidge years would continue.

Chiefs of Staff, Joint. As the immediate military staff of the Secretary of Defense they advise not only the Secretary but are also the principal military advisers to the President and the National Security Council. They prepare strategic plans, plan for military mobilization and review the needs of the armed forces. The Joint Chiefs of Staff consist of the Chairman of the Joint Chiefs of Staff; the Chief of Staff, U.S. Army; the Chief of Naval Operations; and the Chief of Staff, U.S. Air Force. The Commandant of the Marine Corps attends meetings regularly although he is not on the Joint Chiefs of Staff.

Chinese Exclusion Act (1882). The first act of Congress to exclude immigrants, the legislation was aimed at Chinese laborers who entered the U.S. to work for mining and railroad companies. As unemployment in the West mounted in the 1870's, the Chinese were accused of working for "coolie wages."

The Act was extended and made permanent in 1902. In 1943, however, a quota was established that allowed 105 Chinese to enter the U.S. annually and Chinese in the U.S. were made eligible for citizenship.

Chippewa (Ojibwa). Of Algonquian stock, they lived at first at the eastern end of Lake Superior, now Sault Ste. Marie. Eventually, they spread from Lake Erie to North Dakota. The Indians were allied with the French during the French and Indian War, but later sided with the British during the War of 1812. They sold their timberlands to the federal government and have been confined to reservations in Minnesota, Wisconsin and Michigan.

Chippewa, battle of (July 5, 1814). During the War of 1812, the British plan for a push on New York was anticipated by American forces under Gen. Jacob Brown. His subordinate, Gen. Winfield Scott, forced the British to retreat from Chippewa, near Niagara Falls, in Canada.

Chisholm Trail. Cattle were driven over the trail which led from ranches near San Antonio, Tex., to the railhead at Abilene, Kans. The first drive, in 1867, was made when Texas ranchmen were attracted by the high prices brought by cattle in the

North. The trail was used until rail lines were extended south into Texas in the 1880's.

Chisholm v. Georgia (1793). The U.S. Supreme Court upheld the right of a British creditor to collect a debt for which he had sued the state of Georgia.

The creditor never collected because the Georgia legislature passed a law declaring that any federal marshal attempting to enforce the Court's ruling would be guilty of a felony and subject to hanging "without benefit of clergy."

As an outcome of the Supreme Court decision a constitutional amendment was voted for by Congress taking from the federal courts jurisdiction in cases brought against a state by the citizens of other states or of any foreign country. This was ratified in 1798 and became the 11th Amendment.

Choate, Rufus (1799–1859). Statesman. He was born on Hog Island, Mass. He helped organize the Whig party in Massachusetts and was a member of the House of Representatives (1831–34). He served out Daniel Webster's term in U.S. Senate (1841–45). An eminent trial lawyer and orator, his fame rests on his oratorical skill and brilliance as a cross-examiner. He denounced the Republican party as "sectional" and "anti-Union" (1855).

Choctaws. Expert in farming, the Muskhogean-speaking people lived in Mississippi, Alabama and Georgia. They were generally more friendly to the French than to the English. In the early 1830's the Indians ceded their lands to the federal government and moved to the Indian Territory (Oklahoma). They formed the Choctaw Nation and became one of the Five Civilized Tribes. After abandoning their tribal organization in 1906, they became U.S. citizens and continued to live in Oklahoma.

cholera. The first Asian cholera epidemic broke out in New York City, June 28, 1832, and resulted in 2,251 deaths. The epidemic spread to other large cities in the Northeast. In the South, more than 6,000 perished in New Orleans during a 12-day period beginning Oct. 25, 1832. During the next decade the disease swept the Indian Nations of the Great Plains, drastically reducing their numbers and their ability to resist the advance of white settlers.

In 1850 a cholera epidemic fanned out from New Orleans through the Middle West and was checked only by the seasonal cold. In 1866 many cities were ravaged by cholera. About 200 a day died in St. Louis, Mo., during the height of the epidemic. In 1873 epidemics of cholera, yellow fever and smallpox swept through many southern cities.

Christian Churches. Formerly called Disciples of Christ, a Protestant denomination was founded in western Pennsylvania in the early 1800's by Thomas and Alexander Campbell that stressed the simple gospel and the Bible alone as the basis of faith. In 1957 they adopted the denominational name International Convention of Christian Churches. There are almost 2,000,000 members.

Christian Science. The religion is founded upon principles and divine laws expressed in the acts and sayings of Jesus Christ, as discovered and formulated by Mary Baker Eddy. She founded the Mother Church, the First Church of Christ, Scientist (1879), in Boston, Mass. There are now some 2,500 Christian Science churches in the U.S. Each church is self-governing and self-supporting, but all accept the tenets of Mrs. Eddy, who recovered her health in 1866 when she read in the New Testament an account of healing by Jesus. In 1875 her *Science and Health with Key to the Scriptures* was published.

The churches have no individual pastors. Services are conducted by two readers, one reading from the Scriptures, the other from *Science and Health.*

Of the numerous publications directed by the Christian Science Publishing Society, the most important is *The Christian Science Monitor,* a daily newspaper.

Churubusco, battle of (Aug. 20, 1847). Gen. Winfield Scott defeated Santa Anna and captured about one-third of his army in a village about five miles from Mexico City. This victory followed one the previous day at Contreras, also on the road to Mexico City.

Cincinnati, Society of the. Revolutionary War officers formed in 1783 an organization to perpetuate the friendships formed during the war and to provide for the care of widows and orphans. Descendants of the officers were included in its membership. The Society, which has continued to this day, was criticized as having aristocratic tendencies. Washington was its first president.

It was named after Cincinnatus, the Roman general, who returned to his farm following his successful defense of Rome.

circuit riders. The term has been used to describe both ministers and judges who traveled from place to place in performance of their duties.

The ministerial circuit riders helped to bring religion to frontier communities. The Methodists were especially active in recruiting preachers who took to horse and saddlebags, riding the circuit in the second half of the 18th century and first half of the 19th century. A single preacher might have some 20 places on his circuit.

Under the Constitution, the U.S. was at first divided into three judicial districts. It was the duty of U.S. Supreme Court justices to ride the circuit and hold court, sitting with a federal district judge. It was not until 1869 that federal circuit court judges were appointed and the strain of travel to distant places was eased for Supreme Court justices.

City College of New York. Founded in 1847 as the Free Academy, it started granting degrees in 1853. The name was changed in 1866 to The College of the City of New York (popularly known as City College or CCNY). In 1926 when the Board of Higher Education was established, the College of the City of New York became the joint corporate title of all the municipal colleges under the jurisdiction of the Board of Higher Education and the college was given its present name —The City College of New York.

In 1961 the City College of New York became one of the colleges of The City University of New York, created by action of the Board of Higher Education. The system includes City College, Hunter College, Brooklyn College, Queens College, York College and the Community Colleges of Staten Island, Bronx, Queensborough, Kingsborough and Manhattan.

During most of its history financing of City College has been by the City of New York, but it is now shared by the State of New York as well. Traditionally, qualified bonafide residents of New York City have been admitted tuition-free to the baccalaureate program.

The undergraduate program is varied and embraces colleges of liberal arts and science, education, business, technology, etc.

The college has been eminently successful in terms of the end result, as is shown by the fact that a relatively large number of alumni have distinguished themselves in the various professions as well as in public life.

city manager-type government. The plan was first adopted in Staunton, Va. (1908) and later in Dayton, O. (1913), after the city was almost submerged by a flood and the mayor-council-type government found that it was unable to effectively handle the emergency. It has since become the basis of governments of hundreds of small cities in the U.S. The city manager as an expert in government administration is usually hired by an elected city council. He is supposed to remain independent of politics and to run the city's affairs as efficiently as a sound business would be run.

city planning. The planning of urban centers was developed in ancient times. Greek cities, for example, were laid out with the main streets running north and south and east and west to a forum. This gridiron plan was dominant in city planning of U.S. cities, including Philadelphia, planned by William Penn (1682).

America's best-known example of city planning is the

city of Washington laid out from bare land by Pierre L'Enfant (1791)—a rectangular plan with diagonal main streets superimposed and with the Capitol as the central feature. Earlier New England towns were laid out with homes along wide elm-lined central roadways or commons and a large open "green."

Modern city planning in the U.S. dates from the "City Beautiful" movement spurred by D. H. Burnham's "White City," in Chicago at the Columbian Exposition (1893). Some industrial cities such as Gary, Ind., built by the United States Steel Corp. have been planned from the beginning.

City planning has been influenced by the zoning laws of New York City (1916) which control the areas and heights of buildings as related to street widths and the uses to which buildings may be put in various parts of the city.

In the 1920's and 1930's cities were aided in master planning by city planning commissions. City planning became a profession as courses in it were introduced in universities.

Since the 1940's the federal government has helped cities to eradicate slums through urban renewal programs. The crowding of cities, despite the growth of suburbs, is a continuing problem for city planners. They hope to develop better traffic control, highways bypassing city centers, new neighborhoods with recreational areas and open spaces, industrial parks and regional master planning.

Civil Aeronautics Board (CAB). The Civil Aeronautics Act of 1938 created an independent federal agency composed of five members appointed for six-year terms by the President with the consent of the Senate. In general, the Board performs three functions. It regulates the economic aspects of domestic and international U.S. aviation, including fares charged the public for air transportation. It assists the Department of State in the negotiation of agreements with foreign governments for the establishment of air routes. It investigates accidents involving civil aircraft and reports its findings and recommendations to the Administrator of the Federal Aviation Agency (FAA).

civil disobedience. It is an illegal, nonviolent, moral protest against a governmental measure. The persons engaged in the act are willing to accept punishment as lawbreakers. The act must be public.

Direct civil disobedience takes place when a law calls for the separate seating of whites and Negroes and a person violates that very law because he thinks it is wrong. It is indirect civil disobedience when the absence of a law is being protested. Suffragettes, demanding the right to vote before the 19th Amendment (1920) could not disobey the law that disenfranchised them. Their civil disobedience took place in violation of trespass laws and disturbing the peace.

What distinguishes Henry David Thoreau as a practitioner of civil disobedience is the way in which he reflected about the nature of his refusal to pay a poll tax as a gesture of civil disobedience in protest against slavery and the Mexican War. After one night in jail at his own insistence, he was released, the tax being paid by one of his aunts. The incident underlay his essay "Resistance to Civil Government" (later called "Civil Disobedience") first published in Elizabeth Peabody's *Aesthetic Papers* (1849) and retold in *Walden*.

Civilian Conservation Corps (CCC). The Corps was established in 1933 as a New Deal measure to meet the employment needs of young men 18 to 25 during the Great Depression. By the end of 1941 almost 2 million had served in the work camps built by the War Department. City youths worked on such conservation projects as reforestation, fire prevention, road and dam construction, control of mosquitoes and similar tasks.

CCC members earned $30 a month, of which $22 was sent home to their families.

Civil Rights Cases of 1883. The U.S. Supreme Court in a series of five cases ruled that it was not a crime for one person to deprive another of equal accommodations at inns, theaters or public conveyances as provided in the Civil Rights Act of 1875. It held that the law, one of the Force Acts of the Reconstruction period, exceeded powers conferred on Congress by the 13th and 14th Amendments.

Individuals, the Court reasoned, were protected from violation of their civil rights by Congress under the 5th Amendment and from violation by the states under the 13th and 14th Amendments; but the federal government had no jurisdiction over social discrimination practiced by individuals against individuals of a different color.

The effect of the rulings was to open the way to passage of Jim Crow laws that segregated Negroes from whites in public places.

civil rights laws. In 1866 Congress passed a Civil Rights Act forbidding states to discriminate among their citizens because of color or race, as they had in the Black Codes. Since Congress was in doubt about the constitutionality of the legislation, a section on civil rights was included in the 14th Amendment.

In 1957 Congress enacted the first civil rights legislation since the Reconstruction period. The new law set up a federal Civil Rights Commission to investigate alleged violations of civil rights throughout the nation including the right to vote, free speech, freedom of assembly, etc. The law gave the federal government the power to seek court injunctions on behalf of persons who claimed that their voting rights had been violated.

The Civil Rights Act of 1960 created an intricate system of court-appointed "voting referees" to investigate the denial of voting rights to qualified Negroes in the South and elsewhere. Desegregation was ordered in the nation's armed forces, and the voting rights of labor union members were safeguarded.

The Civil Rights Act of 1964 outlawed racial discrimination in public accommodations and facilities; it prohibited voting registrars from applying different standards to white and Negro voting applicants; it prohibited racial discrimination by employers and unions; it empowered the Attorney General to initiate suits or to intervene on behalf of complainants in school desegregation cases and in other cases involving racial discrimination; it permitted halting funds to federally aided programs in which racial discrimination is allowed to persist.

The Civil Rights Acts of 1957, 1960 and 1964 fell short of giving the franchise to southern Negroes. They were largely ineffective because while they gave disfranchised Negroes recourse to the federal government under certain conditions, they required voters to qualify under state voting laws. In the South this meant that arbitrary literacy tests could continue to be used to keep Negroes from the polls. This was corrected in the Voting Rights Law of 1965.

Civil Service Commission. The federal agency was established in 1883 by the Pendleton Act as the culmination of a civil service reform movement that was brought to a head by the assassination of Pres. Garfield. Its fundamental purpose is to maintain a merit system whereby civil service workers get their jobs and are promoted on the basis of competitive examinations. Such personnel are known as classified workers in contrast to unclassified civil service employees.

Prior to 1883 the bulk of federal appointees to government offices were indebted to elected officeholders. Congress had provided for a simple examination system in 1871, but this scarcely affected the scramble for federal jobs that started as early as 1789. The spoils system became the prevailing practice as many workers in the old government were turned out with the advent of a new administration.

Since 1883 the classified list has been extended by Congress and the merit system is generally associated with civil service in both federal and state governments.

Civil War (1861–65). The tragic conflict, also known as the "War Between the States," "War of Secession" and the "Brothers' War" resulted in military casualties of 360,000 Union dead and 258,000 Confederate dead, before the victory of the North restored the Union.

The struggle pitted the 23 states that remained in the Union (population, 22,000,000) against 11 southern states (population, 9,000,000, including 3,-500,000 slaves).

The North had almost 85% of the nation's industries and owned most of the country's gold which could be used to buy war materials abroad. The South depended almost entirely on farming, but believed that cotton, essential to the textile mills of New England, Great Britain and France, would see the Confederacy through to victory.

The South won only partial support in Britain, where manufacturers were inclined to think of an independent South as potentially a better market for their exports than the North. The South purchased from England the cruiser *Alabama* which destroyed considerable Northern shipping. Full English support of the Confederacy was made impossible by Pres. Lincoln's Emancipation Proclamation which committed the North to the eradication of slavery and won the backing of strong anti-slavery forces in England.

Historians differ over the fundamental causes of the war. While the slavery question wound its way into every facet of the struggle, it cannot be said that the war was fought to free the slaves. Before the war the Republican party was opposed to the extension of slavery into the territories and did not seek its abolition. There were, of course, many in the North and the South who deeply hated human slavery and everything it stood for. Some historians take the simple view that the war was a clash between a feudal society with slave labor and the advancing tide of human rights and democracy. Slavery did inflame tempers in the North and South and gave rise to psychological factors as a cause of the war.

Historians who see the war as an "irrepressible conflict" between Northern capitalists and free farmers and the planter aristocracy observe that the conflict was foreshadowed by the clashes in Congress over high tariffs, federal subsidies to railroads and a centralized banking system—all of which were favored by the North and opposed by the South.

The war has also been looked upon as a struggle between the principle of states' rights and a strong central government.

The election of Lincoln (Nov. 1860) was regarded in the South as the triumph of a sectional candidate and the end of the South's chances for equality in the Union. It precipitated the secession of seven states in the lower South. By the time Lincoln took office (Mar. 4, 1861) almost all federal forts in the seceding states had been seized by the Confederates.

The attack on Fort Sumter (Apr. 12, 1861) is usually regarded as the immediate cause of the war. This was followed, in turn, by Lincoln's call for the militia to suppress the rebellion and the secession of the four states in the upper South.

Almost from the first the South's ports were blockaded by the North. As a result the South was prevented from exporting cotton, and munitions and other supplies from Europe were largely cut off.

The land fighting was slow and bloody. Gen. Ulysses S. Grant carried out northern strategy by pushing down the Mississippi. As Grant moved southward, Adm. David G. Farragut advanced northward, following his capture of New Orleans. In other memorable battles in the West, Vicksburg and Chattanooga fell to northern forces (1863). The fall of Vicksburg split the Confederacy. From that time on the chances for a southern victory were slim.

Southern armies in the East fought bravely against superior forces during the four grueling years of the conflict. Under the brilliant generalship of Robert E. Lee and his "right arm," T. J. ("Stonewall") Jackson, the South won numerous victories, including the Second Battle of Bull Run and Chancellorsville. Lee's attempted invasion of the North was turned back at Gettysburg, in southern Pennsylvania (1863).

In 1864 the attack on Richmond, Va., capital of the Confederacy, was resumed. This time it was led by Gen. Grant who had assumed command in the East. Grant's superior forces wore down Lee's battered army.

At Appomattox Courthouse, Va. (Apr. 1865), Union troops saluted the beaten but valiant southern soldiers as they laid down their arms. Within a month, other Confederate armies surrendered. The war was over.

Civil Works Administration (CWA). Established in 1933, the New Deal agency was devoted entirely to work relief. It put four million men to work on such tasks as repairing roads and improving schools and parks. The CWA was disbanded in 1934 and much of its work was absorbed by the Federal Emergency Relief Administration (FERA).

Claims, U.S. Court of. A federal court was established in 1855 to determine the validity of certain kinds of claims against the U.S. Formerly, relief in these cases could be obtained only by special act of Congress. The Court of Claims examines suits filed with it against the U.S. The Court consists of a chief judge and four associate judges. The Court sits *en banc* with all judges present.

Clark, George Rogers (1752–1818). Frontier leader. Born in Charlottesville, Va., he was known as "conqueror of the Northwest." He prevented the British from recapturing Illinois country in the Revolutionary War and assured its cession to the U.S. in the Treaty of Paris (1783). He lost the support of Virginia and the national government in various western projects, including an effort to regain Louisiana for France (1793).

Clay, Henry (1777–1852). Statesman. Born in Hanover Co., Va., he moved to Kentucky where he became the nation's foremost spokesman for the West. He represented Kentucky as U.S. Senator (1806–07, 1810–11, 1831–42, 1849–52); member of U.S. House of Representatives (1811–14, 1815–21, 1823–24, served as Speaker same years, except 1821); U.S. Sec. of State (1825–29). His nationalist program, known as the American System, called for a protective tariff and internal improvements in transportation at federal expense. Efforts to stave off dissolution of the Union over slavery included the Missouri Compromise of 1820 and earned for him the nickname, "Great Pacificator." His last great stand for peace was the Compromise of 1850.

Clayton Antitrust Act (1914). Aimed at plugging the worst loopholes in the Sherman Antitrust Act, the law attempted to state definitely what practices and conditions would be considered interference with free competition. For example, business executives were warned that they could not legally attempt to stifle competition by varying their prices to different buyers, by entering into agreements with other corporations or by choosing the same men to sit on boards of directors of competing corporations (interlocking directorates).

The Act also contained provisions which were intended to benefit organized labor. The law declared that labor unions were not to be considered unlawful combinations in restraint of trade; and that injunctions could no longer be issued by federal courts in labor disputes, except to prevent "irreparable injury."

Clayton-Bulwer Treaty (1850). The U.S. and Great Britain agreed that neither would ever exercise exclusive control over or fortify a canal to be built across the Isthmus of Panama. The Treaty was negotiated by Sec. of State John M. Clayton and Sir Henry Bulwer.

Britain expected the U.S. to seek a canal route through Central America following the Mexican War. The U.S. resented British seizure of territory on the eastern coast of Central America that included a logical terminus of a canal. The Treaty was intended therefore to ease strained relations.

When 50 years went by without any canal being built, agitation by the navy and business interests increased for construction of an American-controlled canal. The way was paved for such a canal by the Hay-Pauncefote Treaty.

Clemens, Samuel Langhorne (1835–1910). Author. Born in Florida, Mo., the great American humorist wrote under the pseudonym Mark Twain. A

116

river pilot on the Mississippi (1857–61), the river played a role in such classics as *The Adventures of Tom Sawyer* (1876) and *Life on the Mississippi* (1883).

A severe critic of the Gilded Age in which he lived, Clemens satirized the life of the period in *The Gilded Age* (1873), written in collaboration with Charles Dudley Warner. The social criticism in Clemens' widely read works did not detract from the human interest. *The Adventures of Huckleberry Finn* (1884), for example, is an attack on social hypocrisy. Huck in trying to escape from "civilization" remains true to his natural goodness. *Innocents Abroad* (1869), the first of Clemens' many successes, is a record of a trip through Europe, Egypt and the Holy Land filled with humorous incidents and observations not found in the usual guidebook.

Other works of Clemens include *The Jumping Frog of Calaveras County* (1867), *Roughing It* (1872), *The Prince and the Pauper* (1882), *A Connecticut Yankee at King Arthur's Court* (1889) and *The Man That Corrupted Hadleyburg* (1900).

Cleveland, Grover (1837–1908). Twenty-second and twenty-fourth President of the U.S. Born as Stephen Grover Cleveland in Caldwell, N.J., he was governor of New York (1883–85) and Democratic President of U.S. twice (1885–89; 1893–97). He supported civil service reform and a low tariff and opposed the currency inflation. He sent troops to stop the Pullman workers' interference with mail in a railroad strike.

Clinton, De Witt (1769–1828). Political leader. Born in Little Britain, N.Y., he was credited with introducing the "spoils system" when, as a member of the New York governor's Council of Appointment (1801), he replaced Federalists with Republicans. Mayor of New York City (1803–15), except for two annual terms, and Republican governor of N.Y. (1817–21; 1825–28), he was a prominent spokesman for public education in New York. He played a major role in construction of the Erie Canal.

Clinton, George (1739–1812). Statesman. Born in Little Britain, N.Y., he was a member of the Continental Congress (1775–76) from New York. He is regarded as "father of the state," by virtue of his seven terms as governor of N.Y. (1777–95; 1801–04). He refused to yield any state sovereignty, and as "Cato" in the N.Y. *Journal* he opposed ratification of the U.S. Constitution. Later, however, he became Vice-President of the U.S. (1805–13). A confirmed anti-Federalist, he opposed Alexander Hamilton's Bank of U.S.

clipper ships. Designers such as Donald McKay of East Boston, Mass., extended the ordinary three-masted packet ship to great length and reduced the ratio of beam to length to give the vessel a graceful look that was accented by the tallest masts that could be found. The large spread of canvas and lean lines made it possible for the ships to travel at an unprecedented clip. These ships were popular in the 1840's and 1850's.

The clippers were used in the coastal trade and made the voyage to California during gold rush years in as little as 89 days. Clippers such as the *Flying Cloud*, *Lightning*, *Andrew Jackson* and *Flying Fish* made record runs from the East to the West Coast when get-rich-quick adventurers were prepared to pay top fares for a speedy run to the goldfields. From the west coast clippers sailed to the Orient, where they picked up cargoes of tea, silk and spices. They often proceeded to Europe. English merchants had clipper ships built for them chiefly in Boston and Baltimore.

The clippers were used less and less in shipping with the further development of steamships in the post-Civil War period.

Coast and Geodetic Survey. In 1807 Congress established a federal bureau that would provide charts for the safe navigation of ships. Duties and functions of the bureau were consolidated when it was reorganized in 1947. In addition to aids to ship and air naviga-

tion it provides basic geodetic, geophysical and oceanographic data for engineering and scientific purposes and for commercial, industrial and defense needs.

Coast Guard, U.S. A military branch of the Armed Forces of the United States, the Coast Guard operates as a service in the Department of Transportation. In time of war it operates as a service in the Navy. Its history goes back to 1790, but it was reorganized by Congress in 1915. Its functions include saving life and property at sea, enforcing maritime laws, providing navigational aids to maritime commerce and to transoceanic air commerce, promoting the efficiency of the American merchant marine and maintaining readiness for military operations.

Code of Laws of the United States of America. All of the permanent laws of general application currently in force in the U.S. are included in the code. After each regular session of Congress a supplement is published cumulating all laws enacted since the basic volume. The code and supplements are published under the supervision of the Committee on the Judiciary of the House of Representatives, printed at the Government Printing Office and procurable from the Superintendent of Documents.

Coercive Acts (1774). To punish the colonists for such re-

118

sistance to British controls as the burning of the *Gaspee* and the Boston Tea Party, Parliament passed a series of acts known as the Coercive or Intolerable Acts. Boston was dealt with severely; its port was closed until the tea was paid for. Officials indicted by Massachusetts courts for capital offenses while enforcing English laws were to be tried in Britain. Massachusetts lost its charter, and officials, formerly elected locally, were to be appointed by the king. A new Quartering Act was imposed on all the colonies specifying that troops could be housed in public inns or deserted buildings.

Coeur d'Alene strikes. The lead and silver mines of northern Idaho were scenes of some of the most violent episodes in American labor history. Union miners struck in 1892. When mineowners sought to continue operations with non-union workers the ensuing battle brought the state militia to the scene. When this was not enough, Pres. Harrison authorized the use of federal troops to restore order.

The following year the Western Federation of Miners was formed. Strikes in 1894 and 1899 brought in federal troops again.

In 1905 Frank Steunenberg, who had been governor of Idaho, was murdered by a former coal miner, Harry Orchard. The president of the union, William D. ("Big Bill") Haywood was accused of complicity in the crime. Orchard was given life imprisonment but Haywood was acquitted. Coeur d'Alene was linked in the public mind with labor violence.

Cohens v. Virginia (1821). The U.S. Supreme Court upheld the Virginia state court of appeals conviction of the Cohens, who had been found guilty of selling lottery tickets in violation of a state law. The Cohens had based their appeal on the ground that the Constitution had been violated. Virginia, for its part, contended that under the 11th Amendment the Supreme Court had no jurisdiction in the case. In this larger issue, Chief Justice Marshall affirmed the Court's right to review the judgment of a state court in accordance with the doctrine of national supremacy.

Cohn, Edward Joseph (1892–1953). Biochemist. Born in New York City, he was granted a Ph.D. by the Univ. of Chicago (1917). He taught at Harvard Medical School (1935–49) and was director of the physical chemistry laboratory at Harvard after 1949. His research in fractionization of blood led to the wide use, by U.S. forces in World War II, of serum albumin as a blood substitute better suited to emergency conditions than whole blood or dried plasma.

Coin's Financial School (1894). In his little handbook, William H. Harvey sought to convince the public that the answer to the depression of 1893 lay in free and unlimited coinage of silver. Harvey created "Professor Coin" who explained that silver was the money of the people and gold was the money of the rich. The book vastly oversimplified the economic problems of the nation. It was distributed free by silver mine-owners during the presidential campaign of 1896.

Cold Harbor (June 3, 1864). Gen. Ulysses S. Grant's forces were disastrously defeated in their assault on Gen. Robert E. Lee's center, near a crossroads shamble of houses in a line defending Richmond, Va. The Confederates were too firmly entrenched in breastworks to be defeated. Horror swept the North, and Grant the victor was named Grant "the butcher"; 12,000 Union troops fell, dead or wounded.

cold war. The alliance of the U.S., Britain, France and the Soviet Union, which had defeated Germany, Italy and Japan, began to fall apart in 1946. The Western powers in general followed the leadership of the U.S. The Soviet Union became the center of a worldwide Communist bloc. The hostility, short of total war, that arose between the two sides became known as the cold war.

The Western democracies had expected that the countries freed from the Nazi dictatorship would be permitted to hold free elections. But the Soviet dictator, Joseph Stalin, kept his troops in the occupied nations of eastern Europe. Communists took over Rumania, Bulgaria, Albania, Poland, Hungary and Czechoslovakia. Within three years of the end of the war, an "Iron Curtain" (the phrase coined by Winston Churchill) had fallen across the heart of Europe.

U.S. answers to Communist advances in Europe included the Truman Doctrine, the Marshall Plan and the North Atlantic Treaty Organization (NATO). In Asia, major clashes between Communists and Western democracies took place in Korea, Laos and Viet Nam. In Africa, the rise of new nations, notably the Republic of the Congo (formerly Belgian), involved cold war contestants who sought to win new non-aligned nations to their sides.

Even the U.S.-Soviet space race to the moon was a dimension by which victory in the cold war was measured. People knew that escalation of the cold war into a nuclear war could mean virtual destruction of man on earth.

Cold war compromises were evident in the continued division of Berlin between East and West, the division of Korea at the 38th parallel and Viet Nam at the 17th parallel. The United Nations, built on the premise that the victorious allies would be in basic agreement on issues that might threaten war, became an arena for defending cold war decisions made elsewhere. Except for intermittent thaws promised by nuclear test bans, the world came to accept the cold war as a necessary though dismaying condition of life in the post-World War II world.

Collector v. Day (1870). The U.S. Supreme Court held the salary of a state judge to be immune from federal taxation. The Court reasoned that such immunity was necessarily implied from the very nature of the federal system in which the governments of the various states and the federal government are each independent within their respective spheres.

The case arose when Judge Day (Mass.) paid the Civil War income tax upon his salary under protest and obtained a judgment to recover it.

Colonial Dames of America. Founded in 1890 the organization is open to descendants of Americans who arrived in the American colonies before 1750 and played some significant role in the nation's development. The members seek in various ways to promote an interest in American history.

Colorado. The "Centennial State," a Mountain group state, was admitted to the Union Aug. 1, 1876, as the 38th State. A land that had been inhabited by prehistoric cliff dwellers, known only through the remains of their villages, it was first explored by Spain in the 16th century. The Spaniards found nomadic Indian tribes on the plains—Utes, Cheyennes, Arapahoes—and made no effort to found settlements. In the 19th century, Lt. Zebulon M. Pike, exploring for the U.S. Army, sighted the peak which bears his name (1806). Later explorations were made by John C. Frémont (1842–48).

Colorado (the Spanish word meaning "red" was first applied to the Colorado River) is comprised of territories acquired by the U.S. through the Louisiana Purchase (1803), admission of Texas (1845) and the Treaty of Guadalupe-Hidalgo at the end of the Mexican War (1848). The Continental Divide, which forms the crest of the continent and separates watersheds of the Pacific Ocean and the Gulf of Mexico, runs through the west-central part in a general north-south direction. The average elevation (6,800 ft.) is higher than that of any other state, but the eastern quarter is part of the Great Plains region. Denver, known as the Mile High City, is the state's capital.

Settlement of Colorado was stimulated by the discovery of gold in 1858. Mining continues to be important, but irrigation has made it possible for agriculture to become of even greater value.

"color of law" statute (1870). The federal statute provides that no person "under color of any law" was, because of race, to be deprived of rights guaranteed by the Constitution or be subjected to punishment

121

other than that provided for other persons. The law was intended to secure for Negroes protection afforded them by the 14th Amendment. It was invoked in 1965 by a federal court judge in Mississippi who upheld one count of an indictment against 17 men accused of murdering three civil rights workers. Maximum penalty under the statute is one year imprisonment and a $1,000 fine.

"Colossus of the North." The term was used in Latin America to describe the U.S., largely in the period between the Spanish-American War and the beginning of F. D. Roosevelt's "Good Neighbor" policy. An expression of hostility, it reflected criticism of the policy of intervention in Latin American affairs by U.S. superior military power, great wealth and determination to enforce the Monroe Doctrine and Roosevelt Corollary.

Colt six-shooter. The "revolving pistol" patented by Samuel Colt in 1836 was used with special effectiveness in the West. Indians who first drew the fire of the white men and then rushed in while the besieged were reloading were now met with a rapid fire. This was made possible by cocking of the hammer of the revolver which firmly aligned the cylinder with the barrel of the weapon. The Colt (.44 caliber) became standard equipment for the U.S. Army. It was used widely by both sides in the Civil War.

Columbia University. One of the oldest American universities, it was founded as King's College by grant of King George II (1754). It was closed down during the Revolution, but reopened as Columbia College (1784). The trustees adopted the name Columbia University (1896). Under the presidency of Seth Low (1889–1901), the University moved to its present site on Morningside Heights, New York City (1897). It was greatly expanded under Nicholas Murray Butler (1901–45).

From the first King's College envisaged widening the field of instruction beyond the classical course usual in the 18th century. The university includes faculties in law, political science, philosophy, pure science, journalism, business, dental surgery, medicine, engineering and library science.

Independent corporations forming part of the university educational system include Barnard College, the undergraduate college for women, and Teachers College.

Columbus Day (Oct. 12). The first celebration of Columbus' discovery of America in 1492 was held in New York City in 1792 under the auspices of the Society of St. Tammany. Since that time it has been celebrated in 35 states and Puerto Rico. It is designated Discovery Day in Indiana and North Dakota; Landing Day in Wisconsin; a memorial day in Arkansas and Oregon.

Comanche. Ranging from Texas to Wyoming, the tribe of Shoshonean stock chiefly menaced settlements in the southern plains. After 1875 they settled down on a reservation in Oklahoma and became cattle raisers.

combine. In a single continuous operation, the machine combines the reaping, threshing, cleaning and bagging of grain. It came into commercial use during the 1880's. A stimulus to the New Agricultural Revolution of the post-Civil War period, it contributed to large scale farming which began to replace the small farming operation.

Commerce, Department of. This executive department was established by Congress in 1913 by removing all labor activities from the Department of Commerce and Labor, created in 1903. The Secretary of Commerce has a place in the President's Cabinet.

The Department of Commerce has jurisdiction over foreign and domestic commerce, the manufacturing and shipping industries and the transportation facilities of the U.S. Activities of the Department include population, agricultural and other census taking, dissemination of commercial statistics, issuance of patents and the registration of trademarks, encouragement of travel from abroad to the U.S., administration of federal funds for highway improvement, promotion of inland waterway transportation,

operation of the St. Lawrence Seaway in U.S. territory and maintenance of a well-balanced merchant marine.

Committee on Public Information. The CPI was set up by Pres. Wilson less than two weeks after the U.S. declared war on Germany in 1917. It was headed by George Creel, a former muckraker, who rallied journalists, scholars and ministers to the Allied cause. The CPI magnified the "depravity" of the Germans and aroused anti-German feeling in the U.S. to a point where pacifists and sympathizers of the Central Powers were persecuted throughout the country.

Committees of Correspondence. In 1772 Samuel Adams set up in Massachusetts an intercolonial organization of committees in and out of legislatures. They kept each other informed about British measures and the kind of resistance taken or planned. They fomented revolutionary activity in the years before the final split between the colonies and England.

committee system of Congress. Standing committees (those which are permanent) were established as early as 1803. They became a practical necessity to insure a preliminary check on the flood of bills introduced. In the 61st Congress (1909–11) a peak was reached when a total of 44,363 measures were introduced in both Houses.

Committee procedure, with its witnesses and cross-examination, offers a much more satisfactory method of reaching the real merits of a measure and presenting it in workable form than the necessarily limited consideration on the floor in a Committee of the Whole (with a possible membership of 435 in the House of Representatives).

Each party has a committee on committees to recommend committee assignments. The proportion of Republicans to Democrats is fixed by the party in the majority for the time being. The House by a strict party vote adopts the slate presented by the two parties. A similar method is used in the Senate.

There are 20 standing committees in the House: Agriculture, Appropriations, Armed Services, Banking and Currency, District of Columbia, Education and Labor, Foreign Affairs, Government Operations, House Administration, Interior and Insular Affairs, Interstate and Foreign Commerce, Judiciary, Merchant Marine and Fisheries, Post Office and Civil Service, Public Works, Rules, Science and Astronautics, Un-American Activities, Veterans' Affairs, Ways and Means.

There are 16 standing committees in the Senate covering essentially the same areas with slightly different titles.

The *Congressional Directory* printed every two years by the Government Printing Office is a major source of reference on the Congress.

commodore. Congress legally established the naval rank of commodore in 1862. From 1775 to 1862 it had not been an actual rank but a courtesy title used ashore or on board when a senior captain cruised with junior officers. The commission, between that of captain and rear admiral, is given in wartime only to officers with special missions.

common law. It is that system of law which has prevailed in England and the U.S., in contradistinction to other great systems such as the Roman law, which is based on an enacted code. Unlike statutory law, a common law is not passed by a legislature. It derives from experience with human affairs. The principles of common law are unwritten and ready to meet every new and unexpected case. This is not to say, however, that common law cannot be adopted or modified by legislatures. In the U.S. the doctrines of the common law are being reduced to the statutory form, with such modifications as the legislatures choose to make.

Basic documents in American history which express common-law rights as inalienable rights of the people, based on tradition and usage, are the Declaration of Independence and the Bill of Rights (first 10 amendments) contained in the Constitution.

Common Sense. Writing in January 1776, Thomas Paine

justified revolution against the widely held belief that conciliation with the mother country was possible and desirable. The pamphlet's large circulation and the force of its argument against "the Royal Brute, a hardened, sullen-tempered Pharaoh," rallied the wavering and gave strength to those who agreed that "nothing but independence" could save America from ruin.

Commonwealth v. Hunt (1842). In an epoch-making decision the Massachusetts Supreme Court established the legality of labor unions. Until that time they were viewed as conspiracies under common law, since they were assumed to be organized for the purpose of injuring someone.

Chief Justice Shaw, instead of abandoning the common law, sought to reshape it. He reasoned that the proper test was whether the combination was "to accomplish some criminal unlawful purpose, or to accomplish some purpose, not in itself criminal or unlawful, by criminal or unlawful means." The purpose of union members was to persuade "all those engaged in the same occupation to become members." This, he said, was not in itself unlawful. Specifically, the Boston Journeymen Bootmakers Society was held to be a lawful organization.

communications revolution. Except when carrier pigeons and smoke signals were used, the speed of early communication was directly related to the pace of human travel. In the late 18th and early 19th centuries in the U.S., pioneer paths gave way to expanded turnpikes and canals. Operation of the first telegraph line (1844), divorcing communication from transportation, heralded a communications revolution. The Atlantic cable, telephone, radio and television extended the sphere of instantaneous electrical communication, creating a revolution in society. The horizons of every community were widened; news, culture, the arts spread rapidly. Greater centralization in industry and government was made possible.

Communications Satellite Corporation (COMSAT). The Corporation was created by Congress in 1962 to handle space communications on a profit-making basis under close government supervision. Half the corporation's shares of stock is owned by communications companies and half by stockholders.

In 1965 "Early Bird," the world's first commercial satellite and the first link in a commercial space communications global network, was launched from Cape Kennedy. The satellite quickly demonstrated its utility for relaying telephone messages and television programs between the U.S. and Europe.

Communist Mail Case (1965). The U.S. Supreme Court held unconstitutional a federal law requiring persons to whom

"Communist political propaganda" from abroad is addressed to make a special request to the Post Office to deliver it (*Lamont v. Postmaster General; Fixa v. Heilberg*).

The statute was passed in 1962 a year after Pres. Kennedy ordered that interception of unsolicited Communist propaganda mail be halted. The interception had been initiated in 1948.

The Court said that the law was contrary to the 1st Amendment's guarantee of freedom of speech and of the press. It was the first time in U.S. history that the Supreme Court nullified a congressional statute on the ground that it violated the 1st Amendment.

Communist party. The American Communist party was founded in 1919 and has maintained a precarious existence since that time. The peak of its voting strength was reached in the presidential election of 1932 when William Z. Foster polled almost 103,000 votes.

Communists are not, however, concerned with power through the ballot. Their teachings are based on Karl Marx's *Communist Manifesto* (1848), written with Friedrich Engels, and Marx's *Das Kapital* (1867–94). Unlike Socialist parties, they believe that violence is necessary to overthrow the capitalist "ruling class" if "dictatorship of the proletariat" is to be achieved.

The party, also known as the Workers' party during its early years in the U.S., urges collective ownership of the means of production. This means ownership by a strong centralized state government under which the traditional freedoms of a democracy would be crushed.

At the beginning of World War II the federal government set out to destroy the Communist party and other organizations deemed to be subversive. The Smith Act (1940), McCarran Act (1950) and Communist Control Act (1954) had the effect of ending the legal status of the party in the U.S.

Community Facilities Administration. A branch of the Housing and Home Finance Agency was created in 1954 to furnish technical and financial assistance to states, public agencies and nonprofit educational and other groups for the planning, construction and financing of group housing and community facilities.

Compromise of 1850. The resolutions offered by Henry Clay, "the great compromiser," sought to prevent the threatened secession of the South by compromising once again the sectional differences which threatened the Union. After bitter debate, five laws, the "Omnibus Bill," were passed by Congress. California was admitted as a free state; the rest of the territory acquired from Mexico was organized without providing for either the introduction of slavery or the exclusion of it; the Texas boundary excluded a part of New Mexico in return for which the federal government assumed the Texas state debt; the slave trade was ended in the District of Columbia; a more effective fugitive slave law was passed.

The principle of "popular sovereignty" was included in the acts establishing territorial governments for Utah and New Mexico. This provided that any states formed out of the territories should be admitted with or without slavery in accordance with the constitutions voted for by the people.

Compton, Arthur Holly (1892–1962). Physicist. Born in Wooster, O., he was granted a Ph.D. by Princeton Univ. (1916). He was professor of physics at the Univ. of Chicago (1923–45) and chancellor of Washington Univ., St. Louis (1945–53). He discovered the change in wavelength of scattered X rays, known as the Compton effect, for which he was awarded the Nobel Prize (1927), with C. T. R. Wilson. He also discovered the electrical nature of cosmic rays. Wartime director of plutonium research for the U.S. atomic bomb project (1942–45), he guided development of first quantities of plutonium.

Comptroller of the Currency. The office was created by Congress in 1863 as an integral part of the National Banking System. The Comptroller is involved in virtually every phase of the organization of national banks, including chartering new national banks and converting state-chartered banks into national banks. Should he deem a national bank to be insolvent, the Comptroller is empowered to appoint a receiver, the Federal Deposit Insurance Corporation, to handle its affairs. The Comptroller also participates in the issue, custody and redemption of Federal Reserve notes. New national bank notes are no longer issued, but the Comptroller is responsible for destruction of these notes as they are retired from circulation.

compulsory education. The origins of state compulsory education laws in the U.S. may be found in the Massachusetts Law of 1642, urged upon the colonial legislature by leaders of the Puritan church. It directed the officials of each town to hold parents responsible for seeing that their children learned "to read and understand the principles of religion and the capital laws of the country." Non-compliance was to be followed by fines. The law did not, however, establish schools. The Massachusetts Law of 1647 was an improvement over the law of 1642 for it gave the state the right to require communities to support schools or be subject to fines.

The first compulsory school attendance law was passed by Massachusetts in 1852. All children between the ages of eight and fourteen were required to attend school for twelve weeks each year, six weeks of which must be consecutive. Other states and territories followed so that by 1900 some form of compulsory school-attendance law had been enacted by most states in the North and West. The laws have since been extended to cover the full school year.

Comstock Lode. A fabulous silver deposit was discovered in Nevada in 1859. It was named after a shiftless miner, Henry Comstock, also known as "Old Pancake," who sold his holdings for almost nothing.

About a half-billion dollars in silver and gold were taken from the lode by the time it petered out after 1880. The wealth derived from it did not benefit Virginia City, jerry-built at the mine site, but was used by mine-owning families to establish palatial homes and banking institutions in San Francisco.

Conant, James Bryant (1893–). Educator. Born in Dorchester, Mass., he was granted a Ph.D. in chemistry by Harvard (1916). Author of works on organic chemistry, he was president of Harvard (1933–53). He played a key role in the World War II production of the atomic bomb. He aided in the creation of the National Science Foundation (1950). He was high commissioner to West Germany (1953–55) and U.S. ambassador there (1955–57). Under a Carnegie grant (1957–58), he published *The American High School Today* (1959); his subsequent reports on Amer-

ican education intended to strengthen public secondary schools.

Concord, battle of (Apr. 19, 1775). After the skirmish at Lexington, the British regulars moved on to Concord, where little of the military stores reported was found.

Harassment of the British by the provincials started at Concord and continued on their march back to Boston. The virtual rout of the British regulars convinced the colonists that armed resistance could be successful. While independence was still more than a year off, Lexington and Concord stirred the militancy of the colonists.

Concord group. The reference is to a group of idealists who gathered about Ralph Waldo Emerson after he had taken up residence in the little town of Concord, Mass. Among the group in the 1830's and 1840's were Henry David Thoreau, Nathaniel Hawthorne, Bronson Alcott and William Ellery Channing. Their books, essays and commentaries on society are part of the American heritage.

Conestoga wagon. The covered wagon, usually pulled by a team of six horses, transported settlers and their possessions across the Alleghenies and made possible settlement of the early West. It was first built in the Conestoga region of Pennsylvania (c. 1725) and was used into the 1850's. The bottom of the wagon sloped upward at both ends so that freight would not fall out on hills. The white canvas top afforded protection from the elements.

The cheap black cigar smoked by the wagon drivers became known as "stogies."

Confederate States of America (1861–65). Even before all 11 states had seceded from the Union, six of the southern states met at Montgomery, Ala. (Feb. 4, 1861) to form a new government; they called themselves the Confederate States of America.

The Montgomery convention adopted a new flag, the "Stars and Bars," and wrote a new constitution. It provided for a Congress in which each state was given one vote. Early in 1862 the Congress unanimously elected Jefferson Davis of Mississippi president and Alexander H. Stephens of Georgia vice-president.

The government of the Confederacy collapsed in 1865.

conflict of interest. This is an ill-defined area, not covered by laws, which affects legislators and other public officials whose personal business interests may be affected by actions they take in their official positions. It is the area where the relationship between official and private interests is often a matter of individual judgment.

Practically no national administration has remained unscathed and public officials have been compelled to resign when their individual judgment proved faulty. Pres. Johnson in 1965 issued an Executive Order requiring most government officials to file complete financial statements listing all assets owned by them and their immediate families. The President also clarified previous Executive Orders prohibiting the acceptance of gifts and restricting outside employment.

Congregationalism. Brought to America on the *Mayflower* in 1620, the doctrine holds that each local Protestant church is free to control its own affairs. Each congregation has Jesus Christ alone as its head and such intermediates as bishops and presbyters have no place in the church. Deacons are the principal assistants of the pastors.

In the 17th century Congregationalism was practically a state religion in New England. The Cambridge Platform (1648) was drafted to clarify interchurch relations and to emphasize their Calvinist views. Church membership increased following the Great Awakening (1734–44) in which Jonathan Edwards was a vital figure. But disputes led to the secession of the Unitarians early in the 19th century.

Congregationalists have been prominent in education. They founded Harvard, Yale, Williams, Amherst, Oberlin and many other colleges. The American Missionary Society was founded in 1846 and devoted itself primarily to the interests of Negroes and Indians. Some of the outstanding Negro colleges in the U.S. are under Congregationalist control.

The first regular National Council of the Congregational Churches of the U.S. met at Oberlin, O. (1871). Since then there have been meetings at stated intervals. Practical Christianity in the social service field has occupied Congregationalists. The trend toward wider cooperation was indicated in the merger of Congregationalists with the Christian Church (1931) to form the General Council of the Congregational and Christian Churches of the U.S. The combined churches have over 2,000,000 members.

Congress, U.S. The legislative (lawmaking) body of the federal government is Congress, consisting of the House of Representatives and the Senate.

The powers of Congress are listed in Art. I, Sec. 8 of the Constitution. They include the power to levy and collect taxes, to regulate commerce among the states and with foreign countries, to coin money and to declare war. The powers of Congress are specifically limited in Art. I, Sec. 9 of the Constitution. Congress cannot, for example, place a tax on exports from any state or withdraw money from the treasury unless the appropriation is made by law. The powers of Congress are also limited by some of the amendments to the Constitution, notably by the 1st Amendment.

A Representative must be at least 25 years of age, a citizen of the U.S. for at least seven years and a resident of the state he represents. Representatives hold office for two years and, like Senators, may be reelected for an indefinite number of terms. After each census, the House seats are reapportioned (redistributed). Congress decides how many seats there shall be in the House. Since 1910 this number has been set at 435. The presiding officer of the House is the Speaker, elected at the beginning of each new Congress. He is always a prominent member of the majority party.

Qualifications for the Senate indicate that the Founding Fathers expected the upper house to have a moderating influence on the lower house. A Senator must be at least 30 years of age, a citizen of the U.S. for at least nine years and a resident of the state he represents. Under the 17th Amendment (1913) Senators are elected directly by the voters of each state. Prior to the Amendment, Senators were chosen by state legislatures. Each state has two Senators. A Senator is elected for a term of six years. One-third of the Senators are elected every two years in even-numbered years. Thus the Senate never changes its entire membership at any one time. The Vice-President of the U.S. (elected every four years with the President) presides over the Senate. He is not one of the 100 members of the Senate and may vote only in case of a tie.

The Senate alone has the power to approve or disapprove major presidential appointments by majority vote. It also ratifies treaties by a two-thirds vote. On the other hand, all bills concerning the raising of money (principally through taxes) must originate in the House of Representatives.

Almost from the first, Congress realized that it could not handle successfully the many matters which came before it unless these were first examined by small groups of members of each House. The method by which a vast mass of legislation is examined and prepared for congressional action is known as the committee system.

Congressional Record. The proceedings of Congress are published daily when Congress is in session. Publication of the *Record* by the federal government began Mar. 4, 1873. It is the successor to the *Congressional Globe*.

Congress of Industrial Organizations (CIO). The failure of the American Federation of Labor (AFL) effectively to organize workers in mass production industries led to formation of the Committee for Industrial Organization (1935). The CIO was ousted from the AFL in 1937 and took the name Congress of Industrial Organizations.

In its early years the CIO was under the leadership of John L. Lewis (president of the United Mine Workers) and Sidney Hillman (president of the Amalgamated Clothing Workers). The CIO grew quickly with the organization of new unions in the steel, automobile, glass, rubber and radio industries. The emphasis was on industrial unionism under which all workers in a given industry, regardless of the kind of work they do, belong to the same union.

The 20-year split was not repaired until 1955, when the CIO and AFL merged to form the American Federation of Labor and Congress of Industrial Organizations (AFL-CIO).

Congress of Racial Equality (CORE). The civil rights organization was founded in 1942 to carry out a program of nonviolent, direct action in many areas to end racial discrimination. It claims 65,000 members in 118 local groups and has strong appeal for youth, recruiting many of its members from college campuses. CORE conducted its first sit-in at Stoner's Restaurant, Chicago. After many demonstrations the restaurant agreed to integrate in 1946. It also organized freedom rides in the 1960's to integrate bus lines and bus stops, utilizing the technique of the sit-in at stations.

Connecticut. One of the New England group, it was first explored by the Dutchman,

Adriaen Block, who sailed up the Connecticut River in 1614. The name is derived from Mohican and other Algonquian words meaning "long river place."

In 1633 Dutch settlers from New Netherland established a trading post near the present town of Hartford. Hartford, Windsor and Wethersfield were founded by groups led by Thomas Hooker, a minister, who left the Massachusetts Bay colony in 1636. The towns were governed for two decades under the Fundamental Orders, which explains why Connecticut is known as the "Constitution State." In 1662 the colony was granted a liberal royal charter with almost complete self-government.

One of the original 13 colonies, Connecticut played a vital role in provisioning and supplying troops for the Continental army. It was the fifth state to ratify the Constitution (Jan. 9, 1788). Hartford is the capital. Connecticut's manfacturing was greatly stimulated by the Civil War. Industry now claims half the employed population. Principal products include aircraft engines, machinery, ball bearings, electrical equipment, silverware and nuclear submarines. Poultry and dairy products yield the chief farm income. Many large insurance companies have their home offices in the state.

conquered province theory. Vigorous opponents of slavery such as Congressman Thaddeus Stevens (Pa.) argued at the end of the Civil War that the southern states should be treated as conquered provinces. They advocated the confiscation of all property of ex-Confederates.

conquistadores. The term is used to designate the Spanish conquerors of the New World in the 16th and 17th centuries. Included among them are Ponce de León, Cortéz, Pizarro, Coronado and De Soto.

"Conscience" Whigs. Many Whigs bolted their party in 1848 because it had not condemned slavery. Their consciences would not permit them to support the party's candidate, Gen. Zachary Taylor. Instead they supported former Pres. Van Buren, the Free Soil party nominee, who had opposed extension of slavery into new territories.

conscription (the "draft"). During the Civil War both North and South conscripted able-bodied men for service in the armed forces. The draft law of 1863 in the North permitted those whose names were drawn in the draft to provide a substitute or pay $300. In 1864 this provision was abolished. About 2% of the men who served in the Union army were drafted.

In World War I, the Selective Service Act of 1917 made possible the registration of about 24,000,000 men between the ages of 18 and 45. About 60%

of U.S. armed forces were raised by the draft during World War I. Conscription ended with the armistice in 1918. Recruitment was voluntary between World Wars.

In 1940 Congress passed the Selective Training and Service Act (Burke-Wadsworth Bill). As in World War I a complicated lottery system was devised to determine the order in which men were called, and local draft boards drew on those eligible for service. Before U.S. entrance into World War II almost one million men were drafted. By the end of the war over 10 million had been inducted. Another five million volunteered, some of whom may have been encouraged to enlist in order to be able to select a particular branch of the service. The 1940 draft law expired in 1947.

U.S. commitments in the post-World War II world compelled passage of the Selective Service Act of 1948 which has been extended several times. Local boards continue to induct men, ages 18½ to 26, for 24 months, to fill those needs of the armed forces that are not met by volunteers.

conservation of natural resources. The conservation movement calls for wisely using the nation's soil, forests, mineral deposits, wildlife and water, and reducing waste to a minimum.

The "pioneer psychology" which viewed the land as inexhaustible lasted long after pioneer conditions were gone in the U.S. The rapid distribution of the public domain through land sales at low prices or free, as in the Homestead Act (1862), contributed to the economic development of the country, but no thought was given to the conservation of the priceless national resources that such land contained.

Interest in conservation began with the appointment of a U.S. commissioner of fisheries (1871) and the passage of the Forest Reserve Act (1891). Presidents Harrison, Cleveland and McKinley acted to set aside forest reserves, but it was Pres. Theodore Roosevelt who set aside almost 150 million acres of unsold government timberland. He dramatized the need for conservation by calling a conference of governors at the White House (1908). Even earlier he had stimulated land reclamation with the Newlands Act (1902). The National Conservation Association was started in 1909.

Interest in conservation subsided during World War I, but the National Park Service was set up in 1917. The Federal Power Commission started work in 1920.

Conservation was spurred again under the New Deal. The Tennessee Valley Authority (1933) and the Civilian Conservation Corps (1937) were major efforts in this direction. The Agricultural Adjustment Act (1938) was committed to soil conservation.

World War II was an especially heavy drain on U.S. natural resources. The drain has continued since the war as the U.S. population has grown and defense needs have risen. Presidential commissions have reported that the situation is serious and that drastic action is necessary to halt pollution of streams, water shortages, depletion of irreplaceable resources, careless farming practices and other threats to the nation's natural resources.

Constitution, U.S. The Constitution of the United States was drafted by the Convention of 1787 and was signed on Sept. 17 by 39 of the 55 delegates who took part in the deliberations. The delegates provided that when nine states ratified the Constitution it could become effective among those nine. The ninth state to ratify was New Hampshire, June 21, 1788. The new government went into effect, Mar. 4, 1789, and George Washington was inaugurated first President on Apr. 30.

The Preamble to the Constitution which begins with the words, "We the people of the United States. . . ." suggests that ultimate authority resides in the people as a whole. The Preamble is introductory and does not grant power to any branch or organization of the national government. The actual grant of power by the people is set forth in the seven articles which follow the Preamble.

Art. I creates a Congress. Sec. 8 is the most important part of Art. I. It contains the 18 paragraphs which grant powers to Congress. Pars. 1 through 17 are called enumerated powers; par. 18 refers to implied powers (the famous "elastic clause").

Art. II creates the executive department headed by the President, who is the responsible executive head answerable for the actions of his subordinates.

Art. III authorizes the federal court system and lists areas that comprise the jurisdiction of the federal courts. Congress creates the courts below the Supreme Court level.

Art. IV, the "Federal-State Relations Article," sets forth the relations of the national government to the states and the relations of the states to each other. Sec. 1 declares: "Full faith and credit shall be given in each State to the public acts . . . of every other State." By this so-called "Friendship Clause" of the Constitution, the states recognize each other's contracts, wills and civil judgments.

Art. V specifies how amendments can be made to the Constitution and what amendments cannot be made. Except for the 21st Amendment, ratified by conventions in the states, all amendments have been ratified by the legislatures of "three-fourths of the several states."

Art. VI contains the important clause which makes the Constitution "the supreme law of the land." It declares that "the judges in every State shall be bound thereby, anything in the Constitution or laws of any

State to the contrary notwithstanding."

Art. VII states when the Constitution goes into effect. It is the only one of the original articles having no present-day significance.

The Constitution is the oldest written document of its kind. By broad use of congressional powers, sustained by the U.S. Supreme Court, a few amendments and the development of custom, the document fashioned by the Founding Fathers has remained a living Constitution.

Constitutional Convention (1787). The men who assembled at Philadelphia met at the call of the Continental Congress and the Annapolis Convention (1786) for the purpose of amending the Articles of Confederation, the supreme law of the land at the time. They soon arrived at a decision to submit a new frame of government to the Continental Congress and to state conventions that would be called to ratify the new Constitution.

Agreement was general that a stronger national government than the one provided for under the Articles was necessary. Differences arose over the best way to accomplish this result, but the conflicts were resolved by the 55 delegates from 12 of the 13 states (Rhode Island was not represented).

About half the delegates were lawyers and eight of them had signed the Declaration of Independence (1776). Delegates included such leaders as George Washington, Benjamin Franklin, Alexander Hamilton, Robert Morris and James Madison.

Thomas Jefferson was not present at the Convention because he was the U.S. minister to France; John Adams was the minister to England; Samuel Adams had not been elected a delegate; Patrick Henry refused to attend because he feared the Convention would devise a strong central government that would interfere with the rights of the states and of the people.

Debates were conducted at a high level and were kept secret because the delegates did not want differences to be exaggerated by the public and undermine acceptance of the final document.

The Constitution which emerged was scarcely a "bundle of compromises," but rather the substantial work of men in essential agreement who recognized the need for give and take in fashioning a workable frame of government. The Virginia Plan, favored by the big states, was countered by the New Jersey Plan, which defended the small states. By the Great Compromise (also known as the Connecticut Compromise) the two-house legislature was evolved. The small states gained equality in the Senate and the population strength of the big states was reflected in the House of Representatives. Compromises over slavery were as ingenious as the agreement by which a slave was to be counted as three-fifths of a person for taxation and representation.

The Convention labored from May to September through a long hot summer. It succeeded in forging the flexible instrument which is the Constitution of the United States of America.

CONSTITUTION OF THE UNITED STATES (*Text*)
(*Adopted in* 1787–88)

THE PREAMBLE*
Establishment of the Union. We the People of the United States, in order to form a more perfect union, establish justice, insure domestic tranquility, provide for the common defense, promote the general welfare, and secure the blessings of liberty to ourselves and our posterity, do ordain and establish this Constitution for the United States of America.[1]

ARTICLE I
THE LEGISLATURE

Section 1. Establishment of the Constitution
All legislative powers herein granted shall be vested in a Congress of the United States, which shall consist of a Senate and House of Representatives.

Section 2. The House of Representatives
1. How Elected. The House of Representatives shall be composed of members chosen every second year by the people of the several States, and the electors in each State shall have the qualifications requisite for electors[2] of the most numerous branch of the State legislature.

2. Qualifications. No person shall be a representative who shall not have attained the age of twenty-five years, and been seven years a citizen of the United States, and who shall not, when elected, be an inhabitant of that State in which he shall be chosen.

3. Basis of Representation and Taxation. Representatives and direct taxes[3] shall be apportioned among the several States which may be included within this Union, according to their respective numbers, [*which shall be determined by adding to the whole number of free persons, including those bound to service for a*

---

* The boldface headings, footnotes and current usage in spelling are added for help in reading.

[1] The Preamble is an introduction to the Constitution and does not grant the federal government any power. However, its clauses have been used to aid in interpreting the Constitution.

[2] "Electors" here means voters.

[3] The income tax is a form of direct tax which is paid by individuals rather than apportioned among the states. The income tax law was passed by Congress after ratification of the 16th Amendment.

term of years, and excluding Indians not taxed, three-fifths of all other persons.][4] The actual enumeration shall be made within three years after the first meeting of the Congress of the United States, and within every subsequent term of ten years, in such manner as they shall by law direct. The number of representatives shall not exceed one for every thirty thousand,[5] but each State shall have at least one representative; [*and until such enumeration shall be made, the State of New Hampshire shall be entitled to choose three, Massachusetts eight, Rhode Island and Providence Plantations one, Connecticut five, New York six, New Jersey four, Pennsylvania eight, Delaware one, Maryland six, Virginia ten, North Carolina five, South Carolina five, and Georgia three.*]

4. Filling Vacancies. When vacancies happen in the representation from any State, the executive authority thereof shall issue writs of election to fill such vacancies.

5. Choosing the Speaker and Impeachment. The House of Representatives shall choose their Speaker and other officers, and shall have the sole power of impeachment.

Section 3. The Senate

1. How Elected. The Senate of the United States shall be composed of two senators from each State, [*chosen by the legislature thereof*][6] for six years; and each senator shall have one vote.

2. Election of One-Third of Senators Every Two Years. Immediately after they shall be assembled in consequence of the first election, they shall be divided as equally as may be into three classes. [*The seats of the senators of the first class shall be vacated at the expiration of the second year; of the second class, at the expiration of the fourth year, and of the third class, at the expiration of the sixth year,*] so that one-third may be chosen every second year; [*and if vacancies happen by resignation or otherwise during the recess of the legislature of any State, the executive thereof may make temporary appointments until the next meeting of the legislature, which shall then fill such vacancies.*]

3. Qualifications. No person shall be a senator who shall not have attained to the age of thirty years, and been nine years a citizen of the United States, and who shall not, when elected, be an inhabitant of that State for which he shall be chosen.

4. Vice President as Presiding Officer. The Vice President of the United States shall be President of the Senate, but shall have no vote, unless they be equally divided.

5. Choosing of Senate's Officers. The Senate shall choose their other officers, and also a President *pro tempore* in the absence of

---

[4] Brackets with italics indicate parts of the Constitution which are no longer in effect.

[5] The number of representatives in 1967 is one for every 450,000 residents.

[6] Replaced by the 17th Amendment.

the Vice President, or when he shall exercise the office of President of the United States.

6. Power to Try Impeachments. The Senate shall have the sole power to try all impeachments. When sitting for that purpose, they shall be on oath of affirmation. When the President of the United States is tried, the Chief Justice shall preside; and no person shall be convicted without the concurrence of two-thirds of the members present.

7. Judgment in Case of Conviction. Judgment in cases of impeachment shall not extend further than to removal from office, and disqualification to hold and enjoy an office of honor, trust, or profit under the United States; but the party convicted shall, nevertheless, be liable and subject to indictment, trial, judgment, and punishment, according to law.

Section 4.   Elections and Meetings of Congress

1. Rules for Holding Elections. The times, places, and manner of holding elections for senators and representatives shall be prescribed in each State by the legislature thereof; but the Congress may at any time by law make or alter such regulations, except as to the places of choosing senators.

2. Meeting Once a Year. [*The Congress shall assemble at least once in every year, and such meeting shall be on the first Monday in December, unless they shall by law appoint a different day.*][7]

Section 5.   Rules of Congress

1. Admission of Members and Quorums. Each House shall be the judge of the elections, returns and qualifications of its own members, and a majority of each shall constitute a quorum to do business; but a smaller number may adjourn from day to day, and may be authorized to compel the attendance of absent members, in such manner, and under such penalties as each House may provide.

2. Determination of Rules. Each House may determine the rules of its proceedings, punish its members for disorderly behavior and, with the concurrence of two-thirds, expel a member.

3. Reports on Meetings. Each House shall keep a journal of its proceedings, and from time to time publish the same, excepting such parts as may in their judgment require secrecy; and the yeas and nays of the members of either House on any question shall, at the desire of one-fifth of those present, be entered on the journal.

4. Ending the Session. Neither House, during the session of Congress, shall, without the consent of the other, adjourn for more than three days, nor to any other place than that in which the two Houses shall be sitting.

---

[7] Changed to January 3rd by the 20th Amendment.

Section 6.   Privileges and Limitations of Congressmen

1. Pay and Special Rights. The senators and representatives shall receive a compensation for their services, to be ascertained by law, and paid out of the Treasury of the United States. They shall in all cases, except treason, felony, and breach of the peace, be privileged from arrest during their attendance at the sessions of their respective Houses, and in going to and returning from the same; and, for any speech or debate in either House, they shall not be questioned in any other place.

2. Limitations of Office Holding. No senator or representative shall, during the time for which he was elected, be appointed to any civil office under the authority of the United States, which shall have been created, or the emoluments whereof shall have been increased during such time; and no person, holding any office under the United States, shall be a member of either House during his continuance in office.

Section 7.   Method of Passing Laws

1. Money Bills. All bills for raising revenue[8] shall originate in the House of Representatives; but the Senate may propose or concur with amendments as on other bills.

2. Veto of Bills by the President. Every bill, which shall have passed the House of Representatives and the Senate, shall, before it becomes a law, be presented to the President of the United States; if he approve he shall sign it, but if not he shall return it with his objections to that House, in which it shall have originated, who shall enter the objections at large on their journal, and proceed to reconsider it. If after such reconsideration two-thirds of that House shall agree to pass the bill, it shall be sent, together with objections, to the other House, by which it shall likewise be reconsidered, and if approved by two-thirds of that House, it shall become a law. But in all such cases the votes of both Houses shall be determined by yeas and nays, and the names of the persons voting for and against the bill shall be entered on the journal of each house respectively. If any bill shall not be returned by the President within ten days (Sundays excepted) after it shall have been presented to him, the same shall be a law, in like manner as if he had signed it, unless the Congress by their adjournment prevent its return, in which case it shall not be a law.

3. Congressional Measures Subject to President's Approval. Every order, resolution, or vote to which the concurrence of the Senate and House of Representatives may be necessary (except on a question of adjournment) shall be presented to the President

---

[8] Revenue bills are those which raise money for governmental purposes. Money-spending bills are not revenue bills. Since either type of bill must be approved by both houses of Congress, they have equal power in raising and spending money.

of the United States; and before the same shall take effect, shall be approved by him, or being disapproved by him, shall be re-passed by two thirds of the Senate and House of Representatives, according to the rules and limitations prescribed in the case of a bill.

Section 8.   Powers Granted to Congress

1. Taxation. The Congress shall have power to lay and collect taxes, duties, imposts and excises, to pay the debts and provide for the common defense and general welfare of the United States; but all duties, imposts and excises shall be uniform throughout the United States;

2. Borrowing. To borrow money on the credit of the United States;

3. Commerce. To regulate commerce with foreign nations and among the several States, and with the Indian tribes;

4. Immigration and Bankruptcy. To establish an uniform rule of naturalization, and uniform laws on the subject of bankruptcies throughout the United States;

5. Money, Weights and Measures. To coin money, regulate the value thereof, and of foreign coin, and fix the standard of weights and measures;

6. Punishment of Counterfeiters. To provide for the punishment of counterfeiting the securities and current coin of the United States;

7. Post Offices. To establish post offices and post roads;

8. Copyrights and Patents.[9] To promote the progress of science and useful arts by securing for limited times to authors and inventors the exclusive right to their respective writings and discoveries;

9. Courfs. To contribute tribunals inferior to the Supreme Court;

10. Punishment of Piracy. To define and punish piracies and felonies committed on the high seas[10] and offenses against the law of nations;

11. War. To declare war, grant letters of marque and reprisal,[11] and make rules concerning captures on land and water;

12. Army. To raise and support armies, but no appropriation of money to that use shall be for a longer term than two years;

---

[9] Authors, composers, and artists are protected by the copyright laws. They are granted exclusive rights of publication and sale of their work for 28 years, with the right of renewal for another 28 years.

Inventors are protected by the patent laws. They are granted protection on the profits of their inventions for 17 years. Patent renewals are rare.

[10] "High seas" are ocean waters more than three miles from shore. No nation has exclusive rights in such waters.

[11] Letters of marque and reprisal are government commissions granted to owners of private vessels to make war on the enemy. They were not granted during the Civil War or since that time.

140

13. Navy. To provide and maintain a navy;

14. Regulation of Armed Forces. To make rules for the government and regulation of the land and naval forces;

15. Calling the Militia. To provide for calling forth the militia to execute the laws of the Union, suppress insurrections, and repel invasions;

16. Rules for the Militia. To provide for organizing, arming, and disciplining the militia, and for governing such part of them as may be employed in the service of the United States, reserving to the States respectively the appointment of the officers, and the authority of training the militia according to the discipline prescribed by Congress;

17. Government of Washington, D.C. To exercise exclusive legislation in all cases whatsoever over such district (not exceeding ten miles square) as may, by cession of particular States and the acceptance of Congress, become the seat of the Government of the United States, and to exercise like authority over all places purchased by the consent of the legislature of the State in which the same shall be, for the erection of forts, magazines, arsenals, dockyards, and other needful buildings; and

18. Implied Powers of Congress.[12] To make all laws which shall be necessary and proper for carrying into execution the foregoing powers, and all other powers vested by this Constitution in the Government of the United States, or in any department or officer thereof.

Section 9.   Powers Denied to Congress

1. Control of Slave Trade. [*The migration or importation of such persons as any of the States now existing shall think proper to admit shall not be prohibited by the Congress prior to the year one thousand eight hundred and eight, but a tax or duty may be imposed on such importation, not exceeding ten dollars for each person.*]

2. Habeas Corpus. The privilege of the writ of *habeas corpus*[13] shall not be suspended, unless when in cases of rebellion or invasion the public safety may require it.

3. Bill of Attainder and Ex Post Facto Laws. No bill of attainder[14] or *ex post facto* law[15] shall be passed.

---

[12] This is the famous "elastic clause" which has permitted Congress to increase its powers greatly. Congress, for example, holds that labor disputes may interfere with its power "to regulate commerce . . . among the several States. . . ." (Article I, Section 8, Paragraph 3); therefore it is "necessary and proper" to pass labor laws.

[13] A writ of *habeas corpus* is an order by a judge that a person being kept in prison be brought before him to determine whether he is being held legally.

[14] A bill of attainder is the act of a legislature which has the effect of punishing a person without a trial.

[15] An *ex post facto* law is legislation which makes unlawful and prescribes punishment for an act which was lawful when it was committed.

4. Direct Taxes. No capitation or other direct tax[16] shall be laid, unless in proportion to the census or enumeration hereinbefore directed to be taken.

5. Export Taxes. No tax for duty shall be laid on articles exported from any State.

6. Trade Between States. No preference shall be given by any regulation of commerce or revenue to the ports of one State over those of another; nor shall vessels bound to or from one State be obliged to enter, clear, or pay duties in another.

7. Accounting for Public Money. No money shall be drawn from the treasury but in consequence of appropriations made by law; and a regular statement and account of the receipts and expenditures of all public money shall be published from time to time.

8. Titles of Nobility. No title of nobility shall be granted by the United States; and no person holding any office of profit or trust under them shall without the consent of the Congress, accept of any present, emolument, office, or title, of any kind whatever, from any king, prince, or foreign State.

Section 10. Powers Denied to the States

1. Foreign Affairs, Money, Undermining of Basic Rights. No State shall enter into any treaty, alliance, or confederation; grant letters of marque and reprisal; coin money; emit bills of credit; make anything but gold and silver coin a tender in payment of debts; pass any bill of attainder, *ex post facto* law, or law impairing the obligation of contracts, or grant any title of nobility.

2. Interstate Trade. No State shall, without the consent of Congress, lay any imposts or duties on imports or exports, except what may be absolutely necessary for executing its inspection laws: and the net produce of all duties and imposts, laid by any State on imports or exports, shall be for the use of the Treasury of the United States; and all such laws shall be subject to the revision and control of the Congress.

3. War. No State shall, without the consent of Congress, lay any duty of tonnage, keep troops, or ships of war in time of peace, enter into any agreement or compact with another State, or with a foreign power, or engage in war unless actually invaded, or in such imminent danger as will not admit of delay.

ARTICLE II
THE EXECUTIVE

Section 1. The President and Vice President

1. Term of Office. The executive power shall be vested in a President of the United States of America. He shall hold his office

---

[16] See footnote 3 (page 136).

during the term of four years and, together with the Vice President, chosen for the same term, be elected as follows:

2. Appointment of Electors. Each State shall appoint, in such manner as the legislature thereof may direct, a number of electors, equal to the whole number of senators and representatives to which the State may be entitled in the Congress; but no senator or representative, or person holding an office of trust or profit under the United States, shall be appointed an elector.

3. Counting of Electoral Votes. [*The electors shall meet in their respective States, and vote by ballot for two persons, of whom one at least shall not be an inhabitant of the same State with themselves. And they shall make a list of all the persons voted for, and of the number of votes for each; which list they shall sign and certify, and transmit sealed to the seat of the Government of the United States, directed to the president of the Senate. The president of the Senate shall, in the presence of the Senate and House of Representatives, open all the certificates, and the votes shall then be counted. The person having the greatest number of votes shall be the President, if such number be a majority of the whole number of electors appointed; and if there be more than one who have such majority, and have an equal number of votes, then the House of Representatives shall immediately choose by ballot one of them for President; and if no person have a majority, then from the five highest on the list the said House shall in like manner choose the President. But in choosing the President, the votes shall be taken by States, the representation from each State having one vote; a quorum for this purpose shall consist of a member or members from two-thirds of the States and a majority of all the States shall be necessary to a choice. In every case, after the choice of the President, the person having the greatest number of votes of the electors shall be the Vice President. But if there should remain two or more who have equal votes, the Senate shall choose from them by ballot the Vice President.*][17]

4. Time for Election. The Congress may determine the time of choosing the electors, and the day on which they shall give their votes; which day shall be the same throughout the United States.

5. Qualifications for President. No person except a natural born citizen, [*or a citizen of the United States, at the time of the adoption of this Constitution,*] shall be eligible to the office of President; neither shall any person be eligible to that office who shall not have attained to the age of thirty-five years, and been fourteen years a resident within the United States.

6. Provisions for Replacement of the President. In case of the removal of the President from office, or of his death, resignation, or inability to discharge the powers and duties of the said office,

---

[17] Replaced by the 12th Amendment.

the same shall devolve on the Vice President, and the Congress may by law provide for the case of removal, death, resignation, or inability, both of the President and Vice President, declaring what officer shall then act as President, and such officer shall act accordingly, until the disability be removed, or a President shall be elected.[18]

7. Salary of the President. The President shall, at stated times, receive for his services a compensation, which shall neither be increased nor diminished during the period for which he shall have been elected, and he shall not receive within that period any other emolument from the United States, or any of them.

8. Presidential Oath of Office. Before he enter on the execution of his office, he shall take the following oath or affirmation:—"I do solemnly swear (or affirm) that I will faithfully execute the office of President of the United States, and will to the best of my ability, preserve, protect, and defend the Constitution of the United States."

Section 2. Powers of the President

1. Commander-in-Chief of Armed Forces and Power of Pardon. The President shall be commander-in-chief of the army and navy of the United States, and of the militia of the several States, when called into the actual service of the United States; he may require the opinion, in writing, of the principal officer in each of the executive departments,[19] upon any subject relating to the duties of their respective offices, and he shall have power to grant reprieves and pardons for offences against the United States, except in cases of impeachment.

2. Treaties and Appointments. He shall have power, by and with the advice and consent of the Senate, to make treaties, provided two-thirds of the senators present concur; and he shall nominate, and by and with the advice and consent of the Senate, shall appoint ambassadors, other public ministers and consuls, judges of the Supreme Court, and all other officers of the United States, whose appointments are not herein otherwise provided for, and which shall be established by law; but the Congress may by law vest the appointment of such inferior officers, as they think proper, in the President alone, in the courts of law, or in the heads of departments.

3. Filling of Vacancies. The President shall have power to fill up all vacancies that may happen during the recess of the Senate, by granting commissions which shall expire at the end of their next session.

---

[18] This provision is expanded by the 25th Amendment (1967). See page 157.
[19] There is no constitutional provision for a cabinet. However, President Washington's practice of meeting with executive department heads gave rise to the cabinet.

Section 3.   Duties of the President
Recommendations to Congress and Enforcement of Laws. He shall from time to time give to the Congress information of the state of the Union,[20] and recommend to their consideration such measures as he shall judge necessary and expedient; he may, on extraordinary occasions, convene both houses, or either of them, and in case of disagreement between them with respect to the time of adjournment, he may adjourn them to such time as he shall think proper; he shall receive ambassadors and other public ministers; he shall take care that the laws be faithfully executed, and shall commission all the officers of the United States.

Section 4.   Impeachment
Grounds for Impeachment. The President, Vice President, and all civil officers of the United States shall be removed from office on impeachment for and conviction of treason, bribery, or other high crimes and misdemeanors.

ARTICLE III
THE COURTS

Section 1.   The Federal Courts
The Supreme Court and Inferior Courts. The judicial power of the United States shall be vested in one Supreme Court, and in such inferior courts as the Congress may from time to time ordain and establish. The judges, both of the supreme and inferior courts, shall hold their offices during good behavior, and shall, at stated times, receive for their services a compensation which shall not be diminished during their continuance in office.

Section 2.   Jurisdiction of the Federal Courts
1. Kinds of Cases. The judicial power shall extend to all cases, in law and equity,[21] arising under this Constitution, the laws of the United States, and treaties made, or which shall be made, under their authority; to all cases affecting ambassadors, other public ministers, and consuls; to all cases of admiralty and maritime jurisdiction; to controversies to which the United States shall be a party; to controversies between two or more States; between a State and citizens of another State; between citizens of different States; between citizens of the same State claiming lands under

---

[20] These messages have been both written and delivered in person by our Presidents. Washington and Adams delivered theirs before joint sessions of Congress. The custom was resumed by President Wilson and has been continued since that time.

[21] Equity law attempts to remedy injustices which the common law cannot correct. For example, if a person believes that his property may be damaged, he may seek to have the court issue an injunction in order to prevent the damage.

grants of different States, and between a State, or the citizens thereof, and foreign States, citizens, or subjects.

2. Original and Appellate Jurisdiction of the Supreme Court.[22] In all cases affecting ambassadors, other public ministers and consuls, and those in which a State shall be a party, the Supreme Court shall have original jurisdiction. In all the other cases before mentioned the Supreme Court shall have appellate jurisdiction, both as to law and fact, with such exceptions and under such regulations as the Congress shall make.

3. Rules for Trials. The trial of all crimes, except in cases of impeachment, shall be by jury; and such trial shall be held in the State where the said crimes shall have been committed; but when not committed within any State, the trial shall be at such place or places as the Congress may by law have directed.

Section 3.   Treason

1. Treason Defined. Treason against the United States shall consist only in levying war against them, or in adhering to their enemies, giving them aid and comfort. No person shall be convicted of treason unless on the testimony of two witnesses to the same overt act, or on confession in open court.

2. Punishment for Treason. The Congress shall have power to declare the punishment of treason, but no attainder of treason shall work corruption of blood or forfeiture except during the life of the person attainted.

ARTICLE IV
RELATIONSHIP OF THE STATES TO THE FEDERAL GOVERNMENT

Section 1.   Recognition of State Laws

States' Respect for Each Other's Acts. Full faith and credit shall be given in each State to the public acts, records, and judicial proceedings of every other State. And the Congress may by general laws prescribe the manner in which such acts, records, and proceedings shall be proved, and the effect thereof.

Section 2.   Rights of Citizens and Return of Fugitives

1. Rights of Citizens in Different States. The citizens of each State shall be entitled to all privileges and immunities of citizens in the several States.

2. Return of Fugitives from Justice. A person charged in any State with treason, felony, or other crime, who shall flee from

---

[22] *Original jurisdiction* refers to the right of the Supreme Court to decide cases before they are presented in any other court. *Appellate jurisdiction* gives the Supreme Court the right to hear cases after they have been decided in lower courts.

justice, and be found in another State, shall on demand of the executive authority of the State from which he fled, be delivered up to be removed to the State having jurisdiction of the crime.

3. Fugitive Slaves. [*No person held to service or labor in one State under the laws thereof, escaping into another, shall, in consequence of any law or regulation therein, be discharged from such service or labor, but shall be delivered up on claim of the party to whom such service or labor may be due.*]

Section 3.   New States and Territories

1. Admission of New States. New States may be admitted by the Congress into this Union; but no new State shall be formed or erected within the jurisdiction of any other State; nor any State be formed by the junction of two or more States or parts of States, without the consent of the legislatures of the States concerned as well as of the Congress.

2. Regulation of Territories. The Congress shall have power to dispose of and make all needful rules and regulations respecting the territory or other property belonging to the United States; and nothing in this Constitution shall be so construed as to prejudice any claims of the United States or of any particular State.

Section 4.   Republican Form of Government

Federal Guarantee to State of Republican Government and Protection. The United States shall guarantee to every State in the Union a republican form of government, and shall protect each of them against invasion; and on application of the legislature, or of the executive (when the legislature cannot be convened), against domestic violence.

ARTICLE V
AMENDING THE CONSTITUTION

Methods of Amendment. The Congress, whenever two-thirds of both Houses shall deem it necessary, shall propose amendments to this Constitution, or, on the application of the legislature of two-thirds of the several States, shall call a convention for proposing amendments, which, in either case, shall be valid to all intents and purposes as part of this Constitution, when ratified by the legislatures of three-fourths of the several States, or by conventions in three-fourths thereof, as the one or the other mode of ratification may be proposed by the Congress; [*provided that no amendment which may be made prior to the year one thousand eight hundred and eight shall in any manner affect the first and fourth clauses in the ninth Section of the first article; and*] that no State, without its consent, shall be deprived of its equal suffrage in the Senate.

ARTICLE VI
THE SUPREME LAW OF THE LAND

1. **Debts.** All debts contracted and engagements entered into, before the adoption of this Constitution, shall be as valid against the United States under this Constitution, as under the Confederation.

2. **Supremacy of the Constitution.** This Constitution and the laws of the United States which shall be made in pursuance thereof and all treaties made, or which shall be made, under the authority of the United States, shall be the supreme law of the land; and the judges in every State shall be bound thereby, anything in the Constitution or laws of any State to the contrary notwithstanding.

3. **Required Support of the Constitution.** The senators and representatives before mentioned, and the members of the several State legislatures, and all executive and judicial officers, both of the United States and of the several States, shall be bound by oath or affirmation to support this Constitution; but no religious test shall ever be required as a qualification to any office or public trust under the United States.

ARTICLE VII
RATIFICATION

Requirements for Ratification. The ratification of the conventions of nine States shall be sufficient for the establishment of this Constitution between the States so ratifying the same.

Done in Convention by the unanimous consent of the States present the seventeenth day of September in the year of our Lord one thousand seven hundred and eighty-seven and of the independence of the United States of America the twelfth. In witness whereof we have hereunto subscribed our names.

GEORGE WASHINGTON,
President and Deputy
from Virginia

WILLIAM JACKSON, Secretary

New Hampshire
JOHN LANGDON
NICHOLAS GILMAN
Massachusetts
NATHANIEL GORHAM
RUFUS KING
Connecticut
WILLIAM S. JOHNSON
ROGER SHERMAN

New York
ALEXANDER HAMILTON
New Jersey
WILLIAM LIVINGSTON
DAVID BREARLEY
WILLIAM PATERSON
JONATHAN DAYTON
Pennsylvania
BENJAMIN FRANKLIN
THOMAS MIFFLIN

ROBERT MORRIS
GEORGE CLYMER
THOMAS FITZSIMONS
JARED INGERSOLL
JAMES WILSON
GOUVERNEUR MORRIS
          Delaware
GEORGE READ
GUNNING BEDFORD, JR.
JOHN DICKINSON
RICHARD BASSETT
JACOB BROOM
          Maryland
JAMES MCHENRY
DANIEL OF ST. THOMAS JENIFER
DANIEL CARROLL

          Virginia
JOHN BLAIR
JAMES MADISON, JR.
          North Carolina
WILLIAM BLOUNT
RICHARD DOBBS SPRAIGHT
HU WILLIAMSON
          South Carolina
J. RUTLEDGE
CHARLES C. PINCKNEY
PIERCE BUTLER
          Georgia
WILLIAM FEW
ABRAHAM BALDWIN

AMENDMENTS

1st AMENDMENT (1791)[1]
Fundamental Freedom
Congress shall make no law respecting an establishment of religion, or prohibiting the free exercise thereof; or abridging the freedom of speech or of the press; or the right of the people peaceably to assemble, and to petition the Government for a redress of grievances.

2nd AMENDMENT (1791)
Right of People to Bear Arms[2]
A well-regulated militia being necessary to the security of a free State, the right of the people to keep and bear arms shall not be infringed.

3rd AMENDMENT (1791)
Quartering Soldiers
No soldier shall, in time of peace, be quartered in any house without the consent of the owner, nor in time of war, but in a manner to be prescribed by law.

4th AMENDMENT (1791)
Searches and Seizures
The right of the people to be secure in their persons, houses, papers, and effects, against unreasonable searches and seizures, shall not be violated, and no warrants shall issue but upon probable

---

[1] The first ten amendments are known as the *Bill of Rights*.
[2] State laws now regulate the use of firearms.

cause, supported by oath or affirmation, and particularly describing the place to be searched, and the person or things to be seized.

5th AMENDMENT (1791)
Protection of Life, Liberty, and Property
No person shall be held to answer for a capital or otherwise infamous crime, unless on a presentment or indictment of a grand jury, except in cases arising in the land or naval forces, or in the militia, when in actual service in time of war or public danger; nor shall any person be subject for the same offense to be twice put in jeopardy of life or limb; nor shall be compelled in any criminal case to be a witness against himself, nor be deprived of life, liberty, or property, without due process of law[3]; nor shall private property be taken for public use without just compensation.

6th AMENDMENT
Rights of Accused in Criminal Cases
In all criminal prosecutions the accused shall enjoy the right to a speedy and public trial, by an impartial jury of the State and district wherein the crime shall have been committed, which district shall have been previously ascertained by law, and to be informed of the nature and cause of the accusation; to be confronted with the witnesses against him; to have compulsory process for obtaining witnesses in his favor, and to have the assistance of counsel for his defense.

7th AMENDMENT
Trial by Jury
In suits at common law,[4] where the value in controversy shall exceed twenty dollars, the right of trial by jury shall be preserved, and no fact tried by a jury shall be otherwise reexamined in any court of the United States, than according to the rules of the common law.

8th AMENDMENT (1791)
Excessive Bail and Punishment
Excessive bail shall not be required, nor excessive fines imposed, nor cruel and unusual punishments inflicted.

---

[3] In the 5th Amendment, the famous "due process of law" clause is a restraint upon the federal government. In the 14th Amendment it is a restraint upon the state governments. Although "due process" has not been exactly defined by the courts, it is intended to protect people and property by a fair trial.

[4] Common law is based on decisions which have been followed by courts since the Middle Ages in England. It was continued in America by the colonists. Unlike statutory law, it is not passed by a legislature; nor is it constitutional law, which is based on the Constitution of the United States.

9th AMENDMENT (1791)
Other Rights of the People
The enumeration in the Constitution, of certain rights, shall not be construed to deny or disparage others retained by the people.

10th AMENDMENT (1791)
Rights Reserved to the States
The powers not delegated to the United States by the Constitution, nor prohibited by it to the States, are reserved to the States respectively, or to the people.[5]

11th AMENDMENT (1798)
Suits Against States
The judicial power of the United States shall be construed to extend to any suit in law or equity, commenced or prosecuted against one of the United States by citizens of another State, or by citizens or subjects of any foreign State.

12th AMENDMENT (1804)
Election of President and Vice President[6]
The electors shall meet in their respective States, and vote by ballot for President and Vice President, one of whom at least shall not be an inhabitant of the same State with themselves; they shall name in their ballots the person voted for as President, and in distinct ballots the person voted for as Vice President, and they shall make distinct lists of all persons voted for as President, and of all persons voted for as Vice President and of the number of votes for each, which lists they shall sign and certify, and transmit sealed to the seat of the Government of the United States, directed to the President of the Senate;—The President of the Senate shall, in presence of the Senate and House of Representatives, open all the certificates and the votes shall then be counted;— The person having the greatest number of votes for President, shall be the President, if such number be a majority of the whole number of electors appointed; and if no person have such majority, then from the persons having the highest numbers not exceeding three on the list of those voted for as President, the House of Representatives shall choose immediately, by ballot, the President. But in choosing the President, the votes shall be taken by States, the representation from each State having one vote; a quorum for this purpose shall consist of a member or members from two-thirds of the States, and a majority of all the States shall be necessary to

[5] This important amendment reserves for the states the greater part of governmental power. Education, marriage laws, control of crime, and health standards are only a few of the matters controlled by the states.

[6] The 12th Amendment replaces Article II, Section 1, Paragraph 3. It was made necessary by the tie vote in the Jefferson-Burr controversy in 1800.

a choice. And if the House of Representatives shall not choose a President whenever the right of choice shall devolve upon them, [*before the fourth day of March next following,*][7] then the Vice President shall act as President, as in the case of the death or other constitutional disability of the President. The person having the greatest number of votes as Vice President, shall be the Vice President, if such number be a majority of the whole number of electors appointed, and if no person have a majority, then from the two highest members on the list, the Senate shall choose the Vice President; a quorum for the purpose shall consist of two-thirds of the whole number of senators, and a majority of the whole number shall be necessary to a choice. But no person constitutionally ineligible to the office of President shall be eligible to that of Vice President of the United States.

13th AMENDMENT (1865)
Abolition of Slavery
Section 1
Neither slavery nor involuntary servitude, except as a punishment for crime whereof the party shall have been duly convicted, shall exist within the United States, or any place subject to their jurisdiction.

Section 2
Congress shall have power to enforce this article by appropriate legislation.

14th AMENDMENT (1868)
Citizenship Defined
Section 1. Rights of Citizens
All persons born or naturalized in the United States, and subject to the jurisdiction thereof, are citizens of the United States and of the State wherein they reside. No State shall make or enforce any law which shall abridge the privileges or immunities of citizens of the United States; nor shall any State deprive any person of life, liberty, or property without due process of law;[8] nor deny to any person within its jurisdiction the equal protection of the laws.

Section 2. Penalty for Restrictions on Voting
Representatives shall be apportioned among the several States according to their numbers, counting the whole number of persons in each State, excluding Indians not taxed. But when the right to vote at any election for the choice of electors for President and Vice President of the United States, Representatives in Congress,

---

[7] This has been changed by the 20th Amendment to "noon on the 20th day of January."

[8] Intended for the protection of Negroes, this "due process of law" clause has been used by many corporations to protect their property. A corporation is a "person" in the eyes of the law.

the executive and judicial officers of a State, or the members of the legislature thereof, is denied to any of the male inhabitants of such State, being twenty-one years of age, and citizens of the United States, or in any way abridged, except for participation in rebellion, or other crime, the basis of representation therein shall be reduced in the proportion which the number of such male citizens shall bear to the whole number of male citizens twenty-one years of age in such State.[9]

Section 3. Penalty for Rebellion
No person shall be a Senator or Representative in Congress, or elector of President and Vice President, or hold any office, civil or military, under the United States or under any State, who, having previously taken an oath as a member of Congress, or as an officer of the United States, or as a member of any State legislature, or as an executive or judicial officer of any State, to support the Constitution of the United States, shall have engaged in insurrection or rebellion against the same, or given aid or comfort to the enemies thereof. But Congress may, by a vote of two-thirds of each house, remove such disability.

Section 4. War Debt of the Confederacy
The validity of the public debt of the United States, authorized by law, including debts incurred for payment of pensions and bounties for services in suppressing insurrection or rebellion, shall not be questioned. But neither the United States nor any State shall assume or pay any debt or obligation incurred in aid of insurrection or rebellion against the United States, or any claim for the loss or emancipation of any slave; but all such debts, obligations, and claims shall be held illegal and void.

Section 5. Enforcement
The Congress shall have power to enforce, by appropriate legislation, the provisions of this article.

15th AMENDMENT (1870)
Right of Negroes to Vote
Section 1
The right of citizens of the United States to vote shall not be denied or abridged by the United States or by any State on account of race, color, or previous condition of servitude.[10]

Section 2
The Congress shall have power to enforce this article by appropriate legislation.

---

[9] This penalty has not been enforced.
[10] Other qualifications for voting are set up by the states.

16th AMENDMENT (1913)
The Income Tax

The Congress shall have power to lay and collect taxes on incomes, from whatever source derived, without apportionment among the several States, and without regard to any census or enumeration.

17th AMENDMENT (1913)
Direct Election of Senators

The Senate of the United States shall be composed of two senators from each State, elected by the people thereof, for six years; and each senator shall have one vote. The electors in each State shall have the qualifications requisite for electors of the most numerous branch of the State legislature.

When vacancies happen in the representation of any State in the Senate, the executive authority of each State shall issue writs of election to fill such vacancies: *Provided* that the legislature of any State may empower the executive thereof to make temporary appointments until the people fill the vacancies by election as the legislature may direct.

[*This amendment shall not be so construed as to affect the election or term of any senator chosen before it becomes valid as part of the Constitution.*]

18th AMENDMENT (1919)[11]
Prohibition

[*Section 1. After one year from the ratification of this article the manufacture, sale, or transportation of intoxicating liquors within, the importation thereof into, or the exportation thereof from the United States and all territory subject to the jurisdiction thereof for beverage purposes is hereby prohibited.*

Section 2. The Congress and the several States shall have concurrent power to enforce this article by appropriate legislation.

Section 3. This article shall be inoperative unless it shall have been ratified as an amendment to the Constitution by the legislatures of the several States, as provided in the Constitution, within seven years from the date of the submission hereof to the States by the Congress.]

19th AMENDMENT (1920)
Woman Suffrage
Section 1

The right of citizens of the United States to vote shall not be denied or abridged by the United States or any State on account of sex.

---

[11] The prohibition amendment was repealed thirteen years later by the 21st Amendment.

Section 2

The Congress shall have power to enforce this article by appropriate legislation.

20th AMENDMENT (1932)[12]
New Time for Beginning of Congressional and Presidential Terms
Section 1.   Ending of Terms of Office

The terms of the President and Vice President shall end at noon on the twentieth day of January, and the terms of Senators and Representatives at noon on the third day of January, of the years in which such terms would have ended if this article had not been ratified; and the terms of their successors shall then begin.

Section 2.   Regular Sessions of Congress

The Congress shall assemble at least once in every year, and such meeting shall begin at noon on the third day of January, unless they shall by law appoint a different day.

Section 3.   Provision for a Temporary President

If, at the time fixed for the beginning of the term of the President, the President-elect shall have died, the Vice President-elect shall become President. If a President shall not have been chosen before the time fixed for the beginning of his term, or if the President-elect shall have failed to qualify, then the Vice President-elect shall act as President until a President shall have qualified; and the Congress may by law provide for the case wherein neither a President-elect nor a Vice President-elect shall have qualified, declaring who shall then act as President, or the manner in which one who is to act shall be selected, and such person shall act accordingly until a President or Vice President shall have qualified.

Section 4.   Power of Congress in Unusual Elections

The Congress may by law provide for the case of the death of any of the persons from whom the House of Representatives may choose a President whenever the right of choice shall have devolved upon them, and for the case of the death of any of the persons from whom the Senate may choose a Vice President whenever the right of choice shall have devolved upon them.

---

[12] The 20th Amendment is known as the "lame duck" amendment. Until it was ratified, defeated candidates for office remained in office for four months after they were rejected by the voters. Some of them went "limping" to the President for an appointive office; others were absent from Congress or carried on their duties in a halfhearted fashion.

Section 5. Date in Effect

[*Sections 1 and 2 shall take effect upon the fifteenth day of October following the ratification of this article.*]

Section 6. Time for Ratification

[*This article shall be inoperative unless it shall have been ratified as an amendment to the Constitution by the Legislatures of three fourths of the several states within seven years from the date of its submission.*]

21st AMENDMENT (1933)
Repeal of Prohibition
Section 1

The eighteenth article of amendment to the Constitution of the United States is hereby repealed.

Section 2

The transportation or importation into any State, Territory, or Possession of the United States for delivery or use therein of intoxicating liquors, in violation of the laws thereof, is prohibited.

Section 3

[*This article shall be inoperative unless it shall have been ratified as an amendment to the Constitution by convention in the several States, as provided in the Constitution, within seven years from the date of the submission hereof to the States by the Congress.*]

22nd AMENDMENT (1951)
No Third Term for Presidents

No person shall be elected to the office of the President more than twice, and no person who has held the office of President or acted as President, for more than two years of a term to which some other person was elected President shall be elected to the office of President more than once.

[*But this Article shall not apply to any person holding the office of President when this Article was proposed by the Congress, and shall not prevent any person who may be holding the office of President, or acting as President, during the term within which this Article becomes operative from holding the office of President or acting President during the remainder of such term.*]

23rd AMENDMENT (1961)
Presidential Vote for District of Columbia
Section 1

The District constituting the seat of Government of the United States shall appoint in such manner as the Congress may direct:

A number of electors of President and Vice President equal to the whole number of Senators and Representatives in Congress to which the District would be entitled if it were a State, but in no event more than the least populous State; they shall be in addition to those appointed by the States, but they shall be considered, for the purpose of the election of President and Vice President, to be electors appointed by a State; and they shall meet in the District and perform such duties as provided by the 12th article of amendment.

Section 2

The Congress shall have power to enforce this article by appropriate legislation.

24th AMENDMENT (1964)
Barring Poll Tax in Federal Elections
Section 1

The right of citizens of the United States to vote in any primary or other election for President or Vice President, for electors for President or Vice President, or for Senator or Representatives in Congress shall not be denied or abridged by the United States or any State by reason of failure to pay any poll tax or other tax.

Section 2

The Congress shall have power to enforce this article by appropriate legislation.

25th AMENDMENT (1967)
Presidential Disability and Succession
Section 1

In case of the removal of the President from office or his death or resignation, the Vice President shall become President.

Section 2

Whenever there is a vacancy in the office of the Vice President, the President shall nominate a Vice President who shall take the office upon confirmation by a majority vote of both houses of Congress.

Section 3

Whenever the President transmits to the President *pro tempore* of the Senate and the Speaker of the House of Representatives his written declaration that he is unable to discharge the powers and duties of his office, and until he transmits to them a written declaration to the contrary, such powers and duties shall be discharged by the Vice President as Acting President.

Section 4

Whenever the Vice President and a majority of either the principal officers of the executive departments, or of such other body as Congress may by law provide, transmit to the President *pro tempore* of the Senate and the Speaker of the House of Representatives their written declaration that the President is unable to discharge the powers and duties of his office, the Vice President shall immediately assume the powers and duties of the office as Acting President.

Thereafter, when the President transmits to the President *pro tempore* of the Senate and the Speaker of the House of Representatives his written declaration that no inability exists, he shall resume the powers and duties of his office unless the Vice President and a majority of either the principal officers of the executive departments, or of such other body as Congress may by law provide, transmit within four days to the President *pro tempore* of the Senate and the Speaker of the House of Representatives their written declaration that the President is unable to discharge the powers and duties of his office. Thereupon Congress shall decide the issue, assembling within 48 hours for that purpose if not in session. If the Congress, within 21 days after receipt of the latter written declaration, or, if Congress is not in session, within 21 days after Congress is required to assemble, determines by two-thirds vote of both houses that the President is unable to discharge the powers and duties of his office, the Vice President shall continue to discharge the same as Acting President; otherwise, the President shall resume the powers and duties of his office.

Constitution and Guerrière (Aug. 19, 1812). In a famous naval engagement in the War of 1812, the U.S. frigate *Constitution* ("Old Ironsides") destroyed the smaller British frigate *Guerrière* off the coast of Massachusetts. The victory established the superiority of the American type of frigate and aroused some enthusiasm among New England merchants who regarded the war as disruptive to their trade.

containment policy. The phrase describes the post-World War II foreign policy of the U.S. which aimed to block the expansion of communism. It was used by George F. Kennan (under the pseudonym of "Mr. X")

158

in an article in the magazine *Foreign Affairs* (July 1947), entitled "The Sources of Soviet Conduct." Kennan had been a counselor in the American Embassy in Moscow and, in 1947, was a member of the Policy Planning Committee of the State Department. He believed that Soviet foreign policy was based on the inevitability of conflict between communism and capitalism. He held, however, that Russia would not risk gaining its objectives by force if it was faced by a strong opposition force. To counteract the Russian objectives, Kennan called for a U.S. policy "of long-term, patient but firm and vigilant containment of Russian expansive tendencies."

Before Kennan's article was published administration leaders had been discussing how the containment he suggested could be accomplished. It had, in fact, been started by Pres. Truman in Mar. 1947 (the Truman Doctrine) under which the U.S., while building up its own armed forces, gave military and economic aid to nations threatened by the USSR. Greece and Turkey, the first to be helped under the policy, did not become Russian satellites.

contempt. Courts of justice have an inherent power to punish for contempt all persons who disregard their orders and proceedings.

Legislative bodies, too, under the state constitutions have the right to punish for contempt.

Under the U.S. Constitution each house of Congress may determine the rules of its proceedings, punish its members for disorderly behavior and with the consent of two-thirds expel a member. A person called before a committee of Congress who refuses to answer questions or who is disrespectful may be held in contempt of Congress. The Department of Justice then proceeds with the prosecution, which may result in fine and imprisonment if the federal court sustains the contempt charge.

Continental army. In June 1775 the Continental Congress appropriated $6,000 for the support of a "Continental army" and appointed George Washington Commander-in-Chief. When he took command at Cambridge, Mass., 1775, he found such a motley array of citizens that he proposed the uniform of the hunting shirt to give some semblance of order. In 1776 he described the difficulty of operating an army "without any money in our treasury, powder in our magazines, arms in our stores. . . ." Throughout the war there was an acute shortage of clothing, blankets, shoes and medical supplies. The French helped by supplying munitions.

To attract troops requested by Congress, the states offered cash bounties or land. In New England this was supplemented by the draft and the hiring of substitutes. In 1781 volunteers were in such short supply that

Virginia offered 300 acres of land and a prime Negro slave or £60 in specie.

Despite seemingly insuperable obstacles the army was kept in the field although short periods of enlistment meant constant training of troops. Washington's resourcefulness, foreign aid, farmers accustomed to firearms and fighting for their homeland, the overextended line of British communications —all help to explain the ultimate victory of the Continental army in the Revolutionary War.

Continental Association (1774). The First Continental Congress organized an economic pressure group to influence British merchants to persuade Parliament to ease tax measures and other punitive acts taken against the colonies. Committees in the colonies were set up to boycott the sale of British goods, halt the export of colonial goods to Britain and discontinue the slave trade.

It was a step short of war— but it did not achieve its aim.

Continental Congress (1774–89). During the period of the American Revolution and up to the time that the Second Continental Congress was replaced by the Congress under the new Constitution, two Continental Congresses managed colonial and later state activities.

The First Continental Congress had a brief but significant life. It met in Philadelphia, Sept. 5–Oct. 26, 1774, to protest colonial grievances, especially measures taken against Massachusetts. It agreed upon "The Association" which revived nonimportation as a means of pressuring Britain into a change of policy. It resolved to meet again if grievances were not redressed by George III.

The Second Continental Congress met May 10, 1775. It appointed George Washington as Commander-in-Chief of all the continental armies and moved toward a declaration of independence. It was this Continental Congress that coordinated the resistance of the newly formed states in the Revolutionary War and won the support of foreign allies in the struggle for independence.

The Continental Congress drafted the Articles of Confederation in 1777 and functioned without a written constitution until they were ratified by the 13 states in 1781.

Congress, under the Articles, was handicapped by lack of power to collect taxes and regulate interstate commerce; but it did settle land disputes among the states and promised equality to new states that were to be carved out of the western lands yielded by the original states for the common good.

The Congress itself called for the Constitutional Convention (1787) that was to replace it with a stronger central government than the one it had provided during its 15-year life.

Continental Divide. Also known as the Great Divide and the "backbone" of the continent, it generally coincides with various ranges of the Rocky Mts. It is the line connecting the highest points of land that separate the streams flowing west from those flowing east. Its central point is Colorado, where many of the peaks are above 13,000 feet.

Continentals. On June 14, 1775, at the beginning of the American Revolution, the Second Continental Congress voted to enlist troops in the Continental army. This was a departure from the usual enlistment in the service of an individual colony. The new troops were referred to as Continentals.

continental shelf. In the post-World War II years the search was intensified for oil and gas in offshore waters of the states bordering the Gulf of Mexico.

The continental shelf—that relatively shallow underwater land mass that lies between the coast and the deep sea—is a transition zone between the continent and the ocean shelf. Generally, it is considered part of the coast out to a point where the water is 600 feet or 100 fathoms deep.

Its width varies greatly. Off Louisiana, where numerous oil wells have been brought in, the shelf extends outward for 100 miles; off New England it extends as far as 200 miles; off the California coast, it extends but a few miles seaward; off the Florida coast it narrows to a mile or so.

The shelf is a submerged portion of the continent. Geological formations on the coast generally continue below the surface of the shelf. Thus, petroleum-bearing strata on land can be followed below the sea.

continuous voyage doctrine. Under international law contraband goods carried by a neutral vessel in time of war are subject to seizure if their "ultimate destination" is enemy territory. The doctrine was applied by the British against the U.S. in the Napoleonic Wars, by the U.S. against England in the Civil War and in World War I when the British expanded the rule to include overland shipments.

contract labor law. In 1864 Congress passed a law allowing businessmen to import immigrants at the cost of transportation and to keep them as employees until repayment of the passage money. Organized labor opposed this form of competition from immigrants, and in 1885 Congress prohibited the importation of contract labor. The law, however, was evaded by some businessmen.

Convention of 1800. By an agreement between the U.S. and France under Napoleon, the Treaty of 1778 was abrogated. In return the U.S. gave up claims on France for damages done to U.S. shipping during the war between France and England. Napoleon did not

161

want war with the U.S. at a time when he was struggling with England.

As an unexpected outcome, it put Napoleon in a frame of mind in which he was willing to sell the Louisiana Territory to a friendly U.S.

Convention of 1818. The agreement between the U.S. and Britain supplemented the provisions of the Treaty of Ghent (1814) which ended the War of 1812.

Americans were granted limited fishing rights in the Atlantic off Newfoundland and Labrador; the disputed northern boundary of the Louisiana Territory was fixed at the 49th parallel and ran from the Lake of the Woods in northern Minnesota to the Stony (Rocky) Mts. Beyond that point there was to be a joint occupation of the Oregon territory.

convoy system. During both World Wars I and II U.S. merchant ships and troop transports traveled in fleets protected from submarines by cruisers and destroyers. This naval strategy made possible valuable additions to the manpower and supplies of U.S. allies.

Conway Cabal. Major Gen. Thomas Conway was appointed general of the Continental army. His letter to Gen. Gates early in 1778 criticizing Washington's conduct of the war contributed to an attempt in Congress by New England representatives to gain control of the Revolution and the army.

Conway had not engaged in the plot, but his conduct led to a duel with Gen. Cadwalader and his resignation from the Army, Apr. 28, 1778. Conway wrote Washington an apology and returned to France.

Cooke, Jay (1821–1905). Banker. Born in Sandusky, O., he entered a banking firm in Philadelphia (1839). He headed Jay Cooke & Co., one of the country's best-known banking houses (1861–73). He marketed $2,500 million worth of government bonds for financing the Civil War at virtually no profit to himself and, after the war, financed construction of western railroads. Failure of the Northern Pacific RR brought about the collapse of his company and precipitated the Panic of 1873. Cooke later recouped his fortune through mining investments in Utah.

Coolidge, Calvin (1872–1933). Thirtieth President of the U.S. (1923–29). Born as John Calvin Coolidge in Plymouth, Vt., he was graduated from Amherst (1895). Vice-President of U.S. (1921–23), he succeeded to the Presidency on the death of Warren Harding. He was the Republican governor of Massachusetts (1919–20) and attracted national attention by his firm stand in the Boston police strike (1919). "Silent Cal" refused to run for a second full term in 1928.

Cooper, James Fenimore (1789–1851). Novelist. Born in Burlington, N.J., his novel *The Spy* (1821) became the best-selling American book up to that time. Best known for his *Leatherstocking Tales* of the American frontier, he created a picture of the wilderness which he later found did not exist. After travel in Europe (1826–33), Cooper became disillusioned with American life, and his attacks on American vulgarity and dishonesty cost him his popularity. He nevertheless remains an important American writer who brought the frontier to life in a highly imaginative way.

Cooper, Peter (1791–1883). Manufacturer and philanthropist. Born in New York City, he erected an iron works in Baltimore where he designed, for the Baltimore and Ohio R.R., *Tom Thumb*, the first steam locomotive built in America. He was the first U.S. iron manufacturer to use the Bessemer converter (1856). He promoted the laying of Cyrus Field's Atlantic cable. A lasting monument to his memory is Cooper Union (founded 1857–59) N.Y.C., a free educational institution "for the advancement of science and art."

cooperatives. The cooperative (or co-op, as it is commonly known) is a type of business enterprise usually organized as a corporation. The first cooperative business was established as a food store by a group of industrial workers in Rochdale, England, in 1844.

Cooperatives work according to principles which distinguish them from ordinary businesses. There is one vote per member no matter how much stock a member owns. Co-ops do not try to undersell their competitors, but co-op members receive a patronage dividend, sharing in the profits according to their purchases.

There are in general two types of cooperatives. Consumers' (purchasers') cooperatives usually take the form of retail selling organizations. They may deal in many different commodities, such as groceries, drugs and farm machinery. They may also operate service facilities, such as banks, laundries and restaurants. Consumers' co-ops are found in the U.S. both in the cities and in farm areas.

Producers' cooperatives are those which serve such producers as farmers and businessmen. In the U.S. their most important field of activity has been the wholesale marketing of agricultural produce. While most farm business is still done with private enterprise, cooperatives market a substantial part of the milk, butter, fruits, poultry, livestock, grains, tobacco and other crops produced in the U.S. Outside of farm areas, producers' cooperatives are not highly developed in the U.S.

As early as 1850, farmers joined together in clubs for the purpose of group buying. But the early plans for eliminating middlemen by buying in large quantities were not successful. The first successful nationally known farmers' cooperative was the Patrons of Husbandry (known as the Grange), founded in 1868. Other farm organizations which have promoted cooperatives include the American Farm Bureau Federation, the Farmers' Alliance and the Farmers' Union. In 1965 there were about 10,000 marketing and purchasing cooperatives in the U.S., serving nearly eight million farmers.

Most students of agriculture in the U.S. would agree that cooperatives have not coped successfully with such farm problems as overproduction and low prices for farm products combined with high prices for industrial goods. Such situations resulted in large-scale government programs in the 1930's.

Cooper Union speech (Feb. 27, 1860). In his address before the Cooper Institute in New York City, Lincoln cited the past actions of Congress excluding slavery from the territories and thus undermined Sen. Douglas' "popular sovereignty" position. While stating that Republicans opposed extension of slavery into the territories, Lincoln made it clear that the institution would be protected "not grudgingly, but fully and fairly" where its "actual presence among us makes that toleration and protection a necessity."

The speech helped establish Lincoln as a national statesman and moved him closer to his party's nomination for President.

Copland, Aaron (1900–   ). Composer. Born in Brooklyn, N.Y., his works include *Symphony for Organ and Orchestra* (1925). He wrote scores for the ballet, including *Billy the Kid* (1938) and *Appalachian Spring* (1944), which won the Pulitzer Prize in music. His film score for *The Heiress* won the Academy Award (1950). He wrote *Our New Music* in 1941.

Copley, John Singleton (1738–1815). Painter. He was born in Boston, Mass. An outstanding portraitist, his subjects included John Hancock, John Adams, Samuel Adams and other colonial figures. The Loyalist sympathies of his family caused him to leave Boston in 1774 and settle in London. Even before this he was elected a Fellow of the Society of Artists of Great Britain (1766). Subsequent portraits and paintings of historical subjects (*The Death of Lord Chatham*) assured his election to the Royal Academy (1783).

Copperheads. The Democratic party in the North during the Civil War included a faction of "Peace Democrats," called "Copperheads" or "Butternuts," who opposed Pres. Lincoln's war policies as tyrannical.

The most prominent Peace Democrat was the Ohio Congressman, Clement L. Vallandigham who was arrested in 1863 for defying a military order against "declaring sympathy for the enemy." He was saved from imprisonment by Lincoln who ordered his banishment to the Confederacy.

Copperhead influence was evident in the Democratic party platform of 1864 which condemned the war as a failure and called for restoration of the Union.

Copperhead activity continued in a secret society, the "Knights of the Golden Circle," also known as the "Order of American Knights" and "Sons of Liberty." Although Copperheads were opposed by "War Democrats," the Democratic party was discredited in the victorious North in post-Civil War years.

copyright. Congress is empowered by the Constitution "To Promote the Progress of Science and useful Arts, by securing for limited Times to Authors and Inventors the exclusive Right to their Respective Writings and Discoveries (Art. I, Sec. 8, Par. 8).

Copyright law in the U.S. is under a 1909 statute, as amended, which protects an author for 28 years with the privilege of renewing for another 28 years. The first purpose of copyright legislation is to foster learning and creative activities for the public benefit. Granting a temporary and limited monopoly to authors and other artists is a means to this end. Without such protection few writers and other creative workers could afford to use their talents, and few distribu-tors of such works would have the incentive to invest their resources.

In 1967 Congress was considering further revision of the copyright law including a change in the length of the copyright term to "life of the author plus 50 years after his death."

Coral Sea, battle of the (May 7–8, 1942). During World War II a naval battle between Japanese and U.S. forces was fought in the Coral Sea that separates Australia from the Solomon Islands. It was the first naval engagement in history in which surface ships did not exchange a shot. U.S. planes from the *Lexington* and *Yorktown* sank seven major enemy warships. American losses included the carrier *Lexington.* The Japanese fleet withdrew northward halting their advance toward Australia.

Cornell University. Founded at Ithaca, N.Y., in 1865 under the terms of the Morrill Land Grant Act, the university received substantial gifts of land and money from Ezra Cornell, financier. In addition to its privately supported units, the non-sectarian institution has administered, since the creation of the State University of New York in 1948, four publicly supported units—the College of Agriculture, College of Home Economics, the College of Veterinary Medicine and the School of Industrial and Labor Relations. Among the other divisions

165

of the university are the medical and nursing schools located in New York City.

Although it is a large university, Cornell is made up of a number of colleges. Each one, in general, is housed in its own group of buildings and operates with considerable autonomy.

Corregidor. On May 6, 1942, a Philippine island fort with its elaborate tunnel system surrendered to Japan after five months' resistance. The heroic fighting by U.S. and Filipino soldiers later inspired American forces in the Pacific during World War II.

Cotton, John (1584–1652). Puritan clergyman. Born in England, he came to the Massachusetts Bay colony in 1633. Known as "The Patriarch of New England," he headed Congregationalism in America. At first he supported Anne Hutchinson and then urged her excommunication; he also opposed Roger Williams. He staunchly upheld the power of the civil magistrate over the conscience of citizens and believed in strong government by the few. A prolific author, his catechism *Milk for Babes* (1646) was a standard text for New England children. In reply to Williams he wrote *The Bloudy Tenent Washed and Made White* (1647).

cotton gin. The machine for removing the seeds from cotton,

invented by Eli Whitney in 1793, revolutionized cotton production in the South. The laborious hand method had placed severe limitations on the amount of cotton that could be cleaned for manufacture into cloth. The gin used spikes on rollers, later replaced by saws, to separate the seed form the cotton.

A significant side effect of the invention was that it increased the demand for slaves in the South and more closely integrated slavery into its economy at a time when emancipation sentiment was growing.

Cotton Kingdom. Between 1830 and 1860 cotton was produced over an area that extended more than a thousand miles westward from South Carolina to central Texas. The region stretched northward about 200 miles from Texas, about the same distance from South Carolina and about 600 miles up the Mississippi Valley. Every aspect of southern life was dominated by what came to be called the "Cotton Kingdom," a land of plantations worked by Negro slaves. Southern exports of the "white gold" mounted and by 1860 represented two-thirds of the world's annual supply.

"cotton Whigs." The term was attached in derision to northern Whigs during the decade before the Civil War because they were willing to overlook the slavery issue in deference to southern Whigs.

coureurs de bois. The term is applied to 17th-century French Canadian "bushrangers" who entered the woods without permission of the government to seek adventure and to profit from the fur trade. The historian, Francis Parkman, branded them "outlaws of the bush."

Gov. Jean de Lauzon of New France had authorized Médart Chouart, Sieur de Groseilliers, to go west with the Indians. His return with a fine supply of pelts in 1656 encouraged other *coureurs* to plunge into the wilderness without French authority. Many of these were gone from French settlements for years and took on Indian ways (romanticized as the life of the "Noble Savage"). One of their leaders, Daniel Greysolon, Sieur Du Lhut, explored the Lake Superior region (Duluth, Minn., is named after him).

The inroads of *coureurs* into the government-controlled fur trade became so deep that the king ordered the execution of anyone going into the woods unlicensed. But evasion was widespread and the activities of these men contributed to the weakening of the French empire in the New World.

Courier 1-B. A U.S. Army satellite, launched Oct. 4, 1960, received, stored and transmitted messages sent to it from several points on earth, effectively proving the feasibility of a satellite communications system.

"court-packing bill." A hostile press gave the name to Pres. F. D. Roosevelt's Judiciary Reorganization Bill sent to Congress, Feb. 5, 1937. The President sought to change the complexion of the federal courts, chiefly the U.S. Supreme Court, which had invalidated a number of New Deal laws. Under the plan new justices were to be added when judges who reached the age of 70 failed to retire within six months. Up to six additional justices were to be added to the U.S. Supreme Court, bringing the total to 15.

The need for the bill disappeared when Justice Roberts began to vote more "liberally." The five to four balance on the Court, which had gone against New Deal laws in several cases, was reversed. In May 1937, conservative Justice Van Devanter announced his retirement and within five years Pres. Roosevelt had made eight new appointments. The bill was buried in the Senate Judiciary Committee.

cowboys. The need for herding cattle in Texas, in the 1820's, produced the American cowboy. It was the cowboys who undertook the hazardous cattle drives from Texas to railheads further north. The work was so tough and dangerous that the average life of a man, once he became an active cowboy, was seven years. Clothes worn by cowboys were adopted from the Mexican *vaqueros.* Leather chaps covering their legs protected them from thorns and goring cattle. High heels kept them from getting entangled in the stirrup. A neckerchief helped to cover the mouth to keep out dust. The lariat was used for catching horses and cattle.

Cowpunchers are cowboys who used poles to prod or punch cattle through chutes into stock cars headed for slaughterhouses. In the 1880's the term began to be applied to cowboys.

cowcatcher. After a few cows were killed by the new steam locomotives of the 1830's, Isaac Drips of the Camden and Amboy (N.J.) line (now part of the Pennsylvania system) invented a little truck bearing two iron bars thrust out like spears, but slanting down toward the track. This device was placed at the front end of the locomotive. When the bars impaled the cows, he substituted a crosswise bar. Eventually the V-shaped cowcatcher came into use to deal with a variety of obstructions on the track.

Cowpens, battle of (Jan. 17, 1781). In a stunning American victory at "the Cowpens," S.C., Gen. Daniel Morgan's militia routed British Col. Banastre Tarleton who lost 900 of his 1,000 men, killed, wounded and captured. The American loss was only 12 dead and 61 wounded.

British Gen. Cornwallis was dismayed by the defeat. It cost him the support of Loyalists in South Carolina who he had hoped would rally to the British cause.

Coxey's army. The Panic of 1893 caused great unemployment and industrial unrest which was dramatized by a march on Washington led by Jacob Coxey, an Ohio businessman. Coxey had called for a gigantic railroad building program to absorb the unemployed and proposed that it be financed by large issues of paper money. His "army" of about 500 reached the capitol building after a march from Ohio. Before he could address the large crowd that had gathered, he was arrested for walking on the grass.

Other "armies" of unemployed were formed on the West Coast and elsewhere in the nation, but they did not reach Washington. They were symbols of a mounting Populist protest.

"crackers." The term has been used contemptuously to describe poor whites in the rural areas of the southeastern U.S. Georgia "crackers" live in the pine barrens of the state. The term seems to have been derived from the cracking of the whip by farmers driving from the rural areas into the towns.

Crane, Stephen (1871–1900). Writer. Born in Newark, N.J., he is best remembered for the Civil War novel, *The Red Badge of Courage* (1895). Despite his early death from tuberculosis, Crane wrote several other novels, including *Maggie: A Girl of the Streets* (1892) and *Wounds in the Rain* (1900). A newspaperman, he covered the Spanish-American War. The freshness and intensity of his single great novel had considerable impact on American writing.

Crédit Mobilier. The name recalls a major financial scandal that left the indelible mark of corruption on the Grant administration. It was exposed in 1872 by the New York *Sun.*

The Crédit Mobilier acted as the construction company for the Union Pacific Railroad which was heavily financed by the government. It charged the railroad huge sums for services. A financial clique were the major stockholders in both corporations and $23,000,000 in profits soon found its way into their pockets.

Several congressmen were "sold" stocks in Crédit Mobilier by Oakes Ames, a member of the Pacific Railroad Committee in the House, in an effort to head off investigation of the company. Vice-President-elect Schuyler Colfax was implicated. A Senate investigating committee whitewashed the congressmen involved, but the scandal gave birth to the term "Grantism."

Creek. Mistreated by the Spanish in the 17th century, the powerful tribe of southern Indians allied themselves with the English during the colonial period. A Muskhogean-speaking people, they were farmers living in villages organized into a confederacy, but each village was autonomous when a decision to make war was required.

They fought against the U.S. in the War of 1812 and were defeated by Andrew Jackson at Horseshoe Bend, yielding much of their land in the Treaty of Fort Jackson (1814). Subsequently, they were forced out of Georgia and settled in the Indian Territory (Oklahoma) in the 1830's, where they were one of the Five Civilized Tribes. They gave up their tribal organization in 1906 and became U.S. citizens.

Creek War (1813–14). A year after the outbreak of the War of 1812, a war faction of the Creeks, known as "Red Sticks," took part in a general uprising in Alabama. The Creek Confederacy was in existence at the time, but some of the Creeks sided with the frontiersmen.

The massacre at Fort Mims, on the Alabama River about 35 miles above Mobile, caused Andrew Jackson, a major general of the Tennessee militia, to call out volunteers. Other frontier armies were organized in Georgia and Mississippi.

Jackson's victory at the Horseshoe Bend of the Tallapoosa River, in Alabama, broke Creek resistance. Under the Treaty of Fort Jackson (Aug. 9, 1814), two thirds of the Creek lands were ceded to the U.S. and the Indians agreed to withdraw from the southern and western part of Alabama.

Creole Affair (1841). A cargo of slaves aboard the American ship *Creole* overpowered the officers killing one white crew member. They took the ship into the British Bahamas. The actual murderers were held for their crime, but the British refused to release either ship or slaves despite protests by the owners and southerners generally.

In 1855 the Anglo-American mixed claims commission awarded $110,330 to the U.S. for slave property lost.

"Crime of 1873." The Coinage Act of 1873 ended the minting of silver dollars which had long been out of circulation. This demonetization did not bother western silver interests at the time because silver was commanding a high price in the open market where it was being purchased for commercial purposes. When, however, new discoveries lowered the price of silver, mineowners wanted to sell it once again to the U.S. Mint for coinage into silver dollars. They were joined by cheap money advocates in charging that the demonetization of silver was the "Crime of 1873."

For more than two decades after 1873 free silver was a campaign issue and many voters believed erroneously that a "crime" had been committed.

Cripple Creek (Colo.) strikes. A mining boom began in 1891 and the town of Cripple Creek was founded in central Colorado in the heart of the gold-producing district. The first strikes took place in 1893 and 1894 and the workers were successful in preventing the lengthening of the working day. In the bitter strikes of 1903–04 the Western Federation of Miners failed to win recognition. Union organizers were driven from the smelting plants of the mining districts by the state militia.

Crisis, The American. Some dozen essays, published by Thomas Paine, appeared between 1776 and 1783. In the first, he opened with: "These are the times that try men's souls. The summer soldier and the sunshine patriot will, in this crisis, shrink from the service of their country. . . ."

In the *Crisis* essays Paine commented on treatment of the Tories, western lands, federal taxes and other current issues. In his final tract, he extolled the United States as "an aggregate that serves for all."

Critical Period, the (1783–89). The historian John Fiske originated the expression in 1888 to describe the years during which the young U.S. was governed under the Articles of Confederation. Serious economic problems and other difficulties faced the new nation. Many farmers could not pay their debts and unrest took the form of Shays' Rebellion in Massachusetts (1786).

Some historians refuse to regard the period as "critical." Toward the end of the period economic conditions improved as trade with other countries revived. Many of the interstate tariff laws were not strictly enforced and business among the states increased. There was, nevertheless, a decided feeling, particularly among men of property, that a strong central government was essential if the new nation was to earn respect abroad and assure a sound economic life.

Crittenden Plan. Amendments to the Constitution were proposed by Sen. John J. Crittenden (Ky.), Dec. 18, 1860, in an effort to head off secession of the southern states. These included federal protection of slavery below the line 36° 30'; a stipulation that future states were to come in slave or free, as they wished; the assurance that no further amendment was ever to be made to the Constitution that would authorize Congress to touch slavery in any of the states.

The Plan was taken under advisement by the Senate "Committee of Thirteen." Pres. Lincoln made known his opposition to any plan that would permit extension of slavery into the territories. Since southerners would not back the Plan unless Republicans were committed to it, it was not adopted.

Croly, Herbert David (1869–1930). Journalist and political philosopher. Born in New York City, he studied at Harvard but did not obtain his B.A. until 1910. Author of *The Promise of American Life* (1909), a progressive manifesto, he influenced Theodore Roosevelt's New Nationalism. He supported Pres. Wilson in World War I but broke with him over the Treaty of Versailles. He was founder (1914) and editor of the *New Republic*.

Crompton's loom. Patented in 1837 by William Crompton, an English weaver who engaged in wool manufacture in Lowell, Mass., the power loom was used to manufacture figured woolens in the 1840's and virtually ended hand weaving in New England.

Crossbow, Operation. The term was the World War II military code name for the Allied air onslaught on German V-bomb rocket sites.

"cross of gold" speech (July 8, 1896). At the Democratic national convention, William Jennings Bryan of Nebraska delivered the speech that won him his party's nomination for President. Bryan stood for free silver as opposed to Pres. Cleveland's support of the gold standard. He closed with the imagery he had perfected in his speeches in the West: "You shall not press down upon the brow of labor this crown of thorns, you shall not crucify mankind upon a cross of gold."

Croswell libel case (1802–05). A New York publisher, Harry Croswell, was convicted of criminal libel for an attack on Pres. Jefferson which appeared in the Hudson (N.Y.) *Wasp.* Alexander Hamilton took an appeal to the N.Y. Supreme Court in which he argued that truth published "with good motives and justifiable ends" was not a libel. A divided court denied the appeal. However, Hamilton's reasoning was later incorporated in the new libel law contained in the New York constitution of 1821. Other states adopted the New York libel law.

Crow (Absaroke). Inhabiting the Yellowstone area of Wyoming, the Siouan-speaking tribe warred with Sioux and Blackfeet, but were friendly with the whites; members of the tribe acted as scouts for the U.S. Army in wars against unfriendly Indians. They lived in lodges and possessed large herds of horses and cattle.

Cuba, intervention in. At the end of the Spanish-American War (1898), U.S. troops remained in Cuba under Gen. Leonard Wood. Cuban finances were placed on a stable basis. Havana was rebuilt and improvements were made in sanitation and schools. U.S. forces withdrew in 1902 after Cuba agreed to add the Platt Amend-ment to its constitution guaranteeing the U.S. special rights in Cuba. With this limitation Cuba became an independent nation.

Revolutionary disturbances in Cuba in 1906 caused Pres. Theodore Roosevelt to intervene. "Necessity," as one New York journal remarked "is the mother of in(ter)vention." U.S. forces remained in Cuba until 1909 when orderly government was reestablished.

American Marines were again landed in Cuba in 1917 following a revolt against the Cuban administration. They remained during World War I to protect foreign interests and Cuban sugar production.

Although there were grave disorders in Cuba in the early 1930's arising from the depression and repression by dictator Gerardo Machado, the U.S. did not intervene. Warships were, however, sent to Cuban waters. Pres. F. D. Roosevelt gave weight to the "Good Neighbor" policy by concluding a treaty with Cuba, May 29, 1934, releasing the island from the restraints of the Platt Amendment.

In 1959 Fidel Castro ousted dictator Fulgencio Batista. By welcoming Communist influence and infiltration into Cuba, Castro came close to bringing about direct U.S. intervention. In 1961 the U.S. severed diplomatic relations with Cuba.

Cuban passport decision. In *Zemel v. Rusk* (1965) the U.S. Supreme Court upheld the right of Sec. of State Dean Rusk to designate areas in which citizens might not travel unless given special permission by the State Department.

Louis Zemel, a ski resort owner from Middlefield, Conn., had been denied permission to visit Cuba as a tourist. The Court in 1958 and 1964 had ruled that persons could not be denied a passport because of their political beliefs or associations. Chief Justice Warren in ruling against Zemel declared that the area restriction is different from the earlier cases because it was based on "foreign policy considerations affecting all citizens" and was not used to penalize individuals for their beliefs. In the case of Cuba, Warren declared, the restrictions are justified because the Communist government there seeks to export revolution through travelers.

Culpeper's Rebellion (1677–79). John Culpeper led a popular uprising against the enforcement of the British trade laws by the proprietary government of North Carolina. Culpeper, who was made governor of the colony by the rebels, was later removed by the proprietors.

Cumberland Gap. The natural pass in the Appalachian Mts. provided a route between Virginia and Kentucky during the 18th and 19th centuries. The historian Frederick Jackson Turner, expounding his frontier theory, wrote in the 1890's: "Stand at Cumberland Gap and watch the procession of civilization marching single file—the buffalo following the trail to the salt springs, the Indian, the fur-trader and hunter, the cattle-raiser, the pioneer-farmer—and the frontier has passed by."

Today a national highway runs through the Gap.

Cumberland Road. The Road, also called the National Road, the first to be built with federal funds, was authorized by Congress in 1806, but construction did not begin until 1811. By 1818 it extended from Cumberland, Md., to Wheeling, West Va., on the Ohio River. Twenty years later it had been extended across Illinois to within 100 miles of St. Louis on the Mississippi. It was the highway most heavily traveled by easterners and immigrants heading for the Old Northwest.

Currency Act (1764). Heeding the British merchants who protested the payment of debts in anything but sterling money "of certain and fixed value," Parliament prohibited the issuance of paper currency in any of the colonies.

A previous Currency Act (1751) had prohibited issuance of paper money in New England. In 1764 this was extended to all of the colonies. The Currency Act made it necessary for the colonial legislatures to raise taxes in order to redeem the bills of credit that had been used to pay debts during the French and Indian War.

Franklin, in 1766, informed British officials that the restraint on paper money was one of the principal causes of colonial unrest.

Currier and Ives. The firm of "Publishers of Cheap and Popular Pictures" was founded by Nathaniel Currier in 1834. He took his bookkeeper, James Merritt Ives, into partnership with him. The inexpensive lithographs were no longer in demand when photographs became available in the 1890's, but they have since become popular with antique hunters.

Cushing, Harvey William (1869–1939). Surgeon. Born in Cleveland, O., he was granted an M.D. by Harvard (1895), where he was professor of surgery (1912–32) and during the same period surgeon-in-chief of the Peter Bent Brigham Hospital in Boston. His successes with brain tumor operations were not equaled by any neurological surgeon of his time. He contributed a classic paper (1918) on wartime injuries to the brain, based on his service with U.S. medical units in World War I. He wrote the Pulitzer Prize-winning biography *The Life of Sir William Osler* (1925).

Cushman, Charlotte Saunders (1816–76). Actress. She was born in Boston, Mass. During her early career in New York and Philadelphia (1837–44) she displayed a strong but untrained talent. Seasoned by experiences on the London stage, she was acclaimed in U.S. as an outstanding Shakespearean actress. Deep-voiced, almost masculine in some respects, she played both male and female roles.

Custer's "last stand." Indian wars of the 1870's reached a climax after the discovery of gold in the Black Hills in 1874. Their opposition to the encroachment by miners led to the Black Hills War. Lt. Col. Custer was detailed to end the resistance of the Sioux and other Indians when he and some 260 cavalrymen were surrounded by forces under Crazy Horse and Sitting Bull. Custer and his men were wiped out to the last man in the battle of the Little Big Horn (June 25–26, 1876) in what is now southern Montana.

Customs, Bureau of. The Bureau was created by Congress in 1927 and operates under the Secretary of the Treasury. It is concerned with the entry of merchandise into the U.S. and export therefrom. Its principal functions include the collection of duties on imports and the prevention of smuggling and frauds on the customs revenue.

Customs and Patent Appeals, U.S. Court of. A federal court was established in 1909 to decide certain questions arising under the customs laws. In 1929 it was given jurisdiction to review certain patent and trademark cases. It reviews decisions of the customs court on the classification of and duties upon imported merchandise and decisions of the Patent Office on applications and interferences as to patents and trademarks. It also considers legal questions based on the findings of the Tariff Commission as to unfair practices in import trade. The court consists of a chief judge and four associate judges. The court sits *en banc* with all judges present.

D

Daily Advertiser. Established in 1785 in New York City, it was the first daily newspaper in America to start publication without previously appearing as a weekly, or at longer intervals. It was founded by Francis Childs.

"Damn the torpedoes! Go ahead!" During the Civil War, Union Adm. Farragut steamed into the harbor of Mobile (Ala.), Aug. 5, 1864, with four ironclads and 13 wooden vessels. Union monitor *Tecumseh* hit a mine (then called "torpedo") and sank. The column of ships was stopped, but Farragut is said to have reacted with his famous order. The fleet then went in to overwhelm the Confederate squadron and silence the forts.

Dana, Richard Henry (1815–82). Author. Born in Cambridge, Mass., he was graduated from Harvard in 1837 after interrupting his student days to sail around Cape Horn as a common seaman. His novel, *Two Years Before the Mast* (1840), records vividly a sailor's life in the days of the sailing ship.

His book helped to end cruel treatment of sailors, such as the practice of flogging. Dana's manual, *The Seaman's Friend* (1841), became a standard work on maritime law.

Danbury Hatters' Case (*Loewe v. Lawlor*, 1908). The U.S. Supreme Court ruled that a secondary boycott acted to restrain trade and was a violation of the Sherman Antitrust Act. The case was brought to the Court by D. E. Loewe & Co., Danbury, Conn., who was suing the United Hatters of North America for calling a nationwide boycott of the firm's hats in support of a strike by a local union to win recognition. The company charged the United Hatters with conspiring against it and claimed triple damages from the individual members of the local union who had gone on strike. The U.S. Supreme Court upheld the company's view.

The case aroused the resentment of labor because it brought secondary boycotts under the ban of the Sherman Antitrust Act and subjected individual members to damage suits. The fines were eventually paid through contributions from the national union and the American Federation of Labor.

Dark Day (May 19, 1780). The day became so dark in New England that by noon many religious people thought the world was coming to an end and fell to their knees praying for forgiveness. Explanations for the phenomenon vary, but it was suggested at the time that the cause was smoke from frontier fires.

"dark horse." The term has been used in American politics to describe major party presidential candidates who were not expected to receive the nomination. James K. Polk, successful Democratic candidate for President in the election of 1844, was the first "dark horse." Three other "dark horse" winners were Franklin Pierce in 1852, James Garfield in 1880 and Warren Harding in 1920. "Dark horses" who were not elected President were Horatio Seymour in 1868, William Bryan in 1896 and John Davis in 1924.

Darrow, Clarence Seward (1857–1938). Lawyer. Born in Kinsman, Ohio, he practiced in Chicago, Ill., and gained a national reputation by virtue of his brilliant defense work. Among the widely publicized cases in which he was the attorney for the defense were those of Eugene V. Debs (1895), William D. Haywood (1906–07), the McNamara brothers (1911), the Loeb-Leopold murder case (1924), the Scopes trial in Tennessee (1925), the Massie trial in Honolulu, Haw. (1932), the Negroes in the Scottsboro case (1932). His jury appeals, especially in criminal cases, developed the idea that men are victims of social circumstances beyond their control.

Dartmouth College. A privately controlled, non-sectarian institution at Hanover, N.H., it is one of the historic colleges which antedate the Revolution. Chartered in 1769 by King George III, it started as an outgrowth of a school founded at Lebanon (now Columbia), Conn., for the Christian education of Indian youth.

The college has held fast to its main mission: instruction of high quality in the liberal arts and sciences.

Dartmouth College Case (*Dartmouth College v. Woodward*, 1819). The U.S. Supreme Court ruled that the New Hampshire legislature had violated its contract with Dartmouth College. This was contrary to the provision of the Constitution which forbade the states to pass laws impairing the obligation of contracts (although the Founding Fathers had in mind the ordinary contracts between man and man). Chief Justice Marshall delivered the opinion.

Dartmouth College had been granted a charter in 1769 by George III which was later acknowledged by the legislature. In 1816 the legislature passed a law entirely reorganizing the government of the college. The trustees of the college brought an action raising the general question of the constitutionality of the statute.

An effect of the decision that a corporate charter is a contract which may not be impaired by legislative enactment was to give those who invested money in corporate enterprises assurance that the corporations would be free from legislative interference. The decision encouraged the expansion of private enterprise in the fields of railroad construction, insurance, commerce and industry.

Daughters of the American Revolution (DAR). When the Sons of the American Revolution was founded in 1889, it voted to exclude women. The aroused Daughters were organized at Washington, D.C., in 1890. They have been accused of attempting to establish an aristocracy based on ancestry, but of the four founding Daughters, two were government clerks.

Members must be "personally acceptable to the Society" from among descendants of patriots who were active in military or government service.

Daughters of the Confederacy, United (UDC). The organization is comprised of the descendants of those "who gave personal service or loyal aid to the Southern cause" during the War Between the States. Founded in Nashville, Tenn.

(1894), it has remained active in social and educational causes long after the United Confederate Veterans, which excluded women, was "lost beyond recovery."

Davis, Jefferson (1808–89). President of the Confederate States of America. Born in Christian (now Todd) Co., Ky., he was raised in Mississippi. A graduate of West Point (1828), Davis served on the frontier and fought in the Mexican War. He represented Mississippi in the U.S. House of Representatives (1845–46) and the U.S. Senate (1847–51, 1857–61) and served as U.S. Sec. of War in Pres. Pierce's cabinet (1853–57). A slave owner, he resigned from the Senate when Mississippi seceded from the Union. As President of the Confederacy from 1861, he was determined to achieve independence despite severe military reverses. Opposition to him within the Confederacy was based, in part, on his loyalty to the South as a whole rather than to the principle of state sovereignty. Though unable to win European support, he sought to keep an army in the field to the very end. Davis was imprisoned (1865–67) but was never brought to trial for treason. His personal account of the war years is contained in *The Rise and Fall of the Confederate Government* (1881).

Davisson, Clinton Joseph (1881–1958). Physicist. Born in Bloomington, Ill., he was granted a Ph.D. by Princeton Univ. (1911). Known for researches in electricity, magnetism and radiant energy, he discovered that the wavelength of electrons depends on their velocity. In 1937 he shared the Nobel Prize for Physics with George Paget Thomson.

Dawes Plan. Devised in 1924 by a commission headed by Gen. Charles G. Dawes, the Plan provided for World War I reparations payments more nearly commensurate with Germany's ability to pay.

Germany's payments to the Allied Powers had been fixed at $33 billion. Under the Dawes Plan, in effect until 1930, annual payments were greatly reduced, but the full amount due was left undetermined.

Dawes Severalty Act (1887). The Act (named for Sen. Henry L. Dawes, Mass.) provided for the breaking up of Indian tribal autonomy even on the reservations. Heads of Indian families were granted 160 acres of land (twice as much if it was fit only for grazing) and comparable allotments were made to unmarried Indians. After 25 years the Indians were to be granted U.S. citizenship and might sell the land. All Indians were granted citizenship in 1924.

The Act did not apply to the Five Civilized Nations living in Oklahoma. They were persuaded by the Dawes Commission (1893–1905) to give up their tribal governments and live under state and federal laws. Provision was made for division of the land on an equitable basis.

daylight-saving time (DST). The idea to adjust clocks to save the daylight hours in summer goes back to the 18th century. Congress adopted DST for the nation during World War I (1918), but it was repealed in 1919, partly because of farmers' opposition. The decision was then left to local authorities. Under DST clocks are moved forward one hour at 2 A.M. on the last Sunday in April and are turned back at 2 A.M. on the last Sunday in October.

Increased congressional awareness of the nation's shift from a largely rural to a predominantly urban society caused Congress in 1966 to require uniform time, either standard or daylight saving, within each state. Cities and localities no longer enjoy local option under the uniform time law of 1966. The effect of the law is to end much of the confusion encountered by large metropolitan business concerns dealing with states in which time patterns varied widely from city to city. It also saves railroads, bus companies and airlines several million dollars a year on timetable revisions.

D-Day (June 6, 1944). On this day in World War II the long-awaited invasion of France commenced when British and

American forces under Gen. Eisenhower crossed the English Channel onto the beaches of Normandy. The landings in northern France were made possible by Allied air supremacy. Previous to the landings German military strength had been sapped by heavy air attacks on German industrial centers and on the Nazis' "Atlantic Wall."

Deacons. A Negro civil rights group organized in Jonesboro, La., in 1964, the Deacons for Defense and Justice are an armed, semi-secret, loosely organized federation. Some of the members who were religiously inclined produced the name "Deacons," the specially chosen protectors of the faith. They organized to resist the Ku Klux Klan and other anti-Negro elements in the South when they realized that they could not count on local police protection.

Death of a Salesman (1949). A social drama by Arthur Miller, one of the foremost playwrights of the post-World War II period, it traces the disintegration of Willie Loman. A salesman who lives in a dream world where his own capabilities and expectations for his sons are concerned, he crumbles under the final humiliation—dismissal by the son of his boss, after the young man has taken over the hosiery business. His wife, the one stable figure in the family, is unable to stave off the final disaster. The play was awarded a Pulitzer Prize (1949).

Debs, Eugene Victor (1855–1926). Socialist leader. Born in Terre Haute, Ind., he became active in the labor movement. As president of the American Railway Union, he led the Pullman Strike (1894). Debs was an organizer of the Social Democratic party of America (1897), and was the Socialist candidate for President of the U.S. (1900, 1904, 1908, 1912, 1920). A defender of those charged with sedition in World War I, he was himself imprisoned (1919–21). His dedication commanded respect.

Debs, In re (1895). The case arose out of the Pullman railway strike which had caused Pres. Cleveland to dispatch troops to Chicago in 1894. Attorney General Olney had obtained an injunction restraining Eugene V. Debs, president of the American Railway Union, and others, from interference with the mails and with interstate commerce. When the injunction was violated the federal court in Chicago found Debs and others in contempt and sentenced them to jail for from three to six months.

The U.S. Supreme Court validated the injunction holding that the government had the right to protect its property in mails and on the broader ground that the "general welfare" of the public at large was involved.

debtor laws. Under English common law a man who did not pay his debts could be sent to prison. This was also the law in the American colonies. However, imprisonment for debt was abolished in England by the Debtor's Act (1869).

In the early 19th century in the U.S. state bankruptcy laws were passed which enabled an unsuccessful businessman to settle his debts with his creditors as best he could, without being sent to debtors' prison. By the beginning of the 1840's, most of the states had ceased imprisoning debtors.

Decatur, Stephen (1779–1820). Naval officer. Born in Sinepuxent, Md., he is one of the best-remembered figures in American naval history. In the Tripolitan War, he captured and burned the frigate *Philadelphia*, held by the Tripolitans (1804). In the War of 1812 Decatur commanded the *United States* in a victory over the British ship *Macedonian* (1812). In 1815 he headed a squadron which forced a peace on the Barbary pirates, ending their demands for tribute. His toast, on returning to the U.S. (1816), "Our Country . . . right or wrong," continues to strike a resounding chord in the nation. He was killed in a duel with another naval officer, Capt. James Barron.

Declaration and Resolves (Oct. 14, 1774). The First Continental Congress drew up a list of grievances and a call to George III for their redress. Revenue measures imposed since 1763 were criticized and

the Coercive Acts against Massachusetts were denounced. A boycott of British imports was promised until the punitive measures and other taxes levied without the consent of the colonists were repealed. On a conciliatory note the Declaration expressed "an ardent desire that harmony and mutual intercourse of affection and interest may be restored."

Declaration of Independence (July 4, 1776). The document was drafted by Thomas Jefferson at the request of the Continental Congress and strengthened by several changes made by Benjamin Franklin. It was altered somewhat by the Congress, and adopted July 4. Two days earlier Richard Henry Lee's first resolution dissolving connections between the colonies and Britain had been approved.

The Declaration falls into three parts. The preamble sets forth a philosophy of human rights which has affected the world's political views ever since. Jefferson summarized the thinking of 18th-century intellectuals when he declared: "We hold these Truths to be self-evident, that all Men are created equal, that they are endowed by their Creator with certain unalienable Rights, that among these are Life, Liberty, and the Pursuit of Happiness. . . ."

The second part of the Declaration enumerates 27 grievances which precipitated the break with Britain. These included stationing standing armies among the colonists in time of peace, dissolving colonial legislatures, cutting off colonial trade with large parts of the world and waging war against the colonies.

The conclusion of the Declaration announced a complete break with Britain. It was a formal declaration of war, signed boldly by John Hancock, President, on behalf of the Congress.

From Aug. 2 on, the remaining 55 signatures were added to a formal copy of the document. The signers pledged their lives, fortunes and honor in support of the Declaration of Independence.

DECLARATION OF INDEPENDENCE (Text)
(July 4, 1776)

The Unanimous Declaration of the Thirteen United States of America

Reasons for the Declaration.[1] When, in the course of human events, it becomes necessary for one people to dissolve the political bands which have connected them with another, and to assume, among the powers of the earth, the separate and equal station to which the laws of nature and of nature's God entitle them, a decent respect to the opinions of mankind requires that they should declare the causes which impel them to the separation.

Fundamental Rights of the People. We hold these truths to be self-evident: That all men are created equal; that they are endowed by their Creator with certain unalienable rights; that among these are life, liberty, and the pursuit of happiness. That, to secure these rights, governments are instituted among men, deriving their just powers from the consent of the governed; that, whenever any form of government becomes destructive of these ends, it is the right of the people to alter or to abolish it, and to institute a new government, laying its foundation on such principles, and organizing its powers in such form, as to them shall seem most likely to effect their safety and happiness. Prudence, indeed, will dictate that governments long established should not be changed for light and transient causes; and accordingly all experience hath shown that mankind are more disposed to suffer while evils are sufferable, than to right themselves by abolishing the forms to which they are accustomed. But when a long train of abuses and usurpations, pursuing invariably the same object, evinces a design to reduce them under absolute despotism, it is their right, it is their duty, to throw off such government, and to provide new guards for their future security. Such has been the patient sufferance of these colonies; and such is now the necessity which constrains them to alter their former systems of government. The history of the pres-

---

[1] The boldface headings and current usage in spelling are added for help in reading.

182

ent King of Great Britain is a history of repeated injuries and usurpations, all having in direct object the establishment of an absolute tyranny over these states. To prove this, let facts be submitted to a candid world.

Grievances Against the King. He has refused his assent to laws the most wholesome and necessary for the public good.

He has forbidden his governors to pass laws of immediate and pressing importance, unless suspended in their operation till his assent should be obtained; and, when so suspended, he has utterly neglected to attend to them.

He has refused to pass other laws for the accommodation of large districts of people, unless those people would relinquish the right of representation in the legislature—a right inestimable to them and formidable to tyrants only.

He has called together legislative bodies at places unusual, uncomfortable, and distant from the depository of their public records for the sole purpose of fatiguing them into compliance with his measures.

He has dissolved representative houses repeatedly, for opposing with manly firmness his invasions on the rights of the people.

He has refused for a long time, after such dissolutions, to cause others to be elected; whereby the legislative powers, incapable of annihilation, have returned to the people at large for their exercise; the State remaining in the meantime exposed to all the dangers of invasion from without, and convulsions within.

He has endeavored to prevent the population of these States; for that purpose obstructing the laws for naturalization of foreigners; refusing to pass others to encourage their migration hither, and raising the conditions of new appropriations of lands.

He has obstructed the administration of justice, by refusing his assent to laws for establishing judiciary powers.

He has made judges dependent on his will alone, for the tenure of their offices, and the amount and payment of their salaries.

He has erected a multitude of new offices, and sent hither swarms of officers to harass our people, and eat out their substance.

He has kept among us, in times of peace, standing armies without the consent of our legislature.

He has affected to render the military independent of and superior to the civil power.

He has combined with others to subject us to a jurisdiction foreign to our constitution, and unacknowledged by our laws; giving his assent to their acts of pretended legislation:

For quartering large bodies of armed troops among us;

For protecting them, by a mock trial, from punishment for any murders which they should commit on the inhabitants of these States;

For cutting off our trade with all parts of the world;

For imposing taxes on us without our consent;

For depriving us in many cases of the benefits of trial by jury;

For transporting us beyond seas to be tried for pretended offences;

For abolishing the free system of English laws in a neighboring province, establishing therein an arbitrary government, and enlarging its boundaries so as to render it at once an example and fit instrument for introducing the same absolute rule into these colonies;

For taking away our charters, abolishing our most valuable laws, and altering fundamentally the forms of our government;

For suspending our own legislatures, and declaring themselves invested with power to legislate for us in all cases whatsoever.

He has abdicated government here, by declaring us out of his protection and waging war against us.

He has plundered our seas, ravaged our coasts, burned our towns, and destroyed the lives of our people.

He is at this time transporting large armies of foreign mercenaries to complete the works of death, desolation, and tyranny already begun with circumstances of cruelty and perfidy scarcely paralleled in the most barbarous ages, and totally unworthy the head of a civilized nation.

He has constrained our fellow-citizens, taken captive on the high seas, to bear arms against their country, to become the executioners of their friends and brethren, or to fall themselves by their hands.

He has excited domestic insurrection among us, and has endeavored to bring on the inhabitants of our frontiers the merciless Indian savages, whose known rule of warfare is an undistinguished destruction of all ages, sexes, and conditions.

Colonial Efforts to Avoid Separation. In every stage of these oppressions we have petitioned for redress in the most humble terms; our repeated petitions have been answered only by repeated injury. A prince whose character is thus marked by every act which may define a tyrant is unfit to be the ruler of a free people.

Nor have we been wanting in our attention to our British brethren. We have warned them, from time to time, of attempts by their legislature to extend an unwarrantable jurisdiction over us. We have reminded them of the circumstances of our emigration and settlement here. We have appealed to their native justice and magnanimity; and we have conjured them, by the ties of our common kindred, to disavow these usurpations, which would inevitably interrupt our connections and correspondence. They, too, have been deaf to the voice of justice and consanguinity. We must, therefore, acquiesce in the necessity which denounces our separation, and hold them, as we hold the rest of mankind, enemies in war, in peace friends.

Independence of the Colonies. We, therefore, the representatives of the United States of America, in General Congress assembled, appealing to the Supreme Judge of the world for the rectitude of our intentions, do, in the name and by authority of the good people of these colonies, solemnly publish and declare, That these united colonies are, and of right ought to be, free and independent states; that they are absolved from all allegiance to the British crown, and that all political connection between them and the state of Great Britain is, and ought to be, totally dissolved; and that, as free and independent states, they have full power to levy war, conclude peace, contract alliances, establish commerce, and do all other acts and things which independent states may of right do. And, for the support of this declaration, with a firm reliance on the protection of Divine Providence, we mutually pledge to each other our lives, our fortunes, and our sacred honor.

[The foregoing Declaration was by order of Congress, engrossed, and signed by the following members:]

JOHN HANCOCK.[2]

New Hampshire[3]—JOSIAH BARTLETT, WM. WHIPPLE, MATTHEW THORNTON.

Massachusetts Bay—SAML. ADAMS, JOHN ADAMS, ROBT. TREAT PAINE, ELBRIDGE GERRY.

Rhode Island—STEP. HOPKINS, WILLIAM ELLERY.

Connecticut—ROGER SHERMAN, SAM'EL HUNTINGTON, WM. WILLIAMS, OLIVER WOLCOTT.

New York—WM. FLOYD, PHIL. LIVINGSTON, FRANS. LEWIS, LEWIS MORRIS.

New Jersey—RICHD. STOCKTON, JNO. WITHERSPOON, FRAS. HOPKINSON, JOHN HART, ABRA. CLARK.

Pennsylvania—ROBT. MORRIS, BENJAMIN RUSH, BENJA. FRANKLIN, JOHN MORTON, GEO. CLYMER, JAS. SMITH, GEO. TAYLOR, JAMES WILSON, GEO. ROSS.

Delaware—CAESAR RODNEY, GEO. READ, THO. M'KEAN.

Maryland—SAMUEL CHASE, WM. PACA, THOS. STONE, CHARLES CARROLL of Carrollton.

Virginia—GEORGE WYTHE, RICHARD HENRY LEE, TH. JEFFERSON, BENJA. HARRISON, THOS. NELSON, JR., FRANCIS LIGHTFOOT LEE, CARTER BRAXTON.

North Carolina—WM. HOOPER, JOSEPH HEWES, JOHN PENN.

South Carolina—EDWARD RUTLEDGE, THOS. HEYWARD, Junr., THOMAS LYNCH, Junr., ARTHUR MIDDLETON.

Georgia—BUTTON GWINNETT, LYMAN HALL, GEO. WALTON.

---

[2] John Hancock signed first as President of the Second Continental Congress.
[3] The names of the states, given here for convenience, do not appear in the original document.

Declaration of Rights and Grievances (Oct. 19, 1765). Issued by the Stamp Act Congress, the resolutions were chiefly the work of John Dickinson, a Pennsylvania delegate to the Congress. While recognizing allegiance of the colonists to the Crown, the resolutions condemned the Stamp Act and claimed for the colonists all the rights of Englishmen, including freedom from taxation except "with their own consent, given personally or by their representatives." The Declaration went on to state that since it was not practical for colonists to be represented in Parliament, they could be taxed only by their own legislatures. Also condemned were recent trade regulations and the increased powers of the admiralty courts.

Declaratory Act (1766). Although economic pressures and colonial resistance forced Parliament to repeal the Stamp Act, it passed the Declaratory Act to emphasize its right to legislate for the colonies in all cases whatsoever. The Act sought to clarify the constitutional relationship between the colonies and the mother country by establishing the supremacy of Parliament. This was regarded by many colonists as a threat to self-government.

Decoration Day (May 30). Also known as Memorial Day, the holiday had its origin in the South. In the spring, before the close of the Civil War, women decorated the graves of their dead soldiers with flowers.

On May 5, 1868, Gen. John A. Logan, commander-in-chief of the Grand Army of the Republic, issued an order fixing May 30 of that year for strewing flowers on the graves of dead soldiers. Most states have since made it a legal holiday for honoring the dead of all wars.

Defense, Department of. Established by the National Security Act of 1947 as an executive department of the federal government, it is headed by the Sec. of Defense, who is a member of the President's Cabinet. The purpose of the new department, which replaced the Navy and Army departments, is to achieve unity in the policies of the Army, Navy (including the U.S. Marine Corps) and Air Force. Each of these military departments has its own secretary, but the three are under the jurisdiction of the Secretary of Defense.

De Forest, Lee (1873–1961). Radio engineer and inventor. Born in Council Bluffs, Ia., he was granted a Ph.D. by Yale (1899). Sometimes called "the father of radio broadcasting," he pioneered in wireless telegraphy and radio telephony. He established a radio station (1916), and he designed the first high power radio stations for the U.S. Navy. He invented the glow-lamp recording of sound on film for motion pictures and contributed to the development of television and high-speed facsimile transmission.

deism. Many educated men, including Thomas Jefferson and Thomas Paine, in late 18th-century America, called themselves deists. They believed in a supreme being who had planned and set in motion a harmonious and self-regulating universe, but rejected the divinity of Christ and the Biblical account of creation as superstitions. Deists preferred scientific findings to revelation, rejected sectarianism and believed that the moral truths of Christianity could be defended on rational grounds. They were not atheists, although they were so labeled by their critics.

Delaware. The "First State," one of the Middle Atlantic group, is named after an English colonial governor, Lord De la Warr, who is said to have anchored in the bay in 1610. Settlement by the Dutch followed in 1631. Swedes landed in 1637 and named the land "New Sweden." When Peter Stuyvesant became governor of New Netherland, he asserted the claim of the Dutch to the territory. The Dutch held on until 1664 when the English captured New Netherland and took over Dutch holdings in the New World.

In 1682 Delaware was granted by the English to William Penn. He wanted it to strengthen his hold on Pennsylvania, and ruled it until 1776 when it became one of the original 13 states. Delaware was the first state to ratify the Constitution (Dec. 7, 1787).

Delaware remained in the Union during the Civil War, although many of its people served in the Confederate army. The state did not ratify the 13th, 14th and 15th Amendments until 1901.

The capital city is Dover. Wilmington, its major city, is a world chemical center and the headquarters of the E. I. du Pont de Nemours & Co. Both industry and agriculture are diversified.

Delaware Indians. Named by the whites because they were found in the Delaware River Valley of New Jersey, New York, Delaware and Pennsylvania, the Algonquian-speaking tribesmen called themselves Leni-Lenape. During the 17th century they traded peacefully with the Dutch and concluded the friendly Treaty of Shackamaxon (1682) with William Penn by which they gave up some of their land.

Part of the tribe moved to the Ohio Valley and sided with the French against the English in the 18th century. In 1794 they and other tribes were defeated by Wayne. In the Treaty of Greenville (1795), they ceded their lands in Pennsylvania and Ohio to the whites. The tribe crossed the Mississippi and eventually joined with the Cherokees in the Indian Territory in Oklahoma.

De Lôme letter. Relations between the U.S. and Spain over Cuba were already bad when Hearst's New York *Journal* (Feb. 9, 1898) printed a letter which it had illegally intercepted. It had been sent by the Spanish minister at Washington, Dupuy de Lôme, to a friend in Cuba. In it he described Pres. McKinley as "weak and a mere popularity seeker."

Publication of the letter further inflamed American public opinion against Spain and brought war closer. The Department of State demanded De Lôme's recall and a *Journal* cartoon showed Uncle Sam pointing to the White House door and saying to the Spaniard, "Git!" The minister resigned even before the demand for his recall could be presented.

Delta. The launch vehicle for U.S. spacecraft, first used in 1960, can rocket 500 pounds into a 300-nautical-mile orbit or about a 60-pound probe to the moon's vicinity.

democracy, world made safe for. On Apr. 2, 1917, Pres. Wilson went before Congress to read his war message. He reviewed the submarine controversy and the threat to international law by Germany's ruthless autocracy. "The world must be made safe for democracy," the President declared.

Democracy in America. The first part of the study of American democracy by Alexis de Tocqueville appeared in 1835 and the second part in 1840. Sent by Louis Philippe's Ministry of Justice to study American penitentiaries, de Tocqueville used the opportunity to travel in the U.S. and observe democracy, not only as a system of government, but as the basic characteristic of an entire society. In his book he discusses the advantages of democracy and the consequences of the unlimited power of the majority. He raises for the first time such enduring topics as the preference of Americans for practical rather than for theoretical science, the taste for physical well-being and the creation of an industrial aristocracy. Few books of social observation have remained so obstinately contemporary.

Democratic party. Its origins are found in Thomas Jefferson's Republican party. It took shape in 1793 when Jefferson left George Washington's Cabinet because Alexander Hamilton's views were being favored. In general, the new party appealed to small farmers, frontiersmen and small shopkeepers. It was partial to personal liberty and opposed too strong a federal government. Strict construction of the Constitution was favored, except when the responsibilities of power (as in the case of the Louisiana Purchase) suggested a broader interpretation. The party opposed a national bank and high tariffs.

The young party was called "Democratic-Republican" by the

Federalist opposition, at a time when "democratic" described the mob rule they saw in the French Revolution. By 1800 the pro-French Republicans had accepted this party name.

When Andrew Jackson was elected in 1828 "Republican" was dropped from the party name and the Democratic label remained. The party, in power since Jefferson's election in 1800, then divided into factions under Jackson, John Q. Adams and Henry Clay. Nevertheless, it remained dominant until division over the slavery issue resulted in the election of Abraham Lincoln, a Republican, in 1860.

From 1860 to 1912, with the exception of Grover Cleveland's interrupted terms (1885–89 and 1893–97), the party kept alive by occasional control of one house in Congress and victories in state and local elections. When Woodrow Wilson took office in 1913 the party leaned toward a strong central government and regulation of business. It was turned out of Washington again at the end of World War I.

It found its way back under the New Deal leadership of Franklin D. Roosevelt starting in 1933. Except for the Dwight Eisenhower years (1953–61), the Democrats have been experiencing a long stay in the nation's capital and in many of the state capitals. John F. Kennedy brought the party back to power by a narrow margin in 1960 and Lyndon B. Johnson's landslide victory in 1964 strengthened the party throughout the nation.

Democratic-Republican party. The party was founded by Thomas Jefferson and James Madison in 1793 when Jefferson left George Washington's Cabinet because of his opposition to Federalist policies. It was at first known as the Anti-Federalist party and then as the Republican party. Its enemies dubbed it the "democratic" Republican party in an effort to rub some of the ill-repute of the democratic excesses of the French Revolution onto Jefferson's party. This wore off, however, and by 1800 the party was known as the Democratic-Republican party and no stigma was attached to the label. In 1828 Jackson dropped the "Republican" and the Democratic party name emerged.

deposit, right of. Westerners needed the use of the port of New Orleans to deposit their bacon and hams, corn and wheat, and tobacco and cotton, while waiting to transfer them to ocean-going or coastwise ships. Since New Orleans was part of the territory owned by Spain, the right or privilege of making such deposits without paying any duties was demanded by the farmers who transported their goods down the Mississippi to its mouth.

The right of deposit was gained for the West in the Pinckney Treaty (1795). When Spain withdrew the right temporarily in 1802, war was

189

threatened. In 1803 the U.S. purchased the Louisiana Territory and western farmers had no further worries about the right of deposit.

Deseret. Meaning "land of the honey-bee," the name was adopted by the Mormons for the territory which they organized to gain admission to the Union as a state in 1849. It was taken from the *Book of Mormon*. Congress refused admission to Deseret and in 1850 included it in the newly organized Territory of Utah.

Desert Land Act (1877). The measure was passed by Congress to stimulate settlement of the West. A settler was permitted to occupy 640 acres at 25 cents an acre. He could gain clear title to the land after three years on payment of an additional $1 per acre provided he could prove that he had irrigated the plot. Thousands of farmers tried but gave up before three years.

Cattlemen used the Act as a device for gaining title to the once open-grazing land. They registered thousands of acres in the names of cowhands who later testified that they "had seen water on the claim."

De Soto expedition (1539–43). Hernando de Soto's appetite for treasure was whetted by his experience as a lieutenant of Francisco Pizarro, conquerer of Peru. After returning to Spain, De Soto received royal permis-

sion to colonize Florida. He set forth with a band of 600 noblemen and arrived at Tampa Bay in 1539. They moved on through the southeastern part of what was later to become the U.S. to Tennessee, where the Mississippi was found at a point near Memphis.

De Soto, however, was not satisfied by his discovery of the "Father of Waters," since it was treasure that he sought. After further exploration of present-day Arkansas and Oklahoma, De Soto died in 1542 and was buried in the Mississippi. Survivors finally reached Mexico.

Dewey, John (1859–1952). Philosopher and educator. Born in Burlington, Vt., he was granted a Ph.D. by Johns Hopkins Univ. (1884). He joined the faculty of Columbia Univ. in 1904. An adherent of pragmatism as formulated by C. S. Peirce and William James, he evolved what he called "instrumentalism," holding that life need not be accepted passively, but could be shaped by man. He laid a philosophical groundwork for the program of liberal reformers. He related his ideas to education, which he thought could be made an instrument of social reform, and urged that democratic values permeate every aspect of educational training. His "progressive" theories of learning greatly influenced American education. Among his numerous works: *The School and Society* (1899), *Democracy and Education* (1916), *Art as Experience*

(1934), *Problems of Men* (1946).

DEW Line. Northernmost of three radar warning lines stretched across Canada in the 1950's, the distant early warning line guards against manned bomber attacks over the North Pole or around the Atlantic and Pacific flanks.

The Line has outlived its usefulness, according to U.S. Sec. of Defense McNamara, who told the House Armed Services Committee in 1965 that a "deliberate determined attack" would come first from missiles "long before the bombers could reach their targets."

Dickinson, Emily Elizabeth (1830–86). Poet. Born in Amherst, Mass., she lived there as a spinster-recluse. Only two of her poems were published during her lifetime. Six volumes of poems published after her death revealed terseness, wit and deep understanding. She dealt with the humble objects about her and with such themes as love, death, God and eternity.

Dickinson, John (1732–1808). Continental congressman. Born in Talbot Co., Md., he became a lawyer and was active politically in Pennsylvania and Delaware. He counseled peaceful opposition to the Sugar Act and Stamp Act in his pamphlet, *The Late Regulations Respecting the British Colonies* (1765) and favored conciliation in his *Letters from a Farmer in Pennsylvania to the Inhabitants of the British Colonies* (1768). Although Dickinson did not sign the Declaration of Independence, he volunteered for the Continental Army and served in the Continental Congress (1774–76, 1777, 1779, 1780). Active in the Constitutional Convention (1787) as a delegate from Delaware, his letters urging adoption of the Constitution were signed "Fabius."

Diesel locomotives. The Diesel engine patented in 1892 was invented by Rudolph Diesel, a German engineer. Since the early 1930's locomotives with Diesel engines have virtually replaced steam locomotives on U.S. railroads. On May 26, 1934, the *Pioneer Zephyr*, owned by the Burlington Railroad, made the run from Denver to Chicago in 13 hours and 5 minutes. The fastest steam schedule for the trip was 26 hours.

The Diesel is an internal-combustion type of engine using crude oil as a fuel. The Diesel locomotive operates quietly and can run long distances without refueling. It eliminated the water stops made by steam locomotives and made ghost towns of the small railroad towns with their coal chutes and water tanks.

Digger Indians. Used contemptuously by pioneers, the term was applied to some western tribes, such as the Shoshone, in the Great Basin, an elevated region between the Wasatch and Sierra Nevada Mts., including most of Nevada and parts of Utah, California, Idaho, Wyoming and Oregon. Indians living in the region, comprising the Great Salt Lake Desert, Mohave Desert and Death Valley, did not eat meat but dug roots and subsisted on wild seeds, grasshoppers and lizards.

dime novels. Paper-backed novels selling for ten cents first appeared in 1860. They were read by millions. The hero was usually a poor boy who became rich through honest industry. If the novel was a story about the West, the hero was a superman figure who could always best any number of bad men.

Horatio Alger wrote more than a hundred books that enthralled a whole generation of American boys. Among them were *Ragged Dick* (1867), *Luck and Pluck* (1869) and the *Tattered Tom* (1871) series. Similarly, Martha Finley's *Elsie Dinsmore* series was read by millions of girls who hoped they would develop the noble character of the heroine.

Edward Z. C. Judson as "Ned Buntline," was another pioneer writer of dime novels and adventure fiction.

Dingley Tariff of 1897. During the Republican administration of Pres. McKinley, Congress raised the protective tariff rates not only above the 1894 rates, but also above those of the McKinley Tariff of 1890. Even the duties on wool, removed by the Wilson-Gorman Tariff of 1894, were restored. The Tariff of 1897 like that of 1890 was "the outcome of an aggressive spirit of protection."

direct primary. Since the party voter and not the nominating convention selects the candidate for office, the power of nominating candidates is taken out of the hands of machine politicians and given to the rank and file voter. The direct primary had its initial trial in Crawford County, Pa., in 1842, where it was used by the Democratic party.

Under Gov. Robert M. LaFollette, the Progressives passed the first statewide direct primary law in Wisconsin in 1903. Its use has since spread so that almost all states have the direct primary for nominating at least some candidates.

The great majority of states have a "closed" primary in which the voter must be a party member who indicates his party affiliation when he registers to vote. A few states have the "open" primary, in which a voter may choose his party at the time of the primary.

Discourse on Davila (1790–91). Published in book form by John Adams in 1805, it originally appeared in the *Gazette of the United States*. Adams proposed a classical view of the social order and advocated a utopia ruled by the wealthy, powerful and talented. His theory was regarded as a reaction toward monarchism.

Discourse on the History, Character, and Prospects of the West (1834). Dr. Daniel Drake, an Ohio physician, foresaw the growth of a literature based on western speech. In his book, he insists that the "great reservoir of spoken language" would strengthen the written word. Western speech might be "inferior in refinement" to the mother tongue, but it was "superior in force, variety, and freshness." Drake was also enthusiastic about American oratory and regarded it as particularly suitable for the untutored multitudes of the West.

Discoverer I. The first U.S. satellite to be placed in polar orbit, it circled the earth at the poles instead of the Equator. It was launched Feb. 28, 1959. Other Discoverers were launched with the primary mission of testing experimental techniques for space cabin recovery either at sea or in midair. The first such recovery—by a ship-helicopter team at sea—was accomplished on Aug. 11, 1960, from Discoverer XII.

Displaced Persons Act (1948). Under this law passed by Congress, 205,000 displaced persons (DP's), beyond the regular quota of immigrants under the National Origins Act, were admitted to the U.S. over a two-year period. The DP's were to be charged against future annual quotas. They came from the million European refugees at the end of World War II.

In 1950 Pres. Truman persuaded Congress to relax the discrimination against DP's from southern and eastern Europe and to increase the total admitted to 415,000.

District Courts, U.S. Each state has at least one District Court (a trial court with general federal jurisdiction), while some of the larger states have as many as four. Altogether there are 87 District Courts in the 50 states, plus the one in the District of Columbia. In addition the Commonwealth of Puerto Rico has a District Court.

At present each District Court has from one to twenty-four federal district judges, depending upon the amount of judicial work within its territory. Only one judge is usually required to hear and decide a case in a District Court.

Cases from the District Courts may be reviewed by the U.S. Courts of Appeals. Those cases which may be appealed from District Courts directly to the U.S. Supreme Court include injunction orders of special three-judge District Courts, certain decisions holding acts of Congress unconstitutional and certain criminal decisions.

Dix, Dorothea Lynde (1802–87). Reformer. Born in Hampden, Me., she taught school in Massachusetts (1821–34). After travel in Europe for her health, she returned to Boston and entered social work. Her *Memorial to the Legislature of Massachusetts* (1843) spotlighted conditions in insane asylums that were medieval in their barbarity. She brought about lasting reforms not only in Massachusetts but in other states. She was also active in the reform of prisons and alms-houses. As superintendent of women nurses during the Civil War, she selected and assigned nurses for hospitals.

Dixie. Various origins have been ascribed to the popular name of the South. One notes that in early Louisiana the ten-dollar bill had the French word *dix* (ten) on it. The pronunciation was corrupted to *dixie* and spread throughout the South.

The song "Dixie" was written in 1859 by Daniel D. Emmett, who sang it for the first time in a minstrel show in New York. The tune captured the imagination of the South and was sung at Jefferson Davis' inauguration in 1861. The words were changed somewhat when it became a marching song for the Confederates during the Civil War.

Dixiecrats. The States' Rights Democratic party was formed in 1948 to protest the Democratic party's plank favoring civil rights for Negroes. Popularly known as the Dixiecrats, the party nominated Gov. J. Strom Thurmond of South Carolina for President and carried South Carolina, Alabama, Mississippi and Louisiana, for a total of 39 electoral votes.

Dodge City, Kansas. In the 1870's a million head of cattle were driven to Dodge City for rail shipment to Kansas City. This "Cowboy's Capital" was so rough that gunmen, among them Bat Masterson, were hired to keep order. Dodge City has enjoyed a revival on television westerns.

"Dollar Diplomacy." In the early 1900's the U.S. intervened in the affairs of Caribbean countries which had become so involved in debt that European powers sought to move in and take over to insure payment. Since this would have violated the Monroe Doctrine, the U.S. decided to act first—thus preventing European powers from encroaching once again in the Western Hemisphere.

In the case of the Dominican Republic a show of force in 1905 permitted the U.S. to take control of the country's finances. The foreign debt was transferred from European to American bankers and a percentage of customs collections was set aside to insure payment of Dominican debts.

There were other instances in Cuba, Honduras, Haiti, Costa Rica and Nicaragua where the U.S. intervened in the hope that "Dollar Diplomacy" would safeguard American investments. The policy aroused antagonism against the U.S. in Latin America.

dollar sign ($). The origins of the symbol for U.S. paper currency is not clear. It came into use about the time the Constitution was ratified and may be an alteration of the symbol for the Spanish combination of the p and s standing for pesos.

The term "dollar" is an English corruption of the German word, "thaler."

Dominican Republic (Santo Domingo). The revolution-rent republic occupies two-thirds of the island of Hispaniola in the West Indies. (Haiti occupies the other third.) It became the object of a challenge to the Monroe Doctrine in 1861 when Spain reannexed it. Spain had ceded Santo Domingo to France in 1795. Touissant L'Ouverture, Haitian leader, overran it in 1801 and Napoleon found control of the island too bloody and expensive. Several native republics came and went.

Sec. of State Seward challenged Spain's right to take back Santo Domingo in 1861. Spain voluntarily withdrew in 1865. In 1869 Congress rejected Seward's proposal for establishing a naval station on the island. In 1870 the U.S. Senate rejected Pres. Grant's treaty for annexing the bankrupt and war-torn republic. In 1905 Pres. Theodore Roosevelt ordered the Dominican customs house to be taken over to assure payment to European creditors who might otherwise have stepped in to collect their debts. In 1916 Pres. Wilson sent in the Marines to quell an insurrection and U.S. troops were not withdrawn until 1924, when U.S. financial interests had been safeguarded. The Dominican Republic soon fell under the Molina Trujillo dictatorship (1930–61).

On Apr. 28, 1965, Pres. Johnson sent in troops to halt what he thought to be a Communist take-over of the government. He then called upon the Organization of American States to aid in establishing a constitutional government to replace the military junta which controlled the Dominican Republic.

Dominion of New England (1686–89). James II sought to consolidate the separate northern colonies into one dominion to lighten the cost of administration and tighten control over the colonists, who were under six separate colonial governments. The short-lived Dominion of New England included Massachusetts, Plymouth, Rhode Island, Maine, New York and New Jersey.

Gov. Edmund Andros, appointed by the King, tried to enforce the Navigation Acts, subordinate the Puritans to the Anglican Church and raise money by reissuing land titles. Although personally able and honest, Andros was denounced as a tyrant.

James II was forced to flee to France as a consequence of the Glorious Revolution (1688) and the Dominion was dissolved as soon as the news reached the colonies.

domino theory. As applied to U.S. foreign policy in the post-World War II world the theory holds that as one country in Asia falls to Communism its neighbor follows until all are lost. Adherents of the domino theory argue that the loss of South Viet Nam, for example, would mean the loss of neighboring countries to Communist Chinese influence.

Donelson, Fort, capture of (Feb. 15, 1862). At the surrender of the Confederate-held fort on the Cumberland River, in Tennessee, Gen. Ulysses S. Grant acquired "Unconditional Surrender" as a substitute for his first and middle name.

The fort was one of the key defenses against the split in the Confederacy toward which the Union forces were driving. When the commanding Confederate officer asked for terms, after four days of siege and heavy fighting, Grant replied with the memorable words that became a catch phrase for the North.

Dongan Charters (1683). Gov. Thomas Dongan of New York, who identified himself chiefly with the upper-class groups in the colony, granted a charter to the city of New York. It gave to the merchant class a larger measure of home rule. Freemen of the town were allowed to elect the aldermen.

Dongan also granted Albany a new city charter which conferred upon that town a monopoly of the fur trade.

Donner party (1846–47). One of the groups moving west from Illinois was trapped south of the Great Salt Lake in early snows in the Sierra Nevada Mts. About half the 87 lived, but only by eating those who had died. Rescue parties brought the survivors to California during the winter.

"Don't fire till you see the white of their eyes." When ammunition was running low for colonists defending Breed's Hill (not Bunker Hill as is commonly thought), in the battle on June 17, 1775, Gen. Putnam is alleged to have given this command.

"Don't give up the ship." The words of dying James Lawrence, commander of the U.S. frigate *Chesapeake*, were uttered before its surrender to the British frigate *Shannon* (1813). The action took place off the coast of Boston during the War of 1812. Capt. Lawrence's words have become an inspiration to the American Navy to this day. They were first flown on a flag from the masthead of Capt. Perry's flagship during the successful battle of Lake Erie.

"Don't tread on me." The motto, along with the figure of a coiled rattlesnake, appeared frequently on flags in the South during the colonial period.

Dooley, Mr. A saloonkeeper character created by the popular humorist Finley Peter Dunne, Mr. Dooley commented on a range of public issues in a thick Irish brogue as penetrating as a scalpel. Mr. Dooley usually hit out at intolerance, sham and the foibles of society in talks with his friend "Hinnissy."

Dunne's book, *Mr. Dooley in Peace and War* (1898) was a great success at home and abroad. The author contributed, also, to a number of journals, including the muckraking *Collier's* and the *American Magazine*.

"Doomsday" statistics. Computer calculations and elaborate analyses of U.S. fatalities in the event of an initial all-out nuclear attack were presented to Congress by Sec. of Defense McNamara in 1965.

According to McNamara some 30 million lives might be saved if a national fallout shelter program costing about $5 billion were undertaken. An additional expenditure of $20 billion—$17 billion for an anti-ballistic missile system, $3 billion for an improved and more extensive anti-bomber defense might save an additional 40 million lives. However, McNamara could foresee nothing that might reduce U.S. fatalities much below 80 million fatalities in the event of a general nuclear war between the U.S. and the Soviet Union in the early 1970's.

Dorchester Company. Organized in the early 1620's, the company founded a fishing settlement at Cape Ann, on Massachusetts Bay. It failed to make a profit and was replaced by the New England Company in 1628. Some of the Dorchester men received stock in the new company and were designated as the "Old Planters" in the new settlement at Salem. In 1629 the New England Company became the Massachusetts Bay Company.

Dorr's Rebellion. In 1841 Rhode Island was still governed under the charter granted in 1663 by Charles II. Voting was restricted to property holders and their eldest sons; over half the adult male population was not eligible to vote.

Thomas Wilson Dorr led insurgents who drew up a new constitution under which he was elected governor in 1842. The official administration called out the state militia and the Dorrite insurgents were routed. Dorr was tried and sentenced to life imprisonment, but his sentence was withdrawn.

The rebellion caused conservatives to recognize the need for reform. In 1843 a new constitution was adopted which provided for almost universal manhood suffrage.

Dos Passos, John (1896–1970). Author. Born in Chicago, Ill., he was graduated from Harvard (1916). His notable trilogy, *U.S.A.*, covers the years 1900 to 1930 and introduces a large number of characters representing every class and a variety of occupations. The people move up and down the social scale. They have no roots, no firm moral anchor, and they seem to flounder in the social maelstrom. The books are a massive indictment of America. Individual titles are *The 42nd Paral-*

lel (1930), *1919* (1932) and *The Big Money* (1936).

Other books by Dos Passos include *Three Soldiers* (1921), *Manhattan Transfer* (1925) and *Midcentury* (1961).

double eagle. The $20 gold piece authorized for coinage as legal tender by Congress in 1849 was popularly referred to as a "double eagle." The name was derived from the fact that the $10 gold piece authorized in 1792 was popularly called an "eagle" because the national bird was stamped on the reverse side of the coin.

doubloon. Worth eight dollars during the colonial period, the Spanish gold coin circulated in the American colonies, West Indies and South America. It was so named because it was double the value of a pistole.

The shortage of English coins and the prohibition on colonial mints made the doubloon hard money saved as cash assets, especially in the South.

doughboys. The source of the popular name for U.S. infantrymen in World War I dates back to mid-19th century and perhaps earlier when the expression was used contemptuously by cavalrymen to describe infantrymen who wore white belts and had to clean them with "dough" made of pipe clay.

doughfaces. In one of his "fire and brimstone" speeches, in 1820, John Randolph of Roanoke, Va., belittled as "dough-faces" the Northern congressmen who voted for extending slavery into the territories.

Douglas, Stephen Arnold (1813–61). Political leader. Born in Brandon, Vt., he moved to Illinois in 1833. A power in the Democratic party, he represented Illinois in the U.S. House of Representatives (1843–47) and U.S. Senate (1847–61). His "popular sovereignty" approach failed to solve the controversy over slavery, and the split in the Democratic party helps to explain his defeat by Abraham Lincoln in the presidential election of 1860. Earlier, his memorable debates with Lincoln, whom he defeated for the Senate (1858), made Lincoln a national figure. In 1860 Douglas favored an amendment to the Constitution protecting slavery in the states where it existed. This effort to stave off the Civil War failed, and he supported the Lincoln administration in its early days.

Douglass, Frederick (c. 1817–95). Abolitionist and journalist. Born a slave in Tuckahoe, Md., he escaped in 1838 and settled in Massachusetts. A powerful advocate of his people's freedom, he was a central figure in the "One Hundred Conventions" of the New England Anti-Slavery Society. Douglass founded the abolitionist newspaper, *North Star* (1847), and assisted in recruiting Negro regiments in the Civil War. In the federal civil service (1877–86), he was appointed U.S.

minister to Haiti (1889–91). A social reformer, he supported woman suffrage.

"doves" and "hawks." The terms were used during the U.S. involvement in the war in Viet Nam during the 1960's. The "doves" favored a negotiated peace at the opportune time and wanted to avoid a confrontation with Communist China and Russia. The "hawks" held that delay and postponement merely darkened the future. They favored vigorous military action to end further encroachment by the Communists in Southeast Asia.

Dow, Neal (1804–97). Reformer. He was born in Portland, Me. "Father of the Maine law" (1851), a prohibition measure, he was a national crusader for temperance reform. As much opposed to slavery as he was to liquor, he served in the Union army and was twice wounded. He was the Prohibition party candidate for President in 1880.

Draft Riots (1863). Resentment in New York City against the conscription (draft) law passed by Congress led to rioting resulting in a thousand casualties, including free Negroes, and destruction of over a million dollars' worth of property.

The draft came at a time when antiwar sentiment in New York was high and voluntary enlistments low. Tempers were inflamed by a provision of the law which permitted men of means to buy substitutes or simply pay the draft officials $300 and leave it to them to find men ready, for a bounty (cash payment), to fight for their country.

The rioting was finally quelled by federal troops.

Drago Doctrine (1902). The Venezuela debt controversy caused the foreign minister of Argentina, Louis M. Drago, to formulate the policy that no European power might use force to collect debts owed by American nations to foreign creditors.

According to Drago, a country invests at its own risk. This position was modified by the Roosevelt Corollary to the Monroe Doctrine. The Drago Doctrine, reinforcing the Monroe Doctrine, was adopted by the Second Hague Peace Conference (1907).

Dred Scott Case (1857). In a decision which brought the Civil War closer, the U.S. Supreme Court held that slavery could not be excluded from the territories.

Dred Scott, a slave, had been taken by his Missouri master to Illinois, a free state, and to the free Wisconsin Territory. After several years, he was returned to Missouri. Scott, with the support of an antislavery group, sued for his freedom on the ground that his residence in a free state and territory had freed him.

Chief Justice Taney went beyond his ruling that a slave was not a citizen and did not have a right to sue in a federal court. In an obiter dictum he broadened his decision to deny the right of Congress to exclude slavery from any territory. In so doing he declared the Missouri Compromise unconstitutional. It had already been replaced by Congress by the Kansas-Nebraska Act which contained the principle of popular sovereignty, giving the people of a territory the right to decide whether the territory should be free or slave. The decision (*Scott v. Sandford*) threatened the principle of popular sovereignty, for if Congress did not have the right to exclude slavery from the territories neither did the territorial legislatures.

The decision struck at the roots of the Republican party which was pledged to oppose extension of slavery into the territories. Republicans, including Lincoln, decided to oppose Taney's ruling peacefully and to seek another judicial ruling.

Dreiser, Theodore (1871–1945). Novelist. Born in Terre Haute, Ind., his early life in a family of 13 children was one of poverty. After several years as a newspaperman in big cities, he became a naturalist writer. In *Sister Carrie* (1900), his first novel, Carrie Meeber comes from a small town to Chicago to look for work. The mistress of two men, she ruins one of them, Hurstwood. The novel was not advertised by the publisher following public protest over its frankness.

During the Progressive era, Dreiser's novels were praised by reformers as searing indictments of unsavory business practices. His works during this period include *The Financier* (1912), *The Titan* (1914) and *The Stoic* (1917), which describe the rise and fall of Frank Cowperwood as he searches for power and wealth in Philadelphia and Chicago.

In the post-World War I period, Dreiser continued to dwell on the forces which control men. In his widely read *An American Tragedy* (1925), he attacked the American race to riches which corrupts a youth who drowns his sweetheart to marry a rich girl. Nothing in the young man's training has enabled him to surmount the driving need to "succeed."

During the 1930's Dreiser became increasingly involved in politics and social questions. Before his death he joined the Communist party.

dry farming. The practice of farming in dry areas without irrigation was undertaken in California beginning in 1850 and in the Pacific Northwest and Great Plains in the 1880's. The growing season of drought-resistant. crops coincided with the limited time when rainfall could be counted on.

Du Bois, William Edward Burghardt (1868–1963). Educator and writer. Born in Great Barrington, Mass., of slave descent, he was granted a Ph.D. by Harvard (1895). Taking a militant position on race relations, he helped to organize (1905) the Niagara Movement for racial equality. He was professor of history, Atlanta Univ. (1896–1910) and head of the department of sociology (1933–44). He had a long-time connection with the National Association for the Advancement of Colored People (NAACP) as director of publicity and research (1910–34) and head of department of special research (1944–48). His friendly attitude toward USSR in the post-World War II period inspired formation of the Du Bois clubs, comprised of Communists. He was author of *The Souls of the Black Folk* (1903) and *Black Reconstruction* (1935).

ducking stool. The chair was attached to a long pole and operated in seesaw fashion for immersing women convicted of prostitution or practicing witchcraft in 17th- and 18th-century colonial America. The court determined the number of times the prisoner was ducked in the pond.

duelling. All the colonies together left records of only about a dozen duels up to the outbreak of the Revolution. The few duels that occurred usually involved military men using swords or pistols to settle disputes. Duels were commonly called "affairs of honor" and the duelling ground was the "field of honor."

By the early 19th century duelling was outlawed on the statute books of most states. In South Carolina, for example, an act of 1812 prescribed a year in prison and a fine of $2,000 for all participants in a duel, including seconds (friends of the challenger and challenged who made arrangements in accordance with a code of procedures). Nevertheless, duelling continued in the South until well after the Civil War.

It was between the American Revolution and the Civil War that duelling had its remarkable growth. Most notorious was the encounter between Aaron Burr and Alexander Hamilton (July 11, 1804), in which Hamilton was killed. Other duelling dramas involving prominent figures were Andrew Jackson v. Charles Dickinson (May 30, 1806); Henry Clay v. Humphrey Marshall (Jan. 19, 1809) and v. John Randolph of Roanoke (Apr. 8, 1826); James Barron v. Commodore Stephen Decatur (Mar. 22, 1820), in which Decatur was killed.

due process clauses. The "due process of law" provision appears in two places in the U.S. Constitution. In the 5th Amendment it places limitations on the federal government, and in the 14th Amendment it places limitations on the state governments. It also appears in most state constitutions.

"Due process" has its origins in British law going back to

the Magna Carta (1215). King John was enjoined from imprisoning a free man, "except by a legal judgment of his peers or by the law of the land."

During the first half of the 19th century litigation in the U.S. involving due process was satisfied by the grand jury and petit jury process. These procedures for protecting accused persons continue as basic to due process. The great expansion of business after the Civil War caused an increase in federal and state regulations. Due process was expanded to include claims by corporations (persons in the eyes of the law) who suffered losses without due process of law allegedly because of the unreasonableness of legislation affecting their property. Since reasonableness is not subject to exact definition, the litigation has been extensive.

Although the 14th Amendment was intended to protect the rights of Negroes, its use for this purpose lapsed. In recent years, however, due process as protection against discrimination has been revived. *Bolling v. Sharpe* (1954), a companion case to *Brown v. Board of Education* (1954), involved the 5th rather than the 14th Amendment. The Court acknowledged that "it would be unthinkable that the same Constitution would impose a lesser duty on the Federal Government." It held that segregation in public schools is not reasonably related to any governmental objective. The Court reasoned that imposition thereof on Negro children attending public schools in the District of Columbia constituted an arbitrary deprivation of their liberty without due process of law.

dugout. The term has two different references in American history. It was a boat hollowed out of a tree trunk and used by Indians and pioneers for travel on waterways.

The dugout was also the name of a cavelike dwelling carved into a hill in the Great Plains. The earth constituted the floor and two sides. The roof, a combination of hay and sod, was held up by a long pole. The front was constructed out of logs or sod with provision for a door and window.

Duke, James Buchanan (1856–1925). Industrialist and philanthropist. He was born near Durham, N.C. With his brother Benjamin Newton Duke (1855–1929), he was triumphant in the "cigarette war" resulting in formation of the American Tobacco Co. (1890) which was subsequently dissolved as a combination in restraint of trade by U.S. Supreme Court (1911). Newly formed companies retained large shares of the tobacco business. The major philanthropy of the brothers was the endowment of Trinity College, renamed Duke University (Durham, N.C.) in their honor.

Duke of York's laws. Drawn up in 1665 by Gov. Nicolls,

then governing New York for the Duke of York, the code conformed to the laws of England and provided for a system of courts, trial by jury, equal taxation and liability for military service. The Duke was a firm believer in autocratic rule and at first refused to grant the settlers a representative assembly. Prior to 1691 the government of New York was more undemocratic than that of any other of the English colonies.

Dulles, John Foster (1888–1959). Statesman. Born in Washington, D.C., he was a prominent international lawyer and headed the firm of Sullivan and Cromwell from 1927. He was a delegate to the UN (1946–50); Pres. Eisenhower's Sec. of State (1953–59), he played a major role in forcing Britain and France to abandon the Suez Canal attack (1956); he was responsible for the Eisenhower Doctrine (1957); and he committed the U.S. to hold West Berlin (1958). As part of the policy of containment of the USSR, he sponsored SEATO and the Baghdad Pact.

Dumbarton Oaks Conference. Proposals for a peace organization (the United Nations) were drafted at an international conference near Washington, D.C., Oct. 1944.

Dunbar, Paul Laurence (1872–1906). Poet. Born in Dayton, O., of slave parents, he was hailed by W. D. Howells as the first man of African descent and

American training to feel Negro life esthetically and express it lyrically. Dunbar is the author of *Oak and Ivy* (1893) and *Majors and Minors* (1895).

Duncan, Isadora (1878–1927). Dancer. She was born in San Francisco, Calif. An interpreter of classical music, performing barefoot and in flowing costumes, she was the first in modern times to make the dance a creative art. She established her reputation in London and Paris and toured Europe and the U.S. (1906–08). She popularized the dance in U.S. thus providing a base for the later successes of Martha Graham and Agnes de Mille. She wrote her autobiography, *My Life* (1926–27). She was killed in an automobile accident.

Dunkards. Derived from the German "to dip," the name refers to a sect of German Baptist Brethren, also called Dunkers or Tunkers, who practice baptism by immersion three times, symbolic of the Trinity. Dunkards dress simply and are opposed to oaths, alcohol, tobacco and war.

The Dunkards fled from Germany and settled in Germantown, Pa., in 1719. They have spread from Pennsylvania to the West and Canada.

Du Pont, Eleuthère Irénée (1771–1834). Industrialist. Born in Paris, he came to the U.S. in 1799. He established a plant for manufacturing gunpowder near Wilmington, Del. (1801–04). Sales were stimulated by the War of 1812. E. I. du Pont de Nemours & Co., founded 1801, continues to this day.

dust bowl. Although dust storms in the Southwest were known early in the 19th century, it was not until 1934 that years of drought made the expression an apt description of the land in adjoining parts of Kansas, Colorado, Oklahoma, New Mexico and the semi-arid plains of Texas.

The demand for wheat in World War I had caused farmers to strip the land of its protective grass cover. The soil lay beneath the burning sun, defenseless against the driving wind. The result was storms that carried dust to the Atlantic coast.

Millions of acres were abandoned by poverty-stricken farmers.

Dutch West India Company. The company was founded in the Netherlands in 1621; its first settlers arrived at Manhattan Island in 1624. They consisted of about 30 families of French-speaking Walloons—Protestant exiles from the Netherlands. Since the company was primarily interested in the fur trade in North America, the settlers established several trading posts. These included Fort Orange, at the present site of Albany, and Fort Nassau, opposite the site of present-day Philadelphia. One band remained at Manhattan to hold the island and build Fort Amsterdam. This became the seat of government for New Netherland (later New York).

The company was also granted a monopoly of the trade of western Africa, the eastern coasts of North and South America and of all the islands in between. It became bankrupt about 1645 and neglected New Netherland, which fell to the English in 1664.

E

Eads, James Buchanan (1820–87). Engineer and inventor. Born in Lawrenceburg, Ind., he invented a diving bell in 1842 and made a fortune in steamboat salvage. He constructed the armor-plated, steam-propelled gunboats used by the Union in the West in the Civil War. The builder of Eads Bridge (1867–74) across the Mississippi at St. Louis, he also devised a system of jetties controlling sediments and kept open a channel for navigation from the mouth of the Mississippi into the Gulf of Mexico.

eagle, American. The huge bird is the U.S. symbol. The American eagle, so named by James Audubon, belongs to the bald, white-headed variety. It was placed on the Great Seal of the U.S. in 1785 and has appeared on various coins since 1776. The $10 gold piece, first coined in 1794, had the American eagle stamped on one side and the coin became known as an "eagle."

Eakins, Thomas (1844–1916). Painter and sculptor. Born in Philadelphia, Pa., his style was influenced by the realist paintings of Velásquez and Goya. The study of anatomy at Jefferson Medical College (Philadelphia) helped to make him a master of the human figure. His paintings include *Clinic of Dr. Gross, The Chess Players* and *Max Schmitt in a Single Scull.* His sculptures include reliefs on the battle monument at Trenton, N.J.

Earhart, Amelia (1898–1937). Aviator. Born in Atchison, Kans., she started flying about 1921 and was the first woman to cross the Atlantic Ocean in an airplane (1928), making a transatlantic solo flight in 1932. She disappeared after leaving New Guinea on a round-the-world flight (1937). Her book, *Last Flight* (1938), was edited by her husband, George Palmer Putnam.

Eastman, George (1854–1932). Inventor and industrialist. Born in Waterville, N.Y., he perfected the dry plate process of film making and paper-backed flexible film and manufactured a small box camera, the Kodak (1888). By 1901 the Eastman Kodak Co., Rochester, N.Y., was the world's largest industrial plant for the manufacture of photographic supplies. His philanthropies include founding of the Eastman School of Music (Rochester, N.Y.).

East St. Louis race riot. Violent race riots erupted in this city in southwestern Illinois, on the Mississippi, in 1917. In the conflict 39 Negroes and nine whites were killed.

In 1919, in Chicago, 23 Negroes and 15 whites lost their lives in a racial battle.

Eaton Affair (1829–31). A social scandal rocked the Jackson administration when John H. Eaton, Jackson's Sec. of War, married Margaret O'Neil Timberlake, an ex-barmaid. As a Senator he had resided with the Timberlakes when in Washington and there had been rumors about his relationship with Peggy Timberlake even before her husband died while serving in the navy in 1828.

When Mrs. John C. Calhoun, wife of the Vice-President, and some other Cabinet members' wives snubbed Mrs. Eaton, Jackson sided with the Eatons, perhaps remembering the attacks on his own wife. Sec. of State Martin Van Buren, a widower, was kind to Mrs. Eaton and this further solidified his position in Jackson's administration.

There were other reasons for the falling out between Jackson and Calhoun, but the affair helped to dissolve the Cabinet. Van Buren offered to resign; others were encouraged to do so and Jackson formed a new Cabinet. Eaton was appointed governor of Florida Territory. Calhoun's supporters found themselves out of the Cabinet.

Echo I. Orbited on Aug. 12, 1960, the satellite proved that it is possible to communicate between distant areas on earth by reflecting radio microwaves from a man-made satellite. Radio signals were literally bounced off the satellite from one point on earth to another.

Echo II, an enormous signal-reflecting balloon as tall as a 13-story building and the first satellite to be used in cooperation with the USSR, was launched Jan. 25, 1964.

Economic Advisers, Council of. Established in the Executive Office of the President by the Employment Act of 1946, the Council consists of three members appointed by the President with the consent of the Senate. It analyzes the national economy, appraises the economic programs and policies of the government, recommends to the President policies for economic growth and stability and assists in the preparation of the economic reports of the President to the Congress.

Economic Stabilization, Office of. The OES was established as a World War II agency, Oct. 3, 1942, after Congress passed an act to lower the ceilings on farm prices. Its first head was James F. Byrnes, who resigned from the U.S. Supreme Court to take the first of a number of wartime administrative assignments.

The OES sought to control inflationary tendencies which threatened the military effort and domestic economic structure. It was abolished in 1945.

Eddy, Mary Morse Baker (1821–1910). Founder of the Christian Science Church. Born in Bow, N.H., she was an invalid who investigated many types of healing and found help in the Bible. Viewing science as another name for the wisdom of God, she explained her spiritual and metaphysical system, known as Christian Science, in *Science and Health with Key to the Scriptures* (1875). The Church of Christ, Scientist, was chartered in 1879. She founded the Christian Science Publishing Society (1898), publisher of *The Christian Science Monitor* (first issue, 1908).

Edison, Thomas Alva (1847–1931). Inventor. Born in Milan, Ohio, he spent his youth in Michigan and his mature years in his laboratories at Menlo Park, N.J. (1876) and West Orange, N.J. (1887). His name is synonymous with the incandescent lamp which he did not invent but made practical so that lamps might be empowered from central stations. Edison was not a theoretician, but concentrated on practical

inventions for commercial use. These numbered over a thousand and include improvements in telegraphy, a "kinetoscope" for showing photographs of moving objects, the phonograph, storage battery, improved dynamos and motors. He organized the Edison General Electric Co., later the General Electric Co. His phenomenal output made him a legend in his own time.

Education, Office of. The federal office was created by an act of Congress in 1867. In 1869 it was absorbed into the Department of the Interior. It became a constituent agency of the Department of Health, Education and Welfare upon the establishment of that department in 1953.

The Office of Education collects statistics related to the condition of education, disseminates information to aid the states in maintaining efficient school systems and in general promotes the cause of education. It is also responsible for federal financial assistance to education and for special studies and programs.

Edwards, Jonathan (1703–58). Congregational clergyman and theologian. Born in East Windsor, Conn., he was graduated from Yale (1720). A powerful preacher and author of numerous works, including *Freedom of the Will* (1754), he is regarded as the first great American philosopher. Edwards held firmly to a belief in predestination and original sin and played an important role in the "Great Awakening" in the 1730's. Forced to resign from his Northampton, Mass., parish because he demanded high criteria for church membership, he became a missionary to the Indians at Stockbridge, Mass., before he was called to the presidency of the College of New Jersey at Princeton (1757–58).

Einstein, Albert (1879–1955). Physicist. Born in Germany, he came to the U.S. in 1932. Deprived of German citizenship by the Nazi government (1934), he became a naturalized American citizen. Granted a Ph.D. by Univ. of Zurich (1905), he published an account of the special theory of relativity (1905) and of the general theory (1916). His $E=mc^2$ is the basis for the modern concept of the atom. He carried on his work at the Institute for Advanced Study at Princeton (1933–45) and sent a historic letter to Pres. Roosevelt (1939) stressing the need for research on the atomic bomb. He formulated a unified field theory (1953).

Eisenhower, Dwight David (1890–1969). Thirty-fourth President of the U.S. (1953–61). Born in Denison, Tex., he was graduated from the U.S. Military Academy, West Point, N.Y. (1915). He was commander of the Allied Expeditionary Force in Western Europe (1944–45) and the Supreme Commander of the Allied Powers in Europe (1951–52), resigning to become Republican candidate for President. He sought to contain Soviet expansion in the Middle East.

Eisenhower Doctrine (1957). Pres. Eisenhower offered to help any country in the Middle East to resist Communist encroachment. Under this Doctrine, the U.S. sent troops into Lebanon in 1958 at that government's request when revolutionary activity was stirred up by Pres. Nasser of the United Arab Republic. At the same time the U.S. supported British intervention in Jordan.

Troops were withdrawn when Arab nations pledged that they would not interfere in one another's affairs.

"elastic clause." This clause in the Constitution (Art. I, Sec. 8, Par. 18) has permitted Congress to increase its powers greatly. It contains the implied powers of Congress: "To make all laws which shall be necessary and proper for carrying into execution the foregoing powers, and all other powers vested by this Constitution in the Government of the United States, or in any department or officer thereof."

Congress, for example, holds that labor disputes may interfere with its power "to regulate commerce . . . among the several States. . . ." (Art. I, Sec. 8, Par. 3); therefore it is "necessary and proper" to pass labor laws.

Election of 1788. George Washington was regarded as the obvious choice to be the first to hold the office of President even as provision for the office was being hammered out in the Constitutional Convention (1787). He was unanimously elected when the electors cast their ballots on the first Wednesday in February 1789. His total electoral vote was 69. There was a possible 91 votes if the electors of all 13 states had voted. However, two states failed to ratify in time; New York did not choose electors and four electors did not vote.

John Adams received most of the electors' second votes (each elector had two votes), a total of 34, and was elected Vice-President. There was a scattering of votes for 11 candidates, including John Jay, John Hancock and George Clinton.

Although there were no party designations, Washington and Adams take their place in political history as Federalists.

Election of 1792. Pres. Washington feared the growth of factionalism. It was his fear of disunity that impelled him to accept a second term for which he was again elected unanimously with 132 votes cast by electors in 15 states.

John Adams for Vice-President had some rough opposition from anti-Federalists but he defeated George Clinton of New York by a vote of 77 to 50.

Election of 1796. The campaign of 1796 was bitter. Newly formed parties contested the role of the U.S. in the French Revolution and disagreed over the Jay Treaty (Treaty of London).

Federalists nominated John Adams of Massachusetts for President and Thomas Pinckney of South Carolina for Vice-President. Republicans nominated Thomas Jefferson of Virginia for President and Aaron Burr of New York for Vice-President. Electors were chosen by 16 states.

Adams was elected President by only three electoral votes. He received 71 votes to 68 for Jefferson.

Hamilton had grown cool to Adams and sought to maneuver Pinckney into the Presidency. The plan backfired and Jefferson got the second largest number of electoral votes and the Vice-Presidency. Since this was prior to the adoption of the 12th Amendment (1804) it was possible for men of opposing parties to gain the number one and two positions in the national government.

Election of 1800. The split in the Federalist party pitted Adams against Hamilton on the issue of war with France. The Republicans (Jeffersonian) were pro-French and embittered by the Alien and Sedition Acts which the Federalists had passed as a curb on the growth of their party.

The Federalists decided on John Adams and Charles C. Pinckney as candidates for

President and Vice-President, respectively. The Republican caucus named Thomas Jefferson and Aaron Burr. Electors were chosen by 17 states.

Jefferson and Burr each received 73 electoral votes. Adams received 65 and Pinckney 64 votes. The intent of the electors was clearly to elect Jefferson as President and Burr as Vice-President. This was the eventual result but not before the Federalists had forced the election into the House of Representatives by seeking to confound the Republicans and make Burr President.

The 12th Amendment has prevented any recurrence.

Election of 1804. Jefferson's first administration record assured him of selection, once again, as the Democratic-Republican (Jeffersonian) party candidate for President. Burr was dropped as Vice-President and George Clinton, also of New York, took his place. The Federalists chose Charles C. Pinckney of South Carolina and Rufus King of New York for President and Vice-President respectively. Electors were chosen by 17 states.

Jefferson was overwhelmingly elected with 162 electoral votes. Pinckney received 14 votes. This was the first election after ratification of the 12th Amendment and each elector voted once for a President and a Vice-President. Clinton was elected with Jefferson, but his designation as Vice-President was clear.

Election of 1808. Differences over the Embargo Act split the Republican party (Jeffersonian) and revived the Federalists' hope of regaining the Presidency.

Jefferson decided to follow the precedent of Washington and declined a third term. He supported Madison, who was chosen by the caucus over Monroe. George Clinton was supported by Independent Republicans on the seaboard who were as much opposed to the embargo as the Federalists. Clinton settled for the Vice-Presidency although he carried New York's six electoral votes for President.

In nominating Pinckney of South Carolina for President, the Federalists sought to show, once again, that they were a national and not a New England party. King was nominated for Vice-President. Electors were chosen by 17 states.

The Republicans (Jeffersonian) won. Madison received 122 electoral votes for President. Clinton ran behind the ticket but won the Vice-Presidency. Pinckney and King each garnered 47 electoral votes. The Federalists made gains in the House of Representatives, but the Republicans retained a majority.

Election of 1812. The Napoleonic Wars split the Republicans (Jeffersonian). Many detested Napoleon as a despot and believed that Madison's neutrality policy was aiding Napoleon. Even more important, disruption of trade alienated the Northeast.

Madison, who wanted peace, became the candidate of the "War Hawks." Anti-administration Republicans nominated De Witt Clinton of New York who was supported by Federalists. Electors were chosen by 18 states.

Madison was reelected, winning 128 electoral votes, with his running mate Elbridge Gerry of Massachusetts, who did not carry his own state. Clinton received 89 electoral votes carrying every northern state, except Pennsylvania and Vermont.

Election of 1816. James Monroe gained the Republican (Jeffersonian) nomination for President over the unsuccessful opposition of William H. Crawford of Georgia who had the support of the old Randolph state-rights contingent. The Federalists nominated the last of their candidates for President, Rufus King of New York. Electors were chosen by 19 states.

Monroe won easily with 183 electoral votes to 34 for King. Daniel D. Tompkins of New York was elected Vice-President.

Election of 1820. The Republicans (Jeffersonian) showed so much concern for protecting manufacturers in the tariff and chartering a national bank that differences within the party that divided New England and the South were reconciled. The

Federalist party, virtually dead, did not nominate candidates.

Electors were chosen by 24 states in 1820 and Monroe, who was unopposed for the Presidency, was reelected with 231 out of 232 electoral votes. A single vote was cast for John Q. Adams by an elector who felt that George Washington alone should have the honor of a unanimous election. Some sources, however, hold that he opposed the Virginia dynasty of Presidents. Daniel D. Tompkins of New York was reelected Vice-President.

Election of 1824. With the completion of Monroe's second term, the Republican party divided over his successor. Sectional candidates were put forward. The South was behind Sec. of the Treasury William Crawford of Georgia, who was the nominee of the Republican caucus. New England supported Sec. of State John Quincy Adams of Massachusetts. Speaker of the House Henry Clay of Kentucky was a spokesman for the West. Andrew Jackson of Tennessee was a westerner but the military hero's supporters cut across regional lines. Sec. of War John Calhoun of South Carolina withdrew as a candidate and was on both the Adams and Jackson tickets as Vice-President. Electors were chosen by 24 states.

The Electoral College vote was Jackson 99, Adams 84, Crawford 41, Clay 37. Jackson also topped the field with his popular vote. Since no candidate had a majority of the

211

electoral vote, the election was decided in the House of Representatives. Clay was eliminated since he had the lowest vote. His views, however, as expressed in the American system, were closest to Adams' to whom he moved his support. Adams was elected President and Calhoun, who had received 182 electoral votes, was Vice-President.

When Adams named Clay as his Sec. of State, a stepping stone to the Presidency, Jackson's supporters screamed "corrupt bargain" and kept the cry up during the course of the clouded administration of Adams.

Election of 1828. The campaign for this election began in 1824 when John Q. Adams' election was attributed to a "corrupt bargain" between him and Clay. The campaign was marked by charges against both Jackson, the candidate of the Democratic-Republican party and Adams, the candidate of the National Republicans. Calhoun was the vice-presidential candidate on Jackson's ticket. A democratic tide was marked by a large increase of voters in the 24 states that chose electors.

Jackson received 178 electoral votes and was elected President. Calhoun became Vice-President. Adams received 83 votes. Jackson carried the South and West and Pennsylvania in the Middle States. The frontier hero accepted his election as vindica-

tion of his charges against Adams.

Election of 1832. The major campaign issue was Jackson's veto of the recharter of the United States Bank, which he charged with being a monopoly. The Bank was defended by Henry Clay, who became the candidate of the National Republicans. Jackson was renominated by the Democratic party and Martin Van Buren was chosen as his running mate. Calhoun was dropped when he split with Jackson in 1830 over the tariff.

This was the first election in which the parties resorted to national nominating conventions. A newly formed Anti-Masonic party nominated William Wirt. Electors were chosen by 25 states.

Jackson was reelected overwhelmingly with 219 electoral votes and an even larger percentage of the popular vote than in 1828. Clay received 49 votes; Wirt, 7. The Nullifiers of South Carolina cast 11 votes for John Floyd of Virginia.

Jackson had accurately sensed the mood of the voters on the bank issue.

Election of 1836. The outgoing Jackson supported Van Buren for the Presidency and thus secured him the nomination of the Democratic party. The opposition was united in their dislike for Jackson and anyone whom he supported. They realized, however, that they could not hope to defeat Van

Buren unless they so divided the electoral vote that the election would again be thrown into the House of Representatives as it had been in 1824.

The newly formed Whig party decided upon the strategy of nominating several sectional candidates. Their strongest candidate was William Henry Harrison of Ohio who was also nominated by the Anti-Masonic party. Other candidates were Judge Hugh L. White, who opposed Jackson in Tennessee, and Daniel Webster, the choice of a Massachusetts legislative caucus. Electors were chosen by 26 states.

Van Buren's popular vote was a small majority over that of his combined opposition. In the Electoral College he won decisively with 170 votes to Harrison's 73, White's 26 and Webster's 14. William P. Mangum, South Carolina's anti-Jackson candidate, received 11 votes.

Since there was no majority for a Vice-President, the election was decided in the Senate. Richard M. Johnson, on Van Buren's ticket, was the only Vice-President to be so elected in the history of the U.S.

Election of 1840. Van Buren was renominated by the Democratic party, but the Panic of 1837 and the ensuing depression were too much of a handicap for him to win reelection.

The recently formed Whig party rejected Clay, their national leader, who was opposed by Webster, and nominated the military hero, William Henry Harrison of Ohio. For Vice-President, in deference to Southern Whigs, they chose John Tyler of Virginia.

The Whig campaign slogan was "Tippecanoe and Tyler Too." They pictured Van Buren as luxuriating in splendor and turned Democratic charges to the advantage of Harrison who was portrayed in a "log cabin and hard cider" posture in complete disregard of his gentlemanly origins.

The Whigs won a smashing victory. Harrison received 234 electoral votes to Van Buren's 60. The candidate of the Liberty party, James G. Birney, did not receive any electoral votes. Electors were chosen by 26 states.

The Whig triumph was short-lived, for Harrison died one month after taking office and Tyler's policies divided the party.

Election of 1844. The major issue was the annexation of Texas, over which the country was divided.

The Democratic convention was deadlocked over choice of a candidate. The first "dark horse" in American politics, James K. Polk of Tennessee, won the nomination. Van Buren's stand against annexation cost him the nomination.

The Whigs nominated Henry Clay of Kentucky, who sought to straddle the annexation issue. Theodore Frelinghuysen of New Jersey was the candidate for Vice-President. The Whigs campaigned for a protective tariff and establishment of a national bank.

Polk was elected President with George M. Dallas as Vice-President. The popular vote provided the Democrats with a narrow margin of victory. This hardly committed the nation to the annexation of Texas and reannexation of Oregon, Polk's campaign pledge.

Electors were chosen by 26 states and Polk received 170 electoral votes to Clay's 105. The antislavery Liberty party, which again chose James G. Birney as its candidate, took away enough votes from the Whigs in New York to give the Democrats the state and perhaps the election.

Election of 1848. Although the controversy over slavery was sharpening, the major parties in this election campaign slurred over the issues.

The Whigs passed over the controversial party leaders, Webster and Clay, to nominate the Mexican War hero, Gen. Zachary Taylor. The Democrats nominated Lewis Cass of Michigan. The Free-Soil party, comprised of dissident elements in both Whig and Democratic parties, united on Van Buren who had repudiated slavery.

Taylor was elected President and Millard Fillmore of New York, Vice-President. The popular vote gave the Whigs a 5% margin of victory. Electors were chosen by 30 states. Taylor received 163 electoral votes to Cass' 127. Van Buren won no electoral votes, but his popular vote caused Cass to lose New York and contributed to the Whig victory.

Taylor died after two years in office and was succeeded by Fillmore, who did not win the Whig presidential nomination in 1852.

Election of 1852. Both major parties, Whigs and Democrats, supported the Compromise of 1850 and hoped the slavery controversy would abate.

The Democrats again selected a "dark horse," Franklin K. Pierce of New Hampshire, when they could not agree on one of the front runners—Lewis Cass and Stephen Douglas, the "popular sovereignty" advocates, or James Buchanan of Pennsylvania who had southern support.

The Whigs were badly split between North and South on the slavery issue. They rejected Pres. Fillmore who had antagonized "Conscience Whigs" by supporting the Fugitive Slave Law. They tried once again to win with a Mexican War hero, Gen. Winfield Scott.

Pierce, the Democrat, was elected President and William R. King of Alabama, Vice-President. They received a heavy popular and electoral vote. Electors were chosen by 31 states. Pierce received 254 electoral votes to Scott's 42. The Free-Soil candidate, John P. Hale, ran a poor third.

The election heralded the dissolution of the Whig party, a consequence of the controversy over slavery which continued to be a divisive force.

Election of 1856.

The growing split in the nation over the slavery issue was evident in the election campaign.

The Democrats passed over Douglas and nominated the conservative James Buchanan of Pennsylvania. As American minister to England during the Pierce administration, he had avoided party squabbles. The newly formed Republican party nominated the soldier-explorer, John C. Frémont. The party opposed extension of slavery and favored free homesteads and a high tariff. The Native American (Know-Nothing) party nominated ex-Pres. Fillmore.

Buchanan was elected President and John C. Breckinridge of Kentucky, Vice-President. Electors were chosen in 31 states. Buchanan received 174 electoral votes, Frémont 114 and Fillmore 8. Buchanan's popular vote was only 45% of the total. New England voted overwhelmingly for Frémont. The sectional character of the voting did not augur well for the unity of the nation.

Election of 1860.

Four parties contested for the Presidency in this election on the eve of the Civil War. The slavery controversy was at its height and the sectional division was sharp enough to create the great split in the Democratic party that made possible a Republican victory.

The Democrats met first at Charleston, S.C., but could not agree on a candidate when Southern extremists insisted on a guarantee for slavery that would prevent any limitation of it in the territories. They moved on to Baltimore where Stephen Douglas of Illinois and Herschel Johnson of Georgia were nominated on a "popular sovereignty" platform. The southern wing of the party left the convention and nominated John C. Breckinridge of Kentucky and Joseph Lane of Oregon.

Republicans meeting in Chicago sensed victory. They avoided nominating the controversial William Seward or Solomon Chase and decided on Abraham Lincoln of Illinois and Hannibal Hamlin of Maine. The party opposed extension of slavery into the territories, appealed to Pennsylvania voters with a high tariff plank and sought western support with the promise of free homesteads.

The Constitutional Union party made up of conservative remnants of Whigs and Know-Nothings (Native American party) nominated John Bell of Tennessee and Edward Everett of Massachusetts who called for preservation of the Union but would not commit themselves to any controversial position on slavery.

Electors were chosen by 33 states. Lincoln won a majority in the Electoral College with 180 votes, but his popular vote (40% of the total) made him a minority President. Douglas with 30% of the popular vote won only 12 electoral votes.

Breckinridge won 72 electoral votes and 18% of the popular votes. Bell did well in the border states, garnering 39 electoral votes, but showed up poorly in the popular vote column.

Although no informed southerner could believe that Lincoln's election meant the abolition of slavery in the states where it had been legal, the threat that his election would mean secession was carried out.

Election of 1864. The military reverses of the Union forces made Lincoln's renomination doubtful for a time. Radical Republicans, however, were divided among themselves and the Chicago convention decided on Lincoln and Andrew Johnson of Tennessee, a "War Democrat," as his running mate. Since the party was augmented by "War Democrats," it called itself the Union party and pledged victory on the battlefield as a means of achieving reunification of the nation.

The Democrats charged the Republicans with "war failure" and called for an end to the war and restoration of the Union on the old basis. They nominated Gen. George McClellan for President and George Pendleton for Vice-President. McClellan, who did not share the "Peace Democrats" view, repudiated the platform.

Sherman's victory at Atlanta gave the Union party the needed lift and Lincoln was re-elected with 55% of the popular vote. There were 36 states, but 11 seceded states did not choose electors. Lincoln won 212 electoral votes to McClellan's 21.

Pres. Lincoln was assassinated less than six weeks after his second inauguration. Vice-President Johnson succeeded to the Presidency on Apr. 15, 1865.

Election of 1868. Congress' Reconstruction plan for the South and cheap money were the issues in this election.

The Republican party, controlled by radicals, rejected Pres. Johnson who unsuccessfully sought the Democratic nomination. Instead, it chose a war hero, Ulysses S. Grant, for President and Schuyler Colfax of Indiana for Vice-President. They "waved the bloody shirt" by labeling the Democrats the party of treason. The Democratic call for payment of the national debt with greenbacks was denounced as disloyalty to the nation's creditors.

The Democrats nominated former Gov. Horatio Seymour of New York for President and Frank Blair of Missouri for Vice-President.

Grant won only 53% of the popular vote but received 214 electoral votes to Seymour's 80.

The victorious Republicans accepted the election as a mandate for continuing the Radical Reconstruction program in the South. The nation's creditors were assured of the repayment of bonds in gold although this form of payment had not been specified.

216

Election of 1872. The corruption with which the Grant administration was charged and dissatisfaction with Radical Republican Reconstruction policy in the South caused a split in the Republican party.

Radical Republicans, for their part, stood behind Grant who was renominated. Henry Wilson of Massachusetts was the candidate for Vice-President.

Liberal Republicans attracted dissidents from all sides and were united only in their opposion to Grant. Horace Greeley was nominated for President. Greeley, editor of the New York *Tribune*, had been embroiled in controversy for 30 years. He was mercilessly lampooned in the press. B. Gratz Brown of Missouri was the nominee for Vice-President. The new party included the civil service reformer Carl Schurz, but gathered in its folds malcontent Republicans who had not shared in the spoils. Democrats endorsed the Liberal Republican party candidates.

Grant was reelected with a resounding 56% majority of the popular vote. He received 286 electoral votes to Greeley's 66.

Election of 1876. Republican scandals, civil service reform and the continuing controversy over hard versus soft money were the issues. Republicans continued to "wave the bloody shirt." The election is memorable because of the dispute over the electoral returns, which was settled without bloodshed. Republican "Stalwarts" would

have liked to renominate Grant for a third term, but a boom for James G. Blaine made this impractical. When the "Stalwarts" rejected Blaine, Gov. Rutherford B. Hayes of Ohio became the compromise candidate of the convention. William A. Wheeler of New York was nominated for Vice-President.

The Democrats had been out of office for 16 years and felt that Republican corruption made this their year. They nominated Samuel J. Tilden, reform governor of New York, on the first ballot. Thomas A. Hendricks of Indiana became the candidate for Vice-President.

As the returns came in, it seemed clear that Tilden was elected. He had a plurality of 250,000 votes and 184 of the 185 electoral votes needed for election. However, election irregularities permitted Republican strategists to question returns from Louisiana, Florida and South Carolina; in addition, Democrats claimed one vote from Oregon. In all there were 20 electoral votes in dispute and only one was needed to assure Tilden's election.

Congress created an electoral commission evenly divided between Republicans and Democrats. The 15th member was a Republican judge acceptable to the Democrats because of some of his decisions. The commission decided by a majority of one that all 20 disputed electoral votes should go to Hayes, the Republican candidate.

Hayes' designation as President might have been delayed by a Democratic filibuster, but southern Democrats accepted Hayes when it was promised that carpetbag government would be ended in the South; that southerners would be represented in Hayes' Cabinet and subsidies would be granted to southern railroads.

Election of 1880. Serious issues such as civil service reform and the tariff were bypassed in the campaign. Veterans' pensions and Chinese exclusion were placed in the forefront.

Republican "Stalwarts" sought to revive and run Grant for a third term. Another faction within the party wanted Blaine. The result was a "dark horse" candidate, James A. Garfield of Ohio. To conciliate the "Stalwart" wing of the party, Chester A. Arthur of New York was named as his running mate.

Democrats nominated a Civil War hero of the battle of Gettysburg, Winfield Scott Hancock. Their candidate for Vice-President was William H. English of Indiana.

Hancock described the tariff as a local issue and was ridiculed for it. Thomas Nast caricatured Hancock asking one of his fellow Democrats, "Who is Tariff, and why is he for revenue only?"

Garfield squeaked through with a slender plurality of 9,464 votes out of a total of almost nine million cast. His electoral majority of 214 to Hancock's 155 was made possible by narrow victories in the pivotal states of Indiana and New York. The candidate of the Greenback party, Peter Cooper, received about 300,000 votes.

Garfield was assassinated in 1881 and Arthur succeeded to the Presidency.

Election of 1884. Currency and tariff, which might have been the chief issues, were subordinated to personal vilification in one of the dirtiest campaigns in American history.

Republicans rejected Pres. Arthur and nominated James G. Blaine of Maine, a long-time aspirant for the Presidency. Blaine's record had been tarnished by financial manipulations. Reformers took the view that he had "wallowed in spoils like a rhinoceros in an African pool." Since Blaine had no war record, the party nominated a political general, John A. Logan of Illinois, for Vice-President. Reformers, known as Mugwumps, bolted the party and became Cleveland Democrats.

The Democrats nominated Grover Cleveland, reform governor of New York, for President. Cleveland had admitted paternity of an illegitimate child and the scandal gave rise to the Republican cry, "Ma, ma! Where's my Pa?" to which unabashed Democrats replied, "Gone to the White House, Ha, Ha, Ha!" Thomas A. Hendricks of Indiana was nominated for Vice-President.

The Prohibition party nominated John P. St. John of Kansas. The Greenback party nominated Benjamin F. Butler of Massachusetts whose name was linked with harsh Reconstruction policies.

Cleveland led the Democrats back to the White House after 24 years in the desert. His popular plurality was only 23,-000 out of 10 million votes cast. In the Electoral College he received 219 votes to Blaine's 182.

Cleveland's victory in New York by a mere 1,149 votes was the deciding factor. Blaine had failed to rebuke a clergyman who had called the Democrats the party of "rum, Romanism and rebellion." The slur alienated Irish voters and probably cost Blaine New York and the Presidency.

Election of 1888. The tariff was the major issue in the campaign with the Democrats standing for lowered duties and the Republicans calling for a high tariff.

Pres. Cleveland was renominated by the Democrats. His new running mate was 75-year-old Allen G. Thurman of Ohio, no help to Cleveland, who did not campaign actively.

Republicans nominated Benjamin Harrison of Indiana, grandson of "Old Tippecanoe." Levi P. Morton of New York was the candidate for Vice-President.

The Prohibition candidate was Clinton B. Fisk of New Jersey. The Union Labor party nominated Alson J. Streeter of Illinois for President and the United Labor party nominated Robert H. Cowdrey of Illinois.

Cleveland received 100,000 more popular votes than Harrison, but lost the election in the Electoral College. Harrison received 233 votes to Cleveland's 168. A fatal factor was the statement by the British minister in Washington that Cleveland would be friendlier to England than Harrison. This was used by the Republicans to buttress their argument that Cleveland's tariff views would favor English industrialists. Irish voters in New York, a key state, moved out of the Democratic column in sufficient numbers to swing the state into the Republican column.

Election of 1892. Republicans stopped "waving the bloody shirt" and stuck to the issues. They defended their shaky positions on the high McKinley Tariff of 1890 and the Sherman Silver Purchase Act against Democratic and Populist party opposition.

Republicans renominated Pres. Benjamin Harrison. Whitelaw Reid of New York was their candidate for Vice-President. Democrats turned to ex-Pres. Grover Cleveland and Adlai E. Stevenson of Illinois for Vice-President. The Populist party nominated James B. Weaver of Iowa and James G. Field of Virginia as candidates for President and Vice-President. The Prohibition candidate for President was John Bidwell. The Socialist-Labor party nominated Simon Wing of Massachusetts.

Democrats, who sensed victory after the congressional elections of 1890, won the election. They were aided by Populists who cut into Republican strongholds in the Midwest. Cleveland won 46% of the popular vote and 277 electoral votes to Harrison's 43% and 145 votes. The farm protest showed vigor in the large popular vote of over a million for Weaver who received 22 electoral votes.

Business was content with the Democrats' return because of their confidence in Cleveland's hard money views at a time when free silver sentiment was rampant in the nation.

Election of 1896. In one of the most dramatic campaigns in American history, conservative business interests in the East furnished the financial support that helped to overwhelm an alliance of free silverites and discontented farmers. Republicans stood for the gold standard and high tariff against a combination of Democrats and Populists who urged free silver, a lower tariff and a host of political reforms, including the direct income tax.

Republicans nominated William McKinley of Ohio whose candidacy and campaign were supported by the Ohio industrialist, Marcus Alonzo Hanna. Garret A. Hobart of New Jersey was the candidate for Vice-President. The Democrats rejected Cleveland and nominated William Jennings Bryan of Nebraska, following his electrifying "Cross of Gold" speech. Some gold Democrats bolted the convention.

Populists also nominated Bryan, rather than divide the free silver vote. They could not, however, stomach the Democratic candidate for Vice-President, Arthur Sewall, a Maine banker, and nominated Thomas E. Watson of Georgia. Bryan was not helped by Vice-Presidential campaigners at odds with each other.

Minor party nominees for President were John M. Palmer, Nationalist (gold) Democratic; Joshua Levering, Prohibition; Charles H. Marchett, Socialist-Labor; Charles E. Bentley, Nationalist.

The Republicans triumphed with McKinley winning a 600,-000 popular vote plurality and receiving 271 electoral votes to Bryan's 176. Bryan carried the Solid South, Great Plains and Rocky Mountain states. McKinley carried all of the thickly populated states of the Northeast and Middle West, plus California and Oregon.

Republicans linked Bryanism with anarchy and revolution during the campaign and employers pressured their workers to save their jobs by voting Republican. This accounts, in part, for Bryan's defeat. Bryan failed to attract urban support and farmers themselves were divided over his candidacy, as evidenced by the loss of such states as Iowa, Minnesota and North Dakota. A rise in wheat prices before the election undercut the agrarian discontent expressed by Bryan in a campaign that took him over 18,-000 miles, while McKinley stayed on his front porch in Canton, O.

Election of 1900. The paramount issue was imperialism, with free silver and the tariff taking subordinate places in this return engagement of the major party candidates. Republicans upheld the gold standard and promised the people of the new territories as much freedom as was consistent with American responsibility. Democrats raised the cry of "imperialism."

Republicans renominated Pres. McKinley and campaigned on "the full dinner pail" slogan, a symbol of Republican prosperity. Gov. Theodore Roosevelt of New York was nominated for Vice-President in a successful move by "Boss" Platt to get Roosevelt out of state politics.

Democrats renominated William J. Bryan. Adlai E. Stevenson of Illinois was the candidate for Vice-President. Fusion Populists also endorsed Bryan.

Other minority party candidates for President were Wharton Baker, People's (Anti-Fusion); Eugene V. Debs, Socialist Democrat; John C. Woolley, Prohibition; Joseph F. Maloney, Socialist Labor; Seth H. Ellis, Union-Reform; Jonah F. R. Leonard, United Christian.

McKinley won handily with a plurality of almost a million popular votes. He received 292 electoral votes to Bryan's 155.

Theodore Roosevelt succeeded to the Presidency in 1901, after McKinley's assassination.

Election of 1904. Businessmen contributed so heavily to Republican campaign funds in this election that Democrats charged it was bribery to suppress impending investigations.

Republicans nominated Pres. Theodore Roosevelt by acclamation. His only possible rival for the nomination, Sen. Marcus Hanna of Ohio, had died earlier in the year. Charles W. Fairbanks of Indiana was chosen for Vice-President.

Democrats rejected Bryanism and nominated conservative Judge Alton B. Parker of New York for President and Henry G. Davis of West Virginia for Vice-President.

Minor party candidates for President were Eugene V. Debs, Socialist; Silas C. Swallow, Prohibition; Thomas E. Watson, People's; Charles H. Corregan, Socialist Labor; Austin Holcomb, Continental.

Roosevelt's popularity was attested to by his huge popular margin of 2,500,000 votes. He received 336 electoral votes to Parker's 140.

Election of 1908. Progressive reforms under Theodore Roosevelt left the Democrats virtually without issues. Roosevelt conformed to the third-term tradition and gave his support for the Republican nomination to William Howard Taft of Ohio. James S. Sherman of New York became the candidate for Vice-President.

Democrats, who had lost badly with conservative Judge Parker, returned to Bryan, the

"Great Commoner," for the third and last time. John W. Kern of Indiana was nominated for Vice-President. They campaigned on a platform that condemned monopolies and pledged a reduction in tariff rates.

Minor party candidates for President were Eugene V. Debs, Socialist; Eugene W. Chafin, Prohibition; Thomas L. Hisgen, Independence; Daniel B. Turney, United Christian; Thomas E. Watson, People's; August Gillhaus, Socialist Labor.

Taft won by more than a million popular votes. He received 321 electoral votes to Bryan's 162.

Election of 1912. This was a three-cornered fight with the conservative position defended by the Republican party and the progressives represented by the Democratic party and newly formed Progressive party.

Republican regulars renominated Pres. Taft and Vice-Pres. Sherman. Progressives bolted and formed their own party. They nominated Theodore Roosevelt for President and Hiram W. Johnson of California for Vice-President. Democrats, too, had a tough fight in the convention before agreeing on Gov. Woodrow Wilson of New Jersey for President and Thomas R. Marshall of Indiana for Vice-President. Bryan, by giving his support to Wilson, helped defeat "Champ" Clark's bid for the nomination.

Minor party nominees for President were Eugene V. Debs, Socialist; Eugene W. Chafin,

Prohibition; Arthur E. Reimer, Socialist Labor.

Wilson won 42% of the popular vote but the Republican split gave him command of the Electoral College in which he received 435 votes. Roosevelt won 28% of the popular votes and 88 electoral votes; Taft 23% and 8 votes. Debs polled over 900,000 votes, the largest proportion of the total votes cast ever achieved by a Socialist presidential candidate.

The nation was clearly committed to progressive legislation.

Election of 1916. Democrats defended their peace program, while yielding to demands for greater preparedness. They defended progressive legislation, including business regulation and a lowered tariff. Republicans united on a candidate, but the party was divided from within between war-minded and pacifist (or pro-German) elements.

Democrats renominated Pres. Wilson and Vice-Pres. Thomas R. Marshall. Republicans nominated Justice Charles Evans Hughes of the U.S. Supreme Court for President and Charles W. Fairbanks of Indiana for Vice-President. Theodore Roosevelt had hoped for the Republican nomination and was nominated by the Progressive party, but he scrapped the party and campaigned for Hughes.

Minor party candidates for President were A. L. Benson, Socialist; J. Frank Hanly, Prohibition; Arthur E. Reimer, Socialist Labor.

The election results fluctuated with Hughes going to sleep thinking that he was President; but California went to Wilson by 4,000 votes and he was reelected with 49% of the popular vote and 277 electoral votes to Hughes' 46% and 254 votes.

Election of 1920. It was Wilson's hope that this election would be "a great and solemn referendum" on the League of Nations, which the Senate had rejected. The Republicans were evasive on the issue, but there was a reaction in the nation against the demands imposed by World War I and Wilson's idealism.

Democrats could not agree on any of the party leaders. On the 44th ballot they nominated Gov. James M. Cox of Ohio for President and young Assistant Secretary of the Navy Franklin D. Roosevelt for Vice-President.

Republicans, casting about for a candidate, hit upon Sen. Warren G. Harding of Ohio. Gov. Calvin Coolidge of Massachusetts was nominated for Vice-President.

Minor party candidates for President were Eugene V. Debs, Socialist, in prison for violation of the Espionage Act; P. P. Christensen, Farmer - Labor; Aaron S. Watkins, Prohibition; James E. Ferguson, American; W. W. Cox, Socialist Labor; Robert C. Macauley, Single Tax. All of the minor parties combined received less than 6% of the total popular vote.

Democrats received only 34% of the popular vote, the worst defeat experienced by a major party candidate up to that time. Harding won 404 electoral votes to Cox's 127.

Since both major party candidates were relatively unknown, the Republican victory was considered a rejection of Wilson and what he stood for. When Harding died on Aug. 2, 1923, Coolidge became President.

Election of 1924. "Coolidge prosperity" counterbalanced the scandals of the Harding administration. Democrats were divided over whether to condemn the Ku Klux Klan in their platform and decided not to do so. The Progressive platform challenged the conservative major parties and created much of the excitement in an otherwise apathetic campaign.

Republicans nominated Pres. Coolidge and Charles G. Dawes of Illinois as his running mate. Democrats were divided over the two front-running candidates, William Gibbs McAdoo of California, Wilson's son-in-law, and Gov. Alfred E. Smith of New York, a Catholic. Party division made the nomination worthless and it went to a New York corporation lawyer, John W. Davis, on the 103rd ballot. Charles W. Bryan of Nebraska was nominated for Vice-President in recognition of growing farm discontent. The Progressive party nominated Senator Robert M. La Follette of Wisconsin for President and Senator Burton K. Wheeler of Montana for Vice-President. They were supported by the Socialists.

Other party candidates for President were Herman P. Faris, Prohibition; Frank T. Johns, Socialist Labor; William Z. Foster, Workers; Gilbert O. Nations, American; William J. Wallace, Commonwealth Land.

Republicans again won by so substantial a majority that the two-party system seemed to be giving way. Coolidge received 54% of the popular vote and 382 electoral votes; Davis 29% and 136 votes; La Follette, 17% and 13 votes.

Election of 1928. Repeal of the Prohibition amendment and the religion of the Democratic candidate were the issues. Basic economic policy was not challenged by either major party. Industrial prosperity quieted the criticism which had produced five million votes for minority party candidates in the previous presidential election.

Pres. Coolidge stated that he did not "choose to run." Republicans then united behind Herbert Hoover, Sec. of Commerce, who had gained an international reputation in administering relief in Europe after World War I. Sen. Charles Curtis of Kansas was nominated for Vice-President. Democrats nominated Gov. Alfred E. Smith of New York. Smith was a "wet" (opposed to prohibition) and Catholic. Sen. Joseph T. Robinson of Arkansas was nominated for Vice-President.

Minority party candidates for President were Norman Thomas, Socialist; William Z. Foster, Communist; William D. Upshaw, Prohibition; William H. Harvey, Liberty; Verne L. Reynolds, Socialist Labor; Jacob S. Coxey, Sr., Farmer-Labor.

Republicans won decisively and carried five states in the "Solid South." Bigotry played a part in Smith's defeat, but it was not likely that any Democratic candidate could have prevailed against Hoover, who won 58% of the popular vote and 444 electoral votes to Smith's 41% and 87 votes.

Election of 1932. Deep depression, part of a worldwide economic decline, made the causes and the proposed cures the major issue of the campaign. Republicans warned against government interference with business. Democrats leaned toward greater government direction of the economy.

Republicans renominated Hoover and Curtis. Democrats nominated Gov. Franklin D. Roosevelt of New York on the fourth ballot. Speaker of the House John Nance Garner of Texas became his running mate. Roosevelt was the first presidential nominee to go to the convention to accept the nomination of his party. It was there that he proclaimed: "I pledge you, I pledge myself to a new deal for the American people."

Minor party candidates for President were Norman Thomas, Socialist; William Z. Foster, Communist; William D. Upshaw, Prohibition; William H. Harvey,

Liberty; Verne L. Reynolds, Socialist Labor; Jacob S. Coxey, Sr., Farmer-Labor.

Democrats turned the Republicans out of office after their 12-year stay. Both houses of Congress fell to Democrats by great majorities. Roosevelt won 57% of the popular vote and 472 electoral votes to Hoover's 40% and 59 electoral votes. Hoover carried only six states.

Election of 1936. Republicans denounced New Deal encroachments on business and American institutions. Democrats pointed to the progress which had been made in getting the country out of the slough of the depression and denounced "economic royalists" who were indifferent to the needs of the people.

Roosevelt and Garner were renominated by the Democrats. Republicans nominated Gov. Alfred M. Landon of Kansas for President and Frank Knox, a Chicago newspaper publisher, for Vice-President.

Minority party candidates for President were William Lemke, Union; Norman Thomas, Socialist; Earl Browder, Communist; John Aiken, Socialist Labor; D. Leigh Colvin, Prohibition and Commonwealth.

The popular vote was the largest up to that time—over 45 million. Roosevelt was overwhelmingly elected with 61% of the popular vote and 523 electoral votes. Landon carried only Maine and Vermont with 37% of the popular vote and eight electoral votes.

Election of 1940. The war in Europe was on and both major parties promised to keep the U.S. out of war. Republicans criticized the secrecy with which aid to the Allies had been undertaken. New Deal reforms were attacked, but the Republicans did not say that they would undo the new legislation.

Republicans rejected isolationist leaders Senators Robert A. Taft of Ohio and Arthur Vandenberg of Michigan. Thomas E. Dewey of New York, who also had isolationist leanings at the time, was turned aside on the sixth ballot for Wendell L. Willkie of New York, former president of the Commonwealth and Southern Corporation, a public utility. Willkie, a magnetic personality, represented the liberal wing of the party in contrast to the "Old Guard." Sen. Charles L. McNary of Oregon was nominated for Vice-President.

Democrats renominated Roosevelt for President, making him the first third-term candidate in the nation's history. This became an issue in the campaign. Henry A. Wallace of Iowa, Sec. of Agriculture, was nominated for Vice-President.

Minor party candidates for President were Norman Thomas, Socialist; Roger Q. Babson, Prohibition; Earl Browder, Communist; John Aiken, Socialist Labor.

Roosevelt triumphed again, but by a smaller margin than in 1936. He won 54% of the popular vote and 449 electoral votes to Willkie's 44% and 82 electoral votes.

Election of 1944. There was no sound issue on which the Republicans could attack since they were committed to the war effort and the war was going well.

Republicans nominated Thomas E. Dewey, youthful governor of New York, for President and Gov. John W. Bricker of Ohio for Vice-President. Democrats renominated Roosevelt for a fourth term. Wallace was dropped as Vice-President when Roosevelt went along with intra-party criticism of Wallace in the South and among city bosses. Sen. Harry S Truman of Missouri gained the nomination on the second ballot. Since Roosevelt died on Apr. 12, 1945, four months after he took office for the fourth time, the nomination for Vice-President had special significance.

Minor party candidates for President were Norman Thomas, Socialist; Claude A. Watson, Prohibition; Edward A. Teichert, Socialist Labor. Texas Regulars voted for unpledged electors.

Roosevelt's popularity continued to be high in his last election. He polled 53% of the popular vote and won 432 electoral votes to Dewey's 46% and 99 votes.

Election of 1948. Republican control of Congress in 1946 seemed to promise victory in 1948. Prospects were enhanced by splits in the Democratic party. A States' Rights Democratic (Dixiecrat) party was organized in the South in protest against the civil rights plank in the Democratic party platform of 1948. Radicals in the party, led by Henry Wallace, seceded to form the Progressive party, which counseled negotiation with Russia to end the cold war.

Republicans for the first time in their history renominated a defeated candidate, Thomas E. Dewey of New York. Governor Earl Warren of California was the party's choice for Vice-President. With little enthusiasm, Democrats nominated Pres. Truman and Sen. Alben W. Barkley of Kentucky for Vice-President. The States' Rights Democratic party nominated Gov. J. Strom Thurmond of South Carolina for President and Gov. Fielding L. Wright of Mississippi for Vice-President.

Minor party candidates for President were Henry Wallace, Progressive; Norman Thomas, Socialist; Claude A. Watson, Prohibition; Edward A. Teichert, Socialist Labor; Farrell Dobbs, Socialist Workers.

In what is regarded as a political miracle, Harry Truman won the election. He received 49.5% of the popular vote and 303 electoral votes to Dewey's 45% and 189 votes. The Dixiecrats with less than 3% of the popular vote won 39 electoral votes.

Election of 1952. Republicans attacked the Democratic party on the grounds of corruption in various executive agencies, negligence in ousting Communists from public office, high costs of government and failure to establish peace in Korea. Democrats had been in the White House since F. D. Roosevelt took over in 1933 and Republicans cried, "It's time for a change." Democrats replied that the Republican party was the "party of reaction" and predicted another depression if the GOP were to win. They defended their New Deal and Fair Deal records.

For their standard bearer, Republicans nominated the enormously popular Gen. Eisenhower who represented the international thinking in the party. Sen. Taft ("Mr. Republican") was turned down by the convention. Sen. Richard Nixon of California was chosen as Eisenhower's running mate.

When Pres. Truman refused renomination, the Democrats turned to Gov. Adlai E. Stevenson of Illinois and Sen. John J. Sparkman of Alabama.

Minor party candidates for President were Vincent Hallinan, Progressive and American Labor; Stuart Hamblen, Prohibition; Eric Haas, Socialist Labor; Darlington Hoopes, Socialist; Farrell Dobbs, Socialist Workers.

The country was not swayed by Stevenson's brilliant speeches. Eisenhower won 55% of the popular vote and 442 electoral votes to Stevenson's 44% and 89 votes.

Election of 1956. Pres. Eisenhower's illness and the controversial character of his running mate permitted Democrats to warn voters about the danger of a Nixon succession. They sought also to capitalize on discontent in the farm belt and weaknesses in foreign policy. They were encouraged by their control of both houses of Congress.

Republicans renominated Eisenhower and Nixon. Democrats put forward, once again, Adlai E. Stevenson and chose Sen. Estes Kefauver of Tennessee to run for Vice-President. The Liberal party supported the Democratic ticket.

Minor party candidates for President were Thomas Coleman Andrews, States' Rights; Harry F. Byrd, Independent; Eric Haas, Socialist Labor; Enoch Holtwick, Prohibition; Darlington Hoopes, Socialist; Henry Krajewski, American Third Party; and Farrell Dobbs, Socialist Workers.

Eisenhower's personal popularity overwhelmed Stevenson with a surge even greater than in 1952. Democrats, however, retained both houses of Congress. Eisenhower polled 57% of the popular vote and 457 electoral votes to Stevenson's 42% and 73 electoral votes.

Election of 1960. Democrats charged that U.S. defenses had lagged; that economic growth had to be increased; that the Republican administration had lowered U.S. prestige abroad.

227

The Republicans defended Eisenhower's record. A much discussed aspect of the campaign was the Democratic candidate's religion.

Democrats nominated Sen. John F. Kennedy of Massachusetts, a Catholic. His running mate was Lyndon B. Johnson of Texas, the powerful Senate majority leader. Republicans nominated Vice-Pres. Richard Nixon who was endorsed by Pres. Eisenhower. His running mate was Henry Cabot Lodge of Massachusetts, former senator and then UN ambassador.

Minor party candidates for President were Eric Haas, Socialist Labor; Farrell Dobbs, Socialist Workers; Rutherford B. Decker, Prohibition; Orval Faubus, National States Rights.

Television debates pitted presidential candidates against each other for the first time. The favorable impression made by Kennedy was a major factor in his narrow victory. Kennedy's popular vote was less than two-tenths of 1% greater than Nixon's. A record high vote of more than 69 million ballots was cast. Kennedy received 303 electoral votes to Nixon's 219. Sen. Harry F. Byrd received 15 electoral votes (unpledged electors in Alabama and Mississippi and one Nixon vote in Oklahoma).

At age 43, Kennedy was the youngest President ever to be elected to that office and the first Catholic to be elected President. He was assassinated on Nov. 22, 1963, and was succeeded by Vice-Pres. Johnson.

Election of 1964. The conservative wing of the Republican party ran the campaign and attacked Democrats for excessive interference in the life of the individual. They called for an end to government competition with private industry. Democrats struck back by accusing Republicans of wanting to undo social reforms that had benefited the great majority of the people. They defended the Kennedy - Johnson administration's accomplishments.

Republicans nominated Sen. Barry Goldwater of Arizona for President and Cong. William E. Miller (N.Y.), an Easterner and a Catholic, for Vice-President. The confidence with which Pres. Johnson took over responsibility following the death of Pres. Kennedy assured him of the Democratic nomination for a full four-year term. Sen. Hubert Humphrey of Minnesota was chosen as his running mate.

Minor party candidates for President were Eric Haas, Socialist Labor; Clifton De Berry, Socialist Workers; Earle H. Munn, Prohibition; John Kasper, National States Rights.

The Johnson-Humphrey ticket rolled up the largest popular vote plurality in U.S. election history. It won 61% of the popular vote and 486 electoral votes to Goldwater's 38% and 52 votes.

Election of 1968. The two major parties were not far apart on the major issues: the war in Viet Nam, the urban crisis (poverty in the city slums) and law and order. Peace talks had started in Paris in May, and the Democrats, in the final weeks of the campaign, indicated that they would take more risks to end the war. The Republicans called for "a progressive de-Americanization" of the war.

President Johnson had withdrawn as a candidate for reelection in March, when he saw the nation deeply divided over his conduct of the war. The Democrats nominated Vice-Pres. Hubert H. Humphrey of Minnesota. Sen. Edmund M. Muskie of Maine, a Catholic, was chosen as his running mate. The nominating convention, held in Chicago (Aug. 26–29), was marred by street fighting in which the Chicago police used considerable force to restrain the anti-war demonstrators from disrupting the convention.

The Republicans nominated former Vice-Pres. Richard M. Nixon, who had been counted as dead politically in 1962, when he was defeated as candidate for governor of California. He then engaged in law practice in New York, while assisting Republicans in local campaigns throughout the nation. The Republican vicepresidential nominee was a surprise candidate, Gov. Spiro T. Agnew of Maryland.

A third-party candidate, George C. Wallace, former Democratic governor of Alabama, campaigned nationally, promising to end riots with troops and bayonets and to revise the guidelines for desegregation. He selected as his running mate on the American Independent party ticket, retired Gen. Curtis E. LeMay, father of the Strategic Air Command.

The election was extremely close. Nixon won only 43.4% of the popular vote to Humphrey's 43%. He gained, however, 302 of the electoral votes to Humphrey's 191. The Wallace candidacy, which for a time threatened to force the election into the House of Representatives, faded in the final weeks, and he carried only five states, all in the South, for a total of 45 electoral votes.

Electoral College. Under the Constitution the President and Vice-President are not elected directly by popular vote of the people, but by electors chosen "as each state legislature should direct." The candidates with a majority of the electoral votes are elected. Only twice in U.S. history has a candidate not been elected although receiving more popular votes than the winning candidate. Hayes received 264,-000 fewer votes than Tilden in 1876, and Harrison received 100,000 fewer votes than Cleveland in 1888. Both Hayes and Harrison won because they polled the larger number of electoral votes.

The electors in each state are equal to the number of that state's representatives plus senators in Congress. Although it has no congressmen, the District of Columbia has three electors (23rd Amendment), the minimum number for a state.

The Founding Fathers did not believe that a scattered and uniform electorate could be entrusted with election of a President. They preferred electors who would exercise their independent judgment. In the event that no one candidate wins a majority of the electoral votes the Constitution provides for election by the House of Representatives from a slate of the leading five candidates (later reduced to three by the 12th Amendment) with each state delegation in the House having a single vote. Only twice in U.S. history, in 1800 and 1824, has an election been decided in the House.

The Founding Fathers failed to anticipate the growth of a party system. Political parties soon nominated candidates and electors have traditionally voted for the candidates nominated by their party. The candidate who wins a majority of the vote in a state receives all of the electoral votes in that state.

At first the electors were chosen by the legislatures in each state, but by 1824 only six of the 24 states failed to choose electors by popular vote. They assemble in their state capitals in mid-December and "vote by ballot" for the President and Vice-President, confirming what was known within a few hours after the balloting ended in early November. The election is officially certified, early in January, at a joint session of the Senate and House of Repre-

sentatives when the President of the Senate counts the ballots received from the Electoral College.

Electoral Count Act (1887). To prevent a repetition of the confusion over electoral votes in the Hayes-Tilden election of 1876, Congress provided that where two sets of electoral returns came in from a state, the governor of the state would decide which set was valid. In short, each state was to be the judge of its own electoral returns.

electric light. The first demonstration of electric home lighting took place at Salem, Mass., 1859. Current supplied by Voltaic battery was conducted to two lamps on the mantelpiece in the home of Prof. Moses G. Farmer. Strips of platinum provided resisting and lighting medium. This was the best artificial light then known but was more expensive than gaslight.

On Oct. 21, 1879, Thomas Edison, working at his Menlo Park, N.J., laboratories, perfected an electric light with a carbonized filament of cotton that would last for about 40 hours.

The first city to be completely lighted by electricity was Cleveland, Ohio, Mar. 31, 1880.

Elementary and Secondary Education Act of 1965. Education history was written when Pres. Johnson signed a law authorizing more than $1.3 billion in federal funds to be channeled into U.S. classrooms to strengthen school programs for educationally deprived children in low income areas. Children in both public and non-public schools are aided under the law. The law also provided additional school library resources, textbooks and other instructional materials. It financed supplementary educational centers and services, broadened areas of cooperative research and strengthened state departments of education.

A major obstacle to school-aid legislation in previous years had been the demand by Roman Catholics that private parochial schools share in the federal-aid program. The Act skirted the conflict by providing that no direct subsidy be given to church-related schools but that needy children be aided by federal funds, whatever school they attend. Books and materials would not be given to church-related schools but to children enrolled in them "on loan." They would remain the property of the public schools. Finally, all aid programs, whether in public or non-public schools, would remain "under the control of the public authority."

elementary school. Generally including the first six or eight grades of the common school system, it has been called the "grade school" or the "grammar school." Its basic purpose has been teaching the fundamentals or the 3-R's—"Readin, Ritin

and Rithmetic." When the British term "primary school" is used in the U.S., it refers to the first two or three grades of the elementary school.

Origins of the elementary or common school in the U.S. may be found in the petty or dame school in 17th-century New England, a carryover from the mother country. The dame school was kept by some woman who had the rudiments of education and for a few pennies a week she taught the children of neighbors in her kitchen or living room. The dame school gave way to the primary school in colonial New England. Children were taught the alphabet and reading and writing became the requirements for admission to the town grammar school. The ungraded school of the 17th and 18th centuries was the so-called common school.

By 1830 a full curriculum had been developed for elementary schools. For younger children it included reading, writing, spelling and good behavior. Older children took advanced reading and spelling, penmanship, arithmetic, geography, grammar, history, manners and morals. For girls, sewing was added to the curriculum.

Up to the end of the 19th century it was expected that most young Americans would end their formal schooling with the completion of the elementary school. Since 1900 the period of compulsory education has lengthened and the proportion of the school population who continue into the secondary school has increased rapidly.

elevated railways. The first "elevated" in America began operation in New York City in 1867 on a single track running from Battery Place through Greenwich Street and Ninth Avenue to 30th Street. It was a financial failure; but other lines, notably the Sixth and Third Avenue "El" lines, were successful, beginning in the 1870's and continuing until the mid-20th century by which time most elevated lines in N.Y.C. were dismantled. At first trains were pulled by a steam locomotive, but the lines were electrified in the early 1900's. Elevated lines wound through other boroughs—Brooklyn and the Bronx—and were constructed in Chicago and Boston.

elevators. The first hydraulic elevator with an adequate safety device for preventing the car from falling was developed in 1852 by Elisha G. Otis of Yonkers, N.Y. This invention has made possible the building of skyscrapers. In 1859 the Fifth Avenue Hotel, N.Y.C., installed the first passenger elevator in a U.S. hotel. In 1868 the Equitable Life Assurance Society built in N.Y.C. the first office building to contain an elevator.

High-speed elevators can now be operated by passengers who simply touch their fingers to an electronic device indicating floor numbers. The hired operator is becoming extinct as automatic operation takes over even in large office buildings.

Eliot, Charles William (1834–1926). Educator. Born in Boston, Mass., he was professor of chemistry, Massachusetts Institute of Technology (1865–69). He was president of Harvard for 40 years, from 1869 to 1909. He developed an "elective system" of undergraduate courses; organized a graduate school of arts and sciences (1890); and raised law and medical school standards. In 1892 he prepared the report of the "Committee of Ten" of the National Education Association, which charged the secondary schools with preparing their students for college. The report prepared the way for the organization of the Board of College Entrance Examinations (1901). He was editor of the widely sold *Harvard Classics* ("five foot shelf").

Eliot, Thomas Stearns (1888–1965). Poet, literary critic and playwright. Born in St. Louis, Mo., he took up residence in London (in 1914) and became a naturalized British citizen (1927). "The Love Song of J. Alfred Prufrock" (1915) irritated American critics, but T. S. Eliot's influence widened as he expressed despair over modern life. Among his many works are *The Waste Land* (poem, 1922), *Elizabethan Essays* (1934), *Murder in the Cathedral* (produced, 1935). He was awarded the Nobel Prize for Literature (1948).

Elkins Act (1903). Rebates (reductions in freight rates) given by railroads to some shippers were forbidden. The law was favored by the railroads themselves. Under the Act both shippers and railroads were liable to punishment if they departed from the published freight rates.

The Act, however, did not give the Interstate Commerce Commission the power to fix rates, which was what farmers and businessmen wanted most.

Emancipation Proclamation. The preliminary proclamation by Pres. Lincoln (Sept. 22, 1862) declared that "persons held as slaves" within areas "in rebellion against the United States" would be free on and after Jan. 1, 1863. When that day arrived, Lincoln's Emancipation Proclamation held that all slaves in areas still in rebellion were freed. Since the Union did not control those areas, the Proclamation did not immediately free any slaves. It did, however, capture the public imagination and made it clear that abolition of slavery was a war aim.

Embargo Act (1807). Rather than involve the young nation in war with either Britain or France or both of these powers, Pres. Jefferson sought through economic pressure to get them to respect U.S. freedom to trade. The Act was his response to the seizure of American ships following the British Orders-

in-Council and Napoleon's Berlin and Milan decrees.

Despite Federalist opposition, Jefferson won Congress' approval of an act that virtually prohibited the export of any goods from the U.S. by sea or land.

Although British labor in cotton mills suffered from unemployment as a result, it 'was too weak politically to bring about a change in U.S. policy. Napoleon favored the Embargo Act, for he felt it was more injurious to Britain than to France.

The Embargo Act was denounced as disastrous by New England merchants. Ships were held in port and sailors and others were unemployed. Smuggling increased, especially to Canada, and British vessels gained the trade given up by the Americans.

The unpopularity of the Act during its 14-month trial forced repeal in 1809, at the end of Jefferson's administration.

emblems, party. The elephant and donkey as the symbols of the Republican and Democratic parties, respectively, were popularized by Thomas Nast. He first used the donkey to represent the Democrats in a cartoon published in the Jan. 15, 1870 issue of *Harper's Weekly*. The elephant as a party symbol was born, Nov. 7, 1874, in a Nast cartoon in the same periodical. The symbols caught the public fancy and they have been emblems of the two major political parties ever since.

Various devices were originally used to help illiterate voters. Many Democratic organizations adopted the rooster or gamecock as the party emblem after 1840. Republicans displayed the eagle as their party emblem soon after the party was organized in the early 1850's. With these emblems printed at the top of party tickets it was easy for the local politicians to tell the Democrats to vote for the "big chick" or the Republicans to vote for "the bird on the dollar."

Emergency Quota Act (1921). Opposition to immigration led to passage of the Act, sponsored by Sen. William P. Dillingham (Vt.), which fixed the maximum number of immigrants that could be admitted from each European country yearly. The quota was three percent of the number of persons of each nationality living in the U.S. in 1910.

Emerson, Ralph Waldo (1803–82). Essayist, poet. Born in Boston, Mass., he was graduated from Harvard (1821), attended the Harvard Divinity School and entered the ministry. Disagreement over doctrine caused him to leave the ministry, although he continued to preach and lecture throughout America. His address, "The American Scholar" (1837), was hailed by Oliver Wendell Holmes as "our intellectual Declaration of Independence."

A leading transcendentalist, he emphasized freedom and self-reliance in essays which make him a continuing force in American life. Emerson was the center of a group including such luminaries as Longfellow, Hawthorne, Motley, Dana, Agassiz and Holmes. Thoreau was one of his disciples. His reputation was international, and he corresponded with Carlyle for over 40 years. An organizer of such utopian experiments as Brook Farm, he also spoke on behalf of the Abolitionists. He drew for his lectures and essays from his *Journals* (begun in 1820). Among Emerson's most famous works are his first book, *Nature* (1836), and *Essays* (1841, 1844). His *Poems* (1847) and *May-Day and Other Poems* (1868) place him in the first rank of American poets.

eminent domain. The state has an inherent right to acquire for the public benefit any property that is privately owned without regard to the wishes of the owner. In the U.S. the right of eminent domain is exercised in accordance with due process of law as provided in the 5th and 14th Amendments. The private owner is given "just" compensation. If either the amount of compensation or the public use to which the property is being put is challenged, the determination may be made by a court, jury or other state agency.

Employment Act (1946). Pres. Truman sought to assure employment for all who wanted to work after World War II. The Full Employment bill would have required federal expenditures in order to guarantee jobs. As passed, it provided only a promise that the federal government would use all its resources in order to bring about full employment. It included provision for a Council of Economic Advisers.

empresario system. After Mexico won its independence from Spain in 1821, the government contracted with Americans, notably Stephen Austin, who were given large land grants to bring in families for permanent settlement. The empresario, or promoter, was expected to build schools and churches as part of his contract.

Between 1820 and 1830 about 20,000 Americans with approximately 2,000 slaves settled in Texas. It was not long before they began to resent Mexican interference with their freedom and an independence movement was started. As early as 1826 one empresario quarreled with the Mexican government over land titles and sought unsuccessfully to establish the Republic of Fredonia.

Empress of China. The first U.S. vessel to sail for China, after the proclamation of peace with Great Britain, it left New York harbor in 1784 with a cargo of ginseng (a plant used in the preparation of medicine by the Chinese). It returned a year later with a cargo that yielded a profit of 25%. This was the beginning of the Old China trade which grew so rapidly that 34 American vessels reached Canton in 1801.

enabling acts. Any territory which sought admission to the Union as a new state petitioned Congress to pass an enabling act. The act provided for the election of delegates to a constitutional convention in the territory. In some cases the act also specified conditions under which the state would be admitted. Utah, for example, was not admitted until it prohibited polygamous marriages.

encomiendas. The king of Spain granted large feudal estates in the New World to favored leaders and the Church. The Spanish overlords used the forced labor of natives to raise such crops as sugar, indigo and Indian corn. Although the workers received wages, they were kept in debt and their status was little better than that of serfs. Foodstuffs grown on the *encomiendas* supplied the workers in the gold and silver mines.

Enlightenment, American. Ideas rejecting religious authority and friendly to scientific progress developed during the colonial period. The Enlightenment fostered humanitarian causes, accepted the idea of progress and emphasized man's capacity for improving himself through reason.

The Enlightenment came to America later than it did to Europe because of the distance from intellectual centers. Even before the Revolution, however, Americans were reading the French philosophers of the Enlightenment — Montesquieu, Rousseau, Voltaire and Diderot. It was in the spirit of the Enlightenment that the natural rights of man—life, liberty, property and the pursuit of happiness—were proclaimed in the Declaration of Independence.

Enlightenment doctrines of economic freedom were especially acceptable to a growing middle class in America. Merchants, manufacturers, small farmers and planters opposed strict religious or governmental controls as restraints on their personal freedom and right to do business.

The ideas of the Enlightenment, although strongly resisted by conservative elements, were advanced during the Revolution and in the decades that followed.

entail. Similar to the system of land ownership in feudal England, an estate in the colonies could not be given or sold, even in part, to any but a specified line of heirs. In Virginia, for example, during the colonial period, any heir who wanted to get rid of such restrictions had to secure in his own name, and for that particular piece of land, a private Act of the House of Burgesses. Between 1711 and 1774 a total of 125 such Acts were passed, chiefly for members of the leading families in the colony. Such private Acts of the House were a necessity for the substantial planter: without them he was not free to deal with his land, to move his labor force or to dispose of worn-out parcels in order to acquire lands farther west.

By 1800 entail was abolished in all of the states.

"entangling alliances." Thomas Jefferson in his first inaugural address (Mar. 4, 1801) called for "peace, commerce, and honest friendship with all nations, entangling alliances with none." The phrase is often mistakenly attributed to George Washington, who advised against "permanent alliances" in his Farewell Address.

enumerated articles. The English Parliament in the 17th- and 18th-century Navigation Acts decreed that certain goods grown or manufactured in the colonies were to be sold only to England or to another colony. Among these commodities were tobacco, sugar, indigo and cotton-wool. The purpose was to make the colonies contribute more to English self-sufficiency and profits.

enumerated powers. Art. I, Sec. 8 of the Constitution explicitly grants Congress certain powers, such as laying and collecting taxes, borrowing money on the credit of the U.S., regulating commerce with foreign nations and among the several states. Paragraph 18 contains the implied powers of Congress and is the famous "elastic clause."

Ephrata Cloister. A communal religious community located 50 miles west of Philadelphia, it was founded in 1735 by Seventh-Day Baptists (Dunkers). It was most famous for its music. Johann Conrad Beissel, whose many hymns were published by Benjamin Franklin in 1730, was one of its leaders. The monastic orders in Ephrata dissolved about 1800, but some of the buildings are still preserved by the state as a historic site.

Episcopal Church, Protestant. The Church of England (Anglican Church) is the parent body. The first Anglican services in America were held in Jamestown, Va. (1607). The few Anglican clergymen in the colonies during this early period were concentrated in Virginia and Maryland. In New England, the Puritans were hostile to Anglicanism. After revocation of the charter of the Massachusetts colony (1686), the first Episcopal churches in the northern colonies were established— King's Chapel, Boston, and Trinity Church, New York City, both consecrated in 1689. Colleges established by the Church during the colonial period were William and Mary College and King's College (now Columbia).

After the American Revolution, at the General Convention in 1789, the name of the church was changed from Church of England in the Colonies to Protestant Episcopal Church. A constitution and *Book of Common Prayer* were adopted.

The structure of the Church includes the parish, the diocese, the province and the General Convention, which is the highest ecclesiastical authority. The ministry is of the three orders: bishops, priests and deacons. The Church maintains that the Holy Scriptures are the ultimate rule of faith.

Conflict developed in the 1840's when the Oxford (Tractarian) Movement sought to restore Catholic ideals in the Church. Later the Church was split by the Civil War, but the breach was healed quickly. Controversy over ritualism died down in the post-Civil War period as unity was achieved on such issues as social reform. Church membership is over 3,500,000.

e pluribus unum. The Latin phrase meaning "one out of many" is the motto of the U.S. It was selected by Benjamin Franklin, John Adams and Thomas Jefferson in 1776 and appears on all U.S. coins.

Equal Rights party. Headed by Mrs. Belva A. Lockwood, self-nominated for the Presidency in 1884 on a woman suffrage platform, the party never polled more than 2,000 votes. The party no longer existed by 1888.

237

"Era of Good Feelings" (1817–24). First appearing as the title of an article in Boston's *Columbian Centinel* (July 12, 1817), the phrase was used to describe the period covered by Monroe's administrations. The two-party system had ended temporarily with the demise of the Federalists and it appeared that all was peaceful in the Republican (Jeffersonian) party. As a matter of fact, there was considerable factionalism, which erupted in full force in the election of 1824.

Ericsson, John (1803–89). Engineer and inventor. Born in Sweden, he established a reputation as an engineer in London where he introduced the screw propeller on a commercial vessel. He came to the U.S. in 1839 and furnished designs for the screw propeller for the warship *Princeton* (1840). He built the ironclad *Monitor* (1861) for the Union and followed with the building of other ironclads. He inaugurated a new era in naval engineering.

Erie, Lake, battle of (Sept. 10, 1813). To make possible the recapture of Detroit during the War of 1812, the task of clearing Lake Erie was entrusted to young Capt. Oliver Hazard Perry.

When his flagship, the *Lawrence*, was all but shot out from under him, Perry transferred to the *Niagara*, from which he directed devastating fire at the British squadron. He returned to the *Lawrence* to receive the British surrender. It was from this ship that he sent his famous message to Gen. William Henry Harrison, the commander of the American Army in the Northwest, "We have met the enemy and they are ours. . . ."

Erie Canal. An era of canal building in the U.S. was stimulated by the success of the Erie Canal, which stretched 363 miles from Albany on the Hudson River to Buffalo on Lake Erie.

Gov. De Witt Clinton of New York pushed the canal project most forcefully. It was begun in 1817 and was completed in 1825. Success was assured when shipping costs along the length were reduced from $100 to $15 a ton and travel time from 20 to 8 days.

Erie Railroad. Chartered in 1832, the six-foot gauge track from Piermont, N.Y., on the Hudson, to Dunkirk on Lake Erie was completed in 1851. In 1869, the Erie boasted of 1,400 miles under one management; 860 miles without change of cars. Profits, however, which should have gone into improving equipment and service were siphoned off. Jay Gould sold out his Erie securities for millions in cash on the eve of the Panic of 1873. The line was badly managed for a long time.

Before merging with the Lackawanna in 1960, the Erie, with its 2,239 miles of track, was one of the four main trunk systems between New York and Chicago.

Esch-Cummins Transportation Act (1920). After World War I, Congress returned the railroads to private operation. The Interstate Commerce Commission was empowered to fix fair rates and returns for railroad investors. All earnings over 6% were to be split between the railroads and the government, with the government's share going to the weaker roads. Railroads were encouraged to consolidate in order to make their operations more efficient. This was a departure from the anti-trust policy of the federal government.

The Act also provided for a Railway Labor Board, whose authority stopped short of compulsory arbitration.

Escobedo v. Illinois (1964). The U.S. Supreme Court ruled that persons seized by the police for interrogation had the right to advice of counsel. Justice Arthur Goldberg, speaking for the Court, held that Escobedo's constitutional rights had been violated because he had been denied the 5th Amendment privilege against self-incrimination. Escobedo's lawyer had not been allowed to see him while the police were questioning him.

The decision freed Danny Escobedo, a Chicago laborer, from an Illinois prison where he was serving a 20-year term for slaying his brother-in-law.

The effect of the decision was to place in question a police method of solving crimes (questioning suspects and extracting confessions) that was to be curtailed further in *Miranda v. Arizona* (1966).

Espionage Act (1917). The law prescribed a fine of up to $10,-000 and a prison term of 20 years for anyone who interfered with the draft or attempted to encourage disloyalty. A few hundred pacifists, including the Socialist party candidate for President, Eugene V. Debs, were imprisoned for violating the Act.

ESSA. The task of the Environmental Survey Satellite is to take and send pictures of the earth's cloud cover. Hatbox-shaped ESSA-II, launched Feb. 28, 1966 from Cape Kennedy, flies about 850 miles above the earth in a near polar orbit and beams pictures down to earth 200 seconds after they are taken. They are received by ground stations operated by the U.S. Weather Bureau across the country. Its continuously transmitted pictures can be used by any country willing and able to build a ground-receiving set.

Previous weather eyes, including ESSA-I, orbited in Jan. 1966, and 11 experimental weather satellites orbited since 1956 took similar pictures, stored them on tape and relayed them back to earth once every orbit.

ESSA-II is of great help to forecasters around the globe, keeping track of local storms and helping in the selection of safe aircraft and shipping routes.

Essex. The U.S. frigate did extensive damage to the British whaling fleet off the west coast of South America during the War of 1812. The ship itself was captured and two-thirds of its crew killed or wounded, Mar. 28, 1814, when it was attacked off the coast of Chile by a superior British naval force.

Essex, case of the (1805). The British wanted to end the practice of "broken" voyages whereby American vessels were evading British regulations. Yankee merchants were aiding Napoleon by engaging in direct trade between the French West Indies and Europe. They did this by carrying their cargoes from the French West Indies to an American port where they paid a token duty, and then after reloading it continued on with the cargo to a European port under French control.

A British tribunal in the case of an American vessel, *Essex,* held that the produce it carried between two enemy ports had not paid a bona fide duty at an American port and thus violated the Rule of 1756 (trade not open in time of peace could not be permitted in time of war). In normal times the French restricted the direct trade to and from their West Indian colonies to their own merchant marine.

Under the ruling, British cruisers seized scores of American merchantmen, chiefly those engaged in the roundabout West Indian trade. Their action aroused a storm of protest in the commercial centers of the U.S.

Essex Junto. Extremist Federalist leaders from Esssex County, Mass., during the early days of the Republic, were accused by Pres. John Adams, himself a Federalist, of trying to force a war with France, 1798–99. The Junto represented the commercial interests, and the name became a synonym for New England Federalism during the embargo period.

The Junto's determination to end the War of 1812 included secession from the Union. More moderate influences prevailed at the Hartford Convention (1814) and the Junto, led by Timothy Pickering, disappeared along with the Federalist party.

European Defense Community (EDC). The military arm of the North Atlantic Treaty Organization, it was created by agreement (May 27, 1952) of the U.S., Britain, France, West Germany, Italy, Belgium, the Netherlands and Luxembourg.

Eutaw Springs, battle of (Sept. 8, 1781). As a result of a battle in South Carolina, the British were forced to retire to Charleston.

American forces were under the command of Gen. Nathanael Greene and included state militia led by Francis Marion, the "Swamp Fox."

Evangelical United Brethren Church. The Protestant denomination was formed in 1946 at Johnstown, Pa., by a merger of the Evangelical Church and the Church of the United Brethren in Christ. Both bodies had their beginnings among the Germans of Pennsylvania, Maryland and Virginia at the time of the evangelistic movement of the late 18th century. Jacob Albright, a Lutheran convert to Methodism, was the founder of the Evangelical Church in 1807. Philip W. Otterbein and Martin Boehm were the joint founders of the United Brethren in 1800. The church has episcopal government, follows Arminian doctrine and stresses individual responsibility. The membership is almost 800,000.

evangelism. The term denotes the efforts of Protestant churches to spread the gospel of Christ among all men. In the American colonies it took the form of revivalism. The Great Awakening of the 1730's increased church membership through the efforts of such evangelists as the Congregationalist Jonathan Edwards (Mass.), the Dutch-Reformed minister Theodore Frelinghuysen (N.J.) and the Presbyterians William Tennent and his sons (Pa.).

On the frontier during the 19th century evangelists preached at camp meetings and stirred non-church members with their exhortations. Baptists and Methodists were especially successful in winning converts in the West.

In the 1820's and 1830's Charles G. Finney, a Congregationalist minister, preached along the lines of eastern and western revivalism. In the latter part of the 19th century Dwight L. Moody carried his message to many cities.

In the 20th century William Ashley (Billy) Sunday was a prominent evangelist. In the 1950's and 1960's William Franklin (Billy) Graham preached at mass meetings in cities all over the world.

The organized churches' acceptance of evangelism as a responsibility is evidenced by the work of the National Preaching Mission of the National Council of the Churches of Christ in the U.S.

Evarts, William Maxwell (1818–1901). Statesman. Born in Boston, Mass., he won acquittal for Pres. Johnson in his impeachment trial before the Senate (1868). He served as Attorney General of U.S. (1868–69). He was counsel for U.S. before the Geneva court of arbitration in the *Alabama* claims (1871–72). As a leading New York lawyer he led the reform movement against the "Tweed Ring" (1870–80). He was Pres. Hayes' Sec. of State (1877–81) and U.S. senator from New York (1885–91).

evening schools. An extension of the public education idea, the first evening school was probably begun in New York City in 1833. One was established in Louisville, Ky., in 1834. Other cities followed.

241

Baltimore established six evening schools as early as 1840. In 1855, Cincinnati, O., opened evening schools for girls. The first public evening high school was opened in Cincinnati in 1856. By 1900, 165 cities were providing evening schools.

Originally, evening schools were begun to provide education for those unable to attend during the day. This continued to be their important function up to about 1900. Subsequently, evening elementary schools have been used chiefly to provide the foreign-born with the elements of an English education. Evening high schools offer those who have completed elementary school but who did not remain in day high school a chance to gain a high school diploma. Evening vocational high schools offer training in a variety of trades.

Everson v. Board of Education (1947). A divided U.S. Supreme Court sustained the right of local authorities in New Jersey to provide free transportation for children attending parochial schools. The use of the tax funds for transporting parochial school pupils was justified by the so-called "child benefit" principle. This implies that benefits conferred on parochial school children (such as textbooks and bus transportation) come within public welfare legislation and are not to be construed as aid to religious schools.

The decision was accompanied, however, with these warning words: "No tax in any amount, large or small, can be levied to support any religious activities or institutions . . . whatever form they may adopt to teach or practice religion."

expatriation. The term describes the act of voluntarily abandoning one's country and becoming the citizen or subject of another. In 1868 Congress declared the right of expatriation to be the right of all people. The U.S. has since entered into treaties with nearly all the nations of Europe by which the contracting powers concede the right of expatriation on conditions and under qualifications. The expatriate may not be involved in any fraud or attempted escape from duties in his home country. A woman who is a citizen of the U.S. does not expatriate herself merely by marriage with an alien.

Explorer I. The first of a series of satellites put in orbit by the U.S., it was launched Jan. 31, 1958. In confirming the existence of the Van Allen radiation belt, it made the most important single contribution of the International Geophysical Year.

Succeeding Explorers have obtained information on meteoroids, temperatures and pressures, radiation and magnetic fields, effects of solar activity on the earth environment, behavior of energetic particles, solar pressure, composition of the ionosphere and gamma rays. Others have mapped the near-earth radiation region and the area of the earth's magnetic influence in space.

Export-Import Bank. An independent agency of the federal government, it is designed to facilitate trade between the U.S. and any foreign country. It was started in 1934 and has been expanded considerably. For the most part it has been helpful in making loans to businesses carrying on trade with Latin America. The Eximport Bank (popular name) supplements and does not compete with private capital.

Exposition and Protest, The (1828). Published anonymously by Vice-Pres. John C. Calhoun as the "South Carolina Exposition," the essay proposed that the tyranny of the majority be countered by each state in the Union using its constitutional right to nullify an unconstitutional act of Congress. The immediate cause of Calhoun's stand was the Tariff of 1828, which he charged destroyed the rights of the South and placed the Union in danger.

extradition. Under the Constitution "A person charged in any State with Treason, Felony or other Crime, who shall flee from Justice, and be found in another State, shall on Demand of the executive Authority of the State from which he fled, be delivered up, to be removed to the State having jurisdiction of the Crime" (Art. IV, Sec. 2, Par. 2).

The U.S. Supreme Court in *Kentucky v. Dennison* (1861) held that extradition was a moral duty and not mandatory and that a federal court could not issue a mandamus to compel the governor of one state to surrender a fugitive to another. In 1934 Congress plugged the loophole exposed by this decision by making it unlawful for any person to flee from one state to another for the purpose of avoiding prosecution in certain cases.

Where a person flees to another country, he may be extradited under the terms of a reciprocity treaty which the U.S. has with that country.

"extremism in defense of liberty. . . ." Sen. Barry Goldwater (Ariz.), in accepting the Republican party's nomination for the Presidency in 1964 told the convention that "extremism in defense of liberty is no vice; moderation in pursuit of justice is no virtue."

Anti-Goldwater forces interpreted the remark as a dangerous defense of the "lunatic fringe" in American politics that included anti-Negro and anti-civil liberties elements.

Defenders of Goldwater held that he was speaking in the tradition of the heroic forerunners in American history who had crusaded for unpopular causes without fear. Goldwater believed that American liberty was being whittled away by excessive concentration of power in the federal government, including the enforcement of Negro rights by federal rather than state governments.

F

Fair Deal. Pres. Truman used the term in his State of the Union Message to Congress, Jan. 1949, to describe the program he called upon Congress to enact. It included proposals for increasing the minimum hourly wage, improved housing for low income groups, a strengthened civil rights law, full employment and expanded social security coverage. In general it was a continuation in spirit of the New Deal.

Fair Employment Practices Committee (FEPC). During World War II Congress set up a committee to guard against discrimination in hiring employees. In Feb. 1946 a bill to make the FEPC permanent was blocked in Congress by a southern filibuster.

There are laws against discrimination in private employment in more than one-third of the states and in some cities. The first such law was passed in New York State in 1945 (Ives-Quinn Act). Under such laws employment agencies, employers and labor unions are forbidden to discriminate against any person in placement procedures, wages, conditions of employment or union membership because of race, creed, color or national origin.

Fairfax proprietary. A great estate in colonial Virginia was held by Lord Fairfax who had inherited the land. Originally a retreat for English Cavaliers, it was granted to Lord Culpeper by King James II in 1688.

Lord Fairfax's title to the land had been confirmed by the Crown in 1745, and he lived as a landed magnate at "Greenway Court" (near present-day Winchester, Va.). He was not molested during the Revolution despite charges (unproved) that he was a Loyalist.

Virginia took possession of Lord Fairfax's domain of more than five million acres between the Rappahannock and the Potomac Rivers (the Northern Neck), after his death in 1781. The action was not the result of Fairfax's political faith, but was evidence of the revolutionary opposition to feudal survivals.

Fair Labor Standards Act (1938). Also known as the Wages and Hours Act, the New Deal law established a minimum wage of 25 cents an hour rising to 40 cents an hour in seven years, a 44-hour week to be reduced to 40 hours in three years and prohibited the labor of children under 16 in industries whose products entered into interstate commerce. Overtime after 40 hours is paid at 1½ times the regular rate. Subsequent amendments moved the minimum up to $1.40 in 1967 and $1.60 in 1968. The act represented the first attempt in U.S. history to place a national ceiling on hours and a floor under wages.

Fair Oaks, battle of (May 31– June 1, 1862). The battle, also known as Seven Pines, took place during the Union's Peninsular campaign. Gen. George McClellan's Army of the Potomac was turned back on the outskirts of Richmond by the Confederates under Gen. J. E. Johnston. When Johnston was wounded in the fighting, Gen. Robert E. Lee came in to command the Army of Northern Virginia, as it was known after this battle.

fair trade laws. Severe price-cutting became widespread during the depression of the 1930's and many merchants were forced out of business. The result was pressure for laws to permit price-fixing. In 1937 Congress passed the Miller-Tydings Act which amended the antitrust laws. It permitted states to pass fair-trade laws under which manufacturers would be able to fix prices on goods in interstate commerce without being considered in violation of federal antitrust statutes. Most states passed such laws.

From the beginning some retailers objected to the plan. They felt that they should be allowed to sell the merchandise on their shelves at any prices they wished. But the system continued in force until 1951 when the U.S. Supreme Court held that the Miller-Tydings Act was not clear and sustained the right of a Louisiana supermarket to charge any price it wanted for the goods it carried.

The decision set off a new wave of price wars all over the country. In 1952 Congress passed the McGuire Act as an amendment to the antitrust laws. This authorized state legislatures to legalize "fair trade" if they chose to. Over the years, 45 states have done so, but courts in many of these states have overruled them. Controversy over the wisdom of fair trade laws has continued.

A substantial amount of retail merchandise is now sold at discount prices—that is, at figures lower than the regular list prices set by manufacturers. This includes sales both in discount houses and in regular retail stores.

Falaise gap, battle of (Aug. 1944). In a key battle in the closing months of World War

II, the 100,000-man German Seventh Army in Normandy, France, was encircled by a British-Canadian army under command of Field Marshal Montgomery and a U.S. Army group under Gen. Bradley. A stretch of 25 miles separated the Canadians from the Americans. Through this gap 40,000 Germans escaped before the route was closed.

Military men have debated command decisions in the battle since it ended.

Fallen Timbers, battle of (Aug. 20, 1794). Gen. Anthony Wayne defeated the Indian tribes of the Northwest in a battle on the banks of the Maumee, O. (near present-day Toledo). The fallen trees did not prevent Wayne from dispersing the Indians, who had twice defeated U.S. Army forces. The Indians' defeat and the subsequent Treaty of Greenville encouraged emigration to the Northwest.

fall line. At a certain point rivers may drop sharply, forming rapids and falls. During the colonial period regions below the fall line were settled first because navigation upstream was halted by the rapids or falls.

Since it was possible for ocean-going vessels from Europe to sail up the river to the fall line, towns were established at the fall line. In addition the towns were able to receive goods transported down the river in small boats.

Cities in the South on the fall line include Richmond, Va.; Raleigh, N.C.; Columbia, S.C.

Falmouth, burning of (Oct. 18, 1775). The town on the coast of Massachusetts was burned by the British in retaliation for the aid given by the townspeople to the people of Boston. The act of violence further inflamed the colonists and hardened their determination to oust the British.

Farewell Address (Sept. 19, 1796). Shortly before he left office, Pres. Washington urged unity upon his countrymen and wrote of the "baneful effects of the spirit of party." Toward the end of the address, he touched upon foreign affairs and said: "It is our true policy to steer clear of permanent alliances with any portion of the foreign world. . . . Taking care always to keep ourselves . . . on a respectable defensive posture, we may safely trust to temporary alliances for extraordinary purposes."

The address was not delivered in person by Washington; instead it was published in the newspapers.

Farm Bloc. The term was used facetiously by a newspaperman in 1921 to describe an informal organization of congressmen in both parties. The Bloc was formed in response to the farm distress which developed after World War I. Its members supported legislation that aided cooperative associations, raised the tariff on farm produce or in general favored farmers. The group was diverse and difficult to hold together after a few years. The term has continued to this day, but the Farm Bloc lacks the unity which characterized it in the early 1920's.

Farm Credit Administration. An independent federal agency, it was established in 1933, but the origins of the Farm Credit System go back at least as far as the Federal Farm Loan Act of 1916.

The FCA supervises a cooperative credit system for agriculture which provides long and short-term credit to farmers and their cooperative marketing and purchasing organizations. All of the expenses of the FCA are paid for by assessments against the banks and associations it supervises.

Farmer-Labor party (1920). The political party attempted after World War I to unite labor unions and farmers in the Midwest on a socialist program. The party platform called for government ownership of railroads, mines and national resources; the lifting of the blockade against Russia; American withdrawal from the Treaty of Versailles; and the enactment of part of the Progressive platform of 1912.

The party failed to gain the support of the Farmer-Labor party of Minnesota which confined itself to local issues during the early 1920's. The party did not win support of the major farm organizations and won a small vote in the presidential election of 1920. It soon disintegrated.

Farmers' Alliance. To relieve farm distress of the 1880's, the farmers in both the North and South formed organizations that sought easier credit, railroad regulation, disposal of public lands to actual settlers and a lower tariff. In addition, they organized cooperatives to reduce purchasing and marketing costs.

Apart from economic demands, the alliances like the Granges held picnics and meetings intended to relieve the bleakness of farm life and stimulate farmers to think about issues of the day.

The Northern Alliance and Southern Alliance differed over organization. The southerners insisted on secrecy and opposed admission of the Colored Alliance to any merged organization.

In the early 1890's both the Northern Alliance and Southern Alliance agreed that national political organization was necessary to extend the local and state political victories that they had begun to enjoy. They met in Omaha, in 1892, in convention with other reformers, and formed the national People's (Populist) party.

Farragut, David Glasgow (1801–70). Naval officer. Born near Knoxville, Tenn., he rose from midshipman in the U.S. Navy, at age 9, to Admiral, a position created for him by Congress (1866). He took New

Orleans (1862) during the Civil War and captured Port Hudson, La., on the Mississippi (1863). In 1864 he forced his way over mines to silence Confederate forts Gaines and Morgan in Mobile Bay, Ala., and his "Damn the torpedoes!" continues to ring in U.S. naval annals.

Farrell, James T. (1904–   ). Novelist. Born in Chicago, Ill., he realistically depicts the effects of the Chicago slums on an American youth of Irish parentage in his trilogy composed of *Young Lonigan: A Boyhood in Chicago's Streets* (1932), *The Young Manhood of Studs Lonigan* (1934) and *Judgment Day* (1935). He allows his young delinquents to speak in their tough vernacular and graphically describes their sordid activities. The sources of ruin were moral and psychological rather than economic in Farrell's work.

"father of his country." George Washington was known by the title even before he became the first President of the U.S. He was referred to in this way in laudatory addresses made in 1783 when he resigned his commission as commander-in-chief of the Continental armies.

"father of the Constitution." James Madison earned the title by virtue of the role he played in establishing the Constitution. He attended every session of the Constitutional Convention

of 1787, helped to frame its provisions and took careful notes of the proceedings. Along with Alexander Hamilton and John Jay, he wrote the brilliant essays in defense of the Constitution that were published as *The Federalist*. Madison's notes on the Constitutional Convention were published in 1841, five years after his death.

Faulkner, William (1897–1962). Novelist. Born in New Albany, Miss., he created the imaginary Yoknapatawpha County as the backdrop for much of his work and earned a worldwide reputation as a commentator on the mind and spirit of the South. He saw the South as a microcosm of a world that rejected the past and abandoned traditional values. His characters, whether aristocrats or the poor white clan of the Snopses, lived in a land doomed by the curse of slavery. His novels include *The Sound and the Fury* (1929), *Light in August* (1932), *Absalom! Absalom!* (1936), *The Unvanquished* (1939), *The Hamlet* (1940), *A Fable* (1954) and *The Reivers* (1962). Faulkner was awarded the Nobel Prize for Literature (1949).

favorite sons. At both Democratic and Republican national conventions nominations for President are sometimes made to honor a leading political figure of a state. He soon withdraws in favor of a candidate who is being seriously considered for the party's nomination.

Federal Bureau of Investigation (FBI). The Bureau in the Department of Justice has jurisdiction over espionage, sabotage, treason and other matters pertaining to the internal security of the U.S. Among the laws related to the jurisdiction of the FBI are the Federal Kidnapping Statute, the White Slave Traffic Act, the Atomic Energy Act of 1946, statutes dealing with interstate transportation of stolen motor vehicles and aid of gambling or racketeering.

Federal Communications Commission. The FCC was created by Congress in 1934. Its purpose is to regulate interstate and foreign communication by telegraph, cable and radio to make the service efficient for the public and the charges reasonable. The act transferred to the FCC the authority of the Interstate Commerce Commission over communications and imposed new regulations for the control of radio broadcasting.

Federal Emergency Relief Administration (FERA). Established in 1933 under Harry Hopkins, the New Deal agency was authorized to provide direct emergency relief to states and localities. The federal government matched the funds put up by the states and the relief was administered by the states. At first cash grants were made, but soon "relief projects" were set up. About half of those who received relief worked for 30 cents an hour on a wide variety of projects that were not in competition with private industry. Ultimately the Relief Administration spent about $4 billion of which about a third came from the states and municipalities.

Federal Farm Loan Act (1916). At a time when Pres. Wilson was seeking Progressive support for reelection, Congress created a Federal Farm Loan Board and 12 regional Farm Loan banks patterned after the Federal Reserve System. The banks were authorized to lend sums to cooperative farm-loan associations on the security of farm lands and buildings. The loans were made for long terms at a maximum of 6% interest. In about a decade over $1 billion in farm mortgages were outstanding.

Federal Hall. The building in New York City, renovated at the time for the first Congress, is now the site of the Old Sub-Treasury Building, made a national historic site under the name Federal Hall Memorial. It contains the slab on which George Washington stood to make his first inaugural address, Apr. 30, 1789.

Federal Housing Administration. The FHA, created by the National Housing Act of 1934, was made a constituent agency of the Housing and Home Finance Agency in 1947. It was established to encourage improvement in housing conditions, to further home ownership, to provide a system of mortgage insurance and to exert a stabilizing influence on the mortgage market. The FHA does not make loans or build housing, but operates insurance programs. If the holder of an FHA insured mortgage defaults on his payment to a private lending agency, the FHA pays the lender and takes over the property for resale.

Federalist, The. Written in 1787 and 1788 by Alexander Hamilton, James Madison and John Jay, the essays supported ratification of the Constitution in New York where strong opposition had arisen. When the articles appeared individually in *The Independent Journal*, they were signed "Publius." Seventy-eight of them were collected in book form as *The Federalist*, 1788. Eight were added the same year, making a total of 85. They continue to be regarded as brilliant essays in political theory and the best commentary on the Constitution ever written.

Federalist party. Supporters of the Constitution before ratification in 1787 were called Federalists. Later, during George Washington's first administration (1789–93), political parties began to develop and the Federalist party took shape under the leadership of Alexander Hamilton and John Adams.

The Federalists favored a strong central government and consequently a loose interpretation of the Constitution which would permit expansion of the national government's powers. They favored a national bank, encouragement of manufacturers and Hamilton's financial plan, which included assumption of state debts.

The party leaned toward support of England in the war with France. Federalists were quick to condemn the excesses of the French Revolution. In general their attitude toward the common people was expressed by John Jay in 1809 when he wrote "that those who own the country are most fit persons to participate in the government of it."

Federalists were critical of the War of 1812 and sponsored the Hartford Convention (1814). The party virtually disappeared a short time later.

Federal National Mortgage Association. Originally chartered in 1938, the association was made a constituent agency of the Housing and Home Finance Agency of 1954. FNMA ("Fanny Mae") provides supplementary assistance to the secondary market for home mortgages. It thereby improves the distribution of investment capital available for home mortgage financing. It may also provide special assistance for selected types of home mortgages for segments of the population which are unable to obtain adequate housing under established home financing programs.

Federal Reserve System. Basically the system which operates today, a central banking system was established by the Glass-Owen Currency Act of 1913 realizing an objective of Woodrow Wilson's New Freedom. Under it there are 12 Federal Reserve Banks in major cities throughout the nation. Each of these Reserve Banks (bankers' banks) deals only with member banks within its district which belong to the system. Overall control of the system is entrusted to the Board of Governors, whose members are appointed by the President.

One of the powers of the Board of Governors is to set the ratio of cash reserves which member banks must keep against deposits. These reserves are deposited with the Federal Reserve Bank. Thus the reserves are centralized and can be used, as provided by the Federal Reserve Bank, to help out banks that need financial assistance or for other constructive purposes.

The Federal Reserve Banks are also able to provide a more *elastic* currency. The amount of money in circulation can be increased or decreased (expanded or contracted) depending upon the needs of business. At various times businessmen and farmers must borrow money from banks to finance their operations. When such a loan is made, the borrower usually gives the bank a promissory note (a written promise to pay). The local bank can take such a note to its Federal Reserve Bank, which may then issue currency (Federal Reserve Notes) backed in part by this kind of "commercial paper." When the loans are paid off the Federal Reserve Notes are retired (withdrawn).

federal system. The U.S. has a federal system of government as provided in the Constitution. Under this system specific powers are delegated by the states to the national government which has three branches—executive, legislative and judicial. Among the powers granted to the national government are the right to coin money, regulate commerce with foreign nations and declare war.

Powers not specifically granted to the federal government are reserved to the states. There is some overlapping. Both federal and state governments, for example, raise revenue through taxation.

Citizens in a federal system are under two jurisdictions—state and federal. Where the jurisdictions conflict the federal courts make the final determination based on the justices' interpretation of the Constitution.

Federal Trade Commission. The basic objective of the FTC, established during Wilson's administration under the Federal Trade Act (1914), is the maintenance of free competitive enterprise as the keystone of the American economic system. FTC "cease-and-desist" orders are numbered in the thousands. They aim to prevent abuse of the consuming public by false or deceptive advertisements of food, drugs, cosmetics

251

and therapeutic devices. The FTC also acts to prevent discriminations in price and corporate mergers and interlocking directorates where the effect of such arrangements may tend toward monopoly.

fencing. In 17th century colonial New England, fenceviewers were town officers who took care that fences protecting crops were four feet high and maintained in reasonable repair. Fencing laws were passed by various states and the fencing of pasture and crop lands became common.

Cattlemen used barbed wire to fence in their land beginning in the 1870's. This led to wire-cutting "wars" by cattlemen who resisted being shut out of grazing land even if it was not their own.

Fenian movement. Irish-Americans who sought to aid Ireland to become independent of Great Britain raised funds in the U.S. They went so far as to attempt an invasion of Canada in 1866. To convince Britain of its neutrality the U.S. government arrested some of the raiders despite the growing importance of the Irish-American vote to the Johnson administration. The Fenian movement died out when its leader, John O'Mahoney, died in 1877.

Fermi, Enrico (1901–54). Physicist. Born in Rome, Italy, he came to the U.S. in 1939. The previous year he received the Nobel Prize for Physics for experiments in radioactivity, using slow neutrons, which led to discovery of uranium fission. He placed the first atomic furnace in operation (1942) and participated in the atomic bomb project at Los Alamos. He was professor of physics at Columbia (1939–45) and later at Chicago. He discovered element 93 (neptunium).

Fetterman massacre (Dec. 21, 1866). Capt. William Fetterman, supposed author of the statement "Give me eighty men and I'll ride through the whole Sioux nation," fell into a trap that brought his 81 men to a sudden end. He was attempting to help a wood-transport train fight off an attack by Indians in northern Wyoming. A force of 2000 warriors was responsible for the destruction. The chief of the Ogallalas, Red Cloud, who was also a leader of the Sioux and Cheyenne tribes, had set up an ambush. He used a party of ten to decoy the band that had set out from Fort Phil Kearny.

Fever War. In the late 1850's Missouri cattlemen claimed that the Texas Longhorns feeding on Missouri grass were poisoning the native Shorthorns that grazed there later. This was America's first bout with tick, also known as Spanish fever or Texas fever. In 1861 a statewide ban against Texas cattle became law in Missouri. Texas men then trailed their cattle through the Oklahoma panhandle to Colorado.

Field, Cyrus West (1819–92). Financier. Born in Stockbridge, Mass., he is remembered as the promoter of the first successful Atlantic Cable (1866). He made his first fortune in paper manufacturing, but suffered financial reverses at various times. Field helped establish elevated trains in New York City, and with Jay Gould developed the Wabash RR.

Field, David Dudley (1805–94). Lawyer. Born in Haddam, Conn., he was counsel in important cases involving constitutional issues (counsel for Milligan in *Ex parte Milligan,* 1867). His major contribution was made in codifying the municipal laws of New York (completed 1865). He drafted an international code that gained recognition by the courts of many nations.

Field, Marshall (1835–1906). Merchant and philanthropist. He was born near Conway, Mass. Starting as a clerk in a drygoods store in Pittsfield, Mass., he moved to Chicago where he became general manager of a wholesale drygoods firm that he expanded into Marshall Field & Co., the largest wholesale and retail drygoods establishment in the world (1881–1906). He donated the site of the Univ. of Chicago, and his will provided funds for the Field Museum of Natural History.

"Fifty-four Forty or Fight!" The Democratic platform of 1844 called for "reoccupation of Oregon, reannexation of Texas." Pres. Polk in his annual message (Dec. 1845) asserted that the American title to the Oregon Territory was "clear and unquestionable" up to latitude 54° 40′ N, which brought it to the Alaskan border. Polk never intended to risk war with England over Oregon at a time when our relations with Mexico were worsening. The British for their part were disposed to compromise following the reduction of American tariffs on British manufactures in 1846.

When Lord Aberdeen proposed to extend the international boundary along latitude 49° N to Puget Sound, leaving Vancouver Island to Canada, Polk accepted. He submitted this offer to the Senate in June 1846, after the war with Mexico had started. It was during this debate that a Western expansionist coined the slogan, "Fifty-four Forty or Fight!" Nevertheless, the Senate, on June 15, consented to a treaty accepting Aberdeen's boundary.

The disputed territory was divided at the 49th parallel by the Oregon Treaty of 1846. This parallel extended to the Pacific Ocean the Canadian-American boundary that had been fixed in 1818 only as far as the Rockies.

"fifty-niners." Gold was discovered in Colorado, 1859, in the Pikes Peak region in the foothills of the Rockies. The gold rush did not produce the sudden wealth of the California gold rush of "forty-niners." It turned out that the gold required mining by skilled engineers.

Also in 1859, fabulous silver deposits were discovered at the Comstock Lode in Nevada and the "fifty-niners" pushed further west.

"fight it out on this line if it takes all summer." Gen. Grant suffered heavy troop losses in the battle of the Wilderness, but was determined to crush Gen. Lee's armies and reach Richmond. On May 11, 1864, having reached Spotsylvania, Va., he made his famous statement, which begins "I propose to . . .," in a letter to Gen. Halleck in Washington.

filibuster, congressional. The right of U.S. Senators to talk endlessly in an effort to prevent a bill from coming to a vote is a Senate tradition. Filibuster tactics range from reading recipes to long-winded talks on the issue. The tactic is always obstructive and it has been looked upon with increasing disfavor by the public which sees it as frustration of the majority will. Efforts to curb the filibuster include threatening cloture (closure) which permits two-thirds of the Senators to vote for closing debate, or keeping the Senate in continuous session in order to exhaust the filibusterers.

Among the bills which have been subject to filibusters have been the anti-lynching bill (1938) and the civil rights bills

of 1960 and 1964. The Civil Rights Law of 1964 was finally passed by the Senate after a three-month southern filibuster —the longest in history. The bill came to a vote only when the Johnson administration leadership successfully invoked the cloture rule. This marked the first time in the history of civil rights legislation that the cloture rule was successfully invoked to halt a Southern filibuster.

filibustering expeditions. The English buccaneers of the 17th century who preyed on Spanish ships had their counterpart in the U.S. in the first half of the 19th century. Although U.S. laws prohibited filibustering, expeditions were organized by adventurers in the U.S. for the purpose of taking over foreign countries.

In the 1850's William Walker, a southerner, led several expeditions to Central America. He established himself as dictator of Nicaragua (1855–57). Northerners looked upon this adventure as an effort to secure more slave territory for the South. The British viewed it as part of U.S. expansionism. Walker fell before a Honduran firing squad, Sept. 12, 1860.

A filibustering expedition was aimed at Cuba in 1851. Gen. Narciso Lopez, a Venezuelan adventurer, and about 500 Americans, stole out of New Orleans in the last of three efforts to seize Cuba. He was captured by the Spanish army and was executed along with 50 of his followers, some of whom were from the "best families" of the South. Public sentiment in New Orleans led to the sacking of the Spanish consulate. U.S. apologies were made to Spain.

The last of the important filibusterers was George Bickley. He won much popular support in the South (1860–61) for his filibustering organization designed to annex Mexico and add as many as 25 slave states to the Union.

Fillmore, Millard (1800–74). Thirteenth President of the U.S. (1850–53). He was born in Summerhill, Cayuga County, N.Y. Vice-President of the U.S. (1849–50), he succeded to the Presidency on the death of Zachary Taylor. He served New York as a member of the U.S. House of Representatives (1833–35; 1837–43). He was the unsuccessful aspirant for the Whig presidential nomination in 1852 and was the unsuccessful "Know-Nothing" candidate for President in 1856.

"fireside chats." The first of the evening radio talks by Pres. F.D. Roosevelt was given Mar. 12, 1933. In them he sought, in simple language, to calm the depression fears of the nation and to win support for the measures being undertaken to establish a sound economy. His opening greeting was "My friends . . . ."; the broadcasts were listened to by huge audiences during those troubled times.

"First in war, first in peace . . . " In a resolution passed by Congress when Washington died in 1799, Henry Lee's characterization of him included the memorable description: "First in war, first in peace, first in the hearts of his countrymen."

Fish, Hamilton (1808–93). Statesman. Born in New York City, he was governor of N.Y. (1849–50); U.S. Senator (1851–57); Pres. Grant's Sec. of State (1869–77). He negotiated settlement of the *Alabama* claims with Great Britain by arbitration; he adjusted the *Virginius* affair with Spain peacefully; and he signed a treaty of commercial reciprocity with Hawaii. His efforts to secure agreements with Colombia and Nicaragua for an inter-oceanic canal failed.

fisheries dispute. Before the Revolutionary War fishermen of the American colonies had free access to the fishing grounds of Labrador, Newfoundland and the Gulf of St. Lawrence. Limitations were placed on these fishing rights by the Treaty of Paris (1783). As a consequence of the War of 1812, U.S. fishing rights in Canadian waters were further limited. By the Convention of 1818 the U.S. was given the right to fish only on the western and northern coasts of Newfoundland and the Magdalen Islands. Rivalry between Canadian and American fishermen was abated somewhat by a reciprocity treaty concluded in

1854. A major settlement was later reached in the Treaty of Washington (1871) which permitted the Americans to engage in the sea fishery virtually without restriction. In return British subjects were permitted to fish along the coast of the U.S. as far south as the latitude of Delaware Bay. This agreement terminated in 1885. It was not until a Hague tribunal decision in 1910 that the disputed fisheries ceased to be a source of continuing controversy.

Fiske, John (1842–1901). Philosopher and historian. He was born in Hartford, Conn., and lectured on philosophy and history at Harvard. After his resignation from Harvard (1879) he became a popular lecturer on history both in the U.S. and abroad. He was America's chief exponent of evolution. The author of many popular books, his works include *Outlines of Cosmic Philosophy* (1874), *Darwinism and Other Essays* (1879), *The American Revolution* (1891), *The Discovery of America* (1892), *Dutch Quaker Colonies* (1899).

Fitzgerald, Francis Scott (1896–1940). Novelist. Born in St. Paul, Minn., he became rich and famous at the age of 24, with the publication of his first novel, *This Side of Paradise* (1920). He was to write about a wildly free, partying age of the 1920's in which the characters somehow arrived at catastrophe. He managed to suggest simultaneously the glitter of American prosperity and the treacherous foundations on which it rested. In *The Great Gatsby* (1925), Jay Gatsby, an idealistic bootlegger, believes every dream can be made real simply by wishing for it intensely enough. He is betrayed by his gangster friends and by the privileged rich who "smashed up things and then retreated back into their money or vast carelessness."

Other novels by Fitzgerald include *Tales of the Jazz Age* (1922), *The Beautiful and Damned* (1922), *Tender is the Night* (1934) and the unfinished *The Last Tycoon* (1941).

five-cent piece. Silver half-dimes were the first coins struck by the U.S. mint in 1795. The silver content was reduced in 1853. In 1866 the coinage of nickel five-cent pieces was authorized. The value of the coin remained one-twentieth of the standard dollar.

Five Civilized Nations. The Cherokee, Choctaw, Chickasaw, Creek and Seminole, who were removed to Oklahoma in the 1820's from their homes in the Gulf Plains, became known in the Indian Territory as the Five Civilized Nations. Each was organized as a republic. All except the Seminole had written constitutions and laws.

Five Forks, battle of (Apr. 1, 1865). In a bloody battle, near Petersburg, Va., during the closing days of the Civil War, Gen. Philip Sheridan cut to pieces Gen. George Pickett's Confederate troops and forced Gen. Robert E. Lee to evacuate Richmond and Petersburg.

Five-Power Naval Treaty (Feb. 6, 1922). At the Washington Conference, the U.S., Great Britain, Japan, France and Italy agreed to accept a 10-year naval holiday during which no new capital ships were to be built and to limit the building of capital ships according to a 5–5–5–1.7–1.7 ratio for tonnage. No agreeement was reached on construction of smaller ships, cruisers, destroyers and submarines. The naval race continued at this level.

Five-Twenties. During the Civil War the Union issued bonds which became redeemable after five years and payable after 20 years. They paid 6% interest. Repayment in gold was not specified. When it was proposed, after the war, that repayment be made in greenbacks, Radical Republicans charged that this would be a betrayal of the nation's creditors who had helped finance the war during desperate times. Eventually the bonds were redeemed either in gold or in paper money that had the confidence of the bondholders.

flag, American. The Continental Congress, June 14, 1777, enacted a resolution ". . . that the Flag of the thirteen United

States be 13 stripes, alternate red and white, that the Union be 13 stars, white in a blue field representing a new constellation." On Jan. 13, 1794, Vermont and Kentucky having been admitted to the Union, Congress added two stars and two stripes. In 1818, however, a congressional law provided that the 13 stripes be restored to represent the original 13 states and that a star be added to the blue canton for each state after its admission to the Union. With the admission of Alaska in 1958 and Hawaii in 1959, the 49th and 50th stars were added to the flag.

Flag Day (June 14). By proclamation in 1916 Pres. Wilson called upon his countrymen to observe June 14 as a day for honoring the American flag. It was on this day in 1777 that the Continental Congress adopted the flag. Flag Day is generally observed in the U.S., but is a legal holiday only in Pennsylvania.

"Flag Salute" Cases. The U.S. Supreme Court sustained the State of Pennsylvania in excluding from its schools children of Jehovah's Witnesses, who in the name of their beliefs refused to salute the flag (*Minersville District v. Gobitis*, 1940). This decision was reversed in *West Virginia State Board of Education v. Barnette* (1943) when a law requiring that the flag be saluted regardless of religious beliefs was held to violate the 1st Amendment.

257

flatboats. Widely used on inland rivers and canals, the raft-like vessels with flat bottoms could be moved along by means of poles in shallow water or floated with the current. They were also pulled by horses or mules walking along the river or canal banks.

Annually, in the early 19th century, thousands of flatboats bearing the produce of the lower Northwest descended the Mississippi to New Orleans. Regular flatboatmen earned about $50 for the voyage. They returned north by sea or by foot or horseback over the Natchez Trace, a 500-mile road running from Natchez, Miss., to Nashville, Tenn.

Flatheads. The Indian tribe lived in western Montana and were properly known as Salish; the name was applied to one of the largest language families of the Northwest—Salishan. They were called Flatheads, however, by neighboring tribes who "pointed" their heads; hence the heads of others looked flat to them. The Flatheads were friendly to whites and in 1841 welcomed the Jesuit missionary, De Smet. According to the terms of the Garfield Treaty (1872), they moved further north to a lake in Montana which was given the name Lake Flathead, where they have remained.

Fletcher v. Peck **(1810).** The U.S. Supreme Court declared that an act of the Georgia legislature had violated the Constitution by impairing a contract. The case arose out of the fraudulent land grants by Georgia to Yazoo stockholders in 1795 and their cancellation by the legislature in 1796.

In the first interpretation of the contract clause in the Constitution (Art. I, Sec. 10, Par. 1) Chief Justice Marshall delivered the Court's opinion. He held that the grant of land, even though made under circumstances of the most scandalous corruption, was a contract within the meaning of the constitutional provision and could not be rescinded after the land in question had passed into the hands of innocent purchasers.

Flexner, Abraham (1866–1959). Educator. Born in Louisville, Ky., he joined the research staff of Carnegie Foundation for the Advancement of Teaching; his reports (1910, 1912) hastened much-needed reforms in medical education. He was influential in guiding the philanthropies of the Rockefeller, Carnegie and George Eastman trusts. He was the first director of the Institute for Advanced Study, Princeton, N.J.

Flintlock, Operation. The code name designated the Allied attack on the Marshall Islands in early 1944 during World War II.

flogging. Thrashing with a whip or lash as a form of punishment was abolished in the U.S. Army by act of Congress, Aug. 5, 1861, and in the Navy, June

6, 1872. It is still legally permitted, though rarely practiced in the punishment of misdemeanors in the state of Delaware.

Flood Control Act (1928). Following the great Mississippi flood of 1927, Congress appropriated $325 million for levee work in the Mississippi Valley over a 10-year period.

The program for control of flooding rivers in flat lands, where the river has not cut a channel deep enough to allow for peak periods of flow, includes building levees, planting trees in watershed areas to slow rapid run-offs, constructing reservoirs or retarding basins and deepening channels.

Florida. A South Atlantic state, known as the "Sunshine State," it was the 27th state admitted to the Union, March 3, 1845. It seceded from the Union on Jan. 10, 1861, and was readmitted on June 25, 1868.

Florida was named by its discoverer, Ponce de León, in 1513. Subsequent Spanish settlements were challenged by the French who were driven out before the 17th century. The Spaniards founded St. Augustine (1565), the oldest city in the U.S. In 1763 Spain was forced to cede Florida to the English, but regained the territory in 1783 at the end of the Revolutionary War.

The U.S. claimed that west Florida was part of the Louisiana Purchase (1803). After Indian troubles had precipitated

an invasion of Florida by U.S. troops under Andrew Jackson (1818), Spain sold Florida to the U.S. (1819). It was organized as a territory in 1822.

Miami Beach, Fla., has the largest concentration of luxury hotels in the U.S.; Tallahassee is the capital. Major agricultural products include citrus fruits and vegetables; industries include food products and chemicals.

Florida Purchase (1819). Spain's cession of Florida to the U.S. for $5,000,000 rounded out the southeastern boundary of continental U.S.

U.S.-Spanish relations had been disrupted by the difficulty of controlling the area. It was a refuge for runaway slaves, a hiding place for smugglers and outlaw bands and a base for Indian attacks on settlements in the Southeast. Gen. Andrew Jackson had pursued Seminole Indians into Florida in 1818.

When it seemed to Spain that either sale or seizure was in the offing, the minister to the U.S. negotiated the sale with Sec. of State John Quincy Adams, an ardent nationalist who had been pressing for the purchase (Adams-Onís Treaty). The treaty settled more than the Florida issue, for it established the boundary between the U.S. and Spanish Mexico, excluding Texas from the Louisiana Territory.

flour milling. About 1785 Oliver Evans put into operation an automatic flour mill which cut labor time required for grinding grain by one-half. The invention spurred the growth of the industry. In the East during the early 19th century Baltimore, Richmond and Rochester became important milling centers. As the Middle West became the nation's granary, large mills were concentrated in St. Louis and Milwaukee. In the 1870's Minneapolis millers substituted rollers for the millstones used in the grinding process since ancient times. Kansas City became a milling center in the 1890's. The state of Kansas remains the leading producer of wheat flour in the U.S. In the post-World War I period, Buffalo became one of the great milling centers, owing to the availability of cheap electric power, nearness to Canadian wheat and great consumer markets.

Flowering of New England, 1815–1865, The (1936). The book is the first in a series of five by the literary historian, essayist and critic, Van Wyck Brooks, who became the genealogist of American literature with this successful series. The other volumes in the series are *New England: Indian Summer, 1865–1915* (1940), *The World of Washington Irving* (1944), *The Times of Melville and Whitman* (1947) and *The Confident Years, 1885–1915* (1952).

Flushing Remonstrance (Dec. 27, 1657). The inhabitants of the Town of Flushing wrote to Gov. Stuyvesant of New Amsterdam that they would not accept his command that they "not receive any of those people called Quakers because they are supposed to be by some, seducers of the people." The signers wrote: "We desire in this case not to judge least we be judged, neither to condemn least we be condemned, but rather let every man stand and fall to his own Master." It was probably the first declaration of religious tolerance by any group of ordinary citizens in American history.

Flying Cloud. Built by a master designer, Donald McKay, and launched in 1851, the clipper ship achieved during her maiden voyage the record distance of 374 miles in a day's run. While conventional sailing ships made the trip from New York to San Francisco in 159 days, the *Flying Cloud* cut the time to 89 days.

food stamps. Persons on relief, 1939–40, were permitted to buy $1 to $1.50 worth of "orange stamps" each week for each family member. For each $1 of these stamps the purchaser was given, in addition, 50 cents' worth of "blue stamps" which were used to buy surplus farm commodities. The purpose of the New Deal plan was to dispose of agricultural surpluses and, at the same time, help the poor.

The food stamp program was revived in 1961 and has been

continued on a limited basis since that time. In 1967 families with the lowest incomes paid about $2 for coupons worth $10 a person. The average family paid about 64% of the coupon value. Commercial banks redeem the stamps and the federal treasury pays the additional cost.

football. English in origin, the sport took approximately its present form in the U.S. when Yale, Harvard, Princeton and Columbia met in 1876 to adopt rules. In 1880, the Intercollegiate Football Association was formed; and through the years there have been many changes in rules. The game is played by 11 players on each side with intricate running plays starting behind the line of scrimmage by half-backs who seek to move the ball forward for a touchdown. The forward pass was first used early in the 20th century; spectator interest has increased to a point where college games and, in recent years, professional games attract huge numbers of spectators.

In some colleges, football revenue supports the whole extra-curricular program. It is not rare for football coaches to be paid more than professors. Many colleges offer athletic scholarships to high school players. Abuse of this practice and the extension of the season, usually from October through December, led the Ivy League to adopt a code of ethics in 1952.

Sunday games by professionals, first organized in 1920, attract rooters whose enthusiasm is comparable to that of college alumni.

Forager, Operation. The code name designated Allied operations in the Mariana Islands in mid-June 1944 during World War II.

Forbes Expedition. During the French and Indian War Gen. John Forbes, to reach Fort Duquesne, later the site of Pittsburgh, cut a road through western Pennsylvania. His force consisted of British regulars, Pennsylvanians, Marylanders and Virginians, including Col. George Washington. The French, however, did not wait for the English attack but burned and evacuated the fort when they lost their Indian allies and learned that they had been cut off from Canada by the fall of Fort Frontenac, in Ontario, Aug. 27, 1758. Fort Duquesne was taken over by the English, Nov. 25, 1758.

The Forbes Road was used as a major highway between the East and Ohio Valley for almost a half-century.

Force Acts. At various times the federal government has found it necessary to demonstrate to the states that it was determined to enforce laws of Congress, if necessary, by armed force. In two notable instances when a Force Act was passed by Congress, it involved Southern states.

In the Force Act (1833) Pres. Jackson was authorized by Congress to use the Army and Navy to collect import duties listed in the Tariffs of 1828 and 1832. South Carolina's Ordinance of Nullification had declared these tariff laws null and void. It became unnecessary, however, to invoke the Force Act when Congress passed the compromise Tariff of 1833. South Carolina, nevertheless, proceeded to nullify the Force Act itself in order to maintain its stand on states' rights.

During the Reconstruction era, Congress passed four Force Acts (1870–75) intended to protect Negro rights guaranteed by the 14th and 15th Amendments. These had been infringed upon by terrorist activity against Negroes by secret organizations such as the Ku Klux Klan. The Force Acts established heavy fines and jail penalties for offenses under either amendment and gave to federal courts rather than to southern courts original jurisdiction over all cases arising out of the amendments. As evidence that the Congress meant business in protecting Negro civil rights, Pres. Grant placed nine counties of South Carolina under martial law.

It was not until 1894 that Congress repealed most of the provisions of the Force Acts.

Ford, Henry (1863–1947). Automobile manufacturer. Born in Greenfield, Mich., he was prominent as an automobile manufacturer by 1908. His Model T, in "any color you choose so long as it's black" (introduced in 1909), sold for $550 in 1913. The sale of 168,000 automobiles (1913) represented about one-third of the whole industry in the U.S. In 1914 he introduced the electric conveyor belt for assembly of cars. By 1925 Ford was turning out a complete car every 10 seconds. The Ford Motor Co. is the second largest manufacturer in the U.S. today (after General Motors). Ford was its organizer and president (1903–19, 1943–45). During World War I, he chartered the Ford Peace Ship, *Oscar II*, and took a group to Europe in an unsuccessful effort to end the war.

Ford Foundation. Founded in 1936 with income largely from Ford Motor Company stock its funds have been used to support education, culture and community welfare in the U.S. and abroad.

By 1965 it had distributed over two billion dollars by underwriting institutions, individuals and communities. About half of the Foundation's funds have been donated as educational grants.

Among the nonprofit corporations with special objectives that the Foundation has financed are the Fund for the Republic, devoted to study of the basic issues underlying a free society, and the National Merit Scholarship Corporation, concerned with subsidizing the college education of outstanding students.

Fordney-McCumber Tariff Act of 1922. The highest protective tariff in American history until that time was passed during the Republican administration of Pres. Harding.

Farmers, traditionally for low tariffs, joined industry in demanding high tariffs. The "Farm Bloc" contended that protection was necessary to protect farmers from "dumping" from abroad. New industries producing chemicals and dye stuffs demanded protection against German firms. Old industries joined in the demand for protection to develop national self-sufficiency, the need for which the past war had indicated.

The President was given flexible power to lower or raise existing duties by as much as 50% to equalize costs of production here and abroad. He was to be advised by a Tariff Commission which studied production costs in the U.S. and foreign countries.

Foreign Service of the U.S. The Department of State ordinarily assigns Foreign Service officers abroad as ambassadors, ministers, counselors of embassy or legation, attachés, diplomatic secretaries, consuls general, consuls or vice consuls.

Forest Reserve Act (1891). The President was empowered by law to close timber areas to settlers and establish them as national parks. A small start was made by Pres. Harrison who set apart about 13 million acres of forest lands. In the early 1900's Pres. Theodore Roosevelt, an ardent conservationist, put aside almost 150 million acres of unsold government timber land and turned over the supervision of the national forests to the Sec. of Agriculture.

"forgotten man, the." The term was popularized in a lecture by William Graham Sumner (1840–1910), professor of political and social science at Yale. It is also a chapter heading in his *What Social Classes Owe to Each Other* (1883). He referred to the man, or woman, who through patient industry supports a family and pays taxes, but is "the only one for whom there is no provision in the great scramble and big divide" of the "political bunglers" and "social quacks."

The phrase was used by Gov. Franklin D. Roosevelt (N.Y.) in a pre-convention campaign speech, Apr. 7, 1932, to describe the "underprivileged man" or the "underdog."

Forrest, Edwin (1806–72). Actor. Born in Philadelphia, Pa., he was the earliest American-born actor to achieve an international reputation for portrayal of Shakespearean roles. His first New York success was as Othello (1826). He encouraged plays by American dramatists by offering prizes and acted in Robert M. Bird's tragedy, *The Gladiator*. His rivalry with the English actor, Macready, led to the Astor Place Riot (1849) at New York. This was followed by Forrest's scandalous divorce proceedings (1851–69). He bequeathed a fortune to establish a home for aged actors (Forrest Home, Philadelphia).

Fort. All forts are listed alphabetically by name (for example, Sumter, Fort).

"forty acres and a mule." Negro slaves mistakenly expected at the end of the Civil War that the plantations of their masters would be confiscated and divided among them. In 1862 the expression was "ten acres and a mule," but the hope was enlarged to 40 acres as a consequence of Gen. William T. Sherman's special field order (Jan. 16, 1865): "Every family shall have a plot of not more than forty acres of tillable ground." The federal government had, however, made no such promise to the slaves.

"forty-eighters." The term is used to describe German-Americans who emigrated to the U.S. as a consequence of the Revolution of 1848. Among the more prominent of these immigrants was Carl Schurz, political reformer and U.S. Senator from Missouri (1869–75).

"forty-niners." The discovery of gold in California in 1848 led to the gold rush of 1849 by people from all walks of life in the U.S. and other parts of the world. Most took the overland route across the Great Plains, along the Oregon or Santa Fe Trails. Others made the six-month trip by sea around Cape Horn. A trip that was a rough combination of sea and land was the one down to Panama, across the Isthmus on horseback, on muleback or on the backs of Indians and up the Pacific coast to Sacramento.

Death and disease claimed many of the "forty-niners" long before they reached the "gold diggings."

Foster, Stephen Collins (1826–64). Composer. Born in Allegheny City, Pa., he began life as a bookkeeper, but after publication of "O Susanna" and "Away Down South," in *Songs of the Sable Harmonists* (1848), he turned to writing ballads for the Negro minstrel troupes popular in his day. He sold E. P. Christy (1851) the privilege of singing his songs from manuscript, but reserved publication rights for himself. Among his greatest songs were "The Old Folks at Home" (1851; also known as "Swanee River"), "My Old Kentucky Home" (1853) and "Old Black Joe" (1860).

Foster probably visited the South only once, but his best songs gave expression to the melancholy of the American Negro and became part of the folk-literature of American music. He died in poverty in a Bowery rooming house in New York City.

"Founding Fathers." Of the 55 delegates who met at Philadelphia in 1787 and framed the new Constitution, only 39 remained to sign the completed document. The signers, known as the "Founding Fathers," included George Washington, Benjamin Franklin, James Madison, Alexander Hamilton and James Wilson.

Four Chaplains. On Feb. 3, 1943, the U.S. troop carrier *Dorchester* was torpedoed by a German submarine off the coast of Greenland. On the ship were four chaplains: Rabbi Alexander Goode, Jewish; Father John Washington, Roman Catholic; the Rev. George Fox, Methodist; and Rev. Clark Poling, Reformed Church.

The chaplains helped men search for life jackets and launch lifeboats. When there were no more life jackets to be found, each chaplain gave away his own. As the *Dorchester* slid under the water, the four chaplains linked arms, braced themselves against the deck railing, and prayed until the seas engulfed them.

The "Chapel of the Four Chaplains," an interfaith memorial, is located on the campus of Temple University, Philadelphia, Pa.

Four Freedoms. During the period 1939–41, between the outbreak of World War II and U.S. entrance into the War, Pres. Roosevelt pointed out again and again what an Axis victory would mean for the democracies. In a speech to Congress (Jan. 6, 1941), he declared that moral world order must include the "Four Freedoms"—freedom of speech, freedom of religion, freedom from want and freedom from fear.

Four-H (4-H) Clubs. First started in 1900 in Illinois for boys and girls in rural areas, the organizations aim to improve methods of farming and home economics and to promote good citizenship. Since then they have become nationwide under the supervision of the Department of Agriculture. There are now about 2,225,000 club members.

The symbol of the clubs is a four-leaf clover with an "H" on each leaf. Members pledge: "My Head to clear thinking. My Heart to great loyalty. My Hands to larger service. My Health to better living. For my club, my community, and my country."

"Four Hundred, The." The list of slightly more than 300 social celebrities was compiled in 1892 by Ward McAllister, a wealthy socialite. He prepared it for Mrs. John Jacob Astor on the occasion of her New York ball, Feb. 1. The list included "two visitors from Baltimore" (the Browns). It was so heavily weighted with bankers, lawyers, brokers, real estate men and railroaders, that a critic remarked: "The Four Hundred would have fled in a body from a poet, a painter, a musician or a clever Frenchman."

Fourteen Points. Pres. Wilson hoped that World War I might end without bitterness. When the Russian Communists who had overthrown Czar Nicholas II released secret agreements revealing how the Allies planned to carve up the German Empire, Wilson gave his answer. In a message to Congress, Jan. 8, 1918, he outlined his Fourteen Points for a just and generous peace. Unfortunately, he failed to obtain in advance agreement from the Allies to support his proposals.

Several of the Fourteen Points dealt with specific territorial settlements, such as the return of Alsace-Lorraine to France. The most significant general ideas included: "open covenants of peace openly arrived at"; guarantee of freedom of the seas; the removal of tariff walls and other barriers that had obstructed trade and encouraged enmity among nations; general disarmament; self-determination for the peoples of Europe, meaning that European boundaries would be adjusted in accordance with the people's wishes; the creation of a League of Nations to preserve the peace.

In Oct. 1918, Germany asked for an armistice based on the Fourteen Points. The Allies agreed after reserving for themselves determination of freedom of the seas and gaining from Germany acceptance of the principle of reparations.

Fox Indians. The tribe, called Renards by the French, was forced from the western shores of Lake Erie to the forests of Wisconsin. They fought relentlessly but unsuccessfully against the French (Fox-French Wars, 1712–18, 1727–38) and sided with the Americans in the Revolutionary War. The Fox, an Algonquian people, joined the British in the War of 1812. They later joined the Sauk against the U.S. in the Black Hawk War. In 1842 they agreed to leave Iowa but later returned. They are now located on reservations in Iowa, Kansas and Oklahoma.

Franciscan missionaries. Many members of a Catholic religious order following the Rule of St. Francis came to preach in the New World. In the 16th century they used New Spain (Mexico) as a base for pushing into what was later to become the U.S. Southwest. Padres Juan de la Asunción and Pedro Nazal are believed to be the first white men to have entered Arizona (1538). In 1582 Fray Bernardino Beltrán was aided by Spanish soldiers in searching for missing missionaries in New Mexico. The Beltrán-Espejo Expedition did not save the missing friars, but it increased Spain's determination to colonize New Mexico and California and convert the Indians to Christianity.

Late in the 18th century the Franciscans under Father Junipero Serra founded nine missions in California. The missions were not only seminaries, but also training schools for Indians who were taught European methods of raising grain and fruits, tending livestock, leather work and other crafts. A complete mission plant included a church, an Indian village, shops, orchards, pastures and living quarters for priests, friars and soldiers.

The Franciscans were also active in French territory in the upper Mississippi and along the Great Lakes.

Frankfurter, Felix (1882–1965). Jurist. Born in Vienna, Austria, he came to the U.S. in 1894. He was granted his A.B. by the College of the City of N.Y. (1902) and his LL.B. by Harvard Law School (1906). He taught administrative law at Harvard (1914–39). His critique of the Sacco-Vanzetti trial (1927) gained him national prominence. He was appointed Associate Justice of the U.S. Supreme Court (1939–62) by Pres. F. D. Roosevelt. He opposed the Black-Douglas position that First Amendment rights were absolute; and in the *Dennis Case* (1951) repudiated the "clear and present danger" doctrine, holding that advocating the overthrow of government merits little protection.

franking privilege. Beginning in 1776 the privilege of sending mail free was accorded to members of Congress. The privilege was extended to the President, Vice-President, Cabinet officers and a few others. By 1873 the privilege was so abused that Congress abolished it for individuals. It has, however, been continued for federal departments and congressmen writing on official business.

Franklin, battle of (Nov. 30, 1864). Confederate forces under Gen. John B. Hood were disastrously repulsed in a direct frontal attack on Gen. John Schofield at a little Tennessee town, south of Nashville. Confederate casualties included six general officers among the 1,750 killed and 3,800 wounded. Union losses were 189 killed and 1,033 wounded.

Franklin, Benjamin (1706–90). Statesman, scientists and philosopher. Born in Boston, Mass., he settled in Philadelphia where he started in printing and gained a wide circle of readers through his *Poor Richard's Almanack* (1732–57). He formed the discussion club, the Junto, which developed into the American Philosophical Society (1743). He invented an improved heating stove (about 1740); his kite experiments (1752) demonstrated the identity of lightning and electricity. As a statesman, he tried for conciliation with Britain but recognized the drift toward war. He helped write the Declaration of Independence and was one of the negotiators of the final peace treaty with Britain (1783). A member of Constitutional Convention (1787), he helped frame a compromise between the large and small states. His popular *Autobiography* covered his early years.

Franklin, State of (1784–88). When North Carolina ceded the Watauga region to Congress, the settlers set up a state which they named Franklin. John Sevier was elected governor, but he became involved in other interests and local leadership failed.

The new state, sometimes referred to as the "lost state," or Frankland, failed to win recognition from either North Carolina or Congress. It collapsed when North Carolina rescinded her cession of the Watauga region. In 1789 the western region was again ceded to Congress, but by this time it had been staked out by private speculators and the movement for independent statehood was dead.

Frayser's Farm, battle of (June 30, 1862). As Union Gen. George McClellan retreated toward the James River, Va., to gain protection of the fleet, southerners came close to victory at Savage's Station (June 29). On the 30th there was another battle referred to as White Oak Swamp, Glendale or Frayser's Farm. Here McClellan held off the Confederates under Gen. James Longstreet and Gen. A. P. Hill. The Confederates lost 7,000 killed, wounded and missing to the Union's 4,000. It was a loss that the South could not afford during this part of the Seven Days' fighting in the Peninsular Campaign.

Frazier-Lemke Act (1934). Intended to aid debt-ridden farmers to save their farms from foreclosure, the Farm Mortgage Moratorium Act stated that a five-year delay before payment of mortgage installments was possible. Even if a mortgage had already been foreclosed, the farmer could buy his farm back if he met the terms set by a federal court. The Act was declared unconstitutional as a violation of property rights under the 5th Amendment (*Louisville Joint Stock Land Bank v. Radford*, 1935).

A revised act (1935) outlining more specifically the protection of the rights of the creditor was upheld by the U.S. Supreme Court (*Wright v. Vinton Branch of Mountain Trust Bank of Roanoke*, 1937).

Fredericksburg, battle of (Dec. 13, 1862). Gen. Ambrose Burnside, newly appointed commander of the Army of the Potomac, was disastrously defeated in Virginia by Gen. Robert E. Lee's Confederate army. Burnside had sought to advance on Richmond but was turned back by Lee.

Pres. Lincoln, disheartened by the failures of his generals, who were being beaten despite superior manpower, had replaced Gen. George McClellan with Burnside. After the slaughter at Fredericksburg, he replaced Burnside with Gen. Joseph Hooker.

Freedmen's Bureau. Although the federal agency was authorized by Congress to help both Negroes and "loyal [white] refugees" in the South during the Reconstruction period, its efforts were concentrated on aiding former slaves.

The Bureau functioned under the War Department from 1865 to 1872, and its immediate task was to prevent people from starving. In addition, the Bureau distributed clothing, housed refugees who had left the fields for the towns, provided transportation for freedmen and refugees making their way back home and established hospitals and schools. The Bureau was also the custodian of abandoned and confiscated land, but this was less than 1% of the land and the purchase price placed it out of the reach of the freedmen.

Most southerners were critical of the Bureau, but its work helped to relieve disaster conditions in the postwar South.

Freedom Democrats. The Mississippi Freedom Democratic party burst dramatically on the national scene in the summer of 1964 at the National Democratic Convention in Atlantic City. Its delegates—all Negroes —demanded to be seated in place of the regular delegation on the ground that Negroes were deprived of the ballot. They refused the offer of two "honorary" seats as merely a token.

The party is part of the great movement of social protest in American history in which the crusaders fail to find full expression in the major political parties.

"Freedom for Puerto Rico!" The cry launched one of the most terrifying incidents in the history of the U.S. House of Representatives. On Mar. 1, 1954, the House was conducting business when the cry was heard from the visitors' gallery overhead; it was followed by the rattle of gunshots. Five representatives were wounded.

The attack had come from four members of the extremist Puerto Rican Nationalist party, demonstrating for Puerto Rican independence from the U.S. Gov. Luis Muñoz Marin of Puerto Rico characterized the attack as "lunacy" and the attackers as fanatics. The assailants were sentenced to long prison terms.

On Nov. 1, 1950 two Puerto Rican Nationalists tried to force their way into Blair House in Washington, D.C., to kill Pres. Truman. Although the attempt was foiled, a guard was killed along with one of the gunmen.

"Freedom Now!" Under the slogan, the Negro civil rights movement of the 1960's sparked demonstrations all over the U.S.

The petition by leaders of the Selma-to-Montgomery Freedom March, prepared for presentation to George C. Wallace,

Mar. 25, 1965, read in part: "We have come to you, the Governor of Alabama, to declare that we must have our freedom NOW. We must have the right to vote; we must have equal protection of the law, and an end to police brutality."

freedom riders. During the civil rights movement of the early 1960's, groups of white and Negro people hired busses in the North and toured the South stopping in various cities and towns to demonstrate against discrimination. In May 1961 white citizens of Anniston and Birmingham, Ala., attacked two racially mixed groups of freedom riders on a bus tour from Washington to New Orleans.

freeholder. During the colonial period suffrage and the right to hold office were largely limited to freeholders or freemen, although in some colonies holders of other forms of property had these rights. Freeholders were estate owners who held tenure on their lands for life and could pass their holdings on to descendants.

Freeholders retained their privileged position until democratic pressures early in the 19th century brought about universal manhood suffrage.

Freeman's Farm, battles of (Sept. 19 and Oct. 7, 1777). In both Revolutionary War battles, also known as Bemis Heights or Stillwater, British Gen. Burgoyne was repulsed when he sought high ground,

south of Saratoga, N.Y., near the headquarters of American Gen. Gates. Burgoyne was thus frustrated in his move south from Canada to Albany. Within two weeks after the second battle, he surrendered to Gen. Gates at Saratoga.

Freeport doctrine. One of the Lincoln-Douglas debates in Illinois, 1858, took place in Freeport. It was here on Aug. 27 that Abraham Lincoln asked how Stephen Douglas could support the Dred Scott decision and the principle of popular sovereignty at the same time. Under the U.S. Supreme Court ruling Congress could not exclude slavery from the territories. Under the principle set forth by Douglas the people of the territories could determine whether or not to permit slavery.

Douglas' reply, known as the Freeport doctrine, was that slavery could not exist anywhere for a day if the territorial legislature did not pass the necessary laws to protect and police slave property.

The answer was realistic but kindled southern opposition to Douglas. It divided the Democratic party, as Lincoln expected it would, and made possible a Republican victory in 1860.

"free ships, free goods." During the wars between France and England, 1793–1815, the U.S. maintained that in time of war all goods whether belonging to neutrals or belligerents were, if carried in neutral vessels, thereby exempted from capture, unless they were by nature contraband of war. This doctrine was opposed by England, regarded by neutral carriers at the time as the "tyrant of the seas." It was one of the differences which led to the War of 1812.

By the Declaration of Paris (1856), which the U.S. did not agree to as a whole, the major powers subscribed to the principle that free ships made free goods and that goods even of belligerents if carried on neutral ships were exempt from capture.

free silver. The movement for the free and unlimited coinage of silver became a major political issue after 1873 and did not leave the political arena until 1900. Free coinage of silver was intended to increase the amount of money in circulation, raise prices and thus aid farmers and other debtors to pay off their debts more easily. For silver miners faced with a surplus of silver after 1873 free silver would have meant purchase by the U.S. Mint of silver at the old ratio of 16 ounces of silver for every ounce of gold (16–1).

Since silver had depreciated in value to a point where 16 ounces of it was worth less than one ounce of gold, its purchase at that ratio was opposed by businessmen and others who felt that free coinage of silver would permit redemption of government bonds and payment of other debts by a cheap currency.

Free silver ceased to be an issue after 1900 when new gold discoveries lowered the value of gold in relation to silver and made possible a cheaper currency without unlimited purchase of silver by the U.S. Mint.

Free Soil party (1848–54). Antislavery elements in both the Whig and Democratic parties combined with the Liberty party to form a new third party. The party opposed admission of any new slave states or the addition of slave territory and called for free homesteads for genuine settlers.

Martin Van Buren, who had indicated opposition to slavery, was the party's nominee for President in 1848. His vote was large enough to contribute to the defeat of Lewis Cass, the regular Democratic nominee. The party elected nine congressmen.

In 1852 the party lost strength. Two years later it merged with the newly formed Republican party.

Frémont explorations. As a consequence of his explorations in the Far West in the 1840's, John C. Frémont became known as "The Pathfinder." He explored the territory north of the Great Salt Lake and areas that were later to enter the Union as Nevada, Idaho, Washington, Oregon and California. In his expedition of 1846, he became involved in the U.S. conquest of California.

Frémont's vivid reports of the Northwest, written with the

aid of his wife, Jessie Benton Frémont, publicized the fertility of the region and were a sound guide for emigrants.

Frémont, John Charles (1813–90). Army officer, explorer and politician. Born in Savannah, Ga., he is remembered as the "Pathfinder." His expeditions along the Oregon Trail and into New Mexico (1843–44) were vividly and accurately reported with the literary help of his wife, Jessie Benton Frémont (1824–1902), daughter of Sen. Thomas H. Benton (1782–1858). Exploring in California, he helped capture Los Angeles (1846) during the Mexican War. Frémont served (1850–51) as one of the first two senators from California, and was the unsuccessful Republican candidate for President (1856). He was given a Western command by Pres. Lincoln in the Civil War but was relieved when he prematurely confiscated the slaves of rebel Missourians. His personal fortunes declined in his later years, and he was rescued from poverty by his wife's writings and his appointment as territorial governor of Arizona (1878–83).

French and Indian War (1754–63). The final struggle in North America between the French and English, each with their Indian allies, was known in Europe as the Seven Years' War. It was the last of a number of wars, beginning in 1689, fought in Europe, Asia and America. It ended in triumph for Britain, with the French virtually ousted from North America.

In an opening skirmish George Washington was turned back in a move on Fort Duquesne, 1754, in western Pennsylvania. The fort was one of a series the French had built extending from Canada to the Ohio Valley. In 1755 Washington headed a group of Virginia militiamen, part of a much larger force of British regulars under Gen. Edward Braddock, in another advance on Fort Duquesne. Gen. Braddock's army was disastrously defeated and the general himself mortally wounded in the Battle of the Wilderness (July 9, 1755).

English reverses were corrected when William Pitt became Prime Minister. He concentrated British strength on the conquest of Canada and the American interior. Land and the fur trade were the great stakes.

In 1758 British Generals Jeffrey Amherst and James Wolfe captured the French fortress of Louisbourg, the key to the St. Lawrence River and the Atlantic fisheries. The same year, another English force took Fort Duquesne. Realizing the fort could not be defended, the French blew it up. The English erected Fort Pitt (later the city of Pittsburgh) on the site.

The greatest triumph of the war was the capture of Quebec in 1759. Gen. Wolfe stormed the Heights of Abraham outside Quebec and took the city from French Gen. Louis Montcalm. Both Montcalm and Wolfe died in the battle. In 1760 the city of Montreal also surrendered to the British. The war in America was over. The Treaty of Paris (1763) ended the dream of a New France.

French spoliation claims. American citizens whose commerce suffered during the wars following the outbreak of the French Revolution sued France for damages.

The first claims were settled by the Convention of 1800 and by the purchase of Louisiana (1803) in which the U.S. government undertook as part of the purchase price to pay the claims of American citizens.

The second series of claims was settled by treaty in 1831, but the delays in payment almost led to war between the U.S. and France when Pres. Jackson in 1834 threatened to seize French property. The British mediated and payments were made in 1836.

Freneau, Philip Morin (1752–1832). Poet and editor. Born in New York, N.Y., he is known as "the poet of the American Revolution." Captured at sea during the Revolutionary War, he described his brutal imprisonment in *The British Prison Ship: A Poem* (1781). After the war Freneau edited the pro-Jeffersonian *National Gazette* (1791–93). The most significant American poet before William Cullen Bryant, he wrote such poems as "The Indian Burying Ground," "The Wild Honeysuckle," "Eutaw Springs" and "A Poem on the Rising Glory of America."

Fries Rebellion (1799). John Fries stirred Pennsylvania Germans to revolt against a land tax. The resistance was also known as the "Hot Water Rebellion" when the farmers' wives poured scalding water on tax assessors who tried to measure the size of their windows.

Fries was found guilty of treason but was pardoned by Pres. John Adams before the death sentence was carried out.

Fritchie, Barbara, legend of. Immortalized in John Greenleaf Whittier's Civil War poem, the little aged lady is supposed to have waved a Union flag and taunted "Stonewall" Jackson's troops as they passed through Frederick, Md., in 1862. Jackson, allegedly impressed with her bravery, saw to it that no harm came her way.

There is no evidence that the flag waving or taunting took place. She may have waved a flag when the Union soldiers came through a week later.

Frobisher's voyages. Martin Frobisher, an English seaman, made three voyages for Queen Elizabeth in search of the Northwest Passage. On his first trip in 1576, he discovered Baffin's land, met Esquimaux, and returned with some of the ore that had gold content. The report of gold and Frobisher's belief that he had found an all-water route to India, led to

273

the second trip in 1577, a trip diverted by the search for a mine. On the third trip in 1578, he brought home 800 tons of worthless ore. When the hope of a gold discovery diminished, interest in finding the Northwest Passage revived.

frontier theory, Turner's. On July 12, 1893, Frederick Jackson Turner, professor of history at the University of Wisconsin, read his famous paper, "The Significance of the Frontier in American History," to the American Historical Association. It explained American history in terms of the influence of the frontier.

Turner's hypothesis, which became a thesis through frequent repetition, held that the frontier stimulated individualism, developed democratic institutions and was a crucible for immigrants. It required special legislation by the national government and thus was a force for nationalism. The availability of free land acted as a "safety valve" for people in more settled areas who could move West. Turner subsequently modified this part of the thesis since skills required on the frontier did not attract industrial workers from the East.

Turner did not always sharply define his use of the term "frontier" and used it in three senses: a moving line separating areas populated by more, and by less than, two persons per square mile; a geographical area, thinly populated but experiencing settlement and development; and a historical process. He viewed the frontier as a process of Americanization and ever-changing. He held that frontier life contributed to the development of "individualism, democracy and nationalism," which "powerfully affected the East and the Old World."

Turner's thesis has been subjected to criticism by historians who have contended that democracy did not come out of the West unless it was first carried there. But his frontier theory, though modified, helps in understanding our nation's development.

Frost, Robert Lee (1874–1963). Poet. Born in San Francisco, he was a professor of English at Amherst (1916–20; 1923–25; 1926–38) and a professor of poetry at Harvard (from 1936). Most of his poetry is based on New England life. Awarded the Pulitzer Prize four times (1924, 1931, 1937, 1943), he was the first poet to participate in a presidential inaugural ceremony (1961). Among his collections are *A Boy's Will* (1913), *North of Boston* (1914), *New Hampshire* (1923), *A Witness Tree* (1943). Among his best-remembered poems are "The Death of the Hired Man," "Mending Wall" and "Birches."

Fugitive Slave Law (1850). As part of the Compromise of 1850 a severe fugitive slave law was enacted to aid in the recapture of runaway slaves. The earlier law of 1793 had proved to be ineffective. Under the new law anyone helping a slave to escape was subjected to a heavy fine and imprisonment. A U.S. marshal who let a slave escape might be sued for his value. The hunt for runaway slaves caused many of them to flee to Canada.

Fulbright Act (1946). Under a law sponsored by Sen. J. William Fulbright (Ark.), the U.S. embarked on a program of international cultural exchanges. The program was at first financed by the sale of U.S. materials remaining in foreign countries at the end of World War II. The foreign currencies were used to pay for the exchange of teachers, training of personnel and cooperative relationships between nongovernmental institutions in scientific and other areas.

Fulbright Resolution (1943). Rep. J. W. Fulbright (Ark.) and Sen. Tom Connally (Tex.) introduced in Congress a peace plan known also as the Connally-Fulbright Resolution. It favored "the creation of appropriate international machinery with power adequate to establish and to maintain a just and lasting peace" and U.S. participation "through its constitutional process."

As an outcome of this resolution the Senate approved U.S. membership in the United Nations Food and Agriculture Organization (July 21, 1945) and ratified the UN Charter by a vote of 89 to 2 (July 28,

1945). Pres. Truman signed the Charter (Aug. 8, 1945).

"full dinner pail." The slogan of the Republican campaign in the election of 1900, the "full dinner pail" was the symbol of prosperity associated with Pres. McKinley's first administration, during which the nation emerged from the depression of 1893 to 1897.

Fuller, Sarah Margaret (1810–50). Social reformer. Born in Cambridgeport, Mass., she was accepted in transcendentalist circles on a par with Alcott and Thoreau. A leader in the women's movement, her "conversations" in 1839 with ladies in Boston society were recorded in *Woman in the Nineteenth Century* (1845). She edited the transcendentalist *The Dial* (1840–42) with Ralph Waldo Emerson and George Ripley. On the staff of Horace Greeley's New York *Tribune*, she won a reputation as one of the ablest literary critics in America (1844–46). She visited Europe (1846) and with her husband, the Marquis Angelo Ossoli, a follower of Mazzini, took part in Italy's unification movement. She and her husband and infant son were drowned in a shipwreck while returning to America.

Fulton, Robert (1765–1815). Artist, civil engineer and inventor. Born in Lancaster Co., Pa., he is best remembered for building the *Clermont* (1807), which navigated the Hudson River between New York City and Albany, N.Y. It proved to be the first of a line of commercially successful steamboats. His early career was devoted to painting portraits and landscapes. Fulton lived in Europe (1786–1806) during which time he invented a machine for sawing marble and a dredge for cutting canal channels. He also wrote on the improvement of canal navigation.

"Fulton's Folly" (1807). When Robert Fulton's steamboat, the *Clermont*, made the trip up the Hudson from New York to Albany against the current in 32 hours, the term of contempt was swallowed by critics. Fulton and Robert R. Livingston had been granted a monopoly for steamboats on New York's waterways and they were successful where others before them, notably John Fitch, had failed.

In 1811 Fulton launched the *New Orleans* on the Mississippi.

Fundamental Orders of Connecticut (1639). The Connecticut planters drew up a frame of government for the towns of Hartford, Wethersfield and Windsor in accordance with the Puritan theory of civil government. Its provisions influenced subsequent state constitutions and explain why Connecticut has been called the Constitution State.

Under the Orders four deputies from each town were sent to a general assembly or court.

A governor was elected by the assembly and might not serve for two years consecutively. If the governor refused to call an assembly, the freemen (voters) of the towns had the power to call one. The assembly also elected an upper house which had the right to veto the legislation of the deputies.

Funk, Casimir (1884–1967). Biochemist. Born in Warsaw, Poland, he was granted a Ph.D. by Berne Univ. (1904) and became a citizen of the U.S. in 1920. In searching for the cause of beriberi, Funk discovered that vitamins were essential to life and reported this in his paper, "The Etiology of Deficiency Diseases" (1912). In the U.S. he continued with his original work on vitamins. He also carried on cancer research and found that two separate substances affected tumor growth and that an imbalance of the substances may be the cause of the disease.

"Fuss and Feathers." Gen. Winfield Scott (1786–1866) who led an army into Mexico City (1847) during the Mexican War was known to his troops as old "Fuss and Feathers." Scott was a stickler for exactness in military procedure. The nickname was used affectionately by Scott's friends.

Scott first gained national prominence during the War of 1812 when his troops were among the only ones to give a good account of themselves in the land fighting. He was the sole author of the revised *Infantry Tactics* (1835), which remained standard until the Civil War. The reputation he gained during the Mexican War led to his nomination as the Whig candidate for President in 1852. He was overwhelmingly defeated by Franklin Pierce. Foreseeing the Civil War, he unsuccessfully urged Pres. Buchanan to reinforce federal forts in the South. His "anaconda" plan for curtailing the war was rejected. He was regarded as too old to give advice.

G

Gabriel's Insurrection (1800). A plot by a Negro slave, "General Gabriel," to incite slaves to attack Richmond, Va., was revealed before the conspirators could strike. Gov. James Monroe called out the militia and the insurgents were arrested. The ringleaders were executed. Fear inspired by the plot caused Virginians to support plans for the colonization of Negroes in other lands.

Gadsden Purchase (1853). A continuing boundary dispute between the U.S. and Mexico was settled when James Gadsden, minister to Mexico, was authorized by Pres. Pierce to purchase a small piece of territory which now comprises the southern part of Arizona and New Mexico. It rounds out the present-day continental limits of the U.S.

The land was particularly desired to provide a southern route for a transcontinental railroad and lobbyists were active in persuading Senators to ratify the Gadsden Treaty (Apr. 25, 1854). It was opposed by senators who saw the land as added slave territory and the $10,000,000 purchase price as bolstering the Santa Anna government.

"gag rule" (1836). The House of Representatives cut off debate on the antislavery petitions which were inundating the Congress by passing a resolution directing that they be completely ignored. The tactic further inflamed abolitionists.

Rep. John Quincy Adams, former President, looked upon the "gag rule" as a restriction on the right of petition guaranteed in the Bill of Rights. He fought it for eight years until it was repealed in 1844.

Gaines' Mill, battle of (June 27, 1862). Gen. Robert E. Lee struck at Union Gen. Fitz-John Porter in one of the Seven Days' Battles in Virginia, also known as First Cold Harbor. Porter was forced to retreat across the Chickahominy River. Both Union and Confederate losses were great, but the South was less able to afford the drain on its manpower.

Gallatin, Albert (1761–1849). Statesman. Born in Geneva, Switzerland, he came to Massachusetts in 1780. He emerged as the leader of Republicans in western Pennsylvania. He was a member of the U.S. House of Representatives (1795–1801). His genius for finance brought recognition as Pres. Jefferson's and Madison's Sec. of Treasury (1801–14). He helped negotiate peace at the end of the War of 1812. He was minister to France (1816–23) and to England (1826–27). He was president of the National (later Gallatin) Bank, N.Y. (1831–39). Author of the pioneer study, *Synopsis of the Indian Tribes . . . of North America* (1836), he has been called "the father of American ethnology."

Gallaudet College. The world's only institution offering higher education for deaf students is in Washington, D.C., and functions under the U.S. Department of Health, Education, and Welfare. The college was originally incorporated in 1857 as the Columbia Institution for the Instruction of the Deaf and Dumb.

galley boats. Small warships using both sails and oars were maintained on the Mississippi River and its tributaries by the French and Spanish during the latter part of the 18th century. The U.S. also constructed some of these vessels for naval operations in the West.

Galloway, Joseph (1731–1803). Colonial statesman. Born in West River, Md., he attempted to restore harmony with England on the eve of the Revolution. His Galloway Plan (1774) for an imperial legislature was defeated by a close vote in the First Continental Congress. He aided the British when Gen. Howe occupied Philadelphia and left for London (1778) when the city was recaptured. He became the spokesman for American Loyalists in exile.

Galloway's Plan of Union (Sept. 28, 1774). A plan to establish a colonial legislature as a branch of Parliament was submitted to the First Continental Congress and was defeated by a single vote. The plan of Joseph Galloway, Pennsylvania delegate, sought to moderate the growing split between colonies and mother country by calling for establishment of a grand council to be chosen by the assemblies of each colony. Either the council or Parliament could propose measures for the colonies, but these would take effect only if approved by both bodies.

The Plan was expunged from the minutes of the Congress.

Gallup poll. A technique for sampling public opinion on various issues was devised by George Horace Gallup, who founded the American Institute of Public Opinion in 1935. Polling public opinion on political campaigns has survived even after the disaster of 1948 when

279

the pollsters erroneously predicted Gov. Dewey's landslide victory over President Truman in the presidential campaign of that year.

Galvanic, Operation. The military code name designated an Allied assault to win back the Gilbert Islands in the Western Pacific in Nov. 1943 in World War II.

Galveston pirates. From 1817 to 1821 Galveston, Tex., was the haunt of the famous pirate, Jean Lafitte. Although the Gulf pirates pretended to be acting as privateers in the service of Mexico operating against Spanish vessels, they were actually engaged in the illegal slave trade and preyed on commerce. They were wiped out by U.S. naval action.

Garcia, message to. Shortly before the outbreak of the Spanish-American War, Pres. McKinley sought to gain information from Gen. Calixto Garcia, a Cuban revolutionist, of the size and disposition of Spanish and Cuban forces. The Army lieutenant who contacted Garcia in Cuba brought a message *from* Garcia. An inspirational but somewhat garbled account by Elbert Hubbard, *A Message to Garcia*, appeared in *The Philistine* (Mar., 1899).

Garfield, James Abram (1831–81). Twentieth President of the U.S. He was born in Orange, O., and was graduated from Williams College (1856). He served Ohio as Republican member of the U.S. House of Representatives (1863–80). Inaugurated as President, Mar. 4, 1881, he was shot by Charles J. Guiteau on July 2 and died Sept. 19, 1881.

Garfield's assassination (1881). Pres. Garfield was shot on July 2 at the Washington railroad station and died on Sept. 19. His assassin was a disappointed office seeker, Charles J. Guiteau, who was executed on June 30, 1882.

The assassination stirred public support for reform of the civil service system.

Garrison, William Lloyd (1805–79). Abolitionist and reformer. Born in Newburyport, Mass., he was one of the first Abolitionists to demand complete and immediate freedom for slaves. The founder of the American Anti-slavery Society (1833), his radical approach to emancipation was set forth for 35 years in his newspaper, *The Liberator* (founded 1831). Refusing compromise, he burned a copy of the Constitution (July 4, 1854), declaring, "So perish all compromises with tyranny." After the Civil War Garrison gave himself to other causes, including prohibition, fair treatment of the Indians and woman suffrage.

Garveyism. A mass movement among Negroes in the 1920's arose as a protest against the anti-Negro reaction of the post-

World War I period. It was led by Marcus Garvey, a Jamaican Negro who came to the U.S. in 1916. Garvey organized branches of his Universal Negro Improvement Association in New York and other large cities. In his publication, *The Negro World*, he told Negroes that it was futile to appeal for justice to white men. He sought unsuccessfully to lead Negroes back to Africa. "To be a Negro," he wrote, "is no disgrace, but an honor, and we of the U.N.I.A. do not want to become white. . . . We are proud and honorable. We love our race and respect and adore our mothers."

In 1923 Garvey estimated membership in his movement at 6,000,000; but his critics held that the number was closer to 500,000. Garvey was imprisoned in 1925 for using the mails to defraud in raising money for his Black Star Line, a steamship company that was an auxiliary of the UNIA. He was pardoned by Pres. Coolidge in 1927 and deported as an undesirable alien. The movement disintegrated. Negro leaders like Dr. DuBois called the UNIA "bombastic and impracticable."

gaslight. Baltimore, Md., became the first city in the U.S. to use coal gas for lighting city streets in 1816. Its use was begun in Boston, 1822; New York, 1823; Philadelphia, 1836. By the 1880's, however, gaslight had become obsolete and electric lights were illuminating many U.S. cities.

Gaspee, burning of the (June 10, 1772). The British revenue cutter which had been seizing smugglers in Narragansett Bay, R.I., was burned by the colonists when it ran aground. A British inquiry got nowhere since the people of Providence refused to cooperate in the investigation.

The incident marked the growing friction between colonial merchants and British customs officials in the years before the American Revolution.

Gatling gun. Richard Jordan Gatling patented a "revolving gun battery" (not a machine gun), Nov. 4, 1862, that fired 350 rounds a minute. It was not used during the Civil War since it was first adopted by the Ordnance Department of the U.S. Army in 1866. It was used during the Spanish-American War but was soon replaced by the machine gun.

Gazette of the United States. Edited by James Fenno, the pro-Federalist newspaper was founded in New York in 1789 and continued publication in Philadelphia, 1790–98, then the nation's capital. Alexander Hamilton wrote for the publication and helped to support it.

Gemini, Project. The U.S. manned space flight program has demonstrated that spacecraft can rendezvous in orbit, an accomplishment which is crucial to the mastery of space. It is part of the technology that must be developed to land

American explorers on the moon and to conduct advanced ventures of the future.

Gemini spacecraft are designed to carry two men who will maneuver their craft in space so that it can join up with an Agena rocket. The first spacecraft to be maneuvered while in orbit was Gemini 3 (the "Molly Brown") in 1965. Major Virgil I. Grissom and Lt. Commander John W. Young were the astronauts. In June 1965 Gemini 4 orbited for four days during which Major Edward H. White 2nd was the first American to leave a spaceship and move about in space while tethered to the ship, manned by Major James A. McDivitt. On Dec. 16, 1965 Gemini 6 (Capt. Walter M. Schirra, Jr., and Major Thomas P. Stafford) and Gemini 7 (Lt. Col. Frank Borman and Commander James A. Lovell, Jr.) met 180 miles above the earth and flew for four hours 6 to 10 feet from each other.

Gemini 8 and 9 did not carry out their major objectives, but the mission of Gemini 10 (Cmdr. John W. Young and Major Michael Collins), in July 1966, was considered an important test of the engineering and navigational techniques that must be perfected before man can make his round trip to the moon.

The Gemini 10 astronauts flew deeper into space—475 miles—than man had ever penetrated, spent the most time— 39 hours—linked with another satellite, fired the rocket engine of the captured satellite for the first manned launching at orbital altitudes and reached yet another satellite for the first dual rendezvous. In addition, Major Collins, "walking" in space, made physical contact with another orbiting object, retrieving a scientific experiment from the side of an Agena rocket.

Gemini 11 and 12, the last of the series, involved rendezvous and docking with Agena rockets.

General Agreement on Tariffs and Trade (GATT). Under the agreement drafted in 1947, the U.S. and other nations negotiate to reduce tariffs and eliminate trade barriers. Member states may make complaints about the trade policies of other members. Often a friendly adjustment has been arranged. GATT is administered by the United Nations.

General Aniline and Film Corporation seizure. The German chemical company was seized in 1942 by the U.S. under trading-with-the-enemy laws. The company had been transferred to Swiss ownership just before World War II, and the seizure was challenged by Swiss owners as illegal on the ground that Switzerland was not an enemy country.

The U.S. contended that the Swiss ownership was a fiction and that the new name Interhandel was actually only a "front" for the German I. G. Farben chemical empire.

In 1963 a settlement was

reached with the Swiss owners under which they would get about one-fourth of the sale price of the company. The public sale was held in 1965. The U.S. government placed its share of the proceeds in a special War Claims Fund that would be used to reimburse American citizens for losses of life and property arising out of World War II.

General Armstrong. Although it claimed protection in the neutral Azores, the American privateer was sunk by the British navy, Sept. 26, 1814. U.S. demand for an indemnity from Portugal was denied in subsequent arbitration proceedings.

General Electric Company. Incorporated in New York, in 1892, as a merger of the Thomson-Houston Electric Co. and the Edison General Electric Co., its first president was Charles A. Coffin, who continued as chairman of board of directors until 1922. The company is the U.S. leader in development, manufacture and sale of products for generation, transmission, utilization and control of electrical power; these products range from lamps to complete utility power plants.

General Motors Corporation. The first successful automobile mergers were completed by William C. Durant in 1908 and 1909. Durant combined Buick, Cadillac and Oldsmobile with many smaller companies under the name of General Motors. He was soon in financial difficulty and had to yield leadership of the company to bankers before he was granted a loan.

The present company was incorporated in Delaware in 1916, succeeding the 1908 consolidation. It is the world's largest manufacturer of motor vehicles, including Chevrolet, Pontiac, Oldsmobile, Buick and Cadillac passenger cars and Chevrolet and GMC trucks and motor coaches. It also makes auto supplies and earth moving equipment, diesel engines, locomotives, refrigerators and household appliances, aircraft engines and many other products. It employs more than 600,-000 people, a figure exceeding the combined payrolls of the state governments of New York, California, Illinois, Pennsylvania, Texas and Ohio.

Durant, seeking to raise money soon after 1900, had boasted that 500,000 automobiles would soon be sold annually. He was ridiculed. In 1965 General Motors sold 5,696,480 cars and trucks produced in the U.S. Other companies sold an additional 2,000,000.

General Services Administration. To establish for the government an economical and efficient system for management of its property and records, an independent federal agency was created in 1949. Its functions included the construction and operation of buildings, distribution of supplies, disposal of surplus property and the stockpiling of critical materials.

"general welfare" clause. According to the Constitution (Art. I, Sec. 8, Par. 1) the Congress has power to tax the people and provide for "the general welfare of the United States." This clause has been interpreted broadly to give the Congress great power.

The expression "promote the general welfare" is also contained in the Preamble, but the Preamble is introductory and does not grant power to any branch of the federal government.

Genêt Affair (1793). During the French Revolution "Citizen" Edmond Genêt was sent to the U.S. to gain support for France. He arrived in Charleston, S.C., and even before presenting himself to Pres. Washington undertook to outfit American privateers to prey on English shipping and to detach Florida and Louisiana from Spain.

At first Genêt enjoyed the friendship of Thomas Jefferson who believed that the U.S. was obligated to aid France under the Treaty of 1778. When Genêt allowed the *Little Democrat* to sail as a privateer, despite Washington's express warning, he alienated even Jefferson.

Pres. Washington asked for Genêt's recall. Genêt did not, however, return to France. The Girondists who had sent him on the mission had been ousted by Jacobins and his return to France would have meant the guillotine. Genêt was permitted to remain in the U.S. He married the daughter of Gov. Clinton of New York and retired to a country estate on the Hudson.

Geneva Conference (Apr. 27–July 20, 1954). The Swiss city of Geneva has been the scene of innumerable international conferences and was the home of the defunct League of Nations, whose buildings have been taken over by the UN.

A major conference was held in Geneva in an effort to settle the war in French Indo-China. Participants included the Western Big Three (U.S., Great Britain and France), Russia, Communist China, the French-sponsored State of Viet Nam, Laos and Cambodia.

It was agreed that Laos and Cambodia were to become independent states within the French Union. Viet Nam was divided in the middle at the 17th parallel. The Communists took the northern half, Viet Minh. The southern half, Viet Nam, became an independent state. France withdrew its forces. It was agreed that an election was to be held in 1956 to create a unified government for the two parts, but the election was not held.

An American Military Assistance Advisory Group (MAAG) to the French forces in Indo-China had been set up as early as 1950. Soon after the Geneva Conference, U.S. involvement in Viet Nam deepened.

Geneva "Summit" Conference (July 1955). Winston Churchill urged "a conference at the highest level" to deal with problems which had given rise to the cold war. The expression "summit conference" was used widely to describe the gathering of heads of government of the U.S., Britain, the Soviet Union and France. The discussion included the unification of Germany, disarmament and improvement of East-West relations through cultural interchanges (greater freedom of travel, exchange of scientific ideas, student visits). It was only in the interchange area that any progress was made.

genteel tradition. American letters during the 19th and early 20th centuries were characterized by optimism, complacency and propriety. Sex was subordinated in Victorian fashion and conventional moral idealism was exalted. The genteel tradition was exemplified, as late as the 1920's in the warmth and quiet heroism of characters in Willa Cather's *Death Comes for the Archbishop*.

In revolt against the genteel tradition were post-World War I writers who emphasized sex themes. Even before the breakdown of inhibitions brought on by World War I, Theodore Dreiser and Edgar Lee Masters were in revolt against the conventional treatment of sex by the writers of the genteel tradition. The philosopher George Santayana wrote *The Genteel Tradition at Bay* (1931).

Gentlemen's Agreement (1907–08). In a series of diplomatic notes, the Japanese government bound itself to issue no more passports to coolies coming directly to the U.S. In return Pres. T. Roosevelt got the San Francisco Board of Education to rescind the school order which prohibited Japanese children from attending school with the whites. The agreement was not a treaty but served as a face-saving device for the Japanese, who deeply resented discrimination against their nationals in California.

The agreement was terminated by the Immigration Act of 1924 (National Origins Act) which excluded Orientals from U.S. citizenship.

The term "gentlemen's agreement" has also been used in business to describe arrangements whereby competing companies agree on prices and division of the market. Such agreements are outlawed under the antitrust laws.

Geological Survey. Established by Congress in 1879 as a federal agency in the Department of Interior, it carries on research covering topography, geology and the mineral and water resources of the U.S. It enforces departmental regulations applicable to oil, gas and mining leases. Among its functions is publication of the National Topographic Map Series covering the U.S. and its outlying areas.

George, Henry (1839–1897). Economist and reformer. Born in Philadelphia, Pa., he worked in San Francisco during his early years as a typesetter and editor. His experiences in the California land boom stimulated the thinking about a single-tax theory that was developed in his classic study, *Progress and Poverty* (1877–79). He believed that the entire tax burden should be laid on land, freeing industry from taxation and destroying monopolies deriving from rising land values. He made a good showing as unsuccessful candidate for mayor of New York City (1886) in a campaign against Abram S. Hewitt (winner) and Theodore Roosevelt. He published *The Irish Land Question* (1881) and lectured widely in the U.S., Ireland, England and Australia.

Georgia. The "Empire State of the South," a South Atlantic state, was the last of the original 13 Colonies to be organized. Its capital is Atlanta. It was first settled in 1733 under the leadership of James Oglethorpe, who named the colony in honor of King George II.

The colony, a haven for English debtors, served as a buffer between the British settlements and the Spanish of Florida and French Louisiana. It received such generous financial grants from the British monarch that it did not send delegates to either the Stamp Act Congress or First Continental Congress. It was, however, represented in the Second Continental Congress and was the first southern and the fourth of all the states to ratify the Constitution (Jan. 2, 1788).

Georgia seceded from the Union, Jan. 19, 1861, and suffered devastation when Sherman marched through. It was first readmitted to the Union in 1868, but was placed under a military governor when the legislature refused to seat Negroes. The state reentered the Union again in 1870.

The Sea Islands, a chain of low islands along the coast of South Carolina, Georgia and north Florida, had great cotton plantations early in the 19th century. The land was divided among the slaves after the Civil War. St. Simons, Sea and Jekyll islands are Georgia resorts. St. Simons Island has the ruins of Fort Frederica, built 1736–54 by James Oglethorpe during the English-Spanish struggle for the southeast colonies.

Cotton is the leading profitable crop in Georgia. The state ranks second only to California in lumber production. It produces more than half the world's supply of turpentine and is the world's largest producer of kaolin and china clay. Industries include textiles, food processing, chemical and apparel.

geriatrics. The increasing number of Americans 65 years old and over has given rise to this new specialty in medicine. Doctors are seeking to combat those illnesses which are especially prevalent among old people—hardening of the arteries, heart trouble, cancer and mental ailments.

Germantown battle of (Oct. 4, 1777). Gen. Washington sought unsuccessfully to dislodge Gen. Howe's army, which had taken the nearby city of Philadelphia. His plan for converging on Howe's forces by four roads was disrupted by fog which caused colonial troops to fire on each other. Washington did, however, keep Howe from sending much-needed help to Gen. Burgoyne in New York and this was a factor in the French decision to come to the aid of the 13 Colonies.

Gerry, Elbridge (1744–1814). Statesman. Born in Marblehead, Mass., he was graduated from Harvard (1762). An early advocate of colonial independence, Gerry was a signer of the Declaration of Independence, served in the Continental Congress (1776–81, 1782–85) and actively sought to supply the Continental Army. He was a delegate to the Constitutional Convention (1787) but refused to sign the final version, charging that it was "full of vices" and would not guarantee the people's liberty. Nevertheless, he represented Massachusetts in the U.S. House of Representatives (1789–93). A member of the XYZ mission to France (1797–98), he broke with his fellow delegates and tried to negotiate separate terms with Talleyrand. Gerry was governor of Massachusetts (1810, 1811) and his name is forever linked to "gerrymandering" following his plan to redistrict Massachusetts in such a way that Republicans would retain control of the state. Vice-Pres. of the U.S. (1813–14) under James Madison, he died in office.

gerrymander. When a state legislature draws the map of a district to gain the maximum number of votes for the party in power, it is gerrymandering. The term was first used in Massachusetts in 1812 when Democratic - Republican Gov. Elbridge Gerry signed a bill that redistricted a county in such a way that a Federalist caricatured it as a salamander. By combining Gerry and salamander he got gerrymander.

Gerrymandered districts have been challenged in the courts as contrary to some state constitutions which require districts to have compact territories and substantial equality in the number of voters.

Gershwin, George (1898–1937). Composer. Born in Brooklyn, N.Y., he first worked as a song plugger in Tin Pan Alley. He wrote the scores for *George White's Scandals* (1920–24); symphonic jazz compositions, such as *Rhapsody in Blue* (1923), *Piano Concerto in F*

(1925); musical comedies, including *Lady Be Good* (1924), *Funny Face* (1927), and *Girl Crazy* (1930); and was awarded the Pulitzer Prize (1931) for *Of Thee I Sing*. His best remembered songs include "Somebody Loves Me" (1924), "It Ain't Necessarily So" (1935), and "Summertime" (1935). He wrote the opera *Porgy and Bess* (1935). His brother Ira (1896–) wrote the lyrics for many of the musical comedies.

Gettysburg, battle of (July 1–3, 1863). In a major battle usually thought of as a turning point of the Civil War, Gen. Robert E. Lee's invasion of the North was turned back at Gettysburg, in southern Pennsylvania. Lee withdrew south of the Potomac River on July 4 but was not pursued by Gen. George Meade, who commanded the Union armies. Praise for Meade's victory was softened somewhat by his hesitancy in pursuing the greatly weakened Confederate army. The overall record—Union: 88,289 engaged, 3,155 dead, 14,529 wounded and 5,365 missing. Confederate: 75,000 engaged, 3,903 dead, 18,735 wounded and 5,425 missing.

Gettysburg Address (Nov. 19, 1863). Beginning with the stirring words "Four score and seven years ago our fathers brought forth on this continent a new nation, conceived in liberty," Pres. Lincoln dedicated the military cemetery at Gettysburg, Pa.

Lincoln had been preceded on the platform by Edward Everett, former president of Harvard and one of the nation's great orators. Despite popular belief at the time, Lincoln's heartfelt words were quickly sensed as unforgettable by many who heard and read them. Everett himself wrote to Lincoln: "I should be glad if I could flatter myself that I came as near the central idea of the occasion in two hours as you did in two minutes."

Ghent, Treaty of (1814). The treaty that ended the War of 1812 between the U.S. and Britain was negotiated in Ghent, Belgium. The American peace commission consisted of John Quincy Adams, Henry Clay, Albert Gallatin, James Bayard and Jonathan Russell. The head of the British commission was Lord Gambier. Both sides retreated from demands that would have prolonged the indecisive struggle. The net effect of the treaty was to restore things to the way that they had been before the war.

The U.S. gained no commitment from the British about neutral rights, especially impressment of seamen, presumably the cause of the war, and no territorial demands of the West were granted. The British for their part were unable to keep American fur traders and settlers out of the Northwest and continued to withhold from New Englanders the right to fish in Newfoundland and Labrador waters.

The U.S. agreed to respect Indian rights and arrangements were made for arbitral commissions to settle disputed boundaries along the northern frontier.

ghost dance. White men gave the name to an Indian ceremonial dance performed in anticipation of the day when Indians would once again be free of white men. In a new world the Indian dead would be resurrected and the buffalo returned to the plains.

Wavoka, the medicine man of the Nevada Paiutes, ordered the dance after a solar eclipse on Jan. 1, 1889, which he saw as a sign from the Great Spirit that he had been chosen to lead the Indians to freedom. He promised the dancers that white men's bullets would never penetrate the shirts they wore in the ceremonial dance.

Because the dance excited the Indians the War Department, which feared that it might lead to violence, prohibited the ghost dance. A disturbance resulted when armed ghost dancers sought to prevent the arrest of Sitting Bull on Dec. 14, 1890. The Sioux chief was killed in the fighting.

Gibbons, James (1834–1921). Roman Catholic cardinal. He was born in Baltimore, Md. An ordained priest (1861), he became the youngest Catholic bishop of his time (1868). He was appointed archbishop of Baltimore, the oldest U.S. archdiocese (1877). He took an active part in civic and humanitarian movements, sympathized with labor's aspirations, and gained assurance from Rome that the Knights of Labor would not be condemned as a secret society. He was made the second American cardinal (1886) by Pope Leo XIII and was the first American to participate in the election of a pope (1903). He promoted the spirit of religious toleration.

Gibbons v. Ogden (1824). The U.S. Supreme Court voided an act of the New York legislature which granted exclusive steamboat navigation on the Hudson River to Fulton and Livingston. Speaking for the Court that struck down the New York licensing act, Chief Justice Marshall held that it violated Congress' right to regulate interstate commerce, which he broadened to include navigation inside the limits of the states.

Ogden, licensed by Fulton and Livingston to operate a ferry between New York and New Jersey, had successfully obtained a New York court order restraining Gibbons from competing with him. Gibbons had operated his ferry under a federal coasting license.

Gibbs, Josiah Willard (1839–1903). Physicist. Born in New Haven, Conn., he was granted a Ph.D. by Yale (1863), where he was professor of mathematical physics from 1871 until his death. In 1876 he wrote an epochal paper, "On the Equilibrium of Heterogeneous Substances." His investigations established the basic theory for physical chemistry. He evolved a system of vector analysis for mathematical physicists. The scientific world continues to apply his ideas.

GI Bill of Rights. Even before the end of World War II (1941–45), Congress passed the Servicemen's Readjustment Act (June 1944), known popularly as the GI Bill of Rights. It entitled veterans to unemployment insurance for a year, guaranteed loans for building homes or establishing businesses and paid a substantial part of the costs of their education in colleges or vocational schools proportionate to the length of their service.

During the war enlisted men in the U.S. armed forces were called GI's. The initials stood for "government issue" which covered a multitude of items issued by supply depots in all parts of the world.

Benefits of the GI Bill of Rights were extended to Korean War veterans by the Veterans Readjustment Assistance Act of 1952 (Korean GI Bill). The Veterans Readjustment Act of 1966 extends similar benefits to individuals, serving in the armed forces, who were discharged after Jan. 31, 1955, the termination date for eligibility of Korean War veterans. Veterans eligible are those who serve on active duty for more than 180 days.

Gideon v. Wainwright (1963). The U.S. Supreme Court held unconstitutional a Florida law which did not give poor defendants the protection of a court-appointed counsel in cases involving less than capital offenses (those for which punishment of death is inflicted). The Court ruled that this was a denial of due process of law. This reversed an earlier decision (*Betts v. Brady*, 1942).

The case arose when a Florida prisoner named Clarence Earl Gideon, who was not represented by a lawyer, was convicted.

Gila Trail. An early 19th century route to California followed the course of the Gila River from western New Mexico across Arizona to the Colorado River.

Gilbert's patent. In 1578 Sir Humphrey Gilbert received a patent from Queen Elizabeth I conferring on him the exclusive right "to inhabit and possess at his choice all remote and heathen lands not in the actual possession of any Christian prince." Sir Humphrey believed that America was an island around whose northern coasts a water passage might be found which would lead to the Pacific Ocean and Asia. His dream of a Northwest Passage was not realized in two voyages to America in 1578 and 1583. In the latter voyage on the *Squirrel*, accompanied by a second vessel, the *Golden Hind*, he took possession of Newfoundland in the name of the Queen and left a small band on its shore while he sought a better site for a station on the anticipated route to India. The settlers disappeared and Gilbert himself was lost at sea, Sept. 1583. His rights passed to his half-brother Sir Walter Raleigh, who received (1584) an almost identical royal patent.

Gilded Age. The period of American life that extended roughly from the end of the Civil War in 1865 to the 1880's gained its name from the novel, *The Gilded Age* (1873), by Mark Twain and Charles Dudley Warner. As in the book, which satirizes corruption in politics and the coarse manners of the *nouveau riche*, the age was characterized by an emphasis on get-rich-quick methods of doing business. Despite its unflattering cognomen, the period was marked by great national growth and impressive cultural achievements.

Gilman, Daniel Coit (1831–1908). Educator. Born in Norwich, Conn., he wrote the plan (1856) for what was to be Sheffield Scientific School at Yale, where he served as professor of physical and political geography (1861–72). He was president of the Univ. of California (1872–75) and first president of Johns Hopkins (1876–1901). He raised the standards of medical education in founding Johns Hopkins Medical School (1893). He placed emphasis on the quality of teachers and insisted on freedom of thinking and teaching. He was first president of Carnegie Institution, Washington, D.C. (1901–04).

Girl Scouts of the U.S.A. The organization for girls 7 to 17 was founded in 1912 in Savannah, Ga., by Mrs. Juliette Gordon Low who had been a leader of Girl Guide troops in England. It aims to build good citizenship through outdoor activities, homemaking and the arts. The girls wear uniforms at troop meetings and are guided by adult leaders. Membership, including adults, is about 3,500,-000.

Gitlow v. New York (1925). The U.S. Supreme Court affirmed the conviction of Benjamin Gitlow, who had been convicted by the state courts of violating the New York Criminal Anarchy Act of 1902 by his publication of *The Left Wing Manifesto*. The pamphlet included calls for "mass strikes," "expropriation of the bourgeoisie" and the setting up of a "dictatorship of the proletariat."

The Court upheld the right of free speech in the abstract but said of the pamphlet that "it is the language of direct incitement." Justices Brandeis and Holmes dissented, with Holmes observing that "every idea is an incitement" and that the Court had been too narrow in its interpretation of the right of freedom of speech.

The importance of the case

lies in the fact that for the first time the Court proceeded on the assumption that freedom of speech and of the press "which are protected by the 1st Amendment from abridgment by Congress—are among the fundamental personal rights and 'liberties' protected by the due process clause of the Fourteenth Amendment from impairment by the states." The Court held, however, that the New York act as applied in Gitlow's case did not unduly restrict freedom of press and was therefore valid.

"Git thar fustest with the mostest." Nathan Bedford Forrest, who rose from private in the Confederate army to lieutenant general, is credited with originating the phrase that the one who gets there first with the most is victorious.

"give me liberty or give me death." The breaking point with England had not yet been reached when Patrick Henry addressed the Virginia Convention, Mar. 23, 1775. In a plea for organizing defense of the colony, he asked: "Is life so dear, or peace so sweet, as to be purchased at the price of chains and slavery? Forbid it, Almighty God! I know not what course others may take, but as for me, give me liberty or give me death!"

glass. The first glass in the colonies was made in Jamestown, Va., in 1607, when glass beads were made for trade with the Indians. A prosperous glass firm was set up in New Amsterdam by Jan Smedes in 1654. In 1739 Caspar Wistar set up his glass works at Allowaystown, N.J., and manufactured the distinctive "South Jersey" glass.

After the Revolution glass manufacturing was carried on widely, especially in Boston, New York, Philadelphia, Pittsburgh and Sandwich, Mass. From 1819, the New England Glass Co. of Cambridge, Mass., made major contributions to the development of the glass industry in the U.S. In the Midwest blown and molded glass, known as "Ohio" because of the busy centers in that state, established a style of American glassware used from 1815 to the Civil War.

Since the post-Civil War period demands for glass have come from virtually every industry. In 1938 James Slayter and John H. Thomas of Newark, O., perfected methods of manufacturing glass wool or fiberglass, a sort of threadlike glass that can be woven.

Glass-Steagall Banking Act (1933). The measure was designed to forestall a recurrence of the kind of banking crisis that faced the nation at the beginning of the New Deal. To prevent, in Roosevelt's words, "speculation with other people's money" the law required commercial banks to divorce themselves from investment banking. The Act increased the regulatory power of the Federal Reserve Banks to prevent banks from extending loans that seemed bad risks. It came closest to meeting the needs of the ordinary bank depositor by establishing the Federal Deposit Insurance Corporation. A depositor in a bank that became a member of the FDIC would receive up to $10,000 of his deposit if the bank failed.

By the Banking Act of 1935 (also sponsored by Sen. Glass, Va., and Rep. Steagall, Ala.) federal control over private banking was increased still more by empowering the Federal Reserve Board to regulate interest rates.

Glorieta, battle of (Mar. 27, 1862). In the far southwest during the Civil War, the Confederates under Henry Hopkins Sibley captured Santa Fe (Mar. 4). But they were halted by the Federals in Apache Canyon at Pidgin's Ranch, near Glorieta Pass, in New Mexico. Their defeat ended the Confederacy's hopes for taking over the Southwest.

Gnadenhutten. The village in Ohio was inhabited by Delaware Indians who had been converted to Christianity by Moravian missionaries. After some of their warriors had attacked a white settlement in western Pennsylvania, they were captured by militia under Col. David Williamson. Although the 100 Indian men, women and children offered no resistance, resentment against the earlier attack led to their execution by the frontiersmen, Mar. 7, 1782.

Goddard's rockets. A momentous landmark for rocket flight was the launching of the first liquid fuel rocket at Auburn, Mass., Mar. 16, 1926, by Robert H. Goddard. Goddard, known as the "father of the modern rocket," was a physics professor at Clark University, Mass. He launched the first instrumented rocket, July 17, 1929, containing a barometer and a thermometer with a small camera focused to record their readings at maximum altitude. Through continual improvement, Goddard's rockets reached 7,500 feet by 1935 and speeds of over 700 miles per hour.

American rocket enthusiasts formed the American Interplanetary Society in 1930, later changing the name to the American Rocket Society. Many members of this early society are responsible for current space programs.

Godey's Lady's Book. The forerunner of the home magazines widely circulated in 20th century America, it first appeared in 1837 when Louis Godey merged his *Lady's Book,* published in Philadelphia beginning in 1830, with *The Ladies' Magazine* (Boston), edited by Sarah Josepha Hale. Mrs. Hale was retained as editor, and circulation reached a monthly peak of 150,000 before 1860.

The magazine staffed largely by women was an arbiter of

fashions, morals and etiquette. It ceased publication in 1892, but did not want for imitators.

Godkin, Edwin Lawrence (1831–1902). Editor. Born in Ireland, he came to U.S. in 1856. He was founder and editor of *The Nation* (1865–1900), a weekly periodical and also edited the New York *Evening Post* (1883–1900). He raised standards of journalism. An independent in politics, he opposed the spoils system and favored civil service reform.

Goethals, George Washington (1858–1928). U.S. army officer and engineer. Born in Brooklyn, N.Y., he was graduated from the U.S. Military Academy (1880). Appointed as chief engineer on the Isthmian Canal Commission by Pres. Theodore Roosevelt, he overcame innumerable construction problems to become known as the "builder of the Panama Canal." He was governor of the Panama Canal Zone from 1914 to 1916 and acting quartermaster general and director of purchase, storage and transportation of U.S. troops in World War I.

Gold Clause Cases (1935). The U.S. Supreme Court sustained the power of Congress to abrogate clauses in private contracts calling for payment in gold coin, although such contracts were executed before the legislation was passed (*Norman v. Baltimore & Ohio RR. Co.*). In another case the Court held that Congress could not abrogate a clause in government bonds calling for payment in gold coin, but the creditor was denied a remedy since he could not prove actual damage (*Perry v. U.S.*).

The cases arose following passage of a joint resolution of Congress (June 5, 1933) designed to benefit debtors which voided any clause in past or future contracts, governmental or private, that required payment of obligations in gold.

Golden Hill riot (Jan. 18, 1770). Protesting against the New York Assembly's vote to supply the soldiers under the Quartering Act, the citizens clashed with the British on a spot above Wall Street in lower Manhattan. The soldiers used bayonets against citizens armed with cutlasses and clubs. Some on each side were seriously wounded.

Alexander McDougall, a leader of the Sons of Liberty, had issued a broadside criticizing the Assembly. The soldiers in retaliation cut down one of the liberty poles. The riot was more serious than a number of other clashes that had taken place in previous months.

Golden Hind. The navigator and freebooter Francis Drake became the first Englishman to circumnavigate the globe (1577–80). Receiving permission from the Queen to attack Spanish holdings on the Pacific coast of South America, Drake sailed his ship, the *Golden Hind*, through the Strait of

Magellan, plundered the coasts of Chile and Peru, named the California coast New Albion and claimed it for Queen Elizabeth. When he could find no passageway through the continent to the Atlantic, he sailed west, rounded the Cape of Good Hope and arrived at Plymouth, England.

"Golden Twenties." The term has been used to describe the 1920's in the U.S. Prosperity was symbolized by a rising stock market, but farm prices were falling. The period was also referred to as the "Era of Flaming Youth." Pocket flasks and drinking parties were commonplace in what was supposed to be a "Dry Decade." It was a "Jazz Age" in which the snappy Charleston was danced to the music of loud saxaphones. In an "Age of the Flapper" girls enjoyed post-World War I freedom and the divorce rate rose. It was a "Lawless Decade" in which rival gangsters, seeking to oust competitors in the illegal liquor market, mowed each other down with machine gun bullets. The 1920's were marked by expanding automobile and radio sales. It was a time when women were enraptured by crooner Rudy Vallee and made to laugh by Charlie Chaplin. It was a day of expanding education as high school enrollment increased by 66% and college enrollment by 75% over the previous decade. It was a time when many predicted that the U.S. would never again see poverty.

Goldfine scandal. In Sept. 1958 it was disclosed that Sherman Adams, the Assistant to the President, had accepted expensive gifts from Bernard Goldfine, a businessman with cases pending before the government. Pres. Eisenhower at first resisted pressure to ask for Adams' resignation but then acquiesced. This was one of several scandals to rock the second Eisenhower administration.

Gold Reserve Act of 1934. The Act prohibited the withdrawal of bank deposits in gold or the exchange of paper money for it. It was intended to prevent the hoarding of gold or its shipment abroad by persons who had lost confidence in governmental policy or were seeking to make profits from fluctuations in foreign exchange. The main intention of the Act was to push up prices.

Under the Act, Pres. Roosevelt cut the value of the dollar in terms of gold from 25.8 grains to 15.24 grains. This meant that an ounce of gold, which had been worth about $20, was now worth $35. The U.S. government thus made a huge profit in terms of dollars on its gold reserves.

The Treasury continued to accept newly minted gold and other stocks of bullion, but gold did not circulate. The country was put on what is sometimes called the gold bullion standard.

gold rush. The California gold rush was set off by a trickle of gold first found at Sutter's sawmill, near Sacramento, Jan. 24, 1848. News reached the East by mid-August and the trek west, of "forty-niners" by land and sea, was in full force early in 1849.

The gold yield was reported as having reached a total of $65,000,000 in 1853. The people who profited most were tradesmen who sold the miners shovels, food and liquor and provided them with services, including hotels and dance halls.

Other gold rushes took place in Nevada in 1859, where the Comstock Lode yielded gold and silver, and in the Klondike in the Yukon territory of Canada, 1897–99.

gold standard. When a country uses only one metal as a standard of value for its currency (monometallism) and that metal is gold, the country is said to be on the gold standard. After the U.S. government promised to redeem greenbacks in gold, beginning in 1879, the U.S. was practically on the gold standard. However, free coinage of silver continued to be an issue until bimetallism was decisively rejected by the voters in the presidential election of 1900.

Under the Gold Standard Act of 1900, the gold dollar was made the standard unit of value in the U.S. There was no limit to the amount of gold that would be accepted by the Treasury. All currencies were maintained at an equal value with gold and were convertible into gold upon request. Gold coins and gold certificates were full legal tender. This meant that all debts, public and private, could be settled in such money. In actual fact there were not a great many gold coins in circulation, but this was not due to any legal limitation.

The nation was taken off the gold standard in 1933. Gold coins as well as gold certificates were withdrawn from circulation. No citizen was allowed to hold gold bullion (refined but unminted gold), except for industrial purposes. Moreover, the government cancelled the "gold clause" found in almost all bonds issued in the U.S. prior to 1933. This was a promise to repay the value of the bond in "gold dollars of the present standard."

The dollar is still defined by law as being worth so many grains of gold and the Treasury will still accept newly minted gold and other stocks of bullion. But gold does not circulate and paper money may not be converted into gold, as before 1933. This is sometimes called the gold bullion standard.

Goliad, massacre at (Mar. 27, 1836). During the Texas Revolution a force of Americans surrendered to Mexican Gen. José Urrea. More than 300 of them were shot, near Goliad, Tex., when the Mexican government chose to regard them as pirates on Mexican soil rather than prisoners of war.

Gompers, Samuel (1850–1924). Labor leader. Born in London,

England, he came to the U.S. in 1863 and rose to leadership of the American labor movement from his activity in the Cigarmakers' Union. President of the American Federation of Labor (1866–1924, except 1895), he abjured theory and concentrated on such everyday issues as wages, hours and working conditions. Gompers opposed independent politics for trade unions and believed that labor should reward its friends and punish its enemies. He pledged the support of labor in World War I and was appointed by Pres. Wilson to the Council of National Defense. His life story and a history of organized labor is contained in the autobiography, *Seventy Years of Life and Labor* (1925).

Gone With the Wind (1936). A novel by Margaret Mitchell, it tells the story of the Civil War in Georgia and Scarlett O'Hara's fight to restore her father's plantation, destroyed in Sherman's march. She fights her way through the business world, becoming obligated to Rhett Butler, who does not share her patriotism. Their marriage ends in tragedy. A modern best seller, the motion picture made from it was an equally spectacular success.

"Good Neighbor" policy. The good neighbor ideal for U.S. relations with Latin America was foreshadowed by Pres. Coolidge, urged by Pres. Hoover and given great impetus by Pres. F. D. Roosevelt. In his first inaugural address, Mar. 4, 1933, Roosevelt dedicated the nation "to the policy of the good neighbor—the neighbor who resolutely respects himself and, because he does so, respects the rights of others." On Dec. 28, 1933, Roosevelt announced, "the definite policy of the United States from now on is opposed to armed intervention." This was matched with deeds when, despite grave disorders in Cuba under the mailed fist of the dictator Machado, the U.S. refrained from landing troops. In 1934 Cuba was released from the terms of the Platt Amendment. Also in 1934 the last Marines were withdrawn from Haiti. In 1938 the "Good Neighbor" policy was severely tested when Mexico expropriated outright all foreign oil holdings.

The policy also extended to Canada. The growing strength of the dictator states in Europe and the possibility that they might attack the Americas served to draw Canada and the U.S. closer together.

Goodnight-Loving Trail. Thousands of Longhorns grazed their way to Colorado and Wyoming over the cattle trail opened in the 1860's by Charles Goodnight and Oliver Loving, Texas ranchers. It ran from Fort Belknap, Tex., to Fort Sumner in eastern New Mexico, up the Pecos River, on through Trinidad and Pueblo, and to Denver, Colo., and Cheyenne, Wyo.

Goodyear, Charles (1800–60). Inventor. Born in New Haven, Conn., he began experiments in the treatment of rubber (1834). He combined Nathaniel M. Hayward's method of spreading sulphur on rubber to eliminate stickiness with his own process. He patented the vulcanization process (1844), the basic patent of the rubber manufacturing industry. Because he sold licenses and accepted absurdly low royalties for his invention, he died in debt.

GOP. The abbreviation of "Grand Old Party" referring to the Republican party has been used lovingly by its adherents and, perhaps unknowingly, by its critics. The term came into use after the Civil War when the party recalled with pride its role in saving the Union.

Gorgas, William Crawford (1854–1920). Sanitarian and army surgeon. Born in Toulminville, Ala., he joined the Army Medical Corps in 1880. He survived an attack of yellow fever at Fort Brown, Tex., and thereafter was in demand for posts ravaged by yellow fever. Chief sanitary officer of Havana (1898), he destroyed the breeding places for yellow fever when he learned from Walter Reed that the *Stegomyia* mosquito was the carrier. He was made a member of the Panama Canal Commission (1906) and rid the Canal Zone of yellow fever. He came to be regarded as the foremost sanitation expert in the world.

Governors Island, N.Y. The military installation in New York harbor south of the Battery was once the property of Dutch Gov. Wouter van Twiller. It was fortified by colonial troops during the Revolution. Fort Jay was built on the island, 1794–1806. During the Civil War Castle Williams on the island was used as a prison for Confederate soldiers. Until 1965 the island was the headquarters of the First U.S. Army which had charge of the military activities in New York, New Jersey and New England. It is now the home of the Eastern Area of the U.S. Coast Guard.

"Go west, young man, go west." The phrase has been ringing in American ears since Horace Greeley used it in an editorial in the New York *Tribune* (July 13, 1865). Greeley at the close of the Civil War urged young Americans in the more settled areas of the East to seek their fortunes in lands beyond the Alleghenies. The advice, "Go west, young man, and grow up with the country," was not original with Greeley, but it captured the public's imagination and was a spur to the westward movement.

grain elevators. Usually located at railroad terminal points and at milling centers, they are warehouses for storing grain. They utilize a continuous belt of buckets that scoop up the grain and carry it to the bins.

Farmers complained of abuses by elevator owners, usually railroads, in the 1870's and state regulation of elevators began in Illinois in 1871.

About one-fourth of the grain elevators are now owned by cooperatives. Elevators have made it possible to store government-owned surpluses of grain.

Grain Futures Act (1922). The Act was intended to curb the grain speculation that was believed to have contributed to the collapse of grain prices in 1920. Previously, the Future Trading Act (1921) had been invalidated by the Supreme Court because the tax used to curb speculation was held to be an improper use of the tax power. The new Act limited the amounts of price fluctuation on the grain exchange in a given trading period.

Grand Alliance. The term designated the Big Three in World War II—the U.S., Britain and the Soviet Union.

Grand Army of the Republic (GAR). Veterans of the Union army formed the GAR and held their first encampment in Indianapolis, in 1866. The organization backed the Republican party in the latter part of the 19th century.

The GAR was instrumental in getting Congress to provide pensions for Union veterans and aided soldiers' widows and orphans.

Grand Banks. Known as the "silver mines of the Atlantic" because of the sleek and shiny fish caught there, the shoals off Newfoundland offer the greatest cod fishing in the world. By the beginning of the 16th century French fishermen were supplying France with cod. Although fishing was not as rewarding as finding gold, it was a good start in the New World. The shoals continue to be frequented by fishing fleets of Canada, Great Britain, France and the U.S.

Grand Canyon. An unusual example of stream erosion, the striking rock formations in north central Arizona have become one of the world's outstanding spectacles. From rim to rim the canyon of the Colorado River varies from four to 18 miles in width; it is 5,700 feet deep, measured from the North Rim. The canyon was discovered by Spanish explorers from Coronado's camp in 1540. The first journey down the Colorado River through the canyon was made in 1869 by nine men under Major John W. Powell. Grand Canyon National Park was established by Congress in 1919.

grandfather clause. Post-Reconstruction efforts to keep the Negro from voting in the South included literacy tests and poll taxes, but these acted to keep poor whites as well as Negroes from the polls. Beginning in 1898 a number of southern states kept Negroes from voting by passing laws which provided that only those eligible to vote in 1867, or the sons or grandsons of those voters, could vote. Since Negroes were not voters in 1867, the effect of the laws was to deprive them of the franchise.

The "grandfather" clauses were struck down by the Supreme Court (*Guinn v. U.S.*, 1915) as violations of the 15th Amendment and therefore unconstitutional.

Grand Portage. The nine-mile overland haul between Lake Superior and the Pigeon River, in the northeast corner of present-day Minnesota, got its name from 17th-century French-speaking Canadian fur traders.

Grangers. In the 1870's and early 1880's farmers, largely in the Midwest, sought to reduce railroad rates and other costs of handling their products. They organized granges which began with the National Grange of the Patrons of Husbandry, founded in 1867 by Oliver H. Kelley. The first granges were lodges of farmers who met both to exchange information on improvement of farming methods and for social purposes. By the mid-1870's the number of granges had grown to 20,000, their peak number.

The decline in farm prices prompted the Granger movement to seek farm reforms. The Illinois legislature responded to Granger demands for laws to fix maximum railroad and grain storage rates, and other states followed Illinois. This led to the "Granger Cases" when businesses protested against rate regulation by the state as interference constituting deprivation of property without due process of law in violation of the 14th Amendment. In *Munn v. Illinois* (1877), a major victory for the Grangers, the state's right to regulate warehouse prices was upheld by the U.S. Supreme Court. A decade later, when the Grangers were on the decline, the decision was modified by *Wabash v. Illinois* (1886).

The granges also organized cooperatives. These were hard hit by the Panic of 1873, especially their investments in the manufacture of farm implements. The failure of the Granger venture in cooperatives contributed to the decline of the Granger movement.

The Grange continues to exist as an organization of farmers' social clubs.

Granite Railway (Mass.). Built in 1826 and the first railway to be chartered in the U.S., it connected the stone quarries at Quincy with a wharf on the Neponset River, three miles away. Over this track, horses hauled stone for the building of Bunker Hill Monument. The horse - drawn wagons had grooved wheels so that the wagons would not run off the rails. The tracks were simply an improvement over the rough highways of the day.

Gran Quivira. The old Spanish church built about 1627 by

Father Letrado and the Indian pueblo ruins, in New Mexico, have become a national monument.

Grant, Ulysses Simpson (1822–85). Eighteenth President of U.S. (1869–77). He was born in Point Pleasant, Ohio and was graduated from the U.S. Military Academy, West Point, N.Y. (1843). After a succession of Union generals, Pres. Lincoln selected Grant to command the armies that finally brought about Gen. Lee's surrender at Appomattox Courthouse (Apr. 9, 1865). The Republicans capitalized on Grant's war record to put him in the White House. He was personally honest, but his administration was marked by scandals.

Grapes of Wrath (1939). The novel by John Steinbeck was one of the most widely read books of the depression years. It tells the story of the Joads, a family of dispossessed Oklahoma farmers ("Okies"), who wandered to California to look for work among the downtrodden fruit-and-vegetable pickers of the Salinas Valley.

Other works by one of the foremost novelists of the 20th century include *Tortilla Flat* (1935), *In Dubious Battle* (1936), *Of Mice and Men* (1937), *The Red Pony* (1937), *The Moon Is Down* (1942), *Cannery Row* (1945), *The Wayward Bus* (1947), *East of Eden* (1952) and *Travels with Charley in Search of America* (1962).

Gray, Asa (1810–88). Botanist. Born in Sauquoit, N.Y., he was one of the world's great botanists. Professor of botany at Harvard (1842–88), a pioneer in the field of plant geography, he did immense service in popularizing botany. His greatest achievement was his elaboration of the descriptive botany of North America in some 350 books, monographs and shorter papers. He was author of the *Botanical Text-Book* (1842, later called *Structural Botany*), the model for many imitations, *How Plants Grow* (1858), and a second *Elements of Botany* (1887).

Gray, Robert (1755–1806). Navigator and explorer. Born in Tiverton, R.I., he served in the American Navy during the American Revolution. He carried the American flag around the world for the first time when he sailed from Boston in Sept. 1787, rounded Cape Horn, loaded sea-otter skins on the Northwest coast and returned home by way of China in Aug. 1790.

Commanding the *Columbia*, he left Boston in Sept. 1790 for the Northwest and arrived at Vancouver Island in June 1791. He discovered Gray's Harbor and the Columbia River (named in honor of his vessel) before sailing to China, again circling the world before returning to Boston in July 1793. His discoveries in the Northwest were the foundation of the American claim to the Oregon country.

"Great American Desert." Major Stephen H. Long who explored some of the area between the Missouri River and the Rocky Mts. in 1820 wrote: ". . . we do not hesitate in giving the opinion that it is almost wholly unfit for cultivation, and of course uninhabitable by a people depending upon agriculture. . . ." On his map he called this expanse of land the "Great American Desert." He was referring to the area now known as the Great Plains. Until the Civil War the maps of the U.S. appearing in school textbooks carried the forbidding name. Moreover, the lack of water and timber did discourage early attempts to settle in that area.

Great Awakening. In contrast to the religious apathy in the colonies in the 1730's, a great revival shook New England. Thousands sought personal conversion which was often expressed in weeping, screaming and bodily gyrations induced by the emotional exhortations of the preachers.

The Great Awakening stimulated the growth of Presbyterians, Baptists and Methodists and broke the hold of conservatives on the churches of the day.

Jonathan Edwards of Northampton, Mass., a Congregationalist clergyman, was one of the great revivalists. His efforts in the early 1730's paved the way for the electrifying English evangelist, George Whitefield, who stirred the colonists in the 1740's.

Great Compromise (1787). An important problem that divided the Constitutional Convention dealt with the method of representation in the legislature. Virginia's plan favored the large states, and New Jersey's plan the small ones. Differences were fortunately settled by the Great Compromise, also called the Connecticut Compromise, proposed by Roger Sherman, a delegate from Connecticut.

Under the terms of the Compromise the large states accepted representation in one legislative house based on size of population. The small states won equal representation in the other legislative house. The two houses of the legislature thus provided for in the U.S. Constitution are the House of Representatives and the Senate.

Great Depression. The Wall Street crash of Oct. 24, 1929 (Panic of 1929), was the forerunner of the deepest economic depression in the nation's history. It persisted virtually to the outbreak in 1939 of World War II in Europe.

Overspeculation in the stock market, a farm depression that reduced farm purchasing power, loss of foreign markets and lack of purchasing power by the masses of the people were some of the factors which contributed to the economic collapse. The resultant depression was characterized by business bankruptcies, bank closings, factory shutdowns, farm foreclosures, low prices, hunger and huge unemployment—13 million in 1933, one out of four workers. As late as 1939 there were 9,500,000 workers unemployed in the U.S.

Great Meadows. The first engagement of the French and Indian War took place in May 1754 near this site in southwestern Pennsylvania. George Washington surprised a party of French, killed their commander and took over 20 prisoners. Washington built Fort Necessity on the Great Meadows.

Great Migration. During the reign of the Stuart King Charles I (1629–40), large numbers of British subjects, chiefly Puritans, migrated to the New World. While most of the migrants sought religious freedom, others left England in the hope of making a better living for themselves in a new country.

Great Northern Railway Co. Originally started in 1862 and named St. Paul and Pacific, it ran only 200 miles west of St. Paul; the line was taken over by James J. Hill in 1878 and took the name Great Northern in 1889. Construction was pushed 2,775 miles west through Minnesota, North Dakota and Montana, and up to Winnipeg in Canada.

Hill constructed track and roadbed with the best materials available and built around mountains rather than over them. The line was able to use long trains and carry heavy trainloads which neither the track nor the mountain routes of other western roads could do. A consequence of Hill's foresight was that the Great Northern alone of all the transcontinentals survived the Panic of 1893.

The northernmost U.S. transcontinental railroad now operates over 8,000 miles of road extending from Duluth and St. Paul to the Pacific Coast and serves ten states, Vancouver and Winnipeg.

"Great Pacificator." Although Henry Clay of Kentucky was not a leader in working out the 36° 30′ line which divided slave and free territory, he left his impression on the Missouri Compromise when he persuaded Missouri to modify its constitution, which had prohibited the entry of free Negroes into the state. Accepting Clay's solution, Missouri amended its constitution to guarantee citizens entering from other states the rights granted to them under the Constitution of the U.S. The Compromise made the Missouri constitution acceptable to the Congress and Missouri entered the Union as a slave state in 1821.

Great Plains. Stretching from western Missouri west to the Rocky Mountains, the so-called last frontier was so forbidding to settlers that it was known

303

as the "Great American Desert." Blazing summers and severe winters discouraged settlement. For decades it was mistakenly believed that the tough soil of the treeless plains could not be farmed.

For the 200,000 plains Indians it was a happy hunting ground on earth. They hunted the millions of buffaloes which provided them with food and hides.

White men crossing the plains in caravans of covered wagons over the Oregon, Santé Fe and other trails were harassed by Indians before their numbers and federal troops overwhelmed the Indians and forced them onto reservations.

The building of the transcontinental railroads in the post-Civil War period aided settlement of the interior plains by farmers. Lumber was brought in so that frame houses replaced their sod huts. Deep wells and irrigation combatted the uncertain rainfall. The invention of barbed wire in 1873 helped win the plains for farmers in their struggle with cattle and sheep ranchers. The hardy farmers who survived made the plains a great corn and wheat producing region.

Great Society, the. In an address at the University of Michigan in 1964, Pres. Lyndon B. Johnson first set forth an ideal which he later identified as a goal of his administration in his State of the Union Message to Congress, Jan. 4, 1965. The Great Society was to be ushered in by an expanded program of education, "a massive attack on crippling and killing diseases," beautification of our cities, prevention of crime and delinquency, establishment of civil rights, support for "achievement of thought and creation of art" and a campaign against waste and inefficiency. The Great Society would "improve the quality of life for all."

Greeley, Horace (1811–72). Editor and political leader. Born in Amherst, N.H., he moved to New York City in 1831. Founder of the *New York Tribune* (1841), which attained national influence, he was an exponent of the kind of personal journalism which made the paper a reflection of his views on the issues of his time. Greeley supported cooperative shops, labor unions, a protective tariff, free land for settlers and popularized the phrase, "Go west, young man. . . ." Opposed to slavery as both immoral and uneconomic, he joined the Free Soil movement. Among the first editors to join the Republican party, he supported Lincoln in 1860, but was lukewarm in 1864 because of the President's efforts to conciliate the border states. After the war Greeley favored full Negro equality and radical Reconstruction views. Regarding the Grant administration as corrupt, he indulged his political ambitions and was the badly defeated Liberal Republican candidate for President in 1872.

greenback movement. The major objective of the movement during the 1870's was to increase the amount of money in circulation and thus help farmers pay off their debts in a cheap currency. Congress was urged to authorize issuance of more greenbacks, paper money issued without gold backing during the Civil War.

A Greenback party formed in 1874 reached its height in 1878 when it elected a number of Congressmen. It remained, however, a minor party where some of its candidates enjoyed major party support.

The party received labor support during the unrest of 1877 and became the Greenback Labor party. To the demands for increased paper currency were added such labor demands as shorter hours, the abolition of Chinese immigration and social reform. James B. Weaver, party candidate for President in 1880, won a very small vote. The party waned as free coinage of silver replaced greenbacks as the avenue to currency inflation sought by the debtor groups.

Greenback party. It had its origins in the farm unrest which followed the deflationary currency measures of 1873 and 1874. The party held its first national convention in 1876, at Indianapolis, Ind., and adopted a platform which called for repeal of the Specie Resumption Act of 1875. The Act obliged the government to resume paying specie on demand for all its paper currency. The party's presidential nominee in 1876, Peter Cooper, received less than 1% of the total ballots cast.

The Greenbackers turned to labor for additional support following the great railroad strikes of 1877. The Greenback Labor party emerged from a national convention in 1878 at Toledo, O. It denounced specie payments, called for more paper money, reduction of hours for industrial workers and restrictions on Chinese immigration. The party polled over 1,000,000 votes in the congressional elections of 1878 and 14 candidates won seats in Congress. James B. Weaver, an Iowa lawyer, became the party's leader in Congress and in 1880, the party's candidate for President.

The party declined as economic conditions for farmers and workers improved. In 1884 it ran its last candidate for President.

Greene, Nathanael (1742–86). Revolutionary officer. Born in Warwick, R.I., he led the left column in Washington's victory at Trenton (1776); as quartermaster-general of the Continental army (1778–80), he established an efficient system of depots. Appointed to command in the South after Gen. Gates' defeat at Camden, S.C. (1780), he forced the British out of Georgia and the Carolinas.

Green Mountain Boys. The land west of the Green Mountains, which run through Vermont, was in dispute between New York and New Hampshire. In 1770 it was granted to New York, which meant that settlers would have to repurchase lands they had received from New Hampshire.

Ethan Allen and his brother Levi organized the Green Mountain Boys and resisted by force the New York sheriffs who sought to dispossess them.

During the American Revolution the Green Mountain Boys sided with the Patriots and gained a victory for the U.S. at Fort Ticonderoga.

Greenville, Treaty of (1790). The Northwest tribes of Indians agreed to a treaty signed at Fort Greenville after their defeat by Gen. Anthony Wayne at Fallen Timbers. He had been sent by Pres. Washington to end Indian attacks on settlers in Ohio. The tribes yielded most of their Ohio land to the U.S., opening the Northwest to immigration.

Greif, Operation. In World War II, the German army disguised special troops in American uniforms to capture the bridges on the Meuse during the battle of Ardennes, Dec. 1944.

Grenville program. At the close of the French and Indian War, the ministry of George Grenville (1763–65) embarked on a new colonial policy of raising revenue in the colonies through such taxes as the Sugar Act and Stamp Act. The determination to enforce the collection of taxes as well as various trade laws was a departure from the old colonial policy ("salutary neglect"). The new colonial policy aroused strong resistance in the American colonies and contributed to the American Revolution.

Grierson's Raid (Apr. 17–May 2, 1863). Gen. Benjamin H. Grierson and his Union cavalry raided an area from LaGrange, Tenn., to Baton Rouge, La. destroying railroads, bridges and telegraph lines, penetrating the heart of the Confederacy.

Griffith, David Lewelyn Wark (1875–1948). Motion picture producer. He was born in La Grange, Ky. A pioneer in the art of the motion picture, he won fame with *The Birth of a Nation* (New York premiere, 1915), based on *The Clansman* (1905), a novel by Thomas Dixon, Jr. The film cost $100,000 to make and by the time Griffith died, earned $48 million. In 1919 he helped found the United Artists Corporation. Other films he produced include: *Intolerance* (1916), *Broken Blossoms* (1919), *Way Down East* (1920), *Orphans of the Storm* (1922) and *America* (1924).

gringo. Originally meaning "gibberish," as applied to foreign speech, the term has been used in Spanish-speaking countries, especially in Mexico, to refer contemptuously to Anglo-Americans.

Gros Ventres Indians. An Algonquian-speaking people,

named by the French, "Big Bellies," they were really two tribes, the Atsina, a band of the Arapaho, and the Hidatsa. The French made contact with them in the Missouri River Valley during the fur-trading days of the colonial period.

Guadalcanal, battle of (Aug. 7, 1942–Feb. 1943). The island, at the southeastern end of the Solomons, an archipelago in the Western Pacific, was the center of a six-month battle. The American victory strengthened the rebuilding of the lifeline to Australia.

The fighting on Guadalcanal gave the U.S. Marines their first taste of jungle warfare in World War II, a special type of fighting that was to take place on scores of Pacific islands. The Marines, after the initial landing on Guadalcanal and the adjacent islands of Florida, Tulagi and Gavatu, were assisted by infantrymen.

Americans at Guadalcanal gave a brilliant demonstration of teamwork by sea, air and land forces in amphibious warfare.

Guadalupe-Hidalgo, Treaty of (1848). The peace treaty which ended the Mexican War (1846–48) was signed in a suburb of Mexico City. The southern boundary of Texas was set at the Rio Grande. Upper California and New Mexico were ceded to the U.S. for a payment of $15,000,000 and the U.S. assumed the claims of its citizens against the government of Mexico.

Guam. The principal Pacific base of the U.S. Air Force Strategic Air Command (SAC), the island is an unincorporated territory under the jurisdiction of the Department of Interior. It is administered under the Organic Act of 1950, which provides for a governor appointed for four years by the President and a 21-member unicameral legislature, elected biennially by the residents (primarily of Chamorro stock). They are American citizens but do not vote for the President.

Guam, the largest of the Mariana Islands in the western Pacific, about 1,500 miles from the Philippines, was ceded to the U.S. by Spain in the Treaty of Paris (Dec. 10, 1898), ending the Spanish-American War. The islands were discovered by Magellan (1521) who called them the Ladrones. They were renamed the Mariana Islands by Spanish missionaries (1668) in honor of a Queen of Spain.

Guggenheim, Daniel (1856–1930). Industrialist and philanthropist. Born in Philadelphia, Pa., he was one of seven sons of Meyer Guggenheim (1828–1905), who interested himself in the copper business. Daniel was in business in Switzerland (1873–84). He joined his father and brothers in the U.S. and planned the "Guggenheim" strategy of integrating copper mining, smelting and refining with exploration for and control of sources of supply. He reorganized the American Smelting and Refining Co. (1901) and extended his interests to gold mines in the Yukon, diamond mines in the Belgian Congo, tin mines in Bolivia and nitrate deposits in Chile. He practiced large-scale philanthropy in the Daniel and Florence Guggenheim Foundation (1924) to "promote the well being of mankind."

Guilford Courthouse, battle of (Mar. 15, 1781). In this Revolutionary War battle in North Carolina, six months before the debacle at Yorktown, the British dream of conquering the South was shattered. Although British Gen. Cornwallis forced Gen. Nathanael Greene and his Continentals to retreat, his losses were so great that Charles Fox, in the House of Commons, remarked: "Another such victory would destroy the British army!"

gunboat system. During Thomas Jefferson's administration, small armed craft were used for the defense of principal harbors. They were manned by trained seamen of the towns and when not in use were drawn up under sheds. Federalists opposed the system, favoring a strong navy. Gunboats saw limited service during the War of 1812.

Guntown, battle of (June 10, 1864). Confederate Gen. Nathan Bedford Forrest defeated a Union attempt to end his daring cavalry raids at Guntown, Miss., also known as Brice's Cross Roads.

H

habeas corpus, writ of. The right to secure a court order to bring an imprisoned person before a judge to determine whether he is being held illegally was guaranteed in England by the Habeas Corpus Act (1679). It was highly valued by the American colonists who objected when it was suspended in special cases. Provision for the writ is set forth in the Constitution (Art. I, Sec. 9, Par. 2): "The privilege of the writ of habeas corpus shall not be suspended, unless when in cases of rebellion or invasion the public safety may require it." It was suspended by Pres. Lincoln. When Chief Justice Taney in *Ex parte Merryman* (1861) held that the President had exceeded his powers, Congress provided for its suspension during the Civil War. The writ remains a basic safeguard of civil liberties. It is also provided for in state constitutions.

Hague Tribunal (Permanent Court of International Arbitration). The international body was organized in 1901 as an outcome of the peace efforts of the First Hague Conference (1899) which was attended by twenty-five nations, including the U.S., at the invitation of Czar Nicholas II of Russia.

Under the convention establishing the Tribunal, the disputing nations select the judges for arbitration from a list provided by the Tribunal. Hence it is not a court in the usual sense. Member nations are not required to submit their disputes to the Tribunal, nor is there power to enforce the decisions of the court. Nevertheless, the Tribunal has settled some serious international disputes, including the Venezuela debt controversy (1904) and the dispute between Britain and the U.S. over North Atlantic coast fisheries (1910). The Tribunal has not been superseded by the World Court.

"Hail Columbia." The song composed in 1798 by Joseph Hopkinson, a Federalist, was a patriotic reaction to the French demand for a bribe in the XYZ affair. The words of what was to be our first national hymn were set to the music of

The President's March, written in 1789 by Philip Roth for the inauguration of Washington.

"hair buyer." The charge that a British official was paying Indian allies to scalp American patriots was made by George Rogers Clark when he recaptured Vincennes (1779) in what was to be southwestern Indiana. The charge was not proved. It was, however, a common practice, both before and after the Revolution, for white men to use Indian allies against hostile Indians and against any other white men's army with which they were in contention.

Haiti, intervention in. Sharing the island of Hispaniola in the Caribbean with the Dominican Republic, the French-speaking Negro republic occupies the western third. Intervention by the U.S. in 1915 followed Pres. Guillaume Sam's butchering of about 160 imprisoned political enemies and his own destruction by a Haitian mob which dragged him from the French legation. When Haitian finances deteriorated, the U.S. feared that the intervention by Germany or some other power would menace the Panama lifeline. Haiti was virtually a U.S. protectorate from 1915 to 1934, when the last American Marines were withdrawn.

Hale, Nathan, execution of (Sept. 22, 1776). "I only regret that I have but one life to lose for my country." These are the famous words, which reflect a line in Addison's play *Cato*, uttered by young Capt. Hale before he was hanged as a spy by the British. He had volunteered to gain information on fortifications in New York and had hidden notes written in Latin in the sole of his shoe. Hale, a Yale graduate and schoolteacher, was captured as he was about to return to George Washington's headquarters.

"Halfbreeds." Factionalism in the Republican party during the 1870's and 1880's gave rise to the contemptuous term "Halfbreeds" to describe a wing led by Sen. Blaine of Maine that supported Pres. Hayes' program for the South and civil service reform. A liberal policy toward the South was regarded as weakness or "Halfbreed" Republicanism by the "Stalwarts" in the party.

Half Moon. Henry Hudson, an English seaman in the service of the Dutch, sailed (1609) up the river which bears his name. The ship, the *Half Moon*, was owned by the Dutch East India Company.

Half-way Covenant (1662). A blow was dealt orthodox Puritan church members when a Massachusetts Synod proclaimed that children of members who had no religious experiences to confess in public when they became adults might nevertheless remain in the church, although without voting privileges, and have their children baptized.

310

Hall of Fame. A national shrine established in 1900 at New York University with the aid of a $250,000 donation by Mrs. Finley J. Shepard. Names of outstanding Americans were inscribed on bronze tablets in 1900 and other names have been added at five-year intervals. Busts and tablets are donated. N.Y.U. acts as trustee for the shrine. A list of Americans honored follows:

1900

John Adams (statesman)
John James Audubon (ornithologist and artist)
Henry Ward Beecher (clergyman)
William Ellery Channing (clergyman)
Henry Clay (statesman)
Peter Cooper (manufacturer and philanthropist)
Jonathan Edwards (clergyman and theologian)
Ralph Waldo Emerson (essayist and poet)
David Glasgow Farragut (admiral)
Benjamin Franklin (statesman, scientist and philosopher)
Robert Fulton (engineer and inventor)
Ulysses Simpson Grant (general and President of U.S.)
Asa Gray (botanist)
Nathaniel Hawthorne (novelist)
Washington Irving (author)
Thomas Jefferson (statesman and President of U.S.)
James Kent (jurist)
Robert Edward Lee (general)
Abraham Lincoln (Civil War President of U.S.)

Henry Wadsworth Longfellow (poet)
Horace Mann (educator)
John Marshall (jurist)
Samuel Finley Breese Morse (artist and inventor)
George Peabody (merchant and philanthropist)
Joseph Story (jurist)
Gilbert Charles Stuart (artist)
George Washington (general and first President of U.S.)
Daniel Webster (statesman)
Eli Whitney (inventor)

1905

John Quincy Adams (statesman and President of U.S.)
James Russell Lowell (poet, essayist and diplomat)
Mary Lyon (educator)
James Madison (statesman and President of U.S.)
Maria Mitchell (astronomer and educator)
William Tecumseh Sherman (general)
John Greenleaf Whittier (poet)
Emma Willard (educator)

1910

George Bancroft (historian)
Phillips Brooks (clergyman)
William Cullen Bryant (poet and editor)
James Fenimore Cooper (novelist)
Oliver Wendell Holmes (author)
Andrew Jackson (general and President of U.S.)
John Lathrop Motley (historian)
Edgar Allan Poe (poet and short story writer)
Harriet Beecher Stowe (author)
Frances Elizabeth Willard (educator and reformer)

1915

Louis Agassiz (naturalist)
Daniel Boone (pioneer)
Rufus Choate (lawyer and orator)
Charlotte Saunders Cushman (actress)
Alexander Hamilton (statesman)
Joseph Henry (physicist)
Mark Hopkins (educator)
Elias Howe (inventor)
Francis Parkman (historian)

1920

Samuel Langhorne Clemens (Mark Twain) (author)
James Buchanan Eads (engineer and inventor)
Patrick Henry (statesman)
William Thomas Green Morton (dentist)
Alice Freeman Palmer (educator)
Augustus Saint-Gaudens (sculptor)
Roger Williams (clergyman and founder of R.I.)

1925

Edwin Booth (actor)
John Paul Jones (naval officer)

1930

Matthew Fontaine Maury (oceanographer)
James Monroe (statesman and President of U.S.)
James Abbott McNeill Whistler (artist)
Walt Whitman (poet)

1935

Grover Cleveland (President of U.S.)
Simon Newcomb (astronomer)
William Penn (founder of Pennsylvania)

1940

Stephen Collins Foster (songwriter)

1945

Sidney Lanier (poet)
Thomas Paine (political philosopher and author)
Walter Reed (army surgeon)
Booker T. Washington (educator)

1950

Susan B. Anthony (woman suffrage advocate)
Alexander Graham Bell (inventor)
Josiah Willard Gibbs (physicist)
William Crawford Gorgas (sanitarian and army surgeon)
Theodore Roosevelt (statesman and President of U.S.)
Woodrow Wilson (statesman and President of U.S.)

1955

Thomas ("Stonewall") Jackson (general)
George Westinghouse (inventor and manufacturer)
Wilbur Wright (pioneer in aviation)

1960

Thomas Alva Edison (inventor)
Edward Alexander MacDowell (composer)
Henry David Thoreau (essayist and poet)

1965

Jane Addams (social settlement worker)
Oliver Wendell Holmes, Jr. (jurist)
Sylvanus Thayer (army officer and educator)
Orville Wright (pioneer in aviation)

Hamilton, Alexander (1755–1804). Statesman. Born in Nevis, British West Indies, he came to New York City in 1772. An aide-de-camp to Gen. Washington, he fought in the Revolutionary War. In 1783 he embarked on a distinguished law career in New York, while deeply involved in politics. Regarding the central government as too weak under the Articles of Confederation, Hamilton was a major mover in the call for the Constitutional Convention (1787). His contributions to *The Federalist* (1787–88) helped to secure the adoption of the Constitution. Differences with Jefferson over domestic policy and foreign affairs led to the formation of the two-party system in which he was a leader of the Federalist party. First Sec. of the Treasury (1789–95), his financial plan for placing the new nation's credit on a sound basis was largely accepted. In his report on manufactures, Hamilton favored protection of infant industries. He advocated strict neutrality between France and Britain, during the wars arising from the French Revolution. Although critical of Jefferson, he supported him over Burr in the election of 1800 and prevented the election of Burr as governor of New York (1804). He was killed by Burr in a duel.

Hamilton's Financial Plans. Alexander Hamilton was determined to strengthen the newly created central government. He urged Congress to assume not only the foreign debt of about $12,000,000 owed to France, Holland and Spain, but also the internal (domestic) debt. Congress passed the Assumption Act (1790).

The internal debt consisted of about $42,000,000 which the national government had borrowed from its citizens to finance the Revolutionary War and $21,000,000 which the states owed individual citizens. Some of the states had already repaid part of their debt when Hamilton made his proposal and most of the bonds representing the internal debt had passed into the hands of speculators. Nevertheless, Hamilton believed that faith in the credit of the U.S. would be established only if the federal government became responsible for all the obligations. Furthermore, the central government would be strengthened since creditors would look to it for payment.

In a compromise arrangement, Thomas Jefferson and his followers agreed to support the assumption of debts in return for locating the capital of the U.S. on the banks of the Potomac on a tract of land donated by Maryland and Virginia.

Hamilton was also a major force in establishing the first Bank of the United States, a central bank which issued sound uniform currency. He was less successful with his "Report on Manufactures" (1791) which was coldly received by Congress. It called for a protective tariff, subsidies to industries in their infancy and conversion of the U.S. into an industrial nation.

Opposition to Hamilton's financial program was usually bitter and vocal. In the case of his tax on whiskey, one of a number of taxes on manufactures by which he sought to raise revenue to pay the debt, objection took a violent turn (the Whiskey Rebellion).

Hamilton had been criticized for favoring the wealthy groups; yet when Jefferson became President he made no substantial changes in the financial policy.

Hamlet Case (1850). James Hamlet, a free Negro, was arrested in New York by a deputy U.S. marshal as a fugitive slave from Baltimore. It was the first recorded action under the Fugitive Slave Act of 1850 and aroused so much public indignation that Hamlet was redeemed and freed.

Hammerstein, Oscar, 2nd (1895–1960). Playwright and librettist. Born in New York City, he was a notable collaborator with composers and helped to develop Broadway musicals as an art form with a serious story line. He won a special Pulitzer award (with Richard Rodgers) for *Oklahoma* (1943). His other notable productions include *Rose Marie* (music by Rudolf Friml, 1924), *Desert Song* (music by Sigmund Romberg, 1926), *Show Boat* (music by Jerome Kern, based on Edna Ferber's novel, 1927), *Carousel*

(based on Molnar's *Liliom,* 1945), *South Pacific* (1949), *The King and I* (1951) and *The Sound of Music* (1960). The songs of Rodgers and Hammerstein which became American classics include "The Surrey with the Fringe on Top" (from *Oklahoma*) and "Some Enchanted Evening" (from *South Pacific*).

Hammer v. Dagenhart (1918). The U.S. Supreme Court in a five to four decision declared unconstitutional the Keating-Owen Child Labor Act (1916) which prohibited the employment of children below the ages of 16 or 14 in various specified industries.

Dagenhart, the father of two children who were employed in a cotton mill in Charlotte, N.C., brought action to enjoin Hammer, the U.S. district attorney for that district, from enforcing the law. The federal district court judge granted the injunction and Hammer took the appeal to the Supreme Court.

The Supreme Court ruled that the link between child labor and interstate commerce was so slight as to be virtually non-existent. Even if there were a connection, the Court reasoned, it would be regulation of commerce within the reserved power of the states.

The decision was overruled in *U.S. v. Darby* (1941).

Hampton Roads Conference (Feb. 3, 1865). Unsuccessful negotiations for ending the Civil

War took place aboard the Union transport *River Queen.* Confederate Pres. Jefferson Davis sent Vice-Pres. Stephens and two other representatives to confer with Pres. Lincoln and Sec. of State Seward. The Confederates insisted on recognition of southern independence. This was unacceptable to Lincoln, who insisted on reunion and emancipation of the slaves but offered considerate treatment of the South.

Hancock, John (1737–93). American Revolutionary statesman. He was born in Braintree, Mass. A leading colonial merchant, he took part in the Stamp Act protest (1765) and was defended by John Adams when his sloop, *Liberty,* was seized by customs on a charge of illegal trading (1768). Identified with the colonial cause, he became President of the Continental Congress (1775–77) and was the first signer of the Declaration of Independence. He was elected first governor of Mass. (1780) and served nine terms.

Hand, Learned (1872–1961). Jurist. He was born in Albany, N.Y. Although he was never appointed to the U.S. Supreme Court, his decisions as judge of the U.S. Circuit Court, 2nd Circuit (N.Y.) from 1924 until his retirement, were influential in the fields of maritime law, taxation, banking, trademarks and labor law. In the antitrust suit against the Aluminum Co. of America, he held that "Congress did not condone 'good trusts' and condemn 'bad' ones; it forbade all." His numerous addresses and epigrams were widely quoted. Aware that judges are human, he kept Cromwell's plea in mind: "I beseech ye in the bowells of Christ, think that ye may be mistaken."

Hanna, Marcus Alonzo (1837–1904). Businessman and politician. Born in New Lisbon, Ohio, he was a partner in his father's grocery business before moving into Great Lakes' shipping, banking, street railways and ownership of the *Cleveland Herald.* A dominant figure in Ohio politics, he supported William McKinley for governor (1891, 1893) and for President of the U.S. (1896, 1900). As chairman of the Republican national committee, Hanna helped assure McKinley's election by making large regular assessments on businesses. An important presidential adviser and U.S. Senator (1897–1904), he used federal patronage to strengthen his party. A conservative who took pride in his "Standpattism," he nevertheless believed in the right of labor to organize and preferred to have big business bargain with responsible labor leaders. He helped to settle disputes in the anthracite coal industry.

"Happy Warrior." Elected governor of New York for four terms (1919–20, 1923–28), Alfred E. Smith, to whom the nickname was given, had a record of liberal reform legislation.

However popular and personable he was, as a Catholic and a "wet" he was badly defeated in the presidential election of 1928.

Harding, Warren Gamaliel (1865–1923). Twenty-ninth President of the U.S. (1921–23). He was born in Corsica, O., and served Ohio as U.S. senator (1915–21). A conservative Republican, he favored high tariffs and opposed U.S. entrance into the League of Nations. His administration was scarred by the corruption of officials he appointed. He died (Aug. 2, 1923) while on a speaking tour.

Hard Labor, Treaty of (Oct. 14, 1768). By agreement signed at Hard Labor, S.C., between England and the Cherokee tribe, the Virginia border was moved a little further west. White settlers, however, still remained on Indian lands, and the Virginians were not satisfied with the Treaty.

hard money. Specie, usually gold or silver, was in short supply during the colonial period and foreign coins were circulated along with English money before the Revolution.

The issuance of paper money when it was not backed by gold invariably led to a monetary struggle. This was so in the 1830's when the paper money issued by banks drove hard money out of circulation. Lack of specie backing for "greenbacks" caused their depreciation during the Civil War. In the post-Civil War period free silver interests, largely debtor farmers, were opposed by hard money advocates who successfully urged gold as a backing for paper money.

"Hards." A Democratic faction in New York politics, 1852–60, sympathized with the proslavery Democrats in other parts of the country. The "Hards" were distinguished from the "Softs" and, in part, were identified with the "Hunkers" of the 1840's.

Harlan, John Marshall (1833–1911). Jurist. Born in Boyle Co., Ky., he served as colonel in the Union army in the Civil War (1861–63). He was attorney general of Kentucky (1863–67). Appointed by Pres. Hayes as associate justice of U.S. Supreme Court (1877–1911), he dissented in 316 cases and is remembered as the "great dissenter." He protested against what he regarded as impairment of the vital power of national taxation in *Pollock v. Farmer's Loan and Trust Co.* (1895). He believed that firm protection should be given police power of the state and dissented from the judgment in *Lochner v. N.Y.* (1905). He denounced judicial legislation in his dissents in the Standard Oil and American Tobacco Co. cases, written a few months before his death.

Harlem, battle of (Sept. 16, 1776). In his retreat from New York, Gen. Washington halted long enough at Harlem Heights, on Manhattan Island, to turn back a British attack. He prepared new fortifications which he held for about three weeks.

Harlem race riots. Racial violence erupted in the predominantly Negro section of Harlem in New York City, July 18, 1964, and continued for several days. It followed a Harlem rally by the Congress of Racial Equality (CORE) in protest against the shooting of a Negro youth by a white police officer. Subsequent investigation made it clear that the officer had been attacked by the knife-wielding youth. Mobs of Negroes roamed the Harlem streets looting stores, attacking white persons and taunting policemen. The toll of the rioting included one Negro shot to death, five other Negroes shot and wounded, 81 civilians and 35 policemen injured, at least 112 stores damaged.

Elsewhere during the "hot summer" of 1964, race riots flared in the predominently Negro Bedford-Stuyvesant section of Brooklyn, N.Y. and in Rochester, N.Y.

A race riot resulting in the death of five persons flared in Harlem (Aug. 1, 1943) after a Negro soldier was wounded by a white policeman.

Harmony Society. Led by George Rapp, German Separatists established a religious communal organization at Harmony, Pa., in 1805. The Society moved to New Harmony, Ind., in 1815, but returned to Economy, Pa., in 1825. Members vowed celibacy and shared their resources. By the end of the century the settlement had disintegrated.

Harper, William Rainey (1856–1906). Educator. Born in New Concord, O., he was granted a Ph.D. by Yale (1874) when he was only 18. A Hebraist, he taught Semitic languages at Baptist Union Theological Seminary, Chicago, Ill. (1879–86). When, with John D. Rockefeller's encouragement, the new Univ. of Chicago was founded, he became its first president (1891–1906) while teaching full time as chairman of his department. He stipulated that there should be entire academic freedom. His plans included a university press, university extension, division of the year into four quarters, and emphasis on graduate study and research. He was the author of *Critical and Exegetical Commentary on Amos and Hosea* (1905).

Harpers Ferry. The little residential town and tourist resort in northeastern West Virginia was the site of a U.S. arsenal established in 1796 and seized in John Brown's raid (1859).

It was regarded as a strategic base early in the Civil War by Gen. Robert E. Lee, who invaded Maryland hoping to bring this border state to the side of the Confederacy. To protect his rear, he sent orders to "Stonewall" Jackson to take the federal arsenal at Harpers Ferry, Va. His dispatch, wrapped around a few cigars, was found by Union soldiers and Gen. George McClellan was alerted to Lee's plans. Nevertheless, Jackson captured Harpers Ferry (Sept. 15, 1862) although he returned to Lee a day later than expected. Fearing that the "Lost Order" was a trick, McClellan had hesitated to attack while Lee's forces were divided.

Harris, Joel Chandler (1848–1908). Writer. Born in Putnam Co., Ga., he wrote for various newspapers (1864–76) and made the *Atlanta Constitution* nationally known with his Uncle Remus stories (1876–1900). A master of Negro dialect and folkways, his stories about Uncle Remus and the world of animals were enormously popular. He published *Uncle Remus: His Songs and His Sayings* (1880), *Nights with Uncle Remus* (1883) and *Mingo and Other Sketches in Black and White* (1884).

Harris, Townsend (1804–78). Diplomat. Born in Sandy Hill, N.Y., he established a family business importing china in New York City. President of N.Y.C. Board of Education (1846–48), he helped establish a free college, the College of the City of New York (CCNY). Following trips to the Pacific on his trading ship, he was named first U.S. consul general to Japan (1855). He negotiated the earliest U.S. commercial treaties with Japan (1857–58).

Harrison, Benjamin (1833–1901). Twenty-third President of the U.S. (1889–93). He was born in North Bend, O., and was graduated from Miami Univ., Oxford, O. (1852). The grandson of William Henry Harrison, he served Indiana as U.S. senator (1881–87). He was defeated by Grover Cleveland for the Presidency in 1892. The first Pan-American Conference was held during his administration.

Harrison, Ross Granville (1870–1959). Biologist. Born in Germantown, Pa., he was granted a Ph.D. by Johns Hopkins (1894); an M.D., Univ. of Bonn (1899). He taught anatomy and biology at Yale (1907–38) and was managing editor, *Journal of Experimental Zoology* (1904–46). He was the first to adapt (1907) the hanging-drop culture method to the study of embryonic tissues and perfected devices for tissue grafting.

Harrison, William Henry (1773–1841). Ninth President of the U.S. He was born in Berkeley, Charles City County, Va. Commanding the army of the Northwest during the War of 1812, he fought against Tecumseh. He was U.S. senator from Ohio (1825–28). The Whig candidate for President in 1836, he was defeated; but he won the Presidency at the age of 67 in 1840 in an anti-Jackson wave. The oldest President to be inaugurated, he died of pneumonia after one month in office (Mar. 4–Apr. 4, 1841).

Harrison Land Act (1800). The government liberalized land sale policy in response to frontier protests that speculators rather than settlers were being favored. Named for William Henry Harrison, active in the Northwest Territory (later President of the U.S., 1841), the Act made it possible for settlers to buy 320 acres rather than the former 640-acre minimum. It retained the $2 per acre price, but made credit terms easier.

Harte, Francis Brett (1836–1902). Writer. Born in Albany, N.Y., he went to California (1854) where he was a teacher, newspaperman and editor. He moved to New York (1871–78), but continued to draw on his Western experience for short stories which became a model for writers using "local color." Known as Bret Harte, he is best remembered for *The Luck of Roaring Camp and Other Sketches* (1870) and his poem "The Heathen Chinee." He ended his career, which included service as U.S. Consul in Prussia (1878–80) and Scotland (1880–85), as a hack writer in London.

Hartford Convention (1814). The Convention of New England Federalists, at Hartford, Conn., called for states' rights and proposed constitutional amendments that reflected its hostility toward the South and West. Near the end of the War of 1812, an unpopular war in commercial New England, it gathered in secret sessions.

The delegates loathed Jeffersonian Republicanism which they saw installed in the nation's capital. Their recommendations would have been even more separatist if the Essex Junto, a group of extremist Federalists, had not been restrained by the moderation of Harrison Gray Otis.

The Convention's recommendations were made at the end of the war. They were buried along with the Federalist party in the general rejoicing at the advent of peace.

"Hartford (or Connecticut) Wits." A group of young conservative writers — all Yale graduates—pilloried Jeffersonian policies (1785–1800). One of their better-known works, *The Anarchiad* (1786–87), satirized mob rule and other alleged aspects of Jeffersonianism. One of the "wits," Joel Barlow, best-known for his humorous poem, *Hasty Pudding* (1796), later became an ardent Jeffersonian. His patriotic poems include *The Vision of Columbus* (1787), expanded into *The Columbiad* (1807). Others dubbed "Hartford Wits" were John Trumbull who wrote *The Progress of Dullness* (1772–73), a satire on education; Timothy Dwight, a Congregational minister, whose *Triumph of Infidelity* (1788) defended orthodoxy; David Humphreys and Lemuel Hopkins who joined with the others in *The Anarchiad*.

Harvard University. In 1636 the Massachusetts General Court agreed to donate £400 "toward a schoole or collidge" which, aided by a bequest two years later by John Harvard, became the college bearing his name. The first classes met in 1638 at New Towne (now Cambridge). The college is the oldest in the U.S. and became a university in 1782.

Although the Puritan community desired an educated ministry, and a religious spirit permeated the college, Harvard was not a theological seminary. A broader type of higher education was advocated by most New Englanders. Only half of Harvard's 17th-century graduates became ministers. The college soon added a medical school (1782) and law school (1815).

Haryou-Act board. The agency was set up in 1964 with New York City, federal and private contributions to relieve the "despair, hopelessness and futility" of Harlem. It combines Harlem Youth Opportunities Unlimited (Haryou) with Associated Community Teams (Act).

Hat Act (1732). Parliament prohibited the exportation of American-made hats from the colony in which they were produced. It restricted each hatmaker to two apprentices. The Act was an example of British colonial policy which discouraged competition with manufacturers in the mother country by preventing the growth of large-scale production in the colonies.

Hatch Act (1887). Agricultural education and research was furthered by passage of the Act, which provided an annual grant of $15,000 to each state for carrying on research in the agricultural sciences. It initiated the system of state agricultural experiment stations which are in most states associated with the state colleges of agriculture.

The first state agricultural college in the U.S. was established in Michigan (1857). Maryland and Pennsylvania followed in 1859, and in 1862 the land-grant college system was made more general through the Morrill Act.

The federal support for state agricultural experiment stations under the Hatch Act was enlarged through passage of the Adams Act (1906), which provided an additional $15,000 per year to each of the states for research on agricultural problems. Additional larger grants were made in the 1920's and in the following decades.

hatchet, burying the. The Iroquois custom of burying their hatchets (tomahawks), scalping knives and war clubs to indicate that all thoughts of hostility had been put aside was continued during colonial times. "Burying the hatchet" became a symbol denoting the establishment of peace between warring tribes or Indians and whites.

Hatfields and McCoys. These feuding families on opposite sides in the Civil War continued their hostilities after the war. In the 1880's their hatred resulted in a series of murders following an alleged theft of a farm animal by a West Virginia Hatfield from the Kentucky McCoys, just across the state border. The feud has become legendary.

"hat in the ring." Entry into a political campaign by a candidate has been described as "throwing the hat in the ring." The expression was popularized by Theodore Roosevelt in 1912 when newspaper reporters asked him whether he planned to run for President in the coming campaign. Roosevelt answered, Feb. 21, "My hat's in the ring; the fight is on and I'm stripped to the buff."

The phrase is derived from Western sporting slang used when a man volunteered to enter a boxing or wrestling match by throwing his hat in the ring. "Ready to fight at the drop of a hat" refers to the same practice.

Hawaii. Known as the "Aloha State," and the first overseas and second non-contiguous U.S. state, Hawaii is separated from the mainland by the North Pacific Ocean, 2,397 miles from San Francisco. It was admitted as the 50th State, Aug. 21, 1959. Honolulu is the capital.

The Hawaiian Islands (there are eight major islands, seven inhabited and 114 minor islands, four inhabited) were called the Sandwich Islands by British Capt. James Cook, who visited them in 1778. By 1820 American whalers were using the islands as a repair station and American missionaries arrived.

Hawaii was a kingdom until Jan. 17, 1893, when Queen Liliuokalani was deposed. Pres. Cleveland opposed annexation because of American collusion in the revolution. A republic was organized in 1894. In 1898 Hawaii was annexed by the U.S. as an outcome of the Spanish-American War when the strategic value of the islands became increasingly evident. The Territory was established in 1900.

The U.S. was forced into World War II when Japan staged a "sneak attack" on our great naval base at Pearl Harbor, Hawaii, Dec. 7, 1941 (the "day of infamy" described by Pres. Franklin D. Roosevelt). "Remember Pearl Harbor!" became a U.S. battle cry.

Although a third of the Hawaiian people are Japanese by descent, the Nisei distinguished themselves in the Italian campaign and became known as the "Purple Heart Battalion" (the purple heart medal was awarded to those wounded in action). Another one-third of Hawaiians are Caucasian. There are lesser numbers of part Hawaiian, Filipino, Chinese, Hawaiian, Negro and American Indian.

The largest industries are sugar, tourism and pineapples. National defense installations also contribute to the economy of the islands.

Hawley-Smoot Tariff Act of 1930. The rates, the highest in U.S. history, were opposed by economists who protested that it would cause higher prices for consumers, destroy international trade, make it impossible for foreign countries to repay their debts to the U.S. since they could not sell to us and would not help the American farmer who was producing great surpluses. One thousand economists signed a petition urging Pres. Hoover to veto the measure.

The President approved the measure thinking that he could use the flexible provision to raise or lower rates up to 50% on advice of the Tariff Commission. Foreign countries retaliated with high tariffs.

Hawthorne, Nathaniel (1804–64). Novelist. Born in Salem, Mass., he trained himself to be a man of letters by extensive reading and travel. Early in his career the *New England Magazine*, founded in 1828 by Samuel Goodrich, was his chief publishing outlet. For a short time he lived with the Transcendentalists who had founded Brook Farm. His best-known work, *The Scarlet Letter* (1850), criticizes the hypocrisy, insensitivity and inhumanity of the New England Puritans. His exposure of their cruelty to the woman who had committed adultery mocked the reformers and scientists who wrote and spoke of progress.

Other novels by Hawthorne include *Twice-Told Tales* (First Series, 1837; Second Series,

1842), *The House of the Seven Gables* (1851) and *The Blithedale Romance* (1852).

A classic figure in American literature, he held various minor federal positions to earn a living. Later in life he was U.S. consul in Liverpool, England (1853–58).

Hay, John Milton (1838–1905). Statesman. Born in Salem, Ind., he practiced law in Illinois. As assistant private secretary to Lincoln (1861–65), he gained an abiding sense of Lincoln's greatness. He held various diplomatic posts abroad (1865–70). He was Pres. McKinley's and Theodore Roosevelt's Sec. of State (1898–1905). He favored the Open Door policy in China (1899), and his masterful dealings with China following the Boxer Rebellion (1900) kept China from being partitioned. He sought to clear the way for the Panama Canal with various treaties. With John Nicolay he was author of *Abraham Lincoln: A History* (10 vols., 1890).

Hay - Bunau - Varilla Treaty (1903). The Treaty, between the U.S. and Panama, gave the U.S. the right to build the Panama Canal. Panama had revolted in 1903 and declared its independence of Colombia. Sec. of State John Hay and Philippe Bunau-Varilla, Panama's first minister to the U.S., signed the Treaty by which the U.S. guaranteed the independence of Panama and leased a zone 10 miles wide—the Panama Canal

Zone—for the projected canal. The U.S. agreed to pay Panama $10,000,000 outright and $250,000 annually beginning nine years after the ratification of the Treaty.

Hayburn's Case (1792). The case, involving the constitutionality of a law of Congress, was the first of its kind to come before the U.S. Supreme Court. It arose when the Pennsylvania Circuit Court of Appeals refused to make a decision involving the claim of William Hayburn for a pension. The Circuit Court held that the pension law was inconsistent with the Constitution because it made the administration of the law nonjudicial in nature by requiring that Congress and the Secretary of War review the judge's decision.

Before the Supreme Court could pass on the act, the pension law was changed by Congress. It has since been the firm practice of the courts to render no judgments that are subject to review or alteration by administrative action.

Hayes, Rutherford Birchard (1822–93). Nineteenth President of the U.S. (1877–81). He was born in Delaware, O., and was graduated from Kenyon College (1842). He served Ohio as member of U.S. House of Representatives (1865–67). In the close election of 1876 he won the Presidency by a single electoral vote when the electoral commission, formed to consider the contested ballots, declared him the winner over Samuel Tilden, who had won the popular vote.

Hay-Herran Treaty (1903). The U.S. proposed to Colombia an agreement which would permit the U.S. to build a canal across the Isthmus of Panama. The U.S. would lease a canal zone six miles wide for $10,000,000 in cash and an annual rental of $250,000. The Treaty was not ratified by Colombia, which wanted part of the $40,000,000 the U.S. was prepared to pay the French company which owned the rights to build the canal.

Leading Panamanians, afraid that the U.S. would switch to a Nicaragua route, revolted. The U.S. quickly recognized the new Republic of Panama and concluded the Hay-Bunau-Varilla Treaty, which permitted the U.S. to go ahead with canal construction.

Haymarket riot (May 4, 1886). Agitation for the eight-hour day, coupled with a protest against police violence in the McCormick Harvester Company strike, led to calling of a mass meeting in Haymarket Square, Chicago, by August Spies, editor of the *Arbeiter-Zeitung*, a semi-anarchist newspaper. Other radical agitators publicized the meeting and addressed it.

Since violence was anticipated, the mayor of Chicago was present with a police detachment. He left believing that the speeches were harmless. As the meeting was breaking up, police moved in to disperse the crowd. A bomb was thrown and the ensuing "massacre" resulted in the death of seven police and the wounding of 67; four workers died and 50 or more were injured.

In the trial that followed, the bomb-thrower was not identified. But eight of the radical agitators were found guilty of inciting the violence which had supposedly caused the bombing. Four were executed. Three of the surviving prisoners were pardoned in 1893 by Gov. John Peter Altgeld of Illinois on the ground that they had not been granted a fair trial. Altgeld was praised by labor and denounced in the conservative press. His political career was ruined. The riot or "massacre" also dealt a blow to labor. It contributed to the downfall of the Knights of Labor and slowed the movement toward an eight-hour day.

Hay-Pauncefote Treaty (1901). Britain and the U.S. abrogated the Clayton-Bulwer Treaty and the former agreed to the construction of a U.S.-controlled canal across the Isthmus of Panama. The canal, however, was to be opened to the ships of all nations on equal terms.

Britain foresaw that the canal would strengthen U.S. naval power and wished to be linked with a friendly U.S. at a time when German naval power was increasing.

head right system. According to the practice introduced in Virginia early in the 17th century, a settler who transported himself to the colony and remained for three years was given title to 50 acres of land. Later, the head of a family could claim an additional 50 acres for any dependent or servant he brought with him.

The system was extended to other colonies and some men who made a business of importing colonists acquired large tracts of land in this way.

Health, Education, and Welfare, Department of. Created by Congress in 1953, the Department was established for the purpose of improving the administration of those agencies of the government which are responsible for the general welfare in the fields of health, education and social security. The Secretary of the Department has a place in the President's Cabinet.

"He kept us out of war." The slogan was used thousands of times by Democratic campaigners for Woodrow Wilson's re-election in 1916. The longer phrase, "With honor, he kept us out of war," appeared on all official literature emanating from the Democratic National Committee.

Helper's *Impending Crisis* (1857). *The Impending Crisis of the South: How to Meet It,* which added to the division of North and South over the slavery issue, was published in New York by Hinton Helper, a small farmer of North Caro-

324

lina. Helper was hailed in the North and denounced as a renegade in the South. He sought to show that slavery was not only economically unprofitable, but that it was ruinous to the non-slaveholders of the South. He made slavery "the root of all the shame, poverty, ignorance, tyranny and imbecility of the South."

Hemingway, Ernest (1899–1961). Novelist. Born in Oak Park, Ill., he worked as a reporter for various newspapers before perfecting the monosyllabic, concrete style "drawn from many vernaculars" that distinguished his writing. War, violence, sport and dissipation were recorded in works that reached a wide audience. In his famous war novel, *A Farewell to Arms* (1929), he tells the story of an American in the ambulance service in Italy during World War I. Frederic Henry falls in love with an English nurse. In the hard realities of war they do not legalize their marriage. The birth of their child results in the mother's death.

Other works by this foremost American novelist include *The Sun Also Rises* (1926), *Death in the Afternoon* (1932), *For Whom the Bell Tolls* (1940) and *The Old Man and the Sea* (1952). Hemingway won the Nobel Prize for Literature in 1954.

Hench, Philip Showalter (1896–1965). Physician. Born in Pitts-

burgh, Pa., he was granted an M.D. by the Univ. of Pittsburgh (1920). He headed the section on rheumatic diseases at the Mayo Clinic, Rochester, Minn. (1926). Awarded the Nobel Prize (1950) for discoveries of hormones of the adrenal cortex, he was a pioneer in work on cortisone and ACTH therapy in crippling rheumatic diseases.

Henry, Fort, capture of (Feb. 6, 1862). To prevent the South's being split, the Confederacy tried unsuccessfully to hold the fort on the Tennessee River. It fell to the gunboats of Commodore A. H. Foote as Gen. Ulysses S. Grant moved up his troops. Grant did not delay but moved on to the next key point in the Mississippi campaign, Fort Donelson.

Henry, Joseph (1797–1878). Physicist. He was born in Albany, N.Y. He was a researcher into the relation of electric currents to magnetism; electromagnets of the present day are precisely like those he designed. The modern unit of inductance is called the "henry" in honor of his research. He was professor of natural philosophy at Princeton, then the College of New Jersey (1832–46). He was first secretary and director of the Smithsonian Institution (1846). He was instrumental in initiating a system of receiving weather reports by telegraph and basing predictions on them.

Henry, Patrick (1736–99). Revolutionary leader. Born in Hanover Co., Va., he practiced law and was an early outspoken critic of England. In opposing the Stamp Act, in the Virginia House of Burgesses, he ended his speech with, "Caesar had his Brutus; Charles the First, his Cromwell; and George the Third—may profit by their example. . . . If this be treason, make the most of it." He was to Virginia what Samuel Adams was to Massachusetts in the years before the final break with Britain; he started an intercolonial committee of correspondence. At the Virginia Convention (Mar. 23, 1775), he uttered the famous phrase, "Give me liberty, or give me death." He was a member of the Continental Congress (1774–76) and governor of Virginia (1776–79; 1784–86). Henry declined to be a delegate to the Constitutional Convention, opposed ratification and urged passage of the first ten amendments (Bill of Rights). He declined positions of responsibility in the new federal government.

"Henry Letters." Reports by a Canadian secret agent, John Henry, to the British, on the extent of disunion sentiment in New England, were made public after their purchase by Pres. Madison who hoped to embarrass his political opposition. The disclosure of these letters angered many Americans and was one of the factors which led Pres. Madison to send his war message to Congress, June 1, 1812.

Hepburn Act (1906). Congress strengthened the Interstate Commerce Commission's power to regulate railroads by giving it the power to fix maximum rates when complaints were made. Under the Act reversal of such action by the courts rested on railroads seeking to change an ICC ruling. The Act also curbed the issuance of free passes.

ICC regulation was extended to terminal facilities, sleeping-car and pipeline companies.

Hermitage, the. Preserved as a memorial near Nashville, Tenn., Pres. Jackson's beautiful home reflects his status as a plantation owner. Jackson, 7th President of the U.S., was born in a log cabin.

Hessians. German mercenaries from petty principalities in south and west Germany were paid to fight on the British side during the Revolutionary War. Specifically, the name was applied to soldiers hired out by the princes of Hesse-Kassel and Hesse-Hanau. There were some 30,000 German mercenaries in all. Their use was exploited by colonial propagandists and opposed by American sympathizers in Parliament.

Hickey plot. A conspiracy to assassinate Gen. George Washington at New York was discovered, and its ringleader, Thomas Hickey, one of the general's guards, was hanged in June 1776. David Matthews, mayor of New York, was implicated and imprisoned.

"higher law." On Mar. 11, 1850, Sen. William H. Seward (N.Y.) electrified the country with a speech denouncing compromise with slavery and appealing to a "higher law" than the Constitution. Critics charged that this was an appeal to lawlessness.

The concept of a "higher law" has its roots in the ethics of the Stoics whose *Jus Naturale* was the way of happiness for all men. According to these ancient Greek philosophers the supreme legislator was Nature herself. This concept of the "higher law" was carried forward into Roman jurisprudence by Cicero, who in his *De Legibus* assigned the binding quality of the civil law itself to its being in harmony with the universal attributes of human nature. "We are born for justice, and right is not the mere arbitrary construction of opinion, but an institution of nature."

The concept of a "higher law" had been developed by antislavery groups for many years, and Seward himself had used it on a number of occasions.

high school. More training than the elementary schools offered was made necessary by the business growth of the second quarter of the 19th century. The demand was for an upward extension of the public school, which would provide academy instruction for the poor as well as the rich.

The first high school in the U.S., known as the English Classical School, was founded in Boston in 1821. In 1824 this school was called the English High School. It was the Massachusetts Law of 1827 that laid the base for the American high school. It required establishment of a high school in every town with 500 or more families and specified a curriculum of U.S. history, algebra, geometry, surveying and bookkeeping. In towns of 4,000 or more inhabitants, added to the curriculum were Greek, Latin, rhetoric and logic. The cost of the schools fell almost entirely on the local taxpayer and maintaining them was a struggle.

Other states followed the lead of Massachusetts. In 1850 there were about 60 high schools in the U.S.; 325 in 1860; 800 in 1870; 1,200 in 1880; 2,526 in 1890. In 1900, 500,000 students attended free public high schools, or 0.7% of the 75 million population. Today high school attendance is universal. The proportion of 14- to 17-year-olds who continue in secondary school is higher than in any other country.

The list of required subjects varies from state to state. With the development of the elective system in the early years of the 20th century, students have a wide choice of subjects in the high schools.

Highways, National System of Interstate and Defense. A federal program of highway construction was begun in 1956 to improve transportation, aid defense readiness and buoy the economy. The Bureau of Public Roads, in the Department of Commerce, supervises the program although private contractors do the work under direction of state highway departments. The federal government pays 90% of the cost and the states pay the remaining 10%.

The road complex links 90% of U.S. cities having a population of 50,000 or more by wide ribbons of limited-access highway, thereby sharply reducing travel time.

The interstate system was originally expected to cost $27.6 billion. But that estimate rose to $46.8 billion in 1965 and is expected to run higher before the completion date in 1972.

Less than 15% of the interstate mileage will lie in urban areas, but these roads will carry 41% of the system's traffic and represent 47% of its cost.

Hill, James Jerome (1838–1916). Railway promoter. Born near Rockwood, Ontario, Canada, he was known as the "empire builder" because of his role in developing the Northwest. Hill had wide interests in railroads, steamship lines, mines and banks. He developed the Great Northern Railroad, which extended from Duluth to Seattle. His clash with Edward W. Harriman over securing an entrance for his lines into Chicago and St. Louis precipitated the Panic of 1901. The Northern Securities Co., designed as a holding company for Hill's railroad interests, was declared illegal by the U.S. Supreme Court (1904). His Great Northern Railroad, a transcontinental carrier, weathered financial crises and made its way without government land grants.

Hillman, Sidney (1887–1946). Labor leader. Born in Lithuania, he came to the U.S. in 1907 and became a clothing worker in Chicago. The agreement which he negotiated with Hart, Schaffner, and Marx (1911), clothing manufacturers, formed the basis for the impartial chairman plan adopted by other industries. He was the first president of the Amalgamated Clothing Workers Union (1914–46). He initiated such union activities as cooperative housing and banking and was cofounder of the CIO (1935). He headed the labor division of the War Production Board (1942). Active in politics, he supported F. D. Roosevelt. At the 1944 Democratic convention, F.D.R. used the expression "Clear it with Sidney" long remembered as indicative of labor's political power. He helped found the World Federation of Trade Unions (1945).

Hindenburg Line. The famous German defensive line in World War I (1914–18), named after Field Marshal Paul von Hindenburg, extended roughly from Arras to Soissons northwest of Paris. He withdrew to it after the battle of the Somme (July 1–Nov. 18, 1916). The line was pierced by American troops in the Meuse-Argonne fighting of

1918 that led to German surrender.

Hiroshima. The first atomic bomb was dropped on Hiroshima, in Honshu, Japan (Aug. 6, 1945), killing or wounding almost half of its population of 400,000. The second target was Nagasaki, in Kyushu, Japan (Aug. 9, 1945). The destruction of these cities hastened Japan's surrender in World War II.

Hiroshima (1946). A powerful work by the novelist, John Hersey, it is an account of the effects upon the inhabitants of Hiroshima, Japan, of the atomic bombing of that city by the U.S. Air Force during World War II. It first appeared in the *New Yorker*, which devoted most of an issue to its publication in 1946.

Other books by Hersey include *A Bell for Adano* (1944), *The Wall* (1950), *A Single Pebble* (1956) and *The Child Buyer* (1960).

Hiss Case. Alger Hiss, a former employee of the State Department, was found guilty (Jan. 21, 1950) of perjury for having denied giving secret State Department documents to Whittaker Chambers in 1937. He had also denied seeing Chambers, then an agent for a Communist spy ring, later than Jan. 1, 1937. Hiss was sentenced to five years in prison.

Hobkirk's Hill, battle of (Apr. 25, 1781). In a skirmish 10 miles north of Camden, S.C.,

Gen. Nathanael Greene was defeated by British Lord Rawdon, but managed to keep the pressure on the British in the Carolinas.

Hoe, Richard March (1812–86). Inventor and manufacturer. Born in New York City, he succeeded his father (1830) in the Hoe printing-press-building establishment and greatly improved an already famous company. Among his inventions were the large cylinder press and the type revolving press (1847) which greatly increased the number of papers printed per hour. His web press (1871), first installed in the New York *Tribune,* printed from a continuous roll of paper both sides of a sheet; this process revolutionized newspaper printing.

Hohokam. Residing in what is now Arizona, the Hohokam Indians were an artistic people whose drawings, found almost entirely on pottery, depict graceful archers and dancers. Engineering diagrams of their aqueducts have not been found. Evidence indicates that their places of abode disappeared at the end of the 15th century. They may have been wiped out by some calamity, but recent scientific thinking is that they were simply scattered by drought and disease and were the ancestors of contemporary Indians.

Holmes, Oliver Wendell (1809–83). Author and physician. Born in Cambridge, Mass., he was granted an M.D. by Harvard Medical School (1836) to which he returned as professor of anatomy (1847–82). He wrote "The Contagiousness of Puerperal Fever" (1843). The first installment of *The Autocrat at the Breakfast Table* appeared in the first issue of the *Atlantic Monthly* (Nov. 1857); published in book form, 1858. His poems include "Old Ironsides," "The Chambered Nautilus" and "Wonderful One-Hoss Shay." His first novel *Elsie Venner* (1861) foreshadowed later psychological fiction. He was author of biographies of *John L. Motley* (1879) and *R. W. Emerson* (1885). Father of Oliver Wendell Holmes, U.S. Supreme Court justice.

Holmes, Oliver Wendell, Jr. (1841–1935). Jurist. Born in Boston, Mass., he served in the Union army in the Civil War. He taught constitutional law at Harvard (1870–82). He was associate justice (1882–99) and chief justice (1899–1902), supreme court of Massachusetts. Pres. T. Roosevelt appointed him associate justice of U.S. Supreme Court (1902–32). A commanding legal figure, his notable dissents have shaped history. In *Lochner v. New York* (1905), he declared that "the 14th Amendment does not enact Mr. Herbert Spencer's *Social Statics.*" He stated the "clear and present danger" doctrine in *Schenck v. U.S.* (1919). He called for "free trade in ideas" in the Abrams Case (1919) and was author of *The*

Common Law (1881). "The life of the law," he wrote, "has not been logic: it has been experience."

Holy Experiment. William Penn used the term to describe the commonwealth he established in Pennsylvania, in 1681. He wanted colonists to live in peace, brotherly love, toleration, sobriety and charity under an orderly, just government that would confer the twin blessings of liberty and property. Penn's ideas, especially his views on religious liberty, became part of the mainstream of American thought. "No man, nor number of men upon earth," he wrote, "hath power or authority to rule over men's consciences in religious matters."

Home Mortgage Credit Program, Voluntary. Authorized by title VI of the Housing Act of 1954, the program is operated by the National Committee of which the Housing and Home Finance Administrator is chairman. Six regional committees are located at HHFA Regional Offices. Committees are composed of representatives of private lenders, lumber dealers, builders and real estate brokers. They help obtain private mortgage credit for FHA-insured and VA-guaranteed loans in areas where there may be a shortage of local capital for such loans. This assistance is available to minority groups in any area where financing for such housing is not available on terms comparable to those offered others.

Home Owners Loan Corporation (HOLC). The New Deal agency set up in 1933 was granted funds to refinance the mortgages of impoverished homeowners threatened with loss of their property through foreclosure. The HOLC also undertook housing development and helped more than a million homeowners.

Homer, Winslow (1836–1910). Painter. Born in Boston, Mass., his early career was as illustrator for *Harper's Weekly* for which he drew Civil War scenes. After settling in Maine (1884), he concentrated on marine paintings in which he captured the dignity and heroism of man in watercolors and oils. His major works include *The Life Line, The Fog Warning, Banks Fisherman,* the deep-sea classic *Eight Bells* and *Summer Night.*

Homestead Act (1862). Agitation for free land resulted in the passage of a law during the Civil War granting land to settlers. Under this basic public lands law, homesteaders after living on the quarter-section allotted to them for five years were to receive the whole 160 acres free, except for a small fee.

The act was a boon to many poor western farmers, but fraudulent promoters faked settlement of the land which they then took over for resale.

Homestead strike (1892). The strike against the Carnegie Steel Company works, at Homestead, Pa., was caused by a cut in wages ordered by Henry Clay Frick, the company's general manager. Carnegie was in England at the time.

When the skilled workers refused to accept the cut, Frick closed the plant. He attempted to bring in by barges towed up the Monongahela River some 300 Pinkerton detectives armed with rifles. They were met at the shore by the workers and in a pitched battle forced to surrender, give up their weapons and entrain for nearby Pittsburgh.

Frick was determined to break the strong Amalgamated Association of Iron, Steel and Tin Workers that had organized the resistance. He gained public sympathy during the strike when an anarchist, who had nothing to do with the union, shot and stabbed him.

Frick prevailed upon the governor of Pennsylvania to send in the militia. The 8,000 troops were effective and permitted Frick to bring in strikebreakers.

After five months the strike was broken. Frick took back about 800 of the original Homestead working force of nearly 4,000. The union was broken and it was not until the 1930's that another strong steel union was formed.

"Home Sweet Home." The song was first heard in the opera *Clari,* or, *The Maid of Milan* (Covent Garden, London,

1823). The words are by John Howard Payne, an American, and the music by Sir Henry Bishop who based it on a Sicilian air. The opera was popular in America for a half-century.

Hoover, Herbert Clark (1874–1964). Thirty-first President of the U.S. (1929–33). Born in West Branch, Ia., he was graduated from Stanford (1895). He was the chairman of Commission for Relief in Belgium (1915–19), the U.S. Food Administrator (1917–19) and the U.S. Sec. of Commerce (1921–28). His administration was scarred by the Great Depression. He created the Reconstruction Finance Corporation and headed the Hoover Commissions to study the reorganization of the executive branch of the government (1947, 1953).

Hoover Commissions. Non-partisan commissions headed by former Pres. Herbert Hoover were set up by Congress in 1947 and 1953. Task forces of experts sought to unravel the "red tape" in which the executive branch was entangled, to streamline operations and reduce overlapping of departments and agencies. More than half of the almost 600 recommendations were adopted, with savings estimated at $10 billion annually.

Operations of the General Accounting Office were improved, the Military Unification Act passed (1949), the General Services Administration created (1949), transfer of civil service

employees among departments encouraged, independent commissions reorganized under appropriate departments and the Department of Health, Education and Welfare created (1953).

Hoover Dam. Authorized by the Boulder Canyon Project Act (1928) the dam was completed in 1936. It is 726 feet high, one of the highest dams ever completed and one of the world's greatest engineering projects. The dam impounds one of the largest artificial lakes in the world, Lake Mead, on the Arizona-Nevada border. Water stored by Hoover (formerly Boulder) Dam, in the Black Canyon of the Colorado River, now irrigates parts of Arizona and southern California. The project has made possible flood control, improved navigation and the establishment of power plants.

Hoover moratorium. In 1931 during a worldwide depression Pres. Hoover recommended a one-year moratorium (postponement) on payment of war reparations and war debts. The reparations were owed by Germany to the Allies as an outcome of World War I. The war debts were owed by the Allies to the U.S. The moratorium was accepted by the 15 governments involved.

Neither reparations nor war debts were ever paid in full.

Hopewell, Treaty of. At Hopewell, S.C., 1785–86, the U.S. concluded separate treaties with the Cherokees, Choctaws and

Chickasaws defining Indian land holdings and granting the U.S. sovereignty over the tribes.

Hopi. When Coronado's men explored the Southwest in 1540, they encountered the Pueblo Indians, also known as Moqui. The Indians resisted missionary efforts until recent times. Living in Pueblos in Arizona, the Hopis, of Uto-Aztecan stock, are expert farmers and famous for such crafts as basket making and pottery. Among their ceremonies is the famed snake dance, which is held in odd years at the pueblo of Walpi.

Hopkins, Mark (1802–87). Educator. He was born in Stockbridge, Mass., and became known as an inspired teacher and lecturer. During most of his career, he served at Williams College where he was a tutor (1825–27), professor of moral philosophy and rhetoric (1830–87) and also president (1836–72). He was elected to the Hall of Fame (1915).

hornbook. Colonial children learned their letters and began to read by means of a device which resembled a rectangular paddle with a short handle. It was a thin board on which a printed page was placed. This was covered with a transparent sheet of "horn" to protect it from dirty fingers. When one page was learned a new page took its place.

Hornet. Commanded by James Lawrence the 18-gun U.S. sloop harassed the British during the War of 1812. It sank the British brig *Peacock* off the coast of British Guiana, Feb. 24, 1813; captured and scuttled the British *Penguin* in the South Atlantic, Mar. 23, 1815; and narrowly escaped capture itself by throwing overboard its guns and heavy stores when chased by the British 74-gun *Cornwallis.*

Hortalez et Cie. A French export firm was organized in 1776 to enable France to supply Washington's army before France openly joined with the American colonies against the British. The company was created by Pierre Augustin Caron who had assumed the name of De Beaumarchais. He was also the playwright who wrote *Le Barbier de Séville* (first performed in 1775) and *Le Mariage de Figaro* (1784).

hospitals. In 17th-century America the patient was often housed in the residence of his physician, a situation that had the advantage of providing a clean environment. Hospitals were very few until the 18th century, when attempts were made to separate the sick from the insane. The Pennsylvania Hospital, founded by Dr. Thomas Bond in 1751, aided by Benjamin Franklin, was superior to most other hospitals of the time. The New York Hospital, sponsored by Dr. Samuel Bard, opened in 1791.

The association between hospitals and medical schools was given impetus when John Warren, professor of anatomy and surgery at Harvard's medical school (started in 1782), founded the Massachusetts General Hospital in 1811. Thereafter hospitals developed as training institutions for medicine and nursing.

The latter half of the 19th century and the first three decades of the 20th century were marked by rapid expansion of hospital construction in the U.S. By 1928 there were 6,850 hospitals. With the onset of the depression in 1929, however, hospital construction dwindled. Not only did construction decrease but from 1928 to 1938 nearly 800 hospitals closed. With the advent of World War II, hospital construction came to almost a complete halt.

To survey the nation's hospital needs a Commission on Hospital Care was organized under the sponsorship of the American Hospital Association in 1944. The Commission found that people in rural areas particularly were not receiving care.

Congress passed the Hill-Burton Act (1946), sponsored by Sen. Lister Hill of Alabama and Sen. Harold Burton of Ohio. It was regularly extended and has provided funds for over 8,000 hospitals, clinics, public health centers, nursing homes, rehabilitation centers and other health facilities.

In 1966 the states estimated that fewer than two million persons are living in areas without acceptable hospital facilities. Despite this progress, many of the larger and better urban hospitals are becoming obsolete and increasingly inefficient to operate.

"House Divided" speech (1858). The phrase appeared in the speech in which Abraham Lincoln accepted the Illinois Republican senatorial nomination. In referring to slavery he used a phrase that had been frequently used before, but it was Lincoln's speech that gave currency to the idea.

"'A house divided against itself cannot stand.' I believe this government cannot endure permanently half slave and half free. I do not expect the Union to be dissolved; I do not expect the house to fall; but I do expect it will cease to be divided. It will become all one thing or all the other."

House of Burgesses. The first representative assembly in the New World met at Jamestown, Va., in 1619, and became a model for other colonial governments. It was formed by the Virginia Company in an effort to make political improvements that would satisfy the discontented settlers. The assembly consisted of the governor and his councilors appointed by the Virginia Company and two burgesses from each plantation, elected by the settlers.

Housing Act of 1965. Congress provided $7.3 billion over a four-year period for the construction of housing for 500,000 families who live in substandard homes. Building is to be done by private builders with guaranteed government-insured mortgage money as well as money from private sources. A controversial feature provides that the government help pay the rent of lower-income tenants. They are to pay 25% of their total income for rent while the government subsidizes the remainder.

The omnibus Act also includes provisions for grants to match sums budgeted by states and localities for water and sewer facilities and for constructing community centers in low-income sections of cities. The Act allows up to $1,500 for low-income homeowners in urban-renewal areas to help them bring their homes up to standard, thus avoiding eviction. It also makes available grants for low-rent housing for domestic farm labor, increased loans for college housing, extension of government insurance programs for middle-income home buyers and extension of low-interest loans for housing for the elderly.

The Act was even broader than the basic Housing Act of 1949 which facilitated slum clearance throughout the nation.

Housing and Home Finance Agency. Established by Reorganization Plan 3 of 1947 the Agency provided a single permanent agency responsible for the principal housing programs of the federal government.

The Administrator of the Agency submitted to the President and to Congress national estimates of housing needs and the progress being made toward meeting them; then he recommended legislative action to further the policy established by the Housing Act of 1949. He also encouraged localities to make studies of their own needs and plans for housing, urban land use and related community development. He saw to it that the relocation requirements for families displaced from urban renewal areas were met.

Constituent units in the HHFA were the Community Facilities Administration, Urban Renewal Administration, Federal Housing Administration, Public Housing Administration and the Federal National Mortgage Association. All are under the Department of Housing and Urban Development created in 1965.

Housing and Urban Development, Department of. The eleventh executive department was created by legislation signed by Pres. Lyndon B. Johnson, Sept. 9, 1965. On Jan. 17, 1966 the Senate confirmed the appointment of Robert C. Weaver as the first Negro Cabinet member in the nation's history. He heads the new Department as its secretary. Establishment of the Department was first proposed by Pres. Kennedy in his State of the Union Message, Jan. 30, 1961.

The Department is intended to give the nation's city dwellers a voice in the President's Cabinet. The Department supervises the programs of the Housing and Home Finance Agency, the Federal Housing Administration, the Public Housing Administration, the Federal National Mortgage Association, the Community Facilities Administration and the Urban Renewal Administration. In addition it will be responsible for federal participation in planning programs to assist metropolitan areas.

Houston, Samuel (1793–1863). Soldier and statesman. Born near Lexington, Va., he served under Andrew Jackson against the Creeks (1813–14). He resigned from the army (1818) to study law and enter politics. He was governor of Tennessee (1827–29). Sent to Texas (1832) by Pres. Jackson to negotiate a treaty with the Indians, he remained to lead Texas to independence from Mexico. He commanded the Texan army (1835) and defeated Santa Anna at San Jacinto (1836). He was president of Texas (1836–38, 1841–44), and one of the first two senators from Texas (1846–59). Elected governor of Texas (1859), opposed secession and was forced to resign in 1861.

Howard University. The university, situated in Washington, D.C., admits students of both sexes of every race, color and national origin, but has a special responsibility for the training of Negro students. It was established by Congress in 1867 and functions under the Department of Health, Education, and Welfare. It is jointly supported by congressional appropriations and private funds.

Howe, Elias (1819–67). Inventor. Born in Spencer, Mass., he became an apprentice in a textile machinery factory. His work on a design for a sewing machine gained a patent for him in 1846. The machine was first marketed in England. Patent infringements in the U.S. led to a long legal fight which Howe won.

Howe, Samuel Gridley (1801–76). Reformer. Born in Boston, Mass., he was granted an M.D. by Harvard (1824). He participated in the Greek war of independence against Turkey (1827–29). A pioneer in the education of the blind, he headed Perkins Institution for the Blind (1832–76). He promoted the public school movement, prison reform and care of the insane. An Abolitionist, he supported Free Soilers in Kansas. With his wife Julia Ward Howe (1819–1910), a leader in the woman suffrage movement, he coedited the antislavery paper *The Commonwealth.*

Howells, William Dean (1837–1920). Novelist, editor and critic. He was born in Martin's Ferry, O. Self-educated, he started work as a compositor in his father's newspaper office. A successful campaign biography for Lincoln (1860) led to his appointment as consul in Venice, Italy (1861–65). Returning to America, he rose to editor-in-chief of the *Atlantic Monthly*

(1871–81). Author of at least 40 works of fiction, a number of plays and volumes of criticism, he led the school of "realists." To him the term simply meant "the truthful treatment of commonplace material." His masterpiece was *The Rise of Silas Lapham* (1885), the story of a self-made businessman in cultured Boston. Other works include *A Hazard of New Fortunes* (1890), in which he examined class problems of the time. He set forth his view of writing as an art in *Criticism and Fiction* (1891).

How the Other Half Lives (1890). The work by Jacob A. Riis, a crusading journalist, offered evidence of the degradation of the tenement districts of New York City. Riis, who helped to effect reforms in housing, found a powerful friend in Theodore Roosevelt.

Hudson's Bay Company. The English fur-trading company was founded in 1670 by two Frenchmen, Groseilliers (called "Gooseberry" by the English) and Radisson, who were unable to persuade the authorities in Canada or France that they had found a safer route for getting furs out of Indian country in the Lake Superior region, by way of Hudson Bay, thus bypassing Quebec. They were able to interest Prince Rupert, a cousin of King Charles II, and the company charter gave the merchants practically sovereign rights in the region drained by rivers flowing into Hudson Bay. Conflict with the French ensued, but the region fell to the British in 1763. The company established forts on U.S. territory and gained influence in Minnesota through its traders in the region.

Rivalry with the North West Company which had made great gains in the Oregon fur trade was resolved by amalgamation in 1821. The name of the older company was retained.

Parts of the U.S., especially Washington and Oregon, were virtually under the control of the company until settlement of the Oregon boundary dispute in 1846. Dr. John McLoughlin, a company man, had encouraged Americans to settle in Oregon and thus reinforced the U.S. claim to the disputed territory.

In 1869 Hudson's Bay Company territory was transferred to the Dominion of Canada and the company changed from fur-trading to diversified interests.

Hughes, Charles Evans (1862–1948). Jurist and statesman. He was born in Glens Falls, N.Y. Counsel for the New York State legislature's Armstrong Commission investigating financial methods of life insurance companies (1905–06), he gained a national reputation. He was governor of N.Y. (1907–10), then was appointed as associate justice of the U.S. Supreme Court (1910) by Pres. Taft. He resigned in 1916 to campaign as Republican candidate for President; he lost a decisive electoral vote in California to

Wilson. He was Pres. Harding's and Coolidge's Sec. of State (1921–26). He was judge on the Permanent Court of International Justice (1930). Appointed chief justice of U.S. Supreme Court by Pres. Hoover (1930–41), he occupied a middle ground and helped reshape the law to meet social change. He wrote the majority decision invalidating NRA (*Schechter Case*, 1935), but sustained the Wagner Act (1937).

Hull House. Jane Addams converted a mansion on Chicago's West Side into a settlement house (1889). The idea of a settlement house to bring relief to poor people in the slums first materialized with the founding of Toynbee Hall in East London (1884). Jane Addams had visited it and decided to devote herself to the "potentially useful citizen who simply needed help."

Other settlement houses included the University of Chicago Settlement (1894), established by Mary McDowell, and Chicago Commons (1894), by Graham Taylor in Chicago; Henry Street Settlement (1893), by Lillian Wald, Hudson Guild (1895), by John L. Elliott, and Greenwich House (1902), by Mary Kingsbury Simkhovitch in New York; and South End House (1892), by Robert A. Woods in Boston.

Humphrey's Executor v. U.S. (1935). The U.S. Supreme Court limited the power of the President to remove officials from office by ruling that William E. Humphrey had been an employee of the Federal Trade Commission. Since this was an administrative body, created by Congress to carry into effect legislative policies, it could not be "characterized as an arm or eye of the executive."

The case arose when Pres. Franklin D. Roosevelt removed from office a member of the Federal Trade Commission because of his views on public policy. Humphrey sued for salary and after his death his executor, Rathbun, carried the case to the Supreme Court and won.

"Hundred Days," the. Pres. F. D. Roosevelt, on Mar. 5, 1933, a day after his first inauguration, ordered a special session of the 73rd Congress to meet. The session which lasted for a hundred days, until June 16, was devoted to passage of bills to combat the depression. Never before in the history of the Congress was such far-reaching social and economic legislation enacted in so short a time. Measures included the Tennessee Valley Authority Act, the Agricultural Adjustment Act, the Home Owners Loan Act, the Securities Act (revised in 1934 to include regulation of stock exchanges), the Glass-Steagall Banking Act and establishment of the Federal Emergency Relief Administration and the Civilian Conservation Corps.

Hunkers. A conservative Democratic faction was generally in control in New York State in the 1840's. They "hunkered" for office and opposed the Barnburners, who were upsetting the Democratic apple cart in Washington by their anti-slavery agitation. The Hunkers themselves split in 1852 over support of Franklin Pierce, Democratic candidate for President.

Hurons. A confederation of four Indian tribes, they lived in Ontario, Canada, and were visited in their villages of bark wigwams by Champlain in 1615. An Iroquoian-speaking people, they were slaughtered by their enemies, the Iroquois, 1648–49, when the latter learned from the Dutch how to use firearms. Some Huron refugees found their way to the Midwest. About 1750 they settled in villages near Detroit and at Sandusky, O. Known as Wyandots, they aided the British in both the Revolution and War of 1812. Ultimately, they settled on a reservation in Oklahoma.

Hutchinson, Anne (1591–1643). Religious liberal. Born Anne Marbury in Alford, England, she married (1612) William Hutchinson and emigrated with her family to America in 1634; they settled in Boston. She held to a faith based on the individual's direct intuition of God's love ("covenant of grace") as opposed to Massachusetts advocacy of the clergy's "covenant of works." At first she was supported by John Cotton, John Wheelwright and Henry Vane; but Cotton recanted, Wheelwright was banished and Vane returned to England. Banished by the Massachusetts General Court, she settled in Rhode Island (1638) and after her husband's death (1642) she moved to what is now Pelham Bay, N.Y. She and all but one of her family were massacred by Indians (1643).

Hutchinson, Thomas (1711–80). Loyalist statesman. Born in Boston, Mass., he served in the Massachusetts legislature (1737–49). Strongly opposed to a "soft" currency, he was a conservative colonial leader. He was a member of the governor's council (1749–66). He opposed the Sugar Act and the Stamp Act as harmful to empire trade, but allowed that Parliament had the right to tax the colonies as it saw fit. His position on legality of the Stamp Act led to the sack of his house by a Boston mob (Aug. 26, 1765). He was Royal governor of Massachusetts (1771–74). Urged to use sterner methods by the British government, he went to England (1774) and remained in exile. He wrote the outstanding *History of the Colony of Massachusetts Bay* (3 vols., Boston, 1764).

Hylton v. U.S. (1796). In the first case to come before it on the issue of direct and indirect taxation, the U.S. Supreme Court upheld the right of Congress to place a tax on carriages and accepted Hamilton's argument that it was an excise tax since it placed a tax on the "use" of the carriage.

A hundred years later the decision was reversed in *Pollock v. Farmer's Loan and Trust Co.* (1895).

I

Icaria. A communistic settlement was founded in 1856 in Corning, Ia., by followers of Étienne Cabet. The Frenchman had written a book, *Voyage en Icarie*, in which the people shared according to need everything they produced. The first settlement in Texas had failed in 1848. Subsequent unsuccessful settlements included one in Nauvoo, Ill. (1849), under Cabet's leadership. Dissension led to Cabet's expulsion from the community in 1856. By the end of the 19th century Icarian experiments were ended.

Idaho. The 43rd state, a Mountain group state known as the "Gem State," was admitted to the Union, July 3, 1890. Its capital is Boise. Idaho in the language of the Shoshone is derived from "ida" (salmon) and "ho" (tribe).

Full of timbered, rugged mountains and beautiful valleys, the country was crossed by Lewis and Clark in 1805 and was exploited by fur companies. It became part of the Oregon Territory in 1848 and was organized as the Idaho Territory

in 1863. Settlement was stimulated by the discovery of gold near Orofino, 1860, and silver at Coeur D'Alene, 1884.

Leading minerals are lead, silver, gold, phosphates, zinc and copper. It is the only state with substantial supplies of antimony. The state produces much lumber, with the world's largest white pine lumber mill at Lewiston. It also ranks high in wool production.

"I do not choose to run." With this laconic announcement Calvin Coolidge rejected any move by Republicans to renominate him for President in 1928.

"If nominated, I will not accept. If elected, I will not serve." Made by Gen. William T. Sherman, the famous political statement was written in reply to a message from the Republican national convention of 1884 asking him to accept the nomination for the Presidency.

"If this be treason, make the most of it." Patrick Henry made the famous retort when cries of "Treason!" interrupted him as

341

he spoke out against the Stamp Act and George III in the Virginia House of Burgesses, 1765. The bold words echoed throughout the 13 Colonies.

"I had rather be right than be President." Henry Clay made the remark in 1839 when he declined to withhold criticism of abolitionism in the North. Clay did not receive his party's nomination in 1840. He did run unsuccessfully in 1844 and at other times.

"I have not yet begun to fight!" In the Revolutionary War, John Paul Jones helped to create a tradition of valor for the U.S. Navy. In 1779 Jones aboard the *Bonhomme Richard* attacked the British ship *Serapis* in English waters. Close to defeat at one point, he was asked about surrender. His reply is memorable. Jones captured the British ship in a savage engagement.

Illinois. The "Prairie State," lying within the East North Central group, was the 21st state admitted to the Union, Dec. 3, 1818. Its capital is Springfield.

Illinois (an Algonquian word for "men," "warriors") was reached by La Salle, who built a fort in the territory in 1679. French settlements were yielded to the British in the Treaty of Paris (1763). In 1778 the British relinquished Kaskaskia (once considered the most powerful fortress in the New World) to George Rogers Clark, who took it in the name of Virginia.

The British ceded Illinois to the U.S. in the Treaty of Peace (1783) and Virginia gave up its claim to the territory to the federal government in 1786. Illinois was part of the Northwest Territory, organized in 1788 under the Northwest Ordinance. Settlement was speeded after the War of 1812.

The state is a leading producer of soybeans, corn and wheat. There are important reserves of coal and oil. Chicago, the country's greatest rail center, became a major midwestern port for overseas shipping when the St. Lawrence Seaway was opened in 1959.

Illinois Central Railroad. Chartered in 1851 the line answered the need of Illinois farmers for a means of transporting their crops from the interior of the state. It was the first railroad to receive federal land grants and the first interstate railroad in the U.S.

The main line of this 6,500-mile system constitutes the shortest route between the Great Lakes and the Gulf of Mexico, connecting Chicago with New Orleans and other large cities in the South and with Omaha, Sioux City and Sioux Falls in the West.

Immigration Act of 1965. On Oct. 3, Pres. Johnson came to New York and signed an historic immigration law at the Statue of Liberty. The new law ended the 41-year-old National Origins Act (1924) quota system which favored northern European countries.

Under the new law an overall quota of 170,000 is assigned annually to all countries, except those in the Western Hemisphere, with a limit of 20,000 that may be admitted annually from any one country. For the first time it sets a ceiling on immigration from the Western Hemisphere for which the allotment is 120,000 annually, exclusive of husbands, wives, unmarried children and parents of citizens or resident aliens.

impeachment of President Andrew Johnson (1868). Under the Constitution the President and other civil officers may be removed on impeachment by the House and conviction in a Senate trial. The charges brought against Pres. Johnson arose from differences over Reconstruction plans between the President and the Radical Republicans in control of Congress. Technically, however, the President was impeached for violating the Tenure of Office Act when he removed Sec. of War Stanton from the Cabinet.

The Senate trial of Pres. Johnson, extending over two months, was presided over by Chief Justice of the Supreme Court Salmon P. Chase. Seven Republicans deserted the Radical leadership and joined with 12 Democrats against Johnson's removal so that the vote was 19 for acquittal and 35 for conviction. Since a two-thirds majority was required for conviction, the President narrowly escaped removal from office by a single vote. Had Johnson been removed, a precedent might have been set that would have destroyed the relationship between the major branches of the federal government.

Impeachment proceedings under the Constitution have been undertaken at various times, usually against federal judges, but convictions have been very few. Comparable impeachment provisions in state constitutions have resulted in the trials of governors and judges. In some instances, these have had partisan political motives. Where the term of office has been short, impeachment procedures are discouraged.

implied powers (elastic) clause. Art. I, Sec. 8, Par. 18 of the Constitution of the U.S. grants Congress power "To make all laws which shall be necessary and proper for carrying into execution" powers previously listed. A broad interpretation of the implied powers of Congress was set forth by Chief Justice John Marshall (*McCulloch v. Maryland,* 1819) in one of the most famous sentences in American constitutional law. Marshall, in upholding the right of Congress to create the Bank of the U.S., wrote: "Let the end be legitimate, let it be within the scope of the Constitution, and all means which are appropriate, which are plainly adapted to that end, which are not prohibited, but consist with the letter and spirit of the Constitution, are constitutional." This

343

interpretation of the Constitution laid the groundwork for a great expansion of the powers of the federal government.

impressment of seamen. The need of the British navy for seamen led to their forcible seizure on foreign vessels from the time of the American Revolution to 1815. Impressment of seamen was based on the British reasoning "Once an Englishman, always an Englishman," a doctrine that clashed with the American idea that naturalization of foreigners made them U.S. citizens.

The drain on British manpower was increased by the better working conditions and pay on American merchant and naval vessels. While thousands of English seamen did sign on American vessels, the British often impressed seamen without any real effort to determine whether they were bona fide American citizens. A notable instance of this policy was the *Chesapeake* Affair.

Impressment of seamen was cited by Pres. Madison as a cause of the War of 1812.

Inchon landing (Sept. 15, 1950). With U.S. forces pinned down at the southern tip of Korea, Gen. Douglas MacArthur determined to surprise the enemy by an amphibious invasion of their rear at Inchon on the west coast of Korea, 30 miles north of Seoul, almost as far north as the 38th parallel.

The plan was daring because the attack would have to be launched at high tide. A few hours afterward the 30-foot tides would recede and there would be no water as far out as two miles from shore. Failure to invade or pull out exactly on time meant that the whole fleet would flounder in mud flats. Furthermore, the attack would have to be launched in broad daylight against the nine-foot-high sea wall at Inchon.

MacArthur carried out his plan and the landing was successful.

indentured servants. The shortage of labor in the colonies was met in part by white servants who contracted to pay their passage to America by working for terms ranging from three to seven years. When these "redemptioners" arrived in a colony, sometimes whole families without a written contract, they arranged to work for established settlers. When their service was completed, they were given clothing, a piece of land and a gun and became freemen.

Other indentured servants were poor men and vagrants kidnapped in English slums and transported to the colonies as contract labor. Convicts (many of them debtors) were also sent to the colonies as indentured servants.

During the 17th century there were more indentured servants in the South than slaves. Over one-third of the members of the Virginia House of Burgesses in 1663 had begun their colonial life as contract laborers. The Middle Colonies received most of the indentured servants in the 18th century.

Independence Hall. The historic building in Philadelphia, Pa., where the Declaration of Independence was signed, was also the meeting place of the Second Continental Congress and the Constitutional Convention of 1787. The Liberty Bell is preserved there.

The Hall was first occupied as the Pennsylvania State House in 1735.

Independent Treasury System. The "divorce of banks and state" as it was called was accomplished by Pres. Van Buren in 1840. Under the plan, government specie (gold and silver) was removed from private banks and placed in sub-treasuries along with tariff revenues and receipts from land sales.

While the plan protected government funds and discouraged speculation, it removed large sums of specie from banks which used them to expand credit necessary for carrying on business.

The sub-treasuries were retained until the establishment of the Federal Reserve System in 1913.

Indian Affairs, Bureau of. Created as part of the War Department in 1824, the Bureau was transferred in 1849 to the newly established Department of Interior. The main functions of the Bureau include work with Indians and natives of Alaska, assisting them in making the most effective use of their lands. The Bureau provides public services such as education, welfare aid and law and order, where these services are not available to Indians from other agencies. Help is given those who wish to leave reservations and enter normal channels of American economic and social life. Assistance is extended to Indian tribes and groups for developing programs to attract industries to reservation areas.

Indian Reorganization Act of 1934. The Wheeler-Howard Act reversed the federal government's Indian policy under the Dawes Act (1887). Tribal lands were no longer allotted to individuals and provision was made for recovering "surplus" reservation lands that had not yet been homesteaded. The law sought to make the Indians independent by encouraging group progress by way of a tribal approach.

Since 1948 Congress has been moving toward a policy of ultimately withdrawing all federal supervision. In 1953 Congress decided to move "as rapidly as possible" to make Indians "subject to the same laws and entitled to the same privileges and responsibilities as are applicable to other citizens of the United States."

In 1961 the Menominees in northern Wisconsin became the first tribe of any size to lose its status as a ward of the federal government. The reservation became Menominee County, Wisconsin's 72nd, its smallest and one of its poorest. The Menominees are chiefly engaged in lumbering.

Indiana. The "Hoosier State," in the East North Central group, was admitted to the Union as the 19th state, Dec. 11, 1816. Its capital is Indianapolis.

Indiana (so named because of its Indian inhabitants) was occupied by the Miami and Wabash tribes when French Jesuits and traders traversed the land in the 17th century. The French were in control until they yielded to the English in 1763. In 1779 George Rogers Clark wrested Vincennes from the British. Indiana then passed to Virginia, which ceded the land to the federal government in 1784. From 1787 to 1800 Indiana was part of the Northwest Territory. It then became part of the Indiana Territory. Colonization was retarded by Indian wars, but was speeded during the War of 1812 when Tecumseh was defeated at Tippecanoe.

The state was greatly aided by a system of internal improvements—canals and railroads—before the Civil War. During the war southern sympathizers were in the minority and the state loyally supported the Union.

Indiana became a leading industrial state despite the fact that some 80% of the land is in farms. It ranks third in steel production and provides two-thirds of the building limestone used in the nation. Diversified crops are combined with livestock.

Indians. The name was mistakenly applied because it was thought that Columbus had reached the Indies—the eastern coast of Asia. At the time of the discovery of America, the number of Indians was about 846,000. It gradually decreased until at the end of the 19th century the estimated Indian population was about 243,000. Since then, the number has increased steadily and is now approximately 555,000.

Indians are divided by language, customs and traditions. Within what is now the U.S. (excluding Alaska) they may be classified according to the way in which they found their food. In the East from the Great Lakes south to the Gulf of Mexico were the "Woodsmen of the Eastern Forests" who, traveling by foot or canoe, lived mostly by hunting, fishing and berrypicking. These were the first Indians encountered by the earliest English settlers in Virginia and Massachusetts.

The second large group were the "Hunters of the Plains." They lived in a vast area west of the Mississippi and east of the Rockies, extending from Montana and the Dakotas south to Texas. These Indians early acquired horses from the Spaniards and by the 18th century were hunting great areas of the West for buffalo. These Indians with their feathered headdresses and their fast riding ponies have become, thanks to popular fiction and movies, the stereotype of American Indians throughout the world.

There were several smaller groups according to this system of classification. Their names indicate how they lived: "the Northern Fishermen" of the forests and river valleys of Washington and Oregon; "the Seed Gatherers" of California, Nevada and Utah; "the Navaho Shepherds" of Arizona; "the Pueblo Farmers" of New Mexico; and "the Desert Dwellers" of southern Arizona and New Mexico who included the first irrigation farmers.

The Indians were almost always in conflict with one another because they moved about frequently. Certain tribes had words in common with certain other tribes—sometimes with tribes living many miles away. On the basis of common words or language ethnologists discovered eight major linguistic families which included almost all American Indians. The major linguistic families were the Algonquian, Iroquoian, Caddoan, Muskhogean, Siouan, Penutian, Athapascan and the Uto-Aztecan.

Relentless pressure on the Indians forced them to cede their lands to the white men. During the colonial period land sales were made to proprietors or other colonial officials. Under the federal government, Indian treaties were made with War Department officials on the tenuous theory that each Indian tribe was an independent nation. In 1871 treaties gave way to agreements requiring the approval of both houses of Congress. The boundaries agreed upon were often uncertain because the Indians had vague concepts of land ownership. Payment for the land was made in hardware, blankets, some trinkets, livestock, guns, ammunition and cash.

Between 1825 and 1840 when it was clear that all lands east of the Mississippi would be carved into states, the removal of Indians was accelerated by the federal government. They were forced to accept land west of the Mississippi. Apart from their less than cordial acceptance by western Indians, their stay in the new lands was brief. The Great Plains, which the federal government had not viewed as habitable by white men, turned out to be a new frontier.

After the Civil War establishment of Indians on reservations became federal policy. The land has been allotted to tribes as common holdings. But the conscience of the nation has been troubled by a record which shows that the natives of the continent were forced from their land. After World War II individual tribes were compensated more generously for land cessions that had been made under pressure by an expanding nation.

Industrial Revolution. About the middle of the 18th century in England, significant changes in production were made to meet the growing demands for manufactured goods. Under the old domestic system farmers and their families made cloth in their own homes and other goods were manufactured in small shops. The work was mainly handicraft. Under the new factory system workers were brought together into special buildings known as factories. They used relatively complicated, power-driven machinery owned by the employer. Goods were manufactured for a wider market that included all of England and even foreign lands. This far-reaching change in industry is known as the Industrial Revolution.

During the Revolutionary War, when Americans could not buy British manufactured goods, infant industries were stimulated in the U.S. In 1793 Samuel Slater, a mechanic who had emigrated from England, constructed textile machines from memory in Pawtucket, R.I. He was to become known as the "father of the factory system" in America. In 1800 Eli Whitney showed how muskets could be built from interchangeable parts. Within a half-century, farm machines, sewing machines, rifles and pistols were being manufactured by means of standardized interchangeable parts.

The War of 1812 further stimulated the growth of the factory system in the U.S. when trade with Britain was largely cut off. It was during the war that Francis Lowell established in Waltham, Mass., the first American factory to combine spinning and weaving.

Other major inventions and developments that brought about an Industrial Revolution in the U.S. were Oliver Evans' (the "Watt of America") factory for the manufacture of steam engines (about 1802), Charles Goodyear's vulcanization process (1844), Elias Howe's sewing machine (1846), the William Kelly-Henry Bessemer steel-making process of the 1860's.

The rapid industrialization of the nation, South and North, in the post-Civil War period has sometimes been described as the New Industrial Revolution. It has been characterized by the growth of mass production, labor saving devices and automation.

Industrial Workers of the World (IWW). Members of the organization, known as "Wobblies," aimed to overthrow the wage system and replace the state with a nationwide industrial syndicate. It was founded in Chicago, in 1905, and was at first comprised of miners, lumberjacks, migratory harvest hands in the West and unorganized industrial workers in the East. It was soon torn by factionalism. William "Big Bill" Haywood remained a leader even though his Western Federation of Miners withdrew in 1906.

The IWW reached a peak in the violent textile strike in Lawrence, Mass. (1912). Subsequent strikes of textile workers in Paterson, N.J., and rubber workers in Akron, O., were unsuccessful. The "Wobblies" were subjected to vigilante attacks and federal prosecution during World War I and dissolved in 1925.

infant school. The first infant or primary school in the U.S. was established in Boston, Mass. (1818). It met the needs of children who could not be admitted to school without knowing how to read. The idea took shape at New Lanark, Scotland, in 1799, where Robert Owen, a manufacturer, established an infant school for the children in his town and factories.

In Boston, four-year-old children were admitted to the infant school where they were prepared for entrance to city schools, known as English grammar schools. As the infant or primary school grew, it became part of the elementary school program in the U.S. which subsequently divided into "primary grades" and "grammar grades."

Information Agency, U.S. The purpose of the USIA is to help the U.S. achieve its foreign policy objectives by influencing public attitudes in other nations. The agency also advises the President and various departments on the implications of foreign opinion for present and contemplated U.S. programs and official statements. This purpose is carried out by means of personal contact, radio broadcasting, libraries, book publication and distribution, press, motion pictures, television, exhibits and English-language instruction.

The agency was established by Reorganization Plan 8 of 1953 to carry out international information activities authorized by Congress in 1948.

"In God we trust." The motto has been appearing since 1864 on U.S. coins produced by the Bureau of the Mint. There is no law which requires that the motto be included in the design of the coins.

Inness, George (1825–94). Painter. Born near Newburgh, N.Y., he was known as one of the last and most talented members of the scenic and literal "Hudson River" school. His style underwent a change as he recognized the value of suggestion in portraying nature. An outstanding American landscapist, his works include *Millpond, Florida Pines, Niagara Falls, Delaware Valley, Rainbow After a Storm* and *Spring Blossoms.*

Inspector General. In the Army, Navy, Air Force and Marine Corps, this officer determines the status of combat readiness, logistic effectiveness, discipline, and efficiency of his branch of the armed forces. He also investigates matters involving crime and subversion.

Insular Cases. The U.S. Supreme Court ruled that the Constitution did not follow the flag, that the rights of U.S. citizens did not automatically belong to the people of overseas territories.

In *DeLima v. Bidwell* (1901)

the Court held that while Puerto Rico did not become an integral part of the federal Union by the mere fact of annexation, it did cease to be a foreign territory. Duties on goods entering the U.S. from Puerto Rico could not be collected without further congressional action. Congress thereupon modified the tariff statutes but retained duties upon goods brought in from Puerto Rico and the Philippines.

In *Downes v. Bidwell* (1901) the Court held that the territories did not come within the clause of the Constitution which requires that "all duties, imposts, and excises shall be uniform throughout the United States." They, therefore, had to pay the duties levied by Congress.

Civil liberties in the territories became an issue in *Hawaii v. Mankichi* (1903). The Court ruled that the constitutional provision for trial by jury did not extend to Hawaii, an unincorporated territory at the time that Mankichi was tried for manslaughter. (Congress determined whether or not a territory was incorporated.) Mankichi's indictment had not been presented by a grand jury and he had been convicted by a verdict rendered by nine of the twelve jurors instead of by a unanimous verdict required in U.S. courts. The Court upheld the conviction.

In *Rasmussen v. U.S.* (1905) the Court held that Alaska was an incorporated territory and that the jury trial of the 6th Amendment applied there and could not be abrogated by any congressional or territorial enactment.

Interior, Department of the. Created by Congress in 1849, the Department changed during the years from being general housekeeper for the federal government to custodian of the nation's natural resources. Under the Defense Production Act of 1950, as amended, the Secretary, who is a member of the President's Cabinet, has been delegated responsibilities relating to petroleum and gas, solid fuels, electric power, fishery products and metals and minerals.

The jurisdiction of the Department extends over the continental U.S., to islands in the Caribbean and the South Pacific and to lands in the Arctic. It includes the custody of 760,-000,000 acres of land, the conservation of mineral resources, promotion of mine safety, conservation of fish and wildlife resources, coordination of federal and state recreation programs, administration of the nation's great scenic and historic areas, reclamation of arid lands of the West through irrigation and the management of hydroelectric power systems. It is also responsible for the welfare of about 180,000 persons in the territories of the U.S. and in the Trust Territory of the Pacific Islands and provides services to 380,000 Indians, nearly all of whom reside on or adjacent to reservations.

internal improvements. The building of canals, roads, harbor improvements and railroads with the aid of federal, state and local funds was a continuing issue in American politics during the first half of the 19th century. Economic interests in all parts of the country stood to gain from improved and lowered costs of transportation. As a consequence the opposition of Presidents Madison, Monroe and Jackson on constitutional grounds halted only momentarily congressional action.

Henry Clay of Kentucky, champion of the West, favored internal improvements as part of his American system. John C. Calhoun of South Carolina, in 1816, when he was a nationalist, defended the constitutionality of internal improvements as an extension of provisions for post roads and the general welfare.

The popularity of internal improvements proved irresistible with the beginning of the Cumberland Road (1806) furthered by federal, state and local funds. On Mar. 3, 1823, the first act for harbor improvement passed Congress. An unlooked for result was the "pork barrel" legislation which later followed as congressmen voted for each other's projects without regard for the national interest. The success of the Erie Canal (completed 1825), financed largely by New York, was a stimulus to canal construction in other states. The canal craze culminated in the Panic of 1837. Too many of them had not been eco-nomically feasible and growing railroad competition in the 1840's and 1850's affected canal companies. The railroads, although privately owned, were aided by federal land grants and state and local funds.

The effect of internal improvements at public expense was to link the nation tightly together more quickly than would have been the case if private local financing had been relied upon.

International Development, Agency for. Set up as a federal agency within the Department of State in 1961, AID is responsible for administering non-military U.S. foreign assistance programs. These include loans and grants to less developed friendly countries and areas.

International Geophysical Year (IGY). The period (actually 18 months) July 1, 1957 to Dec. 31, 1958 was devoted to scientific investigation of the phenomena of the earth. A vast amount of data was accumulated by scientists of 66 nations engaged in a worldwide study of seismology, gravity, meteorology, oceanography, glaciology, solar activity, etc. Congress provided the National Science Foundation with about $42,-500,000 to initiate programs.

Most spectacular were efforts to probe the physical secrets of the upper atmosphere.

International Monetary Fund. The agency affiliated with the United Nations was established in Washington, D.C., in 1946. Some 70 member nations contribute funds in the form of gold and their own nation's currency. Countries may buy currency to settle international debts. The IMF aims to promote expansion of international trade and to avoid competitive exchange depreciations.

Interplanetary Explorers. Often called IMP (Interplanetary Monitoring Platform), these satellites, similar to Explorer XVIII, the first of the series, launched Nov. 27, 1963, provide the data necessary for the planning of the projected Apollo series of manned flights to the moon. The Explorers investigate factors like radiation and magnetic fields that will be encountered by astronauts going to the moon.

Interstate Commerce Act (1887). Under the first important federal statute regulating big business, railroads engaging in interstate commerce were required to establish "just and reasonable" rates. Discrimination on behalf of certain shippers by means of special rates and rebates was forbidden. Pooling agreements by which markets were divided among competing railroads were outlawed. Charging more for a "short haul" than a "long haul" was prohibited. An Interstate Commerce Commission of five members was established to enforce the law.

The Commission, however, had to rely upon the courts for enforcement of its rulings. The courts, particularly during the 1890's, were friendly to big business. As a result the agency was too weak at first to provide effective railroad regulation. The law, however, was strengthened by subsequent amendments.

The ICC's regulatory authority was extended to rail and water routes for transportation of property by the Panama Canal Act of 1912, and amended by the Transportation Act of 1940. Transportation of passengers and property by motor carriers in interstate commerce was provided for by the Motor Carrier Act of 1935. The Transportation Act of 1958 gave the ICC power to approve or disapprove discontinuance of train or ferry service conducted between points in different states or within a single state by railroads subject to the Interstate Commerce Act. The Commission now consists of 11 members appointed by the President and confirmed by the Senate.

"In your heart, you know he's right." The slogan was used by supporters of Sen. Barry Goldwater (Ariz.), Republican candidate for President in 1964. It reflected their feeling that Goldwater's vote against the Civil Rights Act of 1964 was approved widely by Americans who were silent rather than risk abuse for being anti-Negro.

Iowa. The "Hawkeye State," in the West North Central part of the Middle West, was admitted to the Union as the 29th state,

Dec. 28, 1846. Its capital is Des Moines.

Iowa, named after the Indians who lived there, was explored by Jolliet and Marquette in 1673. It was not until after 1785 that Julien Dubuque, attracted by extensive lead deposits, established the first white settlement on the site of the city named in his honor. The territory passed from the French to the U.S. as part of the Louisiana Purchase (1803). From that time it formed part of many territorial government units until it was established as a separate territory in 1838, prior to statehood.

The state leads the Union in the value of its agricultural products. It is first in corn production and ranks high in oats, hogs and cattle. Its industrial growth has also been rapid. Many industries process farm products or produce farm implements.

Iron Act (1750). Parliament sought to restrict the colonial iron industry by prohibiting the manufacture of crude iron into finished products. Iron manufacturers in England had been complaining of growing competition from the colonial iron industry. The Act allowed pig and bar iron manufactured in the colonies to enter England duty-free so that these might be fashioned into nails, tools and other iron wares by English iron manufacturers.

The restriction was resented by colonists who found it increasingly difficult to earn the sterling (British money) with which to pay for imports from England.

Iron Curtain. On Mar. 5, 1946, Winston Churchill speaking at Fulton, Mo., with Pres. Truman beside him on the platform, warned of the Soviet Union's expansionist tendencies. "From Stettin in the Baltic to Trieste in the Adriatic," he said, "an iron curtain has descended across the Continent." The expression is generally understood to refer to the Communist practice of keeping out Western ideas and crushing freedom of the people under Communist control.

"Iron Horse." The metaphor was applied to railroad locomotives in the U.S. when they first replaced horses on railroad tracks, in the early 1830's.

Iroquois League. Founded about 1570, the Five Nations inhabited all of central New York from the Genesee River to Lake Champlain. The League, or Confederacy, reading from west to east, was comprised of Seneca, Cayuga, Onondaga, Oneida and Mohawk. Legend says the League was organized by the saintly statesman, Deganawidah (son of a virgin mother), assisted by the great and noble councilor Hiawatha, a Mohawk, to put an end to wars among the tribes and to establish peace based on justice and a government of law.

The Iroquois, except for the

Oneidas and Tuscaroras (admitted to the League as the sixth "nation" in 1722), were allies of the British against the French and supported Britain during the Revolutionary War.

Many Iroquois continue to live on reservations in New York.

Iroquois Theatre fire (Dec. 30, 1903). The "loop" district of Chicago was the scene of the greatest theater disaster in U.S. history. Some 500 persons, many of them women and children at an afternoon performance during the holiday season, died in the flames.

"irreconcilables." The term reflected the isolationist attitudes of the senators who opposed the League of Nations no matter how it might be modified. William E. Borah said of the League Covenant that it was a "treasonable" document that "should be buried." Other irreconcilables were Hiram Johnson and Robert La Follette.

"irrepressible conflict." Referring to the conflict over slavery between North and South in the years before the Civil War, William H. Seward used the phrase in a speech in Rochester, Oct. 25, 1858. It was hailed by Abolitionists who liked the strong language. Seward was somewhat taken aback when it was inferred that he was counseling a violent solution.

Earlier in 1858 Lincoln in his "house divided" speech of June 16 declared that the government could not permanently endure half slave and half free. Lincoln repudiated the accusation that he planned war against the slaveholders. He hoped for a democratic solution of the conflict.

Irving, Washington (1783–1859). Author. Born in New York City, he practiced law for a short time but soon became the first American man of letters to win an international reputation and to write full time for a living. Some pseudonyms he used include Geoffrey Crayon, Jonathan Oldstyle, Launcelot Langstaff and Friar Antonio Agapida. He was the moving spirit in publication of *Salmagundi* (1807–08), whimsical essays in which the name Gotham was first applied to New York City; and his genially satirical *History of New York . . . by Diedrich Knickerbocker* (1809) gave its name to the Knickerbocker School of writers. In Europe (1815–32), he wrote *The Sketch Book* (1820), which included his best-known tales: "The Legend of Sleepy Hollow" introducing Ichabod Crane, the gawky schoolmaster who became one of the best-known characters in all American literature, and "Rip Van Winkle." On the staff of the U.S. embassy in Madrid (1826–29), he published the *History of . . . Christopher Columbus* (1828). After serving as the U.S. minister to Spain (1842–46), he returned to the U.S. (1846) where he resided at "Sunnyside," his country home near Tarrytown, N.Y. He published the *Life of Washington* (5 vols., 1855–59).

"I shall go to Korea." Toward the end of the election campaign of 1952 Gen. Eisenhower, the Republican candidate, announced: "I shall go to Korea and try to end the war." When elected, Eisenhower did go to Korea; but his visit had little if any effect on the truce negotiations there.

Isis. International Satellite for Ionospheric Studies is a series of spacecraft planned in the mid-1960's to include electron and ion probes to measure the temperature and densities of hydrogen, helium and oxygen present at satellite altitudes.

Island Number 10. The fortified Confederate post on the Mississippi River, below Cairo, Ill., fell to the Union army under Gen. Pope, Apr. 8, 1862. It was the first successful effort in a campaign to split the Confederacy by gaining control of the entire length of the main waterway in the U.S.

isolationism. Both Washington and Jefferson preached an isolationist foreign policy at a time when the young U.S. was too weak to engage in international politics that might involve it in European wars of Continental origin. The tradition of avoiding alliances with foreign powers in peacetime persisted into the 19th century and was reinforced later by the disillusionment following World War I.

With U.S. entrance into World War II, the country turned away from isolationism toward collective security as a more realistic policy. U.S. leadership in organizing the United Nations (1945) and in formation of the North Atlantic Treaty Organization (1949) ended isolationism as a viable foreign policy for the U.S.

Ivy League. The term is popularly used to designate eight major eastern colleges with high admission standards. They are Brown (R.I., established 1764), Columbia (N.Y., 1754), Cornell (N.Y., 1865), Dartmouth (N.H., 1769), Harvard (Mass., 1636), Pennsylvania (1740), Princeton (N.J., 1746), and Yale (Conn., 1701).

Iwo Jima, battle of (Feb. 19–Mar. 15, 1945). The U.S. Marines took the island south of Japan in one of the bloodiest battles of World War II. Only 750 miles from Tokyo it contained three airfields and Japan's "seeing eye" to warn of the approach of bombers. It was heavily fortified with interlocking underground strongholds and fortified caves, all cleverly camouflaged.

The U.S. needed the island as a base for air attacks on Japan; the nearest American bases in the Mariana Islands— Saipan, Tinian and Guam— were 1,300 miles from Tokyo. A round trip by the huge B-29's took some 16 hours, leaving only a tiny fuel margin, and the result was crash landings in the Pacific in bad weather.

After 26 days of fighting the Marines reached the top of Mount Suribachi, the extinct volcano on the island, where the raising of the American flag was photographed by an Associated Press photographer, Joe Rosenthal. His picture, the most talked-about of World War II, became the new "Spirit of '45."

U.S. casualties were 20,196, including 4,189 killed. The Japanese fought almost to the last man; more than 21,000 were killed.

J

Jackson, Andrew (1767–1845). Seventh President of the U.S. (1829–37). He was born in Waxhaw, S.C. "Old Hickory" became a national hero at the battle of New Orleans (1815). He was U.S. Senator from Tennessee (1823–25), and the unsuccessful candidate for President in the bitterly fought campaign of 1824. In 1828 he won the election. The high points of his administration included firm opposition to South Carolina's nullification ordinance and the overthrow of the Bank of the U.S.

Jackson, Thomas Jonathan (1824–63). Confederate general. He was born in Clarksburg, Va., now West Va. Lee's greatest lieutenant, he was graduated from the U.S. Military Academy (1846). He won the name "Stonewall Jackson" at the first battle of Bull Run (1861). A brilliant field tactician, he led the Confederates in the Shenandoah Valley campaign (1862). He died after routing the federal right wing at Chancellorsville (1863), where he was accidentally wounded by fire from his own troops.

Jacksonian democracy. Andrew Jackson, seventh President of the U.S. (1829–37), placed the imprint of his background and personality on the Democratic party. Jackson's origins were humble, but by the time he ran for the Presidency he had become a planter whose business and law practice linked him with large propertied interests of Tennessee.

Jackson's reputation as the hero of the battle of New Orleans helped him to cut across class and regional lines in his march toward the Presidency. He knew that the common people wanted him to "turn the rascals out" and he did so with relish that won for him their continued support. Jackson believed in rotation in office and held that common sense was qualification enough for the highest offices in the land.

The Jacksonian era (1829–41), which included Martin Van Buren's administration, was marked by reform movements. Jackson deserves some of the

357

credit for the growth of political democracy. He was in tune with times enlivened by reformers demanding free public schools, more rights for women, better working conditions in factories and the abolition of slavery.

Jackson, however, had little understanding of the democratic movement named for him. Some revisionist historians have gone so far as to question whether there ever was a movement or force which can properly be called "Jacksonian democracy."

Jackson's Valley Campaign (May–June 1862). In the Shenandoah Valley of Virginia, Gen. "Stonewall" Jackson marched about 300 miles in 35 days and fought several battles (Middletown, Newton, Winchester, Front Royal, Strasburg, Cross Keys, Port Republic), some of them small encounters. Invariably he was outnumbered but managed to mass a sufficient force at the point of attack. He threatened Washington from the west and kept 60,000 Federals under Gen. Irvin McDowell occupied. Jackson thus weakened Gen. George McClellan's army in the peninsula, aimed at Richmond.

Jacobin clubs. The French Revolution inspired supporters in the U.S. who formed clubs in Philadelphia and other cities after the arrival of Citizen Genêt in 1793. The members were bitter in their attacks on Pres. Washington for failure to support the French revolutionary government against England. They were named after the Jacobins, a political club of the French Revolution whose original meeting place was a monastery of the Jacobins (Parisian name of Dominicans).

James, Henry (1843–1916). Novelist. Born in New York City, he attended Harvard Law School and, from about 1865, devoted himself to writing. He critically observed and wrote about the strains in upper-class society. He lived much of his life abroad, and while his novels invariably have a European setting, the plots are international and involve Americans. In *Roderick Hudson* (1876), *The American* (1877) and *The Portrait of a Lady* (1881) he subjected his characters to moral tests which they either passed or failed.

James, William (1842–1910). Philosopher and psychologist. Born in New York City, he was granted an M.D. by Harvard (1869), where he lectured on anatomy, physiology and hygiene before transferring to the Department of Philosophy in which he served as a professor (1885–1907). He established the first psychology laboratory in America and published the immensely popular *Principles of Psychology* (1890). His *Talks to Teachers on Psychology* (1899) gave impetus to the new subject of educational psychology. Known especially as one of the founders of pragmatism, he held that truth should properly be applied as a term, not to reality, but to our beliefs about it. A particular truth must "work," that is satisfy the purpose for which it was adopted. A leader in American thought, his works include *The Varieties of Religious Experience* (1902), *Pragmatism* (1907) and *A Pluralistic Universe* (1909).

Japanese-American Treaty of 1951. Renewed in 1960 for a ten-year period, the Treaty, a mutual security pact, provides for U.S. defense of Japan in case of attack. However, the U.S. is pledged to consult with Japan before bringing atomic arms into U.S. bases in Japan.

Java Sea, battle of (Feb. 1942). The Allies attempted, unsuccessfully, to save the island of Java, the most populous of the Dutch East Indies, rich in rice, quinine, oil and manganese. The entire Allied fleet of five cruisers and nine destroyers, including the U.S. *Houston,* all under command of Dutch Admiral Helfrich, was destroyed by a Japanese fleet superior in numbers and firepower.

Jay, John (1745–1829). Jurist and statesman. He was born in New York City where he later practiced law. Active in pre-Revolutionary agitation, he became a member of the Continental Congress (1774–77) and its president (1778–79). He helped to negotiate peace with Britain (1782–83) and was U.S. Sec. of Foreign Affairs (1784–89). He wrote five of the *Federalist Papers* supporting the Constitution (1787–88). As Chief Justice of the U.S. Supreme Court (1789–95), his ruling in *Chisholm v. Georgia* (1793), giving a citizen of one state the right to sue another state, led to the 11th Amendment. He negotiated the Jay Treaty (1794) which settled differences with Britain and avoided war, but was attacked by Jeffersonian Republicans. He was governor of N.Y. (1795–1801). "An able man, but not a genius, he brought intellectual vigor and moral tone into every office which he held."

Jay-Gardoqui negotiations (1785–86). Discussions were held in New York, then the capital, between John Jay and Don Diego de Gardoqui, the Spanish diplomatic representative. In return for the U.S. yielding to the Spanish the right to navigate the Mississippi freely for two or three decades, Spain promised trade concessions in its European ports. Interests of American merchants in the East were thus pitted against western farmers. Jay recommended that Congress go along with such arrangements. However, the South and West combined against it. Since nine of the 13 states had to ratify a treaty under the Articles of Confederation, the treaty was never approved.

Jayhawkers. Unionist guerrilla bands carried on irregular warfare in eastern Kansas before and during the Civil War. Their activities earned them the southerners' hatred.

Jay Treaty (1794). The Treaty prevented war between the U.S. and Britain at a time when France and Britain were engaged in a war following the French Revolution.

Pres. Washington sent John Jay to London on a special mission to settle differences arising from failure to carry out settlements agreed upon in the Treaty of Paris (1783) and from the maritime conflict which began in 1793.

The Treaty negotiated by Jay provided for evacuation of the British frontier forts in the Northwest; a commission to settle boundary disputes between the U.S. and Britain, especially in the area of Maine and Canada; a commission to agree on the amounts to be paid English merchants whose pre-Revolution debts had not been paid; settlement of debts still outstanding of Loyalists who had lost their property during the Revolution; settlement of damages owed Americans whose ships had been seized by the British.

The Treaty was so unpopular in the U.S. that Jay was burned in effigy. It made no provision for guaranteeing our maritime neutrality and said nothing about the impressment of American seamen. Washington signed the Treaty reluctantly. It did keep the young U.S. out of war and preserved essential tariff revenues for support of the national government, most of which were derived from British imports.

"jazz age." The term is just one of many that describe the 1920's, also known as the "roaring decade" or "golden daze." Young people were disillusioned after the idealism of the war years. Dancing to jazz music (four beats to the bar) became a popular form of recreation. The unconventional rhythm and exciting tempo were spread from New Orleans throughout the land by the greats among jazz musicians, including Red Nichols, Bix Beiderbecke, Louis Armstrong, Count Basie and Duke Ellington.

jeep. The four-wheel drive vehicle was widely used by the armed forces in World War II. The word jeep is taken from the letters G.P., U.S. Army parlance for "general purpose"; this describes the use of the vehicle by the military services. A more romantic explanation of the origin of the term is that it was taken from Eugene the Jeep, a small, fanciful wonder-working animal created in 1937 by Elzie C. Segar, the American cartoonist, for the comic strip Thimble Theatre starring Popeye.

Jefferson, Thomas (1743–1826). Third President of the U.S. (1801–09). Born in Shadwell, Goochland County (now Albemarle County), Va., he was graduated from the College of William and Mary (1762). A Virginia member of the Continental Congress, he was chairman of the committee that wrote the Declaration of Independence. He served as U.S. Minister to France (1785–89), U.S. Sec. of State (1790–93), and Vice-President of the U.S. (1797–1801). The high point of his administration as President was the Louisiana Purchase (1803).

Jeffersonian democracy. Thomas Jefferson's trust in the common man distinguished him from such contemporaries as Alexander Hamilton. Concerned with the welfare of farmers, Jefferson feared all rulers and the rise of an industrial proletariat.

In his first inaugural address, he spoke of "honor and confidence from our fellow citizens . . . resulting not from birth, but from our actions. . . ."

Jefferson's faith in democracy encompassed a firm belief in education, evidenced by his labors on behalf of the University of Virginia. Although he was abused by the press, he believed in its freedom. He abhorred religious intolerance. His tolerance was extended to his political enemies when he said on becoming President: "We are all Republicans, we are all Federalists."

Although Jefferson was opposed to a strong central government and favored states' rights, the responsibility of high office sometimes caused him to modify his philosophy in deference to the practical.

Jefferson was a firm defender of human liberty. His political philosophy is contained in the Declaration of Independence.

Jehovah's Witnesses. Highly evangelistic, the Protestant sect was founded in the U.S. in 1872 by Charles Taze Russell, a Congregationalist layman. In its early days members were known as Russellites. Its doctrine centers on the second coming of Christ, when Satan's rule will be destroyed and God's theocracy established. Each Witness is considered a minister of God. Its publications include the monthlies *Watchtower* and *Awake*. The denomination has over 315,000 members.

Jenkins' Ear, War of (1739–43). Trade rivalry and differences over the ownership of Georgia were the causes of this strangely named war between England and Spain. It was precipitated when a British officer, Capt. Jenkins, appeared before Parliament with a little box in which he carried a human ear. He claimed that it had been cut from his head by a Spanish officer as a warning to Britain.

During the war a Spanish invasion of Georgia was turned back, as was an invasion of Florida by the Georgia governor. The British were unsuccessful in attacks on the Atlantic and Pacific coasts of Spanish America. The war was part of the continuing struggle among Britain, Spain and France for supremacy in the New World.

Jersey prisonship. An unseaworthy British warship lying off the Brooklyn shore of New York Harbor from 1776–83 was used as a prison for captured American sailors. Conditions were so vile that thousands of Americans died on board.

Jesuit missionaries. Members of a Catholic religious order, the Society of Jesus, founded by St. Ignatius Loyola, they were active in the New World as explorers and founders of missions among the Indians. In the 1640's and 1650's they established French missions and claims in present-day Wisconsin. They explored the Great Lakes region from mission bases at Michilimackinac and Green Bay on Lake Michigan and Sault Ste. Marie on the portage between Lake Huron and Lake Superior. Their missions among the Hurons were especially successful. They were called "Black Robes" by the Indians and traveled as far west as Oregon. Many suffered martyrdom, especially at the hands of the Iroquois.

The requirement that Jesuit missionaries report annually to the chief of their order in France or Rome resulted in compilation of the Jesuit *Relations,* an invaluable source of information about Indian tribes, explorations and conditions in North America in the 17th and 18th centuries.

Jesuits helped to found Maryland (1634) and remained active in the American colonies and in the U.S. A primary interest of the group has been education. Jesuits founded such centers of higher learning as Georgetown (1789), St. Louis University (1829) and Fordham (1841).

Jews in the U.S. The first Jewish community in North America was established in 1654 in New Amsterdam by 23 refugees. They had fled Brazil when the Dutch lost it to the Portuguese. At first Jews were denied the civil rights of New Amsterdam citizens, but Peter Stuyvesant soon granted them the right to stand guard duty for the protection of the towns. When the English assumed control in 1664, the right of public worship for all creeds was recognized. In 1729 the New York Congregation Shearith Israel built a synagogue.

For the next century Jews filtered into other seaboard settlements—New York, Newport, Philadelphia, Charleston and Savannah. By the time of the Revolution about 2,500 Jews had established congregations. Almost without exception they were committed to the Revolutionary cause; in Philadelphia, Haym Salomon worked ceaselessly to help finance the struggle. Jewish names in the lists of dead and wounded tell the story of their participation in the Revolutionary War and in all other wars in which the U.S. has fought.

The Constitution established religious liberty, but discrimination continued and had to be removed by legal action. The

Board of Delegates of American Israelites (1865–78) labored to obtain the removal from several state constitutions of the remaining relics of legal discrimination against Jews. During the Civil War when more than 700 Jews fought with both the Confederate and Union armies, rabbis were permitted to serve as chaplains only after persistent efforts.

During the two decades preceding the Civil War about 200,000 German Jews settled in America. Some of them settled on the Atlantic coast. Others moved into the interior, developing communities in Chicago, Cincinnati, Memphis and St. Paul. From 1840 to 1880, these German Jewish immigrants founded religious, philanthropic and fraternal organizations that are still basic to Jewish communal life in America.

By the time the German Jews outnumbered the Sephardic Jews (Spanish and Portuguese), the American-born Sephardim had achieved social prominence, wealth and considerable influence. Soon the German Jews, who had started out in the main as peddlers with packs on their backs, opened retail stores, went on to establish great firms dealing with varied merchandise and became quickly absorbed in the American middle class.

German Jews, led by Rabbi Isaac Meyer Wise, introduced the Reform movement in the U.S. in 1885. The Sephardim clung largely to strict observance and to their particular ritual in the synagogue.

Between 1880 and 1920, 2,000,000 Jews came to America from eastern Europe, refugees from persecution in Czarist Russia, Rumania and Hungary. The eastern Jews (Ashkenazim, as were the German Jews) took to peddling, worked in sweatshops and gradually established themselves. They created trade unions in the garment industries, emerged from the sweatshops and turned to a pursuit of education. Large numbers of their children entered the professions. Eastern Jews built up religious institutions and a Jewish educational system culminating in *yeshivot* and seminaries. Under the leadership of Solomon Schechter, the Conservative movement (midway between Orthodoxy and Reform Judaism) took root and developed.

With immigration reduced to a trickle since the early 1920's, American Jewry has become largely native-born. Before World War I the majority of American Jews were laborers. Since then the occupational pattern has changed and most Jews have become middle-class professional and businessmen. B'nai B'rith, an organization dedicated to safeguarding Jewish rights, continues to report evidence of discrimination against Jews in various industries. In government Jews have been represented in all political offices other than the Presidency and Vice-Presidency.

Since the Nazi destruction of 6,000,000 Jews in Europe, American Jewry has become the largest Jewish body in the world and has thus accepted great responsibilities. American Jews are the chief contributors to support of the state of Israel. Rescue, relief and reconstruction are shouldered by American Jews under the leadership of such organizations as the United Jewish Appeal and the American Joint Distribution Committee.

There are about 5,500,000 Jews in the U.S.

Jim Crow laws. The expression applies to laws and practices which aim to keep Negro and white separated in American life. It seems to have been first used as the title of a popular minstrel song in 1830 in which white actors used blackface make-up.

Although Negroes and whites were separated in practice in the antebellum South, Jim Crow laws were enacted chiefly in the 1890's. They were passed as a reaction to 30 years of "freedom" which the Negro gained during the Reconstruction era. The discriminatory legislation was characterized by critics as Jim Crow laws. It deprived the Negro of his right to vote and established segregation in the schools, public transportation, restaurants, other public places and employment.

The Negro civil rights movement has sought the repeal of Jim Crow legislation. U.S. Supreme Court decisions have set aside such laws as unconstitutional, as in the case of *Brown v. Board of Education* (1954).

John Birch Society. The ultraconservative, semisecret political organization was founded in 1958 by Robert Welch, Jr., a Massachusetts businessman. He named the Society after a Georgia Baptist missionary serving as a U.S. intelligence officer who was killed by Chinese Communists in 1945.

The organization maintains that Communist penetration of American life is deep and alleges that a number of the highest officials in U.S. government are under Communist influence. Birchers inveigh against expanded federal controls and call among other things for the repeal of social security laws.

John Brown's Body (1928). A narrative poem of the Civil War, awarded the Pulitzer Prize for Poetry (1929), it was written by Stephen Vincent Benét. The poem's title was that of a song written by William Steffe about 1852. The tune was used by Julia Ward Howe in her "Battle Hymn of the Republic" (1862).

John Brown's raid (1859). By seizing the federal arsenal at Harpers Ferry, Va., with an armed band of 18 (five of them Negroes), the Abolitionist John Brown hoped to arm the slaves and start an insurrection. Brown was captured by a Marine detachment under the command of Col. Robert E. Lee.

William Seward, Abraham Lincoln, Stephen Douglas—men of all parties—condemned Brown's action, but he was deified by the foremost American writers, Ralph Waldo Emerson and Henry Thoreau.

After the trial and execution, Thoreau observed that John Brown became "more alive than ever he was."

The raid inflamed the South, fearful of slave insurrections. It helped to bring on the Civil War by weakening the ties between the North and South.

Johnny Appleseed. John Chapman (1775?–1847) dedicated himself to planting appleseeds and pruning the growing trees in the Ohio Valley in preparation for the new settlers. They would have been without fruit if he had not preceded them with his good work. He is the subject of many legends and is celebrated in literature, as in Vachel Lindsay's *In Praise of Johnny Appleseed* (1921).

Johnson, Andrew (1808–75). Seventeenth President of the U.S. (1865–69). He was born in Raleigh, N.C. Vice-President of the U.S. (Mar. 4–Apr. 15, 1865), he succeeded to the Presidency on the death of Pres. Lincoln. He served Tennessee as a member of the U.S. House of Representatives (1843–53) and U.S. Senator (1857–62, 1875). He was loyal to the Union during the Civil War. His differences with Congress over Reconstruction policies led to his impeachment (1868) and acquittal.

Johnson, Lyndon Baines (1908–73). Thirty-sixth President of the U.S. (1963–69). Born near

Stonewall, Tex., he was graduated from Southwest Texas State College (1930). Vice-Pres. of U.S. (1961–63), he succeeded to the Presidency on the death of Pres. Kennedy (Nov. 22, 1963). He served Texas as a Democratic member of U.S. Senate (1948–60), and was Senate majority leader (1953–60). He signed civil rights bills and headed the nation during the war in Vietnam.

Johnson, Sir William (1715–74). British official in American colonies. Born in Ireland, he came to America about 1738 and settled in Mohawk River Valley of N.Y. During King George's War (1744–48), he was largely responsible for preventing the Six Nations from joining the French. He failed to capture Crown Point (1755), but prevented the northern colonies from falling to the French. He sought to centralize control of the fur trade and prevent a westward rush of settlers; he aided projects for education and religious training of Indians. An imperialist loyal to the Crown, he helped draw the French from North America.

Johnson Act (1934). Sen. Hiram W. Johnson (Calif.) sponsored the ban on federal loans to governments in default on their war debts. The Act, also known as the Foreign Securities Act, signified growing isolationist sentiment in the U.S.

Johnson doctrine. "The American nations cannot, must not, and will not permit the establishment of another Communist government in the Western hemisphere." This statement by Pres. Johnson, May 2, 1965, was referred to in some quarters as the "Johnson doctrine." It was made a few days after the President ordered U.S. troops into the Dominican Republic to stop what was described as a Castro-type takeover.

At the same time as he used U.S. troops in Santo Domingo, the President had stepped up military aid to South Vietnam. The doctrine meant that emphasis was to be placed on resisting with military force the advance of Communism anywhere in the world.

Johnston, Joseph Eggleston (1807-91). Confederate general. He was born in Prince Edward Co., Va. A graduate of the U.S. Military Academy (1829), he was wounded five times in the Mexican War. He resigned from the U.S. Army (1861) to join the Confederacy. His tactical skill at the first Bull Run (1861) won him a promotion to general and the command in northern Virginia. He commanded in Tennessee and Mississippi (1862), where he lost Vicksburg. He ordered withdrawal from Chattanooga to Atlanta but failed to halt Gen. Sherman's advance. He refused Jefferson Davis' order to continue the war in the interior and surrendered to Sherman (Apr. 26, 1865). He was congressman from Virginia

(1879-81) and U.S. commissioner of railroads (1885-91).

Johnstown Flood (May 31, 1889). The collapse of the Conemaugh Reservoir resulted in the disastrous flooding of the Pennsylvania town, southeast of Pittsburgh. More than 2,000 people were killed and damage was estimated at $10,000,000. It was charged that the dam holding back the waters was badly constructed but the state legislature did not investigate.

Jolliet and Marquette discovery (1673). For more than a century before the "discovery" of the Mississippi River, explorers knew of the "great water." It was not, however, until the voyage of Louis Jolliet, the French explorer, and the Jesuit missionary, Father Jacques Marquette, that the upper Mississippi was mapped. Jolliet was commissioned by Jean Talon, the governor of New France (French empire in Canada) to undertake the trip. Marquette accompanied him "as chaplain and Christian spokesman."

They set out from the Michigan peninsula for the Wisconsin River and entered waters of the Mississippi, sailing down almost to the Arkansas River. They did not proceed farther for fear of falling into the hands of the Spanish, but determined from Indians that the river flowed into the Gulf of Mexico and did not turn east toward Virginia as had been thought.

In Quebec Jolliet reported

the news of an almost all-water route from the St. Lawrence to the Spanish Gulf. The French perceived that by controlling this route they could confine the English within narrow limits and split the Spanish empire in two.

Jones, John Paul (1747–92). Naval officer. Born in Scotland, he served in the British mercantile marine before settling in Fredericksburg, Va. (about 1773). He entered the American Navy at the outbreak of the Revolution. In command of the *Bonhomme Richard* (named in honor of Benjamin Franklin), he forced the surrender of the more heavily armed British *Serapis* (1779). He is reported to have said, when asked if he was surrendering, "Sir, I have not yet begun to fight." After the Revolution he served briefly in the Russian Navy (1788). Although he was buried in Paris, his remains were brought to the U.S. (1905) and placed in the crypt of the U.S. Naval Academy chapel in Annapolis, Md. (1913).

Judge Advocate General, Office of. Existing in the Army, Air Force and Navy departments, the office administers military justice and provides the legal services for the branches of the armed forces.

judicial review. Although the right of federal courts to declare acts of Congress unconstitutional is not stated explicitly in the Constitution or in the Judiciary Act of 1789, this right was asserted early in the history of the U.S. Supreme Court. The concept of judicial review was discernible in the colonial period when laws of colonial legislatures were subject to review by the Privy Council in England. This is not, however, regarded as a firm precedent for Chief Justice Marshall's decision in *Marbury v. Madison* (1803) when he not only ruled that a section of the Judiciary Act of 1789 was unconstitutional, but also asserted that it is "emphatically the province and duty of the judicial department to say what the law is."

Judicial review was also extended by the U.S. Supreme Court under Marshall to an act of a state legislature which was held to be in conflict with the Constitution in *Fletcher v. Peck* (1810) and to revision of a state court decision in *Cohens v. Virginia* (1821). Authority for review in these latter two cases is, however, contained in the Judiciary Act of 1789.

After *Marbury v. Madison* the Supreme Court did not again declare an act of Congress unconstitutional until the Dred Scott Case (1857). In the post-Civil War period, the Court found a number of state statutes invalid, but in those cases where laws of Congress were reviewed found them to be valid. In the period 1890–1937 the Court was more active in finding federal laws unconstitutional, notably during the early years of the New Deal.

State courts have also exercised the right of judicial review, but the comparative ease of amending state constitutions has moderated the impact of judicial action on state legislation.

The power of judicial review held by U.S. courts is a unique contribution of the American judiciary to political science.

judiciary. The federal court system is provided for in the Constitution (Art. III) which calls for one Supreme Court and inferior courts. In 1789 Congress set up a court system whose general plan has been followed ever since. The states provide for their own court systems.

Federal courts below the Supreme Court include Circuit Courts of Appeal and District Courts. There are, in addition, special federal courts which consider matters relating to patents and claims against the federal government. Most cases involving federal laws are tried in the District Courts.

A major weakness of the federal government under the Articles of Confederation had been the lack of a court system. Under the new Constitution the federal government could force individual citizens to obey it.

Juilliard v. Greenman (1884). The U.S. Supreme Court held valid legal tender laws passed in time of peace. The Court ruled that the Congress may make treasury notes legal tender in payment of debts previously contracted as well as those subsequently contracted, whether that authority be exercised in course of war or time of peace.

The case arose when Juilliard refused to accept payment in U.S. notes of a debt owed to him by Greenman and demanded payment in gold or silver. The effect of the Court's decision was to affirm the constitutionality of the Legal Tender Act of 1862. Juilliard had to accept payment in U.S. notes.

Jungle, The (1906). The muckraking novel by Upton Sinclair exposed the foul conditions in the Chicago meat packing plants. It led to passage of the Pure Food and Drug Act.

junior college. Offering two years of education beyond the high school, it is often called a community college. Where the 13th and 14th years of education are equivalent to the first two years of college, the junior college is a higher educational institution. Where it is an upward extension of the high school, it is administered by the local school system.

The first private junior college was organized in Joliet, Ill., in 1902. The movement developed rapidly in the 1920's and by 1930 there were public junior colleges in 29 states. California assumed the lead in establishing the junior college. It served the needs of students who did not plan to complete a full four-year course, or who could not finance a college education away from home.

The terminal function of the junior college has become important, since many students do not intend to transfer to a four-year institution. Many vocational courses of a semiprofessional or highly skilled nature have developed.

There are now over 700 junior colleges in the U.S.

junior high school. Part of the secondary school program, it was organized to meet the needs of early adolescents—ages 12 to 14—usually in the seventh, eighth and ninth grades. The first formally organized junior highs were established in Columbus, O., in 1909, and in Berkeley, Calif., in 1910. The 8–4 plan (eight years of elementary school and four years of high school), prevalent in most states by 1890, had been criticized as requiring too long a period in elementary school.

Since 1920 the junior high schools, usually organized in separate buildings, have grown so that three-fourths of all secondary school students attend them. Exploration of the interests, abilities and aptitudes of the pupils is a function of the junior highs. Pupils take work in the major subject areas, various shops (industrial arts) and engage in an extracurricular program. It is claimed that the junior highs offer leadership opportunities to ninth-grade pupils who would otherwise be submerged in a four-year high school.

Justice, Department of. Headed by the Attorney General, the department of the federal government was created by Congress in 1870. Prior to 1870 the Attorney General had been a member of the President's Cabinet, but not as the head of a department. The office of Attorney General had been created by Congress in 1789.

The chief functions of the Department of Justice are to provide means for the enforcement of federal laws, to furnish legal counsel in federal cases and to construe the laws under which other departments act. It conducts all suits in the Supreme Court in which the U.S. is concerned, supervises federal penal institutions and investigates federal law violations. It represents the government in legal matters and offers legal advice to the President and to the heads of executive departments. The Attorney General directs activities of U.S. attorneys and marshals in various judicial districts.

K

Kalamazoo Case (1874). The Supreme Court of Michigan upheld the rights of the city of Kalamazoo to establish a high school, employ a superintendent of schools and levy additional taxes to cover the expense.

A citizen by the name of Stuart had brought suit to prevent the collection of additional taxes, contending that high schools were not included among "common schools" and that the district board should supervise the schools.

The court reviewed the educational history of the state and found that school districts were not confined to the primary grades. It confirmed the right of the voters to tax themselves for the education of children in whatever "branches of knowledge" the school district officers "may cause to be taught. . . ."

The decision was one of the important milestones in the establishment of the American public high school.

Kanagawa, Treaty of (Mar. 31, 1854). A treaty of peace, friendship and commerce, signed by Commodore Matthew C. Perry, opened the Japanese ports of Shimoda and Hakodate to U.S. trade and made provision for shipwrecked U.S. seamen.

Kansas. The "Sunflower State," in the West North Central group in the Great Plains, was admitted to the Union as the 34th state, Jan. 29, 1861. Its capital is Topeka.

The territory was part of France's claim to the land drained by the Mississippi, based on La Salle's explorations (1682). All but a small part of Kansas was included in the Louisiana Purchase (1803) when Kansas (Sioux word for south wind people) became part of the U.S. It was organized as a territory in 1854 and was fought over by proslavery and free-soiler groups until it entered the Union as a free state.

Farms covering 95% of the land area produce the biggest winter wheat crop in the nation. Cattle number over five million and Kansas City, Kan., has the second largest number of stockyards and packing plants in the U.S.

Kansas-Nebraska Act (1854). The Act repealed the Missouri Compromise of 1820 by permitting residents of the territories of Kansas and Nebraska to decide for themselves whether their states would permit slavery. This principle of popular sovereignty was advanced by Sen. Stephen A. Douglas, who was most influential in getting the Act passed by Congress. What he thought to be a peaceful approach to settling the slavery issue produced "bloody Kansas" and further inflamed the sectional controversy over slavery that led to the Civil War.

The debate over the bill split both the Democratic and Whig parties. Antislavery sentiment against the bill was so strong that Douglas said he could travel from Boston to Chicago by the light of his burning effigies. The party splits led to the formation of the Republican party, pledged to oppose extension of slavery into the territories.

Kearsarge and *Alabama* (June 19, 1864). In a naval battle off the coast of Cherbourg, France, the Confederate warship *Alabama*, which had been preying on Union ships in European waters, was sunk. The *Kearsarge* had been dispatched in search of the *Alabama*.

keelboats. The boats were used extensively on western rivers during the 18th and early 19th centuries to carry freight and passengers. About 50 feet long and as narrow as seven feet, they were propelled by oars, sails or poles in shallow water. Keelboatmen and flatboatmen had many a brawl on the Mississippi.

Kellogg-Briand Pact (1928). The treaty, officially known as the Pact of Paris, outlawed war as "an instrument of national policy" but was so interpreted as to permit defensive wars. Negotiated by U.S. Sec. of State Kellogg and French Foreign Minister Briand, it was signed originally by 15 nations and later by almost all nations.

The Pact was hailed as a major step toward lasting peace. Critics, however, observed that nations invariably alleged that they were fighting defensively and that the treaty had no teeth.

Kellogg himself declared that "the only enforcement behind the pact is the public opinion of the people."

Kelly's Industrial Army. The march on Washington via boxcar from California was led by "General" Charles T. Kelly at the head of some 1,500 unemployed as a result of the Panic of 1893. A few arrived in the nation's capital on foot. No relief was voted by the Congress.

Kendall, Edward Calvin (1886–1972). Biochemist. Born in South Norwalk, Conn., he was granted a Ph.D. by Columbia (1910). He headed the biochemistry section at Mayo Foundation, Rochester, Minn., beginning 1914. He won the

Nobel Prize in 1950 (with Hench and Reichstein) for isolating and synthesizing the principal hormone of the adrenal cortex (cortisone).

Kendall v. U.S. (1838). The U.S. Supreme Court held that Postmaster General Kendall was required to perform a duty imposed upon him by statute even if the President did not desire him to do so.

The case arose when the Postmaster General, at Pres. Jackson's instigation, refused to pay a claim made by one Stokes. Congress passed a special act ordering payment. Stokes sought and obtained a mandamus in the U.S. Circuit Court for the District of Columbia and on appeal this decision was affirmed by the U.S. Supreme Court. The Court recognized the underlying question to be whether the President's duty to "take care that the laws be faithfully executed" made it constitutionally impossible for Congress to enact laws requiring subordinates of the President to carry out the laws. The Court held that Congress had such power and Kendall was required under the law to perform the duty imposed by Congress despite the President's objection.

Kenesaw Mountain, battle of (June 27, 1864). Gen. William Sherman's march through Georgia was delayed by the Fabian tactics of Confederate Gen. Joseph E. Johnston. In this battle Sherman, instead of continuing his flanking tactics, attacked frontally and was repulsed with over 2,000 killed and wounded compared with 270 Confederate casualties. The delay was temporary and Sherman took Atlanta on Sept. 2.

Kennebec expedition. In 1775 Gen. Washington sent Benedict Arnold to cooperate with Gen. Richard Montgomery in a Canadian campaign in which Montreal was captured. Arnold then proceeded along the Kennebec River in Maine and through the wilderness to Quebec. In an assault on that city (Dec. 31, 1775) Montgomery was killed. Arnold failed to penetrate the defense of Gen. Guy Carleton.

Kennedy, John Fitzgerald (1917–63). Thirty-fifth President of the U.S. (1961–63). Born in Brookline, Mass., he was graduated from Harvard (1940). The first Roman Catholic to be elected President, he aroused enthusiasm with his New Frontier program. Earlier in his career, he served Massachusetts as Democratic member of the U.S. Senate (1953–60). He was assassinated in Dallas, Tex. (Nov. 22, 1963).

Kennedy assassinations (1963 and 1968). Pres. John F. Kennedy, the 46-year-old chief executive of the U.S., was shot and fatally wounded by an assassin as he rode in a motorcade through Dallas, Tex., on Nov. 22, 1963 while on a three-day political tour of the state.

He died in Parkland Hospital without regaining consciousness.

Lee Harvey Oswald, a 24-year-old former Marine, was charged with the murder. Oswald himself was shot and fatally wounded (Nov. 24, 1963) by Jack Rubenstein, also known as Jack Ruby, a Dallas nightclub operator. Ruby was found guilty of murder by a jury in the Texas District Court in Dallas (Mar. 14, 1964). The conviction was reversed by the Texas Court of Criminal Appeals (Oct. 5, 1966), which ordered the case transferred out of Dallas County. Ruby died of cancer before a new trial could take place.

Pres. Johnson appointed a seven-man commission headed by Chief Justice Earl Warren to investigate the assassination of Pres. Kennedy and the murder of his alleged assassin. After ten months of inquiry the commission released a controversial report which concluded that Oswald was solely responsible for the killing of the President.

On June 5, 1968 while in Los Angeles, Calif., campaigning for the Democratic nomination for the Presidency, Sen. Robert Francis Kennedy (b. Nov. 20, 1925) of New York, Pres. Kennedy's brother, was shot. He died the next day and was buried near the gravesite of his brother in Arlington National Cemetery.

Kennedy Round. The name was given to the tariff-cutting talks at Geneva in 1965 held under the General Agreement on Tariffs and Trade (GATT). Pres. Kennedy was no longer alive but the name of the talks reminded negotiators that he had planned ahead for the conference, which he hoped would liberalize trade.

Kensington Stone. Alleged to be a runic record of a Norse exploration party in America in 1362, the stone on which the writing is inscribed was found near Kensington, Minn., in 1898.

Kent, James (1763–1847). Jurist. He was born in Fredericksburg, now Southeast, N.Y. Admitted to New York bar (1785), he practiced in New York City (from 1793). He was first professor of law at Columbia College (1793–98, 1823–26) and judge of the New York Supreme Court (from 1798) and chief judge (1804), introducing the practice of written opinions. Chancellor, New York Court of Chancery (1814–23), he practically created equity jurisdiction in the United States, preserving the best features of English law. He wrote the foremost American legal treatise, *Commentaries on American Law* (1826–28, 1830).

Kentucky. The "Blue Grass State," in the East South Central group, was admitted to the Union as the 15th state, June 1, 1792. Its capital is Frankfort.

Kentucky (Wyandot word meaning "plain") was originally part of Virginia. Because the Iroquois and Cherokee Indians struggled for its possession, it was known as the "Dark and Bloody Ground" or the "Middle Ground." White settlers entered in increasing numbers after Daniel Boone's visit in 1767. The Cumberland Gap and the Ohio River were the chief routes into Kentucky.

During the American Revolution the resources of Virginia were so strained that Kentuckians had to fend for themselves against the Indian menace. Virginia agreed to separation when the federal government accepted Kentucky as a state.

Although there was strong proslavery sentiment in Kentucky, the state remained within the Union.

The soil is generally good. Corn, tobacco and potatoes are the chief crops. Industrial centers manufacture tobacco, lumber and oil products. Bituminous coal is a principal resource. The state is best known for its thoroughbred horses.

Kentucky Gazette. One of the principal newspapers in the West was founded at Lexington, Ky., Aug. 11, 1787, by John Bradford of Fauquier County, Va.

Within a few years Bradford, like other colonial and early national period printers, was issuing both almanacs and books, since income from newspaper publishing was not adequate to maintain the printing plant.

Kettering, Charles Franklin (1876–1958). Electrical engineer and manufacturer. Born in Londonville, Ohio, he made no-

table improvements in automobile ignition and perfected the self-starter, first installed in Cadillacs. He was General Manager of General Motors Research Corporation (1925–47). Inventor of a starting, lighting and ignition system, later known as "Delco," for automobiles and other lighting and power equipment, he also developed a new high compression engine (1951). He was co-founder of the Sloan-Kettering Institute for Cancer Research.

Kickapoo. An Algonquian people, they resisted the advance of whites in Wisconsin until forced southward into Illinois and Indiana about 1765. They sided with the British against the Americans in both the Revolutionary War and War of 1812. By the Treaty of Edwardsville (1819) they ceded their lands to the U.S.

Some Kickapoos moved to northern Mexico where they raided the Texan border. They were induced to settle in the Indian Territory in Oklahoma in 1873 where they were joined by tribesmen from Kansas. Survivors continue to live in Oklahoma.

Kilbourn v. Thompson (1881). The U.S. Supreme Court held that the House of Representatives had exceeded its powers in directing one of its committees to make a particular investigation.

The case arose when Kilbourn refused to produce certain papers relating to the bankruptcy of Jay Cook & Co. Thompson, sergeant-at-arms of the House, was ordered to arrest and imprison him for 45 days in the common jail of the District of Columbia. Kilbourn was released on a writ of habeas corpus and brought suit before the Supreme Court against Thompson on the plea of illegal imprisonment.

The Court decided that the Constitution did not invest either House with a general power of punishment for contempt. It concluded that the purpose of the inquiry was an improper one—to pry into private affairs and matters with which the judiciary alone was empowered to deal.

kindergarten. A term for early childhood education, it was coined in 1840 by the German educator Friedrich Wilhelm Froebel. The educational program included games, songs, plays and various kinds of self-activity.

A Froebel disciple, Mrs. Carl Schurz, wife of the prominent German refugee, established a German kindergarten at Watertown, Wis., in 1855. Elizabeth Peabody opened the first English-speaking kindergarten in Boston in 1860. Both of these early kindergartens were privately operated. The first public school kindergarten in the U.S. was opened by Susan Blow in St. Louis, Mo., in 1873, under the sponsorship of Superintendent of Schools William T. Harris. St. Louis became a center for the diffusion of kinder-garten ideas. After 1890 U.S. school systems began to adopt the kindergarten as an additional rung in the educational ladder.

King, Martin Luther, Jr. (1929–68). Clergyman. Born in Georgia, he acquired a worldwide reputation as a Negro leader in the civil rights movement. An advocate of passive resistance, a Ghandi-inspired philosophy of direct, nonviolent mass protest, King led the boycott (1955–56) which forced desegregation of Montgomery, Ala., city bus lines. He became an international figure when he was awarded the Nobel Peace Prize in 1964. An assassin shot and killed him in Memphis, Tenn. (Apr. 4, 1968), where he had come to lead a march on behalf of striking sanitation workers. On Sunday, April 7, the nation officially began a period of mourning that extended to Tuesday, Apr. 9, the day of the funeral.

"King Andrew." Andrew Jackson was so styled by his political enemies during his Presidency (1829–37) because of his vigorous party leadership, his dismissal of non-Democrats from political office, his resounding veto of a renewal of the charter of the Bank of the United States, his announced intent of using force to suppress secession of South Carolina and other evidences of presidential power.

"King Caucus." The party system which arose after Washington's retirement led to the congressional caucus, a meeting of party members in Congress. The caucus decided on the candidates for President and Vice-President. This method of nomination was practiced from 1796 to 1824, when divisions within the Republican (Jeffersonian) party toppled "King Caucus." It gave way to more democratic methods of nominating candidates for high office.

"King Cotton." The South had high hopes before secession that its famous staple would be in such demand that need for it would bring about speedy recognition of the Confederacy. It was also expected that cotton exports would pay for manufactures, thus freeing manpower needed for the fighting. These hopes were dashed by the large supply of raw cotton held by British textile mills which had anticipated outbreak of the Civil War.

Cotton had been hailed as king by Sen. Hammond (S.C.), who declared in 1858, "You dare not make war upon cotton! No power on earth dares make war upon it. Cotton is king." Earlier, *Cotton Is King* (1855) appeared as the title of a book by David Christy.

King George's War (1744–48). The war between France and Britain in North America was known in Europe, where it had started four years earlier, as the War of the Austrian Succession. The hostilities were started by French efforts to seize part of Nova Scotia and by the desire of Massachusetts merchants to protect their trade and Canadian fishery against the French.

A high point in the war was the capture of Louisbourg, key to the St. Lawrence River, by the British with New England assistance. It was, however, returned to the French, in order to regain for the British East India Company the post of Madras in India which the French had taken during the war.

By the Treaty of Aix-la-Chapelle (1748) all conquered territories were returned to their former possessors.

King Philip's War (1675–76). Indians led by King Philip, chief of the Wampanoags, resisted the growing encroachment of New England settlers on their land. They raided and burned numerous New England towns and massacred hundreds of settlers. New Englanders organized and drove the Indians out of southern New England. Many escaped to Canada where they joined the French in opposing English colonists. The war ended when King Philip was killed in action.

King's Mountain, battle of (Oct. 7, 1780). A British force, most of whom were Loyalists, was wiped out by frontier patriots in the South Carolina hills. Even after white flags were hoisted, the frontiersmen went on slaughtering the enemy.

King William's War (1689–97). The first of a long series of wars between France and England in North America, it was known as the War of the League of Augsburg in Europe. In America, French forces captured York Factory on Hudson Bay and disrupted the trade of the English. Aided by Indian allies, the French launched ferocious attacks on Schenectady, N.Y., and the New England settlements. The Iroquois were the Indian allies of the British in the war. An English attack on Quebec led by the Massachusetts Governor Sir William Phips was turned back.

The fighting was ended by the Treaty of Ryswick (1697), but it did little more than give the combatants a breathing spell in the war for the control of land, fisheries and furs in North America.

Kiowa. A small tribe of warlike Indians, whose language origin is not definitely known, was the scourge of the southern plains. They signed their first treaty with the U.S. in 1837. Subsequently, they raided Texas and Mexico until subdued. By the Treaty of Medicine Lodge (1867), they were forced onto a reservation in the Indian Territory in Oklahoma, where they remained except for sporadic outbreaks.

kit and kaboodle. Soldiers carried their shaving gear and knife and fork in their kit. The boodle was the box in which they carried prizes and loot from campaigns. The word "boodle" was perhaps derived

from the Dutch "boedel" meaning property or possessions. The expression came into use in the U.S. during the early 19th century.

Kit Carson. "Kit" was the nickname for Christopher Carson (1809–68), a trapper and guide, who accompanied Frémont on his Western expeditions, including the one associated with the conquest of California (1846–47).

A noted Indian fighter, Carson organized the 1st New Mexican Volunteer Infantry and campaigned successfully against Apaches, Navajos and Comanches during the Civil War. He was made a brigadier general in the Union Army in 1865.

"kitchen cabinet." The uncomplimentary term was applied to a small group of Pres. Jackson's advisers and personal friends who were especially influential during the early years (1829–31) of Jackson's first administration. He conferred with them rather than with his regular Cabinet.

Amos Kendall, one of the group, also called the "lower cabinet," was denounced as Jackson's "thinking machine" and his "lying machine." Others were Martin Van Buren, Francis P. Blair, Sr., John H. Eaton, William B. Lewis and Andrew J. Donelson.

Klamaths. Several Indian tribes of the Lutuami linguistic stock, living in Oregon and California, resisted the influx of whites in the early 1850's. They went on a reservation in 1864, after ceding large tracts of land to the federal government.

Klondike gold rush. The discovery of gold in 1896 on the Klondike River, a tributary of the Yukon, in the Northwest Territory of Canada, precipitated a mass migration to that area. The rush was given impetus, 1897–99, by the ships that arrived at San Francisco with millions of dollars in gold.

Adventurers arriving late on the Klondike found little and moved on to Nome, Fairbanks and other places in Alaska where gold had been discovered. The settlement of Alaska was stimulated by the gold rush.

Knights of Labor. The "Noble and Holy Order of the Knights of Labor" was founded in 1869 in Philadelphia by a group of nine tailors. At first the organization was secret, but the broader vision of Uriah S. Stephens, leader of the tailors, expanded the aims of the society to include all workers without regard to creed, sex, nationality or party. Lawyers, bankers, saloon keepers and gamblers were excluded.

Stephens soon turned to politics and left the Knights. Terence V. Powderly, a Scranton, Pa., machinist, became "Grand Master" in 1878. He pushed the one big union idea and the formation of producers' cooperatives. Although the Knights opposed strikes, their membership was boosted to a peak of 700,000 following a successful strike against Jay Gould's Missouri Pacific Railroad in 1895 by affiliated unions.

The Knights were plagued by internal dissension, failure of the producers' cooperatives, growth of trade unions organized around single skills and the unrelenting opposition of employers. Although the Haymarket riot of 1886 was not the fault of the Knights, public opinion turned against them and contributed to their collapse.

Knights of St. Crispin. An organization of shoemakers was established on industrial lines in 1867. It reached a peak membership of 50,000, becoming the largest labor organization in the U.S. at the time. Through a series of successful strikes, it was effective in enforcing the closed shop. By 1878, however, it had virtually disappeared. Its members joined the Knights of Labor.

Knights of the Golden Horseshoe. In 1716 Gov. Alexander Spotswood of Virginia led a party on an exploring expedition into the Shenandoah Valley. The men's horses, normally unshod in coastal Virginia, were shod for this rough journey. To commemorate the trip, Spotswood later gave pins shaped like a small gold horseshoe to the members of the party— hence the name.

Knights of the White Camelia.
One of the secret organizations
which grew up in the South
during the Reconstruction era,
its aim was to preserve white
supremacy in the South. It replaced the Ku Klux Klan in
Louisiana.

A number of lesser organizations like the Red Jackets, Native Sons of the South, Society
of the White Rose, Knights of
the Black Cross, the White
Brotherhood and others, operated in many parts of the South.
They were lumped together in
the popular imagination as the
Klan.

Know-Nothing party. Later becoming a third party, it had its
origins in the 1840's in "The
Order of the Star Spangled Banner," a merger of several secret
nativist societies such as the
Sons of '76, the Sons of America,
the Druids, the Order of United
Americans and many others. In
secret rites members replied "I
know nothing" when ques-
tioned; hence the popular name
of the American party (known
earlier as the Native American
party).

The Know-Nothings opposed
immigration and resented German and Irish Catholics whose
religious beliefs contrasted with
Protestantism. They advocated
a 21-year residence requirement
for citizenship. It was hoped by
some politicians that this kind
of bigotry might unite Americans and cause them to forget
the slavery issue.

At the party's national convention the Know-Nothings split
over the vote to support the
Kansas-Nebraska Act. Its candidate for President in 1856,
Millard Fillmore, carried only
the state of Maryland. The
party disintegrated with the advent of the Civil War.

Knoxville Road. One of the
early U.S. turnpikes, constructed
1791–95, it linked the Wilderness Road to the Cumberland
settlements in Tennessee.

Korean War (1950–53). Korea
was freed from 50 years of
Japanese rule at the end of
World War II. It was occupied
north of the 38th parallel by
the Soviet Union. U.S. troops
were stationed in the southern
half. In 1948 the UN created a
Korean Commission to supervise
an election throughout the nation but the Soviet zone refused
to participate. The election was
held in the south and the Republic of Korea was established
with UN approval. The Russians then established a Communist government in the north.

On June 25, 1950, North
Korean troops trained and
equipped by Russia invaded
South Korea. The UN Security
Council declared North Korea
to be an aggressor and approved
military action to repel the aggression. After initial reverses
the UN forces (largely U.S.
troops) drove the North Ko-
reans to the Manchurian border. Late in 1950, hopes of
peace were shattered by the
sudden entrance into the war

of large numbers of Chinese Communist troops on the side of their defeated North Korean "comrades." UN forces were pushed back to the 38th parallel where fighting seesawed for months.

A change in UN command was ordered by Pres. Truman in 1951 when he recalled Gen. Douglas MacArthur and named Gen. Matthew B. Ridgway to succeed him. The change was made, Pres. Truman asserted, primarily because Gen. MacArthur was out of sympathy with the administration's plan for limiting the war to Korea.

Truce negotiations begun in 1951 dragged on for years as did the fighting. Finally, in 1953, at Panmunjom near the 38th parallel, UN and Communist representatives signed an armistice agreement. An uneasy peace has prevailed, with UN truce teams on the scene to enforce the armistice terms.

In 1954 the U.S. entered into a treaty with South Korea to come to the aid of that country if it is attacked again.

Ku Klux Klan (KKK). Operating secretly through the South at the end of the Civil War, the society's purpose was to intimidate Negroes and prevent them from voting or seeking equality with whites.

Klansmen rode at night, covered with sheets, and claimed to be the ghosts of Confederate soldiers. At first the Klansmen played pranks on the Negroes but soon their violence, including lynchings, caused with-drawal of the respectable element of southerners who had joined the order. The KKK in the hands of low elements continued to terrorize Negroes.

Congress in 1870 and 1871 passed the Ku Klux Klan Acts which provided severe penalties for violations of the 14th and 15th Amendments. Under these laws, Pres. Grant introduced martial law in several southern states where the rights of freedmen had been violated. Federal rather than state courts were given jurisdiction in such cases.

The Klan died as carpetbag governments were ousted toward the end of the Reconstruction era (about 1877).

A new Ku Klux Klan, organized in 1915, adopted the methods of the Klan which had flourished in Reconstruction days. Its hate program was directed against Negroes, Jews, Catholics and internationalists. The secret ritual of the KKK revolved around "wizards," "goblins" and "Kleagles." The burning of a cross as a warning of impending violence became the Klan's symbol. Its brutal methods included floggings, tar and feather parties and even murder.

The Klan wielded considerable political power in the 1920's and abandoned its secrecy in 1928. At its peak in 1924 its membership was estimated at around 4,500,000, concentrated in the small towns of the South, the Middle West (especially in Indiana) and the Pacific Coast. It survived in the

1930's by stressing anti-Communism and anti-union activities.

In the 1940's state and federal governments, ably reinforced by civil rights organizations, shattered the Klan into local fragments. These have lived on in some southern communities by reverting to the anti-Negro preoccupation of the first Klan.

L

Labor, Department of. The ninth executive department of the federal government was created by Congress in 1913. The Secretary of Labor has a place in the President's Cabinet.

A Bureau of Labor was first created by Congress in 1884 under the Department of the Interior. The Bureau of Labor later became independent as a Department of Labor without executive rank. It again returned to Bureau status in the Department of Commerce and Labor, created in 1903.

The Department of Labor is charged with administering and enforcing laws that promote the welfare of the wage earners of the U.S. and impove their working conditions.

Labor Day. On June 28, 1894, Pres. Cleveland signed a bill making the first Monday in September a legal holiday. It was first celebrated in New York City in 1882 with a parade sponsored by the Central Labor Union.

La Farge, John (1835–1910). Artist. Born in New York City,

he painted chiefly landscapes (1860–76). His mural, *The Ascension* (1876–77), decorating Trinity Church, Boston, led to other commissions, including panels in St. Thomas' Church, N.Y.C., and lunettes in the Supreme Court room of the Minnesota State Capitol at St. Paul. A worker in stained glass, he developed opalescent glass and wrote the pamphlet, *The American Art of Glass* (1893). His paintings include *Christ and Nicodemus* (Trinity Church, Boston), *The Three Kings* (Boston Art Museum), *The Arrival of the Magi* (Church of the Incarnation, N.Y.C.). An example of his work in stained glass is in Columbia Univ. Chapel, N.Y.C.

"Lafayette, we are here." The arrival of the American Expeditionary Force (AEF) in France during World War I was a great stimulant to the French. The right note was struck by Col. Charles E. Stanton on Gen. Pershing's staff when he uttered the famous line at the tomb of Lafayette, July 4, 1917. The sentiment was popularly attributed to Gen. Pershing himself.

Lafayette had served with distinction in the Continental army during the American Revolution, and French aid in the struggle against Britain had been vital to American victory.

La Follette, Robert Marion (1855–1925). Political leader. Born in Primrose, Wis., he became a state and national leader of the progressive movement in American politics. His "Wisconsin Idea" of reform encompassed control of party bosses and expansion of business regulating agencies. He lost the Progressive party nomination for President in 1912 and never forgave Theodore Roosevelt for wresting it from him. La Follette served his state as a member of the U.S. House of Representatives (1885–91); governor of Wisconsin (1901–05) and U.S. Senator (1906–25). He opposed the U.S. entry into World War I, the League of Nations and the World Court. He was the presidential candidate of the League for Progressive Political Action, in 1924, and was defeated.

His son, Robert Marion La Follette, Jr. (1895–1953) succeeded him as U.S. Senator from Wisconsin (1925–47).

La Follette Seamen's Act (1915). The law raised the safety requirements on American ships. It abolished the crime of desertion and released American merchant seamen from bondage to labor contracts upon their return to American ports.

Seamen had become the prey of the "crimp," a combination shipping master and boarding-house keeper. The crimp obtained control of the sailor's employment by taking the sailor into his boardinghouse between jobs and keeping him there until he ran up a huge board bill. The crimp then provided the sailor with a voyage, making him sign over several months' pay which the shipping company paid as soon as the ship cleared, keeping the sailor in a perpetual state of peonage.

Even after the legislation sponsored by Sen. La Follette (Wis.) was passed, the methods of signing on crews remained corrupt and chaotic. Conditions aboard ship remained tyrannical until the 1930's.

La Guardia, Fiorello Henry (1882–1947). Political leader. Born in New York City, he is best remembered as its colorful reform mayor (1934–45), a Republican elected on a Fusion ticket. He served in the U.S. Air Service in World War I, on the Italian front and was a member of the U.S. House of Representatives (1917–21, 1923–33); chief of the U.S. Office of Civilian Defense (1941–42) and Director of U.N. Relief and Rehabilitation Administration (1946).

laissez-faire. The French phrase "let alone" applied to the American economic scene meant "let business alone." This philosophy was expressed by Pres. Van Buren, who did not believe that the government should take steps to end the depression following the Panic of 1837. He stated: "The less government interferes with private pursuits, the better for the general prosperity."

Although this view was typical of the day, it is inaccurate to think of the federal government as following a policy of laissez-faire during the 19th century. The protective tariff and government land grants to railroads were examples of government assistance to business. The growth of regulatory agencies started with the Interstate Commerce Act of 1887 and Sherman Antitrust Act of 1890. The Great Depression of the 1930's made untenable for both political parties a hands-off policy in matters affecting the economic welfare of the nation.

Lake George, battle of (Sept. 8, 1755). Early in the French and Indian War, Gen. William Johnson, commanding a force of 3,500 British regulars and New England militiamen, turned back a French and Indian attack. He was unable however to achieve his purpose of taking Crown Point, N.Y., on Lake Champlain.

"Lame-duck" Amendment. Under the Constitution, before adoption of the 20th Amendment (in effect after 1933), during even-numbered years, congressmen defeated in November met in December with the rest of Congress to make laws, or were inactive right up to Inauguration Day (Mar. 4). This short session of the Congress was called the lame-duck (ducks whose wings had been clipped) session and such defeated congressmen were called lame ducks.

Unless the President called a special session after Mar. 4 in the odd years, the newly elected congressmen did not take seats in the Congress until 13 months after they had been elected.

In Pres. Washington's time, when communication and transportation were slow, delaying the inauguration of the newly elected President and congressmen made sense. But Sen. George W. Norris of Nebraska and many others felt that there was no excuse for such delays in the 20th century. As a result of Norris' efforts, the 20th Amendment (Lame-duck Amendment) was adopted. Under its provisions, the Congress elected in November takes office on Jan. 3 and the newly elected President takes office on Jan. 20.

The term "lame duck" has been applied to executives and legislators defeated for reelection, or non-candidates in a November election, who can still legally act for several weeks until their term of office is ended.

Lancaster Pike. The 62-mile turnpike from Philadelphia to Lancaster, Pa., was a pioneer road-building effort. Construction of this privately financed toll road was begun in 1791 and completed in 1797. It was not freed from tolls until the state purchased the road in 1917.

Lancastrian school system. A system of instruction in which pupil monitors taught small groups, it was first introduced in the U.S. in New York City in 1806. The system was popular from about 1810 to 1830, but went out of use as its defects became evident.

Under the system pupil monitors were first taught a lesson from a printed card by the teacher. They then taught other children in groups of ten what they had learned. The monitors went up and down the rows. In this way groups of from 200 to 1,000 were taught. From the teaching of reading and the catechism, the plan was extended to the teaching of writing, arithmetic, spelling and higher subjects.

The plan was devised by Joseph Lancaster, an English schoolmaster, who needed more teachers in his school but could not afford to pay them. It was developed independently by Andrew Bell, also in England, who described the system in *An Experiment in Education* (1797). The plans of the two men are frequently referred to as the Bell-Lancastrian school.

Land Act of 1796. In accordance with the law, Congress provided for the sale of public lands to the highest bidder with a minimum price of $2 per acre and a minimum purchase of 640 acres. Payment had to be made within a year. The Act provided for the new office of Surveyor General and the division of land into township units six miles square. Land offices were established at Cincinnati and Pittsburgh, but sales went slowly until the terms and size of purchase were lowered by the Land Act of 1800 (Harrison Land Act).

Land Act of 1820. The legislation was intended to curb the speculation in public lands which had resulted from the Land Act of 1800. By eliminating credit provisions, it insured payment to the government for the land sold. The price of the land was reduced from $2 to $1.25 an acre and minimum purchases were reduced from 320 to 80 acres. The full cash payment proved to be a handicap to the pioneer and a boon to the speculator.

land grant colleges. Early in U.S. history the federal government demonstrated its interest in furthering free public education by a policy of generous land grants to the states. The Land Ordinance of 1785 included a provision for the support of local education.

After 1848 new states entering the Union were given sections of land to establish "seminaries of learning." Great universities which benefited from such land grants include Michigan, started in 1817 at Detroit by territorial legislation and moved to Ann Arbor in

1837; Indiana, at Bloomington and Indianapolis, started in 1820, became a university in 1838. Wisconsin, founded in 1848, with its main campus at Madison, has centers throughout the state.

Land grant colleges were given a great boost by the Agricultural College Land Grant Act (1862), popularly known as the Morrill Act, sponsored by Sen. Justin S. Morrill of Vermont. It granted 30,000 acres of public lands for each senator and representative to the states and territories to aid in establishing colleges where agriculture, the mechanical arts and military science and tactics would be taught. The states added the land grant to the endowment of existing state universities, gave the land to private institutions within the state, or established separate agricultural and mechanical colleges.

Land Management, Bureau of. The Bureau was established in 1946 as part of the Department of Interior through consolidation of the General Land Office (created in 1812) and the Grazing Service (formed in 1934). The Bureau is concerned with the use and disposal of public lands and the conservation of natural resources on public lands. It is partially responsible for administration of mineral resources on 800 million acres, approximately one-third of the area of the U.S., and has exclusive jurisdiction for the management of lands and resources on some 477 million acres.

Landrum-Griffin Act (1959). A major labor law amending the Taft-Hartley Act, it is significant as the first real attempt by the federal government to regulate the internal affairs of labor unions. The law is officially known as the Labor-Management Reporting and Disclosures Act.

The "Bill of Rights" for individual union members contained in the Act includes the right to participate fully in meetings and elections. Union members are granted the right to a notice and a fair hearing before any disciplinary action is undertaken by the union.

Each union must file an annual financial report with the Secretary of Labor. Union officers must report any interest they may hold in companies with which their union has dealings. Picketing may not be employed for organizational purposes. Various safeguards protect union funds.

Critics charge that the law is still not tough enough to carry out the wholesale housecleaning that American labor unions require. Labor spokesmen maintain that the law is not intended to reform labor unions but rather to prevent them from carrying on their proper functions in a vigorous way.

Langdell, Christopher Columbus (1826–1906). Lawyer and educator. Born in New Boston, N.H., he was a professor of law at Harvard Law School (1870–1900) and introduced (1870) the "case system" of teaching law, now the system generally used in the U.S. His works include *Cases on the Law of Contracts* (1871) and *A Summary of Equity Pleading* (1877).

Langmuir, Irving (1881–1957). Chemist. Born in Brooklyn, N.Y., he was granted a Ph.D. by the Univ. of Gottingen (1906). He was an associate director (1932–51) of the General Electric Research Laboratory, Schenectady, N.Y. He developed the gas-filled tungsten electric lamp, electron-discharge apparatus, a high vacuum pump, a process of welding using atomic hydrogen. He originated the Lewis-Langmuir atomic theory of atomic structure and valence with Gilbert N. Lewis. He was awarded the Nobel Prize (1932) for his work in surface chemistry.

Lanier, S i d n e y (1842–81). Poet. Born in Macon, Ga., he served in the Confederate Army. He was captured in 1864 and was confined to a federal prison (described in *Tiger-Lilies,* 1867). His poems "Corn" and "The Symphony" (1875) marked the beginnings of his poetic career. He produced verses in accordance with his theories of identity between laws of music and poetry and played the flute in the Peabody Symphony Orchestra, Baltimore, Md. A lecturer on English literature at Johns Hopkins Univ. (1879), his works include *The Science of English Verse* (1880) and *The English Novel* (1883).

Long troubled by ill health, he died of tuberculosis.

Lansing-Ishii Agreement (Nov. 2, 1917). In an exchange of notes Sec. of State Lansing recognized Japan's "special interests" in China in return for reaffirmation of the Open-Door policy in China. Lansing asserted that he meant "economic interests," but the Japanese claimed it as a diplomatic victory and the Chinese condemned it. The agreement was the price for keeping Japan in World War I on the side of the Allies.

The agreement was annulled in 1923 at the Washington Conference.

Laramie, Fort. The fort on the Oregon Trail in what is now Wyoming was established by fur traders in 1834. It was later purchased by the federal government and maintained as a military fort (1849–90), serving as a post in the Indian fighting during much of this period.

By the first Treaty of Fort Laramie (1851) boundaries were established for Indians hostile to each other. In return for presents and cash the Sioux and Shoshone, among others, agreed to permit construction of roads and forts in their territory.

By the second Treaty of Fort Laramie (1868) the federal government agreed to abandon certain forts, restrain settlement of unceded Indian territory and set up a Sioux reservation in

South Dakota with food, clothing and other supplies. In return the Indians agreed to halt their attacks on white settlers and railroad workers.

Late George Apley, The (1937). A novel by John P. Marquand, it satirizes the traditional, conventional life of the Boston brahmins as represented in the person of George Apley, whose habits and sayings are recorded in the book, which won a Pulitzer Prize (1938).

Marquand, a prolific writer, recorded business, society and politics with a satirical touch in his many novels, including *Lord Timothy Dexter* (1925), *Haven's End* (1933), *H. M. Pulham, Esquire* (1941) and *Point of No Return* (1949).

Latin grammar school. Important in the early school development of 17th- and 18th-century New England, it was a school for beginners in Latin. A carryover from England, it was found in the large towns of the middle and southern colonies. The school was aristocratic in type and maintained by the towns for boys who were going on to higher education. The boys started school at age seven and were readied for college at age 15 or 16.

The curriculum was comprised largely of Latin and Greek, with some concession to reading, writing and arithmetic.

Latrobe, Benjamin Henry (1764–1820). Architect and engineer. Born in Yorkshire, England, he came to the U.S. in 1796. He led the Greek revival in America, beginning with his design for the Bank of Pennsylvania (completed 1801) at Philadelphia. He was the engineer for the first city water supply system in America, in Philadelphia (1801–15). Appointed surveyor of U.S. public buildings (1803) by Pres. Jefferson, he revised the plans for the national Capitol drawn up by William Thornton. He took charge of rebuilding the Capitol after the destruction of the War of 1812. He designed numerous homes and institutional buildings, apart from his government work. He made architecture a profession in the U.S.

Lawrence, Ernest Orlando (1901–58). Physicist. Born in Canton, S.D., he invented the cyclotron (1931), an atom-smashing machine, which enabled him to make researches into the structure of the atoms. During World War II he participated in atom bomb research in which the cyclotron was used to separate U-235 from natural uranium. He was awarded the Nobel Prize (1939) for Physics.

League of Nations. Provision for this international peacekeeping organization was made in the fourteenth of Wilson's Fourteen Points. The League Covenant (constitution) was included in the Treaty of Versailles (1919). Wilson looked upon it as "a definite guarantee of peace."

League members pledged themselves to preserve "the territorial integrity" and "political independence" of all other members. The Covenant provided for military, naval and economic sanctions against nations that resorted to war in violation of their League agreements. The League Assembly was composed of all members. The Council was composed of the Great Powers—England, France, Italy and Japan, later also Germany and the U.S.S.R. —and other non-permanent members.

The U.S. never joined the League. Wilson was unsuccessful in winning the two-thirds vote of the Senate required for ratification of the Treaty of Versailles. Sen. Henry Cabot Lodge (Mass.) led the opposition. Wilson was adamant in refusing to accept any of the Lodge Reservations to the League Covenant. "The Senate must take its medicine," Wilson said. It didn't.

The U.S. did participate in a number of League activities, including conferences on control of opium, disarmament and economic affairs. When Japan moved to take over Manchuria in 1931, Sec. of State Stimson's notes of protest supported those from the League Council, to no avail.

The League gradually disintegrated as the world plunged toward World War II. It surrendered its assets, including its headquarters at Geneva, to the United Nations in 1946.

Leatherstocking Tales. James Fenimore Cooper wrote a series of novels dealing with the American frontier. Leatherstocking is the old scout, probably drawn in part from Daniel Boone, whose adventures bind the stories together. He is the immortal type of American frontiersman, strong, self-reliant and devoted to the open country. His retreat before the advance of civilization gives him a touch of tragedy that adds to his stature.

The novels in the chronological order of the events they describe follow: *The Deerslayer* (1841) relates the scout's adventures as a youth in the Lake Otsego (N.Y.) settlement; *The Last of the Mohicans* (1826) deals with the scout in his prime under the name of Hawkeye in the French and Indian War; *The Pathfinder* (1840) narrates his unrequited love for a girl whom he surrenders to a more successful suitor; *The Pioneers* (1823) tells of the return of the old scout, here known as Natty Bumpo, to his boyhood home in the Otsego region; *The Prairie* (1827) concludes the narration of the scout's days as a trapper in the plains west of the Mississippi.

Leavenworth, Fort. The U.S. Army fort was built in 1827 on the Missouri River in northeast Kansas to protect the trade on the Santa Fe Trail. It was used during the Mexican War as the headquarters of the Army of the West and remained an important Union outpost during the Civil War. At present it includes a command and general staff school and a federal penitentiary.

Leaves of Grass (1855). Walt Whitman continued to add to and revise the *Leaves* until his death. His first volume of poetry, it captured the hurly-burly life of working America. The poems broke in content and form from the New England school of poetry and expressed the new democracy of a nation finding itself. Whitman looked to the people for his inspiration. His love of people explains his unprecedented use of words ordinarily excluded from polite verse ("I recken," "gallivant," "duds," "folks," "blab"). Whitman's democratic credo is contained in his book of essays, *Democratic Vistas* (1871).

Lecompton Constitution (1857). The constitution of the Kansas Territory, drawn up at Lecompton, Kan., guaranteed slavery. It was written by proslavery men who had been chosen as delegates in an election from which free-state men abstained. When the constitution was presented to the electorate of Kansas, it was turned down. It was not until 1861 that Kansas entered the Union as a free state.

Lederberg, Joshua (1925–   ). Geneticist. Born in Montclair, N.J., he was granted a Ph.D. by Yale (1947). In 1958 he was awarded the Nobel Prize for Medicine/Physiology for discoveries relating to genetic material of bacteria. His research in virus breeding is basic to the control of virus diseases.

Lee, Richard Henry (1732–94). Revolutionary statesman. Born in Westmoreland Co., Va., he entered the House of Burgesses in 1758 and became a leading defender of colonial rights. He organized the "Westmoreland Association" (1766) against the importation of British goods until the Stamp Act should be repealed. He helped to initiate intercolonial committees of correspondence. As a Virginia delegate to the Continental Congress (1774–79), he introduced the resolution calling for a declaration of independence. A member of Congress (1784–89), he opposed the new Constitution. His *Letters of the Federal Farmer* (1787, 1788) became an anti-Federal textbook. As U.S. Senator from Virginia (1789–92), he was active in adding the Bill of Rights to the Constitution.

Lee, Robert Edward (1807–70). Commander-in-chief of Confederate armies. He was born in Stratford, Va. Graduated from the U.S. Military Academy (1829), he was its superintendent (1852–53). Offered a field command by Pres. Lincoln, he declined and resigned from the U.S. Army. He took command of the Army of northern Virginia (1862); he was checked at Antietam, Md. (Sept. 17, 1862). Almost always outnumbered, he turned back Federal attacks at Fredericksburg (Dec. 13, 1862) and Chancellorsville (May 2–4, 1863). He was decisively defeated at Gettysburg, Pa. (July 1–4, 1863). A great strategist, he fought doggedly but was finally overwhelmed by Grant and surrendered to him at Appomattox Courthouse, Va. (Apr. 9, 1865). He became president of Washington College, in Lexington, Va. (Sept. 1865), rebuilding the college which was renamed Washington and Lee University.

Lee's Resolutions (June 7, 1776). Three resolutions that cast the die for revolution were introduced into the Continental Congress by Richard Henry Lee of Virginia. The first announced the right of the colonies to be free and independent of the British Crown. The second urged the colonies to conclude arrangements for foreign alliances. The third proposed that the colonies form themselves into a confederation under a constitution to be approved by each state.

The Congress adopted the resolutions and appointed a committee that included Jefferson to draft a declaration of independence.

legal tender. The term designates currency that the government authorizes for business transactions and payment of taxes and debts, public and private. During the American Revolution the states issued paper currency that they declared to be legal tender. It was fiat money for it was not convertible into specie (gold, for example), and it declined sharply in value. Under the Constitution the power of issuing currency was taken away from the states and granted to the national government.

During the Civil War the federal government issued treasury notes (paper money known as "greenbacks") without gold or silver backing and not redeemable in coin. This currency was declared to be legal tender, but it soon depreciated in value. Businessmen did not want to accept it in payment of debts.

After the Civil War greenbacks continued to circulate. When businessmen refused to accept them as legal tender, their legality was tested in the U.S. Supreme Court. In *Hepburn v. Griswold* (1870) the Court decided that Congress did not have the right to require that the currency issued be legal tender, especially in payment of debts contracted before the greenbacks were issued in 1862. Pres. Grant then appointed two new justices to the Supreme Court. When the question came up again, the Court in the Legal Tender Cases reversed itself (*Knox v. Lee* and *Parker v. Davis*, both 1871) and held that Congress could declare paper money legal tender. It is legal tender today.

Lehman, Herbert Henry (1878–1963). Banker and political leader. Born in New York City, he was graduated from Williams College (1899). He left the banking firm of Lehman Brothers to enter New York politics where he made a notable record sponsoring social and welfare legislation, while reforming the state administration. A Democrat, he was lieutenant governor of New York (1928–32) and governor (1932–42). Before entering the national political scene, Lehman served as director of foreign relief and rehabilitation (1942). His liberal record was continued in the U.S. Senate (1949–57), where he was among the first to speak out against McCarthyism.

Leisler's Rebellion (1689). Jacob Leisler, a German-born merchant, seized control of southern New York when news was received of the overthrow of King James II. Leisler's revolt against aristocratic families with trade monopolies in New York was supported by small farmers and city workers.

Although Leisler yielded control of the fort in New York when a new governor arrived, he had refused to yield to troops preceding the governor. He was tried for treason in 1691 and hanged before he could appeal to the Crown. Four years later Parliament recognized that an injustice had been done and restored his estate to his family.

Lend-Lease Act (Mar. 11, 1941). When Britain could no longer pay cash for goods transported in her own vessels, Pres. F. D. Roosevelt told the nation, "We must be the great arsenal of democracy." The President asked and received from Congress power to "lend or lease" to governments resisting Hitler any American materials that they needed. Before World War II ended the amount distributed in this way reached a value of $50 billion of which 69% went to Britain, 25% to the Soviet Union, and lesser quantities to other Allies. In exchange the U.S. received goods and services valued at about $6 billion, most of which came from Britain.

Letters from a Farmer. . . . (1767). John Dickinson of Pennsylvania published a popular pamphlet, *Letters from a Farmer in Pennsylvania to the Inhabitants of the British Colonies*, in which he attacked the Townshend Acts as unconstitutional and decried Parliament's action against the New York assembly as a danger to colonial liberty. One of the Acts had suspended the assembly's law-making powers until it accepted the Quartering Act.

Letters from an American Farmer (1782). In a series of essays the French writer, J. Hector St. John de Crèvecoeur, depicted rural life in minute detail. He saw the American as "a new man, who acts upon new principles." De Crèvecoeur was one of the first in a long line of foreign commentators on the American character.

Lewis, Gilbert Newton (1875–1946). Chemist. Born in Weymouth, Mass., he was granted a Ph.D. by Harvard (1899). His work includes studies on thermodynamic theory and its application to chemistry. He collaborated with Ernest O. Lawrence in inventing the cyclotron (atom-smashing machine) and with Irving Langmuir on the Lewis-Langmuir theory of atomic structure and valence. He is author of *The Anatomy of Science* (1926).

Lewis, John Llewellyn (1880–1969). Labor leader. Born in Lucas, Ia., he was president of United Mine Workers (1920–60). He resigned from the AFL (1935) and worked with Sidney Hillman and David Dubinsky to form the Committee for Industrial Organization and became president of the CIO (1935–40). With Hillman he organized (1936) Labor's Non-Partisan League, to mobilize the working-class vote in industrial centers for reelection of Pres. F. D. Roosevelt. Later, he split with Roosevelt and kept his promise to resign from the presidency of CIO if Roosevelt were elected for a third term. He broke with Philip Murray, new president of CIO, in 1942, and took the UMW out of the CIO. He led the coal strike (Apr. 1946) in which the U.S. government seized the mines, but won labor's demands when mines were returned to owners.

Lewis and Clark Expedition (1804–06). The expedition was authorized by Congress at Pres. Jefferson's urging to explore not only the Louisiana Territory but far beyond it. Although its purpose was partially scientific, it also aimed to seek new supplies and outlets for American fur-trappers and traders.

The party of about 45 men was headed by Meriwether Lewis, an experienced wilderness explorer who took as his colleague William Clark, younger brother of George Rogers Clark and an experienced frontiersman in his own right. Also in the group was the wife of one of the interpreters, Sacajawea (the Bird Woman), a beautiful Snake girl, who became a heroine in the journals of Lewis and Clark.

The group started near St. Louis and ascended the Missouri. They then crossed the Continental Divide and followed the Snake and Columbia rivers to the Pacific Ocean, thereby establishing the U.S. claim to the Oregon country. On the return voyage the party broke into three groups in order to expand their report on the territory they explored. Their journal became a vital source of information for mapmakers and settlers.

Lexington, battle of (Apr. 19, 1775). The first battle of the American Revolution was fought more than a year before the colonists definitely decided on independence; 700 British regulars marching toward Concord to seize provincial military stores met resistance from Minutemen at Lexington. Eight of the Minutemen were killed and ten wounded.

The British were only briefly delayed on the march to Concord, but the skirmish aroused colonial militancy.

Lexow Committee. Denunciation of conditions under Tammany's rule of New York City led the New York State legislature to establish an investigating committee in 1893. It uncovered vice and graft and led to the defeat of the Tammany candidate for mayor in 1894. William L. Strong, head of the "Fusion" ticket, was elected mayor.

Leyte Gulf, battle of (Oct. 1944). In one of the great naval actions of World War II the U.S. Navy defeated the Japanese Navy and virtually ended whatever chance Japan might have had of winning the war in the Pacific.

The Navy's primary objective was to protect troop landings on Leyte, in the Philippines. Approximately 166 American and 70 Japanese warships, 1,280 American and 716 Japanese warplanes were engaged. The U.S. had the Seventh Fleet under Vice-Adm. Thomas C. Kincaid and the Third Fleet under Adm. William F. ("Bull") Halsey, Jr. in direct support in the Leyte area. The Japanese fleets avoided complete annihilation.

The great naval battle left the Japanese in a critical position in the Philippines. Gen.

Douglas MacArthur now had a land wedge, and the Japanese could no longer provide reinforcements or supplies for their picked troops scattered in isolated pockets over the Philippines.

Libby prison. Warehouses were converted into a Confederate prison in Richmond, Va. to hold captured Union officers. It was notorious for crowding and generally bad conditions. The prison got its name from the company that owned the warehouses.

Liberal party. A trade union-oriented organization in New York, it was formed in 1942 following a split in the American Labor party. A minor political party, its weight has at times been considerable in determining the nomination and election of major party candidates in city and state elections. In 1966, for the first time, it failed to support the Democratic candidate for governor and nominated its own candidate, who was defeated.

Liberal Republican party. In 1872 a reform wing of the Republican party left the regulars who supported Pres. Grant for a second term. At a national convention in Cincinnati they nominated Horace Greeley for President. The Democrats, knowing their own candidate could not win, also nominated Greeley.

The new party had its origins

in Missouri where Liberal Republicans under the leadership of Carl Schurz had ousted the carpetbag government. The national party attracted civil service reformers, critics of the Grant administration scandals and regular Republicans disgruntled with their share of the spoils. The diverse assemblage was united only in its opposition to Grant. It erred in nominating Horace Greeley, who was ridiculed as a crackpot in the press. Liberal Republicans were overwhelmingly defeated in the election of 1872 and the party disintegrated.

Liberator, The (1831–65). The antislavery weekly was published in Boston under the editorship of the radical abolitionist, William Lloyd Garrison. Garrison kept the promise printed in his first issue: "I am in earnest—I will not equivocate—I will not excuse—I will not retreat a single inch—AND I WILL BE HEARD."

Liberty Bell. The bell first reached Philadelphia in 1752 after it had been ordered to commemorate the 50th anniversary of Penn's Charter of Liberties. It was cast in London and bore an inscription from Leviticus xxv. 10: "Proclaim liberty throughout the land unto all the inhabitants thereof." While being tested the bell cracked. It was recast but cracked again when tolling for the funeral of John Marshall in 1835.

The bell, rung at the time the Continental Congress met in Philadelphia, became known as the Liberty Bell. It is on exhibition in Independence Hall, Philadelphia.

"liberty cabbage." Sauerkraut was renamed soon after the U.S. declared war on Germany in 1917. It was as nonsensical as renaming the dachshund "liberty pup," but it indicated the extent of anti-German feeling in the U.S.

Liberty League. The shortlived organization was financed by conservative millionaires who were united by their hatred of F. D. Roosevelt and the New Deal. In 1936 it supported Alfred Landon for President. Al Smith, a disaffected Democrat and prominent Liberty League member, led in denouncing the New Deal as socialistic.

Roosevelt ridiculed the League for attributing to him "the worst features of Ivan the Terrible, Machiavelli, Judas Iscariot, Henry VIII, Charlotte Corday, and Jesse James."

Liberty party. One of the many third-parties in U.S. history, it was comprised of moderate Abolitionists who favored political action to do away with slavery. Its candidate for President, James G. Birney, garnered only 7,069 votes in 1840 and 62,300 votes in 1844, less than one-half of 1% of the total vote. In 1848 it merged with the Free Soil party.

liberty poles. Poles and trees were used by the Sons of Liberty as symbols of the protest against British misrule. In Boston, New York, Philadelphia, Charleston and other colonial cities, meetings were held around them and handbills were posted on them. On Jan. 13, 1770, the liberty pole set up by patriotic citizens in New York was cut down by British soldiers.

Liberty Tree. A Boston mob hanged the effigy of Andrew Oliver who had agreed to distribute stamps under the Stamp Act. The tree from which the effigy was hung was consecrated, Aug. 14, 1765, as "The Tree of Liberty."

libraries. Personal libraries were acquired by some plantation owners, merchants, clergymen, physicians and lawyers during the colonial period. Books were imported from abroad and tastes included the classics, science, theology and popular writers of the day. By the time of his death in 1728, Cotton Mather, Puritan clergyman, had acquired a library of 3,000 volumes. William Byrd II, who died in 1744, had a library of 4,000 volumes.

In the 18th century merchants supported proprietary libraries (owned by shareholders) in many large towns. Nonshareholders were admitted on payment of an annual fee. In practice, these libraries were used by the professional and merchant groups that supported them.

Free circulating parish libraries were established in the late 17th and early 18th centuries in Annapolis, New York City, Charleston and other towns, by the Rev. Thomas Bray, cofounder of the Society for the Propagation of the Gospel in Foreign Parts. Later, these parish or "social" libraries multiplied in New England. Their volumes of theology, biography and history provided the foundations for the learning of boys like Elihu Burritt, called the "Learned Blacksmith."

Semipublic subscription libraries of the colonial period included the Library Company of Philadelphia (1731), Redwood Library, Newport, R.I. (1747), Charleston Library Society (1748) and New York Society Library (1754). Libraries suffered pilfering and reduction of funds during the Revolutionary War.

The Library of Congress, established in 1800, was enriched in 1815 by the purchase of Thomas Jefferson's collection of rare books. In 1825 the Library was damaged by fire, but it soon went on to become "a great national monument to learning." State libraries were established by New York and New Hampshire in 1820.

By 1800 there were 50 semipublic proprietary libraries in the U.S. with 80,000 volumes. By 1825 there were that many libraries and 20 times the number of books in the four largest cities alone. In the West, small libraries appeared in Lexington (1795), Cincinnati (1802), Vincennes (1808), Louisville (1816), Detroit (1817) and St. Louis (1824). In 1814 the several circulating libraries in Pittsburgh formed the Pittsburgh Permanent Library. In 1830 Transylvania University (Lexington, Ky.), with its 2,000 volumes, had the largest library in the West. In general, western libraries followed the eastern pattern of proprietary, subscription and "social" libraries. But books reached only a small proportion of the people in town and country. The days of the free public library had not yet arrived.

The desire of the middle classes in the cities for more reading matter took form in the founding in 1820, in New York City, of the Mercantile Library Association and the Apprentices' Library Association. Boston and Philadelphia soon had comparable libraries. The lower ranks of the middle class were served by the growth of mechanics' and apprentices' libraries in many cities in the 1820's and later.

In 1833 the New Hampshire legislature was the first to permit towns to establish tax-supported libraries. Even earlier some New England towns acquired shares in proprietary libraries. Government support of public libraries was spurred in 1838 when New York State provided funds for district school libraries. By 1850 there were

over 12,000 such libraries, chiefly in New York and New England, and they held more than 1,500,000 books. In 1848 Boston was permitted by the state legislature to use public funds for the support of the projected Boston Public Library, the first institution like the public library today. Between 1825 and 1850 the number of libraries of all sorts doubled over the preceding 25 years bringing the total to 550.

The Civil War stimulated reading and expansion of libraries in the North. In the post-Civil War period, free public libraries reached many who could not afford lecture fees. Library building was aided by the philanthropies of Enoch Pratt of Baltimore, Samuel J. Tilden of New York and, above all, by Andrew Carnegie. In 1881 Carnegie made his first offer to donate public library buildings to municipalities, provided that each agreed to finance the library by annual taxes.

In 1876 the American Library Association held its first convention, and in that year the *Library Journal* was established. Library cataloguing was made efficient by Melvil Dewey who originated the Dewey "decimal classification." He founded the New York State Library School in 1887.

By 1900 there were over 1,700 free public libraries in the U.S. with 5,000 or more books. The New York Public Library was founded (1895) out of the consolidation of the Astor (1848) and Lenox (1870) Libraries and funds provided in the Tilden Trust (1886). It became the largest public library in the U.S. with over 5,000,000 volumes.

Library of Congress. The library, in Washington, D.C., was established by Congress in 1800 under a law appropriating $5,000 "for the purchase of such books as may be necessary for the use of Congress." As it has developed the Library serves the public and the entire governmental establishment so that it has become a national library for the U.S. Its first responsibility however remains service to Congress. One department, the Legislative Reference Service, functions exclusively for the legislative branch of the government.

licks. A lick is either a saline stream or a muddy deposit impregnated with salt. Both men and animals have worn trails to find the salt so essential to their diet. It is probable that if licks had not been discovered in the trans-Appalachian region, settlement of the West would have been delayed or severely handicapped.

Place names in the U.S. have been identified with licks, especially in Kentucky where the Licking River flows into the Ohio. Big Bone Lick, Ky., was first discovered early in the 18th century and contained the skeletons of mastodons.

Lightning. One of the famous clipper ships designed by Donald McKay of East Boston, Mass., it was launched in 1854. The *Lightning* made a day's run of 436 miles on her maiden voyage, a record run.

"lily-whites." The term arose in Reconstruction days and was used by Negroes to describe Republicans who did not want Negroes in the party. Republicans who accepted Negroes in the party were known as "black and tans."

The term was widely used in newspapers covering the Republican national convention of 1888. A Negro national committeeman, N. Wright Cuney, "boss" of Texas, said that Republicans bolting the party regarded themselves as too good to clasp their "lily-white" hands with those of Negroes.

Lincoln, Abraham (1809–65). Sixteenth President of the U.S. He was born in Hodgenville, Hardin County (now Larue County), Ky. He practiced law in Illinois and was elected to the state legislature (1834–41). He was a member of the U.S. House of Representatives (1847–49). Although he was the unsuccessful candidate for U.S. Senate (1858), his debates with Sen. Stephen Douglas made him the leading Republican candidate for President (1860). He firmly opposed the extension of slavery before the Civil War and determined to unite the nation as an outcome of the war. He made the immortal Gettysburg Address and signed the Emancipation Proclamation in 1863. He was shot on Apr. 14, 1865 and died the next day.

Lincoln County War. In the 1870's a factional struggle broke out among cattlemen in New Mexico. On one side was John Chisum, King of the Pecos, who was the biggest cattle owner in the world. He gave his backing to Billy the Kid (William H. Bonney) in the struggle against farmers and small ranchers. The war on the flatlands between gunmen of both sides became a battle between the forces of so-called law and outlawry when a sheriff handpicked by the small ranchers was killed.

Pres. Hayes appointed Gen. Lew Wallace, Governor of the Territory of New Mexico (1878–81), for the express purpose of ending the killings. When it was all over, after a major fight in July 1878, John Chisum was still the boss of the narrow Pecos River valley.

Lincoln-Douglas debates (1858). The seven debates, each in a different congressional district in Illinois, were part of the campaign for a seat in the U.S. Senate.

Stephen Douglas, the "Little Giant," attacked Abraham Lincoln's "house divided" position, contending that it would lead to a "war of extermination." Lincoln replied that he did not propose to interfere with slavery where it already existed but that he opposed its extension. His position was in accord with the Republican platform of 1854. Furthermore, he denied Douglas' allegation that he favored social equality for Negroes.

At Freeport, Lincoln asked how Douglas could support the Dred Scott decision and yet advocate popular sovereignty. Douglas answered in a practical vein that slavery could not exist anywhere unless it was protected by local law.

Senator Douglas was re-elected by the state legislature where his supporters outnumbered Lincoln's. But his Freeport statement caused him to lose support in the South, divide the Democratic party and be defeated in the presidential election of 1860.

Lincoln's assassination (Apr. 14, 1865). The President was shot in the head at about 10:13 P.M. while seeing a play called *Our American Cousin* in Ford's Theater, Washington, D.C. The same night, Sec. of State Seward was shot and wounded in his home. Lincoln died without regaining consciousness at 7:22 A.M., Apr. 15. Following a prayer by Lincoln's pastor, the silence was broken by Sec. of War Stanton's calm sentence: "Now he belongs to the ages."

The assassin, John Wilkes Booth, a mentally deranged actor, had jumped from Lincoln's theater box to the stage, paused a moment to brandish a gun and shout *Sic semper tyrannis!* He fled to Virginia where he was shot Apr. 26, during a siege of his hiding place. Nine others implicated in the plot were tried before a military commission and either hanged or imprisoned.

The national tragedy was given added dimension by the failure of Pres. Johnson to gain congressional acceptance of the lenient Reconstruction plan advanced by Lincoln before his death.

Lind, Jenny, tours America. Jenny Lind, the "Swedish nightingale," was the most popular singer in America in 1850. She enjoyed an enormously successful tour of the U.S. under the management of P. T. Barnum, before returning to Europe in 1852.

Lindbergh Kidnapping Case. The infant son of Col. Charles A. Lindbergh (famous for his non-stop solo flight to Paris, 1927) was kidnapped from his home in Hopewell, N.J., Mar. 1, 1932. A ransom of $50,000 was paid but the baby's dead body was found on May 12. In Sept. 1934, Bruno Hauptmann, a carpenter, was arrested when he attempted to pass a $20 bill of the ransom money. More of the ransom money was found in his home and the ladder used in the kidnapping was identified as his. Hauptmann was executed, Apr. 3, 1936.

linotype. Invented by Ottmar Mergenthaler, a Baltimore machinist, the keyboard method of typecasting revolutionized newspaper publishing. It was first used successfully in the composing room of the New York *Tribune* in 1886.

linsey-woolsey. Colonial settlers in coastal towns and on the frontier spun at home a coarse fabric woven from linen warp and coarse wool filling. Its use for rough work clothes was continued into the 19th century. The term is British in origin.

Lipmann, Fritz Albert (1899–   ). Biochemist. Born in Königsberg, Prussia, he became a U.S. citizen in 1944. He was awarded the Nobel Prize (1953) for Medicine and Physiology for isolating coenzyme A, vital in the body-building process, and demonstrating how it produces fatty acids and steroids essential to the body's growth.

Lisa, Manuel (1772–1820). Fur trader. Born in New Orleans, La., he led an expedition up the Missouri River (1807–08) and explored the region. He built Fort Manuel, on the upper Missouri, the first structure of its kind and established a trading post at the mouth of the Big Horn River (other posts established in successive trips). He joined with Andrew Henry, first to trap west of the Rockies, Pierre Chouteau and others in the Missouri Fur Co. (1808).

Literacy Test Act (1917). The bill requiring immigrants to pass a literacy test was passed over Pres. Wilson's veto. It stated that no alien over 16 would be admitted to the U.S.

unless he could read some language. Since relatively few immigrants from southern and eastern Europe could meet the requirement, the purpose of the law was "restriction, not selection," the President stated. Four earlier Presidents had been successful in vetoing similar literacy test bills.

Little Belt affair (1811). As an outcome of U.S. efforts to protect American commerce, the American frigate *President* mistakenly attacked the British corvette *Little Belt* killing nine British seamen and wounding 23. The *President* had been seeking the *Guerrière,* a larger British raider.

Britain protested the attack on the *Little Belt.* The U.S. offered a settlement if the British would revoke the Orders-in-Council. The British refused and the U.S. public hailed the attack on the *Little Belt* as a warning to "the mistress of the seas" that the U.S. was prepared to defend its commerce. A year later the U.S. was at war with Britain (War of 1812).

Little Crow. The Minnesota Sioux, the four Dakota subtribes known as the Santee, believed themselves cheated by a treaty they had signed and, under Little Crow in 1862, murdered some 650 settlers and killed 100 soldiers before they were driven out of Minnesota to join the other Dakotas on the plains. In 1863 Little Crow was shot by a farm youth while he was foraging for berries.

Little Giant. Stephen A. Douglas (1813–61) of Illinois was nicknamed the "Little Giant" because of his small stature and great abilities.

Little Magician. The nickname was fastened on Pres. Martin Van Buren, who was small in stature but dexterous in his political maneuvers in New York and on the national scene.

Livingston, Edward (1764–1836). Lawyer and statesman. He was born in Columbia Co., N.Y. Mayor of New York City (1801–03), he was held responsible when a customhouse clerk stole funds. He gave up his property to make restitution, and moved to New Orleans, La. He completed a new Louisiana penal code (1825) which aimed at the prevention rather than punishment of crime. Sir Henry Maine called him "the first legal genius of modern times." He served in U.S. House of Representatives (1823–29) and was U.S. Senator from Louisiana (1829–31). As Jackson's Sec. of State (1831–33), he drafted the 1832 proclamation to the South Carolina nullifiers.

Livingston, Robert R. (1746–1813). Lawyer and diplomat. Born in New York City, and member of Continental Congress (1775–79, 1779–81, 1784–85), he helped to draft the Declaration of Independence but favored its postponement. He was secretary of the Department of Foreign Affairs (1781–83). Deeply involved in New

York affairs, he was active on behalf of ratification of the Constitution, and became chancellor of New York State (1777–1801). He was a U.S. minister to France (1801–04) and successfully negotiated the Louisiana Purchase (1803). He aided Robert Fulton in building his steamboat and obtained a monopoly of steam navigation on the Hudson, terminated by *Gibbons v. Ogden* (1824). The steamboat *Clermont* was named for his estate in New York.

lobbying. The term describes the efforts of pressure groups to influence the passage of legislation on federal, state and local levels. Sometimes the lobbyist uses reason to get a legislator to favor or oppose a bill. He may be an expert in the legislative area and can supply the legislator with valuable information. At other times the lobbyist may entertain legislators lavishly or promise them jobs when they no longer hold elective office. Lobbyists represent diverse groups. Some speak for tobacco, liquor or other business interests. Others act on behalf of labor unions, teachers, war veterans and hundreds of other interests. Lobbyists have so much influence that they are sometimes said to make up a "third house of Congress."

Under Title III of the Legislative Reorganization Act of 1946 "lobbyists" seeking to influence Congress are required to register with the government and give an accounting of the money they spend and where it comes from. While the law has not effectively controlled lobbying, it reflects the concern of Congress with the problem.

Lochner v. N.Y. (1905). The U.S. Supreme Court held unconstitutional a New York law which limited the work week in the bakery industry to 60 hours. Lochner, owner of a Utica bakery, had been convicted of violating the law.

In overruling the conviction, the Court held that the "right to make a contract in relation to his business is part of the liberty of the individual protected by the Fourteenth Amendment. . . . Clean and wholesome bread does not depend upon whether the baker works but ten hours per day or only sixty hours a week. The limitation of the hours of labor does not come within the police power on that ground."

In a dissent from the majority opinion, Justice Holmes, whose dissents shaped history, argued: "The Fourteenth Amendment does not enact Mr. Herbert Spencer's *Social Statics* . . . a constitution is not intended to embody a particular economic theory, whether of paternalism . . . or of laissez-faire." Holmes stated that the word "'liberty' in the 14th Amendment is perverted" when it is used to prevent the state from limiting hours of work as "a proper measure on the score of health."

Locofocos. The name designated a Democratic faction in New

York that opposed conservative Tammany leadership and gained control of a regular party meeting in 1835. When the regulars turned off the gaslight, the radicals lit candles with "locofoco" matches. The name was used derisively by opponents of the Democratic party for two decades after the incident.

The Locofocos, comprised largely of city workers, favored hard money rather than the depreciated paper money with which they were paid wages. They opposed the Bank of the United States as a force which kept the little man down and prevented him from climbing the economic ladder. Locofocos were linked with Jacksonian democracy and had a role in persuading Van Buren to adopt the Independent Treasury System.

Lodge corollary. The Monroe Doctrine was expanded to include an Asian power and a foreign company. The resolution was proposed by Sen. Henry Cabot Lodge (Mass.) and approved by the Senate, Aug. 2, 1912. It stated that the U.S. disapproved of the transfer of strategic spots in the Americas to non-American private companies which might be acting for a foreign power.

The declaration was regarded as unnecessary and provocative by Pres. Taft. It was made when a Japanese company sought to obtain a tract of land in the vicinity of Magdalena Bay in lower California but was dissuaded from completing the project by the U.S. State Department. The tract had potentialities as a naval base and could have threatened California, the Panama Canal and the line of communications between these two points.

Lodge Reservations. Republican Sen. Lodge (Mass.) formulated his opposition to the League of Nations in 14 reservations. He believed that U.S. membership in the League without qualifications would threaten America's interests. He did not want the U.S. to use its armed forces to sustain any article of the Treaty of Versailles without the specific approval of Congress. One of the reservations opposed Article X, which insured the permanence of the territorial boundaries agreed upon at Versailles. Wilson regarded this as "the heart of the Covenant." Other modifications by the reservationists stated that the League had no right to interfere in any question involving the Monroe Doctrine or the domestic affairs of the U.S.

Wilson feared, perhaps mistakenly, that acceptance of any of the reservations would indicate weakness and invite additional reservations. He urged his supporters not to vote for the reservations. On Nov. 19, 1919, Wilson's supporters, joined by opponents of the League, rejected the Treaty and with it the League.

logrolling. The settlement of intersectional differences in Congress has been managed by what has been called logrolling. It means "I will vote for what you want, if you will vote for what I want," or sometimes "I will abandon my demands if you will give up yours."

The term was borrowed from the frontier where pioneers helped a neighbor clear the land, roll the logs and build his cabin.

Logstown, Treaty of (June 13, 1752). Iroquois and Delaware Indians ceded to Virginia lands south of the Ohio River and permitted the Ohio Company to build a fort and settle that area. The agreement encouraged settlement of the lands west of the Allegheny Mts.

London, Jack (1876–1916). Novelist. Born in San Francisco, his early years included experience as a seaman, janitor and hobo. He became a socialist before joining the gold rush to the Klondike (1897–98). After his return, he devoted himself to writing and produced some 50 books, most of them fiction.

He was deeply concerned with the brute struggle of men in the capitalist society he condemned. *The Call of the Wild* (1903), a novel about a pack of dogs in the Yukon, depicts the struggle in the animal world. *The Iron Heel* (1907) portrays a bitter fight to the death between workers and capitalists. The autobiographical *Martin Eden* (1909) tells the story of the bitter struggle of a working-class youth who seeks respectability and a literary career.

London was widely read early in the 20th century. His works continue to be popular in the Soviet Union.

London Company (Virginia Company of London). In 1606 a group of English promoters obtained from King James I a grant of land in America fronting 100 miles along the sea and extending 100 miles inland with the exclusive right to colonize between the 38th and 34th parallels. In 1607 the London promoters established at Jamestown, Va., the first permanent English settlement in the area. The Company was dissolved in 1624.

London Economic Conference (June–July 1933). The World Monetary and Economic Conference sought to check the world depression by means of international financial and economic agreements. Commodity agreements were reached by silver and wheat producing nations, but the Conference foundered on currency stabilization. It broke up when Pres. Roosevelt refused to halt devaluation of the dollar which he permitted to sink in relative value to foreign currencies by taking the U.S. off the gold standard.

London Naval Treaty of 1930. At a conference called by Great Britain, at the suggestion of Pres. Hoover, the U.S., Great Britain and Japan agreed on the respective number of smaller ships—cruisers, destroyers and submarines that each nation might maintain. This had been left unlimited by the Washington Conference of 1922 and naval competition had continued. The ratio agreed upon in 1930 was generally 10–10–7 with the Japanese winning equality in submarines. France and Italy did not sign the Treaty. An "escalator clause" provided that if any power believed itself endangered by a growth in tonnage of a non-signatory power, it could increase its tonnage.

As Japan's involvement in Manchuria deepened, she demanded parity. When this was refused in 1934, Japan notified the other powers that on Dec. 31, 1936, she would no longer be bound by any part of the Washington or London agreements. A naval race followed.

Japan did not sign the London Naval Treaty of 1936; nor did Italy, angered by the application of sanctions by the League of Nations in the Ethiopian War. The U.S., Great Britain and France agreed to minor limitations, largely made ineffective by numerous "escape" clauses. In 1938 Congress voted a billion-dollar naval-building program.

Lonely Crowd, The (1950). In analyzing modern American life the sociologists David Riesman, Nathan Glazer and Reuel Denney contrast the 19th-century and the 20th-century American. They suggest that the former was "inner-directed," driven by personal ambition, highly competitive and sometimes ruthless in seeking mastery of the world in which he lived. The 20th-century American they believe to be "other-directed," seeking to get ahead by working within a "group" and attuning himself to the needs of others. The change in "direction" of American individuals, they allege, explains the change in the economy's emphasis from new departures in production to efficient administration of established businesses and deft salesmanship.

Long, Huey Pierce, assassination of (Sept. 8, 1935). The U.S. Senator from Louisiana, known as the "Kingfish," was shot to death by Dr. Carl A. Weiss, a Louisianan who had a personal grievance against him. Long, who had been governor, was the virtual dictator of the state. He had won a national following through his vaguely developed "share the wealth" plan.

Long Drive. The first attempt to herd Texas cattle northward to a profitable market was made in 1866. The drive through the Red River country in the Texas Panhandle to the railhead at Sedalia, Mo. was not a complete success. The following year a better trail was laid out and the Texans herded thousands of cattle north with fewer losses. The Long Drive was always a hazardous undertaking for the cowboys who acted as drovers.

Longfellow, Henry Wadsworth (1807–82). Poet. Born in Portland, Me., he became a professor of modern languages at Bowdoin College (1829–35) and at Harvard (1836–54). He achieved an international reputation as a poet. Except for his interest in abolition of slavery (*Poems on Slavery*, 1842), he was not active in social reform. Influenced by Goethe and the German romantic lyricists, he introduced hexameters, successful in German narrative poems, into American verse.

Longfellow wrote *Hyperion* (1839), which describes the journey of a young man in search of his soul; *Evangeline* (1847), the story of the expulsion of the Acadians from Grand Pré in Nova Scotia; *The Song of Hiawatha* (1855), based on the hero myths and customs of American Indians; *The Courtship of Miles Standish* (1858), which recorded the Pilgrims' first memorable romance, containing Priscilla's often quoted remark to John Alden, "Why don't you speak for yourself, John?"

Among his other works were *Ballads and Other Poems* (1841), which contains "The Village Blacksmith," "Excelsior" and "The Wreck of the Hesperus"; *Tales of a Wayside Inn* (1863), which includes "Paul Revere's Ride"; *The Divine Comedy of Dante Alighieri* (a translation issued 1865–67); and *In the Harbor* (1882).

Longhorns. Texas steers predominated on the ranges of northern Mexico and the Great Plains in the 19th century. They were developed from Spanish cattle introduced at Vera Cruz about 1521. Longhorns were rangy and recognized by horns which spread from about three to five feet from tip to tip. They were cross-bred with other strains which have now become valuable for their beef.

Long Hunters. Daniel Boone was one of that legendary frontier breed. They were so-called because of the duration of their stays in the transmontane wilderness. The principal goal of the Long Hunters was deerskin. In the late 18th century the hide of a doe was worth 50 cents or more. The skin of a buck brought a dollar and up— hence the term "buck" as slang for currency. A band of hunters could bring back several hundred skins in a season, a stimulus to the cash-starved economy of the frontier.

Long Island, Battle of (Aug. 1776). Early in the Revolution Gen. Washington came close to losing his army and the war. He had fortified Brooklyn Heights, on Long Island, hoping that it would give him command of Manhattan where half of his troops were encamped. He had thus divided his army when Gen. Howe came over from Staten Island with a large force, outflanked Washington and crushed his forces. If the

British had pressed their advantage despite a rainstorm, on the 27th of Aug., Washington would have been unable to evacuate his men across the East River to New York City.

long rifle. The frontier rifle noted for its reliability was made famous by the exploits of Kentucky and Tennessee backwoodsmen. It was used with special effectiveness against the British at the battle of New Orleans (1815). It has been called the "Kentucky rifle," "American rifle" and "Pennsylvania rifle" after the state (Pennsylvania) where it was first assembled.

Frontier boys learned to use the long rifle as soon as they were old enough to hold a long rifle steady. By the age of 12 many of them were helping to furnish meat for the table and fighting against an Indian attack.

Looking Backward (1888). The novel by the utopian socialist author, Edward Bellamy, tells of Julian West, a wealthy young Bostonian, who is put into hypnotic sleep in 1887 and wakes up in the year 2000. The utopian world in which West finds himself contrasts sharply with 19th-century social problems.

Lookout Mountain, battle on (Nov. 24, 1863). In one of the actions in the War in the West, Gen. Joseph Hooker led a Union force in a successful assault in the mists, which gave it the name "the Battle Above the Clouds." Grant, in complete charge of the Chattanooga campaign in Tennessee, was thus enabled to dig Confederate Gen. Braxton Bragg out of what had seemed to be an impregnable position.

loose construction. The powers of Congress are listed in Art. I, Sec. 8 of the Constitution. A final clause in this section, the famous "elastic clause," authorizes Congress "to make all laws which shall be necessary and proper" for carrying out the other powers. This provision made possible a loose construction of the Constitution favored by the Federalists who wanted a strong national government. Establishment of a national bank, for example, was held to be implied by the expressed powers of Congress. Since Congress is expressly given the right to borrow money and also "to coin money, regulate the value thereof. . . ." Congress has the power to create a national banking system, for banks are closely tied up with all phases of money management.

Los Angeles race riot (Aug. 11–17, 1965). The rioting was touched off when a white police officer arrested a drunken Negro driver. The burning, looting and shooting in Watts, a 98% Negro section of the city, spilled over into adjacent areas and resulted in the death of 34 persons, 1,032 wounded, 3,952 arrests and destruction resembling national disasters. The National Guard was needed to restore order.

The wave of summertime rioting, which had begun in 1964, reached a new peak in the Detroit riot (July 22-26, 1967) where 38 persons were killed and property damage was in excess of $200 million, compared with $40 to $50 million in Watts. The Detroit riot had been preceded, earlier in July 1967, by rioting in Newark, N.J. and, after Detroit, spread to 18 other cities. Another "long, hot summer," threatened by militants and feared by observers of the national scene, had scarred the nation's urban areas.

Some sociologists seeking to explain the riots held that there was a widening gap between Negro reality and Negro expectations. The gap had become greater during the 1960's, and because of improvements in communications like television and improvements in education, the Negro feels the gap more intensely.

The riots occurred after the federal government had passed the Civil Rights Act of 1964 and the Voting Rights Act of 1965 and had launched a war on poverty, but little of the movement had penetrated to the lower depths of Negro deprivation.

Lost Battalion. The 1st Battalion, 308th Infantry, of the 77th Division in World War I was never lost. It was surrounded by Germans after breaking through to its objective in the Meuse-Argonne offensive (Oct. 1918) and was almost wiped out, losing about 400 of 600 men before American troops were able to reach them.

Lost Colony. A third expedition to Virginia, sponsored by Sir Walter Raleigh, landed on Roanoke Island, off the coast of present-day North Carolina, in 1587. John White, appointed governor by Raleigh, returned to England after only a month's stay in the colony. He left behind his daughter and his granddaughter, Virginia Dare, the first English child born in America, as pledges of his return with supplies.

White was not able to get back until 1591 and found no trace of the 117 persons, except the word "Croatoan," referring to an island to the south, carved in a doorpost.

"lost generation." The expression has been used to describe novelists of the 1920's and others who shared their disillusionment with post-World War I America. Some fled what they considered vulgar, dollar-chasing Americans to live in Paris or on the Riviera.

lotteries. The selling of tickets under a plan that returns to the holder of the winning tickets a windfall of goods or money was widely practiced in colonial America. A lottery was held by the Dutch authorities in 1655 to aid the poor in New York. Its prizes were a certain quantity of Bibles, but no cash. Public lotteries were used to avoid taxation. Privately operated lotteries were also common, but colonial lawmakers saw that these were "pernicious."

In the 19th century the movement against gambling in all forms grew stronger. Between 1830 and 1860 a lottery reform movement swept the country. The concept urged upon legislatures was that "man should and could better his condition by hard work and prudence." Under the Lottery Act of 1895 the federal government denied lotteries the use of the mails.

In recent years there has been a revival of government-sponsored lotteries. In 1966 New York State authorized a public lottery to aid the public schools.

Lottery Case (1903). In *Champion v. Ames* the U.S. Supreme Court ruled that Congress has the right to prohibit the use of interstate or foreign commerce as a means of encouraging objectionable trade or as a way of distributing harmful products.

The case arose when the constitutionality of the Lottery Act of 1895 was challenged. Under the Act Congress forbade the sending of lottery tickets through interstate commerce or the mails. The Court held that lottery tickets were articles of commerce and that Congress had the right to protect the people of the U.S. from the "widespread pestilence of lotteries" by preventing operation across state lines.

Congress proceeded to use the police power thus established. Laws have been enacted excluding from interstate trade impure food and drugs, improperly inspected meat, obscene literature, prizefight films and other harmful products.

Louisiana. The state, known as the "Creole State," "Pelican State" and "Sugar State" in the West South Central region was admitted to the Union as the 18th state, Apr. 30, 1812. Its capital is Baton Rouge.

Louisiana was named after King Louis XIV of France by La Salle, who sailed down the Mississippi to its mouth in 1682. Even before this, in 1542, Spain laid claim to the region on the basis of De Soto's explorations. The territory bounced back and forth between Spain and France before the American Revolution, the Creole being a descendant of either of these groups of settlers. Spain held the upper hand during the Revolution and aided the American colonies.

After the war reluctance to permit western settlers free navigation of the Mississippi spawned plots either for detaching Louisiana from Spain or the West from the U.S. The Pinckney Treaty (1795) assured U.S. access to the port of New Orleans.

In 1801 Spain found it convenient to cede the colony to France. But Napoleon's ambitious plans in the New World evaporated and he sold the whole Louisiana Territory, including vastly more than what was to become the state of Louisiana, to the U.S. (1803).

Louisiana, a slave state, seceded from the Union, Jan. 26, 1861. It was readmitted, June 25, 1868, but not before almost 200 Negroes were killed during Reconstruction in a riot (1865) arising from resentment over giving the vote to the freedmen.

The state leads the nation in the production of sugar cane and is second only to Texas in oil production. Immense reservoirs of oil are being tapped offshore.

Louisiana Purchase (1803). The vast region between the Mississippi River and the Rocky Mts. was transferred by Napoleon to the U.S. for $15,000,000. Napoleon needed the money and it seemed that England might wrest from him the territory he had regained from Spain in 1800.

Pres. Jefferson had wanted New Orleans in order to insure control of the mouth of the Mississippi for western farmers who sent their crops to the East coast and to Europe by way of the Gulf of Mexico. Jefferson's representatives in Paris, James Monroe and Robert Livingston, had not been authorized to purchase the entire territory unexpectedly thrust upon them. When Jefferson learned of the offer to sell the entire Louisiana Territory, he hesitated, thinking that a constitutional amendment was necessary to permit the purchase. But he relaxed his strict interpretation

of the Constitution and the Senate ratified the treaty.

With the purchase of the ill-defined but huge Louisiana Territory the European policy of containing the U.S. was dealt a fatal blow. The future greatness of the U.S. was virtually assured by one of the great bargains in history.

Lovejoy riots. Elijah P. Lovejoy, antislavery editor, was the first martyr to the Abolitionist cause. He was killed in 1837 defending his press against a mob in Alton, Ill. Before moving across the river to Alton, Lovejoy's presses had been destroyed in St. Louis, Mo., after his fearless report of the burning of a mulatto sailor. He continued his activity in Illinois where he organized a state antislavery society and edited *The Observer* until his death.

Lowell, James Russell (1819–91). Poet, essayist and diplomat. He was born in Cambridge, Mass. The foremost American man of letters of his time, he wrote for the antislavery publications *Pennsylvania Freeman* and the *National Anti-Slavery Standard*. In 1848 he published *Poems by James Russell Lowell* (Second Series), *A Fable for Critics, The Vision of Sir Launfal* and *The Biglow Papers* (First Series), a satire on the Mexican War in Yankee dialect. In 1864 *The Biglow Papers* (Second Series; first published in book form in 1867) appeared; it dealt with equal skill with the Civil War.

Lowell succeeded Longfellow

410

as professor of modern languages at Harvard (1855–86). He was the first editor of the *Atlantic Monthly* (1857–61) and co-editor with Charles Eliot Norton of the *North American Review* (1864–72). Literary essays of this leading critic of his day were gathered in *Among My Books* (1870, 1876) and *My Study Windows* (1871). A high point in his poetic achievement was *Ode Recited at the Harvard Commemoration* (1865). A diplomat, he was U.S. Minister to Spain (1877–80) and Great Britain (1880–85).

Loyal League. The organization was established in the North during the Civil War and brought into the South during the Reconstruction era as part of the effort to gain Republican voters. At first both Negroes and whites joined the Union League of America (ULA) or, as it was often called, the Loyal League. But it soon became an organization in which Negroes were taught to vote the Republican ticket and to assert their right to equality with whites. The Ku Klux Klan did much to destroy the League.

Loyalists. Those loyal to Great Britain during the American Revolution were scornfully called Tories by the patriots. The Loyalists were generally more conservative than the patriots. While many of them objected to British taxes and other controls, they did not feel that rebellion was the answer. They were confident that British authority would crush the opposition and aided the British during the Revolution.

Loyalists cut across social classes and included rich merchants, lawyers, those in the service of the Crown, Anglican clergymen, farmers and workers. It is estimated that one-third of the colonists were loyal to the Crown and opposed the final break with Britain.

During the Revolution, Loyalists lost their property under laws passed by state legislatures. They were harassed in countless ways, including imprisonment and tar and feathers, but few lost their lives. Many obtained protection in New York City and Philadelphia when these cities were held by the British; others fled to Canada.

At the end of the war the British government spent about £3 million in compensating the Loyalists for their losses.

"lulu." The term is a short form of the phrase "payments in lieu of expenses" and was originated by Gov. Alfred E. Smith in the early 1920's. It represents a tax-free expense fund for chairmen and ranking minority members of certain powerful committees in the New York State legislature.

Lunar Orbiter. The name was given to a series of spacecraft planned by the National Aeronautics and Space Administration for obtaining photographs of the moon's surface. The pictures help scientists select landing places for the Surveyor spacecraft and the Apollo lunar expedition. Orbiters provide a means of expanding man's knowledge of the moon.

Lunar Orbiter 1, a satellite launched Aug. 10, 1966, from Cape Kennedy, Fla., was the first U.S. vehicle to circle the moon. The 850-pound camera-bearing spacecraft snapped the first high-quality photographs of sites being considered for landings by astronauts.

Lundy's Lane, battle of (July 25, 1814). During the War of 1812 the British movement toward New York was met by Gen. Jacob Brown, who took the initiative and met the British at Lundy's Lane, near Niagara Falls, in Canada. Brown outfought the enemy but fell back when he learned that strong British reinforcements were on the way. Both sides claimed victory.

Lusitania. The sinking of the British Cunard liner on May 7, 1915, by a German submarine resulted in the loss of 128 of the 197 Americans on board. These were among the 1,198 men, women and children who drowned. The ship was carrying rifle cartridges and other contraband.

The sinking outraged American citizens although the German embassy in Washington had published a warning that Americans traveled at their own risk in British or Allied ships. The New York *Nation* declared:

"The torpedo that sank the *Lusitania* also sank Germany in the opinion of mankind."

Pressure on Pres. Wilson mounted, but he determined to send sharp notes of protest to Germany rather than a war message to Congress. The U.S. stayed out of the war for another two years.

Lutherans. The large Protestant denomination in the U.S. has its roots in the teachings of Martin Luther, 16th-century German leader of the Protestant Reformation. Luther emphasized the "responsibility of the individual conscience to God alone" with the Scriptures as the one standard for judging doctrines and institutions and the only necessary guide to truth.

The first Lutheran settlers in North America came to Manhattan Island from the Netherlands in 1623. The first congregation was established in 1638 by Swedish settlers at Fort Christina (Wilmington, Del.). In the 18th century exiles from the Palatinate established German Lutheran churches in New York, Pennsylvania, Delaware, Maryland and the South. In 1748 Heinrich Melchior Mühlenberg formed the first synod in Pennsylvania. A great number of small synods were formed in the West and Northwest following the great German migration of the 1830's and the Scandinavian migration of the 1860's. As language differences were submerged, these were absorbed by larger synods.

412

A split in the Lutheran church arising from the Civil War was healed in 1918. Various mergers of Lutheran churches took place in the early 1960's. Lutheran bodies in the U.S. have a membership of over 8,500,000.

lyceums. Associations of urban workers and villagers who had no time to acquire formal education but hungered for learning spread rapidly in the 1830's and 1840's. They were stimulated by the influence in America of an Englishman, Lord Henry Brougham, founder of the Useful Knowledge Society.

Josiah Holbrook, a New Englander, spurred the movement with publication (1826) of his recommendations on adult education. The National American Lyceum organization coordinated the activities of member groups (1831). By 1839 the 137 lyceums of Massachusetts alone drew some 33,000 citizens to lectures on the arts, sciences and the live issues of the day. About 3,000 lyceums were established between 1820 and 1860 in New England, New York and the upper Mississippi Valley. The movement declined after the Civil War and was replaced by the Chautauqua movement.

Lyon, Mary (1797–1849). Educator. Born in Buckland, Mass., she was a pioneer in the higher education of women and opened the Mount Holyoke Female Seminary (1837; later Mount Holyoke College) at South Hadley, Mass., for girls of moderate means. She was president of the seminary (1837–49).

M

MacArthur, Douglas (1880–1964). Soldier. Born in Little Rock, Ark., he was graduated from the U.S. Military Academy (1903) to which he returned as Superintendent (1919–22). He commanded the 42nd (Rainbow) division in France during World War I. After service in the Philippines he retired from the Army in 1937 to become a field marshal in the Philippine Army. Recalled to service in 1941 as commander of U.S. forces in the Far East, he resisted the Japanese on Bataan Peninsula, escaping to Australia. He led U.S. forces in the southwest Pacific in World War II and accepted the formal surrender of Japan (1945). He commanded occupational forces in Japan (1945–51), and was Supreme Commander of UN forces in Korea (1950–51) until removed by Pres. Truman.

Macassar Strait, battle of (Jan. 23–28, 1942). The Japanese made their first strike at Java in the Dutch East Indies in these waters. Four American destroyers, assisted by units of the Dutch navy, inflicted serious losses on a Japanese convoy, but their victory was only momentary.

McCardle, Ex parte (1869). William H. McCardle, editor of the Vicksburg *Times*, was arrested for criticizing the military authorities of Mississippi and held by a military commission for trial. Through a writ of habeas corpus, his case reached the U.S. Supreme Court on appeal. The Court had previously decided in *Ex parte Milligan* that a civilian could not be tried in a military court when the civil courts were functioning. It was about to hand down its decision when Congress passed a special statute taking away its jurisdiction.

McCarran Internal Security Act (1950). Also known as the Subversive Activities Control Act, the law required all members of the Communist party to register with the Attorney General. It barred the employment of Communists in defense plants, prohibited issuance of passports to Communists and barred aliens who had been

Communists from entering the U.S.

Pres. Truman vetoed the Act, charging that it punished opinions rather than actions, but it was passed over his veto.

Between 1950 and 1965 the Justice Department brought registration actions against the party itself, 22 alleged front organizations and 44 individuals. None registered with the Subversive Activities Control Board.

In 1965 the U.S. Supreme Court declared unconstitutional the section that allowed the State Department to deny a passport to a Communist. In 1966 the Court ruled that individuals may invoke their constitutional privilege against self-incrimination (5th Amendment) and refuse to register with the government as a member of the Communist party. The effect of the decision was to make the registration requirement unenforceable.

McCarran-Walter Act (1952). Passed over Pres. Truman's veto, the Immigration and Nationality Act aimed to replace the 150-year-old patchwork of regulations with a single code, covering all immigration, naturalization and deportation procedures.

Under the Act immigration was limited to 154,657 persons per year. The basic quota provisions of the National Origins Act (1924) were kept; the total each year was divided among European nations by a method which favored northern and western Europe. The flat ban against admitting immigrants from Asian and other Pacific nations was removed. However, the quotas assigned these nations were so small that they were of little practical value.

Aliens admitted to the U.S. can obtain citizenship after five years without "first papers." Screening measures to keep out subversives and other undesirables are strengthened. Special powers are granted the Attorney General to deport immigrants for "Communist and Communist-front" affiliations even after they have been granted citizenship.

Dissatisfaction with the McCarran-Walter Act was stated in general terms in the Democratic party platform of 1960: "We shall adjust our immigration, nationality and refugee policies to eliminate discrimination and to enable members of scattered families abroad to be united with relatives already in our midst. The national origin quota system of limiting immigration contradicts the founding principles of this nation." Presidents Kennedy and Johnson called upon Congress to carry out this pledge. The Immigration Act of 1965 revised the quota system.

McCarthy-Army dispute. In 1954 the U.S. Army charged Sen. Joseph McCarthy (Republican, Wis.) and members of his staff with trying to gain favored treatment for G. David Schine, a young assistant of McCarthy who had been drafted into the Army. McCarthy replied that the Army was seeking to interrupt his investigation of subversion at Fort Monmouth, N.J. He accused the Army of "coddling" Communists.

The charges were aired before millions at the televised hearings of the Subcommittee on Investigations of the Senate Committee on Government Operations (Apr. 22–June 17, 1954).

McCarthy first gained the national limelight in 1950 when he charged that the State Department was infested with Communists. From that time to 1954, as Chairman of the Senate Committee on Government Operations he made a variety of accusations against government agencies and individuals. He attacked such widely respected Americans as former General of the Army George C. Marshall, whom he accused of treasonable disloyalty.

The term "McCarthyism" found its way into the language. It is an expression of reckless and indiscriminate charges of political disloyalty.

At the McCarthy-Army hearings, the Army counsel, Joseph B. Welch, provoked McCarthy into a number of attacks on individuals. McCarthy's methods were so discredited that the Senate voted to "condemn" him, Dec. 2, 1954, for conduct "unbecoming a member of the United States Senate."

McClellan, George Brinton (1826–85). Soldier. Known as "Little Mac," he was gradu-

ated from the U.S. Military Academy (1846). Influential in keeping Kentucky in the Union, he was called upon by Pres. Lincoln to reorganize the Union troops after the defeat at Bull Run (1861), succeeding Winfield Scott as general-in-chief. He commanded the Army of the Potomac and directed the Peninsular Campaign (Mar.–Aug. 1862) which failed to take Richmond. He was regarded as overcautious by Lincoln who damned him with faint praise when he said of McClellan, "If he can't fight, he excels in making others ready to fight." He was denied any field command after Antietam (Sept. 17, 1862) when he failed to follow up Gen. Lee's forces. His concepts of strategy were sound, but he always felt that he needed more time. He was looked upon by Lee as the best commander who faced him during the war.

McClellan was the Democratic candidate for President in 1864 and was badly defeated by Lincoln. He was governor of New Jersey (1878–81).

McClure's Magazine. The muckraking journal founded in 1893 was edited and published by Samuel S. McClure. McClure financed the research of journalists who undertook to expose corruption in industry and politics. He estimated that each of Ida Tarbell's articles on the Standard Oil Company cost $4,000 and that each of Lincoln Steffens' articles on corruption in American cities cost $2,000.

McCormick, Cyrus Hall (1809–84). Inventor and manufacturer. Born in Walnut Grove, Va., he invented a mechanical reaper which he patented in 1834. He erected his own factory in Chicago and, by 1850, built up a national business for the McCormick Harvesting Co., adding such devices to the reaper as a mowing attachment. A pioneer in the creation of modern business methods, he was among the first to use field trials, guarantees and testimonials in advertising.

McCrea, Jane, murder of (1777). The daughter of a Loyalist was entrusted to two Indians to bring her to Gen. Burgoyne's camp where her fiancée, Capt. Jones, awaited her. She was tomahawked when they quarreled over the rum they were to receive for the mission. Burgoyne failed to punish the Indians, fearing that his Indian scouts would turn against him. Thousands throughout New York and New England flocked to join Gen. Horatio Gates.

McCulloch v. Maryland (1819). The U.S. Supreme Court ruled the Maryland law taxing the Bank of the U.S. unconstitutional. Chief Justice Marshall held: "The power to tax involves the power to destroy." If states were permitted to nullify acts of Congress by attacking its agencies, they could "defeat and render useless the power to create."

The Court upheld the consti-tutionality of the Bank of the U.S. created by Congress. Although there was no specific provision in the Constitution for such a bank, Marshall held that it was appropriate for carrying out powers granted to Congress. The decision was a blow against strict construction of the Constitution, for it sustained the doctrine of the implied powers of Congress. It established the principle that states may not interfere with the functioning of federal agencies.

MacDowell, Edward Alexander (1861–1908). Composer. Born in New York City, he studied in Paris and Frankfurt. Before returning to America (1888), he composed his *First Modern Suite* (1882). He also composed and taught in Boston (1888–96). To this period belong his *Indian Suite, Sonata Eroica* and *Woodland Sketches*. He received a degree of international acclaim not previously accorded any American composer. He was professor of music at Columbia Univ. (1896–1904). His symphonic poems include *Hamlet, Ophelia, Lancelot and Elaine, Lamia* and *The Saracens*. "To a Wild Rose," one of his small pieces, became popular.

mace. Its origin as a symbol of government authority goes back to the "fasces" of Republican Rome—the bundle of rods and an ax which were carried by the lictors who attended each Roman magistrate as he held court and administered justice. The rods were used for administering whippings and the ax for beheading.

The mace was adopted by the House of Representatives by resolution, Apr. 14, 1789. There is no mace in the Senate. The original mace was burned in the Capitol in 1814. The present mace dates from 1841 and is a reproduction of the original. It consists of a bundle of 13 ebony rods bound with silver and terminating in a silver globe, surmounted by a silver eagle with wings outspread. The sergeant-at-arms is its custodian and is charged with its use when necessary.

McGuffey's Readers. The standard elementary school textbooks for nearly a century were written by Prof. William Holmes McGuffey. A First and Second Reader was published for use in public schools in 1836. The series of *Eclectic Readers*, revised five times, last in 1901, grew to six readers. More than 120,000,000 copies were sold. They were still in use in U.S. schools in 1927.

McKinley, William (1843– 1901). Twenty-fifth President of the U.S. (1897–1901). He was born in Niles, O., and served Ohio as a member of U.S. House of Representatives (1877–83, 1885–91) where he played a major part in framing the McKinley Tariff (1890). He was governor of Ohio (1892–96). His presidential campaigns were directed by Republican leader Marcus Alonzo Hanna. He led the nation in the Spanish-American War. Shot by Leon Czolgosz, an anarchist, at Buffalo, N.Y. (Sept. 6, 1901), he died on Sept. 14.

McKinley Tariff of 1890. The highest protective tariff in the history of the U.S. until that time, it was passed during the Republican administration of Benjamin Harrison.

Apart from raising duties on manufactured goods to new highs, the act of 1890 admitted sugar free and provided a bounty for U.S. sugar growers who then could undersell Hawaiian sugar growers. The action produced a depression in Hawaii.

Another feature of the act providing for reciprocity was intended to permit retaliation against Latin American countries that would not reduce their tariffs on manufactured goods from the U.S. even though the U.S. admitted their coffee, sugar and other products duty free.

Since "infant" industries had outgrown their swaddling clothes, the protective nature of the Tariff of 1890 was justified as a means of assuring high wages for American workers. In the depression of 1893, however, the high tariff was blamed for discouraging trade and contributing to unemployment.

MacLeish, Archibald (1892–). Poet and librarian. Born in Glencoe, Ill., he was the librarian of Congress (1939– 44) and assistant Sec. of State

(1944–45). He was awarded the Pulitzer Prize for Poetry in 1933 and 1953 and drama in 1959 for the play *J.B.* Among his volumes of verse are *The Happy Marriage* (1924), *The Pot of Earth* (1925), *Streets in the Moon* (1926), *Conquistador* (1932), *Land of the Free* (1938), *Act Five* (1948), *Sons for Eve* (1954). He has been a professor of rhetoric at Harvard (since 1949).

McMillan, Edwin Mattison (1907–). Physicist. Born in Redondo Beach, Calif., he was granted a Ph.D. by Princeton (1932). Long associated with the Radiation Laboratory at the Univ. of California, he has been its director since 1958. His discovery of neptunium (element 93) made possible production of plutonium (element 94). He was awarded the Nobel Prize (1951) (with Glenn T. Seaborg) for discoveries in the chemistry of transuranic elements.

McNamara dynamite case. On Oct. 1, 1910, the Los Angeles *Times* was dynamited; 20 people were killed and 17 injured. The *Times* had been a consistent and fervent opponent of unionism. Labor leaders James B. McNamara and his brother, John J. McNamara, were accused. Ortie McManigal, an ironworker, confessed to the crime and implicated the others. Their "irregular" extradition from other states to California helped to convince organized labor that they were being "framed." A defense fund was raised by the American Federation of Labor and Clarence Darrow was hired to defend the McNamara brothers.

To the consternation of labor, the McNamara brothers confessed their crimes after the trial began. James B. admitted blowing up the *Times* and was sentenced to life imprisonment. John J. admitted only to blowing up an iron works in Los Angeles and was given a 15-year sentence.

McNary-Haugen Bill. The measure provided for the purchase of wheat, cotton and corn surpluses by the government and their sale abroad at world prices. Disposal of surpluses in this manner was intended to raise domestic prices and permit farmers to pay the special tax thus compensating government for its outlay.

The Farm Bloc reacting to the farm depression of the 1920's supported the measure. The Bill, passed by Congress in 1927 and 1928, was vetoed both times by Pres. Coolidge. He held that the dumping of surpluses would be resented by foreign countries and that the plan was socialistic because it put the government in the farming business.

Macon's Bill No. 2 (1810). Under this Bill, named for the chairman of the House Committee on Foreign Affairs, the Non-Intercourse Act was repealed. The Macon Bill reopened trade with both England and France and contained the proviso that the U.S. would restore non-intercourse with one of the two nations if the other repealed the measures which allowed seizure of American ships.

Napoleon announced repeal of the French decrees while continuing to seize American ships, but the promise was accepted by Pres. Madison. Congress renewed non-intercourse against Britain (1811), thus aggravating relations which were to culminate in the War of 1812.

"Mad Anthony" Wayne. Gen. Anthony Wayne (1745–96) gained the name and reputation for his reckless heroism during the Revolutionary War. At George Washington's direction he undertook a brilliantly successful surprise attack on the British at Stony Point on the Hudson (1779).

Madison, James (1751–1836). Fourth President of the U.S. (1809–17). Born in Port Conway, Va., he was graduated from the College of New Jersey, now Princeton Univ. (1771). Known as the "father of the Constitution," he was one of the authors of *The Federalist*. He was a member of U.S. House of Representatives (1789 –97). A leader of the Democratic-Republican party, he opposed Alexander Hamilton's financial measures. With Thomas Jefferson, he drafted the Virginia Resolutions (1798) in opposition to the Alien and Sedition Laws. He was U.S. Sec. of State (1801–09), and President during the War of 1812.

Mafia. The national crime organization, known variously as the Mafia, Cosa Nostra and the Syndicate, has been involved in gambling, usury, murder, narcotics and other flagrantly criminal enterprises. Profits from criminal activity have been invested in legitimate businesses taken over by the Mafia and these have often been drained of their capital. The organization in the U.S. is limited to men of Italian birth or descent. In the 1960's the Mafia was investigated by Congress. Individual Mafia members have been prosecuted by the federal and state governments, but the organization has continued.

The modern American Mafia is neither a branch nor a counterpart of the centuries-old Sicilian secret society. The U.S. did, however, become involved in an incident, in 1891, arising from Sicilian Mafia (or Black Hand) activity in New Orleans, La. Mafia members were tried for assassinating the chief of police, but were acquitted despite overwhelming evidence. Citizens descended on the jail and put to death 11 persons (including three Italian nationals). The government of Italy protested and the U.S. paid a small indemnity.

magazines. A dozen short-lived magazines were published by enterprising colonial printers in the years between 1741 and

1776. The first magazine published in America was Andrew Bradford's *American Magazine* or *A Monthly View of the Political State of the British Colonies* (Feb. 13, 1741). Three days later came Benjamin Franklin's *General Magazine and Historical Chronicle, For all the British Plantations in America.* Both magazines were dated Jan. 1741, in Philadelphia. Bradford's magazine lasted only three months; Franklin's six. The *American Magazine and Historical Chronicle*, edited by Jeremy Gridley, appeared Sept. 1, 1743, in Boston. Devoted largely to politics, it lasted more than three years. Most admired of early literary magazines was *The American Magazine* (Oct. 1757–Oct. 1758), which found space for original problems in mathematics and for scientific papers. Other magazines of the period discussed theories of British and French deists and rationalists. Horticulture and mechanics also received attention. Two of the three magazines being published in the colonies on the eve of the Revolution did not survive the War; the third both started and ended during the conflict.

During the first quarter of the 19th century about 100 periodicals appeared, but their circulations were limited and their lives were short. Many were specialized, indicating the intellectual advances in medicine, law, the theater and science. Other factors which explain the limited appeal of periodicals were the high postal rates adding 40% to subscription costs and inability of presses to make long runs.

Probably the earliest legal periodical in the U.S., the *American Law Journal*, founded in Baltimore, Md., in 1808, by John Elihu Hall, professor of rhetoric at the Univ. of Maryland, continued until 1817. The first agricultural magazine in the U.S., the *Agricultural Museum*, was published in Georgetown, in the District of Columbia, in July 1810 and lasted until May 1812. The *Christian Disciple* was a liberal Protestant magazine, founded in 1813 by William Ellery Channing, a world famous Congregationalist Unitarian minister, as a challenge to the more conservative Protestant press. The first journal entirely devoted to temperance was *The National Philanthropist*, founded in 1826 by the Rev. William Collier, a Baptist missionary. Such specialized periodicals as the *Medical Repository* had a subscription list of 300 and Silliman's *American Journal of Science* did not reach 1,000. The *North American Review*, founded in Boston in 1815, had fewer than 600 subscribers in 1820. The *Port-Folio*, the only general literary magazine of the first quarter of the 19th century, reached a circulation of only 2,000.

In the second quarter of the 19th century the popularization of knowledge, made possible by the penny newspaper, the lyceum platform and the public library, was further extended by inexpensive magazines. Dozens of new periodicals appeared, aided by the cheap and uniform postage rates adopted by Congress in 1851. They included the *Magazine of Useful and Entertaining Knowledge*, *The Spirit of the Times*, *Graham's*, *Peterson's* and *Parley's Magazine*. Other magazines of general interest that appeared in the three decades before the Civil War included *Godey's Lady's Book*, the *New York Ledger*, the *Atlantic Monthly* and *Harper's*. A sectional note on the literary front was struck by the editor of the *Southern Literary Journal* (Sept. 1835), who declared that the periodical would "at all times, breathe a Southern spirit, and sustain a strictly Southern character." Magazine mortality was high because of delinquent subscribers, competition of the penny press and cheap imprints of pirated English books.

During the Civil War periodicals in the South suffered from shortages of paper, ink, type, slow communications and the high cost of postage. *De Bow's Review* was suspended in 1862. *The Southern Literary Messenger*, a leading magazine of the antebellum days, closed its office in 1864. The *Southern Presbyterian Review* and the *Southern Cultivator* survived the war.

Northern periodicals were affected by the Civil War. *Godey's Lady's Book* and *Harper's* lost their southern subscribers. But coverage of the war by *Harper's* and *Frank Leslie's Illustrated*

Newspaper led to an increase in their subscribers. New periodicals, *The Continental Monthly* and the *United States Service Magazine* offered military news, stories, verse and articles on the larger issues in the conflict.

In the post-Civil War period there was a great expansion of the periodical press. *The Ladies' Home Journal*, founded by Cyrus Curtis in 1883, sold for only ten cents a copy and dealt with household matters, advice to the lovelorn and with the growing civic interests of women. Edward W. Bok, who began editing it in 1889, did much to stimulate its great circulation.

The popular muckraking magazines made their appearance with *McClure's*, founded in 1893 by Samuel S. McClure. Along with the *Cosmopolitan*, *Forum*, *American*, *Everybody's*, *Munsey's* and *Pearson's*, it excited a multitude of readers in the first decade of the 20th century with "the literature of exposure."

In the post-World War I period long-established general magazines like *Collier's* (1888) and *The Saturday Evening Post* (1821) became mass circulation "slicks" and reached millions with their glossy covers and shallow stories. Pulp magazines, printed on cheap paper and catering to low tastes, appeared under such titles as *True Romances*, *True Story Magazine*, *Paris Nights* and *Medical Horrors*. Intellectual tastes were met by the *Saturday Review of Lit-*

erature (1924) and the *Partisan Review* (1934), among others. Picture magazines, notably *Life* (1936) and *Look* (1937), held millions of readers weekly. News magazines such as *Time* (1923) and *Newsweek* (1933) won large followings.

In 1973 there were about 4,500 periodicals. *Look* ceased publication in 1971 and *Life* died in 1972. The top 15 in circulation (1972 figures) were the *Reader's Digest* (17,827,-661), *TV Guide* (16,410,858), *Woman's Day* (8,191,731), *Better Homes & Gardens* (7,996,-050), *Family Circle* (7,889,-587), *McCall's* (7,516,960), *National Geographic* (7,260,-179), *Ladies' Home Journal* (7,014,251), *Playboy* (6,400,-573), *Good Housekeeping* (5,-801,446), *Redbook* (4,761,477), *Time* (4,287,348), *American Home* (3,676,364), *Senior Scholastic Unit* (2,800,573), *American Legion* (2,682,025). There were, in addition, 36 magazines with a circulation of over 1,000,000.

Mahan, Alfred Thayer (1840–1914). Naval officer and historian. Born in West Point, N.Y., he was graduated from the U.S. Naval Academy (1859). The first "philosopher of sea power," he was president of the Naval War College, Newport, R.I. (1886–89, 1892–93). He published his lectures in 1890 as *The Influence of Sea Power Upon History, 1660–1783* and won immediate recognition in Europe and America. He was made world famous by *The Influence of Sea Power Upon the French Revolution and Empire, 1793–1812* (1892), showing how British victories at sea nullified Napoleon's land conquests. His other works include *Sea Power in Its Relation to the War of 1812* (2 vols., 1905), *Naval Strategy* (1911) and biographies of Farragut and Nelson. His works were influential during a period of naval expansion.

Mahanism. The writings of Capt. (later Admiral) Alfred Thayer Mahan were influential in support of the "big navy" forces in the U.S. Mahan included the U.S. in the ideas he set forth in *The Influence of Sea Power upon History (1660–1783),* published in 1890. He believed that the U.S. could not be a great nation without sea power accompanied by the acquisition of colonies and bases throughout the world.

Mahican. The confederacy of Indians, an Algonquian people, occupied the upper Hudson Valley, New York. The Dutch provided firearms to their enemies and hastened their dispersal. Some became part of the Stockbridge (Mass.) Indians and came under the influence of the missionary John Sergeant in 1736.

Maine. The "Pine Tree State," largest of the six New England states, was admitted to the Union as the 23rd state, Mar. 15, 1820. Its capital is Augusta.

Maine, named after an ancient province in France, was explored by Verrazano for

Francis I (1524). John Smith mapped the coast and called the region "New England". (1614). The Council of New England (successor to the Plymouth Company) granted the territory to Sir Ferdinando Gorges and John Mason (1622). The claims of their heirs were bought by Massachusetts (1677) and a royal charter confirmed Massachusetts' possession of Maine (1691).

A movement to break away from Massachusetts was under way in 1783, but it was not until the admission of Missouri as a slave state in 1820 that the break was made. Maine was admitted as a free state to preserve the balance in Congress.

Maine produces wood products, from ships to toothpicks. Aroostook potatoes lead the nation's production. Fisheries and the canning of vegetables are important.

Main Street (1920). The novel by Sinclair Lewis is a literary landmark. It presents a sardonic view of Gopher Prairie, an imaginary small town in the Midwest. The chief character, Carol Kennicott, is imbued with the desire to bring culture to the town but antagonizes its smug leaders. In the end she has to compromise with them. Lewis' picture of village America is scarcely tender.

Other works by one of the foremost American novelists include *Babbitt* (1922), *Arrowsmith* (1925), *Elmer Gantry* (1927), *Dodsworth* (1929) and *It Can't Happen Here* (1935).

Mandans. A Siouan linguistic group strategically located on the Missouri River, the Mandans lived in stockaded villages in dome-shaped lodges made of packed earth supported by poles. They relied on agriculture for subsistence, but also hunted buffalo and fished. The Lewis and Clark expedition (1804–06) made contact with them after their numbers had been greatly reduced by a smallpox epidemic. Another epidemic in 1837 virtually wiped them out.

Manifest Destiny. The phrase was the theme of the expansionists who believed that it was God's will for the U.S. to spread democracy from the Atlantic to the Pacific.

The term "Manifest Destiny" first appeared in the *Democratic Review* (July–Aug. 1845) in an article on the annexation of Texas. Manifest Destiny was extolled by orators who urged acquisition of the territories as a result of the Mexican War. It was heard again and again in demands for Oregon, the desire for Cuba in the 1850's, the purchase of Alaska and the annexation of Hawaii.

Manifest Destiny combined the idealism of a confident, growing population, pride in "Anglo-Saxon" achievement and opposition to European absolutism. But it did have racist, imperialist and mercenary overtones.

Manila Bay, battle of (May 1, 1898). In the first military action of the Spanish-American War, Commodore George Dewey destroyed the Spanish naval squadron in Manila Bay and made possible the capture of the city of Manila in the Philippines by an army unit.

Mann, Horace (1796–1859). Educator. He was born in Franklin, Mass. A member of the Massachusetts legislature, he pioneered in the establishment of public schools. As president of the state senate, he signed the epoch-making education bill of 1837. Secretary of the state board of education (1837–48), he advocated nonsectarian instruction, established state teacher-training institutions, increased teacher salaries, founded 50 new high schools, improved curriculum and provided a minimum school year of six months. He started and edited the *Common School Journal,* and prepared a series of annual reports that helped the growth of public education in the nation. An antislavery Whig, he served in the U.S. House of Representatives (1848–53) and then was president of Antioch College (1853–59).

Mann-Elkins Act (1910). The Interstate Commerce Commission was empowered to suspend general increases in railroad rates and granted the initiative in revising rates. A Commerce Court was established to speed up court actions by hearing appeals directly from the ICC.

Mann White Slave Act (1910). The Act of Congress prohibited interstate transportation of women for immoral purposes.

Manpower Development and Training Act (1962). Under the MDTA Congress authorized federal grants for training programs, particularly for persons dislocated by automation and technological changes. The 1963 amendments to the MDTA provided that unemployed youths, 16–21 years of age, may receive training in institutional or on-the-job training programs.

A significant amendment provided for training in basic education under the Multi-Occupational Manpower Program (Umbrella Project) to aid chronically unemployed and unemployable youths and adults to attain realistic vocational goals and the necessary basic educational and vocational skills. The program is for those with a literacy level of eighth grade or less.

Marbury v. Madison (1803). In this landmark case the important doctrine of judicial review, or the power of the Supreme Court to declare acts of Congress unconstitutional, was established.

The U.S. Supreme Court refused Marbury's request for a writ of mandamus (an order by a superior authority instructing an inferior one to redress a wrong) ordering Sec. of State Madison to deliver a judge's commission to Marbury. The Court held that while Marbury had a right to the writ, the law under which the Supreme Court might issue the writ (Section 13 of the Judiciary Act of 1789) was unconstitutional. According to the Court, the Constitution gave the Supreme Court original jurisdiction only in certain special cases. The power to issue mandamuses was not among them. Chief Justice Marshall, himself a Federalist, wrote the decision.

The immediate impact of the decision was to prevent the Federalist Marbury and other "midnight judges" from retaining control of the judiciary after the Federalist party had been defeated by Jefferson's Republicans in the election of 1800.

Mardi Gras. The carnival was first celebrated in New Orleans in 1827 when French-American students organized a procession of mummers on Shrove Tuesday, the last day of a season of merrymaking before Lent.

Marin, John (1872–1953). Painter. Born in Rutherford, N.J., he is noted for his Maine seascapes. A water colorist of distinction, his work reflected the method of abstract cubism and expressionism.

Marine Corps, U.S. The Continental Marines, a forerunner of the present Corps, was organized by the Continental Congress in 1775. The present Corps was established by Congress in 1798. It provides forces for service with the Navy to seize advanced naval bases and to conduct land operations essential to the prosecution of a naval campaign. It is also charged in coordination with the Army and Air Force with developing amphibious operations used by landing forces.

Mariner. A series of U.S. spacecraft have been designed to fly in the vicinities of Venus and Mars and send back to earth information about these planets. On Dec. 14, 1962, NASA's Mariner 2 flew as close as 21,648 miles to Venus, giving man his first relatively close-up observation of earth's cloud-covered neighbor. On July 14, 1965, Mariner 4, after a seven-month flight, came within range of Mars and sent back photographs over 134 million miles of space, one of the great scientific feats of history.

Maritime Administration. The federal agency was established in 1950 as one of the successor agencies to the former U.S. Maritime Commission. It is responsible for administering programs authorized by the Merchant Marine Act, 1936, as amended. It aids in developing an American merchant marine that is adequate to carry the nation's domestic waterborne commerce and a substantial portion of its foreign commerce during peacetime and would be capable of serving as a naval and military auxiliary in time of war.

"Mark Twain." The chant, by the men on Mississippi River steamboats who called the soundings, indicated the sounding at two fathoms, or twelve feet. The term was made famous by the novelist, Samuel Clemens, who took it as his pen name.

Marne, battles of. In the First Battle of the Marne (Sept. 1914), on which the fate of France depended, infantry reinforcements were sent to the front by taxicab. The Germans were forced to fall back behind the Aisne. The victory presaged the end of the mobile war on the Western Front and the beginning of a trench stalemate.

The Second Battle of the Marne, which included both the Champagne-Marne and the Aisne-Marne offensives, was launched by the Germans, July 15, 1918. "Ils ne passeront pas!" was again the rallying cry, as it had been in the First Battle of the Marne. Unlike 1914, however, there were nine American and two Italian divisions, plus 23 French divisions to stem the tide. By July 18, the drive had failed and the Germans were moving north of the river again.

marque and reprisal, letters of. One of the powers granted to Congress under the Constitution is to grant letters of marque and reprisal (Art. I, Sec. 8, Par. 10). These are government commissions granted to private vessels (privateers) to make war on the enemy. They were not granted during the Civil War or since that time.

Marshall, George Catlett (1880–1959). Soldier and statesman.

Born in Uniontown, Pa., he was graduated from the Virginia Military Institute (1901). The principal Allied strategist in World War II, he was U.S. Army Chief of Staff (1939–45), and then U.S. ambassador to China (1945–47). As Pres. Truman's Sec. of State (1947–49), he was responsible for the European Recovery Program (Marshall Plan). While Sec. of Defense (1950–51), he planned the defense of Korea. He was awarded the Nobel Peace Prize (1953).

Marshall, John (1755–1835). Jurist. He was born in Fauquier Co., Va. After service in the Continental army, he became a leading Federalist in Virginia. He was a member of the House of Burgesses (1782–88), and served as one of the commissioners to France (1797). He was Pres. John Adams' Sec. of State (1800–01) and appointed by him as Chief Justice of U.S. Supreme Court (1801–35). He established the Court's right of judicial review in *Marbury v. Madison* (1803). His decisions curbed state interference with property rights. His other notable opinions include establishing the fundamental doctrines of constitutional law (*McCulloch v. Maryland, Dartmouth College v. Woodward, Cohens v. Virginia, Gibbons v. Ogden*).

Marshall Plan. The European Recovery Program (ERP) was proposed by Gen. George C.

Marshall in an address at Harvard University, June 5, 1947. At the time Marshall was Sec. of State. The underlying purpose of the program was to help the European nations recover from the devastation of World War II. Eighteen nations taking part grouped themselves into the Organization for European Economic Cooperation (OEEC). They were Austria, Belgium, Britain, Denmark, France, West Germany, Greece, Iceland, Ireland, Italy, Luxemburg, the Netherlands, Norway, Portugal, Sweden, Switzerland, Trieste and Turkey. Spain was not invited to join. Russia and her satellites refused to join.

ERP cost the American people about 14 billion dollars from 1948 to 1952. Almost 70% of the supplies involved came from the U.S.; the remainder, from Canada, Latin America, the participating countries and other parts of the world. No military aid was given under ERP. Some of the projects completed included hydroelectric plants, roads, bridges, land reclamation schemes, irrigation systems and large-scale housing facilities.

Politically, ERP succeeded in halting and rolling back the tide of Communism within the countries of Western Europe. Socially, the program meant improved standards of living, including better food, clothing and housing. Economically, ERP stimulated production and created jobs. The manufacturing industries of Western Europe reached all-time highs in production. Agriculture, in general, returned to prewar levels.

martial law. While there is no provision in the Constitution for the establishment of martial law, it has been the practice in the U.S. for the federal or state governments to establish martial law by using the military when the civil law enforcement body is unable to keep the peace. It is also possible for a military commander to declare martial law in an area he is occupying. This was done by Gen. Andrew Jackson in New Orleans, Dec. 1814. Several state governors declared martial law during the Railroad Strikes of 1877, and Pres. Hayes sent in federal troops to protect U.S. property.

Martin v. Hunter's Lessee (1816). The U.S. Supreme Court asserted its supremacy over state courts in interpreting the Constitution. The Court reasoned that the Constitution was established by the people of the U.S. and not by the states. It ruled, therefore, that under the Constitution the U.S. Supreme Court had the right to review state court decisions. It was necessary also that final decision must rest somewhere. Justice Story spoke for the Court in ruling against Virginia.

The Virginia state court of appeals had denied the right of the U.S. Supreme Court to review its decision involving the confiscation of the Fairfax land grants and its statute prohibiting an alien from inheriting land.

Maryland. "The Old Line State," one of the Middle Atlantic states, was one of the original 13 Colonies. Its capital is Annapolis. The colony was first settled in 1634 by Leonard Calvert, a son of the first Lord Baltimore who had been given the grant of land by King Charles I of England. Maryland was named after Queen Henrietta Maria, wife of Charles I.

The Calverts were threatened by claims of Virginia and Pennsylvania and lost control of the colony in 1649 when the Puritans came to power in England. There were further changes in power and Maryland was returned to the Calverts in 1715.

Although Maryland was founded as a refuge for Roman Catholics, it included Protestants from the very first. The principle of religious toleration was set forth in Maryland's Act of Toleration (1649).

Maryland was an important source of provisions for the Continental army during the Revolutionary War. It was the seventh state to ratify the Constitution (Apr. 28, 1788). Since it had no western land claims, the state was strongly pro-national in urging other states to relinquish their western lands to the federal government.

The state did not secede from the Union during the Civil War, but there was strong southern sentiment which resulted in curbs on popular rights by the federal government.

The state has become primarily industrial with iron and steel works, oil and copper refineries, meat packing plants and canneries. It is known agriculturally for its vegetables and fruits, especially tomatoes. Baltimore, its major city, is one of the nation's great seaports.

Maryland! My Maryland! The marching song of the Confederacy was a poem set to the music of the old German song, "O Tannenbaum." It was written by James R. Randall, a native Marylander who hoped that his state would join the Confederate cause. He was inspired to write it in 1861 when he learned that Massachusetts troops had been attacked as they passed through Baltimore.

Mason, George (1725–92). Revolutionary statesman. Born in Fairfax Co., Va., he drew up the nonimportation resolutions which Virginia adopted at the time of protest over the Townshend duties. He wrote the Fairfax Resolves (July 1774), adopted by the Continental Congress, defining the constitutional position of the colonies as against the Crown. He framed the Declaration of Rights (June 1776) for the Virginia Convention, which later became the basis for the first 10 Amendments to the Constitution. He sketched the plan by which Virginia ceded her western lands to the U.S. A member of the Constitutional Convention (1787), he did not sign the final document and led opposition to ratification in Virginia. A consistent opponent of slavery, he denounced the compromise on the slave trade.

Mason and Dixon Line (1763–69). Two English surveyors, Charles Mason and Jeremiah Dixon, surveyed the disputed boundary between Maryland and Pennsylvania. The line agreed upon was extended westward in 1784. It became the northern boundary of Maryland, Delaware, and a part of Virginia which became West Virginia.

In the period before the Civil War the line and the Ohio River came to be considered the boundary in the East between free and slave states. The Mason and Dixon Line continues as a symbolic division between North and South.

Masons. The secret fraternal society was introduced into the American colonies in the 18th century with the establishment of Masonic lodges in such cities as Philadelphia and Boston. Benjamin Franklin and George Washington were Freemasons.

In 1826 there was a strong reaction against Masonry when William Morgan of Batavia, N.Y., became embroiled in disagreements with his fellow Masons. He left the order and wrote a book exposing its secret rituals. He was kidnapped and was never again seen alive. A body tentatively identified as his was washed up from the shores of Lake Ontario.

A short-lived Anti-Masonic party was formed in the late 1820's but disappeared within a decade, after its candidate for President was crushingly defeated in the election of 1832.

Many political leaders and judges were Masons before 1826 and many of these repudiated the Masons following the Morgan incident.

The Anti-Masonic movement soon subsided and by the end of the 19th century the order had reestablished itself. Its membership includes many people in political life, lawyers and businessmen.

Massachusetts. The "Bay State," one of the six New England states, was one of the original 13 Colonies. The name is that of an Indian tribe.

The Massachusetts coast was visited by several early explorers, including John and Sebastian Cabot in 1498. The first permanent settlement was established by the Pilgrims, sailing from Plymouth, England, on the *Mayflower* and landing in 1620 at the point on the coast they called Plymouth.

The Massachusetts Bay colony and Boston were founded in 1630. The charter of the colony was revoked in 1684. The administration of the new royal governor, Sir Edmund Andros (1686–89) proved unpopular and a new charter was granted in 1691 that united Massachusetts Bay, Plymouth and Maine as a royal colony.

The merchants of Massachusetts were especially vigorous

in their opposition to British restrictions and the colony played a vigorous role in the American Revolution. Samuel Adams, John Adams, John Hancock and James Otis were among the leaders of the Revolution. The early battles of the Revolutionary War were fought around Boston. Massachusetts was the sixth state to ratify the Constitution (Feb. 6, 1788).

The state pioneered in the shoe and textile industry and leads the nation in shoe production. Paper is an important industry. Dairy products are first in order of cash receipts in agriculture.

Boston, the state's capital, is the great cultural, industrial, fishery and wholesale center of New England. The city is a leading financial center.

Massachusetts Institute of Technology. Established at Cambridge, Mass., in 1859, the Institute held its first classes in 1865. It is one of the outstanding institutions in the world for students who hope to become leaders in science, teaching, engineering and industry. An independent, endowed institution, it possesses unrivaled laboratories on its campus. Its greatest claim to distinction lies in its faculty, a group which includes scholars, scientists and engineers of world renown. Essentially an undergraduate college, though research and graduate instruction are also vital to its work, M.I.T. has a current combined enrollment of about 7,200.

mass media. By the end of the 19th century the U.S. had more than half the newspapers of the world. Tabloid newspapers, after World War I, reached a mass audience of millions. Magazines, too, notably those which emphasized pictures along with text, sold in the millions by World War II. Between World Wars, the silent film and then the talking film reached huge audiences. Radio in the 1930's and television in the 1950's added to the mass media which deeply influenced the business and culture of the nation.

Critics charged that mass media, controlled largely by advertisers, sought the lowest common denominator of public taste. Optimists conceded that mass media promoted uniformity, but that it also permitted a rise in the cultural level. Television, for example, had given a single performance of Shakespeare's *Richard III* a larger audience than all the theater audiences that had seen it since its opening in 1597. And the rise of the low-priced paperback book, selling more than 300,-000,000 copies annually by 1960, meant that every family could stock its shelves not just with thrillers and westerns, but with scholarly works and classics.

mass production. An enormous increase in goods available at lowered prices was made possible by the application of machinery to the production of standardized products. The process was evolved by Eli Whitney, who introduced the interchangeable parts system in the manufacture of firearms (1798).

The classic example of mass production, or large-scale production, as it is sometimes called, was its application to the manufacture of automobiles by Henry Ford, early in the 20th century. Ford planned assembly lines on which materials were brought to a large number of men who each performed a specific simple operation as the product moved forward on a belt and parts could be added as it moved in order to form the finished automobile.

In the early days of mass production, water power was used directly to operate machines. But with the coming of steam and electric power, and of gasoline and diesel engines, mass production boomed. The operation has been applied to the manufacture of steel, sewing machines, clothing, shoes, television sets and a huge variety of products.

Mass production is possible where there is mass consumption by large numbers of people who have the purchasing power that enables them to buy the products.

Mather, Cotton (1663–1728). Puritan clergyman. Born in Boston, the son of Increase Mather, he was graduated from Harvard (1678). Ordained an American Congregational clergyman (1685), he assisted his father (1685–1723) before succeeding him in the Second Church pastorate, Boston (1723–28). Active in politics, he helped oust the Royal Governor, Sir Edmund Andros (1689) and supported the new governor, Sir William Phips. He did not protest publicly against the witchcraft trials, although he favored fairer rules of evidence. He defended some of the verdicts in his *Wonders of the Invisible World* (1693). Defeated for the presidency of Harvard, he came to favor Yale as a bastion of Congregational education. He was among the first to recommend smallpox vaccination when an epidemic broke out in Boston (1721). Of some 450 books he authored, his *Magnalia Christi Americana* (1702) was a great literary achievement; also popular in its day was his *Bonifacius* (1710), later titled *Essays to do Good*. A Calvinist and a conservative, his tolerance grew as he recognized the changed standards of his last years.

Mather, Increase (1639–1723). Puritan clergyman. Father of Cotton Mather, he was born in Dorchester, Mass. As president of Harvard (1685–1701), he encouraged the study of science while retaining Congregationalism. He was active in colonial politics; he took petitions to King James II (1688) requesting return of the charter to Massachusetts and secured exception of his colony from Gov. Andros' rule from King William III (1689). He returned to Boston (1692) with Sir William Phips whom he had nominated the royal governor. During the Salem witchcraft trials, he issued the earliest criticism of the witchcraft courts in New England in *Cases of Conscience Concerning Evil Spirits* (1693) and is credited with halting the trials. He was "unequaled in reputation and power by any native-born Puritan of his generation."

Maury, Matthew Fontaine (1806–73). Naval officer and oceanographer. He was born near Fredericksburg, Va. Superintendent of the Dept. of Charts and Instruments and of the Naval Observatory (1842–61), he began a series of researches on winds and currents. He advocated a uniform system of recording oceanographic data which was adopted for naval and merchant ships of the world at the Brussels International Congress (1853). He published *The Physical Geography of the Sea* (1855), the first textbook of modern oceanography and served as a consultant in the laying of the Atlantic Cable. He resigned from the U.S. Navy (1861) and joined the Confederacy, serving as an agent in England (1862–65) where he was instrumental in securing warships. He was professor of meteorology at the Virginia Military Institute (1868–73). Maury Hall, U.S. Naval Academy, Annapolis, is named in his honor.

maverick. Unbranded cattle in Texas came to be known as "one of Maverick's." Samuel A. Maverick, a Texas lawyer, had acquired some cattle in 1845 but his help were too shiftless to brand the cattle.

After the Civil War thousands of unbranded cattle wandered the range and they became known as "mavericks." A cattleman was free to brand any such cattle he found.

The term has been extended to dissenters who take pride in standing alone.

Maximilian Affair. During the Civil War France joined with Spain and Great Britain in using force to collect debts from Mexico. When the debts were collected, Spain and Great Britain withdrew. France, however, remained to set up an empire in Mexico to satisfy Emperor Napoleon III's imperial ambitions. He persuaded an Austrian prince, Archduke Ferdinand Maximilian, to accept the throne in 1864. This was a clear violation of the Monroe Doctrine and the U.S. protested.

When the Civil War ended the U.S. moved troops to the Mexican border to support the demands that France withdraw from Mexico. The Mexicans themselves, under the leadership of Benito Juárez, actively resisted French domination. This resistance, the threat of U.S. intervention and the possibility of war in Europe convinced Napoleon III that he "had a bear by the tail" and that the best thing to do was to "let go." He withdrew his troops and Maximilian was soon captured by the Mexicans and executed (1867).

Maxim machine gun. The gun was invented in 1884 by Sir Hiram Maxim, who was born in Maine but moved to England. It used a belt of cartridges and an early model fired 10 shots per second.

Mayflower Compact (Nov. 11, 1620). The 41 male passengers on the sailing vessel, the *Mayflower*, which brought them to Plymouth, signed an agreement to "frame such just and equal laws . . . as shall be thought most meet and convenient for the general good of the colony. . . ." The only males who did not sign were those who were under age and the two sailors who had agreed to stay only a year.

The Mayflower Compact did not outline a plan of government, but the historic document is a landmark on the road to democracy because it did commit the Pilgrims to a government based on consent of the governed.

Mayo, William Worrall (1819–1911). Physician. He was born in Manchester, England, and came to the U.S. in 1845. He developed St. Mary's Hospital, Rochester, Minn., in which his sons William James (1861–1939) and Charles Horace (1865–1939), surgeons, organized the Mayo Clinic (1889) which became world famous. At a time when new methods of antiseptic surgery were developing, based on principles of Joseph Lister, they traveled widely and brought the newest techniques to Rochester, Minn. William was known especially for operations for cancer and gallstones; Charles for operations for goiter. As the number of patients grew, the Mayo brothers engaged some 200 trained specialists in the cooperative private practice of medicine. In 1915 they established the Mayo Foundation for Medical Education and Research in affiliation with the Univ. of Minnesota to further study leading to an advanced degree in medicine.

Maysville Road Bill (1830). The Bill provided for construction at federal expense of a road from Lexington to Maysville, Ky., in the heart of Henry Clay's country. It was vetoed by Pres. Jackson, who had no love for Clay. Furthermore, he was swayed in this instance by Martin Van Buren who pointed out to the President that transportation improvements in New York and Pennsylvania had been paid for by the states concerned. Jackson vetoed the bill as "a measure of purely local character." In other instances, however, Jackson signed bills which permitted internal improvements at federal expense.

Mazzei letter. Thomas Jefferson's criticism of George Washington and the Federalists became public knowledge in 1797 when his letter of Apr. 24, 1796 to Philip Mazzei was published in Florence, Italy. Jefferson's break in personal relations with Washington, arising from the "Mazzei letter" incident, dates from this time.

Meat Inspection Act (1906). Publication of Upton Sinclair's novel, *The Jungle,* brought to a head mounting criticism of the meat packing industry. The industry had already been castigated after the exposure of the "embalmed beef" sold to U.S. troops in the Spanish-American War.

After determining that Sinclair's charges were based on fact, Pres. Theodore Roosevelt supported passage of the Act. Power was granted to the Secretary of Agriculture to inspect meat and to condemn any found "unwholesome or otherwise unfit for human food."

Mechanicsville, battle of (June 26, 1862). Confederate Gen. Robert E. Lee was repulsed north of Richmond, Va., when he tried to turn Gen. George McClellan's right flank in a battle also known as Beaver Dam Creek.

Mecklenburg Resolutions (May 31, 1775). Citizens meeting in this county in North Carolina denounced the authority of the King and Parliament in the colony. They called upon the Continental Congress to give direction to the Provincial Congress or representative body in each colony. One of the 20 resolutions branded as an enemy anyone who accepted a royal commission.

After the American Revolution it was claimed that a Mecklenburg Declaration of Independence had been proclaimed, May 20, 1775, but the claim is unsupported by historical evidence.

Mediation and Conciliation Service, Federal. Created by the Labor Management Relations Act (1947), the Service possesses no law enforcement authority. Its mediators who are located in seven regional offices rely wholly on persuasive techniques of mediation and conciliation to perform their duties. The Service seeks to prevent or minimize interruptions of the free flow of commerce growing out of labor-management disputes. Mediators assist representatives of labor and management to settle disputes about wages, hours and other aspects of the employment relationship that arise in the course of negotiations. The mediator's basic function is to promote better day-to-day relations between labor and management. He thereby reduces the incidence of work stoppages resulting from disputes about the terms of collective bargaining agreements.

Medicare. Legislation, signed by Pres. Johnson, July 30, 1965, added a program of health insurance to the Social Security Act passed in 1935. Medicare provides health insurance for persons over 65 years old under two plans, one designated as "basic" and the other as "supplementary." The insurance is financed by increases in the Social Security payroll tax.

Under the basic plan provision is made for hospitalization up to 90 days, up to 100 days in a nursing home and up to 100 days of home nursing visits for each spell of illness. Payments by the patient are small (e.g., the first $72 of hospital costs and $18 for each day after 60 days up to the 90-day limit).

Under the supplementary plan, persons enrolling will pay $6.30 a month in premiums for covering most other major medical expenses, except those for dental services, medicines and drugs. Insurance covers physicians' services, including surgery.

Medicaid, also enacted in 1965, is a federal–state–county program that provides health care for needy persons under 65. The federal government pays about 50 percent of the costs with state and local governments sharing the balance. The program was approved by Congress as Title 19 when Medicare was added to the Social Security Act of 1935. Title 19 eliminated the over-65 age requirement of Medicare and extended coverage to disabled adults, children of families on relief and the blind.

megalopolis. The term describes chains of metropolitan areas that have been formed by the overflow of population from cities into areas between that had previously been distinct and separate urban centers. The term was applied by Prof. Jean Gottman of the University of Paris in his Twentieth Century Fund study, *Megalopolis* (1961), to the urban complex which is the Boston-Washington axis. Population experts now see similar megalopolises forming in other parts of the U.S., notably along the California coast from San Francisco to the Mexican border and around lower Lake Michigan from southern Wisconsin to northern Indiana.

"melting pot." This concept of the assimilation of immigrants concentrated in the cities was popular in the decades immediately preceding World War I. The expression was derived from Israel Zangwill's *The Melting Pot* (1908), a drama of race fusion in America. By 1910 most large cities had well-defined "Little Italys" or "Little Polands."

The concept was applied especially to the "new" non-English-speaking immigrants from southern and eastern Europe who had supplanted the "old" immigrants from northern and western Europe. The melting-pot idea was symbolic of the belief that the foreign born would intermingle quickly with the native stock and a new type of American would result. Sociologists now hold that the theory shows little insight into the actual process of adjustment. According to a more recent theory, cultural pluralism, each group has a right to maintain its own cultural life without interference. It points to the enrichment of community life that comes from a variety of cultures and the dignity of the immigrant whose way of life is respected.

Melville, Herman (1819–91). Novelist. Born in New York City, he claims fame largely on the classic, *Moby Dick* (1851). His experiences as a seaman provide a base for much of his work. His life among cannibals, after he deserted the whaler *Acushnet* in 1842, is captured in *Typee* (1846). The first major literary figure to write of South Sea island life, Melville's books on Polynesia include *Omoo* (1847), *Mardi* (1849), *Redburn* (1849) and *White-Jacket* (1850). Working as a customs inspector in New York, he completed his last novel, *Billy Budd* (1891; not published until 1924). His poetry, *Battle Pieces* (1866) and *Clarel* (1876), has been reassessed in the wake of renewed appreciation of his merit as a literary artist.

Mencken, Henry Louis (1880–1956). Editor and literary critic. He was born in Baltimore, Md. A satirist, cynical about democracy, he coined the term "Boobus Americanus." He was associated with various Baltimore newspapers, especially the *Sun*. As the literary critic of the *Smart Set* (1908–23), he helped to gain attention for such writers as Theodore Dreiser, D. H. Lawrence, Ford Maddox Ford and Sherwood Anderson. He was editor (1924–35) of the *American Mercury* which he founded with George Jean Nathan. His most lasting contribution is *The American Language* (several editions, 1919–48).

Mennonites. The sect of Protestant Christians derived its name from Menno Simons, a Dutch reformer. A group migrated from Germany to the American colonies and established Germantown, Pa., in 1683. They have continued as a rural farming people in eastern Pennsylvania, where they are known as Pennsylvania Dutch. Other settlements exist in various parts of the Midwest.

Mennonites take the Bible as their only rule of faith. They keep apart from the world, preserve simplicity of dress and habits and refuse to bear arms or take oaths.

The Amish constitute a conservative division within the Mennonite Church.

mercantilism. According to the economic philosophy practiced by England and other colonial powers during the 17th and 18th centuries, colonies existed for the benefit of the mother country. They were to supply the mother country with raw materials and carry on trade, industry and agriculture in such a way that the trade of the mother country would be increased.

Tariffs protected both the mother country and colonies from foreign competition. The general aim was to bring about a favorable balance of trade that would result in gold and silver coming into the mother country's treasury. English Navigation Acts expressed the mercantilist approach to trade.

The American colonists were not opposed to mercantilism in principle. In general, they benefited from bounties paid them for the production of certain raw materials—naval stores, for example—and evaded the more oppressive restrictions on colonial manufactures.

merchant marine. Privately owned shipping in the U.S. began in the colonial period when New England merchants built ships and engaged in foreign and coastwise trade. There was a shipping boom in the years before the War of 1812 when the struggle between France and England (the Napoleonic Wars) made possible great profits for American shippers willing to risk the loss of vessels to either power in return for high prices for needed cargoes.

After a period of decline the American clipper ship in the 1840's and 1850's placed the U.S. merchant marine in the front rank among the maritime nations of the world. This was followed by another decline because shippers failed to shift quickly enough from wooden sailing vessels to iron steamships. Americans preferred to put their money into railroads, mines, factories and farms.

A merchant marine revival was stimulated by World War I and for the first time a federal agency, the U.S. Shipping Board, was established by Congress (1916) to supervise the merchant marine. Needed encouragement was given in the Jones-White Act (1929) which provided subsidies in the form of mail contracts for shippers who could not meet low operating costs of foreign competition. The Merchant Marine Act (1936) further expanded subsidies. The investment paid off in World War II when the need for shipping reached new heights and the federal government financed the building of "Liberty ships."

In the post World War II period the merchant marine again faced high costs and competition with foreign shippers. There has been a precipitous decline since 1945 in the percentage of imports and exports carried under the U.S. flag (about 8% in 1967). Coastal trade between ports in the U.S. and traffic on the Great Lakes, stimulated by the St. Lawrence Seaway, present a brighter picture.

The U.S. is a close second to the British Commonwealth of Nations in the tonnage of its merchant fleet.

"merchants of death." The term was used to describe munitions makers who profited from U.S. involvement in World War I. Isolationist sentiment which

438

reached a peak in the 1930's was reflected in the Senate investigation (1934), headed by Gerald P. Nye of North Dakota. Committee findings tended to confirm the belief of isolationists that the U.S. had entered World War I to safeguard the interests of munitions makers and bankers whose loans might otherwise have been lost.

Mercury, Project. On Oct. 5, 1961, exactly three years after the inception of the project, Astronaut Alan B. Shepard, Jr., was rocketed into space. The first American to actually orbit the earth was Astronaut John H. Glenn, Jr. His Mercury spacecraft, "Friendship 7," circled the earth three times, Feb. 20, 1962.

Mercury flights have revealed important facts about man's capabilities in space and indicate the real need in space travel for man, who is capable of dealing with the unexpected, in addition to machines that have been set up to deal only with what is known or expected. This project, which explored such basic problems as the possibility of eating while in a state of weightlessness, was the successful beginning of many such projects.

Merryman, Ex parte (1861). John Merryman, a civilian in Maryland, was arrested by the military authorities and imprisoned at Ft. McHenry because of his statements in opposition to the Union cause. He peti-

tioned Chief Justice Taney, sitting in his capacity as a circuit judge, for a writ of habeas corpus. Taney issued the writ but it was ignored by the fort commander. Taney then wrote to Lincoln that it remained for the President to enforce the laws and release Merryman. Lincoln made no answer to Taney's letter but Merryman was later released and turned over to the civilian authorities.

The Merryman case was one example of Lincoln's invasion of private constitutional rights in wartime.

Methodists. The movement originated in 1729 with the teachings of John and Charles Wesley, Oxford students. The name is derived from their resolution to conduct their lives and religious study "by rule and method."

Their ideas were carried to America in 1760 by emigrants from Ireland. In 1766 Philip Embury began preaching in New York. Robert Strawbridge organized a congregation in Maryland. American Methodists were momentarily set back when the Wesleys supported King George III during the Revolutionary War. After the war John Wesley established the American Methodists as an independent body. Francis Asbury and Dr. Thomas Coke were elected bishops of the Methodist Episcopal Church in 1784.

Methodist preachers helped to make religion a vital personal experience. Lay preachers were given "circuits" and moved among different congregations. Their freedom of movement was especially helpful in building congregations on the frontier during the 18th and 19th centuries.

In the early 19th century Negro Methodists withdrew from congregations in the Middle Atlantic states and formed denominations of their own such as the African Methodist Episcopal Church. The controversy over slavery split the Methodists. The Methodist Episcopal Church, South, was formed in 1845. A substantial step toward unity was taken in 1939 with the merger of the church in the South with churches in the North. Methodist bodies in the U.S. have a membership of almost 13,-000,000.

metropolis. Specialists in urban affairs speak of "metropolis" or "metropolitan area" to cover both the old cities and their expanding suburbs. In an attempt to measure them the Census Bureau in 1960 defined a "standard metropolitan statistical area" (SMSA) as a "county or group of contiguous counties (except in New England) which contains at least one city of 50,000 inhabitants or more or 'twin cities' with a combined population of at least 50,000."

With people continuing to flock to the urban fringes since 1960, it seems likely that suburban dwellers now outnumber residents of the traditional cities.

Meuse-Argonne offensive (Sept. 26–Nov. 11, 1918). The last great offensive of World War I was under the overall command of Gen. Foch. American army groups under Gen. Pershing cleared the Argonne Forest, west of Paris, and crossed the Meuse River, driving the Germans northward toward their own borders. The advance was the biggest battle in American history to that time. In the offensive that brought the war to an end, 120,000 of the 1,200,-000 Americans involved were killed or wounded.

Mexican Cession. The territory acquired from Mexico for $18,-250,000 as an outcome of the Mexican War (1846–48) included today's California, most of New Mexico and Arizona, Nevada, Utah and parts of Colorado and Wyoming.

Mexican War (1846–48). The annexation of Texas by the U.S. in 1845 aggravated relations with Mexico, which had never recognized the independence of Texas. At the same time the U.S. was pressing claims against Mexico for injuries and property damages suffered by American citizens. Mexico refused to receive John Slidell as a minister empowered to negotiate the claims and purchase New Mexico and California. In response Pres. Polk ordered American troops under Gen. Zachary Taylor into a disputed area between the Nueces River and the Rio Grande, an act which aroused Mexico. When Gen.

Taylor reported that Mexicans attacked his troops, Polk asked Congress for a declaration of war.

Major military actions of the war included Gen. Taylor's invasion of northern Mexico; the capture of California by a naval force under Capt. Robert F. Stockton, aided by the insurgent army captain and explorer John C. Frémont; and the capture of Mexico City (the "halls of Montezuma") by Gen. Winfield Scott.

The war came to an end with the signing of the Treaty of Guadalupe-Hidalgo (1848). U.S. westward expansion to the Pacific was assured. In his *Memoirs*, Ulysses S. Grant, who had been a second lieutenant in Taylor's army, wrote that it was "the most unjust" war in American history. The war has been justified by those who argue that it was provoked by Mexico's refusal to negotiate with the U.S. and the Mexican attack on Gen. Taylor's troops. The war scarred United States relations with Latin America.

Miami Indians. In general the Algonquian tribe aided the French against the British and put up strong resistance against American advances into their territory in Ohio, Indiana, eastern Illinois and southern Michigan. Their chief, Little Turtle, signed the Treaty of Greenville (1795) when combined Indian tribes were defeated by Wayne. The Miami soon lost all unity and ceded more of their lands to the U.S. in the early 19th century. Some of them found their way to the Indian Territory in Oklahoma where they merged with other tribes.

Michelson, Albert Abraham (1852–1931). Physicist. Born in Prussia, he was brought to the U.S. as an infant (1854). He was graduated from the U.S. Naval Academy (1873) and was a professor of physics at the Univ. of Chicago (1892–1929). He determined with a high degree of accuracy the speed at which light travels and invented an interferometer for measuring distances by means of the length of light waves. He performed an experiment (with E. W. Morley) which showed that the absolute motion of the earth through the ether is not measurable. The Michelson-Morley findings contributed to the development of the theory of relativity. In 1907 he was awarded the Nobel Prize for Physics.

Michigan. The "Wolverine State," an East North Central state, was admitted to the Union as the 26th state, Jan. 26, 1837. Its capital is Lansing.

Michigan (from the Chippewa word micigama, "large water") was first visited by French missionaries and fur traders. Jean Nicolet in 1634 was probably the first white man to explore the Upper Peninsula. He was followed by Jolliet and Marquette. La Salle may have been the first to penetrate the Lower Peninsula.

The French yielded the region to the British in 1763 who ceded it to the U.S. in 1783. It became part of the Northwest Territory in 1787 and was organized as the Michigan Territory in 1805. There was much wrangling over boundaries with the other states that were carved out of the Northwest Territory until Michigan achieved statehood.

The state has access to four out of the five Great Lakes. The Sault Ste. Marie Ship Canal (Soo) connecting Lakes Huron and Superior, conveys the greatest amount of canal traffic in the country.

Michigan leads the world in production of motor vehicles. Detroit, founded by the Frenchman Antoine Cadillac in 1701, is the motor car capital of the world. The state is also a great fruit producer, especially of tart cherries. It is one of the great resort states of the Middle West.

"middle passage." The term refers to the notorious leg of the triangular trade route along which slaves were transported in sailing vessels from Africa to the West Indies or Continental American colonies. Conditions on board were inhuman and many Negroes died en route. The profits were so great that the slave trade continued even after it was legally abolished in 1808.

"midnight judges." In an effort to keep control of the courts in the hands of the Federalist party, Pres. John Adams, on the night before his term of office expired, signed commissions for federal judges. The positions these judges were to fill had been created—also at the last minute—by the outgoing Federalist Congress.

The appointments were cancelled early in Jefferson's administration when the Judiciary Act of 1801 was repealed. The episode led to the famous decision in *Marbury v. Madison*.

Midway, battle of (June 3–6, 1942). The battle was the turning point of the naval war in the Pacific in World War II. Midway, a strategically important island under U.S. control, lay between the Philippine archipelago and Hawaii, about 1,100 miles west of Hawaii. A Japanese armada under Adm. Yamamoto advanced on Midway with the intention of converting it into a huge air base.

Advance knowledge of the attack was had by U.S. intelligence which had broken the main Japanese diplomatic code. The Japanese were met by Adm. Chester W. Nimitz, Commander-in-Chief of the U.S. Pacific Fleet. The naval vessels never came within sight of each other, but planes from U.S. aircraft carriers sank four Japanese carriers, a heavy cruiser and inflicted other damage. The Japanese lost 322 planes. The Americans lost the carrier *Yorktown*, sunk by an enemy submarine, a destroyer and 147 aircraft.

The victory at Midway ended all threats to Hawaii and the

West Coast. It forced the Japanese to take the defensive. Adm. Nimitz commented: "Pearl Harbor has been partially avenged."

"milk for the Hottentots." Political enemies of Vice-President Henry A. Wallace distorted part of his address, May 8, 1942, when he said: "The object of this war is to make sure that everybody in the world has the privilege of drinking a quart of milk a day."

Millay, Edna St. Vincent (1892–1950). Poet. Born in Rockland, Me., she entered into Bohemian life in Greenwich Village, N.Y.C. During that period she published *A Few Figs from Thistles* (1920) and was awarded the Pulitzer Prize (1923) for *The Harp Weaver and Other Poems*. Active in the protest against the Sacco-Vanzetti trial, she wrote the poem "Justice Denied in Mass." (1927). Recognizing the Nazi threat to the democracies she wrote *There Are No Islands Any More* (1940) and *The Murder of Lidice* (1942). Her poetic works include *The Buck in the Snow* (1928) and *Huntsman, What Quarry?* (1939). She also wrote the libretto for *The King's Henchman*, an opera composed by Deems Taylor (produced at Metropolitan Opera House, N.Y.C., 1927).

Miller, Arthur (1915–). Playwright. Born in New York City, he is generally recognized as being among the first dramatists of his time. *Death of a Salesman* (1949) has the proportions of a classic. Other works include *All My Sons* (1947), *The Crucible* (1953), *A View from the Bridge* (1953), *The Misfits* (1961), *After the Fall* (1964), *The Price* (1967).

Miller, Samuel Freeman (1816–90). Jurist. Born in Richmond, Ky., he was appointed associate justice of the U.S. Supreme Court (1862–90) by Pres. Lincoln. A strong supporter of national authority, he upheld the constitutionality of the loyalty oath in the Test-Oath Cases (1867) and voted with the majority in the Legal Tender Cases (1870–71). In the Slaughterhouse Cases (1873) he denied that the 14th Amendment was applicable to business corporations and restricted it to Negroes. He voted with the Republican majority in the Electoral Commission (1876). He was the dominant personality on the bench in his time.

Milligan, Ex parte (1866). The U.S. Supreme Court decided that Lambdin P. Milligan had been unlawfully convicted of treason by a military court established in Indiana on the authority of Pres. Lincoln. The Court reasoned that the President did not have the right to set up military tribunals except in the actual theater of war where civil courts were no longer functioning. The Court held that Milligan, a civilian, had been deprived of his constitutional right to trial by jury in

443

a state where the civil courts were functioning.

The decision was denounced by Radical Republicans who feared that it might be used to oppose the military governments in the South provided for in the congressional reconstruction plans. Congress went forward with its plans in contemptuous disregard of the decision. The constitutionality of the Reconstruction Acts was never passed upon by the Supreme Court.

Millikan, Robert Andrews (1868–1953). Physicist. Born in Morrison, Ill., he was granted a Ph.D. by Columbia (1895). Director of the Norman Bridge Laboratory of Physics, California Institute of Technology (from 1921), he was credited with being the first to isolate the electron and measure its charge. He investigated the penetrating power of cosmic rays, the absorption of X-rays and the effect of temperature on photoelectric discharge. He was awarded the Nobel Prize (1923) for Physics. He wrote *The Electron* (1917) and *Protons, Photons, Neutrons and Cosmic Rays* (1935).

"millionaire's club." The name was applied by critics of big business to the U.S. Senate in pre-World War I years when senators were elected by the state legislatures, prior to adoption of the 17th Amendment (1913).

"Millions for defense, but not one cent for tribute" (1798). The ringing phrase was occasioned by the refusal of representatives of Pres. John Adams to pay a bribe to Talleyrand, Foreign Minister of the French Directory.

It is not true that Charles Pinckney flung this challenge at the emissaries of Talleyrand. It was made as a toast at a dinner honoring one of the representatives on his return from the diplomatic mission to persuade the French to stop their raids on American shipping.

Minnesota. Nicknamed the "North Star State" because its boundary extends further north than any other state, it is also known as the "Gopher State." One of the West North Central states, Minnesota was admitted to the Union as the 32nd state, May 11, 1858. Its capital is St. Paul.

The region was first explored by the Frenchmen Radisson and Groseilliers (1660). The site of the Twin Cities (Minneapolis and St. Paul) was reached in 1680 by La Salle. The territory east of the Mississippi River was ceded by France to England in 1763. The territory west of the Mississippi was in Spain's hands but was joined to the U.S. as part of the Louisiana Purchase.

Indian troubles marked the territory. During the Civil War 650 white people were killed in a Sioux uprising (1862) led by Little Crow. The Indians were crushed in 1863 and forced to move across the Missouri River. In the 1870's thousands of

Scandinavian and German settlers arrived in the state.

Minnesota (from the Dakota Sioux word for "cloudy water," applied first to the river, then to the state) is a leading producer of iron ore. The "biggest man-made hole" is the iron mine in the Mesabi Range. The state has great slaughtering and flour-milling industries. Agriculture is diversified, with production high in oats and butter. Known as the "Land of 10,000 Lakes," the state is noted as a recreation and sports land.

minority Presidents. Under the Electoral College system a candidate may be elected President of the U.S. without winning a majority of the popular vote. This has happened most frequently when three strong candidates competed for the office. Minority Presidents were John Q. Adams, Polk, Taylor, Buchanan, Lincoln, Hayes, Garfield, Cleveland, Harrison, Wilson and Truman.

minstrel shows. A popular form of entertainment in the 19th century and into the 1920's, it involved singing, dancing, comic sketches and acrobatics by white actors who blackened their faces.

One of the earliest origins of Negro minstrelsy is found in a play, *Oroonoko,* produced in Boston (1799) when an actor made himself up as a Negro and sang "The Gay Negro Boy," accompanying himself on the banjo.

E. P. Christy of the famous Christy Minstrels claimed that he organized his minstrels in 1842, a year before his rivals, the Virginia Minstrels, opened at the Chatham Theater in New York City. In the latter part of the 19th century, when minstrel shows were at the height of their popularity, scores of troupes toured the country.

The cakewalk became a popular feature of all minstrel shows after 1877 when the New York musical comedy team of Harrigan and Hart presented a number called "Walking for Dat Cake," an imitation of antebellum plantation "cakewalks."

Mint, Bureau of the. The Mint of the U.S. was established by act of Congress, Apr. 2, 1792, and went into operation in Philadelphia. Silver, gold and copper were coined. When the Coinage Act of 1873 was passed, all mint and assay office activities were placed under the newly organized Bureau of the Mint in the Department of the Treasury. The Mint manufactures all domestic coins and coins for some foreign countries, receives and disburses gold and silver bullion and directs the distribution of coins from the Mints among the Federal Reserve Banks. It also manufactures medals for the armed services.

Minuit, Peter (1580–1638). Colonial governor. Born in Wesel, Duchy of Cleves (Germany), he is remembered as the Dutch director–general of New Netherland who purchased

Manhattan Island (1626) from the Indians for 60 guilders ($24). Dismissed by the West India Co. in 1631 because of differences with Dutch Reformed ministers in New Amsterdam, he next led a Swedish company in the settlement of the right bank of the Delaware (now Trenton, N.J.) and called it New Sweden (1638). He built Fort Christina (now the site of Wilmington, Del.). Minuit was lost at sea.

Minuteman. The name designates a series of intercontinental nuclear-tipped ballistic missiles. In 1965 there were 800 Minuteman I missiles, first-generation solid-fuel weapons, in firing position in the U.S. They are capable of hurling a nuclear warhead with the explosive equivalent of one million tons of TNT at targets about 6,300 miles away. Minuteman II was expected to have a range of 9,000 miles with twice the accuracy and 30% more of a warhead.

Minutemen. A special force was authorized by the Continental Congress in 1775 to be ready to spring to arms on a moment's notice. They were organized in Massachusetts and several other colonies.

Minutemen and militia were lined up on the village green at Lexington (Apr. 19, 1775) to resist the march of British regulars on Concord.

Miranda v. Arizona (1966). In a detailed opinion by Chief Justice Warren, the U.S. Supreme Court in a five to four ruling declared that the 5th Amendment's privilege against self-incrimination rules out confessions by persons in police custody, unless careful steps are taken to protect a suspect's rights. In the atmosphere of the police station, the Court reasoned "no statement obtained from the defendant can truly be the product of his free choice."

According to the ruling, the police must warn all persons in their custody that they have a right to counsel and to remain silent, and must provide lawyers for those too poor to pay.

The Court's conclusion was based on a new and refined view of the "coercion" necessary to violate the 5th Amendment's command that "no person . . . shall be compelled in any criminal case to be a witness against himself." Warren's majority report was presented with the concurrence of Justices Black, Brennan, Douglas and Fortas.

Justice Harlan dissented, denouncing the majority decision as "dangerous experimentation" at a time of a "high crime rate that is a matter of growing concern."

Mischianza ball. The elaborate entertainment was provided for Gen. Howe by his officers on his departure from Philadelphia (May 18–19, 1778). The celebration arranged by Major John André was attended by distinguished Loyalists in the city.

Missionary Ridge, battle of (Nov. 25, 1863). A Confederate force under Gen. Braxton Bragg was defeated in the mountains of Tennessee, east of Chattanooga. They were forced from the Ridge by Union troops led by Gen. George Thomas, who was under orders of Gen. Ulysses S. Grant.

Mississippi. The "Bayou State," also called the "Magnolia State," is an East South Central state in the Deep South. It was admitted to the Union as the 20th state, Dec. 10, 1817. Its capital is Jackson.

The region was crossed by De Soto in 1540 but Spain did nothing about colonizing it. La Salle sailed down to the mouth of the Mississippi in 1682 and claimed its valley for France. The French established permanent posts near the present cities of Biloxi and Natchez about 1700. The land was ceded to England in 1763 and Spain captured it in 1781. The U.S. took over in 1798 and established the Mississippi Territory. The boundaries were changed several times before its admission as a slave state.

The state seceded from the Union, Jan. 9, 1861. Jefferson Davis, a citizen of Mississippi, became Pres. of the Confederacy. With the capture of Vicksburg by the Union in 1863 most of the state came under federal control. It was readmitted to the Union, Feb. 23, 1870.

Mississippi (meaning great river in Algonquian) is primarily an agricultural state. Cotton is the major crop. It is one of the chief states in lumber production and leads the nation in tung oil, used in paint and varnish.

"Mississippi Bubble." A company was organized in 1718 in France by John Law, a Scotsman, to develop the French territory of Louisiana. Law's business reputation was so substantial that when the company expanded to include trade operations in the Indies, China and Africa, prices of its stock skyrocketed. The "bubble" burst in 1720 when public confidence in the venture was impaired. Many were financially ruined.

Mississippi River. The "Father of Waters" is the principal waterway in the U.S. and stretches about 2,350 miles from northern Minnesota to the Gulf of Mexico. It was discovered by Hernando de Soto in 1541 and claimed for France by Robert La Salle in 1682. The French controlled it until the end of the French and Indian War (1763). It became the western boundary of the U.S. at the end of the Revolutionary War (1783). Western farmers were dependent upon it to get their crops to the East and to Europe. When the Spanish closed the mouth of the river to them in the 1790's it led to the threat of war with Spain and possible secession of the West from the U.S. These threats evaporated when the river became part of the U.S. with the Louisiana Purchase (1803).

447

River traffic was boosted by steamboats from 1830–60, and St. Louis, Mo., became the greatest river port in the U.S.

During the Civil War control of the river was vital to the South. When New Orleans was captured by the Federals in 1862 and other points on the river were lost in 1863, the Confederacy was divided.

The flooding of the river has caused great damage. Engineering projects are usually under way to make the "Great River" manageable. Its major tributaries are the Missouri, Ohio, Arkansas and Red rivers.

Missouri. The "Show Me State," a West Central state, was admitted to the Union as the 24th state, Aug. 10, 1821. Its capital is Jefferson City.

Missouri (meaning muddy river) was probably traversed by de Soto in 1541 but it was the French missionaries and traders Marquette, Jolliet and La Salle who reached the area in 1682 and made permanent settlement possible. The French claimed Missouri as part of the province of Louisiana, ceded it to Spain in 1762 and regained it in 1800. The U.S. acquired it in the Louisiana Purchase (1803). Missouri was organized as a territory in 1812 and was later admitted to the Union as a slave state as provided in the Missouri Compromise (1820).

Since most of the settlers in Missouri were from free states, Missouri did not secede from the Union during the Civil War. A "border state," it was subject to guerrilla warfare and regular army raids.

Missouri has been one of the principal agricultural states, raising corn, cotton and wheat. It is the nation's chief source of lead and zinc. St. Louis is a great railroad center and Kansas City is important for grain milling and meat packing.

Missouri Compromise (1820). The 22 states in the Union were equally divided when Missouri applied for admission as a slave state in 1819. The South was infuriated when it was proposed that importation of slaves be prohibited as a condition of admission. The North was aroused by the prospect that the balance in the Senate would be tipped in favor of the South.

A compromise was achieved when Maine (formerly part of Massachusetts) was admitted as a free state. Missouri came in as a slave state but slavery was prohibited in the remaining parts of the Louisiana Territory above 36° 30′ (the southern boundary of Missouri).

Bitterness was diminished by the compromise but Jefferson, reflecting on the temper of the times, wrote that it was "like a fire bell in the night. . . . I considered it at once as the knell of the Union. It is hushed, indeed, for the moment. But this is a reprieve only, not a final sentence."

Missouri-Kansas-Texas Railroad Co. ("Katy"). The road started in 1865 and took its present name in 1870. It now operates about 3,000 miles of road extending from St. Louis and Kansas City through Missouri, Kansas and Oklahoma to San Antonio, Houston and Galveston, Tex. The road serves many important oil producing and refining centers.

Mitchell, Maria (1818–89). Astronomer and educator. Born in Nantucket, Mass., she discovered comets (1847) and studied sunspots. She was the first professor of astronomy at Vassar College (from 1865), and the first woman elected to American Academy of Arts and Sciences.

Mitchell, William (1879–1936). Army officer and aviator. Born in Nice, France, of American parentage, he entered the U.S. Army as a private (1898) and attained the rank of brigadier general (1920). He commanded the aviation section of the Signal Corps, AEF (1917–18). Between World Wars, "Billy" Mitchell urged establishment of the Air Force as an independent branch of the Armed Forces. His outspoken criticism of the War and Navy Departments resulted in his conviction by a court-martial (1925). He resigned his commission and advocated his ideas as a civilian. In advance of his times, his ideas are reflected in the establishment of the U.S. Air Force as a separate branch (equal to the Army and Navy) of the Department of Defense.

Mitchell, William, court martial (1925). Brig. Gen. William ("Billy") Mitchell made a brilliant record in World War I as a pilot and strategist. After the war he urged establishment of a separate air arm and demonstrated the capacity of airplanes by sinking obsolete warships in test bombing attacks. His criticism of the War and Navy Departments led to his court martial, and he was suspended from the service. He resigned in 1926 and carried on his campaign as a civilian. His confidence in the military potential of airplanes was justified by the Army Air Force of World War II.

Moby Dick (1851). One of America's greatest literary masterpieces, the novel by Herman Melville describes the pursuit by a Yankee whaling captain, Ahab, a godlike but ungodly man, of a gigantic white whale that symbolized the beauty, the wickedness and the mystery of nature.

Melville rejected the optimism of the transcendentalists and felt that man faced a tragic destiny. His views were not popular in his day but less hopeful generations have accepted his gloomy insights.

Melville also wrote popular sketches of life in the South Seas: *Typee* (1846) and *Omoo* (1847).

Modoc War (1872–73). The final resistance of the Indians in the Northwest was led by Capt. Jack (Kintpuash) of the Modocs. He clashed with white settlers over the Lost River country south of Upper Klamath Lake in southern Oregon. He resisted the troops which sought to force him onto a reservation on the lake and fought them in the lava beds below the California line, killing both settlers and soldiers. Attack after attack failed to dislodge Capt. Jack and he killed the peace commissioners who came out to him, including the noted Gen. E. R. S. Canby. Pres. Grant was outraged and ordered his commander of the Army, Gen. William T. Sherman, to end the Modoc uprising. The Modocs were finally shelled out of the lava beds with field guns. Capt. Jack and three of his lieutenants were hanged. The rest of the band were sent to a malaria-infested corner of the Indian Territory.

Mohave. Living in the Colorado River region the Indians, of Yuman linguistic stock, were nomads although they practiced farming. They resisted the advance of the whites but were finally subdued and forced in 1865 to settle on a reservation in Arizona.

Mohawk and Hudson Railroad. The line started laying tracks in the summer of 1830 and the *DeWitt Clinton* pulled a train of cars over its tracks between Albany and Schenectady, Aug. 9, 1831. The locomotive was built by the West Point Foundry, the same company that had provided the South Carolina Railroad with its first two engines. The Mohawk and Hudson was the first link in the New York Central System.

Mohawks. These Indians, members of the Iroquois League, occupied the Mohawk Valley in New York. The name "Mohawk" came from an Algonquian term meaning "maneaters" and early accounts of the tribe describe its ferocity. It may be, however, that they were the most easterly of the Five Nations and had the closest contacts with the first European colonies in the 17th century. Some of the early accounts refer to the Five Nations as the Mohawk, who were thus given the onus for attacks by other tribes in the League. Some of the survivors live near Hogansburg, N.Y.

Mohawk Trail. During the colonial period the Trail through the Appalachians was a gateway to the West. It followed the Mohawk River in New York from Schenectady to Rome and then continued on lesser trails to the Great Lakes region. The Trail declined in importance with the opening of the Erie Canal (1825) and the growth of railroads. The Genesee Road from Albany to Buffalo, an early 19th-century route to the West, ran parallel to it.

Mohegans. The chief village of the Indians during the colonial period became the site of the present town of Mohegan, Conn., on the Thames River. Under the leadership of Uncas they split off from the Pequots and helped the English colonists. The Mohegans, an Algonquian people, eventually surrounded by white settlements, accepted a reservation on the Thames.

Molasses Act (1733). The Act placed prohibitive duties on rum, molasses and sugar imported by the American colonies from the French and Spanish West Indies. Parliament wanted the Continental Colonies to buy these products from the British West Indies. The British West Indies could not, however, meet the demand and there was widespread evasion of the law. It was repealed by the Sugar Act (1764).

Molino del Rey, battle of (Sept. 8, 1847). In the march on Mexico City, Gen. William J. Worth under Gen. Winfield Scott's orders attacked the gun foundry of Molino del Rey just outside the gates of the city. The heavily entrenched Mexicans resisted strongly before surrendering.

Molly Maguires. The notorious secret organization of coal miners allegedly was a faction of the Ancient Order of Hibernians, founded in Pennsylvania in 1871 as a charitable association.

The Molly Maguires were charged with terrorizing the coal fields and preventing miners who wished to return to work during "the long strike" (1874–75) from doing so. They were also charged with intimidation of the coal operators, as the secret society of the 1840's once intimidated Irish landlords under the leadership of the widow Molly Maguire, from whom the organization took its popular name.

A Pinkerton detective, James McParlan, was planted among the Molly Maguires by the Philadelphia and Reading Railroad, owner of mines in the anthracite fields. McParlan's testimony made possible the trial and conviction of 24 of the Molly Maguires in 1875. Ten of them were hanged for murder and the others imprisoned for terms of two to seven years. An end result was the breakup of the miners' union and the end of the strike.

Monitor and *Merrimac*. The first ironclad vessels built in the United States were pitted against each other during the Civil War.

The *Merrimac* (renamed the *Virginia*) was the Confederate ironclad that had been converted from the hull of a Union ship scuttled in Norfolk Harbor during the Union evacuation. This "cheesebox on a raft" was sent out to clear Hampton Roads of Union naval support for armies preparing for the Peninsular Campaign. It proceeded to destroy two Union warships and was waiting to demolish a third when the Union answer arrived.

The *Monitor* came down Hampton Roads and met the *Merrimac* in a five-hour fight, Mar. 9, 1862. The shells bouncing on iron did only slight damage and the engagement was a draw. The *Merrimac* headed back into Norfolk and was destroyed when the port was evacuated in May. It had served the Confederate cause by permitting Gen. Robert E. Lee to shift forces from the Potomac to the defense of Richmond. It had never really been a threat to the Union blockade because it could not navigate in the open Atlantic.

The battle of the ironclads signaled the end of wooden naval vessels. Northern shipyards proceeded to turn out dozens of ironclads.

Monmouth, battle of (June 28, 1778). In the battle in New Jersey, Gen. Washington sought to disrupt the movement of Gen. Henry Clinton's forces from Philadelphia to New York. Gen. Charles Lee failed to carry out Washington's orders and retreated too soon. Washington arrived in time to check the flight of Lee's forces. Lee was court-martialed and suspended from the service. Clinton's forces reached New York. Washington took a position at White Plains, above New York City.

Monroe, James (1758–1831). Fifth President of U.S. (1817–25). Born in Westmoreland County, Va., he was graduated from the College of William and Mary (1776). A Virginia member of the Continental Congress (1783–86), U.S. Senator (1790–94), minister to England (1803–07), he helped negotiate the Louisiana Purchase. He was U.S. Sec. of State (1811–17), and then President during the "Era of Good Feelings." The high points of his administration include the Florida Purchase (1819) and the Monroe Doctrine (1823).

Monroe Doctrine (1823). The basic statement of American foreign policy was made by Pres. Monroe in a message to Congress. The words and ideas were in large part those of Sec. of State John Quincy Adams who had warned Russia against attempting to exclude all but Russian vessels from the northwest coast of North America.

Monroe made four main points: (1) that the American continents were not open to any further European colonization; (2) that the U.S. would oppose any attempt to extend the European system of monarchy to the Americas; (3) that the U.S. would not interfere with existing colonies; (4) that the U.S. would not meddle in the internal affairs of any European country.

The immediate occasion for Monroe's message was Russia's threat to extend its holdings south of Alaska and the report that Spain might seek to regain control of the newly independent colonies in South America. Britain had proposed joining with the U.S. in a warning to European powers planning to help Spain recover the colonies. Adams, however, insisted that the U.S. make its own declaration rather "than to come in as a cock-boat in the wake of the British man-of-war."

The Doctrine was cited by the U.S. on major occasions such as British and French interference in the U.S. annexation of Texas, France's attempt to establish the empire of Maximilian in Mexico during the Civil War, Britain's dispute with Venezuela over the latter's boundary and efforts of European powers to collect debts from Caribbean countries early in the 20th century.

At first the Monroe Doctrine was regarded contemptuously by European powers. It never became international law but the growing military power of the United States gave it practical effectiveness. Lafayette, in France, sensing what the Monroe Doctrine could mean, called it "the best little bit of paper that God ever permitted any man to give to the world." It gave Americans new self-esteem and continues to carry emotional force.

Montana. The "Treasure State" or "Bonanza State," a Mountain group state, was admitted to the Union as the 41st state, Nov. 8, 1889. Its capital is Helena.

The first white men to explore Montana (meaning mountainous in Latin) were the French Vérendryes, father and sons (1743). Lewis and Clark traversed part of the region when they followed the Missouri River to its source (1805). The land was passed back and forth between France and Spain. The eastern part, three-fifths of which is in the Great Plains, became part of the U.S. with the Louisiana Purchase (1803). The Continental Divide runs through the western third of the state. The part west of the Rockies was in the Oregon Territory. Montana was organized as a territory in 1864.

The popular names for the state are explained by the finding of gold in the 1850's and 1860's. The discovery of silver and copper followed that of gold. The state's biggest smelter is at Anaconda. Mineral production includes coal. Agriculture, manufacturing and tourism are major sources of income. The state is a big producer of spring wheat.

Monterey, battle of (Sept. 1846). Early in the Mexican War Gen. Zachary Taylor with 6,600 men captured the city of Monterey in northeastern Mexico, although outnumbered by a Mexican force of 10,000. This ended the campaign on the Rio Grande.

Monticello. The home and burial place of Thomas Jefferson is on a hill three miles southeast of Charlottesville, Va. It was designed by Jefferson himself. The magnificent estate is open to the public.

Moody, Dwight Lyman (1837–99). Evangelist. Born in Northfield, Mass., he was a shoe salesman in Boston and Chicago before giving up business to devote himself to city missionary work. Accompanied by the organist and singer Ira D. Sankey, he preached to millions in urban Great Britain, U.S. and Canada (1873–99). He founded the Northfield Seminary for girls (1879), the Mount Hermon School for boys (1881) and the Chicago Bible Institute (1889, now called Moody Bible Institute). He stimulated Young Men's Christian Associations on college campuses as well as in Chicago. He believed in personal evangelism with emphasis on God's fatherly love.

Moore's Creek Bridge, battle of (Feb. 27, 1776). Early in the Revolution a Loyalist force in North Carolina, near Wilmington, was defeated by Whigs in an action that has been described as the "Lexington and Concord of the South." The Loyalist defeat dissuaded Gen. Henry Clinton, who had arrived off Cape Fear, N.C., from landing with a British expeditionary force.

Moravians. Members of the Renewed Church of the Brethren, or *Unitas Fratrum*, are followers of John Huss, the Czech religious reformer who broke with the Roman Catholic Church early in the 15th century. They first settled in Georgia in 1735 but moved on to Pennsylvania where they founded Nazareth and Bethlehem, about 1741. About a decade later some moved to the South where they founded Salem, in North Carolina, now part of Winston-Salem.

This evangelical Protestant sect was active in missionary work among the Indians. They are conscientious objectors to war and have laid heavy stress on education. Moravians in the U.S. now number about 70,000.

Morey letter. Two weeks before election day in 1880 a letter was published allegedly written by James A. Garfield, the Republican nominee for President, to "H. L. Morey" of the Employers' Union of Lynn, Mass. Calculated to alienate labor from Garfield, the fictitious letter favored continued immigration of Chinese.

Morgan, Daniel (1736–1802). Revolutionary soldier. Born in Hunterdon Co., N.J., he moved as a youth to Virginia. He served under Benedict Arnold in the unsuccessful assault on Quebec (1775) and commanded the sharpshooters opposing Gen. Burgoyne at Saratoga (1777). As brigadier-general in North Carolina, he decisively defeated the British at Cowpens (1781). He commanded the Virginia militia in helping to suppress the Whiskey insurrection (1794) in western Pennsylvania.

Morgan, John Pierpont (1837–1913). Banker and financier. Born in Hartford, Conn., he was the son of Junius S. Morgan. He acted as New York agent for his father's firm (1860–64). He gained prominence in 1873 when he broke Jay Cooke's monopoly in the refunding operations of the government. He managed a long series of railroad and other corporate reorganizations, notably that of the U.S. Steel Corp. (1901). He aided Pres. Cleveland's administration by forming a syndicate which halted a drain of gold from the U.S. Treasury (1895). He formed J. P. Morgan & Co. in 1895. He helped to overcome the money Panic of 1907 and became a symbol of financial power in the nation. A major collector of books and art, his collections are now housed in the Pierpont Morgan Wing of the Metropolitan Museum of Art and the Pierpont Morgan Library, both in New York City.

Morgan, Lewis Henry (1818–81). Ethnologist and anthropologist. Born near Aurora, N.Y., he practiced law in Rochester, N.Y., but interested himself in the study of American Indian culture. The "father of American anthropology," his works include *The League of the . . . Iroquois* (1851), the first scientific account of an Indian tribe; *Systems of Consanguinity and Affinity of the Human Family* (1871); *Ancient Society* (1877, 1878) and *Houses and House-Life of the American Aborigines* (1881).

Morgan, Thomas Hunt (1866–1945). Zoologist. Born in Lexington, Ky., he was granted a Ph.D. by Johns Hopkins Univ. (1890). He was a professor of experimental zoology at Columbia (1904–28) and, from 1928, director of biological science at California Institute of Technology. His experiments with fruit fly (Drosophila) mutations added to the knowledge of the genes and provided the basis for the development of the science of genetics. In 1933 he was awarded the Nobel Prize for discoveries relating to the laws and mechanisms of heredity.

Morgan's raiders. Col. John Hunt Morgan, a Kentucky Confederate officer, caused considerable damage by his cavalry raids in Kentucky and Tennessee during the Civil War. "Morgan and his terrible men" were captured in Ohio, July 1863, but escaped from the penitentiary at Columbus, Nov. 27, to continue raiding. He was killed at Greenville, Tenn., Sept. 4, 1864, when his headquarters was surrounded.

Mormons. The Church of Jesus Christ of Latter-Day Saints was founded at Fayette, in western New York, in 1830, by Joseph Smith after revelations which he claimed led him to the golden plates on which was printed the *Book of Mormon.* In his translation the Indians were viewed as descendants of the lost tribes of Israel. Smith and his followers undertook the task of converting them.

The Mormons settled in Kirtland, Ohio, where they practiced communal living. Business reverses in 1837 forced them to move to Jackson County, Mo., from which they were driven in 1838 because of their Abolitionist views. They then moved to Nauvoo, Ill., where the sect itself divided over Smith's revelation that plural marriages (polygamy) were permissible. When Smith smashed the press of the faction attacking him, he was thrown into prison by the non-Mormon authorities. Although the Mormons had enjoyed five years of prosperity in Nauvoo, the sect was generally unpopular. A mob took the Prophet from jail and shot him and his brother (June 27, 1844). Relations with the non-Mormons at this point deteriorated into disorders known as the Mormon War (1844-46).

In 1846 a new leader, Brigham Young, "The Lion of the Lord," led the Mormons over a route that became known as the Mormon Trail from Nauvoo, across Iowa, along the north side of the Platte River, over part of the Oregon Trail, through South Pass in the Rockies, to Fort Bridger in Wyoming and on to the "Great Basin" (Salt Lake Valley). Salt Lake City became the Mormon's Zion, famous for its great temple. The community was cooperative rather than competitive. Plural marriage was made a doctrine of the church in Utah by Young in 1852. In 1890, however, the head of the Mormon Church issued a manifesto to the Saints calling upon them to respect the marriage laws of the U.S.

The Mormons have always placed emphasis on missionary work and their heavy expenses are met chiefly by "tithing." A convert pays in one-tenth of his property and afterward annually one-tenth of the "increase." There are now about 2,000,000 Latter-Day Saints in the U.S.

Morrill Land Grant Act (1862). The Act, introduced into Congress by Rep. Justin S. Morrill (Republican, Vt.) and signed by Pres. Lincoln, enabled the states to establish colleges for agriculture, the mechanical arts and military science. The program had long been urged by Jonathan Baldwin Turner, an Illinois educational and agricultural reformer.

Under the Act each state received 30,000 acres of land for each representative and senator in Congress. The grants made possible the establishment of new colleges and revitalized some of the existing ones. The institutions became known as land grant colleges.

Morrill Tariff (1861). Tariff levels moved upward in the first of a number of tariff acts passed during the Civil War. Protectionists were in the saddle again. The Morrill Tariff sought to attract to the Republican party Pennsylvania and some of the Western states by raising duties on iron and wool.

The war necessitated heavy internal revenue taxes on manufacturers. The raised tariff duties were intended as compensation for the internal taxes.

During the post-Civil War period, tariff schedules were slightly reduced but the country was clearly committed to the protective tariff.

Morris, Gouverneur (1752–1816). Statesman. Born in Morrisania, N.Y., he was graduated from King's College (now Columbia Univ.) in 1768. At first reluctant to break with Britain, he was a member of the Continental Congress (1778–79). As Assistant Superintendent of Finance (1781–85), he planned our decimal coinage system. Morris was a Pennsylvania delegate to the Constitutional Convention (1787) and favored a strong central government in the hands of the rich and well born. Extensive business experience in Europe qualified him for service as U.S. commissioner to England (1790–91) and U.S. minister to France (1792–94), where he sympathized with the French monarchy. A staunch member of the Federalist party, he served New York in the U.S. Senate (1800–03) and was Chairman of the Erie Canal Commission (1810–13).

Morris, Robert (1734–1806). Financier of the American Revolution. Born near Liverpool, England, he came to America about 1747. He was successful in the export-import business in Philadelphia and signed the non-importation agreement of 1765, opposing the Stamp Act. A member of the Continental Congress, he thought the Declaration of Independence premature; but he signed it in Aug. 1776. He arranged for financing the purchases of supplies for Washington's armies (1776–78) and served as superintendent of finance (1781–84). He was virtually the nation's financial dictator during difficult times. He founded and organized the Bank of North America (1782). A delegate to the Constitutional Convention (1787), he favored a strong central government. He served as U.S. Senator from Pennsylvania (1789–95). Financially ruined by speculation in western lands, he was confined in Philadelphia's debtor prison (1798–1801). He died a nearly forgotten man.

Morse, Samuel Finley Breese (1791–1872). Inventor and artist. Born in Charlestown, Mass., his name is linked permanently with the Morse Code devised by him for use in the telegraph for which he filed a patent in 1837. After much litigation, his rights to the telegraph were established and he made a fortune from its commercial application. Prior to his interest in telegraphy, he had made a reputation as a portrait painter and was the first president (1826–42) of the National Academy of Design. His public image was marred by brief activity in Nativist and anti-Catholic agitation.

Morton, William Thomas Green (1819–68). Dentist. He was born in Charlton, Mass. At the suggestion of a Boston chemist, Charles T. Jackson, he employed drops of ether as a local anesthetic during the filling of a tooth (1844). He tested ether on animals and himself. It was used successfully in a surgical operation (Oct. 16, 1846) when Dr. John C. Warren removed a tumor from the neck of a patient anesthetized by Morton's process. Morton and Jackson received the patent for the use of "letheon" (1846). Morton insisted that the discovery was entirely his. A rival claimant, Dr. Crawford W. Long (1815–78) of Athens, Ga., published accounts (1848, 1853) of independent discoveries he had made with sulphuric ether in operations on patients. But Morton assumed full responsibility for the first use of ether in an operation on a human being and is credited with the discovery of ether for surgical use.

Mosby's rangers. Col. John S. Mosby, a Confederate cavalry officer, operated behind Union lines in Virginia and Maryland during the Civil War. He captured Federal Brig. Gen. Edwin H. Stoughton at Fairfax Court House, Va., March 9, 1863. In the "greenback raid" (Oct. 14, 1864), Mosby seized $168,000 dividing it among his men to buy new uniforms and equipment. Union forces regarded the rangers as robbers. Mosby survived until 1916 and published *Mosby's War Reminiscences* (1887).

Moscow Conference (Oct. 19–30, 1943). The spokesmen for the Allies were their foreign ministers: Sec. of State Cordell Hull for the U.S., Anthony Eden for Britain and V. M. Molotov for the Soviet Union. They set the machinery in mo-

tion for a new world organization—the United Nations.

Italy was promised aid in establishing democracy after "Fascism and all its evil influence . . . shall be completely destroyed." Austria was promised liberation from the Nazis; the annexation of Austria by Germany in 1938 was declared null and void. Severe punishment was promised for the "atrocities, massacres and cold-blooded mass executions which are being perpetrated by Hitlerite forces."

motion pictures. Experimentation with moving pictures (serial photographs) was carried on in the 1870's and was spurred by Thomas Edison's invention of a workable camera in the late 1880's. His Kinetograph camera and viewer were patented in 1893. This development was one step away from projecting moving images on a screen, and this was done in France in 1895. By the late 1890's motion pictures were being shown in Europe and the U.S. The early theaters built in the U.S. charged five cents admission and were known as "nickelodeons."

Motion picture production was moved from New York City to Hollywood, favored by better weather, shortly before World War I. The first full-length film made in Hollywood was "The Squaw Man" (1913), with Dustin Farnum, produced by Jesse Lasky, Cecil B. De Mille and Samuel Goldwyn. A star system developed when Mary

Pickford and Charles Chaplin became world famous in the post-World War I period. The silent film gave way to talking pictures with the advent of Al Jolson in "The Jazz Singer" (1927). Color films came in during the mid-1930's and "Gone With the Wind" (1939) assured their predominance.

Motion pictures were jolted by the competition of television in the 1950's, but fought back with wide screens and spectaculars such as "The Robe" (1953). Drive-in theaters attracted large audiences. In the 1960's the better foreign films enjoyed a market in the U.S. while American film producers continued to count on exports for a substantial part of their revenue.

Motley, John Lothrop (1814–77). Historian and diplomat. Born in Dorchester, Mass., he interested himself in the history of the Netherlands and worked in archives in Germany and Holland. *The Rise of the Dutch Republic* (3 vols., 1856), a dramatic interpretation of the Netherlands' fight for liberty, won immediate acclaim. His other works include *The History of the United Netherlands* (4 vols., 1860, 1867) and *The Life and Death of John of Barneveld* (1874). He was U.S. Minister to Austria (1861–67) and to Great Britain (1869–70).

Moultrie, Fort, battle of (June 28, 1776). The palmetto log fort on Sullivan Island, in Charleston Harbor, was named after its defender, Col. William Moultrie. It successfully resisted British warships under Sir Peter Parker. British Gen. Henry Clinton's troops were also turned back from Charleston the same day. These defeats dissuaded the British from fighting in South Carolina for two years.

"Mountain Men." The name was applied to fur trappers in the Rocky Mountain region in the early 19th century. Christopher ("Kit") Carson was one of the most celebrated of these trappers.

Mount Vernon. The home and burial place of George Washington overlooks the Potomac River, 16 miles south of Washington, D.C. The buildings, gardens and grounds have been restored and are open to the public.

Mount Vernon conference (1785). The meeting, a forerunner of the Constitutional Convention, was held at the invitation of George Washington. The representatives of Virginia and Maryland met in Alexandria, Va. (Alexandria conference), late in March, and laid plans for the use of the Potomac River that was a boundary between the two states and also a water route leading to the western lands. On Mar. 28 they continued the conference at Mount Vernon. They agreed to a conference to be held the following year—to include Delaware, Maryland, Virginia and Pennsylvania—to discuss still other problems of commerce (Annapolis Convention). This meeting, in turn, led to the Constitutional Convention of 1787.

muckrakers. The term was coined in a speech by Pres. Theodore Roosevelt in 1906 to describe the writers who were uncovering corruption in business and politics during the early 1900's. He compared them to the man in Bunyan's *Pilgrim's Progress* "who was offered the celestial crown for his muck-rake, but would neither look up nor regard the crown he was offered, but continued to rake the filth on the floor."

The leading muckraking journals were *McClure's Magazine, Everybody's, Cosmopolitan, Collier's* and the *American Magazine.* Some of the great muckraking books were *The Shame of the Cities* (1904) by Lincoln Steffens, *History of the Standard Oil Company* (1904) by Ida Tarbell, *The Jungle* (1906) by Upton Sinclair.

In contrast to Roosevelt's fear that the muckrakers would arouse dangerous discontent, the people's reaction was to accept the revelations as a challenge to clean up politics and to press for the regulation of business in the public interest.

Mugwumps. The derisive name designated the Independent Republicans who opposed James Blaine, the candidate of the party regulars in 1884. They bolted their party and supported Grover Cleveland. Their desire for change was confined largely to civil service reform and tariff reduction.

The term originated in an Algonquian word, mugwump, meaning chief, but was used in the 19th century to describe people who acted with self-importance.

Mulligan letters. On the basis of letters written by him, Republican aspirant for the Presidency James G. Blaine was accused of using his position as Speaker of the House of Representatives for personal gain by issuing a land grant to the Little Rock and Fort Smith Railroad.

James Mulligan, an employee of the Boston businessman to whom Blaine had written, testified about the letters before a congressional committee on May 31, 1876. Their publication in 1884 contributed to Blaine's defeat in the election.

Multilateral Force (MLF). The phrase denotes a U.S. proposal in 1963 to share control of nuclear weapons among the North Atlantic Treaty Organization (NATO) powers. The idea, calling for a fleet armed with Polaris missiles and manned by crews of various nations, was endorsed by Presidents John F. Kennedy and Lyndon B. Johnson but was not adopted by NATO.

Munn v. Illinois (1877). The U.S. Supreme Court affirmed the right of the state to fix maximum storage rates for grains. The warehouse firm of Munn and Scott had appealed to the courts on the grounds that it was being deprived of its property without due process of law guaranteed by the 14th Amendment. Chief Justice Waite held that the state regulation was warranted because the storage of grain affected the public interest.

The decision, the first of The Granger Cases, was a high point in the Granger movement which had pressed for passage of the state law. It was reversed in the Wabash Case (1886).

Murchison letter. During the presidential campaign of 1888, when Pres. Cleveland and Benjamin Harrison were the Democratic and Republican candidates, respectively, Charles F. Murchison, inspired by Republican politicians, wrote a letter to the British minister at Washington, Lord Sackville-West. In effect he asked whether the election of Cleveland would be helpful to Britain. The minister rose to the bait and replied that Britain would prefer Cleveland. The correspondence was released to the press at Los Angeles, Oct. 21, 1888. It probably contributed to Cleveland's defeat by alienating the Irish and other voters and confirming the Republican charge that the British were behind the reduction in tariff. Pres. Cleveland forced the minister's withdrawal after the election.

Murfreesboro, battle of (Dec. 31, 1862–Jan. 2, 1863). In the battle fought near Nashville,

Tenn., Confederate Gen. Braxton Bragg failed to defeat Union forces under Gen. William Rosecrans, who had been sent south by Gen. Ulysses S. Grant. Losses were heavy on both sides with Rosecrans losing almost a third of his army. Bragg retreated to Chattanooga.

The battle, known also as Stone's River, was hailed by the North as a victory. It encouraged Pres. Lincoln, who had been hearing little but bad news from the East.

Myers v. U.S. (1926). The U.S. Supreme Court sustained the power of the President to remove a postmaster from his job. In so doing the Court held unconstitutional an act of Congress in 1876 which required removal to be made with the consent of the Senate. The law was declared to be in conflict with the Constitution since it interfered with the President's duty to "take care that the laws be faithfully executed" (Art. II, Sec. 3).

In 1917 Pres. Wilson had appointed Myers first-class postmaster in Portland, Ore., for a term of four years. In 1920 he ordered the Postmaster General to remove him from office. Myers sued for about 18 months of salary. Chief Justice Taft ruled that Congress may not restrict the President's power to remove officers appointed by him with consent of the Senate.

The Court limited the President's power to remove office holders in *Humphrey's Executor v. U.S.* (1935).

N

Narcotics, Bureau of. Created in the Treasury Department by act of Congress in 1930, the Bureau is charged with preventing violations of the federal narcotic and marihuana laws and the Opium Poppy Control Act of 1942. It issues permits to import the crude narcotic drugs and to export preparations manufactured therefrom. It determines the quantities of crude opium and coco leaves to be imported into the U.S. for medical and scientific uses.

Narragansetts. The Indians, of Algonquian linguistic stock, inhabited what is now Rhode Island. They deeded part of their land to Roger Williams, who founded Providence (1636). Williams won the tribe over as allies against the hostile Pequots.

The Narragansetts joined in King Philip's War but were overwhelmed by a colonial force in the "Swamp Fight" (1675). Remnants of the tribe joined other Indians. A few were permitted to return to Rhode Island to settle on a tract near Charlestown.

Nashville, battle of (Dec. 15–16, 1864). Union Gen. George Thomas routed Confederate Gen. John B. Hood and brought to a successful end the operation in Tennessee which was part of the War in the West.

Nashville Convention (1850). Southern leaders assembled in Tennessee (June 3) at the call of the Mississippi legislature to consider a program for protecting slavery. Henry Clay's proposals for compromise on extension of slavery were being considered in Congress at the time. Advocates of secession were overruled by moderates and the Convention (June 10) voted for extension of the Missouri Compromise line westward to the Pacific.

The Convention reassembled (Nov. 11–18) after the passage of the Compromise of 1850. It was poorly attended and the right to secession was affirmed. Southern support for the Compromise was, however, growing.

Nast, Thomas (1840–1902). Cartoonist. Born in Landau, Germany, he was brought to

New York City as a child. A staff artist of *Harper's Weekly* (1862–86), he was hailed by Lincoln during the Civil War as "our best recruiting sergeant." A master of political caricature, Nast's drawings of the Tammany tiger mauling the republic helped overthrow the "Tweed Ring" (1869–72). His Democratic donkey and Republican elephant have become fixed political symbols.

Natchez Indians. The tribe, of Muskhogean linguistic stock, lived near the present city of Natchez in Mississippi. They warred unsuccessfully against the French early in the 18th century and were scattered among other tribes. Some were sold into slavery in the West Indies.

The Natchez were farmers who constructed mounds for temples and houses.

Nation, Carry Amelia Moore (1846–1911). Temperance agitator. Born in Garrard County, Ky., she lived in Kansas (from 1889), a prohibition state. Her fierce hatred of saloons was vented with a hatchet which she used to destroy the premises and liquor. Carry Nation theorized that since saloons were illegal in Kansas, they could be destroyed by any citizen; the violence she practiced in major American cities was often turned against her. She paid court fines from the sale of souvenir hatchets, stage appearances and lectures.

Nation, The. The weekly magazine of dissent was founded in New York City in 1865 with the aim of making "an earnest effort to bring to the discussion of political and social questions a really critical spirit. . . ." Its first editor was E. L. Godkin, an Anglo-Irish journalist who came to America in 1856 to write a series of articles on the South. Among its other founders were Frederick Law Olmstead, the architect of Central Park in New York City; Charles Eliot Norton, the Harvard scholar; and James Miller McKim, the Philadelphia Abolitionist.

The second editorial of the first issue was concerned with civil rights, a subject to which the magazine has continued to devote itself.

National Aeronautics and Space Administration (NASA). The federal agency was established by Congress in 1958 to supervise activities related to the use of outer space. It promotes research for the solution of problems of flight within and outside the earth's atmosphere and for the development of space vehicles.

National Association for the Advancement of Colored People (NAACP). Known as the "N-double-A," this is a leading civil rights organization in the U.S. with 500,000 members of all races and religions in 1,600 local groups. The NAACP seeks to achieve equal citizenship rights for Negroes through peaceful and lawful means. Its most historic legal victory was the 1954 Supreme Court order on school desegregation (*Brown v. Board of Education*). Its long fight against lynching helped to reduce the number of murders from 90 a year to only a few.

The NAACP was founded in 1909 by whites headed by a woman crusader, Mary White Overton. Later it affiliated with the Niagara movement, a Negro movement led by the scholar W. E. B. Du Bois.

National Bank Act (1863). Revised in 1864, the Act helped finance the Civil War and made possible establishment of a more uniform currency in the U.S.

Congress authorized issuance of federal charters to bankers who organized national banks. The banks were required to invest part of their money in government bonds as security for national bank notes issued by them. The national bank notes were lent to customers of the bank who paid interest on the loans. The notes themselves circulated as national currency.

In 1865 Congress placed a 10% tax on paper money issued by state banks and drove this type of paper money out of circulation. National bank notes, all backed by government bonds, became the uniform currency of the country until the Federal Reserve System was established in 1913.

National Baptist Convention. The largest Negro religious body in the U.S. was founded in 1880

and claims 5.5 million members in 26,000 churches. The leadership has opposed demonstrations, including the March on Washington in 1963, and took the position: "We must not sacrifice constructive human relations in a meticulous contention for the letter of the law."

National Council of the Churches of Christ in America. The organization comprises 33 Protestant denominations embracing over 40,000,000 church members in the U.S. It was formed in 1950 by merging the Federal Council of the Churches of Christ in America, Foreign Missions Conference of North America, Home Missions Council of North America, International Council of Religious Education, Missionary Education Movement in the U.S. and Canada, National Protestant Council on Higher Education, United Council of Church Women and the United Stewardship Council.

Among the objectives of the National Council are the promotion of cooperation among local churches and the coordination of the missionary work of the denominations through area offices for Africa, Latin America and the Middle and Far East.

National Defense Education Act (NDEA). Legislation was enacted in 1958 and extended several times to increase federal support for schools and colleges, public and private.

NDEA establishes student loan funds with the federal government contributing up to 90% and the participating institutions supplying the remainder. It seeks to strengthen instruction in subject areas of critical importance by providing grants to states and loans to private schools for the purchase of equipment and for the repair of classrooms. It provides fellowships for graduate students to improve instruction in colleges and grants to state agencies for improvement of guidance services. The program supports teaching of modern foreign languages, English, reading, history and geography and the training of teachers of disadvantaged youth.

National Gazette (1791–93). The first issue of the anti-Federalist newspaper was issued in Philadelphia, then the national capital, in Oct. 1791. It was edited by the poet, Philip Freneau, who had been James Madison's classmate at Princeton.

National Housing Act (1934). In the measure Congress sought to stimulate residential construction, improve housing standards and help finance building. It established the Federal Housing Administration (FHA) for the purpose of insuring loans by lending institutions for new construction and housing repairs. It aided modernization of farm properties and small business plants. The Act also increased the borrowing power of the Home Owners

Loan Corporation (HOLC) to $3 billion.

National Industrial Recovery Act (1933). The Act provided for the National Recovery Administration (NRA), directed by Gen. Hugh Johnson. "Codes of fair competition" were devised by businessmen, labor and consumers in various industries. Once such a code was approved by the President, it became binding on the entire industry. Cooperating companies were authorized to display the "Blue Eagle," a symbol indicating that they were helping in national recovery. Code participants were assured exemption from the antitrust laws.

In general the codes outlawed child labor, limited production, provided for the control of prices and sales practices, and established a 40-hour workweek and minimum wage scales of $12 to $15 a week. The famous Section 7a of the NIRA guaranteed workers the right to bargain collectively with employers.

For a time the NRA was popular but soon there was considerable dissatisfaction, especially among consumers and smaller businessmen. In 1935 the NIRA was declared unconstitutional by the Supreme Court in *Schechter v. U.S.*

nationalism, American. At the end of the War of 1812, the U.S. was a nation of 8,000,000 people. Hundreds of thousands of Americans were crossing the

Appalachian Mt. Range and new states were being formed. Between the end of the war (1815) and 1820, Indiana, Mississippi, Illinois and Alabama were admitted to the Union as new states.

There was the general feeling that the U.S. was no longer an "infant nation." While the U.S. had not beaten England in the war just ended, neither had it been conquered. Measures to strengthen the nation in the period between the War of 1812 and the Civil War took form not only in the territorial expansion of the U.S., but in the adoption of a protective tariff policy to help American industry, federal aid to internal improvements—making it easier for western crops and eastern manufactures to be interchanged —and a centralized banking system. In this period, subsequent to the early national period, there grew up a school of native American writers—Irving, Cooper, Longfellow and Hawthorne — whose themes were American and whose talents were respected abroad.

After the Civil War there was abundant evidence of nationalism in the growth of transcontinental railroads and expansion of businesses with national and international markets. Late in the 19th and early 20th centuries, the nation embarked upon a program of territorial expansion beyond the Continental limits, and the U.S. became a world power.

The feeling of American "nationhood" was based initially on several factors: Americans spoke the same language; the U.S. had natural boundaries on the Atlantic, the Gulf of Mexico, the Great Lakes and the Rockies; vigorous economic prosperity was provided by the growth of agriculture and industry; and more important than all, perhaps, was the common history which Americans shared.

National Labor Relations Act (1935). Also known as the Wagner Act (named for Sen. Robert F. Wagner, N.Y.), the most important of the New Deal labor laws guaranteed to workers the right to organize and join labor unions and to bargain collectively through representatives of their own choosing. A National Labor Relations Board (NLRB) was set up to enforce this right. Employers were forbidden to engage in practices which were considered "unfair" because they interfered with the right of collective bargaining. The constitutionality of the law was sustained by the U.S. Supreme Court in *N.L.R.B. v. Jones and Laughlin Steel Corp.* (1937).

The Wagner Act came under severe criticism. Critics claimed that it was one-sided because it specified "unfair" labor practices on the part of employers but said nothing about union abuses. Labor spokesmen replied that employers had long enjoyed an unfair advantage over workers and that all this law did was to redress the balance.

A new basic labor law was

enacted soon after World War II, the Taft-Hartley Act.

National Labor Union. The short-lived post-Civil War national labor organization which reached a peak of 650,000 members was founded in 1866 in Baltimore by union leaders. It was conceived by William H. Sylvis, who became its president in 1868, but died after a year of whirlwind activity.

The organization was open to men and women workers, skilled and unskilled, and farmers. Negroes were encouraged to form their own unions. Consumers' and producers' cooperatives were promoted and objectives included the eight-hour day, abolition of convict labor, restriction of immigration, disposal of public lands only to actual settlers and the establishment by the national government of a department of labor.

Reformist and political interests outweighed trade union objectives and the organization transformed itself into the National Labor Reform party. It nominated Judge David Davis of Illinois for President in 1872. When Davis withdrew his name the party and union collapsed.

National Origins Act. Known also as the Immigration Quota Act of 1924 or the Johnson Bill (sponsored by Sen. Hiram W. Johnson, Calif.) the law cut further into the number of immigrants admitted to the U.S. It limited the total number to 164,447 and reduced from 3% to 2% the quota permitted to enter the country under the Emergency Quota Act of 1921. It changed the base year from 1910 to 1890 in deference to the "old" immigration (1776–1890) from northern and western Europe. The 1910 base had permitted greater entry of "new" immigrants (1890 to the present) from southern and eastern Europe.

The 1924 Act barred immigration from Asian countries entirely and embittered the Japanese who felt that they were lumped with the mentally ill, paupers and criminals who were also excluded under U.S. immigration laws.

In 1929 total immigration from all European countries was limited to 150,000. The 2% quota for each country was the proportion of this total that its nationals represented in the U.S. in 1920. Each European nation was entitled to send a minimum of 100 immigrants a year regardless of its quota. Quota restrictions did not apply to immigrants from Canada or Latin America.

The effect of the quota law of the 1920's was to stem the flow of a million immigrants a year before World War I to a trickle.

National Republican party. Developing as an outcome of the election of 1824, a faction of the Democratic-Republican party joined the forces of J. Q. Adams, Henry Clay and Daniel Webster in opposition to Andrew Jackson.

The party favored such nationalistic measures as recharter of the Bank of the United States, a high tariff and internal improvements at national expense. Its supporters were mainly merchants, manufacturers, bankers and wealthy landowners—groups especially influential in the Northeast.

In 1828 it was unsuccessful in bringing about the reelection of Pres. J. Q. Adams. In 1832 it again suffered defeat when Clay was the party's nominee. The party merged with the Whigs in 1836.

National Science Foundation. The NSF was established by Congress in 1950 for the purpose of strengthening basic research and education in the sciences in the U.S. It awards contracts to universities in support of basic scientific research and disseminates information relating to scientific resources, including manpower. NSF recommendations guide national decisions on strengthening the scientific effort of the nation.

National Union party. The name was temporarily adopted by the Republican party in the election of 1864 in an effort to secure the support of the War Democrats. In the congressional elections of 1866 Pres. Johnson attempted to join all moderates in a National Union (Arm-in-Arm) Convention meeting in Philadelphia (Aug. 14). He convinced many northerners that his supporters were primarily ex-rebels and Copper-

heads. In opposition to the President, Radical Republicans contended that the South was unregenerate. In the fall elections the Republicans captured two-thirds of each house giving the Radicals effective control of Reconstruction.

National Urban League. A voluntary community service agency of civic, professional, business, labor and religious leaders, the organization is dedicated to the removal of "all forms of segregation and discrimination based on race or color." The League uses research, conciliation and negotiation to obtain equal job opportunities for Negroes, better schools and housing and improved family life and neighborhood conditions. It was founded in 1910 and now has a membership of 50,000 in 64 local groups.

National Youth Administration (NYA). Established in 1935, the New Deal agency gave young people between 16 and 25 part-time employment in high schools, colleges and universities that kept them in school and out of the labor market. They assisted almost all the branches of the institutions, including the faculty.

Naturalization Act (1798). Passed at the time of the Alien and Sedition Acts, the Act increased from two to 14 years the residence requirement for American citizenship. It was passed by a Federalist Congress hostile to aliens, especially the

468

French whom they viewed as potential Republican voters.

During Jefferson's administration in 1802 the residence requirement for citizenship was reduced to, and has remained, five years.

natural rights. According to this theory man has inalienable rights. Jefferson in the Declaration of Independence drew upon John Locke, 17th-century English philosopher, and others when he identified such rights as "self-evident." He included among them "life, liberty and the pursuit of happiness." These rights could neither be granted by governments nor taken away since man was endowed with them before governments were formed. The theory was popular in the colonies before the American Revolution and served the colonists well in their dispute with the Crown.

Nautilus. The first U.S. submarine to use nuclear power was launched at Groton, Conn., Jan. 21, 1954. H. G. Rickover, then a Rear Admiral, was responsible for the development and construction of the *Nautilus.*

Navaho. Although the tribe of Southwest Indians, of Athapascan linguistic stock, first made contact with the Spanish in the 17th century, they resisted white encroachments until subdued (1863–64) by Kit Carson. After their release from imprisonment in Fort Sumner, N.M., they were given a supply of sheep for stock raising (1868). They have been peaceful since that time. Two major crafts in which they excel are silver metalwork and weaving. Their blankets are known for their beauty.

Navigation Acts. Beginning in 1650 Parliament passed a series of Acts aimed at regulating colonial trade. All colonial exports and imports were to be carried in English ships. Since ships belonging to American colonists were regarded as English, no hardship was worked on the colonists by this feature of the Acts.

Other provisions enumerated products (tobacco, sugar, indigo, cotton, wool, rice, molasses, beaver skins, lumber, etc.) which had to be brought to England before they could be shipped elsewhere. There was evasion by colonial ships and enforcement efforts led to conflicts between colonial merchants and England.

The Acts were not intended to hurt colonial trade, but to eliminate foreign competition and to confine the trade to England and her colonies. American tobacco farmers, for example, benefited by a provision which gave colonial grown tobacco a virtual monopoly of the English market by discouraging tobacco growers in England and placing prohibitive duties on foreign tobacco. In general the Navigation Acts were not oppressive. While the controls were elaborate, evasion made the more onerous provisions largely unenforceable. The defiance of English law contributed to a growing spirit of independence in the colonies.

Navy, Department of the. Headed by the Secretary of the Navy, the Department was established by Congress in 1798. For nine years prior to that the conduct of naval affairs was under the Secretary of War.

The Department of the Navy was incorporated in the National Military Establishment by the National Security Act of 1947 and is under the Secretary of Defense. Its mission is to maintain combat and service forces, and such aviation as may be essential to operations, for sea combat as well as such land operations by the Marine Corps as may be necessary to the naval campaign.

Neagle, In re (1890). The U.S. Supreme Court extended the definition of a law of Congress to include an executive order by the President who, in the exercise of his duty to see that the laws are faithfully executed, may without special statutory authority appoint an officer to protect the life of a federal judge. The ruling extended the doctrine of federal supremacy over the states.

The case arose when a U.S. deputy, Neagle, detailed by the Attorney General to protect the life of Justice Field, shot and killed a man who made an attempt on the justice's life when he was in Stockton, Calif., on Circuit Court business. Neagle was arrested by the California authorities and charged with murder. He was released upon a writ of habeas corpus by the federal Circuit Court on the ground that he was held in custody for "an act done in pursuance of a law of the United States." The Supreme Court held against California and freed Neagle.

Near v. Minnesota (1931). The U.S. Supreme Court ruled a Minnesota law of 1925 prohibiting publication of a "malicious, scandalous and defamatory newspaper, magazine or other periodical" to be unconstitutional. Under the law, known as the "Minnesota gag law," a "padlock" injunction could be issued to halt any publication deemed to be in violation of the law. The judge might remove the injunction if he were satisfied that the offending publication would not be objectionable in the future.

The Court held that this constituted prior censorship and reversed the conviction of Near. This was the first case in which provisions of a state law were held to restrict personal freedom of speech and press without due process. The provisions of the 1st Amendment were thus incorporated into the 14th Amendment as restrictions upon the states.

Nebbia v. N.Y. (1934). The U.S. Supreme Court upheld the constitutionality of a New York law setting a maximum and minimum price for milk sold at retail.

Nebbia, the proprietor of a grocery store in Rochester, sold milk for less than the minimum price and was convicted of violating the law. He contended that the milk business was not affected with a public interest and that the state regulation of milk prices violated the due process clause of the 14th Amendment.

The Court noted that the milk industry in N.Y. had undergone "destructive and demoralizing competitive conditions . . . which . . . reduced the income of the farmer below the cost of production." It ruled that price control is merely a phase of the police power of the state subject only to the limitations of due process of law upon arbitrary interference with liberty and property.

Nebraska. The "Cornhusker State," a West North Central state, was admitted to the Union as the 37th state, Mar. 1, 1867. Its capital is Lincoln.

Nebraska (the Omaha Indian name for the Platte River; both names mean "flat") was reached by Pierre and Paul Mallet, who went up the Platte in 1739. It was claimed by the French, who ceded it to Spain in 1763 and then regained it in 1800. The U.S. acquired it as part of the Louisiana Purchase (1803). Lewis and Clark passed through on their way up the Missouri (1804). One of the principal trails to the West Coast, the Oregon Trail passed through Nebraska, as did the Mormon and Denver Trails. After a number of adjustments in its boundaries, Congress created the Territory of Nebraska by the Kansas-Nebraska Act (1854). Settlement was stimulated by the Homestead Act (1862). The Union Pacific began its transcontinental railroad at Omaha, 1865.

Nebraska is a great wheat, corn and livestock state. Omaha is the nation's largest livestock and meat packing center.

In 1934 the state adopted a unicameral, or one-house, legislature with its members elected on a nonpartisan ballot.

Necessity, Fort. The fort was built by George Washington in 1754 early in the French and Indian War. He had been sent out by the Virginia governor to occupy a newly built fort and encountered a small French force which he defeated. Since he expected an attack by the main French force from Fort Duquesne (later Pittsburgh), he ordered his men to establish a strong point which he called Fort Necessity. The French found his party of men and drove them out of the Ohio country back into Virginia.

Negro American Labor Council. The organization of Negro trade unionists was founded in 1960 by A. Philip Randolph, head of the Brotherhood of Sleeping Car Porters and originator of the March on Washington, 1963. It "promotes equality in employment and apprenticeship opportunities for Negro workers." The Council has 10,000 members out of 1.5 million Negroes in the labor movement.

Negro Conspiracy (1741). In March and April a number of fires of unknown origin broke out in New York City. Public suspicion fell on Negro slaves only because they were present in the area. The wild charge was made that a plot was afoot to burn the town and that the Negroes were being incited by Roman Catholic priests incited by Spain. Before the public fury subsided four whites and 18 Negroes were hanged, and 13 Negroes were burned at the stake.

Negro in America. The first 250 years of Negro life in America, dating from the arrival of the first Negro slaves at Jamestown, Va. to the end of the Civil War, is tied inextricably to the institution of slavery. At the time of Lincoln's Emancipation Proclamation (1863) there were about 2,000,000 Negro slaves in the U.S. and 200,000 free Negroes. Even free Negroes in the North were subject to the various kinds of discrimination which have given rise to the "Negro Revolution" of the 1960's.

The 13th, 14th and 15th Amendments which seemed to promise the Negroes a greater measure of freedom and equality in the post-Civil War period were bypassed when Jim Crow practices in the 1890's in the South became commonplace. Reconstruction gains of Negroes in the political arena were eroded.

In the World War I period a huge migration of Negroes from the South started. An exodus to the North of 500,000 took place as the flow of European immigration ceased and the need for industrial labor opened jobs for Negroes. The migration continued in the 1920's when restrictive immigration laws cut off the supply of white immigrant labor in northern cities.

During the Great Depression, World War II and the postwar period concerted efforts to improve conditions for Negroes were made by federal and state governments. The Armed Forces were desegregated and discrimination in employment was combated by law. National labor unions also sought to open their rolls to Negroes. The reaction to segregation practices was given great stimulus by the 1954 Supreme Court decision (*Brown v. Board of Education*).

Although Negroes have been severely handicapped by slavery and discriminatory practices, a number of Negro leaders have contributed to American life. In science, George Washington Carver is preeminent; in education, Booker T. Washington; in the Abolitionist movement, Frederick Douglass; in statesmanship, Ralph Bunche; in letters, William E. Du Bois and Richard Wright; in music, Marion Anderson and Paul Robeson; in sports, Jesse Owens, Joe Louis and Jackie Robinson.

Negro gains since World War II are registered in the number of high school and college graduates, in expanding opportunities for those qualified for professional and clerical jobs, in increased purchasing power, savings accounts and insurance policies. In politics the new status is evident in the appointment of scores of Negroes to high-level federal posts as well as their capture of 280 elective offices, including six in Congress and 90-odd in state legislatures —10 of them in Georgia (1965). A Negro U.S. Senator, Edward W. Brooke (Mass.), the first since Reconstruction days, was elected in 1966. Negro mayors were elected in Gary, Ind., and Cleveland, O., in 1967.

Negroes must still overcome the unemployment gap between races. The Department of Labor in 1964 reported that Negroes constituted 20.6% of the unemployed though they accounted for only 10% of the population. It also reported that nearly a fourth of all Negro children are born illegitimate. No husband is present in 20% of the homes of "nonwhite" married women; by the time they are 18 more than half of all Negro children have lived in broken homes at least part of their lives. Dependent-children relief checks go to more than half of all Negro children at some time during their childhood compared with 8% of white children. Disintegration of families, said the report, is the principal cause of low intellig-

ence test scores, the swollen crime rate and narcotics addiction.

There remains much for both the Negro and the white man to do to bring about equality for the Negro in America.

nesters. The term was used by cattlemen in the post-Civil War period to describe farmers who sought to settle on range lands. Congressional action was necessary in 1885 to protect the farmers from being driven off the land by cattlemen who had hired gunmen to oust grangers from range land.

Neutrality Acts of the 1930's. Before fighting began in Europe in 1939 Congress enacted neutrality legislation aimed to keep the U.S. out of any world war. The legislation was a compromise between Pres. Roosevelt and the isolationists.

The Neutrality Act of 1935, passed at the time of the Italo-Ethiopian crisis, made it illegal for anyone in the U.S. to sell or to transport munitions to the belligerents. No distinction was made between the aggressor and the invaded nation. In 1936 the munitions embargo was extended to include loans. The Neutrality Act of 1937 continued to prohibit loans and the sale of munitions and extended the prohibition to travel on ships of belligerents. But the President was permitted to help any nation to buy food and other non-military supplies provided the nation paid cash and carried the goods in its own vessels.

When the war in Europe broke out the President declared: "Let no one imagine that America will escape, that it may expect mercy, that this western hemisphere will not be attacked." As the brutality of Nazi aggression became clear, public opinion in the U.S. grew strongly sympathetic to the cause of the Allies. The Neutrality Act of 1939 lifted the embargo on arms so that aid might be given to France and England. But the law required that they pay cash and carry the arms in their own vessels ("cash and carry" provision).

Nevada. The "Silver State" or "Sagebrush State," a Mountain group state, was admitted to the Union as the 36th state, Oct. 31, 1864. Its capital is Carson City. Pres. Lincoln speeded Nevada's admission because he wanted the state's three votes for ratification of the 13th Amendment.

Nevada (meaning "snow covered" in Spanish) was first entered by Spanish missionaries in 1776. It was explored by John C. Frémont, 1843–44, and was part of the territory ceded to the U.S. at the end of the Mexican War in 1848. Nevada was in the Utah Territory, organized in 1850. The demand for separate territorial status was stimulated by discovery of the Comstock Silver Lode (1859). The miners did not want to be under Mormon con-

trol and separate territorial status was arranged in 1861.

The state has yielded vast amounts of silver, copper and gold. Irrigation is expanding agriculture. Two of its cities receive national attention—Reno, where the law makes divorce comparatively easy; and Las Vegas, a legal gambling center.

New Albion. Albion is a poetic name for England, and thus the name (Nova Albion) given to what is now upper California and Oregon by Sir Francis Drake in 1579.

It was also used as the name of a grant of territory to Sir Edmund Plowden, June 21, 1634. The boundaries of this New Albion were defined so as to include all of New Jersey, Maryland, Delaware and Pennsylvania. Little effort was made at settlement and nothing came of the grant.

Newburgh Addresses (1783). On March 10 an anonymous address directed to officers of the Continental Army awaiting demobilization at Newburgh, N.Y., called for direct action against a Congress that had not paid the men for their war service. Years later, John Armstrong on Gen. Gates' staff professed to have written the address.

In an address of his own at Newburgh, Mar. 15, 1783, Gen. Washington urged the officers to have confidence in the Congress and not to "open the floodgates of civil discords." As he read Washington was forced to take out his eyeglasses, which he had never before worn in public. He remarked quietly, "You have seen me grow gray in your service. Now I am going blind." The assembled officers responded with a resolution stating their "unshaken confidence in the justice of the Congress" and their "abhorrence" and "disdain" for the "infamous propositions contained in the late anonymous address."

Newcomb, Simon (1835–1909). Astronomer. He was born in Nova Scotia. Internationally renowned, he masterfully treated a wide range of subjects in astronomy. He was commissioned professor of mathematics in the U.S. Navy (1861–97); Superintendent, American Ephemeris and Nautical Almanac (1877–97); professor of mathematics and astronomy at Johns Hopkins (1884–94 and 1898–1900). He made celebrated studies of the moon's motion (beginning 1868). With the assistance of A. A. Michelson, he redetermined the velocity of light by the revolving-mirror method. He published a catalogue of some 1,500 fundamental star positions. He wrote *Popular Astronomy* 1878, *The Stars* (1901), *Astronomy for Everybody* (1902) and some books on economics.

New Deal. Pres. Franklin D. Roosevelt promised the country a "new deal" when he accepted the Democratic nomination for President in 1932. In many ways the New Deal program was not really "new." Theodore Roosevelt and Woodrow Wilson had led the way in regulating business; conserving natural resources, helping working people and introducing other social and economic reforms.

In another sense the New Deal did represent a break with the past for never had so many reforms been undertaken in so short a time after a President came into office. In "the first hundred days," the early months of 1933, Congress almost without debate passed numerous far-reaching acts. These laws and others adopted during the period of 1933–38 comprise the New Deal. They may be classified under the "three R's," which made up the main objectives of the program—relief, recovery and reform.

Relief measures were undertaken by the Works Progress Administration (WPA) and National Youth Administration (NYA). Recovery and reform were intertwined in a host of measures establishing the Social Security Administration (SSA), Federal Deposit Insurance Corporation (FDIC), Securities and Exchange Commission (SEC), National Labor Relations Board (NLRB), Federal Housing Administration (FHA), Tennessee Valley Authority (TVA) and Agricultural Adjustment Administration (AAA).

There was scarcely a phase

of American life that was not affected by New Deal measures.

New England. The name was first given to the region by Capt. John Smith in his map of 1616. Though organized into separate colonies or states the region has always maintained a certain degree of uniformity in its religion as well as in its economy. The states now comprising New England are Maine, New Hampshire, Vermont, Massachusetts, Rhode Island and Connecticut.

New England Confederation. In an effort to meet the threatening French and Indian attacks and to promote progress in their settlements Massachusetts, Plymouth, Connecticut and New Haven joined together in 1643 to form "The Confederation of the United Colonies of New England." It was the first in a series of colonial attempts to work together. Representatives from the four colonies were empowered to negotiate with the Indians and foreign powers—French and Dutch—and to settle differences among themselves. The Confederation broke up in 1684 over opposition to the growing domination by Massachusetts.

New-England Primer, The. A textbook for beginning readers, it first appeared about 1690 and was used in the schools of all the colonies except those under the control of the Church of England. Since the reading matter was religious in nature and included the catechism it was also read in the churches. The 88-page book, only 3¼ by 4½ inches in size, was used for almost a century and a half. It has been said of it that "it taught millions to read, and not one to sin."

New Freedom. The expression describes Pres. Wilson's political philosophy. He spoke of it in his political campaigns and during his years in office (1913–21). Wilson wanted to destroy monopoly by promoting fair competition. "The men who have been ruling America," he said, "must consent to let the majority enter the game." He titled his ideas for bringing back the old days of equal opportunity for all the "New Freedom."

New Frontier. The expression was used during the short and tragically terminated administration of Pres. Kennedy (1961–63). In the 1960 election campaign Kennedy urged that the federal government spend large sums on education, housing, transportation, relief of unemployment in chronically depressed areas and projects to spur economic growth. He summed up his program as the "New Frontier." In his inaugural address, Jan. 20, 1961, Kennedy called upon the people of the U.S. to show renewed vigor and devotion in defense of American ideals. "My fellow Americans," the President said, "ask not what your country can

476

do for you—ask what you can do for your country."

New Hampshire. The "Granite State," one of the six New England states, was named by Capt. John Mason for a county in England. The land, including Maine, was granted to Mason and Sir Ferdinand Gorges in 1622. Later grants established New Hampshire as Mason's. It was settled in the 1630's by Massachusetts Bay emigrants and was absorbed by the Bay colony in 1644. Other changes in control included status as a royal province in 1679, rule again by the Bay colony after the fall of Gov. Andros in 1688 and permanent separation in 1692. There were boundary disputes with New York and Massachusetts. Indian attacks severely menaced the settlers.

During the American Revolution the colony contributed to the victories at Bennington and Saratoga. New Hampshire, one of the original 13 Colonies, was the ninth state to ratify the Constitution (June 21, 1788), making it possible for the U.S. government to start operating. Its capital is Concord.

In politics the state was generally Federalist until 1816. It was less violently opposed to the War of 1812 than the rest of New England. With the demise of the Federalists the state became Democratic. Since it was strongly antislavery, however, it adhered to the Republican party after 1856.

Known as the "Switzerland of America," the state is an important resort area in the East. Dairy cattle, hay, vegetables and apples are the chief agricultural products. The principal industries are textiles, paper, leather goods, machinery, printing and electronics items.

New Harmony. The utopian colony was founded in Indiana in 1825 by Robert Owen, the English philanthropist and industrialist. Its one thousand members were supposed to live and work on the basis of complete equality. It attracted a diversified group, ranging from the lazy and unprincipled to the hard working and idealistic. Many desired a better order of things and some simply wanted an education for their children.

The colony lacked firm direction and failed after two years. It did, however, inspire other socialist communities.

New Jersey. The "Garden State," the smallest of the Middle Atlantic states, was one of the original 13 Colonies. Its capital is Trenton.

The first explorations were made by Henry Hudson, and the first settlement by Swedes early in the 17th century. In 1655 it was taken over by the Dutch as part of New Netherland. When the English took over from the Dutch in 1664, the land west of the Hudson to the Delaware River was granted by the Duke of York to Lord John Berkeley and Sir George Carteret. It was named Nova Caesaria or New Jersey in honor of the island of Jersey of which

Carteret had been governor. New Jersey became a royal colony in 1702.

Although sentiment was divided in the colony, it broke with England in 1776. The state was a major theater in the Revolution because of the struggle for control of the Hudson and Delaware rivers. It was the third state to ratify the Constitution (Dec. 18, 1787).

New Jersey became industrialized after the Civil War and ranks high in manufacturing. Chief agricultural products are fruits, vegetables, milk, poultry and eggs.

The state has one of the finest highway systems in the U.S. Its shipping facilities make it a large freight terminal. Its chemical products have the highest dollar value in the U.S.

New Jersey Plan (1787). The Plan preferred by the small states was presented to the Constitutional Convention by William Paterson of New Jersey. It proposed equal representation for the states in a single-house legislature. Congress was to be given the right to regulate commerce, levy certain taxes, name the executives and a supreme court.

The Plan contrasted with the Virginia Plan of the big states. Both plans were modified by the Great Compromise.

newlanders. Agents were employed by merchants and ship captains in the 18th century to encourage emigration from Germany to America. The newlanders visited peasants and persuaded them to leave the fatherland. They posed as American settlers temporarily sojourning in Germany, wearing flashy clothes and jewelry. The money for the voyage was advanced to the migrants who had to agree to allow the ship captain to sell their labor in the colonies for a term of years.

New Mexico. The "Cactus State," or "Spanish State," a Mountain group state, was admitted to the Union as the 47th state, Jan. 6, 1912. Its capital is Santa Fe.

Spaniards in Mexico gave the land north and west of the Rio Grande the name. It was explored by Cabeza de Vaca, 1528–36. In 1539 Friar Marcos de Niza saw from a distant height the "Seven Cities of Cibola," the first Indian pueblos (villages) discovered by the Spaniards. He returned to Mexico with tales of fabulous wealth in the region. In 1540 Coronado started his vain search for riches. Between 1605 and 1609, Juan de Oñate founded Santa Fe, the second oldest city in the U.S.

The land became a province of Mexico in 1821 when that country broke away from Spain. It was ceded to the U.S. in 1848 at the end of the Mexican War. The Territory of New Mexico, including the present states of Colorado and Arizona, was formed in 1850. The Territory was settled by Americans who joined those of Spanish descent with the eventual result that laws in New Mexico are published in both English and Spanish. Indian citizens include Apache, Navaho, Ute and Pueblo.

The raising of livestock is important. The chief industry is mining, including uranium, in which the state leads the nation. Atomic and space research centers are at Los Alamos and White Sands.

New Nationalism. In 1910, in a speech in Kansas, ex-Pres. Theodore Roosevelt used this phrase to describe his progressive views on social and political reform. He believed that the states could not legislate the reforms that were needed and called for bold federal action on behalf of all the people.

New Netherland. The colony which was to become New York in 1664 was first settled by the Dutch. Families were sent out by the Dutch West India Company in 1624 and established New Amsterdam (later New York City) and Fort Orange, near the present site of Albany.

Peter Minuit, who was sent by the company as director-general, purchased Manhattan Island from the Indians (1626) for 60 guilders' (about $24) worth of trinkets. The tip of the island had already been occupied by the Dutch. A system of patroonships was established by the company in an effort to stimulate settlement. The patroon was given a large grant of land for settling a specified number of families.

Relations with the Indians were especially bad under one of Minuit's successors, Willem Kieft. Kieft was succeeded by Peter Stuyvesant, whose autocratic control was moderated somewhat after the colonists complained to the company. It was Stuyvesant, beset by Indian troubles and rebellion, who yielded New Netherland to the English fleet under the Duke of York.

New Orleans, battle of (Jan. 8, 1815). In the final battle of the War of 1812, fought two weeks after the peace treaty had been signed (Treaty of Ghent), Gen. Andrew Jackson defeated a British army under Sir Edward Packenham.

The British had decided to take New Orleans, gain control of the Mississippi Valley and, perhaps, detach the Southwest from the U.S. The British veteran army, placed in position for attack by a naval squadron, attempted a direct assault on breastworks held by Jackson's motley collection of Creoles and militiamen from Kentucky, Louisiana and Tennessee. The devastating defeat and retreat of the trained army led the American public to believe that the victory had beaten the British into submission, since news of the peace treaty did not arrive in the nation's capital until more than a month after the battle. Peace was so welcome that the terms of the treaty did not disturb the general rejoicing. Jackson was called "the hero of New Orleans."

New Orleans, capture of (May 1, 1862). The gateway to the Confederacy in the West was captured by Adm. David G. Farragut, who cut through the heavy chains that linked forts on either side of the Mississippi, 90 miles below New Orleans.

The city itself was penetrated by Gen. Benjamin F. Butler, whose forces were carried by Farragut's squadron. Resistance in New Orleans was attempted by a weak force of 3,000 Confederates for the river defenses had been counted on to withstand a Union attack on the strategically located port city.

Butler's harsh rule of the city caused him to be hated in the North as well as in the South.

New South. The Old South of the plantation system and slavery was ended by the Civil War. The New South was slow in finding itself. By the late 1870's, however, there was evidence of a changing economic life with industry and commerce taking their place beside agriculture. Northern capital was attracted to the South and invested in the construction of railroads; an iron industry developed around Birmingham, Ala.; cotton mills began to appear. Throughout the states of the former Confederacy, steps were taken to repair war damage.

newspapers. The first regularly published newspaper in the American colonies was the weekly *Boston News-Letter*,

founded in 1704. Boston's example was followed by other colonial cities and between 1713 and 1745 twenty-two papers were established. By 1775 there were 37 newspapers in 11 of the 13 Colonies. They were usually 12 by 18 inches in size and consisted of four pages. They contained political letters on current issues in the colonies and England, foreign news, contributors' letters, shipping news, stories of crime and accidents, poems, moral advice and bits of useful information.

The Revolution interrupted publication of all colonial newspapers at various times, largely because colonial presses were poorly equipped and most type and supplies were imported from England. The first American type casting foundry was established in 1772.

Between 1801 and 1833 the number of newspapers in the country rose from 200 to 1,200, of which 65 were dailies; most of the rest were weeklies. Acrimonious political debate was usual in their pages and many newspapers were tied to political factions. By 1820 there were 250 newspapers in the West. The agricultural press also developed rapidly and, apart from articles on the evils of the city and the glory of farming, contained useful articles on farming practices, politics and events of interest.

In the 1830's newspaper competition, especially in the larger cities, became keen. There were 47 newspapers in New York City in 1830. They were not, however, mass circulation papers and had a combined circulation of only 90,000; the largest among them had a circulation of 4,000. Established papers sold for six cents a copy. The founding of Benjamin Day's *New York Sun* (1833) as the first "penny newspaper" boosted circulation greatly. It started newsboys hawking papers on street corners.

The introduction of the cylinder press in 1830 made larger sheets possible. Larger press runs followed from the use of power-driven presses that could produce 1,000 papers an hour. Other publishers followed the *Sun* in reducing the price of their papers to one cent and competed with it in sensationalism. Advertising men, catching the spirit of the times, discarded staid copy for more eye-catching layouts.

The press did not, however, pander to low tastes exclusively. Reporting the news to an educationally and politically awakened people was carried on by such papers as the *New York Tribune,* the *Cincinnati Gazette,* the *Brooklyn Eagle,* the *Cleveland Plain Dealer,* the *Baltimore Sun* and the *Philadelphia Ledger.*

In the 1840's the telegraph had an enormous impact on newspapers. The demand for presses that could turn out 10,-000 an hour was met in 1847 by the cylindrical press developed by Richard March Hoe.

The demand for news during the Civil War increased newspaper reading enormously and led to the appearance of Sunday editions of newspapers. After the war there was further expansion in the size of newspapers. About 1870, expensive rag paper, fed to the presses sheet by sheet, gave way to rolls of paper made from wood pulp and fed to new rotary presses. Syndicated matter was sold to newspapers beginning in the 1870's. Newspapers were enlivened by photographs made possible by the new photoengraving process first used by the *New York Daily Graphic* in 1873. Typesetting by hand gave way to the linotype in the late 1880's. Steady improvement in presses and printing equipment has continued to a point where automation promises a revolution in newspaper production in the last quarter of the 20th century.

The daily circulation of newspapers increased from 2,800,000 in 1870 to 24,000,000 in 1899. Revenues mounted from sales and advertising, enabling editors to become powerful forces in shaping public opinion. Joseph Pulitzer, owner of the *St. Louis Post-Dispatch* and later of the *New York World,* boosted circulation of his papers in the closing years of the 19th century by combining sensationalism with exposés of civic corruption and by adopting the newest printing improvements. His methods were emulated by E. W. Scripps' papers in Cleveland, St. Louis and Cincinnati and, in sensationalism, they were topped by William Randolph Hearst. The Spanish-

American War (1898) afforded a field day for this brand of newspaper reporting. The "yellow journalism" which predominated at the turn of the century was effectively answered by *The New York Times*. The moribund *Times* was taken over by Adolph S. Ochs in 1896. He revived its circulation when he cut its price to a penny, introduced new features and promoted trustworthy coverage of foreign and domestic news.

In the 20th century newspapers have ranged from tabloids featuring pictures and the sensational to responsible journals vital to the growth of an informed electorate. Their pages are varied and include columns devoted to news, editorials, letters to the editor, business and finance, sports, entertainment, art, music, books, comics, fashions, food, society, television and radio.

The great newspaper publishers, styled "lords of the press"— the Hearsts, Gannetts, Howards, Pattersons and McCormicks— have been subjected to their share of criticism. The Commission on the Freedom of the Press (1947), headed by Chancellor Robert M. Hutchins of the University of Chicago, in its report, *A Free and Responsible Press*, concluded that near-monopoly conditions in newspaper publishing, exacerbated by newspaper ownership of two-thirds of the radio stations in the country, endangered freedom of the press. While noting the excellence of the leading journals and that the American press is less "venal and subservient to political and economic pressures than that of many other countries," the Commission nevertheless found newspaper publishers largely responsible for interference with the free flow of ideas.

The number of daily newspapers in the U.S. has been declining from a peak of 2,042 in 1920 to about 1,750 today. "The most sensational merger in an era of mergers," according to Frank Luther Mott in his book *American Journalism* (1941, 1962), was the 1931 consolidation of Roy W. Howard's New York *Telegram* with Joseph Pulitzer's *World* and *Evening World*. Pulitzer had died 20 years earlier. The *World-Telegram* added the New York *Sun* in 1950 and the Scripps-Howard newspaper was published as the *World-Telegram and The Sun*. In 1966 this newspaper merged with the *New York Herald Tribune* and *The New York Journal-American* to form the *World Journal Tribune*, but the new paper ceased publication in 1967, less than eight months after its start. New York City's daily newspapers, 15 in general circulation in 1900, have dropped to three: *The New York Times*, the *New York Post* and the *Daily News*.

The demise of so many daily newspapers in the U.S. has been due to rising costs of every kind, population shifts away from the cities, fiercer competition from television, radio, news magazines and the growth of suburban dailies.

New Sweden. The only Swedish colony to be founded in the New World was established in the Delaware River Valley in 1638. It was sent out by the South Company, primarily interested in the fur trade, which established Fort Christina (named after the Queen) on the site of present-day Wilmington, Del. The Swedish companies' settlements never included more than 400 people or extended more than 35 miles along the Delaware.

The Dutch who claimed the region tolerated New Sweden since they were allies during the Thirty Years' War (1618–48), one result of which was Dutch independence from Spain. In 1655 the Dutch took over easily and New Sweden was absorbed by New Netherland. Swedish farmers were allowed to keep their land or return to Sweden.

New York. The "Empire State," a Middle Atlantic state and one of the original 13 Colonies, was called New Netherland when it was under Dutch control. The name was changed to New York when the Dutch yielded it in 1664 to the forces of the Duke of York, who had been granted the land by his brother King Charles II.

New York Bay and the lower part of the Hudson were first explored by the Florentine navigator Verrazano in 1524. The first Dutch settlement in New Netherland was made at Fort Nassau, near the present site of Albany, in 1614.

In 1664 New York had a varied population with some 18 languages being spoken such as Dutch, English, Flemish, French, German, Italian, Norwegian, Portuguese, Spanish and Yiddish. In response to the popular demand for greater self-rule, the first representative assembly met in 1683.

New York attracted not only New Englanders but the French, who contested for control of the northern and central parts of the colony in the 18th century. They were defeated by the English in the French and Indian War (1756–63).

After 1763 growing insistence on self-rule sharpened the struggle with Britain. Although sentiment was divided, the colony cast for independence in 1775. The first state constitution was adopted in 1777. During the Revolution the state was a hotly contested theater of action. British Gen. Howe held New York City during most of the struggle.

New York was the 11th state to ratify the Constitution (July 26, 1788), after Alexander Hamilton, James Madison and John Jay persuaded the majority with their arguments in the *Federalist*. New York City was the nation's first capital (1789–90). Albany has been the state's capital since 1797.

The state's commercial and industrial growth was stimulated by completion of the Erie Canal in 1825 and by a fresh tide of immigration in the 1850's. The state supported the Union during the Civil War although there were draft riots in 1863. After the war the state became an increasingly strong industrial area.

New York is the financial capital of the nation and has the largest deep-sea port. The head offices of the largest corporations, insurance companies and a variety of industries are located in New York City. Although the state is troubled by a decline in employment in manufacturing it remains a great center for workers in the apparel trades, printing and publishing. In agriculture the state is especially noted for its dairy cattle.

New York Central Railroad. A leader in forming trunk (main) lines linking the East and Middle West, the system was started in 1853 by the consolidation of 11 short roads between the Hudson River and Buffalo. The resulting road was able to operate more cheaply and offer continuous service. The system was expanded in a series of mergers by Cornelius Vanderbilt after 1866. Until these mergers took place it was not unusual for a passenger to change trains eight or ten times on a trip from New York to the "Windy City" (Chicago).

The system now operates about 10,600 miles of track. The main line runs from New York to Chicago; subsidiaries serve St. Louis, Cleveland, Detroit, southern Canadian cities and other points. A merger with the Pennsylvania Railroad was approved by the U.S. Supreme Court in 1968. The combined company is the Pennsylvania–New York Central Transportation Company (Penn-Central).

New York Herald Tribune, The. The newspaper was formed in 1924 by the merger of *The Herald,* founded in 1835 by James Gordon Bennett, and the *Tribune,* founded in 1841 by Horace Greeley. The merged paper, published by Ogden M. Reid, established itself as the eastern voice of the Republican party. Reid died in 1947 and the paper declined. In 1958 John Hay Whitney, then Ambassador to London, took it over from the Reid family. The paper was weakened by a 114-day newspaper strike in New York City that began in Dec. 1962.

In Mar. 1966 Whitney agreed to the merger with two afternoon papers, *The New York Journal-American,* owned by the Hearst Corporation, and *The World-Telegram and The Sun,* one of the Scripps-Howard newspapers. A four-month strike against the new company by the Newspaper Guild of New York and other newspaper unions prevented publication planned for Apr. 25. On Aug. 15 the *Herald Tribune* announced that it would not resume publication. A new afternoon paper, the *World Journal Tribune,* appeared on Sept. 12, 1966, but ceased publication in 1967.

New York Times, The. The first issue of *The New York Daily*

Times appeared on Sept. 18, 1851; the word *Daily* was dropped from the title in 1857. The paper was founded by Henry J. Raymond, George Jones and Edward B. Wesley. It sold for a penny during its first year, but this was raised to two cents after *The Herald* and *Tribune* raised their price.

The paper was, at first, pro-Whig party. When the Whigs declined, it turned to the Free Soilers and then the Republicans. It was critical of Lincoln, but supported him during the Civil War. In 1884 it left the Republican party and, although considered Democratic, it has been independent in politics.

The *Times* was a powerful force in exposing the Tweed Ring in the 1870's and, beginning in 1881, the Star Route frauds in the Post Office Department. In 1891 it helped to clean up abuses in the conduct of the New York Life Insurance Co.

In 1896 the *Times* was purchased by Adolph S. Ochs, a Tennessee newspaperman. He dealt a blow to yellow journalism by showing how a paper could build up a large circulation merely by being a good newspaper. In 1898 the price per copy was cut from three cents to one cent, thus challenging the yellows at their own price level.

Upon Ochs' death in 1935 his son-in-law and nephew came into the management of the *Times*—Arthur Hays Sulzberger, president and publisher. The paper has remained preeminent in the field of American journalism.

New York University. Chartered in 1831 as the University of the City of New York, it adopted its present name in 1896. A coeducational institution, it is privately controlled. Divisions include undergraduate colleges of arts and sciences, engineering, education and commerce. There are graduate schools of law, engineering, education, business administration, medicine, dentistry, arts and sciences, retailing, public administration and social work. There is also a division of general education for adult education. It is the largest university in the U.S., with a full-time and part-time, day and evening enrollment of 60,000.

Nez Percé Indians. The Indians of Shahaptin stock in the Pacific Northwest, some of whom wore nose pendants, were given their name ("pierced nose") by the French. They made friendly contact with the Lewis and Clark expedition (1804–06) and accepted settlers until an effort was made to oust them from their reservation in the Wallowa Valley in Oregon. In the Nez Percé War (1877) Chief Joseph with a force of only 300 resisted 5,000 soldiers until he was forced to surrender by Gen. Nelson A. Miles. The tribe is now scattered among several reservations.

Niagara Falls. Called by the Iroquois "thunder of water," it was described in 1678 by a

French missionary, Father Hennepin. Since that time it has probably been visited by more people than any other scenic spot on the American continent. Located in northern New York, near Buffalo, on the Canadian border, the American falls are 167 feet high and about 1,300 feet wide. The Canadian falls are 158 feet high with a crest of over 2,500 feet outlining a deep curve named Horseshoe Falls.

Nicaraguan intervention. The outstanding instance of "Dollar Diplomacy" took place in 1911 when a revolution broke out in Nicaragua in Central America. American investments were comparatively small but Nicaragua contained an alternate canal route which the U.S. could not permit to fall under foreign control.

In 1912 the revolution threatened American lives and property. Pres. Taft sent in Marines and troops remained in the country until 1925. By that year the financial policies of about half of the 20 Latin American states were in some measure directed by the U.S.

In 1926 during another outbreak, Marines were sent back to Nicaragua by Pres. Coolidge. His critics called it a "private war." Coolidge replied that the U.S. had a "moral responsibility" in Nicaragua, insisting that "we are not making war on Nicaragua any more than a policeman on the street is making war on passersby." Followers of Gen. Sandino, one of the rebel leaders, refused to be pacified and harassed American Marines until 1933 when the last troops were withdrawn.

Nick Carter. The great detective appeared in the dime novels of the late 19th and early 20th centuries. John R. Coryell created the character and used "Nick Carter" as one of his pen names. Two of the titles were *Nick Carter's Clever Protégé,* and *Nick Carter Down East.* Other writers also wrote many of the Nick Carter stories.

Nicola proposal (May 1782). Col. Lewis Nicola, active as a recruiting officer and commander of the Philadelphia home guard, wrote to George Washington proposing that Washington serve the nation as King of the United States. Nicola, who had emigrated from Dublin, Ireland, about 1766, professed to speak for the Army.

Washington, appalled by the proposal, wrote back sharply: "I am at a loss to conceive what part of my conduct could have given encouragement to an address, which seems to me big with the greatest mischiefs, that could befall my Country . . . banish these thoughts from your mind, and never communicate as from yourself or any one else, a sentiment of the like nature."

Niebuhr, Reinhold (1892–1971). Theologian. Born in Wright City, Mo., he was graduated from the Yale Divinity School (1914) and ordained a minister in the Evangelical Synod of

North America (1915). The editor of *Christianity and Crisis*, he has stressed sinful man's dependence on the goodness of God. A liberal in politics, he has been a professor of applied Christianity (since 1930) at the Union Theological Seminary in New York. His works include *Does Civilization Need Religion?* (1927), *Reflections on the End of an Era* (1934), *Christianity and Power Politics* (1940), *The Irony of American History* (1952) and *The Structure of Nations and Empires* (1959).

Nimbus. One of a series of meteorological satellites, it stores cameras and infrared sensors which always face the earth. The near-polar orbit of Nimbus 1 in 1964 enabled it to take the first photographs ever of the earth's nighttime cloud cover.

Nimitz, Chester William (1885–1966). Naval officer. Born in Fredericksburg, Tex., he was graduated from the U.S. Naval Academy (1905). In World War I, Nimitz served as Chief of Staff to the Commander of the U.S. Atlantic submarine fleet. In peacetime, he advanced through the grades to Rear Admiral (1938). Commander of the U.S. Pacific Fleet in World War II, he was promoted to Admiral of the Fleet (1944) and became U.S. Chief of Naval Operations (1945–47). An advocate of "island hopping" as the way to the main islands of Japan, he directed amphibious landings at Guadalcanal (1942) and subsequent offensives in the Solomon, Gilbert, Marshall and Bonin Islands. He headed (1949) the UN mediation commission in the dispute between India and Pakistan over Kashmir.

Ninety-Six, Fort. The fort in the interior of South Carolina was so named by the Indians because it was 96 miles from the nearest Indian village. During the Revolution it was held by the British until they decided to evacuate it in 1781 and retreat to Charleston after a siege by Gen. Greene.

Nobel Prizes. Annual awards for outstanding work for physics, chemistry, medicine, literature and for the promotion of international peace were made possible by a fund established by Alfred Bernhard Nobel, a Swedish chemist and inventor.

The Nobel Peace Prize of 1964 was awarded to Martin Luther King for advancing Negro civil rights through nonviolent means. Other Americans who have won this Peace Prize include Linus C. Pauling (1962), who also won the prize for chemistry (1954), George C. Marshall (1953), Ralph J. Bunche (1950), Cordell Hull (1945) and Theodore Roosevelt (1906).

American writers who have won the Nobel Prize for Literature are John Steinbeck (1962), Ernest Hemingway (1954), William Faulkner (1949), T. S. Eliot (1948), Pearl Buck

(1938), Eugene O'Neill (1936) and Sinclair Lewis (1930).

Americans have also been the recipients of prizes in the other fields.

No Man's Land. The strip of land was ceded by Texas to the U.S. at the time of its admission to the Union in 1845. It lay north of 36° 30′ North Latitude and was without government until 1890 when it became part of Oklahoma.

During World War I the expression was applied to any stretch of soil in the cross fire between German and Allied trenches.

nonimportation agreements. To force repeal of various acts of Parliament that taxed the colonists and curbed their freedom, colonial merchants made nonimportation agreements to boycott British goods. They were effective in bringing about the repeal of the Stamp Act (1765) and the Townshend Acts (1767).

Nonintercourse Act (1809). During the final days of Jefferson's administration the Act replaced the Embargo Act as a means of pressuring Britain and France into permitting U.S. vessels to trade freely with foreign nations. It legalized American commerce with all parts of the world except those under British and French control. The Act provided that the U.S. would restore its trade with either Britain or France, whichever of these nations first withdrew its

orders or decrees against American shipping.

The Act was part of an evolving diplomatic policy of the U.S. by which it sought through economic pressures to preserve American rights while avoiding war. The Nonintercourse Act was soon replaced by Macon's Bill No. 2, an even more moderate restriction on U.S. commerce during the Napoleonic Wars.

Norfolk and Western Railway Co. Greatly dependent upon transporting bituminous coal, the line was incorporated in Virginia, 1896, as a reorganization of an established company. In time it acquired, among others, the Tug River & Kentucky Railroad and the Buck Creek Railroad. In 1964 it absorbed the New York, Chicago & St. Louis (Nickel Plate) Railroad and leased the Wabash Railroad. This consolidation also included leasing the Pittsburgh & West Virginia Lines as well as the purchase of the Akron, Canton & Youngstown and the Sandusky lines of the Pennsylvania Railroad. The combined system operates more than 7,400 miles of road and serves industrialized areas. The main line of the Norfolk and Western extends from the tidewater at Norfolk, Va., to Columbus and Cincinnati, Ohio.

In 1968 the U.S. Supreme Court upheld an Interstate Commerce Commission directive requiring the Norfolk and Western to acquire control of three smaller roads that could be hurt by the merger of the Pennsylvania and the New York Central railroads. The three roads are the Boston & Maine, the Delaware & Hudson and the Erie-Lackawanna. The planned merger of the Norfolk and Western and Chesapeake & Ohio, announced by their directors in 1965, continued to await approval of the ICC.

normal schools. A French term, schools for the training of teachers were first established in France in the late 17th century. In the American colonies, as early as 1756, one of the purposes specified in the establishment of Franklin's academy at Philadelphia was "that others of the lesser sort might be trained as teachers."

The first school for training teachers in the U.S. was established in 1823 at Concord, Vt. The Rev. Samuel R. Hall gave a three-year course reviewing common school subjects and adding a new study, the "Art of Teaching." Practice teaching was carried on in the rural school. Hall's *Lectures on School-keeping* (1829) was the first professional book in English.

The first state to provide for the professional education of teachers in the common schools was New York in 1834. The first state normal school in the U.S. was established at Lexington, Mass. in 1839. Horace Mann aided in founding it. A new feature was a model school where the teacher trainees observed and practiced teaching. In 1844 the State Normal School, at Albany, N.Y., was founded.

In a series of developments the normal school courses changed from one to three years. They became teachers' colleges and offered a bachelor's degree. In recent years it has become desirable to speak of the "education" rather than the "training" of teachers. The term "teachers' college" is being dropped and is being replaced by "state college." Increasingly, schools of education are emphasizing the general education of teachers and professional courses in methodology have decreased in relative time in the curriculum. Professional courses and supervised teaching experience have been delayed until the third and fourth years, or even until the fifth year.

Normandie fire (Feb. 9, 1942). France's greatest ocean liner, the world's fastest, burned and capsized at her New York pier. U.S. Naval officers found no evidence of sabotage.

Norris, Frank (1870–1902). Novelist. Benjamin Franklin Norris, known as Frank Norris, was born in Chicago, Ill. A naturalist writer, he dealt with great forces that moved men. In *McTeague* (1899), he told the story of man's reversion to brutishness in a way that was new in American fiction. Two volumes in a planned trilogy, the "Epic of Wheat," were completed before his death. *The Octopus* (1901) presents an epic struggle between California wheat growers and the railroad. It was a turn of the century protest against huge forces that seemed to be grinding down the little man. *The Pit* (1903) is based on the speculative frenzy of the Chicago wheat market, known in the financial world as "the pit."

Norris, George William (1861–1944). Statesman. Born in Sandusky County, O., he moved to Nebraska (1885) and represented that state in the U.S. House of Representatives (1903–13) and the U.S. Senate (1913–43). A progressive Republican, he fought the arbitrary House rule of Speaker Joseph G. Cannon (1910). Norris opposed U.S. entry into World War I and the League of Nations, but favored U.S. entry into World War II. A liberal legislator, he sponsored an anti-injunction law (Norris-La Guardia Act, 1932) and was a major force in establishing the Tennessee Valley Authority (1933). The first TVA-built dam (1936) is called Norris Dam (near Knoxville, Tenn.) in his honor. He is also known as the "Father of the Twentieth Amendment" (the "Lame-duck" Amendment, 1933).

Norris-LaGuardia Act (1932). The measure declared it public policy for labor to have full freedom of association without interference by employers. It outlawed yellow-dog contracts and prohibited federal courts from issuing injunctions in labor disputes except under carefully defined conditions.

The Act was sponsored by Sen. George W. Norris (Neb.), "Father of the Twentieth Amendment," and Rep. Fiorello LaGuardia (N.Y.), who as the vigorous Mayor of New York (1934–45) was known affectionately as the "Little Flower."

North American Air Defense Command (NORAD). The international command couples the air defense forces of Canada and the U.S. An "eyes and ears" organization of the space age, it was activated in 1961. Its mission is alerting the Free World to a missile or satellite-launched attack on the North American continent or Western Europe. The first warning of an attack would come from NORAD's combat operations center built in tunnels and chambers inside Cheyenne Mountain, Colo.

North Atlantic Treaty Organization (NATO). One of the largest peacetime alliances the world has ever known was formed in 1949 to counter the threat of Soviet military power. The U.S., Canada and 10 nations of western Europe—Belgium, Denmark, France, Great Britain, Iceland, Italy, Luxemburg, the Netherlands, Norway and Portugal—were charter members. Greece and Turkey joined NATO in 1952. West Germany became a member in 1955 making a total of 15 nations in all. Spain is not a member of NATO but is linked to the U.S. by the Pact of Madrid (1953), under which the U.S. has built air bases and a naval base in Spain.

NATO serves notice on the world that an armed attack against one member nation would be considered an attack against them all. The Treaty does not affect the primary responsibility of the UN Security Council for the maintenance of international peace.

In 1951 a military arm of NATO called SHAPE (Supreme Headquarters of Allied Powers in Europe) was set up near Paris.

Within the Atlantic Alliance there are serious divisions of opinion as to the best way of meeting the lessened threat of Soviet aggression. In 1966 France withdrew its troops from the integrated military command and required that all NATO bases and headquarters be removed from French soil. In 1967 SHAPE was moved to Brussels, Belgium. France, nevertheless, remained a member of NATO.

North Carolina. The "Tar Heel State," a South Atlantic state, was one of the original 13 Colonies. It was named after Charles I (Carolus, Latin name for Charles) who granted the land to Sir Robert Heath in 1629.

Verrazano touched the coast in 1524 and De Soto went into the Great Smoky Mts. in 1540. The first settlement was promoted by Sir Walter Raleigh, who sent an expedition to Roanoke Island in 1584. These colonists returned to England, and another settlement, 1587, disappeared (the Lost Colony). In 1656 several Virginians came to the area and bought land from the Indians. In 1663 Charles II made an extensive grant to eight of his favorites, who became known as the lords proprietors. They divided the territory into North and South Carolina. When the colonists rebelled against excessive taxation, the territory became a royal colony in 1729.

The next great rebellion was the Revolution and North Carolina broke with England in 1775. It was invaded in 1776 and again in 1780–81. It was the 12th state to be admitted to the Union and ratified the Constitution (Nov. 21, 1789), after the new government had begun to function. Its capital is Raleigh.

North Carolina seceded from the Union, May 20, 1861 and was readmitted in 1868. It lost more soldiers in the Civil War than any other state.

It is an important agricultural state with tobacco, peanuts, sweet potatoes, vegetables, fruits and cotton among its chief crops. The state is one of the main sources in the country for feldspar and mica. It is especially important for the manufacture of cotton goods and tobacco products and produces furniture and other lumber products.

North Dakota. The "Sioux State" or "Flickertail State," in the West North Central group, was admitted to the Union as the 39th or 40th state (with South Dakota), Nov. 2, 1889. Its capital is Bismarck.

It was first explored by French-Canadians (1742). The Lewis and Clark expedition (1804–06) passed through the territory. Fur-trading posts and forts were erected along the Missouri and Red rivers.

Dakota (Sioux for friend or ally) was part of the Louisiana Purchase (1803). It was included in the Dakota Territory, organized in 1861. Settlement was slow and in 1870 there were only 2,400 white inhabitants. Railroad construction hastened settlement, especially in the productive Red River Valley.

Agriculture is the principal industry in the state, with spring wheat, barley and rye important crops. Minerals include lignite coal, natural gas and crude petroleum. Uranium production began in 1962.

Early in the 20th century cooperative state banks, grain elevators and other enterprises were organized, giving the state a reputation for progressive economic experimentation.

Northeast power blackout. On Nov. 9, 1965, shortly after 5 P.M., a network of power lines broke down and left a large part of the Northeast virtually paralyzed. Homes, factories, offices and farms were left without light or power. A population of 30,000,000 in an area of 80,000 square miles was plunged into darkness.

The power went out first somewhere along the Niagara frontier. Then the blackout hurtled eastward to New York City and into New England and parts of New Jersey and Pennsylvania and northward into Canada's Ontario province. A malfunction in the Northeast's huge CANUSE (Canadian-U.S. Eastern interconnection) power grid caused the cascading effect which shut down power plants as automatic switches tripped one another to prevent damage to the electrical equipment.

The blackout lasted from an hour or two in some areas to more than 13 hours in parts of New York City, depending upon the time required for local systems to start auxiliary power or restart their main generators.

Northern Pacific Railway Co. The transcontinental line, the first to reach the Pacific Northwest, was chartered by the federal government in 1864. It received lavish land grants—about 40 million acres. Jay Cooke financed the start of construction in 1869 but met disaster in the Panic of 1873. In 1881 the N.P. was captured by Henry Villard who pushed construction from the head of the Great Lakes to Portland, Ore., and by 1883 to Tacoma, Wash.

James J. Hill acquired the N.P. with the help of J. P. Morgan in 1896. E. H. Harriman sought to win control of the road by purchasing its shares in the open market. The clash of the Hill-Morgan and Harriman-Kuhn, Loeb factions sent N.P.

stock soaring. The crash that followed was the Panic of 1901.

The N.P. extends from the head of the Great Lakes and St. Paul-Minneapolis through states bordering Canada to Pacific Northwest cities. It operates about 7,000 miles of road. Jointly with the Great Northern it controls the Chicago, Burlington and Quincy Railroad and holds 50% interest in the Spokane, Portland & Seattle Railway.

Northern Securities Case (1904). The U.S. Supreme Court ordered dissolution of the Northern Securities Company which was held to restrain trade under the Sherman Antitrust Act. The holding company, formed to monopolize the railroads of the Northwest, had been organized by the James J. Hill and J. P. Morgan interests, managers of the Great Northern and Northern Pacific railroads, and the Edward H. Harriman and Jacob H. Schiff interests, directors of the Union Pacific and Southern Pacific railroads.

These rival groups had competed for control of the Chicago, Burlington and Quincy which commanded the best connections with Chicago from the West. When Hill gained control of this road Harriman launched a counterattack by seeking control of Hill's Northern Pacific. This caused a boom in Northern Pacific stock followed by the bust which helped to bring the financial Panic of 1901. Pres. T. Roosevelt ordered his Attorney General to proceed against the Northern Securities Company which had been formed by the competing giants as a peaceful settlement of their expensive contest. Roosevelt regarded dissolution of the Northern Securities Company as a major victory in his campaign to control abuses by big business.

Northwest Ordinances. The Ordinances of 1784, 1785 and 1787, passed by Congress under the Articles of Confederation, provided the basis for admitting new states into the U.S. They applied to the "Old Northwest," the territory north of the Ohio River that became known officially as the Northwest Territory.

The Ordinance of 1785 called for the scientific survey and establishment of clear-cut boundaries. The Ordinance of 1784 was never put into effect by Congress but it was the basis for the famous Northwest Ordinance of 1787. This provided for the division of the territory into from three to five states and their admission to the Union on the basis of full equality with the original states. It guaranteed freedom of religion, speech and press, barred slavery and reserved part of the public lands for development of public education.

The Northwest Ordinances marked a fundamental break with the colonial policy of Great Britain. They made certain that the new nation would grow by admitting new states which would share all the powers of government equally with the older states.

Northwest Passage. The search for an all-water route from the Atlantic to Asia across North America started in the 17th century. Champlain was among the notable explorers. He founded Quebec (1608) and used it as a base on the St. Lawrence River from which he pushed westward to Lake Huron. Henry Hudson sailing for the Dutch discovered Hudson Bay (1610). Many other explorers sought the link between Atlantic and Pacific unsuccessfully.

In the mid-19th century Robert McClure, a British naval officer searching for Sir John Franklin, an explorer, discovered the Northwest Passage by traveling eastward over the ice from Bering Strait. The route was, however, blocked by ice. Roald Amundsen, Norwegian polar explorer, was the first to navigate the Northwest Passage from the Atlantic to Alaska (1903–06).

Norumbega. The New England coast was known by that name when it was explored by the Frenchman Champlain early in the 17th century.

"not worth a Continental." During the American Revolution the Continental Congress issued great amounts of paper money without backing in gold or silver. The paper money depreciated so rapidly that by 1781 a pair of shoes cost $100 and a barrel of flour $1,575. The inflation of the currency gave rise to the expression "not worth a Continental." The states, too, were issuing paper money without specie backing, contributing to inflation of the currency.

nullification. The doctrine held that the Union was a compact of states each of which had the right to declare null and void any act of the federal government that it deemed a violation of the Constitution.

An outstanding attempt at nullification occurred in South Carolina, which opposed the protective tariffs of 1828 and 1832. A state convention passed the Ordinance of Nullification (1832) declaring the tariff acts null and void.

Pres. Jackson responded with his famous Nullification Proclamation (1832) warning South Carolina that he would meet treason with force. Federal force, however, became unnecessary when the compromise tariff of 1833 provided for gradual reduction of tariff rates. The nullifiers in South Carolina, who had received no support from other southern states, rescinded the Ordinance of Nullification.

O

Ocala Platform. The National Farmers Alliance and Industrial Union, meeting together in Ocala, Fla., Dec. 8, 1890, drew up a program of reforms. They called for abolition of national banks, free coinage of silver, low tariffs, establishment of subtreasuries to lend money directly to the people at low rates of interest and a graduated income tax.

Ochs, Adolph Simon (1858–1938). Newspaper publisher. Born in Cincinnati, O., he began his publishing career by purchasing the Chattanooga *Times* (1878), with which he enjoyed great success. When *The New York Times* was nearing bankruptcy, he purchased it and was its publisher (1896–1935), using principles he had practiced in Chattanooga and making no concessions to yellow journalism. It became a "news" paper in which editorial opinion was subordinate and the news was treated with freedom from personal bias. Ochs selected the motto for the *Times*: "All the news that's fit to print" and made it "the newspaper of record" because of its extensive coverage of public events.

Odets, Clifford (1906–63). Playwright. Born in Philadelphia, Pa., he started his theater career as an actor in minor roles. In *Awake and Sing* (1935) he dramatized the impact of the depression on a lower-middle-class Jewish family in the Bronx. His other significant works include *Waiting for Lefty* (1935), *Paradise Lost* (1935) and *Golden Boy* (1938).

Ohio. The "Buckeye State" (after the buckeye tree), one of the East North Central group, was admitted to the Union as the 17th state, Mar. 1, 1803. Its capital is Columbus.

Ohio (meaning "great" in Indian, referring to the river) was explored before 1700 by the French. It was a battleground in the French and Indian War (1754–63), at the end of which it was ceded to the English. The region was won by George Rogers Clark in the Revolution and became part of the Northwest Territory in 1787. Marietta, the first permanent settlement in the state, was founded in 1788. The territory was torn by conflict with the Indians prior to statehood.

After 1850 railway construction linked the towns of the state. Industrial development during the next century made the state a leader in manufacturing, particularly of motor vehicles, automobile tires, iron and steel products. Most of the land lies within the Corn Belt and agricultural production includes Indian corn, wheat and other small grains. Ohio leads the states in output of lime, clays and ferro-alloys.

Ohio and Erie Canal. Opened in 1833 the canal connected Cleveland, on Lake Erie, with the Ohio River at Portsmouth. It gave Ohio farmers an outlet to the Mississippi River and to the markets of the South.

Ohio Company (1747). Although one of the promoters was a London merchant, the land company was organized chiefly by Virginians. (English capitalists were also looking to the Ohio Valley as a field of investment.) In 1749 the company obtained from King George II a grant of 200,000 acres on both sides of the Ohio, between the Monongahela and Kanawha rivers, together with a promise of 300,000 acres more if 200 families were settled upon the first tract within seven years. Christopher Gist was sent out to explore the region.

Land speculation, settlement and trading with the Indians were the principal objects of the company. Its grant was not renewed in 1770, but it had played a role in pushing the frontier over the mountains into the country's interior.

Ohio Company of Associates (1787). The enterprise was organized in Boston by Revolutionary War officers and soldiers with a major assist from New York land speculators interested in lands north of the Ohio River. The Rev. Manasseh Cutler, a Massachusetts clergyman with a keen business sense, and William Duer, a veteran speculator, were instrumental in getting Congress to sell the group some 1,500,000 acres, at about nine cents an acre, payable mostly by Continental certificates. These had greatly depreciated in value but were accepted at par in exchange for public lands.

As soon as the land purchase was made by the company it pressed for adoption of the Northwest Ordinance of 1787 so that the government of the new territory might be organized. When this was accomplished the company sent out its first group of 47 settlers. In 1788 they founded Marietta, O., at the junction of the Ohio and Muskingum rivers. By the 1830's all of the company's land had been sold.

Ohio Idea. The Democratic platform of 1868 proposed that greenbacks be reissued to pay off the war bonds. Thus a two-fold purpose would be served: retiring the national debt and cheapening the currency to the advantage of debtor farmers. The author of the "soft money" plan was George H. Pendleton of Ohio, who sought but did not obtain the presidential nomination.

Republicans attacked the Ohio Idea as repudiation of a sacred trust to the people who had purchased bonds during the Civil War. They urged payment of the war bonds in gold; they promised that the redemption of greenbacks would proceed slowly to avoid hurting the credit structure of the country. The Republicans won the election and the Ohio Idea was never adopted.

Okinawa, battle of (Mar. 22–June 22, 1945). The U.S. forces won a costly but vital victory in the Pacific in World War II. Okinawa, the main island in the Ryukyu archipelago, is virtually on the doorstep of the main Japanese islands, only 362 miles southwest of Kyushu.

The Japanese had strengthened the island's natural rugged defenses by adding concrete blockhouses, pillboxes and inter-communicating tunnels.

The Marines, commanded by Gen. Buckner, landed after a ten-day bombardment of the island by Adm. Spruance's Fifth Fleet. At first they encountered little resistance, but the Japanese made their stand in the southern part of the large island. Before surrender their casualties, including thousands of suicides, amounted to 109,629 killed. U.S. losses were 12,520 killed and missing, 36,-631 wounded. The casualty rate was almost twice that on Iwo Jima.

The victory practically cut off all Japanese positions to the southward. Their position in China, Burma and the Dutch East Indies became untenable and they withdrew. Okinawa was set as the final base for Operations Olympic and Coronet, the invasion of the Japanese home islands; however, the war ended before the operations were necessary.

Oklahoma. One of the West South Central group, it was admitted to the Union as the 46th state, Nov. 16, 1907. Its capital is Oklahoma City.

Oklahoma (meaning "home of the red man" in Choctaw) was first explored by Coronado of Spain in 1541. Settlement by the French occurred the next century. The land, except the panhandle, which did not become part of the U.S. until the annexation of Texas, was part of the Louisiana Purchase (1803).

Part of Oklahoma was reserved by the U.S. (1834) as Indian Territory for tribes sent out of the southern states. The "Unassigned Lands" were opened to white settlers in "runs." One such "run" was set by Congress for Apr. 22, 1889 when 50,000 people were poised for the "Land Rush" which helped speed settlement of the country.

Oklahoma is popularly called the "Sooner State" because settlers had rushed into the new territory sooner than they were officially admitted. The portion opened up in 1889 was organized as a territory. In 1890 it was joined with the Indian Territory to form the Oklahoma Territory.

The state is a great poultry and egg center and has become an important cotton and wheat growing area. Its most valuable mineral products are petroleum and gas.

The state voted, Apr. 7, 1959, to end 51 years of liquor prohibition.

Old Colony. In Massachusetts history the name refers to the territory formerly occupied by the Plymouth colony and absorbed into that of Massachusetts Bay in 1691.

Old Dominion. The name was adopted by the Virginia House of Burgesses in 1660 when Charles II returned to the throne. Its members had so enthusiastically accepted the Restoration that the King made Virginia, the oldest of the New World settlements, a dominion.

Old Glory. The U.S. flag was probably first given this name by William Driver, master of the brig *Charles Daggett*, who raised the flag on his ship, Aug. 10, 1831, saying: "I name thee Old Glory!" He also said: "My ship, my country and my flag, Old Glory!"

Old Guard. The term was used by Republican Progressives to describe the conservative group in the party during the Taft administration (1909–13). The Old Guard, led by "Uncle Joe" Cannon, Speaker of the House, opposed progressive legislation, pushed through a high tariff, obtained the dismissal of Gifford Pinchot, an ardent conservationist, and controlled the party. The term still signifies the conservatives in the Republican party.

Old Hickory. Andrew Jackson's endurance during the War of 1812 earned for him the nickname "Old Hickory." He carried it with him into political life and through his Presidency (1829–37).

Old Ironsides. The U.S.S. *Constitution* which fought notable engagements in the War of 1812 gained the name during the fight with the British frigate *Guerrière* when a seaman seeing a shot rebound from her side shouted that her sides were made of iron.

The *Constitution* was to be scrapped but the poem, "Old Ironsides," by Oliver Wendell Holmes, aroused public opinion and the ship was rebuilt. The ship has been preserved in Boston Harbor and remains a reminder of the glory of the early days of the Republic.

"Old Joe Clark." The post-Civil War ballad records the wry lament of the white residents of a southern town suffering under the insolence of a turncoat town marshal, a scalawag appointed by Pres. Andrew Johnson.

Old Lights. The name was applied to the orthodox colonial churchmen to distinguish them from New Lights, or revivalists, followers of Jonathan Edwards and George Whitefield during the period of the Great Awakening in the American colonies in 1734.

Old Man Eloquent. The title was earned by John Quincy Adams in 1828 after his defeat for reelection as President. He served in Congress, 1831–48, where his voice never seemed to be stilled in his opposition to slavery. His complete independence of party control enabled him to speak and vote in accordance with firmly held convictions.

Old Public Functionary. Pres. Buchanan was known by the nickname he used when he alluded to himself in a message to Congress in 1859.

Old Rough and Ready. The commanding general in the field during the Mexican War (1846–48) was Gen. Zachary Taylor. Beloved by his men, he had during his 40 years of army service earned the nickname, Old Rough and Ready.

Old South Church. The Boston church, first built in 1670, appears in colonial history as the scene of Boston massacre anniversary orations and the Tea Party meeting which preceded the dumping of British tea into the harbor.

Olive Branch Petition. Led by John Dickinson in 1775, moderates in the Second Continental Congress hoped, by petitioning George III, to achieve peaceful reconciliation with Britain even after the fighting at Lexington, Concord and Bunker Hill.

The petition put the blame for colonial disorders on the King's ministers and asked George III to keep Parliament from further tyranny.

The King refused to receive the petition on the grounds that it came from a disloyal group. He declared that the Americans were in rebellion and that Loyalists should give them no support.

Olmstead, Frederick Law (1822–1903). Landscape architect. Born in Hartford, Conn., the results of his travels in the South were collected in *The Cotton Kingdom* (2 vols., 1861), a classic picture of the planter-slavery system. Appointed superintendent of Central Park in New York City (1858), he became the first American park's chief architect. He also planned Prospect Park in Brooklyn, South Park in Chicago, the grounds of the Capitol at Washington and the Boston park system. He tenaciously sought to protect quiet, sylvan retreats to be used by busy urban residents.

Olney Doctrine (1895). U.S. Sec. of State Richard Olney expanded the Monroe Doctrine during the Venezuela Boundary Dispute. He held Britain's seizure of territory in dispute between Venezuela and British Guiana to be, in effect, further colonization, an action in violation of the Monroe Doctrine. He then went beyond the Doctrine in maintaining that the U.S. because of "its infinite resources combined with its isolated position, is practically sovereign on this continent, and its fiat is law" in any matters on which it chooses to interfere. Britain rejected Olney's claim to U.S. sovereignty in the Western Hemisphere but accepted arbitration of the dispute.

Olney-Pauncefote Treaty (1896). Sec. of State Richard Olney and Sir Julian Pauncefote, the British ambassador in Washington, entered upon negotiations for a general arbitration treaty as a by-product of the Venezuela boundary dispute. They agreed that the cause of peace would be served if varied disputes that might arise between the two countries were subject to binding arbitration. The Treaty was, however, rejected by the U.S. Senate.

Omaha platform (1892). In a stinging statement of aims the People's party, familiarly known as the Populist party, expressed the farm resentment that had accumulated in the 1880's.

The preamble, by Ignatius Donnelly of Minnesota, excori-

ated governmental corruption, capitalist control of government and pauperization of the people. The Populists saw gold interests as "a vast conspiracy against mankind . . . rapidly taking possession of the world. If not met and overthrown at once, it forbodes terrible social convulsions. . . ."

The platform called for easier credit, free coinage of silver and government land for settlers only. Resolutions supplementing the platform endorsed the secret ballot, restriction of immigration, an eight-hour day for government workers, initiative and referendum and direct election of U.S. Senators.

Oneida colony. The utopian colony was founded in central New York in 1848 by John Humphrey Noyes, Vermont-born social reformer. He led a society of Bible communists, known as Perfectionists, who had returned to the communism of the early Christian church. The Oneida Community was formed as a social experiment. Free love or complex marriage was abandoned in 1879, along with communism, after Noyes had to flee to Canada to escape prosecution for adultery. The community continued to thrive as a joint stock company and became known especially for the manufacture of mousetraps and so-called Community silverware.

Oneida Indians. The Indian tribe, one of the Iroquois League, inhabited the area around Oneida Lake, N.Y. They aided the Americans against the British in the Revolutionary War. Some of them may still be found in the area of central New York, where they first made contact with white men.

O'Neill, Eugene (1888–1953). Playwright. Born in New York City, he worked as a common seaman before settling down to write plays in which his characters struggled against uncontrollable natural forces. In one of his psychological dramas, *Strange Interlude* (1928), each character's thoughts are revealed by the device of the stage "aside."

Other plays by this distinguished dramatist include *Beyond the Horizon* (1920), *The Emperor Jones* (1920), *Anna Christie* (1921), *The Hairy Ape* (1922), *Desire Under the Elms* (1924), *The Great God Brown* (1926), *Marco Millions* (1928), *Mourning Becomes Electra* (1931), *Ah, Wilderness!* (1933), *The Iceman Cometh* (1946) and *Long Day's Journey Into Night* (1956). The last-named play, autobiographical in theme, was produced after the author's death.

"one-third of a nation." In his second inaugural address, Jan. 20, 1937, Pres. F. D. Roosevelt made it clear that much remained to be done to raise the living standards of Americans. "I see one-third of a nation ill-housed, ill-clad, ill-nourished," the President said.

Onondaga. One of the original five tribes of the Iroquois League, they were guardians of the council fire of the confederacy. The great council of the League was held each summer at the principal Onondaga town in New York. The Onondaga also furnished 14 of the 50 councilors and the council's presiding officer.

Open-Door policy. In keeping with traditional American policy, the U.S. sought equal commercial opportunity for all—rather than special privileges for a few—in China. This policy was set forth in almost identical notes which Sec. of State John Hay sent to England, Germany, Russia, France, Italy and Japan in 1899, expressing what is known as the Open-Door policy.

Hay asked that all countries "enjoy perfect equality of treatment for their commerce and navigation" in the parts of China that some nations had carved out for themselves. Some of the answers were not direct, but Hay announced that all of the countries had accepted the principle.

A group of fanatical Chinese, called "Boxers" in the Western world, rose up against the "foreign devils" in 1900. Hay feared that the powers would take advantage to do violence to the Open Door. In his Circular Note, July 3, 1900, which did not call for an answer, he declared that the U.S. stood for the territorial integrity of all China and for commercial equality in "all parts" of China.

The Open Door proved to be very much of an empty phrase, for the U.S. made no military plans to defend the principle against violations by European powers and, especially, by Japan.

Oppenheimer Case. On Dec. 23, 1953, the Atomic Energy Commission suspended the security clearance of Dr. J. Robert Oppenheimer (1904–67), father of the atom bomb. The AEC action astounded the nation. On June 29, 1954, the AEC voted four to one against reinstating the scientist because of his association with known Communists. No proof was unearthed that he had ever been disloyal to his country.

Subsequently, Oppenheimer was appointed director of the Institute for Advanced Study at Princeton. In 1963 the AEC erased the stigma by selecting him to receive the $50,000 Enrico Fermi Award for his contributions in the field of nuclear science.

Orders-in-Council (1806–07). The British authorized the seizure of any vessel that attempted to trade on the continent of Europe without first having secured British permission. The Orders, which sought to cut France off from outside aid, were countered by Napoleon's Berlin and Milan Decrees.

The U.S. as a neutral was thus subjected to seizure of its ships by both England and France. Although losses grew, the profits for ships which ran the blockades encouraged continuation of the traffic.

The Orders were resented and resisted by the U.S. They were repealed by the British before Pres. Madison's war message to Congress, but their repeal was not enough to avert the War of 1812.

Oregon. The "Beaver State," a Pacific group state, was admitted to the Union as the 33rd state, Feb. 14, 1859. Its capital is Salem.

Wauregan, Algonquian for "beautiful water," probably referring to the Columbus River, is the origin of the name of the state. Early in the 17th century the Spanish explored the territory but did not settle there. About a century later the Russians from the north and the British searching for the Northwest Passage appeared. The Northwest coast then became important to both English and U.S. fur trappers who exported furs to Canton, China. U.S. claim to the area rested on the voyage of Robert Gray, who reached the Columbia River (1792), and the Lewis and Clark expedition (1804–06). John Jacob Astor founded a fur depot at Astoria (1811). U.S. missionaries, including Dr. Marcus Whitman, helped settle the area (1835), and the first emigrant train made its way over the Oregon Trail (1842).

The territory, which extended from northern California to Alaska, was disputed by Great

Britain, the U.S., Russia and Spain. In 1818 the U.S. and Britain agreed to joint occupation of Oregon. Spain withdrew its claim in 1819. Russia withdrew its claims below 54° 40′ North Latitude by treaty with the U.S. (1824). Pres. Polk pledged himself to "reoccupy Oregon" in 1844. In the Oregon Treaty (1846) a compromise with Britain drew the boundary between the U.S. and Canada at the 49th parallel. Congress established the Oregon Territory (1848).

The lumber industry ranks first in Oregon. The chief crops are wheat and other grains. Leading manufactures are light metals and wood products.

Oregon. In the most remarkable run ever made by any steam vessel the U.S. battleship raced from the Mare's Island Navy Yard, San Francisco, through the Straits of Magellan, halting at Rio de Janeiro for coal and arrived in Cuban waters after 66 days. It then participated in the destruction of Cervera's fleet off Santiago, July 3, 1898, in a Spanish-American War action.

Oregon Parochial School Case (1925). In *Pierce v. Society of Sisters* the U.S. Supreme Court invalidated the Oregon Compulsory Education Law which required every parent to send his child to a public school. The Court ruled that this was an unconstitutional interference with the liberty of parents and guardians to direct the upbringing of their children and violated due process guaranteed by the 14th Amendment.

Oregon system. In 1902 the progressive legislation was introduced in Oregon to encourage direct voter participation in law making. Under a constitutional amendment provision was made for "initiative" (introduced in South Dakota in 1898) whereby legislation must be introduced in the legislature if a specified number of voters, usually 5% to 10%, petition for it. Under a "referendum" the same percentage of voters can require that a bill rejected by the legislature be placed before the voters to decide whether or not it is to become law. Under "recall" a specified number of voters, usually 20% to 30%, can petition for an election to decide whether an official should be removed from office. These political devices—initiative, referendum and recall—were adopted by a number of state legislatures, especially in the West.

Oregon Trail. "Oregon fever" swept the Mississippi Valley frontier by 1843 and thousands of emigrants in their covered wagons moved toward the fertile Willamette Valley in Oregon.

The 2,000 mile Trail wound its way from Independence, Mo., and took a northwest course to Fort Kearney on the Platte River. It followed the Platte to Fort Laramie. Here the Trail entered mountain

503

country. It crossed the Continental Divide at South Pass at an elevation of 7,500 feet. At Fort Bridger, after going through the pass, the emigrants usually rested and refitted themselves for the final stage of the journey. The Trail now bent northward to Fort Hall on the Snake River and passed Fort Boise. From there it led into the Columbia River Valley which led in turn to the Willamette. Shallow graves, the bones of horses and oxen and abandoned precious personal possessions marked the Trail.

One of the "Great Migrations" in American history, it is described in Francis Parkman's *Oregon Trail* (1849).

Organization for Economic Cooperation and Development (OECD). The 20-nation international economic organization replaced the Organization for European Economic Cooperation (OEEC) in 1961. It is comprised of the U.S., Canada and 18 European nations. Its purpose is to "promote economic stability and the orderly growth of the economies of member countries" and to distribute equitably the burden of aiding less developed countries.

Organization Man, The (1956). A popular book by William H. Whyte, Jr., is concentrated on the plight of the individual in the new collective world. Whyte argued that the old Protestant-individualist code was giving way before a new collective ethic. The new ethic, arising from the bureaucratization of society, lent approval to the pressures of society against the free-wheeler. Assumptions in the collective ethic were that the group, rather than the individual, was the source of creativity; "belongingness," rather than personal fulfillment, the ultimate need of the individual.

Organization of American States (OAS). The OAS Charter was signed in 1948 at Bogota, Colombia, by the 21 republics of the Western Hemisphere. (Canada is not included.) It gave permanent form to the Inter-American Treaty of Reciprocal Assistance drafted in Rio de Janeiro and commonly known as the Rio Pact (1947).

The major purpose of the OAS, according to the U.S. Department of State, is to protect the Hemisphere "against the interventionist and aggressive designs of international communism."

The Pan American Union is the secretariat of the OAS with headquarters in Washington, D.C.

Oriskany, battle of (Aug. 6, 1777). In the battle in central New York, British Lt. Col. Barry St. Leger was prevented from joining Gen. Burgoyne, who desperately needed his help.

St. Leger, commanding a force of Loyalists and Iroquois Indians, laid siege to Fort Stanwix. The fort was relieved by the New York militia under Gen. Nicholas Herkimer. After a bloody battle St. Leger retreated to Oswego, misled by a stratagem of Benedict Arnold into believing that a superior American force was on the way. Arnold then joined Gen. Horatio Gates to defeat Burgoyne at Saratoga.

Osage Indians. Plains Indians of Siouan linguistic stock, the tribe migrated from the Ohio Valley to the Osage River in Missouri, where Marquette met them in 1673. They were allied with the French during the colonial period. In 1808 when they ceded their lands in Missouri and Arkansas to the U.S., they were given land in northern Oklahoma. Oil strikes made the Osage one of the richest tribes in the U.S.

Osage Trace. The western trail blazed by the Osage Indians became part of the principal wagon road between St. Louis and the Texas frontier in the early 19th century. After leaving St. Louis the Trace went up the north side of the Missouri River to within a few miles of Jefferson City where it crossed the river and struck off to the southwest. The name first applied to the trans-Missouri section of the great trail. Later it covered the important north-south trail of the Osage Nation, running through eastern Oklahoma to the Red River where it merged with the Texas Road or Shawnee Trail.

Ostend Manifesto (1854). To consolidate their efforts to pur-

chase Cuba, James Buchanan, John Y. Mason and Pierre Soulé, American ministers to England, France and Spain, met in Ostend, Belgium, in October. Their recommendations were contained in a memorable dispatch to Sec. of State Marcy. They urged that Spain be offered a price not to exceed $120,000,000, and if Spain refused to sell "Then, by every law, human and divine, we shall be justified in wresting it from Spain. . . ."

Antislavery elements in the U.S. were outraged by the brazen plan set forth in the dispatch, mistakenly considered as an ultimatum to Spain. Hostile comment was also provoked in Europe. Marcy refused to accept the recommendations of the ministers.

"O Susanna." Published in 1848, the popular song by Stephen Foster caught the country's imagination at a time when many were on the move to Oregon and California. The words were: "O, Susanna! O, don't you cry for me, I've come from Alabama, wid my banjo on my knee." But Oregon and California were sometimes substituted when voices were raised at campfires and on ships rounding Cape Horn.

Other People's Money (1914). Before he was appointed to the U.S. Supreme Court by Pres. Wilson in 1916, Louis D. Brandeis wrote a number of essays on the "money trust," indicting banking and corporate practices that fostered monopolies.

Otis, James (1725–83). Pre-Revolutionary leader. Born in West Barnstable, Mass., he represented Boston merchants (1761) in their opposition to writs of assistance applied for by the royal customs collectors seeking to enforce the Sugar Act of 1733. His defense provided the base for continuing attacks upon acts of Parliament which regulated colonial commerce and taxation. His political pamphlet, *A Vindication of the Conduct of the House of Representatives* (1762), detailed the rights of Englishmen. While he was the recognized political leader of Massachusetts Bay (1761–69), his pamphlet *The Rights of the British Colonies Asserted and Proved* (1764) summarized his position on natural rights. The Stamp Act Congress (1765) accepted his constitutional position but rejected his argument that the colonies should have representation in Parliament. Struck in the head and seriously injured by a Crown official (1769), he took no part in the Revolution.

Ottawas. An Algonquian people claiming the Ottawa River region, they controlled the Indian traffic to the French on that Canadian river. Their alliance with the Huron made them enemies of the Iroquois who forced them to flee further west, 1648–49. Some Ottawas continue to live in Kansas, Oklahoma and Michigan.

"Our Country . . . right or wrong." Stephen Decatur after distinguishing himself in naval action against the Barbary pirates in the Mediterranean returned to the U.S. in 1816. At a dinner in his honor, he offered a toast that reflected the growing nationalism of the day: "Our Country! In her intercourse with foreign nations may she always be in the right and always successful, right or wrong."

"Our federal union! It must and shall be preserved!" The toast was made by Pres. Jackson at the Jefferson anniversary dinner, Apr. 13, 1830. Jackson thus made it clear to the nullifiers that he would resist the states rights proponents' claim to void the tariff law—an issue at the time.

Vice-President Calhoun's reply to Jackson's toast was: "The Union, next to our liberty, most dear."

outer space. The U.S. joined with UN Committees on the Peaceful Uses of Outer Space in 1958 and 1959 to avoid projecting national rivalries into this new field.

overland mail. In 1858, John R. Butterfield established a stagecoach line that provided twice-a-week service between San Francisco in the West and St. Louis and Memphis in the East. The U.S. government paid $600,000 a year for carrying the mail by stagecoach. Butterfield constructed 160 stations where horses could be changed and meals served. He charged

$200 for the westward trip which included 40 pounds of baggage. There was less demand for the eastward trip for which he charged $150. The trip from St. Louis to San Francisco could be made in 25 days by anyone who wanted to travel day and night.

Overlord, Operation. The code name designated the Allied invasion of the Normandy coastline which began June 6, 1944.

Ox-Bow Incident, The (1940). A novel by Walter Van Tilburg Clark, it is a story of violence and quick justice in the Old West. A high point in the psychological study of men in action is the conflict among the members of the lynch-posse over the lives of three men.

P

Packers and Stockyards Act
(1921). The Act prohibited
such "unfair" practices as ap-
portioning supplies among packers, dividing territory and creating conditions tending toward
monopoly of the livestock and
poultry business. Rates and
practices of the stockyards regarded as public corporations
were regulated. Enforcement
was lodged with the Secretary
of Agriculture rather than in
the Federal Trade Commission.

packet lines. In 1818, transatlantic vessels commenced sailing regularly from New York
to Liverpool, England. They
were scheduled for three sail-
ings weekly and carried passengers and freight. Improved
efficiency of ship design was
reflected in the average time
for crossing which was reduced
from 39 days (1818–22) to 33
days (1848–52). The packet
lines were also used in the
coastal trade. Their scheduled
service was taken over by steamships after the mid-19th century.

pack trains. Settlers in the West
loaded horses or mules with
furs or other items for trade
and drove them along regular
trails to more settled centers to
exchange their goods for articles which could not be produced on the frontier.

Some pack trains were run by
the Army to supply outposts.
They made camp in late afternoon and started moving at sun-
rise. Personnel were subject to
the command of officers. They
were formed into messes which
ate together and rotated routine
jobs.

Paine, Thomas (1737–1809).
Political philosopher. Born in
Thetford, England, he emigrated
to Philadelphia (1774). Quickly
aligning himself with the patriot
cause, his widely read pamphlet, *Common Sense* (Jan.
1776), called for an immediate
break with Britain. During service in the Continental army
(1776), he started the first of
his twelve issues of *Crisis*, a
periodical supporting the colonial cause. In Europe, after the
war, Paine hailed the French
Revolution and wrote *The
Rights of Man* (1791–92). He
called for the overthrow of the
British monarchy and was out-

lawed in Britain. Imprisoned in Paris (1793–94), he was released on the request of James Monroe, who said Paine was an American citizen. He lived in Paris until 1802, during which time he wrote *The Age of Reason* (1794–96), a defense of deism which was praised by Jefferson. Upon his return to America, Paine became involved in a political conflict between Jefferson and John Q. Adams. He died in obscurity and poverty.

pairing of votes. In the House of Representatives a pair is a written agreement between members on opposite sides not to vote on a specified question or during a stipulated time. It is in effect equivalent to a vote on the part of each against the proposition favored by his colleague. The practice appeared in the House as early as 1824. It was not officially recognized in the House rules until 1880. Pairing is also permitted in the Senate although not recognized by the rules.

Paiutes. The name is commonly given to a large number of Indians of Shoshonean linguistic stock who live in Nevada, Utah, Arizona and southeastern California. They were peaceful, except for a few instances of fighting with miners, and adapted themselves to working for the whites. They were allied with the Bannocks against U.S. soldiers in the Bannock War (1878), a protest against reservation policies in Idaho and Oregon.

Palatines. German Protestants in the Palatinate, part of the Rhine country, emigrated to the New World to escape persecution and heavy taxes at home. The voyage to New York of some 3,000 Palatines in 1710 was financed by the English Board of Trade, which wanted them to develop a naval stores industry (the manufacture of tar, pitch and resin, used to plug gaps between planks to make vessels more seaworthy). They settled at German Flats, N.Y., south of the Mohawk River, but ran out of funds. Some stayed in New York, but Pennsylvania was friendlier. Other Palatines who sought to settle in North Carolina early in the 18th century suffered from disease, hunger and Indian attacks.

Palmer, Alice Elvira Freeman (1855–1902). Educator. She was born in Colesville, N.Y. As president of Wellesley (1882–87), she developed it into a first-rate woman's college. She was appointed to the Massachusetts board of education (1889); she served as dean of women at the new Univ. of Chicago (1892–95). She was the author of a book of verse, *A Marriage Cycle* (1915) and was elected to the Hall of Fame (1920).

Palmer raids. Pres. Wilson's Attorney General, A. Mitchell Palmer, in 1919 and early in 1920 organized a series of raids on homes and offices to arrest and deport aliens who were Communists. The action was part of the Red scare stimulated by the threat of Communism in post-World War I Europe, the increased number of strikes in the U.S., mounting immigration (nearly a million immigrants came to the U.S. in 1920) and the newspaper reports which fanned the flames of public intolerance. Of the thousands arrested, more than 500 were deported under an Alien Act that gave the Secretary of Labor the power to deport any alien he held to be a radical.

Personal rights were violated by the raids, but they were generally supported by the public. A few prominent citizens raised their voices against violations which "savor of the worst practices of tyranny."

Palo Alto, battle of (May 8, 1846). In one of the first battles of the Mexican War, Gen. Zachary Taylor with a force of about 2,000 troops defeated a Mexican force that was three times greater. The superiority of U.S. artillery pieces was clearly demonstrated. The battle took place on the prairie at the southern tip of Texas, near the water hole of Palo Alto.

Panama Canal. The 50-mile waterway across the Isthmus of Panama, connecting the Atlantic and Pacific oceans, was started in 1904 and was opened to commercial traffic in 1914. The military need for this short cut was dramatized during the Spanish-American War (1898) when the battleship *Oregon*, at San Francisco, took 66 days to make its way around Cape Horn, and north to Cuba, its destination. The commercial value was equally evident.

An earlier effort to build a canal, begun in 1881, by a French company owned by Ferdinand de Lesseps, collapsed. The U.S. purchased the French right for $40,000,000 in 1902 over the opposition of Colombia of which Panama was a part at the time.

Pres. Theodore Roosevelt aided a "revolution" in Panama and the U.S. quickly recognized the new government of Panama. The Hay-Bunau-Varilla Treaty (1903) permitted canal construction to get under way.

Another obstacle to the building of the canal was the Clayton-Bulwer Treaty (1850), but this was set aside by the Hay-Pauncefote Treaty (1901). Even more serious were the engineering obstacles to completing the "Big Ditch." George W. Goethals, an Army engineer, is credited with the successful construction. William C. Gorgas, a health officer, eradicated yellow fever which had decimated workers on the canal.

Roosevelt's intervention in Panama was deeply resented in Latin America. He justified his role by holding that Colombia must not be permitted "permanently to bar one of the future highways to civilization." In 1921 the U.S. paid Colombia $25,000,000 as a gesture of goodwill.

Annual rental payments to Panama have been increased, but long-standing resentment against U.S. sovereign control "in perpetuity" in the Canal Zone was reflected in anti-American rioting in 1963.

In 1964 the U.S. notified Panama that it intended to proceed with the building of a new sea-level canal in Central America or northern Colombia and to renegotiate the 1903 canal treaty. The Canal itself has become inadequate in an era of big ships and heavy interocean traffic.

Panama Refining Co. v. Ryan (1935). The U.S. Supreme Court invalidated the oil control provisions of the National Industrial Recovery Act (NIRA) on the ground that they delegated legislative power to the President. This section of the NIRA had given the President power to forbid the transportation in interstate commerce of "hot oil" (oil produced or withdrawn from storage in violation of state law). The Court pointed out that the statute did not contain any definition of the circumstances under which the transportation was to be permitted or prohibited, that no legislative policy was outlined to guide the President and that too much was left to his discretion.

Pan American Union. The First International American Conference was a gathering of 17 Latin American nations and the U.S., in Washington, D.C.

(1889). U.S. Sec. of State Blaine was host to the Conference. A direct outcome was establishment of the Pan American Union, an organization designed as a clearinghouse for disseminating information and encouraging cooperation among the constituent nations.

Subsequent Pan American Conferences were intended to establish closer ties among the 21 American Republics. At Montevideo, Uruguay (1933), the U.S. formally abandoned the (Theodore) Roosevelt Corollary to the Monroe Doctrine. The U.S. agreed that "no state has the right to intervene in the internal and external affairs of another." At Lima, Peru (1938), the U.S. departed from its unilateral view of the Monroe Doctrine and adopted the multilateral view that the nations composing the Pan American Union (now the secretariat of the Organization of American States) would join together "against all foreign intervention or activity."

Panay incident (Dec. 12, 1937). The U.S. gunboat *Panay*, on the Yangtze River, above Nanking, was bombed by Japanese planes attacking China. The vessel sank killing three men and wounding thirty. In response to Sec. of State Hull's protest, Japan agreed to pay indemnities of over $2 million.

panhandle. The term is used to describe northern Texas, which projects like the handle of a pan. Other states with a pan-

511

handle are Oklahoma, Idaho and West Virginia.

Panic of 1819. The financial collapse following the War of 1812 boom was triggered by the credit contraction of the second Bank of the U.S., which sought to curb the land speculation of the day. The depression continued until 1823 when there was a revival of trade and manufacturing.

The panic was not confined to the U.S. It was worldwide; with a glut of wheat and cotton in the markets, prices plummeted to low levels. The panic followed the agricultural and textile boom which had taken place at the end of the Napoleonic Wars.

Panic of 1837. During Andrew Jackson's administration investments in land, cotton, slaves and internal improvements, such as canal and road building, greatly expanded. The boom was encouraged by the establishment of state banks in which government funds withdrawn from the Bank of the United States were deposited. These "pet banks" issued paper money and financed wild speculation, especially in the purchase of federal lands at $1.25 an acre.

Hard-money advocates recognized the danger and prevailed upon Jackson to issue his Specie Circular (1836) which required payment for public lands in gold or silver. The land speculation bubble was punctured and a number of state banks collapsed. A European depression at this time caused bankers to call for repayment of loans and liquidation of investments in American business. A panic ensued which included the failure of Nicholas Biddle's Bank of the United States.

The resultant depression involved falling cotton prices, business bankruptcies, unemployment and general distress. Martin Van Buren who inherited the panic was defeated for reelection in 1840. Soon after, the fog of depression lifted.

Panic of 1857. The bubble of speculation in land, railroads, manufacturing, wheat and state banking burst a decade after the Mexican War. The financial panic was heightened by the bankruptcy of the Ohio Life Insurance Co. which precipitated bank closings in New York and other parts of the nation. The resultant industrial unemployment and farm unrest were factors in the growth of the new Republican party which defeated the Democrats in the election of 1860.

Panic of 1873. The failure of Jay Cooke and Co., the most famous banking house in the U.S., triggered the panic. It was preceded and followed by thousands of business bankruptcies that plunged the nation into a six-year depression. Unemployment created widespread destitution and violence marked labor unrest. The depression was worldwide.

Fundamental causes of the

panic in the U.S. included over-expansion in railroads, mining, manufacturing and western wheat, unscrupulous manipulation of stocks of many businesses and currency inflation.

Panic of 1893. One of the most disastrous panics in American history, it plunged the nation into a four-year depression during Pres. Cleveland's second administration. The number of bank and business failures reached new highs. Among the most staggering collapses were those of the Union Pacific and Northern Pacific railroads.

Fundamental causes of the panic included withdrawal of gold from the U.S. by European investors who sold their American stocks because of unstable conditions in their own countries. Further drains on the gold supply were caused by the government's need to purchase silver under the Sherman Silver Purchase Act (1890) and this contributed to the fear that the U.S. would be forced off the gold standard. There was over-expansion of railroads and uncontrolled stock market speculation. A farm depression, under way before the panic, contributed to the loss of purchasing power in the nation and the business decline.

Panic of 1907. A stock market crash clouded the final months of Pres. T. Roosevelt's administration. The Knickerbocker Trust Co., a major bank in New York, closed. Other banks, businesses and railroads collapsed.

Roosevelt sought to stem a long decline by permitting the U.S. Steel Corp. to acquire the Tennessee Coal and Iron Co. The securities of this firm were held by brokerage houses which might fail if the securities were not underwritten. It was understood that U.S. Steel would not be subject to antitrust prosecution.

The crisis, which has been called the "Rich Man's Panic," subsided and the memory of the Roosevelt administration was not darkened by a subsequent depression. Pres. Taft did, however, authorize antitrust action against U.S. Steel in 1911 and this contributed to the bitterness between Roosevelt and Taft.

Papal Line of Demarcation (1493). The so-called papal line, agreed to by Portugal and Spain and decreed by Pope Alexander VI, set apart areas in which discovery would confer title to land. Spain felt that such papal sanction was necessary to guarantee claims arising from the voyage of Columbus. The line was drawn through a point a hundred leagues (about 300 miles) west and south of the Azores and the Cape Verde Islands. Spain was to have title to and a monopoly of the commerce with the lands she had discovered or might discover as far to the west of this line as the Indies, provided they did not already belong to a Christian prince. Portuguese subjects were not to pass beyond the line without consent of Spain.

The line was changed by the Treaty of Tordesillas (1494) between Spain and Portugal. The change permitted Brazil later to fall within the Portuguese sphere of influence.

"paper tiger." The Chinese Communists, beginning in the 1950's, steadily contended that "United States imperialism is a paper tiger" that would collapse when pushed. The expression of contempt was picked up in other Communist states, including Cuba. The tendency to minimize the effectiveness of U.S. intervention was, however, curbed by Raúl Castro, brother of Fidel Castro, and himself the Armed Forces Minister of Cuba, when he declared (1965): "United States imperialism is no paper tiger."

Paris, Treaty of (1763). By the Treaty ending the French and Indian War (1754–63), Britain acquired Canada and France's territory east of the Mississippi River, except New Orleans. Martinique and Guadeloupe, important sugar-producing islands in the West Indies, and Haiti were returned to France to satisfy English sugar planters, who feared competition. Britain gave back Cuba and the Philippines to Spain and received Florida in exchange.

France gave New Orleans and the land west of the Mississippi to Spain. France got fishing privileges off Newfoundland and the islands of Saint Pierre and Miquelon useful for drying fish.

The Treaty capped the great victory of Britain over France after a series of wars that had lasted almost a hundred years.

Paris, Treaty of (Sept. 1783). England recognized U.S. independence. Although France hoped to keep the young nation confined by the Appalachian Mts., in order to assure continued dependence, the American negotiators, Benjamin Franklin, John Adams, John Jay and Henry Laurens, gained the Mississippi River as the western boundary of the U.S. To the north the line was fixed approximately where it is today. The southern boundary was Spanish Florida. Americans were permitted to continue to use the Newfoundland fisheries. The thorny question of debts resulted in agreement that the British merchants should "meet with no lawful impediment" in attempting to recover legitimate debts. In the matter of Loyalist claims, Congress pledged to recommend to the states that any properties they had confiscated during the war should be returned to the former owners.

These liberal terms were granted by Lord Shelburne, the King's Prime Minister, because England was still at war with France, Spain and the Netherlands. The Anglo-American Treaty did not go into effect until peace treaties with England's enemies were concluded. Such treaties were signed earlier in 1783.

Paris, Treaty of (1898). The Treaty ending the Spanish-American War provided that Spain free Cuba and cede the Philippines, Guam and Puerto Rico to the U.S. Spain received $20 million for improvements it had made in the Philippines.

The Treaty, signed Dec. 10, 1898, was ratified by the Senate, Feb. 1899, with a margin of two votes. The country had divided over the issue of imperialism versus anti-imperialism. Anti-imperialists argued that the acquisition of colonies was a denial of freedom to others—a repudiation of U.S. traditions. Imperialists held that timidity on the part of the U.S. would mean that the islands would be gobbled up by foreign powers and that they were necessary for future expansion.

Parker, Theodore (1810–60), Unitarian clergyman. He was born in Lexington, Mass. Skeptical of orthodoxy, he believed that religious truths were drawn from individual intuition rather than from revelation. His transcendentalist views brought him into conflict with orthodox Unitarians. He became minister of a new free church in Boston (1852). Active in humanitarian movements, he aided fugitive slaves to escape, supported the New England Emigrant Aid Society and was a member of a committee that abetted John Brown's raid on Harpers Ferry (1859). An immensely popular lecturer and essayist, his writings were collected in *Theodore Parker's Works* (14 vols., 1863–70).

Parkman, Francis (1823–93). Historian. He was born in Boston, Mass. After graduation from Harvard Law School (1846), he made a trip over the old Oregon Trail westward out of St. Louis and wrote an account of it, *The California and Oregon Trail* (1849). Although bordering on blindness and physically ill the rest of his life, he became the leading American historian. He used source materials and wrote with a flowing prose style. His great series of historical works deals with the struggle of England and France for control of North America. His works include *History of the Conspiracy of Pontiac* (1851), *Pioneers of France in the New World* (1865), *The Jesuits in North America* (1867), *The Discovery of the Great West* (1869), retitled in 1879 *La Salle and the Discovery of the Great West*, *The Old Regime in Canada* (1874), *Count Frontenac and New France under Louis XIV* (1877), *Montcalm and Wolfe* (1884), and to complete the series, *A Half-Century of Conflict* (1892).

"parson's cause." A colonial dispute between Virginia clergy and taxpayers arose over the method of paying the unpopular Anglican clergy. Their pay had been in pounds of tobacco, but when the price of tobacco rose the colonial government passed

515

a law allowing taxpayers to pay the ministers (parsons) in currency at the rate of two cents for each pound of tobacco due (two-penny act).

The clergy protested and the Crown disallowed the law. When the clerics sued for back salary, Patrick Henry, representing the taxpayers, denounced the clergy and argued that the King by disallowing the Virginia law of 1758 had "degenerated into a tyrant. . . ." The jury awarded only one penny in damages to the clergyman who had sued for back pay.

The case made Patrick Henry famous in Virginia. His arguments exemplified the growing opposition to English interference in colonial government.

Patent Office. The Constitution provides that Congress shall have the power "to promote the progress of science . . . by securing for limited times to . . . inventors the exclusive right to their . . . discoveries" (Art. I, Sec. 8). The first law protecting patents was enacted Apr. 10, 1790, but the Patent Office as a distinct bureau in the Department of State dates from 1802. It was removed to the Department of Interior in 1849 where it remained until 1925 when it was transferred to the Department of Commerce.

General revisions of the patent laws were made in 1836 and 1870. These and other acts of Congress relating to patents were codified and made effective in 1953.

In addition to the patent laws, the Patent Office administers federal trademark laws.

Pauling, Linus (1901–   ). Chemist. Born in Portland, Ore., he was granted a Ph.D. by the California Institute of Technology (1925) where he has been a professor of chemistry since 1931. He was awarded the Nobel Prize (1954) for Chemistry for discovery of forces holding proteins and molecules together. He is known for his application of quantum mechanics to chemistry and has done important work in the theory of electrolytes. In 1963 he received another Nobel award, the Prize for Peace.

Pawnees. A Caddoan family of plains Indians, settled around the forks of the Platte River in Nebraska and beyond, they were generally friendly to whites. In 1859, however, the Pawnee War broke out, and the defeated Indians retired to a reservation on the Platte. A famous "Pawnee battalion" was used as scouts to protect workers during construction of the Union Pacific Railroad.

The Pawnees were hard hit by the smallpox epidemic of 1832. They were disastrously defeated by the Sioux in 1873 and gave up their reservation. The few survivors settled in the Indian Territory of Oklahoma. In 1893 they gave up their tribal holdings and became U.S. citizens.

Paxton Boys. The frontiersmen in Paxton, Pa., organized to protect settlers against Indian raids during the French and Indian War (1754–63). They deeply resented failure of the Assembly to afford them protection but they were dissuaded from marching on Philadelphia by Benjamin Franklin. Their hostility to the Indians led them to kill (Conestoga Massacre, 1763) some 20 peaceable Indians engaged in handicrafts near Lancaster.

"pay-as-you-go" policy. Since 1958 a withholding tax, applicable to federal income tax payment, has been deducted from wages at the time they are paid. Taxpayers thus do not have large sums to pay when income taxes are due and the federal government receives billions in revenue earlier than under the former method.

Payne-Aldrich Tariff of 1909. The act continued the high protection of previous tariffs with average rates of 37 to 40%. Some of the reductions, especially the abolition of the duty on hides, were hailed as a promise of moderation in the U.S. protective trade policy. Greater reductions were promised than were delivered, for Sen. Aldrich piloted through Congress some 800 amendments raising rates. Western Republican insurgents were outraged by passage of the act.

The rift in the Republican party yawned wider when Pres. Taft ineptly spoke of the Tariff of 1909 as "the best tariff bill that the Republican party has ever passed and, therefore, the best that has been passed at all."

Peabody, George (1795–1869). Merchant, financier and philanthropist. Born in South Danvers, Mass., his early career was in the wholesale dry-goods business. He settled permanently in London (1837), where he specialized in foreign exchange and American securities. After the Panic of 1837, he helped restore confidence in the U.S. economy. Founder of the Peabody Institute at Baltimore and at Peabody, Mass., advancing libraries, music and art, he also established the Peabody Museum of Natural History at Yale and the Peabody Education Fund for the promotion of education in the South.

Peabody Education Fund. Established in 1867 with a one-million-dollar contribution by George Peabody, Massachusetts financier, the foundation's purpose was to advance education in the South. The George Peabody College for Teachers, Nashville, Tenn., was endowed when the Fund capital was divided in 1914.

Peace Corps. Pres. Kennedy in 1961 established the organization which enrolls and trains American men and women to help undeveloped nations "meet their urgent need for skilled manpower." These volunteers, who serve mostly in Africa and South America, fill the gap between technical advisers and local experts on the one hand and relatively unskilled local labor on the other.

peaceful coexistence. The expression seems to have been used first by Nikita Khrushchev in 1956 when he was Premier of the Soviet Union. The policy is aimed at keeping the peace between Communist and non-Communist countries. In the U.S. it was feared that the policy was a carefully planned peace offensive to lull the West into cutting down on its defense preparations.

"Peace, it's wonderful." Father Divine, Negro leader of the Kingdom of Peace movement, preached the message to his followers who were both Negro and white. He is believed to have been born as George Baker, in Georgia. His movement grew rapidly in the 1930's and 1940's when he spoke frequently and when *New Day*, his weekly, was circulated.

"Peace, it's wonderful" was the theme preached at the movement's meetings and "peace," rather than "hello" and "good-bye," was the word of greeting and departure for members of the Kingdom.

"peace without victory." After Pres. Wilson's reelection in 1916 he renewed his efforts to end the war in Europe. In a speech before the Senate, Jan. 22, 1917, which was an appeal to the world, he called for a lasting peace. "It must be a peace without victory," the President said. "Only a peace between equals can last."

Peale, Charles Willson (1741–1827). Painter. He was born in Queen Anne Co., Md. A Revolutionary War officer, he fought at battles of Trenton and Princeton. Best known for his portraits of George Washington, who sat for him repeatedly, he left scores of portraits of distinguished men and families of his day. Also a naturalist, he opened Peale's Museum of Natural History Objects and Portraits (1802, later the Philadelphia Museum).

Pea Ridge (Elkhorn), battle of (Mar. 7–8, 1862). Union Gen. Sam Curtis defeated the Confederates in northern Arkansas, ending the war west of the Mississippi River.

Peary, Robert Edwin (1856–1920). Arctic explorer. Born in Cresson, Pa., he was graduated from Bowdoin College (1877). He served in the U.S. Navy and retired as a rear-admiral (1911). The first of his seven expeditions to the Far North, in which he made significant meteorological, tidal and ethnological observations, took place in 1886. He succeeded in reaching the North Pole (Apr. 6, 1909). Peary's claim to be the first was blighted by Dr. Frederick A. Cook, who had announced five days before Peary that he had reached the North Pole a year earlier. Cook's claim was false.

Pegasus. The giant winged satellite was put into orbit

around the earth in 1965 to measure the potential hazards of meteoroids to astronauts and spacecraft.

The satellite was named Pegasus for the horse in Greek mythology that ascended to live among the stars.

Peirce, Charles Sanders (1839–1914). Philosopher and scientist. Born in Cambridge, Mass., the son of Benjamin Peirce (1808–80), the mathematician and astronomer, he was graduated from Harvard Univ. (1859). His priority in setting forth the philosophy of pragmatism was acknowledged by William James. Peirce's "How to Make Our Ideas Clear" appeared in the *Popular Science Monthly* (Jan. 1878) as one of a series of six articles on logic. He referred to his system as pragmaticism to distinguish it from James' pragmatism. He was on the staff of the U.S. Coast Survey (1861–91) and lectured on logic at Johns Hopkins (1879–84). An original thinker, he contributed to the theory of probability and the logic of scientific methodology and laid the foundation for the logical analysis of mathematics.

Pelican. The ship carried Sir Francis Drake in his famous voyage around the world, leaving England, Dec. 13, 1577, and returning to that country, Sept. 26, 1580. The ship was renamed the *Golden Hind* by Drake during the voyage.

Pemaquid. The first permanent settlement in Maine was established on the peninsula on the Maine coast by John Brown who bought lands from Algonquin Chief Samoset, July 15, 1625. Pemaquid was also originally the name given to the Kennebec River near which the settlement was located. Pemaquid was fortified by the British during the Indian wars of the late 17th century but was captured by the French and Indians.

Pendleton Act (1883). The assassination of Pres. Garfield by a disappointed office seeker led to the passage of a law which, for the first time, provided a practical basis for civil service reform. It authorized the President to appoint a three-man civil service commission to give competitive examinations for certain positions in government service. This classified list could be extended by the President. About 12% of the 110,000 employees then in government service were classified under the Act. Furthermore, it prohibited political assessments of federal office holders.

The Act cut into the spoils system and paved the way for a civil service system based on merit examinations.

Peninsular Campaign (Apr. 4–July 1, 1862). During the Civil War the Union Army of the Potomac under Gen. McClellan sought to capture Richmond, Va., the Confederate capital, by way of the peninsula formed by the York and James rivers. Furious battles were fought in the hills before Richmond against the opposing forces commanded by Gen. Lee; these included actions at Mechanicsville in which Lee was routed and the Seven Days' Battles during which McClellan retreated.

The Peninsular Campaign was a failure. Lincoln removed McClellan and placed Gen. Henry W. Halleck in command of the Union's land forces. Halleck withdrew the Army of the Potomac from the peninsula.

Pennsylvania. The "Keystone State," so named because of its position with regard to the 13 original Colonies, is a Middle Atlantic state. Its capital is Harrisburg. Pennsylvania was named (Latin for Penn's woodland) by King Charles II in honor of William Penn's father, to whom he owed some £16,-000. The land was granted in partial settlement of the debt (1681) to Penn, who became the proprietor.

Swedes were the first white settlers at New Gottenberg (1643). However, this and other Swedish settlements in the Delaware River Valley were seized by the Dutch in 1655 and by the English in 1664.

Penn established the colony as a refuge for the English Friends (Quakers), who were experiencing religious persecution. His "Frame of Government" (1681) provided for friendly relations with the Indians, representative government and religious freedom. Other immigrants to the colony included Germans and Scotch-Irish. During the colonial period Pennsylvania's borders were in constant controversy.

Although there existed considerable Loyalist sentiment on the eve of the Revolution, Philadelphia became the seat of both the First and Second Continental Congress. The Constitution was drawn up there (May 25–Sept. 17, 1787). The historic city was the nation's capital, 1790–1800. Pennsylvania was the second state to ratify the Constitution (Dec. 12, 1787).

The state's development was spurred by extensive canal building. By 1840 there were 600 miles of canal, with the main canal from Philadelphia to Pittsburgh. Railroad building then developed.

In the Civil War, Pennsylvania was the first state to send troops to Washington in response to Pres. Lincoln's call (Apr. 15, 1861). Invasion of the North was turned back at Gettysburg (1863).

Pennsylvania is one of the greatest industrial states of the Union. Its great fuel resources, especially coal, enable it to manufacture more iron and steel than any other state. Agriculture is also a major industry, with dairy products most important.

Pennsylvania, University of. Inspired by Benjamin Franklin's pamphlet on education (*Proposals Relating to the Education of Youth in Pensilvania,* 1749), 24 citizens of Philadelphia joined to found an Academy, with Franklin as first president of the trustees. In 1755 it became the College, Academy, and Charitable School of Philadelphia and awarded its first degrees in 1757. The first college in the country to become a university (1779), it took its present name in 1791. It was the first college in North America to establish a school of medicine (1765); also the first to start a university school of business—the Wharton School of Finance and Economy (1881), reflecting the rising academic prestige of business.

The university, a privately endowed nonsectarian institution, is currently comprised of 22 undergraduate, graduate and professional schools.

Pennsylvania Gazette. The semiweekly newspaper was established at Philadelphia, Dec. 24, 1728, by Samuel Keimer, but he turned it over to his apprentice, Benjamin Franklin, who made it the most valuable newspaper property in the American colonies. Franklin retired from the management of the *Gazette* in 1766. It was of service to the Revolutionary cause until the British occupation of Philadelphia. Publication was resumed after the war. The *Gazette* was merged with the *Daily North American* in 1845.

Pennsylvania Railroad (the "Pennsy"). The line was chartered in 1846 and within a decade was handling the important traffic between Philadelphia and Pittsburgh. The system expanded and reached Chicago about the same time as the New York Central (1869), and also secured a route to St. Louis. In addition, there are connections with the leading cities on the eastern seaboard — Wilmington, Baltimore, Washington, Norfolk and Richmond. When the line completed a tunnel under the Hudson River in 1910 its trains finally could enter New York City directly.

The line, one of the world's larger railroad systems, is the largest coal carrier in the U.S. It operates about 10,000 miles of road. A merger with the New York Central was approved by the U.S. Supreme Court in 1968. The combined company is the Pennsylvania-New York Central Transportation Company (Penn-Central).

Penobscot. Champlain ascended the central Maine river in 1604. It became the center of an area over which the French and British disputed in the 17th and 18th centuries.

Pentagon. Completed in 1943 and located on the Potomac River, across from Washington, D.C., the building houses the U.S. Department of Defense. It is the largest office building in the world and derives its name from its shape, a formation of five concentric buildings.

Pequots. Indians in Connecticut under their chief, Sassacus, were involved in a war against the New England colonists in

1637. The Pequot town on the Mystic River was burned down and the inhabitants slaughtered by an army of English aided by other Indians. The remaining Pequots, an Algonquian people, were scattered among New England tribes.

Perry, Oliver Hazard (1785–1819). Naval officer. Born in South Kingston, R.I., he was immortalized when he reported at the end of the battle of Lake Erie (Sept. 10, 1813): "We have met the enemy and they are ours." He first entered the U.S. Navy as a midshipman (1799) and was given command of the American fleet on Lake Erie in the War of 1812. His victory gave the U.S. a strong claim to the Northwest at the peace negotiations in Ghent, Belgium.

Perry's mission to Japan. Mistreatment of shipwrecked American sailors, the need for a coaling station on the route to China and the possibility of new markets in Japan inspired the mission of Commodore Matthew C. Perry, which was authorized by Pres. Fillmore. In 1853 Perry's four ships, to the consternation of the people, steamed into the Bay of Yedo (later called Tokyo) belching black smoke and moving against a strong head wind. Perry was instructed not to use force unless attacked. He opened negotiations in preparation for a return visit in 1854 with a squadron of seven vessels.

Perry arrived at a time when Japan was in ferment and the feudal system was breaking down. This circumstance combined with his diplomatic skill enabled him to win agreement for the opening of two ports for American trade. This entering wedge was given perspective years later by the humorist, Finley Peter Dunne (Mr. Dooley), who reflected: "Whin we rapped on the dure, we didn't go in, they come out."

Pershing, John Joseph (1860–1948). Army commander. Born in Linn County, Mo., he was graduated from the U.S. Military Academy (1886). He served in Cuba (1898), the Philippines (1899–1903) and commanded the expeditionary force sent into Mexico in pursuit of Pancho Villa (1916). Commander of the American Expeditionary Forces (1917–18) in World War I, he demanded that Americans be given a place in the lines as a separate force, rather than as replacements, and called for an offensive that would take the Allies out of the trenches. Promoted to general (1917), Pershing was the U.S. Army Chief of Staff (1921–24). His book *My Experiences in the World War* (1931) was awarded the Pulitzer history prize.

"personal liberty" laws. The laws were passed in northern states in the 1850's as a protest against the provision for a fugitive slave law in the Compromise of 1850. Because the laws made difficult the return of runaway slaves who had reached the free states, they were viewed in the South as examples of northern hostility to the institution of slavery.

"pet banks." The term was used by anti-Jacksonians to describe the state banks in which federal funds were deposited in 1833 after Pres. Jackson had vetoed recharter of the second Bank of the United States. The implication was that the banks had been selected purely on political grounds.

Petersburg, siege of (June 15, 1864–Apr. 2, 1865). During the final months of the Civil War, Gen. Ulysses S. Grant sought to take Richmond from the rear by way of Petersburg, 20 miles to the south. He was repulsed and dug in for a nine-month siege, the longest of the war. In the final days, Gen. Robert E. Lee sought to break through by hitting Grant's left flank at Five Forks, near Petersburg, but was repelled by Gen. Philip Sheridan. Lee then evacuated Petersburg and Richmond.

Pewter Muggers. The New York faction of the Democratic party was opposed to the Tammany candidates in 1828. While the members met in a Frankfort Street tavern, they drank from pewter mugs. The name was affixed to them by their opponents.

Philadelphia Cordwainers' Case (1805). Philadelphia shoemakers, organized as the Federal Society of Journeymen Cord-wainers in 1794, have been called the first continuous organization of wage earners in the U.S. When they struck for higher wages, their leaders were arrested and the strike broken. The judge in the Mayor's Court of Philadelphia held that they were engaged in criminal conspiracy and levied a small fine. The grounds for such a decision were found in the old common law principle that wherever two or more persons conspired to do something jointly even though they were individually entitled to take such action, the public interest was endangered.

The Journeymen Cordwainers of New York in 1809 and Pittsburgh shoemakers in 1815 were indicted on similar charges of criminal conspiracy. On both occasions the court again found for the employers. These judicial decisions aroused widespread resentment among the workingmen.

Philanthropist. First edited by James G. Birney in Ohio (1836) as the *Cincinnati Philanthropist,* he removed it to New York in 1837 and edited it as the *Philanthropist.* From its inception, the newspaper attacked slavery.

When Birney increased his lecture and organization work, the editorship was taken over by Gamaliel Bailey, who continued editing it until 1847 when the paper gave way to the new antislavery *National Era,* also edited by Bailey.

philanthropy. Giving away money for the purpose of improving mankind has had a long tradition in the U.S. Such giving has been organized through philanthropic foundations built on sums of money left by wealthy individuals and administered by trustees. Early examples of this kind of philanthropy were the funds provided for in the will of Benjamin Franklin (1791) making loans available to deserving "young married artificers" in Boston and Philadelphia. During the 19th century other foundations were established, notably the Peabody Education Fund (1867) to aid the South after the Civil War and the Baron de Hirsch Fund (1890) to aid Jewish immigrants.

Philanthropic foundations became a multibillion-dollar venture in the 20th century, spurred by Andrew Carnegie, who set up his first foundation, the Carnegie Institution of Washington (1902). The most heavily endowed of the early 20th-century foundations was the Rockefeller Foundation (1913). The greatest of all foundations in terms of endowed capital is the Ford Foundation (1936).

The freedom which trustees have enjoyed to dispense tax-free foundation money has invited a range of criticism and even investigation by the federal government. A Senate investigation (1915) looked into the charge that the foundations were run by big businessmen who used the funds to further reactionary ends. A later investigation (1953–54) sought to determine whether foundation money was being used to undermine confidence in the capitalist system.

Foundation grants to individuals and institutions have been heaviest in the field of education, but medical science, international peace, social welfare and government research have received substantial aid. In general, the major foundations have sought to make funds available for research and to further "the well-being of mankind" where private or governmental funds are not forthcoming or are in need of supplementation.

Philippine Islands. The archipelago off the coast of Southeast Asia was visited by Ferdinand Magellan in 1521 and conquered by Spain in 1565. It was ceded to the U.S. by Spain in the Treaty of Paris (1898) ending the Spanish-American War. Pres. McKinley himself confessed: "When we received the cable from Admiral Dewey telling of the taking of the Philippines I looked up their location on the globe. I could not have told where those darned islands were within 2000 miles!"

Filipino resistance to American rule developed under Emilio Aguinaldo and was not ended until 1902. The U.S. then began a program of developing industry and agriculture in the islands while preparing the people for the establishment of an independent democracy. In 1901 William Howard Taft became the first civil governor. By 1907 the Filipinos had gained the right to elect the lower house of the legislature and in 1916 the Jones Act gave them virtual autonomy over their domestic affairs. In 1934 Congress passed the Philippine Independence (Tydings-McDuffie) Act providing for independence after ten years. World War II and Japanese occupation of the islands delayed independence until July 4, 1946.

The U.S. has continued to maintain military bases on the islands and has extended considerable economic aid to the Republic of the Philippines. The government quelled the Hukbalahap (Huks) movement (1946–50) which was pro-Communist and anti-U.S. The extreme nationalists oppose the U.S. bases in the islands. But the Republic maintains close economic ties with the U.S. and is a member of SEATO.

Philippine Sea, battle of (June 1944). Following a disastrous air battle over Guam in the Marianas (known as the Great Marianas Turkey Shoot), the Japanese carrier force, stripped of its planes, was driven halfway to the Philippines. Opposing warships did not exchange a single shot in a battle that was fought entirely by aircraft. It was a crushing defeat for Japan and assured American conquest of the Marianas.

Phillips, Wendell (1811–84). Reformer. He was born in Boston, Mass. An ardent Abolitionist, he denounced the murder of Elijah P. Lovejoy in a speech in Faneuil Hall, Boston (1837). He succeeded William Lloyd Garrison as president of the American Antislavery Society (1865–70). After the Civil War he turned to other causes and advocated prohibition, penal reforms, fair treatment for the Indians, woman suffrage, regulation of corporations and organization of labor unions. An outstanding orator, he traveled extensively on the lyceum circuit.

Pickett's Charge (July 3, 1863). The heroism of Confederate forces was nowhere more evident than in the men who sought in a single charge to turn the tide at the battle of Gettysburg.

In an assault on the Union's center, Gen. Lee ordered Gen. Pickett and other division and brigade commanders to advance with 15,000 men from Seminary Ridge, across an open plain and up the slant of Cemetery Hill. They faced fire from three sides, and 6,000 men fell in an assault that doomed the Confederate advance into the North.

pieces of eight. The Spanish silver coins (equal to eight bits at 12½ cents each), also known as pesos or dollars, circulated in the American colonies. The first U.S. dollars minted in 1786 contained about the same amount of silver bullion as the Spanish pieces of eight.

Piedmont. A hilly, rolling region in the South, west of the fall line, it reached the first ridges of the Appalachian Mts. It was sometimes called upcountry or back country, and was settled early in the 18th century by small farmers whose interests often clashed with the wealthier plantation owners in the Tidewater region below the fall line.

When the Tidewater lands were depleted, plantation owners in South Carolina and Georgia moved into the Piedmont region and by 1816 produced 60% of the nation's cotton crop. When the Piedmont soil gave out in the 1820's, the planters pushed on into Alabama and Mississippi.

Numerous small cities are now scattered throughout the Piedmont. They manufacture a variety of metalware, household goods, furniture and textiles.

Pierce, Franklin (1804–69). Fourteenth President of the U.S. (1853–57). He was born in Hillsboro, N.H., and was graduated from Bowdoin (1824). A Jacksonian Democrat, he served New Hampshire in the U.S. House of Representatives (1833–37) and the U.S. Senate (1837–42). The high point of his administration was the passage of the Kansas-Nebraska Act (1854).

Pike, Zebulon Montgomery (1779–1813). Soldier and explorer. He was born in Lamberton, N.J. Ordered by Gen. James Wilkinson to lead a party from St. Louis, Mo., to headwaters of the Mississippi, he explored the upper Mississippi region of the Louisiana Purchase (1805–

06). He then explored the source of the Arkansas and Red rivers, moved up the Arkansas and reached the site of the present Pueblo, Colo., but failed to reach the peak of the summit that bears his name. Raised to rank of brigadier-general, he commanded the troops attacking York (now Toronto), Canada, in Apr. 1813 and was killed in the assault.

"Pikes Peak or Bust!" The slogan was painted on many covered wagons heading in 1859 for Pikes Peak, a landmark in the Rockies of Colorado, about 75 miles from a gold strike. Many of the fortune hunters soon headed back with another slogan on their wagons, "Busted by Gosh!"

Pilgrims. The first permanent English settlement in New England and the second on the American mainland was the Pilgrim colony at Plymouth. It was established in 1620 by the 102 colonists who crossed the Atlantic on the *Mayflower* with William Bradford as one of the leaders.

The Pilgrims had separated from the "popish" Anglican Church and had fled to Holland where they remained for about 12 years before embarking for America.

The Pilgrims or Separatists were bent on establishing a place where they might worship God in their own fashion. Their voyage was backed financially by the London merchants of the Virginia Company of

Plymouth, one of two companies incorporated in the first Virginia charter of 1606. The Pilgrims were expected to work for the company for seven years at the end of which time profits from fishing or trading with the Indians would be divided between the settlers and the merchants.

The Pilgrims landed at a point far north of the boundaries of the Virginia Company. They succeeded, however, in gaining the right to settle from the Council of New England (the former Plymouth Company). Plymouth merged with the Massachusetts Bay colony in 1691.

There is doubt about which of the Pilgrims was the first to step on Plymouth Rock in what is now Provincetown Harbor. The rock is displayed in Plymouth, Mass.

Pimas. Although peaceful, the tribe of Indians from the Southwest, of Piman (Uto-Aztecan) linguistic stock, showed courage in defending their Arizona holdings against Apache attacks in the 19th century. They have long practiced irrigation of crops. Pima women are noted for the beauty of their basketry.

Pinckney Treaty (1795). Also known as the Treaty of San Lorenzo, the Treaty between the U.S. and Spain was negotiated for the U.S. by Thomas Pinckney. It gave the U.S. free navigation of the Mississippi River in Spanish territory and the right of deposit at New Orleans for a period of three years subject to renewal. The Treaty was hailed by western farmers, whose trade with the East Coast and Europe had been menaced by the lack of the rights now guaranteed by the Treaty.

In addition, both powers agreed to try to prevent Indian attacks from the territory of one against the territory of the other. The boundary between the U.S. and Florida was fixed at the 31st parallel, a decision favorable to the U.S., for Spain had been claiming territory which was part of Georgia.

Spain was prompted to make these concessions because of the possibility that the U.S., which had recently concluded the Jay Treaty with Britain, might take over Spanish holdings in North America.

pine tree flag. The first naval flag of the U.S. carried the symbol of the pine tree. It was flown in 1775 on American ships attacking Boston by order of Gen. Washington. The pine tree represented the sturdy New Englanders. In 1776 Massachusetts adopted a white flag, with a green pine tree and the inscription, "An Appeal to Heaven," for its sea service.

pinetree shilling. Minted in Boston in the mid-17th century the coin was so named because of the pine tree pattern on it. Since they contained less silver than the English shilling, the government hoped that the pinetree coins would remain in the colony which suffered a shortage of coins. Since, however, importers raised their prices in order to obtain as much silver for their wares as formerly, the pinetree shillings were exported as bullion in order to pay for European goods.

Pinkertons. Alan Pinkerton was the founder of the Pinkerton National Detective Agency. The Pinkertons were employed to protect railroad property and solved a $700,000 robbery for the Adams Express Agency (1866). They foiled a plot to assassinate Pres. Lincoln (1861). Alan Pinkerton's espionage activity on behalf of the Union during the Civil War led to the establishment of the federal secret service.

The agency was employed by corporations combating union activity. In 1875 a Pinkerton detective working among coal miners was instrumental in gaining the conviction of the Molly Maguires. Pinkertons were employed by the Carnegie Steel Co. to help break the 1892 Homestead strike. They served as labor spies and were detested by unions.

The agency has since engaged in protecting property and supplying uniformed guards and private detectives for employers whose needs are not met by public police forces.

Pinkster. The Dutch pentecost was celebrated in colonial New York by pinkster flowers (wild azaleas with pink flowers) especially on Pinkster Hill (Capitol Hill), Albany. The celebration was forbidden in Albany early in the 19th century after it had been taken over by Negroes who climaxed their version of Pinkster with election of a Negro governor, "King Charley."

Pioneer I. The unmanned interplanetary exploration vehicle was launched on Oct. 11, 1958 to determine the radial extent of the Van Allen Radiation Region. It made the first determination of the density of micrometeoroids in space.

Other Pioneer experiments sought to advance understanding of the sun and of interplanetary space for planning manned interplanetary flights.

Pitt, Fort. Named after the British Prime Minister, the fort was built in 1759 just above Fort Duquesne, which had been destroyed by the French. It was located at a point between the Monongahela and Allegheny rivers and was used as a base for the protection of western settlers and for Revolutionary War operations. The fort was not used after 1800. It is the site of the city of Pittsburgh.

Pittsburgh Gazette. The first newspaper west of the Appalachian Mts., it was founded in 1786 by John Scull and Joseph Hall, printers from Philadelphia. They were helped in establishing the newspaper by Hugh Henry Brackenridge, a lawyer and author, who recognized its value to the new town.

"Pittsburgh of the South." Birmingham, Ala., has been called by this name because of the great expansion of its heavy industry, notably steel manufacture, in the post-Civil War period.

Plains of Abraham. A decisive French and Indian War battle that doomed the French empire in the New World was fought here in 1759 on the heights above Quebec on the west side of the city. The generals of both sides, Montcalm (French) and Wolfe (English), were killed in the battle. The site is now a Canadian national park. Its name is derived from that of its former owner, Abraham Martin.

plantation system. In the Tidewater (coastal region) of the South during the colonial period the agricultural estates were mainly plantations. William Byrd II of the Virginia colony, one of the richest planters, owned an estate of 200,000 acres worked by thousands of slaves. Planters like Byrd practically controlled the governments of southern colonies. Most plantations, however, consisted of a few hundred acres and small plantation owners lived in modest homes, not the large white mansions, with tall, columned porches, traditionally associated with plantation life. The majority of southern farmers worked smaller plots with few or no slaves.

Major plantation crops were rice, tobacco and indigo (a blue dye valuable to the English textile industry at a time when there were no synthetic dyes). In the 19th century cotton was added as a major crop on southern plantations. In 1791 the U.S. had produced two million pounds of cotton. By 1860 it was producing two billion pounds. The plantation system had spread throughout the South, moving inland from the coastal regions into the Gulf states.

The old plantation system based on slave labor was destroyed by the Civil War. In the postwar period planters divided up their plantations into many small farms.

Platt Amendment. The amendment to an Army appropriations bill (named for Sen. Orville H. Platt, Conn.), passed by Congress in 1901, established a policy for Cuban-U.S. relations after the Spanish-American War. Cuba was compelled to sign a treaty by which she granted the U.S. the right to intervene "for the protection of life, property, and individual liberty." In addition, the U.S. was given the right to buy or lease coaling and naval stations; Cuba's right to borrow money was limited; a sanitation program started by the U.S. was to be continued; and Cuba was to make no treaty affecting either its territory or independence.

Cuban patriots looked upon the Platt Amendment as an infringement of sovereignty. It was replaced by a new treaty in 1934.

Plattsburg, battle of (Sept. 11, 1814). During the War of 1812, a British force of 14,000 under Gen. Sir George Prevost was turned back from northern New York by an American force of 4,000 under Gen. Alexander Macomb. At the same time, in the battle on Lake Champlain, Commander Thomas Macdonough defeated a British naval force. The effect of these victories was to prevent the British from gaining the Great Lakes in the treaty of peace at the end of the war.

Plessy v. Ferguson (1896). The U.S. Supreme Court sustained the validity of the segregation practices of the southern states. The Court held that a Louisiana statute requiring railroads to "provide equal but separate accommodations for the white and colored races" did not constitute a denial of the equal protection of the laws in violation of the 14th Amendment. Such a law, the Court held, is a proper exercise of the state's police power aimed at maintenance of peace and order. The Court dismissed the contention that "the enforced separation of the two races stamps the colored race with a badge of inferiority" and observed: "If this be so, it is not by reason of anything found in the act, but solely because the colored race chooses to put that construction upon it."

In a blistering dissent, Justice Harlan of Kentucky took exception to the majority support of Jim Crow laws. In holding all men equal before the law, Harlan declared "The Constitution is color-blind."

The majority's reasoning was reversed as it applied to education in *Brown v. Board of Education* (1954) and specifically reversed in *Gayle v. Browder* (1956) which voided an ordinance requiring segregation on motor buses operated within a city.

Plumed Knight. James G. Blaine of Maine, a prominent political figure of the 1870's and 1880's, was so described at the Republican convention of 1876 by the famous orator Robert Ingersoll. Blaine's own oratorical power, magnetic personality and unblemished family life made the title seem appropriate. But Blaine, whose reputation had been tarnished by the "Mulligan letters," lost the nomination to Rutherford Hayes.

Plummer Gang. Henry Plummer was leader of a gang that terrorized a Montana mining district. The gang was broken up by vigilante action in 1863.

pocket veto. The Constitution allows the President 10 days (exclusive of Sundays) from the date of receiving a bill to give it his approval; if, within 10 days, Congress adjourns and so prevents the return of a bill to which the President objects, that bill does not become law. In many cases, where bills have been sent to him toward the close of a session, the President has taken advantage of this provision. He has held until after adjournment measures which he disapproves but which for some reason he does not wish to return with his objections to Congress. His action is the so-called pocket veto.

Poe, Edgar Allan (1809–49). Poet, author and critic. Born in Boston, Mass., he studied at the U.S. Military Academy but was dismissed for neglect of duties (1831). A major lyrical poet, he first won fame with "The Raven" (1845), in which he tries to forget his lost love, Lenore, in a rather lengthy philosophical discussion with a "grim . . . bird of yore." His reviews, poems and stories boosted the circulation of the *Southern Literary Messenger,* Richmond, Va. (1835–37), *Burton's Gentleman's Magazine,* (1839–40), *Graham's Lady's and Gentleman's Magazine* (1841–42), both published in Philadelphia, Pa., and the *Broadway Journal* (1845–46), New York City. Commonly considered the originator of the "detective" story, he published "The Gold Bug" (1843) and "Murders in the Rue Morgue" (1843). Near the end of his short life, troubled by illness and alcoholism, he wrote some of his best-known poems: "The Bells," "Annabel Lee" and "El Dorado."

Point Four. In his inaugural address of Jan. 20, 1949, Pres. Truman asked for support of a program of technical assistance to underdeveloped countries. This proposal for a "bold, new program" was the fourth major point in his address. Congress appropriated necessary funds, and U.S. contributions generally consisted of technicians plus the cost of equipment they needed. The technical aid program was continued by subsequent administrations although the name was dropped.

Point Pleasant, battle of (Oct. 10, 1774). Shawnee Indians were repulsed in an attack on frontiersmen at the juncture of the Ohio and Great Kanawha rivers in West Virginia. By the Treaty of Camp Charlotte the Indians yielded hunting rights in Kentucky and agreed to allow transportation to go unmolested on the Ohio.

Polaris. The name was given to missiles carried by U.S. submarines in the 1960's. One version, the A-3, bearing a thermonuclear warhead with an explosive power of about 800 kilotons, was reported to have a 2,800-mile range. A kiloton is the equivalent of a thousand tons of TNT.

Polaris is also the name given to the fleet of nuclear-powered missile-firing submarines armed with the Polaris missile that can be fired from underwater or surface.

police powers. Under the Constitution powers not delegated to the federal government "nor prohibited by it to the States, are reserved to the states" (10th Amendment). Among the most vital of powers reserved to the states are the police powers. State, county or city governments may pass laws regulating the health, safety, welfare and morals of the people. Examples of such regulations include rules enforced by policemen, firemen, housing, factory and health inspectors. The licensing of dogs, peddlers, barber shops, even medical doctors, are exercises of the police power. The right of a state to pass minimum wage laws was justified as an exercise of the police power by the U.S. Supreme Court in *West Coast Hotel Co. v. Parish* (1937). The exercise of police power is subject to review in the courts.

Polk, James Knox (1795–1849). Eleventh President of the U.S. (1845–49). Born near Pineville, Mecklenberg County, N.C., he was graduated from the Univ. of North Carolina (1818). He served Tennessee as a member of the U.S. House of Representatives (1825–39), Speaker of the House (1835–39) and governor of Tennessee (1839–41). A successful "dark horse" candidate (Democrat) for the Presidency, he favored the annexation of Texas and led the nation in the Mexican War.

Polk Doctrine. Pres. Polk elaborated on the Monroe Doctrine in his first annual message to Congress in 1845. Polk, a Democrat, had campaigned on the slogan "54° 40′ or fight," in pursuit of the northernmost limit of the Oregon Territory, which was in dispute with England. Polk declared: "The people of *this continent* alone have the right to decide their own destiny." He opposed any interference on the part of European countries who might seek to prevent an independent state from entering the Union. He stated, also, that no European colony should be established in North America without American consent.

Pollock, Jackson (1912–56). Painter. Born near Cody, Wyo., he studied under Thomas Hart Benton at the Art Student's League, N.Y.C. His early paintings are marked by controlled violence (*Wounded Animal*). He broke away from realism in the 1940's and became a leading abstract expressionist. He died in an auto accident.

Pollock v. Farmer's Loan and Trust Co. (1895). The U.S. Supreme Court declared that the income tax provision of the Wilson-Gorman Tariff Act of 1894 was unconstitutional. The Court in a five to four vote decided that the income tax was a direct tax and, therefore, had to be apportioned among the states in accordance with the population.

The income tax was denounced as a "communist march" and defended as a fair burden on the rich since most taxes fell on goods consumed by the poor. The controversy led to the 16th Amendment.

poll tax. By the 1890's a number of southern states devised ways of keeping Negroes from voting, including a special tax called a poll tax. The effect of the tax was to keep poor Negroes and poor whites from voting.

As late as 1963 five southern states retained a poll tax as a requirement for voting. Poll taxes in elections for federal office were abolished by the 24th Amendment to the Constitution (1964). In 1966, poll taxes in elections for federal declared unconstitutional by the U.S. Supreme Court, which held that Virginia's $1.50 tax as a prerequisite for voting in state elections violated the equal protection of the law guaranteed by the 14th Amendment. The decision brought to a successful conclusion a long campaign by civil rights advocates to abolish poll taxes as a prerequisite for voting.

Pomeroy Circular (1864). Pres. Lincoln's uncertainty about his party's renomination inspired a circular by Sen. Pomeroy of Kansas which stated that Lincoln could not win and that the Union could be saved only by Salmon P. Chase, Lincoln's Sec. of the Treasury.

This political disloyalty could not be softened by Chase's disavowal of the circular, and the ambitious Chase offered his resignation. It was not accepted at first, but a second offer was accepted by Lincoln, to Chase's surprise.

Poncas. The tribe of Dakota Indians, of Siouan linguistic stock, suffered greatly from hostile Indian attacks which drove them beyond the Missouri. In 1858 they sold their lands to the federal government and went on a reservation in the Dakota Territory. In 1865 they were assigned a reservation on the Missouri River.

Pontiac's Conspiracy. In 1763 the Ottawa chieftain Pontiac organized a confederation to drive the English settlers eastward over the Appalachian Mts. He captured all but three forts in the West—Forts Pitt, Niagara and Detroit. The British were finally victorious and forced Pontiac to make peace in 1765 but not before more settlers had been slaughtered than at the peak of the French and Indian War.

Pony Express. Developing political and economic interests required speedier methods of communication between the East and the newly acquired regions of California and Oregon. A Pony Express route was established to carry mail between St. Joseph, Mo., and San Francisco. It was started in 1860 and ended in 1861 when the opening of the transcontinental telegraph ended the need for it.

The Pony Express kept 80 lightweight riders in the saddle on fast Indian ponies, 40 racing west in relays and 40 returning. At each of the 190 stations, about ten miles apart, the mail pouches were switched to a fresh pony and rider in two minutes. Mail was carried at the rate of $2 to $10 an ounce, depending on distance. The run from the Mississippi to California took about ten days.

Although the Pony Express was short-lived and unprofitable, the riders captured the public imagination, and they are celebrated in western novels.

Poor Richard's Almanack (1732 –57). The almanac, first published by Benjamin Franklin in Philadelphia, soon became the most widely sold in the colonies—10,000 copies a year. In addition to the usual items of interest to farmers—weather forecasts, eclipses, tides, listing of religious days—Franklin included witty sayings and proverbs, not all of them original. It did, however, put in the shade many of the competing almanacs in the colonies.

Franklin continued to write for his almanac until about 1748 and continued to publish it until 1757 after which it was carried on by another publisher.

Poor Richard's sayings were collected by Franklin from various editions of the almanac and appeared as *The Way to Wealth* (also known as *Father Abraham's Speech*).

Popham colony. The first attempt to colonize New England was sponsored by Sir John Popham, Chief Justice of England, who believed that England's paupers might profitably be sent to build settlements in northern America.

George Popham, brother of Sir John, headed 120 colonists who established themselves at the mouth of the Kennebec River in Maine (1607–08). The expedition had been sent out by the Plymouth Company of Virginia encouraged by reports of lucrative fishing, fur trade with friendly natives and fine timber resources.

The colony collapsed following a severe Maine winter, difficulties among the colonists ("out of all the gaols of England") and the death of both Pophams.

popular sovereignty. The term, meaning the right of the people to rule, was introduced into the slavery controversy in the U.S. before the Civil War. Under the Missouri Compromise of 1820 Congress prohibited slavery in part of the territories of the U.S. This prohibition was ended by the Kansas-Nebraska Act (1854) which contained the principle of popular sovereignty (called "squatter sovereignty" by its opponents) permitting the residents of the territory to provide in their constitution for acceptance or rejection of slavery.

Sen. Stephen A. Douglas (Ill.) was the foremost proponent of popular sovereignty. He found himself defending it in his debates against Abraham Lincoln in the face of the Dred Scott decision, which held that the people could not exclude slavery from the territories.

population. The estimated population, not including Indians, at the end of the first decade of settlement in the American colonies was 2,000. Net immigration and a high rate of natural increase brought the U.S. population at the time of the first official census in 1790 to 3,929,000.

Up to 1830 when the population was 12,866,000 immigration played a small role in the increase. After 1830 immigration was an important factor in the net increase of the population accounting for as much as 43% of the population growth, 1880–90. This declined to 22% of the population growth, 1920–30.

In 1850 the total number of foreign born in the U.S. was about 10% of the population. By 1970, it was about 5%.

In 1900 the population was 75,995,000; in 1950, 150,697,-000. On Nov. 20, 1967, the "Census Clock" in the Commerce Department ticked past the 200,000,000 mark. On Apr. 1, 1970, the total population was 204,765,770. There was a big bulge of some 74,000,000 between the ages of 5 and 23.

In 1972 U.S. birth and fertility rates dropped to their lowest level in history—2.03 children a family, significantly below the "replacement level" of 2.1 children. However, there is no likelihood of "zero" population growth because there are so many potential mothers in the population. The Census Bureau estimates that the population in the year 2000 will be between 251 million and 300 million.

During the 1960–70 decade the proportion of Americans living in towns and cities continued to grow. In 1790 only 3.35% of the population lived in towns of 8,000 or more. By the end of the 19th century a third of the population was classified "urban" by this definition. By 1920, for the first time in American history, more than half the population lived in the cities. By 1970, 73.5% of the nation's population lived in urban areas.

A major finding of the 1970 census reports was the changed view of the suburbs. The view that people live in the suburbs but work in the cities is obsolete. Overall in the 15 largest metropolitan areas, 72% of the workers who live in the suburbs also work in the suburbs.

The U.S. center of population has been moving ever westward. In 1790 its approximate location was Baltimore, Md. In 1970 the center was near East St. Louis, Ill. On a regional basis, the West continued to grow at the fastest rate—24.1%, compared to 14.2% for the South, 9.7% for the Northeast and 9.6% for the North Central region. California had the greatest gain in population among the individual states during the 1960's to become the most populous state for the first time (Apr. 1, 1970) with a total of 19,953,134. Gains of more than 1 million were also registered by Florida, Texas, New York, New Jersey, Michigan and Illinois.

Another dramatic change has been the population movement of blacks. In 1940 the South contained 77% of the black population. By 1970 the proportion had dropped to 53%. In the same period the population of the Northeast and North Central states went from 11% to about 20% black. The black population as a whole has declined from about 20% of the total population in 1790 to 11.1% in 1970. Their proportion fell almost steadily because of the large immigration of whites during the 19th century and the higher death rate among blacks. Since 1930 the death rate of blacks has declined and their birth rate has declined more slowly than that of the white population.

Populist party. The People's party was organized in 1892 to voice the farmers' protest against falling prices, farm foreclosures and the general farm discontent in the South and West. Its Omaha platform called for easier credit, free coinage of silver and a host of reforms intended to curb the "money power" in the East and extend political democracy.

As a third party in the election of 1892 the Populists polled over one million votes and carried five states. It achieved representation in Congress and in

state governments. But this threat to the major parties evaporated in 1896 when it joined with the Democrats in support of William Jennings Bryan rather than split the vote for free silver. The emphasis on free silver was resented by some Populists who held that it was subordinate to other demands set forth in the Omaha platform.

The defeat of Bryan was the death knell of the Populists. Although they ran candidates in the next three elections the party ceased to be a threat as farmers moved back into the major parties.

port authority. A self-supporting public corporation may be established by a city or joint action of state legislatures for the purpose of improving efficiency of port and other terminal and transportation facilities. One of the best known is the Port of New York Authority, created in 1921 by the states of New York and New Jersey to administer terminal and transportation facilities and promote commerce. It was organized to make best use of the Hudson River, which runs between the two states. Since this involves interstate commerce, approval was given by Congress.

The Port of New York Authority operates marine and inland terminals, airports, bridges and tunnels. Its revenue is derived from tolls and rentals for the use of its facilities. The authority may also borrow money to finance its construction program by sale of tax-free bonds.

Port Royal. The port in Nova Scotia, now Annapolis Royal, changed hands between French and British during the colonial period. It was founded by the French in 1605 and was long viewed as a potential base of naval operations against New England. Among the many exchanges are the following: It was captured by the English in 1628 but restored to the French in 1632. It was again captured by the British in 1690 when it was taken by an expedition of Massachusetts troops under Sir William Phips. In 1691 it was retaken by the French. It was finally captured by the British in 1710 and renamed Annapolis.

Port Royal, S.C. The island north of the mouth of the Savannah River was first settled by the French Huguenots in 1562 but was taken by the Spanish in 1565. A settlement of Scotsmen under a patent from the Carolina proprietors took over briefly, 1684–86, despite resentment of Spain and the Charleston settlers who saw a rival for Indian trade.

During the Revolution the Americans defeated the British in the battle of Port Royal Island (Feb. 3, 1779). In the Civil War the Confederates were prevented from defending the Sea Islands below Charleston when they were defeated in a naval action at Port Royal, Nov. 7, 1861.

Portsmouth, Treaty of (Sept. 5, 1905). The conference which settled the Russo-Japanese War (1904–05) was held at the Portsmouth Navy Yard, N.H. Pres. Theodore Roosevelt agreed to mediate in the hope that the balance of power might be preserved in the Far East with neither Russia nor Japan gaining the ascendancy and threatening the Open Door policy in China.

Japan, under Roosevelt's prodding, bitterly gave up its demand for a financial indemnity. It did gain the southern half of the island of Sakhalin and an improved position in Korea and southern Manchuria. Japan emerged as the dominant power in the Far East.

Poseidon. The name was given to a missile with a thermonuclear warhead. It was announced in 1965 that the Poseidon would replace the Polaris missile carried by submarines. With about twice the explosive power and double the accuracy of the Polaris, the Poseidon is intended for effective use against a broader range of possible targets and to give added insurance of penetrating enemy defenses.

postage currency. Early in the Civil War (1862), before Congress authorized issuance of fractional currency ("shinplasters") Sec. of the Treasury Chase authorized the use of postage stamps as legal tender. He sought to aid retail trade which was being strangled by the shortage of silver coins caused by hoarding. When the post office ran out of stamps, which had become sticky messes in pockets and purses, Chase authorized issuance of "postage currency" in small denominations.

postage stamps. The first adhesive stamps were authorized by Congress, July 1, 1847. The five-cent stamp bore the head of Franklin and the ten-cent stamp the head of Washington. These, along with stamps printed earlier by individual postmasters, are rarities which philatelists treasure today. Postage stamps were also issued by express companies using their own designs after the adhesive stamp was invented in England in 1840. On May 1, 1873 the first penny postcards were issued by the U.S. Post Office.

Postage stamps in the U.S. have been used to commemorate great events, but it was not until 1893 that the first commemorative series was issued celebrating the World's Columbian Exposition. The first airmail issue was a 24-cent stamp in 1918. A three-color stamp was issued for the first time in 1965.

Post Office Department. Benjamin Franklin, appointed postmaster at Philadelphia in 1737, became the first Postmaster General under the Continental Congress, July 26, 1775. He is credited by historians with having laid much of the foundation for the development of the present U.S. Postal System. The Constitution of the U.S. (Art. I, Sec. 8) provides that "The Congress shall have Power . . . To establish Post Offices and Post Roads."

On Sept. 26, 1789, when Samuel Osgood was appointed the first Postmaster General under the Constitution, there were only 75 post offices. From that small beginning, the Postal Service has developed into what is now the largest business in the world. There are 35,000 post offices in the U.S.

The Post Office Department became an executive department by an act of Congress in 1872 although it had been known as a department for many years. The Postmaster General has been a member of the President's Cabinet since 1829 when he entered it on invitation from Pres. Jackson.

While the original purpose of the Postal System was to provide "the best means of establishing posts for conveying letters and intelligence through this continent" (Journal of the Continental Congress, May 27, 1775), the Post Office Department was ultimately enlarged to include several services. Among the more important, in the order of their establishment, are postage stamps, 1847; registered mail, 1855; railway mail service, 1862; city delivery service, 1863; postal money orders, 1867; special delivery, 1885; rural delivery, 1896; postal savings, 1911 (ended, 1967); village delivery, 1912; parcel post, including insurance and collect-on-delivery service, 1913; air mail, 1918; and certified mail, 1955.

post roads. In colonial times certain roads between cities were designated as post roads for the carrying of mail, first by horseback and later by coach. Two famous roads were the Albany Post Road between New York City and Albany and the Boston Post Road between New York City and Boston. The federal government allowed private companies to hold a monopoly for mail delivery on these roads up to about 1860. Navigable rivers and city streets were designated as post roads at various times in the early 19th century in order to eliminate private companies and steamboat captains as mail carriers. Post roads were given a priority in road improvements authorized by Congress.

Potawatomie Massacre (1856). The clash of proslavery and antislavery forces in Kansas led to the murder of five proslavery men who were hacked to death by the fanatical Abolitionist John Brown and six of his followers. The "massacre" took place in a proslavery settlement at Potawatomie Creek and started a guerrilla war that gave substance to the name by which the territory became known— "Bleeding Kansas."

Potawatomi Indians. Living around the southern end of Lake Michigan, the tribe, of Algonquian linguistic stock, sided with the French against the English. They warred against the U.S. and aided the British in the War of 1812. They settled on a reservation in Kansas, but many moved to the Indian Territory in Oklahoma.

Potomac Company. Chartered in 1784 with George Washington as president, the company sought to connect the Potomac Valley with the West by means of short canals. Several of these were completed and were helpful to farmers trying to get their products to the coast. The company however, was not successful financially and sold out to the Chesapeake and Ohio Canal Company in 1828.

Potsdam Conference (July 17– Aug. 2, 1945). Pres. Truman, Prime Minister Churchill and Premier Stalin met in Potsdam, Germany, to deal with the world situation after the surrender of Germany. During the Conference Churchill was replaced by Clement R. Attlee, who had become Prime Minister when the Labour party defeated the Conservatives in an election (July 1945).

At Potsdam, the Council of Foreign Ministers was ordered to prepare treaties of peace with Italy, Rumania, Bulgaria, Hungary and Finland and to draw up a peace settlement with Germany.

Germany was to be divided into four occupation zones, administered by the U.S., the Soviet Union, Britain and

France. Germany was to be demilitarized and pay reparations for the damage her invading armies had done. Such payments were to be in kind (that is, in materials and equipment) rather than in cash. About half of all reparations would go to the Soviet Union. Moreover, German labor would be used to repair some of the damage in the occupied countries. The schools and courts of Germany were to be democratized, local self-government encouraged and a basis for social and political democracy established. De-Nazification was to include punishment of war criminals. Free elections were to be held in Poland.

Russia had not yet entered the war against Japan, but the U.S. and Britain issued the Potsdam declaration (July 26) calling on Japan to surrender or be destroyed.

Pound, Ezra Loomis (1885–1972). Poet. Born in Hailey, Ida., he left the U.S. (1907) to travel in Europe and as an expatriate lived for long periods in London and Rome. His *Ripostes* (1912) contain the earliest examples of "imagist" verse. Pound praised the work of T. S. Eliot and Robert Frost when those poets were largely unread. He is known for his *Cantos* (1925–48) which draw upon legend. The award to Pound of the Bollingen Prize (1949) for his *Pisan Cantos* stirred controversy because of his broadcasting for Mussolini in World War II. Treason charges against him were subsequently dropped.

Powderly, Terence Vincent (1849–1924). Labor leader. He was born in Carbondale, Pa. A machinist by trade, he headed the largest labor organization of the day, the Knights of Labor (1879–93). An idealist and reformer, he laid little stress on immediate demands. He urged government ownership of public utilities, reform of the currency and land system, abolition of child labor and establishment of producers' cooperatives in which every man would be his own employer. Opposed to strikes as an outmoded weapon, he called for labor bureaus and public arbitration systems. He was the mayor of Scranton, Pa. (1878–84), U.S. commissioner-general of immigration (1897–1902) and chief of the Division of Information of the Bureau of Immigration (1907–21). He wrote the autobiography *Thirty Years of Labor, 1859–1889* (1889).

Powell, John Wesley (1834–1902). Geologist. Born in Mt. Morris, N.Y., he served in the Union army during the Civil War and lost an arm at the battle of Shiloh (1862). He was the pioneer explorer of the Green and Colorado rivers (1869–75). On the staff of the U.S. Geological Survey (1875–94), he became its director (1880). The recommendations in his *Report on the Lands of the Arid Region of the United*

540

States (1879) became a part of national land policy.

Powhatan Confederacy. At the time of the Jamestown, Va., settlement in 1607, the Indian league numbered some 200 villages. About 50 years later the league was virtually extinct; only a few Indians survived the English attacks and expansion from the coast inland to satisfy the need for tobacco-producing land.

King Powhatan, so called by the English, was the father of Pocahontas who married John Rolfe in 1614. The marriage helped to establish peaceful relations for a time between the English colonists and Indians. After Powhatan's death in 1618, relations with the Indians worsened, and the English who survived a massacre in 1622 vowed to scourge the Powhatans from the face of the earth. They kept their vow.

prairie dogs. The rodents, over a foot long, burrowed into the grazing lands of the plains and were the bane of cattlemen. The holes not only ruined grass lands but broke horses' legs. They have been controlled by poisons.

prairie schooner. A lighter wagon than the Conestoga, it came into use in the 1820's for transporting families and freight across the plains and even to the Far West. It was usually drawn by oxen or mules. The white canvas top stretched over wooden bows gave the wagon the appearance of a schooner when seen from a distance.

"Praise the Lord and pass the ammunition." The famous wartime phrase was pronounced, Dec. 7, 1941, by Howell M. Forgy, Chaplain on the U.S. cruiser *New Orleans*, under attack at Pearl Harbor by the Japanese. While sweating sailors kept up a continuous barrage, he kept up their spirits with the phrase. It became a popular war song.

Praying Indians. The name was given to those New England Indians who were among the first Christian converts. During King Philip's War (1675–76) they remained friendly to the colonists, acting as scouts and spies.

pre-emption acts. Federal laws were passed giving squatters on government-owned land the right to buy at minimum prices before it went on public sale. This pre-emption right was intended to help settlers who had occupied land and improved it before government surveys were completed. Without the pre-emption acts the squatters could be outbid, often by speculators. A series of temporary bills were passed in the 1830's giving the squatters pre-emption rights for two-year periods.

The Pre-emption Act (1841) permitted squatters to buy 160 acres at $1.25 an acre when the land was officially opened to settlement. This Act was hailed in the West, but it did not help the settler without the $200 to purchase the land. The law was abused by speculators who had "floaters" pre-empt land for them. The law soon outlived its usefulness, but it was not repealed until 1891.

Presbyterians. The nucleus of the Protestant denomination in the American colonies was comprised of Scotch-Irish settlers. Their first church was established about 1640 and was governed by its presbyters—minister and lay elders. The first presbytery or assembly of local ministers and elders met in 1706 in Philadelphia.

Pennsylvania was most friendly to the Presbyterians after their cold reception by Puritans in New England. They grew rapidly in the colonies and were second in numbers only to the Congregationalists at the time of the Revolution. Almost all Presbyterians were on the patriot side.

Although Presbyterians had a doctrinal split in the 18th century, at the time of the Great Awakening, in general they adhered to John Knox's views on predestination (derived from Calvin) and insisted on a literal interpretation of the Bible. A serious split took place in 1861 with the establishment of a southern division—a split that is not yet fully healed.

As a consequence of a merger in 1958 three-fourths of the more than three million Presbyterians are joined in the United Presbyterian Church in the U.S.A. A general assembly adopted "The Confession of 1967," which makes social action a part of church doctrine. It also rejects the idea that the Bible is "inerrant" and therefore not subject to criticism in the light of new knowledge.

Prescott, William Hickling (1796–1859). Historian. He was born in Salem, Mass. When he was a Harvard undergraduate an accident destroyed the sight of his left eye and a subsequent inflammation so weakened the right eye that he was virtually blind for the rest of his life. Secretaries who read to him, a tenacious memory and a special writing device permitted him to pursue historical studies of Spain and the Spanish conquest of the New World. He is recognized as the first scientific historian in the U.S. His literary narratives, based on primary sources, include *History of the Reign of Ferdinand and Isabella the Catholic* (3 vols., 1838); *History of the Conquest of Mexico* (3 vols., 1843); *History of the Conquest of Peru* (2 vols., 1847) and *History of the Reign of Philip the Second* (3 vols., 1855, 1858).

president (of a state). The first constitutions of Pennsylvania and New Hampshire (1776) provided not for a single executive head but for an executive council, one member of which was president. Delaware, South Carolina and New Hampshire constitutions of 1784 provided for a single head and called him president. South Carolina in 1778, Pennsylvania in 1790, Delaware and New Hampshire in 1792 changed the title to governor.

President of the U.S. The executive branch of the federal government is headed by the President. His office and powers are described in Article II of the Constitution. After the experience with the Articles of Confederation, which had no provision for an executive, the Founding Fathers agreed to an executive with considerable power. At the same time they provided for curbs on the power of the President.

The President must be a natural-born citizen and must be at least 35 years of age. He has the authority to appoint virtually all officers of the U.S. who are not elected. Most important appointments such as ambassadors, judges and heads of departments must be approved by the Senate. The President is Commander-in-Chief of the armed forces. He directs foreign relations through his power to make treaties and to speak for the country in its dealing with other nations.

The President is expected to provide leadership by drawing up a legislative program on which Congress can act. The program is presented in his regular annual message at the opening of Congress and in special messages which he may deliver during the session. As the choice of the entire nation and as the leader of his party, the President usually is in a strong position to line up support for the measures he wants to see enacted. He has a chance to approve or to veto each bill passed by Congress. If he vetoes a bill, it does not become law unless passed over his veto by a two-thirds vote in each house of Congress. As part of his judicial powers, he can grant pardons, except in cases of impeachment.

The President is elected for a four-year term and may be reelected once. From the first, strong personalities made the Presidency a powerful office. In the 20th century the President's access to mass media, radio and television, for direct talks to the nation, has added to the authority of the office and made possible leadership that sometimes bypasses Congress.

The following is a list of Presidents in the order of inauguration, dates of birth and death, state from which each came at the time of his election, party affiliation, years in office:

1.	George Washington	1732–1799	Va.		1789–1797
2.	John Adams	1735–1826	Mass.	Fed.	1797–1801
3.	Thomas Jefferson	1743–1826	Va.	Rep.	1801–1809
4.	James Madison	1751–1836	Va.	Rep.	1809–1817
5.	James Monroe	1758–1831	Va.	Rep.	1817–1825
6.	John Quincy Adams	1767–1848	Mass.	Rep.	1825–1829
7.	Andrew Jackson	1767–1845	Tenn.	Dem.	1829–1837

8. Martin Van Buren	1782–1862	N.Y.	Dem.	1837–1841
9. William H. Harrison	1773–1841	Ohio	Whig	1841
10. John Tyler	1790–1862	Va.	Whig	1841–1845
11. James K. Polk	1795–1849	Tenn.	Dem.	1845–1849
12. Zachary Taylor	1784–1850	La.	Whig	1849–1850
13. Millard Fillmore	1800–1874	N.Y.	Whig	1850–1853
14. Franklin Pierce	1804–1869	N.H.	Dem.	1853–1857
15. James Buchanan	1791–1868	Pa.	Dem.	1857–1861
16. Abraham Lincoln	1809–1865	Ill.	Rep.	1861–1865
17. Andrew Johnson	1808–1875	Tenn.	Rep.	1865–1869
18. Ulysses S. Grant	1822–1885	Ill.	Rep.	1869–1877
19. Rutherford B. Hayes	1822–1893	Ohio	Rep.	1877–1881
20. James A. Garfield	1831–1881	Ohio	Rep.	1881
21. Chester A. Arthur	1830–1886	N.Y.	Rep.	1881–1885
22. Grover Cleveland	1837–1908	N.Y.	Dem.	1885–1889
23. Benjamin Harrison	1833–1901	Ind.	Rep.	1889–1893
24. Grover Cleveland	1837–1908	N.Y.	Dem.	1893–1897
25. William McKinley	1843–1901	Ohio	Rep.	1897–1901
26. Theodore Roosevelt	1858–1919	N.Y.	Rep.	1901–1909
27. William H. Taft	1857–1930	Ohio	Rep.	1909–1913
28. Woodrow Wilson	1856–1924	N.J.	Dem.	1913–1921
29. Warren G. Harding	1865–1923	Ohio	Rep.	1921–1923
30. Calvin Coolidge	1872–1933	Mass.	Rep.	1923–1929
31. Herbert Hoover	1874–1964	Calif.	Rep.	1929–1933
32. Franklin D. Roosevelt	1882–1945	N.Y.	Dem.	1933–1945
33. Harry S Truman	1884–1972	Mo.	Dem.	1945–1953
34. Dwight D. Eisenhower	1890–1969	N.Y.	Rep.	1953–1961
35. John F. Kennedy	1917–1963	Mass.	Dem.	1961–1963
36. Lyndon B. Johnson	1908–1973	Tex.	Dem.	1963–1969
37. Richard M. Nixon	1913–	Calif.	Rep.	1969–

Presidential Succession Act. When Pres. Garfield was shot, July 2, 1881, he was totally incapacitated for 10 weeks prior to his death. During this time the Vice-President did not take over the duties of the President. A similar situation prevailed when, because of a stroke, Pres. Wilson was bedridden for nearly all of the last 18 months (1919–21) he was in office.

After Garfield's death, Congress realized that if Vice-President Arthur, who succeeded to the office of President on Sept. 20, 1881, had also died or been disabled, the country would have been without a President. While the law in force from 1792 to 1886 had provided that the president pro tempore of the Senate and then the Speaker of the House would be in line of succession to the Presidency, neither of these officials had been elected.

The Presidential Succession Act (1886) provided that, in the event the President and Vice-President should die, resign, be removed from office or be unable to serve, the members of the Cabinet should succeed to the Presidency in the order in which their positions had been created, beginning with the Secretary of State.

After Pres. F. D. Roosevelt died (1945) he was succeeded by Vice-President Truman and the country again had no Vice-President. Since succession by a non-elected official, such as the Secretary of State, a Cabinet member, to the office of President did not seem to be in accordance with the democratic process, Congress passed the Presidential Succession Act (1947). It provided for an order of succession in which the Speaker of the House of Representatives would be first in line for the Presidency, followed by the president pro tempore of the Senate, then the members of the Cabinet in the order in which their positions were created.

The heart attack of Pres. Eisenhower in 1955 and the assassination of Pres. Kennedy in 1963 invited reexamination by Congress of presidential disability and succession. In 1965 Congress passed a proposed constitutional amendment on presidential disability and succession and sent it to the states for ratification. It became the 25th Amendment in 1967.

presidios. Spain established military settlements in California and other parts of the Southwest. The soldiers at the posts or forts were accompanied by their families and did some farming while protecting the religious missions and holding the frontier for Spain. One was established at Los Angeles before 1795. The commander of a *presidio* exercised no influence in the management of the province.

Presque Isle, Fort. The fort on the present site of Erie, Pa., was first established by the French in 1753. In 1759 during the French and Indian War the British captured it. They held it as a frontier outpost until it was burned by the Indians in 1763. A new fort was built in 1795.

Price Administration, Office of. The World War II agency was created, Apr. 11, 1941, with limited powers to recommend price control measures. The first OPA head was Leon Henderson. Price ceilings were set on a wide variety of consumer goods. A few products, such as sugar, coffee and meat were rationed without causing undue hardship. Prices had already risen about 25% over the 1937–39 base when controls were first authorized, Jan. 1942. They continued to rise slightly but serious inflation was avoided.

Congress renewed the Price Control Bill in 1946 and extended the life of the OPA for one year, but it so crippled the powers of OPA that Pres. Truman vetoed the bill and permitted price controls to lapse, July 1. Congress put through a second bill, but in Nov. 1946 all controls except those on rents, sugar and rice were ended.

Prigg v. Pennsylvania (1842). The U.S. Supreme Court invalidated a Pennsylvania statute (1826) which prohibited an owner from seizing a runaway slave. The Court ruled that this violated the federal Fugitive Slave Act of 1793.

The case arose when Edward Prigg, an agent, returned a runaway slave to her Maryland owner and was indicted for kidnapping in Pennsylvania.

In striking down the Pennsylvania law, Justice Story's decision seemed to make it appear that any state regulation on fugitive slaves was invalid. The South resented this as a threat to states' rights and northern states reacted by passing "personal liberty" laws.

primogeniture. One cause for large colonial estates was primogeniture, a carry-over from feudal days in England, under which the eldest son received all of his father's landholdings.

Even before the Revolution there was increasing sentiment for equality of inheritance or at least freedom of the freeholder to determine for himself how to distribute his estate. By 1798 primogeniture had been abolished in all of the states.

Princeton, battle of (Jan. 3, 1777). In the battle, Gen. Washington defeated Gen. Cornwallis and freed most of New Jersey.

Cornwallis thought that he had Washington cornered but waited until morning to "bag the fox." Washington left campfires burning but moved his main force out by a little-known road and outflanked Cornwallis, forcing him to retreat to New Brunswick. Washington then set up winter headquarters at Morristown.

The victory at Princeton followed upon Washington's rout of the Hessians at Trenton and buoyed patriot morale.

Princeton University. Founded by Presbyterian ministers, the university was chartered as the College of New Jersey in 1746. The first classes were held in New Brunswick. The college was moved to Princeton in 1756 but was not named Princeton University until 1896.

A distinctive feature of its administration is the preceptorial system, under which small groups of students meet with their professor to discuss assigned readings. This was introduced by Woodrow Wilson after he became president of the university in 1902.

Privacy Case (1965). The U.S. Supreme Court struck down the Connecticut birth control law of 1879 which forbade the use of contraceptives by anyone, including married couples (*Estelle T. Griswold v. Connecticut*). In the majority ruling, written by Justice William O. Douglas, the Court held that "the specific guarantees in the Bill of Rights have penumbras" that reached areas not specifically mentioned in the Amendments—the 1st, 3rd, 4th, 5th, 9th and 14th—that create a "zone of privacy" violated by the law's restrictions on married couples. Justice Arthur J. Goldberg said in a concurring opinion, signed by Chief Justice Earl Warren and Justice William J. Brennan, that the 9th Amendment protected "fundamental rights," such as the right of privacy, not specifically mentioned in the Bill of Rights.

Dissenting justices in the seven to two ruling charged that the decision revived the Court's earlier policy of striking down legislation that it considered unreasonable even when the law did not violate a specific provision of the Constitution.

The case arose when two leaders of the Connecticut Planned Parenthood League were fined $100 each for operating a birth control clinic in New Haven. Mrs. Estelle T. Griswold, executive director of the League, and Dr. C. Lee Buxton, a professor at the Yale Medical School and medical director of the clinic, had been arrested on Nov. 10, 1961 and charged with aiding and abetting their patients to violate the law.

Privy Council. In the 17th century the King's advisers received complaints from the colonies, disallowed colonial laws, heard appeals from colonial courts, appointed the royal governors, put the seal of approval to the instructions to the governors and settled disputes among royal agents in the colonial service.

After 1700 the influence of the Privy Council declined partly because a new council of ministers, the Cabinet, evolved who were responsible to Parliament rather than to the King. The Privy Council became increasingly an honorary body.

Prize Cases (1863). The U.S. Supreme Court sustained the seizure of neutral vessels that had sought to penetrate the blockade of Confederate ports proclaimed by Pres. Lincoln, Apr. 19, 27, 1861. The Court did not accept the argument that the U.S. was not at war. It reasoned that insurrection was in fact war and that Pres. Lincoln had declared that an "insurrection" existed, Apr. 15, 1861. The President, the Court ruled, was doing his duty.

prize courts. During colonial times courts were established to determine the amount of money to be awarded to privateers or naval vessels that captured enemy ships. They were presided over by governors or judges appointed by them. Under the Judiciary Act of 1789 federal district courts were made prize courts. Prize money was usually shared proportionally by the victorious crew in accordance with rank and pay. During the Civil War Union blockaders had a harvest of prizes. In 1899 Congress abolished prize money.

Proclamation Line of 1763. In an effort to head off continued Indian wars the British Parliament drew a line along the crest of the Appalachian Mts. and forbade settlement west of it. This outraged the colonies with claims to the western lands. Fur traders did not object since settlers drove game out of the region, but land speculators and settlers set about to violate the Proclamation Line.

"proclamation money." In 1704 the English government issued a royal proclamation establishing uniform coin values in the colonies. Foreign coins were rated proportionately depending on their bullion content.

The purpose of the proclamation was to benefit English merchants. They complained that the higher valuation placed on foreign coins by the northern colonies was attracting trade from the southern colonies that might otherwise be carried on directly with England.

The proclamation was not enforced and it was ignored by the colonies.

Proclamation of Neutrality (Apr. 22, 1793). Following France's declaration of war on Britain, Pres. Washington announced that the U.S. would be impartial in the struggle arising from the French Revolution.

Thomas Jefferson had at first argued against the Proclamation because of our Treaty of 1778 with France. Alexander Hamilton countered that the Treaty had been made with the French monarchy which had been overthrown. The French for their part were content for the U.S. to be neutral if this permitted foodstuffs to get through the British blockade to the French West Indies and France.

The Proclamation did not in fact use the word "neutrality" although this was its intent. It set a precedent for later pronouncements when other nations were at war and U.S. maritime interests were involved.

Proclamation of Neutrality (Aug. 19, 1914). With the outbreak of World War I Pres. Wilson publicly appealed to Americans to be "impartial in thought as well as in action."

Progressive movement (1901–17). The reform movement gained wide popular support from the time Theodore Roosevelt became President to U.S. entry into World War I. The leadership of Roosevelt, Woodrow Wilson, Robert M. La Follette, Hiram Johnson and a host of muckraking journalists gave impetus to the movement.

Progressives aimed to correct abuses which had accompanied the growth of big business in the post-Civil War period. Federal regulatory agencies were established in an effort to curb monopolies and restore competition.

"Trust busting," not necessarily successful, was the order of the day. Tariff and banking reform and improvement of working conditions were undertaken. Laws were passed protecting the consumer against abuses by meat packers and food and drug manufacturers.

New government devices intended to provide direct democracy—direct primary, initiative, referendum, recall—were adopted by states. With passage of the 17th Amendment senators were directly elected by the people.

The "Square Deal" and "New Freedom" were battle cries of progressives. Their purpose was reform—not radical change or revolution.

Progressive party. The name has been adopted by several separate parties at different times in the 20th century. All, however, have sought reform of existing institutions.

In 1911 the National Republican Progressive League was formed and backed Robert M. La Follette of Wisconsin against Pres. Taft in the election of 1912.

When former Pres. Theodore Roosevelt failed to win the Republican party nomination, he withdrew with his progressive followers and formed the Progressive (Bull Moose) party which nominated him for President. The Progressive party was defeated in 1912 by the Democrats led by Woodrow Wilson.

In 1916 Roosevelt again sought the Republican nomination. When the party united behind Charles Evans Hughes, Roosevelt scrapped the Progressive party and supported Hughes against Wilson.

In 1924 the Progressive party was revived and ran Robert M. La Follette as a third-party candidate for President on a platform calling for government ownership of railroads, abolition of the injunction in labor disputes, relief for farmers and other reforms. La Follette received over 4,000,000 popular votes, but the party (also known as the Progressive Socialist party) disintegrated when he died in 1925.

In 1948 a newly formed Progressive party nominated former Vice-Pres. Henry Wallace for President. Communists sought to control the party. Wallace received a mere 1,000,000 popular votes. The party collapsed.

prohibition. Agitation against drinking dates back to the colonial period. Temperance was one of the reform movements of the 1830's and 1840's. A major success was achieved when Maine passed a prohibition law in 1846. Within the next five years 13 states passed prohibition laws.

Major organizations that spearheaded the drive included the Prohibition party (1869) which has run candidates for President since 1872, the Women's Christian Temperance Union (WCTU, 1874) and the Anti-Saloon League (1893).

During World War I the grain shortage caused Congress to prohibit the use of grains for the manufacture of intoxicating beverages. This encouraged the prohibitionists, who had already brought about passage of prohibition laws in 26 states. The ultimate was attained when the 18th Amendment (1919) established prohibition in the nation.

In the same year Congress passed the Volstead Act in which an intoxicating liquor was defined as any beverage containing one-half of one per cent alcohol.

The 1920's were marked by the greatest contempt for federal law in the nation's history. "Bootleggers" (sellers of illegal whiskey) smuggled liquor into the country from Canada, the West Indies and elsewhere, or sold locally manufactured liquor which was often poisonous. Law enforcement efforts were met with widespread indifference or even hostility. Bootleggers and allied criminals extended their operations to large-scale "racketeering," including extortion, kidnapping and gambling.

Although Pres. Hoover called prohibition "a great social and economic experiment, noble in motive," many Americans became convinced that it was doing more harm than good. The 18th Amendment was repealed by the 21st Amendment (1933), thus ending the "dry era."

Prohibition party. The party's first national convention was held in 1872 in Columbus, O. Its origins lay in the crusade for temperance which started early in the century. Although the party has concentrated on prohibition, it has also favored other reforms. It split over the free silver issue in 1896.

The oldest third party in existence, it has nominated presidential candidates in every election since 1872, but it has never won an electoral vote. A voting peak was reached in 1892 when 271,000 votes were cast for the party's standard bearer.

proprietary colonies. When trading companies failed to complete the job of settling new colonies in the 17th century, the King made large land grants to individuals or small groups who were known as proprietors. They had the right to sell part or all of their holdings and some of them did so.

Under the charters granted by the Crown the proprietary provinces were ruled by the owners, but court decisions and laws were subject to review in England. The proprietors appointed the governor and council and almost all officials. Representative assemblies, elected by the more substantial property owners among the colonists, curbed the power of the proprietors. At the beginning of the American Revolution the proprietors' vast lands were confiscated and little compensation was allowed by the new state governments.

Among the proprietary provinces were Maryland granted to Lord Baltimore (1632), Maine to Sir Ferdinando Gorges (1639), New York, New Jersey and Delaware to the Duke of York (1664), Carolina to a small group (1663 and 1665) and Pennsylvania to William Penn (1681).

Except for Maryland and Pennsylvania, the proprietary colonies became royal colonies before the Revolution.

"public be damned." The expression was attributed to William Henry Vanderbilt, president of the N.Y. Central RR, who was interviewed by reporters, Oct. 8, 1882. Vanderbilt had been asked about his plans for meeting the competition of the Pennsylvania RR which had introduced "express service" for passengers. His alleged response was made when he was asked about "the public benefit" of such a service. Public criticism of Vanderbilt's arrogance caused him to deny using the expression.

public domain. The term refers to land owned by the federal or state governments. The first great federal land acquisitions came when the states yielded their claims to western land during the period 1781–1802. Other great acquisitions came with the Louisiana Purchase (1803), purchase of Florida (1819), annexation of Texas (1845), Oregon Compromise (1846), Mexican Cession (1848), Gadsden Purchase (1853) and Alaska Purchase (1867).

Much of the public domain was granted to new western states to aid them in establishing schools and making other improvements, made available to railroads to help finance construction, and offered for sale to settlers and speculators. It was not until the National Forest Reservation Act (1891) that Congress decided to retain parts of the public domain. Subsequent conservation measures have led to the preservation of valuable government-owned land for its natural beauty, mineral resources, water power and related national defense purposes.

Public Housing Administration. Established in 1947 as an organ of the Housing and Home Finance Agency, it is the successor of two agencies—the Federal Public Housing Authority and the United States Housing Authority.

The PHA's basic responsibility is to administer the program of federal assistance to low-rent public housing authorized by the U.S. Housing Act of 1937, as amended. This law authorizes federal financial assistance to local communities "to remedy the unsafe and insanitary housing conditions and the acute shortage of decent, safe, and sanitary dwellings for families of low income. . . ."

Publick Occurrences. The first newspaper in the American colonies, published by Benjamin Harris in Boston, lasted exactly one day, Sept. 25, 1690. It was suppressed by the authorities.

public schools. The movement to establish free, tax-supported, non-sectarian common schools was under way by 1825. In 1850 they existed in almost every northern state. Among the early organizations which won public support for the free school idea were the Free School Society of New York (later known as the Public School Society), chartered in 1805; the Pennsylvania Society for the Promotion of Public Schools (1827); the Hartford (Conn.) Society for the Improvement of Common Schools (1827); the Western Academic Institute and Board of Education (1829), at Cincinnati, O.

Opponents of public schools included church and private school interests and those who argued that it would make education too common and that it was unfair to tax one citizen to educate another citizen's child.

Proponents included humanitarians, trade unions and statesmen with vision. They rejected the pauper school idea as harmful to the public interest and held that education increases production; that immigrants can best be assimilated in a system of publicly supported common schools; and that free education is a natural right of children in a republic.

Among the cities which were the first to obtain school-tax legislation from the state were Providence, R.I. (1800) and Philadelphia, Pa. (1812 and 1818). States passing general school laws included New York (1812), Rhode Island (1828), Indiana (1824), Pennsylvania (1834) and Alabama (1854).

Public Works Administration (PWA). Established in 1933 under Sec. of Interior Harold L. Ickes, the agency, unlike the Federal Emergency Relief Administration (FERA), made contracts with private companies, joining with cities and states to finance public works projects. By 1939 about $6 billion were spent putting to work 500,000 people who might otherwise have been unemployed. The projects approved and completed after careful surveys, included Boulder (later Hoover) Dam, the Triborough Bridge in New York City and the aircraft carriers *Yorktown* and *Enterprise*.

Pueblo Indians. The tribe which now lives in Arizona and New Mexico once was more widely spread in the Southwest. They were named by the Spanish for the towns (pueblos) in which they lived. Missionary work among these Indians was under way by 1580. In 1680 the Pueblos drove the Spanish out. The Spanish were back in 1692 when the Pueblos were defeated and some of their towns demolished by Diego de Vargas.

The Pueblos built their houses in canyons or in the sides of rock cliffs. In open territory they used stone or adobe for building material. They are good basket makers and weavers, excel in making pottery, and practice irrigation in raising corn, beans, onions and other crops. The four Pueblo linguistic stocks are Tanoan, Keresan, Zuñian and Shoshonean.

Pueblo seizure (Jan. 23, 1968). The U.S.S. *Pueblo*, an electronic intelligence ship, was seized by North Korean patrol boats and forced into the North Korean port of Wonsan. North Korea charged that the U.S. had been warned against violating the 12-mile limit claimed as its territorial waters. The U.S. denied that the *Pueblo* had been in territorial waters. The seizure came at a time when North Korean military pressure against South Korea had been increasing and served also as a diversionary effort by North Korea to aid the Vietnamese Communists. The U.S. brought the seizure before the UN Security Council, sought also to induce third countries to put diplomatic pressure on North Korea. But the 83-man crew (one dead) was not released for 11 months. The officers and men were not court-martialed for their surrender of the *Pueblo*.

Puerto Rico. The easternmost island of the West Indies group known as the Greater Antilles was discovered by Columbus (Nov. 19, 1493). Ponce de León conquered it for Spain (1509). It fell to the U.S. at the end of the Spanish-American War (1898). Spanish continues to be the official language although English is widely spoken.

Under the Foraker Act (1900) the President appointed the governor. The inhabitants were granted U.S. citizenship under the Organic Act of 1917 (Jones Act). They do not, however, vote for President unless they move to the U.S. The islanders were given the right to choose their own chief executive in 1947. In 1952 they adopted a constitution providing for a two-house legislature. It was approved by Congress and elevates Puerto Rico to the status of a free commonwealth associated with the U.S. Supporters of statehood and independence are in the minority in Puerto Rico.

The economy of the island has been stimulated by "Operation Bootstrap" which has encouraged the diversification of industry by attracting mainland companies to the island. Income from manufacturing is most important and products include textiles, electrical equipment and chemicals. Agriculture, the second largest source of income, includes dairying and livestock, sugar, tobacco, pineapples and garden truck.

Migration to the U.S. has helped to relieve population pressure. About 650,000 people of Puerto Rican origin live in New York.

Pujo Committee (1912). The Banking and Currency Committee of the House of Representatives authorized Rep. Arsène Pujo (La.), with Samuel Untermeyer (N.Y.) as counsel, to investigate the financial affairs of the Morgan and Rockefeller interests. It found that persons who belonged to these interests held 341 directorships in 112 corporations having aggregate resources of $22,245,000,000. This huge concentration of power, according to the majority report of the committee, was a threat to American free enterprise.

Its findings led to the Federal

Reserve Act (1913) and the Clayton Antitrust Act (1914).

Pulitzer, Joseph (1847–1911). Journalist and newspaper publisher. Born in Mako, Hungary, he came to the U.S. in 1864. After service in the Union army, he settled in St. Louis where he practiced law and entered politics. He purchased the St. Louis *Dispatch* (1878) and merged it with the *Post* to form the St. Louis *Post-Dispatch*, which became an outstanding midwestern newspaper. He moved to New York and bought the New York *World* (1887). Along with Hearst's *Evening Journal*, it practiced the kind of "yellow journalism" that helped bring on the war with Spain (1898). Later, the *World* settled down to more responsible journalism. He endowed the school of journalism at Columbia and established the Pulitzer Prizes "for the encouragement of public service, public morals, American literature, and the advancement of education."

Pulitzer Prizes. The prizes in journalism, letters (fiction, biography, history), drama and music were established by the will of Joseph Pulitzer, publisher of the St. Louis *Post-Dispatch* and the New York *World*. They are administered by Columbia University's Graduate School of Journalism and have been awarded annually since 1917.

Pullmans. George M. Pullman, a cabinetmaker, started by improving accommodations on railroad coaches in the 1850's. In 1864, he built the first modern sleeping car. The Pullman Palace Car Company was formed in 1867, and the continuous improvement of its cars revolutionized rail travel on transcontinental trips.

Pullman strike (1894). When the Pullman Palace Car Company cut wages sharply and dismissed many workers, members of the newly formed American Railway Union went on strike. An additional cause of the strike was the refusal of the company to make comparable reductions in rents and prices in the company town near Chicago. The strike spread throughout the country as workers boycotted railroads using Pullman cars.

Hoodlums took advantage of the stoppage to loot railroad stores and freight trains. A federal court, at Attorney General Olney's request, issued a "blanket injunction" restraining all interference with movement of trains and the U.S. mail. The workers defied the injunction.

Pres. Cleveland sent federal troops to Chicago over the protest of Gov. Altgeld. Cleveland justified his action as necessary to end defiance of the injunction and to move the mails. Violence intensified as troops tried to operate the trains, but the federal action broke the strike.

Eugene V. Debs, the union president, was held in contempt of court for defiance of the injunction and was jailed for six months.

Industry saw the court injunction as a valuable weapon in curbing unions and organized labor started a long campaign to end this use of the injunction.

Pupin, Michael Idvorsky (1858–1935). Physicist and inventor. Born in Austria-Hungary, he came to the U.S. in 1874. He was granted a Ph.D. by the Univ. of Berlin (1889). He was professor of electromechanics, Columbia (1901–31). He received 34 patents for his inventions, which included a system of multiplex telegraphy accomplished by electrical tuning (1894) and the "Pupin coil," which extended the range of long-distance telephony. He discovered a means of overcoming static resistance to wireless telegraphy; obtained the first X-ray photograph in America (Jan. 2, 1896) and also discovered secondary X-radiation. He was awarded the Pulitzer Prize (1924) for his autobiography *From Immigrant to Inventor* (1923).

Pure Food and Drug Acts. The "embalmed beef" scandal of the Spanish-American War and the writings of such muckraking journalists as Upton Sinclair on meat packing and Samuel Hopkins Adams on patent medicines led to passage of the Meat Inspection Act and then the Pure Food and Drug Act (both, 1906).

The latter Act laid the foundation for protecting the national food and drug supply. Its aim was to remove harmful and poisonous products from the market and to protect the consumer from being deceived by misrepresented products. To accomplish this purpose, the law forbade fraudulent adulteration and misbranding.

From time to time Congress has passed laws to strengthen the original Act. The Wheeler-Lea Act of 1938 plugged serious gaps in the legislation. It extended the Pure Food and Drug Act to include misleading advertisements in newspapers and magazines and on the radio. A major omission, cosmetics, came under federal control. Penalties were made heavier, including fines and imprisonment.

Between 1958 and 1960 Congress authorized the Food and Drug Administration to supervise the addition of chemical preservatives and artificial coloring agents to food and to insist on warning labels on such household products as waxes and detergents. The Federal Trade Commission proceeded against misleading advertisers.

Puritans. Part of a broad movement in 17th-century England, they were religious dissenters who sought to purify the Church of England (Anglican Church) of its Catholic vestiges. Puritans supported the middle-class party in Parliament that wanted to limit the power of the Stuarts who believed in the divine right of kings.

The main body of 1,000 Puritans who founded the Massachusetts Bay colony in 1630 was led by John Winthrop. The company charter placed the powers of government in a small group of Puritan leaders who hoped to make money from the fur trade, fisheries, lumbering and possibly gold mining. They settled such towns as Boston, Salem, Lynn, Roxbury and Dorchester.

Puritans, in general, were English followers of Calvin. They believed that man was born and lived in sin and could not effect salvation of his soul. The emphasis of New England Puritans on Covenant theology distinguished them from other religious dissenters of the period. God, in effect, made a convenant (agreement) with those who accepted his offer of regeneration (grace). Those who accepted the covenant demonstrated their salvation by giving up sinful ways and living a godly life. The clergy prepared the sinful for their conversion and then determined who might be admitted to the church.

In the Massachusetts Bay colony only those who belonged to the church enjoyed the right to vote for the governor and members of the legislature, called the General Court. Church and state were virtually one in the "Bible Commonwealth." Ministers, chosen by the congregation, spoke with authority, and their word was enforced as law. Although the Puritans were themselves dissenters, they did not tolerate dissent from their beliefs and practices. The power of the Puritan ministers declined with the growing secularization of colonial society and the great increase in immigration during the 18th century.

Too much may be made of the autocratic ways of the Puritans. They did develop a system of representative government and by distributing land among freemen (church members) helped spread the settlement of New England.

Q

Quakers. The followers of George Fox, who began to preach in England in the 17th century, trembled when they prayed and so gained the name Quakers. Every Quaker regards himself as a member of the priesthood since all men possess the "inner light" that enables them to hear God's voice. At their meetings, Quakers meditate silently unless moved to exhort others through sermons and prayers. They are members of the Religious Society of Friends.

Quakers who migrated to New England were persecuted by the Puritans. They were driven out of Massachusetts Bay colony in 1656 but were accepted in Rhode Island where they held their first "Yearly Meeting" in Newport in 1661.

The Friends found a home in Pennsylvania in 1681 where William Penn, a convert to Quakerism, welcomed them. After the Revolution they spread to the free soil of the West since they strongly opposed slavery. A split in the Society developed in the 1820's with one group following Elias Hicks (the Hicksites), stressing "inner guidance," and the other an "Orthodox" policy.

Quakers have emphasized education in their independent schools and have been active in humanitarian causes. Since they refuse to swear oaths or bear arms, they organized the American Friends Service Committee in 1917 so that they might serve the nation in relief work. They did notable relief work in Europe during and after both World Wars and have maintained a remarkable overseas aid program. From the first, mission efforts took them to Asia, Africa and America.

The Friends have abandoned their special clothes and forms of address ("thee" and "thou") but have held to their basic principles. There are about 127,-000 Friends in the U.S.

Quantrill's Raid (Aug. 21, 1863). The widespread devastation of Lawrence, Kan., was carried out by a Confederate guerrilla leader, William Clarke Quantrill, a former resident of the town, who had been forced to leave as an undesirable.

Quantrill carried on raids in Missouri and Kansas, robbing mail coaches and sacking Unionist communities and farms. He made a raid into Kentucky early in 1865 and was killed.

quarantine. The method of controlling the spread of disease by public authority was used by colonial legislatures. The first national quarantine act (Feb. 23, 1799) required federal officers to aid in the execution of state or municipal quarantine regulations. On Sept. 1, 1892, Pres. Harrison proclaimed a 20-day quarantine of New York City to prevent the spread of cholera.

"quarantine speech" (Oct. 5, 1937). The invasion of North China by Japan caused Pres. F. D. Roosevelt to tell a Chicago audience that peace-loving nations must act together to isolate the aggressor. "When an epidemic of physical disease starts to spread, the community approves and joins in a quarantine of the patients in order to protect the health of the community against the spread of the disease. . . ." He called for measures to protect the nation against the "contagion" of war. In Jan. 1938, the call took specific shape when he asked Congress for a billion dollars to build a two-ocean navy.

quarter eagle. A two-and-a-half-dollar gold coin was authorized by Congress in 1792. Coinage was begun in 1796. The coin's name represents its relationship to the eagle, the $10 coin which also had the national bird on the reverse side.

Quartering Act (1765). An Act of Parliament provided that in areas in the American colonies where barracks were not available for British troops, they were to be housed in public inns or private barns. The persons who furnished the quarters were to be paid by the colony in which the troops were stationed. The Act was resented by those colonists who opposed paying for the quartering of "foreign" soldiers.

A new Quartering Act (1774) was one of the Coercive Acts.

Quebec Act (1774). Parliament extended the Province of Quebec to the Ohio River on the south and the Mississippi River on the west. In doing so, it ignored the western land claims of Massachusetts, Connecticut and Virginia.

The Act also sought to conciliate French Canadians by granting political and religious freedom to the Catholics of Quebec, a move that alarmed American Protestants.

The aim of the Quebec Act was to improve administrative efficiency, but its timing caused it to be lumped by the colonists with the Coercive Acts which led to the calling of the First Continental Congress.

Queen Anne's War (1701–13). On the continent of Europe

the war was known as the War of the Spanish Succession. England, the Netherlands and the Holy Roman Empire were ranged against France and Spain in a quarrel over the succession to the throne of Spain.

In America fighting broke out in the West Indies, the Carolinas and New England. In the West Indies the fighting was reduced to French and Spanish privateering which hurt English colonial trade. In the South the Carolina Assembly authorized an expedition to seize St. Augustine, Fla., before it could be reinforced by the French. A force of 500 colonists and Indians burned the town but was unable to take the fort. The Choctaws prevented the Carolinians from penetrating the French Gulf settlements. New Englanders bore the brunt of the French and Indian attacks. The Abnakis raided Maine settlements and destroyed Deerfield, Mass. (Feb. 28–29, 1704). In retaliation a force of 500 New Englanders under Col. Benjamin Church destroyed two French Canadian villages. In 1710 Acadia fell to the British.

By the Treaty of Utrecht (1713), Newfoundland, Acadia and Hudson Bay were ceded to Britain. However, boundaries of the interior of the continent were not clearly defined and the door was left open for further conflict.

Queenstown Heights, battle of (Oct. 13, 1812). The British defeated American forces on the Niagara River, overlooking the village of Queenstown, Ontario. Over 900 Americans were captured during this engagement in the War of 1812.

Quids. The name was applied to a faction of the Republican party, led by John Randolph of Roanoke, Va., in the years from 1805 to 1811. They opposed the nomination of James Madison, Thomas Jefferson's choice for succession, and resisted what they regarded as the party's movement toward centralization and federal encroachment. The "quids" or *tertium quids* were distinguished from the two chief parties.

quint. A silver coin equal in value to about 35 cents was presented to the Continental Congress in 1783 by Gov. Robert Morris for consideration as a national coin. It was not accepted.

quitrent. During the colonial period landowners paid a fee to proprietors or to the Crown. The practice was carried over from feudal days in England when a quitrent or fee was paid to the Crown in place of produce or service.

In the colonies, because of the shortage of specie, quitrent (when collected) was paid in produce such as wheat or tobacco. Payment, often evaded, was resented by freeholders right up to the outbreak of the Revolution. After the American Revolution the states abolished quitrents.

Quivera. Indians described to Francisco Vásquez Coronado a golden realm lying north and east of Arizona where the Spanish explorer had been disappointed in his search for cities of gold. Coronado took a band of 20 picked men and passed on to what is now central Kansas. He reached Quivera in 1641 to find miserable Indian villages destitute of gold.

R

Rabi, Isidor Isaac (1898–).
Physicist. Born in Austria, he
was brought to the U.S. as an
infant. He was granted a Ph.D.
by Columbia (1927). He was
on the teaching staff of Columbia from 1929 and professor
from 1937. Especially known
for the study of the frequency
spectra of atoms and molecules,
he was awarded the Nobel Prize
(1944) for Physics for his precision work in neutrons. He engaged in radar research during
World War II and was a consultant to the Los Alamos atom
bomb laboratory.

Radical Republicans. A segment
of the Republican party regarded the Civil War as a war
to end slavery. They clashed
with so-called "conservatives"
who sided with Lincoln in his
view that the Civil War was a
war for the restoration of the
Union. The Radicals earned the
epithet "Vindictives" by their
incessant criticism of what they
regarded as Lincoln's timid conduct of the war.

The break between Radical
and Conservative Republicans
became final after the assassination of Lincoln who had worked
with both factions of the party.
So severe was the Radical indictment of Pres. Johnson's Reconstruction plan that they attempted, unsuccessfully, to impeach him.

Radical rule of state legislatures in the South during the
Reconstruction era advanced the
program of civil rights for Negroes and disfranchisement of
the former Confederate leaders.

Radical leaders on the national level included Sen.
Charles Sumner (Mass.) and
Rep. Thaddeus Stevens (Pa.).
Radical Republicanism faded
toward the end of the Reconstruction era as more moderate
counsel in the party prevailed.

Railroad Brotherhoods. Although organized along craft
lines an important group of labor unions did not affiliate with
the American Federation of Labor. They are the Locomotive
Engineers (founded 1863), the
Railroad Conductors (1868),
Locomotive Firemen and En-
ginemen (1873) and the Railway Trainmen (1883).

Railroad Retirement Board. The
Board was established by the
Railroad Retirement Act of

1935. It administers a retirement system for railroad employees, the payment of disability annuities, unemployment insurance and sickness and death benefits.

The Railroad Retirement Act of 1937 provides pensions after a specified length of service to employees of U.S. railroads.

An earlier law, the Railroad Retirement Act of 1934, was declared unconstitutional by the U.S. Supreme Court in *Retirement Board v. Alton Railroad Co.* (1935). The Court ruled that Congress had exceeded its right to regulate interstate commerce and the requirement that the railroad companies pay pensions to employees was a violation of due process under the 5th Amendment.

The subsequent legislation, sustained in *Railroad Board v. Duquesne Co.* (1946), provided for payments by both the interstate carriers and their employees and the creation of a fund in the Treasury Department out of which pensions are paid.

Railroad Strikes of 1877. The first of the strikes was triggered on July 17 by a Baltimore and Ohio Railroad wage cut which followed other cuts imposed during the depression that had developed after the Panic of 1873. The strike spread to railway workers on the Pennsylvania, the New York Central and the Erie. The country was confronted with its first industrial outbreak on a national scale.

Apart from low wages, workers complained of high prices charged by company-owned railway hotels used by men away from home; also, the railways were putting together "double-headers," trains with twice the number of cars, without adding trainmen.

The strikes interrupted railroad traffic throughout the country. They were for the most part spontaneous and lacked union leadership. Rioting flared up dangerously in Baltimore, Pittsburgh, Chicago, St. Louis and San Francisco where mobs looted and pillaged railway and other properties. "It is wrong to call this a strike," the St. Louis *Republican* exclaimed. "It is labor revolution." Public sympathy for the railway workers evaporated as the menace to life and property from uncontrolled elements became widespread.

Pres. Hayes authorized the use of federal troops to halt rioting and pillaging and to get the trains running. The strikers realized they were beaten and returned to work in August. The business community realized the potential power of industrial workers and increased efforts to curb labor union activity. Labor realized the need for better organization to prevent strikes from developing into uncontrolled mob action.

"Rail Splitter." The term was used to describe Abraham Lincoln at the Republican convention (1860) and helped to make him popular. As a young man

Lincoln had split tree trunks for rail fences.

Railway Express Agency. The shipping of merchandise by railway was started in 1839 as a personal service by a conductor on a road between Boston and Worcester. The express business soon developed with companies operating under contract with railroads. Two such companies were Wells, Butterfield & Co. and Livingston, Fargo & Co., both in the Northeast and both organized in 1850. Wells, Fargo & Co., organized in 1852, operated in the West. The various railway express companies merged in 1918 to form the American Railway Express Co. This was taken over in 1929 by the Railway Express Agency, owned by participating railroads.

Railway Labor Acts. The 1926 law, also known as the Watson-Parker Act, set up a Board of Mediation, an independent agency of five members appointed by the President, for the purpose of settling railway labor disputes.

In 1934, under the New Deal, a National Railroad Adjustment Board was established to guarantee the right of employees to organize and to bargain collectively through representatives of their own choosing.

Raisin River massacre (Jan. 22, 1813). A division of the American Army under Gen. James Winchester, including about 700 Kentuckians, was defeated at the battle of Frenchtown by a force of British and Indians at Raisin River in what is now Michigan. The Americans aimed to take Detroit, which had been captured by the British in Aug. 1812. American wounded at Frenchtown were scalped and butchered by the Indians in what has been called the Massacre of the River Raisin. The survivors were dragged off to Detroit. "Remember the River Raisin" was long a war cry of Kentuckian soldiers.

"Raleigh Letter." Henry Clay, who was to be the Whig candidate for President in 1844, in a letter written in April explained his opposition to the annexation of Texas. He argued that it would involve us in an unwanted war with Mexico and probably with other foreign powers at a time when the country's financial condition did not make such a war expedient.

Rambouillet decree (Mar. 23, 1810). Napoleon ordered the confiscation of scores of American ships in French ports. The decree was issued in retaliation for the Non-intercourse Act passed by Congress which was aimed at both France and England.

Ramona (1884). In her historical novel Helen Hunt Jackson (Mass.) describes the last days of Spanish rule in California. Ramona, the heroine, marries an Indian rather than the son of a wealthy Spanish family. The author depicts mission work among the Indians in California as well as U.S. policy toward the Indians.

The book was the source of a movie and a popular song hit in 1927.

rams, Confederate. Considerable damage was inflicted by warships whose bows were fitted with iron beaks to ram Union ships. The *Virginia* was the first such ship constructed in the South early in the Civil War.

Randolph, John (1773–1833). Born in Prince George Co., Va., he was known as John Randolph "of Roanoke." At first a Jeffersonian, he was elected to Congress from Virginia and served in the House of Representatives (1799–1813, 1815–17, 1819–25, 1827–29) and the U.S. Senate (1825–27). He split with Thomas Jefferson over secretive efforts to acquire Florida and came into open opposition with his "Decius" letters (beginning in the *Richmond Enquirer*, Aug. 15, 1806). Randolph bitterly opposed the War of 1812.

A master of invective, he castigated the Adams-Clay alliance as a combination of the "puritan and the blackleg" and excoriated northern members of Congress who voted for the Missouri Compromise (1820). A strict-construction man, he denounced the chartering of the second Bank of the United States, the tariff and other nationalistic measures. A champion of lost causes, he seemed demented at times after 1818. But he was one of the most brilliant public figures in national life.

Randolph's commission. In 1676 Edward Randolph was sent to New England as an agent of King Charles II to investigate colonial trade. In 1678 he was appointed collector of the King's revenue in Massachusetts. As a "watchdog" of the English merchants, he had the task of exposing and stamping out all illegal trade. In 1680 he drew up 29 charges against the colony, 23 of which related to violations of the Navigation Acts. He concluded that the King's revenues and the English merchants could be protected only if the charter of Massachusetts were revoked and the locally elected officers of the colony were replaced by agents appointed by the King. The charter was annulled in 1684.

Ranger. The project culminated on July 31, 1964, in the extraordinary mission of Ranger VII, which provided over 4,000 pictures of the lunar surface. This program is a step on the road to lunar exploration. The project as a whole is aimed at gathering as much information about the moon and its surfaces as is possible by utilization of spacecraft carrying television equipment. The Rangers do not attempt a return flight; after performing their mission, they crash to the surface of the moon.

rangers, colonial. A special force of provincial troops was used by England in the American colonies to guard against Indian attacks on the frontiers. They were organized into both mounted and foot companies. During the Revolution some of the rangers sided with the British; others were used on the frontiers by the colonies.

Rayburn, Sam (1882–1961). Political leader. Born near Kingston, Tenn., he was taken to Texas by his family when he was five years old. "Mr. Sam," as he was known to his intimate friends, served in the U.S. House of Representatives for nearly 49 years (1913–61), longer than any man. A Democrat, he was Speaker for 17 years (1940–46, 1949–53, 1956–61), reelected in every term except when the House was Republican, and held the post more than twice as long as the previous record holder, Henry Clay. Regarded as a strong speaker, his success was attributed to his powers of persuasion. He acted as floor leader in Sen. Lyndon B. Johnson's presidential bid in 1960 and counseled Johnson to accept the nomination for Vice-President on the Kennedy ticket.

reapportionment decisions. In *Baker v. Carr* (1962) the U.S. Supreme Court, for the first time, held that failure to re-apportion seats in a state legislature was a denial of the "equal protection" guarantee of the 14th Amendment. In that decision arising from a redistricting case in Tennessee where the seats in the state legislature had not been reapportioned for 61 years, the Court held that the federal courts had jurisdiction. The Court ruled that the appellants were entitled to appropriate relief and could challenge the Tennessee apportionment statutes.

In *Reynolds v. Sims* (1964) the Supreme Court held that the equal protection clause of the 14th Amendment requires that both houses of a bicameral state legislature must be apportioned on a population basis as nearly as is practicable. Chief Justice Warren in his "one man, one vote" opinion held, "Legislators represent people, not trees or acres. Legislators are elected by voters, not farms or cities or economic interests."

Justices Stewart and Harlan dissented; Stewart held: "The court's Draconian pronouncement, which makes unconstitutional the legislatures of most of the 50 states, finds no support in the Constitution, in any prior decision of this court, or in the 175-year history of our federal union."

Six decisions relating to legislative apportionment in six different states, including Alabama (*Reynolds v. Sims*), were laid down the same day, June 15. The rulings also affected New York, Colorado, Delaware, Maryland and Virginia.

In *Wesberry v. Sanders* (1964), a case involving the election of congressmen in Georgia, Justice Black, speaking for the majority, concluded: "While it may not be possible to draw congressional districts with mathematical precision, that is no excuse for ignoring our Constitution's plain objective of making equal representation for equal numbers of people the fundamental goal of the House of Representatives. That is the high standard of justice the Founders set for us."

The apportionment decisions resulted in an outburst of activity in state legislatures which sought to redistrict in a way that would stand up in the courts. Congress also considered the possibility of a constitutional amendment which would allow each state to apportion legislative seats according to factors other than population.

rear-admiral. Created by Congress in 1862, it was the highest grade in the U.S. Navy. The higher ranks of vice-admiral and admiral were created in 1864 and 1866, respectively, for David Farragut. Both were subsequently abolished, but the rank of admiral was revived for George Dewey as a distinction for his victory in Manila Bay, 1898.

Reciprocal Trade Agreement Act (1934). The President was authorized to enter agreements with foreign nations for reciprocal (two-way) tariff reductions. The law was urged by Sec. of State Hull as a means of improving trade relations. Under the Act, extended many times until 1962, the average tariff rate was cut from about 47 to 12%.

The President acting on the advice of the Tariff Commission could lower any rates by as much as 50% without approval of Congress. The reduced rates applied to imports from all nations with which the U.S. had trade agreements. This most-favored-nation principle, as it is called, helps to promote multilateral or many-sided trade.

After the program began Congress added the "peril point" provision which authorized the Tariff Commission to recommend higher rates to the President if the tariff rates in any case endangered the well-being of an American industry. An "escape clause" permitted a business to appeal to the Tariff Commission if a tariff rate hurt it.

Reconstruction (1865–77). The post-Civil War period in the U.S. is known as the Reconstruction era.

A major problem which faced the nation was the restoration of the devastated economy of the South. The end of slavery meant the end of the plantation system. In addition, the war had impoverished the southern plantation owners. Lack of cash led to the sharecropping system with resulting widespread exhaustion of the soil. It was not until the late 1870's that industry and commerce began to develop alongside agriculture. The southern economic advance was slight compared with the growing industrialism of the North.

A major controversy arose

over the conditions under which the seceded states might gain readmission to the Union. All returned to the Union by 1870, but not without bitterness.

Pres. Lincoln's Reconstruction plan was based on the theory that the southern states had not seceded but had rebelled. He expected to pardon all southerners other than Confederate leaders. Each state was to be readmitted to the Union after 10% of its voters (based on the 1860 elections) had taken the oath of allegiance and had elected a new state government.

After Lincoln's assassination, Pres. Johnson added the requirement that the southern states accept the 13th Amendment. The hostile attitude of Radical Republicans toward Johnson's "soft peace" policy led to his impeachment and near removal from office in 1868.

The Radical Republicans, led by Sen. Charles Sumner of Massachusetts and Rep. Thaddeus Stevens of Pennsylvania, took the view that the southern states had seceded from the Union and needed congressional approval for readmission. They argued that the former rulers could not be trusted and pointed to the "black codes" which southern legislatures had passed.

The congressional plan for Reconstruction and not the Lincoln-Johnson plan was adopted and set the tone of Reconstruction. It divided the South into five military districts under the control of federal troops. Many southerners were disqualified from voting because of their previous Confederate activities. Negroes were given the right to vote and hold office; this was to be guaranteed in the new state constitutions. The newly elected southern state governments would have to ratify the 13th and 14th Amendments. The 15th Amendment was also added to the Constitution during this period.

The northern armies of occupation in the South insured control of southern state governments by carpetbaggers, scalawags and former slaves. In five of the southern states Negroes held a majority of the seats in the state legislature. In many cases the carpetbag-Negro governments were corrupt and piled up huge debts for the taxpayers. It should be borne in mind, however, that during Reconstruction state governments in other sections of the country were also inefficient and corrupt.

Too frequently the constructive achievements of the carpetbag-Negro governments are overlooked: laws were passed to protect homes and farms against arbitrary foreclosure; imprisonment for debt was ended; the burden of taxation was spread more equally; women were granted property rights; and most important of all, free tax-supported schools for both races were set up.

Even with troops on the scene, southerners organized secret societies. The Ku Klux Klan used violence to keep the Negroes "in their place" — in

567

particular to keep them from voting.

Gradually, the carpetbag governments lost control of the southern states. Moderate Republicans in Congress turned against the harsh congressional program. Other northerners saw that troops could not remain indefinitely in the South if the nation's wounds were to be healed. Northern businessmen believed that under peaceful and "normal" conditions the South would be a better market for manufactured goods and a safer field for investments. In 1877, after the election of Pres. Hayes, the last federal troops were withdrawn from the former states of the Confederacy. Reconstruction had not, however, erased the wounds of the Civil War.

Reconstruction Finance Corporation (RFC). The RFC was created by Congress in 1932 at the request of Pres. Hoover. During its first year it lent $1,500,000,000 to more than 5,000 banks, railroads, life insurance companies and other business organizations to keep them from going into bankruptcy. The agency was continued and expanded under the New Deal but passed out of existence during the Eisenhower administration.

Red Badge of Courage, The (1895). In his novel set in the Civil War, Stephen Crane depicts naturalistically both the fear under fire of a young Union soldier and his psychological recovery. The story has become a classic of American literature.

Redcoats. The American colonists gave this name to the British troops because of their bright red military jackets. They were also called "lobsters" and "bloody backs."

Red Cross. The international organization was founded at the Geneva Convention (1864) in which the U.S. participated. Four years later a convention provided for neutralization of humanitarian agencies helping the war-wounded.

The American National Red Cross, founded in 1881 by Clara Barton, has provided relief in civil disasters and war. It is financed largely by voluntary contributions.

The recognized symbol of mercy and neutrality throughout the world is the Red Cross flag with its red cross on a white field.

Red River Campaign (1864). The Union expedition in the Southwest failed to seize the cotton-growing regions in eastern Texas, Arkansas and Louisiana. Union Gen. Nathaniel Banks headed a strong land force supported by a fleet under Admiral David Porter. Confederate defensive action under Gen. E. Kirby-Smith frustrated the superior Union forces. He held the area until his surrender to Gen. Edward Canby at the war's end, May 26, 1865.

Red scare. Strikes in 1919 and 1920 increased anti-Communist feeling in the U.S. Strikers were accused of radicalism and disloyalty by anti-labor groups. When bombs killed about 40 people in Wall Street the Communists (Reds) were accused. Pres. Wilson's Attorney General, A. Mitchell Palmer, warned that "free expression of opinion was dangerous to American institutions." Feelings became so intense that many non-radicals were afraid to voice opinions.

Red Shirts. In 1900 a political organization was formed in North Carolina to promote passage of an amendment to the state constitution that would disfranchise Negro voters by requiring a poll tax. The Red Shirts were so violent that the governor had to use troops to suppress them. The amendment was adopted by a large majority.

Reed, Walter (1851–1902). Army surgeon and bacteriologist. Born in Belroi, Va., he was granted an M.D. by the Univ. of Virginia (1869) and Bellevue Hospital Medical College, N.Y.C. (1870). Commissioned in the U.S. Army Medical Corps (1875), he was detailed as professor of bacteriology at Johns Hopkins Hospital. He headed a commission (1900–01) of U.S. Army medical officers (including James Carroll, Jesse W. Lazear and Aristides Agramonte) assigned to investigate the cause and mode of transmission of yellow fever in Havana, Cuba. The commission established by experimentation on human subjects that the disease was transmitted by mosquitoes classified as *Aëdes ægypti.* Dr. Carroll was crippled and Dr. Lazear died as a result of the experiments. An outcome of the findings was the virtual ending of yellow fever in the U.S.

Reformed Church in America. Better known as the Dutch Reformed Church, the first congregation was formed in 1628 by Dutch Protestant settlers in New Amsterdam. In 1766 the Church obtained a charter for Queen's College (now Rutgers). The Church took its present name in 1867.

In 1857 dissenters formed the Christian Reformed Church and its membership exceeded that of the parent body. The membership of all Reformed bodies in the U.S. is about 660,000.

Refugee Relief Act (1953). Under this law Congress provided for the admission to the U.S. of 214,000 German, Italian, Greek, Far Eastern and other refugees from Communist - dominated countries.

In 1957 Congress permitted the allocation of 18,656 visas that remained unissued when the Act expired in 1956. They were issued to refugees from Communism of German and Dutch ethnic origins and those unable to return to the Middle East because of race, religion or political opinion.

In 1958 a law made it possible for Hungarian refugees to become aliens qualified for residence if they lived in the U.S.

for two years, even if they were without documents. Another law in 1958 provided 1,500 special non-quota visas to earthquake victims in the Azores and 3,000 visas for displaced Dutch nationals from Indonesia.

regicides in New England. When Charles II was restored to the throne in England, three members of the High Court of Justice which had condemned Charles I were not granted amnesty. Known as regicides, the three—Edward Whalley, William Goffe and John Dixwell—escaped separately to New England where they were granted refuge by ministers and farmers. The King's agents never caught up with them.

Register of Debates. Congressional proceedings from Dec. 1824 to Oct. 1837 were published in 29 volumes. It contains many state papers and public documents besides the debates and routine congressional work. It is a continuation of the "Annals of Congress" and was succeeded by the *Congressional Globe.*

Regulators. An association of small farmers in North Carolina's western counties was formed in 1768 to protest land monopolies and unfair taxes. They arose violently against the courts and government in general. Their badly equipped forces were routed by government militiamen at Alamance in 1771.

The resentment of these small farmers against the Tidewater planters was such that many sided with the English in the Revolutionary War.

Relay, Project. The National Aeronautics and Space Administration (NASA) developed this project as a means of testing intercontinental communication (telephone, television, teleprint). Relay is an "active-repeater" satellite; that is, it not only receives and transmits signals, but also amplifies before transmission.

On Dec. 13, 1962, Relay I was launched; it performed successfully, as did Relay II, which after its launching on Jan. 21, 1962, provided the first communications satellite transmission between the U.S. and Japan.

released time. In some school districts provision has been made for releasing children during regular school hours so that they may receive religious instruction. In Champaign, Ill., the Board of Education permitted the religious classes to be conducted in the school building by outside teachers.

The U.S. Supreme Court in *McCollum v. Board of Education* (1948) held that the Champaign regulation violated the 1st and 14th Amendments. Justice Black, speaking for the Court, said that the state's tax-supported public school buildings were being used "for the dissemination of religious doctrines. . . . This is not separation of Church and State."

In *Zorach v. Clauson* (1952) the released time program of New York was sustained by the U.S. Supreme Court. The Court distinguished it from the *McCollum* case because no approval of religious teachers was involved and instruction was outside the public school building.

Relief party. Existing as a political party in Kentucky between 1820 and 1826, it advocated relief for delinquent debtors and succeeded in getting a bill passed to this end in 1824.

"Remember the Maine!" The slogan became the rallying cry that swept the U.S. into war with Spain (Apr. 1898). U.S. anger at Spain reached the boiling point, Feb. 15, 1898, when the U.S. battleship *Maine* exploded in the harbor of Havana, Cuba's capital. The explosion took 260 U.S. lives. No one could prove the cause of the disaster, but "yellow" journals, such as Hearst's New York *Journal* and Pulitzer's *World*, placed the blame on Spain and aroused the public's emotions.

Remington, Frederic (1861–1909). Painter, sculptor and author. Born in Canton, N.Y., he became an animal painter and illustrator of scenes from American West. He is unsurpassed in his studies of western Indians, cowboys, frontiersmen, soldiers in the field. His sculptures in bronze accented human figures in action, as did his paintings. His sculptures include *Bronco Buster* (Metropolitan Museum of Art, N.Y.C.), and his paintings include *Cavalry Charge on the Southern Plains, The Last Stand* and *The Emigrants.* He was the author and illustrator of *Pony Tracks* (1895), *Crooked Trails* (1898) and *The Way of an Indian* (1906).

removals. The Constitution gives the President power to appoint officers with the consent of the Senate, but does not state whether the power of removal is also to be exercised with the consent of the Senate. Debate on this arose in 1789 and it was decided to allow the power of removal to rest with the President alone. This remained the policy until the passage of the Tenure of Office Act (1867).

reparations. Under the Treaty of Versailles (1919) Germany agreed to make payments to the Allies for war damages caused by German aggression. In 1921 the Reparations Commission set the total bill at $33 billion. Reparations were scaled down by the Dawes Plan (1924) and Young Plan (1929). Germany's reparations payments were made possible largely through U.S. loans. When these ceased at the beginning of the Great Depression, reparations payments halted.

Although there was no legal connection between German reparations payments and war debts owed by the Allies to the U.S., in practice the one became dependent on the other.

Reparations were repudiated by Germany soon after Hitler came to power in 1933.

Republican party. The party was born in Ripon, Wis., Feb. 28, 1854, at a local meeting. It gained strength with the mounting opposition to the Kansas-Nebraska Act on the part of disaffected Democrats, who had joined the Free Soil party, and northern Whigs. The new party was dedicated to preventing the further spread of slavery. They took the name "Republican" because Thomas Jefferson had founded a party of that name early in the nation's history and because he had also drawn up the Northwest Ordinance (1787) which excluded slavery from the territory north of the Ohio River. Jefferson's party had become known as the Democratic-Republican party, but the Republican part of the name was dropped in 1828.

The new Republican party's first candidate for President was John C. Frémont. He lost the election of 1856 but carried 11 states. A subsequent split in the Democratic party made possible the election of the Republican candidate, Abraham Lincoln, in 1860. Since that time, party leaders have turned to Lincoln, rather than Jefferson, for inspiration in more than a century of campaigning. After slavery ceased to be an issue, the party did not let the nation forget that it—and not the Democratic party—was the party that kept the Union together.

Party platforms usually included planks advancing the protective tariff and sound money. Republican Presidents held office from 1861 to 1913, except for Grover Cleveland's two terms (1885–89, 1893–97).

Republicans received substantial support from big business especially in the election of 1896 when Mark Hanna, an Ohio industrialist, swamped William Jennings Bryan's bid for the Presidency. Under Theodore Roosevelt the party became more progressive, but it reverted to conservatism after World War I when Warren Harding, Calvin Coolidge and Herbert Hoover led the nation. In the minds of many people, Hoover's administration, and by extension, the party, is connected to the Great Depression. The American electorate banished it from the White House for 20 years of New Deal and Fair Deal until it was restored to national power by Dwight D. Eisenhower in the election of 1952. Even under Eisenhower Congress was controlled by the Democrats in three out of four elections. The party narrowly lost the election of 1960 when John F. Kennedy edged out Richard Nixon, but it was overwhelmed when Barry Goldwater became its standard-bearer in 1964. The party retained some strength in Congress and held more than half of the state governorships in 1968 as conservative and liberal rivals within the party sought to rejuvenate it on the national level.

requisitions. Under the Articles of Confederation the only method by which the Continental Congress could raise money was by requisitioning it. From 1782 to 1786 Congress called upon the states for sums amounting to more than $6,-000,000, but only a million of this had been paid by the end of Mar. 1787.

Resaca de la Palma, battle of (May 9, 1846). In one of the early battles of the Mexican War, Gen. Zachary Taylor pursued a larger force of Mexicans to a ravine in southern Texas, near the Rio Grande River. He forced their retreat across the river and later crossed with his troops to occupy the town of Matamoros (May 17–18, 1846).

resolutions in Congress. There are three kinds of resolutions acted upon by Congress: a simple resolution which is passed by one House only, a concurrent resolution which must pass both Houses and a joint resolution, which requires the action of both Houses and the signature of the President, that is, unless it is a proposed amendment to the Constitution.

Restraining Act (Mar. 30, 1775). Parliament cut off New England commerce from all countries outside the empire and closed North Atlantic fisheries to New England fishermen. The Act made conciliation between England and the American colonies even more remote.

Resumption Act of 1875. In accordance with the Act, the government, for the first time since the Civil War, resumed payments in gold specie for paper currency. Greenbacks issued during the Civil War were included. They were to be withdrawn from circulation, beginning Jan. 1, 1879, until only $300,000,000 were still circulating. By that time, however, there was sufficient gold in the Treasury for backing paper money and few people bothered to redeem their greenbacks.

The Act was a victory of "hard money" advocates who wanted a stable currency backed by gold. The Act was opposed by debtor farmers.

"return to normalcy." Warren G. Harding's campaign slogan in the election of 1920 touched a sensitive chord in the American people. They wanted relief from the problems created by World War I and were disillusioned with Pres. Wilson's idealism. Harding was elected by a landslide.

Revere, Paul (1735–1818). Patriot, silversmith and engraver. Born in Boston, Mass., his great skill as a silversmith has been dwarfed by the memory of his "midnight ride" (Apr. 18, 1775) warning patriots that the British troops were marching. Deeply committed to the revolutionary cause, he had shared in the Boston Tea Party (Dec. 16, 1773). He was given no military command in the Revolution but participated in the unsuccessful Penobscot expedition (1779) in Maine. He designed and printed the first Continental currency, made the first official seal for the colonies and designed the Massachusetts State Seal. He directed the manufacture of gunpowder (1779) and was the discoverer of a process for rolling sheet copper.

Revere's "midnight ride." "Paul Revere's Ride," a poem by Henry Wadsworth Longfellow, celebrates the ride (Apr. 18, 1775) which served to warn the colonists that the British were on the way to seize military stores at Concord. Although Revere did not reach Concord, he did arrive at Lexington about midnight and roused patriot leaders John Hancock and Samuel Adams, who escaped capture. William Dawes also rode that night. A third rider, Samuel Prescott, did reach Concord.

Revolutionary War (1775–81). The opening skirmishes at Lexington and Concord (Apr. 1775) scarcely promised the long war ahead. It took five more years before the independence proclaimed at Philadephia (July 4, 1776) was won. The British failed in their plan to cut off the various groups of colonies and then destroy the opposition piecemeal.

Gen. Washington made his famous crossing of the Delaware on Christmas night, 1776. He attacked and captured the sleep-

ing Hessians at Trenton, N.J. The next year, Gen. Burgoyne came down from Canada in anticipation of Gen. Howe's coming up from New York. They hoped to split the New England and Middle colonies by controlling the Hudson. Howe never made it and Burgoyne was forced to surrender at Saratoga, N.Y. (Oct. 1777). Victory at Saratoga brought France into active participation on the American side. This battle is considered the turning point of the war. There followed the bitter winter at Valley Forge near Philadelphia.

In the South, large sections of the Carolinas and Virginia were devastated by the British. Not until 1780, when Gen. Greene took over the command, were the Americans able to put up effective resistance in this region.

In 1781, the British forces under Lord Cornwallis abandoned North Carolina and surrendered to Gen. Washington at Yorktown, Va. Cornwallis' surrender (Oct. 1781) virtually brought the War of Independence to an end.

Revolution of 1800. Although not a revolution in the sense of a violent uprising, control of the government did shift from the Federalist party of John Adams and Alexander Hamilton to Thomas Jefferson's Republican party, which had more faith in the people.

Some historians deny that the Revolution of 1800 represented any fundamental change in the federal government because Jefferson retained the tariff and U.S. Bank and tried to practice an isolationist foreign policy.

Revolution of 1828. A so-called "revolution" took place when Andrew Jackson was elected President. Jackson's humble origins contrasted with those of his predecessors. His rise to a position of wealth and his standing as a war hero made many Americans feel that they were voting for a man who could help the American dream come true.

Jacksonian Democrats felt that the Republicans (Jeffersonians) had adopted the Federalist program and had not opened up political and economic opportunities for the many.

When the White House was overrun by plain people who were appointed to government positions by Jackson, the "revolution" was under way. Jefferson's emphasis on the welfare of farmers gave way to Jackson's broader appeal to city workers and small businessmen, as well as farmers.

Revolution of 1910. Congress revolted against the rule of Joseph Cannon, the tyrannical and reactionary Speaker of the House of Representatives. Under the House rules then in force, the Speaker had the power to select all committees. In his appointments in 1909 Cannon had ignored such insurgent leaders as Sen. George Norris of Nebraska, whose seniority entitled him to impor-

tant posts. In 1910 the insurgents pushed through a resolution that the Democrats also supported. It stripped the Speaker of his absolute powers and gave the House the duty to elect the important Committee on Rules, which would then appoint the other House committees.

Rhea letter. In 1817 Gen. Andrew Jackson was authorized by Pres. Monroe to pursue the Seminole Indians across the Spanish boundary, and if necessary, into Florida. On Jan. 6, 1818, Jackson wrote to Monroe requesting permission to seize east Florida "without implicating the government." Rep. John Rhea (Tenn.) was to be the secret channel through which Monroe's approval might be given.

Jackson claimed that Monroe did give his assent through Rhea. This was denied by Pres. Monroe. The evidence favors Monroe, but the administration knew Jackson's intent and it did nothing to discourage him from seizing east Florida.

Rhode Island. "Little Rhody," the smallest and most densely populated state, is in the New England group. It was one of the original 13 Colonies. Verrazano, noting the similarity of the island in Narragansett Bay to the Island of Rhodes (1624), gave the island's name to the colony.

The colony was founded in 1636 by Roger Williams, who had been forced to leave Massachusetts Bay colony when he challenged the Puritan doctrine of inseparability of church and state. Williams named his settlement Providence; it later became the state capital. Dissenters in other colonies were attracted to Rhode Island because they were free to worship as they pleased in accordance with the doctrine of toleration set forth in Williams' tract *The Bloudy Tenent of Persecution for Cause of Conscience.*

The colonists of Rhode Island made their living chiefly by farming, but trade was increasingly important in the 18th century. Newport became a cultural center and was the fifth largest city in the colonies. Its merchants played a vital role in the profitable triangular trade with Africa and the West Indies.

Rhode Island was critical of the Constitution and was the last of the original 13 Colonies to join the United States. It ratified the Constitution (May 29, 1790), after the new government was in operation.

The largest single industry in the state is textiles, dating back to Samuel Slater's cotton mill built in 1793. The state also pioneered in jewelry and silverware manufacture. Recently its industries have become more diversified. Agricultural output includes dairy products and poultry, notably those chickens known as Rhode Island Reds.

rice. The production of rice is said to have begun in 1695 in South Carolina when the captain of a brigantine from Mada-

gascar, which touched at Sullivan's Island, presented one of the colonists with a small bag containing the vegetable. In any event rice culture developed in the lowlands of South Carolina and in neighboring Georgia and North Carolina during the early 17th century. Cultivation of the crop on plantations with slave labor was disrupted by the Civil War and never fully recovered. Rice culture became successful in Louisiana, Arkansas, Texas and California, areas which now produce the bulk of the rice crop in the U.S.

Richardson, Henry Hobson (1838–86). Architect. He was born in St. James Parish, La. He won the competition for plans for Trinity Church, Boston (1872), employing his own style of modified French and Spanish Romanesque architecture. Starting as a church architect, he turned to more modern problems and created outstanding innovations in commercial buildings of interior richness, notably the Marshall Field Building, Chicago (1885). He led in the Romanesque revival that set an architectural fashion in the eastern U.S. in the 1880's. Charles F. McKim and Stanford White served in his office. Toward the end of his career, he evolved a functional architecture that was a forerunner of Louis H. Sullivan's modernism.

riders. Measures likely to be vetoed on their own merits are sometimes added to important bills to secure their passage. Since, under the Constitution, the President cannot veto part of a measure, riders are sometimes used to get legislation through Congress when the main bill is too important to be held up. Some state constitutions prevent riders by allowing the governor to veto (the item veto) separate items in bills.

Riff incident. On May 18, 1904, Ion Perdicaris, believed to be an American citizen, was kidnapped by the Riff chieftain Raisuli. This created an international incident and the warship *Brooklyn* was rushed to Morocco. Pres. Roosevelt consulted with Sec. of State Hay, who sent a telegram to the American consul at Tangier insisting that the U.S. must have "Perdicaris alive or Raisuli dead." On June 22 Perdicaris was released. This use of the "big stick" by the President enhanced his popularity in the U.S.

"right to work" laws. Under Section 14 (b) of the Taft-Hartley Act (1947) states are allowed to pass laws banning the union shop and other union-management agreements that make union membership a condition for keeping a job. Nineteen states had such laws in 1967.

rings, political. Honest administration of American government has at times been made difficult by little groups who enter politics for financial gain. They corrupt elected officials, police and other agencies of government.

Among the notorious political rings in the U.S. were the Tweed Ring in New York City in the 1870's, the Philadelphia Gas Ring in power from 1865 to 1897, the Butler Ring in St. Louis in the 1890's, the Ames Ring in Minneapolis about 1900 and the Ruef Ring in San Francisco in the early 1900's.

Rio Pact (Sept. 2, 1947). According to the agreement, known also as the Inter-American Treaty of Reciprocal Assistance, an attack on any American nation is regarded as an attack on all even if the aggression comes from a nation in the Western Hemisphere. The Pact was signed by 19 American Republics (Nicaragua and Ecuador did not participate) at Rio de Janeiro, Brazil. This regional collective security agreement was the first to be established under the provisions of Article 51 of the United Nations Charter.

Rise of American Civilization, The (1927). Charles and Mary Beard's survey of American history influenced a generation of American historians. It is a broad, critical interpretation of American history with emphasis on economic factors. Its literary grace made it eminently readable.

In their *Basic History of the United States* (1944), the Beards modified their emphasis on the economic interpretation of history. Charles Beard also wrote *The Republic* (1943), an analysis of American political practices in which he warned Americans to avoid Old World wars and intrigues.

Rivington's Gazette. Pro-royalist in its sympathies, the newspaper was established in New York City, Apr. 22, 1773, and circulated in several colonies. Its full name was the *Connecticut, New Jersey, Hudson's River and Quebec Weekly Advertiser*. Rivington was forced to suspend publication in 1775 when patriots destroyed his press. Publication of the Tory newspaper was renewed in 1777 under the title *Rivington's Gazette*. The publication was finally suspended in 1783 when the British withdrew from New York.

road working days. The practice was feasible in rural America during the 19th century before the construction of modern roads for automobiles. Farmers in off-season used to work a certain number of days on improving the roads in lieu of paying the road tax in cash.

Robinson, Edwin Arlington (1869–1935). Poet. Born in Head Tide, Me., his problem of earning a living while trying to write was solved by Pres. T. Roosevelt, who reviewed his work in the *Outlook* (1905). Roosevelt helped him get a clerkship in the customs service in New York (1905–09). Continuing his career, the poet won wide recognition with *The Man Against the Sky* (1916). He won three Pulitzer Prizes for his works: *Collected Poems* (1921), *The Man Who Died Twice* (1924) and *Tristram* (1927).

Robinson-Patman Act (1936). Also known as the Federal Anti-Price Discrimination Act, the law was aimed at chain stores in interstate commerce that paid lower prices to producers because of large purchases. The Federal Trade Commission was authorized to abolish such price discrimination because it tended to promote monopoly and reduce competition by favoring chain stores.

Rockefeller, John Davison (1839–1937). Industrialist and philanthropist. Born in Richford, N.Y., he started in the oil refining business in Cleveland, O., in 1863. He formed the Standard Oil Co. of Ohio (1870) and came to dominate the American oil industry and the foreign oil market. He organized the Standard Oil trust (1882) and competed ruthlessly to gain absolute control of oil refining in the U.S.

The Standard of Ohio's trust agreement was dissolved by court order (1892). Standard Oil Co. of N.J. was formed (1899) as a holding company, but it was dissolved by the U.S. Supreme Court (1911). After 1897 Rockefeller was wholly occupied with the distribution of his vast fortune. Public opinion of him was changed by his philanthropies, which include the Rockefeller Institute for Medical Research (1901), the General Education Board (1902) and the Rockefeller Foundation (1913) "to promote the well-being of mankind throughout the world."

Roebling, John Augustus (1806–69). Engineer and industrialist. Born in Germany, he came to the U.S. in 1831. He established a factory in Pennsylvania manufacturing the first wire rope made in America (1841). Ranked as the greatest American bridge builder of the 19th century, he designed suspension bridges, including one at Niagara Falls, N.Y. (opened 1855). He suggested and made preliminary plans for the Brooklyn Bridge (1869) spanning the East River and connecting Brooklyn and Manhattan. The bridge was completed in 1883 by his son, Washington Augustus Roebling (1837–1926).

Rogers' Rangers. Commanded by Maj. Robert Rogers, a New Englander, the frontier Rangers were popular in both America and Britain because of their exploits during the French and Indian War. In 1758 they narrowly escaped extinction in the Battle on Snowshoes, at Rogers' Rock, Lake George, N.Y. In 1759 Rogers and his men wiped out a village of St. Francis Indians and later were sent to receive the surrender of the French posts on the Great Lakes (1760–61). In 1763 the Rangers joined in the expedition to crush Pontiac's Conspiracy.

roorback. The name is given to a fictitious story or forged report circulated to injure a candidate on the eve of an election when refutation is difficult if not impossible. The roorback lie receives its name from a story published in 1844 to injure the reputation of James K. Polk, the Democratic candidate for President and a slaveholder. Just before the election the *Ithaca* (N.Y.) *Chronicle* printed what was supposed to be an extract from *A Tour Through the Western and Southern States*, by Baron Roorback. Baron Roorback did not exist and the story that Polk had purchased 43 slaves and branded his initials into their skins was false.

Roosevelt, Anna Eleanor (1884–1962). Lecturer and writer. Born in New York City, a niece of Theodore Roosevelt and a distant cousin of Franklin D. Roosevelt, she was more than "first lady" of the land during F.D.R.'s Presidency (1933–45). Both during and after her husband's death, she worked for social betterment as a lecturer, newspaper columnist ("My Day"), worldwide traveler and author. A U.S. delegate to the UN (1945, 1949–52, 1961–62), she was made chairman of the Commission on Human Rights (1946). Her books include *This Is My Story* (1937), *This I Remember* (1949), *On My Own* (1958), *Autobiography* (1961).

Roosevelt, Franklin Delano (1882–1945). Thirty-second

President of the U.S. (1933–45). Born in Hyde Park, N.Y., he was graduated from Harvard (1904). He was the first President to be reelected for a third term. He served as Democratic governor of New York (1929–33). His legislative reform program was known collectively as the New Deal. He led the nation during World War II, and joined with Churchill (1941) to draw up the Atlantic Charter.

Roosevelt, Theodore (1858–1919). Twenty-sixth President of the U.S. Born in New York City, he was graduated from Harvard (1880). He was Republican governor of New York (1899–1900). Vice-President in 1901, he succeeded to the Presidency on the death of McKinley (Sept. 14, 1901). Elected to the Presidency in 1904, he thus served from 1901 to 1909. The high points of his administration included construction of the Panama Canal, ending the Russo-Japanese War, curbing trusts and conserving natural resources.

Roosevelt Corollary (1904). When the Dominican Republic failed to pay its debts and there was danger of its occupation by foreign powers, Pres. T. Roosevelt expanded the Monroe Doctrine.

Roosevelt intervened to obtain payment of the debts. He explained to Congress that adherence to the Monroe Doctrine forced the U.S. "to the exercise of an international police power" where nations in the Western Hemisphere could not keep order or meet their obligations.

Other instances in which the Roosevelt Corollary was applied include intervention in Nicaragua (1909), Haiti (1915), again the Dominican Republic (1916) and again Nicaragua (1926–27). This policy of forcible intervention aroused Latin American resentment. The practice was repudiated by Pres. F. D. Roosevelt's "Good Neighbor Policy" (1933).

Root, Elihu (1845–1937). Statesman. Born in Clinton, N.Y., he was acknowledged as leader of the American Bar. He was Sec. of War (1899–1904) in Pres. McKinley's and Roosevelt's administrations and Sec. of State (1905–09) under Roosevelt. He was counsel for the U.S. in the North Atlantic Fisheries Arbitration (1910). He was awarded the Nobel Peace Prize (1912) for strengthening friendly relations between U.S. and South American countries and U.S. and Japan. He served as senator from New York (1909–15). His position in the League of Nations fight was that the treaty should be accepted with reservations. He helped frame the statute for the Permanent Court of International Justice and devised a formula (1929) to permit U.S. entry into the World Court.

Root Formula. Opposition of the U.S. Senate to membership in the World Court caused Elihu

Root, jurist and diplomat, to offer a compromise in 1929 whereby the Court would not without U.S. consent render an advisory opinion touching any dispute to which the U.S. was a party. Although Court members agreed, isolationist sentiment in the Senate continued to block ratification.

Root-Takahira Agreement (Nov. 30, 1908). In an exchange of notes between Sec. of State Root and the Japanese ambassador in Washington, both powers agreed to accept the status quo in the Pacific, to respect each other's territorial possessions in that region (e.g., Philippines, Hawaii, Formosa), to uphold the Open Door in China and to support by peaceful means the "independence and integrity of China. . . ."

The Agreement relieved the growing tension between the U.S. and Japan. It was regarded favorably in Europe, but it displeased the Chinese who had not been consulted. Some critics charged that Pres. T. Roosevelt had in effect given the Japanese a free hand in Manchuria.

Rosa Americana. The name was applied to coins issued in 1722 by Great Britain for America. They were also called Wood's money after their manufacturer, William Wood. The coins were of mixed metal resembling brass and in twopence, pence and halfpence pieces. The obverse was stamped with a laureated head of George I; the reverse with a double rose from which projected five barbed points and the legend, "Rosa Americana Utile Dulci, 1722."

Rosenberg Case. In an espionage case Julius Rosenberg and his wife Ethel, native New Yorkers, were executed at Sing Sing (N.Y.), June 19, 1953, after having been found guilty in a federal court (Apr. 5, 1951) of giving information on the atom bomb to Soviet agents. Their trial received international attention as an aspect of the embittered relations between the U.S. and Soviet Union during the cold war.

Roth v. U.S. (1957). The first time the U.S. Supreme Court was called upon to review the constitutionality of obscenity measures, it sustained convictions under the federal postal obscenity law and a California statute.

The test of obscenity for the Court was "Whether to the average persons, applying contemporary community standards, the dominant theme of the material taken as a whole appeals to prurient interests." The Court standard for obscenity required that the material be "patently offensive" and "utterly without redeeming social value." It declared that obscenity, as distinguished from ideas having even the slightest redeeming social importance, is not within the area of constitutionally protected freedom of speech or press.

In the Ginzburg Case (1966) the Court upheld the obscenity conviction of Ralph Ginzburg, publisher of *Eros* and other erotic literature, and decided that "titillating" advertising could be one factor in proving that advertised material was obscene.

In the Mishkin Case (1966) the Court affirmed the conviction of Edward Mishkin on charges of publishing material admitted to be "sadistic and masochistic." The Court denounced "those who would make a business of pandering to the widespread weakness for titillation by pornography."

In the Fanny Hill Case (1966) the Court reversed a Massachusetts ruling because it had admitted that the book, *Fanny Hill* (*John Cleland's Memoirs of a Woman of Pleasure*), had a "modicum of literary and historical value." It was emphasized by the Court that under the Roth test, a publication must be utterly without redeeming social value.

Rough Riders. The charge up San Juan Hill by the Rough Riders, led by Theodore Roosevelt, July 1, 1898, was dramatized in the press and in Roosevelt's book *The Rough Riders* (1899).

The formal name for the unit in the Spanish-American War was the First Volunteer Cavalry Regiment, but the horses were left behind in Florida when only part of the Regiment embarked for Cuba. The men were recruited largely from western cattle ranges. Roosevelt had done some ranching in the Dakota Territory, 1884–86, and had an affinity for the rough life of the men whom he led. The Regiment was at first commanded by Col. Leonard Wood.

Rowland, Henry Augustus (1848–1901). Physicist. Born in Honesdale, Pa., he became the first professor of physics at Johns Hopkins Univ. (1875–1901). His findings "On Magnetic Permeability, and the Maximum of Magnetism of Iron, Steel, and Nickel" (*Philosophical Magazine*, Aug. 1873) were the starting point for calculations for the design of dynamos and transformers. He invented the concave grating for the spectroscope and determined the mechanical equivalent of heat and of the ohm. He was consultant for the installation of equipment at the Niagara Falls power plant.

Royal African Company. Organized in 1672 in England, the trading company was granted a monopoly of the African slave trade. It profited immensely from the sale of slaves to English planters in the West Indies until independent merchants, including those from Rhode Island, were allowed to compete. The company was dissolved in 1750.

royal colony. By 1776 all of the 13 Colonies except Connecticut, Rhode Island, Pennsylvania and Maryland had become royal colonies; that is, they were directed by officials appointed by the King.

The King appointed a governor, judges and other officials and thus had great control over the executive and judicial branches of the colonial governments. The colonists, however, elected their own legislatures and these retained considerable control over the governor because they paid his salary and levied taxes.

After 1760, to check the growing independence of the colonies, the Crown paid the governors' salaries out of taxes raised in the royal provinces.

royal disallowance. The power of the Privy Council and the Board of Trade, in England, to disallow colonial laws applied to all the colonies except Connecticut and Rhode Island. A colonial act might be disallowed (voided) on the ground that it was contrary to a parliamentary statute, a colonial charter or a governor's instructions.

The few colonial laws that were disallowed were usually laws that inflated colonial currency, discriminated against English trade, fostered colonial manufactures or usurped the powers of the royal governors.

Royce, Josiah (1855–1916). Philosopher and educator. Born in Grass Valley, Calif., he was granted a Ph.D. by Johns Hopkins (1878). He taught philosophy at Harvard for 34 years (1882–1916; professor from 1892). During his early career he was greatly influenced by William James, but later varied from him in matter and doctrine. After James' death (1910), Royce was the most influential American philosopher of his day and the leading exponent of post-Kantian idealism, emphasizing individuality and will rather than intellect. His philosophical writings include *The Religious Aspect of Philosophy* (1885) and *The Conception of God* (1897). *The World and the Individual* (1900, 1901) is the most important of his systematic works.

"rugged individualism." The term was used by Herbert Hoover during his campaign for President in 1928 and his period in office. "The man who builds a factory" or starts any business was regarded by Hoover as a "rugged individualist." He believed that if the government aided the "rugged individualist" it would benefit the entire nation. He did not want government to interfere with the economic freedom of businessmen for to do so might endanger the free enterprise system.

"rule of reason." Pres. Theodore Roosevelt's attitude toward trusts was that they should be "not prohibited but supervised, and within reasonable limits, controlled." This approach was accepted by the Supreme Court in *Standard Oil Co. v. U.S.* (1911). The Court announced that only "unreasonable . . . restraint of trade" was in violation of the Sherman Antitrust

Act. According to this "rule of reason" a trust was not bad just because it was big. It was bad if it practiced monopolistic policies that harmed the public.

Rule of 1756. British policy established by British courts when the French opened their colonial ports to the neutral Dutch at the beginning of the Seven Years' War stated that trade not open in time of peace could not be permitted in time of war. Ships belonging to the Netherlands were seized under this British rule.

The rule was invoked by Britain in 1805 when the French opened their West Indies to American trade to break the British blockade which was starving the inhabitants. Britain in return seized American ships trading with the French colonies.

Rules Committee. Bills reported out of other committees come up before the powerful Rules Committee of the House of Representatives. Its main function is to decide whether or not to grant special consideration to bills which otherwise might be long delayed on various calendars of the House. When the Rules Committee recommends a special rule to the House, it is usually adopted and the bill to which it refers is considered under the provisions of that rule.

"rum, Romanism, and rebellion." The slogan contributed to the defeat of James G. Blaine,

Republican candidate for President in 1884. Reverend Samuel D. Burchard, speaking on behalf of Blaine's candidacy at a dinner in New York, coined the phrase to describe the Democratic party's antecedents. When Blaine failed to rebuke the minister, a Democratic reporter was quick to inform Irish voters. Blaine lost New York by a narrow margin and with it the Presidency.

Rural Electrification Administration (REA). The REA was created by an executive order of Pres. Roosevelt in 1935 and was provided for in the Rural Electrification Act (1936). The agency makes loans, preferably to public bodies and cooperatives, to bring electric services to rural areas.

rural free delivery. In 1896 the postal service was extended to permit delivery of mail to farmers in rural areas. By 1900 the number of Americans served by RFD was 185,000; by 1924 the number rose to 6,500,000. The delivery of newspapers reduced the isolation of farmers in out-of-the-way regions while the service enabled large mail order houses to reach new patrons.

Rush, Benjamin (1745–1813). Physician and Revolutionary leader. Born in Byberry, Pa., he was granted an M.D. by the Univ. of Edinburgh (1768). He practiced in Philadelphia and published the first American chemistry text, *A Syllabus of a*

Course of Lectures on Chemistry (1770). A member of the Continental Congress (1776–77), he was a signer of the Declaration of Independence. He was a surgeon in the Continental army (1777–78), and established the first free dispensary in U.S. (1786). He was Treasurer of the U.S. Mint (1797–1813). Believing that diseases were due to spasm in the blood vessels, his practice of bloodletting is believed to have added to the mortality rate in Philadelphia's yellow fever epidemic (1783). He was the first American to write on *cholera infantum* and the first to recognize focal infection in the teeth. A pioneer in psychiatry, he wrote *Medical Inquiries and Observations upon the Diseases of the Mind* (1812).

Rush-Bagot Agreement (1817). The U.S. and Britain agreed that no more than four small armed vessels were to be maintained on the Great Lakes by each country. The treaty was negotiated by Acting Sec. of State Richard Rush and the British representative in Washington, Charles Bagot. The principle of demilitarization of the Great Lakes was extended to the land and resulted in an undefended frontier line of 3,000 miles.

Russell, Majors, and Waddell. In the late 1850's the famous partnership was engaged in carrying government supplies from Fort Leavenworth, Kan., to western outposts. The company employed thousands of wagons, mules and oxen. It also operated the Pony Express, 1860–61, before getting into financial difficulties which caused dissolution of the business in 1862.

Rutgers University. Founded in 1766, under the auspices of the Dutch Reformed Church, as Queen's College, it was renamed Rutgers, in 1825, in honor of its benefactor Col. Henry Rutgers, a landed proprietor. In 1864 it was designated by the legislature as the land-grant college of New Jersey, and in 1917 the land-grant college was designated as the state university.

Now the State University of New Jersey, Rutgers College, oldest division of the university, is located in New Brunswick. Various branches of the university are located in Newark and Camden; the Evening Division holds classes in each city.

Douglass College, founded in 1918 as the New Jersey College for Women, is the women's college of Rutgers.

Ryder, Albert Pinkham (1847–1917). Painter. Born in New Bedford, Mass., he lived principally in New York City. His small marines are most representative of his limited output of a rare kind of poetic painting. He also excelled in landscapes and figure paintings. His *Toilers of the Sea, The Curfew Hour* and *The Bridge* hang in the Metropolitan Museum of Art (N.Y.C.).

Ryswick, Treaty of (Sept. 30, 1697). The Treaty settled King William's War (1689–97) in North America (known as the War of the League of Augsburg in its European phase). The English and French had clashed in the region of Hudson Bay. Under the Treaty the *status quo ante* was restored and a commission was to settle rival claims. It met in 1699 but reached no agreement.

Ryukyu Islands. The western Pacific islands lying between southern Japan and Taiwan (Formosa) were annexed in 1874 by Japan. Okinawa, largest of the group, became a valuable Japanese base in World War II until taken by the U.S. in 1945.

Administration of the islands was vested in the U.S. by the Japanese peace treaty (1951), but Japan retains "residual sovereignty." The Ryukyus are an important American base. Naha, Okinawa, is the seat of the U.S. civil administration headed by a High Commissioner responsible to the Secretary of Defense. The local Ryukyuan government has a popularly elected legislature, an appointive chief executive and an independent judiciary.

S

Sacco-Vanzetti Case. Two alien Italian anarchists, Nicola Sacco and Bartolomeo Vanzetti, were accused of murdering a paymaster and his guard in a robbery of a shoe company in South Braintree, Mass., in 1920. They were found guilty in 1921 and sentenced to death. A worldwide clamor against the trial developed as the feeling grew that the men were being convicted for their radical views rather than any alleged crime.

Execution was delayed by appeals until 1927 when both men were electrocuted. Decades later the guilt or innocence of Sacco and Vanzetti is still debated. The trial is recalled by some as an example of the lengths to which organized society in a mood of intolerance can go.

Sackett's Harbor, battles of. The American naval base where ships were being constructed during the War of 1812 was attacked twice. The base, located on Lake Ontario, N.Y., successfully resisted a British attack, July 19, 1812. The second operation, May 27–29, 1813, was a near victory for England. Six British vessels and 40 bateaux with 1,000 troops aboard, under Gov. Gen. Sir George Prevost, attacked the militia and regulars under Gen. Jacob Brown. The New York militia were scattered initially, but were aided by the accurate fire of the regulars, forcing the British to retreat to their ships. When capture had seemed certain, the Americans burned about $500,000 worth of supplies.

Sacs. The tribe of Algonquian linguistic stock lived near the Detroit River. They were driven beyond Lake Michigan by the Iroquois and settled near Green Bay, where they subsequently joined with the Foxes. They aided Pontiac and during the Revolution supported the British. In 1812 the Rock River Sacs aided Great Britain. In 1804 and 1816 they ceded their lands to the U.S. Their later history is that of the Foxes.

"sage of Monticello." The reference was made to Thomas Jefferson after his retirement from the Presidency in 1809 to Monticello, in Virginia. Jefferson continued his active life counseling his Republican successors and maintaining a voluminous correspondence with friends in America and Europe until his death in 1826.

Saint-Gaudens, Augustus (1848 –1907). Sculptor. Born in Dublin, Ireland, of French and Irish descent, he was brought to the U.S. as an infant. He studied in France and Italy before establishing studios in New York (1873–85) and Cornish, N.H. (1885–1907). A gift for portraiture and imaginative design is attested to by his *Hiawatha* in marble (Saratoga, N.Y.) and *Silence* (Masonic Temple, N.Y.C.). His full-length *Admiral Farragut* (unveiled 1881) was a landmark in the history of American sculpture. In work characterized by simplicity and dramatic power, he interpreted major American historical figures: *Sherman* (N.Y.C.) a great equestrian monument; and two statues of Lincoln (Chicago, Ill.).

St. Lawrence Seaway. In 1954 the U.S. and Canada, after some 50 years of negotiation, agreed to the joint construction of a seaway that would make it possible for oceangoing vessels to proceed from the Atlantic to American and Canadian ports on the Great Lakes. During this time, and for many years before, improvements had been made in cutting canals and in deepening channels. Finally in 1959 the Seaway, with a minimum depth of 27 feet, was opened for a length of 2,342 miles from the Atlantic to Duluth, at the western end of Lake Superior. The new locks and linking channels now accommodate all but the largest ocean carriers. The Seaway is the largest inland navigation system on the continent. It is part of a combined navigation - power project.

St. Louis *Post-Dispatch*. Joseph Pulitzer founded the paper in 1878 by combining the St. Louis *Dispatch*, founded in 1864, with the *Post*, founded in 1875. John A. Dillon, who had owned the *Post*, remained as Pulitzer's partner for about a year until John A. Cockerill, an experienced newspaperman, became Pulitzer's chief editorial assistant. Under Pulitzer the *Post-Dispatch* sought to improve city government. It became St. Louis' leading evening paper, reaching a circulation of 100,000 in 1903.

The St. Louis *Star-Times* (a consolidation of the *Star* and *Times* in 1932) was absorbed by the *Post-Dispatch* in 1951. Later, the *Post-Dispatch* and *Globe-Democrat* combined their mechanical operations while remaining highly competitive newspapers. Circulation of the *Post-Dispatch* in 1966 was 364,118 for the daily evening edition; 593,669 for the Sunday paper.

St. Mihiel, battle of (Sept. 12–16, 1918). The salient, or bulge, fn the Allied lines across the Meuse River below Verdun was held by the Germans from the beginning of their initial offensive in 1914. The task of reducing the salient was given to the American First Army under Gen. Pershing (with one French corps attached). This was its first operation as an independent army and it proved its capacity for planning and executing a major military undertaking. The American Army of 550,000 men pinched off the tip of the salient and captured 16,000 prisoners and 443 guns. U.S. casualties were about 7,000.

Salary Grab Act (1873). Congress raised salaries of its own members 50% from $5,000 to $7,500 and made the increase retroactive for two years, thus giving each member of Congress a $5,000 windfall. Increases were also provided for the President, Cabinet members and the Supreme Court. The Act was considered another scandal in the Grant administration.

Salk vaccine. The immunizing agent against poliomyelitis was developed under the direction of Dr. Jonas E. Salk of the University of Pittsburgh. Beginning in 1954 it was widely used to effectively combat infantile paralysis.

"salutary neglect." The term describes Britain's old colonial policy toward the American colonies during most of the 17th and 18th centuries. The laws of Parliament, especially those regulating colonial trade, were weakly enforced. The practice was in large part due to the mother country's desire to keep the loyalty of the colonies during the long wars with France. When France was finally driven from North America at the end of the French and Indian War (1754-63), Britain sought to raise revenue in the colonies and embarked upon a policy of strict law enforcement. By this time, however, a spirit of independence had developed in the colonies and the new British policy met with increasingly bitter resistance culminating in the American Revolution.

Salvation Army. The work in the U.S. of the international philanthropic and religious organization began in 1880 when a branch was established in Pennsylvania. Its military features developed when evangelists at seaports in England came to be called "captain." The London founder, William Booth, a Methodist minister, held the title "General." Officers are prepared in training colleges. A candidate for membership must sign "Articles of War," pledging himself to abstain from liquor and harmful drugs and to live a Christian and humane life. The official publication is *The War Cry*.

The Army attacks the "fortresses of sin" and offers practical help to those not likely to be reached by other religious bodies. It operates settlements, hotels, homes and hospitals.

No religious creed is required, but members are generally in agreement with beliefs of the Evangelical churches. Funds are raised by voluntary contributions.

Samoa. The archipelago in the South Pacific is 2,300 miles southwest of Hawaii. American Samoa became a possession of the U.S. by agreement with Germany and Great Britain (Dec. 2, 1899). It seemed a logical addition to the far-flung empire acquired by the U.S. at the end of the Spanish-American War. The U.S. obtained the seven eastern islands of the Samoan group, including Tutuila, with the harbor of Pago Pago, on which the U.S. had kept an eye since Pres. Grant's day.

In 1878 the U.S. had made an agreement with a Samoan chief, Le Mamea, who came to Washington, which provided that in return for the rights to a naval station at Pago Pago the U.S. would employ its good offices to adjust any differences between Samoa and a foreign power. Differences mounted and war vessels of the three interested powers (U.S., Germany, Great Britain) converged in Apia Harbor where they experienced a disastrous hurricane (Mar. 16, 1889). In the meantime, a conference at Berlin, concluded on June 14, 1889, established a condominium or three-power protectorate over Samoa. Subsequent dissension led to the division of Samoa in 1899.

Formerly under the jurisdiction of the Navy, American Samoa is administered by the Department of Interior which appoints a governor. It has a bicameral legislature. The residents, who are of Polynesian origin, are U.S. nationals.

Western Samoa, lost by Germany in World War I, became a New Zealand mandate and UN trusteeship. It achieved independence, Jan. 1, 1962. The rest of the islands constitute American Samoa.

Sandburg, Carl (1878–1967). Author. Born in Galesburg, Ill., he crowded into his verse much of the turbulent life he had observed in the small prairie towns of Illinois and in the raw metropolis of Chicago. He first gained a reputation with his *Chicago Poems* (1915) written in broken free-verse rhythms. He turned to journalism and by 1919 had become a feature writer for the *Chicago Daily News*. His poetic volumes include *Cornhuskers* (1918), *Smoke and Steel* (1920), *Slabs of the Sunburnt West* (1922). He was awarded the Pulitzer Prize (1951) for his *Collected Poems*. He was also the author of a distinguished multivolume biography of Lincoln: *The Prairie Years* (1926), followed by *The War Years*, for which he was awarded the Pulitzer Prize (1939) for History.

Sand Creek massacre (1864). Col. J. M. Chivington, commander of the Colorado militia, leading a thousand volunteers, fell upon a camp of Cheyennes and Arapahoes on a reservation at Sand Creek and butchered about 200 of them brutally—men, women and even children. The attack was in retaliation for the raiding and pillaging by the Indians when the federal government broke an agreement with them.

Sane Nuclear Policy, National Committee for (SANE). The original purpose of the organization, set up in 1957, was to build public sentiment for a nuclear test ban treaty. Since that goal was achieved in 1963, SANE has broadened its focus to worldwide disarmament.

San Francisco, Calif., earthquake (Apr. 18, 1906). The disaster, including the fire which followed, resulted in 452 deaths and losses of $350,000,000. Other great earthquakes in the U.S. were felt most severely in New Madrid, Mo., Dec. 16, 1811 and Alaska, Mar. 28, 1964.

Recent quakes have been measured by the Richter scale, named for Charles F. Richter of California Institute of Technology. It is a measure of the energy of the earthquake at its source. The scale is logarithmic so that a recording of 7 signifies a disturbance 10 times as powerful as a recording of 6, and so forth. The Good Friday earthquake in Alaska, the most powerful ever recorded in North America, was put at 8.3.

San Francisco Chronicle. Founded in 1865 as the *San Francisco Dramatic Chronicle*, the word *Dramatic* was dropped from its title in 1868. Within three years, the brothers who founded it, Charles and Michael H. De Young, had changed the paper from a free theater-program sheet to a full-fledged newspaper at two cents a copy. By 1900 the *Chronicle* had become the city's leading newspaper. It led in "boosting California" and in opposition to political corruption. M. H. De Young, active in Republican party politics, lent the paper's support to the high protective tariff.

Circulation of the *Chronicle* in 1966 was 486,330 for the daily morning edition. On Sept. 8, 1965, three San Francisco dailies merged—the *Examiner* (founded 1865), the *News-Call Bulletin* (the *Call* founded 1856; the *Bulletin*, 1855) and the *Chronicle*. The former *Examiner* now publishes six days as an afternoon paper; the *Chronicle* publishes six days in the morning. The Sunday paper is called the *Examiner and Chronicle* (1966 circulation, 690,230).

San Ildefonso, Treaty of (1800). By this Treaty Spain transferred the vast Louisiana Territory she received from France by the Treaty of Fontainebleau (1762) back to France.

In 1802 Spanish officials, who had not yet turned over their posts to the French, withdrew permission from the Americans to deposit their goods in New Orleans. Spain had granted American citizens this right by the Treaty of San Lorenzo (1795). Westerners who had been shipping their produce down the Mississippi to New Orleans were furious at the economic blockade which prevented shipment of farm goods to the East and Europe.

Jefferson sought a solution by opening negotiations with Napoleon for the purchase of New Orleans. Although he regarded France as a "natural friend" of the U.S., he said neither she nor anyone else could be permitted perpetual possession of New Orleans.

When Napoleon's dream of empire in the New World was shattered, he sold the entire Louisiana Territory, including New Orleans, to the U.S. (1803).

San Jacinto Creek, battle of (Apr. 21, 1836). In the Texas Revolution, Gen. Sam Houston surprised and decimated a superior Mexican force. Santa Anna himself was captured and signed a treaty guaranteeing the independence of Texas. The treaty was repudiated by the Mexican Congress, but this did not change the fact of Texan independence.

San Juan Hill. The vantage point overlooking Santiago, Cuba, was stormed and taken by American forces under Col. Theodore Roosevelt, July 1, 1898, during the Spanish-Ameri-

can War. Admiral Cervera, rather than risk an artillery attack on his fleet from the high ground held by the Americans, sailed from the harbor to his destruction. He was decisively defeated by the American fleet under Rear-Admirals Sampson and Schley.

San Marco. The U.S.-Italy cooperative satellite project of the mid - 1960's successfully launched a satellite to measure atmospheric density and ionosphere propagation. The satellite was placed in an equatorial orbit.

Santa Fe Trail. A trade route in the early 19th century, the Trail began at Independence, Mo., and ended nearly 800 miles to the west and southwest, in Santa Fe, N.M. Wagons moving westward were crammed with manufactured goods needed in Santa Fe. On the way back they carried buffalo robes, beaver skins and silver from Mexico. The growth of railroads in the West ended the usefulness of wagon trains.

Santiago, battle of. In the Spanish-American War, Gen. William Shafter drove the Spanish army into Santiago in two actions, July 1–2, 1898. On July 3, the Spanish fleet comprised of the *Cristobal Colon, Vizcaya, Almirante Oquendo, Maria Teresa, Furor* and *Pluton*, under Admiral Cervera, attempted to escape from the harbor and was met and destroyed by the American fleet comprised of the

Brooklyn, Oregon, Texas, Iowa, Indiana, Gloucester, Vixen and New York under Rear-Admirals William Sampson and Winfield Schley. The Spanish lost about 600 killed and 1,700 prisoners; Americans, one killed. Santiago surrendered to Shafter, July 17. The decisiveness of American naval power commanded respect in Europe.

Sarah Constant. The 100-ton vessel was the flagship of the Jamestown settlers, 1607. The crossing from England to Virginia took over four months (Dec. 20, 1606, to Apr. 26, 1607). Two other vessels making the crossing were the *Goodspeed* and *Discovery.* The little fleet was under the command of Christopher Newport.

Saratoga, surrender at (Oct. 17, 1777). The defeat of British forces under Gen. Burgoyne was a "turning point" in the Revolutionary War. It convinced the French that they could come to the aid of the U.S. with a good chance for victory.

Burgoyne had marched south from Canada expecting to meet Gen. Howe's forces coming up from New York City. Howe, however, moved south to Philadelphia. Burgoyne marching through rugged country was decimated by attacks of militia, Indians and the regular Continental army forces under Gen. Horatio Gates.

Only 5,000 of his battered army were left when Burgoyne surrendered to superior patriot forces at Saratoga.

Sargent, John Singer (1856–1925). Painter. Born in Florence, Italy, of American parentage, he painted in Italy, Spain and England. He also went on frequent visits to the U.S. and opened a studio in Boston (1903). His portraits include *Carmencita,* the Wertheimer family, Theodore Roosevelt, Henry James and Woodrow Wilson. Among his best-known works are the mural decorations in the Boston Public Library. The masterpieces of his later years are the water colors *Melon Boats* and *White Ships.*

Satanta's Wars. Satanta, a noted speaker and warrior, led his Kiowa tribe in raids into Texas and other states in the Southwest during the early 1870's. He sought to resist the advance of the buffalo hunters. After capture he killed himself in the Texas state prison, 1878.

satellite. Since 1957 the designation includes man-made bodies placed in orbit around the earth or around any other celestial body. In revolving about the earth, an artificial satellite must obey the same laws that the natural moon does, and artificial bodies circling the sun must obey the natural laws that rule the planets.

Saturn I. First launched successfully Oct. 27, 1961, it is part of a family of launch vehicles that NASA developed for its exploration of the moon (Project Apollo).

Sauk Indians. Of Algonquian linguistic stock, and allied with the Fox, they warred against the French early in the 18th century. One of their warriors, Black Hawk, was a leader in the war (1832) with the U.S. The Sauks were forced to settle on reservations in Kansas and Oklahoma.

Sault-Ste. Marie Ship Canal. Popularly known as the Soo Canal, the canal bypasses St. Mary's Falls which blocked the passage of ships between Lake Superior and Lake Huron. It was built on the U.S. side by Michigan with federal aid. Opened in 1885, it quickly became a valuable link between the iron ore of the Marquette Range in northern Michigan and the steel mills of Pittsburgh, Cleveland and Chicago.

The Sault-Ste. Marie Ship Canal was ceded by the state of Michigan to the U.S. in 1881, four years before its completion and its operation was taken over by the War Department (now Department of Defense). In 1895 the Canadian canal with one large lock was completed. Both the American and Canadian canals are free and their combined commerce is greater in tonnage than that of any other canal in the world. The principal products carried through the canals are iron ore, coal, copper, oil and wheat.

The canal, along with the Canadian-built Welland Canal, which bypassed Niagara Falls, helped win for the Great Lakes the struggle for western commerce. Rivalry with the Mississippi River system was carried on for the 15 years before the Civil War and paralleled the struggle between the free and slave states for control of the West itself.

Savannah. Built in New York and purchased by a Savannah, Ga., shipping company, the steamship was the first to cross the Atlantic. The crossing in 1819 took 29 days.

Its name was given to the world's first atomic-powered merchant ship, the *N.S.* (nuclear ship) *Savannah,* launched in 1959 at the Camden, N.J. yard of the New York Shipbuilding Corp.

"save the last bullet for yourself, pardner." The advice was customarily given by soldiers and frontiersmen who fought the Indians in the Great Plains during the 19th century. It was commonly believed that plains Indians practiced sadistic torture of captives. However, researchers in their ethnology have shown that captive torture was not traditional among the people of the plains as it was among the Indians of the eastern forest.

Indians, for their part, regarded hanging as a most barbarous sort of death. One Indian was said to have cut off his own feet and one of his hands to escape from the shackles in which he had been chained, fearing that he was going to be hanged.

Saybrook Platform. To strengthen the clergy a plan of church organization called Consociation was adopted by a synod meeting at Saybrook, Conn., 1708. Each church joined a county association and the congregation so affiliated became the established church. A uniform doctrine and discipline were imposed on all the church members by the ministers and important laymen formed as a council in the association. This was a change from the congregationalism fostered by the Cambridge Platform (1648) under which individual churches retained a great deal of authority and were merely advised by the synods.

scalawags. The name was given to southerners who cooperated with ex-slaves in establishing a new order in the South during the Reconstruction era. They joined with the freedmen in conducting the Reconstruction governments in the states which had been readmitted to the Union after the Civil War.

The motives of scalawags and carpetbaggers were mixed. Some were adventurers and opportunists. Others were sincere in wanting to help the newly freed Negroes and cooperated with the Congress in carrying forward its Reconstruction plan.

Schechter Corp. v. U.S. (1935). The U.S. Supreme Court declared the National Industrial Recovery Act to be unconstitutional. The Court held that the act improperly delegated legislative power to the President, thereby violating the fundamental doctrine of the separation of powers. It ruled also that the Act went beyond the delegated powers of Congress by extending codes of competition to local business transactions; therefore, the Act was no longer concerned solely with interstate commerce.

The Act sought to combat the Great Depression by stimulating business and improving working conditions through the establishment of "codes of fair competition" in various industries. The codes usually limited output, required the filing of fixed price schedules, prohibited false advertising, price discrimination and similar excesses in competitive practices. The codes were drawn up by representatives of the industries and government officials. The government selected the Schechter Case (also known as the "Sick Chicken Case") arising under the poultry code, as the one on which to stake the constitutional fortunes of the National Recovery Administration. The effect of the Supreme Court decision was to cause the codes to crumble and end the NRA.

Schenck v. U.S. (1919). The U.S. Supreme Court upheld the conviction of Schenck, a socialist, for obstructing the wartime draft. The decision sustained the Espionage Act (1917) punishing anyone who interfered with the draft or attempted to encourage disloyalty. Justice Holmes while upholding the constitutionality of the Act sought to limit the restriction of free speech by stating that it might be curtailed only when there was a "clear and present danger" to the government. "The most stringent protection of free speech," he wrote, "would not protect a man in falsely shouting fire in a theatre and causing a panic."

Schurz, Carl (1829–1906). Statesman. Born near Cologne, Germany, he was active in the revolutionary movement in Prussia (1848–49) before emigrating to the U.S. (1852). Drawn into Republican politics in Wisconsin, he supported Lincoln for the Presidency. He attained the rank of major-general in the Union Army and saw action on various fronts. In the post-Civil War period, he was a journalist (1865–68) and represented Missouri in the U.S. Senate (1869–75). He attacked political corruption in the Grant administration and sought to establish a civil service merit system. A Liberal Republican, he supported the presidential candidacies of Greeley (1872) and Hayes (1876) and was Secretary of the Interior (1877–81) in Hayes' cabinet. He was a co-editor of the N.Y. *Evening Post* and the *Nation* (1881–83) and wrote editorials for *Harper's Weekly* (1892–98). He opposed the Spanish-American War and U.S. overseas expansionism.

Scioto Company. The enterprise was organized in New York in 1787 to take over from the Ohio

Company an option on some five million acres of land between the Ohio and Scioto rivers, north and west of the 1,500,000 acres owned by the Ohio Company. The Scioto Co. sold shares in France and about 600 Frenchmen sailed to America and settled in Gallipolis, O., on land which they thought was owned by the Scioto Co. but which was actually Ohio Co. land. The Scioto Co. was unable to raise the purchase price for the land it held on option and the company collapsed in the financial panic of 1792.

Scopes trial (1925). In what has been called the "monkey trial" a biology teacher in Tennessee was found guilty of violating a state law which prohibited the teaching of evolution in the schools. He was fined but the fine was set aside on a technicality by the state supreme court.

The clash between fundamentalist Christian sects and modernists aroused worldwide attention. Scopes was defended by the nationally prominent lawyers, Clarence Darrow, Dudley Field Malone and Arthur Garfield Hays. The associate counsel for the state was William Jennings Bryan, an ardent fundamentalist.

The fundamentalists were shaken by inconsistencies in their position developed under cross-examination. Modernists were aroused to more vigorous defense against fundamentalist attacks on science and education.

Score. For 30 days (from Dec. 18, 1958) transmission of the human voice from space was possible. Score, operated by chemical batteries of limited duration, relayed messages such as the President's Christmas message from ground stations.

Scotch-Irish. From the early part of the 18th century immigrants came to the American colonies from Ulster in Northern Ireland, to which they had emigrated from Scotland early in the 17th century. They left Ulster for America when Parliament, discriminating against them, excluded their meat, dairy products and woolens from England. Furthermore, as Presbyterians they resented paying taxes to support the Anglican Church.

In America they settled chiefly in Pennsylvania and the Carolinas and took easily to frontier life. They were active in politics and vigorously opposed to the mother country on the eve of the American Revolution.

Scout. The launch vehicle for U.S. spacecraft in the 1960's is planned for rocketing small satellites and probes. It can place a payload of about 220 pounds into a 300-mile orbit or can lift useful payloads as high as 4,000 miles in vertical probe experiments.

Scrooby group. The Pilgrims who settled at Plymouth in 1620 were English Separatists from Scrooby, a village in Nottinghamshire.

"scrub race." The expression was used to describe the presidential election of 1824 in which there were four major candidates. The candidates were not nominated by a congressional caucus as had been the custom. William H. Crawford of Georgia was put forward by a quasi-caucus; New England's candidate was John Q. Adams; Henry Clay was nominated by Kentucky, Louisiana, Missouri, Illinois and Ohio; and Andrew Jackson by Tennessee and other states.

Seaborg, Glenn Theodore (1912–   ). Chemist. Born in Ishpeming, Mich., he was granted a Ph.D. by the Univ. of California (1937) where he became a professor in 1945. He shared in the discovery of plutonium, the fuel for the atomic bomb, and he shared the Nobel Prize (1951) for Chemistry for work in the transuranic elements. In 1961 he became chairman of the Atomic Energy Commission.

sea dogs. The term is applied to sailors with long experience. It has been used to describe English navigators and explorers of the 16th and 17th centuries who preyed on Spanish gold ships and plundered the Spanish coasts of South America. A famous sea dog was Sir John Hawkins, or Hawkyns, who helped to defeat the Spanish Armada (1588). He was joint commander with Sir Martin Frobisher, another sea dog, on the Portuguese coast (1590), and second in command to yet another sea dog, Sir Francis Drake, on an expedition to the West Indies (1595).

Sealab. Experiments were performed in sea laboratories to see how well men can live and work underwater for extended periods of time. In one such experiment in 1965 American aquanauts, including U.S. Navy personnel, descended 205 feet below sea level off the coast of California. They lived within a steel cylinder in an artificial atmosphere consisting mainly of helium and worked outside the Sealab in a sharkproof chamber.

One of the goals of the experiment is to tap the enormous food reserves in the oceans and incalculable mineral wealth under them and thus relieve the strain increasing population has put on the resources of the land.

Seal of the U.S. On July 4, 1776, Congress appointed Benjamin Franklin, John Adams and Thomas Jefferson to prepare a device for the Great Seal of the U.S. A Great Seal was adopted, June 20, 1782, combining various designs of William Barton of Philadelphia and Sir John Prestwich, an English antiquarian.

The face of the Great Seal appears on the right-hand side of the back of every U.S. $1 bill. It shows an American eagle with wings and talons outstretched. The right talon holds an olive branch and the left a bundle of 13 arrows. The beak holds a ribbon on which is inscribed *E Pluribus Unum* (Out of Many, One), a reference to the union of the 13 states. Above the eagle's head is a circle containing 13 "pieces argent," or silver buttons.

The reverse side of the Seal appears on the left-hand side of the back of the $1 bill. It shows a pyramid with 13 steps, the base being marked MDCC-LXXVI (1776). Above the unfinished pyramid, there is a burst of light in which the apex of the pyramid appears as the Eternal Eye of God, capped by the words *Annuit Coeptis* (He Has Favored Our Undertaking). Beneath the base of the pyramid are the words *Novus Ordo Seclorum* (A New Order of the Ages).

The face of the Great Seal is now affixed chiefly to foreign affairs documents. It is kept by the Secretary of State.

secession. The right of secession was finally tested in 1860 when South Carolina seceded from the Union to be followed by the other southern states constituting the Confederate States of America during the Civil War.

The right of secession had been maintained from the early days of the United States. James Madison wrote that the Union was a compact of states. It followed that the states were sovereign and might nullify acts of Congress.

The first serious threat of secession was made when Federalist efforts to control criticism of the government caused Jefferson and Madison to formulate the Kentucky and Virginia Resolutions (1798). In their turn the Federalists threatened secession during the War of 1812 which they opposed. Another major threat of secession was ended when South Carolina withdrew its Ordinance of Nullification (1832) after the protective tariff to which it objected was modified. When secession finally did take place and precipitated the Civil War, southern convention delegates who opposed secession did so not because they questioned the right of secession but because they thought it was not a wise action to take at the time.

sectionalism. From the earliest days of the nation the East, South and West were often divided on issues where their economic interests were at stake. These differences had their origins in climate, geography and traditions. In general the South was opposed to the protective tariff, favored by the industrial East and acceptable to the West. Slavery did not become a major sectional issue until the Compromise of 1820. From this time until the end of the Civil War, slavery was defended by the South as vital to its economic and social structure. The South opposed a national bank as did the West. Most support for the first and second United

States Bank came from the East. Internal improvements at federal expense were favored by the East and West. These sectional differences were the subjects of vigorous debate in Congress and were sometimes compromised.

Sectionalism did not die with the Civil War. It has, however, been subordinated to nationalism as a major force in shaping federal policies.

Securities and Exchange Act (1934). An early New Deal reform measure set up an agency of the federal government known as the Securities and Exchange Commission (SEC) to supervise and regulate the issuance of new securities. Before any new stocks or bonds are placed on the market, the SEC requires the filing of full and accurate information on the financial condition and the plans of the issuing corporation. Everyone involved in the marketing of securities—issuers, underwriters and dealers—is under the scrutiny of the SEC. The agency also watches over the stock exchanges themselves and can move to forbid or correct practices which are not in the public interest.

Although the SEC and other government agencies have been effective in getting rid of some of the worst abuses of earlier days, it is still true that every purchaser of securities must look out for his own interests. The SEC does not say that any stock issue is actually worth the money at which it is bought or sold. Its basic purpose is to give the purchaser a chance to base his judgments on full and accurate information.

Sedition Act (1918). The law, amending the Espionage Act (1917), prescribed a fine of up to $10,000 and a prison term of 20 years for anyone who obstructed the sale of U.S. bonds, incited insubordination, discouraged recruiting or who would "wilfully utter, print, write or publish any disloyal, profane, scurrilous, or abusive language" that interfered with "prosecution of the war." Hundreds of persons were arrested and imprisoned for disloyalty under the Act.

segregation. The term is used to describe the practice of keeping the Negro and white races apart. In the Reconstruction period, southern states enacted Black Codes and individuals discriminated against Negroes who were denied equal privileges in the use of public facilities.

To counteract segregation Congress passed a series of Force Acts. The last of these, passed Mar. 1, 1875, made it a crime for one person to deprive another of equal accommodations at inns, theaters or public conveyances. The U.S. Supreme Court found the law to exceed the powers conferred on Congress by the 13th and 14th Amendments and hence to be an unlawful invasion of the powers reserved to the states by the 10th Amendment (Civil Rights Cases, 1883).

Segregation received further support from the U.S. Supreme Court in *Plessy v. Ferguson* (1896) and segregation continued not only in the South but in other parts of the nation.

The "separate but equal" doctrine in the *Plessy* case was overturned more than a half-century later in *Brown v. Board of Education.* Efforts to end various forms of discrimination were advanced by the Civil Rights laws of the 1960's.

selectmen. The chief officers of a New England town were selected at the town meeting and were responsible to it. The title is now used for officials given authority by state law to supervise local highways, assess property, issue licenses and carry on other duties.

self-governing colonies. There were three types of English colonies in the New World—royal, proprietary and chartered. The colonists preferred the chartered type because it came closest to permitting them to be self-governing. Charters granted by the British monarch permitted the founders of Massachusetts, Rhode Island and Connecticut virtual self-government. For many years they were almost independent of the English King and Parliament.

In these self-governing colonies, the colonists elected their own governor, usually for a year, so that they could dismiss him if they did not approve his policies.

Selma, Alabama. In an address to a joint session of Congress, Mar. 15, 1965, Pres. Johnson spoke of events in Selma, a town with a tradition of segregation, as "a turning point in man's unending search for freedom." He compared events in Selma with Lexington, Concord and Appomattox. The events to which the President referred occurred when Alabama state troopers, using clubs, whips and tear gas, assaulted civil rights demonstrators attempting to march to Montgomery as part of a voter registration drive, Mar. 7, 1965.

Demonstrations across the country dramatized the mounting pressure for action by the federal government. In a message to Congress, Pres. Johnson called for a federal law to enforce the 15th Amendment by striking down restrictions to voting in all elections—federal, state and local—"which have been used to deny Negroes the right to vote."

Seminole Wars (1816–18, 1835 –42). In the first of these wars Gen. Andrew Jackson crossed into Florida, Spanish-held territory, in pursuit of Seminoles who had scalped Americans. He defeated the Indians, burned a number of villages and executed two British subjects, Alexander Arbuthnot and Robert Ambrister, whom he believed to be inciting the Indians. An out-come of this action was the sale of Florida to the U.S.

Florida became a refuge for runaway slaves who sought asylum among the Seminoles. Refusal of the Seminoles to leave Florida in accordance with the treaties of Payne's Landing and Fort Gibson led to the Second Seminole War. Early in the struggle their leader Osceola was captured and died in prison. Pres. Van Buren, in the White House during most of the war, was accused of defending the slaveholding interests. The removal to Oklahoma of the surviving Seminoles was finally accomplished after a long, bloody war.

Senecas. Occupying the region around Seneca Lake, N.Y., the Indians, members of the Iroquoian linguistic group, were members of the Iroquois League. Warlike, they destroyed such enemies as the Hurons, but absorbed captives into their tribe. They sided with the British against the French in 18th-century colonial wars and supported the British in the American Revolution, suffering greatly in the aftermath of the war.

seniority rule. Customarily a member of Congress who has served longest on the majority side of a committee becomes chairman and otherwise acquires additional influence. Members are ranked for the chairmanship according to length of continuous service. If a member loses his seat in Congress, and then returns, he starts at the bottom of the list again, except that he outranks those members who are beginning their first terms.

The Senate adopted the seniority system in 1847; the House of Representatives in 1910.

separation of Church and State. In 1802 Pres. Jefferson wrote a letter to a group of Baptists in Danbury, Conn., in which he declared it was the purpose of the 1st Amendment to build a "wall of separation between Church and State." In *Reynolds v. U.S.* (1879), the first anti-Mormon case, Chief Justice Waite speaking for the unanimous Court characterized this statement as "almost an authoritative declaration of the scope and effect of the amendment. . . ."

In recent times Justice Black in the Everson Case (1947) gave Jefferson's "almost authoritative" pronouncement a greatly enlarged application. He wrote: "Neither a state nor the Federal Government can, openly or secretly, participate in the affairs of any religious organizations or groups and vice versa. In the words of Jefferson, the clause against establishment of religion by law was intended to erect 'a wall of separation between Church and State. . . .' The First Amendment has erected a wall between Church and State. That wall must be kept high and impregnable. We could not approve the slightest breach. . . .'"

sergeant at arms. The office exists in both the House of Representatives and the Senate. The sergeant at arms is the chief disciplinary officer and is empowered to enforce order upon the floor. He is also the disbursing officer for members' salary and mileage (the cost of several trips each session to and from the member's home constituency) and acts as purchasing officer for the body. By the direction of the presiding officer, he may compel the attendance of absent members. Both sergeants at arms share such joint responsibilities as policing the Capitol and grounds.

"Seven Days' Battle" (June 25–July 1, 1862). During the Civil War, an unbroken series of battles, including actions at Mechanicsville, Gaines' Mill and Frayser's Farm, was fought as part of the Union's unsuccessful Peninsular Campaign to take Richmond. The Confederates under Gen. Robert E. Lee had a force of about 85,000 against Gen. George McClellan's army of 100,000. Lee forced McClellan to retreat down the James River to Harrison's Landing. Richmond was saved. But the Confederates could ill afford their greater losses.

Seven Ranges. Under the Land Ordinance of 1785 the land south of the Geographer's Line which began at a point where the Pennsylvania boundary intersected the Ohio River and ran due west was surveyed and divided. The Seven Ranges were laid out along the line and extended 42 miles to the west. Townships six miles square were measured out within each of the ranges. Each township was then divided into consecutively numbered sections, one square mile or 640 acres in size.

The survey was intended to speed the sale and settlement of public lands so that Congress might pay off pressing debts.

"Seven Sisters" Colleges. The designation is popularly given to seven Eastern women's colleges whose high standards for admission are comparable to those of the Ivy League. They are Barnard (N.Y., established 1889), Bryn Mawr (Pa., 1885), Mount Holyoke (Mass., 1837), Radcliffe (Mass., 1879), Smith (Mass., 1875), Vassar (N.Y., 1861) and Wellesley (Mass., 1875).

"seven-thirties." By act of July 17, 1861, U.S. Treasury notes bearing interest at the rate of 7.30% per annum were first authorized in order to meet the expenses of the Civil War. The total amount issued before the war's end was $830,000,000.

"Seventh of March" speech (1850). Daniel Webster in support of Henry Clay's Compromise of 1850 made the most important speech of his career. Webster announced to the Senate chamber that he spoke "not as a Massachusetts man, not as a Northern man, but as an American." He understood the seriousness of the crisis and chose to disregard the sentiments of his section, supporting a stronger fugitive slave law in an effort to conciliate the South. At the same time, he castigated the South for its tirades against the North and condemned the Abolitionists for embittering the nation over slavery. John Greenleaf Whittier painted Webster in a powerful poem, "Ichabod," as a fallen and tarnished hero, but Webster foresaw that secession would be violent and frightful.

Seward, William Henry (1801–72). Statesman. Born in Orange Co., N.Y., he became governor of the state (1839–43). A U.S. Senator (1849–61), he won Abolitionist support when he spoke of "a higher law than the Constitution" (1850). He looked upon the slavery struggle as "an irrepressible conflict" (1858). A leading Republican candidate for President (1860), he failed to win the nomination but served as Pres. Lincoln's and Johnson's Sec. of State (1861–69). He failed to dominate Lincoln, as he had hoped. He handled the seizure of Mason and Slidell on the *Trent* in masterly fashion and helped end effectively the French intervention in Mexico. An expansionist, he negotiated the purchase of Alaska (1867). Wounded by Lewis Powell, a conspirator with John Wilkes Booth in the Lincoln assassination plot, he carried on his official duties. He advocated a conciliatory policy toward the South.

sewing machines. The first sewing machine in the U.S. with an eye-pointed needle was patented in 1846 by Elias Howe, known as the father of the modern sewing machine. In 1851 Isaac Merrit Singer was granted a patent for a practical sewing machine and organized a company. The unique feature of Singer's machine was its continuous stitching, but Howe, whose machine was then the most popular, initiated a royalty suit against Singer for producing a machine based in part on Howe's own machine. Singer lost and was forced to make a settlement of $15,000; but his machine had in the meantime achieved a leading position. It was improved in the next decade by additional patented devices. In 1889 the Singer Manufacturing Co. of Elizabethport, N.J., produced and marketed the first electric sewing machine known in the U.S.

Rapid expansion of the sale of sewing machines in the latter part of the 19th century revolutionized the making and repairing of clothing in the home. The machines were also adapted for industrial production of ready-made garments.

Shackamaxon, Treaty of (1683). Also known as the "Great Treaty," the agreement between William Penn and the Delaware Indians was signed at Shackamaxon (near Philadelphia), Pa. According to its terms Penn purchased what is now southeastern Pennsylvania.

Shakers. The religious sect was founded in America in 1787 by followers of Ann Lee of England. They established several colonies, including one at New Lebanon, N.Y., based on communal ownership of property and were excellent farmers. The Shakers believed in equality of the sexes and celibacy. Known as the United Society of Believers in Christ's Second Appearing, the society waned by the 20th century. The name is derived from the peculiar dance with which the Shakers accompanied their worship.

Shame of the Cities, The (1904). In his muckraking book, the journalist Lincoln Steffens exposed the dishonesty in American city politics during the early 20th century. Steffens contended that the people were not innocent since it was their representative government that was corrupt. His book helped to stimulate a reform movement.

sharecropping system. Farm tenants who have no equipment or livestock of their own may become "share tenants" or sharecroppers. The system is confined largely to the South and includes both Negro and white farmers. They are generally found in the lowest income groups.

The system developed in the South after the Civil War when the plantation owners found they could not afford to pay their former slaves in money wages. Accordingly, they agreed to let the Negroes (and later "poor whites") cultivate small plots of land independently in exchange for a part of the crop. That is essentially how the system works today. The landowner supplies not only the land but also a cabin, tools, seed, work animals and at least part of the fertilizer. He may arrange for the tenant to obtain credit from a local storekeeper so that he will have food during the long growing season. The tenant supplies the labor. Landlord and tenant share the crop, usually on a 50–50 basis. Sharecropping has usually been associated with backward farming methods, poor yields, extreme poverty and unsatisfactory social conditions.

Sharecropping has declined since World War II when many tenant farmers migrated to the North and obtained jobs in industry. Also, use of machinery in cotton cultivation has displaced many sharecroppers.

Sharecropping is being replaced by a new system that sociologists are calling "owner-renter." The owner-renter owns tractors, other mechanized equipment and a small farm. He rents additional land to make maximum use of the equipment.

share-the-wealth movements. Several extreme solutions were offered during the depression of the 1930's. Their supporters, largely the aged and unemployed in the South and Middle West, hoped to gain from the federal government some payments that would in effect redistribute the wealth of the nation. Among the plans were the Townsend Plan, Upton Sinclair's EPIC (End Poverty in California), Father Coughlin's National Union for Social Justice and Huey Long's Share-Our-Wealth Clubs in Louisiana. Most of the plans were inflationary, but their appeal to the discontented was strong.

Shaw, Lemuel (1781–1861). Jurist. Born in Braintree, Mass., he became Chief Justice of Massachusetts (1830–60). He drew the first charter of the city of Boston (1822). He deeply influenced commercial and constitutional law throughout the U.S. in decisions on matters affecting water power, railroads and other public utilities. In *Commonwealth v. Hunt* (1842) he supported legitimate trade union activity, and in *Lombard v. Stearns* (1849) he ruled that a water company was obligated to serve the public.

Shawnee. The Indians of Algonquian linguistic stock migrated from the South and settled in Ohio and Indiana during the 18th century. They were allied with the French against the English in the war which ended in 1763. They then shifted allegiance to the English and aided them against the American colonists.

The Shawnees, determined to resist further white advances in the West, united under their leaders Tecumseh and his twin brother, the Shawnee Prophet (Tenskwatawa) in a war against the U.S. Their village on the Tippecanoe, in Indiana, was destroyed by William Henry Harrison (1811). The Shawnee were forced onto reservations in Oklahoma.

Shawnee Mission government. In Mar. 1855, when a territorial government was to be chosen in Kansas Territory 5,000 men, called "Border Ruffians," poured into Kansas from Missouri. A proslavery legislature was elected fraudulently and met at Shawnee Mission in northeastern Kansas close to the Missouri border. Among laws passed were some severely punishing any antislavery activity in Kansas.

Shawnee Trail. Somehow the cattle trail known as the Texas Road, which led from Dallas up to the Red River, had its name changed although it had never been used by the Shawnees. The name may have been suggested by an Indian village, called Shawneetown, on the Texas bank of the Red River, or the Shawnee Hills which the route skirted. In any event the Trail was a highway for Texas Longhorns in mid-19th century.

Shays's Rebellion (Aug. 1786–Feb. 1787). The discontent of debtor farmers in Massachusetts who were being dispossessed for failure to pay debts led to an uprising which forced the closing of some courts. The farmers demanded issuance of paper money, easier credit and a halt to foreclosures.

Daniel Shays, a Revolutionary War veteran, emerged as a leader of the rebellion and attempted to seize the arsenal at Springfield. Conservative merchants and landowners in the state financed a militia, headed by Gen. Benjamin Lincoln, and the rebellion was crushed. Shays and some of his men were captured but were released when tempers cooled.

The unrest stimulated property owners to support the movement for a stronger national government that could help curb such uprisings. The event contributed indirectly to the establishment of the Constitution.

Shenandoah. Built in England during the Civil War the Confederate cruiser preyed on Union commerce with great success. It was never overtaken by the Union navy, but finally surrendered in Liverpool, England, Nov. 6, 1865, after the war was over. The British turned the ship over to the U.S.

Sheridan, Philip Henry (1831–88). Army officer. Born in Albany, N.Y., he was graduated from the U.S. Military Academy (1853). A captain at the outbreak of the Civil War, he compiled a brilliant record and rose to major-general in the U.S. Army (1864). Commander of the cavalry of the Army of the Potomac, he raided (1864) Confederate communication lines around Richmond. He also commanded the Army of the Shenandoah (in Virginia) in the drive through the Shenandoah Valley, made famous by his ride from Winchester (Sheridan's ride). In the final days of the war, his troops cut off Lee's retreat from Appomattox, forcing his surrender to Grant. The military governor of Louisiana and Texas (1867), his severity caused Pres. Johnson to transfer him to Missouri. He succeeded W. T. Sherman as Commander-in-Chief of the U.S. Army (1884) and was promoted to full general (1888)—the highest rank possible.

Sheridan on Indians. "The only good Indians I ever saw were dead," was the response of Gen. Philip Sheridan in 1869 when the Comanche chief, Tochoway (Turtle Dove), introduced himself to Sheridan saying that he was a "good Indian." At the time Sheridan was touring the West testing the temper of the tribes. The frontier attitude he expressed was adopted by the general public. It was the philosophy of extermination given the sanction of high rank.

Sheridan's ride. Union Gen. Philip Sheridan was away on a staff conference when his troops at Cedar Creek in the Shenandoah Valley of Virginia were routed by one of Gen. Jubal A. Early's raids. Sheridan, riding back Oct. 19, 1864, came on straggling columns and rallied

them to counterattack successfully against Early. The famous ride from Winchester "twenty miles away" is celebrated in Thomas Buchanan Read's poem, "Sheridan's Ride."

Sherman, William Tecumseh (1820–91). Army officer. Born in Lancaster, Ohio, he was graduated from the U.S. Military Academy (1840). He served with distinction under Gen. Grant at Shiloh (1862) and led a corps in the successful advance on Vicksburg (1862). He succeeded Grant as Commander of the Union Army in the West. With Grant's approval, he started his "March to the Sea" (1864) through Georgia. After taking Savannah (Dec. 21, 1864), he marched northward through the Carolinas, continuing his policy of destroying property rather than lives in the hope of shortening the war. The Confederate commander in the Carolinas, J. E. Johnston, surrendered to Sherman (Apr. 26, 1865) a few days after Lee's surrender to Grant (Apr. 9, 1865). In the post-Civil War period, he was commanding general of the U.S. Army (1869–84). Attempts to make him the Republican presidential candidate in 1884 culminated in his absolute veto: "If nominated, I will not accept; if elected, I will not serve."

Sherman Antitrust Act (1890). The law stated: "Every contract, combination in the form of trust or otherwise, or conspiracy in restraint of trade or com-

607

merce among the several states, or with foreign nations is hereby declared to be illegal. . . ." Violators of the law were liable to fine and imprisonment and the injured party might collect triple damages from the offenders.

The Act did not define "restraint of trade" and it was left to the courts to interpret the intent of Congress. In 1895, for example, the Supreme Court refused to dissolve the American Sugar Refining Company, which had obtained control of about 95% of the sugar-refining business of the country. Under Presidents Theodore Roosevelt and Wm. H. Taft trusts were proceeded against more vigorously. Strengthening amendments, such as the Clayton Act (1914), made the antitrust legislation somewhat more effective.

Sherman Silver Purchase Act (1890). The U.S. Treasury was required to purchase 4,500,000 ounces of silver a month, practically all of the output of the silver mines of the West. The Treasury issued legal tender notes to pay for the silver and these notes were redeemable on demand in either gold or silver. It was hoped that this would halt the falling price of silver, increase the amount of money in circulation, raise prices and help debtor farmers. It accomplished none of this. The silver purchased did, however, drain the Treasury of gold that Pres. Cleveland believed was needed at a time of mounting financial

panic. The Act was repealed in 1893.

Sherman's march to the sea (1864). Gen. William T. Sherman cut a 60-mile swath through Georgia for the announced purpose of demonstrating to the world that the Confederacy could no longer resist the Union armies. He started by burning Atlanta and his troops pillaged and lived off the land on the march to Savannah.

Sherman practiced total war although he expressed sorrow over its "sad realities." He observed, after the march to the sea, "To realize what war is one should follow in our tracks."

Shiloh, battle of (Apr. 6–7, 1862). The Union victory at Shiloh (also known as Pittsburgh Landing), in southwestern Tennessee, threatened to split the Confederacy in two.

It was clear to Gen. Ulysses S. Grant from the heavy fighting in which Confederate Gen. Albert S. Johnston was killed that no single victory would crush the Confederacy, but that "complete conquest" would be necessary to save the Union.

Shimonseki, Convention of (1864). A Japanese feudal lord whose cannon commanded the straits of Shimonseki began to fire upon "barbarian" (foreign) ships. The offended powers organized a joint punitive expedition. The U.S. sent only one warship because of the Civil War. The Japanese government agreed to an indemnity of $3,-

608

000,000. The share of the U.S., $785,000, was grossly disproportionate to the loss sustained. In 1883 Congress voted to return this sum to Japan. The gesture made for goodwill between the U.S. and Japan.

shinplasters. The name was popularly and derisively used for fractional paper currency issued during the Civil War, in denominations of 3, 5, 10, 15, 25 and 50 cents. The money was authorized by Congress in 1862 when subsidiary silver coins were hoarded. The fractional currency, essential to retail trade, became grimy and torn quickly. Cost of replacement was high, but its use persisted until 1876 when confidence in greenbacks was restored sufficiently to halt the hoarding of silver coins.

ships-of-the-line. At various times in the 18th and 19th centuries, before the introduction of steam power and armor plate, Congress authorized the construction of battleships—ships that would have sufficient capability in guns to face enemy ships in battle line. The first such ship, the *America*, was built in 1782.

Shockley, William Bradford (1910–   ). Physicist and inventor. Born in London, he was granted a Ph.D. by the Massachusetts Institute of Technology (1936). He directed antisubmarine warfare research (1942–44) at Columbia. In 1958 he shared the Nobel Prize for Physics for developing the transistor, a semiconductor and substitute for the vacuum tube.

Shoshone. Indians of Uto-Aztecan linguistic stock, they were widely scattered by the early 19th century all the way from the Panamint Mts. and Death Valley in California through Nevada, Utah and Idaho into the Rocky Mts. in Wyoming. The desert Shoshone were miserably poor, but the Rocky Mountain Shoshone had acquired horses by the end of the 17th century. They hunted buffalo and antelope and dressed gorgeously. The Shoshone were sometimes called Snake Indians.

"Shot heard round the world." The phrase occurs in Ralph Waldo Emerson's "Concord Hymn" (1836), written to dedicate the monument at Concord Bridge where "the embattled farmers" stood in 1775 and fired on British regulars. The shots they fired soon led to the Declaration of Independence.

sic semper tyrannis. Translated from the Latin, meaning "thus ever to tyrants," it became the motto of Virginia in 1776. The phrase was shouted by John Wilkes Booth when he leaped to the stage of the Ford Theatre after firing a bullet into the head of Abraham Lincoln, Apr. 14, 1865.

"Sighted sub, sank same." The memorable laconic statement was radioed from the South

Pacific by U.S. Navy flyer David F. Mason, Jan. 8, 1942. He swooped down on a surfaced Japanese sub, dropped a depth charge and stayed to observe the wreckage.

Silliman, Benjamin (1779–1864). Chemist and geologist. Born in Trumbull, Conn., he became professor of chemistry and natural history at Yale (1802–53). He profoundly influenced collegiate education by establishing science as a study on a basis of equality with older disciplines. He delivered the first course of lectures in chemistry ever given at Yale (1804) and began a course in geology (1813). He helped organize the Yale Medical School (1813) and delivered the first series of Lowell Institute scientific lectures (1839–40). He laid the foundations for the Sheffield Scientific School at Yale. He founded (1818) and edited what became under his guidance one of the world's great scientific journals, *The American Journal of Science and Arts,* usually called *Silliman's Journal.* He published *Elements of Chemistry* (1831). He was the first president of the Association of American Geologists, forerunner of the American Association for the Advancement of Sciences.

silver. The metal was popular in the colonies by the middle of the 17th century. The silversmithing of Paul Revere in the late 18th century is almost as well known as his "mid-night ride." Craftsmen fashioned various styles of cups, candelabra, baptismal basins and other works in such silversmithing centers as Boston, Philadelphia, Newport and Baltimore.

The metal has been intimately involved in the currency history of the U.S. The Founding Fathers favored bimetallism and expected that both gold and silver would provide the currency base for coins and paper. Until 1873, however, silver generally commanded higher prices than the U.S. Mint paid for the metal and it was sold largely for commercial uses.

Silver mining in the American West increased its output substantially in the late 1850's and discoveries after 1873 glutted the market with silver. The "silver kings" then demanded that the U.S. purchase silver for coinage. Their demand was echoed by debtor farmers who favored bimetallism as a means of cheapening the currency, raising farm prices and paying off mounting debts.

Although the government yielded in part to the pressure of free silver interests in the 1870's, silver purchases did not reach a level that satisfied either mineowners or debtor farmers. The issue of bimetallism became central in 1896 when "silver Democrats" gained control of the national convention and nominated William Jennings Bryan for President. His resounding defeat in both 1896 and 1900 ended bimetallism as an issue in American politics.

Silver continued, however, to be purchased for minting into coins and for commercial uses. Its price has fluctuated widely. During the Great Depression the price fell so low that the "silver bloc" in the Senate threatened to oppose much of the New Deal legislation unless the government supported the price of silver. Under the Silver Purchase Act of 1934 the Treasury was obliged to buy the entire output of the domestic silver mines at an artificially high price. Silver certificates, first issued in 1878, were made full legal tender in 1933. In 1963 the silver used by the Treasury to back the certificates was needed for coins. Silver certificates were withdrawn from circulation.

Simms, William Gilmore (1806–70). Author. He was born in Charleston, S.C. The most prolific and widely known novelist of the antebellum South, he wrote romantic novels, poetry, histories and biographies, all of which loyally defended the institutions of slavery. His best-remembered novel, *The Yemassee* (1835), was a story of colonial and Revolutionary South Carolina.

single tax. In his book *Progress and Poverty* (1879), Henry George expounded the idea that a single tax on land values would make unnecessary all other taxes and would assure progress with social justice. He explained that owners of land added nothing to its worth which was derived from its location and the population. Therefore, the owners should not have the economic rent derived from land, but the rent should go to the state for the public benefit in the form of taxation. Other property might be privately owned.

The single tax continues to have its followers.

Sioux. Also known as the Dakotas, they were the most numerous on the northern Great Plains. Of Siouan or Dakotan linguistic stock, they supported the English against the U.S. in the Revolution and in the War of 1812. They resisted the advance of settlers in the West and were involved in numerous wars during the 19th century. In 1862, for example, Little Crow led a massacre of whites in Minnesota. The Sioux were forced to sign a treaty in 1867 and accepted a reservation in South Dakota. The peace was destroyed, however, when gold was discovered in the Black Hills and miners overran Sioux land. Fighting was led by Sitting Bull, Red Cloud, Rain-in-the-Face and Crazy Horse. The famous last stand of Custer (1876) took place during these wars. It was not until 1891 that Sioux opposition was finally broken by Gen. Miles. They were settled on reservations in Minnesota, Montana, Nebraska, North Dakota and South Dakota.

"Skinners." The name was given to bands of marauders in the Revolution who ravaged the "Neutral Ground" of Westchester County in lower New York State. They were named after Gen. Cortland Skinner's brigade of New Jersey volunteers and were continually skirmishing with the Loyalist "cowboys."

Skin of Our Teeth, The (1942). A play by Thornton Wilder, it is an allegorical comedy of a New Jersey family who represent the first created men and women, in Biblical analogy, and overcome cataclysmic disasters to continue the advance in culture of the human race. It won the Pulitzer Prize for drama (1943).

Other works by Wilder include *The Bridge of San Luis Rey* (1927), a novel, and *Our Town* (1938), a play.

Slater, Samuel (1768–1835). Industrialist. Born in Belper, England, he emigrated to the U.S. in 1789, after memorizing the details of making cotton textile machinery. (It was illegal under English law to export such machinery.) Regarded as the founder of the American cotton industry, he established, with partners, his first cotton textile factory (1793) in Pawtucket, R.I. This was the forerunner of his expanded mill operations in New England.

Slaughterhouse Cases (1873). The first cases involving interpretation of the 14th Amendment had nothing to do with the rights of freemen. The Supreme Court took the narrow view, no longer the position of the Court, that the due process of law clause was not a limitation of the state's police power and that the equal protection of the law clause would probably never be invoked except for protection of the Negro.

The cases arose when the Reconstruction government in Louisiana, unquestionably under corrupt influence, granted a monopoly of the slaughterhouse business to a single concern, thus preventing over one thousand other persons and firms from continuing in that business. The validity of the law was attacked under the 14th Amendment.

The Court by a five to four majority ruled that the state of Louisiana had the right to restrain the exercise of their trade by the butchers of New Orleans and that this was not a deprivation of property within the meaning of the due process of law clause in the 14th Amendment.

slavery. The first Negro slaves in the English colonies were brought to Jamestown, Va., in a Dutch ship in 1619. As ships of all nations entered the trade, the route to America became known as "the middle passage." The trade was notorious for the cruel treatment of the shackled slaves who could not even stand in the confines of the crowded holds. Although many Negroes died en route, the slave trade was highly profitable. It flourished in Rhode Island early in the 18th century.

The demand for slaves increased in the mid-17th century as tobacco cultivation increased in the South. Slavery was not, however, confined to one region. It was given legal recognition in all of the colonies by the end of the 17th century.

By the time of the American Revolution, there were 500,000 slaves in the American colonies in a population of 2,500,000. They were distributed throughout the colonies, with more than half in Virginia and South Carolina.

Antislavery sentiment developed in the 18th century and was implicit in the Declaration of Independence (1776), which held that "all men are created equal." The word "slave" is not mentioned anywhere in the Constitution, but one of the compromises provided that "three-fifths of all other persons" be counted for both representation and for direct taxation. In another compromise, Congress was denied the power to legislate against the importation of slaves for 20 years (until 1808).

In the North, slaves were freed by legislative action during and after the American Revolution. Slavery was excluded from the old Northwest Territory by the Northwest Ordinance of 1787.

Slavery was in decline when the invention of the cotton gin (1793) stimulated anew the demand for slave labor. From this time forward the "peculiar institution" was defended with increased vigor in the South where it became essential to the plantation economy. Most slaves were field hands, but some were house servants, and others became skilled handicraft workers. Extensive smuggling of slaves followed prohibition of their importation after 1808. Slave breeding became an industry in the upper South and slave markets were commonplace.

Slave insurrections were deeply feared in the South. There were hundreds of small revolts, but the major ones were Gabriel's uprising (1801), the plot of Denmark Vesey (1822) and Nat Turner's insurrection (1831).

Slave codes were enacted which limited the freedom of assembly of Negroes, forbade anyone to instruct them in reading and writing and allowed compensation to owners whose slaves were executed for capital crimes.

Notable efforts to prevent slavery from spreading into the territories were contained in the Missouri Compromise of 1820, the Compromise of 1850, the Kansas-Nebraska Act of 1854 and the Dred Scott decision (1857).

As a war measure, Pres. Lincoln's Emancipation Proclamation (1862) freed the slaves in areas in rebellion after Jan. 1, 1863. It was not, however, until after the Civil War that slavery was abolished completely by the 13th Amendment to the Constitution (1865).

Slidell Mission (1845). When Pres. Polk learned that the Mexican government was in desperate straits and might sell California, he sent a representative, John Slidell, to Mexico. The shaky Mexican government feared that negotiation would be unpopular and refused to receive Slidell, who wrote Polk that nothing could be done with the Mexicans "until they shall have been chastised."

Smith, Alfred Emanuel (1873–1944). Political leader. A poor boy from the sidewalks of New York, he rose to political greatness. A leader of Tammany Hall, he served in the New York Legislature (1903–15) and compiled an impressive record of liberal legislation during his four terms as governor of New York (1919–20, 1923–28). The Democratic candidate for President (1928), he was badly defeated with such factors weighing against him as his Catholic religion, unsophisticated speech and opposition to prohibition. A strong supporter of F. D. Roosevelt in the early days of the New Deal, he later broke with the President. When his political career ended, he became president of the company which managed the Empire State Building in New York.

Smith, Jedediah Strong (1798–1831). Fur trader and explorer. Born in Bainbridge, N.Y., he was the first explorer of the Great Basin, an elevated region between the Wasatch and Sierra Nevada Mts., including most of Nevada and parts of Utah, California, Idaho, Wyoming and Oregon. He penetrated the Oregon country from California. After he moved from the Rocky Mts. to the Santa Fe trade, he was killed on the trail by Comanche Indians.

Smith, John (1580–1631). Colonist. Born in Willoughby, Lincolnshire, England, legend as well as genuine accomplishment have perpetuated his name. A promoter of the Virginia Company of London, he was among the first colonists to settle Jamestown, Va. (1607). Taken prisoner by the Indians, he was condemned to death, but he escaped and told the story of his rescue by the Indian princess, Pocahontas, daughter of the chieftain, Powhatan, in his *The Generall Historie of Virginia, New-England, and the Summer Isles* (1624). He saved the colonists from starvation by obtaining corn from the Indians and served as president of the council (1608–09) before he left for England. In 1614 he explored the New England coast and urged that it be settled. His maps were useful and his works include *The True Travels, Adventures and Observations of Captaine John Smith, in Europe, Asia, Affrica, and America* (1630).

Smith, Theobald (1859–1934). Medical scientist. Born in Albany, N.Y., he was granted an

M.D. by Albany Medical College (1883). A pathologist, his researches in such animal diseases as Texas fever and hog cholera were of incalculable help to the American livestock industry. He directed the department of animal pathology at the Rockefeller Institute for Medical Research (after 1915). He wrote far-reaching studies on the relationship between bovine and human tuberculosis.

Smith Alien Registration Act (1940). In an effort to guard internal security at a time when World War II was being fought in Europe, Congress required the registration and fingerprinting of all aliens in the U.S. The Act also made it illegal for anyone to teach or advocate the overthrow of any government in the U.S. by force or to organize or join any group teaching such a doctrine.

In 1949 the Truman administration invoked the Smith Act to convict 11 leading Communist party officials. The constitutionality of the Act was sustained in *Dennis et al. v. U.S.* (1951).

Smith-Hughes Act (1917). Congress provided for federal aid to schools offering vocational education. The Act authorized continuing appropriations to be expended under state plans for the promotion of vocational education. Under this program agricultural and other vocational courses have been widely established in the U.S.

Smith-Lever Agricultural Extension Act (1914). The Act resulted in a far-flung organization for off-campus instruction and service to farm people. A network of county farm advisers, extending throughout the nation for the purpose of guiding and stimulating food production, became the key contacts between the federal government and the farmers.

Smithsonian Institution. The Institution was created by Congress in 1846 under the terms of the will of James Smithson of London, a chemist and mineralogist. He bequeathed his fortune to the U.S. to found, at Washington, an establishment for the "increase and diffusion of knowledge among men." The Institution sponsors scientific research, explorations, museum and art gallery exhibits and publications.

soap opera. The term designates a broad spectrum of radio and television shows that appeal to housewives and family viewers because of the family problems they explore. Each show is usually part of a series presenting the same actors for many weeks and even years. The name came to be applied because many of these shows, the despair of critical viewers, were sponsored by soap companies.

Soapsuds, Operation. The code name refers to a World War II military action in which the Allied air forces bombed the

Ploesti oil fields in Rumania, Aug. 1, 1943.

Social Darwinism. In *The Origin of the Species* (1859) Darwin set forth the idea that man evolved through a process of "natural selection" by which the fittest survived. Over a long period of time this process resulted in new species.

This theory was applied to the American scene by William Graham Sumner (1840–1910), a Yale sociologist, who hailed American millionaires as products of natural selection. An American Darwinian, he regarded reformers as meddlers who tried to save the misfits unable to survive in the struggle for existence.

Socialist Labor party. Founded in 1874, it is one of a long series of parties in the American socialist movement. In the 1890's and early 1900's it was dominated by Daniel DeLeon, editor of its weekly, *The People*. DeLeon's attacks on American trade unions caused a major split in the socialist movement in 1899, leading to the formation of the Socialist party. The two groups have continued to be at odds.

Socialist party. The major faction of the socialist movement came into existence in 1901. It split away from the Socialist Labor party and, under the leadership of Eugene V. Debs, sought to win American trade unions over to the socialist program of abolishing capitalism by democratic means.

Socialists reject the profit system. They believe in government ownership of the means of production and hold that private ownership of property makes possible capitalist control of the workers, who do not get their fair share of the value of their production.

Debs was the Socialist party candidate for President at intervals from 1900 to 1920. A high point in Socialist party organization was reached in 1920 when he polled almost one million votes. Debs gave way as the perennial Socialist party candidate for President to Norman Thomas, who headed the ticket from 1928 to 1948.

Since American trade unionism rejected socialist principles for improvement of working conditions under capitalism, the Socialist party has remained insignificant.

Social Justice, National Union for. The Social Justice movement was organized by the Rev. Charles E. Coughlin, "radio priest" of the Shrine of the Little Flower, in Royal Oak, Mich. Father Coughlin, who became bitterly anti-Roosevelt in the 1930's, charged that capitalism was doomed and wasn't worth saving because it had failed the people. Instead he advocated "state capitalism."

In 1935 Father Coughlin, whose radio audience was estimated at 40 million, started a third-party movement with Dr. Francis E. Townsend and Gerald L. K. Smith. The party lost its most potent candidate for President when Sen. Huey Long (La.), the "Kingfish," was assassinated the same year. The Union party nominated Rep. William Lemke (N.D.), who polled 883,000 votes, less than 2% of the total votes cast in the election of 1936.

The movement passed into oblivion with the outbreak of World War II. Father Coughlin's newspaper, *Social Justice*, was forced by national security officials to cease publication in 1941 because of its tone in a time of national crisis. It opposed U.S. entry into the war on the side of the Soviet Union.

Social Security Act (1935). A major undertaking of the New Deal, the law established the responsibility of the government for the security and better life for the "men, women, and children of the nation." The original law has been changed several times, but the essential features of the three main categories remain.

The most important part of the program provides for a system of Old Age and Survivors Insurance (OASI) with benefit payments to workers who retire at age 62 or later, or to their dependents in the event of death. Totally disabled workers may begin drawing pensions at 50. The money for all pensions comes from a tax on payrolls shared equally by employer and employee. Since 1951 OASI has been extended to include self-employed persons (except phy-

sicians), some employees of state and local governments, farm owners, farm employees and other workers not included in the original act.

Each state administers its own system of unemployment insurance. Although the size of the payments and the number of weeks for which benefits are paid vary widely, all state systems must meet federal standards. The funds needed are raised by a tax on payrolls.

A public assistance program is also provided for in the Act. Federal grants match state and local expenditures up to specified amounts per individual not covered by old age insurance. In addition, similar federal grants-in-aid help dependent and crippled children and needy blind persons. A program of mother and child health services and of general public health is also included.

sod house. Since there was neither enough wood nor stone on the Great Plains to build houses, sod was used during the 19th century. It was plowed in strips from the prairie and cut into three-foot bricks with a spade. The houses provided shelter until the settlers could afford to buy timber brought in by the railroads.

Softs or Softshells. The name was given to a faction of the Democratic party in New York from 1852 to 1860. It opposed any alliance with the proslavery Democrats of the South.

Soil Bank plan (1956). During the Eisenhower administration farmers received benefit payments for withdrawing some of their allotted acreage from basic crops and for an agreed number of years planting grass, trees and other soil-conserving plants. The purpose, like that of the New Deal program of the 1930's, was not only to reduce production and to raise farm income, but also to promote soil conservation.

Soil Conservation Act (1935). The Soil Conservation Service was established as a permanent unit of the Department of Agriculture for the control and prevention of soil erosion.

Soil Conservation and Domestic Allotment Act (1936). The New Deal farm law was passed when the Agricultural Adjustment Act of 1933 was declared unconstitutional. It sought to keep farm production down by allowing benefit payments to farmers who withdrew acreage from production of soil-depleting crops, such as corn, cotton, tobacco, wheat and oats. Payments depended on the number of acres withdrawn from soil-depleting crop production and turned over to soil-conserving crops.

When the Act proved ineffective in curbing farm surpluses and price declines during the recession of 1937–38, it was replaced by the second AAA of 1938.

Solicitor General, Office of the. The federal office was created in 1870 when Congress provided for establishment of the Department of Justice. The Solicitor General is the third ranking official in the Department, after the Attorney General and Deputy Attorney General. He supervises all government cases before the Supreme Court, arguing many of them personally. Since the government appears in about half the cases that come before the Court, he argues far more cases there than any other lawyer.

In 1965 Pres. Johnson appointed Thurgood Marshall to be the 33rd Solicitor General. Since the office was founded, he was the first Negro to serve either in that post or even in the office of the Solicitor General.

Solid South. The Radical Republican Reconstruction program in the South following the Civil War caused the South to vote solidly Democratic. Nomination by the Democrats virtually assured a candidate of carrying the voting districts in the South. Republicans were held responsible for legislation favoring Negroes and laws that promoted the prosperity of other sections of the country at the South's expense.

The Solid South was broken in the election of 1928 when anti-Catholic prejudice against Alfred Smith permitted Herbert Hoover to capture Tennessee, Texas, Florida, North Carolina and Virginia. Except for Tennessee, not one of these states had voted for a Republican since Reconstruction. The Solid South was broken again in the landslide election of Eisenhower in 1952. In 1960 the Democratic candidate, Sen. Kennedy, a Catholic, was able to hold most of the Solid South, but the section is no longer considered solidly Democratic.

Sons of Liberty. Leaders of street demonstrations against the Stamp Act (1765) were members of a newly formed, radical, patriotic organization that agitated against British restrictions in the years preceding the Declaration of Independence.

Especially vigorous chapters of the Sons of Liberty functioned in Boston and New York. Membership included not only workers, but middle-class leaders like Boston propagandist Samuel Adams and the New York merchant Isaac Sears. Paul Revere often served as a courier for the Sons of Liberty.

Sons of the American Revolution. Male descendants of soldiers, sailors and conspicuous patriots during the Revolution organized the society in California, July 4, 1876. It now has several state branches.

Sons of the Revolution is an organization of the same nature, first established in New York in 1876.

sounding rockets. Used in the U.S. space program, they explore space (up to about 4,000 miles) and return data either by telemetry or when the capsule is recovered. Typical of sounding rockets employed in scientific programs are: Aerobee, first fired Nov. 14, 1947; Nike, employed largely in upper atmosphere experiments. Others are Argo, Arcas and Loki.

South Carolina. The "Palmetto State," a South Atlantic state, was one of the original 13 Colonies. It was first settled by Spaniards in 1526. A French settlement, Port Royal (1562), was destroyed by the Spanish. The English held claims on the strength of Cabot's voyage (1497) and King Charles I granted Carolina (Carolus, Latin for Charles) to Sir Robert Heath in 1629. It was regranted in 1663, by Charles II, to eight of his favorites, who divided it into North and South Carolina. A constitution, known as the Grand Model (1669), drafted by John Locke, proved to be unworkable. It sought to establish a feudal system that would insure the growth of large plantations. The colony came under royal control in 1719 and retained this status until the royal governor was ousted in 1775. Charleston, the colony's major port, was held by the British during most of the Revolutionary War. It was the eighth state to ratify the Constitution (May 23, 1788). Its capital is Columbia.

South Carolina, a leading slave state, was the first to secede from the Union, Dec. 20, 1860. The first action of the war took place at Fort Sumter. Sherman marching through the state in 1865 burned Columbia.

The state was readmitted in 1868.

South Carolina is a major producer of tobacco and cotton. Lumber is plentiful. Industrial growth since the end of World War II has been speeded by establishment of plants by such major industries as General Electric, Westinghouse Air Brake, Firestone, Allied Chemical and Owens-Corning Fiberglas.

South Carolina Canal and Rail Road Co. Chartered Jan. 30, 1828, the line operated the first commercially adequate American-built locomotive in Dec. 1830. *Best Friend of Charleston* made 30 miles an hour alone and pulled four cars containing from 40 to 50 passengers at 21 miles per hour. The boiler exploded, Jan. 17, 1831, destroying the engine. The line's second engine, the *West Point*, enabled operations to continue.

The South Carolina Railroad (now included in the Southern Railway System) never used horse-drawn equipment. It was a steam railroad from the beginning and when the line was completed from Charleston to Hamburg, Sept. 1833, it was the longest railroad in the world—136 miles.

South Dakota. The "Coyote State" in the West North Central group was admitted to the Union as the 39th or 40th state (with North Dakota), Nov. 2, 1889. Its capital is Pierre.

The first white men to reach the region were the La Véren-

drye brothers, French-Canadians, on their search for the route to the western ocean (1742). The Lewis and Clark expedition (1804–06) traversed the region which is divided by the Missouri River. The Dakota Territory was established in 1861. Settlement was hindered by the Sioux rising of 1862 and later troubles with the Indians. The state has seven Indian reservations, the largest being the Rosebud, the Pine Ridge and the Cheyenne River. Dakota, in Sioux, means "friend" or "ally."

Gold was discovered in the Black Hills in 1874 and the state continues to lead in gold production. Agriculture is the chief industry, with wheat and corn the chief crops. Cattle, sheep and hogs are raised. Most of the manufactures are related directly to agriculture and include meat packing, flour, feed and lumber mills.

Sculptured on the granite face of Mount Rushmore in the Black Hills are the heads of Washington, Jefferson, Lincoln and Theodore Roosevelt.

Southeast Asia Treaty Organization (SEATO). When Communist expansion in Europe was checked by NATO, the Communists turned their attention to the Far East. They succeeded in taking over North Viet Nam (1954) and fought a guerrilla war in rubber-rich Malaya. Communist China took over Tibet (1951) and put pressure on its neighbors.

Against this background, the

U.S. and seven other governments—Australia, Britain, New Zealand, Thailand, Pakistan, France and the Philippines—joined in 1954 to form SEATO (the Manila Pact). They are pledged to meet any "common danger" in the treaty area in accordance with their "constitutional processes." A protocol to the Pact includes Laos, Cambodia and South Viet Nam in the treaty area. SEATO has no military force comparable to that of NATO.

Southern Christian Leadership Conference. Founded in 1957 by the late Rev. Martin Luther King, Jr., Atlanta Baptist minister, as a Negro civil rights organization, it seeks "full citizenship rights, equality and the integration of the Negro in all aspects of American life." King successfully led the Montgomery, Ala., bus boycott in 1955-56. His impassioned "I have a dream" speech was the peak of the 1963 summer civil rights "March on Washington." The SCLC works primarily in 16 southern and border states. After his assassination in 1968, his plan for a Poor People's Campaign in Washington, D.C., was carried forward by his successor as head of the SCLC, the Rev. Ralph David Abernathy.

Southern Pacific Co. The railroad company was chartered in California in 1865 to connect San Francisco and San Diego. After 1876 it was pushed east through the two best mountain passes, through Needles in California and Yuma in Arizona, thereby controlling the access routes leading into California as well as the lines within the state itself. By 1881 El Paso became the Southern Pacific's eastern terminus. Colis P. Huntington replaced Leland Stanford as president of the road in 1890. In 1900 at Huntington's death, E. H. Harriman acquired 45% of the stock of the Southern Pacific. Harriman's backers were the bankers, Kuhn, Loeb and Company.

The Southern Pacific Co. is the second largest transportation company in the U.S. in point of mileage operated—about 13,-450 miles. It extends from New Orleans to Los Angeles and up the Pacific Coast to Portland, Ore. The St. Louis Southwestern ("Cotton Belt"), which it controls, extends the system from Texas to Mississippi gateways at Memphis and St. Louis.

Southern Railway Co. Incorporated in Virginia (1894), the system joined all of the large cities on the Mississippi with the important eastern-seaboard cities from Washington southward. It has about 8,000 miles of track.

South Improvement Company. The company was chartered in 1870 by Tom Scott of the Pennsylvania Railroad for the purpose of eliminating cutthroat competition among the railroads. It was reorganized as an oil company in 1872, headed by Standard Oil chiefs under John

D. Rockefeller He planned to have the railroads—the Erie, New York Central and the Pennsylvania and their affiliates—double their charges for hauling oil products. The South Improvement Company alone was not to pay the increased charges and was, in fact, to receive as "drawbacks" most of the increase paid by the oil companies in competition with Rockefeller's interests.

News of the plan leaked out and the public outcry forced its abandonment. Rockefeller did, however, get rebates from railroad lines and by 1879 he had cornered about 95% of the refining capacity of the country.

South Pass. The historic gateway through the Rocky Mts. was utilized by pioneer wagons in the early 1830's on the trip to Oregon and California. The pass, a sagebrush plain about 20 miles wide, located in Wyoming, was an important part of the Oregon Trail.

space program. The U.S. space program was spurred when the Soviet Union put the first man-made satellite, Sputnik I, into orbit. On Jan. 31, 1958, the U.S. launched its first satellite, Explorer I. With these two launchings the world entered the Age of Space. The program was accelerated in 1961 since Presidents Eisenhower and Kennedy and the Congress considered it basic to national strength and continued leaderhip of the free world. The project includes operations in the near-earth orbit,

exploration of the moon and search for extraterrestrial life on the planets and beyond.

Spanish-American War (1898). U.S. sympathy for the Cuban insurgents against Spanish rule was aroused by the harsh policies of Gen. Valeriano Weyler (the "Butcher"), who had been sent to Cuba by the Spanish government, Jan. 1896. He herded Cubans into concentration camps and some 200,000 Cubans were victims of his ruthlessness. Gen. Weyler was recalled by Spain in 1897.

U.S. public opinion was particularly inflamed by the sinking of the battleship *Maine* in Havana Harbor, Feb. 15, 1898. This followed publication by the New York *Journal* of a letter by the Spanish minister to the U.S. criticizing Pres. McKinley (the De Lôme letter). War fever, kept at a high pitch by the "yellow press," became difficult to control. Two great newspaper publishers, William Randolph Hearst and Joseph Pulitzer, competed with each other in sensationalism.

The clamor for war forced the State Department to send an ultimatum to Spain demanding the end of hostilities in Cuba. Spain agreed to an armistice shortly before Pres. McKinley sent his war message to Congress. This constituted virtual surrender by Spain, but McKinley chose to give it no weight. Perhaps he had no confidence in Spain's promises; or perhaps he gave in to the pressure for war by such prominent

Republicans as Assistant Sec. of the Navy Theodore Roosevelt; John Hay, Ambassador to Great Britain; Senators Beveridge and Lodge; Whitelaw Reid, editor of the New York *Tribune*; and Walter Hines Page, editor of the *Atlantic Monthly*.

In general American business interests in Cuba and on the mainland wanted peace and restoration of normal business activity. U.S. businessmen had invested some $50,000,000 in Cuban sugar and tobacco plantations, railroads and business establishments. U.S. trade with Cuba amounted to more than $100,000,000 annually. Another complication was provided by Cubans who became U.S. citizens and then returned to Cuba to aid the revolution. When these Cubans were captured they claimed the protection of the U.S. There were also Spanish protests against arms and recruits that were raised in the U.S. and sent to Cuba. The rebels sought U.S. intervention and even mounted attacks against American property in order to force the U.S. to declare war.

The war declared by Congress, Apr. 25, 1898, lasted only four months. The tottering Spanish monarchy was no match for the U.S. Although the U.S. Army was small, and there was much inefficiency and unpreparedness, the Spanish forces were too weak to offer much resistance. The battle of San Juan Hill, which preceded the capture of the city of Santiago in Cuba, made a popular hero of Theodore Roosevelt. The Atlantic fleet, under Adm. William Sampson, made short work of the Spanish fleet which sought to break out of Santiago Harbor. The Pacific fleet under Adm. George Dewey was equally successful in smashing another Spanish fleet in Manila Bay, in the Philippine Islands.

In the "splendid little war," as Hay called it, the U.S. lost 5,462 men of whom only 379 fell in combat. The rest died from disease and other causes. Spain's casualties were much higher and in the Treaty of Paris she lost whatever had remained of a once imposing empire in the New World.

Speaker of the House. The Constitution (Art. I, Sec. 2) provides that the House of Representatives "shall choose their speaker and other officers." The officers include Speaker, Chaplain, Clerk, Sergeant-at-Arms, Doorkeeper and Postmaster.

The Speaker is nominated at a party caucus and chosen by the members of the majority party in the House. He presides over the House, appoints the chairmen to preside over the Committees of the Whole, appoints all special or select committees, recognizes a member who wishes to address the House and makes many important rulings and decisions. The Speaker may vote, but usually does not, except in case of a tie. The Speaker and majority leader often confer with the President and are regarded as spokesmen for the administration if they and the President belong to the same political party.

Specie Circular (July 11, 1836). Issued by Pres. Jackson, the circular was intended to curb land speculation caused by the paper money printed by state banks without adequate specie backing. It required that all purchases of public lands be paid for in specie (gold or silver). This punctured the land speculation bubble and the sale of public lands declined sharply. The Panic of 1837 followed.

Spindletop oil strike (Jan. 10, 1901). The first great oil strike in Texas launched a fabulous era in the Southwest. The Spindletop claim near Beaumont, owned by Anthony F. Lucas, opened up savage financial struggles over oil.

"Spirit of St. Louis." Charles A. Lindbergh, known as "Lucky Lindy" or the "Lone Eagle," made the first nonstop solo flight across the Atlantic, May 20–21, 1927. The flight from New York to Paris covered 3,610 miles and took 33 hours, 39 minutes. The plane, "Spirit of St. Louis," is on exhibit in the Smithsonian Institution, in Washington, D.C.

Spiritualists. The name is applied to believers in the theory that spirits can and do act through sensitive individuals known as mediums. The theory first achieved prominence in the U.S. through the manifestations of the Fox sisters, at Hydeville, N.Y., 1848. The phenomena include the moving of physical objects, rapping and spirit-photographing.

spoils system. With the introduction of the two-party system in the U.S., the practice developed whereby office holders were turned out when the political party in power was defeated and the new party took over.

Pres. John Adams was careful to appoint Federalists to office. The "midnight judges," whom he appointed just before leaving the Presidency, illustrated his determination to keep Federalists in office. Pres. Jefferson, with equal determination, cleaned house of the Federalists and replaced them with Democratic-Republicans loyal to his administration.

Andrew Jackson, who believed firmly in rotation in office, is mistakenly credited with being the founder of the spoils system. He was not even its foremost practitioner, since he replaced only one-fifth of the office holders when he was President. The Whig housecleaning in 1841 was a prime example of spoilsmen in action.

The merit system did not make any headway in the federal government until passage of the Pendleton Act (Federal Civil Service Act) in 1883.

State and local governments have been no less prone than the federal government to reward loyal party men with appointive office. "To the victor belong the spoils" is a slogan practiced to this day, but with less intensity since an increasingly large number of government positions are held on the basis of merit examinations.

Spoon River Anthology (1915). Satirical imaginary epitaphs of various people in a drab village of the Middle West make up this book of poems by Edgar Lee Masters. One of the most widely quoted epitaphs is that about Ann Rutledge, Abraham Lincoln's fiancée, who died suddenly of malarial fever in 1835.

"Spot Resolutions." As justification for the U.S. declaration of war on Mexico, Pres. Polk stated that American blood had been shed on American soil. Abraham Lincoln, Illinois Congressman, submitted a series of resolutions in 1847 attacking the President's statement and asking that the spot be identified. These "Spot Resolutions," as they were derisively called, made Lincoln unpopular back home and, subsequently, forced him into temporary political oblivion. Later, in 1858, when Lincoln campaigned for a Senate seat, Sen. Douglas referred to him as "Spot" Lincoln and disparaged his record on the Mexican War.

"spy flights." The expression was used to describe the flight of a U.S. plane, a U-2, high over the Soviet Union in 1960. American officials admitted that the plane, brought down in Soviet territory, had been sent to gather military intelligence about the USSR. The "spy flights" infuriated Khrushchev, then Premier of the Soviet Union. He cancelled an invitation that had been extended to Pres. Eisenhower to visit Russia and broke up a "summit conference" in Paris.

Square Deal. Pres. Theodore Roosevelt coined the expression to designate his policy. He promised fair treatment for capital, labor and for every segment of society. The expression became a symbol of his endorsement of "equality of opportunity and reward."

squatters. Settlers who occupied land before it was surveyed and placed on sale by the federal government were known as squatters. Since many improved the land on which they squatted, its loss was an additional hardship. Often, the improvements did not indicate that cash for purchase could be raised and speculators were able to outbid the squatters when the land was placed on sale. To help squatters during the course of the westward movement, Congress passed laws in the 1830's and 1840's allowing preemption of the land. This permitted squatters to claim the land in advance of the sale and to buy it at the minimum price.

Stalwarts. A faction of the Republican party was firmly committed to the spoils system and bitterly opposed to the civil service reform efforts of the Hayes administration. It was led by Sen. Roscoe Conkling of New York who sought unsuccessfully to gain a third-term nomination for Grant in 1880. The Stalwarts contemptuously referred to their opponents within the Republican party as "Halfbreeds."

Stamp Act (1765). During the ministry of George Grenville, Parliament imposed a stamp tax on all colonial purchases of legal and commercial documents, licenses, newspapers, pamphlets, almanacs, playing cards, dice and liquor permits. The stamp tax was intended to raise revenue in the colonies to defray mounting costs of defending the colonies against Indian attacks.

The tax was resisted by the most vocal forces in the colonies —lawyers, printers, editors and tavern owners.

Stamp Act Congress (1765). Delegates from nine colonies met in New York City to protest Parliament's Stamp Act. The Congress asserted the right of the colonies to freedom from taxation except "with their own consent, given personally, or by their representatives." Parliament was petitioned for repeal of the Stamp Act, but there was no threat of independence. The Stamp Act was repealed by Parliament (1766) under the Rockingham ministry. Opposition to the stamp tax included boycotts, which hurt British merchants, and refusal to use the stamps.

Standard Oil Company. As early as 1867, John D. Rockefeller had become the greatest oil refiner in Cleveland. In 1870 he organized, in Ohio, the Standard Oil Co., started with a capital of $1 million. Large stockholders included Samuel Andrews, an experienced oil-refining technologist, Henry M. Flagler, William Rockefeller and Stephen V. Harkness. By 1872 Standard Oil was refining one-fifth of the "Black Gold" extracted from the oil fields of Pennsylvania, West Virginia and Ohio. By 1879 it owned about 95% of the refining capacity of the U.S. and had won most of the world market for its products.

The company was a vertical combination integrating the various phases of the petroleum industry. It made its own sulphuric acid for use in the refining process; established its own cooperage plants for barrels, even buying forests to provide the lumber; made its own tank cars, tin cans and other supplies; set up its own draying service and warehouses. Its ownership of pipelines lessened the company's dependence upon railroads. In addition to organization of production, Rockefeller set up a system of distribution involving licensed dealers all over the nation and in foreign countries.

Business efficiency was not alone responsible for Standard's rise to a monopolistic position in the oil industry. In an age of ruthless competition, Rockefeller was able to force railroads into giving him greater secret rebates than those won by his competitors. He would charge high rates in an area where he had at first lowered rates to drive out competition. He made large contributions to political campaign funds to insure the election of friendly legislators. Standard Oil's methods were much like those of the largest industries which developed after the Civil War.

To achieve more effective control over the far-flung operations, Rockefeller organized the Standard Oil Trust in 1879 and reorganized it in 1882. The trust agreement was an arrangement whereby the refineries, pipeline companies and other related industries turned over their voting stock to trustees in return for trust certificates. While the trust certificates paid dividends, the voting stock of the related companies was now in the hands of a few men who could manage the various operations of refining and distributing oil in a unified way. Since the trustees controlled a majority of the voting stock in the constituent companies, the trust, unlike the pool, had no difficulty in controlling its members and was a highly successful form of combination used in various industries.

In 1892 an Ohio court decision dissolved the Standard Oil Trust and caused a general abandonment of the trust agreement as a form of combination. The name trust, however, continues to be a popular name for all forms of large-scale business combinations.

In 1899 the Standard Oil Co. reorganized as a holding company. New Jersey, in 1899, was the first state to allow this practice. The holding company was a corporation organized for the purpose of owning the securities of other corporations. In cases where stock ownership was widely distributed, effective control could be exercised with control of less than 50% of the voting stock. The acquired companies could continue to operate as separate corporations. In the case of Standard Oil there were 20 companies.

In 1911 the U.S. Supreme Court (*Standard Oil Company of New Jersey et al. v. United States*) found that Standard Oil had engaged in an unreasonable combination. It ruled that the industrial holding company was a combination in restraint of trade and as such a violation of the Sherman Antitrust Act. It forced the company to split into 29 parts, but they continued to function with such synchronization that they might almost have remained one company.

The different Standard Oil companies continue to play major roles in the oil business. Among the top 100 corporations in the U.S. today, as measured by total revenues, are the Standard Oil Company of New Jersey, the Standard Oil Company of California and the Standard Oil Company of Indiana.

Stanford, Leland (1824–93). Railroad builder. Born in Watervliet, N.Y., he was admitted to the bar in New York. He moved west and entered the merchandising business in California. As Republican governor of California (1861–63), he held the state in the Union. He was a U.S. Senator (1885–93). His reputation rests chiefly on his promoting and financing of the Central Pacific R.R., the western link in the transcontinental line (built 1863–69). He founded (1885) Stanford Univ. in memory of his son.

Stanford University. Chartered in 1885, it opened in 1891 as the Leland Stanford Junior University. A privately endowed, coeducational, nonsectarian university, 30 miles south of San Francisco, in Stanford, Calif., it is organized into six schools, offering both undergraduate and graduate work in education, engineering, humanities and sciences, law, medicine (including nursing) and mineral sciences. The large campus of more than 8,000 acres gives Stanford a unique character among universities. There are extensive library, laboratory and research facilities in this "Harvard of the West."

Stanley, Wendell Meredith (1904–). Biochemist. Born in Ridgeville, Ind., he was granted a Ph.D. by the Univ. of Illinois (1929). He did notable work on viruses and was the first to isolate a virus (the tobacco mosaic virus). In 1946 he shared the Nobel Prize for Chemistry with J. H. Northrop.

Stanton, Elizabeth Cady (1815–1902). Reformer. Born in Johnstown, N.Y., she organized, with the aid of Lucretia C. Mott, the first woman's rights convention at Seneca Falls, N.Y. (July 19–20, 1848), launching the woman's suffrage movement. She was closely associated in suffrage work with Susan B. Anthony. President of the National Woman Suffrage Association (1869–90), she was also active in the abolition and temperance movements.

Stanwix, Fort. The fort in the Mohawk Valley of New York, on the site of present-day Rome, was named after Gen. John Stanwix who built it in 1756 during the French and Indian War on the ruins of another fort. Two major treaties with the Indians were concluded here.

In the first Treaty of Stanwix (1768) Sir William Johnson negotiated with the Iroquois a new boundary line that moved the Indians farther back than the Proclamation Line of 1763. The line agreed upon extended south and west to where it meets the Tennessee River. The effect of the Treaty was to encourage white settlers to move even farther west.

In the second Treaty of Fort Stanwix (1784) the Iroquois yielded a large part of northwestern Pennsylvania and a section of western New York to the U.S. They were compelled to do so after they were defeated several times during the Revolution.

Star Route Frauds. During the Garfield and Arthur administrations federal investigations showed that the government was being defrauded of about $4,000,000 by Post Office Department officials, contractors and an ex-senator. The swindle developed in the distribution of U.S. mail, by horse and wagon, over routes mainly in the South and West. The "gang" conspired to gain more congressional appropriations for fictitious routes and for expensive improvements in routes which carried virtually no mail. Although the fraud was clear, the government was unable to obtain convictions in the trials, held in 1882 and 1883.

Stars and Bars. The flag of the Confederacy from 1861 to 1863 consisted of a red field with a white space extending horizontally through the center and equal to one-third the width of the flag. Also part of the flag was a white star for each state on a field of blue. It first flew over the State House, Montgomery, Ala., Mar. 4, 1861, when Lincoln was inaugurated.

The first Confederate flag appeared to be too similar to the Stars and Stripes and was modified in 1863 and again in 1865.

Stars and Stripes. The alternating red and white stripes of the U.S. flag have their origin in the family crest of the Washington family in England. George Washington had the design on the panels of his carriage. The first flag of the U.S. was raised at Cambridge, Mass., by Washington, Jan. 2, 1776. It consisted of 13 stripes, alternate red and white, with a blue canton bearing the crosses of St. George and St. Andrew.

The legend that the flag adopted by the Congress was sewed by Betsy Ross, at the direction of Washington, is colorful but unsupported by historical evidence.

"Star Spangled Banner." The poem was written by Francis Scott Key, a young Baltimore lawyer, following the bombardment of Fort McHenry in Baltimore Harbor (Sept. 13–14, 1814). Key could scarcely believe that the American flag was still flying at dawn, after the intermittent 25-hour bombardment to which the fort had been subjected. The opening line of the four-stanza poem expresses his reaction: "Oh, say can you see by the dawn's early light."

Key's vantage point for watching the bombardment was the British fleet. He and a group of friends were being detained temporarily by the British naval commander. They had gone out to the fleet, under a flag of truce, with a note from Pres. Madison requesting the release of a prominent Baltimore physician. Their arrival conflicted with the commander's plan for moving to an attack on the fort.

The poem was quickly adapted to the popular English drinking song, "Anacreon in Heaven," and caught on as a patriotic ballad. More than a hundred years later it was designated the national anthem by Act of Congress, Mar. 3, 1931.

"starving time." The Jamestown colonists had settled on difficult to clear wooded land because they feared Indian attack in open fields. The winter of 1609, after Capt. Smith departed, was the "starving time." When relief came in the spring of 1610 only 60 of the 500 left by Smith had survived.

State, Department of. Prior to Mar. 4, 1789, the foreign affairs of the U.S. were conducted by the Continental Congress' Committee of Secret Correspondence (1775–77), the Committee for Foreign Affairs (1777–81) and the Department of Foreign Affairs (1781–89).

The Department of Foreign Affairs was reconstituted, following the adoption of the Constitution, by an act of Congress approved July 27, 1789. The name of the Department was changed to "Department of State" and its activities were extended to include some of a purely domestic nature.

The President, as Chief Executive, has overall responsibility for the direction of the foreign policy of the U.S. The Secretary of State, who heads the Department of State, has a place in the President's Cabinet and is his chief adviser in this field. He thus has primary responsibility for initiating and implementing foreign policies.

Since 1789 the Department has had custody of the Great Seal of the U.S., but use of the Great Seal is now restricted chiefly to matters pertaining to foreign affairs.

state fairs. Exhibitions of farm produce, livestock and new inventions are now annual gatherings in many states. The fairgrounds are usually located conveniently for city and rural people and enlivened by dining and entertainment. The annual state fair with the longest record of continuity is the one in Syracuse, which was first held in 1841.

Staten Island, N.Y. Bought from the Indians by Michael Pauw in 1631, the island was later transferred to the Dutch West India Co. It was settled by colonists under De Vries in 1637; two years later the settlement was burned by the Raritan Indians. The West India Co. acquired the patroon titles on the island, but in 1665 it was taken over by the Duke of York. Today, the island, also known as Richmond, is one of New York City's five boroughs.

State of the Union message. At each of the opening sessions of Congress, the President delivers a message on the state of the union, in accordance with Art. II, Sec. 3 of the Constitution which states: "He shall, from time to time, give to the Congress information of the state of the union, and recommend to their consideration, such measures as he shall judge necessary and expedient. . . ." Pres. Washington started the practice by appearing before the Congress in person. With the outbreak of the French Revolution, the ceremonies surrounding the address were attacked as "monarchical." Pres. Jefferson, aware of his limitations as a speaker and sympathetic to the criticism, determined to replace "the speech from the Throne." The precedent established by Jefferson was not upset until Pres. Wilson appeared in person before both Houses of Congress in Apr. 1913 to deliver his first message. Pres. Kennedy, at the start of his message (Jan. 11, 1962), observed: "It is my task to report the State of the Union —to improve it is the task of all of us."

states' rights. The colonial experience with Parliament made the newly formed states jealous of their rights and reluctant to yield them to a central government. As a consequence, the Articles of Confederation guaranteed each state its sovereignty. This principle was maintained in a more limited way in the Constitution, which reserved to the states any powers not specifically granted to the federal government (10th Amendment).

The principle of states' rights was adhered to in numerous instances in American history. It was set forth in the Virginia and Kentucky Resolutions (1798), which held that a state had the right to nullify laws of Congress that restricted freedom to criticize the government. The Hartford Convention (1814) asserted states' rights when New England threatened secession in opposition to the War of 1812. South Carolina was emphasizing states' rights in its Ordinance of Nullification (1832) challenging the tariff acts of 1828 and 1832. The principle is cited down to present times whenever the powers of the federal government are challenged as being excessive. The principle of states' rights has not been linked with the right of secession since the Civil War.

state universities. Dissatisfaction with the colleges of colonial origin, largely attended by the rich and under denominational control, led to the establishment of state institutions of higher learning. Their growth was stimulated, beginning about 1820, by the rise of a new democratic spirit.

The failure of the New Hampshire legislature to transform Dartmouth into a state institution was confirmed by the U.S. Supreme Court in the Dartmouth College Case (1819). It became clear that states could not hope to change old establishments and that they would have to create new state universities.

Virginia created its state university in 1819. The University of North Carolina, established in 1789, was taken over by the state in 1821. The University of Vermont, originally chartered in 1791, became a state university under a new charter in 1838. The University of Indiana was established in 1820. The University of Alabama was opened for instruction in 1831. Wisconsin, while still a territory, provided for a state university in 1836 and included the idea in its first constitution when it entered the Union in 1848. Missouri provided for a state university in 1839; Mississippi in 1844; Iowa in 1847; Florida in 1856.

There is a state university in almost every state.

Statue of Liberty. The statue in New York Harbor has been a symbol of liberty to immigrants arriving in the U.S. since it was dedicated, Oct. 28, 1886, by Pres. Cleveland. It was a gift of France to the U.S. and was to have been delivered in 1876, the 100th anniversary of the signing of the Declaration of Independence; but the arrival of the statue, built by the French sculptor Frederic Auguste Bartholdi, was delayed by the Franco-Prussian War.

It stands on Liberty Island (formerly Bedloes Island, renamed by Congress in 1956). It is 152 feet tall and stands on a 150-foot-high pedestal. The right arm, the one that carries the torch, is 42 feet long.

steel traps. By the beginning of the 18th century they were being widely used in the American colonies and in unsettled areas for trapping beavers and other animals. Indians obtained them from traders and used them to increase the supply of pelts. The Newhouse traps, American made, set a standard for quality by the middle of the 19th century.

steering committee. The committee in the House of Representatives is chosen by the majority caucus to exercise supervision over the handling of business by the House. Its main function is to select from the large number of bills on the House calendars those which the majority's leaders wish to advance to final consideration.

Steffens, Lincoln (1866–1936). Journalist and social reformer. Born in San Francisco, Calif., he was graduated from the Univ. of California (1889). After reporting and editorial work for the New York *Evening Post* and New York *Commercial Advertiser* (1892–1901), he gained prominence as a muckraking journalist at war with the civic corruption and social evils of the first decade of the 20th century. On the staff of *McClure's Magazine,* he wrote "Tweed Days in St. Louis" (1902). His book, *Shame of the Cities* (1904), collected his articles linking business and politics with corruption. After the Bolshevik Revolution (Nov. 1917), he looked for a time to the Soviet Union for a better world. His *Autobiography* (1931) reflects his doubt that it is attainable.

Stephens, Alexander Hamilton (1812–83). Statesman. Born

632

near Crawfordville, Ga., he was a member of the U.S. House of Representatives (1843–59), first as a Whig and later as a Democrat (1852). He opposed immediate secession, but joined his state and accepted the vice-presidency of the Confederate States of America (1861–65). His support of civil liberties and constitutional restraints caused him to be critical of President Davis' policies. He headed the Confederate peace mission at Hampton Roads Conference (Feb. 1865). Elected to U.S. Senate (1866), he was refused a seat along with others from the "rebel" states. He was a member of the U.S. House of Representatives (1873–82) and governor of Georgia (1883). He was author of *A Constitutional View of the Late War Between the States* (2 vols., 1868, 1870).

Stevens, Thaddeus (1792–1868). Political leader. Born in Danville, Vt., he was graduated from Dartmouth (1814). He began practicing law in Pennsylvania (1816) and defended fugitive slaves without fee. A strong member of the Pennsylvania legislature (1833–41), he favored extension of free public education. As a member of the U.S. House of Representatives (1849–53, 1859–68), Stevens favored the protective tariff, opposed any compromise with slavery in the territories and sought to maintain Republican supremacy in the Union. While supporting Lincoln in the financing of the war, he urged sterner measures toward the

South and viewed the returning states as "conquered provinces." Regarding Pres. Johnson as too conciliatory to the South, he helped to manage his impeachment. A master of invective, he forced his program of military Reconstruction through Congress and was untiring in his efforts to achieve rights and economic aid for the newly emancipated Negroes.

Stevenson, Adlai Ewing (1900–65). Statesman. Born in Los Angeles, Calif., he practiced law in Chicago (1927–41). He performed varied governmental service during World War II. He was a member of the U.S. delegation to the UN Conference at San Francisco (Apr. 1945). He was governor of Illinois (1949–53). Democratic nominee for President (1953, 1956), he was defeated both times by Pres. Eisenhower. A witty, eloquent speaker, as U.S. Ambassador to the UN (1961–65), he sought to raise the level of political discussion.

Stieglitz, Alfred (1864–1946). Photographer. Born in Hoboken, N.J., he gave new dimensions to commonplace scenes and raised photography to a fine art. He was editor and publisher of *Camera Work* (from 1903).

Stimson, Henry Lewis (1867–1950). Statesman. Born in New York City, he was graduated from Yale (1888). A lawyer by profession and a Republican in politics, he was the first American to serve in the Cabinets of

633

four Presidents — Republican and Democratic. Stimson was Sec. of War (1911–13) under Taft and Sec. of State (1929–33) under Hoover, during which time he announced the "Stimson Doctrine" (1932) of not recognizing territories obtained by acts of aggression. In World War II, he served the Democratic administrations of F. D. Roosevelt and Truman as Sec. of War (1940–45).

Stimson Doctrine (Jan. 7, 1932). After Japan invaded Manchuria in 1931 it set up the puppet state of Manchukuo. Sec. of State Stimson declared that the U.S. would not recognize Manchukuo because it had been set up by force in violation of treaties. The League of Nations Assembly adopted a resolution incorporating this doctrine of non-recognition.

The League appointed the Lytton Commission, which included an American representative, to investigate Japan's action. The Lytton Report (Oct. 4, 1932) condemned Japan as an aggressor.

Japan did not, however, quit Manchukuo; it quit the League in 1933.

Stone, Harlan Fiske (1872–1946). Jurist. Born in Chesterfield, N.H., he practiced law in New York City. Dean of Columbia Law School (1907, 1910–23), he was appointed to U.S. Supreme Court as an associate justice (1925) by Pres. Coolidge and became Chief Justice in 1941. He joined Justices Holmes and Brandeis as a frequent dissenter on social issues. He generally supported the New Deal. He dissented when the Agricultural Adjustment Act processing tax was declared unconstitutional (*U.S. v. Butler*, 1935) holding that "Courts are not the only agencies of government that must be assumed to have capacity to govern."

Stony Point, capture of (July 16, 1779). "Mad Anthony" Wayne, under orders of Gen. Washington, captured the strategic site on the Hudson River, which controlled the roads leading from New England to Pennsylvania. Although the point was yielded two days later by Washington, the victory in the surprise attack boosted morale in the Continental army.

Story, Joseph (1779–1845). Jurist. Born in Marblehead, Mass., he was graduated from Harvard (1798). The youngest justice ever to be appointed to the U.S. Supreme Court (1811–45), he extended the admiralty jurisdiction of the federal courts after the War of 1812 and significantly extended appellate jurisdiction of the Supreme Court over state courts (*Martin v. Hunter's Lessee*, 1816). He upheld the sanctity of contracts in a notable dissenting opinion (*Charles River Bridge v. Warren Bridge*, 1837). Story's *Commentaries*, through which he acquired an international reputation, were a result of his teaching methods at Harvard (1829–45). They began with bailments (1832) and ended with promissory notes (1845). Included also were his *Commentaries on the Constitution of the United States* (3 vols., 1833). Together with Chancellor James Kent, he is remembered as the founder of the system of equity practice in U.S. courts.

Stourbridge Lion. The first to run on any American railroad (Aug. 8, 1829), this seven-ton English-made steam locomotive was tried by the Delaware and Hudson Canal Company, the line built to transport anthracite coal in northeastern Pennsylvania. The locomotive was too heavy for the company's track and was not used again.

Stowe, Harriet Elizabeth Beecher (1811–96). Author. Born in Litchfield, Conn., she was the daughter of a prominent clergyman, Lyman Beecher, and the sister of the widely influential clergyman, Henry Ward Beecher. An ardent Abolitionist, she won enduring fame in her own right with the publication of *Uncle Tom's Cabin; or, Life Among the Lowly* (first published as a serial in the *National Era,* 1851–52, and in book form, 1852). It was the first novel with a black man as a hero and aroused the North against slavery as a moral wrong. The *Southern Literary Messenger* described the book as a "criminal prostitution of the high functions of the imagination." Her other works include *Dred, a Tale of the Great*

Dismal Swamp (1856), *The Minister's Wooing* (1859) and *The True Story of Lady Byron's Life* (1869) in which she accused Lord Byron of incest with his sister Augusta. Her works were collected in *The Writings of Harriet Beecher Stowe* (16 vols., 1896).

strawfoot. The nickname was given to the farm boys recruited in the Union army during the Civil War. They did not seem to know their left foot from their right. Drill sergeants licked the problem of teaching them to march by having them tie hay to the left foot and straw to the right foot. The marching commands which then rang out were "Hayfoot! Strawfoot!"

streetcars. The first streetcar in the world began operation, Nov. 26, 1832, in New York City. It was the "John Mason," a horse-drawn car on rails slotted deeply into the streets, operated on lower 4th Avenue by the New York and Harlem RR. This street railway was a financial failure, but there was a considerable growth of street railways in the 1850's.

In 1873 the cable streetcar, invented by Andrew S. Hallidie, was used on the steep hills of San Francisco, Calif. The car was attached to an electric cable slotted under the surface of the street. In 1874 the first electrically powered streetcar, invented by Stephen Dudley Field, was run successfully in New York City. Electric streetcars were widely used in American cities until the 1930's, after which they were gradually replaced by motor buses.

Stuart, Gilbert Charles (1755–1828). Painter. He was born in North Kingstown Township, R. I. A pupil of Benjamin West in London (1776–81), he attracted favorable public notice with his *Portrait of a Gentleman Skating* (1782). He became one of the leading portrait painters of London before sailing for the U.S. (1793). He is best known for his portraits of Washington. Other lifelike portraits were made of Jefferson, Madison, Monroe and other notable contemporaries. West is reported to have said of him: "It's no use to steal Stuart's colors; if you want to paint as he does you must steal his eyes."

Stuart, James Ewell Brown (1833–64). Born in Patrick Co., Va., he was graduated from the U.S. Military Academy (1854) and resigned from the U.S. Army to join the Confederacy. Known as "Jeb" Stuart, he was promoted to brigadier general following his contribution to the victory at the first battle of Bull Run (1861). His brilliant cavalry sweeps around the Union forces in subsequent actions caused Gen. Lee to praise him as the "eyes of the army." He distinguished himself in the Seven Days' Battle (1862) and was promoted to major general. Stuart succeeded the wounded Stonewall Jackson as commander at Chancellorsville (1863) and played a disputed role at Gettys-

burg (1863) because of his failure to join the main body of the Confederate Army until the second day of the battle. A dandy in appearance, he was a dramatic figure who was at times accused of seeking credit that belonged to others. He was mortally wounded in the defense of Richmond.

Student Nonviolent Coordinating Committee (SNCC). Popularly pronounced "snick," the agency for nonviolent direct action to eliminate segregation was founded in 1960. In 1964 it had 520 volunteers in Mississippi, including 150 lawyers and law students, Negro and white, working on voter registration or operating "Freedom Schools" where Negro history and voter registration skills were taught. The organization had backers on many college campuses. By 1967 the leadership disavowed nonviolence, and white members were discouraged from continuing in the organization.

Stuyvesant, Peter (1592–1672). Colonial governor. Born in West Friesland, the Netherlands, he served in the Dutch army and lost a leg in its service. Appointed director-general in New Netherland (1646) by the Dutch West India Co., he arrived in New Amsterdam the following year. His stern rule of the colony included restrictions on alcohol, enforced Sunday observance (Dutch Reformed Church) and restrictions on freedom of worship.

The people of New Amsterdam protested and won independent municipal government (1653). Stuyvesant ousted the Swedes from Delaware and improved relations with the Indians and English. He reluctantly surrendered New Netherland to the English (1664). A large landowner, he spent his remaining years in New York on his farm on the "Bouwerij" (Bowery).

submarines. The first American submarine, *American Turtle*, was built in 1775 by David Bushnell. It nearly succeeded in blowing up a British frigate in New York Harbor (1776). During the Civil War, the Confederate *Hunley* was the first to sink an enemy ship. The "father of the modern submarine" is John P. Holland, who won the U.S. government's competition for a practical submarine in 1893.

U.S. submarines were scarcely active in World War I, but the example of German World War I submarine (U-boat) activity was not ignored. In World War II, U.S. submarines of the *Flasher* type sank over 1,300 vessels in the Pacific.

In the post-World War II period the emphasis has been concentrated on the construction of nuclear-powered submarines.

Suffolk Resolves (Sept. 9, 1774). Delegates from Boston and other towns in Suffolk County met to protest British coercive measures against Massachusetts. The resolutions formulated by Dr. Joseph Warren set forth grievances against Britain, called for the colonies to raise troops of their own and urged a boycott of trade with Britain and the West Indies. The Resolves were sent to the Continental Congress meeting in Philadelphia, where they were endorsed. The final break with Britain was brought closer.

Sugar Act (1764). The Act reduced the duty on foreign molasses and provided for strict collection of the lowered duties. It raised duties on foreign refined sugar. The Act was part of a broad Revenue Act, a new phase of British colonial legislation, for it aimed to raise revenue to defray the cost of governing and protecting the colonies rather than to regulate trade. The Act dealt a blow to the profitable colonial trade with the foreign West Indies.

The colonists protested that they were being taxed without their consent and demanded repeal of the Sugar Act. While Parliament was not moved by colonial arguments on basic freedoms, nonimportation agreements begun by colonial merchants forced Parliament in 1766 to reduce from three cents to a penny a gallon the duty on all molasses (whether British or foreign).

Sugar Trust Case (1895). In *U.S. v. E. C. Knight Co.*, the U.S. Supreme Court held that although the American Sugar Refining Co. had acquired "nearly complete control of the manufacture of refined sugar in the United States," it was not in restraint of trade. The case was the first to come before the Court under the Sherman Antitrust Act of 1890 and made the statute a dead letter for several years.

The Court reasoned that the refining of sugar was a manufacturing process carried on within a state. Transportation of the sugar was incidental. It was, therefore, a matter for the states to regulate and did not come within the interstate commerce clause of the Constitution.

Sullivan, Harry Stack (1892–1949). Physician and psychiatrist. Born in Norwich, N.Y., he was granted an M.D. by Chicago College of Medicine and Surgery (1917). He made intensive studies of schizophrenia and obsessional neurosis. According to his theory of interpersonal relations, psychoanalysis needed to be supplemented by consideration of the impact of cultural forces upon personality. He taught psychiatry at Maryland Medical School (1923–39), and practiced psychiatry in N.Y.C. He edited *Psychiatry* (1939–49). He collected some of his papers in *Conceptions of Modern Psychiatry* (1940).

Sullivan, Louis Henri (1856–1924). Architect. Born in Boston, Mass., he was a leading figure in the so-called Chicago school of architecture. His designs for skyscrapers mark him as the father of modernism in architecture.

Sumner, Charles (1811–74). Statesman. Born in Boston, Mass., he became a leading antislavery advocate who represented Mass. in the U.S. Senate (1851–74). A powerful orator, he was assaulted in the Senate (May 22, 1856) by a kinsman of a congressman whom he had excoriated for his position on the Kansas-Nebraska Act. A founder of the Republican party, Sumner was among the first to urge emancipation of the slaves. He favored control of Reconstruction by Congress, not the President, and took the lead in impeachment of President Johnson. He remained a firm advocate of civil rights for Negroes in the post-Civil War period. In foreign affairs, he earned Pres. Grant's displeasure by opposing the annexation of Santo Domingo and did not support Grant's reelection. His writings were published as *The Works of Charles Sumner* (15 vols., 1870–83).

Sumner-Brooks Affair (May 22, 1856). The boiling point reached in the slavery controversy was dramatized by the brutal beating given the Abolitionist Sen. Charles Sumner of Massachusetts, by Rep. Preston S. Brooks of South Carolina.

In his speech, "The Crime Against Kansas," Sumner had inveighed against the "harlot slavery" and the "incoherent phrases" spoken in its defense by Sen. Andrew P. Butler of

South Carolina, a cousin of Brooks.

While Sumner sat at his desk in the Senate chamber, Brooks struck him repeatedly over the head with a cane and almost killed Sumner, who took more than three years to recover. The North was revolted by the attack, but the South applauded it. Brooks was reelected to his seat in the House.

Sumter, Fort. The firing on Fort Sumter (Apr. 12, 1861) by southern troops under Gen. Pierre Beauregard did more than previous acts to bring on the Civil War. It caused Lincoln to summon the militia to suppress the rebellion which was under way.

The fort, in Charleston Harbor (S.C.), surrendered when the bombardment caused fires and the defenders ran out of food. An earlier effort to provision the fort by sending in a merchant ship, *Star of the West*, had failed when it was fired upon by Fort Moultrie, which Confederate troops under Beauregard had taken over without encountering resistance.

In Feb. 1865, the Union flag was once more raised over Fort Sumter.

Supreme Court of the U.S. The Constitution of the U.S. (Art. III, Sec. 1) provides that "the judicial power of the United States shall be vested in one Supreme Court and in such inferior Courts as the Congress may from time to time ordain and establish." The Supreme Court of the U.S. was created in accordance with this provision and by authority of the Judiciary Act of Sept. 24, 1789. It was organized, Feb. 2, 1790.

The Supreme Court comprises the Chief Justice of the U.S. and such number of Associate Justices as may be fixed by Congress. John Jay was the first Chief Justice and there were five Associate Justices. The number of Justices has varied from five to ten. In 1869 the number was fixed at nine and has remained at that number.

Justices are nominated by the President and appointments are made with the consent of the Senate. The Justices hold office for life "during good Behaviour."

The Supreme Court has original jurisdiction in all cases affecting ambassadors and consuls and those in which a state is a party. In all other cases the Supreme Court has appellate jurisdiction. These include controversies to which the U.S. is a party and where citizens of different states are involved. Since the Judiciary Act of 1925 the Court determines for itself which cases it will hear on appeal.

The Court's vital power of judicial review was established under Chief Justice John Marshall who presided 1801–35. The Court can void laws of Congress and state laws where it holds that these are in conflict with the Constitution. A Supreme Court decision can be reversed by an amendment to the

Constitution, but this has been a rare recourse. The Court's power remains a unique feature of U.S. government.

The Court has been attacked over the years for decisions which affect political and economic relationships; but, in general, it has enjoyed wide respect.

Surveyor. A stride beyond Ranger, the spaceship is designed to land softly on the moon rather than crash into it. Surveyor 1, launched June 2, 1966, was equipped with television cameras to take pictures both before and after landing. It carried instruments to analyze lunar surface material and measure meteorite bombardment and moonquakes. It helped to verify the suitability of sites for manned landings and furnished information that aided in designing protective shielding for the manned spacecraft and astronauts' space suits.

Surveyor 2, launched Sept. 20, 1966, failed and crashed into the moon. Surveyor 7, the most fully equipped scientifically of all Surveyor probes, completed the series with a soft landing on the moon, Jan. 9, 1968. The last probe in the NASA Surveyor program, it began transmitting TV pictures back to earth 45 minutes after landing.

Sussex **pledge.** In 1916 a German submarine torpedoed an unarmed French ship, the *Sussex*, and several Americans on board were injured. The U.S. sent a strong note of protest to Germany and threatened to sever diplomatic relations unless Germany abandoned her methods of submarine warfare.

Germany pledged that no more merchant ships would be sunk without warning, provided that the U.S. also held England accountable for her violations of international law.

Wilson chose to ignore the proviso and accepted the pledge by which Germany restricted the use of a powerful maritime weapon rather than risk war with the U.S. at the time.

Sutter's Mill. On Jan. 24, 1848, at a sawmill near Sutter's Fort, on the site of present-day Sacramento, Calif., millwright James W. Marshall accidentally found grains of a yellow mineral. The mill was owned by Capt. John A. Sutter who tried to keep his employees silent about the discovery. The news leaked out and the result was the California gold rush.

"swamp fox." The nickname was earned by Francis Marion of South Carolina whose guerrilla operations against the British prevented effective organization of South Carolina Tories during the Revolutionary War.

Swedish West India Co. Founded in 1624 by William Usselinx of Antwerp under a charter granted by Gustavus Adolphus, the company held special trading privileges with New World colonies. Also known as the South Co., it combined later with Dutch merchants and established settlements along the Delaware River. The charter was terminated in 1646.

Swiss. Early in the 18th century economic conditions in Switzerland led to emigration to the American colonies. In 1711 a number of Swiss and Germans led by Jean Pierre Purry emigrated to South Carolina. In 1732 an extensive tract along the Savannah River was granted to a new body from Neufchâtel.

When emigration became general, the Swiss cantons cracked down. The outflow meant to noblemen the loss of mercenaries who could be hired out to European princes. Swiss emigrants had to steal out of the country to Holland or France for embarkation to America.

Syncom. In experiments for a global communications system, "synchronous" satellites are orbited at 22,300 miles above the Equator, traveling around the earth in the same time that it takes the earth to rotate around its axis. The high altitude of these satellites makes it possible, in theory, to provide worldwide coverage with only three satellites.

On Feb. 14, 1963, Syncom I was launched and lost. Syncom II, launched July 26, 1963, was successful. Orbiting over Brazil, it relayed a telephone conversation between the heads of state of the U.S. and Nigeria.

T

Taft, Robert Alphonso (1889–1953). Statesman. He was born in Cincinnati, O. Known as "Mr. Republican," he consistently opposed the New Deal. He was a member of the Ohio state House of Representatives (1921–26) and in the U.S. Senate (1938–53). He cosponsored the Taft-Hartley Act (1947).

Taft, William Howard (1857–1930). Twenty-seventh President of the U.S. Born in Cincinnati, O., he was graduated from Yale (1878). He practiced law in Ohio and was a U.S. circuit court judge (1892–1900). He was the first civil governor of the Philippine Islands under American control (1901–04) and U.S. Sec. of War (1904–08). The high points of his administration included support of the unpopular Payne-Aldrich Tariff Act (1909); prosecution of trusts; and the dismissal of Gifford Pinchot, a leading conservationist, which caused him to lose the support of Theodore Roosevelt and eventually brought about his defeat for reelection (1912). He served as Chief Justice on the U.S. Supreme Court (1921–30).

Taft-Hartley Act. The Labor-Management Relations Act of 1947 was sponsored in Congress by Sen. Robert A. Taft (O.) and Rep. Fred A. Hartley (N.J.) and passed over the veto of Pres. Truman. Commonly known as the Taft-Hartley Act it reaffirmed the Wagner Act by guaranteeing the right of workers to form unions and to engage in collective bargaining. The National Labor Relations Board is continued to protect labor's rights.

In contrast to the Wagner Act, however, it lists unfair practices by labor unions including mass picketing and secondary boycotts.

The Act outlaws the closed shop: an employer may not sign a contract with a union which requires membership in the union as a condition of employment. The law, however, does authorize contracts establishing the union shop. Under such an arrangement an employer may hire workers who are not members of the union but these workers must join the union within a specified period of time in order to hold their jobs.

There are a number of provisions in the Act to protect "rank and file" union members against unfair treatment by union officials.

To reduce the likelihood of strikes the Act provides for a 60-day "cooling-off" period at the end of a contract during which no strike or lockout may go into effect. It provides further for an additional 80 days of "cooling-off," if the President is of the opinion that the strike or lockout may imperil the national health or safety. He may appoint a fact-finding commission to help settle the dispute.

Labor spokesmen denounced the law as "a slave labor act," a criticism which later seemed extreme. Employers defend the Act's basic approach.

Tallmadge Amendment (1819). Missouri's request for admission to the Union as a slave state threatened to upset the equal balance between free and slave states. Rep. James Tallmadge (N.Y.) amended the bill permitting the entry of Missouri to forbid further importation of slaves into that state. It provided, too, for the emancipation of resident slaves at the age of 25 who were born after the state's admission to the Union. The amendment was defeated in the Senate where the South was in control. Missouri's entrance into the Union as a slave state in 1821 was effected by the Missouri Compromise.

Tammany. A political organization that dominated New York City politics from the second half of the 19th century to 1932, when it failed to support Franklin D. Roosevelt and lost much of its political strength. It is now known as the New York County Democratic Committee.

The Society of Tammany, or Columbian Order, a patriotic and charitable organization, was formed about 1786. It took its name from the Delaware chief, Tammany, and followed Indian rituals. Its leaders were known as sachems.

In the early 1820's the society became active in politics as the franchise was expanded to include the propertyless class. Beginning in 1854 Tammany dominated New York City politics. The organization became notorious under the control of Boss Tweed in the 1860's and 1870's. Although it fostered such political leaders as Gov. Alfred E. Smith, Tammany is generally linked with boss-ridden machine politics.

Tampico incident (1914). The crew of an American whaleboat was arrested by the Mexican government when they landed at Tampico without permission. Relations between the U.S. and Mexico were already strained by the refusal of Pres. Wilson to recognize the Huerta regime.

Although the Americans were released quickly, the commander of the American squadron near Tampico demanded an apology. Wilson chose to regard Huerta's reply as an insult to the nation's dignity and asked Congress for authority to use armed forces.

Taney, Roger Brooke (1777–1864). Jurist. He was born in Calvert Co., Md. Fourth Chief Justice, U.S. Supreme Court, his name is indelibly linked with the Dred Scott decision (1857). As Pres. Jackson's Attorney General (1831–33), he helped the President crush the Bank of the United States.

tariff. Under the U.S. Constitution, Congress may place a tariff on goods coming into the country from foreign lands (imports). It may not place a tariff on goods leaving the country (exports).

The many tariff acts passed in U.S. history have been described as either revenue or protective tariffs, depending on the size of the duty (tax) levied on imports. Specific duties are stated in terms of the units of measurement of the goods being imported. For example, the duty on a certain grade of tobacco may be five cents a pound. Ad valorem duties are placed on the money value of the goods imported. The duty on glassware may be 30% of its wholesale value.

Early tariffs were intended primarily to raise revenue from customs duties but contained protective features. The first unmistakably protective tariff intended to protect American "infant" industries was passed in 1816. In the period before the Civil War, the industrial North was the stronghold of

high tariff supporters. The South, in general, was opposed to the protective tariff. U.S. tariffs were protective in the post-Civil War period, except for occasional reductions when Democratic administrations were in office.

In the post-World War I period U.S. tariffs were very high. In 1934 the U.S. embarked on a program of reciprocal trade agreements to lower tariff barriers as a means of stimulating foreign trade. In 1962 sharp cuts in U.S. tariffs were made possible by the Trade Expansion Act.

Tariff legislation has remained highly controversial.

Tariff of 1789. In the first tariff act passed by Congress under the Constitution, James Madison's simple proposal for a revenue tariff was modified by a more complicated schedule of duties. A general duty of 5% was placed on all goods not otherwise enumerated. Higher ad valorem rates were fixed on luxury articles. Specific duties were imposed on hemp, cordage, nails and glass. These articles were selected with the clear intent of stimulating domestic production and were protective in nature. The major purpose of the tariff was, however, to raise revenue.

Tariff of 1816. When the War of 1812 ended early in 1815, British manufacturers "dumped" their goods on the American market at low prices in an effort to stifle American manufactures which had grown during the war. The new tariff, the first to be imposed primarily to protect American industry, was intended to meet the complaints of distressed manufacturers.

It was not, however, passed without opposition. New England was not yet fully committed to manufacturing, and commercial interests, represented by Daniel Webster, opposed the protective features. The Middle Atlantic states were for protection. The South was generally opposed, but John C. Calhoun favored protection in the hope that manufacturing might be stimulated in the South. The West was for protection and hoped that manufacturing would be encouraged in its section.

The Act failed to gain the kind of protection for manufacturers that was needed. Tariff interests moved for still higher protection.

Tariff of 1824. Duties imposed by the protective Tariff of 1816 were raised, but still not high enough to satisfy the manufacturing interests.

The most important changes increased duties on imported iron, lead, wool, hemp, cotton-bagging and other articles whose domestic manufacture the Middle Atlantic and western states wished to protect. New England was still divided between manufacturing and commercial interests. The South opposed the tariff.

Tariff of 1828. Protection of manufacturers was boosted still further by the "Tariff of Abominations," as it was called by its severe critics, especially in the South. It raised the tariff not only on manufactured goods but on raw materials, such as raw wool and pig iron, to the distaste of New England.

The tariff was as much concerned with the "manufacture of a President" as with protecting manufactured goods. Andrew Jackson's supporters in the North and South hoped to gain votes by standing for a high tariff in the North, but one so high that it would be rejected. Southern supporters might then say that they had defeated the high tariff principle opposed in the South.

The plan backfired because protective tariff interests were unwilling to back away from the principle of protection and swallowed the high duties on raw materials.

Tariff of 1832. The high rates of the "Tariff of Abominations" (1828) were reduced. The Tariff of 1828 had raised revenues to a point where Treasury surpluses could not be justified by the Jackson administration. Protectionists realized that moderation was necessary if sectional controversy was not to disrupt the nation.

Some of the "abominations" were done away with. Flax, for example, which had been subjected to a duty of $60 a ton in 1828, was placed on the free list. The duties on pig and bar iron were brought back to the rates of 1824.

Even in modified form, however, the protective tariff was assailed in the South. South Carolina adopted an ordinance of nullification declaring the Tariffs of 1828 and 1832 null and void and threatened secession if the federal government attempted to enforce the tariffs.

Tariff of 1833. A compromise tariff devised by Henry Clay conciliated the South and caused South Carolina to withdraw her ordinance nullifying the Tariffs of 1828 and 1832. The protectionists accepted gradual reduction of high rates over a nine-year period until no rate would be higher than 20%. Opponents of the protective principle were mollified by additions to the free list.

taxables. The term was used in the southern colonies for persons for whom a poll tax was paid (called tithables in Virginia). In Maryland, for example, taxables included all males and all slaves 16 years and older, excepting clergymen of the Church of England, paupers and disabled slaves.

Taxation No Tyranny (1775). In his pamphlet, Dr. Samuel Johnson attacked the cause of the American colonies.

Taylor, Zachary (1784–1850). Twelfth President of the U.S. He was born in Montebello, Orange County, Va. His record as a general in the Mexican War catapulted "Old Rough and Ready" into the Presidency. A Whig, he died after only a year and four months in office (Mar. 4, 1849–July 9, 1850).

Teapot Dome scandal. The disclosures created the most spectacular of the Harding administration scandals. In 1921 the Department of Interior was entrusted with disposal of the oil reserves for the Navy. A year later, Sec. of the Interior Albert B. Fall leased the Teapot Dome Reserve in Wyoming to Harry F. Sinclair's Mammoth Oil Co. and the Elk Hills Reserve to Edward F. Doheny's Pan-American Petroleum Co. Both arrangements were made without competitive bidding. Fall recived $223,000 in Liberty Bonds from Sinclair, along with a herd of cattle for his ranch, and a "loan" of $100,000 from Doheny.

In 1929 Fall was convicted of accepting a bribe and sentenced to a year in prison. Sec. of the Navy Denby resigned from office. The leases were voided by the U.S. Supreme Court. Pres. Harding had died, Aug. 2, 1923, before the scandal was known to the public. His memory was tarnished by the subsequent revelations.

Technocracy. The short-lived movement had its birth in the depression of the early 1930's. Industrial technicians who studied the capitalist system in the U.S. concluded that much of the productive capacity was unused and that improved efficiency in production would eventually make manual labor unnecessary. The technocrats envisaged abandonment of the distribution system with its use of money once the maximum capacity of industry could be unleashed.

Teheran Conference (Nov. 28– Dec. 1, 1943). The leaders of the Allies met in the capital city of Iran. It was the first conference in which Premier Stalin joined Pres. F. D. Roosevelt and Prime Minister Churchill. Stalin was deeply disturbed by the delay in opening a second front in western Europe.

The Allied leaders announced their determination to destroy "the German armies by land, their U-boats by sea, and their war plants from the air." "And as to the peace," they stated, "we are sure that our concord will make it an enduring peace."

telegraph. Samuel F. B. Morse patented the first practical telegraph in the U.S. in 1832. Following a large number of experiments, with the assistance of Alfred Vail, he established the first line between Baltimore and Washington, D.C. It was federally owned and started operation in 1844. In 1847, Congress turned over the line to the newly founded Magnetic Telegraph Co. of Maryland, the first telegraph company in the U.S.

New instruments were patented in the 1840's and 1850's and the telegraph business was enmeshed in litigation. Some order was derived after formation of the Western Union Co. in the late 1850's.

By 1860 there were over 50,000 miles of telegraph lines in operation in the U.S. Today there are over a million miles of wire in the U.S. Messages are now rarely sent by Morse code (invented in 1838) but are teletyped.

telephone. Rival claims to invention of the telephone have largely been resolved in favor of Alexander Graham Bell who patented his instrument in the U.S. in 1876. The first private home installation was made in 1877, and service between New York and Boston was in effect in 1884.

Improvements in the 1960's brought about coast to coast service (started in 1915) by direct dialing. Transatlantic telephone service between New York and London was begun in 1927. Worldwide service by radio telephone and oceanic cables was available thereafter.

television. The transmission of pictures and sound together by electrical impulses was first accomplished in 1927 between New York and Washington. On May 11, 1928, Station WGY, Schenectady, N.Y., began the first program of scheduled television broadcasts. Television was demonstrated at the New York World's Fair in 1939. In 1941 the Federal Communications Commission authorized a number of channels for commercial use, but television did not become established in the home until the end of World War II. About four out of five households in the U.S. now have television sets; they are often also portable. Color television was first demonstrated in 1950, and the sale of color sets, which received both black and white and color, was well under way in the 1960's. The FCC has reserved channels for use by educational institutions.

Teller, Edward (1908–   ). Physicist. Born in Budapest, Hungary, he was granted a Ph.D. by Univ. of Leipzig (1930). He left Germany when Hitler came to power and came to the U.S. in 1935. He worked on the A-bomb project (1941–45) and was known as "the principal architect of the H-bomb." He was in charge of the H-bomb laboratory of the Atomic Energy Commission at Livermore, Calif. (1952). In a controversy over the testing of atomic and hydrogen bombs, he opposed cessation of the tests.

Teller Resolution (1898). Sen. Henry M. Teller (Colo.) offered an amendment to Congress' joint war resolution against Spain (Apr. 19). It was adopted by Congress and pledged that the U.S. would leave Cuba in control of the Cuban people.

Telstar 1. On July 10, 1962 and July 11, 1962, by utilization of this satellite the U.S. and England were able, for the first time, to view live telecasts across the Atlantic.

Telstar 2, launched May 7, 1963, was projected into a higher orbit to reduce the period that the satellite spends in the most intense portion of the Van Allen Radiation Region. Telstar 1's transistors were damaged by radiation and eventually were silenced. Telstar 2 has been redesigned to avoid this difficulty.

temperance movement. Until abolition of slavery aroused the country, the movement for "temperance" was the most intense reform activity in the U.S. Agitation against excessive use of liquor was begun during the colonial period and gained impetus from publication of Dr. Benjamin Rush's *Inquiry into the Effect of Ardent Spirit upon the Human Mind and Body*, written during the American Revolution.

Whereas Rush regarded drinking as bad for the health, reformers of the 19th century regarded it as sinful. In 1826 local Bible and Tract societies were coordinated in the American Temperance Union. By 1830 more than 2,000 "teetotaling" societies had been formed. Anti-drinking propaganda was carried on in tracts and at evangelical meetings. A famous temperance book, *Ten Nights in a Bar-Room and What I Saw There*, by T. S. Arthur, was published in 1854. By 1880 it had sold about 100,000 copies and was often dramatized.

Prohibition laws were enacted in 13 northern states by 1851, with Neal Dow, known as

"Father of the Maine Law," leading the way. Prohibition made little headway in the South and was not too well enforced even in those states which enacted laws.

Temporary National Economic Committee (TNEC). The joint legislative-executive committee under the chairmanship of Sen. Joseph C. O'Mahoney (Wyo.) conducted public hearings (Dec. 1, 1938–Apr. 26, 1940) following Pres. Roosevelt's recommendations for curbing the monopolies and the growing concentration of economic power. In its final report (Mar. 31, 1941) the TNEC recommended stronger antitrust laws, allocation of defense funds in such a way as to eliminate monopoly control of basic products and legislation prohibiting the use of "basing point" and other industrial pricing systems resulting in the elimination of competition.

Some antitrust suits initiated as a direct result of the TNEC's hearings were suspended during World War II.

"ten-forties." In 1864, to help finance the Civil War, the U.S. government issued bonds bearing 5% interest. They were redeemable any time after 10 years from the date of issue and payable in full at the end of 40 years.

ten-hour laws. During the 19th century the working day extended from sunup to sundown. In the 1830's workers organized for a 10-hour day. In 1835 the Philadelphia common council established a 10-hour day for public servants. Employers fell into line until the 10-hour day prevailed throughout the city.

In 1840 Pres. Van Buren issued an executive order establishing 10 hours as the workday on all government projects.

New Hampshire passed the first state 10-hour law in U.S. history in 1847; Pennsylvania followed in 1848 with a 10-hour day or 60-hour week "in cotton, woolen, silk, paper, bagging and flax factories." During the 1850's, Maine, Connecticut, Rhode Island, Ohio, California and Georgia passed some sort of 10-hour laws. There was a catch, however, in almost every case. The 10-hour provision could be circumvented by "special contracts." The employer could virtually disregard the law by refusing to hire anyone unless he was willing to accept a longer working day.

Tennessee. The "Volunteer State," so-called because of its response to the call for soldiers in the Mexican War, is in the East Central group. It was admitted to the Union as the 16th state, June 1, 1796. Its capital is Nashville.

The region was first visited by De Soto (1541). La Salle built Fort Prud'homme (1682). It remained, however, Indian hunting grounds until the French and English clashed in the mid-18th century. The name Tennessee is derived from the name of the Cherokee villages,

"'Tanasi," on the Little Tennessee River. France ceded the region to England in 1763. It was part of North Carolina when the short-lived state of Franklin was carved out of it (1784–88). North Carolina finally ceded the land to the federal government in 1790, and it became part of the Territory south of the Ohio until it entered the Union as a slave state.

Tennessee was the last of the southern states to leave the Union, June 1861, and the first to regain admission, 1866. It experienced some of the hardest fighting of the Civil War.

Tennessee is chiefly industrial. Principal industries are chemicals, textiles, foods, apparel and lumber products. It leads the South in a variety of minerals, including coal. Its agricultural output is about equally divided between field crops and livestock; the former include cotton, corn and tobacco.

Tennessee Valley Authority. In 1933, Congress authorized the construction of some 30 dams along the Tennessee River and its tributaries. The undertaking was designed to prevent floods and raise the standard of living in the Tennessee Valley, an area which includes parts of seven states—Tennessee, Kentucky, Virginia, North Carolina, Georgia, Alabama and Mississippi.

The dams have made it possible not only to control floods and promote navigation, but also to supply hydroelectric power to a region where the average farmer and city worker were without electricity prior to 1933. TVA also is concerned with soil erosion, the manufacture of fertilizer and the development of recreational areas. Factories have moved into the area, providing jobs for workers in the region.

tennis. The first mention of tennis in the New World appeared in a proclamation issued by Peter Stuyvesant in 1659 forbidding tennis playing, among other things, on a certain day. The game, as we know it today (net, ball, racquets and two to four players on a court), was brought to America from Bermuda in 1874 by Mary Ewing Outerbridge. She set up her net on the lawn of the Staten Island Cricket and Baseball Club where she and a friend played the first game in the U.S.

The game in its early days was on the genteel side, played by members of society. In 1881 the U.S. Lawn Tennis Association was formed, and a pattern of play was set up and adopted all over the world. A national championship tournament was held at Newport, R.I., Aug. 31, 1881. Richard D. Sears won the first men's singles crown. International competition got under way with the establishment of the Davis Cup matches in 1900. The national tennis championships were moved to Forest Hills, N.Y., in 1915. William T. Tilden, Jr. ("Big Bill" Tilden) became the U.S. and world's champion in the 1920's. In 1931 he turned professional and toured the U.S. with a group of players.

The game is one of the most popular amateur sports, and tennis courts are open to the public in virtually every community in the U.S. Professional tennis, with outstanding players recruited from among amateur champions, has also become popular since the end of World War II.

"Tennis Cabinet." The name was given by journalists to a group of Pres. Theodore Roosevelt's unofficial advisers with whom he played tennis or exercised during his administration (1901–09).

Tenure of Office Act (1867). Congress, controlled by the Radical Republicans, passed a law severely limiting the President's right to remove officials appointed by the President without the consent of the Senate. It required that they be removed only with the Senate's approval. The Act, passed over Pres. Andrew Johnson's veto, was part of the constant struggle between the President and Congress over Reconstruction plans.

When the President removed Sec. of War Stanton from the Cabinet, he was impeached in the House.

The Act was modified during Grant's administration and repealed in 1886 when Pres. Cleveland refused to permit Congress to curb his power of appointment.

Tesla, Nikola (1856–1943). Inventor. Born in Austria-Hungary, he came to the U.S. in 1884. He was employed by the Edison Co., West Orange, N.J. for several years. He applied the principle of the rotating magnetic field to an induction motor. Principally known for his researches in alternating currents of high frequency, his inventions include a system of arc lighting (1886) and a high-potential magnifying transmitter (1897).

Texas. The "Lone Star State," in the West South Central group, was admitted to the Union as the 28th state, Dec. 29, 1845. Its capital is Austin.

Texas (meaning "friends" or "allies" in the language of the Caddo Indians) was in Spanish hands until the 19th century. The coast was explored by Alonso de Pineda (1519). Other Spaniards who explored the region were De Vaca (1536) and Coronado (1541). The Frenchman La Salle founded Fort St. Louis (1685). The French were ousted by the Spanish, who made Texas a province (1691). Americans were invited to settle in 1821 and Stephen F. Austin, the "father of Texas," brought in settlers. The same year, Mexico revolted successfully from Spain and Texas became Mexican territory. Relations with the Americans became bitter and Texas declared its independence as a republic (Mar. 2, 1836). The action was followed by Mexican annihilation of a Texan force at the Alamo and the Texas victory under Sam Houston at San Jacinto.

The Lone Star State remained independent while seeking to join the U.S. It was annexed by the U.S. (1845) and joined the Union as a slave state. Despite Gov. Houston's opposition, Texas joined the Confederacy Mar. 2, 1861, and was not readmitted to the Union until Mar. 30, 1870.

In the post-Civil War period, the cattle industry thrived as cattle were driven north over the "long trail." Texas continues to lead the nation in cattle and sheep. The longest pipeline in the U.S. starts in Texas and carries oil 1,600 miles to Staten Island, N.Y. Texas is a major producer of petroleum and natural gas. The fertile black lands of central Texas are a fine cotton-growing region. Chemical production is the largest manufacturing industry in the state. Houston is the second largest deep-sea port in the nation. Dallas is a major cotton market and center for textile manufacture, petroleum products, meat packing, oil machinery and aircraft.

Texas & Pacific Railway Co. Chartered by Congress in 1871, the line was one of three transcontinentals given land grants by the federal government. The other two were the Northern Pacific (1864) and the Atlantic and Pacific (1866). Only the Northern Pacific was ever completed to the coast.

The T & P operates over 1,800 miles of main line extending from New Orleans to El Paso, via Shreveport, Texarkana, Dallas and Fort Worth.

Texas Rangers. The Texas government established a semi-military organization of picked men who were used against marauding Indians in the 1830's and against Mexicans in the 1840's. They were without uniforms but always carried a six-shooter and a saddle gun for their forays against cattle thieves, desperadoes and others who threatened the peace in Texas. The Rangers fought for the Confederacy during the Civil War. In the 1870's they resisted Indians who ravaged the state's frontiers. Rangers are widely respected and continue to keep law and order in Texas.

Texas v. White (1869). The U.S. Supreme Court ruled that secession was not possible under the Constitution and that Texas had never ceased to be a state in the Union. Radical Republicans had contended that Texas was not in the Union and could not bring any action before a federal court. While not ruling on the constitutionality of the Reconstruction acts, Chief Justice Chase said that the Constitution was intended "to form a more perfect union" and that "the Constitution, in all of its provisions, looks to an indestructible union composed of indestructible states." The Court accordingly took jurisdiction in the case.

The question was whether,

after the war, actions undertaken by Texas while it was in the Confederacy should be enforcible in U.S. courts. Chase held that the answer depended on the nature of the case. If the Confederate state's action was merely one "necessary to peace and good order among citizens," he said, "it should later be legally respected. But if it was an action designed to further the rebellion, the courts should not enforce it."

The case arose from an action by the governor of Texas against White and others to enjoin them from receiving payment for war expenses from bonds. The bonds had required the endorsement of the governor until 1862, when the state legislature repealed the act. The Court held that Texas was entitled to recover the bonds.

TFX (tactical fighter experimental). In 1965, a revolutionary military plane, the F-111, designated as the TFX, was built for the U.S. Air Force. Its outstanding feature is its wings —they can move from a conventional position to an angle of 18 degrees from the fuselage. In this position turbulence at high speeds is minimized, and the plane can fly at twice the speed of sound.

Thames, battle of the (Oct. 5, 1813). Gen. William Henry Harrison, aided by a Kentucky mounted regiment under Col. Richard Mentor Johnson, defeated a British force under Gen. Henry Procter. England's Indian ally, Tecumseh, was slain in the battle, which took place at the Thames River in Canada in the Lake Erie area. The effect of the victory was to regain for the Americans all that had been lost by Gen. Isaac Hull at Detroit in 1812. The Indian confederacy collapsed and deserted the British cause. The U.S. military frontier in the Northwest was made secure.

"Thanatopsis." The theme of the best-known poem of William Cullen Bryant is death. It appeared anonymously in the *North American Review* (Sept. 1817).

Thanksgiving Day. In 17th-century New England, the holiday was celebrated not only by religious observance but also by a week-long harvest festival of feasting. A day for thanksgiving was set aside by Gov. Bradford of the Plymouth colony in 1621. The first public thanksgiving day was a fast day in the Massachusetts Bay colony (Feb. 22, 1631).

Several Presidents, beginning with Washington, proclaimed thanksgiving days. Pres. Washington proclaimed a thanksgiving day in 1789 as an expression of gratitude for the establishment of the new government. Other Presidents proclaimed such days for various reasons.

On Oct. 3, 1863, it was proclaimed by Pres. Lincoln as a national holiday to be observed on the last Thursday in November. The states were under no obligation to accept the proclamation but many of them cooperated. In 1939 Pres. F. D. Roosevelt moved the day to the third Thursday in November to stimulate business activity by separating it more widely from Christmas. In 1941 he moved it forward again to the last Thursday and conceded that there had been no rise in holiday buying.

Thayer, Sylvanus (1785–1872). Military engineer and educator. Born in Braintree, Mass., he was graduated from the U.S. Military Academy, West Point (1808). He served as its superintendent (1817–33) and became known as "Father of the Military Academy." He established military organization, academic standards and methods of instruction which have endured. The engineer in charge of fortifications at Boston Harbor, he made improvements in New England harbors (1833–63). He endowed (1867) the Thayer School of Engineering at Dartmouth.

theater. During the colonial period there was considerable church opposition to public performance of plays. Nevertheless, the theater grew. It was stimulated by British actors, who toured America in the 18th and 19th centuries. Shakespearean plays were presented, and even American authors began to write for the stage. The actor rather than the play, however, attracted playgoers in the 19th century. The star still continues to draw Americans to plays and musicals that might otherwise not attract an audience.

The first theater in the colonies was built in Williamsburg, Va., 1716, but it was short lived. A much longer life was granted the Dock Street Playhouse, established in Charleston, S.C., 1736. In 1750 plays were banned in Boston. The ban was repealed in 1794, and the Boston Theater was opened. Philadelphia, too, became hospitable to plays, which were housed in the Chestnut Street Theater and Southwark Theater. The latter showed Thomas Godfrey's *The Prince of Parthia,* 1767. It was the first full-length play of note by an American writer.

Plays, along with cock fighting and "other expensive diversions and entertainments" were discouraged in 1774 by the Continental Congress, but the British enjoyed the theater during their occupation of Boston.

A celebrated actor of the 19th century, Edwin Forrest, made his debut at the Walnut Street Theater, Philadelphia, 1820. Other popular actors of the century include Edwin Booth, Charlotte Cushman, Joseph Cushman, E. L. Davenport, Fannie Davenport and Joseph Jefferson.

William Dunlap, the "father of the American drama," wrote over 50 plays by 1832 when he published his *History of the American Theatre.* During the 20th century American playwrights have established worldwide reputations. These include Eugene O'Neill, Thomas (Tennessee) Williams, Maxwell Anderson and Arthur Miller.

Although Broadway (N.Y.C.) remains the capital of the American theater, there are road companies of hit shows and countless little theater groups in the nation. Repertory groups, comprised of a permanent staff of actors who perform classics and new plays, are also receiving more public support.

third-term tradition. The Founding Fathers made no provision in the Constitution limiting the Presidency to two terms. George Washington, however, set the precedent that was followed until Pres. Franklin D. Roosevelt was elected to a third term in 1940 and a fourth term in 1944. World War II undoubtedly influenced this change in tradition. Pres. Grant had sought a third-term nomination but did not win it from his party.

In the postwar reaction to the New Deal, Congress passed the Bricker Amendment (1947), which prohibited a third term. This was ratified by the states and became the 22nd Amendment (1951).

Thirteen Colonies. The "Thirteen United States of America," declared unanimously, July 4, 1776, that they end their status as colonies and state their independence of Great Britain. They were New Hampshire, Massachusetts, New York,

Rhode Island, Connecticut, New Jersey, Pennsylvania, Delaware, Maryland, Virginia, North Carolina, South Carolina and Georgia. The 13 Colonies were also the original 13 states that ratified the Constitution of the United States.

Thomas, Christian Friedrich Theodore (1835–1905). Known as Theodore Thomas. Musician. Born in Essens, Germany, he was brought to the U.S. in 1845. A great influence on the development of appreciation for classical music in the U.S., he joined William Mason in 1855 in the first of a long series of Mason-Thomas chamber music concerts. A kind of musical missionary, he took orchestras on tours of the U.S. He was conductor of the Chicago Symphony Orchestra from 1891 to 1905.

Thomas, Isaiah (1750–1831). Printer and publisher. Born in Boston, Mass., he was the official printer for the patriots of the Massachusetts colony. He founded the *Massachusetts Spy* (1770) and became the leading book and periodical publisher of his day. He printed books noted for the beauty of their typography, including the first English illustrated folio Bible in the U.S. and William Perry's dictionary, the first printed in America. He was the first publisher in U.S. to do a large amount of printing of music type. He was known, also, for a long list of children's books, among them the first American issues of *Mother Goose's Melody* (1786) and illustrated editions of the *New England Primer*. After retirement he wrote the *History of Printing in America* (1810), a standard authority. He founded and incorporated (1812) the American Antiquarian Society, of which he became the first president.

Thor-Agena B. The U.S. Air Force developed and NASA adapted it to civilian space programs. The launch vehicle, first used in 1959, can rocket 1,600 pounds into a 300-nautical-mile orbit, or about 600 pounds into a 1,200-nautical-mile orbit.

Thoreau, Henry David (1817–62). Essayist and poet. He was born in Concord, Mass. Regarded as one of the most original and finest minds of the New England renaissance, he was a close friend of Ralph Waldo Emerson and one of the transcendentalists. He was arrested (1845) for non-payment of the poll tax as a protest against slavery and the Mexican War. His essay "Civil Disobedience" (1849), a classic of individualism, inspired believers in passive resistance. He recorded his simple life on Walden Pond, Concord (1845–47) in *Walden* (1854), his greatest achievement. He also wrote *A Week on the Concord and Merrimack Rivers* (1849). Thoreau advised his countrymen to simplify their private lives and their government, too, for he was a supreme indivi-

dualist. He defended John Brown after his arrest in 1859.

Thorndike, Edward Lee (1871–1949). Educator. Born in Williamsburg, Mass., he was professor for most of his career at Teachers College, Columbia. He influenced the development of educational psychology with his testing methods which were employed by the U.S. Army in World War I. He observed innate differences in the aptitudes of pupils, leading to modifications in the idea of equality of educational opportunity. He stressed practical education. His works include *Educational Psychology* (1903), *The Principles of Teaching* (1905) and *The Measurement of Intelligence* (1926).

"three acres and a cow." The expression was widely used by Populists in the 1890's to designate the meager wealth of the common man.

three-cent piece. This silver coin was issued in 1851. Three-cent pieces made of nickel began to be coined in 1865. The coinage was discontinued by act of Congress in 1873.

"three-fifths compromise" (1787). Differences between northern and southern states at the Constitutional Convention over the counting of slaves for the purpose of representation and taxation were resolved by a compromise.

The South wanted slaves to be given less weight than free

men, if they were to be given any weight at all, in apportionment of taxes. The North wanted them to be given less weight only in representation in the House of Representatives. The compromise provided that for both representation and taxes slaves were to be counted as three-fifths of a free man.

Ticonderoga, Fort. The fort on Lake Champlain, in New York, played a role in 18th-century military actions. During the French and Indian War, it was captured by a British force under Gen. Jeffrey Amherst who was proceeding north to Canada. Early in the American Revolution Massachusetts and Connecticut sent expeditions which united under the command of Ethan Allen and took the fort from the British in 1775. Washington had the fort's heavy cannon pulled all the way to a point overlooking Boston, thus making Gen. Howe's position untenable and forcing him to evacuate the city, Mar. 1776.

Tidelands oil. Ownership of mineral deposits in the ocean off the shore line has been in dispute between the federal and state governments for some time. The first producing oil well was dug one mile off the coast of Louisiana in 1938. A second well, 11 miles off the coast, started production in 1947. It has been estimated that oil deposits off the Gulf Coast may amount to 50% of the proved reserves for the whole of the U.S.

In Jan. 1953, Pres. Truman issued an executive order "setting aside the submerged lands of the continental shelf as a naval petroleum reserve." This policy was reversed by the Eisenhower administration. In May 1953, Congress gave the states title to submerged lands and the federal government jurisdiction over the resources of the outer continental shelf.

In 1960 the U.S. Supreme Court decided that Mississippi, Alabama and Louisiana owned the rights to the offshore submerged lands for a distance of 3½ miles from their coasts. Florida and Texas rights were held to extend 10½ miles offshore.

Tidewater. The term describes the fertile coastal plain which was America's first frontier in the South. Tobacco cultivation flourished in the 17th century in the Tidewater region of Virginia and Maryland. Tidewater lands of the Carolinas grew such staple crops as rice and indigo. The region, extending along the southern coastal plain, lay below the fall line. It became the center of the plantation aristocracy during the 18th century.

Depletion of Tidewater lands caused small farmers to push out of the older sections into the interior and the frontier kept moving westward.

Tilden, Samuel Jones (1814–86). Statesman. He was born

in New Lebanon, N.Y. Chairman of the New York State Democratic Committee (1866–74), he successfully fought the "Tweed Ring." Governor of New York (1875–77), he broke the "Canal Ring," a bipartisan group of politicians who profited illegally from the repair and extension of the state canal system. He won the Democratic nomination for President in 1876, and although he received about 250,000 more votes than Hayes in the election, all contested electoral votes went to Hayes. Tilden lost the Presidency by a strict party vote in the electoral commission and accepted the result to avoid civil war. He left a fortune derived from his law practice to Tilden Trust and thus made possible the New York Public Library.

Tillmanism. Toward the end of the 19th century, agrarian discontent was strengthened by Benjamin R. Tillman of South Carolina. He advocated a Populist program while remaining within the Democratic party. "Pitchfork Ben" gained control of the state government in 1890. "Send me to Washington," he told his audiences at the height of his dissatisfaction with Pres. Cleveland, "and I'll stick my pitchfork into his fat old ribs." He was elected to the U.S. Senate in 1895.

Tillman pitted the rural white farmer against businessmen, urged higher taxes on corporations, regulation of railroads and vocational education for white farm boys. He expanded democracy for the whites while depriving Negroes of suffrage they had gained during the Reconstruction era.

Timber Culture Act (1873). Congress offered an additional quarter section (160 acres) to any settler who would plant trees on 40 acres of it. By doubling the size of the tract available under the Homestead Act (1862), Congress sought to attract farmers or farm corporations capable of making the investment in machinery necessary in the arid, treeless plains. Few settlers were attracted and the Act was repealed in 1891.

"Tin Lizzie." Henry Ford's *Model T*, nicknamed "Tin Lizzie," sold in the 1920's, was cheap enough to enable millions to buy it.

Tippecanoe, battle of (Nov. 7, 1811). Anticipating Shawnee chief Tecumseh's plan to unite the tribes against further encroachment on their lands, Gov. William Henry Harrison of Indiana Territory advanced against the Indians.

The Shawnee braves attacked Harrison's men at Tippecanoe Creek and were repulsed with heavy losses on both sides. Harrison went on to burn Prophet's Town, the Indian village on the Wabash River.

Tecumseh, who had been away seeking the support of southern tribes, increased his determination to wipe out the American frontier settlements.

He joined forces with the British in the War of 1812.

"Tippecanoe and Tyler Too!"
The Whig campaign slogan carried Gen. William Henry Harrison of Ohio, who headed the ticket, and John Tyler of Virginia, the candidate for Vice-President, into office in 1840.

Americans looked back at the battle of Tippecanoe (1811) through rose-colored glasses and discerned a "victory" which made Harrison a war hero. In a demagogic campaign which subordinated the issues, "Old Tippecanoe" was given log cabin credentials in contrast to his gentlemanly origins. Harrison died of pneumonia a month after taking office.

TIROS. The name is an acronym for television and infrared observation satellites. About 350,000 usable cloud pictures have been obtained from TIROS satellites since the launching of TIROS I, Apr. 1, 1960.

TIROS Operation Satellites (TOS), projected for 1966, were to be used in weather forecasting, sea ice reconnaissance, locust control and storm warning.

Titan. Powerful rockets are used in the U.S. Air Force's program for launching men into space. In 1965 Titan 3-C, a solid-fuel rocket, propelled 21,000 pounds of test payload into an orbit 100 miles above the earth.

Titanic, sinking of (Apr. 14, 1912). The British White Star ocean liner struck an iceberg and went down while on its maiden voyage from Liverpool to New York. The company was blamed for poor equipment and for the order to speed through dangerous waters. Of 2,223 people aboard, only 706 were saved and brought to New York by the *Carpathia,* which had come to the rescue. The public's anger at the disaster led to better patrol of the iceberg belt and more lifeboats on vessels.

tithingmen. Colonial New England town officers helped get the colonists to the church on time and maintained order when they got there.

"Toledo War." In the boundary controversy in 1835 between Ohio and Michigan, each claimed the territory which contained the city of Toledo. Michigan appealed to the federal government. An armed collision was averted when it was agreed that Michigan would be admitted to the Union and compensated with territory in the north for yielding the Toledo region.

Toleration Act (1649). The Maryland Assembly confirmed the policy of Lord Baltimore (Cecilius Calvert) who had founded the colony as a refuge for Roman Catholics. The influx of Puritans from Virginia increased the Protestant majority and Catholics feared the growth of intolerance. The Act granted liberty of conscience only to those who believed in the divinity of Jesus Christ. Although it did not recognize the principle of toleration for all, it was nonetheless a step forward in establishing freedom of conscience.

Tombstone, Arizona. Millions of dollars in silver and gold were mined in the few years following the original strike in 1878 by Ed Schieffelin, one of the earliest prospectors in the region. He had come under the protection of soldiers scouting for Apaches and when he decided to strike out for himself was told, "You'll find your tombstone." Schieffelin gave that name to his first location. Tombstone soon became a boom town of tents, shacks, saloons and dance halls. The famous old mining camp went into decline as rising underground waters forced suspension of operations.

The town cemetery was called Boot Hill because so many men who came for business or fun died with their boots on. A cemetery of the same name is in Dodge City, Kan. Both Tombstone and Dodge City have enjoyed a revival on television westerns.

Tom Thumb. The steam locomotive weighing only one ton was built by Peter Cooper for the Baltimore and Ohio Railroad. In a test run against a horse-drawn car in 1830, *Tom Thumb* lost a pulley and limped to defeat, but horses were taken off the double track out of Baltimore just the same.

"too proud to fight." The sinking of the *Lusitania* (1915) increased pressure on Wilson to call for war against Germany. He resisted and in a public address declared: "There is such a thing as a nation being too proud to fight. There is such a thing as a nation being so right that it does not need to convince others by force that it is right."

Militant Americans regarded this as cowardice, but Wilson did no more than send vigorous protests to Germany.

Topeka Constitution. Drawn in 1855 by Free State Kansas, it specifically excluded slavery from the territory and left to the vote of the people the decision whether free Negroes would be admitted to Kansas.

Although the House of Representatives in 1856 passed a bill admitting Kansas to the Union under the Topeka Constitution, the Senate substituted its own bill calling for a constitutional convention in Kansas.

Controversy over admission of Kansas as a slave or free state earned for the territory the name "Bleeding Kansas."

Torch, Operation. The code name designated the Allied landings along the coasts of North Africa which began Nov. 8, 1942 during World War II.

"To the victor belong the spoils. . . ." New Yorker William L. Marcy who supported Andrew Jackson for President thus summed up the politician's credo.

As U.S. Senator, Marcy defended Van Buren's appointment as minister to London, stating that he could see "nothing wrong in the rule that to the victor belong the spoils of the enemy" (1832). The term "spoils system" in American politics originated in Marcy's speech.

town meeting. According to the "Body of Liberties" which was adopted by the Great and General Court of Massachusetts in 1641, "Every man . . . shall have liberty to come to any Town meeting, and either by speech or writing to move any lawful, seasonable and material question." These words have the same binding force in Massachusetts today as they did in 1641, and since the other five New England states have similar provisions in their constitutions, the annual town meeting remains the local governmental event of the year. Citizens assemble to elect officials and pass laws for the community. New England town meetings are examples of direct or pure democracy, rather than representative democracy.

Where New England townsfolk found that no hall was large enough to hold more than a fraction of those qualified, they adopted the limited or representative town meeting. Brookline, Mass., adopted it in 1915 and 40 other Massachusetts towns followed suit. The representative town meeting is like the traditional town meeting in all respects but the actual voting is restricted to a certain number of elected town-meeting representatives.

New Englanders moving west carried with them the town meeting and this type of local government was practiced in the northernmost row of western states.

Townsend Plan. Announced by a California physician, Dr. E. Townsend, Jan. 1, 1934, the plan called for outright federal grants of $200 a month to everybody over 60 years of age, provided he "shall not engage in any gainful pursuit." The money was to be raised by a 2% national sales tax.

The Plan was widely supported as a cure for the economic ills of the Great Depression. Its popularity may have influenced Congress to retain old age insurance in the Social Security Act as a means of arresting growth of the Townsend movement.

Townshend Acts (1767). The Townshend Act that aroused deepest resentment in the colonies was the import duties on glass, lead, paints, paper and tea. Charles Townshend, finance minister, persuaded Parliament that since the colonists objected to the Sugar Act that regulated trade and "internal" taxes, such as the Stamp Act, they would accept "external" taxes on imports. These would be collected before the goods reached the colonists. Another of the Townshend Acts provided for customs collection at Boston.

The colonists responded with nonimportation agreements that cut sharply into British trade with America. As a consequence of this economic pressure, Parliament repealed all the duties except the one on tea, which was kept to assert the principle that Parliament was still supreme.

Trade Expansion Act of 1962. The "bold new program" was introduced by Pres. Kennedy when the Reciprocal Trade Agreement Act of 1934 came up for renewal for the twelfth time. It gives the President full authority to slash all existing tariffs by as much as 50%. His negotiating authority now covers whole categories of products instead of individual items and bargaining can be carried on with blocs of nations rather than nation by nation.

The President may eliminate all tariffs on any product of which 80% is supplied to the world markets by the U.S. and the Common Market (formed in 1958 by France, West Germany, Italy, the Netherlands, Belgium and Luxembourg to eliminate tariffs and import quotas among themselves). The Act authorizes a special fund for "adjustment assistance" to firms and workers injured by new tariff-cutting negotiations.

trademark. The sole right is given by the federal government for the use of a distinctive name, slogan or artistic device (such as the "GE" for General Electric products). Registration of trademarks was first permitted by Congress in 1870. It identified the owners of a product.

"Trail of Tears." The Cherokee thus named their terrible journey in the winter of 1838–39 when federal troops under Gen. Winfield Scott evicted them from their homes in Georgia and escorted them to Indian country in Oklahoma.

A minority of the tribe, over the protest of the majority, had surrendered the Cherokee land in Georgia by the Treaty of New Echota (1835).

transcendentalism. This philosophy, formulated in the essays and lectures of Ralph Waldo Emerson, held the view that the individual is in direct communication with God and nature and therefore has no need for complacent or rigid churches and creeds. Emerson urged man to be self-reliant and non-conformist.

Transcendentalism was not a systematic faith. Its organ, *The Dial,* was edited by Margaret Fuller. It appealed to "all those who contend for perfect freedom, who look for progress in philosophy and theology, and who sympathize with each other in the hope that the future will not always be as the past."

Emerson's ideas stimulated a cultural revival in New England, 1830–45, and contributed to the formation of such utopian experiments as Brook Farm and Fruitlands.

Transit I-B. The U.S. Navy satellite, launched Apr. 13, 1960, proved the feasibility of a worldwide all-weather navigation satellite system. Accurate data for navigational fixes to ships and aircraft throughout the world will be provided by the Transit operational system.

Transportation, Department of. Created by Congress in 1966, this executive Department became the 12th Department in the President's Cabinet. It brought together 31 large and small government agencies and bureaus. The main previously autonomous agencies included in the Department are the Coast Guard, Federal Aviation Administration, Bureau of Public Roads and St. Lawrence Seaway. In 1967 Alan S. Boyd became the first Secretary of Transportation.

traveler's check. An American-invented "international currency" that has gained universal acceptance, the idea was copyrighted by the American Express Co. (1891). It is a piece of negotiable paper that is just as acceptable as money. The double signature required safeguards it against loss. If the checks are lost or stolen, the company issuing them replaces the checks.

treason. "Treason against the United States shall consist only in levying war against them, or in adhering to their enemies, giving them aid and comfort. No person shall be convicted of treason unless on the testimony of two witnesses to the same overt act, or on confession in open court" (Constitution, Art. III, Sec. 3, Par. 1).

The Founding Fathers saw treason as the most serious crime against the nation and defined it carefully in the Constitution rather than leave it to the discretion of Congress. The Constitution goes on to grant Congress the right "to declare the punishment of treason."

Treasury, Department of the. Created by Congress in 1789, the Department was established to manage the national finances. With the expansion of the country and its financial structure, frequent amendments to the original act have so broadened the scope of the Department that it now embraces a score or more of diversified bureaus, divisions and offices. Besides managing the financial affairs of the nation, the Department now controls the coinage and printing of money. The Bureau of Narcotics and the Secret Service have been placed under the jurisdiction of the Department.

The Secretary of the Treasury, who has a place in the President's Cabinet, is required by law to submit periodic reports to Congress on the fiscal operations of the government, including an annual report upon the condition of the nation's finances.

treaty-making power. Under the Constitution, the President "shall have power, by and with the advice and consent of the Senate, to make treaties, provided two-thirds of the senators present concur" (Art. II, Sec. 2, Par. 2). Treaties are usually negotiated by the State Department, though the President may take part in the proceedings, as Pres. Wilson did in the formulation of the Treaty of Versailles.

The Senate may accept the whole or reject the whole treaty or accept it in part and reject it in part. The Senate rejected in toto the Treaty of Versailles in 1919 and 1920 and accepted all but Article XII of the Jay Treaty in 1794. When part of a treaty is not accepted, the President does not have to agree to the Senate's changes, nor does the foreign nation involved. Presidents have found it advisable to keep influential senators informed during the treaty's negotiation in order to smooth its path in the Senate.

Treaty of 1778. The Franco-American Alliance was concluded during the Revolutionary War and brought France to the aid of the newly independent United States.

Under the Treaty both nations agreed to fight until American independence was "formally or tacitly assured." Neither France nor the U.S. would conclude a "truce or peace" with Britain without the "formal consent of the other first obtained." Each of the two nations guaranteed the possessions of the other in America "mutually from the present time and forever against all other powers."

Tredegar Iron Works. A prime target for the Union army, the iron works, in Richmond, Va., was the backbone of the South during the Civil War. It not only produced cannon but manufactured the machinery for scattered munitions plants throughout the South. It had been a major iron-producing company before secession and sparked the building of the New South after the war.

Trent **Affair** (1861). During the Civil War, U.S. and British relations were threatened when two Confederate diplomats, John Y. Mason and John Slidell, were removed from a British ship, the *Trent*. This action by a U.S. naval captain was hailed as a victory in the North.

When British protests reached Pres. Lincoln, he acted to prevent a break in diplomatic relations. Sec. of State Seward freed the Confederate commissioners on the ground that their arrest had been unauthorized and violated the U.S. policy of freedom of the seas.

Trenton, battle of (Dec. 26, 1776). Gen. Washington's victory at Trenton, early in the American Revolution, came at a time when morale had been lowered by a number of defeats suffered by the patriot armies around New York.

On Christmas night, in a surprise move later memorialized

on canvas, Washington crossed the Delaware, and defeated the sleeping Hessians who had been celebrating the night before. The victory gave the Continental army the morale boost it needed.

Trevett v. Weeden (1786). The Rhode Island legislature passed a law making it a crime punishable by fine, without trial by jury, for anyone to refuse to accept payment of a debt in paper money. Paper money had been depreciating rapidly and influential debtors, when they found creditors refusing to accept payment of debts in paper money, persuaded the legislature to pass the law.

John Weeden, a butcher, appealed his conviction under this law to the state supreme court. The court dismissed Weeden's complaint on the ground that it had no jurisdiction over the case, but went on to declare the law a violation of the state charter.

Triangle Fire (Mar. 25, 1911). A disastrous fire in a New York City loft building occupied by the Triangle Waist Co. resulted in the loss of 146 lives (mostly women and girl workers trapped on the three top floors). The proprietors were indicted but acquitted.

After the disaster which led to a revised building code and a revision of the labor laws, the International Ladies Garment Workers Union made notable strides in eliminating evils in sweatshops in the shirtwaist trade.

triangular trade. "Three cornered" trade during the 18th century linked the West Indies, New England and Africa. Molasses and sugar were carried from the West Indies to New England and made into rum. The rum was transported to the African Gold Coast where it was bartered for slaves. The slaves were sold in the West Indies for molasses and sugar. Items in the trade varied, but a major effect was to produce a source of revenue which New Englanders used to purchase manufactured goods in England. Surplus capital derived from the trade was also invested in American business enterprise. There were other triangular trade routes.

Truman, Harry S (1884–1972). Thirty-third President of the U.S. (1945–53). He was born in Lamar, Mo. Vice-President of U.S. (1944), he succeeded to the Presidency on the death of F. D. Roosevelt (Apr. 12, 1945). He served Missouri as Democratic member of U.S. Senate (1934–44). He led the nation during final months of World War II, authorizing the use of the atomic bomb against Japan. He sponsored Fair Deal legislation.

Truman Doctrine (1947). When Pres. Truman saw that Britain was no longer able to maintain troops in Greece and Turkey, he placed the U.S.

squarely behind these countries in an effort to prevent a Communist take-over by the Soviet Union. Congress on May 15 granted the President's request for $400,000,000 in support of his declaration that it was American policy "to help free peoples to maintain . . . their national integrity against aggressive movements that seek to impose upon them totalitarian regimes." This doctrine made it clear to the world that the U.S. had abandoned its policy of non-entanglement in European affairs and that the U.S. would use its resources to prevent the overthrow of any democratic government through outside interference.

Trust Territory of the Pacific Islands. The 96 atolls and island units in the western Pacific, including the Caroline, Marshall and Mariana islands (except Guam), were formerly under Japanese mandate. They were placed under the trusteeship of the United Nations by an agreement approved by the Security Council and the U.S. in 1947. The islands are administered by the U.S. Department of Interior.

Some of the islands had been seized by Germany in 1885; others were under control of Spain until the end of the Spanish-American War (1898), when they were sold to Germany. In 1914, at the beginning of World War I, the islands were taken over by Japan, which later received the mandates from the League of Nations. It was from these western Pacific Islands that Japan launched her attack on Pearl Harbor (Dec. 7, 1941).

Turner, Frederick Jackson (1861–1932). Historian. Born in Portage, Wis., he received his B.A. at the Univ. of Wisconsin (1884) and was granted a Ph.D. by Johns Hopkins Univ. (1890). A professor of history at Harvard Univ. (1910–24), he wrote little; but his frontier theory of American history had enormous influence on historical scholarship. Apart from the seminal essay, "The Significance of the Frontier in American History" (read to the American Historical Association, July 12, 1893), he wrote *The Rise of the New West* (1906), *The Frontier in American History* (1920) and *The Significance of Sections in American History* (1932) which won a Pulitzer Prize.

Turner's rebellion. The most widely known of the slave revolts in the South was organized by a fanatic Negro preacher, Nat Turner, who led about 70 slaves in a massacre of 57 whites in southeast Virginia, Aug. 1831. The revolt was crushed by the militia with the death of about 100 Negroes.

The effect of the uprising was to pass laws to restrict slaves and to discourage any efforts to educate the Negro in the South.

Tuscaroras. A confederation of Iroquoian linguistic stock, these North Carolina Indians engaged in a savage war with the colonists in 1711 after some of their land had been seized and their children sold in the slave trade. The colonists, aided by other Indian allies, crushed the Tuscaroras. The remnants migrated north to a new home in the Five Nations country. In the American Revolution, they sided with the colonists.

Tuskegee Institute. Founded in 1881 by Booker T. Washington, the famous Negro college, in Alabama, first sought to prepare Negroes for agriculture, domestic service and lower-paid factory jobs since better jobs were not open to them. Its curriculum has long since been broadened.

Tweed Ring. William M. Tweed, boss of Tammany Hall, headed a ring of notorious grafters who mulcted New York City taxpayers of millions of dollars in the period between 1869 and 1871 and forced the city to the verge of bankruptcy.

Contractors who worked for the city padded their bills and the difference went into the pockets of Tweed and his henchmen. He bribed legislators, judges and newspapermen and kept on the city or his own payroll Republican opponents and others who might bring his train of robberies to a halt. Tweed sought to appear as a public benefactor by giving handouts to the poor and helping immigrants get their naturalization papers.

Public reaction was built up by editorials in the *Times* and by Thomas Nast's devastating cartoons, which appeared in both the *Times* and *Harper's Weekly*. Some of the wealthy citizens of the city helped to get the law enforcement agencies to work on prosecuting Tweed and other city officials. Tweed himself was finally convicted and died in jail in 1877.

Twenty-One Demands (Jan. 18, 1915). With the Western world involved in World War I, Japan sent a startling ultimatum to China threatening that nation's sovereignty and making it appear that Japan was preparing to lock the Open Door.

Sec. of State Bryan sent a note to both Japan and China, May 11, 1915, in which he foreshadowed the later Hoover-Stimson doctrine by declaring that the U.S. "cannot recognize any agreement . . . impairing the treaty rights of the U.S. and its citizens in China, the political or territorial integrity of the Republic of China, or the international policy . . . commonly known as the open door policy."

"two bits." The colloquial term was first used to describe the U.S. quarter (25 cents) authorized in 1792. It is an old monetary term derived from the colonial six-penny "bit," which was equal to one Spanish *real*. The U.S. quarter was equal to two Spanish bits.

two-cent piece. Initially issued in 1864, the coin was the first to display the motto "In God

We Trust." The issue was discontinued in 1873, but the motto has been retained on U.S. coins.

Tyler, John (1790–1862). Tenth President of the U.S. Born in Charles City County, Va., he was graduated from the College of William and Mary (1807). Vice-President of the U.S. (1841), he succeeded to the Presidency on the death of William H. Harrison. Elected as a Whig, he lost the support of his party and was not nominated in 1844. He remained loyal to Virginia when it seceded.

typewriter. Writing machines appeared in Europe during the 18th century, but it was not until 1829 that the first patent in the U.S. was issued to William A. Burt of Mt. Vernon, Mich. for his "typographer." It was unworkable. The first successful typewriter was invented by Christopher Latham Sholes of Milwaukee and a patent was issued in 1868 to him, Samuel W. Soule and Carlos Glidden. The slogan, "Now is the time for all good men to come to the aid of the party," was created by Charles Weller, a court reporter, to test the efficiency of Sholes' typewriter in 1867. In 1873 Sholes sold his rights to the Remington Arms Company for $12,000. Remington mechanics converted Sholes' invention into a product marketed as the "Remington typewriter." The invention played a major role in bringing more women into the working world and contributed to their economic emancipation.

U

ugly American. The term became a common part of the language following publication in 1958 of the novel, *The Ugly American*, by Eugene Burdick and William J. Lederer. The novel annoyed the State Department as it appeared to describe the actions of officials administering the foreign aid program in Southeast Asia.

It was fictionalized reporting that used as its locale the fictitious nation of Sarkahn; but the depiction of stupid, tactless, ignorant and arrogant American officials was found by many Americans to be all too plausible.

Un-American Activities Committee. Established by the House of Representatives in 1938, and later becoming a standing committee, HUAC has been a center of controversy since its start under the chairmanship of Martin Dies of Texas. The Committee's function was to investigate un-American propaganda activities and help prepare legislation to combat them.

Over the years the major criticism directed against the Committee has been that it practices exposure for the sake of exposure rather than to help in preparing legislation. Its defenders claim the Committee has helped uncover Communist subversion and alerted Congress and the nation to the need for internal security safeguards.

Uncle Sam. The letters "U.S." appeared on the uniforms of soldiers in the War of 1812. They were interpreted as standing for "Uncle Sam" by those who opposed the war and ridiculed the soldiers. The first reference to "Uncle Sam" in print appeared in the Troy (N.Y.) *Post*, Sept. 7, 1813.

Although the first known cartoon of Uncle Sam did not appear until 1853, the words "Uncle Sam" had long before been commonly used as a synonym for the United States.

Uncle Tom. The expression is used contemptuously to describe any Negro who appears to be unduly subservient to white men. It is derived from a character in Harriet Beecher Stowe's novel, *Uncle Tom's Cabin*

(1852). In the novel, Uncle Tom, an old Negro slave, tried to please even a harsh master.

Uncle Tom's Cabin (1852). The widely read novel, by Harriet Beecher Stowe, quickened northern resistance to slavery. Episodes which described Negro mothers forcibly separated from their children aroused strong sentiment against slavery. It was Mrs. Stowe's hope that once the sinfulness of slavery was revealed, southerners would give it up voluntarily. The effect of the book was to widen the breach between North and South.

"under-belly of the Axis." The term was used by Prime Minister Churchill of Britain early in 1944, when he proposed that the Western powers (Britain and the U.S.) invade Italy and the Balkans, "the under-belly of the Axis." Apart from military considerations, Churchill hoped to decrease Russian influence in the Balkans.

underground railroad. A system was devised to help slaves escape from the South into the free states and Canada. It was called the underground railroad because most of the traveling was done at night and all of it was secret. The fugitives, always aided by antislavery people, fled from station to station using many routes and all sorts of hiding places. It is estimated that about 75,000 Negroes found freedom this way between the War of 1812 and the Civil War.

Underwood Tariff of 1913. With the Democrats in power Woodrow Wilson set about to change the protective tone of American tariff policy. His public blast at the lobbyists working to defeat the tariff bill helped to get the downward revision of the tariff through Congress. The Act, sponsored by Rep. Underwood (Ala.), reduced rates on hundreds of items, added to the free list and raised rates on comparatively few items. The average rate was about 29%. This was still protective, but the downward trend promised to encourage international trade. The promise became an idle one with the outbreak of World War I and the disruption of world trade.

The Act made provision for a graduated income tax, beginning at 1% of incomes of $4,000 and rising to 6% to compensate for loss of revenue expected to follow from reduced tariff rates. The income tax law followed upon adoption of the 16th Amendment.

Union, Fort (N. Dak.). Completed in 1834, the "king of the trading forts" was owned by the American Fur Co. It continued in use until 1867. Its name was derived from its function of unifying the scattered trading posts in the region which is now North Dakota.

Union Labor party. Despite its name, when the party (a third party) was formed in Cincinnati, 1887, comparatively few of the delegates who attended the convention were workingmen. Farmers predominated. The party platform, however, endorsed substantially all of the distinctly wage earners' demands of the preamble of the Knights of Labor. Among these was a plank calling for reduction of hours of labor commensurate with the improvements effected in machinery.

The party nominated Alson J. Streeter of Illinois for President in 1888. It polled a little over 1% of the popular vote. The party was a bridge between the Greenback party and the Populist party of the 1890's.

Union Pacific Railroad. When the Union Pacific was incorporated by Congress, July 1, 1862, the federal government agreed to lend the company $16,000 per mile for that part of the line built on level ground, $32,-000 per mile for somewhat more difficult terrain and $48,000 per mile for mountain sections. In addition the company was deeded 20 sections of land per mile of railroad. The U.P. used a 4-feet, 8½-inch-gauge track that was to become standard all over the country and eventually ensured that the cars of one road could ride on the tracks of all roads.

The Union Pacific broke ground at Omaha, Dec. 1863, and laid four to seven miles of track per day with a work force comprised chiefly of Irish laborers and ex-soldiers. The Union Pacific met the Central Pacific at Promontory Point, near Ogden, Utah, May 10, 1869, after laying 1,086 miles through Indian country and over the Rockies.

In 1897 E. H. Harriman acquired control of the U.P. which now owns about 10,000 miles of line and is one of the nation's most important transcontinental railroad routes. Lines extend from Kansas City and Omaha to the Pacific Coast. One main branch terminates in the Pacific Northwest, the other at Los Angeles.

Unitarians. Christians of this faith affirm the unity of God and reject the doctrine of the Trinity, the Father, the Son, the Holy Ghost (Trinitarianism). The Unitarian Church has its origins in the Protestant Reformation of the 16th century. In America, Unitarianism developed as early as 1785 when liberals withdrew from the Congregational churches of New England. The Rev. Joseph Priestley, discoverer of oxygen, founded a Unitarian society in Philadelphia in 1796. The platform of Unitarianism was set forth by the Rev. William Ellery Channing at Baltimore in 1819. He rejected the Calvinist doctrine of human depravity and a vengeful God. The American Unitarian Association was formed in 1825 for mutual counsel and missionary efforts. Each congregation, however, controls its own affairs.

In 1961 the Universalist Church of America merged with

the American Unitarian Association to form the Unitarian Universalist Association. There are about 165,000 Unitarians in the U.S.

United Church of Christ. The Protestant religious denomination was formed in 1957 through the union of the Congregational Christian Churches with the Evangelical and Reformed Church. It is the first union in the U.S. of churches with differing forms of church government — Congregational and modified Presbyterian — and with different historical backgrounds. Congregationalism was brought to America by the Pilgrims. Later, Puritans from England made Congregationalism the dominant religion of New England. The Evangelical and Reformed group originated with immigrants from Germany and Switzerland.

The United Church of Christ is active in Christian education, church extension, health and welfare, mass communications, race relations, social action and foreign missionary work. The denomination has over 2,000,-000 members.

United Colonies of New England. In 1643 the colonial governments of Massachusetts Bay, Connecticut, Plymouth and New Haven formed a confederation for their mutual protection against the Indians and the French and Dutch settlers of Canada and New York. Each colony had one vote in the league. Eight commissioners

(two from each colony) comprised the board to deal with common problems. The confederation was ended by 1684.

United Empire Loyalists. About 50,000 Tory expatriates fled from the 13 Colonies at the end of the Revolution and formed societies in Canada. The enmity of these associations toward Americans kept border controversies alive for decades.

"United Front." The term was used in the 1930's by the Communist party in the U.S. which sought to muster the strength of liberals and left-of-center groups against the rising fascist powers.

United Labor party. Sponsored by trade unions, the party (a third party) was formed in 1877, in Pittsburgh, Pa. Its platform called for protective tariff legislation, labor bureaus in the state and national governments, abolition of contract convict labor, workmen's compensation legislation, child labor laws, abolition of conspiracy laws applying to labor organizations, distribution of public lands to settlers only and the establishment of courts of arbitration for the settlement of disputes between labor and capital.

It fused with the Greenback party in some campaigns. In 1888 the United Labor party's candidate for President, Robert H. Cowdrey, withdrew from the campaign, except in New York, and polled fewer than 3,000 votes.

United Mine Workers (UMW).
Organized in 1890 on industrial lines, the union soon won full recognition by the operators in the bituminous mines of Pennsylvania, Ohio, Indiana and Michigan. Under the leadership of its president, John Mitchell, it made gains in the anthracite coal strike in 1902. By the time Mitchell resigned from the presidency in 1908 the union boasted a membership of over 300,000 making it the strongest union in the country.

The UMW under the presidency of John L. Lewis played a major role in organizing the Congress of Industrial Organizations. It withdrew from the CIO in 1942, rejoined the AFL in 1946 and left it again in 1947. Thomas Kennedy succeeded Lewis as president in 1960. Membership is about 450,000.

United Nations. Soon after World War II began, Allied statesmen began to think of what could be done to keep the peace after the hoped-for defeat of the Axis Powers. The Atlantic Charter (1941) contained a clear reference to an international peace organization. The name of the organization was first officially used ("Declaration by United Nations"), Jan. 1, 1942, when 26 nations, including the U.S., pledged "not to make a separate armistice or peace with the enemies." The need for an international body was affirmed at the Moscow Conference (1943). A proposal for the UN charter was drafted at Dumbarton Oaks (1944). At

the San Francisco Conference (Apr. 25–June 26, 1945) the UN Charter was signed by 50 nations (June 26). It was ratified by the required number on Oct. 24 (UN Day).

In contrast to U.S. rejection of the League of Nations, the U.S. became a charter member of the UN and is by far the largest contributor to the support of its operations. The UN occupied its permanent headquarters in New York City in 1952.

The effectiveness of the UN as a peace-keeping organization has been impaired by differences between the East and West which took the form of a "cold war" at the end of World War II.

United Press. The worldwide news agency was formed in 1907 by Edward W. Scripps and Milton A. McRae as a rival of the older Associated Press and sold news stories to any newspaper. The UP merged with International News Service in 1958. As United Press International, it continues to cover the news.

Some newspapers subscribe to the AP, UPI and other services in an effort to gain the widest possible coverage for readers.

United Service Organizations. USO clubs were created in 1941 to provide recreation, relaxation and a place for servicemen to socialize. They have served more than 20 million Americans in World War II and after. With the reduction of the

Armed Forces between 1945 and 1950, the USO shrank to a handful of clubs. It was rejuvenated during the Korean War and shrank again in 1953, after the truce.

It is supported entirely by funds contributed to Community Chests and similar groups. The organization's member agencies are the Young Men's Christian Association, the National Catholic Community Service, the National Jewish Welfare Board, the Young Women's Christian Association, the Salvation Army and the National Travelers Aid Association.

United States Air Force Academy. The federal institution for educating and training officers for the U.S. Air Force was established at Colorado Springs, Colo., in 1954, by act of Congress. Nominations for appointment are made chiefly by congressmen, and the successful candidates must pass a stiff entrance examination. Graduates receive a B.S. degree and are commissioned 2nd lieutenants in the regular Air Force. Those who are physically qualified go into pilot training after graduation.

United States Merchant Marine Academy. The federal institution for educating and training officers for the Merchant Marine and Naval Reserve was established in 1942 following the organization in 1938 of the U.S. Merchant Marine Cadet Corps. It is located at Kings Point, on Long Island Sound, N.Y.

Tuition is free to those winning appointments after receiving congressional designations and passing entrance examinations. A B.S. degree is conferred on graduates.

United States Military Academy. The federal institution for educating and training officers of the U.S. Army was established in 1802. It is located at West Point, N.Y., the oldest U.S. military post now in use, first occupied by troops in 1778.

Tuition is free, students receive Army pay and rations. Nominations for appointment are made largely by the President, Vice-President and congressmen. Candidates take a stiff competitive examination. Graduates of West Point receive a B.S. degree and are commissioned as 2nd lieutenants in the regular Army.

United States Naval Academy. The federal institution for educating and training officers of the U.S. Navy was established in 1845 by George Bancroft, the historian, when he was Secretary of the Navy. It is located at Annapolis, Md., but was moved temporarily to Newport, R.I., during the Civil War.

Tuition is free, students receiving naval pay and rations. Nominations for appointment are made largely by the President, Vice-President and congressmen. Candidates take a stiff competitive examination. Graduates of Annapolis receive a B.S. degree and are commissioned as ensigns in the Navy.

United States of America. The name was first used officially in the Declaration of Independence (July 4, 1776) to replace "United Colonies." The word "colonies" implied dependence and "states" was substituted for it. In the treaty with France (Feb. 6, 1778) the title "United States of North America" was used, but the "North" was dropped from the name by action of the Continental Congress, July 11, 1778.

United States Steel Corporation. By 1900 the Carnegie Steel Company was making about one-fourth of the nation's steel. Andrew Carnegie himself was ready to retire from the business. He and his associates, Henry Clay Frick, Henry Phipps and Charles Schwab, sold out to the J. P. Morgan group for $447 million. The newly formed holding company, named United States Steel Corporation, was capitalized at $1.4 billion, about half of which was "watered stock." Schwab became its first president. The Bureau of Corporations estimated the total value of assets at less than $700 million. Nevertheless, the company showed substantial profits from 1901 to 1910.

In 1912 the Justice Department started an antitrust action against U.S. Steel and in 1920 the U.S. Supreme Court found that while the company controlled 40% of the steel industry, it had not engaged in any unreasonable practices. The Court ruled that the company was not in violation of the Sherman Act (*United States v. United States Steel Corporation*). The Court said that "the law does not make mere size an offense, or the existence of unexerted power an offense."

U.S. Steel in 1968 was the largest steel company in the U.S., normally producing about 25% of domestic rolled steel. Other major steel corporations are Bethlehem Steel, Republic Steel, Jones and Laughlin Steel and Inland Steel.

"United we stand, divided we fall!" First expressed in John Dickinson's "The Liberty Song," published in the *Boston Gazette*, July 18, 1768, the phrase became popular as a toast among patriotic orators from Benjamin Franklin to Abraham Lincoln. The words also appear in George Pope Morris' "The Flag of Our Union," a poem written before the Civil War.

Universalists. A Protestant denomination, it was formed in the U.S., in the late 18th century, to oppose the preaching of eternal damnation and the predestination of the elect. Universalists believe in salvation for every soul through divine grace of Jesus Christ. In Gloucester, Mass., John Murray became pastor of the first Universalist Church. In 1790 a general convention, in Philadelphia, agreed on Congregational articles of faith. The denomination veered from Calvinism to Unitarianism in the 19th century. Most of its churches have been in New England and New York, although some were established in the West. In 1961 the Universalists merged with the American Unitarian Association to form the Unitarian Universalist Association. The denomination has about 165,000 members.

university education. Higher education has deep roots in the American past. Harvard College was established in 1636; next came the College of William and Mary, which opened in 1693 at Williamsburg, Va. Other colleges were founded in the 18th century, but all remained small schools until well into the 19th century. Students entered at about age 14 and remained until they were 18. The curriculum, while classical and academic, was by modern standards largely secondary in content.

Private colleges and universities were established in the various states under charters granted by the legislatures incorporating them as nonprofit charitable institutions. Since 1850 most of the new institutions have been chartered by state education departments. Most of the private institutions began as colleges which offered liberal arts instruction. Those which added professional and graduate courses and schools became universities. Both broad fields— liberal arts and professional— may be further subdivided into undergraduate and graduate levels.

There are now about 2,000 institutions of higher education

in the U.S. About one-third are publicly controlled and the remainder are private or church-connected institutions.

American universities conceive of their purpose as being instruction, research and service. The great growth in college and university enrollment since the end of World War II has created a continuing problem of expansion of facilities, recruitment of personnel and maintenance of standards.

"unwritten Constitution." The Constitution has been made flexible not only by Supreme Court interpretations of the implied powers, but also by customs and usages. These are long-established practices of government which make up the so-called "unwritten Constitution." Examples include the entire system of political parties, including the nomination of presidential candidates by conventions; the practice of senatorial courtesy, which requires the President to consult the senators from any state in which he plans to make an appointment, such as a postmaster or collector of internal revenue; presidential leadership in the law-making process. The President is expected to work out a legislative program and to help put it through Congress by means of messages to that body, appeals to public opinion and use of his influence as leader of his party.

urban renewal program. Title I of the Housing Act of 1949 provided that the federal government would pay two-thirds of the cost (prohibitive for any private agency or for government at a lower level) of buying, clearing and reselling slum land. This made it possible to tear down one set of private properties (tenements, flop houses, run-down businesses), compensate the owners and resell the land to another set of private developers and owners for office buildings, housing projects, hotels and business "plazas."

The program prospered and was improved by further legislation, especially by the 1954 Housing Act, which provided for commercial redevelopment, rehabilitation of existing buildings and comprehensive urban planning. By 1965, 5 billion dollars had been provided for renewal projects dramatically visible in the center of many cities from Boston, Hartford, New York and Pittsburgh to San Francisco.

The Urban Renewal Administration, a constituent unit of the Housing and Home Finance Agency, was created in 1954 to administer the slum clearance and urban renewal program.

Urey, Harold Clayton (1893–). Chemist. Born in Walkerton, Ind., he was granted a Ph.D. by the Univ. of California (1923). On the teaching staff of Columbia Univ. (1929–45; professor from 1934), Univ. of Chicago (1945–58), Univ. of California (since 1958), he was awarded the Nobel Prize for Chemistry (1934) for his discovery of heavy hydrogen. He was the research director (1942–45) for the Manhattan District project that produced the atomic bomb and is an outstanding authority on isotopes, the structure of atoms and molecules, thermodynamics of gases and absorption spectra.

Useful Manufactures, Society for Establishing. The tax exempt corporation was founded by Alexander Hamilton and chartered by the state of New Jersey in 1791. It soon gave up financing manufacturing enterprises, but has continued to foster manufacturing by leasing lands and supplying water and electric power to other companies.

Utah. The "Beehive State," in the Mountain group, was admitted to the Union as the 45th state, Jan. 4, 1896. Its capital is Salt Lake City.

Utah (named after the Utes, a Shoshone Indian tribe) was crossed in the 18th century by Escalante and other Spanish explorers. It was not settled until the Mormons, led from hostile Illinois by Brigham Young, reached Utah (July 24, 1847). The region passed to the U.S. at the end of the Mexican War (1848) and became the Utah Territory (1850). The Mormons had requested the name Deseret, land of the honey bee, but this was rejected by Congress. Admission to the Union was long delayed by hostility to the Mormon practice of polygamy. After the practice was abolished by the Mormon

Church, the territory gained admission to the Union.

Utah was one of the earliest states to establish an irrigation system. Alfalfa, potatoes and sugar beets are profitable crops. The state ranks second in production of copper, gold and silver and supplies large amounts of uranium. About 20% of the newly mined copper in the U.S. is produced in the nation's largest open-pit copper mine at Bingham Canyon. Kennecott and International operate copper smelters. Potash is abundant along the shore line of Great Salt Lake, which has a salt density second only to the Dead Sea. The state is an important center for research and production of intercontinental missiles and high-speed aircraft.

Utes. Remnants of the warlike Indians, of Shoshonean linguistic stock, live on reservations in Colorado and Utah. They clashed frequently with whites—the Spanish in the 17th and 18th centuries and the Americans in the 19th century. They did not make their first treaty with the U.S. until 1849. In 1854 they raided the San Luis Valley of Colorado which brought retribution by U.S. soldiers the following year.

V

vaccination. The method of immunization against disease was developed by Edward Jenner, an English physician, in 1796. Benjamin Waterhouse of Boston, a Harvard professor, communicated Jenner's findings to the American newspaper-reading public in the *Columbian Centinel*, Mar. 12, 1799. In 1800 he vaccinated his young son with vaccine virus he had obtained from Jenner's supply. Within a decade vaccination was widely practiced in America. State governments began subsidizing it and Congress authorized a Federal Vaccine Agent to send the virus post-free anywhere in the U.S.

The right of a state to enact a compulsory vaccination law was sustained by the U.S. Supreme Court in *Jacobson v. Massachusetts* (1905). The Court held that such a law was the exercise of the state's police power to protect inhabitants against the spread of smallpox.

Valley Forge. The Continental army under Washington was encamped in this strategic location, 22 miles northwest of Philadelphia, during the bitter winter of 1777–78. Failure of the commissary to keep the troops supplied caused cruel hardships. This period is regarded as a low point in the colonial effort to gain independence. Nevertheless, the time was used for drilling under Baron von Steuben and the army emerged from winter headquarters ready to continue the war against the British.

Van Allen Radiation Belt. The zone of high-intensity radiation surrounding the earth beginning at altitudes of approximately 500 miles is named for James A. Van Allen, the U.S. space program scientist who located the zone. Spacecraft are designed to get through the region without damage to men or equipment.

Van Buren, Martin (1782–1862). Eighth President of the U.S. He was born in Kinderhook, N.Y. The "Little Magician" was a power in New York politics and a loyal supporter of Pres. Jackson. He was U.S. Senator (Democrat) from New

679

York (1821–28); U.S. Sec. of State (1829–31); and Vice-President of the U.S. (1833–37). President during the Panic of 1837, he failed to be re-elected in 1840.

Vanderbilt, Cornelius (1794–1877). Financier, steamship and railroad promoter. He was born in Staten Island, N.Y. Known as "Commodore Vanderbilt," he was founder of the family fortune. He was successful in steamboat operations on the Hudson, establishing his own service (1829). Anticipating a transportation need following the gold rush (1849), he financed a line to California via Nicaragua (1850–59), cutting passage time and fare. He gained controlling interest in the New York & Harlem Railroad (1862–63) when he was victorious over Daniel Drew in a financial struggle for the road. He won control of New York Central Railroad in 1867 and improved it. Adding the Lake Shore & Michigan Southern Railroad (1873) and the Michigan Central and Canada Southern roads (1875) to his holdings, he created one of the great American systems of transportation. He gave $1 million to Vanderbilt Univ. (previously Central Univ.) at Nashville, Tenn.

Vanguard, Project. The first Vanguard satellite went into orbit on March 17, 1958 as part of the U.S. program for the International Geophysical Year. It is expected to continue circling the earth for several hundred years. It has transmitted geodetic observations, including the determination that the earth is slightly pear shaped. Other Vanguard satellites have transmitted data about the weather and surveyed the earth's magnetic field.

Veblen, Thorstein Bunde (1857–1929). Economist and social theorist. Born in Manitowoc County, Wis., he was granted a Ph.D. by Yale (1884). A keen critic of established social and economic institutions, he achieved overnight prominence upon publication of *The Theory of the Leisure Class* (1899), a savage attack upon the business class and their pecuniary values. His basic economic theory is contained in *The Theory of Business Enterprise* (1904), which deals with the influence of business ideas and pressures upon law and politics. *The Higher Learning in America* (1918) is a bitter attack on the conduct of universities by businessmen. He joined the faculty of the New School for Social Research, N.Y.C. (1919). His writing helped mold the trend toward social control in an age dominated by business enterprise.

V-E Day (May 8, 1945). Victory in Europe for the Allies was achieved with the unconditional surrender of Germany in Rheims, France. The surrender was also signed in Berlin. World War II in Europe was ended.

Venezuela Boundary Dispute (1895). Britain had been unable to agree on the boundary line between Venezuela and British Guiana. The British extended their claims, 1885–86, beyond the Schomburgk line (a boundary line surveyed by a British agent in 1840) into a region where gold was reported. Venezuela broke off relations.

Sec. of State Olney pointed out that if Britain seized the disputed territory by force it would be a violation of the Monroe Doctrine. Pres. Cleveland called for arbitration of the dispute and appointed a commission. Britain accepted arbitration. It was having more serious difficulties in South Africa. Besides, at a time when Germany was becoming a power in Europe, Britain felt the need for U.S. friendship.

The arbitration commission returned the land to Venezuela, but established the boundary approximately along the Schomburgk line.

Venezuela Debt Controversy (1902). The ruinous financial policies of the Venezuelan dictator, Cipriano Castro, led Britain, Germany and Italy to blockade Venezuela in an effort to collect debts.

When the Allies seized several gunboats and sank two, Castro informed the U.S. that he would accept the arbitration previously rejected. The message was communicated to the powers concerned.

Since Pres. Theodore Roosevelt had been consulted in advance of the blockade, the U.S. was not involved in the diplomatic crisis. He wrote, in 1901, "If any South American country misbehaves toward any European country, let the European country spank it." This attitude was changed however by the Roosevelt Corollary (1904).

The Venezuela claims were settled by the Hague Court in 1904.

Vermont. The "Green Mountain State," a New England state, was the 14th state to be admitted to the Union, Mar. 4, 1791. Its capital is Montpelier.

The area was first visited by Champlain (1609). The words *vert mont* mean "green mountain" in French. The Green Mountains bisect Vermont, north to south. In the 17th and 18th centuries the French and British clashed in the region. New Englanders in the mid-18th century settled on land granted them by New Hampshire. The grants were contested by the New York colony. When it appeared that the settlers might be ousted, Ethan Allen organized the Green Mountain Boys to protect the claims.

During the Revolution the Green Mountain Boys won victories at Ticonderoga and Bennington. In 1777 Vermont declared its independence and adopted the first constitution providing universal manhood suffrage without property qualifications. New York relinquished its land claims in 1790 prior to Vermont's admission as the first state after the original 13.

The state was vigorously antislavery and supported Abraham Lincoln in opposition to a native son, Stephen Douglas. In the Civil War, Vermont was invaded by Confederates from Canada.

Vermont is rural in character. It has a large dairy industry and leads in the production of maple syrup. Marble and granite are important. Principal industries are stone, clay and wood products, including furniture and paper.

Versailles, Treaty of (June 28, 1919). The Treaty was signed by the Allied Powers and Germany at the Paris Peace Conference at the end of World War I. Germany was disarmed except for a small army of 100,-000 men and a few naval vessels. She lost all her colonies. Large cash reparations (later greatly reduced and even then paid in very small part) were demanded. Alsace-Lorraine was ceded to France. In addition, Germany gave up other territories to Poland, including a strip through East Prussia known as the "Polish Corridor." The rich coal-producing Saar Basin was placed under administrative control of the League of Nations and the economic control of France. Finally, Germany was compelled to accept responsibility for the war (the "war-guilt clause").

German representatives protested that the Versailles Treaty did not conform to Pres. Wilson's Fourteen Points. Wilson was well aware of this; but the Treaty did contain provision for the League of Nations and he was hopeful that in the years to come, the League would "iron out" those features of the settlement which might disturb the peace.

The U.S. Senate did not ratify the Treaty of Versailles and the U.S. war with Germany did not officially end until the Treaty of Berlin was ratified (1921).

Vesey Rebellion. In 1822 Denmark Vesey, a free Negro, planned a slave insurrection in Charleston, S.C. He was betrayed and arrested along with 35 other Negroes and they were tried and hanged.

Fear inspired by the plot resulted in legislation in the South isolating slaves from free Negroes.

Veterans Administration. The VA was established as an independent agency in 1930 to consolidate federal agencies especially created to provide benefits for veterans.

The VA administers laws authorizing benefits for former members of the Armed Forces and for the dependents and other beneficiaries of deceased veterans. Benefits available under various acts of Congress include compensation for disabilities suffered while in service or later; pensions; education and training; war orphans' educational assistance; insurance of home, farm and business loans; life insurance; hospitalization; prosthetic appliances; automobiles for certain disabled veterans; burial allowances.

veto. The word "veto" is derived from the Latin and means "I forbid." The President may, according to the Constitution, refuse his assent to any measure presented by Congress for his approval. In such case, he returns the measure to the House in which it originated, at the same time indicating his objections—the so-called veto message. The veto applies to the entire measure; the President may not, unlike governors of some states, veto separate items in a bill.

Vice-President. Under the Constitution (Art. II, Sec. 1, Par. 5), "In case of the removal of the President from office, or of his death, resignation, or inability to discharge the powers and duties of the said office, the same shall devolve on the Vice-President. . . ." The Vice-President presides over the Senate and can vote in case of a tie (Art. I, Sec. 3, Par. 4). Under the 12th Amendment the electors vote for the President and Vice-President separately. Under the 25th Amendment the Vice-President's succession to the Presidency is further defined.

The Founding Fathers had envisioned the office of Vice-President as being filled by the second most respected figure in the nation. The office, however, was soon relegated to a minor place in the executive branch with the Vice-President completely dependent upon the President for any duties or responsibilities conferred upon him. Martin Van Buren as Vice-President (1833–37) enjoyed the confidence of Pres. Jackson. It was not, however, until Pres. Eisenhower entrusted Vice-President Nixon (1953–61) with responsibility and a place in the National Security Council that the office came out of the shadows. The illnesses of Pres. Eisenhower and the assassination of Pres. Kennedy aroused public concern about the caliber of the Vice-President.

The eight Vice-Presidents who succeeded to the Presidency following the death of the President are: Tyler, who succeeded Harrison (1841); Fillmore, Taylor (1850); A. Johnson, Lincoln (1865); Arthur, Garfield (1881); T. Roosevelt, McKinley (1901); Coolidge, Harding (1923); Truman, F. D. Roosevelt (1945); L. B. Johnson, Kennedy (1963).

Vicksburg, battle of (May 22–July 4, 1863). The key Confederate Mississippi city finally fell before the siege undertaken by Gen. Ulysses S. Grant, aided by the Union navy which controlled the river. Gen. John Pemberton surrendered July 4, 1863, when his food gave out and there was no prospect of relief. Six weeks later, the Confederacy was forced to yield Port Hudson, La. and, in the words of Lincoln, the Mississippi "ran unvexed to the sea."

By this vital victory the trans-Mississippi states of Missouri, Arkansas, Louisiana and Texas were split from the rest of the Confederacy.

Victoria. Only one ship of Magellan's fleet of five vessels returned to Spain in 1522 after having set sail in 1519 on a trip that was to take it around the world. Magellan himself was killed in the Philippines in 1521.

Viet Nam. Cambodia, Laos and Viet Nam in Southeast Asia constituted French Indo-China from the mid-19th century to the mid-20th century. In 1940, during World War II, the Japanese occupied Indo-China. The leading guerrilla group that opposed the Japanese was the Viet Minh, headed by Ho Chi Minh, a Moscow-trained Communist. When Japanese rule collapsed in 1945, the Viet Minh promptly declared Viet Nam independent—and turned to fight against the returning French. A brutal, searing war followed with a final Viet Minh victory in 1954 at Dien Bien Phu, a French stronghold.

Under the Geneva agreements, Viet Nam was split in two. The Communists were recognized as the official government north of the 17th parallel.

Within South Viet Nam the French helped set up Emperor Bao Dai as head of government. In 1955 when it became apparent that Bao Dai preferred a playboy life on the French Riviera, Ngo Dinh Diem, who had returned from self-exile in the U.S., asked voters to decide between a republic headed by himself or a monarchy. Diem won handily and became president of the Republic of South Viet Nam.

With the help of a U.S. military mission Diem's army was able to resist stepped-up Communist agitation. In 1956 Diem refused to hold the free election to unify the country promised at Geneva. He charged that the Communists could not be trusted to conduct free elections in the North. With this, the Viet Cong, as the Communist-led guerrillas in South Viet Nam now came to be called, launched a systematic campaign of assassination and terrorism against local village chiefs and others loyal to Diem.

By 1960 the Viet Cong raids caused Diem to ask the U.S. to step up its assistance. Behind U.S. agreement was a belief that if Viet Nam fell to the Communists, the rest of Southeast Asia would be imperiled. In 1961 Pres. Kennedy decided to take a stronger stand against the guerrillas. Instead of just training the South Vietnamese (a policy followed by Pres. Eisenhower), U.S. pilots began ferrying the South Vietnamese into battle with helicopters. U.S. "Special Forces" troops began directing Vietnamese defense of remote villages and military outposts.

By the end of 1961 the U.S. had 2,000 military advisers in Viet Nam. By the end of 1963 the number had grown to 15,-

500. Yet, as the U.S. stepped up its aid, the South Vietnamese government deteriorated. By late 1963 Diem, a Catholic, was accused of being autocratic and discriminating against Viet Nam's Buddhists. Military leaders stepped in and overthrew Diem. He and his brother Nhu were killed. Numerous changes of government followed. No leader has been able to unify the country, thoroughly divided and weakened by 25 years of war.

The burden of struggle against the Viet Cong was increasingly assumed by the U.S. In 1964 Pres. Johnson ordered U.S. planes to bomb specific military targets in North Viet Nam in retaliation for an attack against U.S. warships in the Gulf of Tonkin. In 1965 U.S. air attacks against targets in both North and South Viet Nam were supplemented by arrival of U.S. ground combat units. In 1965 Pres. Johnson made what he called a "most agonizing and most painful" decision. He threw the whole weight of U.S. prestige into keeping South Viet Nam out of Communist hands. Early in 1969 the total of U.S. troops in Viet Nam and in offshore forces reached 540,000.

Opposition to escalation of the war was vehement even among Democratic senators. J. William Fulbright (Arkansas), Chairman of the Senate Foreign Relations Committee, held that U.S. foreign policy should re-

main "one of determination to end the war at the earliest possible time by a negotiated settlement involving major concessions by both sides." Pres. Johnson in 1968 said that North Viet Nam is no more ready to negotiate than it was three years earlier.

Pres. Nixon embarked upon a policy of U.S. troop reduction following the beginning of peace negotiations in Paris in 1968. Henry Kissinger, who became Secretary of State in 1973, was the chief American negotiator. In 1971 with the seemingly interminable war still on, Pres. Nixon reduced troop strength in Viet Nam substantially. As late as Dec. 1972 he ordered round-the-clock bombing of North Viet Nam when the cease-fire, expected before the Nov. 1972 presidential election, failed to materialize.

On Jan. 27, 1973, a detailed cease-fire agreement ending the war in Viet Nam was signed in Paris. Provision was also made for the neutrality and independence of Laos and Cambodia. The war was the longest in which the U.S. had ever been engaged. The total of American casualties was 45,000 dead and 300,000 wounded. Within 60 days of the war's end, the U.S. withdrew its remaining 23,700 troops, but sporadic fighting continued in Indo-China. The bombing by the U.S. of Communist insurgents in Cambodia continued until the Aug. 15, 1973, deadline set by Congress.

vigilantes. In the frontier communities of the West law enforcement and strengthening the courts to deal with crime were major problems. Citizens often organized committees to suppress outlaws. A notable example of vigilante action was the San Francisco Vigilance Committee (1851). It successfully stopped the desperadoes who had been attracted by the gold rush of 1849 to what was called the Barbary Coast of San Francisco. Other western communities followed the lead of San Francisco.

Vigilantes acting extralegally hanged many murderers and thieves, but some injustice resulted from the mob violence they aroused. The name has been applied to later groups who have used force to impose their will on others.

Vinland. The name has been given to the shores of America somewhere between Labrador and Cape Cod which were visited between 986 and 1003 by the Northmen (Norsemen or Scandinavian Vikings), Bjarni Herjulfson and Leif Ericsson, on separate voyages. Several later voyages failed to accomplish colonization of the wooded, vine-covered shore which Ericsson first explored.

Vinson Naval Act (1938). Also known as the Naval Expansion Act, it provided for building a "two-ocean navy" in the next 10 years. Authorization was given for an increase of 135,000 tons in capital ships, bringing them to 660,000 tons. Cruiser tonnage might be increased by 68,754 tons, bringing them to 412,500 tons. The aircraft tonnage increase allowed was 40,000 tons, bringing them up to 175,000 tons.

Virginia. The "Old Dominion," a South Atlantic state, was one of the original 13 Colonies. It was named after Queen Elizabeth, the "Virgin Queen." Its capital is Richmond.

The first permanent settlement in North America was made at Jamestown (1607) by the London Company. The colony began to prosper under John Smith. The first representative assembly in the New World, the House of Burgesses, met at Jamestown in 1619. In the same year the first slaves arrived in the American colonies. The tobacco industry, established in the new colony by John Rolfe, developed rapidly.

Virginia played an important part in the French and Indian War (1754–63) and was a center of resistance to Parliament in the years before the American Revolution. A state constitution was adopted June 29, 1776. Among Virginia's radical leaders of the day were Patrick Henry, Thomas Jefferson and Richard Henry Lee. George Washington was appointed Commander-in-Chief of the Continental army. The state was a major theater of the Revolutionary War.

Virginia was the tenth state to ratify the Constitution (June 25, 1788). The state is known as the "mother of presidents" because until 1825 all U.S. Presidents except John Adams came from Virginia.

The quarrel over secession divided the state. The western part of the state broke away to form West Virginia when Virginia seceded from the Union, Apr. 17, 1861. Richmond became the capital of the Confederate States and Robert E. Lee became Commander-in-Chief of the Confederate army. The state was a bloody battleground during the Civil War. It was not readmitted to the Union until Jan. 26, 1870.

Virginia is one of the largest tobacco producers. Other crops are corn, oats, winter wheat and apples. Smithfield hams from peanut-fed hogs are world famous. Livestock, dairying and turkey raising are important industries and the Piedmont is noted for its thoroughbred horses. Leading industrial products are cigarettes, chemicals, furniture, lumber, cotton, textiles and ships. Newport News, at the mouth of the James River, has a large shipbuilding plant. Hampton Roads is the major port.

Virginia and Kentucky Resolutions. Passed by the legislatures of Virginia and Kentucky in 1798 and 1799, the Resolutions opposed the Alien and Sedition Acts by which the Federalist-controlled Congress sought to curb the opposition of Thomas Jefferson's Republican party.

Jefferson drafted the Kentucky Resolution, which was based on the compact theory of government. It declared that the states had the right to declare void measures which went beyond the agreement between a state and the national government. James Madison, in the Virginia Resolutions, held that the states together might "interpose" to check the exercise of unauthorized powers.

The Resolutions developed the states' rights position that later was to be used as justification for nullification and secession.

Virginia Companies. In 1606, two groups of English promoters of colonization in the New World obtained grants of 10,000 square miles each from King James I. One group resided chiefly in Plymouth, the other in London. The Virginia Company of Plymouth (North Virginia) received the exclusive right to colonize between the 45th and 41st parallels; the Virginia Company of London (South Virginia) could operate between the 38th and 34th parallels. The space between the 41st and 38th parallels was open to occupancy by either group, provided however that the two colonies should be at least 100 miles apart.

The companies are usually referred to as the London Company and the Plymouth Company.

Virginia Declaration of Rights (June 12, 1776). Written by George Mason a month before the Declaration of Independence was signed, the document gave classic expression to the general philosophy of the natural rights of the individual. It was a restatement of English principles of individual rights and liberties and served as a model for the other states and for the Bill of Rights.

"Virginia dynasty." The term was applied to the Virginians who became President of the U.S. during the early years of the Republic—Washington, Jefferson, Madison and Monroe.

Virginian, The (1902). In the novel by Owen Wister, a Virginian goes to the wilds of Wyoming and falls in love with a Vermont schoolteacher, Molly Wood. The difference in their cultural background is a barrier which love finally overcomes.

Wister, who contributed to the cowboy legend in America, defended the free open life of the range against the homesteaders. He created the literary cliché of the gentle cowpuncher who respected virtuous womanhood.

Virginia Plan (1787). Edmund Randolph of Virginia presented at the Constitutional Convention a plan for representation that was supported by the large states. He proposed a two-house legislature based on size of population. The lower house, elected by the people, would elect the members of the upper house. The two houses combined would elect an executive and judges for courts. A council made up of the executive and some judges would have the power to veto acts of the legislature.

The Virginia Plan ignored the principle of separation of powers. It was countered by the New Jersey Plan of the small states. Both plans were modified by the Great Compromise.

"Virginia Resolves" (1769). Virginia supported the views expressed by Massachusetts on the colonists' right to be taxed only by their own legislature and denounced the manner in which the British had responded to colonial protests. The resolutions gained additional force by virtue of their introduction in the Virginia legislature by George Washington.

Virgin Islands. Formerly the Danish West Indies, the islands were purchased by the U.S. in 1917 for $25,000,000. Previous negotiations for their purchase had fallen through, but World War I and the fear that Germany might claim them for a foothold in the Caribbean hastened the final transfer.

They include some 50 islands lying east of Puerto Rico. The largest and most populous are St. Thomas, St. John and St. Croix. Sugar and rum are the principal products.

The inhabitants have been U.S. citizens since 1927, but do not vote in U.S. elections. The islands are administered by the Department of Interior.

The governor is appointed by the President.

Virginius Affair. Owned by Cubans, but fraudulently registered in the U.S. and flying the American flag, the *Virginius* was being used to supply Cuban rebels who were seeking to overthrow Spanish rule. On Oct. 31, 1873, it was captured on the high seas by a Spanish warship. Passengers and crew were brought to Santiago, Cuba, where some of them, including Americans, were executed.

War sentiment was aroused both in the U.S. and Spain. Sec. of State Hamilton Fish sent a virtual ultimatum to Spain, but moderated his demands when he learned of the questionable character of the *Virginius*. Later, he reflected that there should be "no unnecessary war undertaken for a dishonest vessel." Spain eventually paid an indemnity of $80,000,000 to the families of the executed Americans, but promoted the Spanish officer responsible for the executions.

VISTA. Volunteers in Service to America, organized in 1965 under the Economic Opportunity Act, is the domestic version of the Peace Corps. The volunteers are trained to work in city slums, aid social workers, act as mental health assistants, teach hobbies and crafts to the elderly, tutor children, help in struggling farm communities, Indian reservations and migrant labor camps. They do whatever is needed to encourage people to escape from poverty.

Vittorio-Veneto, battle of (Oct. 24–Nov. 4, 1918). About 1,200 U.S. troops participated in an offensive on the Italian front in World War I. It ended in the rout of the Austrian army.

V-J Day (Sept. 2, 1945). Victory over Japan in World War II was achieved with the formal surrender on board the U.S.S. *Missouri.*

vocational education. In 1850 public interest in education centered on free public schools for all children and technical training for farmers and workers. Technical education was stimulated by passage of the Morrill Act (1862), which provided a federal subsidy for land-grant colleges of agricultural and mechanical arts. Interest in better vocational programs for younger students followed. It was not, however, until passage of the Smith-Hughes Act (1917) that a comprehensive program was evolved.

The Smith-Hughes Act provided federal funds to match state and local appropriations for the support of high school courses in agriculture, home economics and trades and industries. This stimulated the establishment of vocational education departments in high schools in all the states.

Demands for funds mounted, and Congress increased appropriations and the fields covered in the original law by the George-Reed Act (1929), the George-Elzey Act (1934), the George-Dean Act (1936) and the George-Barden Act (1946). To the three original vocational areas was added the distributive occupations which included retail selling, marketing and merchandising.

In addition to the vocational education programs of the federal, state and local governments, there are private trade schools and institutions. Also, many industrial plants operate their own training courses.

Von Neumann, John (1903–57). Mathematician. Born in Budapest, Hungary, he came to the U.S. in 1930. He was granted a Ph.D. by Budapest Univ. (1926). After 1933, he was a member of the Institute of Advanced Study, Princeton, N.J. He worked on the A-bomb and H-bomb projects and was a member of the Atomic Energy Commission (1954–57). He helped develop MANIAC (mathematical analyzer, numerical integrator and computer), utilized in testing the H-bomb.

voting. Methods of voting range from the oral declaration in favor of a candidate that prevailed in England in the 17th century to the use of voting machines in the U.S. in the 20th century. As early as 1634 the paper ballot was used in the Massachusetts colony and by 1800 was adopted in all the states. The Australian ballot, which afforded the voter secrecy, came into use in the U.S. in the latter part of the 19th century.

Suffrage (voting) laws in the colonies commonly provided for religious and property qualifications. In 18th-century colonial Pennsylvania, for example, the vote was granted to any Christian male who had resided two years in the colony and owned 50 acres of land (12 of them cleared) or property valued at £50. Under the new state constitutions of the 1780's the franchise (voting privilege) was exercised by property holders in some states and taxpayers in others. In conservative New York, no one could vote for members of the upper house of the legislature who did not own land worth £100. In democratic Georgia, all white male inhabitants who paid taxes (whether they owned property or not) could vote for all state legislators.

Between 1810 and 1820, six new states entered the Union with constitutions that did not establish property qualifications for voting. By 1841 Rhode Island was the only state that had not accepted almost universal white male suffrage. In 1843 this was rectified by a new Rhode Island constitution.

The states continue to set the requirements for voting and these generally include an age limitation, literacy and a residence requirement. The 15th, 19th and 24th Amendments to the Constitution struck down certain state limitations on voting.

Voting Rights Act of 1965. This measure was hailed by Pres. Lyndon B. Johnson, who signed it on Aug. 6, as the means of making the 15th Amendment a reality. It provides for the suspension of literacy tests and for the directed registration of Negro voters by federal examiners whenever the Attorney General certifies that a state or county had literacy tests on Nov. 1, 1964 and had less than 50% of its voting-age population registered or voting in the 1964 presidential election. This so-called "automatic trigger" immediately brought under the law the states of Alabama, Louisiana, Mississippi, Georgia and South Carolina, plus a large number of counties in North Carolina and Virginia.

The law did not ban outright the payment of a poll tax as a prerequisite for voting in state and local elections. It declared that Congress finds that the payment of such a tax has been used in some areas to abridge the right to vote, and it directs the Attorney General to initiate suits immediately to test the constitutionality of such taxes.

Under section 4(E)(2) of the Act Puerto Ricans in New York and foreign-language-speaking citizens in any state must be registered to vote if they can show they have had the required number of grades in a school although the predominant classroom language was other than English. They need not satisfy any state's requirement that they read and write English.

W

Wabash and Erie Canal. The construction of the canal by Ohio and Indiana commenced in 1832 and soon encountered financing difficulties and flood damage. Nevertheless, by 1856 it connected Toledo on Lake Erie with Evansville, Indiana, 452 miles to the south, making it the longest canal in the U.S. The canal was not successful financially and railroad competition forced its abandonment by 1875.

Wabash Case (1886). In *Wabash, St. Louis and Pacific Railway v. Illinois* the U.S. Supreme Court declared unconstitutional the Illinois law outlawing discrimination in rates between long hauls and short hauls. The Wabash Railroad, charged with violating the law, had sued the state.

The Court held that railroads, as corporations, were "persons" in the eyes of the law and were protected against deprivation of property without due process of law by the 14th Amendment. The state regulation constituted such deprivation of property. The power to regulate railroads bringing in goods from outside the state or destined to points outside it rests with the federal government under the interstate commerce clause.

Wade-Davis Bill (1864). In opposition to Pres. Lincoln's 10% policy, the Radical Republicans in Congress proposed that the seceded states gain readmission to the Union only if a majority of the white male citizens take the oath of allegiance and submit a constitution acceptable to Congress. The new state constitutions were required to abolish slavery, repudiate state debts and disfranchise ex-Confederate leaders.

Since the bill was passed an hour before the session of Congress ended, Lincoln permitted the bill to die by a pocket veto. Subsequently, Congress overrode Pres. Johnson and imposed its comparatively harsh Reconstruction program on the South.

Wagner-Steagall Housing Act (1937). Officially named the National Housing Act of 1937, the New Deal measure aimed to improve housing conditions for low-income groups. It established the U.S. Housing Authority (USHA) which extended 60-year loans, at low interest, to local public agencies. These were required to meet about 10% of the slum clearance cost. Provision was also made for federal subsidy of rents in the projects.

Wagon Box Fight (Aug. 2, 1867). A wood chopping detail from Fort Phil Kearny, Wyo., was attacked by a band of Sioux cavalry under Chief Red Cloud. Thirty-two of the 36 soldiers under Capt. James Powell managed to reach the shelter of a wagon box corral. Armed with new breech-loading rifles, they fought off repeated and suicidal charges throughout the day. Twenty-nine were alive and still fighting when relief arrived from the fort. About 180 Indians were killed and wounded.

Waite, Morrison Remick (1816 –88). Jurist. Born in Lyme, Conn., he was admitted to the Ohio bar (1839). He was the American counsel in the Geneva Arbitration (1871–72), serving with Caleb Cushing and William M. Evarts. He was Chief Justice of U.S. Supreme Court from 1874 to 1888. In *Munn v. Illinois* (1877), he upheld the power of the state to regulate the charges of grain elevators— businesses that were "clothed with a public interest." He laid the foundation for the modern interpretation of due process as a limitation on state power in *Stone v. Farmers' Loan and Trust Co.* (1886): "From what has been said it is not to be inferred that this power . . . of regulation is itself without limit. . . . It is not a power to destroy. . . . The State cannot do that which . . . amounts to a taking of private property . . . without due process of law."

Wakarusa War (Nov. 26–Dec. 7, 1855). Free State and proslavery men fought a brief battle with few casualties along the Wakarusa River, near Lawrence, Kansas. The "Border Ruffians" from Missouri refrained from attacking Lawrence which was defended by Free State settlers. The "War" was terminated by the intervention of Gov. Wilson Shannon.

Waksman, Selman Abraham (1888–1973). Microbiologist. Born in Russia, he came to the U.S. in 1910. He was granted a Ph.D. by the Univ. of California (1918). He was awarded the Nobel Prize (1952) for Medicine and Physiology for discovery of streptomycin, an antibiotic. He taught soil microbiology at Rutgers Univ. (1918 –58).

"Wakwak" tree. In an effort to attract settlers to America in the 18th century, promoters resorted to devices that would stun 20th-century advertising men. In 1729 Ibrahim Effendi, a Turkish writer, lured emigrants to America with his account of the "Wakwak" tree, a tree whose fruit was beautiful women.

Walden (1854). In his chief work, which is subtitled *Life in the Woods*, Henry David Thoreau tells of his simple, healthy, hermitlike life on the shores of Walden Pond, near Concord, Mass., where he built himself a hut, cultivated a garden and lived for years on an annual outlay of eight dollars. The book is noted for its descriptions of nature.

Walker, Joseph Reddeford (1798–1876). Trapper and guide. Probably born in Virginia, his knowledge of the geography of the West was outstanding. He is believed to have led the first party of whites across the Sierra Nevada Mts. from the East (1833) and was probably the first to see the Yosemite Valley. Walker Lake in Nevada and Walker's Pass in southern California are named for him. He guided John Frémont's third expedition (1845–46) to California and was among the first of the Forty-niners to reach California.

Walker Tariff of 1846. During the Democratic administration of Pres. Polk a new tariff law pleasing to the South and West reduced sharply the existing tariff rates. It incorporated the principle of tariff for revenue only. Industrialists in the Northeast, many of them Democrats, protested unsuccessfully against the reductions.

walking purchase. Indians in ceding lands to colonists were vague about boundaries and often measured distances in terms of how far a man could walk in a day or in some other specified time. In 1686, for example, William Penn obtained by treaty from the Delaware Indians a tract of land in the fork of the Delaware and Lehigh rivers that was 40 miles deep ("as far as a man can go in a day and a half").

Walk-in-the-Water. The first steamboat to enter service on the Upper Great Lakes was launched, May 28, 1818, and ceased operation after a wreck on Nov. 1, 1821.

Wall Street. The history of the street in downtown Manhattan as the financial center of the U.S. goes back to about 1790. The most powerful banking and brokerage houses are located there. The street is so named because in the 17th century the Dutch built a wall in lower New York to protect themselves from Indian attacks.

Walsh-Healey Government Contracts Act (1936). The New Deal law established the 40-hour week and minimum wages for all employees of contractors making supplies for the federal government.

wampum. Before 1660 these shells or beads were much sought after by the Indians and figured largely in the currency system of New England and New Netherland. The term came from the Algonquian word *wampompeag.*

Wampum belts were exchanged by Indians on ceremonial occasions and at treaty-making times well into the 19th century.

Wanghia, Treaty of (1844). Negotiated for the U.S. by Caleb Cushing, first American commissioner to China, the commercial treaty opened five Chinese ports to American trade and contained a clear statement of extraterritoriality. Americans accused of crimes in China were to be tried before an American official, not by a Chinese judge or court.

war crimes trials. Following World War II, German and Japanese war leaders were tried as war criminals by International Military Tribunals established at American insistence. The most famous were the Nuremberg trials of 22 top Nazis in Germany, who were convicted of war crimes, Sept. 30, 1946. Eleven of the 22 were sentenced to death. They were found guilty not only of waging aggressive warfare but of "crimes against humanity." The proceedings revealed the full story of Nazi barbarity. In all, over 500,000 war criminals were found guilty in the American zone of occupied Germany and received sentences of varying severity.

Similar trials were held in Tokyo (June 1946–May 1948). Premier Tojo and six other war leaders were executed. Further trials led to sentencing of over 4,000 other Japanese war criminals.

Ward, Lester Frank (1841–1913). Sociologist. Born in Joliet, Ill., he was professor of sociology at Brown Univ. from 1906 to 1913. A pioneer of evolutionary sociology in the U.S., he held that the intellect, when rightly informed with scientific truth, enables the individual or the social group to plan for future development. He looked forward to an age of systematic planning for human progress in which government will stress social welfare. His works include *Dynamic Sociology* (1883), *Pure Sociology* (1903) and a "mental autobiography," *Glimpses of the Cosmos* (6 vols., 1913–18).

war debts. During World War I and later the U.S. lent more than $10 billion to the Allies to help finance the war and to facilitate postwar reconstruction. The money for the loans was raised in the U.S. during the war through Liberty Loan and Victory Loan "drives." The loans were to be repaid in 62 years.

The U.S. collected less than a quarter of the loans. Allied repayment was dependent on German payment of reparations to the Allies and these were slow in coming. After the Hoover moratorium (1931) there was virtual cessation of both reparations and war debt payment, except for payment in full by Finland.

Warehouse Act (1916). The Act sought to aid farmers obtain credit by authorizing licensed warehouse operators to issue receipts against farm products deposited with them. Farmers could use the warehouse receipts as negotiable paper to obtain bank loans.

"War Hawks." The congressmen from the South and West who clamored for war against Britain were branded as "War Hawks" by easterners who opposed what was to be the War of 1812.

The "War Hawks" were aroused by what they believed were British-supported Indian attacks on frontier settlements. They urged conquest of Florida and Canada as a means to safeguard the frontier and to satisfy their expansionist desires.

The leading "War Hawk" was Henry Clay of Kentucky. Others included John Calhoun of South Carolina and Felix Grundy of Tennessee.

War Industries Board (1918–19). Under the direction of Bernard Baruch the Board, established during World War I, sought to conserve limited materials and expand production in an orderly way through close regulation of the economy. Manufacturers in key industries were told what to produce and priorities on materials and transportation were established. Items produced for the Armed Forces were standardized to prevent waste.

War Information, Office of (OWI). Created by an executive order of Pres. F. D. Roosevelt, June 13, 1942, the agency consolidated the information activities, both foreign and domestic, of the government. Elmer Davis, a prominent news broadcaster, was made director.

"war . . . is all hell." The view was expressed by Gen. William T. Sherman in a speech at Columbus, Ohio, Aug. 11, 1880. Sherman in his famous "march through Georgia" (1864) lived off the land he devastated and thus helped to crush southern resistance.

War Labor Disputes Act (1943). Also known as the Smith-Connally Anti-Strike Act, the World War II law was passed over Pres. F. D. Roosevelt's veto. It broadened presidential power to seize plants where interference with war production was threatened by a labor disturbance. It made illegal the instigation of strikes in plants seized by the government and made unions liable for damage suits for failure to give 30 days' notice of intention to strike in war industries.

War Mobilization, Office of. The agency was established May 27, 1943, to assume responsibility for the conduct of the war on the home front. It was headed by James F. Byrnes. The OWM unified the activities of federal agencies engaged in the production or distribution of civilian supplies.

On Oct. 3, 1944, Byrnes was named head of the newly established Office of War Mobilization and Reconversion.

War of 1812 (1812–15). The war between the U.S. and Great Britain was fought during the final years of Britain's struggle to end Napoleon's rule of Europe and threat to England. Pres. Madison's war message (June 1, 1812) to Congress stressed the British Orders-in-Council which led to Britain's impressment of American seamen and her interference with American commerce.

The geographical distribution of the vote for and against the war raises some difficult questions about its causes, but recent emphasis has been on the violation of neutral rights and impressment as important issues. Neutral rights involved economic interests, too; as Madison explained, British policy struck not only at commerce but at agriculture as well. Farmers cut off from European markets by the British blockade suffered even though they may never have seen an oceangoing vessel.

Opposition to the war was most pronounced in New York, New Jersey and the New England maritime states. The Federalist commercial interests looked upon war as a greater threat to trade than the Orders-in-Council. Sharing these views with the Federalists was a handful of Republicans representing southern coastal districts. New England's opposition took form in the Hartford Convention.

Support for the war declaration by Congress (June 18, 1812) came from the West and Southwest. Westerners believed that if Canada could be wrested from Britain, the source of supplies for Indian attacks and the valuable fur trade would be in American hands. Americans in the Southwest were anxious to drive Spain, an ally of Britain, from Florida which was a haven for runaway slaves and a source of supplies for Indians of the Southwest. The congressmen who protested against British support of Indian uprisings and urged territorial expansion into Canada and Florida were known as "War Hawks." They were opposed by those who argued that "agrarian cupidity, not maritime right, urges the war."

The "War Hawks'" prediction of an easy victory in Canada was not realized. Few regular troops were ready to fight and the state militia were poorly trained and reluctant to cross the borders of their state. Moreover, Canadian nationalism was aroused. There were more Canadian troops at border points than Americans. Some New England governors refused to furnish any troops at all because they were opposed to "Mr. Madison's War."

Canadian forces crossed the border and took Detroit, which was later retaken by Americans. On Lake Erie, Capt. Oliver Hazard Perry won a bloody but decisive victory over the British lake squadron (1813). Another attempted British invasion failed when Comm. Thomas Macdonough won an overwhelming victory on Lake Champlain (1814).

One British expedition landed near Washington and went on to burn the White House and Capitol (1814) in retaliation for the destruction by American troops of the Parliament buildings in Toronto. When the British fleet moved on to Baltimore, it was turned back by tough resistance put up by American forces in Fort McHenry. The British fleet was, however, largely successful in blockading the U.S. coast during the war.

The greatest victory of American forces was won at the battle of New Orleans (1815) after the Treaty of Ghent had been signed. The peace treaty restored matters to where they had been at the beginning of the war.

"war on poverty." The dramatic phrase was used by Pres. Johnson in 1964 to launch an antipoverty program in the U.S. Congress enacted the Economic Opportunity Act of 1964 which gave high priority to youth. Under the Office of Economic Opportunity (OEO) provision was made for job training and remedial education in Job Corps camps in both rural and urban centers. Cities, states and communities received federal grants to conduct community-wide action programs to help the poor break the cycle of poverty. VISTA, the domestic Peace Corps, recruited workers in migrant camps and city slums. Teen-agers were given part-time work under the Neighborhood Youth Corps program. Part-time jobs were provided for high school, college and university students. Persons on relief and others were placed in jobs under a work-experience program.

War Production Board (WPB). In 1942 Pres. F. D. Roosevelt appointed Donald M. Nelson chairman of the WPB with authority to mobilize the nation's resources for a total war effort. WPB was the principal agency in the field of production and supply. It absorbed the Office of Production Management.

The WPB halted non-essential residential and highway construction to conserve materials for the war effort. In Aug. 1944, Nelson permitted limited reconversion of industry from war to civilian output. The WPB was terminated, Oct. 4, 1945, and its functions transferred to the Civilian Production Administration.

Warren, Earl (1891–   ). Jurist. Born in Los Angeles, Calif., he was attorney general of California (1939–43); governor of California (1942–53); Republican nominee for Vice-President of U.S. (1948); appointed Chief Justice of U.S. Supreme Court (1953) by Pres. Eisenhower; resigned 1968. Generally aligned with the liberals, his notable opinion

(*Brown v. Board of Education*, 1954) struck down the separate-but-equal doctrine permitting racial segregation in the schools.

Warsaw Convention (1934). The agreement in which the U.S. is a participant provides a uniform liability code and uniform documentation on tickets and cargo for international air carriers. Under its provisions liability for loss of life or injury is limited to only $8,300, except where willful misconduct is proved. The treaty was drawn in the early days of air transport when airlines could have been put out of business by sizable damage suits.

Personal injury insurance in the U.S. provides compensation proportionate to the injury sustained, so that the family of an executive who dies in the prime of life usually gets more than the survivors of a retired person.

War Shipping Administration. The agency was established within the Office for Emergency Management, Feb. 7, 1942, to insure most effective use of U.S. shipping in the prosecution of the war. It was terminated Sept. 1, 1946, and its functions transferred to the U.S. Maritime Commission.

Washington. The "Evergreen State," northernmost of the Pacific states, was admitted to the Union as the 42nd state, Nov. 11, 1889. Its capital is Olympia.

The Spaniard Juan Perez was the first white man known to have entered the region. He discovered Nootka Sound and Mt. Olympus (1774). The English claim to the region was based on Capt. Cook's voyage (1778) and the fur trade in the area. Spain and England clashed over Nootka Sound in 1790 and the English won. U.S. claims to the region were based on Robert Gray's navigation of the Columbia River (1792), which he named after his ship. The Lewis and Clark expedition (1804–06) traversed the area.

Washington was part of the Oregon Territory until 1853 and figured in the controversy between the U.S. and Britain dramatized by Polk's "Fifty-four forty or fight" threat. The Washington Territory, named after George Washington, was organized by Congress, Mar. 2, 1853. Completion of the Northern Pacific Railroad (1883) hastened settlement and led to statehood.

The Columbia River Basin, which contains the Grand Coulee system, is the largest power-irrigation development in the U.S. Manufacturing has increased greatly with the use of hydroelectric power. Fisheries and forest products remain important. The state is a leader in growing hops, apples, cherries and winter wheat. Principal mineral products are cement, gold, silver and lead. Puget Sound harbors, especially Seattle, are the nearest American gateway to the ports of Asia. They handle the bulk of the shipping to and from Alaska and a heavy trade via the Panama Canal.

Washington, Booker Taliaferro (1856–1915). Educator. Born a slave in Franklin Co., Va., he gained national recognition as educational leader of the Negro people in the U.S. He worked his way through Hampton Institute, Va. (1872–75). Chosen (1881) to head a school at Tuskegee, Ala., he opened Tuskegee Institute with 40 students in a dilapidated shack. It grew under his leadership into the foremost institution for practical training of Negroes in trades and professions. He stressed immediate improvement of his race from a material point of view but opposed agitation. His best-known book is his autobiography, *Up From Slavery* (1901).

Washington, D.C. The city of Washington, the nation's capital, is coextensive with the District of Columbia. The District was originally given to the nation (1790) by Virginia and Maryland, but Virginia's portion, south of the Potomac, was returned in 1846.

George Washington, who selected the site, appointed Pierre Charles L'Enfant, a French engineer who had come over with Lafayette, to plan the capital on an area not over 10 miles square. His grandiose plans, revised about 1900, have guided the development of the expanding capital.

John Adams was the first President to move to Washington (Nov. 1800). The first Congress to sit in Washington met Nov. 17, 1800. Philadelphia ceased to be the temporary capital.

Congress in 1878 created a government for the city comprised of three commissioners, two of whom live in the District and are appointed by the President with the Senate's consent. One is detailed from the Corps of Engineers of the Army. Each House of Congress has a Committee on the District of Columbia. The residents are taxed although it was not until passage of the 23rd Amendment (1961) that residents of the District gained the right to vote for the President and Vice-President.

The capital is a magnet for Americans. The major federal office buildings and cultural centers are on diagonal avenues radiating from the Capitol and White House. Slums in the shadow of the Capitol are being erased and beautification of the city is a continuing project.

Washington, George (1732–99). First President of the U.S. (1789–97). He was born in Pope's Creek, Westmoreland Co., Va. His military experience in the French and Indian War led eventually to his command of the Continental army in the Revolutionary War. He was the leader of the Virginia opposition to English colonial policy and presided at the Constitutional Convention, 1787. When he declined a third term as President, he set a precedent that stood for more than 140 years.

Washington, Treaty of (1871). The Treaty settled a number of disputes between the U.S. and Great Britain. Sec. of State Hamilton Fish was the chief negotiator for the U.S. and the British group included the Canadian Prime Minister, Sir John A. MacDonald.

The U.S. agreed to refer its claims for destruction by the Confederate cruiser, *Alabama*, to arbitration in Geneva. The British inserted in the Treaty a frank expression of regret for the escape of the *Alabama* from a British port, an unusual international apology.

Also submitted to arbitration was the northwest boundary dispute over the San Juan Islands, a strategic group lying between British Columbia and the state of Washington. The U.S. claim to the islands was subsequently upheld by the German Emperor, who arbitrated the dispute.

The perennial fisheries controversy in the Northeast was settled to the satisfaction of the U.S. Americans were given more extensive fishing rights than had been granted in the Convention of 1818.

Washington Conference (Nov. 12, 1921–Feb. 6, 1922). The disarmament conference was called to avert a mounting naval race and to curb the demands of Japan on China. The American delegation included Sec. of State Charles Evans Hughes, Elihu Root, Henry Cabot Lodge and Oscar Underwood. At one of the first meetings Hughes proposed a 10-year holiday in the construction of capital ships. This led to the Five-Power Treaty in which the U.S., Britain, Japan, France and Italy accepted a 5–5–3–1.7–1.7 ratio of tonnages for capital ships (battleships).

The Anglo-Japanese Alliance of 1902 was abrogated and was replaced by a Four-Power Treaty. The U.S., Britain, France and Japan pledged to respect each other's rights in the Pacific.

In a Nine-Power pact including the five nations, as well as China, Belgium, the Netherlands and Portugal, the territorial integrity of China was affirmed.

At the time, the results of the Conference seemed satisfactory, but in less than a decade Japan invaded Manchuria.

Washington Monument. Construction of the marble shaft in Washington, D.C., honoring George Washington, was begun in 1836 and completed in 1884 from plans by Robert Mills. It is outstanding for its absolute lack of ornamentation in a period when popular taste preferred the ornate. The shaft soars to a height of 555 feet and the top can be reached by both an elevator and a stairway of 898 steps.

Wasp. The 18-gun American sloop-of-war (*Wasp* No. 1) captured the British brig *Frolic* off the coast of Virginia, Oct. 18, 1812. It was, however, so disabled that it was easily taken by the British ship-of-the-line *Poictiers* within a few hours of its victory. The Americans were taken to Bermuda as prisoners.

Wasp (No. 2), a second 18-gun American sloop-of-war harassed British merchant ships in the English Channel. On June 28, 1814, she captured the *Reindeer* and on Sept. 1 conquered the *Avon*. On Sept. 21, near the Azores, she captured and sent home a valuable prize, the *Atlanta*. *Wasp* (No. 2) was never heard from after Oct. 9. Her disappearance remains one of the mysteries of the sea.

"wasp." The letters stand for white Anglo-Saxon Protestant. The term has been used in recent years to refer to the Protestant candidate on a balanced ethnic ticket in election campaigns. This balance is sought in cities where no single religious group is dominant. Party managers urge as a requirement for victory the nomination of a Catholic, Jew and "wasp" for the three top offices.

"watchful waiting." The policy was adopted by Pres. Wilson when the Mexican government of the liberal idealist Pres. Madero was overthrown by Gen. Huerta in 1913. Wilson refused to grant recognition to the Huerta government although he was urged to do so by American businessmen who had invested almost a billion dollars in Mexican oil fields, mines and railroads. Wilson said, "We can have no sympathy for those who seek to seize the power of government to advance their own personal interests or ambition." He adopted a policy of "watchful waiting," hoping that Huerta would fall as had the dictatorship of Pres. Díaz in 1911. The Huerta government did fall in 1914 and the U.S. recognized the Carranza government.

Water Power Act (1920). Under the Act Congress sought to develop water power reserves on public lands of the U.S. It established the Federal Power Commission which was empowered to issue licenses, limited to 50 years, for the construction and operation of dams, power houses, reservoirs and transmission lines, which were to be used for improving navigation and utilizing power. Upon expiration of the lease, the government reserved the right to appropriate and operate these facilities. The FPC was authorized to regulate rates of licensees under its jurisdiction.

"wave the bloody shirt." After the Reconstruction era, the Republican party continued to "wave the bloody shirt" in an effort to gain votes. It kept the wounds of the Civil War open by describing itself as the party of Lincoln and victory and belabored the Democrats as the party of treason.

Waxhaw Creek, battle of (May 29, 1780). A force of cavalry under Col. Tarleton destroyed a Virginia regiment under Col. Buford in South Carolina. Buford was marching from Charleston where he had been too late to help prevent its capture by British Gen. Clinton. After the battle with Tarleton, Buford and about a hundred of his infantry escaped, but the remainder of his force asked for quarter. They were nevertheless decimated by Tarleton's cavalry, giving rise to the expression "Tarleton's quarter."

Wealth Tax Act. The New Deal measure also known as the Revenue Act of 1935 was designed to stop the growth of big business and great individual fortunes. Taxes on individual incomes above $50,000 rose steeply to 75% on incomes over $5 million. Estate and gift tax rates were raised. Holding companies for the management of private fortunes were heavily taxed and corporation income taxes were moved upward.

The Tax Act won the applause of organized labor but resulted in an outcry from business which charged that the measure was punitive and not designed to raise revenue. Pres. Roosevelt held that the Act was intended to "create a broader range of opportunity," but promised business a "breathing spell."

"We are coming, Father Abraham, three hundred thousand more." The opening line of a poem by James S. Gibbons, an Abolitionist, who was inspired by Pres. Lincoln's call for 300,000 more volunteers for the Union army. It first appeared in the *New York Evening Post*, July 16, 1862. Set to music, it became a popular Civil War song.

Webster, Daniel (1782–1852). Statesman. Born in Salisbury, N.H., he was graduated from Dartmouth (1801) and admitted to the bar in Boston (1805). He first attracted national attention with his brilliant legal work on behalf of the Dartmouth College trustees in the Dartmouth College Case (1819) and in defense of the Bank of the United States in *McCulloch v. Maryland* (1819). A member of the U.S. House of Representatives from New Hampshire (1813–17), from Massachusetts (1823–27), a member of the U.S. Senate from Massachusetts (1827–41, 1845–50) and U.S. Sec. of State (1841–43, 1850–52), he supported the Union in the famous Webster-Hayne debate (1830) and favored compromise measures on slavery in his "Seventh of March" speech (1850), although he considered slavery "a great moral and political evil." An advocate of New England industrial interests, he was a leading Whig who was the party's unsuccessful presidential candidate in 1836 and failed to win the nomination in 1852. He is remembered as a "defender of the Constitution."

Webster, Noah (1758–1843). Lexicographer and author. Born in West Hartford, Conn., he had an outstanding success with his

Spelling Book, first composed in 1782, which under various titles continued to be issued well into the 20th century. It helped to standardize American spelling. Pirating of his book caused him to become active on behalf of a uniform copyright law. An ardent Federalist, he favored a strong central government. He published his first dictionary, *A Compendious Dictionary of the English Language*, in 1806. He devoted 20 years to a larger work, *An American Dictionary of the English Language* (2 vols., 1828), a scholarly achievement of the first order; it took first place at once among the English dictionaries.

Webster - Ashburton Treaty (1842). In the Treaty negotiated by Sec. of State Daniel Webster and Lord Ashburton of Britain, the U.S. and England compromised a number of differences between them. The Maine boundary was finally settled by permitting Canada to have approximately 5,000 of the 12,000 square miles of territory in dispute. The British were able to keep their coveted military road, but an adjustment at the 45th parallel permitted the U.S. to keep a fort at Rouses Point, at the head of Lake Champlain, that would otherwise have been in Canadian territory. (In 1932 Benjamin Franklin's "Red Line Map," marking the Maine boundary, was discovered. It would have made unnecessary the concession of territory to Canada.)

The Treaty also included seven extraditable offenses of a non-political nature. Embezzlement was not included until later, which explains why, during this period, "Gone to Canada," told the story of many an absconding bank clerk.

In the matter of Britain's practice of searching vessels suspected of engaging in the slave trade, it was agreed that each nation would keep a squadron off the African coast and enforce its own laws on those merchantmen flying its flag.

It was also agreed that governors of British colonies would be ordered to avoid "officious interference" with American vessels driven by accident or violence into their ports.

Although the Treaty of 1842 was criticized on both sides of the Atlantic as "capitulation," it had the effect of easing tensions and facilitated peaceful settlement of other controversies that arose in the forties and fifties.

Webster-Hayne debate (Jan. 1830). The great debate commenced over a proposal to limit the sale of public lands in the West to new settlers. Sen. Hayne (S.C.) came to the defense of the West and attacked the North which he charged sought to prevent emigration to the West in order to keep cheap labor for its factories. Hayne hoped thereby to win the West's support for the South's opposition to the tariff law, which John C. Calhoun had denounced as unconstitutional in

The Exposition and Protest (1828).

As the debate warmed up, the public lands issue was dropped and Hayne expounded the states' rights doctrine of nullification. Thus, the fundamental nature of the Union was challenged.

Daniel Webster (Mass.), in one of the great dramatic speeches in Senate history, demonstrated the danger of a states' rights doctrine that would permit each of 24 states to decide for itself which of the laws of Congress was unconstitutional. This, he held, would lead to civil war. In support of nationalism, he denounced as "words of delusion and folly, 'Liberty first and Union afterwards.'" He proclaimed "that other sentiment, dear to every true American heart,—Liberty *and* Union, now and forever, one and inseparable!"

"We have met the enemy and they are ours. . . ." The opening words of one of the most famous messages in American military history were written during the War of 1812 by young Capt. Oliver Hazard Perry. He had just defeated a British squadron in the battle of Lake Erie thus making it possible for American forces in the Northwest to recapture Detroit.

The whole message to Gen. William Henry Harrison, commanding in the West, was: "Dear Gen'l: We have met the enemy and they are ours, two ships, two brigs, one schooner and one sloop. Yours with great respect and esteem. O. H. Perry."

"We like Ike!" Dwight D. Eisenhower, who won the Presidency by landslides in both 1952 and 1956, had become somewhat of a folk hero in World War II by the time he became Supreme Commander of the Allied Expeditionary Force in western Europe (Jan. 1944). Known as "Ike" to his friends, his circle of admirers encompassed the nation when he returned from Europe to campaign for the Presidency in 1952. His open, friendly, engaging personality was more important than anything he said or did. "We like Ike" appeared on campaign buttons and the expression has become part of American folklore.

"We Shall Overcome." The American civil rights song was set to a traditional Baptist hymn tune about 1955 by the American folk singer Pete Seeger. It has been sung by marchers and demonstrators (Negro and white) on countless occasions in all parts of the nation.

The expression was used by Pres. Johnson in his address to a joint session of Congress, Mar. 15, 1965, when he said "we shall overcome" the obstacles Negroes have faced in achieving equal voting rights in the U.S.

Wesleyan University. Founded by Methodists in 1831 at Middletown, Conn., and named for John Wesley, it is a privately endowed, nonsectarian men's college. It granted its first degrees in 1833. From the first it has been a small college of the liberal arts and sciences, with a current enrollment limited to about 1,200 students. One of the "Little Three," along with Amherst and Williams, it has one of the highest per capita endowments in the U.S.

West Coast Hotel Company v. Parrish (1937). The U.S. Supreme Court upheld the constitutionality of a Washington law establishing minimum wages for women and children. The law was held to be a just exercise of the police powers of the state to protect the health and morals of its citizens.

The hotel, relying on the decision in *Adkins v. Children's Hospital* (1923), argued that the chambermaid, Elsie Parrish, was not entitled to the difference between the wages paid her and the minimum wage fixed by state law. The law, it contended, violated due process as provided in the 14th Amendment.

The Court overruled (5 to 4) the Adkins decision. Justices Brandeis, Stone, Roberts and Cardozo concurred with the majority opinion of Chief Justice Hughes. Dissenters were Justices Sutherland, Van Devanter, McReynolds and Butler.

Western Pacific Railroad Co. The newest of the transcontinental lines was first incorporated in 1903. It operates 1,189 miles of road extending from San Francisco to Salt Lake City and connects with the Union Pacific and the Denver & Rio Grande Western. The northern California extension connects with the Great Northern.

Western Reserve. In the 1780's when the seaboard states yielded the western lands they owned according to their charters to the newly formed national government, Connecticut retained (reserved) a part in an area of what is now northeast Ohio. It was purchased by the Connecticut Land Company in 1795, whose general agent, Moses Cleaveland, planned and named the city of Cleveland.

Difficulty in selling the land to settlers led to an agreement in 1800 by which the Western Reserve was added to the Ohio Territory. Settlement was speeded by the Erie Canal (1825), and the county became in effect an extension of New England in the West. After European immigrants populated it, reminders of the Western Reserve were preserved chiefly in the names of the historical society and university.

Western Trail. One of the great American cattle trails which flourished in the 1870's and 1880's started in Belton, Tex. and moved north past Fort Griffin and Doan's Store on the north fork of the Red River (all in Texas) and on to Dodge City in southern Kansas.

Western Union Telegraph Co. The chief telegraph company in the U.S. had its origins in a company formed in 1851. In 1856 it was reorganized to consolidate unstable western telegraph lines. Ezra Cornell suggested the name of the company. In 1866 Western Union moved from Rochester, N.Y., to New York City and absorbed the U.S. Telegraph Co. This action made it the first complete monopoly servicing all parts of the country with uniform rates. In 1943 it absorbed the Postal Telegraph Co., which had been formed in 1881. The system now comprises practically all domestic telegraph business in the U.S.

West Ford. Millions of short fine copper wires, called dipoles, were orbited by the U.S. Air Force project in May 1963, creating a radio-reflective band around the world. Experiments will determine whether long-distance communication can be accomplished by bouncing radio waves from the band.

Westinghouse, George (1846–1914). Inventor and manufacturer. Born in Central Bridge, N.Y., he took out his first air-brake patent (1869). The air-brake was of revolutionary importance in making high-speed railroad travel safe. He invented electrical control of signals manufactured by his Union Switch and Signal Co. (1882). He was a pioneer in introducing to America the high-voltage alternating-current single-phase system for transmission of electricity and organized Westinghouse Electric Co.

(1886) for manufacturing and marketing purposes. He took out more than 400 patents in his lifetime in such diverse fields as air-brakes, signals, natural-gas production and electrical power transmission.

West Virginia. The "Mountain State," or "Panhandle State," in the South Atlantic group, was admitted to the Union as the 35th state, June 20, 1863. Its capital is Charleston.

The early history of the state is linked to Virginia. There were, however, differences between the eastern and western parts of Virginia as early as the American Revolution. In 1776 the Continental Congress was petitioned to establish a separate state, Westsylvania, beyond the Alleghenies. The westerners complained of being forced to pay a disproportionate share of the taxes and suffering discrimination in representation in the legislature.

The Civil War furnished an opportunity for separation. When Virginia seceded from the Union, trans-Allegheny delegates met at Wheeling, June 11, 1861, and declared independence from Virginia.

West Virginia leads the nation in production of bituminous coal. It produces more natural gas than any other state east of the Mississippi. Wheeling and Weirton are big steel centers. Supplies of silica, salt brine and limestone have made possible mounting production of glass. There is some sheep raising, and profitable farm products are apples, peaches and grapes.

westward movement. Early in the 18th century colonists started to move westward over the crests of the Appalachian Mts., impelled in part by the feeling that the best lands along the coast had already been taken. By the end of the 18th century a steady stream of settlers had moved across the mountains and rapidly filled up the river valleys.

By 1820 the American march westward reached the Missouri River. Across its waters lay a new west to conquer, the Great Plains. Since this region between the Missouri River and the Rocky Mts., known as the "Great American Desert," seemed too rugged settlers passed over it for a time and pressed on to the Far West, between the Rockies and the Pacific Coast. By the mid-19th century half the continent had been mastered. The population of the Old Northwest, stimulated by the California gold rush of 1849, had grown to almost five million people in 1850.

The "last West" that remained for occupation was the Great Plains. In the 1860's it contained only isolated areas of settlement and was fiercely defended by the plains Indians. In the sixties and seventies the bloodiest Indian fighting in American history took place in the vast area of the Great Plains. By 1876, with the surrender of the Sioux, the major Indian wars were ended. Their resistance had become hopeless in the face of the new Hotchkiss rapid-fire guns.

The westward movement extended over a period of almost 300 years until all the vacant land was distributed (about 1890). It had been encouraged by the federal government which provided cheap land and assured settlers of self-government in the territories. Under the conditions of frontier life, class distinctions were meaningless. A man's success depended on his strength and skill—not on his social position. Thus the West became a center of democracy and political and social equality. Settlement of the West also did much to build up the nation economically. It provided an outlet for restless and discontented elements in the older sections and other countries. It helped establish the U.S. as a "land of opportunity."

"Westward the course of empire takes its way. . . ." The Irish philosopher, Bishop George Berkeley, lived in America, 1728–31. He described his impressions of the English settlement in a poem called "On the Prospect of Planting Arts and Learning in America," which begins with this line.

whaling. A decade before the American Revolution American seamen set out from Nantucket, Mass. and ranged the Atlantic, even south of the equator, in the hunt for whales. They were gone for a year or two at a time.

Their hardiness caused Edmund Burke to warn Parliament not to trifle with a people who could develop men of such courage.

Whale oil was used for lamps or the manufacture of candles. Whalebone was used for whips or for stiffening in ladies' corsets. After the War of 1812 New Bedford, Mass., became a great whaling port and whales were hunted in the Pacific and the Arctic as well as the Atlantic.

The industry declined sharply with discoveries of petroleum in the latter part of the 19th century and the growing use of electricity. Whale oil continues to be used in soap making, as leather dressing and as a lubricant.

"What hath God wrought!" Samuel F. B. Morse, inventor of the telegraph, sent the message from Washington, D.C. to Baltimore when the experimental line between the two cities was formally opened, May 24, 1844.

Wheeler-Rayburn Act (Public Utility Holding Company Act, 1935). The New Deal law was a response to the public outcry against huge business consolidations, especially of gas and electric companies, that raised prices after achieving virtual monopolies.

A holding company purchased enough of an operating company's stock to place its directors in control of the company. By pyramiding one holding company on top of another, intricate financial structures were erected and investors were milked of their funds.

The Act granted the Securities and Exchange Commission the right to supervise the financial operations of holding companies and provided for the breaking up of big public utility holding companies. It contained a "death sentence" clause requiring dissolution of holding companies which could not within five years demonstrate that they had brought about economies in management.

Whig party. Opposition to Jackson during his second administration took form in the Whig party. It assumed the name of the Whigs who had opposed King George during the American Revolution. This time it was "King Andrew" Jackson who was the enemy.

There were diverse elements in the party which was national rather than sectional. In general, however, conservative propertied interests dominated the party which included pro-Bank of the United States forces in the North and plantation owners in the South. The core of the new party was in the National Republican party led by Henry Clay and Daniel Webster. John C. Calhoun was in the fold for a time, but soon rejoined the Democratic party. Anti-Masons, too, came under the banner of Whiggery.

In 1834 the Whigs elected 98 members in the House against 145 Democrats. Since this did not augur well for the election of 1836, they advanced a number of sectional candidates in the vain hope of defeating Martin Van Buren. One of their candidates, William Henry Harrison, emerged as a popular figure and they won with him in the election of 1840. Harrison died after one month in office. His successor, Tyler, split the party when he vetoed a bill to establish a new Bank of the United States.

The party dissolved as the controversies over annexation of Texas, the Mexican War and extension of slavery into the territories became the dominant issues. Southern Whigs could no longer stand with northern Whigs. Northern Whigs were themselves divided between "Conscience Whigs," who opposed extension of slavery, and an almost proslavery group castigated as "Cotton Whigs."

The death of both Clay and Webster in 1852 left the party without leaders of national stature. By 1855 there were no Whigs in Congress. The party had disappeared.

whip, party. Political parties in both Houses of Congress have party whips who keep informed of their colleagues' intentions and eventual votes on roll calls. They help the floor leader hold party members in line.

The party whip in the U.S. was the product of the close, hard-fought party battles of the late 19th century. The first party whip was designated in the House in 1899 and in the Senate in 1913.

A whip in the House now has

15 to 18 assistant and deputy whips, all House members, who know their geographical regions. They are able to promptly inform the chief whip of the intentions of their area colleagues once the party caucus has adopted a policy on a given bill.

The term derives from the English fox-hunting term "whipper-in." It describes the man responsible for keeping the hounds from leaving the pack. The British Parliament adopted the term about 1770.

Whiskey Rebellion (1794). In 1791 Alexander Hamilton obtained passage of a tax on every gallon of liquor distilled in the U.S. This worked a special hardship on farmers who sometimes distilled grain into liquor since the latter was cheaper to transport. The tax was evaded and resentment mounted even higher when farmers had to travel from points as far west as Pittsburgh to Philadelphia to stand trial. The cost of the journey was in itself a substantial fine.

In 1794 frontiersmen in western Pennsylvania took up arms to prevent collection of the tax. A force of 13,000 militiamen, accompanied by Hamilton, soon crushed the insurrection. Although not much money was collected from the tax, the incident helped to establish the authority of the federal government.

Whiskey ring. One of the scandals of the Grant administration, it involved whiskey distillers, chiefly in St. Louis, Mo., and internal-revenue collectors who were allowing the government to be defrauded of whiskey taxes. The ring was broken up in 1875.

Grant's private secretary, Gen. Orville B. Babcock, was among the accused. He was not, however, convicted. It was alleged that Grant had received the gift of a team of horses from the ring and that part of the ring's gain was to be used to finance Grant's bid for a third term.

Whistler, James Abbott McNeill (1834–1903). Painter and etcher. He was born in Lowell, Mass. A West Point cadet (1851–54), he was dismissed for failure in chemistry. He departed for Paris (1855) to study painting and never returned to the U.S. He had studios in Paris and London. His most famous painting is *Arrangement in Gray and Black*, a portrait of his mother (first exhibited in 1872; now in the Louvre). His other notable paintings are *Rose Whistler, Lady in a Fur Jacket, Trafalgar Square* and *Westminster Bridge*. He produced paintings "very rich in sheer beauty, partly through the simplicity characterizing his design and his arrangement of color, and partly through the display of a mysterious and elusive feeling." Excelling as an etcher, he published his *Thames Series* (1871) and first *Venice Series* (1880). He was author of *The Gentle Art of Making Enemies* (1890).

White, Andrew Dickson (1832–1918). Educator and diplomat. He was born in Homer, N.Y. A member, N.Y. Senate (1864–67), he helped to create the state's normal schools. He worked with Ezra Cornell to open Cornell Univ. and served as its first president (1867–85) and a teacher of European history. He was the first president of the American Historical Association (1864); U.S. minister to Germany (1879–81); minister to Russia (1892–94); ambassador to Germany (1897–1902); and headed the American delegation to the Hague Conference (1899). He was author of *History of the Warfare of Science with Theology in Christendom* (1896) and an *Autobiography* (1905).

"white backlash." The term was used to describe the anticipated reaction of white people to various measures taken to improve the status of Negroes in the U.S. The "white backlash" was talked about in the Campaign of 1964 as part of the vote expected for Sen. Barry Goldwater, Republican candidate for President. He had been critical of special legislation for Negroes and had voted against the Civil Rights Act of 1964. It was not possible, however, to determine accurately the "white backlash" vote in the 27 million cast for Goldwater.

White House. The President's residence was designed by James Hoban, an Irish-born architect. The site was chosen by Pres. Washington and was included in the plan of the Federal City prepared by the French engineer, Major Pierre Charles L'Enfant. The cornerstone was laid Oct. 13, 1792. The first President to live in the White House was John Adams, in 1800.

The building was badly damaged when the British burned Washington, D.C., in 1814. Repairs were supervised by Hoban. In 1817 Pres. Monroe moved in and had the gray sandstone walls painted white to obliterate marks of the fire.

A major renovation was undertaken by Pres. Theodore Roosevelt in 1902. Pres. Truman had the mansion rebuilt, 1947–48, because it had become unsafe.

White Plains, battle of (Oct. 28, 1776). When Gen. Washington was unable to hold Manhattan (N.Y.) he retreated up the island to White Plains. British Gen. Howe followed. Washington fought a delaying action at White Plains but was forced to retreat across the Hudson into New Jersey.

Whitman, Walt (1819–92). Poet. Born in West Hills, Long Island, N.Y., he moved to Brooklyn, N.Y. (1823). A journalist associated with at least 10 newspapers (editor, *Brooklyn Eagle*, 1846–48), his fame rests on *Leaves of Grass,* 12 poems which were first published in 1855 and revised and enlarged many times up to the time of his death. During the Civil War, he worked on his own in hospitals, writing letters for the wounded and helping to dress wounds. This work is described in *Memoranda During the War* (1875). Employed briefly in a minor government post, he was moved by Lincoln's death to write the memorable "When Lilacs Last in the Dooryard Bloom'd" (1865). Acceptance of Whitman as a major poet came slowly, although by 1868 he was published in England. In the prose, *Democratic Vistas* (1871), he discussed the weaknesses of American democracy. Whitman thought of himself as the "poet of democracy," but his poetry was too strange to win wide popularity. As a phrase and image maker and master of rhythm, his highly original work places him in the top rank of American poets.

Whitney, Eli (1765–1825). Inventor. Born in Westboro, Mass., he was graduated from Yale (1792). A guest on a Georgia plantation, he turned his mechanical mind to the invention of a machine that could separate the seeds from cotton. His cotton gin (patented, 1794) revolutionized cotton farming and expanded the need for slaves to pick the cotton. Patent infringements prevented Whitney from profiting from his invention. He was subsequently successful in developing the principle of interchangeable parts in the manufacture of rifles and obtained profitable government contracts for the factory he established in what is now Whitneyville, near New Haven, Conn.

Whittier, John Greenleaf (1807–92). Poet. Born in East Haverhill, Mass., he was known as "the Quaker poet" and ranked with Henry Wadsworth Longfellow and William Cullen Bryant. Whittier came under the influence of William Lloyd Garrison and as an Abolitionist devoted himself to the antislavery cause. He edited several publications including the *Pennsylvania Freeman* (1838–40). Whittier contributed most of his poems (1847–60) to the *National Era*, Washington, D.C., including the famous "Ichabod" (1850) in which he poured out scorn on Daniel Webster for the "Seventh of March" speech. He reached the height of his poetic career in the 1860's during which time appeared *Home Ballads* (1860) and *In War Times and Other Poems* (1864, containing "Barbara Frietchie"). *Snow-Bound* (1866) is usually considered his masterpiece.

Wild Bill Hickok. James Butler Hickok (1837–76) was a frontier scout in the Union army during the Civil War and became a U.S. Marshal in Kansas (1869–71). He fought the McCanles gang, at Rock Creek Station, Neb., killing McCanles and two of his gang (July 12, 1861). He joined Buffalo Bill's "Wild West" show, 1872–73. Wild Bill was murdered in Deadwood, Dakota Territory, Aug. 2, 1876.

Recent researchers regret that Hickok has been glamorized in the movies and on television because they have found that he was a professional gambler.

"wildcat banks." In the pre-Civil War days, private commercial banks usually derived their right to go into business from the states and many of these bankers were not too scrupulous in the way they operated. Almost anything could pass as money and very often these banks would set up their offices in some remote and inaccessible places "where only the wildcats could find it" (hence the term "wildcat banking") so that people could not redeem bank notes and any sort of state regulator would find it inconvenient to check on the banks' operations.

"Wildcat banking" helped to make possible the land speculation which contributed to the panics of 1819 and 1837.

Wilderness, battle of (May 5–7, 1864). In a thrust toward Richmond during the final stages of the Civil War, Gen. Ulysses S. Grant's Army of the Potomac engaged smaller Confederate forces under Gen. Robert E. Lee in the "Wilderness," a densely forested region of northeastern Virginia.

Grant's superior artillery and cavalry were neutralized by the forest and dense underbrush. In the indecisive but gruesome fighting, the woods caught fire and wounded soldiers were burned to death.

Grant did not retreat as had Union commanders before him. He pressed past Lee's flank southward toward Spotsylvania, which lay to the north of Richmond.

"wilderness," the. Puritans who came to New England early in the 17th century compared themselves with the Jews who reached Canaan after wandering in the wilderness of Sinai and Palestine. For the Puritans, as John Winthrop put it, America was to be "the good land," a veritable Canaan which they had reached after crossing their Red Sea (the Atlantic).

The Puritans who thought they had emerged from the "wilderness" when they left England were not prepared for the "thicke Wood" inhabited by "wild beasts and beastlike men." If this were the promised land, the task of building Zion proved greater than had been foreseen. America had become the wilderness itself.

By the mid-17th century, the wilderness was seen to serve a moral purpose. Cotton Mather contended that New England's faith was the greater because "a wilderness was a place where temptation was to be met withal." Success in the struggle might be a mark of grace. The difficulties in the wilderness served to reinforce the Puritans' belief that they were the chosen of God. They expected that the New Jerusalem would lie in America.

Wilderness Road. First traveled by Daniel Boone in 1769, the route extended from eastern Virginia through the Cumberland Gap into Kentucky. In 1775 Boone and other woodsmen marked the 300-mile trail for the pioneers who were to use it as a major avenue to the West.

Wild West Show. Inspired by the American West, the exhibitions offered cowboys and Indians in riding and shooting entertainments. The first show was presented by William F. Cody (Buffalo Bill) in 1883. In 1885, he added Annie Oakley ("Little Sure Shot") to his company. It toured Europe during the latter part of the 19th and early 20th centuries.

Wilkes, Charles (1798–1877). Naval officer and explorer. Born in New York City, he was appointed midshipman in 1818. He commanded an exploring expedition to the Antarctic (1838–42) surveying the coast, islands of the Pacific Ocean and American northwestern coast; Wilkes Land in the Antarctic continent is named in his honor. He published *Narrative of the United States Exploring Expedition* (1844). In command of the *San Jacinto* in the Civil War, he halted the British mail steamer *Trent* and removed the Confederate agents, Mason and Slidell (*Trent* Affair, 1861).

Willard, Emma Hart (1787–1870). Educator. She was born in Berlin, Conn. A pioneer in the field of higher education for women, she also worked with Henry Barnard and others for improvement of the common schools. In 1821 she founded the Troy (N.Y.) Female Seminary, now known as the Emma Willard School. She proved that girls could master such subjects as mathematics and philosophy without detracting from their health or charm. She published textbooks in history and geography and a volume of poems which included "Rocked in the Cradle of the Deep."

Willard, Frances Elizabeth Caroline (1839–98). Reformer. She was born in Churchville, N.Y. After resigning from the presidency of Evanston (Ill.) College for Ladies (1871–74), she devoted her life chiefly to the temperance crusade. Elected president of the National Woman's Christian Temperance Union (WCTU) in 1879, she enlisted her society in the cause of woman's suffrage. She was president of the World's WCTU (1891) and aided in organizing the Prohibition party (1882).

William and Mary, College of. The college was chartered by King William and Queen Mary in 1693 at the urging of the Rev. James Blair, who became its first president. He managed to see the college well established despite the disastrous fire which burned the Wren building (1705).

The campus in Williamsburg borders on the restoration of Colonial Williamsburg, begun in 1928 and financed by John D. Rockefeller, Jr. The Wren building was included in the restoration.

A state-controlled liberal arts college, William and Mary became coeducational in 1918. The college's alumni include Thomas Jefferson and James Monroe.

Williams, Roger (1603?–83). Clergyman. Born in London, England, he came to the Massachusetts Bay colony in 1631 and criticized Puritan church leaders for using civil government to enforce religious beliefs. Found guilty by the Massachusetts General Court (Oct. 9, 1635) for spreading "dangerous opinions," he fled from Massachusetts. Founder of Providence (1636), the earliest settlement in Rhode Island, he espoused principles of democracy and religious freedom. Jews and Quakers were safe in the colony. When Massachusetts Bay sought to gain control of its neighbors, he went to England and obtained a charter for the Providence Plantations (1644). Subsequently, he became president of the colony (1654–57). While accepting the fundamentals of Christianity, he identified with no sect. In his best-known works, *The Bloudy Tenent of Persecution* (1644) and *The Bloudy Tenent Yet More Bloudy* (1652), he held that people and religious bodies were entitled to religious liberty as a natural right. A religious liberal, he is one of the fathers of American democracy.

Williams, Tennessee (1914–   ). Playwright. He was born in Columbus, Miss., as Thomas Lanier Williams. One of the foremost American playwrights of the 20th century he has peopled his plays with strange, deeply troubled characters. In *The Glass Menagerie* (1944) a crippled girl escapes from reality by fixing her feelings on her collection of glass animals. The incidents in the play represent a southern family's incapacity to adapt to the modern world.

Other plays by Williams include *A Streetcar Named Desire* (1947), *Summer and Smoke* (1948), *The Rose Tattoo* (1950), *Camino Real* (1953), *Cat on a Hot Tin Roof* (1954), *Orpheus Descending* (1957), *Sweet Bird of Youth* (1959) and *The Night of the Iguana* (1962).

Williams College. Founded in 1793 at Williamstown, Mass., its entrance requirements reflected the current vogue for learning French, a result of close ties between France and America formed during the Revolution. French was accepted as a substitute for classical languages as a prerequisite for admission.

It is a small, independent, privately endowed, nonsectarian liberal arts institution for men. The current enrollment is about 1,200.

Wilmot Proviso (1846). When Pres. Polk requested funds from Congress for purchase of territories that might be acquired from Mexico at the end of the war, Congressman David Wilmot of Pennsylvania proposed an amendment to the bill (a proviso) that would have excluded slavery from such territory. Previous limitation on extending slavery into territories above 36° 30′ N (the southern boundary of Missouri) had applied to the Louisiana Territory.

The Wilmot Proviso was defeated and further embittered the sectional controversy over slavery. Later, it became the fundamental principle on which the modern Republican party was founded and part of the platform on which Lincoln was elected President.

Wilson, James (1742–98). Revolutionary statesman. Born in Scotland, he came to the U.S. in 1765. He practiced law in Pennsylvania and speculated heavily in lands. He was a member, Continental Congress (1775, 1776, 1782, 1783, 1785–87). He was author of the pamphlet *Considerations on the Nature and Extent of the Legislative Authority of the British Parliament* (1774), in which he denied to Parliament the least authority over the colonies and anticipated a British commonwealth. A signer of the Declaration of Independence, he later participated in the Constitutional Convention (1787) and its ratification in Pennsylvania. He was appointed associate justice of the Supreme Court (1789–98). In *Chisholm v.*

Georgia (1793) he upheld the national authority against the states' authority.

Wilson, Woodrow (1856–1924). Twenty-eighth President of the U.S. Born Thomas Woodrow Wilson in Staunton, Va., he was graduated from Princeton Univ. (1879). His political career in New Jersey developed after he served as president of Princeton Univ. (1902–10). He was governor of New Jersey (1911–13). He was successful as the Democratic candidate for President and served two terms (1913–21). He led the nation in World War I, but failed to bring the U.S. into the League of Nations. The high points of his administration were the Clayton Antitrust Act and the establishment of the Federal Reserve System. Three Amendments were added to the Constitution (17th, 18th, 19th) while he was in office.

Wilson-Gorman Tariff of 1894. The tariff act was intended to reduce the high rates of the protective McKinley Tariff of 1890 but was so amended that its effect was slight. High tariffs on iron and coal were retained and high rates were placed on both refined and raw sugar. Pres. Cleveland regarded the Tariff of 1894 as "party perfidy and dishonor." It became law without his signature.

The act also included an income tax of 2% on all incomes above $4,000, but this was declared unconstitutional by the Supreme Court in 1895.

windmills. The settlers on the Great Plains took advantage of the winds on the treeless interior plains in digging wells for water. They constructed windmills to supply the power required to pump the water to the surface.

Winnebago. The Indians, of Siouan linguistic stock, first made contact with the French in Wisconsin in 1634. They aided them against the British and opposed Americans in the 19th century. They are now found on reservations in Wisconsin and Nebraska.

Winthrop, John (1588–1649). Colonial Puritan statesman. Born in England, he sailed for New England in 1630. He was elected first governor of Massachusetts Bay colony (1629) before he emigrated with his family, and was reelected several times. He opposed Anne Hutchinson and presided at the court that banished her and others in the Antinomian controversy that rocked the colony. He led in organizing the New England Confederation and was its first president (1643). His journal was published as *The History of New England* (2 vols., 1825–26).

Wisconsin. The "Badger State," a Midwestern state in the East North Central group, was admitted to the Union as the 30th state, May 29, 1848. Its capital is Madison. Wisconsin is an Indian name; Ouiscousin and Misconsing were the early chroniclers' versions of the spelling of the Chippewa name that means "grassy place."

French explorers, notably Jean Nicolet (1634) and La Salle (1679), explored the region. Fur trading was important though disrupted from time to time by Indian wars. The French lost the territory to the British during the French and Indian War (1760) and the British ceded the land to the U.S. at the end of the Revolutionary War (1783). However, the British continued to hold fur-trading posts until 1816.

Wisconsin was included in the Northwest Territory (1787) and then, successively, became part of the Indiana, Illinois and Michigan Territory. The Wisconsin Territory was formed by Congress (1836). An influx of German settlers in the late 1830's added to the earlier migration of farmers from New England and New York.

The state was staunchly antislavery and a movement was organized at Ripon (1854) that later became the Republican party. During the 20th century Robert M. La Follette, governor (1901–05) and senator (1905–25), advanced progressive reforms (called the Wisconsin Idea).

Wisconsin is the cheese capital of the nation and is second in the production of butter. It ranks high in growing oats and is a heavy producer of cranberries, sour cherries and green peas. Its Great Lake ports, notably those on Lake Michigan, receive transatlantic shipping via the St. Lawrence Seaway. Milwaukee is one of the leading manufacturing areas, producing many kinds of machinery.

Wise, Isaac Mayer (1819–1900). Religious leader. Born in Bohemia, he came to the U.S. in 1846. The rabbi in congregations in Albany, N.Y. (1846–54) and Cincinnati (1854–1900), he advocated adjusting Judaism to American institutions, including use of English in religious services. The founder of Reformed Judaism in the U.S., he led the organization of the Union of American Hebrew Congregations (1873). He founded Hebrew Union College (1875), the first institution for training rabbis in the U.S., and was its president (1875–1900).

witchcraft trials. Excitement in England over witches spread to the colonies. Even William Penn presided over a witchcraft trial, but dismissed the case finding "that there was no law in Pennsylvania against riding on broomsticks." At about the same time, humor gave way to terror in Salem Village (now Danvers), Mass., 1692, when two girls had fits and accused townspeople of bewitching them. Both Increase and Cotton Mather had encouraged the outbreak by publishing books proving the existence of witches (emissaries of the Devil).

Before the ministers and magistrates came to their senses, 19 of the accused were hanged (none were burned) and hundreds were imprisoned. Witchcraft trials virtually disappeared from the colonies after the Salem Village experience.

Witherspoon, John (1723–94). Presbyterian clergyman. Born in Scotland, he held pulpits there until 1768 when he came to America. He was president of the College of New Jersey, now Princeton Univ. (1768–94). He helped heal a factional schism between "Old Side" and "New Side" Presbyterians, contributing to the rapid growth of the Presbyterian Church in the Middle Colonies. A member of various Revolutionary committees, he was a signer of the Declaration of Independence. In 1781, in an article on language in the *Pennsylvania Journal,* he coined the term "Americanism."

"With malice toward none, with charity for all. . . ." The opening words of the final paragraph of Lincoln's Second Inaugural Address (Mar. 4, 1865) sounded the noble note of compassion which was to have marked his acceptance of the seceded states back into the Union at the end of the Civil War.

"wizard of Kinderhook." The nickname was earned by Pres. Martin Van Buren before he entered the White House in 1837. His birthplace was Kinderhook, N.Y. and his political shrewdness had made him a power in New York and a close adviser of Pres. Jackson.

Wolfe, Thomas (1900–38). Novelist. Born in Asheville, N.C., he was a teacher of English at New York Univ. (1924–30). In *Look Homeward, Angel* (1929), he describes the revolt of youth against provincial life. Other books in which he spelled out the story of his family life, his literary aspirations and his friendships are *Of Time and the River* (1935), *The Web and the Rock* (1939) and *You Can't Go Home Again* (1940). The last parts of his personal saga were posthumously published.

woman's rights movement. The feminist movement was under way by the time the Seneca Falls Convention (July 19–20, 1848) which included some men, met. In a Declaration of Independence for Women, it was pointed out that all women, as well as all men, are "created equal" and that women, too, are entitled to "Life, Liberty, and the pursuit of Happiness." The Declaration proclaimed that women would never be free until they won the right to vote, to own property in their own names, to get a thorough education, to work at any job or profession and to be treated as the equals of men in the world outside and inside their homes.

Convention leaders were Lucretia Mott and Elizabeth Cady Stanton. Other feminist leaders were Fanny Wright, who advocated birth control, emancipation of slaves and free public schools; Emma Willard and Mary Lyon, pioneers in higher education for women; Elizabeth Blackwell, the first woman doctor of medicine in modern times; Susan B. Anthony and Carrie Chapman Catt, who campaigned for woman suffrage. The 19th Amendment has been called the "Susan B. Anthony Amendment," although she did not live to see it adopted.

Women gained many more rights after 1865 with the expansion of industries and cities. They got jobs as stenographers and typists, telephone and telegraph operators, bookkeepers, salesclerks and factory workers. Some even opened their own businesses. Women soon began to enter such professions as law and medicine.

Women have gone far toward achieving feminist goals, but there continues to be discrimination in wages. Comparatively few women have achieved executive positions in business or elective office.

woman suffrage. Beginning in the 1840's reform leaders, such as Susan B. Anthony and Elizabeth Cady Stanton, included woman suffrage among their demands. The movement was stimulated when Negro males were enfranchised by the 15th Amendment. By 1898 four of the newest states, Wyoming, Colorado, Utah and Idaho had granted full voting rights to women and, by 1914, 11 states had extended suffrage to women.

Early in the 20th century women entered the working force in large numbers and some made their way into the professions. Suffragette leaders Carrie Chapman Catt and Anna Howard Shaw continued to employ quiet persuasion, while Alice Paul adopted the demonstrations of English suffragettes. The Progressive party endorsed woman suffrage.

The role of women in World War I helped to get Congress to pass a constitutional amendment by a narrow margin. It was ratified by the states and women were granted the right to vote by the 19th Amendment (1920).

Women's Army Corps (WAC). During World War II Congress relieved the manpower shortage in the Armed Forces by authorizing women to join on a volunteer basis. On May 15, 1942, the Women's Army Auxiliary Corps (WAACS) was authorized. The "auxiliary" status was dropped for women in the Army and in other branches of the Armed Forces in 1943 in order to indicate that women were full-fledged members of the branch of service in which they had enlisted. Some 250,000 women served in the Armed Forces in non-combat positions during the war.

Other women's organizations included the Navy WAVES (Women Accepted for Voluntary Emergency Service), authorized by Congress, July 31, 1942; Women's Reserve of the Marine Corps, with no official nickname; the Coast Guard SPARS with the initials standing for the motto, "Semper Paratus; Always Ready"; Women's Auxiliary Ferrying Squadron (WAFS). When the Air Force became a separate service in 1948, women were designated as WAF.

Nurses were the first to gain regular status in the Armed Forces. The Army Nurse Corps was organized in 1901 and the Navy Nurse Corps in 1908. In 1947 nurses were granted permanent commissioned status in the newly organized Women's Medical Specialists Corps. Women's status in the Armed Forces was regularized by the Women's Armed Services Integration Act of 1948. Armed Forces careers have been opened for women and a nucleus is retained for expansion of women volunteer services should they be needed.

women's colleges. In 1821 Emma Willard opened a seminary for girls at Troy, N.Y., the first college for women in the U.S.; in 1837 Mary Lyon opened Mount Holyoke Seminary, Mass. In the twenty years from 1840 to 1860, 54 institutions of higher learning for women were opened, bringing the total of such schools to 61; and by 1901, there were 128 women's colleges.

However, women's colleges like Rockford Seminary, Ill. (1849); Elmira College, N.Y. (1855) and Vassar College, also N.Y. (1865) were, after 1833, no longer the only means of obtaining an education available to women; with the opening of Oberlin (1833) coeducational institutions began to flourish, especially among the state universities. By 1902 women made up 25% of the undergraduate classes, 26% of the graduate students and 3% of professional enrollment. These increases have continued, and today women have the same opportunity that men do in the area of education.

Woolen Act (1699). The Act prohibited the exportation of wool, woolen yarn and woolen cloth from any colony. It was one in a long train of measures by which England sought to restrict the growth of colonial manufactures that might compete with industries in the mother country.

Woolman, John (1720–72). Quaker leader and Abolitionist. Born in Rancocas, West Jersey (now N.J.), he was a tailor by trade. Called to the ministry (about 1743), he traveled throughout the colonies, influencing Quakers and others to give up their slaves. His famous work, published posthumously and often reprinted, is his *Journal* (1774).

Woolworth, Frank Winfield (1852–1919). Merchant. Born in Rodman, N.Y., his name is synonymous with the "5 & 10¢ store." His first successful retail store, offering goods at a fixed price of five cents, was opened in Lancaster, Pa. (1879). He later added ten-cent and higher priced items. The F. W. Woolworth Co., a national chain of stores which he founded, continues to offer a variety of low-priced consumer goods. The Woolworth Building in New York City was erected by him in 1913 and was for a time the world's tallest building (792 feet high).

Worcester v. Georgia (1832). The U.S. Supreme Court held that Georgia had no jurisdiction over the Cherokee reservations. It reversed the conviction of two missionaries, Samuel A. Worcester and Elizur Butler. They had been arrested for residing among the Indians without a license. Chief Justice Marshall wrote the decision.

Georgia refused to enforce the decision. Pres. Jackson, who disliked both Marshall and the Indians, did not support the Court. Worcester and Butler were, however, released from prison after they had promised to drop legal proceedings and leave the state. They were then pardoned by the governor.

Workingmen's party. The New York Workingmen's party, organized in 1829, was typical of the local workingmen's parties organized in the 1820's and 1830's. It was led in its early stages by Thomas Skidmore, a machinist by trade, who had developed a radical agrarian philosophy that questioned the entire basis for existing property rights.

The party's original platform condemned both the private ownership of land and the inheritance of wealth. It then set forth objectives which were common to the workingmen's movement everywhere. The platform demanded communal education, abolition of imprisonment for debt, mechanic's lien laws and the elimination of licensed monopolies.

A second leader of the party was George Henry Evans, a printer by trade, who founded the *Working Man's Advocate,* the organ of the party. It was, perhaps, the most important labor journal of the 1830's. The party itself was divided by internal dissension in its very first year and most of the workers' votes in New York City went to Tammany.

Works Progress Administration (WPA). The New Deal agency was established in 1935 with Harry Hopkins as director. In 1939, its name was changed to Works Projects Administration. By the time the operation ended in 1943, it had provided work for 8 million people who supported 30 million more, at a cost of about $11 billion. Wages were higher than relief payments, but lower than what might have been earned in private industry.

Among the WPA projects were waterworks, sewage plants, street and highway improvements, hospitals, bridges, municipal power plants, school buildings and slum clearance. Employment opportunities were also made available in the fine arts and theater. Many a mural was painted in public buildings. The Federal Writers Project put unemployed writers to work collecting documents, writing local histories and making surveys.

On the whole WPA work was constructive despite the charge of "boondoggling" made by critics who felt that there were waste and frivolity in some of the projects.

World Court (Permanent Court of International Justice). First established in 1921 as the judicial arm of the League of Nations the Court is located at The Hague, in the Netherlands. As the International Court of Justice, it became an agency of the United Nations in 1945. The U.S. did not adhere to the World Court when it was linked to the League.

The Court gives advisory opinions on legal questions at the request of the UN and gives binding judgments, in accordance with international law, in all disputes submitted to it by states which have voluntarily accepted its jurisdiction. The U.S. has accepted World Court jurisdiction but with a reservation, known as the Connolly Amendment, which provides that the U.S. will determine for itself whether or not a matter falls within the jurisdiction of the International Court of Justice.

World's Fairs. International expositions are usually intended to exhibit the progress that has been made in industrial and fine arts and to project possibilities for the future.

The first major World's Fair in the U.S. opened at New York's Crystal Palace, July 14, 1853. Some critics have charged that it stimulated architectural absurdities in city building for the next half century. The World's Columbian Exposition in Chicago (May 1–Oct. 30, 1893) was intended to celebrate the 400th anniversary of the discovery of America, but it opened later. It also stirred controversy over its impact on architecture; and its beautiful lagoons excited favorable comment.

Other U.S. World's Fairs include the Centennial Exposition, Philadelphia (1876); Pan American Exposition, Buffalo (1901); Louisiana Purchase Exposition, St. Louis (1904); New York World's Fairs (1939–40, 1964–65).

World War I. The event that touched off World War I was the assassination at Sarajevo of Archduke Francis Ferdinand, the heir to the Austrian throne, by a Serb nationalist, June 28, 1914. Pres. Wilson sought to maintain U.S. neutrality and said this was "a war with which we have nothing to do." He proclaimed neutrality and warned Americans to be "impartial in thought as well as in action."

As in the Napoleonic Wars, neutrality offered American businessmen opportunities for profitable trade with the warring nations. Our exports more than doubled in the period between 1914 and 1916. J. P.

Morgan, American financier, became purchasing agent for all the Allies. England, France, Russia, Belgium, Serbia, Montenegro and Japan were among the powers known as the Allies. The Central Powers included Germany, Austria-Hungary and the Ottoman Empire. Both sides violated U.S. neutrality.

Although there was no single reason for the U.S. declaration of war against Germany, the German submarine campaign led directly to that step. In the two months preceding Pres. Wilson's war message to Congress, Apr. 2, 1917, U-boats sank eight U.S. vessels, causing the loss of 48 American lives. Antagonism toward Germany mounted in the U.S. when it was revealed, Mar. 1, 1917, that the German Foreign Sec., Alfred Zimmerman, was seeking Mexico's help against the U.S. in the event of war.

Aside from all the other factors, millions of Americans sincerely believed that Germany was a menace to U.S. security and that defeat of the autocratic government headed by the Kaiser was the only way to make the world safe for democracy.

Even before the U.S. declaration of war, Apr. 6, 1917, American money and supplies had been an important factor in strengthening the Allies. After the U.S. entered the conflict, the Allies received material help amounting to about an additional $9.5 billion.

But money and supplies were not enough. The war-weary Allies were in desperate need of manpower. Under the Selective Service Act, the U.S. registered over 24,000,000 men between the ages of 18 and 45. Almost 5,000,000 men were enrolled for military training. More than 2,000,000 U.S. troops reached France. There, the supreme commander of the Allied armies, Marshal Ferdinand Foch, granted the request of Gen. John Pershing, leader of the American Expeditionary Force, that the American units be allowed to constitute a separate army with its own sector of the front.

The first American contingents helped halt Germany's last great offensive in the spring of 1918 at Château-Thierry and Belleau Wood. Later, American troops swept the Germans out of the St. Mihiel salient and the Argonne Forest, in the Allied counteroffensive that ended the war. The fresh American troops gave the Allies the upper hand. As British, French and American forces prepared to invade Germany (Russia had been forced out of the war by Germany, Dec. 1917), the German government gave up and the Armistice was signed, Nov. 11, 1918.

Although Pres. Wilson had been reelected in 1916 on a Democratic platform stating "He kept us out of war," the nation, in general, rallied strongly behind the war effort. Fear that a German victory would doom democracy united the nation. Congress readily granted Wilson emergency powers. Under Pres. Wilson's direction new federal agencies were created to control almost every phase of American life: Food Administration supervised rationing; industry and labor were mobilized under the leadership of Bernard Baruch, whose War Industries Board attempted "to operate the whole United States as a single factory dominated by one management."

The immediate cost of the war to the U.S. exclusive of the loss of life and suffering, which cannot be measured in dollars and cents, was about $22 billion. This was three times the total expenditures of the federal government during the first 100 years of national existence. Of this total about $10 billion went to the Allies as loans. If the immediate costs were added to later payments to veterans and their families, the overall cost would probably be close to $100 billion. About a third of the money needed in 1917–18 was raised by taxation; the remainder was borrowed.

There were 53,402 battle deaths, 63,114 other deaths, and 204,002 wounded. This loss of life, terrible though it was, comprised only a small fraction of the 8 million killed in battle, exclusive of civilian losses, in war-ravaged Europe.

Wilson outlined his Fourteen Points for a just and generous peace, Jan. 1918. At the end of the war he was forced to compromise some of his principles in order to protect American interests and gain support for the League of Nations. But Wilson was unable to obtain the two-thirds Senate majority needed for ratification of the Treaty of Versailles, which had been signed June 28, 1919.

World War II. Germany, defeated in World War I, yielded to the blandishments of the Nazis, under Hitler, who promised the restoration of German glory. In 1933 Pres. von Hindenburg invited Hitler to become chancellor. There followed a series of aggressions, 1935–39, which moved the world inexorably toward World War II. In 1939 Hitler demanded that Poland give up the "corridor" which separated East Prussia from Germany proper. The Allies then realized that appeasement, whereby one country after another fell to Hitler in an effort to satisfy German expansionism, had failed. The Nazis invaded Poland, Sept. 1, 1939, and on Sept. 3, Britain and France declared war on Germany. The greatest of wars had begun— a war which was to involve virtually the entire world.

Before fighting began in Europe in 1939, Congress enacted a series of Neutrality Acts (1935–37) to keep the U.S. out of any world war. Once the war started, Pres. Roosevelt declared: "Let no one imagine that America will escape, that it may expect mercy, that this Western Hemisphere will not be attacked." As the brutality of Nazi aggression became clear, public opinion in the U.S. grew strongly sympathetic to the cause of the Allies. After the fall of France, June 1940, it was clear that the U.S. policy of "neutrality" would have to be given up if German aggression was to be halted short of invasion of the Western Hemisphere. The U.S. became the "arsenal of democracy" and Congress passed the Lend-Lease Act. American merchant ships were armed, destroyers helped to convoy cargoes to Allied ports and U.S. troops were landed in Greenland and Iceland to safeguard the North Atlantic against Nazi attacks.

On June 22, 1941, Hitler attacked the Soviet Union bringing Russia into the war on the side of Britain. In Aug. 1941, Pres. Roosevelt met with Prime Minister Churchill and signed the Atlantic Charter, which outlined a program for a lasting peace. It called for "final destruction of the Nazi tyranny."

On Dec. 7, 1941, the Japanese attacked Pearl Harbor, crippling the U.S. Pacific fleet. On the same day, Japan declared war on Britain and the U.S. On Dec. 8, Britain and the U.S. declared war on Japan. On Dec. 10–11 Germany and Italy declared war on the U.S. and the U.S. declared war on both those countries. The epic struggle was now fully joined.

The high water mark of Japan's military advance in the Pacific was probably reached with the fall of the Bataan fortress of Corregidor, in the Philippines, May 6, 1942. Soon afterward, carrier-based planes

from a British-American naval force sank part of the Japanese fleet moving southward in the Coral Sea, near Australia. The first real offensive by the Allies in the Pacific occurred when Marines stormed ashore at Guadalcanal (Aug. 17, 1942). From that time forward, U.S. forces in the Pacific were involved in a slow, bloody series of island battles until Okinawa was taken in 1945. The U.S. was poised for invasion of Japan, when on the morning of Aug. 6, 1945, a solitary American plane flew over the city of Hiroshima and dropped an atomic bomb. On Aug. 14, 1945, Japan surrendered unconditionally.

The success of the Allies in the Pacific was matched by their victory in the battle of the Atlantic, achieved by 1943. Radar and other plane and submarine detecting devices made possible a halt in the severe losses inflicted on Allied shipping by the Germans.

Even before the battle of the Atlantic had been won, Churchill and Roosevelt approved the attack on the "soft underbelly" of Europe. The invasion of North Africa (Oct. 1942), under Gen. Eisenhower, was the greatest massing of land, air and sea forces up to that time. German and Italian troops were caught in the jaws of a great pincers as British forces under Gen. Montgomery advanced westward from Egypt and Gen. Eisenhower's forces pushed eastward from French Morocco and Algeria. In May 1943 all

German and Italian forces in North Africa surrendered.

From their newly won bases in North Africa, the Allies launched an offensive against Italy. Early in July 1943, they landed in Sicily and quickly overran the island. In July Mussolini fell from power and on Sept. 8, 1945, Italy surrendered to the Allies. But the campaign for Italy proved long and costly as veteran German troops filled the gaps left by the Italians. It was not until June 1944 that the Allies entered Rome. From Italian bases, Allied airmen bombed southern Germany and the German-held Balkans.

By mid-1944 Allied plans for the invasion of western Europe were ready to be carried out. The Russians had been demanding a "second front" in the West, but the Allies did not believe that it would be feasible to make a direct attack on strongly entrenched German forces in western Europe until North Africa and southern Europe had been won.

On D-Day, June 6, 1944, Gen. Eisenhower, Supreme Commander of the invasion forces, ordered 11,000 planes and an invasion fleet of nearly 4,000 transports, landing craft and warships to cross the English Channel. The Allied armies landed in Normandy, in northeastern France, won a beachhead and in spite of tough resistance pushed steadily eastward. The Germans did mount a strong but unsuccessful counteroffensive, remembered as the Battle of the Bulge (Dec. 1944).

Meanwhile Russia had been advancing on the eastern front. The race to Berlin began. The Russian and the combined British and American forces met at the Elbe River in Germany (Apr. 1945). On May 1 Hitler took his own life in the burning ruins of Berlin. On the night of May 7, 1945, the German High Command accepted unconditional surrender. The war in Europe was over.

American workers during the war manned a vast industrial machine whose output astonished the world and even surprised Americans. From 1940 to 1945, U.S. factories produced about 300,000 military planes; 86,000 tanks; 16,000 armored cars; 88,000 scout cars and carriers; 2,500,000 trucks; 990,000 light vehicles, such as jeeps; 123,000 tractors; 18,000,000 rifles and sidearms; 2,700,000 machine guns; 315,000 pieces of field artillery; and corresponding amounts of ammunition. In addition, American shipyards launched more than 7,000 naval vessels and 45,000,000 tons of merchant ships, thus creating the greatest Navy and Merchant Marine the world had ever seen. At the same time enough consumer goods were produced to keep living standards at a high level. This program of military and civilian production was under the overall supervision of the War Production Board.

The peak strength of the U.S. Armed Forces during the war

was 12,300,000 with a total of 16,353,659 serving between Dec. 7, 1941 and Dec. 31, 1946, when hostilities were officially terminated by Presidential Proclamation. There were 291,557 battle deaths, 113,842 other deaths and 670,846 wounded. Total U.S. casualties were three times greater than in World War I.

Wounded Knee, battle of (Dec. 29, 1890). Some 200 Sioux men, women and children were slaughtered by federal troops in the battle at a creek in South Dakota. They had performed their Sun Dance which had been prohibited. The Indians were surrounded, and when some of the Sioux refused to disarm, the "battle" ensued.

Wright, Chauncey (1830–75). Philosopher and mathematician. Born in Northampton, Mass., he was graduated from Harvard (1852). A remarkable thinker, he anticipated the pragmatism of William James and was one of the first to introduce British methods of empiricism to America. Author of the essay "Evolution of Self-Consciousness," his articles describing an instrumentalist conception of mental activities appeared in the *North American Review* (1864). A lecturer on psychology, he also taught mathematics and physics and was a computer for the *American Ephemeris and Nautical Almanac*.

Wright, Frank Lloyd (1869–1959). Architect. Born in Richland Center, Wis., he practiced

in Chicago, where he developed his "prairie" style in a series of homes built with low horizontal lines and with strongly projecting eaves. He practiced radical innovation in structure; he was the first to produce open planning in houses, in a break from the traditional closed volume. Among his notable works are the Imperial Hotel (1916–20), Tokyo, Japan, which survived the 1923 earthquake; his studio homes "Taliesen," near Spring Green, Wis., and "Taliesen West," near Phoenix, Ariz.; the Johnson Building and Tower, Racine, Wis.; Millard House, Pasadena, Calif.; Guggenheim Museum, N.Y.C.; and many private dwellings in and near Chicago.

Wright, Richard (1908–60). Novelist. Born near Natchez, Miss., his autobiographical *Black Boy* (1945) throws much light on the Negro intellectual of the 1930's. Other books by Wright include *Uncle Tom's Children* (1938) and *Native Son* (1940).

Wright, Wilbur (1867–1912). Aviation pioneer and inventor. Born near New Castle, Ind., he and his brother Orville (1871–1948) made the first successful motor-powered airplane. They previously experimented with gliders. Orville, in the longest of the first flights at Kitty Hawk, N.C. on Dec. 17, 1903, stayed aloft for 59 seconds and traveled 852 feet. Continued experiments and improvements led to successful Army tests (1909). The brothers organized the American Wright Co. (1909) to manufacture airplanes under their patents.

writs of assistance. Colonial courts issued general search warrants which authorized customs officials to enter houses and ships, to break down doors and to open containers in their search for smuggled goods. The writs were protested by colonists, who held that they authorized unreasonable searches and seizures.

Massachusetts merchants in 1760 employed James Otis as their attorney to challenge the legality of the writs in court. Otis denied that Parliament had the power to authorize the use of the writs and asserted that British subjects had rights which even Parliament could not take away. The writs remained a grievance not only in Massachusetts but in other colonies as well.

Wyandotte Constitution (1859). The Constitution prohibiting slavery was ratified by the voters of the Kansas Territory, Oct. 4. It confirmed the dominance of free soilers in territory that had earned the name "Bleeding Kansas." Under this Constitution Kansas was admitted to the Union in 1861, before the outbreak of the Civil War. Its admission further aroused southern extremists.

Wyoming. The "Equality State," so called because voting rights were extended to women (1869), was admitted to the Union as the 44th state, July 10, 1890. The name was taken from Wyoming Valley, Pa. A Mountain group state, its capital is Cheyenne.

The first white men known to traverse the area were in the Lewis and Clark expedition (1804–06). On the return trip, John Colter remained in Wyoming and joined Manuel Lisa in fur trading. Colter explored much of the Yellowstone. Most of the state entered the U.S. as part of the Louisiana Purchase. Other parts were added with the annexation of Texas, the settlement of the Oregon question and the Mexican Cession. Wyoming was made a territory in 1869. The Big Horn Expedition of gold seekers in 1870 led to trouble with the Indians.

Mining was replaced by cattle raising as the major industry when it was found that cattle could fend for themselves on the ranges in the winter. Farmers who fenced the land and sheepraisers whose animals cropped the grass too closely, spoiling it for cattle, ran into friction with the ranchers.

Most of Wyoming's people gain their livelihood from farming or ranching. Crops include beans, corn, wheat, sugar beets and hay. Great mineral resources include coal, petroleum, iron, copper and uranium. The state receives both irrigation and power from dams and plants of the Missouri River Basin Project.

Wyoming Valley Massacre (July 3–6, 1778). John Butler's Rangers, a Tory force aided by

Indians, defeated the outnumbered settlers in a Revolutionary War battle in northeastern Pennsylvania. Butler lost control of the Indians, who massacred the settlers after they had surrendered. Gen. Washington was moved by the massacre to send Sullivan's Expedition (1779) against the Iroquois.

X

X-15. The vehicle, part airplane and part spacecraft, made its first flight Sept. 17, 1959. It was carried aloft by a B-52 aircraft and launched at about 42,000 feet. It holds the altitude record (66,000 feet) and has a speed of more than 4,000 miles an hour.

It provides a means of testing the possible physiological and psychological behavior of man in space.

XYZ affair (1797). French interference with U.S. commerce led Pres. John Adams to send envoys to France in the hope of avoiding war. They were not received by the Directory, then in power; but three go-betweens were sent by French Foreign Minister Talleyrand to demand an apology for Adams' critical remarks about France, a bribe for Talleyrand and a loan to France.

The U.S. envoys Charles C. Pinckney, John Marshall and Elbridge Gerry turned the French demands down. They could not have been shocked by the proposed bribe, not unknown in the diplomacy of the day, but reported it to Adams, identifying Talleyrand's emissaries as "X," "Y" and "Z." Adams published their report and the American public was outraged by the affair. There followed an undeclared naval war with France.

Y

Yakima Indian Wars (1855–58). Opposition to confinement on a reservation was led by Chief Kamaiakin of the Yakimas in the Pacific Northwest. The discovery of gold in the regions of Colville and Coeur d'Alene had caused miners and settlers to pour into the treaty lands. They were attacked, and when an Indian agent was killed, Gov. Stevens of Washington Territory sent troops into the area.

The Yakimas and their allies engaged in various actions including an assault on Seattle, turned back by a naval force in the harbor, and attacks on river steamers. Regular Army troops suffered some defeats before a force of 700 infantry, cavalry and artillery troops gained control. Kamaiakin fled to Canada and some of the Indian leaders were hanged.

Yale University. One of the great universities in the U.S., it was formed by a group of Congregational ministers in 1701, at Saybrook, Conn. It was known as the "Collegiate School within his Majesties Colony of Connecticot" until 1718. In that year, the campus was moved to New Haven and the name was changed to honor Elihu Yale, an East India merchant whose gift of valuable goods helped finance the college.

Under the presidency of Timothy Dwight (1795–1817), the curriculum was much enlarged. The institution became Yale Univ. in 1887.

Yalta Conference (Feb. 4–11, 1945). Important decisions reached at Yalta (in the Russian Crimea) by Pres. Roosevelt, Prime Minister Churchill and Premier Stalin were not published until after the war. The secret provisions included Russia's promise to enter the war against Japan within two or three months after the defeat of Germany. In return for such participation in the war against Japan, Outer Mongolia was to remain under the influence of the Soviet Union. The USSR was to regain former territories and rights which had been taken from her as a result of the Russo-Japanese War (1904–05). Specifically, it was agreed that the southern part of the island of Sakhalin was to be returned to Russia; that the port of Dairen in Manchuria was to be internationalized; and that the Soviet lease of Port Arthur (also in Manchuria) as a naval base was to be restored. The Kurile Islands were to be handed over to Russia.

In Europe, the USSR was to receive the eastern part of Poland, roughly a third of pre-war Poland, according to the Curzon Line of 1919. In return Poland was to be compensated in the west with German territory. Provision was also made for Germany to be occupied by the U.S., Britain, the USSR and France.

The U.S., Britain and the USSR also agreed on the formation of a United Nations organization to be set up later in 1945.

Critics of the Yalta Agreement have charged that concessions to the Soviet Union were too great and were unfair to China. Defenders reply that Roosevelt and Churchill were faced with the prospect of a long and bloody campaign to crush Japan and that Russian participation seemed essential to shorten the war and save untold thousands of lives. The concessions in Poland were necessary because the USSR had already occupied eastern Poland and could be pushed back only by force.

Yamasee War (1715–16). The South Carolina frontier was torn by a war between Indians and American colonists. Two hundred whites were massacred by the Yamasees, who had been stirred by the Spaniards at St. Augustine. Surviving farmers, feeling that they had been abandoned by the proprietors of the colony, fled to Charleston, S.C. The colonists, under Gov. Craven, aided by North Carolina and Virginia troops, drove the Yamasees into Florida.

Yancey - Rost - Mann mission (1861). The three-man mission was sent to England by Pres. Davis of the Confederate States of America a month before Gen. Beauregard's bombardment of Fort Sumter. The envoys sought to implement the South's "cotton diplomacy," but found that English textile mills were heavily stocked with cotton. They were unsuccessful in their efforts to win recognition of the Confederacy by England, conclude a commercial treaty or get England to denounce the northern blockade of southern ports.

They did, however, gain from Queen Victoria, May 13, 1861, a proclamation taking note of hostilities between the U.S. "and certain states styling themselves the Confederate States of America" and declaring the "royal determination to maintain a strict and impartial neutrality in the contest between the contending parties." The French, Spanish and other Europeans followed the British lead and refused to accept the Union definition of the Confederates as treasonable rebels.

Their action meant refusal to condemn Confederate privateers as "pirates" (not ordinary prisoners of war).

Yankee. The name was used by Confederates to describe Federal soldiers during the Civil War. The term antedates the war and describes anyone who lives in New England or one of the northern states. The precise origin is unclear although it has been suggested that it started as a mispronunciation of a term used by Indians to describe the English settlers.

"Yankee Doodle." The marching song of the Revolution came from England about 1750. There are various rhymes, the best known of which is:
Yankee Doodle came to town,
Riding on a pony
Stuck a feather in his cap
And called it Macaroni.

Yap Treaty (1922). Japan agreed to grant the U.S. cable rights on the strategically located Pacific island. It was included among the islands mandated to Japan by the League of Nations as an outcome of a secret agreement with Britain by which the Japanese were to take over Germany's North Pacific islands. The Department of State sent vigorous notes to Tokyo in support of America's claims and the Treaty was the result.

Yazoo Land Frauds. In 1795 parts of Alabama and Mississippi through which the Yazoo River flowed were sold by the state of Georgia to four companies. These, in turn, sold the land to purchasers, mainly in the Middle States and New England. The sale was tainted with fraud because of the very low price and the fact that all but one of the Georgia legislators obtained some of the land.

In 1795 the Georgia legislature rescinded the sale of its western lands. Purchasers, however, claimed their share of the land and sought congressional aid.

In 1802 Georgia ceded the disputed land to the U.S. A commission appointed by Pres. Jefferson recommended that Yazoo claimants be reimbursed, but Rep. John Randolph of Virginia bitterly fought against any compensation.

The case finally came before the Supreme Court (*Fletcher v. Peck*, 1810), which decided in favor of the claimants. Congress, in 1814, awarded the Yazoo claimants almost $5 million.

"yellow-dog" contracts. Beginning in the 1890's employers, in an effort to halt the growth of unions, forced employees to promise not to join a union. In 1898 Congress passed the Erdman Act, which prohibited any discrimination by the interstate railways against workers because of union membership.

In *Adair v. U.S.* (1908) the U.S. Supreme Court held this provision of the Erdman Act unconstitutional as an invasion of both personal liberty and the

734

rights of property under the 5th Amendment. A comparable state statute was outlawed in *Coppage v. Kansas* (1915) as a violation of the 14th Amendment. The Supreme Court then proceeded to uphold an injunction granted at the request of the Hitchman Coal and Coke Co., in West Virginia, which prohibited the United Mine Workers from seeking to organize company employees who had been compelled to agree not to join the union under "yellow-dog" contracts.

The decisions upholding and enforcing "yellow-dog" contracts stood until passage of the Norris-LaGuardia Act in 1932.

yellow fever. The dreaded disease was a scourge in the American colonies and struck repeatedly in American cities during the 18th and 19th centuries. It devastated Philadelphia in 1793 and caused over 2,000 deaths (in a population of 50,000) in New York City in 1798. Other great epidemics struck in New Orleans, La., and Vicksburg, Miss. (1853); Jacksonville, Fla., and the South (1888); Brunswick, Ga. (1893).

The source of infection was finally identified in 1900 as the stegomyia mosquito. The discovery was made by a commission sent by the U.S. government to Cuba to track the killer. It included Walter Reed, Aristides Agramonte, Jesse W. Lazear and James Carroll. Dr. Lazear died as a direct result of the effects of yellow fever contracted during experiments.

"yellow journalism." The term describes sensationalism in newspapers. It was first used in the 1880's when the "Yellow Kid," one of the comic strips in Joseph Pulitzer's New York *World*, featured a character who was always dressed in yellow. By 1900 the yellow press was thriving on a diet of war atrocities and scandal. The stories were characterized by general disdain for accurate news reporting when a twist in the truth could produce a screaming headline.

At the time newspapers sought to boost circulation to get increased revenue from advertising. In 1895 competition in New York was heightened when William Randolph Hearst, publisher of the San Francisco *Examiner*, purchased the New York *Morning Journal*. The Cuban insurrection occurred opportunely for a sensational press that stirred the nation into a frenzy with its reports of "Butcher" Weyler's atrocities in Cuban concentration camps. The sinking of the battleship *Maine* in Santiago Harbor in 1898 was the kind of event that the yellow press seized upon with a frenzy that characterized vigilantes determined to shoot first and ask questions afterward.

Publishers who rejected the low standards of the yellow press did adopt some of its innovations, such as Sunday features, comic strips, human interest features and a livelier approach to news writing.

Yellowstone National Park. The largest and best-known national park in the U.S. was established by Congress in 1872. The park, whose area is about 3,472 square miles, is located in northwestern Wyoming. There are about 3,000 geysers and hot springs in the park, the most famous of which is Old Faithful, which spouts at quite regular intervals.

The Grand Canyon of Yellowstone is one of the great scenic features because of its marvellously colored rock formations.

Besides the bears, which are always in evidence, the park contains elk, deer, moose, antelope, mountain sheep and buffalo.

Yorktown, battle of (Aug. 30–Oct. 19, 1781). In the final great battle of the Revolutionary War, Lord Cornwallis' army was maneuvered into a highly unfavorable position on the Yorktown Peninsula, Va. French Admiral De Grasse's fleet blockaded Cornwallis' army, while Gen. Lafayette cut off his escape by land. In a naval action, Sept. 5-9, a British naval force was unsuccessful in breaking the blockade. De Grasse's ships were then used to transport Washington's and Rochambeau's troops to Williamsburg (Sept. 14-24). The siege of Yorktown began as a combined American-French army of over 16,000 faced Cornwallis' 7,000. Cornwallis' position was hopeless

and he surrendered on Oct. 18. His troops laid down their arms the next day. British Gen. Clinton's reinforcements arrived off Chesapeake Bay, Oct. 24, too late to be of aid to Cornwallis and they returned to New York.

Yosemite National Park. The park area is about 1,189 square miles on the west slope of the Sierra Nevada Mts. in middle eastern California. Established by Congress, in 1890, the park contains inspiring gorges, many waterfalls of extraordinary height and three groves of giant sequoias.

Young, Brigham (1801–77). Mormon leader. Born in Whitingham, Vt., he was converted to the Mormon faith in 1832. When the Mormons were ousted from Missouri, he directed their settlement in Nauvoo, Ill. (1838). After Joseph Smith was killed by a mob in Carthage, Ill. (June 27, 1844), Young became head of the Mormon Church and was duly elected in 1847. He guided the mass migration of Mormons to the Great Salt Lake Valley in Utah (1847). A genius as a colonizer, he established virtual dictatorial control over the settlement. First governor of the Territory of Utah (1849–57), he placed the colony on a firm financial footing based on agriculture. His advocacy of the practice of polygamy caused his removal from the governorship by Pres. Buchanan in 1857, but his successors were mere figureheads. His arrival with his followers is celebrated as Pioneers' Day (July 24), a legal holiday in Utah.

Young Men's Christian Associations (YMCA). The current emphasis of the organization is to stimulate the interest of young men in good government and renew the attention of older men to physical fitness. Programs include housing facilities, vocational guidance, sports and recreation. Objectives are the growth of sound citizenship, character building through the development of leadership, interracial understanding and the study of social and political questions in the light of Christian faith and principles.

The organization was founded in London in 1844. The first Associations in North America were formed in Montreal and Boston in 1851. During World Wars I and II the YMCA handled welfare work among American troops. There are now over 1,830 YMCA's in the U.S. and YMCA's in 83 countries. The movement extends into the high schools of the U.S. and Canada through Hi-Y clubs for boys and Tri-Y clubs for girls.

Young Plan. Owen D. Young, an American corporation executive, headed an international committee in 1929 that devised a plan to scale down the German reparations payments arising from World War I. A Bank for International Settlements was established to facilitate payments.

Young Women's Christian Association (YWCA). The organization was founded in London in 1855 to improve the conditions of working girls by providing a place to live and good food for those who lived away from home. In 1858 the first American YWCA was started in New York City as the Ladies Christian Association. Today the YWCA functions in more than 70 countries.

YWCA work in the U.S. is carried on in more than 1,000 cities and towns. It has three main groups: Y Teens, aged 12 to 18; Young Adults, employed girls, 18 to 30; and YW Wives, young married women and mothers of preschool-age children.

The emblem of the YWCA is an inverted triangle signifying mind, body and spirit. The organization tries to develop the potentialities of the individual through promoting physical and mental health and training for useful citizenship. It urges cooperation among all regardless of race or creed.

Ŷpres-Lys offensive (Aug. 19–Nov. 11, 1918). About 108,000 U.S. troops participated in the British offensive in northwestern France and Belgium in the final months of World War I.

Yukon. The river is formed by the union of the Lewes and Pelly rivers in southwest Yukon Territory, Canada. It is about 2,300 miles long, the fifth largest river in North America. The flow is northwest across the Yukon border into Alaska, then southwest across central Alaska to the Bering Sea. It is the third longest river highway in North America since its entire course of 1,260 miles in Alaska is navigable.

The Yukon Territory in Canada was formed from the Northwest Territories in 1898 soon after the Klondike gold rush. The land area is 205,346 square miles, bounded on the north by the Arctic Ocean, on the east by the MacKenzie District, Northwest Territories, on the south by British Columbia and on the west by Alaska. The upper Yukon flows through the Territory before entering Alaska.

Yuma, Fort. Established in 1852 on the California side of the junction of the Colorado and Gila rivers, the fort was a station on early stagecoach lines until these were supplanted by the Southern Pacific Railroad in 1877. Originally, the site of the fort was a ferrying station for Yuma Indians who operated a service for travelers at the junction of the two rivers. Today, Yuma, Ariz., is near the old fort which lies within the Yuma Indian Reservation.

Z

Zenger trial (1735). John Peter Zenger, printer of the *New York Weekly Journal,* was imprisoned for seditious libel at the order of Governor William Cosby of New York.

Under British law a printed attack on a Crown official was libelous. In defending Zenger, Andrew Hamilton of Philadelphia, a distinguished colonial lawyer, argued that Zenger's statements had been true and, therefore, not libelous.

The jury brought in a verdict of not guilty and thereby established a landmark in the history of freedom of the press.

Zimmerman Note (1917). German Foreign Sec. Alfred Zimmerman sent a telegram to the German minister in Mexico advising an alliance between Mexico and Germany in the event of a U.S. declaration of war against Germany. Mexico was also to attempt to bring Japan into the war on the side of Germany. In return, Germany would support Mexico in an effort to recover "her lost territory in New Mexico, Texas, and Arizona."

The telegram was intercepted by British naval intelligence and given to the U.S. When Pres. Wilson released it (Mar. 1917), U.S. public opinion was further aroused against Germany.

Zouaves. The name brings to mind the picturesque Oriental uniforms of hardy soldiers in the French Foreign Legion during the early 19th century. Col. Elmer E. Ellsworth, a former clerk in Abraham Lincoln's law office, organized a Zouave regiment of volunteer firemen in New York early in the Civil War. The men could not, however, adapt to field conditions and the regiment was disbanded after the death of Col. Ellsworth in 1861.

Zuñi. The Indians, of Zuñian linguistic stock, were the first who lived in pueblos to be discovered by the Spaniards (1539). Their seven villages, the "Seven Cities of Cibola," were mistakenly believed to contain great wealth. The Zuñi irrigate their land in New Mexico and are noted for their basketry, pottery and weaving.

Zworykin, Vladimir (1889–). Electronics engineer. Born in Russia, he came to the U.S. in 1916. He was research engineer with Westinghouse Electrical and Manufacturing Co. (1920–29); Radio Corporation of America Manufacturing Co. (1929–42); and RCA Laboratories since 1942. A pioneer in the development of television, he applied for the patent on the iconoscope (1925), basic to the electronic television camera; he successfully demonstrated television between New York and Philadelphia (1933). Author of *Photocells and Their Application* (1932) and *Television* (1940).

CONTEMPORARY
SUPPLEMENT 1969-

Items which appear below in **boldface** type are new.

Items which appear in under-scored **boldface** type update items which appear in the main section.

abortion. In landmark decisions, the U.S. Supreme Court in 1973 limited the power of the state to regulate abortion. Dealing with an emotional and sensitive issue, the Court struck down a Texas law which made abortion a crime unless performed to save a woman's life (*Roe v. Wade*) and a Georgia law strictly limiting the circumstances under which an abortion could be performed (*Doe v. Bolton*).

The Court's pronouncement climaxed a movement toward more liberal abortion laws. New York, Hawaii, Washington and Alaska had removed almost all restrictions on abortion.

Writing for the 7-2 majority, Justice Harry A. Blackmun held that the Constitution's mention of personal liberty is broad enough to include the right to privacy—a woman's decision whether to bear a child. The Court declined to find that the word "person" as used in the Constitution included unborn children. It would not resolve the question of when life actually began. The decision left the states free to place increasing restrictions on abortion as the period of pregnancy lengthens.

Justice Byron R. White dissenting said: "The Court apparently values the convenience of the pregnant mother more than the continued existence and development of the life or potential life which she carries." The ruling, he said, was an "improvident and extravagant exercise of the power of judicial review."

The Catholic Church had led the opposition to the liberalizing of abortion laws. Catholic leader John Cardinal Krol described the decision as "unspeakable tragedy."

Agnew, Spiro Theodore (1918–). Vice-President of the U.S. (1969–73). The son of a Greek immigrant whose name was Anagnostopolous, he was born in Maryland. He attended Johns Hopkins and was graduated from the Univ. of Baltimore law school (1947), after serving four years in the Army during World War II. He was considered a liberal Republican and reformer at the time of his election as Governor of Maryland (1964). As Vice-President, he gained prominence as a defender of law and order and for his criticism of the press. His political career was terminated abruptly as an outcome of a criminal investigation by the Justice Department into his alleged acceptance of kickbacks from consulting engineers and others when he was Baltimore County Executive and Governor of Maryland. He resigned from the Vice-Presidency on Oct. 10, 1973, pleading "no contest" to charges of failing to report $29,500 of income in 1967.

Amendments to the Constitution

Twenty-fifth Amendment

(1967). The Amendment was first brought into play in 1973 when Vice-President Agnew resigned and Pres. Nixon nominated Congressman Gerald R. Ford (Rep., Mich.) to be Vice-President.

Twenty-sixth Amendment

(1971). Some 11,000,000 citizens, aged 18 to 20, cast their first votes in the Nov. 2, 1971, off-year elections. The 26th Amendment gave citizens 18 years of age and older the right to vote in all elections—federal, state and local.

A stimulus to ratification of the Amendment was the draft requirement that 18-year-olds register for military service during the Viet Nam war. The incongruity of requiring men to fight for their country while denying them the right to vote influenced public opinion. Although the 21-year age minimum for voting had predated the Viet Nam war, the demand for 18-year-old voting rights was part of the youth movement of the 1960's.

Amtrak. A contraction of "American" and "track," the nation's new rail passenger system went into effect on May 1, 1971. The number of passenger trains was cut by about half throughout the country to eliminate duplication of services and inefficient and unprofitable trains. Many old favorites like the Wabash Cannonball, the San Francisco Chief and other once-famous trains were dropped.

The National Railroad Passenger Corporation, which operates Amtrak with the goal "to get people back on trains," planned innovations to attract passengers lost to the airlines, buses and automobiles.

Angela Davis case. A black militant and avowed Communist, Angela Davis was indicted for murder, kidnapping and conspiracy stemming from an attempted escape in the Marin County Courthouse, Calif., in

Aug. 1970. The judge and three other persons were shot to death. She was accused of furnishing guns and helping to plot the abortive escape of the "Soledad Brothers" charged with killing a white guard in prison.

The subject of a worldwide "Free Angela" movement, she had fled and was recaptured in New York City six months after the crime. She was returned to California. Acquitted by an all-white jury in San Jose, Calif., on June 4, 1972, the former philosophy instructor at the Univ. of California, at Los Angeles, said: "The only fair trial would have been no trial."

"Archie Bunkerism." A weekly television series, "All in the Family," seen nationally during the early 1970's, made Archie Bunker, played by the actor Carroll O'Connor, a household name. Bunker's loudly voiced prejudices against minorities were proclaimed in a humorous family setting. America laughed at the absurdity of Archie's name-calling and uncritical acceptance of stereotypes. His malapropisms, intended to demean minorities, revealed the shallowness of old prejudices that often surface. His barbs when used in everyday life are often "put down" as "Archie Bunkerism."

Attica prison rebellion (1971). The bloodiest prison clash of the 20th century took place in the Attica State Correctional Facility (N.Y.) where 1,200 inmates held 38 guards hostage. The death toll of 43 included nine prison guards who had been held as hostages and 30 convicts. Eighty others suffered gunshot wounds. The four-day rebellion was ended on Sept. 13 when more than 1,000 New York State troopers and police stormed the prison. Shockwaves were felt around the country as civil rights groups criticized the handling of the revolt by Gov. Nelson Rockefeller.

"Black is beautiful." The expression appears in slightly modified form in the Douay version of the Old Testament (Solomon's "Canticle of Canticles"): "I am black but beautiful. . . ." It was used widely in the late 1960's by black people and taken up in the media.

At the time, young militants favored "black" as a name change to indicate racial pride growing largely out of the civil rights movement and the emergence of independent nations in Africa. Others soon came to accept "black" as preferable to "Negro," to which "a slave connotation" was ascribed by advocates of the change.

While there is no agreement among Americans of African ancestry as to whether "African-American," "Afro-American," "colored," "Negro" or "black" is to be preferred, "black" has become dominant. It continues, however, to be used interchangeably with "Negro."

Organizations founded before

743

the preference for "black" asserted itself have continued to retain their old names (e.g., National Association for the Advancement of Colored People, *Journal of Negro History*).

Brownsville Riot (1906). In 1972 the discharges were changed to honorable by the Secretary of the Army. Only one known survivor was alive to receive vindication.

busing. Perhaps the most controversial approach to achieving school integration since the *Brown* decision (1954) has been the forced busing of public-school children. In Pontiac, Mich., a violent struggle erupted in 1971 in response to a federal court busing order desegregating the schools. Buses were burned, workers stayed off the job to protest and white "freedom schools" were established. About 9,000 of Pontiac's 21,000 students were bused to school, mostly to create a black population of 20% to 49% in each of the city's 31 schools.

Few American cities (for example, Berkeley and Riverside, Calif., and Evanston, Ill.) have voluntarily established two-way busing programs aimed at achieving racial balance. Most of the programs have been court-directed and involve the busing of black children into predominantly white schools.

In the *Swann* Case (1971) a unanimous U.S. Supreme Court, in an opinion written by Chief Justice Warren E. Burger, or-

dered busing to correct the racial imbalance in the Charlotte-Mecklenburg County, N.C., school system. The Court noted that about 30% of the public-school children in the nation are bused and that there had been no objection to busing in Charlotte until it was proposed that busing be used to end the dual school system which prevailed in the county. "All things being equal, with no history of discrimination," the Court reasoned, "it might well be desirable to assign pupils schools nearest their homes." But, the Court found that there had been discrimination in the Charlotte school system.

Two-way busing was prescribed for Detroit, Mich., and its metropolitan area by a U.S. Sixth Circuit Court of Appeals decision (1973). The Court ruled that black children from Detroit must ride buses out to the suburbs and white suburban children must ride them in to Detroit to achieve racial balance in the schools. In approving the principle of metropolitan-area busing, the Court set itself in diametric opposition to the U.S. Fourth Circuit Court of Appeals (1973). The Fourth Circuit invalidated a similar busing plan in the Richmond, Va., area. The U.S. Supreme Court in a 4 to 4 decision let the Richmond decision stand.

The busing issue gave rise to a movement for a constitutional amendment to prohibit involuntary assignment of children to schools on the basis of race, color or national origin. In 1973 New York became the tenth state, the first major industrial state in the Northeast, to call upon Congress for a constitutional convention to ratify the amendment.

capital punishment. In the *Furman* decision (1972) the U.S. Supreme Court ruled that capital punishment (the death penalty) as it was imposed in the U.S. violated the 8th Amendment prohibition against "cruel and unusual punishments." The Court found that the penalty was being "meted out in a random and unpredictable manner. . . ."

At the time of the *Furman* decision, 11 states had abolished the death penalty while five others limited its use to "extreme" crimes. Some legislatures in response to the decision sought to draft laws on capital punishment that would meet the criticism of the Court.

Proponents of the death penalty see it as a deterrent that protects the lives of the innocent. Opponents argue that inflicting capital punishment is barbaric and inhumane.

Congress has been considering legislation that would reinstate the death penalty for certain "specific" crimes like kidnapping, assassination, bombing a public building, airline hijacking and killing a prison guard.

Chappaquiddick. A car driven by Sen. Edward M. Kennedy (Dem., Mass.) plunged off a bridge into a tidal pool on Chappaquiddick Island, Mass., about midnight on July 18, 1969. The body of Mary Jo Kopechne, a 28-year-old secretary, was found in the car. The young senator described his failure to report the accidental death promptly as "indefensible." A grand jury voted to indict no one and the press was barred from the inquest hearing. Kennedy's driving license was revoked. He was given a two-month suspended jail sentence and put on probation for a year after he pleaded guilty to a charge of leaving the scene of an accident.

Kennedy was reelected to the Senate in 1970, but his political career is shadowed by Chappaquiddick.

computers. Research initiated during World War II led to development of the first electronic computer. By 1970 there were 60,000 computers in use and almost every consumer is indirectly acquainted with computers. The machines handle the vast majority of the nation's banking transactions, as well as the customer accounts of utilities, credit-card companies and large department stores.

Although businessmen find the computers indispensable, worrisome aspects include their vulnerability to sabotage and theft of electronically stored information, especially where computers are shared. There is also the factor of human error in programing computers, and many people have encountered errors in a computerized bill. The process of getting the error corrected can be frustrating.

The bottomless capacity of computers for storing information has aroused fears among civil libertarians who charge that the U.S. is moving toward a "dossier society" in which all important details of an individual's life are being stored in computer "memories." Justice Department officials deny that the information contained in its data banks is abused.

The computer industry continues to develop machines with greater speed and capacity. They are sometimes bought by companies who have not yet made full use of the computers which they have.

conscription (the "draft"). In Dec. 1972 the government stopped the draft. Reliance was placed on an all-volunteer force —AVF or VOLAR to military officials. The word VOLAR derives from volunteer armed forces. As of June 30, 1973, the requirement that 18-year-olds register with the Selective Service System remained. However, inductions of nonvolunteers are not possible until a new law is passed.

To encourage voluntary enlistments, Congress in 1972 offered a $1,500 bonus, later increased to $2,500, to recruits who were willing to specify combat duty for four years as "grunts," or foot soldiers. This was the first resort to such payments since the Spanish-American and Mexican wars. The bonus was withdrawn after a year.

It soon became apparent that it was difficult to recruit on a volunteer basis, especially for the Army. To ease a serious manpower shortage, enlistment requirements were relaxed. The policy of enlisting at least 70% high school graduates was changed to permit non-high school graduates "to prove themselves by their performance in training."

VOLAR has been criticized as leading to a military force that does not represent a cross section of society. Few middle-class youths, or members of affluent families, have volunteered.

Constitution of the United States (*Text*)
26th AMENDMENT (1971)
Lowering Voting Age to 18 Years
Section 1
The right of citizens of the United States, who are 18 years of age or older, to vote shall not be denied or abridged by the United States or any state on account of age.
Section 2
The Congress shall have power to enforce this article by appropriate legislation.

consumerism. Everyone who buys any good or service is a consumer. The consumer movement was stimulated by publication of *Unsafe at Any Speed:*

The Designed-in Dangers of the American Automobile (1965) by Ralph Nader.

Consumer concern for automobile safety took shape in the National Traffic and Motor Vehicle Safety Act (1966). Other legislation affecting product safety and a wide range of consumer interests included increased protection from hazardous toys (Child Protection and Toy Safety Act, 1969); reduction of poisoning of children by requiring marketing of products in safety containers (Poison Prevention Packaging Act, 1970); and curbing evasive formulas designed by creditors to make interest charges "sound good" (Truth in Lending Act, 1969). Critics of proliferating legislation contend that consumer laws with teeth have a way of becoming defanged when it comes to enforcement.

Consumer consciousness is evident in criticism of such government agencies entrusted with consumer protection as the Food and Drug Administration, Federal Trade Commission and Federal Power Commission.

The General Services Administration (GSA) made public for the first time in 1971 a list of 350 brand-name products it buys for the federal government. The information had long been sought by consumer groups as a guide to quality.

The average American's quality consciousness has expanded in direct proportion to the number of his vulnerable possessions. More than 90% of all families now possess a washing machine, a refrigerator and at least one television set.

The "ideology of consumerism" has been criticized for ignoring the balancing of costs and benefits and for its prejudice against big business. It is assumed, according to critics of consumerism, that large corporations prefer hazardous products over safe ones.

Copernicus. The last and fourth orbiting astronomical observatory (OAO) was launched on Aug. 21, 1972. The 4,900-pound satellite is equipped with the largest ultraviolet telescope ever orbited. It is the most expensive, complicated and heaviest unmanned satellite ever launched by the U.S. Copernicus observes interstellar gases and young hot stars and X-rays stars and other phenomena.

dollar devaluation. On August 15, 1971, Pres. Nixon took the historic step of denying foreign central banks the right to convert dollars into gold, clearing the way for an 8.57% devaluation of the dollar in Dec. 1971. A second dollar devaluation was reported to the International Monetary Fund in Feb. 1973.

The value of the U.S. dollar prior to these monetary moves had been artificially high in relation to other currencies, especially the West German mark, French franc and Japanese yen. This meant that American exports were too high priced to compete in foreign markets and the cost of imports was high. The high exchange rate of the U.S. dollar contributed to the unfavorable U.S. balance of trade which showed a deficit in 1971 for the first time since 1893.

Dollar devaluation by the U.S. is intended to make U.S. exports cheaper and U.S. imports more expensive with a view to improving the overall U.S. balance of payments.

drug abuse. Addiction to narcotics has become a major problem in the U.S. since the end of World War II. Heroin accounts for 90% of the narcotic addiction problem. Estimates of the number of opiate addicts in the U.S. in the early 1970's are between 100,000 and 200,000.

Among the drugs being abused are marijuana, amphetamines, hallucinogens such as LSD (lysergic acid diethylamide), mescaline and cocaine. Some of the factors in the great "turn on" of recent years are: the numbers of young people who have lost faith in the prevailing social system; the tendency of persons with psychological problems to seek easy solutions with chemicals; the easy access to drugs of various sorts; the development of an affluent society that can afford drugs; the statements of proselytizers who proclaim the "goodness" of drugs.

As an outcome of drug abuse, a subculture has developed in the U.S. Members of the subculture congregate in a particular geographic area, such as the Haight-Asbury district in San Francisco. Drug abuse is not, however, confined to any one geographic area, social class or age group. It is pervasive and has moved from the ghetto areas to the highest reaches of our society.

Users who want help can seek it from physicians, mental-health professions or school counselors. Some community self-help groups, run by ex-users, are effective. Many community mental-health centers have special drug-abuse units. The centers provide service or referral to an appropriate source.

Major drug traffickers are the organized criminal elements based in major metropolitan areas throughout the U.S. These organizations have the manpower, financial ability and international connections with which to procure and successfully smuggle large quantities of drugs, especially heroin, into the country. To a lesser extent, numerous individuals and independent groups smuggle illicitly produced drugs.

Many addicts had criminal records before they became addicted. Nevertheless, a direct relationship between the addicted person and criminal activity does exist because of the need for large sums of money to support his "habit."

Penalties for drug dealing vary throughout the U.S., and modifications of the existing laws are often before the legislatures. Most of the state penalties, compiled by the Federal Bureau of Narcotics and Dangerous Drugs, give a judge ample discretion in sentencing. In Illinois, for instance, a pusher can be sentenced to from 1 to 20 years and a $25,000 fine for sale of hard drugs. If more than 30 grams of heroin, cocaine or morphine is involved, the penalties are 10 years to life with a $200,000 fine and are even harsher when the sale is to a minor.

Despite the massive public education program about drug use, the drug problem has not abated.

ecology. The upsurge of public concern in the 1960's and 1970's over the quality of the environment has heightened interest in human ecology—the study of man's relationship with his environment. Earth Day (Apr. 22, 1970) dramatized for millions the American concern with pollution of air, water and land.

Ecology falls within the scope of conservation, which traditionally emphasized wildlife and fisheries, forests and rangelands, soils and river basins, minerals and fuels. These old problems remain, but the emphasis has been shifted to towns and cities where some 70% of the U.S. population lives.

Ecological problems are not only local; they are regional, national and international. Thus, air pollution from California's coastal cities affects the health of pine trees in the distant Sierra Nevada. Pesticides from the factories of America or Europe appear in the tissues of Antarctic penguins.

A major pesticide, DDT, was subject to a near-total ban in 1973 by the federal Environmental Protection Agency. EPA, established in 1971, has also promulgated air-quality standards and has required auto makers to reduce car emissions of pollutants.

Ecological reform requires the expenditure of billions of dollars to reduce pollution of air and waterways, improve sewage treatment, dispose of industrial wastes, desulphurize fuel oil used in generating electric power, etc.

The public has become conscious of some of the conflicts between convenience on the one hand and environmental preservation on the other. The environmental movement has raised disturbing questions about the desirability of unrelenting economic growth. A momentous choice may have to be made between increasing production and preserving the environment. Unlimited use of cars, innumerable electrical conveniences, vast production of consumer goods—all contribute to the pollution problem. To solve ecological problems, the traditional way of life in the U.S. may have to be modified.

Election of 1972. The major issue was the continuing Viet Nam war. Pollution, school busing for integration and trust in government were other issues confronting the contenders.

Pres. Richard M. Nixon was renominated by the Republican party at its Miami Beach national convention. Also renominated was Vice-President Spiro T. Agnew.

The Democratic convention, also in Miami Beach, reflected changes in delegate selection that provided greater grass-roots representation of young people, blacks and other minorities. The Democrats nominated Sen. George McGovern of South Dakota for President and Sen. Thomas F. Eagleton of Missouri for Vice-President.

About two weeks after his July 13 nomination, Sen. Eagleton admitted that he had undergone hospitalizations in 1960, 1964 and 1966 for nervous exhaustion and mental depression. There ensued a public debate as to the significance of such a medical record and the fact that Eagleton had not disclosed it to McGovern prior to the nomination.

On July 26, McGovern promised Eagleton "1,000%" support. Five days later, he asked Eagleton to become the first American in history to resign the vice-presidential nomination. McGovern's credibility thus became an issue in the campaign.

On Aug. 5, following a search by McGovern for a replacement, the Democratic National Committee nominated for the vice-presidency, Robert Sargent Shriver, Jr. (a Kennedy in-law).

Before the national conventions met, Gov. George Wallace of Alabama, campaigning at a Laurel, Md., shopping center, was shot (May 15, 1972) by an assassin, Arthur Bremer. Paralyzed from the waist down, Wallace was forced to withdraw from the campaign at a time when he held second place among Democratic contenders in the number of committed convention delegates.

With the campaign under way, McGovern branded the Nixon administration as "the most morally corrupt in American history," charging big-business favoritism and political sabotage in the wake of the Watergate bugging raid on Democratic party headquarters. He accused Nixon of "prolonging the Viet Nam war."

Nixon ran his campaign with a low profile stressing his role as a statesman rather than a partisan candidate. He won maximum media exposure with historic trips to China and Russia. On the Viet Nam war, he pointed to the great reduction of American troops, lowered casualty figures and a determination to bring home the prisoners of war. He asked voters to send Hanoi the message that "you back the President of the United States as he insists that we seek peace with honor and never peace with surrender."

The election ended in victory for Pres. Nixon, dealing McGovern the worst Democratic defeat in the nation's history. Nixon carried 49 of the 50 states and 521 out of 538 electoral-college votes. Only Massachusetts went for McGovern. Despite the landslide, in which he became the first Republican President to win all 11 southern states, Nixon failed to win "the new American majority" he had asked for. In a national epidemic of ticket splitting, Democrats retained their majorities in both the Senate and House of Representatives.

Minority party candidates fared badly. John Schmitz, the American party candidate for President, and Dr. Benjamin Spock, the People's party candidate, together got less than 1% of the vote.

energy crisis. Use of energy in the U.S. from all sources has been doubling about every 16 years. The so-called energy crisis of the 1970's is based on the mounting consumption of all forms of energy, especially oil and natural gas which together accounted for more than 75% of the U.S. energy consumption in 1972.

The demand for energy in the U.S. is not being met by current production. Projections indicate that the U.S. must find sources of energy by 1980 that will permit consumption to be about 55% higher than in 1970, assuming that everything else remains the same.

Currently, the U.S. with about 6% of the world's population uses more than 40% of the world's scarce or nonreplaceable resources and a like part of its energy output.

Factors that affect the energy crisis include population growth, foreign oil imports, development of new sources of energy, economy in the use of energy (smaller cars, less wasteful heating and lighting practices) and higher prices and taxes to restrain excessive use of gasoline and electricity. Also relevant to the energy crisis is the need for reassessing the relationship between pollution controls and the increased energy consumption required.

Equal Employment Opportunity Commission (EEOC). Created by an act of Congress in 1972, the Commission is authorized to go to the federal courts to enforce remedies in cases of employment discrimination against women and minorities. Courts are authorized to order an employer to halt discrimination and to remedy past practices by reinstating or hiring the employees with or without awarding them back pay limited to a two-year period.

Equal Rights Amendment. First proposed by the National Women's party in 1923, the proposed amendment to the U.S. Constitution won the approval of Congress in 1972 and by mid-1973 had been approved by 29 of the 38 states required for its adoption. Proponents of the amendment have until March 22, 1979, to convince reluctant states to ratify the amendment.

Those who favor the amendment allege that it will provide the basis for elimination of various kinds of discrimination against women in employment and legal and social relationships. Opponents hold that the amendment will deprive women of the protection of the law in these very areas and that the objectives of the amendment can be accomplished by the passage of specific laws.

The text of the proposed amendment follows:

Section 1. Equality of rights under the law shall not be denied or abridged by the United States or by any State on account of sex.

Section 2. The Congress shall have the power to enforce, by appropriate legislation, the provisions of this article.

Section 3. This amendment shall take effect two years after the date of ratification.

executive privilege. The separation of powers provided for in the Constitution makes it possible for the President to be independent of the other branches of government—legislature and judiciary. Although in practice the powers have overlapped, the Chief Executive has from time to time exercised the doctrine of executive privilege. It holds that the internal, advisory communications of the executive branch are protected from public disclosure to preserve the President's frank recommendations, opinions and considerations.

Until the Watergate affair, the federal courts had never been faced with a case that might have defined the scope of executive privilege, and historians disagree over the extent to which past Presidents used the doctrine. The term itself was first used by Pres. Eisenhower.

In the Watergate affair, Pres. Nixon became the first Chief Executive to be served with subpoenas by Congress. He refused to honor them and the matter was referred to the federal courts.

flying saucers. Unidentified flying objects (UFOS), or "flying saucers," have been dismissed as a threat to national security. In a check of 12,618 UFO sightings reported, during a 21-year study by the U.S. Air Force, ending in 1969, no evidence was found that any of them were extra-terrestrial spaceships.

Fortas resignation (May 14, 1969). The resignation of U.S. Supreme Court Justice Abe Fortas was the first made under public pressure in the tribunal's history.

A *Life* magazine article reported that Fortas had accepted $20,000 from a charitable foundation created by the family of a financier who was serving a year in prison for stock manipulation. The payment was for law lectures and had been the first in an annual lifetime arrangement. Fortas had returned the money.

Ten days after the article appeared, Fortas resigned.

gold standard. The U.S. was first taken off the gold standard in 1933, but gold continued to be used by the government to settle its international accounts at $35 an ounce. On Aug. 15, 1971, the U.S. announced that the dollar is no longer convertible into gold. The move followed the decline in the value of the dollar in relation to foreign currencies. The U.S. raised the value of gold to an official intergovernmental rate of $38 an ounce and then to $42.22 an ounce. There was, however, no link between the official rate and the free-market price which soared above $100 an ounce in 1973.

Wealthy individuals, speculators, hoarders and industrial users from all over the world are among the buyers of gold on the free market. Those who are buying gold think there is too much unconvertible paper money circulating and believe there must be a final reckoning in which gold can only rise in value. American corporations and individuals are specifically forbidden by law from trading or owning gold—except when the metal is used in manufacturing or medical processes. The U.S. continues to hold the world's largest stocks of gold. At the official price of $42.22 an ounce, the U.S. owns about $12 billion of gold.

gun control. As part of a crime-control program Congress, in 1963, passed a gun-control act banning mail-order interstate sales of rifles and shotguns and prohibited their sale to persons under 18. Congress did not act on Pres. Johnson's request for registration of all guns and for licensing of gun owners.

Some proponents of gun-control legislation propose more emphasis on punishment than prohibition. They cite the British law which provides for prison sentences of up to 14 years over and above the sentence for the offense itself for those convicted of possession of a firearm while committing an offense. Such laws have been experimented with in the U.S. as well. Washington, D.C. law provides for a mandatory prison sentence of at least five years over and above any other sentences for someone who has been convicted more than once of possessing a firearm during the commission of a crime.

Hall of Fame.
    1970
Albert Abraham Michelson (physicist)
Lillian D. Wald (social worker)

Hatch Acts. Under the first Hatch Act (1939) candidates for federal elective office were forbidden to accept contributions from relief workers. The second Hatch Act (1940) sought to supplement state laws by prohibiting the assessment of state and local employees for political purposes, if the employees were paid in full or in part with federal funds.

In *Civil Service Commission v. National Association of Letter Carriers* (1973) the U.S. Supreme Court, after its first reexamination of the policy in 26 years, upheld the constitutionality of the Hatch Acts and comparable state statutes which prohibit partisan political activity by federal and state government employees. The Court concluded that the limits on free speech and associations that the law imposes on civil servants were not so broad and unclear as to be unconstitutional.

More than 5.5 million public employees are forbidden to run for public or party office, solicit campaign funds, manage a campaign or solicit votes under the Hatch Acts and state laws.

Hughes hoax. Multimillionaire Howard Hughes, formerly a motion-picture producer, whose fortune is based largely on the manufacture of tools and aircraft, was the subject in 1972 of a purported biography by the writer Clifford Irving. Hughes, who shunned publicity while remaining a subject of avid media comment, denied ever having met with Irving or knowledge of the biography. The McGraw-Hill publishing company had paid Irving $750,000 as an advance for a biography of Hughes that Irving alleged was based on numerous interviews with the inaccessible Hughes. After a four-month spree of headlines, Irving admitted the hoax, pleaded guilty in federal court of conspiracy to defraud McGraw-Hill and made partial restitution of the money. He was given a prison sentence.

Hurricane Agnes. Eastern seaboard states were devastated by a June 1972 hurricane that unleashed the most extensive floods in the nation's history, causing 118 deaths and more than $3 billion in property damage. Florida, Virginia, Maryland, Pennsylvania and New York were declared "major disaster areas," making the five states eligible for federal relief and recovery aid. It was the first time that so many states were classified thus in a single day.

Hurricane Agnes was the first hurricane of 1972. The National Weather Service has been using girls' names to identify hurricanes since 1953. A semipermanent list of 10 sets of names in alphabetical order was established in 1971. The hurricane season in the U.S. begins June 1 and ends Nov. 30.

impoundment. Under the Anti-Deficiency Act (1905) Congress recognized the right of the President to withhold appropriated funds in order "to effect savings whenever savings are made possible by or through changes in requirements, greater efficiency of operations or other developments." Most Presidents have impounded money because government agencies had achieved operating economies or decided to defer spending on particular projects.

A clash developed between Congress and Pres. Nixon over the amounts of money impounded. Critics of the President charged that he had, in effect, transformed a President's managerial discretion into an absolute-item veto. In the fiscal year ended June 30, 1973, Pres. Nixon impounded $18 billion, about 7% of the total federal budget, most of it in the environmental and social welfare program.

jury trial. The U.S. Supreme Court ruled in 1970 that no one may be denied a jury trial in a prosecution that could result in more than six months' imprisonment. Also in 1970, the Court held that criminal-case juries may be of less than 12 members, upholding a conviction in a Florida court by a six-member jury.

As an outcome of the Supreme Court decisions, federal and state courts in various parts of the nation instituted trial by juries of 6 members in civil cases instead of the traditional 12. Extension of the six-member jury to some criminal cases seemed imminent.

In *Colgrove v. Battin* (1973), the Court ruled that the use of six-member juries in civil cases in federal courts did not violate constitutional and statutory guarantees of the right to fair trial.

Kent State. Four students at Kent State College (Ohio) were shot and killed on May 4, 1970, by National Guardsmen acting to quell a protest against the U.S. "incursion" into Cambodia. The soldiers, part of a 600-man contingent, had been summoned to the campus after Kent's ROTC building had been burned to the ground during two nights of disruptions.

As a reaction to the tragedy, more than 400 colleges suspended classes in the first general student strike in the nation's history. A demonstration was held in Washington, D.C. on May 9, 1970, by some 100,000, mostly young people.

Ten days after the shooting at Kent two black students were killed at Jackson State College in Mississippi. The students were part of a group facing city and state highway policemen.

Pres. Nixon appointed a Commission on Campus Unrest, headed by former Pennsylvania governor William W. Scranton. The commission found that the shootings at Kent State and Jackson State were unwarranted. As late as the summer of 1973, the Justice Department reopened the inquiry into the deaths at Kent State.

Kitty Hawk riot (1972). Racial troubles aboard the U.S. aircraft carrier *Kitty Hawk* erupted in rioting on Oct. 15 while the carrier's planes were attacking North Vietnamese targets. Blacks and whites battled for 15 hours with knives and clubs with resultant injury to 46 crew members. Earlier in the year comparable strife had broken out on another aircraft carrier, the U.S.S. *Constellation.*

A Congressional inquiry was concerned with new permissiveness in the regulations of the Navy that might have contributed to the riots. Also of concern to the Congress was the evident racial unrest which took form in the refusal of 123 blacks in Nov. 1972 to report for duty aboard the *Constellation.*

The Navy explained that the lack of education of young blacks accounted for their assignment to messes, laundries and deck duties rather than to duty with electronics or weapons systems that offer better opportunity for advancement and more pay. Black sailors countered: "The Navy gets you to join by telling you they'll teach you a trade and when you go aboard ship they hand you a 'dream sheet' (job preference request), but then they tell you that you're not qualified and you end up in the laundry or polishing brass."

Model Cities. City Demonstration Agencies, known popularly as Model Cities, under the Department of Housing and Urban Development, are part of the effort to meet the urban crisis of the 1960's and 1970's. A selected number of cities have been provided with federal funds to deal with blighted areas. Federal, state and local public and private resources are involved in the program, including residents of the designated Model Cities (inner-city slums). The programs include economic development, rehabilitation or replacement of dilapidated housing, job training and placement, improvement of health, education, recreation, crime control, welfare and other public services. As is often the case in projects of such dimensions, funding, coordination of effort and involvement of the people immediately concerned limit achievement of the recognized goals.

My Lai massacre. On Mar. 16, 1968, a U.S. Army platoon attacked the hamlet of My Lai in the South Vietnamese village of Songmy and killed men, women and children. Stories of the slaughter provoked a national and international furor.

Charges were brought against some 14 officers and enlisted men. In the ensuing court-martial proceedings (1969–71) only one man, Lt. William L. Calley, Jr., was found guilty and sentenced to life imprisonment (Mar. 31, 1971). Calley admitted shooting civilians in the hamlet, but said he had followed orders from superior officers.

The Calley case became a symbol for debating the morality of the war in Viet Nam. Some saw Calley as a "scapegoat" for higher-ups. An Army panel probing the massacre found the entire command structure of the American division guilty of misconduct. The panel concluded (June 3–4, 1972) that many high-ranking officers had learned of the massacre, which took the lives of some 300 civilians, but did nothing about it.

Pres. Nixon announced that he would personally review the Calley conviction "before any final sentence is carried out."

Nixon, Richard Milhous (1913–). Thirty-seventh President of the U.S. (1969–). He was born in Yorba Linda, Calif. Vice-President of U.S. (1953–61). He served California as a Republican member of U.S. House of Representatives (1947–51) and Senate (1951–53). He won the Republican presidential nomination in 1960 and was defeated by Democrat John F. Kennedy in a close race. In 1962 Nixon was defeated in his race for governor of California. He moved to New York City in 1963 and practiced law. He continued to campaign hard for Republicans in 1964 and 1966. He won the Republican nomination in 1968 and defeated Democrat Hubert H. Humphrey in one of the closest presidential elections ever held. In 1972 he was reelected overwhelmingly, carrying 49 of the 50 states. As President, he brought the war in Viet Nam to an end, shattered precedents by visiting mainland China, altered the Supreme Court's balance by appointing four new justices and sought to prevent major newspapers from publishing a

secret Pentagon history of the war in Viet Nam. His second administration was beclouded by the Watergate scandal.

Nixon's "Journey for Peace." After 23 years of bitter confrontation, the U.S. President visited mainland China and conferred in Peking in Feb. 1972, with Chairman Mao Tse-tung and Premier Chou En-lai. General agreement was reached on ways of avoiding war in the Pacific and the "normalization of relations" between the two countries. Plans were launched for bilateral trade, and an exchange of scientists, artists, journalists and sportsmen. In the matter of Taiwan, the People's Republic of China affirmed that Taiwan is part of China. The U.S., while not yielding its commitment to the defense of Taiwan, off the coast of Communist China, reaffirmed its ultimate objective of withdrawal of all U.S. forces.

As part of the 1972 détente with the major Communist powers, Pres. Nixon journeyed to the USSR in May 1972. It was the first time a U.S. President had visited Moscow. He conferred with Communist party General Secretary Leonid I. Brezhnev, who returned the President's visit in 1973 when meetings were held in Washington, D.C. The Moscow meeting ended with agreement on a pact aimed to end the missile race between the two great nuclear powers. Agreements were also reached on health and environmental problems, a joint space flight in 1975 and a five-year science pact. Plans were launched for an overall trade agreement.

The foreign trips by Pres. Nixon were described by him as a "Journey for Peace." Together with the agreement to end the Viet Nam war in 1973, they marked the end of the cold war.

obscenity cases. A clear, unequivocal position has not been taken by the U.S. Supreme Court in "obscenity-pornography" cases. However, Chief Justice Burger averred in *Miller v. California* (1973): "This much has been categorically settled by the Court: that obscene material is unprotected by the First Amendment."

The Court rejected the earlier *Roth* (1957) standard that for a work to be obscene it must be "utterly without redeeming social value." In *Miller* it sought for the first time "to isolate 'hard-core' pornography from expression protected by the First Amendment." Without attempting to dictate statutory language to the states, the Court observed that "Under a national constitution" there need not be "fixed, uniform national standards of precisely what appeals to the 'prurient interest' or is 'patently offensive.' It is neither realistic nor constitutionally sound to read the First Amendment as requiring that the people of Maine or Mississippi accept public depiction of conduct

found tolerable in Las Vegas or New York City."

Critics of the *Miller* decision charged that it made it virtually impossible for producers and distributors of books, national magazines and motion pictures to have any advance assurance that their products will not subject them to criminal penalties in one locality although they are unobjectionable in another.

In *Paris Adult Theater v. Slaton* (1973), the Court held that states may permit commercialized obscenity if they wish but that they have the right to conclude that that obscene material encourages crime and antisocial behavior. It decided that obscenity is not protected by the constitutional doctrine of privacy and that its limitation is not "thought control." Chief Justice Burger observed: "Conduct or depiction of conduct that the state police power can prohibit on a public street does not become automatically protected by the Constitution merely because the conduct is moved to a bar or a 'live' theater stage, any more than a 'live' performance of a man and woman locked in a sexual embrace at high noon in Times Square is protected by the Constitution because they simultaneously engaged in a valid political dialogue."

Okinawa. A major military base for the U.S. in the western Pacific for 26 years after the end of World War II, Okinawa, along with 72 tiny islands in the Ryukyu chain, were returned to Japan. Under the U.S.-Japan treaty, ratified by the Senate in 1971, Okinawa continues to be a link in the U.S. defense chain from Alaska to Thailand. Nuclear weapons are banned from the islands.

Omnibus Crime Control Act (1970). Several anticrime bills were incorporated into one package. It permitted the FBI to investigate campus bombings and widen federal authority over illicit transportation of explosives. This provision was in response to Pres. Nixon's call for "urgently needed powers to control the epidemic of terrorist bombings and nihilist destruction which has suddenly become a feature of American life. . . ." The Act made it a federal crime to kill, kidnap, assault or attack a member of Congress or a member-elect; permitted the government to appeal all rulings in criminal cases except acquittals; made it a federal crime to enter a place where the President was residing or visiting in order to attack him, deface property, attack anyone else or impede others from entering or leaving.

The Act also provided that persons using or unlawfully carrying guns during commission of a federal crime could receive 1 to 10 years in prison for the first offense and 2 to 25 years for the second in addition to punishment for the crime itself.

The Safe Streets Act (1970) extended an existing law for three years with $3.55 billion for law enforcement grants to the states and localities.

open enrollment. As part of the effort to achieve greater integration of schools stemming from the *Brown* decision (1954), some school districts in the nation provide for the voluntary transfer of black children to predominantly white schools.

In practice, open enrollment programs usually give students who live near a school the right to attend it and admit "outsiders" only if there are still vacancies. Where the program exists, only 5% to 15% of black parents usually exercise the right to leave the neighborhood school, even when transportation is free and places are available.

parochial school aid. Some 80% of the five million non-public-school students in the U.S. attend Catholic institutions. Catholic school officials report a variety of reasons for nationwide troubles in parochial schools. They cite inflation, rising teachers' salaries and a decline in the number of brothers and nuns in religious orders. They attribute decreased enrollments to rising tuition, a declining birth rate and changing values.

Parochial schools obtain government financial assistance for nonreligious books, pupil transportation, student health and remedial programs. Efforts to

759

obtain additional money received sharp blows from the U.S. Supreme Court in 1973. The Court struck down aid programs in New York and Pennsylvania.

In *Committee for Public Education and Religious Liberty v. Nyquist*, the Court declared unconstitutional, because of its interference with the separation of church and state, a 1972 New York law. It had provided direct grants to private schools for maintenance and repair, tuition reimbursement for parents of private-school pupils and tax credits for those parents who did not qualify for tuition reimbursement.

In *Levitt v. Committee for Public Education and Religious Liberty*, the Court affirmed a lower-court decision declaring unconstitutional a 1970 New York program for reimbursing private schools for testing and record-keeping expenses.

In *Sloan v. Lemon*, the Court invalidated a Pennsylvania law that provided for reimbursement of a share of tuition paid by parents who send their children to private schools.

Also in 1973, but on a more promising note, the Court in *Hunt v. McNair* upheld a South Carolina law that authorizes state bond issues to help private colleges and universities build facilities. Although some of the institutions are controlled by religious sects, the Court justified the bond issues on the grounds that it is basically a secular aid program.

Pentagon papers. Classified as "top secret" by the Department of Defense, the papers are the department's own study of U.S. involvement in the Viet Nam war. Parts of the study were copied and made public by Daniel Ellsberg, a department analyst, who made them available to *The New York Times*. Publication by the *Times* began on June 13, 1971.

The Department of Justice, contending that national security was endangered, brought suit in federal court to prevent continued publication. The *Times*, momentarily prevented from continuing publication, defended its right to publish the papers on 1st Amendment grounds. The government failed in its suit. Parts of the study were published not only in the *Times*, but in other papers and in book form.

Ellsberg freely admitted copying the papers without authorization. He held that the parts that he had released should never have been stamped secret in the first place. Publication, he said, was his personal effort to end the war by informing Congress and the people of their own government's actions.

A federal grand jury in Los Angeles indicted Ellsberg and Anthony J. Russo, Jr., who had assisted him. They were charged with espionage, theft and conspiracy. The case was dismissed in May 1973. U.S. District Court Judge William M. Byrne found that "bizarre events have incurably infected the prosecution of this case." He was referring to burglary of the office of Ellsberg's psychiatrist by persons in the pay of the White House.

Release of the papers and the trial were subjects of worldwide interest involving U.S. conduct of the Viet Nam war. Related issues included controversy over the government's classification of documents, the clash of government and press over national security versus 1st Amendment rights and the inability of the government to prosecute successfully persons who had admittedly stolen secret papers.

Phases 1-4. Pres. Nixon imposed price and wage controls on a peacetime economy in a historic move taken on Aug. 15, 1971. The 90-day freeze on all wages and prices (only raw agricultural products were exempted) soon came to be called "Phase 1," as Phases 2, 3 and 4 unfolded in the following two years.

Phase 2 was introduced Nov. 14, 1971. It established an elaborate system of wage and price controls to limit wage increases to 5.5% a year and to keep inflation at an annual rate of 2% to 3%. A Cost of Living Council, under the Economic Stabilization Act of 1970, set policy and coordinated the controls program.

On Jan. 11, 1973, Pres. Nixon announced Phase 3, a program of quasi-voluntary restraints on wages and prices. Controls were largely self-administered by labor and management. During the five months of Phase 3 prices advanced at an annual rate of about 9%.

On June 13, 1973, Pres. Nixon was impelled by rising prices to institute Phase 4, a new 60-day price freeze. Wages and raw agricultural prices were exempted from the new freeze. The objective was to "spread out the bulge" by slowing price rises. Nevertheless, food prices rose sharply and beef shortages developed quickly. Retailers, generally, were permitted to pass along the higher costs of goods they bought, but they could add no more than their usual markup. Large companies had to justify any price increases.

Through it all, Pres. Nixon affirmed his deep philosophical opposition to controls, but urged a policy of patience. By April 1974, when federal controls were scheduled to expire, Phase 4 had been transformed into "Phase Out" as one economic sector after another was released from rigid wage/price controls.

Philadelphia Plan. The plan which got under way in Philadelphia in 1970 requires companies that bid on federal construction contracts to promise to hire specific numbers of workers from minority groups. The constitutionality of the federally approved program was upheld by the U.S. Supreme Court in 1971.

The plan is part of an "affirmative action" hiring program

stemming from Executive Order 11246 which was signed by Pres. Johnson in 1965, pursuant to the Civil Rights Act of 1964. Although the word "minority" is not used in either the Act or Executive Order, the Department of Labor has defined minority to mean "Negro, Oriental, American and Spanish Surnamed American."

The principle of the Philadelphia Plan has been extended to colleges and universities by the Office of Civil Rights of the Department of Health, Education, and Welfare. As a condition of retaining federal grants, institutions of higher learning are required to undertake by "some form of positive action" the recruitment of women and minorities.

"Affirmative action" is criticized as discrimination in reverse by those who regard it as a quota system favoring unqualified people who are poor, or black, or disadvantaged in some way, over qualified people who are not.

Pledge of Allegiance. As set forth in the U.S. Code, the present form of the salute to the flag is: "I pledge allegiance to the flag of the United States of America and to the Republic for which it stands, one Nation under God, indivisible, with liberty and justice for all." The words "under God" were added in 1957 by an act of Congress.

The Pledge was first published in an issue of a Boston weekly magazine, the *Youth's*

Companion (Sept. 8, 1892). Controversy over authorship was resolved by the Library of Congress in a report (1957) which attributed the Pledge to Francis Bellamy, a Baptist minister. He wrote it to be used at the Chicago World's Fair in Oct. 1892, on the 400th anniversary of the discovery of America.

The Pledge became a nationally accepted symbol of patriotism. Refusal of some to salute the flag reached the U.S. Supreme Court in the "Flag Salute" Cases of the early 1940's. Controversy flamed anew in the late 1960's when some public-school children refused to salute the flag.

The U.S. Second Circuit Court of Appeals, in *Goetz v. Ansell* (1973), upheld the right of a high school student to remain quietly seated and not participate in the Pledge. In upholding the student's 1st Amendment rights, the Court stated: "If the state cannot compel participation in the pledge . . . it cannot punish nonparticipation . . . and being required to leave the classroom . . . may reasonably be viewed as having that effect."

"plumbers." Established in 1971 as a Special Investigations Unit within the White House, the so-called plumbers sought to stop national security leaks.

One unsuccessful mission, connected with the Pentagon papers, was publicized widely during the Watergate hearings. The "plumbers" failed to uncover anything when they burglarized the office of Daniel Ellsberg's psychiatrist. The burglary was planned by G. Gordon Liddy and E. Howard Hunt, Jr., both of whom were subsequently found guilty of the break-in of Democratic national headquarters.

Post Office Department. After almost two centuries, Congress relinquished its grip on the postal service. The department was reorganized as an independent agency within the executive branch. The newly created U.S. Postal Service, inaugurated on July 1, 1971, is headed by an 11-member board of governors, including a Postmaster General who is no longer a member of the President's cabinet. A Postal Rate Commission recommends rate increases. The Postal Service is expected to be self-supporting.

POWs and MIAs. Prisoners of war (POWs) and the missing in action (MIAs) ranked high in the agreement which ended the Viet Nam war. Among the 587 U.S. troops captured in Indo China, many had been imprisoned for four to seven years. The total MIAs were estimated at 1,335 by the Defense Department.

Arrangements for the prisoner exchange were described by Henry Kissinger, the principal American negotiator, as "one of the thorniest issues" in the peace negotiations. The compromise provided for release of POWs "simultaneously with" the "total withdrawal from South Vietnam of troops." The release was to match the pace of withdrawal.

Efforts to locate MIAs included questioning of returned POWs and inspection of grave sites by neutral observers.

revenue sharing. The State and Local Assistance Act of 1972 provided for a total of $30.2 billion to be distributed among state and local governments over a five-year period. The basic idea behind the revenue-sharing legislation was to help state and local governments finance public services with federal money, on the theory that the federal government can raise money more easily than state and local governments. One-third of the money went to states and two-thirds to local governments.

The Act contains no restrictions on the purposes for which state allocations may be used. It does, however, require local governments to use their share of the money to attack problems in several broadly defined "priority" areas: public safety, environmental protection, public transportation, health, recreation, libraries and social services for the poor and aged.

The complex formulas that Congress devised for distributing the money were intended to give relatively more of the revenue-sharing funds to low-income areas than to high-income sections.

All of the money was to

come on top of various other funds that state and local governments receive from the federal government under an array of aid programs.

rock music. Rock music began in the mid-1950's. The expectation that it would be short-lived is denied by its development during the 1960's and 1970's. At first a hybrid of blues and country-Western, rock became a school of music that incorporates widely ranging styles, including the electronic sound and "noise collages" that can be deafening to the uninitiated.

Rock lyrics often consist of social comment—war protest, overdue social justice. The words reflect disenchantment with much of the traditional in society. Rock has been described as a "music of revolt even if that revolt is frequently patternless and inchoate." Together, rock music and lyrics form a major cultural phenomenon.

The music of young people, increasingly enjoyed by the not-so-young, rock stirs active participation. But, it remains disquieting to the many unreceptive who link it to the life-style of rock groups and audiences— the hair, costumes, volume, sexual "liberation" and drugs.

Rock lyricists, singers and instrumentalists include Chuck Berry, Ray Charles, Elvis Presley, Bob Dylan, The Beatles, Mick Jagger and The Rolling Stones. They have been part of a billion-dollar a year industry built on performances and recordings.

Major rock festivals in which up to 600,000 young people gathered in one place at one time include Woodstock (N.Y., 1969) and Watkins Glen (N.Y., 1973). Undaunted by the incredible crowding and physical discomforts, they came because it was "the place to be" and "where it's at."

SALT Talks. The U.S. and USSR began Strategic Arms Limitation Talks (SALT) in Helsinki, Finland, in 1970. In over a hundred sessions, held at various times and places, the gamut of arms limitations proposals was considered. As an outcome of the talks, the Senate ratified strategic arms treaties in 1972 that placed on each of the powers a limit of two anti-ballistic missile (ABMs) sites, limited land-based and submarine-borne nuclear forces, and froze offensive nuclear missiles at current levels for five years. The accords were first steps in an attempt to defuse the threat of nuclear war and decrease the defense costs of both nations.

searches and seizures. The 4th Amendment prohibition of "unreasonable searches and seizures" has given rise to controversy over the degree to which the prohibition has been interpreted by the courts to favor criminals.

In *Mapp v. Ohio* (1960) the U.S. Supreme Court ruled out

evidence obtained by police officers who broke into an apartment without a valid search warrant after the occupant refused to admit them. The Court held that searches and seizures valid under the 4th Amendment must comply with one of three prerequisites: a valid search warrant, grant of permission to search or a search incident to a legal arrest.

Chief Justice Warren Burger in 1971 called upon Congress to enact a law to stop setting guilty criminals free because police erred in their method of obtaining evidence. He observed that a 1914 Supreme Court ruling—extended to state courts in 1961—holding that evidence obtained by improper search should be suppressed had "never really worked" and has cost "a monstrous price."

The Court itself has become more realistic. In *Terry v. Ohio* (1968) the U.S. Supreme Court upheld the "stop-and-frisk" rule under which policemen have the right to stop and frisk persons for weapons when such action seems necessary for the safety of policemen and others present.

In *Cupp v. Murphy* (1973) the Court made it clear that reasonable and limited intrusions on the privacy of the accused will not be adjudged as violative of the 4th Amendment prohibition against searches and seizures. The defendant in this case was convicted of strangling his wife. Part of the evidence against him—fingernail scrapings—was taken from him without a warrant. The lower courts would have required the officers to secure a search warrant to take this evidence.

Under the *Cupp* ruling police do not now have to risk destruction of evidence for the purpose of adhering to technical search warrant rules.

shield laws. Twenty-four states have laws which afford newsmen some measure of immunity from the duty to testify, mostly by giving them the right not to disclose the identities of confidential sources.

In the *Caldwell* Case (1972) the U.S. Supreme Court ruled that the 1st Amendment does not give journalists the right to conceal the identity of their sources from a grand jury. Earl Caldwell, and another reporter, had gained access to the inner workings of the revolutionary Black Panther party. The party, which originated in Oakland, California, in 1966, draws its membership from among black youths in big-city slums.

Justice Byron R. White, in requiring reporters to give their sources, wrote for the 5-4 majority: "We cannot accept the argument that the public interest in possible future news about crime from undisclosed, unverified sources must take precedence over the public interest in prosecuting those crimes reported to the press by informants. . . ."

Caldwell stated that his extensive coverage of the Black Panthers (about 2,000 members in 38 chapters) came to an end the day the subpoena ordering him to produce documents, tapes and notes was issued because of the Panthers' fear that he would become an unwilling agent of the government. Caldwell refused to honor the subpoena.

Dissenters in the *Caldwell* Case argued that the Court "invites state and Federal authorities to undermine the historic independence of the press by attempting to annex the journalistic profession as an investigative arm of Government. . . ."

skyjacking. Airline hijacking in the U.S. became a major menace to airline safety in the late 1960's. In the years 1968–72, inclusive, there were 147 skyjacking attempts of which 91 were successful. A peak period was reached in 1969. The loss of life, damage to property and freight, and ransoms paid by airlines of up to $2 million caused the Nixon administration in 1972 to impose the strongest antiskyjacking security system in the history of commercial aviation.

Security was tightened at every one of the nation's 531 airports serving scheduled air carriers. The new orders also applied to boarding procedures on U.S. airlines at foreign airports. The new orders required screening before boarding of all passengers by metal-detecting devices, inspection of all carry-on items that would be accessible to passengers during the flight and stationing of armed local law enforcement officers at all passenger checkpoints. The U.S. also sought to negotiate with Cuba and other countries for the return of skyjackers to the U.S. for trial and for sanctions by other countries against skyjackers.

Skylab. The forerunner of a permanent space station, the 85-ton Skylab, launched unmanned in 1973, orbits the earth at an altitude of about 270 miles. Three astronauts, within two days of the launching, rode a modified Apollo ship to the Skylab and occupied the laboratory for 28 days, conducting medical, solar astronomy, earth resources and other studies.

The National Aeronautics and Space Administration (NASA) intends to use the space station for solution of problems closer to earth (*e.g.*, weather forecasting). With its sensing equipment, the orbiting laboratories can locate schools of fish, distinguish between diseased and healthy crops, locate mineral deposits, detect dumping of manufacturing wastes, measure soil fertility and predict crop yields.

Another three-man crew orbited to Skylab and remained aloft for 84 days, returning to earth in February 1974. This was man's longest voyage in space, again without any apparent serious effects from prolonged weightlessness.

Soviet grain deal. In 1972 the USSR anticipated a disastrous grain harvest that would necessitate huge purchases abroad. Soviet traders came to the U.S. and quietly purchased 11 million tons of wheat—a quarter of the U.S. crop—from about six grain companies at prices that did not reflect the real supply-demand situation. After the Soviet purchases of over $1 billion had been made, financed by a U.S. credit of $750 million, U.S. wheat prices rose over 50%.

At the time of the Soviet purchases the Department of Agriculture, acting as though there were a U.S. grain surplus, supported the low export price with $300 million in export subsidies.

The effect of the huge purchases was to leave the U.S. with a tight supply situation in wheat and feed grains and resultant price increases on food items from bread to beef.

A Congressional investigation of the grain deal was undertaken.

Students for a Democratic Society (SDS). The organization came into existence in 1962 when young members of the old Socialist League for Industrial Democracy quit the parent group and set up their own unit, SDS. Deriving its membership largely from alienated youth on college campuses, SDS opposed the Viet Nam war. It charged the universities with subservience to the "corporate military elite."

From the first, SDS had little control over its campus chapters. A major rift took place in 1969 when a revolutionary faction, the Weathermen, bombed public buildings as part of its world revolution program. It derived its name from Bob Dylan's song, "Subterranean Homesick Blues": "You don't need a weatherman to know which way the wind blows."

By the early 1970's SDS had virtually disappeared from U.S. college campuses.

Tinker v. Des Moines Independent Community School District (1969). The U.S. Supreme Court ruled that Iowa public-school officials had violated the 1st Amendment rights of the Tinker children who were attending the public elementary and high schools by suspending them from school for wearing black armbands to protest the Viet Nam war. The Court majority saw the armbands as an exercise of free speech and did not discern any immediate threat to conduct in the schools. The Court, however, affirmed "the comprehensive authority of the States and of school officials, consistent with fundamental constitutional safeguards, to prescribe and control conduct in the schools."

Trident. The name given to a new generation of missile-launching submarines and to the missile itself. Trident is planned as a replacement for Polaris and Poseidon missile-launching submarines expected to remain operational into the

767

1980's. Trident missiles with their longer range of 4,000 nautical miles are expected to increase the operating area of submarines, thus making them less vulnerable to detection by enemy forces.

urban crisis. Violence in the cities peaked in 1968 following the assassination of the Rev. Dr. Martin Luther King, Jr. In the rioting 43 were killed, 3,500 injured and 27,000 arrested, according to records kept by the Center for the Study of Urban Violence at Brandeis University (Waltham, Mass.).

In 1968 Pres. Johnson appointed Dr. Milton Eisenhower to head the National Commission on the Causes and Prevention of Violence. It reported that "violence is gnawing at the vitals of urban America" and that crime would turn the cities into armed camps "in a few years" unless the nation changed its priorities and embarked on a massive spending program ranging from improving local law enforcement to cleaning up the slums.

Another Johnson presidential commission, headed by Otto Kerner, The National Advisory Commission on Civil Disorders, stated in a supplementary report in 1971 that if present trends continued in inner-city racial problems, "most cities by 1980 will be predominantly black and brown and totally bankrupt."

The Watergate. The name of a complex of hotels and offices in Washington, D.C., is given to the scandal which rocked the second Nixon administration.

On June 17, 1972, five men were arrested in the Democratic National Headquarters in the Watergate. The five and two others who helped plan the break-in were in the pay of the Committee for Re-Election of the President. The seven stood trial in the U.S. District Court for the District of Columbia and were found guilty (Jan. 30, 1973) of conspiracy, burglary and eavesdropping. They testified that they had been motivated to break the law by considerations of national security.

Pres. Nixon denied prior knowledge of the break-in and attempts to cover it up.

Stemming from Watergate were Senate, House and grand jury inquiries into a range of possible crimes connected with the President's reelection. Former Attorney General John N. Mitchell described the campaign tactics as "White House horrors." They included bugging of "enemy" offices, burglary, plans to use call girls to compromise Democratic convention delegates, fraudulent leaflets, harassment of speakers and, in general, sabotage of political opponents. Mitchell absolved the President of any direct involvement in illegal campaign activities.

Especially extensive hearings on Watergate and the campaign were conducted by the Senate Select Committee on Presidential Campaign Activities, headed by Sen. Sam J. Ervin, Jr. (Dem., N.C.). A controversy over efforts by the committee and special Watergate prosecutor Archibald Cox to obtain presidential tapes and other papers bearing upon Watergate led to the dismissal of Cox by the President. Attorney General Elliot L. Richardson resigned in protest.

Following the departures of Cox and Richardson, the President changed his mind and agreed to obey a federal court order to turn the tapes over to Judge John J. Sirica of the U.S. District Court. In so doing, Pres. Nixon sought to make it clear that he did not place himself above the law. Editorial calls for the President's resignation brought a firm response from the President who reiterated his determination to serve out the term of office to which he had been elected. The House Judiciary Committee, in Nov. 1973, proceeded with an investigation of grounds for the President's impeachment.

Watergate thus came to encompass not only the break-in of June 17, 1972, but a range of issues including the privacy of presidential papers, confidence in the electoral process and the degree to which wiretaps and other types of surveillance were being abused in the interests of national security.

wiretapping. It was brought out at the Senate Watergate hearings in 1973 that nearly all of Pres. Nixon's official meetings and telephone conversations had been recorded secretly. The President, before discontinuing the practice, explained that the use of recording devices was for historic purposes.

The U.S. Secret Service, which had installed the listening devices, made it known that similar work had been done for Pres. Johnson and Pres. Kennedy. Tape recordings of these Presidents are preserved among their private papers for scholarly use.

The making of such recordings is not illegal. The U.S. Code (Title 18, Section 2511) provides that "it shall not be unlawful for a person not acting under color of law to intercept a wire or oral communication where such person is a party to the communication or where one of the parties to the communication has not given prior consent."

A small attachment with a suction cup allows a tape machine to record from a telephone receiver without the "beep" signal every 15 seconds required by the Federal Communications Commission and the tariff schedules of all U.S. telephone companies.

A key factor in the growing use of wiretapping is the passage by Congress in 1968 of a statute permitting electronic surveillance against specified crimes, such as gambling and bribery attempts. Until 1968 the "taint" of bugging to obtain evidence was often enough for federal judges to dismiss a case. However, wiretapping with advance judicial approval has been authorized in the U.S. since 1942 when a New York State law first permitted it.

women's liberation. The unfinished business of the women's rights movement of the 19th century and first decades of the 20th century is being carried on in the 1960's and 1970's. It has given rise to a new term in the English language, *women's lib*. The new feminists aim for complete legal emancipation, elimination of all forms of sex discrimination in employment, politics and home life.

The largest of the women's lib organizations is NOW (National Organization for Women), formed in 1966 by Betty Friedan, author of *The Feminine Mystique* (1963). The main points in its program are enforcement of equal pay and opportunity for working women at all levels, child care for all mothers desiring it and free abortions for all women on request.

MAPS

—

INDEX

LIST OF MAPS

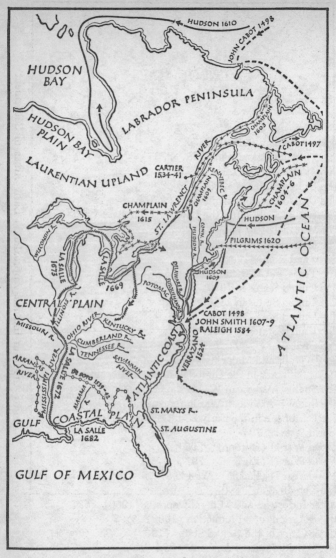

The Discovery of America. Explorations of Eastern North America

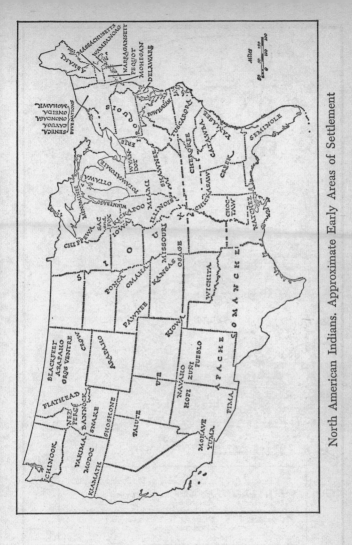

North American Indians. Approximate Early Areas of Settlement

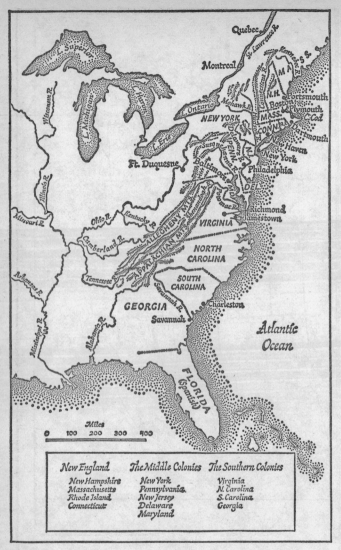

The Thirteen Colonies in 1775. Major cities and natural boundaries are noted

The American Revolution. Major military movements and places of conflict are noted

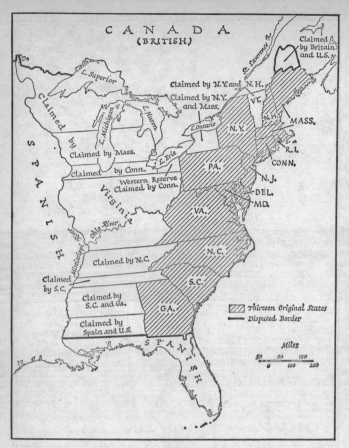

The United States in 1783. Boundaries after the Treaty of Paris. The growth of the United States can be seen by comparison with the map of the Thirteen Colonies

The United States Early in 1803. The Northwest Territory was created by the Ordinance of 1785. Dates of cessions are given

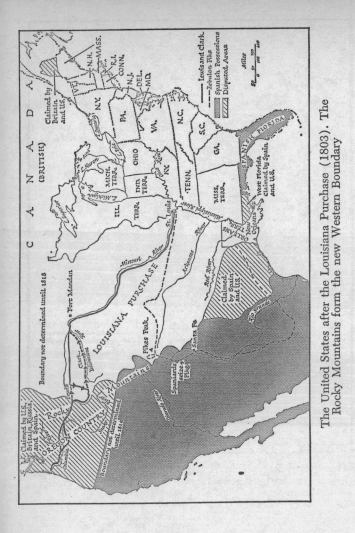

The United States after the Louisiana Purchase (1803). The Rocky Mountains form the new Western Boundary

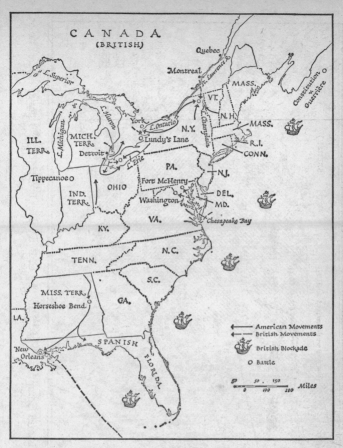

The War of 1812. The Major Battles are indicated. The battle of New Orleans actually took place two weeks after the war was officially over

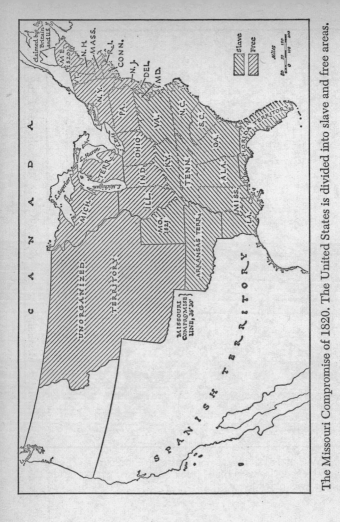

The Missouri Compromise of 1820. The United States is divided into slave and free areas.

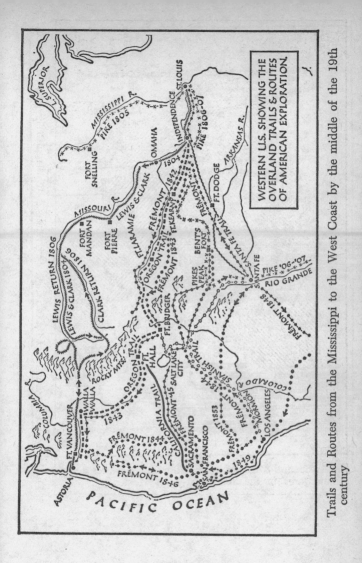

Trails and Routes from the Mississippi to the West Coast by the middle of the 19th century

The Texas and Mexican Wars. The United States acquires a major area of the Southwest from Mexico.

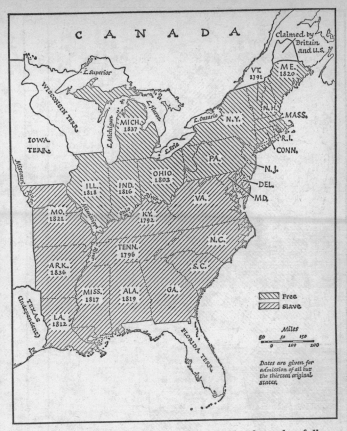

The United States in 1840. This map and the three that follow show the growth of the nation and the division into slave and free areas

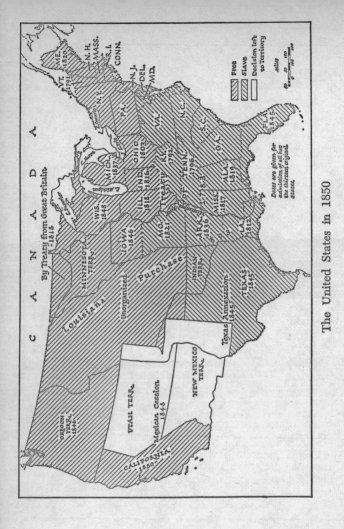

The United States in 1850

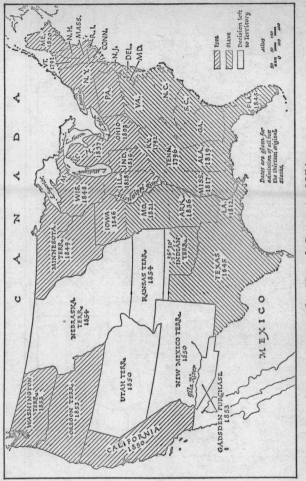

The United States in 1854

Free
Slave
Decision left to territory

Miles
50 0 50 100 150 200

Dates are given for admission of all but the thirteen original States.

CANADA

MEXICO

WASHINGTON TERR. 1853

OREGON TERR. 1853

CALIFORNIA 1850

UTAH TERR. 1850

NEW MEXICO TERR. 1850

GADSDEN PURCHASE 1853

Gila River

NEBRASKA TERR. 1854

KANSAS TERR. 1854

INDIAN TERR.

36°30'

TEXAS 1845

MINNESOTA TERR. 1849

IOWA 1846

MO. 1821

ARK. 1836

LA. 1812

WIS. 1848

ILL. 1818

IND. 1816

OHIO 1803

KY. 1792

TENN. 1796

MISS. 1817

ALA. 1819

GA.

FLA. 1845

S.C.

N.C.

VA.

PA.

N.Y.

N.J.

DEL.

MD.

CONN.

R.I.

MASS.

N.H.

ME. 1820

VT. 1791

MICH. 1837

L. Michigan

L. Huron

L. Ontario

L. Erie

Mississippi River

787

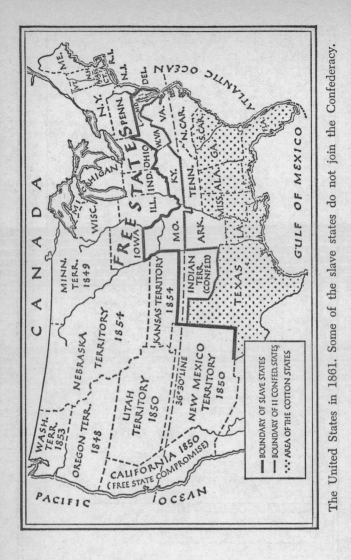

The United States in 1861. Some of the slave states do not join the Confederacy.

788

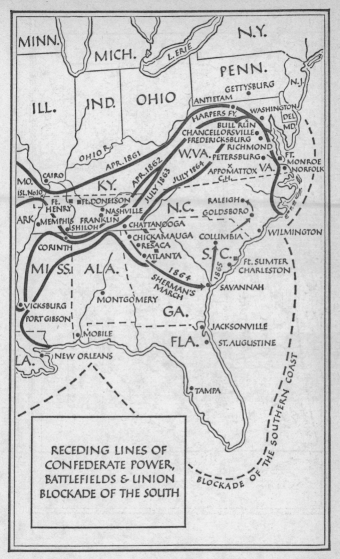

The Civil War. The North advances further into the South
each year of the war. Major areas of conflict are noted

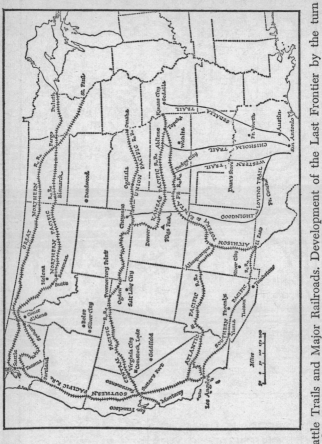

Cattle Trails and Major Railroads. Development of the Last Frontier by the turn of the Century

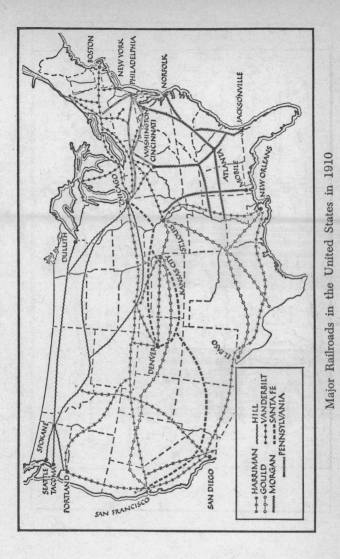

Major Railroads in the United States in 1910

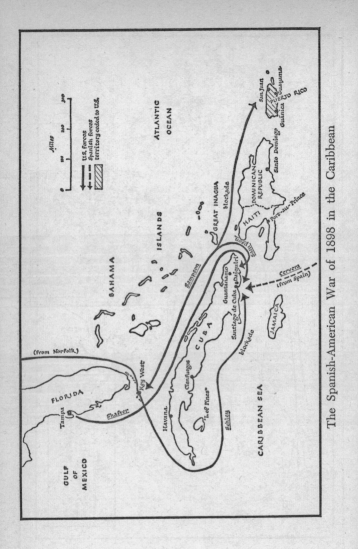

The Spanish-American War of 1898 in the Caribbean

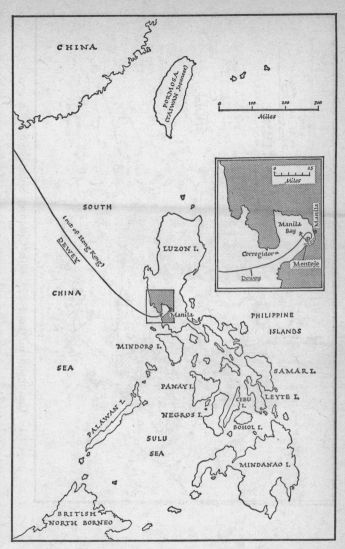

The Spanish-American War of 1898 in the Pacific

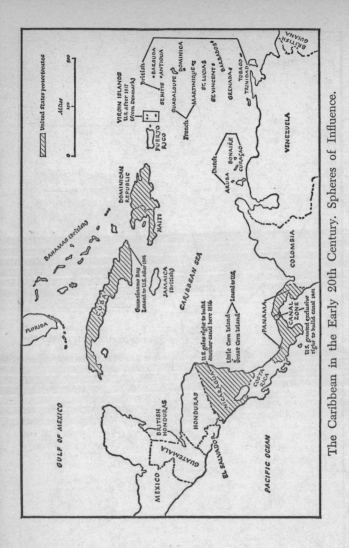

The Caribbean in the Early 20th Century. Spheres of Influence.

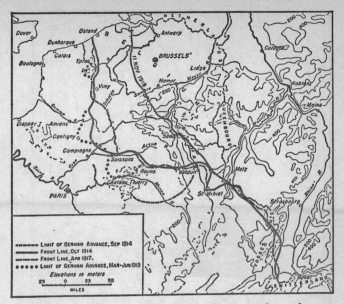

World War I. The Western Front. The Front lines do not change rapidly until after the United States entry into the war in 1917

The maps of World War I and II and the Korean War are reproduced from a publication of the U.S. Government Printing Office, Washington, D.C. The maps are part of the volume *American Military History, 1607–1958* issued as a Department of the Army ROTC Manual (July 1959)

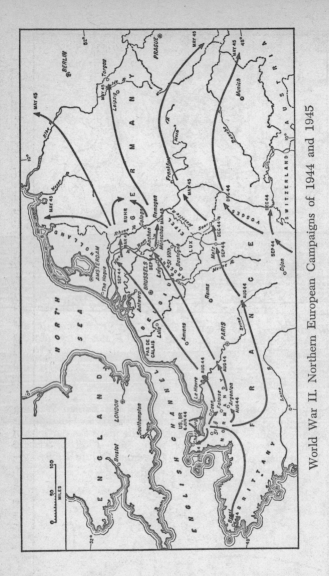

World War II. Northern European Campaigns of 1944 and 1945

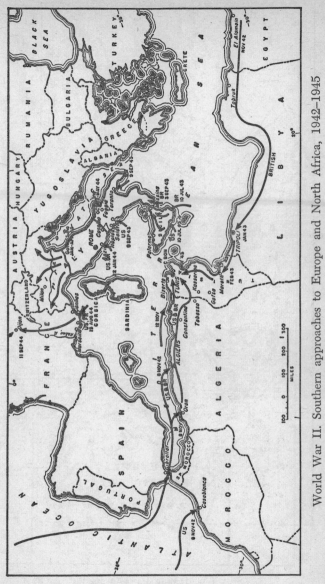

World War II. Southern approaches to Europe and North Africa, 1942–1945

World War II. The Pacific. Areas in which

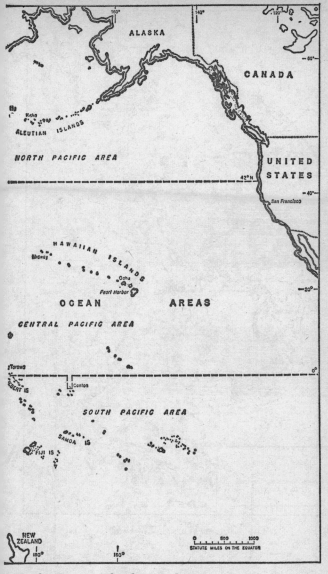

major battles were fought are shown.

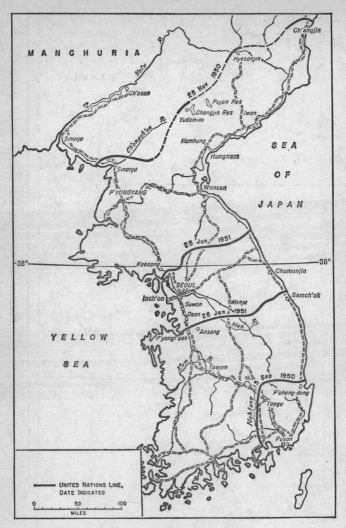

The Korean War, 1950–1951

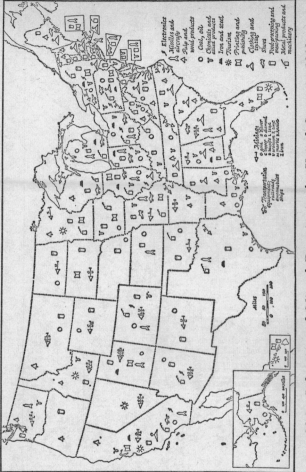

Major Industries and Mineral Deposits in the United States in 1960

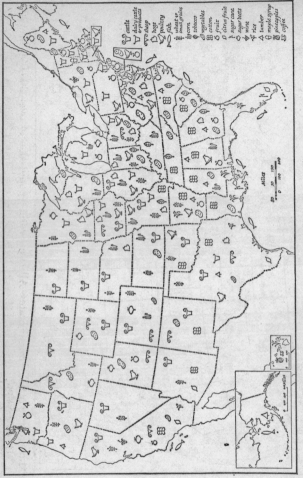

cattle
dairy cattle
& products
sheep
hogs
poultry
fish
wheat &
small grains
corn
tobacco
vegetables
cotton
fruit
citrus fruit
sugar cane
sugar beets
wine
rice
lumber
maple syrup
pineapples
coffee

MILES
0   50   100   150   200

Major Agricultural Production in 1960

802

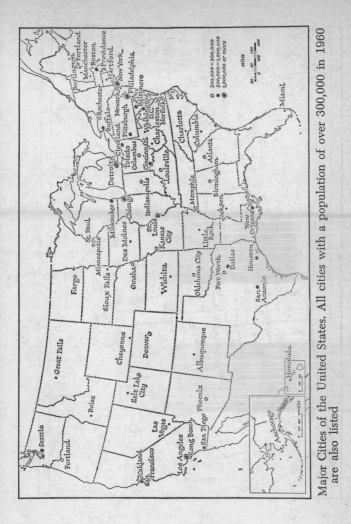

Major Cities of the United States. All cities with a population of over 300,000 in 1960 are also listed

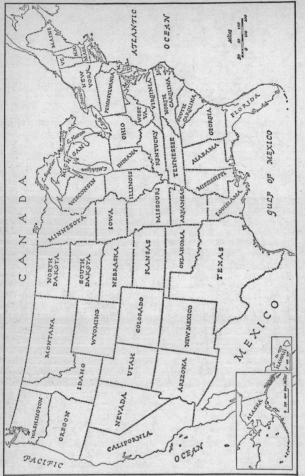

The United States of America

INDEX

Page references refer only to the initial appearance of the subject within each item. Boldface numbers indicate a main entry.

American Expeditionary Force, 9, 60, 382, 522, 724

American Express Co., 663

American Farm Bureau Federation, 164

American Federation of Labor, 25, 26, 74, 131, 177, 393, 419, 673

American Federation of Labor and Congress of Industrial Organizations, 25, 131

American Fur Co., 670

American High School Today, The, 128

American Historical Association, 26

American Home, 423

American Hospital Association, 334

American Institute of Public Opinion, 279

American Interplanetary Society, 293

"Americanism," 719

American Joint Distribution Committee, 364

American Journalism, 482

American Journal of Education, 55

American Journal of Science, 421

American Labor party, 26, 394

American Language, The, 437

American Law Journal, 421

American League, 56

American Legion, 27, 29, 30

American Liberty League, 27

American Library Association, 397

American Magazine, 197, 421, 460

American Magazine and Historical Chronicle, 421

American Medical Association, 27

American Mercury, 437

American Missionary Society, 129

American party, Election of, *see* year of election (*e.g.,* "Election of 1920")

American Philosophical Society, 27, 267

American Protective Association, 27

American Railway Express Co., 563

American Railway Union, 180, 554

American Revolution, 4, 28, 42, 53, 160, 305, 411, 494; *map,* 777; *see also* "Revolutionary War"

American Revolution, The, 256

American rifle, *see* "long rifle"

American Rocket Society, 293

"American Scholar, The," 233

American Society of Composers, Authors, and Publishers, *see* "ASCAP"

American Speaking Telephone Co., 29, 112

American Sugar Refining Co., 608, 637

American system, 28, 116, 351

American Telephone and Telegraph Co., 29

American Third party, 227

American Tobacco Co. v. U.S., 29, 202, 316

American Tragedy, An, 200

American Turtle, 637

American Veterans Committee, 29

American Veterans of World War II and Korea, 30

Ames, Oakes, 169

Ames Ring, 577

Amherst, Jeffrey, 272, 657

Amherst College, 30

Amish, 437

Amistad Case, 30

Amnesty Act, 30

Among My Books, 411

Amos v. U.S., 17

Amsterdam, Fort, 204

Amtrak, 742

Amundsen, Roald, 494

AMVETS, *see* "American Veterans of World War II and Korea"

Anaconda Copper, 30

"anaconda" plan, 30, 277

"Anacreon in Heaven," 629

Ananias Club, 31

Anarchiad, The, 319

anarchism, 31
Anatomy of Science, The, 393
Ancient Order of Hibernians, 451
Ancient Society, 455
Anderson, Carl David, **31**
Anderson, Marian, 472
Anderson, Maxwell, 655
Anderson, Sherwood, 32, 437
Anderson v. Dunn, 32
Andersonville, 32
André, John, 41, 446
Andrew Jackson, 118
Andrews, Samuel, 626
Andrews, Thomas Coleman, 227
Andros, Edmund, 102, 195, 430, 432, 477
Angela Davis case, 742
Anglican Church, *see* "Episcopal Church, Protestant"
"Annabel Lee," 531
Anna Christie, 501
"Annals of Congress," 570
Annapolis, *see* "United States Naval Academy"
Annapolis Convention, 32, 135, 460
Annapolis Royal, 537
Annie Get Your Gun, 62
Antarctic, 87
Antarctica Treaty, 32
Anthony, Susan B., 33, 628, 720
Anthracite Coal Strike, 33, 673
anti-ballistic missiles, 764
Anti-Deficiency Act (1905), 754
Antietam, battle of, 33
Anti-Federalists, 33, 189, 209; *see also* "Democratic-Republican party"
Anti-Fusion party, *see* "Populist party"
Anti-Masonic party, 34, 212, 213, 430, 709; Election of, *see* year of election (*e.g.,* "Election of 1832")
Antinomian controversy, 34, 39
Antirent War, 35
Anti-Saloon League, 549
antislavery movement: Abolition, 2; Adams, John Quincy,

499; Barnburners, 55; Beecher, Henry Ward, 59; *Biglow Papers,* 64; "Bleeding Kansas," 70; Civil War, 113; "gag rule," 278; Garrison, William Lloyd, 280; "higher law," 327; Howe, Samuel Gridley, 336; Liberty party, 213, 214; Stephens, Thaddeus, 633; Sumner, Charles, 638; underground railroad, 670; Vermont, 682; Woolman, John, 721; *see also* "slavery"
antitrust, *see* "Capper-Volstead Act"; "Clayton Antitrust Act"; "Esch-Cummins Transportation Act"; "Gentlemen's Agreement"; "Justice, Department of"; "McGuire Act"; "Miller-Tydings Act"; "monopolies"; "Sherman Antitrust Act"; "Temporary National Economic Committee"
ANZUS Pact, 35
AP, *see* "Associated Press"
Apache, 35, 38, 527
Apache Canyon, 293
Apollo Project, 35, 352, 412, 593
"Apostle of Unitarianism," 101
Appalachia Aid, 36
Appalachian Mountains, 36, **71**, 173, 547
Appalachian Spring, 164
Appeals, U.S. Courts of, 36, 193
Appomattox Courthouse, 36, 115, 301, 391
Apprentices' Library Association, 397
aquanauts, 598
ARA, *see* "Area Redevelopment Act"
Arabic incident, 37
Arapaho, 37, 121, 307, 591
Arbeiter-Zeitung, 323
Arbella, 37
Arbor Day, 37
Arbuthnot, Alexander, 601
Arcas, 619
Archangel intervention, 37
"Archie Bunkerism," **743**
architecture, 82

Archives, National, **37**
Arctic, 87
Ardennes, battle of, 306
Area Redevelopment Act, **37**
Argentina; ABC conference, 1
Argo, 619
Argonne Forest, 440
Ariel I, **37**
Arizona, **37**
Arkansas, 38
"Arkansas Traveler," 38
Arlington National Cemetery, 38, 373
Armed Forces of the United States, 9, 107, 144, 186, 349, 674; *see also* by name (*e.g.*, "Women's Army Corps"; "World War I"; "World War II")
Armed Forces Policy Council, 9
Arm-in-Arm Convention, 468
Arminianism, 39
Arminius, Jacobus, 39
Armistice (Nov. 11, 1918), **39**
arms, bearing of, 16
Arms Control and Disarmament Agency, U.S., **39**
arms limitations, 764
Armstrong, Edwin Howard, **40**
Armstrong, John, 474
Armstrong, Louis, 360
Armstrong, Neil A., 36
Army, Confederate, **40**; *see* "Civil War" listing for battles, etc.
Army, Continental, *see* "Continental army"
Army, Department of the, **40**
Army, Union, **40**; *see* "Civil War" listing for battles, etc.
Army Corps of Engineers, 46
Army of Northern Virginia, 245
Army of the Potomac, 41, 101, 268, 519, 713
Arnold, Benedict, 41, 372, 505
Arnold's treason, 41
Aroostook "War" (1839), **42**
Arrangement in Gray and Black, 711
Arrival of the Magi, The, 382
Arrowsmith, 424

"arsenal of democracy," **42**, 392, 726
Art, National Gallery of, **42**
Art as Experience, 190
Arthur, Chester Alan, 42, 544; elections of 1880 and 1884, 218
Arthur, Timothy Shay, 648
Articles of Confederation, 16, 28, 32, 42, 103, 135, 160, 170, 359, 368, 543, 573, 631
"Articles of War," 589
Arts of Life in America, The, 61
ASCAP, 43
Asbury, Francis, 439
"As goes Maine, so goes the Union," 43
Ashburton, Lord, 704
Ashkenazim, 363
Ashley, William Henry, 43
assembly line, *see* "mass production"
Assiento (1713), 43
Associated Community Teams, 320
Associated Press, 44, 356, 673
Assumption Act, 313
Astor, John Jacob, 44, 502
Astor, Mrs. John Jacob, 265
Astoria, 44, 502
Astor Library, 398
Astor Place riot, 44, 264
astronauts, *see* "space projects" and project by name (*e.g.*, "Apollo Project")
Astronomy for Everybody, 475
Asunción, Juan de la, 266
A.T.&T., *see* "American Telephone and Telegraph Company"
Atchison, Topeka & Sante Fe Railroad, 44
Atlanta, 702
Atlanta Constitution, 44, 318
Atlanta Journal, 44
Atlanta Journal Constitution, 44
Atlantic, battle of, 726
Atlantic and Pacific Railroad, 652
Atlantic and Pacific Tea Company, 100

810

Atlantic Cable, 44, 163
Atlantic Charter, 45, 580, 673
Atlantic Coast Line Railroad, 45
Atlantic Monthly, 64, 330, 336, 411, 422
"Atlantic Wall," 180
Atlas, 45, 99
Atlas-Agena B., 45
atom bomb, 45, 127, 128, 208, 252, 329, 388, 502, 561, 648, 665, 690, 726
Atomic Energy Act of 1946, 46, 249
Atomic Energy Commission, 46, 502
"atoms for peace" plan, 47
Atsina, 307
Attica prison rebellion (1971), 743
Attlee, Clement R., 539
Attorney General, *see* "Justice, Department of"
Attorney General's list of subversive organizations, 47
Audubon, John J., 47, 48, 205
Audubon Societies, 47
Aunt Jo's Scrap-Bag, 13
Aurora, 48
Austin, Stephen Fuller, 48, 234, 651
Australia, 35
Austrian Succession, War of the, 10, 376
Autobiography, by Benjamin Franklin, 268
Autobiography, by Anna E. Roosevelt, 579
Autocrat at the Breakfast Table, The, 330
automation, 48
automobiles, 262, 283, 374, 432, 747, 749
"Autumn Woods," 81
AVC, *see* "American Veterans Committee"
AVF, 746
Avon, 702
Awake, 361
Awake and Sing, 495
"Away Down South," 264
Axis powers, 65, 95

B

Babbitt, 49, 424
Babcock, Orville B., 711
Babson, Roger Q., 225
Bache, Benjamin Franklin, 48
Backus, Isaac, 54
Bacon, Nathaniel, 49
"Bacon's Laws," 49
Bacon's Rebellion, 49
"Badger State," 717
Badlands National Monument, 49
Badlands of South Dakota, 49
Baekeland, Leo Hendrik, 50
Baer, George F., 33
Baffin's land, 273
Baghdad Pact, *see* "Central Treaty Organization"
Bagot, Charles, 585
Bahamas, 23
bail, excessive, 18
Bailey, Gamaliel, 523
Bailey, James Anthony, 55
Bailey, Thomas A., 62
Bailey v. Drexel Furniture Co., 50
Baker, Edward D., 51
Baker, George, *see* "Father Divine"
Baker, Wharton, 221
Baker v. Carr, 565
balance of trade, 50, 438, 748
Balboa, Vasco Nunez de, 23
Ballads and Other Poems, by Henry Wadsworth Longfellow, 406
Ballinger, Richard A., 51
Ballinger-Pinchot controversy, 50
Ballistic Missile Early Warning System, 51
Ball's Bluff, battle of, 51
Baltimore, Lord, *see* "Calvert, George"; "Calvert, Cecilius"
Baltimore & Ohio Railroad, 51, 163, 660
Baltimore Sun, 437, 481
Bambino, the, *see* "Ruth, George Herman"
Bancroft, George, 52, 674
Bank for International Settlements, 737

813

Boot Hill, Arizona, 660
Booth's Theatre, 72
bootleggers, 550
Bootstrap, Operation, 553
Borah, William Edgar, 72, 354
"Border Ruffians," 73, 606, 693
Border States, 70, 73
Border War, 73
Borgne, Lake, battle of, 73
Borman, Frank, 282
boss, political, 73, 667; *see also* "Tammany"
"Boss" Platt, *see* "Platt, Thomas Collier"
Boston Gazette, 675
Boston Journeymen Bootmakers Society, 125
Boston Massacre, 74
Boston News-Letter, The, 74, 480
Boston police strike, 74, 162
Boston Port Bill, 74
Boston Post Road, 539
Boston Public Library, 397
Boston Tea Party, 75, 119, 499
Boston Theater, 654
Boston Whig, 4
Botanical Text-Book, 301
Boulder Canyon Project Act, 332
Boulder Dam, 552
bounties, 41, 75, 199
Bouresches, battle of, 60
Bowditch, Nathaniel, 75
Bowery, 637
Bowie, James, 11, 76
Bowie, Rezin P., 76
bowie knife, 76
Boxer Rebellion, 76, 501
boycott, 176
Boyd, Alan S., 663
Boy Scouts of America, 76
Boy's Will, A, 274
Bozeman, John M., 76
Bozeman Trail, 76
braceros, 76
Brackenridge, Hugh Henry, 528
Braddock, Edward, 272
Bradford, Andrew, 421
Bradford, John, 374
Bradford, William, 77, 526, 653
Bradley, Omar, 246

Bradstreet, Anne Dudley, 77
Bragg, Braxton, 407, 447, 461
Bragg, Thomas, 106
"Brain Trust," 77
Brandeis, Louis Dembitz, 77, 93; *Abrams v. U.S.*, 2; *Gitlow v. New York*, 291; *Muller v. Oregon*, 77; *Other People's Money*, 505; *West Coast Hotel Company v. Parrish*, 706
Brandeis University, 768
Brando, Marlon, 59
Brandywine Creek, battle of, 78
Brannan, Charles, 78
Brannan Plan, 78
Brant, Joseph, 104
Bray, Thomas, 396
Brazil: ABC conference, 1; America, discovery of, 23; Rio Pact, 577
bread colonies, 78
Bread Riots, 78
Breckinridge, John C., 215
Breed's Hill, 84, 196
Bremer, Arthur, 750
Brennan, William J., 446, 547
Brest-Litovsk, Treaty of, 39
Bretton Woods Conference, 78
Breuckelen, *see* "Brooklyn, New York"
Brezhnev, Leonid I., 757
Briand, Aristide, 371
Brice's Cross Roads, 308
Bricker, John W., 78, 226
Bricker Amendment, 78, 655
Bridge, The, 585
Bridge of San Luis Rey, The, 612
Bridger, Fort, 78, 504
Bridger, James, 78
British East India Company, 75, 376
British Expeditionary Force, 100
British Prison Ship: A Poem, The, 273
British West Indies, 451, 665
Broadway (N.Y.C.), 655
Broadway Journal, 531
Broken Blossoms, 306
"broken" voyages, 240
Bronco Buster, 571

815

"Butcher" Weyler, 735
Butler, Andrew P., 638
Butler, Benjamin F., 86, 218, 480
Butler, Elizur, 722
Butler, John, 104, 729
Butler, Nicholas Murray, 5, 86, 122
Butler, Pierce, 706
Butler Ring, 577
Butler's General Order No. 28, 86
Butler's Rangers, 729
Butte, Mont., 30
Butterfield, John R., 506
Butternuts, 86, 164
Buxton, C. Lee, 547
Byrd, Harry F., 227, 228
Byrd, Richard Evelyn, 86
Byrd, William, II, 396, 529
Byrne, William M., 760
Byrnes, James F., 207, 696

Calley, William L., 756
Call It Sleep, 90
Call Me Madam, 62
Call of the Wild, The, 404
Calvert, Cecilius, 659
Calvert, George, 96, 429
Calvert, Leonard, 429
Calvin, John, 90, 556
Calvinism, 90, 101, 129
Cambodia, 685, 755
Cambridge agreement, 91
Cambridge Platform, 129, 595
Camden, battle of, 91
Camden and Amboy line, 168
camels, 91
Camera Work, 633
Camino Real, 716
Campaign of, *see* "Election of" by year of election
campaigning by civil service workers, 753
Campbell, Alexander, 109
Campbell, Thomas, 109
Camp Charlotte, Treaty of, 531
Camp O'Donnell, 57
Campus Unrest, Commission on, 755
Canada: Alaskan boundary dispute, 11; Aroostook "war," 42; Bering Sea dispute, 61; *Caroline* affair, 94; defense forces, 490; fishery dispute, 57; power blackout, 492; satellite launched, 15; St. Lawrence Seaway, 588; Sault-Ste. Marie Ship Canal, 594; War of 1812, 697; Webster - Ashburton Treaty, 704; Welland Canal, 594
Canadian-U.S. Eastern interconnection, 492
"Canal Ring," 658
canal (Panama) tolls controversy, 91
Canal Zone, *see* "Panama Canal"
Canby, Edward R. S., 450, 568
Cannery Row, 301
Cannon, Joseph Gurney ("Uncle Joe"), 490, 498, 575
Cantigny, Americans attack at, 92

819

820

laws, 364; King, Martin Luther, Jr., 375; *Plessy v. Ferguson,* 81; segregation, 600; Selma, Ala., 601; Southern Christian Leadership Conference, 621; Student Nonviolent Coordinating Committee, 636; "We Shall Overcome," 705; *see also* "Negro in America"

eral Departments and branches of the Armed Forces by name; various laws and acts by name (*e.g.*, "Hill-Burton Act"); Supreme Court cases involving laws of Congress

De Berry, Clifton, 228
De Bow's Review, 442
Debs, In re, 180
debtor laws, 180
Decatur, Stephen, 181, 201, 506
"Decius" letter, 564
Decker, Ruthford B., 228
Declaration and Resolves, 181
Declaration of Independence, 28, 124, 181, 182 (text), 236, 345, 361, 469
Declaration of Independence for Women, 719
Declaration of Paris (1856), 271
Declaration of Rights (1776), 429
Declaration of Rights and Grievances (1765), 186
Declaratory Act, 186
Decoration Day, 186
Deere, John, 8
Deerslayer, The, 389
Defense, Department of, 9, 40, 47, 88, 107, 186, 470, 521
Defense Production Act of 1950, 350
De Forest, Lee, 186
Deganawidah, 353
deism, 187
de Kalb, Johann, 91
de Lauzon, Jean, 167
Delaware, 187
Delaware and Hudson Canal Company, 635
Delaware Indians, 187, 293, 404, 604, 694
Delaware Valley, 349
De la Warr, Lord, 187
DeLeon, Daniel, 616
DeLima v. Bidwell, 349
De Lôme Letter, 188, 622
Delta, 188
De Mille, Agnes, 203
De Mille, Cecil B., 458
democracy, world made safe for, 188; types of, 661
Democracy and Education, 190
Democracy in America, 188
Democratic party, 188, 233, 575; Butternuts, 86; Civil War, 164; conventions, 248;

Copperheads, 164; Dixie-crats, 194; Election of, *see* year of election (*e.g.,* "Election of 1836"); factions in New York, 55, 316, 339; Freedom Democrats, 269; Free Soil party, 271; Locofocos, 402; origins, 34; Pewter Muggers, 523; Softs, 617; Solid South, 618; *see also* "Tammany"
Democratic-Republican party, 34, 55, 98, 103, 189, 210, 212, 467; *see also* "Democratic party," "Election of," *see* year of election (*e.g.,* "Election of 1804")
Democratic Review, 424
Democratic Vistas, 390, 712
demonitization of silver, *see* "Crime of 1873"
Denby, Edwin, 646
Denney, Reuel, 405
Dennis et al. v. U.S., 267, 615
Denver, Colo., 121
Denver & Rio Grande Western, 706
Departments, federal, 88; *see also* departments by name (*e.g.,* "Agriculture," "Army," "Commerce," etc.)
deposit, right of, 189, 527
depression, 86, 120, 275; *see also* "Great Depression"
desegregation, *see* "segregation"
Deseret, 190, 677
"Desert Dwellers," 347
Desert Land Act, 190
Desert Song, 314
Desire Under the Elms, 501
De Smet, Pierre Jean, 258
de Soto, Hernando or Fernando, 10, 23, 38, 104, 132, 190, 409, 447, 491, 649
De Soto expedition, 190
détente with China and Russia, 757
de Tocqueville, Alexis, 188
Detroit riot, 408
devaluation, *see* "dollar devaluation"
"Devil Dogs," 60
De Vries, David Pietersen, 630

Dewey, George, 425, 524, 566, 623
Dewey, John, 190
Dewey, Melvil, 397
Dewey, Thomas E., 225, 226, 280
DeWitt Clinton, 450
DEW Line, 191
De Young, Charles, 591
De Young, Michael H., 591
Dial, The, 275, 662
Díaz, Porfirio, 702
Dickinson, Charles, 201
Dickinson, Emily Elizabeth, **191**
Dickinson, John, 186, **191**, 392, 499, 675
Dien Bien Phu, 684
Dies, Martin, 669
Diesel, Rudolph, 191
Diesel locomotives, 191
Digger Indians, 191
Dillingham, William P., 233
Dillon, John A., 588
dime novels, 192, 486
Dingley Tariff of 1897, **192**
direct election, 20
direct primary, **192**
direct tax, 20
disability of President, *see* "Twenty-fifth Amendment"
disarmament, 39, 701
disaster areas, *see* "Hurricane Agnes"
Disciples of Christ, 108
Discourse of Davila, 193
Discourse on the Constitution and Government of the United States, 89
Discourse on the History, Character, and Prospects of the West, 192
Discoverer I, 193
Discovery, 593
Discovery Day, *see* "Columbus Day"
Discovery of America, The, 256
Discovery of the Great West, The, 515
discrimination, 751, 752, 761, 770
Displaced Persons Act, 193
Disquisition on Government, 89

distant early warning line, *see* "DEW Line"
District Courts, U.S., 193
District of Columbia, 5, 21, 36, 700
Divine Comedy of Dante Alighieri, The, trans. by Henry Wadsworth Longfellow, 406
Dix, Dorothea Lynde, 193
Dixie, 194
"Dixie," 194
Dixiecrats, 194, 226, 227
Dixon, Jeremiah, 430
Dixon, Thomas, Jr., 306
Dixwell, John, 570
Doan's Store, 706
Dobbs, Farrell, 226, 227, 228
Dock Street playhouse, 654
Dodge City, Kan., 194, 660, 706
Dodsworth, 424
Doe v. Bolton, 741
Does Civilization Need Religion?, 487
Doheny, Edward F., 646
dollar devaluation, 747
"Dollar Diplomacy," 81, **194**, 486
dollar sign ($), 194
domestic system, 347
Dominican Republic, 65, 194, 195, 366, 580
Dominion of New England, 102, 195
domino theory, 195
Donelson, Andrew J., 377
Donelson, Fort, capture of, **196**, 325
Dongan, Thomas, 102, 196
Dongan Charters, 196
Donnelly, Ignatius, 500
Donner party, 196
"Don't fire till you see the white of their eyes," 196
"Don't give up the ship," 196
"Don't tread on me," 196
Dooley, Mr., 196, 522
"Doomsday" statistics, 197
Dorchester, 265
Dorchester Company, 197
Dorr, Thomas Wilson, 197
Dorr's Rebellion, 197
Dos Passos, John, 197

Emergency Management, Office of, 699
Emergency Quota Act, 233, 467
Emerson, Ralph Waldo, 101, 128, 233, 275, 365, 609, 656, 662
Emigrants, The, 571
eminent domain, 234
Emma and Her Children, 61
Emmett, Daniel D., 194
Emperor Jones, The, 501
"empire builder," 328
"Empire State," 483
"Empire State of the South," 286
Employers' Union, 454
Employment Act (1946), 206, 234
empresario system, 234
Empress of China, 234
enabling acts, 234
encomiendas, 234
Enderbury island, *see* "Canton and Enderbury islands"
energy crisis, 751
Engels, Friedrich, 126
Engel v. Vitale, 64
English, William H., 218
English Classical School, 327
English High School, 327
English Novel, The, 387
Enlightenment, American, 235
entail, 235
"entangling alliances," 236
Enterprise, 552
enumerated articles, 236
enumerated powers, 236
"enumeration. . . . of certain rights," 18
Environmental Survey Satellite, 239
Ephrata Cloister, 237
EPIC, 605
Epic of America, The, 25
"Epic of Wheat," 489
Episcopal Church, Protestant, 237; Anglican in Colonial Period, 195, 526
e pluribus unum, 237, 598
"equal but separate," 530
Equal Employment Opportunity Commission (EEOC), 751

"Equality State," 729
"equal protection," 565
Equal Rights Amendment, 751-52
Equal Rights party, 237
"Equilibrium of Heterogeneous Substances, On the," 290
environmental movement, 751
"Era of Good Feelings," 238, 452
Erdman Act, 3, 734
Ericsson, John, 238
Ericsson, Leif, 23, 686
Erie, Lake, battle of, 238
Erie Canal, 51, 117, 238, 351
Erie Railroad, 238
Eros, 582
Ervin, Sam J., Jr., 769
Escalante, Juan de, 677
"escalator clause" in London Naval Treaty of 1930, 405
"escape clause," 566
Esch-Cummins Transportation Act, 239
Escobedo v. Illinois, 239
Eskimo (Esquimaux) 12, 273
Espionage Act (1917), 239, 595, 600
ESSA, 239
Essays (Emerson), 233
Essays to do Good, 432
Essex, U. S. frigate, 240
Essex, case of the, 240
Essex Junto, 240, 319
"establishment clause," *see* "First Amendment"
Estelle T. Griswold v. Connecticut, 546
"Etiology of Deficiency Diseases, The," 276
European Defense Community, 240
European Recovery Program, *see* "Marshall Plan"
"Eutaw Springs," 273
Eutaw Springs, battle of, 240
Evangelical Church, 241, 672
Evangelical United Brethern Church, 240
Evangeline, 3, 406
evangelism, 54, 241
Evans, George Henry, 722
Evans, Oliver, 259, 348

lin Blockade, 63; Black Tom explosion, 68; Dawes Plan, 179; General Aniline and Film Corporation seizure, 282; *Lusitania*, sinking of, 660; reparations, 571; submarine controversy, 188; *Sussex* pledge, 640; Venezula Debt Controversy, 681; Versailles, Treaty of, 682; Zimmerman Note, 739; *see also* "World War I"; "World War II"

Geronimo, 35

Gerry, Elbridge, 211, 287, 731

gerrymander, 287

Gershwin, George, 287

Gershwin, Ira, 288

Gettysburg, battle of, 288, 525

Gettysburg Address, 288, 399

Ghent, Treaty of, 162, 288, 479, 698

ghost dance, 289

Gibbons, James, 289, 703

Gibbons, Thomas, 289

Gibbons v. Ogden, 289, 402, 427

Gibbs, Josiah Willard, 289

GI Bill of Rights (Servicemen's Readjustment Act of 1944), 27, 290

Gideon, Clarence Earl, 290

Gideon v. Wainwright, 290

Gila Trail, 290

Gilbert's patent, 290

Gilded Age, 117, 291

Gilded Age, The, 117, 291

Gillhaus, August, 222

Gilman, Daniel Coit, 291

Ginzburg Case, 581

Girl Crazy, 288

Girl Scouts of the U.S.A., 291

GI's, 290

Gist, Christopher, 496

Gitlow, Benjamin, 291

Gitlow v. New York, 291

"Git thar fustest with the mostest," 292

"Give me eighty men and I'll ride through the whole Sioux nation," 252

"give me liberty or give me death," 292, 326

Gladiator, The, 264

glass, 292, 382

Glass Menagerie, The, 716

Glass-Owen Currency Act of 1913, 251

Glass-Steagall Banking Act, 292, 338

Glazer, Nathan, 405

Glendale, battle of, 268

Glenn, John H., 93, 439

Glidden, Carlos, 668

Glidden, Joseph F., 55

Glimpses of the Cosmos, 695

Glorieta, battle of, 293

Glorious Revolution, 195

Gnadenhutten, 293

Goddard, Robert H., 293

Goddard's rockets, 293

Godey, Louis, 293

Godey's Lady's Book, 293, 422

Godfrey, Thomas, 654

Godkin, Edwin Lawrence, 294, 463

"God Save the King," 22

Goethals, George Washington, 294, 510

Goetz v. Ansell, 762

Goffe, William, 570

gold: attempt to corner (1869), 66; Black Hills, discovery of gold in, 174, 620; California gold rush, 90, 264, 295, 708; Colorado, discovery in, 121; Colville and Coeur d'Alene discovery, 729; "cross of gold" speech, 171; "fifty-niners," 253; "forty-niners," 264, 296; Gold Clause Cases, 294; Gold Reserve Act of 1934, 295; hard money, 316; Klondike gold rush, 11, 296, 378; Orofino, 341; Panic of 1893, 513; Pikes Peak, 105; Sutter's Mill, 640; Tombstone strike, 660; Virginia City, Mont., 76; *see also* "bimetallism"; "free silver"

Goldberg, Arthur J., 238, 547

"Gold Bug, The," 531

gold bullion standard, 295, 296

"gold clause," 296

Gold Clause Cases, 294

Golden Boy, 495

Golden Hill riot, 294

Golden Hind, 290, 294, 519
"Golden State," 90
"Golden Twenties," 295
Goldfine, Bernard, 295
Goldfine scandal, 295
Goldman, Emma, 31
Gold Reserve Act of 1934, 295
gold rush, 11, 296, 378
gold standard, 65, 171, 295, 296, 404, 747, 753
Gold Standard Act of 1900, 296
Goldwater, Barry, 228, 243, 352, 711
Goldwyn, Samuel, 458
Goliad, massacre at, 296
Gompers, Samuel, 25, 296
Gone With the Wind, 297, 459
Goode, Alexander, 265
Good Housekeeping, 423
"Good Neighbor" policy, 122, 172, 297, 580
Goodnight, Charles, 297
Goodnight-Loving Trail, 297
Goodrich, Samuel, 322
Goodspeed, 593
good works, 91
Goodyear, Charles, 298, 348
GOP, 298
"Gopher State," 444
Gorgas, William Crawford, 298, 510
Gorges, Ferdinando, 424, 477
Gosnold, Bartholomew, 92
Gottman, Jean, 436
Gould, Jay, 61, 66, 238, 253, 378
Government Printing Office, 118, 124
Governor's Island, N.Y., 298
"Go west, young man, go west," 298, 304
grade school, *see* "elementary school"
Grady, Henry W., 44
Graham, Martha, 203
Graham, William Franklin (Billy), 241
Graham's, 422
Graham's Lady's and Gentleman's Magazine, 531
grain elevators, 298
Grain Futures Act, 299

grammar school, *see* "elementary school"
Grand Alliance, 299
Grand Army of the Republic, 186, 299
Grand Banks, 299
Grand Canyon, 299, 736
Grand Canyon National Park, 299
Grand Canyon of Yellowstone, 736
"Grand Canyon State," 37
Grand Coulee system, 699
grandfather clause, 299
Grand Jury, 17, 202
Grand Model, 619
"Grand movement," 41
"Grand Old Party," *see* "GOP"
Grand Portage, 300
Granger Cases, 300, 461
Grangers, 164, 247, 300
Granite Railway (Mass.), 300
"Granite State," 477
Gran Quivira, 300
Grant, Ulysses Simpson, 301; Appomattox Courthouse, 36; Army, Union, 41; Belknap scandal, 60; Black Friday, 67; Bloody Angle, battle of, 71; Cold Harbor, battle of, 120; Crédit Mobilier, 169; Donelson, Fort, capture of, 196; Elections of 1868, 1872, 1876, and 1880, 216, 217, 218; "fight it out on this line . . . ," 254; Force Act, 262; Henry, Fort, capture of, 325; Ku Klux Klan, 380; Lee, overcome, 391; Legal Tender Cases, 391; Liberal Republican party, 394; Lookout Mountain, battle of, 407; Memoirs, 441; Mexican War, 441; Missionary Ridge, battle of, 447; Mississippi, push down the, 115; Modoc War, 450; Murfreesboro, battle of, 461; Petersburg, siege of, 523; Salary Grab Act, 589; Santo Domingo, 195; Shiloh, battle of, 608; "Unconditional Surrender," 196; Vicksburg, battle of, 683; Whiskey

843

Greenville, Treaty of, 187, 246, 306, 441
"Greenway Court," 244
Greenwich House, 338
Greif, Operation, 306
Grenville, George, 306, 626
Grenville program, 306
Greysolon, Daniel (Sieur Du Lhut), 167
gridiron plan, 110
Gridley, Jeremy, 421
Grierson, Benjamin H., 306
Grierson's Raid, 306
Griffin, Fort, 706
Griffith, David L. W., 66, 306
gringo, 306
Grinnell, George Bird, 48
Grissom, Virgil I., 282
Griswold, Estelle T., 546
Groseilliers, Sieur de, 167, 337, 444
Gros Ventres Indians, 306
Groves, Leslie R., 46
Grundy, Felix, 696
"grunt," 746
Guadalcanal, battle of, 307
Guadalupe-Hidalgo, Treaty of, 38, 121, 307, 441
Guam, 307
Guerrière, 158, 401, 498
guerrilla warfare, 9, 640, 684
Guggenheim, Daniel, 307
Guggenheim, Meyer, 307
Guilford Courthouse, battle of, 308
Guinn v. U.S., 300
Guiteau, Charles J., 280
gunboat system, 308
gun control, 753
Guntown, battle of, 308
Gustavus Adolphus, King of Sweden, 640

H

Haas, Eric, 227, 228
habeas corpus, writ of, 2, 309, 414
Hague, Frank, 74
Hague Conference, *see* "Hague Tribunal (Permanent Court of International Justice)"
Hague Peace Conference, Second, 199

Hague Tribunal (Permanent Court of International Justice), 57, 256, 309, 681, 723
Haight-Asbury, 748
"Hail Columbia," 309
"hair buyer," 310
Hairy Ape, The, 501
Haiti, intervention in, 310
Hale, John P., 214
Hale, Nathan, execution of, 310
Hale, Sarah Josepha, 293
"Halfbreeds," 310, 626
Half-Century of Conflict, A, 515
Half Moon, 310
Half-way Covenant, 310
Hall, Charles Martin, 15
Hall, Fort, 504
Hall, John Elihu, 421
Hall, Joseph, 528
Hall, Samuel R., 489
Halleck, Henry Wager, 41, 254, 520
Hallidie, Andrew S., 635
Hallinan, Vincent, 227
Hall of Fame, 311, 753
"halls of Montezuma," 441
Halsey, William F. ("Bull"), 394
Hamblen, Stuart, 227
Hamilton, Alexander, 32, 53, 85, 135, 172, 188, 201, 209, 248, 250, 265, 281, 313, 361, 548, 574, 677, 710
Hamilton, Andrew, 739
Hamilton's Financial Plans, 313
Hamlet (MacDowell), 417
Hamlet, James, 85, 314
Hamlet, The, 248
Hamlet Case, 314
Hammerstein, Oscar, 2nd, 314
Hammer v. Dagenhart, 314
Hammond, James Henry, 376
Hampton Roads, 451
Hampton Roads Conference, 314
Hancock, John, 182, 209, 315, 431, 574
Hancock, Winfield Scott, 218
Hand, Learned, 315
"hands-off" policy, 58
Hanford Engineer Works, 46
Hanly, J. Frank, 222

Hanna, Marcus Alonzo, 220, 221, **315**, 418
Hannibal, Hamlin, 215
Happy Marriage, The, 419
"Happy Warrior," **315**
Harding, Warren Gamaliel, **316**; "dark horse," 177; death, 74; Election of 1920, 223; Fordney-McCumber Tariff Act of 1922, 263; "return to normalcy," 573; Teapot Dome scandal, 646
Hard Labor, Treaty of, **316**
hard money, **316**, 573
"Hards," **316**
"Hard Shells," 54
Harkness, Stephen V., 626
Harlan, John Marshall (1833–1911), **316**, 530, 565
Harlan, John Marshall (1899–): *Miranda v. Arizona,* 446; *Reynolds v. Sims,* 565
Harlem, battle of, **316**
Harlem race riots, **317**
Harlem Youth Opportunities Unlimited, 320
Harmony Society, **317**
Harper, William Rainey, **317**
Harpers Ferry, **317**, 365
Harper's Weekly, 233, 331, 422, 463, 596, 667
Harp Weaver and Other Poems, The, 443
Harrigan and Hart, 445
Harriman, Edward Henry, 328, 492, 493, 621, 671
Harris, Benjamin, 551
Harris, Joel Chandler, **318**
Harris, Townsend, 318
Harris, William T., 375
Harrison, Benjamin, **318**; Coeur d'Alene strikes, 119; conservation, 133; Elections of 1888 and 1892, 219; Electoral College, 229; Forest Reserve Act, 263; McKinley Tariff of 1890, 418; Murchison letter, 461; quarantine, 558
Harrison, Ross Granville, **318**
Harrison, William Henry, **318**, 710; Anti-Masonic party candidate, 34; Elections of 1836 and 1840, 213; Electoral Col-

lege, 229; Harrison Land Act, 319; Lake Erie, battle of, 237; Thames, battle of, 653; Tippecanoe, battle of, 606, 658; "Tippecanoe and Tyler Too!," 659
Harrison Land Act, **319**, 385
Hart, Schaffner, and Marx, 328
Harte, Bret, *see* Harte, Francis Brett
Harte, Francis Brett, **319**
Hartford Convention, 240, 250, 319, 631, 697
Hartford Society for the Improvement of Common Schools, 552
"Hartford (or Connecticut) Wits," **319**
Hartley, Fred A., 642
Harvard, John, 320
Harvard Classics, 232
"Harvard of the West," 628
Harvard University, **319**, 334
Harvey, William H., 119, 224
Haryou-Act board, 320
Hasty Pudding, 319
Hat Act, **320**
Hatch Act (1887), **320**
Hatch Act (1939), **753**
hatchet, burying the, 320
Hatfields and McCoys, **320**
"hat in the ring," 321
Hauptmann, Bruno, 400
Haven's End, 388
Hawaii, **321**; controversy over statehood, 12
Hawaii v. Mankichi, 350
"Hawkeye State," 352
Hawkins, Sir John, 597
"hawks," 199
Hawley-Smoot Tariff Act of 1930, **322**
Hawthorne, Nathaniel, 79, 128, 322
Hay, John Milton, 76, 322, 501, 577, 623
Hay-Bunau-Varilla Treaty, **322**, 323, 510
Hayburn's Case, 323
Hayes, Rutherford B., **323**; civil service reform, 626; Election of 1876, 217; Electoral College, 229; "Half-

847

IGY, see "International Geophysical Year"
"I had rather be right than be President," 342
"I have not yet begun to fight!" 342, 367
ILGWU, see "International Ladies Garment Workers Union"
Illinois, 342
Illinois Central Railroad, 342
"imagist" verse, 540
immigration: Chinese Exclusion Act, 107; contract labor law, 161; Displaced Persons Act, 193; Emergency Quota Act, 233, 468; Gentleman's Agreement, 285; Immigration Act of 1965, 342; Jewish, 363; Literacy Test Act, 400; McCarran-Walter Act, 415; "melting pot," 436; National Origins Act, 193, 285, 342, 467; Naturalization Act, 468; population growth caused by, 536; Refugee Relief Act (1953), 569; Scotch-Irish, 597; Swiss, 641; symbol, 632; see also "population"
Immigration Act of 1924, see "National Origins Act"
Immigration Act of 1965, 342, 415
Immigration and Nationality Act (1952), see "McCarran-Walter Act"
Imigration Quota Act of 1924, see "National Origins Act"
impeachment of President Andrew Johnson, 241, 343
impeachment trial, Chase, 103
Impending Crisis of the South: How to Meet It, 324
Imperial Hotel, 728
imperialism and Spanish-American War, 515
implied powers (elastic) clause, 53, 134, 208, 343, 417, 676; see also "loose construction"
impoundment, 754
imports, 50; see also "tariffs"
impressment of seamen, 344
Incas, 23

Inchon landing, 344
income tax, see "Sixteenth Amendment"
indentured servants, 344
Independence Hall, 345, 395
Independence party, Election of, see year of election (e.g., "Election of 1908")
Independent Journal, The, 250
Independent Treasury System, 345, 403
Indiana, 346
Indian Affairs, Bureau of, 345
"Indian Burying Ground, The," 273
Indian Nations of the Great Plains, 108
Indian paintings, 98
Indian Reorganization Act of 1934, 345
Indians, 12, 23, 28, 49, 72, 82, 83, 100, 104, 179, 256, 266, 289, 304, 306, 310, 320, 345, 346, 350, 362, 374, 377, 387, 404, 417, 454, 479, 487, 527, 560, 564, 565, 594, 607, 620, 652, 653, 694, 697, 708, 722, 727, 730; Abnaki, 2, 559; Algonquian, 2, 14, 37, 66, 105, 107, 187, 266, 306, 374, 423, 441, 451, 462, 506, 522, 539, 587, 594; Apache, 36, 38, 527; Arapaho, 37, 121, 307; Athapascan, 469; Atsina, 307; Blackfeet, 66, 172; Caddoan, 516; Catawba, 96; Cayuga, 98, 353; Cayuse, 98; Cherokee, 104, 187, 256, 316, 332, 662; Cheyenne, 105, 121, 591; Chickasaw, 106, 256, 333; Chippewa, 107; Choctaws, 108, 256, 332; Comanche, 123; Creek, 256, 336; Creek Confederacy, 10; Crow (Absaroke), 172; Dakota, 401, 532, 611; Delaware, 187, 293, 404, 604, 694; Digger, 191; Five Civilized Nations, 104, 106, 108, 169, 179, 256; Five Nations, 353, 450; Flatheads, 258; Fox, 67, 266, 587, 594; Gros Ventres, 306; Hidatsa, 307;

Hohokam, 329; Hopi, 38, 333; Hurons, 339, 506, 601; Iroquois, 96, 320, 339, 353, 404, 504, 506, 601, 628, 666, 730; Kickapoo, 374; Kiowas, 377, 593; Klamaths, 377; Leni-Lenape, 187; Mahican, 423; Mandans, 424; Miami, 441; Mohave, 38, 450; Mohawks, 353, 450; Mohegans, 450; Moqui, 333; Muskhogean, 106, 108, 169, 463; Narragansetts, 462; Natchez, 463; Navaho, 38, 469; Nez Percé, 485; Ogallalas, 252; Ojibwa, 107; Oneida, 353, 500; Onondaga, 353, 501; Osage, 505; Ottawas, 506, 533; Paiutes, 289, 509; Papago, 38; Pawnees, 516; Pequots, 450, 462, 521; Pimas, 38, 527; Poncas, 532; Potawatomi, 539; Powhatan Confederacy, 541; Praying Indians, 541; Pueblo, 333, 552; Raritan, 630; Renards, 266; Sacs, 587; Salish, 258; Santee, 401; Sauk, 67, 266, 594; Seminole, 256, 601; Senecas, 353, 601; Shawnee, 96, 531, 605, 658; Shoshone, 37, 123, 191, 387, 509, 609, 678; Siksika, 66; Sioux, 76, 96, 172, 174, 252, 289, 387, 401, 424, 444, 505, 516, 533, 611, 693, 717; Saint Francis Indians, 599; Snake, 609; Tuscaroras, 354, 666; Utes, 121, 678; Wampanoags, 376; Winnebago, 717; Wyandots, 339; Yakima, 732; Yamasee, 733; Yuma, 38, 450; Zuñi, 739; *map,* 775

Indian Suite, 417

Indian Territory (Oklahoma), 104, 106, 108, 169, 187, 256, 374, 377, 441, 450, 497, 516, 662

Indian Wars, 75, 518, 519; Black Hawk War, 67, 96, 266, 444, 547, 594; Black Hills War, 174; Cayuse War, 99; Creek War, 169; Fallen Timbers, battle of, 246; Fetterman massacre, 252; Fox-French Wars, 266; King Philip's War, 376, 462; Modoc War, 449; Nez Percé War, 485; Pawnee War, 516; Pequot, battles with, 521; Queen Anne's War, involved in, 559; Sand Creek massacre, 105, 590; San Luis Valley, raid of, 678; Satanta's Wars, 593; Seminole Wars, 601; Tippecanoe, battle of, 658; Wagon Box Fight, 693; Wounded Knee, battle of, 728; Wyoming Valley massacre, 730; Yakima Indian Wars, 732; Yamasee War, 733; Wars of the 1870's, 174

Indo-China, *see* "Viet Nam"

In Dubious Battle, 301

Industrial Revolution, 32, **347**

industrial unionism, 131

Industrial Workers of the World, 72, 348

Industry in the United States in 1960, *map,* 801

"infant" industries, protection of, 418, 644

Infantry Tactics, 277

infant school, 349

inflation, 761

Influence of Sea Power Upon History, 1660–1783, The, 423

Influence of Sea Power Upon the French Revolution and Empire, 1793–1812, The, 423

Information Agency, U.S., **349**

Ingersoll, Robert, 530

"In God we trust," 349, 667

initiative, 503

injunction, 116, 180, 490, 554

Inness, George, 349

Innocents Abroad, 117

In Praise of Johnny Appleseed, 365

Inquiry into the Effect of Ardent Spirit upon the Human Mind and Body, 648

Inspector General, 349

"instrumentalism," 190

Insular Cases, 349

851

Bank of the United States,
53, 61; Creek War, 169, 336;
Democratic-Republican party,
34, 189; duel, 201; Eaton Affair, 206; Election of 1824,
1828, 1832, and 1836, 211,
212; Florida, pursuit of Seminoles into, 259; Force Act,
262; French spoilation claims,
270, 273; Hermitage, the,
326; Jacksonian democracy,
357; *Kendall v. U.S.*, 372;
"King Andrew," 375; "kitch-
en cabinet," 377; martial law,
428; Maysville Road Bill,
434; New Orleans, battle
of, 73, 479; nullification, 494;
Old Hickory, 488; opposition
to internal improvements,
350; "Our federal union!"
506; Panic of 1837, 512; "pet
banks," 523; Revolution of
1828, 575; Rhea letter, 575;
"scrub race," 597; Seminole
Wars, 259, 601; Specie Circular, 61, 624; spoils system,
624, 660; Tariffs of 1828 and
1832, 645; Whig opposition
to, 709; *Worcester v. Georgia*,
722

Jackson, Charles T., 457
Jackson, Helen Hunt, 100, 563
Jackson, Thomas ("Stonewall"),
83, 101, 115, 273, 317, 357,
358
Jackson State College, 755
Jacksonian democracy, 357, 403
Jackson's Valley Campaign, 358
Jacobin clubs, 358
Jacobson v. Massachusetts, 679
Jagger, Mick, 764
James, Henry, 358
James, William, 190, 358
James I, King of England, 404,
687
James II, King of England, 102,
195, 202, 244, 392, 432, 477,
479, 483, 630
Jamestown, Va., 49, 237, 404,
630, 686
Japan: atom bomb, 45; Cairo
Conference, 89; Gentlemen's
Agreement, 285; Hiroshima,

329; Kanagawa, Treaty of,
370; Lansing-Ishii Agreement,
387; Lodge Corollary, 403;
London Naval Treaty, 404;
Okinawa, 758; opening of,
522; *Panay* incident, 511;
Portsmouth, Treaty of, 537;
Root-Takahira Agreement,
581; Shimoneseki, convention
of, 608; Stimson Doctrine,
634; Twenty-one Demands,
667; U.S. treaty with, 759;
Washington Conference, 701;
Yap Treaty, 734; *see also*
"World War II"
Japanese-American Treaty of
1951, 359, 586
Java Sea, battle of, 359
Jay, Fort, 298
Jay, John, 209, 248, 250, 359,
360, 514, 639
Jay-Gardoqui negotiations, 359
Jayhawkers, 359
Jay Treaty, 209, 360, 527, 664
"jazz age," 295, 360
"Jazz Singer, The," 459
J.B., 419
jeep, 360
Jefferson, Joseph, 654
Jefferson, Thomas, 360; Alien
and Sedition Acts, 14, 420;
Anti-Federalists, 33; Bank of
North America, 52; Bank of
the United States, 52; Burr's
Conspiracy, 86; *Chesapeake*
Affair, 105; choice for succession, 559; Constitutional
Convention, 135; Croswell
libel case, 172; Declaration of
Independence, 181; deism,
187; Elections of 1796, 1800,
1804 and 1808, 209, 210;
Embargo Act, 232; "entan-
gling alliances," 236; exploration urged by, 393; "fire bell
in the night," 448; French
Revolution, 548; Genêt Affair, 284; Hamilton's Financial Plans, 313; isolationism,
355; Jeffersonian democracy,
361; Kentucky Resolution,
687; Lee's Resolutions, 391;
library, 396; Louisiana Pur-

chase, 410, 592; Mazzei letter, 434; Missouri Compromise, 448; Monticello, 453, 588; motto of the U.S., 237; natural rights, 469; Nonintercourse Act, 488; Revolutions of 1800 and 1828, 574, 575; role in parties, 188, 189; "sage of Monticello," 587; Seal of the U.S., 598; succession, 599; separation of Church and State, 602; spoils system, 624; State of the Union message, 631; Twelfth Amendment, 19; Yazoo Land Frauds, 734

Jeffersonian democracy, 361

Jeffersonian Republicans, 48, 209, 210, 211, 319, 426; see also "Democratic-Republican party"; "Democratic party"

Jehovah's Witnesses, 257, 361

Jekyll Island, 286

Jenkins' Ear, War of, 361

Jenner, Edward, 679

"Jerry," 85

Jersey prisonship, 362

Jesuit missionaries, 362

Jesuits, 96

Jesuits in North America, The, 515

Jews in the U.S., 362, 718

Jim Crow laws, 112, 364, 530

Job Corps, 698

John Birch Society, 364

John Brown's Body, 57, 80, 364

John Brown's raid, 317, 364, 515

John L. Motley, 330

"John Mason," 635

Johnny Appleseed, 365

Johns, Frank T., 224

Johnson, Andrew, 365, 499, 692; Elections of 1864 and 1868, 216; impeachment trial of, 241, 343; Lincoln's assassination, 400; National Union party, 468; Radical Republicans oppose, 561; Reconstruction, 567; veto of Tenure of Office Act, 651

Johnson, Herschel, 215

Johnson, Hiram W., 222, 354, 365, 467, 548

Johnson, Hugh, 465

Johnson, Lyndon Baines, 365; "affirmative action" hiring, 761; Alliance for Progress, 14; Appalachia Aid, 36; conflict of interest, Executive Order on, 129; Democratic party, 189; doctrine, 366; Dominican Republic, 195; Elections of 1960 and 1964, 228; Elementary and Secondary Education Act of 1965, 230; Great Society, the, 304; gun control, 753; Housing and Urban Development, 335; immigration, 342, 415; Kennedy assassination, 373; Medicare, 435; Multilateral Force, 460; Rayburn, Sam, 656; Speech on Selma, 601; Viet Nam, 685; violence and civil disorders, 768; Voting Rights Act of 1965, 691, 705; "war on poverty," 698; "We Shall Overcome," 705; wiretapping, 769

Johnson, Richard Mentor, 213, 653

Johnson, Samuel, 646

Johnson, Sir William, 365, 384, 628

Johnson Act (1934), 365

Johnson Bill, see "National Origins Act"

Johnson (Lyndon B.) doctrine, 365

Johnston, Albert S., 608

Johnston, Joseph E., 40, 245, 366, 372, 607

Johnstown Flood, 366

Joint Chiefs of Staff, see "Chiefs of Staff, Joint"

Joint Committee on the Conduct of the War, 51

Jolliet, Louis, 38, 353, 366, 441, 448

Jolliet and Marquette discovery, 353, 366

Jolson, Al, 459

Jones, George, 485

Jones, John Paul, 342, 367

Jones Act, 524, 553
Jones-White Act, 438
Jordan, 208
Joseph, Chief, 485
Journal (John Woolman), 721
Journal (New York), 117, 188
Journal of Commerce, New York, 44
Journal of Experimental Zoology, 318
journalism, shield laws and, 765
"Journey for Peace," Nixon's, 757
Juárez, Benito, 433
Judge Advocate General, Office of, 367
Judgment Day, 248
judicial circuits, 36
judicial review, 367, 425, 741; *see also* "Supreme Court of the U.S."
judiciary, 368; Appeals, U.S. Courts of, 36; Chase impeachment trial, 103; Circuit Court, U.S., 86; circuit riders, 109; Claims, U.S. Court of, 115; "court-packing bill," 167; Customs and Patent Appeals, U.S. Court of, 174; District Courts, U.S., 193; federal court system, 134; judicial legislation, 316; judicial review, 367; "midnight judges," 442; state legislature's act unconstitutional, 57; *see also* "Constitution of U.S." (relevant portions); "Supreme Court of the U.S."
Judiciary Act of 1789, 367, 368, 426, 547, 639
Judiciary Act of 1801, 442
Judiciary Reorganization Bill, 167
Judson, Edward Z. C., 192
Julliard v. Greenman, 368
Jumbo, African elephant, 55
Jumping Frog of Calaveras County, The, 117
Jungle, The, 368, 435, 460
junior college, 368
junior high school, 369
jury trial, 17, 443
"just" compensation, 234

Justice, Department of, 14, 16, 88, 159, 249, 369, 415, 618, 675, 760
"Justice Denied in Mass.," 443

K

"Kaddish Symphony," 63
Kaiser Wilhelm II, 724
Kalamazoo, Case, 370
Kamaiakin, Chief, 732
Kanagawa, Treaty of, 370
Kansas, 60, 70, 73, 370, 390, 539
Kansas City, Kan., 1, 194
Kansas-Nebraska Act, 70, 200, 371, 471, 534, 613
Kansas Pacific Railway, 1, 82
Kansas territory, 73, 390, 606, 660, 729
Kaskaskia, Fort, 342
Kasper, John, 228
Kearney, Fort, 504
Kearsarge and *Alabama,* 371
Keating-Owen Child Labor Act, 314
keelboats, 371
Kefauver, Estes, 227
Keimer, Samuel, 521
Kelley, Oliver H., 300
Kellogg, Frank Billings, 371
Kellogg-Briand Pact, 371
Kelly, Charles T., "General," 371
Kelly, Edward J., 74
Kelly, William, 63, 348
Kelly's Industrial Army, 371
Kendall, Amos, 377
Kendall, Edward Calvin, 371
Kendall v. U.S., 372
Kenesaw Mountain, battle of, 372
Kennan, George F., 158
Kennebec expedition, 372
Kennedy, Edward M., 745
Kennedy, John Fitzgerald, 372, 545, 683; Alliance for Progress, 14; Arlington National Cemetery, 39; Bay of Pigs, 58; Cape Kennedy, 93; Communist propaganda mail, 126; Democratic party, 189; Election of 1960, 228; Housing

Ku Klux Klan, 66, 180, 262, 379, 380, 411, 567

L

Labor, Department of, 88, 382
Labor Day, 382
Labor Management Relations Act, see "Taft-Hartley Act"; "Mediation and Conciliation Service, Federal"
Labor - Management Reporting and Disclosures Act, see "Landrum-Griffin Act"
Labor movement, 31, 540
Labor's Non-Partisan League, 393
labor unions: American Federation of Labor, 25; American Federation of Labor and Congress of Industrial Organizations, 25; Anthracite Coal Strike, 33; Clayton Antitrust Act, 116; Coeur d'Alene strikes, 119; *Commonwealth v. Hunt*, 125; Congress of Industrial Organizations, 131; contract labor law, 161; Cripple Creek (Colo.) strikes, 170; Danbury Hatters' Case, 176; Homestead strike, 331; Industrial Workers of the World, 348; international, 25; International Ladies Garment Workers Union, 665; Knights of Labor, 378; Knights of St. Crispin, 378; Landrum-Griffin Act, 386; local, 25; Mc-Namara dynamite case, 419; Molly Maguires, 451; national, 25; National Labor Relations Act, 466; National Labor Union, 467; Negro American Labor Council, 471; Norris-LaGuardia Act, 490; Philadelphia Cordwainers' Case, 523; Pullman strike, 180, 554; Railroad Brotherhoods, 561; Railroad Strikes of 1877, 562; "right to work" laws, 577; Socialist party, 616; Taft-Hartley Act, 386, 642; ten-hour laws, 649;

United Labor party, 672; Western Federation of Miners, 119; "yellow-dog" contracts, 734
Lackawanna Railroad, 238
Ladies' Home Journal, The, 422
Ladies' Magazine, The, 293
Ladrones, 307
Lady Be Good, 288
Lady in a Fur Jacket, 711
Lady's Book, 293
La Farge, John, 382
Lafayette, Marquis de, 383, 453, 736
"Lafayette, we are here," 382
Lafitte, Jean, 280
LaFollette, Robert M., 192, 223, 354, 383, 548, 549, 718
LaFollette, Robert Marion, Jr., 383
LaFollette Seamen's Act, 383
LaGuardia, Fiorello, 383, 490
laissez-faire, 93, 383
Lake Borgne, battle of, 73
Lake Champlain, battle of, 530
Lake Erie, battle of, 196, 238, 705
Lake George, battle of, 384
Lake of the Woods, 162
"lame-duck" Amendment, 21, 384
Lamia, 417
Lamont v. Postmaster General, 126
Lancaster, Joseph, 385
Lancaster Pike, 384
Lancastrian school system, 385
Lancelot and Elaine, 417
Land Act of 1796, 385
Land Act of 1800, 385
Land Act of 1820, 385
land grant colleges, 320, 385, 456, 585, 689
land grants for railroads, 492, 652
Landing Day, see "Columbus Day"
Land Management, Bureau of, 386
"Land of 10,000 Lakes," 445
"Land of Opportunity," 38, 708
Land of the Free, 419
"land of the honey-bee," 190

857

Sheridan blocks retreat, 607;
Wilderness, battle of, 713
Lee's Resolutions, 391
Left Wing Manifesto, The, 291
legal tender, 391
Legal Tender Act of 1862, 368
Legal Tender Cases, 391, 443
"Legend of Sleepy Hollow,
The," 354
Legislative Reference Service,
398
Legislative Reorganization Act
of 1946, 402
legislature, the, *see* "Congress"
Lehman, Herbert H., 391
Leisler, Jacob, 392
Leisler's Rebellion, 392
Le Mamea 590
LEM, *see* "lunar excursion mod-
ule"
LeMay, Curtis E., 229
Lemke, William, 225, 617
Lend-Lease Act, 392, 726
L'Enfant, Pierre Charles, 111,
700, 712
Leni-Lenape, 187
Lenox library, 398
Leonard, Jonah F. R., 221
Leopard, 104
Leo XIII, Pope, 289
Lesseps, Ferdinand Marie de,
510
Letrado, Father, 301
Letters from a Farmer. . . .
(1767), 191, 392
*Letters from an American
Farmer*, 392
Letters of the Federal Farmer,
390
Levering, Joshua, 220
*Levitt v. Committee for Public
Education and Religious
Liberty*, 760
Lewis, Gilbert Newton, 387,
393
Lewis, John Llewellyn, 131,
393, 673
Lewis, Meriwether, 341, 393
Lewis, Sinclair, 49, 424
Lewis, William B., 377
Lewis and Clark Expedition,
341, 393, 424, 453, 471, 485,
492, 502, 620, 699, 729

Lewis-Langmuir theory, 387,
393
Lexington, 165
Lexington, battle of, 28, 128,
393, 446, 574
Lexow Committee, 394
Leyte Gulf, battle of, 394
liability of airlines, 699
Libby prison, 394
libel law, *see* "Croswell libel
case"
Liberal party, 27, 227, 394
Liberal Republican party, 217,
394
Liberator, The, 280, 395
Liberia, 2, 24
Liberty, 31, 315
"Liberty and Union, now and
forever . . . ," 705
Liberty Bell, 345, 395
"liberty cabbage," 395
Liberty Island, 632
Liberty League, 395
Liberty Loan "drives," 695
liberty of contract, 3, 5
Liberty party, 213, 214, 271,
395; *see also* "Election of" by
year of election (*e.g.*, "Elec-
tion of 1840")
liberty poles, 294, 396
"liberty pup," 395
"Liberty ships," 438
"Liberty Song, The," 675
Liberty Tree, 396
libraries, 396, 398
Library Journal, 397
Library of Congress, 396, 398
licks, 398
Life, 423, 752
"life, liberty and the pursuit of
happiness," 469
Life Among the Indians, 98
*Life and Death of John of
Barneveld, The*, 459
Life Line, The, 331
"Lifelong Learning," 6
Life of Sir William Osler, The,
174
Life of Washington, 355
Life on the Mississippi, 117
Light in August, 248
Lightning, 118, 398
Liliom, 314

859

Ludendorff, Erich Friedrich Wilhelm, 100
"lulu," 411
lunar excursion module, 35
Lunar Orbiter, 411
Lundy's Lane, battle of, 412
Lusitania, 412, 660
Luther, Martin, 412
Lutherans, 412
lyceums, 6, 413
Lyon, Mary, 413, 719, 721
Lytton Commission, 634

M

McAdoo, William Gibbs, 223
McAllister, Ward, 265
MacArthur, Douglas, 57, 72, 344, 380, 394, 414
Macassar Strait, battle of, 414
McAuliffe, Anthony, 56
Macauley, Robert C., 223
Macbeth, 44
McCall's, 423
McCanles gang, 713
McCardle, Ex parte, 414
McCarran Internal Security Act, 126, 414
McCarran-Walter Act, 415
McCarthy, Joseph, 415
McCarthy-Army dispute, 415
McCarthyism, 416
McClean farmhouse, 36
McClellan, George Brinton, 33, 41, 216, 245, 268, 318, 358, 416, 435, 519, 602
McCloskey, John, 97
McClure, Robert, 494
McClure, Samuel S., 416, 422
McClure's Magazine, 96, 416, 422, 560, 632
McCollum v. Board of Education, 570
McCormick, Cyrus Hall, 8, 417
McCormick Harvester Company strike, 323
McCormick publishing, 482
McCormick's reaper, 8
McCoy's, *see* "Hatfields and McCoys"
McCrea, Jane, murder of, 417
McCulloch v. Maryland, 343, 417, 427, 703

McDivitt, James A., 282
MacDonald, John A., 701
Macdonough, Commander Thomas, 503, 698
McDougall, Alexander, 294
MacDowell, Edward Alexander, 417
McDowell, Irvin, 41, 83, 358
McDowell, Mary, 338
mace, 417
Macedonian, 181
McGovern, George, 749
McGraw-Hill, 754
McGuffey, William Holmes, 418
McGuffey's Readers, 418
McGuire Act, 245
Machado, Gerardo, 172, 297
McHenry, Fort, 629, 698
machine gun, 434
McKay, Donald, 117, 260, 398
Mackay, John W., 61
McKim, Charles F., 576
McKim, James Miller, 463
McKinley, William, 418; American Protective Association support, 28; anarchist shoots, 31; conservation, 133; Elections of 1896 and 1900, 220, 221; "full dinner pail," 275; message to Garcia, 280; McKinley Tariff, 418; Philippine Islands, 524; Spanish American War, 622; tariffs, 192
McKinley Tariff of 1890, 192, 219, 418, 717
MacLeish, Archibald, 418
McLeod, Alexander, 94
McLoughlin, John, 337
McMahon Act, 46
McManigan, Ortie, 419
McMillan, Edwin Mattison, 419
McNamara, James B., 177, 419
McNamara, John J., 177, 419
McNamara, Robert, 191, 197
NcNamara dynamite case, 419
McNary, Charles L., 225
McNary-Haugen bill, 419
Macomb, Gen. Alexander, 530
Macon's Bill No. 2, 419, 487
McParlan, James, 451
McRae, Milton A., 673

Macready, William Charles, 44, 264

McReynolds, James C., 706

McTeague, 489

"Mad Anthony" Wayne, 187, 246, 306, 420, 441, 634

Madero, Francisco Indalecio, 702

Madison, James, **420**; Alien and Sedition Acts, 14; Anti-Federalists, 33; Bank of the United States, 53; Bonus Bill, 72; "compact of states," 598; Constitutional Convention, 135; Democratic-Republican party, 189; Elections of 1808 and 1812, 210; "father of the Constitution," 248; *Federalist, The,* 250; "Founding Fathers," 265; "Henry Letters," 326; impressment of seamen, 344; Macon's Bill No. 2, 420; *Marbury v. Madison,* 425; neutrality policy, 210; opposition to internal improvements, 350; proposes a tariff, 644; Quids, 559; Virginia Resolution, 687; war message, 502, 697

Mafia, 420

Magazine of Useful and Entertaining Knowledge, 422

magazines, 420, 431; *see also* various magazines by name

Magellan, Ferdinand, 23, 307, 524, 684

Maggie: A Girl of the Streets, 169

Magna Carta, 202

Magnalia Christi Americana, 432

Magnetic Telegraph Co., 647

"Magnolia State," 447

Mahan, Alfred Thayer, **423**

Mahanism, **423**

Mahican, **423**

mail, 533, 538, 584; *see also* "Post Office Department"

Maine, 3, 42, 43, **423**, 534, 704

Maine, 519, 521, 571, 622, 735

Maine, Sir Henry, 401

Main Street, **424**

Majors and Minors, 203

Malcolm X, 6

Mallet, Paul, 471

Mallet, Pierre, 471

Malone, Dudley Field, 596

Maloney, Joseph F., 221

Mammoth Oil Co., 646

Man Against the Sky, The, 578

Manassas, battle of, *see* "Bull Run, battle of"

Manchukuo, 634

Manchuria, and take-over by Japan, 389

mandamus, writ of, 425

Mandans, 424

Mangum, William P., 213

Manhattan District project, 677

Manhattan Island, 79, 204, 479

"Manhattan Project," 46

Manhattan Transfer, 198

Manifest Destiny, 424

Manila Bay, battle of, **424**

Manila Pact, *see* "Southeast Asia Treaty Organization"

Mann, Horace, 425, 489

Mann-Elkins Act, 425

Mann White Slave Act, **425**

Manpower Development and Training Act, 425

Man That Corrupted Hadleyburg, The, 117

Manuel, Fort, 400

Man Who Died Twice, The, 578

Mao Tse Tung, 757

Mapp v. Ohio, 764

Maps, 771-804

Marais des Cygnes, massacre at, 73

Marbury v. Madison, 367, 425, 427, 442

Marchett, Charles H., 220

"March on Washington," 464, 471, 621

"march through Georgia," 696

"March to the Sea," 84, 608

Marco Millions, 501

Marcy, William L., 12, 68, 505, 660

Mardi, 437

Mardi Gras, 426

Mariage de Figaro, Le, 333

Mariana Islands, 261, 307, 355, 525, 666

marijuana, 749
Marin County Courthouse, California, 742
Marin, John, 426
Marin, Luis Muñoz, 269
Marine Corps, 426
Mariner, 426
Marion, Francis, 240, 640
Maritime Administration, 426
maritime jurisdiction, 6
maritime law, 176
marketing cooperatives, *see* "producers' cooperatives"
marketing quotas, 7
Mark Twain, *see* "Clemens, Samuel Langhorne"
"Mark Twain," the chant, 426
Marne, battles of, 100, 427
Marne River, 9, 10, 103
Marquand, John P., 388
marque and reprisal, letters of, 427
Marquette, Jacques, 38, 353, 366, 441, 448, 505
Marriage Cycle, A, 509
Marshall, George Catlett, 416, 427
Marshall, Humphrey, 201
Marshall, James W., 640
Marshall, John: *Barron v. Baltimore,* 55; Burr's Conspiracy, 86; *Cohens v. Virginia,* 119; Dartmouth College Case, 177; *Fletcher v. Peck,* 258; *Gibbons v. Ogden,* 289; judicial review, 639; *Marbury v. Madison,* 367, 426; *McCulloch v. Maryland,* 343, 417; *Worcester v. Georgia,* 722; XYZ affair, 731
Marshall, Thomas R., 222
Marshall, Thurgood, 618
Marshall Field & Co., 253
Marshall Islands, 258, 666
Marshall Plan, 120, 427
martial law, 380, 428
Martin, Abraham, 529
Martin Eden, 404
Martin v. Hunter's Lessee, 428, 634
Marx, Karl, 126
Maryland, 96, 429, 659
Maryland! My Maryland! 429

Maryland's Act of Toleration, *see* "Toleration Act (1649)"
Mason, Charles, 430
Mason, David F., 610
Mason, George, 65, 429, 687
Mason, John Y., 424, 477, 505, 664
Mason, William, 655
Mason and Dixon Line, 430
Masons, 34, 430; *see also,* "Anti-Masonic party"
Massachusetts, 430, 661
Massachusetts Bay Colony: charter problems, 432; includes Old Colony, 498; Pilgrims, 527; Puritans, 556; Quakers, 557; religious issues, 34, 39
Massachusetts Bay Company, 91, 197, 556
Massachusetts General Hospital, 334
Massachusetts Institute of Technology, 431
Massachusetts Law of 1642, 1827 and 1852, 127, 327
Massachusetts Spy, 655
Massie trial, 177
mass media, 431
mass production, 431, 432, 348
Masters, Edgar Lee, 285, 625
Masterson, Bat, 194
Mather, Cotton, 396, 432, 714, 718
Mather, Increase, 432, 718
Matthews, David, 326
Maury, Matthew Fontaine, 433
maverick, 433
Maverick, Samuel A., 433
Maxim, Sir Hiram, 434
Maximilian, Emperor (Ferdinand Maximilian Joseph), 94, 433
Maximilian Affair, 433
Maxim machine gun, 434
Max Schmitt in a Single Scull, 205
May, Samuel J., 2
May-Day and Other Poems, 233
Mayflower, 77, 129, 430, 434, 526
Mayflower Compact, 434
Mayo, Charles Horace, 434

Mayo, William James, 434
Mayo, William Worrall, 434
Mayo Clinic, 434
Maysville Road Bill, 434
Mazzei, Philip, 434
Mazzei letter, 434
Meade, George Gordon, 41, 288
Meany, George, 25
Measurement of Intelligence, The, 656
Meat Inspection Act, 435, 555
meatpacking, *see* "Beef Trust Cases"
Mechanicsville, battle of, 435, 520, 602
Méchanique céleste, 76
Mecklenburg Resolutions, 435
Mediation and Conciliation Service, Federal, 435
Medical Horrors, 422
Medical Inquiries and Observations upon the Diseases of the Mind, 585
Medical Repository, 421
Medicare, 27, 435
Medicine Lodge, Treaty of, 377
Medill, Joseph, 106
megalopolis, 436; *see also* "metropolis"
Megalopolis, 436
Meionaon Hall, 84
Mellon, Andrew William, 15, 42
Melon Boats, 593
"melting pot," 436
Melting Pot, The, 436
Melville, Herman, 437, 449
Memoirs of John Quincy Adams, 4
Memoirs v. Massachusetts, see "Fanny Hill Case"
Memoranda During the War, 712
Memorial Day, *see* "Decoration Day"
Memorial to the Legislature of Massachusetts (1843), 193
Mencken, Henry Louis, 437
"Mending Wall," 274
Mennonites, 437
Menominees, 346
Mercantile Library Association, 397

mercantilism, 437
merchant marine, 118, 383, 426, 438, 674
"merchants of death," 438
Mercury, Project, 45, 439
Meredith, James, 68
Mergenthaler, Ottmar, 400
merit system, *see* "civil service reform"
Merrimac, 451
Merryman, Ex parte, 309, 439
Merry's Museum, 13
Message to Garcia, A, 280
Methodists, 109, 241, 439
METO, *see* "Central Treaty Organization"
metropolis, 440; *see also* megalopolis"
metropolitan area busing, 744
Meuse-Argonne offensive, 328, 408, 440
Mexican Cession, 440
Mexican War, 440; Biglow Papers, 64; bounties, 75; Buena Vista, battle of, 82; California, independent, 90; Cerro Gordo, battle of, 100; Chapultepec, battle of, 101; Churubusco, battle of, 109; Contreras, battle of, 109; Guadalupe-Hidalgo, Treaty of, 307; Lincoln, Abraham and the "Spot Resolutions," 625; Mexican Cession, 440; Molino del Rey, battle of, 451; Monterey, battle of, 453; Palo Alto, battle of, 510; Resaca de la Palma, battle of, 573; San Jacinto Creek, battle of, 592; *map*, 784
Mexico: ABC conference, 1; Alamo, 11; America, discovery of, 23; "Bear Flag" Republic, 58; braceros, 76; Carlotta, 94; empresario system, 234; Gadsden Purchase, 38, 278; Guadalupe - Hidalgo, Treaty of, 38, 307, 441; imprisons Austin, 48; Maximilian, Emperor, 94; Maximilian Affair, 433; Mexican Cession, 440; Mexican War, 440; Monroe Doctrine, 453; Slidell

865

Mosby's rangers, **458**
Mosby's War Reminiscences, 458
Moscow Conference (1943), 458, 673
Moslems, *see* "Black Muslims"
Mosque No. 1, 67
Most, Johann, 31
Mother Earth, 31
Mother Goose's Melody, 656
"mother of presidents," 686
motion pictures, 90, 431, **458**
Motley, John Lothrop, **459**
Motor Carrier Act of 1935, 352
Mott, Frank Luther, 482
Mott, Lucretia C., 628, 719
Moultrie, Fort, 639
Moultrie, Fort, battle of, **459**
Moultrie, William, 459
"Mountain Men," 45, **459**
"Mountain State," 707
Mount Hermon School, 454
Mount Holyoke College, 413
Mount Rushmore, 620
Mount Suribachi, 356
Mount Vernon, **459**
Mount Vernon conference, **459**
Mount Whitney, 90
Mourning Becomes Electra, 501
movies, *see* "motion pictures"
Mr. Dooley in Peace and War, 197
"Mr. Madison's War," 697
"Mr. Republican," 227, 642
"Mr. Sam," 565
"Mr. X," 158
muckrakers, 197, 368, 416, **460**, 548, 555, 604, 632
Mugwumps, 218, **460**
Muhammed, Elijah, 6, 67
Mühlenberg, Henrich Melchior, 412
Muller v. Oregon, 78
Mulligan, James, 460
Mulligan letters, **460**, 530
Multilateral Force, 460
Multi-Occupational Manpower Program, 425
Mundus Novus, 23
Munn, Earle H., 228
Munn v. Illinois, 300, **460**, 693
Munsey's, 422
Murchison, Charles F., 461

Murchison letter, **461**
Murder in the Cathedral, 232
Murder of Lidice, The, 443
"Murders in the Rue Morgue," 531
Murfreesboro, battle of, **461**
Murray, John, 675
Murray, Philip, 393
Muskhogean, 106, 108, 169, 463
Muskie, Edmund M., 229
Muslims, *see* "Black Muslims"
Mussolini, Benito, 727
My Antonia, 96
"My country 'tis of thee," *see* "America"
"My Day," 579
Myers v. U.S., 461
My Experiences in the World War, 522
My Lai massacre, 756
"My Old Kentucky Home," 264
My Study Windows, 411

N

NAACP, *see* "National Association for the Advancement of Colored People"
Nader, Ralph, 747
Nagasaki, Japan, 45, 329
Naismith, James A., 56
Napoleon I (Napoleon Bonaparte), 62, 161, 195, 210, 232, 239, 409, 410, 420, 502, 563, 592
Napoleon III, Emperor, 433
Napoleonic Wars, 62, 104, 161, 210, 438
narcotic addiction, *see* "drug abuse"
Narcotics, Bureau of, 462, 663
Narragansetts, 462
Narrative of the United States Exploring Expedition, 714
NASA, *see* "National Aeronautics and Space Administration"
Nashville, battle of, 462
Nashville Convention, 462
Nassau, Fort, 483
Nasser, Gamal Abdel, 208
Nast, Thomas, 218, 233, 462, 667

Niagara Movement, 201, 464
Nicaraguan intervention, 81, 486
Nicholas II, Czar of Russia, 266, 309
Nichols, Red, 360
Nick Carter, 486
"nickelodeons," 458
Nicola, Lewis, 486
Nicola proposal, 486
Nicolay, John, 322
Nicolet, Jean, 441, 718
Nicolls, Richard, 202
Niebuhr, Reinhold, 486
Night of the Iguana, The, 716
Nights with Uncle Remus, 318
Nike, 619
Nimbus, 487
Nimitz, Chester W., 442, 487
Niña, 23
Nine-Power Treaty, 701
1919, 198
Nineteenth Amendment, 21, 690, 720
Ninety-Six, Fort, 487
Ninth Amendment, 18, 547
Nisei, 321
Nixon, Richard M., 757; dollar devaluation, 747; Election of 1952, 227; Election of 1956, 227; Election of 1960, 228; Election of 1968, 229; Election of 1972, 749-51; executive privilege, 752; impoundment, 755; "Journey for Peace," 757; My Lai massacre, 756; Phases 1-4, 761; skyjacking, 766; Vice-President, 683; Viet Nam war, 685; Watergate, 768
Niza, Marcos de, 478
N.L.R.B. v. Jones and Laughlin Steel Corp., 466
Nobel, Alfred Bernhard, 487
Nobel Prizes, 487
"Noble Savage," 167
No Man's Land, 488
nominating conventions, 98
non-aligned nations, 120
nonimportation agreements, 487
Non-Intercourse Act, 419, 487, 563
Nootka Sound, 699

NORAD, *see* "North American Air Defense Command"
Norfolk and Western Railway Co., 105, 488
normal schools, 3, 489
Normandie fire, 489
Normandy, France, 180; landing of Allies, 727
Norman v. Baltimore & Ohio RR Co., 294
Norris, Frank, 489
Norris, George W., 384, 490, 575
Norris-LaGuardia Act, 490, 735
Norsemen, 23, 373, 686
North, Lord Frederick, 75
North American Air Defense Command, 490
North American Review, 4, 411, 421, 653, 728
North Atlantic Treaty Organization, 120, 240, 460, 490
North Carolina, 11, 491, 570
North Dakota, 491
Northeast power blackout, 492
Northern Alliance (farmers), 247
Northern Baptist Convention, 54
"Northern Fishermen," 347
Northern Pacific Railway Co., 162, 492, 513, 652, 699
Northern Securities Case, 493
Northfield Seminary, 454
Northmen, 686
North of Boston, 274
North Pole, 87, 518
Northrop, J. H., 628
North Star, 198
"North Star State," 444
North West Company, 337
Northwest Ordinances, 342, 493, 496, 613
Northwest Passage, 290, 494
Northwest Territory, 342, 345, 442, 493; *map*, 779
Norton, Charles Eliot, 411, 463
Norumbega, 494
"not worth a Continental," 494
Nova Caesaria, 477
Nova Scotia, 3
NOW, *see* "National Organization for Women"

Noyes, John Humphrey, 500
NRA, *see* "National Industrial Recovery Act"
"nuclear club," 46
nuclear power, 472, 637
nuclear test ban, 40, 46, 120, 591, 764; *see also* "atom bomb"
nullification, 243, 262, 494, 598, 631, 646, 705
Nullification Proclamation, 494
Nullifiers, 212
Nuremberg trials, 695
Nurse Corps, 721
"Nuts!" 57
Nye, Gerald P., 439
nylon, 95

O

Oak and Ivy, 203
Oakley, Annie, 714
Oak Ridge, Tenn., 46
OASI, *see* "Old Age and Survivors Insurance"
Oberlin rescue, 85
obscenity cases, 758
Observer, The, 410
Ocala Platform, 495
Ochs, Adolph S., 482, 485, 495
O'Connor, Carroll, 743
Octopus, The, 489
Ode Recited at the Harvard Commemoration, 411
Odets, Clifford, 495
OES, *see* "Economic Stabilization, Office of"
Of Mice and Men, 301
Of Thee I Sing, 288
Of Time and the River, 719
Ogallalas, 252
Ogden, Aaron, 289
Oglethorpe, James, 286
"Oh, How I Hate to Get Up in the Morning," 62
Ohio, 495, 659
Ohio and Erie Canal, 496
Ohio Company, 404, 496, 596
Ohio Idea, 496
Ohio Life Insurance Co., 512
oil, 624, 626, 646, 657
oil industry, 161
"Okies," 301
Okinawa, battle of, 497

Okinawa, island of, 586, 758
Oklahoma, 314
Oklahoma, 72, 497
Old Age and Survivors Insurance, 617, 661
"Old Black Joe," 264
"Old Bullion," 61
Old China trade, 234
old colonial policy, 306
Old Colony, 498
Old Dominion, 498, 686
Old Faithful, 736
"Old Folks at Home, The," 264
Old Glory, 498
Old Guard, 225, 498
Old Hickory, 357, 498
Old Ironsides, 158, 330, 498
"Old Ironsides," 498
"Old Joe Clark," 498
Old Lights, 499
"Old Line State, The," 429
Old Man and the Sea, The, 325
Old Man Eloquent, 499
"Old Northwest," 493
"Old Oklahoma," 72
"Old Pancake," 128
"Old Planters," 197
Old Public Functionary, 499
Old Regime in Canada, The, 515
Old Rough and Ready, 499, 646
"Old School" Baptists, 54
Old South, 10, 480
Old South Church, 499
"Old Tippecanoe," 659
O'Leary, Mrs., and Chicago fire, 106
"O Little Town of Bethlehem," 79
Olive Branch Petition, 499
Oliver, Andrew, 396
Olmstead, Frederick Law, 463, 499
Olney, Richard, 180, 500, 554, 681
Olney Doctrine, 500
Olney-Pauncefote Treaty, 500
Omaha platform, 500, 536
O'Mahoney, Joseph C., 649
O'Mahony,, John, 252
Omnibus, 63
"Omnibus Bill," *see* "Compromise of 1850"

879

692; Wabash Cannonball, 742; Western Pacific, 706; *maps*, 790, 791

Railroad Strikes of 1877, 305, 428, 562

"Rail Splitter," 562

Railway Express Agency, 563

Railway Labor Acts, 563

Railway Labor Board, 239

Rainbow After a Storm, 349

Rain-in-the-Face, 611

Raisin River massacre, 563

Raisuli, Ahmed ibn-Muhammed, 577

Raleigh, Walter, 291, 408, 491

"Raleigh Letter," 11, 563

Rambouillet decree, 563

Ramona, 563

rams, Confederate, 564

Randall, James R., 429

Randolph, A. Philip, 471

Randolph, Edmund, 688

Randolph, Edward, 564

Randolph, John (of Roanoke), 198, 201, 559, 564, 734

Randolph's commission, 564

Ranger, 564

rangers, colonial, 564, 730

Rapp, George, 317

Raritan Indians, 630

Rasmussen v. U.S., 350

"Raven, The," 531

Rawdon, Lord, 329

Rayburn, Sam, 565

Raymond, Henry J., 485

Read, Thomas Buchanan, 607

Reader's Digest, 423

realists, 338

reaper, McCormick's, 8

reapportionment decisions, **565**

rear-admiral, 566

rebates, 232, 627

"rebels without a cause," 59

recall, 503

recession, 86

Reciprocal Trade Agreement Act (1934), 566, 622

reclamation, *see* "conservation"

Reconstruction, 566; ab-initio movement, 1; *Birth of a Nation, The,* 66; "Black Codes," 66; Black Republican, 68; carpetbaggers, 95; conquered province theory, 132; constitutionality of Acts, 444; election issue, 216, 217; Fifteenth Amendment, 20; Force Acts, 112, 262; Fourteenth Amendment, 19; Freedmen's Bureau, 269; impeachment of Pres. Andrew Johnson, 343; Jim Crow laws, 364; Ku Klux Klan, 380; laws upheld, 102; Loyal League, 411; scalawags, 595; Solid South, 618; Wade-Davis Bill, 692; *see also* "Civil War"

Reconstruction Finance Corporation, 332, 568

Record, 24

recordings, *see* "wiretapping"

recovery, in business cycle, 86

Red Badge of Courage, The, 168, 568

Redbook, 423

Redburn, 437

Red Cloud, 252, 611, 693

Redcoats, 568

Red Cross, 56, 568

"redemptioners," 344

Redfield, William C., 24

redistricting, *see* "reapportionment decisions"

Red Jackets, 379

"Red Line Map," 704

Red Pony, The, 301

Red River Campaign, 568

Red scare, 510, 568

Red Shirts, 569

Redskins, The, 35

"Red Sticks," 169

red tape, 332

Reed, Walter, 298, 569, 735

referendum, 503

Reflections on the End of an Era, 487

Reformed Church in America, 569, 672

Reform Judaism, 363

Refugee Relief Act, 569

regicides in New England, **570**

Register of Debates, 570

Regulators, 11, 570

Reichstein, Tadeus, 372

Reid, Ogden M., 484

Reid, Whitelaw, 219, 623

Reimer, Arthur E., 222
Reims, attempt to capture, 100
Reindeer, 702
Reivers, The, 836
Relations, Jesuit, 362
Relay, Project, 570
released time, 570
Relief Administration, *see* "Federal Emergency Relief Administration"
Relief party, 571
relief payments, 722
relief program, *see* "New Deal"
"relief projects," 249
relief work, *see* "Civil Works Administration"
Religious Aspect of Philosophy, The, 583
religious freedom, 261, 330; First Amendment, 16, 63, 92; Toleration Act, 659
religious instruction, 570
religious schools, *see* "parochial schools, aid to"
Religious Society of Friends, 557
"Remember," 62
"Remember Pearl Harbor!" 321
"Remember the Alamo!" 11
"Remember the Maine!" 571
Remington, Frederic, 571
Remington typewriter, 668
removals, 571
Renards, 266
Renewed Church of the Brethren, 454
Reorganization Plan 3 of 1947, 335
Reorganization Plan 8 of 1953, 349
reparations, 332, 571, 695; Chesapeake Affair, 105; World War I, 179, 266, 737
"Report on Manufactures," 313
Report on the Lands of the Arid Region of the United States, 540
Republic, The, 578
Republican party, 271, 572; Alien and Sedition Acts, 14, 687; Black Republican, 68; caucus, 98; Civil War, 113; conventions, 248; Dred Scott

Case, 200; Election of, *see* year of election (*e.g.*, "Election of 1800") emblem, 233; factionalism, 310; founded, 34; GOP, 298; Jeffersonian, 48, 103, 189, 238; Mugwumps, 460; National Union party, 468; Old Guard, 498; origin in Democratic-Republican party, 189; Quids, 559; Reconstruction, 398; Revolutions of 1800 and 1828, 574, 575; slogan, 107, 275; Stalwarts, 625; "wave the bloody shirt," 702; *see also* "Radical Republicans"
requisitions, 573
Resaca de la Palma, battle of, 573
reserved powers, *see* "Tenth Amendment"
Reserve Officers Training Corps (ROTC), 755
"Resistance to Civil Government," 112
resolutions in Congress, 573
Restraining Act (1775), 573
Resumption Act of 1875, 305, 573
Retirement Board v. Alton Railroad Co., 562
"return to normalcy," 573
Reuther, Walter, 26
Revenue Act (1764), 637
Revenue Act of 1919, 50
Revenue Act of 1935, *see* "Wealth Tax Act"
revenue sharing, 763
Revere, Paul, 572, 573, 610, 619
Revere's "midnight ride," 573, 574
revivalism, 241, 302, 449
Revolutionary War, 574; Arnold's treason, 41; Bennington, battle of, 61; bounties, 75; Brandywine Creek, battle of, 78; Bunker Hill, battle of, 84; Camden, battle of, 91; Cherokee, 104; Cherry Valley massacre, 104; Clark, G. R., 115; Concord, battle of, 128; Continental army, 159; Con-

Robinson, Edwin Arlington, **578**
Robinson, Jackie, 472
Robinson, Joseph T., 224
Robinson-Patman Act, 100, **578**
Rochambeau, Comte de, 736
Rochdale, England, 163
rock music, **764**
"Rocked in the Cradle of the Deep," 715
Rockefeller, John D., Jr., 715
Rockefeller, John Davison, **578**, 621, 626
Rockefeller, Nelson, 743
Rockefeller, William, 626
Rockefeller Foundation, 524
Rockingham, Marquis of, 626
"Rock of Chickamauga," 106
"Rock of the Marne," 100
Rocky Mountains, 76, 161, 162
Roderick Hudson, 358
Rodgers, Richard, 314
Roe v. Wade, 741
Roebling, John Augustus, **579**
Roebling, Washington Augustus, 579
Rogers, Robert, 579
Rogers' Rangers, **579**
Rolfe, John, 541, 686
Rolling Stones, The, 764
Roman Catholics, *see* "Catholicism in United States"
Romberg, Sigmund, 314
roorback, **579**
Roosevelt, Anna Eleanor, 579
Roosevelt, Franklin Delano, 545, **579**; alphabet agencies, 15; American Labor party, 27; "arsenal of democracy," 42; Atlantic Charter, 45; atom bomb, 46; Bank Holiday (1933), 52; Bataan, battle of, 57; Black, Hugo La Fayette, 66; "Brain Trust," 77; Cairo Conference, 89; Casablanca Conference, 95; "court packing bill," 167; "day of infamy," 321; Democratic party, 189; Elections of 1920, 1932, 1936, 1940 and 1944, 223, 224, 225, 226; "fireside chats," 255; "forgotten man, the," 263; Four Freedoms, 265; Glass-Stea-

gall Banking Act, 292; Gold Reserve Act of 1934, 295; "Good Neighbor" policy, 122, 172, 297, 580; Hillman, Sidney, 328; "Hundred Days," the, 338; labor support, 393; Lend-Lease Act, 392; Liberty League, 395; London Economic Conference, 404; monopolies, 649; Neutrality Acts of the 1930's, 473; New Deal, 475; Office of War Information created, 696; "one-third of a nation," 501; power of removal, 338; "quarantine speech," 558; Rural Electrification Administration, 584; Teheran Conference, 647; third-term tradition, 655; Twenty-second Amendment, 21; Wealth Tax Act, 703; World War II, role in, 725; Yalta Conference, 732
Roosevelt, Theodore, 578, **580**; Algeciras Conference, 13; American Tobacco Company Case, 29; Ananias Club, 31; Anthracite Coal Strike, 33; antitrust proceedings, 608; Ballinger-Pinchot controversy, 51; Beef Trust Cases, 60; "big stick" policy, 64; Brownsville Riot, 80; "Bull Moose" party, 83, 549; conservation, 133, 263; Cuba, intervention in, 172; Dominican Republic, 195; Elections of 1900, 1904, 1908, 1912 and 1916, 221, 222; Forest Reserve Act, 263; Gentlemen's Agreement, 285; "hat in the ring," 321; mayoral campaign, 186; Meat Inspection Act, 435; muckrakers, 460; New Nationalism, 171, 479; Northern Securities Case, 493; Panama Canal, 510; Panic of 1907, 513; Portsmouth, Treaty of, 537; Progressive movement, 548; Progressive party, 549; regulation of business, 475; Riff incident, 577; Riis, Jacob A., 337; Roosevelt Corollary,

886

Schine, G. David, 415
Schirra, Walter M., Jr., 282
Schley, Winfield Scott, 592, 593
Schmidt, Kaspar, 31
Schmitz, John, 750
Schofield, John, 267
Schomburgk line, 681
school aid, *see* "Elementary and Secondary Education Act of 1965"
School and Society, The, 190
School District of Abington Township v. Schempp, 63
school integration, 744
school tax, 552
Schurz, Carl, 217, 264, 395, 596
Schurz, Mrs. Carl, 375
Schwab, Charles, 675
Science and Health with Key to the Scriptures, 109, 207
Science of English Verse, The, 387
Scientific Research and Development, Office of, 46
Scioto Company, 596
Scopes trial, 81, 177, 596
Score, 597
Scotch-Irish, 597
Scott, Tom, 621
Scott, Winfield, 30, 42, 100, 101, 107, 109, 214, 276, 441, 451, 662
Scottsboro case, 177
Scott v. Sandford, see "Dred Scott Case"
Scout, 597
Scranton, William W., 755
Scripps, Edward Wyllis, 481, 673
Scripps-Howard, 482, 484
Scrooby group, 597
"scrub race," 597
Scull, John, 528
SDS, *see* "Students for a Democratic Society"
Seaborg, Glenn Theodore, 419, 597
sea dogs, 597
Sea Islands, 286
Sealab, 598
sealing, *see* "Bering Sea dispute"
Seal of the U.S., 205, 598, 630

Seaman's Friend, The, 176
Sea Power in Its Relation to the War of 1812, 423
searches and seizures, 17, 764
search warrants, 729
Sears, Isaac, 619
Sears, Richard D., 650
"seasonal" work, 77
SEATO, *See* "Southeast Asia Treaty Organization"
SEC, *see* "Securities and Exchange Act"
"secesh," 41
secession, 171, 598; *see also* "states' rights"
Second Adventists, 6
Second Amendment, 16
secondary school, *see* "high school"; "junior high school"
Second Continental Congress, *see* "Continental Congress"
"second front," 727
"second industrial revolution," 48
Secret Service, 663, 769
sectionalism, 599
Securities and Exchange Act, 338, 599, 709
Securities and Exchange Commission, 36
Sedition Act (1798), 14, 48
Sedition Act (1918), 2, 600
"Seed Gatherers," 347
Seeger, Pete, 705
Segar, Elzie C., 360
segregation, 600; *Brown v. Board of Education,* 81, 202; civil rights laws, 112; due process laws, 202; Fourteenth Amendment, 20; Jim Crow laws, 112; *Plessy v. Ferguson,* 530
seizures, searches and, 764
Selective Service Acts, *see* "conscription"
selectmen, 600
self-governing colonies, 600
Selma, Ala, 601
Selma-to-Montgomery Freedom March, 269, 601
Seminary Ridge, 525
Seminole, 256, 886
Seminole Wars, 575, 601

Senate, U.S., 130, 137, 254, 446, 602; *see also* "Congress, U.S."

Senate Committee on Government Operations, 416

Senate Judiciary Committee, 167

senatorial courtesy, 676

Senators, election of, 20

Seneca Falls Convention, 719

Senecas, 353, **601**

seniority rule, **601**

Senior Scholastic Unit, 423

"separate but equal," 600, *see also* "*Plessy v. Ferguson*"; "segregation"

separation of Church and State, 570, **602**

separation of powers, 688, 752

Separatists, *see* "Pilgrims"

Sephardic Jews, 363

Sequoias, 736

Sequoya, 104

Serapis, 342, 367

Sergeant, John, 423

sergeant at arms, **602**

Serra, Junipero, 266

Service Center for Teachers of History, 26

Servicemen's Readjustment Act of 1944 (GI Bill), *see* "GI Bill of Rights"

settlement houses, *see* "Hull House"

Seven Cities of Cibola, 23, 478, 739

"Seven Days' Battle," 268, 278, 520, **602**

Seven Pines, battle of, *see* "Fair Oaks, battle of"

Seven Ranges, **602**

"Seven Sisters" Colleges, **603**

Seventeenth Amendment, 20, 130, 444, 549

Seventh Amendment, **17**

Seventh-Day Adventists, 6

Seventh - Day Baptists, *see* "Dunkards"

"seven-thirties," **603**

"Seventh of March" speech, **603**, 703

Seventy Years of Life and Labor, 297

Seven Years' War, *see* "French and Indian War"

Sevier, John, 268

Sewall, Arthur, 220

Seward, William Henry, 11, 35, 84, 195, 215, 315, 327, 354, 364, 399, **603**, 664

"Seward's folly," 11

"Seward's icebox," 11

sewing machines, 336, **604**

sex discrimination, 751, 770

Seymour, Horatio, 177, 216

Shackamaxon, Treaty of, 187, **604**

Shadows on the Rock, 96

Shadrach, 85

Shafter, William, 592

Shakers, **604**

Shame of the Cities, The, 460, **604**, 632

Shannon, 196

Shannon, Wilson, 693

SHAPE, *see* "Supreme Headquarters of Allied Powers in Europe"

sharecropping system, **604**

share - the - wealth movement, 405, **605**

Sharpsburg, *see* "Antietam, battle of"

Sharps rifle, 59

Shaw, Anna Howard, 720

Shaw, Lemuel, 125, **605**

Shawnee, 96, 531, **605**, 658

Shawnee Mission government, **606**

Shawnee Trail, 505, **606**

Shays, Daniel, 606

Shays's Rebellion, 171, **606**

Shelburne, Lord, 514

Shenandoah, 10, **606**

Shepard, Alan B., Jr., 439

Shepard, Mrs. Finley J., 311

Sheridan, Philip, 257, 523, **606**, 607

Sheridan on Indians, **607**

Sheridan's ride, **607**; poem by Read, 607

Sherman, 588

Sherman, James S., 221, 222

Sherman, Roger, 302

Sherman, William Tecumseh,

Brown v. Board of Education, 80, 202, 364, 464, 472, 530, 600, 698; Caldwell Case, 765; Cantwell v. Connecticut, 92; Champion v. Ames, 409; Charles River Bridge v. Warren Bridge, 101, 634; Chisholm v. Georgia, 18, 108, 359; Civil Rights Cases of 1883, 112, 600; Civil Service Commission v. National Association of Letter Carriers, 754; Cohens v. Virginia, 119, 367; Colgrove v. Battin, 755; Collector v. Day, 391; Comity Cases, 52; Committee for Public Education and Religious Liberty v. Nyquist, 760; Commonwealth v. Hunt, 605; Communist Mail Case, 125; Communist registration, 415; Coppage v. Kansas, 735; "court-packing bill," 167; Danbury Hatters' Case (Loewe v. Lawlor), 176; Dartmouth College Case (Dartmouth College v. Woodward), 177, 631, 703; Debs, In re, 180; DeLima v. Bidwell, 349; Dennis et al v. U.S., 267, 615; Doe v. Bolton, 741; Downes v. Bidwell, 350; Dred Scott Case (Scott v. Sandford), 199, 270; Engel v. Vitale, 64; Escobedo v. Illinois, 239; Estelle T. Griswold v. Connecticut, 546; Everson v. Board of Education, 242, 602; fair trade laws, 245; Fanny Hill Case, 582; Fixa v. Heilberg, 126; "Flag Salute" Cases, 257; Fletcher v. Peck, 258, 367, 734; Furman decision, 745; Gayle v. Browder, 530; Gibbons v. Ogden, 289; Gideon v. Wainwright, 290; Ginzburg Case, 581; Gitlow v. New York, 291; Goetz v. Ansell, 762; Gold Clause Cases, 294; "grandfather" clauses, 300; Granger Cases, 300, 461; Guinn v. U.S., 300; Hammer v. Dagenhart, 314; Hawaii v. Mankichi, 350;

Hayburn's Case, 323; Hepburn v. Griswold, 391; Humphrey's Executor v. U.S., 338, 461; Hunt v. McNair, 760; Hylton v. U.S., 339; Insular Cases, 349; Jacobson v. Massachusetts, 679; judicial districts, 109-10; jury trial, 755; Juilliard v. Greenman, 368; Justice, Department of, 369; Kendall v. U.S., 372; Kentucky v. Dennison, 243; Kilbourn v. Thompson, 374; Knox v. Lee, 391; Lamont v. Postmaster General, 126; Legal Tender Cases, 391, 443; Levitt v. Committee for Public Education and Religious Liberty, 760; Lochner v. New York, 316, 330, 402; Loewe v. Lawlor, 176; Lombard v. Stearne, 605; Lottery Case, 409; Louisville Joint Stock Land Bank v. Radford, 268; Mapp v. Ohio, 764; Marbury v. Madison, 367, 425; Martin v. Hunter's Lessee, 428, 634; McCardle, Ex parte, 414; McCulloch v. Maryland, 343, 417, 703; McCollum v. Board of Education, 570; Merryman, Ex parte, 253, 414, 443; Miller v. California, 758; Milligan, Ex parte, 253, 414, 443; Minersville District v. Gobitis, 257; Miranda v. Arizona, 239, 446; Mishkin Case, 582; Muller v. Oregon, 77; Munn v. Illinois, 300, 460, 693; Myers v. U.S., 461; Neagle, In re, 470; Near v. Minnesota, 470; Nebbia v. N.Y., 470; NLRB v. Jones and Laughlin Steel Corp., 466; Norman v. Baltimore & Ohio RR. Co., 294; Northern Securities Case, 493; obscenity cases, 758; Oregon Parochial School Case, 503; Panama Refining Co. v. Ryan, 511; Paris Adult Theater v. Slaton, 758; Parker v. Davis, 391; Perry v. U.S., 294;

Philadelphia Plan, 761; *Pierce v. Society of Sisters*, 503; *Plessy v. Ferguson*, 81, 530, 600; *Pollock v. Farmers' Loan and Trust Co.*, 20, 316, 340, 532; poll taxes, 533; *Presser v. Illinois*, 17; *Prigg v. Pennsylvania*, 546; Privacy Case, 546; Prize Cases, 547; *Railroad Board v. Duquesne Co.*, 562; railroad mergers, 484, 488; *Rasmussen v. U.S.*, 350; *Retirement Board v. Alton Railroad Co.*, 562; *Reynolds v. Sims*, 565; *Reynolds v. U.S.*, 602; *Roe v. Wade*, 741; *Roth v. U.S.*, 581; *Schechter Corp. v. U.S.*, 465, 595; *Schenck v. U.S.*, 330, 595; *School District of Abington Township v. Schempp*, 63; searches and seizures, 764; Slaughterhouse Cases, 443, 612; *Sloan v. Lemon*, 760; *Springer v. U.S.*, 20; *Standard Oil Company of New Jersey et al. v. U.S.*, 29, 583, 627; *Stone v. Farmers' Loan and Trust Co.*, 693; subversive list, 47; Sugar Trust Case, 637; Test Oath Cases, 443; *Swann Case*, 744; *Terry v. Ohio*, 765; *Texas v. White*, 652; *Tinker v. Des Moines Community School District*, 767; *U.S. v. Butler*, 7, 634; *U.S. v. Darby*, 314; *U.S. v. E. C. Knight*, 6, 637; *U.S. v. United States Steel Corp.*, 675; *Vicksburg & Co. Railroad Co. v. Putnam*, 18; *Wabash v. Illinois*, 300, 461; *Wesberry v. Sanders*, 565; *West Coast Hotel Co. v. Parrish*, 5, 532, 706; *West Virginia State Board of Education v. Barnette*, 257; *Worcester v. Georgia*, 722; *Wright v. Vinton Branch of Mountain Trust Bank of Roanoke*, 268; *Zemel v. Rusk*, 172; *Zorach v. Clauson*, 571

Supreme Courts: of Massachu-

setts, 125; of Michigan, 370; of New York, 172; of Rhode Island, 665

Supreme Headquarters of Allied Powers in Europe, 491

"supreme law of the land, the," 134

"Surrey with the Fringe on Top, The," 314

Surveyor, 412, 640

"Susan B. Anthony Amendment," 720

Susanna and the Elders, 61

Sussex pledge, 640

Sutherland, George, 706

Sutter, John A., 640

Sutter's Mill, 295, 640

Swallow, Silas C., 221

"Swamp Fight," 462

"Swamp Fox," 240, 640

"Swanee River," 264

Swann Case, 744

"Swedish nightingale," 400

Swedish West India Co., 640

Sweet Bird of Youth, 716

Swift and Armour, 60

Swiss, 641

"Switzerland of America," 477

Syllabus of a Course of Lectures on Chemistry, A, 584

Sylvis, William H., 467

symbol, party, *see* "emblems, party"

"Symphony, The," 387

Symphony for Organ and Orchestra, 164

Syncom, 641

Syndicate, *see* Mafia

Synopsis of the Indian Tribes . . . of North America, 279

Systems of Consanguinuity and Affinity of the Human Family, 455

T

tactical fighter experimental, *see* TFX

Taft, Robert Alphonso, 225, 227, 642

Taft, William Howard, 642; antitrust legislation, 29, 513,

898

902

907

909

White, John, 408
White, Stanford, 576
"white backlash," 711
White Brotherhood, 379
"White Christmas," 62
"White City," 111
Whitefield, George, 302, 499
"white gold," 166
White House, 69, 711
White-Jacket, 437
White Oak Swamp, battle of, 268
White Plains, battle of, 712
White Ships, 593
White Slave Traffic Act, 249
White Star Line, 37, 659
Whitman, Marcus, 98, 502
Whitman, Walt, 390, 712
Whitney, Eli, 166, 348, 432, 712
Whitney, John Hay, 484
Whittier, John Greenleaf, 273, 603, 713
Whole Booke of Psalmes Faithfully Translated into English Metre, The, 58
Whyte, William H., Jr., 504
Wild Bill Hickok, 713
"wildcat banks," 713
Wilder, Thornton, 612
Wilderness, battle of (1864), 71, 254, 713
Wilderness, battle of the (1755), 272
"Wilderness," the, 714
Wilderness Road, 379, 714
Wilderness Trail, 72
"Wild Honeysuckle, The," 273
"Wild West," 82
Wild West Show, 713, 714
Wilkes, Charles, 714
Wilkins, Roy, 68
Wilkinson, James, 85, 526
Willamette Valley, 503
Willard, Emma Hart, 714, 719, 721
Willard, Frances Elizabeth Caroline, 715
William and Mary, College of, 237, 715
Williams, Castle, 298
Williams, Roger, 54, 80, 166, 462, 575, 715

Williams, Tennessee, 655, 716
Williamsburg, 715
Williams College, 716
Williamson, David, 293
William III, King of England, 432
Willkie, Wendell L., 225
Wilmot, David, 716
Wilmot Proviso, 716
Wilson, C. T. R., 127
Wilson, Henry, 217
Wilson, James, 265, 716
Wilson, Woodrow, 544, 573, 717; ABC Conference, 1; Adamson Act, 5; Archangel intervention, 37; Bryan-Chamorro Treaty, 81; Committee on Public Information, 123; democracy, world made safe for, 188; Democratic party, 187; Dominican Republic, 195; Elections of 1912, 1916 and 1920, 222, 223; Federal Reserve System, 251; Flag Day, 257; Fourteen Points, 39, 45, 266, 388; "He kept us out of war," 324; League of Nations, 388, 403; Literacy Test Act, 400; *Lusitania*, 412; New Freedom, 476; Panama Canal tolls controversy, 92; Paris Peace Conference (1919), 64; "peace without victory," 518; power of appointment, 461; Princeton University, 546; Proclamation of Neutrality, 548; Progressive movement, 549; regulation of business, 475; State of the Union message, 631; *Sussex* pledge, 640; Tampico incident, 643; "too proud to fight," 660; treaty-making power, 664; Treaty of Versailles, 682; Underwood Tariff of 1913, 670; "watchful waiting," 702; World War I, 723; Zimmerman Note released by, 739
Wilson-Gorman Tariff of 1894, 192, 532, 717
Winchester, battle of, 358
Winchester, Gen. James, 563

910

Yamamoto, Admiral Isoroku, 442
Yamasee War, 733
Yancey-Rost-Mann mission, **733**
Yankee, 734
"Yankee Doodle," 734
Yap Treaty, 734
Yazoo Land Frauds, 258, **734**
"yellow-dog" contracts, 490, **734**
yellow fever, 108, 298, 569, 585, **735**
"yellow journalism," 106, 482, 554, 571, 622, **735**
"Yellow Kid," 735
Yellowstone National Park, **736**
"Yellow Violet, The," 81
Yemassee, 611
YMCA Training College, 56
"Yoknapatawpha County," 248
York, 51
York, Duke of, *see* James II, King of England
Yorktown, 165, 442, 552
Yorktown, battle of, **736**
Yosemite National Park, **736**
You Can't Go Home Again, 719
Young, Brigham, 456, 677, **736**
Young, John W., 282
Young, Owen D., 737

Young Lonigan: A Boyhood in Chicago's Streets, 248
Young Manhood of Studs Lonigan, The, 248
Young Men's Christian Association, 454, 737
Young Plan, 571, **737**
Young Women's Christian Association, 737
Youth's Companion, 762
Ŷpres-Lys offensive, **737**
Yukon, **737**
Yuma, 38, 450, 738
Yuma, Fort, **738**

Z

Zangwill, Israel, 436
Zemel v. Rusk, 172
Zen Buddhism, 59
Zenger, John Peter, 739
Zenger trial, 739
Ziegfeld's Follies, 62
Zimmerman, Alfred, 724, 739
Zimmerman Note, **739**
zoning laws, 111
Zorach v. Clauson, 571
Zouaves, **739**
Zuñi, 739
Zworykin, Vladimir, 740